2e

Essentials of Marketing

Second Edition

Dana-Nicoleta Lascu
University of Richmond

Kenneth E. Clow
University of Louisiana, Monroe

ATOMICdogPUBLISHING
Cincinnati, Ohio
www.atomicdog.com

Book Team

Vice President, Publisher Steve Scoble
Managing Editor Kendra Leonard
Director of Interactive Media and Design Joe Devine
Director of Quality Assurance Tim Bair
Production Coordinator Jana Staudt
Web Production Editor Joyce Powers
Quality Assurance Editor Dan Horton
Marketing Manager Mikka Baker
Cover Design Zach Hicks

When ordering this title, use ISBN 1-59260-271-1.

ISBN 1-59260-270-3

Library of Congress Control Number: 2005936500

Printed in the United States of America by Atomic Dog Publishing,
35 East Seventh Street, Suite 405, Cincinnati, Ohio 45202

10 9 8 7 6 5 4 3 2 1

This book is dedicated to the multitudes of the deprived, neglected, persecuted, and forgotten, for whom marketing is barely relevant.

Dana-Nicoleta Lascu

This book is dedicated to my sons—Dallas, Wes, Tim, and Roy—who always provide me with the encouragement to do another project, and especially to my wife, Susan, who was patient and understanding of the long hours it took to complete this project.

Kenneth E. Clow

Brief Contents

Contents

Appendixes

Preface

Marketing is a central component of every business and organizational structure. Through marketing, customers are identified and contacted using a variety of means. Everyone in an organization needs a basic understanding of marketing. *Essentials of Marketing, Second Edition,* was written to offer a basic understanding of and appreciation for marketing.

This text has a number of unique characteristics that set it apart. First, this is a condensed version of marketing principles. The authors have provided a concise, yet thorough, introduction to the field of marketing, presenting basic concepts and current theory along with memorable and up-to-date marketing practice examples.

Second, Dr. Lascu's international heritage and experience provide a higher level of understanding of marketing within the global environment. The international environment affects all companies, regardless of size, that often either sell to or purchase materials from international firms. As the world continues to shrink through advances in telecommunication technology and infrastructure, an understanding of marketing within a global context becomes even more critical.

Third, Dr. Clow's extensive business experience provides compelling examples, added understanding and valuable perspectives of business-to-business marketing principles. With the majority of marketing dollars spent on trade promotions and business-to-business activities, it is essential that students understand the business-to-business marketing environment. Numerous examples and references aid students in their understanding of this sector of the market, as well as of marketing through channel structures from the producer to the end consumer.

Essentials of Marketing, Second Edition, reveals to students that marketing is both a science built on a complex theoretical framework and an art that engages marketing practitioners and consumers alike, while creating value for each. In the process of illustrating these two aspects of marketing, the text provides extensive and engaging applications and illustrations that together create an integrated marketing experience for students. The text examines current developments in marketing and other functional areas that have a profound impact on marketing and offers current examples from an operating environment that the Internet has redefined and profoundly affected.

Pedagogical Aids

Essentials of Marketing, Second Edition, enhances learning with the following pedagogical devices:

1. Each chapter opens with a *Chapter Outline* and a list of *Chapter Objectives.*
2. Beautifully rendered two-color illustrations and photos throughout the text clarify and enhance chapter concepts.
3. In both the print book and the Online Edition, *Key Terms* are highlighted and defined. In the print book, key terms are also defined in the text margins and listed in alphabetical order with page references at the end of each chapter. A *Glossary* at the end of the print book presents all the definitions alphabetically. The Online

Edition has "pop-up" definitions of key terms, as well as a key term matching quiz in each end-of-chapter Study Guide.

4. *Marketing Illustration* boxes within each chapter enhance students' understanding of a variety of topics.
5. A comprehensive *Summary* at the end of each chapter reviews the *Chapter Objectives,* and content appropriate to each objective is summarized.
6. *Review Questions* at the end of each chapter allow students to check their comprehension of the chapter's major concepts.
7. End-of-chapter *Discussion Questions* suggest possible essay topics or in-class discussion issues.
8. *Cases* at the end of each chapter provide a wide range of scenarios and real-life situations along with questions to help guide student analysis.

Online and in Print

Essentials of Marketing, Second Edition, is available online as well as in print. The Online Edition demonstrates how the interactive media components of the text enhance presentation and understanding. For example,

- Animated illustrations help to clarify concepts.
- QuickCheck interactive questions and chapter quizzes test students' knowledge of various topics and provide immediate feedback.
- Clickable glossary terms provide immediate definitions of key concepts.
- Highlighting capabilities allow students to emphasize main ideas. Students can also add personal notes in the margin.
- The search function allows students to quickly locate discussions of specific topics throughout the text.

Students may choose to use just the Online Edition, or both the online and print versions together. This gives them the flexibility to choose which combination of resources works best for them. To assist those who use the online and print versions together, the primary heads and subheads in each chapter are numbered the same. For example, the first primary head in Chapter 1 is labeled 1-1, the second primary head in this chapter is labeled 1-2, and so on. The subheads build from the designation of their corresponding primary head: 1-1a, 1-1b, etc. This numbering system is designed to make moving between the Online Edition and the print book as seamless as possible.

Finally, icons like those shown in the margin on the left appear next to a number of figures and tables in the print version of the text. These icons indicate that this figure or table in the Online Edition is interactive in a way that applies, illustrates, or reinforces the concept.

Ancillary Materials

Atomic Dog is pleased to offer a competitive suite of supplemental materials for instructors using its textbooks. These ancillaries include a *Test Bank, PowerPoint Slides, Instructor's Manual,* and *Lecture Animations.*

The Test Bank for this book has been created by the authors and includes multiple-choice questions in a wide range of difficulty levels for each chapter. All Atomic Dog Test Banks offer not only the correct answer for each question, but also a rationale or explanation for the correct answer and a reference—the location in the chapter where materials addressing the question content can be found. This Test Bank comes with ExamViewPro software for easily creating customized or multiple versions of a test, and includes the option of editing or adding to the existing question bank.

A full set of PowerPoint Slides, written by the authors, is available for this text. This is designed to provide instructors with comprehensive visual aids for each chapter in the book. These slides include outlines of each chapter, highlighting important terms, concepts, and discussion points.

The Instructor's Manual for this book has also been written by the authors and offers suggested syllabi for 10- and 14-week terms; lecture outlines and notes; in-class and take-home assignments; recommendations for multi-media resources such as films and websites; and long and short essay questions and their answers, appropriate for use on tests.

Lecture Animations allow instructors to use the animations from our online edition in their own PowerPoint slideshows. These include all of the animated figures from each chapter of the text in an easy-to-use format.

Acknowledgments

We would like to express our gratitude to the staff at Atomic Dog Publishing for having the vision to put us together for this project. Even though we had never met or written together, the staff at Atomic Dog believed that we each had unique abilities that would allow us to be successful with this project. We want to especially thank Kendra Leonard and Steve Scoble, who have been excellent editors. In addition to their editorial duties, they provided encouragement and necessary assistance so we could meet our deadlines. Chuck Hutchinson had essential input into this second edition, helping us create a quality and current new edition. Many thanks also go to Victoria Putman, Lori Bradshaw, and Jana Staudt. We would also like to thank all the reviewers for this text for their input into the text material.

Ken would like to thank his wife, Susan, for all of her devotion, faith, and patience. She was especially understanding of the short deadlines and the multiple projects Ken had to accomplish while working on this textbook.

Dana would like to thank her family and students for their tolerance and inspiration.

About the Authors

Dana-Nicoleta Lascu is Associate Professor of Marketing and Chair of the Marketing Department at the University of Richmond. She has a Ph.D. in marketing from the University of South Carolina, a Master's of International Management from Thunderbird, and a B.A. in English and French from the University of Arizona. She was the 2005–2006 Fulbright Distinguished Chair in International Business at the Johannes Kepler University of Linz, Austria. She has published in *International Marketing Review, International Business Review, European Journal of Marketing, Journal of Business Research, Journal of Business Ethics,* and *Multinational Business Review,* among others. She has organized international conferences, such as the 1996 World Business Congress in Bermuda; the Sixth Conference on Marketing and Development, 1997, in Romania; and the Global Business and Technology Association International Conference, 2003, in Hungary. Dr. Lascu was a simultaneous and consecutive translator in English, French, and Romanian in Romania and Rwanda, and she worked as an international training coordinator in the United States, teaching managerial skills to civil servants from developing countries.

Kenneth E. Clow is Professor of Marketing at the University of Louisiana at Monroe. He has a Ph.D. in marketing from the University of Arkansas and has spent time at Pittsburg State University and the University of North Carolina at Pembroke. Dr. Clow's primary research activities are in the areas of services marketing and advertising. He has published more than 120 articles and six textbooks, including second editions of *Services Marketing* and *Integrated Advertising, Promotion, and Marketing Communications.* His articles have been published in many journals, such as *Journal of Services Marketing, Journal of Professional Services Marketing, Marketing Health Services, Journal of Business Research, Journal of Marketing Education, Journal of Restaurant and Foodservices Marketing, Journal of Hospitality and Leisure Marketing,* and *Journal of Marketing Management.* Dr. Clow also operated and owned a contract cleaning service for eight years.

Part 1

Introduction to Marketing

Scope and Concepts of Marketing

1

CHAPTER OBJECTIVES

1. Address the central role of marketing in the twenty-first century.
2. Define marketing and identify its key concepts.
3. Address the different marketing philosophies and explain them in view of the historical development of marketing.
4. Discuss the key elements of the societal marketing concept and the importance of these elements in meeting the needs of consumers, society, and the organization.

CHAPTER OUTLINE

Until a few years ago, Charles M. Harper, chairman of ConAgra Inc., had about as much interest in eating right as the average middle-aged guy: not much (his diet consisted primarily of pork chops, roast beef, and ice cream). As he lay in the hospital recuperating from a heart attack, he contemplated his new personal goal (to improve his eating habits) and his old company goal (profit) and came up with a vision for a new line of health foods called Healthy Choice. After he returned to work, Harper enlisted the help of his product development team to create a healthy product that wouldn't compromise taste. The researchers overdelivered on taste, packaged the product in a distinctive green color that stood out, and advertised it in traditional channels, rather than positioning it as health or diet food. With strong support from retailers, Healthy Choice today dominates the frozen dinner and entrée market. Healthy Choice is a marketing success.[1]

Capable companies today, such as Procter & Gamble, Microsoft, Siemens, and Wal-Mart, rely on marketing to ensure the success of their products and services in the marketplace. What is marketing? Many people—including some management professionals—think of marketing simply as advertising and/or selling. Indeed, promotion in the form of selling and advertising is omnipresent, arriving in neat packages in our mailboxes at home and at the office, resonating on our television screens and radios, popping up in our emails and websites, calling for our attention from billboards on the side of the road, and enchanting us with catchy slogans, such as "where's the beef?" and "just do it!" Promotion is, in fact, part of marketing: It is an important marketing function.

Yet, marketing is much more. It is an integral part of contemporary life. Marketing is pervasive, permeating many aspects of our daily existence, from our selection of the neighborhoods where we live, to the brands we purchase, to our choice of retailers and service providers (see Figure 1-1), and to our selection of television and radio programs. Marketing profoundly affects our decisions and features prominently in our lives.

1-1 Chapter Overview

This first chapter introduces marketing and its components. It presents marketing as an engine of the modern economy and as an important determinant of our high standard of living in the Western world. Section 1-2 addresses the importance of marketing in the twenty-first century economy, as a driver of economic growth and development, and as a

Figure 1-1
Sleek shopping carts in a super-clean store with just the right lighting and enticing bakery aromas announce a delightful shopping experience.

Source: Courtesy of Ukrop's Super Markets, Inc.

vehicle for enhancing buyers' well-being and quality of life in general. Section 1-3 offers a definition of marketing and describes the important concepts of marketing. Section 1-4 addresses the different marketing philosophies—the product/production concepts, the selling concept, the marketing and societal marketing concepts, and their historical underpinnings. Section 1-5 addresses the key elements of the societal marketing concept: a market orientation and an integrated marketing approach, a focus on consumer and society needs, a value-based philosophy, and an organizational goal orientation.

1-2 The Importance of Marketing in the Twenty-First Century Economy

Gross domestic product (GDP): The sum of all goods and services produced within the boundaries of a country.

Marketing constitutes an ever-growing, important driving force of today's modern society. In the United States alone, there are more than 275 million consumers living in 100 million households, spending $5 trillion on products and services, or two-thirds of the national **gross domestic product (GDP).** A significant number of all Americans are employed entirely or in part in assisting the marketing system to perform its functions. More than 30 million Americans work directly within the aggregate marketing system, with salespeople accounting for the largest segment.[2] There are almost 20 million business-to-business buyers, three million of which are retailers that resell to consumers, and another one-half million wholesalers. Firms in general spend more than $200 billion per year on advertising (see Figure 1-2), and all these figures do not account for the marketing expenditures of professional practices, such as doctors, lawyers, and other service providers who must engage in marketing to attract and maintain their clients.[3]

Thus, the broad marketing system is integral to a society's economic system, offering employment and income for millions working in the marketing field, enabling them to be productive and earn money needed for consumption. In this process, private investments for the marketing system further assist in the development of the national infrastructure, in such areas as transportation, telecommunication, medical care, and finance. In turn, companies engaged in marketing pay taxes that further fund public programs. The system's mass-market efficiencies allow for lower costs, lower prices, and increased overall consumer access, fostering innovation that ultimately benefits consumption.[4]

Marketing enhances economic development. Nations with higher proportions of their populations involved in marketing, and with a developed marketing system, also have a higher GDP. It is important to note, however, that the roles of the marketing system differ by stage of economic development.[5] For example, in developing countries, the focus of production is to satisfy basic needs, such as hunger and shelter; here, the limited excess production is traded in local markets. In developed countries, marketing is manifest in all aspects of production and consumption, and all marketing functions are essential for a company to survive.

Figure 1-2
This advertisement by the Family Care Clinic encourages people to use the clinic.

Source: Courtesy of Newcomer, Morris and Young.

Marketing also enhances consumers' well-being and quality of life. In many organizations, marketing practitioners represent consumers' interests, influencing the decisions on the products and services offered. The marketing system then informs consumers about the offering through advertising campaigns and supports the delivery of products and services in a manner that is convenient to consumers. Competition leads to a broader spectrum of product choices as well as to an improved distribution system that reduces product costs. These efforts further help improve the overall national infrastructure, such as telecommunications and transportation.[6] Social marketing in particular focuses on benefiting society as a whole by encouraging behavior that enhances individual and societal health, and by tackling issues from literacy to civil rights to cancer research.

1-3 Defining Marketing

Marketing is described by management guru Peter Drucker as "the most effective engine of economic development, particularly in its ability to develop entrepreneurs and managers."[7] He defines marketing as a systematic business discipline that teaches us to go about, in an orderly, purposeful, and planned way, to find and create customers; to identify and define **markets;** and to integrate customers' needs, wants, and preferences. Marketing also is the intellectual and creative capacity and skills of an industrial society to facilitate the design of new and better products and new distribution concepts and processes.[8]

Markets: All of the actual and potential consumers of a company's products.

Perhaps a more succinct definition of marketing is the one developed by the American Marketing Association:[9]

> **Marketing** is defined as an organizational function and a set of processes for creating, communicating, and delivering value to customers and for managing customer relationships in ways that benefit the organization and its stakeholders.

Marketing: An organizational function and a set of processes for creating, communicating, and delivering value to customers and for managing customer relationships in ways that benefit the organization and its stakeholders.

Exchange is at the heart of marketing. The objective of marketing is to satisfy the needs, wants, and demands of consumers and businesses through providing value, quality, and satisfaction. Exchange of ideas, goods, and services becomes possible through the effective planning and execution of the production, pricing, promotion, and distribution functions. In the following sections, the definition of marketing is explained in more detail.

1-3a Needs, Wants, and Demands

Successful marketers must be able to identify target consumers, as well as their needs, wants, and demands. **Needs** are defined as basic human requirements: physiological needs, such as food and water; safety needs; social needs, such as affection and acceptance; self-esteem needs, such as the need for recognition; and self-actualization needs, such as the need for self-improvement. (A hierarchy of these needs will be addressed in Chapter 5, "Business-to-Business Behavior.") Marketers attempt to address consumer needs with the different goods and services they offer.

Needs: Basic human requirements, such as food and water.

Needs become **wants** when they are directed to a particular product. Wants are shaped by one's culture. Shelter in the United States typically consists of frame housing with Tyvek (synthetic) insulation. In much of Europe, it consists of brick homes, while in Sub-Saharan Africa, it consists of round huts. In each format, the home meets the consumers' need for shelter. Self-esteem needs can be addressed in the United States and Europe through education or through luxury possessions, such as a home in the right neighborhood with the right furnishings (see Figure 1-3), or an automobile that qualifies as appropriate for the individual's aspirations. In Sub-Saharan Africa, self-esteem needs are addressed by the number of cattle owned or the number of servants helping with housework.

Wants: Needs that are directed at a particular product—for example, to meet the need for transportation, consumers may purchase an automobile or a bus ride.

Wants become **demands** when they are backed by the ability to buy a respective good or service. Discerning adults with deep pockets can buy San Pelegrino mineral water, drive a BMW M-class, or take the Queen Mary 2 ultramodern gigantic cruise ship introduced in 2004 to Europe. Busy fathers who do not want to take time cooking can appease their own hunger with Hot Pockets and feed their kids Hot Pockets Juniors.

Demands: Wants backed by the ability to buy the good or service brand.

Figure 1-3
Inside a Romanian home: Plush rugs everywhere denote elegance and create a cozy atmosphere.

1-3b Value, Quality, and Satisfaction

Value: The overall price given the quality of the product; perceived as important for the first purchase decision.

Companies are successful because they provide products of value. That **value,** defined as the overall price given the quality of the product, is especially important in the first purchase of a product. However, how consumers define value will vary. To one consumer, a good value may be a cheap price. To another consumer, the value may be a quality product at a moderate price. To a third consumer, value may be an expensive product that conveys an image of prestige. While each consumer defines value differently, each makes a purchase because in the exchange process he or she perceives something of value is being obtained.

Quality: Overall good or service quality, reliability, and the extent to which a product meets consumers' needs; has the greatest impact on satisfaction.

Closely tied with the concept of value is **quality,** which is the overall product quality, reliability, and the extent to which it meets consumers' needs. Perceived quality has the greatest impact on satisfaction. Again, successful companies sell products that are perceived to be of high quality relative to the price being charged. The quality of food served at a four-star restaurant is higher than what is served at McDonald's. But for the amount a consumer pays at McDonald's, it is perceived to be a quality meal. Indeed, fast-food restaurants are quickly bridging the quality gap by providing food of the highest quality. For example, Hardee's sells a line of premium Thickburgers made from Angus beef, and Arby's is offering quality entrée salads and a line of low-carb wraps, all for a reasonable price of around $5.

Companies that do not provide quality that is reflective of the price may get someone to try the product once, but that consumer will not come back. A business cannot survive without repeat customers.

One reason the Edsel failed in the late 1950s was the poor quality of the automobile. In contrast, a major reason the Mustang succeeded a few years later was the superior quality of the automobile. Both cars were made by Ford: One is used as an example of failure, whereas the other has become an icon of American cars.

Satisfaction: A match between consumer expectations and good or service performance.

Satisfaction is the key to whether consumers or businesses purchase again. If you're satisfied with the taste and quality of a new flavor of potato chips, you will purchase them again. If not, you will purchase another brand. The same is true for a business that is purchasing raw materials or components to manufacture a vacuum cleaner. The level of satisfaction is a function of the quality and perceived value and whether it adequately meets the need or want for which it was purchased.

1-3c Goods, Services, Ideas, and Experiences

As the definition of marketing states, the primary focus of marketing is on the creation and distribution of goods, services, ideas, and experiences that satisfy consumer needs and wants. **Goods** generally refer to tangible products, such as cereals, automobiles, and clothing. **Services** refer to intangible activities or benefits that individuals acquire, but that do not result in ownership. Airplane trips, a massage, and the preparation of a will are examples of services. **Ideas** and **experiences** refer to concepts and experiences that consumers perceive as valuable because they fulfill consumer needs and wants: Watching a movie, riding Dumbo the Elephant at Disneyland, and going on a safari in Kenya fulfill consumers' needs for adventure and exploration. See Table 1-1 for more examples of goods, services, ideas, and experiences.

In this text, goods, services, ideas, and experiences will be collectively referred to as products. Products represent the first ***P*** of marketing. Marketing has four ***P***s that jointly shape the marketing strategy for a particular brand, as the chapters that follow illustrate.

Goods: Tangible products, such as cereals, automobiles, and clothing.

Services: Intangible activities or benefits that individuals acquire, but that do not result in ownership, such as an airplane trip, a massage, or the preparation of a will.

Ideas: Concepts that can be used to fulfill consumer needs and wants.

Experiences: Personal experiences that consumers perceive as valuable because they fulfill consumer needs and wants.

1-3d Exchanges and Transactions, Relationships and Markets

Exchanges and transactions refer to obtaining a desired good or service in exchange for something else. Exchanges involve at least two parties that mutually agree on the desirability of the traded items. Shelter in New York City can be obtained by renting a tiny one-bedroom apartment in one of the city's expensive co-ops in exchange for about $4,000 a month, renting a room at a hotel in Times Square in exchange for about $350 per night, renting in Queens for about $150 per night, or going to a homeless shelter. Other examples of exchanges involve voting for a particular political candidate for a promise of lower taxes, or offering donations to charity in exchange for the comfort of knowing that others will be better off as a result. All of these are examples of transactions in which an exchange of something of value was given in return for something else of perceived equal value.

The exchange process is central to marketing. Ultimately, an exchange takes place between consumers and manufacturers or service providers. Consumers pay money for the goods and services produced by manufacturers or service providers. In reality, the exchange is more complicated because it usually involves a complex distribution process and middlemen:

Exchanges and transactions: Obtaining a desired good or service in exchange for something else of value; involving at least two parties that mutually agree on the desirability of the traded items.

- The first level of the exchange takes place between the manufacturer and a wholesaler: The wholesaler buys the product from the manufacturer.
- A second exchange takes place between that wholesaler and another wholesaler who is closer to the consumer; there could be several levels of wholesalers in the distribution chain, and at each level, an exchange will take place.

TABLE 1-1

Examples of Goods, Services, Ideas, and Experiences

INTERACTIVE TABLE

1. A tennis racquet is a ...	...good.
2. A beauty salon provides a ...	...service.
3. A political candidate is an example of an ...	...idea.
4. A dentist provides a ...	...service.
5. A trip to the beach is an ...	...experience.
6. Toothpaste is a ...	...good.
7. A college textbook is a ...	...good.
8. A college education is an example of an ...	...idea.
9. A haircut is a...	...service.
10. Bungee jumping is an ...	...experience.

- Yet another exchange takes place between the wholesaler and the retailer where the target consumer will purchase the product.
- The final exchange takes place between the consumer and the retailer when the consumer pays the retailer for the product.

At each level, products (goods, services, or ideas) are exchanged for a monetary sum. Each product has a price (cost) at each level of distribution, with the consumer paying the final price for the good or service at the end of the distribution channel. Price is the second ***P*** of marketing.

At all these levels, important relationships of mutual benefit develop. Consumers develop loyalty or preference for the brand and/or the retailer. The retailer develops relationships with wholesalers, and wholesalers develop relationships with manufacturers. The manufacturer nurtures a relationship with all the parties involved in marketing its products and with the final consumer. This is known as **relationship marketing,** which is defined as the process of developing and nurturing relationships with the parties participating in the transactions involving a company's products. The parties involved in the exchange are part of the distribution process; distribution is referred to as place—the third ***P*** of marketing.

Relationship marketing: The process of developing and nurturing relationships with all the parties participating in the transactions involving a company's products.

The manufacturer develops these relationships by communicating with the wholesalers, retailers, and especially, with its market. A market is the set of all the actual and potential buyers of the company's products whose needs can be satisfied with the respective products. The company needs to understand its markets in order to produce goods that address the markets' needs and wants and to communicate with them effectively about their products. Communication with the market is accomplished through promotion in the form of advertising, personal selling, sales promotion, or public relations. Promotion is the fourth ***P*** of marketing (see Figure 1-4).

Hence, products, place, price, and promotion are used to address the needs and wants of the final consumer (see Figure 1-5 on page 10).

1-4 Marketing Philosophies

Marketing has evolved over time. A firm can take five different approaches to marketing. The first approach is for a company to place a heavy emphasis on producing the best product it can, hoping someone will buy it. A second approach is for the company to reduce costs through improved manufacturing processes and technological development, thus selling its products at a lower cost than its competition. A third approach is for the company to put a heavy emphasis on selling its products to consumers and businesses, striving to convince customers of the superiority of its product. A fourth approach is for the company to find out what customers want first and then develop a product that meets that want. The last approach is similar to the fourth, but in addition to finding out what customers want, the company produces and markets the product in the way that will best benefit society.

1-4a The Product/Production Concepts

Production concept: A marketing philosophy that assumes consumers prefer products that are easily accessible and inexpensive.

Product concept: A marketing philosophy that assumes consumers prefer products that are of the highest quality and optimal performance.

The **production concept** assumes that consumers prefer products that are easily accessible and inexpensive. The **product concept** assumes that consumers prefer products that are of the highest quality and optimal performance. For the company, the product and production concepts both focus strategies on the production process and delivery, devoting significant resources to research, product development, manufacturing, and engineering. The Zytec/Artesyn example in Marketing Illustration 1-1 on page 10 offers the example of a company whose focus is on both the product and production concepts. In terms of the product concept, Zytec/Artesyn's goal is to manufacture better quality products. In terms of the production concept, Zytec/Artesyn is concerned with faster production time and lower production costs.

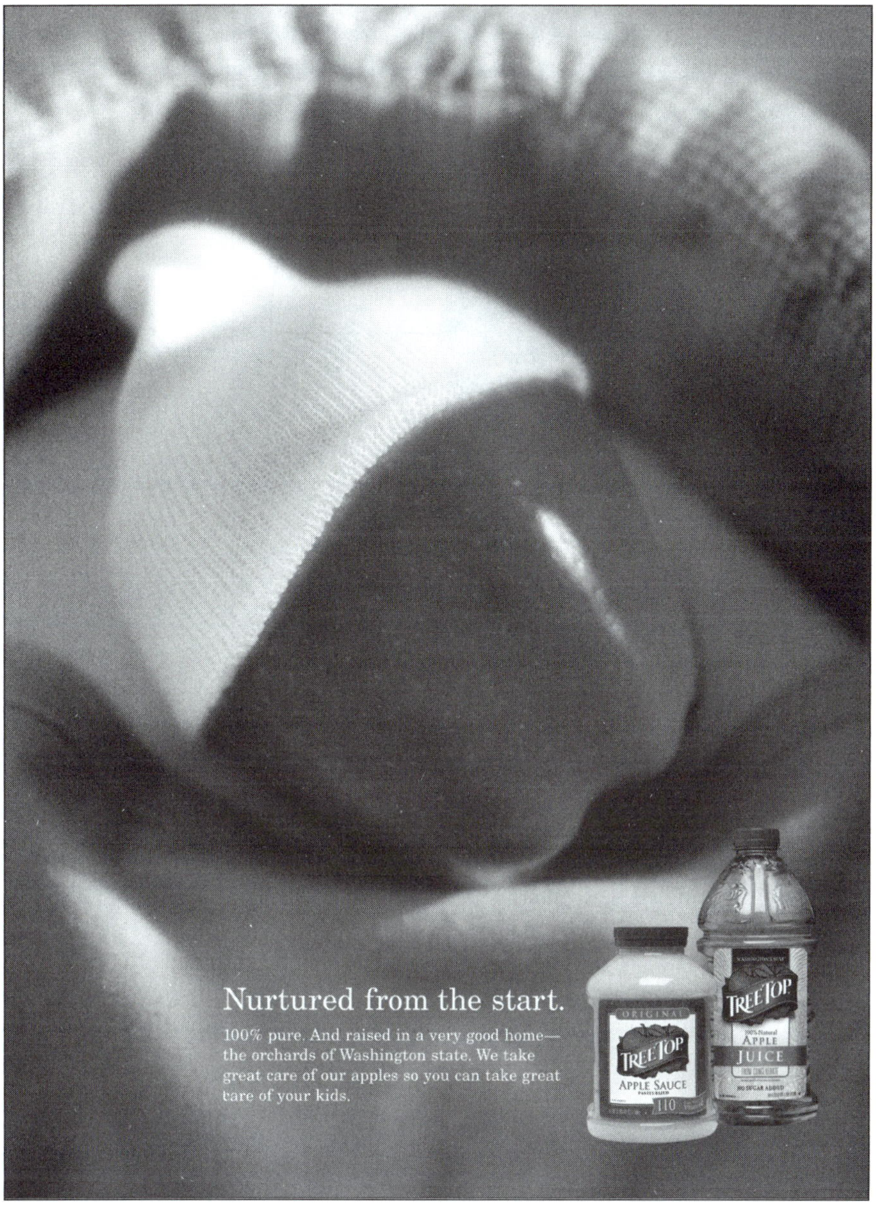

Figure 1-4
Tree Top uses advertising to encourage consumers—in this case, mothers—to serve Tree Top apple juice to their children from the time they are infants.

Source: © Tree Top, Inc., 2002, Yakima, WA. Created by Cole & Weber / Red Cell, Seattle, WA.

Certainly, there are trade-offs between a production orientation, especially when the goal is to cut costs, and a product orientation, where the goal is to provide a high-quality product. The production orientation works well for mass-market service organizations, such as fast-food providers and retailers; for people-processing government agencies; and in developing countries in general. Consumers in developing countries cannot afford high-priced products.

Other organizations, such as medical and dental practices and law firms, may also attempt to optimize their use of resources. However, their primary goal is to provide the highest quality service using the latest techniques. Given this goal, they are more likely to focus on the product first and production second. As such, they are guided primarily by the product concept, but still are very cognizant of the production process and costs.

Firms at the forefront of technology introducing new products to the market are most likely to adopt the product concept. Pharmaceutical firms developing drugs that revolutionize the treatment of formerly incurable illnesses and manufacturers developing the latest communication and computing technology tend to have a product focus. However,

Figure 1-5
The Four *Ps* of Marketing

Product: Any offering that can satisfy consumer needs and wants; products include goods (tangible products), services, ideas, and experiences.

Place: The physical movement of products from the producer to individual or organizational consumers and the transfer of ownership and risk.

Promotion: All forms of external communications directed toward consumers and businesses with an ultimate goal of developing customers.

Price: The amount of money necessary to purchase a product.

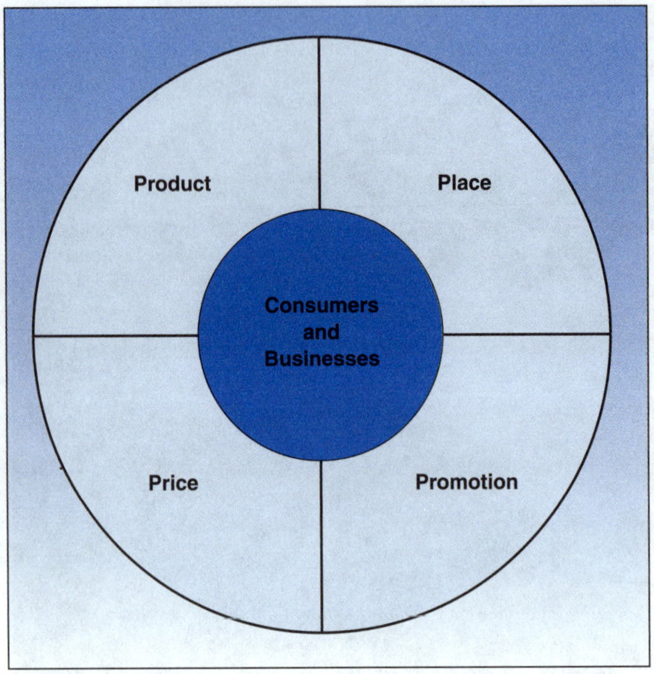

INTERACTIVE FIGURE

even these firms have to fend off competition and broaden their customer base when patents expire and competitors appropriate their new technology. At that point, firms with a product orientation are very likely to shift to a production orientation. For example, patent expiration presented challenges to Claritin, a popular allergy medicine. Competitors were allowed to offer generic allergy medicine using its identical formula at significantly lower cost. As a result, Claritin had to adapt its entire marketing strategy by obtaining approvals for the brand's over-the-counter distribution and offering it to the mass market.

The main disadvantage of the product and production orientations is that the focus is on the product and production processes, rather than the consumer. It is manufacturing,

Marketing Illustration 1-1

Production and Product Focus at Zytec/Artesyn

Zytec Corporation, a medium-size manufacturer of power supplies based in Eden Prairie, Minnesota, boasted in the early 1990s a customer base that included industry giants such as IBM, Fujitsu, Unisys, and AT&T. Zytec's product quality was considered a benchmark against which all its competitors were measured, and constituted an important competitive advantage. Zytec built on its capabilities, with an additional competitive advantage: just-in-time production management, a novel manufacturing and distribution strategy at that time. Just-in-time production refers to a system used to simplify and redefine manufacturing, from the raw materials stage to delivery, so that every part arrives in guaranteed working order at every stage of the assembly line, just in time to be installed. The outcome of this approach to manufacturing was better quality products, reduced production time, and lower production costs.

Zytec merged with Computer Products Inc. in 1997, forming Artesyn, a successful company that ranks as the fifth largest among power-supply companies. The primary focus of the new company is on communications. Artesyn is currently attempting to meet the challenges involved in becoming the lowest-cost provider in the world. To this end, it attempts to gain additional competitive advantage by turning to low-cost areas for manufacturing, such as China and Hungary, where it has 3,500 and 1,000 employees, respectively.

Sources: Tom Murray, "Just-in-Time Isn't Just for Show—It Sells," *Sales and Marketing Management*, vol. 142, no. 6 (May 1990): 62–66; Robert Bellinger, "Artesyn Reclaims Growth Track—Focus on Internet, Wireless Leads to Strong Turnaround," *Electronic Buyers' News*, no. 1229 (September 18, 2000): pg. 44.

Marketing Illustration 1-2

Hard Sell at the Hilton? The Hilton International Grand Vacations Company

Hilton International Grand Vacations Company offers "care-free vacations in your own holiday lodge" for two adults at a very low price in different locations worldwide. For Hilton Honors (the Hilton loyalty program) members in the United States, the company periodically sends emails offering, for two adults, a three-day, two-night vacation for $147 in Las Vegas or a four-day, three-night vacation for $249.

One such offer is for accommodations at the Hilton Hawaiian Village in Waikiki. Here, the company entices consumers to spend six days and five nights in a one-bedroom suite and receive a $100 gift certificate for shopping and dining for a price of $1,199. The regular retail value of the package is up to $2,795. Typically, the offer either flashes on the Hilton website, or it is sent in an email solicitation to Hilton Honors members. Once at the resort, the guests have to attend a two-hour presentation on the resort premises. Hilton Grand Vacations also solicits regular hotel guests at the Hilton Hawaiian Village, who find on their pillows an invitation to take a tour of the rooms in the time-share section of the hotel complex and attend a two-hour presentation on the premises in return for a substantial number of Hilton Honors points (30,000). Guests are invited to the Hilton Grand Vacation tower in the resort, where they have the opportunity to admire the elegant lobby area; from there, they go to the hospitality and waiting area, where enticing refreshments are displayed. The area has a playroom for children and informal babysitting services. In the presentation room, guests are presented with the advantages of time-share ownership and given a tour of typical rooms. Then the hard-sell process begins, with different individuals attempting to persuade guests about the long-term benefits of vacation ownership and the importance of committing immediately and signing on the dotted line.

Source: www.hgvcoffers.com.

engineering, research, and development that dictate what products should be made, rather than the needs, preferences, and interests of the final consumer. That can lead to marketing myopia, whereby marketing efforts ignore specific consumer needs, or important markets, which will be further examined in Section 1-4f.

1-4b The Selling Concept

The **selling concept** assumes that consumers left alone will normally not purchase the products the firm is selling, or not purchase enough products. Consumers, according to the selling concept, need to be aggressively targeted and approached with personal selling and advertising in order to be persuaded to purchase the company's products. Although firms may focus on aggressive selling when they have excess inventories at the end of the year or when new models must replace the old on the retail floor, companies are more likely to embrace the selling concept when their products are unsought goods, such as time-shares and insurance services.

Selling concept: A marketing philosophy that assumes consumers, if left alone, will normally not purchase the products the firm is selling, or not purchase enough products; as a result, consumers need to be aggressively targeted and approached with personal selling and advertising in order to purchase.

In the process of selling time-shares, companies such as Fairfield Resorts identify prospective buyers, approach them with an offer of two nights close to the resort location, and then require those who choose to take advantage of the offer to spend about two hours in a hard-sell environment. Marketing Illustration 1-2 addresses Hilton's strategy to sell time-shares in Hawaii to target consumers.

Even mainstream department store retailers such as Hecht's and Lord and Taylor's adopt the selling concept toward the end of the year, just before the Thanksgiving holiday. At that time, they aggressively promote their merchandise, increasing their advertising in local newspapers and sending direct mail to their target consumers. The mailers advertise the "Biggest SALE of the year, look for our lowest prices of the season" in large white letters against a bright red background. These communications also offer different types of promotions, such as 15-percent-off coupons, an all-day shopping pass, a 0 percent finance charge, and other attractive deals. In their deluge of communications, retailers are often assisted by manufacturers, who offer additional promotional incentives to consumers, thus reinforcing the selling strategy (see Figure 1-6).

Figure 1-6
Retailers are increasingly promoting their own brands. Here, Ukrop's, a large supermarket chain in Virginia, is promoting its own margarine for a fraction of its competitors' price.
Source: Courtesy of Ukrop's Super Markets, Inc.

In both examples, the time-share and the retailers, the focus is on persuading consumers, rather than offering them the products that best fit their needs and interests. In the case of the time-shares, consumers might respond to the offer only to obtain the subsidized stay at the hotel or the loyalty points. In the case of the retailers' holiday blitz, consumer response will be short term and most likely focused on the promotions offered.

1-4c The Marketing Concept

Marketing concept: A marketing philosophy that assumes a company can compete more effectively if it first researches consumers' generic needs, wants, and preferences, as well as good- or service-related attitudes and interests, and then delivers the goods and services more efficiently and effectively than competitors.

The **marketing concept** assumes that a company can compete more effectively if it first researches consumers' generic needs, wants, and preferences, as well as product- or service-related attitudes and personal interests. With this knowledge of the consumer, the firm is able to deliver the goods and services that consumers want more efficiently and effectively than the competition. This marketing philosophy entails a company-wide consumer focus across all functional areas.

Marketing Illustration 1-3 offers an application of the marketing concept philosophy at Arby's. However, adopting the marketing concept is not limited to the product offering or the restaurant ambience. Arby's restaurants are located conveniently to target consumers, typically close to shopping centers that are frequented by its target market. Its prices are somewhat higher than those at a McDonald's or Burger King. Sandwiches, for example, cost about $4 or more, but they are marketed as being of superior quality and match the taste desires of older Americans. Convenient location, appropriate pricing, and well-targeted promotion are indicative of a consumer focus, hence reflecting a marketing concept philosophy.

The marketing concept has five principal components that are essential to a company's performance. They are a market orientation, an integrated marketing approach, a focus on consumer needs, a value-based philosophy, and an organizational goal orientation—as illustrated in Figure 1-7. Each will be discussed in detail in Section 1-5.

The marketing concept is in many ways superior to the selling concept. The outcomes of a focus on aggressive selling lead to short-term results (sales), whereas adopting the marketing concept leads to a long-term relationship with the customer. Selling has as its primary goal increasing sales volume, whereas a marketing philosophy has as its primary goal addressing customer needs and wants. Figure 1-8 on page 14 illustrates the differences between a selling philosophy and a marketing philosophy.

1-4d The Societal Marketing Concept

Societal marketing concept: A marketing philosophy that assumes the company will have an advantage over competitors if it applies the marketing concept in a manner that maximizes society's well-being.

The **societal marketing concept** assumes that the company will have an advantage over competitors if it applies the marketing concept in a manner that maximizes society's well-being. Thus, the societal marketing concept assumes that a company can compete more effectively if it first researches consumers' generic needs, wants, and preferences, as well as product or service-related attitudes and interests, and then delivers the products and services more efficiently and effectively than competitors in a manner that maximizes society's

Marketing Illustration 1-3

The Marketing Concept at Arby's: Appealing to Adult Consumers

Arby's is a fast-food company that has a keen understanding of its target consumers. The first Arby's opened in Ohio in the 1960s, serving roast beef sandwiches, chips, and drinks. Today, the company has more than 500 licensees operating more than 3,000 restaurants worldwide. Arby's is known for a number of successful firsts for fast-food restaurants, such as offering adult fast food like the Market Fresh deli-style sandwiches (chicken, turkey, ham, and beef on thick-sliced honey-wheat bread, with mustard, among others). In late 2002, Arby's created a Restaurant of the Future prototype, with warmer tones and a more contemporary look to appeal to its adult audience.

Arby's focus on adults results from its research of the baby boomer generation, a generation brought up on fast food. As baby boomers have grown up, their preferences have shifted toward healthier adult food and toward a comfortable contemporary ambience, rather than a lively, children-oriented environment. However, their need for convenience and fast food preparation has remained the same. Given their busy lifestyles, Arby's is addressing these new preferences and needs.

Arby's communicates these changes to its fast-food consumer through well-targeted advertising campaigns aimed at reaching its upscale demographic segment. To promote its Market Fresh sandwich line, for example, Arby's aired a four-week, $17-million flight of testimonial ads touting this sandwich line, using the theme "Satisfy your adult tastes." In the advertisements, consumers were asked to taste a sandwich, and then they were asked how they would react if they were told that the sandwiches were from a fast-food restaurant. The ad was aired on about 15 to 20 cable television networks, including Discovery Channel, USA, and ESPN. Currently, the company is using an innovative lead advertising agency, Merkley + Partners in New York, for its integrated marketing communications.

Sources: Kenneth Hein, "The Heat Is On to Remake Fast-Feeder Menus," *Brandweek* vol. 46, no. 1 (January 3, 2005): 9; Bob Sperber, "Arby's Gets Fast-Casual Makeover," *Brandweek*, vol. 43, no. 41 (November 11, 2002): 14; Bob Sperber, "Arby's Sandwiches Get Slice-of-Life Tack," *Brandweek*, vol. 42, no. 29 (December 20, 2002): 6; Arby's website (www.arby.com).

well-being. Companies are expected to be good citizens of society and to build societal considerations into their marketing endeavors while they pursue organizational profit goals.

Arby's has established an exemplary record of following the societal marketing concept through its social involvement. It supports Big Brothers and Big Sisters of America, the Boys & Girls Clubs of America, and various other causes through the Arby's Foundation. Ben & Jerry's, a Unilever subsidiary, has positioned itself as a supporter of social causes. The company ensures that none of its ice cream products are made with milk from hormone-fed cows and takes a strong stand against it. "We oppose recombinant bovine growth hormone" is a statement found on most of the Ben & Jerry's packages. It also supports environmental efforts, such as those involving Vermont's Lake Champlain Watershed, peace in the world, and other causes. Among other examples of societal involvement are the Ronald

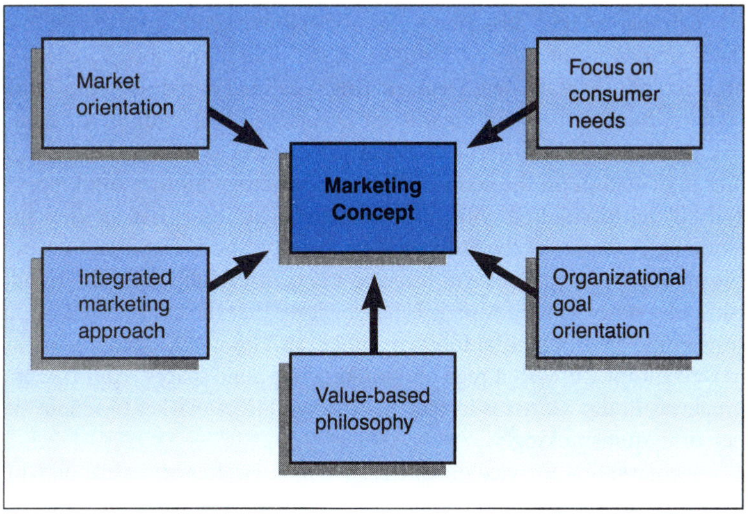

Figure 1-7
The Marketing Concept

INTERACTIVE FIGURE

Figure 1-8
The Focus of Selling and Marketing Philosophies

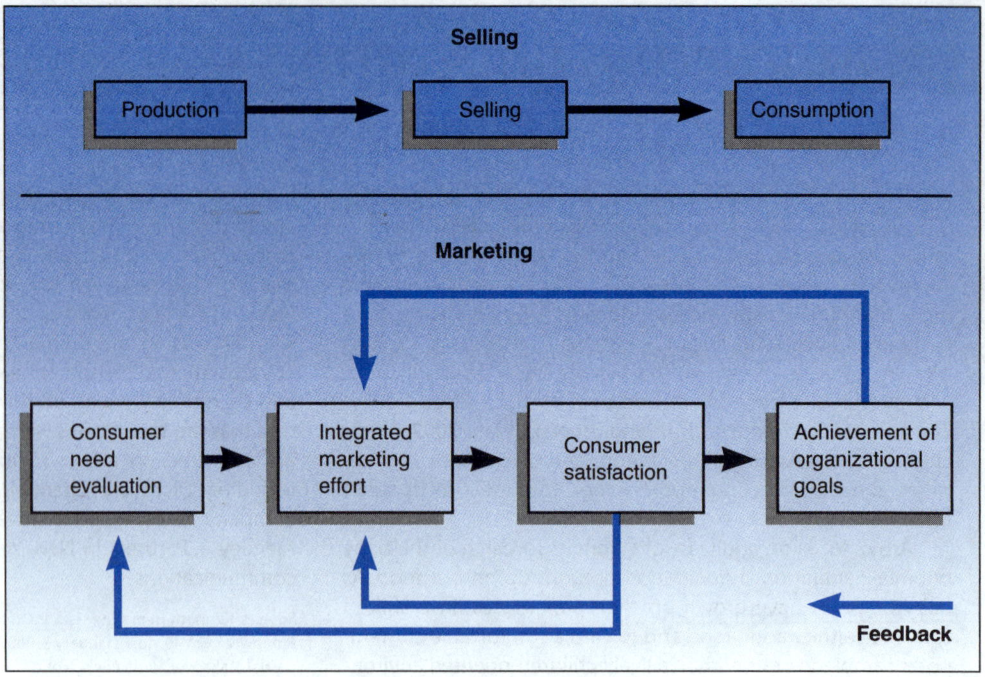

McDonald House Charities, which provide comfort to children in need and their families, and the Avon Breast Cancer Crusade.

Many companies, in the process of adopting the societal marketing concept, partner with nonprofit firms to engage in cause-related marketing. Cause-related marketing refers to a long-term partnership between a nonprofit organization and a corporation that is integrated into the corporation's marketing plan. This topic will be further addressed in Section 3-4a, "Cause-Related Marketing." Examples of corporate societal marketing programs abound. BMW promoted the "Drive for the Cure" test drive program, which donates $1 for every test-driven mile to the Susan G. Komen Breast Cancer Foundation to fund cancer research. This cause-related program is targeted toward women, who are not traditionally BMW's target market.[10] In another example, a number of prominent companies are actively compaigning against domestic violence (see Figure 1-9), in partnership with Glenwood Regional Medical Center in Louisiana.

The societal marketing concept can be illustrated as a modified version of the marketing concept (see Figure 1-7). Its principal components are a market orientation, an integrated marketing approach, a focus on consumer and society needs, a value-based philosophy, and an organizational goal orientation.

Demarketing: A company strategy aimed at reducing demand for its own products in order to benefit society.

Companies that subscribe to the societal marketing concept philosophy will engage in the demarketing of their own products, if demarketing solves societal problems that their products may have created. **Demarketing** is defined as reducing the demand for a company's own products, if that is in the interest of society. Philip Morris, for example, uses an expensive, sleek newspaper insert that directs consumers to its website, www.philipmorris.com, to find information on the serious effects of smoking, quitting smoking, cigarette ingredients, and talking to children about not smoking. The insert has articles, such as "Women and Smoking: A Report of the Surgeon General 2001," and "National Cancer Institute—Low-Tar Cigarettes: Evidence Does Not Indicate a Benefit to Public Health." In one of the articles, the pamphlet states: "Philip Morris U.S.A. believes that the conclusions of public health officials concerning environmental tobacco smoke, also known as secondhand smoke, are sufficient to warrant measures that regulate smoking in public spaces" (p. 13).[11] In effect, through this brochure, Philip Morris is instructing its own target market to reduce demand for its product, or to quit smoking.

Demarketing for vice products, such as cigarettes and alcohol, while especially focusing the messages on vulnerable populations, such as children, the elderly, and the poor,

Figure 1-9
Domestic Violence
This advertisement, created by French Creative Group, highlights the problems with domestic violence. The ad was sponsored by French Creative, the News-Star, TV8, Glenwood Regional Medical Center, Philip Morris Company, Inc., and the YMCA.

Source: Courtesy of French Creative Group, Monroe, LA.

demonstrates social concern on the part of the company and may diffuse public scrutiny of the sponsor's products and practices.

1-4e The History of Marketing Philosophies

The product/production concept, the selling concept, and the marketing concept can be traced historically to the **production era,** the **sales era,** and the **marketing era**—the periods when the respective philosophies were dominant. The production era, between 1870 and 1930, was characterized by firms focusing their attention on physical production and the production process. Firms attempted to fit products within their production capabilities, rather than focusing on customer needs. Output consisted of limited product lines and, because demand exceeded supply, competition was minimal. Retailers and wholesalers were only of peripheral concern because the products practically sold themselves.[12]

Production era: Period between 1870 and 1930, when the primary focus of marketing was on producing the best products possible at the lowest price.

Production efficiency led to a new phenomenon: overproduction. Companies turned to marketing professionals to sell their products during the sales era, between 1930 and 1950. The sales era was characterized by a focus on selling, based on the assumption that, if the customer were left alone, he or she would not purchase the product, or not purchase enough products. Also, supply exceeded demand. With excess supply, companies had to persuade consumers and other businesses to buy their brand instead of the competitors'.

Sales era: Period between 1930 and 1950, when the primary focus of marketing was on selling.

In the 1950s, scholars were concerned that marketers were not paying enough attention to the customers' needs and wants. Thus, the marketing concept emerged as the dominant marketing paradigm. It was then agreed that the main task of the marketing function should not be "to be skillful in making the customer do what suits the interests of the business . . . but to be skillful in conceiving and then making the business do what suits the interests of the customer."[13]

Marketing era: Period from 1950 until the present, when the primary focus of marketing shifted to the needs of consumers and society.

The marketing concept is the dominant philosophy for today's successful companies, such as Unilever, Wal-Mart (see Figure 1-10), McDonald's, and Gateway.

Figure 1-10
A major reason for Wal-Mart's success is its use of the marketing philosophy.
Source: Reprinted by permission of Wal-Mart and Bernstein-Rein Advertising, Inc.

1-4f Beyond the Marketing Philosophies: Avoiding Marketing Myopia

The danger of the product, production, and selling concepts is that they may lead to marketing myopia.[14] This term is attributed to Theodore Levitt, one of the most notable early marketing theorists, who noticed that marketers at the time (in the 1950s) were ignoring an important market—seniors. The term **marketing myopia** is defined here as the tendency of marketing efforts to focus on products, production, or sales and ignore specific consumer needs or important markets.

Marketing myopia: The tendency of marketing efforts to focus on products/production or sales and ignore specific consumer needs or important markets.

Even companies that embrace the societal marketing concept could experience marketing myopia. A case in point is the limited attention, relative to potential, that the ethnic market receives in the United States. Ethnic Americans—African Americans, Hispanic Americans, and Asian Americans—have a spending power of more than $1 trillion; the projected growth of these three ethnic population is 115.2 million by the year 2020.[15] And yet, for marketing practitioners, they primarily represent an afterthought.[16] Marketers need to redefine their target markets with a more precise focus, strengthening their advertising presence in ethnic media vehicles, such as cable channels Telemundo and Black Entertainment Television, and magazines such as *Latin, Vibe,* and *A,* in order to gain both the recognition and loyalty of these markets. Indeed, even in the general media, a full racial palette and representation is still rare: a survey of 471 magazine covers from 31 magazines published in 2002 conducted by the *New York Times* reveals that only one in five depicted nonwhites.[17]

These examples illustrate that, even if companies do focus on consumers and society, they need to follow developments in the marketplace and give due focus to traditionally overlooked consumer segments, such as the elderly and ethnic markets.

1-5 Key Elements of the Societal Marketing Concept

Marketing managers today understand that their firms can no longer afford to limit their focus on the needs of their consumers and the needs of their organizations. The marketing concept alone cannot lead to optimal firm performance in the marketplace. As corporate citizens of society and as employers, companies must meet the needs of their consumers and society, as well as those of their employees, and achieve their own organizational goals in the process.

1-5a A Market Orientation and an Integrated Marketing Approach

Today, marketing managers agree on the importance of a firm-wide focus on customer needs and on delivering high quality to consumers and other businesses in the process of achieving company objectives (i.e., on the importance of adopting a market orientation). A market orientation should be part of the company culture. The company should systematically seek marketing information at the organization level; disseminate that information to the other departments, such as finance, research and development, engineering, manufacturing, and purchasing; and ensure that the entire organization can respond to this information in a manner that best meets customers' needs.[18] A **market orientation** is defined as a company-wide culture creating the necessary behaviors for delivering superior value to buyers.[19] It is a systematic quest for and dissemination of information across departments, and subsequent organization-wide response in a manner that best addresses customers' needs and preferences. In other words, a marketing orientation calls for an integrated marketing approach.

Market orientation: A firm-wide focus on customer needs and on delivering high quality to consumers in the process of achieving company objectives.

Adopting a marketing orientation necessitates top management commitment. Without the involvement and commitment of top management, it would be difficult to create an environment where information is openly and systematically disseminated across departments, where organizational response is aimed at delivering quality goods and services to customers, thereby increasing customer satisfaction.

Chef America has followed its target consumers very closely over the decades, and has been changing with them. The company first launched the frozen stuffed sandwich in 1977. Since then, it has kept pace with all the consumer trends relevant to its business, such as the growth of grazing (eating small portions all day long, rather than the traditional three big meals); the increasing need for convenience, primarily attributed to the return of women to the workforce in the past decades; and the need for smaller portions for adult consumers and children alike.[20]

Like manufacturers, retailers also have to adapt to meet the needs of consumers and to adopt a market orientation in order to succeed. Especially today, in the Information Age, consumers want to quickly find the merchandise they need in stock and at an attractive price. To meet this need, retailers are learning more about their consumers' needs and desires by using a tactic called **data mining,** which is the systematic data analysis procedure of compiling personal, pertinent, and actionable information about the purchasing habits of current and potential consumers.[21] Through data mining, retailers hope to:

Data mining: The process of compiling personal, pertinent, actionable information about the purchasing habits of current and potential consumers.

- Increase sales from a company's existing customers, and hence solidify and increase market share
- Determine purchase habits of consumers with regard to price preferences, sale or regular prices, fashion, and size

Figure 1-11
The Ukrop's Valued Customer Card provides good deals for customers at Ukrop's Super Markets, while also delivering a wealth of information to the company.

Source: Courtesy of Ukrop's Super Markets, Inc.

- Find out who customers are, what they buy, where, and how often
- Obtain information about products, services, and marketing practices of competition[22]

Retailer credit cards or loyalty cards are widely used to find out the types of products consumers are likely to buy. For example, Ukrop's Super Markets, a very popular family-owned supermarket chain in the state of Virginia, uses its Valued Customer Card to better target promotions to area households and to more effectively address the needs of its consumers in general (see Figure 1-11). To illustrate, as Ukrop's was renovating one of its stores in Richmond, Virginia, it offered consumers in the area a coupon valid for two months for a daily small ice cream at a neighboring store. This strategy created goodwill in the community and, in the process, it ensured that consumers shopped at Ukrop's Super Markets, rather than at competitors' stores. Ukrop's did not want to lose its customers while the renovation was taking place.

1-5b A Focus on Consumer Needs and the Needs of Society

For optimal performance in the marketplace, marketers need to address consumer needs and wants more effectively than competitors. That is, they have to use a marketing strategy using the four *P*s of marketing in a manner that optimally addresses consumer needs. This requires that a company:

- Offers the goods or services that best satisfy consumer needs
- Offers a price the consumer perceives as fair in return for the value received
- Makes the product available at retailers that are conveniently located close to the consumer
- Promotes its marketing efforts through vehicles that effectively reach the target consumer

For example, Gap is very successful in its marketing campaign. The company has undertaken substantial research of its target market, younger consumers, and provides fashions that appeal to them, being careful to follow the trends that are popular with this market. Gap combines a relaxed shopping environment with bold brand expressions, which enhances sales associates' ability to provide outstanding service. Its goal is to make every customer's experience the best of any retailer.[23] Gap advertises using lively, bold ads in fashion magazines and on television at prime time. Gap stores are conveniently located in regional malls, within easy access of target consumers. And Gap brand prices are in line with consumers' ability to pay—for example, about $30 for a sweater, $50 for a pair of jeans. The Gap website (www.gap.com) also serves as a venue for promoting Gap to consumers, as well as a retail venue that offers convenience at a fair price. For orders over $100, Gap offers free shipping.

Gap also communicates with its consumers through its social marketing endeavors. Its donations focus on the Boys & Girls Clubs of America and the Lorraine Monroe Leadership Institute, which aims to help students to develop self-esteem, stay in school, and succeed academically so that they can lead rewarding and fulfilling lives. Gap emphasizes the importance of a code of conduct that it requires of its vendors and other distributors, such as compliance with local labor laws, working conditions, and the environment; expectations regarding wages, child labor, safety, and respect of the right of workers to unionize. Finally, it communicates to employees the importance of reducing waste in its packaging materials, and of recycling and purchasing products that contain high percentages of recycled material.[24]

Value-based philosophy: A philosophy that focuses on customers, ensuring that their needs are addressed in a manner that delivers a product of high quality and value, leading to consumer satisfaction.

1-5c A Value-Based Philosophy

A value-based philosophy is essential to organizational success. Companies with a **value-based philosophy** ensure that their consumers' needs are addressed in a manner that delivers a good or service of high quality and value that ultimately leads to consumer satisfaction, and it does so while also enhancing consumers' and society's quality of life. In fact, successful companies that adopt a value-based philosophy are also likely to invest in society, primarily for altruistic reasons that benefit society, not the company—even if, ultimately, there is an expectation of commercial return.[25]

Product quality and value, as well as consumer satisfaction, are interrelated. One measure that addresses both quality and consumer satisfaction is the American Consumer Satisfaction Index, a national economic indicator of the quality of goods and services from companies producing about one-third of the national GDP. The following are the dimensions related to consumer satisfaction,[26] and they will be further addressed in Section 9-5a, "Measuring Service Quality," which discusses the gap theory related to the discrepancy between expectations and performance:

- **Customer expectations** occur when consumers anticipate product performance based on their experiences, on information received from the media, and on information from other consumers. Expectations influence the evaluation of good or service quality and predict how the good or service will perform on the market.
- *Quality* refers to overall product quality, reliability, and the extent to which it meets consumers' needs. Perceived quality has the greatest impact on satisfaction (see Figure 1-12).
- *Value* refers to the overall price given the quality of the product; perceived value is important in the purchase decision.
- **Consumer complaints** are measured as the percentage of consumers that report a problem with a good or service; complaints are related to dissatisfaction.
- **Consumer retention** refers to the likelihood to purchase the product in the future.

Customer expectations: Anticipated good or service performance based on consumers' experiences, on information received from the media, and from other consumers.

Consumer complaints: The registering of a problem with a good or service.

Consumer retention: The ability to retain consumers as customers in the future.

The index over time has demonstrated that companies rating highly are more profitable and have greater shareholder value. These companies are in a better position to reach their organizational goals, as is addressed in the next section.

Goods manufacturers, service providers, retailers, and wholesalers frequently conduct consumer satisfaction surveys to assess their own performance. Historically, consumer satisfaction has been defined as a match between consumer expectations and good or service performance:

- If a product or service performs better than expected, then consumers are likely to be satisfied with it. If satisfied, consumers are likely to purchase the good or service in the future.

Figure 1-12
This advertisement by Haik Humble Eye Center highlights the importance of quality in terms of using the "most advanced eye surgery" techniques.

Source: Sartor Associates, Inc. for Haik Humble Eye Center.

- If performance matches expectations, consumers are somewhat satisfied (psychologists refer to this as "satisficing"—meaning that the consumer is satisfied but would switch to another good or service without much persuasion).
- If expectations are greater than performance, then consumers are likely to be dissatisfied with the good or service and may never purchase the product again. These consumers are expected to engage in negative word-of-mouth communications about the good or service as well as firm switching behavior.

To understand these concepts, take the test in Table 1-2 to evaluate your recent experience with a retail website. Were you satisfied?

1-5d An Organizational Goal Orientation

The ultimate organizational goal is creating profit for the company and wealth for its shareholders. In that sense, increasing productivity and production volume, maximizing consumption, and as a result, increasing sales constitute primary objectives for the company, which can be accomplished with the appropriate marketing strategies. In the process of achieving organizational goals, companies offer quality and value to consumers and businesses, leading to a higher level of consumer satisfaction. They compete to offer a wide variety of goods and services and a maximum of choices for consumers. As they compete, they lower prices that consumers pay for their products in order to gain market share. Ultimately, the marketing system creates a higher standard of living for consumers, while improving their quality of life.

1-5e The Next Level of Marketing: Integrating Societal Marketing Practices Through Customer Relationship Management (CRM)

Customer relationship management (CRM): A database application program designed to build long-term loyalty with customers through the use of a personal touch.

Societal marketing practices are formally integrated into a process known as customer **relationship management** (CRM). Customer relationship management is defined as a database application program designed to build long-term loyalty with customers through the use of a personal touch. Its eight building blocks are vision, strategy, customer experience, organizational collaboration, CRM processes, CRM information, CRM technology, and CRM metrics.[27]

As a direct outgrowth of the marketing concept, customer relationship management[28]:

- Incorporates an organizational focus on the behavior of, and communication with, the customer
- Uses technology for mining data related to customer preferences and behaviors; that is, the company codes/grades customers based on these data
- Shares the collected data across the entire enterprise
- Uses the technology to design business processes that enhance efficiency and effectiveness
- Boosts customer satisfaction by providing consistent, seamless, quality experiences

The customer database is particularly valuable. It provides a unified customer view across the enterprise, tying together all the interaction between the company and a particular customer. For example, the call center can find out about web transactions or direct mail pieces sent to a particular customer, and the customer thus does not have to repeat or reenter information to engage in a new transaction.

CRM allows for multichannel marketing so that customers can deal with the firm when they want to. In a retailing example, the customer can go to the store during store hours to purchase a product, he or she can go to the website, or he or she can order the product by phone. Ultimately, CRM leads to more efficient customer targeting and retention, improving cost management and increasing profitability and thus shareholder equity.

TABLE 1-2 Website Satisfaction Self-Test

How would you rate the retailer website you have used most recently? Take the following test. Indicate the extent to which you agree or disagree with the following statements by circling one of the following numbers:

5= you strongly agree 4= you agree 3 = you neither agree nor disagree
2= you disagree 1= you strongly disagree

Please answer EVERY question.

Expectations **Excellent retailer websites:**		**Performance** **The most recent website you visited:**	
Have an attractive design and other visuals.	5 4 3 2 1	Has an attractive design and other visuals.	5 4 3 2 1
Have little clutter.	5 4 3 2 1	Has little clutter.	5 4 3 2 1
Have few or no banners.	5 4 3 2 1	Has few or no banners.	5 4 3 2 1
Are easy to navigate and allow rapid access to the different pages and links.	5 4 3 2 1	Is easy to navigate and allows rapid access to the different pages and links.	5 4 3 2 1
Are easy to access day or night.	5 4 3 2 1	Is easy to access day or night.	5 4 3 2 1
Require customers to fill in only a minimum of necessary information.	5 4 3 2 1	Requires customers to fill in only a minimum of necessary information.	5 4 3 2 1
Allow customers to reach a customer service center at all times.	5 4 3 2 1	Allows customers to reach a customer service center at all times.	5 4 3 2 1
Have a customer service center that is always willing to help clients.	5 4 3 2 1	Has a customer service center that is always willing to help clients.	5 4 3 2 1
Have a customer service center that will promptly respond to customer inquiries.	5 4 3 2 1	Has a customer service center that will promptly respond to customer inquiries.	5 4 3 2 1
Have a customer service center that is consistently courteous.	5 4 3 2 1	Has a customer service center that is consistently courteous.	5 4 3 2 1
Have a knowledgeable customer service center that can address client questions.	5 4 3 2 1	Has a knowledgeable customer service center that can address client questions.	5 4 3 2 1
Let consumers know exactly when they will receive their products.	5 4 3 2 1	Lets consumers know exactly when they will receive their products.	5 4 3 2 1
Deliver their products when they promise to do so.	5 4 3 2 1	Delivers their products when it promises to do so.	5 4 3 2 1
Deliver the quality products that are accurately described on the website.	5 4 3 2 1	Delivers the quality products that are accurately described on the website.	5 4 3 2 1
Sell products at a fair price.	5 4 3 2 1	Sells products at a fair price.	5 4 3 2 1
Allow you to compare prices with other sites.	5 4 3 2 1	Allows you to compare prices with other sites.	5 4 3 2 1
Show a sincere interest in solving customers' problems.	5 4 3 2 1	Shows a sincere interest in solving customers' problems.	5 4 3 2 1
Protect customers' personal information.	5 4 3 2 1	Protects customers' personal information.	5 4 3 2 1
Offer safe transactions.	5 4 3 2 1	Offers safe transactions.	5 4 3 2 1
Offer customers personal attention when needed.	5 4 3 2 1	Offers customers personal attention when needed.	5 4 3 2 1
Have the customers' interests at heart.	5 4 3 2 1	Has the customers' interests at heart.	5 4 3 2 1
Tailor their offering based on customer preferences and/or purchase history.	5 4 3 2 1	Tailors their offering based on customer preferences and/or purchase history.	5 4 3 2 1
Add the circled numbers in the expectations column:	______	Add the circled numbers in the expectations column:	______

Subtract the expectations score from the performance score. If the number is positive, you are satisfied with the website and will continue to use it. If the number is zero, you are sort of satisfied (psychologists refer to this as "satisficing"—meaning that you are satisfied but could switch to another site without extensive persuasion). If the number is negative, expectations are greater than performance; you are somewhat dissatisfied with the website and may not use it again.

Source: Adapted from Dana-Nicoleta Lascu, "Development of an Ethic Measure of Interactivity." Presented at the 2004 Marketing Science Conference, Rotterdam, the Netherlands (July 2004).

However, the Gartner Group, which specializes in CRM applications, predicts that most companies will use CRM to increase revenue or customer loyalty, rather than use them to save money.[29]

For customer relationship management to be profitable, companies must retain their customers for long periods. At the heart of customer relationship management is the concept of **customer lifetime value** (LTV), defined as the estimated profitability of the customer over the course of his or her entire relationship with a company. Companies that understand customer value have been shown to be 60 percent more profitable than those that do not.[30]

Customer lifetime value: The estimated profitability of the customer over the course of his or her entire relationship with a company.

Customer relationship management has proven itself as a key ingredient in the value creation strategy. Yet, even though CRM technologies have matured in the past decade, their implementation failure rates are high, ranging from 55 to 75 percent.[31] Some of the reasons behind their failure are: implementing CRM before creating an adequate customer-focused strategy or before making the appropriate organizational transformation, assuming that more CRM technology is better, rather than focusing on the appropriate technology, and stalking, rather than wooing customers.[32]

The keys to CRM success are:[33]

- Getting executive buy-in
- Determining why and where CRM is needed
- Defining objectives
- Setting measurable goals
- Taking an incremental approach
- Building and training the right teams
- Managing and selling change internally
- Having an outside marketing specialist monitor the program
- Developing effective feedback mechanisms
- And conducting ongoing systematic customer research

Summary

1. *Address the central role of marketing in the twenty-first century.* Marketing constitutes an ever-growing, important driving force of today's modern society. In the United States alone, there are more than 275 million consumers living in 100 million households, spending $5 trillion on products and services or two-thirds of the national gross domestic product. A significant portion of all Americans are employed entirely or in part in assisting the marketing system to perform its functions. Thus, the broad marketing system is integral to a society's economic system, offering employment and income for millions working in the marketing field, enabling them to be productive and earn money needed for consumption, and leading to an improved national infrastructure in such areas as transportation, telecommunication, medical care, and finance. Companies engaged in marketing pay taxes that further fund public programs. The system's mass-market efficiencies allow for lower costs, lower prices, and increased overall consumer access, fostering innovation that ultimately benefits consumption. Marketing enhances economic development, buyers' well-being, and general quality of life.

2. *Define marketing and identify its key concepts.* Marketing is defined as the process of planning and executing the conception, pricing, promotion, and distribution of ideas, goods, and services to create exchanges that satisfy individual and organizational objectives. Important concepts in marketing are needs (basic human requirements), wants (directed to a particular product), and demands (wants backed by the ability to buy the respective product or service brand). The four *P*s of marketing are products (goods, services, ideas, and experiences), price, place (distribution), and promotion. At each level of distribution between the manufacturer, wholesaler, retailer, and consumer, an exchange takes place: A desired good or service is obtained in exchange for something else. Exchanges involve at least two parties that mutually agree on the desirability of the exchange.

3. *Address the different marketing philosophies and explain them in view of the historical development of marketing.* The different philosophies are the production concept, which assumes that consumers prefer products that are easily accessible and inexpensive; the product concept, which assumes that consumers prefer products that are of the highest quality and optimal performance; the selling concept, which assumes that consumers left alone will not buy, or not buy enough (they need to be aggressively sold in order to purchase); the marketing concept, which focuses on consumers' needs and works to create a good/service that matches those needs; and the societal marketing concept, a philosophy that applies the marketing concept in a manner that maximizes society's well-being. Historically, the product/production concept can be traced back to the product era

(1870–1930), when the focus was on products and production; the selling concept to the sales era (1930–1950), when the focus was on selling overproduction to consumers; and the marketing concept to the marketing era (1950–present), when the focus shifted to the needs of the consumer and, later, to the needs of society.

4. *Discuss the key elements of the societal marketing concept and the importance of these elements in meeting the needs of consumers, society, and the organization.* The first key element is a market orientation and an integrated marketing approach, which is a firm-wide focus on customer needs and on delivering high-quality products to consumers. The second key concept is the achievement of company objectives. The third key element is the dissemination of marketing information across departments using an integrated marketing approach. The fourth key element is a focus on consumer and societal needs. The fifth key element is a value-based philosophy that puts value, quality, and consumer satisfaction first. This is accomplished through the last key, which is an organizational goal orientation that creates profit and shareholder wealth, while offering goods or services that are desirable, competitively priced, and delivered within easy consumer access.

Key Terms

consumer complaints (p. 19)
consumer retention (p. 19)
customer expectations (p. 19)
customer lifetime value (p. 22)
customer relationship management (CRM) (p. 20)
data mining (p. 17)
demands (p. 5)
demarketing (p. 14)
exchanges and transactions (p. 7)
experiences (p. 7)
goods (p. 7)
gross domestic product (GDP) (p. 4)
ideas (p. 7)
marketing (p. 5)
marketing concept (p. 12)
marketing era (p. 15)
marketing myopia (p. 16)
market orientation (p. 17)
markets (p. 5)
needs (p. 5)
product concept (p. 8)
production concept (p. 8)
production era (p. 15)
quality (p. 6)
relationship marketing (p. 8)
sales era (p. 15)
satisfaction (p. 6)
selling concept (p. 11)
services (p. 7)
societal marketing concept (p. 12)
value (p. 6)
value-based philosophy (p. 18)
wants (p. 5)

Discussion Questions

1. You take an aspirin and you feel better. You take Claritin, an allergy medicine, and you have fewer allergy symptoms. When you purchase these drugs, do you buy the products or the reaction to the products? In that sense, are they goods, services, ideas, or experiences?
2. Are the aspirin and the Claritin in the previous question wants? Demands? What need do they address?
3. Explain the process of exchange that takes place at different levels of distribution from the manufacturer to the final consumer.
4. What marketing philosophy is likely to be embraced in general by the manufacturer of Claritin, the allergy medicine mentioned in question 1? Explain. Now that Claritin's patent has expired and the brand is available over-the-counter, along with countless generic copies, how should the company philosophy change?
5. As described in the chapter, Philip Morris, the manufacturer of Marlboro and the creator of the legendary Marlboro Man, is attempting to reach consumers with pamphlets of information on the dangers of smoking. Does Philip Morris subscribe to the social marketing concept? Explain.
6. Develop an exercise that helps you calculate your degree of satisfaction with a prime-time television program. Use the website satisfaction survey in Section 1-5c as a model.

Review Questions

True or False

1. Marketing is a process of exchange at different levels.
2. The production concept assumes that consumers prefer products of the highest quality and performance.
3. The societal marketing concept assumes that the company will have an advantage over competitors if it is applied in a manner that maximizes society's well-being.
4. The selling concept assumes that, if consumers are left alone, they will normally purchase the product.
5. Overall product quality is a set of norms used by the manufacturer to meet the production specification.
6. The marketing concept emerged in the 1950s as a dominant marketing paradigm.
7. Either product or production orientation constitute the best approaches to satisfying consumers.
8. The selling concept is superior to the marketing concept.
9. A market orientation is defined as a company-wide culture creating the necessary behaviors for delivering superior value to buyers.
10. Companies that adopt a value-based philosophy offer high-priced products.

Multiple Choice

11. Which of the following refers to demands?
  a. basic human requirements
  b. needs directed at a particular product
  c. wants backed by customer ability to buy a product
  d. obtaining a product in exchange for something else

12. A haircut is an example of a(n):
  a. good.
  b. service.
  c. idea.
  d. none of the above

13. Demarketing is defined as a
  a. decline in retail distribution.
  b. reduction in demand for the company's own product for the well-being of society.
  c. a process of changing advertisements in the media.
  d. none of the above

14. The production era corresponds to
  a. 1850–1870.
  b. 1870–1930.
  c. 1930–1950.
  d. 1950–present.

15. Companies provide products of value. Value is defined as
  a. a low price guarantee.
  b. product quality at moderate price.
  c. an expensive product that conveys prestige.
  d. a product's overall price given its quality.

16. The marketing mix consists of the following four main components:
  a. product, people, place, price
  b. product, perception, price, place
  c. product, price, place, promotion
  d. prosperity, product, potential, price

17. Marketing myopia is defined as
  a. considering an important market segment.
  b. selling a new brand product within a short period.
  c. a marketing philosophy that is rooted in price and promotion.
  d. a tendency of marketing efforts to focus on product, production, and sales.

18. Components of consumer satisfaction are
  a. customer expectations and product quality.
  b. value and consumer retention.
  c. consumer complaints.
  d. all of the above

19. To gain a competitive advantage in the marketplace, the company should
  a. offer products that satisfy consumers at a perceived fair price.
  b. make products available to consumers.
  c. use effective promotion to reach a target consumer.
  d. all of the above

20. The ultimate organizational goal is
  a. providing high-quality products at low prices.
  b. creating profit for the company and wealth for its shareholders.
  c. offering products that consumers deem as satisfactory.
  d. increasing marketing efforts.

Notes

1. Louise Driben, Bill Kelley, Richard Szathmary, Betsy Wisendanger, and Kerry Rottenberger, "Sales & Marketing Management's Marketing Achievement Awards," *Sales and Marketing Management*, vol. 144, no. 9 (August 1992): 40–41.
2. William L. Wilkie and Elizabeth S. Moore, "Marketing's Contribution to Society," *Journal of Marketing*, vol. 63, no.1 (1999): 198–218.
3. Ibid.
4. Ibid.
5. Ibid.
6. Ibid.
7. Peter Drucker, "Marketing and Economic Development," *Journal of Marketing*, vol. 22, no. 1 (July 1957–April 1958): 252–259.
8. Ibid.
9. Lisa M. Kiefe, "What Is the Meaning of Marketing?" *Marketing News* (September 15, 2004): 17–18.
10. Steve Hoeffler and Kevin Lane Keller, "Building Brand Equity Through Corporate Societal Marketing," *Journal of Public Policy & Marketing*, vol. 21, no. 1 (Spring 2002): 78–89.
11. "Where Can You Find Information On …?" Philip Morris Newspaper Insert (November 2002).
12. Robert A. Fullerton, "How Modern Is Modern Marketing?" vol. 52, no. 1 (January 1988): 108–126.
13. J. B. McKitterick, "What Is the Marketing Management Concept?" in *Frontiers of Marketing Thought and Action*, ed. F. Bass, (Chicago: American Marketing Association, 1957): 71–82.
14. Term coined by Theodore Levitt, "Marketing Myopia," *Harvard Business Review* (July–August 1960): 45–56.
15. Cultural Access Group, *U.S. Ethnic Markets*, (http://www.accesscag.com/hispanic.htm, April 20, 2005).
16. "Media Matters," *Adweek*, vol. 42, no. 9 (February 26, 2001): 44–50.
17. David Carr, "On Covers of Many Magazines, A Full Racial Palette Is Still Rare," *New York Times* (November 18, 2002): C1, C5.
18. Ajay K. Kohli and Bernard J. Jaworski, "Market Orientation: The Construct, Research Propositions, and Managerial Implications," *Journal of Marketing*, vol. 54 (April 1990): 1–18.
19. J. C. Narver and S. F. Slater, "The Effect of a Market Orientation on Business Profitability," *Journal of Marketing*, 54 (October 1990): 20–35.
20. Howard Riell, "A Hot Hand," *Frozen Food Age*, vol. 50, no. 3 (October 2001): 52–54.
21. Tom Hicks, "Data Mining Offers Mother Lode of Information," *Sporting Goods Business*, vol. 33, no. 13 (August 23, 2000): 16–17.
22. Ibid.
23. See www.gap.com.
24. Ibid.
25. Marylyn Collins, "Global Corporate Philanthropy: Marketing Beyond the Call of Duty?" *European Journal of Marketing*, vol. 27, no. 2 (1993): 46–55.
26. Adapted from www.theacsi.org.
27. Sudhir H. Khale, "CRM in Gaming: It's No Crapshoot!" *UNLV Gaming Research & Review Journal*, vol. 7, no. 2 (2003): 43–54.
28. Ibid.
29. Ed Thompson and Michael Maoz, "Grow Revenue Again," Gartner Research (January 7, 2005) www.gartner.com.
30. Khale, "CRM in Gaming: It's No Crapshoot!"
31. Joseph O. Chan, "Toward a Unified View of Customer Relationship Management," *Journal of the American Academy of Business*, vol. 6, no. 1 (March 2005): 32–38.
32. Khale, "CRM in Gaming: It's No Crapshoot!"
33. Ibid.

Case 1-1: Madonna and Corporate Endorsers: Has Madonna Finally Adopted the Marketing Concept?

Madonna Louise Ciccone, raised in an Italian-American Catholic family and brought up by her father, a car welder who raised six children on his own, is the epitome of marketing success. While her fans found her leap from music to movies too complex, and her critics have cringed at many of her reinventions, Madonna reigns in the rankings—"Die Another Day" was Madonna's 35th top-10 hit (she surpassed the Beatles and is second only to Elvis in top-10 rankings)—and in the hearts of her fans. She has more fan websites than most other contemporary performers: Madonnarama, Madonnapower, Little Star, Madonna Internet, Madonna Lyrics Archive, Madonna Song Index, MadonnaShots, Madonna-online.ch, Madonna Electronica, MadonnaWeb, Madonna Rio, Xtreme Madonna Greeting Cards, and Madonna Photogenic, just to mention a few. For more than two decades, Madonna has kept her eyes on the ball—her market of younger consumers and their continuously changing interests—transforming herself successfully and sequentially into a virgin, Marilyn Monroe, material girl, boy toy, dominatrix, media maven, and working mom. And she has achieved her organizational goals at every step of the way, as shown by her movies and record sales of her CDs, as well as her lucrative product endorsements.

Although her music and some of her movies have had great success, her endorsements have been more problematic, due to her daring reincarnations. Her critics berate her for her blatant use and abuse of Christian symbols, her constant exhibitionism, and her frequent graphic depictions of extreme sexual permissiveness. Scandalous headlines in the late 1980s led to a failed relationship with Pepsi—and ever since, Pepsi has been very careful when selecting celebrity endorsers. Madonna signed on to promote Pepsi just before releasing her video, "Like a Prayer," considered blasphemous by religious viewers. Under fire from the Christian advocacy group American Family Association and Fundamentalists Anonymous, Pepsi-Cola Co. had to discontinue its association with the rock singer. Complaints launched against her by conservative groups focus on her video "Like a Prayer"; on her "Blond Ambition" tour, which was opposed by the Vatican; and on her "Justify My Love" video, which was so offensive that the BBC and MTV banned it. She was also criticized for her 1992 book *Sex,* launched just in time for Christmas purchases and containing graphic depictions of degrading sexual practices.

The merchants cried out for *Evita.* Before the movie's release, Walt Disney Co., Bloomingdale's, and fashion designers and cosmetics companies cashed in substantially on the Broadway musical's adaptation, in which Madonna played the lead role. Bloomingdale's created whole "Evita" shops in nine of its stores, carrying Evita jewelry, cosmetics, tango dresses, and 1940s-inspired inaugural gowns; Estee Lauder released a line of 25 Evita cosmetics, and Salvatore Ferragamo, Victor Costa, Nicole Miller, and other designers developed Evita-inspired clothing.

In other partnerships, Madonna starred in a campaign to promote Procter & Gamble's new Max Factor Gold cosmetics line, cementing the brand's position as the technically sound make-up of make-up artists. The advertising campaign, created by Leo Burnett, was launched only in the European and Asian markets, primarily because P&G has no plans to launch the Gold line in the United States in the near future—its strategy was to strengthen its hold on mass-market color cosmetics, battling Unilever and L'Oreal in these markets. Consultants believe that Madonna is a good fit for Max Factor, as she appeals to younger consumers as a pop singer, but also to older consumers as a mother. Of all current celebrity endorsers, she comes closest to an old-style Hollywood star, and would be good for P&G, provided she behaves. Her behavior has improved, and her RE-INVENTION tour of 2004 was a big money maker, grossing $125 million, with 55 of the 56 shows being sellouts.

Questions

1. What needs does Madonna address with the entertainment she offers? How do those needs translate into wants and demands?
2. Is Madonna using the marketing concept?
3. Focus on the key elements of the marketing concept—a market orientation and an integrated marketing approach, a focus on consumer needs, a value-based philosophy, and an organizational goal orientation. Describe Madonna's approach to each element. Does she also focus on societal needs?
4. Could Madonna be guilty of marketing myopia by ignoring more conservative and religious potential fans? Explain.
5. What risks does Procter & Gamble take using Madonna as a spokesperson for its Max Factor Gold cosmetic line?

Sources: www.madonna.com; Madonna Digest, at www.eecs.harvard.edu; Sean D'Souza, "Like a Virgin: Is Your Marketing as Fresh as Madonna's?" www.marketing-profs.com; Richard Yao, "The Other Cola War: A Tale of Two Boycotts," *Business and Society Review,* no. 72 (Winter 1990): 44–47; www.facingthechallenge.org; *The Washington Post,* "The Merchants Cry for 'Evita,'" (November 3, 1996): 1; Alexandra Jardine, "Max Factor Strikes Gold with Madonna Link," *Marketing* (April 29, 1999): 14; Shanda Deziel, "Year in Review/More Tube, Less Boob," *Maclean's,* vol. 117/118, no. 52/1 (December 27, 2004): 99.

Case 1-2: Kraft Foods: Changing the Focus from Yummy to Healthy

It is hard to be the manufacturer of yummy food nowadays, and Kraft knows that only too well: Its Oreo and Nila cookies, its Tobler chocolate, and its Oscar Mayer hot dogs have been washed down with Kool-Aid to create a very profitable bottom line for the company. Kraft further bet on the cookie business in 2000 with its $15 billion acquisition of Nabisco. However, a few years later, the nation's largest food manufacturer is cutting back on its indulgence food. Its Oreos in particular have become the bad poster child for trans fats and Atkins and South Beach diet devotees, and growing obesity and the popularity of low-carbohydrate diets have severely eaten into the company's profits.

As a reaction to the falling profits, the company cut 6,000 jobs and closed 20 plants in 2004 in an effort to reduce operating costs and placed the savings into marketing. In addition, Kraft decided to change its marketing strategy, to focus on social responsibility as its main theme. Kraft Chief Executive Officer, Roger Deromedi, admitted that the company has been hurt lately, particularly in four businesses: cereal, cookies, frozen pizza, and candy. He hosted analysts and reporters for a day-long presentation at the company's headquarters north of Chicago to inform them about changes in its offerings: healthier, better-for-you food choices. In a radical move toward socially responsible marketing, the company decided to help fight obesity around the world by instituting limits on portion sizes, offering nutritional guidelines for its products, and ending all in-school marketing efforts aimed at boosting consumption.

Today, social responsibility efforts at Kraft go beyond its partnership with Save the Children USA: Kraft boasts a broad Sensible Solution program as part of a strategy to improve its customers' health. Sensible Solution is a labeling program to help consumers easily identify better-for-you choices from the company's product mix. The company has formed a global council of advisers to develop policies, standards, measures, and timetables to address the obesity issue. The council boasts experts, mostly academic, in obesity, nutrition, physical activity, behavior, lifestyle education, and intervention programs. The council developed standards in line with the 2005 U.S. Dietary Guidelines, authoritative statements from the U.S. Food and Drug Administration, National Academy of Sciences, and other public health authorities. Kraft then labeled its food with Sensible Solution flags.

To qualify for bearing a flag, the product must provide beneficial nutrients such as protein, calcium, or fiber/whole grain at nutritionally meaningful levels, or deliver a functional benefit, such as hearth health or hydration. At the same time, it must meet specific limits in terms of calories, fat, sodium, and sugar. Alternatively, the product must meet specifications for *reduced, low,* or *free* in calories, fat, saturated fat, sugar, or sodium. Among the products bearing the flag are Crystal Light ready-to-drink beverages, Kraft 2% Milk Mild Cheddar Reduced Fat cheese shreds, Minute Rice Instant whole grain brown rice, Post Shredded Wheat cereal, and Triscuit Original baked whole grain wheat crackers.

In other efforts to be socially responsible, Kraft had already reduced the fat content in 200 of its products. In its current health drive, it has stocked shelves with new snacks that cater to diet-conscious consumers pursuing a healthy lifestyle. Among Kraft's new offerings are 100-calorie packages of Chips Ahoy, Cheese Nips, and Wheat Thins Minis. The company also introduced its CarbWell line of cereals, salad dressing, and barbecue and steak sauce.

The company also reformulated products to meet the U.S. Food and Drug Administration standard of zero grams of trans fat per serving. Among the products that have been reformulated are reduced fat Oreo cookies, Golden Oreo cookies, Triscuit crackers, Back to Nature organic and natural products, and the Boca line of meat alternatives.

Questions

1. Kraft eliminated a number of jobs and closed its plants, thus cutting costs and improving the stockholders' bottom line. It also used some of its profits to enhance its marketing communications. Is Kraft endorsing the societal marketing concept?
2. How is Kraft demonstrating social responsibility in its new health-oriented strategy? Or is the company simply jumping on the current health fad?
3. Will the current new-health focus bring long-term success for Kraft? Justify your response.
4. Suggest how Kraft could incorporate the concepts of consumer relationship management (CRM) in its new health drive.

Sources: "Diets Force Kraft to Change Marketing Approach" *Marketing News* (September 15, 2004): 37; www.kraft.com; "Kraft Launches Initiatives to Fight Obesity," *Nation's Restaurant News,* vol. 37, no. 28 (July 14, 2003): 46.

The Environment of Marketing in the Twenty-First Century

2

CHAPTER OBJECTIVES

1. Provide an overview of the marketing microenvironment and all of its components.
2. Provide an overview of the socio-demographic and cultural environment components of the macroenvironment and related trends.
3. Address the economic and natural environment components of the macroenvironment and the topic of economic development.
4. Examine changes in the technological environment component of the macroenvironment.
5. Address the political environment component of the macroenvironment and discuss indicators of political risk and company approaches to political risk management.

CHAPTER OUTLINE

Through savvy marketing, author Francine Pascal netted $15 million from the *Sweet Valley* book series. Aimed at young adolescents, this 400-book series is set in a fictional California suburb. Pascal was successful because she understood her readers, what they wanted to read, and how to reach them. But despite the 250 million copies in print, the popularity of the *Sweet Valley* series began to wane. The readers of Pascal's books were getting older, and their interests changed. Pascal understood that she also needed to change her approach, so she has moved to a new series, titled *Fearless*. The heroine of this series, Gaia Moore, is a brooding, daredevil teenager who lives in New York. She is the daughter of an undercover CIA antiterrorist agent and a Russian mother who was murdered. This new series resonates well with a slightly older target market (see Figure 2-1).[1]

Pascal's success illustrates the importance of marketing and the need to understand both the microenvironment as well as the macroenvironment, and to follow changes as they occur in each. The microenvironment consists of the company, its consumers (target market), its suppliers and distributors, and the competition. The macroenvironment operates at a more distant level but still has a substantial impact on the success of a business organization. The macroenvironment consists of the socio-demographic and cultural environment, the economic and natural environment, the political environment, and the technological forces that affect a company or organization.

Microenvironment: Environment of the firm, which includes the company, its consumers, suppliers, distributors, and other facilitators of the marketing function and competition.

Macroenvironment: Environment of the firm, which includes the socio-demographic and cultural environment, the economic and natural environment, the political environment, and the technological environment.

2-1 Chapter Overview

Marketing managers need to constantly monitor the environment, evaluating strengths and weaknesses related to the company, consumers, suppliers, middlemen, and other facilitators of marketing functions and to the competition (i.e., the **microenvironment**). For the **macroenvironment,** marketing managers need to examine threats and opportunities in the socio-demographic and cultural environment, the economic and natural environment, the technological environment, and the political and legal environment. Section 2-2 addresses each of the elements in the microenvironment: consumers, suppliers, middlemen and other facilitators of marketing functions, and competition.

Section 2-3 addresses the macroenvironment components. The socio-demographic and cultural environment, discussed in Section 2-3a, focuses on important demographic changes among key demographic market segments and on cultural change. The economic and natural environment, discussed in Section 2-4, focuses on the phenomenon of inter-

Figure 2-1
Young women are avid readers. Marketers who know what young women enjoy reading are able to reach them effectively.

dependence in the world economy, on economic development, and on the impact of the economy on the consumer. The technological environment, discussed in Section 2-5, focuses on the fast pace of technological change and the impact of technology on competition and consumers. The political environment, discussed in Section 2-6, addresses the risks related to economic performance, government economic policy, labor and political action groups, and terrorism. The legal environment, which is a component of the macroenvironment, is addressed in Chapter 3, "Marketing Ethics, Regulations, and Social Responsibility."

2-2 The Microenvironment

A major function of marketing is to develop a company's customer base. Potential customers must be identified, targeted with appropriate marketing strategies, and persuaded to purchase a company's goods or services. While this task may appear to be rather simple, it becomes daunting when the company's microenvironment is considered. Strengths and weaknesses of internal company dynamics, current and potential customers, suppliers, and competing firms can influence how successfully the marketing function is performed. It is the responsibility of the marketing department to manage these various components of the microenvironment, addressing their weaknesses and focusing on their strengths in a manner that is congruent with the company's marketing and organizational goals.

2-2a The Company

Within the company itself, the marketing manager or marketing department will be involved in three arenas: battling for limited resources, seeking a voice in company strategies, and developing a marketing mindset. To succeed, the marketing manager must successfully interact with the various departmental representatives in the company to ensure the marketing function is appropriately stressed and promoted.

First is the battle for limited resources. Every department within a firm is seeking resources to carry out its role within the company. Most departments feel they do not have enough money or people to accomplish the work assigned to them. Most marketing departments reflect the same sentiment. Seldom are there enough funds to satisfy everyone. On the average, most firms spend around 10 percent of their sales revenue on the marketing function. Figure 2-2 provides an idea of how the marketing budget relates to a firm's overall revenue.[2]

The second internal factor affecting the marketing function is gaining a share of the voice in developing corporate strategies. Because marketing strategies are derived from

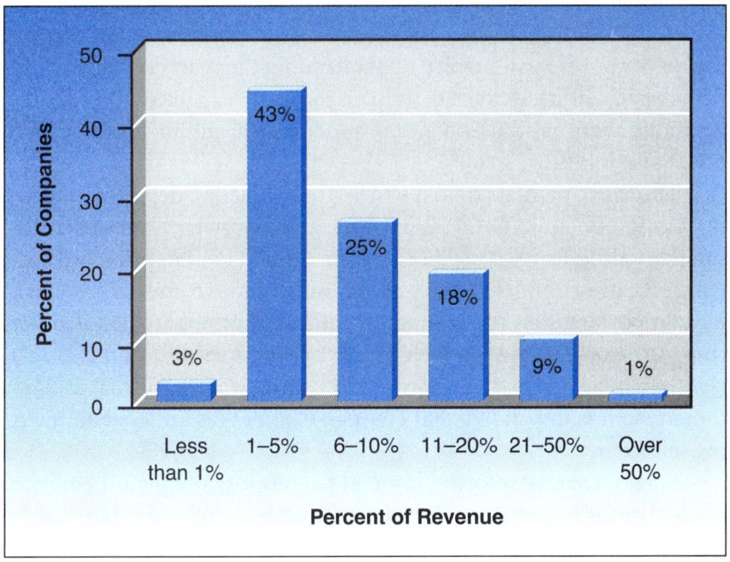

Figure 2-2
Marketing Budget as a Percentage of a Company's Revenue

Source: Susan Greco, "How to Benchmark Sales-and-Marketing Budgets," *Inc.*, 21 (2) (February 1999): 1c.

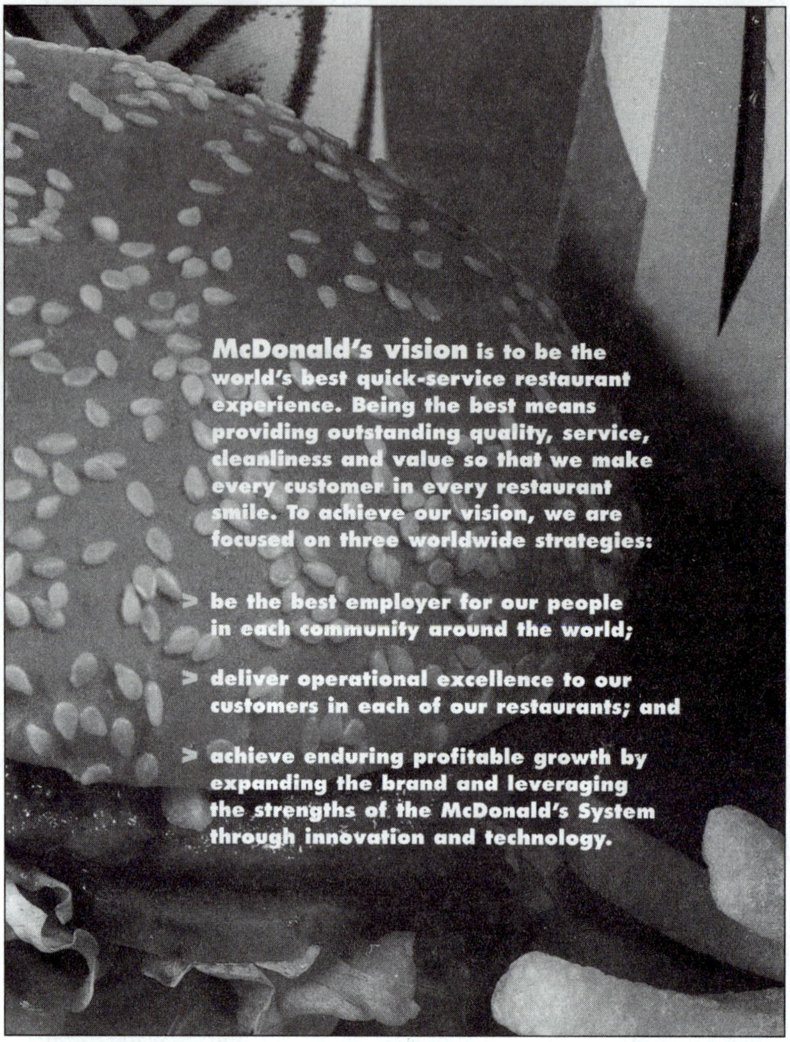

Figure 2-3
This advertisement by McDonald's stresses the corporate vision of being the world's best quick-service restaurant and of its employees delivering operational excellence.

Source: Used with permission from McDonald's Corporation.

corporate goals and objectives, it is important that the marketing department be involved in developing corporate strategies—even in the development of the company's mission statement. By having a voice at the corporate level, marketing managers can ensure that top-level executives understand the marketing function and the importance of marketing in developing plans for the corporation. For example, a decision to expand into another region or country will involve understanding the market potential and the capability of the firm to gain sufficient market share to make the expansion profitable. Marketing influences decisions about production and product modifications based on understanding customer needs and wants.

The third internal company force the marketing department has to address is developing a marketing mindset. It is important for every employee in the organization to understand who the firm's customers are and what is being promised to them (see Figure 2-3, which illustrates a McDonald's ad focusing on the company's vision). While product quality is important, so is the manner in which customers are handled. A bad experience with a company worker can send a customer to a competitor as quickly as a defective product. It costs approximately six times more to gain new customers as it does to keep current customers, so it is imperative that company employees understand the marketing goals of the organization.

Finally, sharing information and promoting interaction between the functional areas of the firm is essential for company success. Companies that rate highly on interdepartmental connectedness; sharing marketing information with all the other functional areas, such as research and development, engineering, finance and accounting, and purchasing; and sharing nonmarketing information with the marketing department are more successful in reaching overall organizational sales and profit objectives.[3]

2-2b Suppliers, Distributors, and Other Facilitators of Marketing

While it is the purchasing department that primarily deals with suppliers, the outcome of this relationship is important to the marketing department. For example, if the cost of raw materials and supplies increases, it will usually reverberate into price increases for the company. The marketing department has to decide how much of a price increase is necessary to cover the additional costs, what the impact will be on customers, and how it will affect competition. The marketing department may even be responsible for communicating the price increase to the customer and providing justification for why it is necessary. Any disruptions in the supply, such as a labor strike, or a natural disaster, such as a drought or hurricane, can impact the marketing function.

Similarly, a delay in product delivery can lead consumers to switch to competitors. The fall of Lotus 1-2-3, which was the leading business software package in the 1980s, is largely attributed to the delay in delivery of a much-publicized improved version. While the marketing area is primarily looking toward customers, it must keep an eye on suppliers and distributors to ensure that customers will always have the product when and where they want it.

Distributors are middlemen whose task is to ensure the convenient, timely, and safe distribution of the product to consumers. Manufacturers rely on distributors to deliver their products, to advertise and promote the products, and, often, to offer financing to other distributors down the channel, or to the consumer, and thus facilitate purchase. Often, they use the services of physical distribution firms, such as warehousing firms, transportation firms, and other facilitators of the marketing function, such as banks, insurance companies, advertising firms, and market research firms.

Distributors: Middlemen whose task is to ensure the convenient, timely, and safe distribution of the product to consumers.

2-2c Customers

Not all customers are alike. Not only are there individual differences among customers, but there are also different types of customers. Each requires a different marketing plan. The primary customer groups are consumers, manufacturers, governments, institutions, other businesses, and retailers. To make the situation more complex, each of these entities can exist in the firm's domestic market, as well as in its international market.

Because of differences in these customer groups, companies have to be very diligent in developing their marketing plan. They must make sure that their marketing plan meets customer needs and, if more than one group is targeted, that additional marketing plans are developed. To understand these differences, think about the marketing of office supplies such as pens, notebooks, paper, folders, and staplers. For consumers, a firm would need to advertise the location of its stores, as well as the attributes of its products. If these companies were selling the office supplies over the Internet, then the site would have to be designed to be attractive and easy to use for consumers. If the company were selling office supplies to a manufacturer or another business, then it would require a salesperson calling on the customer. Once a relationship has been established, the manufacturer or other business may then purchase using the Internet, telephone, or even fax.

Selling office supplies to the federal, state, or local government would require the office-supply company to submit a bid. To make the sale, it would have to outbid its competitors either on price or some other designated criterion. Most institutions such as schools and hospitals also use a bidding process.

The marketing method used to sell to retailers depends on whether the office supplies are for resale or would be used by the retailer's employees. If the office supplies are for resale by the retail store, then the office supply business would have to compete with other

Figure 2-4
This advertisement by Ol'Man highlights the superiority of its tree stand for deer hunting over the competition. It is more comfortable, easier to use, of highest quality, and the safety leader.
Source: Courtesy of Newcomer, Morris and Young.

firms on the basis of price and marketing deals it would offer the retailer to stock its brand. If the office supplies are just being used by the retailer and not resold, as would be the case with a florist or bakery, then the office-supply firm may use salespeople for large retailers, but a catalog and direct mail for the smaller firms.

For the international market, all of these scenarios are repeated, but they become more complex because of potential language and cultural differences. For each country, the office-supply business would have to identify the marketing strategies that would work best in the respective market. While advertising may work in one country, sending direct-mail pieces or offering coupons may not be an option if the mail system is unreliable and couponing is illegal.

2-2d Competition

In developing a marketing strategy, a company must take into consideration its competitors. The task of marketing is to meet the needs and wants of consumers more effectively and efficiently than competitors. Marketers must ask the question, "What do we offer customers that the competition does not?" When making a brand selection, consumers often have many choices and will readily compare one brand to another. The brand chosen will be the one the consumer feels is superior in some way or offers the best value (companies stress the superiority of their product over that of the competition—see Figure 2-4).

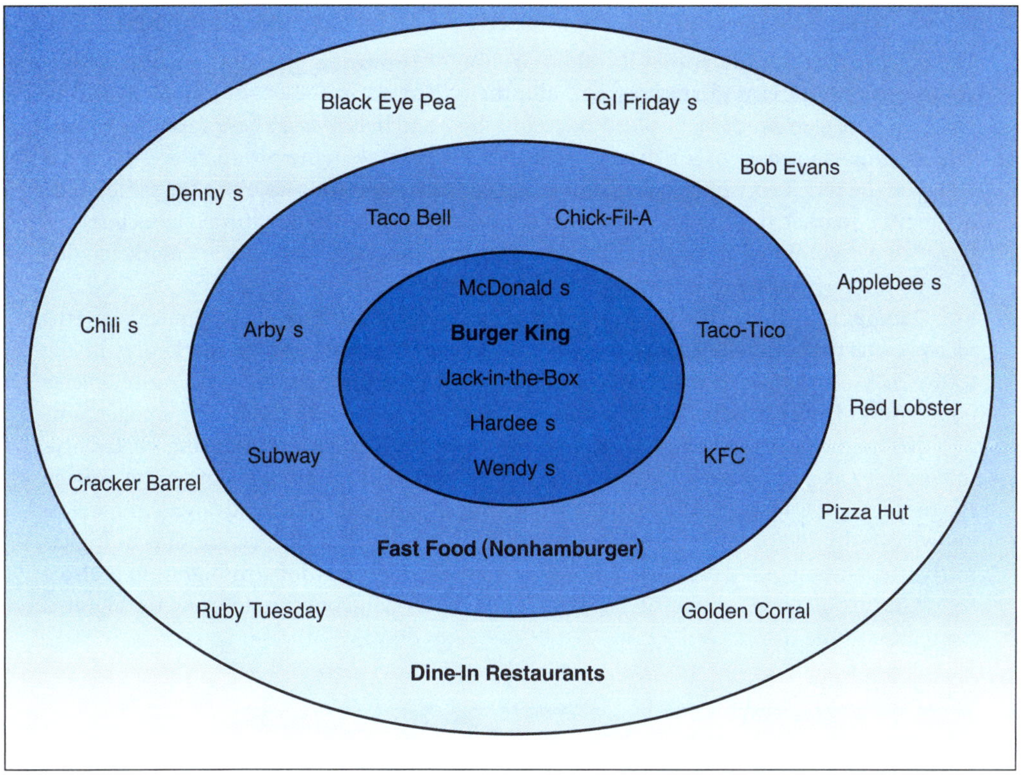

Figure 2-5
Burger King's Competitors

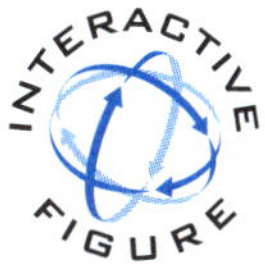

In evaluating competitive forces, it is important to understand there are several layers of competition. Consider the case of Burger King (see Figure 2-5). Burger King's primary competitors are those fast-food operations that sell hamburgers, such as McDonald's, Wendy's, and Hardee's. At a second level are fast-food franchises such as Kentucky Fried Chicken, Taco Bell, and Subway. These businesses sell products other than hamburgers but are still fast-food outlets. At a third level are all of the dine-in restaurants. While they are not shown in the figure, you could argue for other layers, such as grocery stores that have a café serving hot lunch or dinner food, or convenience stores, such as 7-Eleven, which offer sandwiches and wraps to go. Yet another layer could consist of various types of food stores that do not have a sit-down café, nor offer sandwiches to go.

The key to understanding the impact of competition on marketing is to examine it from the consumer's point of view. As a consumer, you are hungry. For Burger King to be considered as an option, you would think about it in terms of the competition. Do I want to eat at Burger King, McDonald's, Hardee's, or another fast-food outlet that sells hamburgers? Is there one close to me? If you decide you want chicken or Mexican food, then you may consider Burger King but you would also consider all of the other options in the second layer. If you are not particular whether it is fast food or dine-in, then all of the options in layer three come into play. Consequently, in developing a marketing plan, Burger King would have to consider all of the options that you, as a consumer, would.

2-3 The Macroenvironment

The macroenvironment encompasses the elements of the broader environment that affect the firm. Marketing managers have no control over the macroenvironment but must continuously monitor it to identify changing threats and opportunities that might affect the firm. The elements of the macroenvironment include the socio-demographic and cultural environment, the economic and natural environment, the technological environment, the political environment, and the legal environment. The legal environment will be addressed in Chapter 3, "Marketing Ethics, Regulations, and Social Responsibility."

2-3a The Socio-Demographic and Cultural Environment

Socio-demographic and cultural environment: A component of the macroenvironment that comprises elements such as demographics, subcultures, cultural values, and all other elements in the environment related to consumers' backgrounds, values, attitudes, interests, and behaviors.

Demographics: Statistics that describe the population, such as age, gender, education, occupation, and income.

The **socio-demographic and cultural environment** comprises elements such as demographics, subcultures and cultures, and all other elements in the environment related to consumers' backgrounds, values, attitudes, interests, and behaviors. These variables constitute an important part of a marketing plan. Consider how many products are marketed based on the target consumer's gender, age, social class, or subculture. Even the same product may be marketed differently based on socio-demographic and cultural characteristics. For example, common products such as deodorant, shampoo, and razors are marketed differently to males than they are to females (see Figure 2-6).

Demographics are the statistics that describe the population, such as gender, age, ethnicity, education, and income. Demographic trends that will impact marketing in the future include a slower population growth rate, an aging population, and a more diverse population.[4] Because individuals are waiting longer to get married and having smaller families than in the past, the U.S. population is not expected to grow as fast during the twenty-first century as it did during the twentieth century. While the growth is slower, the average age of the American population will increase. This is primarily due to advances in medical knowledge. In addition, the diversity of the U.S. population will increase due to higher birth rates among minorities than among the Caucasian population. Immigration is also a factor in this increase in diversity, as the United States will continue to draw immigrants from around the world.

Figure 2-6
When advertising to males, Gillette uses a different advertising approach than when it is advertising its razor to females.

Source: Reprinted by permission of the Gillette Co.

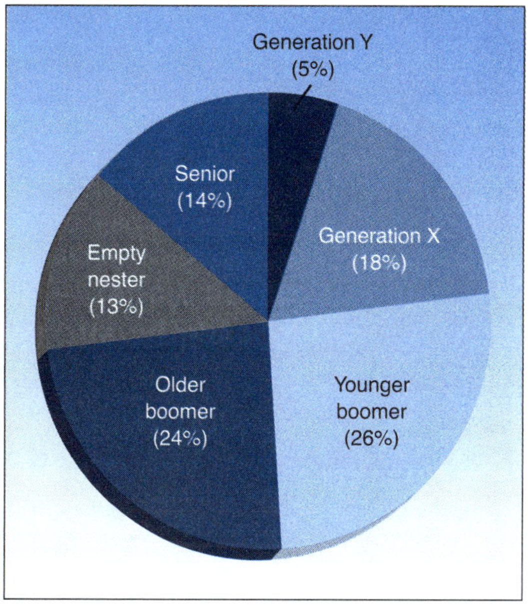

Figure 2-7
Spending Power of U.S. Demographic Age Groups

For many marketers, age is an important characteristic in examining the U.S. population. Spending habits, media preferences, and interests vary among the different age categories. Figure 2-7 divides the population into six different age groups based on the spending power of each group. Table 2-1 provides some additional comparative statistics for each of the demographic groups.

2-3b An Age Categorization of Socio-Demographic Groups

Generation Y **Generation Y** (individuals age 18–24) contributes only 5 percent of the total spending power and is the smallest of the six demographic segments, but it is growing both in size and wealth. Clothes, automobiles, and college are the big-ticket items for this group, which spends 3.3 times more on education than the average person and 1.5 times more on vehicles and apparel than the average person. Nearly 90 percent of this group is either living in a rental or living with parents; spending on homes and home furnishings is a low priority for this market. Generation Y spends substantial amounts on television sets and stereo systems, rather than on refrigerators (the representatives of Generation Y in Figure 2-8 have invested in musical instruments). The collective spending priorities of Generation Y revolve around personal appearance and fun.[5]

Generation Y: A segment of consumers between the ages of 18 and 24 that spends substantial amounts on clothing, automobiles, and college education; they live in rental apartments or with parents.

INTERACTIVE TABLE

TABLE 2-1 **Spending Power of U.S. Demographic Age Groups**

Demographic Group	Age	Total Number of Households (millions)	Average Number in Household	Spending Power (billions)	Annual Average Household Income	Annual Average Spending Per Household
Generation Y	18–24	8.3	1.9	$187	$19,744	$22,563
Generation X	25–34	18.9	2.9	$736	$45,498	$38,945
Younger boomer	35–44	23.9	3.3	$1,100	$56,500	$45,149
Older boomer	45–54	21.9	2.7	$1,000	$58,889	$46,160
Empty nester	55–64	14.1	2.1	$557	$48,108	$39,340
Senior	65+	22.1	1.7	$588	$25,220	$26,533

Figure 2-8
Generation Y consumers are more interested in stereos and music equipment than in home furnishings.

Figure 2-9
Generation X consumers focus on family life, such as shopping with children on the weekend.

Generation X: A segment of consumers between the ages of 25 and 34, whose focus is on family and children, striving to balance family with work, and outsourcing household chores and babysitting.

Younger boomers: A segment of consumers between the ages of 35 and 44, whose focus is on family and home, who pay a large proportion of their income for mortgages, furnishings, pets, and children's toys.

Older boomers: A segment of consumers between the ages of 45 and 54 that spends money on upgrading the family home, on taking vacations, and on ensuring children's education and independence.

McMansions: Super-sized, expensive tract houses on relatively small lots in suburban neighborhoods.

Generation X Contributing 18 percent of the total spending power of consumers in the United States, **Generation X** (individuals age 25–34) focuses on the family and children. Food, housing, transportation, and personal services are the important categories for this market segment. Generation X-ers spend 78 percent more on personal services than the average consumer. Time is at a premium as they strive to balance work and family, so they outsource daily tasks such as house cleaning, lawn mowing, babysitting, and other domestic chores (Figure 2-9 illustrates Generation X-ers shopping with children). Dan Bishop, founder and CEO of The Maids, stated, "Customers are asking us to do more things. They want the laundry done, the carpet cleaned, the light bulb changed that's 20 feet in the air, the patio furniture cleaned, and the furnace filters changed."[6]

Younger Boomers Baby boomers represent 42 percent of the population in the United States, but account for 50 percent of the total spending. Because of the size of this group, it has been divided into **younger boomers,** ages 35–44, and **older boomers,** ages 45–54. The estimated spending power of the younger boomers is $1.1 trillion. The home and family are the focus of younger boomers' spending. The majority, 60 percent, own their own home—many upper class boomers are purchasing the **McMansions** described in Marketing Illustration 2-1; consequently, a considerable amount of their income is allocated to mortgage expenditures and home furnishings and renovation. The remaining

Marketing Illustration 2-1

What Do Boomers Want? McMansions

Boomers are purchasing super-sized houses on relatively small lots in suburban neighborhoods. These McMansions (see Figure 1) cost $750,000 and up and include features such as columned entrances, two-story grand foyers with marble floors and ten-foot-high fireplaces, bathrooms with "his" and "her" dressing rooms, three-car garages, double-sized whirlpool tubs, steam showers, granite kitchens with industrial-quality steel appliances, double wall ovens, sub-zero refrigerators, hard-wired home offices, media rooms, and nanny suites. What these McMansions do not have is much land: Buyers do not want the chores involved in maintaining a large yard, nor the isolation that goes with a big spread. They also want to get the most home for their money in areas where land is quite expensive—the bedroom communities of larger cities.

The McMansion buyer looks for a house that makes a statement. It says that the people living there are sober and conventional, rich and important. Neighborhood critics refer to them as the "fast-food version of the American dream" and to the garages attached to McMansions as "garage Mahal." A website created to parody this type of home and its owners (www.swineopia.com) describes the McMansion as a fake Georgian with bastardized continental touches, lots of Palladian windows, and large, shiny brass fixtures on the outside. With names such as L'Ambiance and the Mews, Foxgrove, Ridings, and Wilshyre, their streets and neighborhoods sound like "English with horses," or like "French air freshener." The splash page of the site asks, "Do you own a McMansion, one of those houses made out of flimsy boards, sawdust, and glue that have sacrificed everything—shrubbery, style, comfort, even structural integrity for the sake of the really big impression?"

McMansions in gated neighborhoods, often located on or close to a golf course, offer comfort, social status, and separate safe communities, physically isolated from lower-priced residences. Inflation for luxury goods hovers around 7 percent, at more than twice the overall U.S. inflation rate—the real rise is not in trinkets for the mass affluent, such as handbags, clothes, and shoes; it is in the big ticket items for the wealthy, such as McMansions, Bugatti sports cars, Patek Philippe watches, and the accoutrements that fit well in or around McMansion communities.

Figure 1

Made out of brick-front veneer or Dryvit, a material that imitates plaster, with their ever-present Palladian windows, McMansions line the exclusive bedroom communities of larger cities.

Sources: Robert Frank, "Making Waves: New Luxury Goods Set Super-Wealthy Apart from the Pack; Rising Riches Stir Rivalry for Ever-Bigger Yachts; Waiting for Maybach; An Echo of Louis XIV's Court," *The Wall Street Journal* (December 14, 2004): A1; Alf Nucifora, "McMansion Mania and Other Trends That Are Affecting Americans," *Shoestring Marketing* (July 24, 1998); Robert Marchant, "Communities in Region Debate 'McMansion' Laws," *The Journal News* (December 10, 2002); www.swineopia.com/mcmansionpage.

Figure 2-10
Boats, recreation, and vacations are major expenditures for the older baby boomers.

disposable income is spent on family purchases such as pets, toys, playground equipment, and large recreational items such as a boat or four-wheel-drive vehicle.[7]

Older Boomers Older boomers account for 24 percent of the total spending—or an estimated $1 trillion. Among priorities of this demographic group are upgrading their homes, ensuring education and independence of their children, obtaining luxury items like boats, and going on vacation. In spite of the higher cost of children's education, this group can afford to remodel their home, purchase better furniture, and buy higher-quality clothing for themselves (older boomers' passion for boating is illustrated in Figure 2-10). Insurance and investments are high-ticket items as they begin to think about their later years and retirement. With fewer responsibilities at home, older boomers spend considerably more on vacation and recreation than any of the other demographic groups.[8]

Empty nesters: A segment of consumers between the ages of 55 and 64 with a large proportion of disposable income, who tend to purchase fancy automobiles, new furniture, and appliances.

Empty Nesters **Empty nesters** are between the ages of 55 and 64. Their children have left home, and they have already paid the college bills. Home mortgages, new furniture, new automobiles, and personal indulgence items represent priorities for this segment. More than 80 percent own their home, and many have paid their mortgage in full. Investments and insurance are high-ticket items, and their attention is now focused on fancy, nice automobiles they could not afford earlier. New furniture, appliances, and china are purchased to enhance the appearance of their home.[9]

Seniors: A segment of consumers, age 65 and older, who live on fixed incomes and spend large amounts on home-related expenses and groceries.

Seniors **Seniors,** individuals over age 65, account for 14 percent of all spending in the United States—that is, approximately $588 million a year. But fixed incomes mean tighter budgets, so household income and spending decline sharply. Health care becomes the number one priority, as seniors spend six times more than the average person (see Figure 2-11). Drugs, health insurance, and health care constitute the top three categories of spending for this group, followed closely by medical supplies and medical expenses. This group tends to reside at home more and spend large amounts on home-related expenses and groceries. Seniors spend 50 percent more than the average consumer on fruits, vegetables, and other food items.[10]

Culture: A continuously evolving totality of learned and shared meanings, rituals, norms, and traditions among the members of an organization or society.

2-3c Ethnic Diversity and Subcultures

The United States is often described as a melting pot. It is indeed a country where many subcultures are maintaining their old traditions but also building common new traditions—a national culture. **Culture,** a society's personality, is defined as a continuously

Figure 2-11
This advertisement by Lincoln General Hospital is directed at seniors, who spend six times more on health care than the average person.

Source: Courtesy of Newcomer, Morris and Young.

evolving totality of learned and shared meanings, rituals, norms, and traditions among the members of an organization or society. The **elements of culture** are language, religion, **cultural values** (beliefs about a specific mode of conduct or desirable end-state that guide the selection or evaluation of behavior),[11] and **norms** (which are derived from values and are rules that dictate what is right or wrong, acceptable or unacceptable). These elements will be addressed at length in Chapter 4, "Consumer Behavior."

Elements of culture: Elements such as language, religion, cultural values, and norms.

Cultural values: Beliefs about a specific mode of conduct or desirable end-state that guide the selection or evaluation of behavior.

Norms: Rules that dictate what is right or wrong, acceptable or unacceptable.

Culture is continuously changing: Until recently, individualism and materialism were dominant values in the United States. Since the September 11, 2001 terrorist attacks, individuals are turning their attention more and more to family and nurturing relationships in general. The message that resonated well during the 1980s' quest for material possessions, "greed is good," sounds shallow today. Family values, the home, and religion are making a comeback.

Ethnic subcultures have shaped and continue to shape culture in the United States. Bagels and tacos, sushi and filet mignon are part of the daily American fare. Hispanic music, hip-hop, and rap have wide appeal beyond the Hispanic and African-American subcultures. Marketing managers study the different subcultures in order to provide goods and services that meet their needs most effectively. They advertise to Hispanic consumers in Spanish-language cable television programs. Using ethnic newspapers, companies offer cosmetic product lines that are specifically designed to address the needs of African-American women. Sensitized to the religious needs of consumers, companies have identified products as Kosher or Pareve, and inform consumers that a product might contain beef or pork byproducts, or alcohol.

2-4 The Economic and Natural Environment

The economic environment encompasses all the factors in the environment that affect the use of resources, including the limited natural resources, the production of goods and services, and their allocation to individual and organizational consumers. Marketing is an important driver of the economy; in turn, the economy has a profound impact on marketing decisions and on consumers, determining consumer income and spending, borrowing decisions, and savings—which, in turn, affect the economy.

2-4a Interdependence in the World Economy

The United States is an important player in the world economy. It is common today to hear that, when the United States sneezes, Europe and Japan catch a cold. When the United States is experiencing a downturn in the economy, reverberations echo throughout the world. Central and South American countries need to be rescued by the International Monetary Fund, all the Asian economies flounder, and banks in developing countries default on their debt. The United States is equally affected by the world economy. The Asian crisis of the late 1990s sent stock markets tumbling in the United States and in the rest of the world. The tsunami and earthquake that impacted Southeast Asia in late 2004 directly affected numerous U.S. business interests. Indirectly, the resulting political instability in the region affected the security of U.S. business involvement in the area and the viability of small and medium enterprises in the United States that had substantial dealings with businesses in the affected countries.

In the Internet Age, countries are becoming more and more connected by trade, by capital markets, by the flow of technology and ideas across national borders, and by psychology. Rather than rising and falling separately, national economies increasingly respond to the same forces.[12] Interdependence has become the leading principle of globalization.

For example, an excess of steel in the world markets attributed to overproduction in Russia led to restructuring of the industry elsewhere in the world, leaving only a few players in the world steel oligopoly. In addition, underproduction of oil, attributed to the controls of the Organization of Petroleum Exporting Countries (OPEC) (www. opec.org), has historically led to inflation worldwide. The boom in technology stocks in 1999 led to much—albeit short-lived—prosperity in many developed countries, as well as in developing countries such as India that stress technical training and software design. During this period of economic prosperity fueled by the technology boom, consumers in developed countries spent more discretionary income on travel and luxuries. Yet, while economies and markets worldwide are interdependent, some markets and economies are more advanced than others, and tend to grow more rapidly. There are many competing classifications of countries from an economic development perspective. Historically, the informal and frequently used classification in the West has referred to highly industrialized, developed countries as the First World, to socialist countries as the Second World, and to developing countries as the Third World. Of this classification, only the term "the Third World" has been used widely, and it is still being used. A United Nations (www.un.org) classification contrasts least-developed, lowest-income countries (LLDCs) and less-developed, lower-income countries (LDCs) to developed countries. Yet other classifications bring in other dimensions, such as newly industrialized countries (NICs), in reference to what used to be known in the 1980s and 1990s as the Asian Tigers (Taiwan, Singapore, South Korea, and Hong Kong [now part of China]), and **emerging markets** (such as Brazil, Argentina, Chile, Peru, and the transitional economies of Central and Eastern Europe). For the purposes of this textbook, we will refer to three categories of countries, based on the classification used by the World Bank (www.worldbank.org):

Emerging markets: Markets that are developing rapidly and have great potential.

Developed countries: Highly industrialized countries that have well-developed industrial and service sectors.

- **Developed countries**—These highly industrialized countries have well-developed industrial and service sectors. NICs fall in this category, as well as countries that have had a developed status for many years (see Figure 2-12). Although these countries present great potential because they have consumers with the highest per capita

Figure 2-12
This photo shows infrastructure-related advances made by developed countries; tall, modern buildings and bridges that appear to defy gravity are the norm in large cities.

income, they also present challenges to international firms because their markets are in a mature stage, consumers have established preferences, and competition is intense. The World Bank refers to the countries in this category as high-income countries, with a GNP per capita of US$9,266 and above.

- **Countries with emerging markets**—Countries considered as emerging markets are both developing rapidly and have great potential. They are countries in Latin America, such as Argentina, Brazil, Uruguay, Paraguay, Chile, Peru, and Bolivia; countries in Asia, such as China, with its immense market, and India, with its substantial middle class; and the transition economies of Central and Eastern Europe, which are rapidly privatizing state-owned industries and adopting market reforms. Important in this category are **big emerging markets (BEMs),** such as Brazil and China, which present the greatest potential for international trade and expansion. The World Bank refers to the countries in this category as middle-income countries, with a GNP per capita of US$756 to US$9,265.
- **Developing countries**—Countries in this category are primarily agrarian, have low per capita income levels, and are located in different regions in Asia and in Sub-Saharan Africa. Developing countries are often neglected or underserved by large multinationals and consequently present great potential as niche markets. Even the countries with the lowest per capita income have a stratum of society that can afford global products. Furthermore, because they are primary recipients of international development aid, they present important opportunities for firms operating in the areas of infrastructure development and industrial sector development, and for related consultancies. The World Bank refers to the countries in this category as low-income countries, with a GNP per capita of less than US$755. Throughout the textbook, there are examples of marketing challenges and opportunities in emerging markets and in developing countries.

Countries with emerging markets: Countries that are developing rapidly and have great potential.

Big emerging markets (BEMs): Markets that present the greatest potential for international trade and expansion.

Developing countries: Countries that are primarily agrarian and have low per capita income.

The discrepancy between the countries in the three categories is evident: With regard to the GNP distribution worldwide, developed, highly industrialized countries account for close to 80 percent of the world's GNP, while only accounting for less than 15 percent of the population.

TABLE 2-2 An Illustration of Human Development in Select Low-Human-Development Countries

Rank (of Total 175 Countries)	Country	Birth Probability of Not Surviving to Age 40	Adult Illiteracy (%)	Population Without Adequate Water Access (%)	Children Underweight for Age (5)	Population Living on Less Than $1 Per Day (%)
158	Rwanda	54.3	32.0	59	24	35.7
159	Benin	34.6	61.4	37	23	—
160	Tanzania	46.4	24.0	32	29	19.9
161	Cote d'Ivoire	51.7	50.3	19	21	12.3
162	Malawi	59.6	39.0	43	25	41.7
163	Zambia	70.1	21.0	36	25	63.7
168	Central African Republic	55.3	51.8	30	24	66.6
169	Ethiopia	43.3	59.7	76	47	81.9
170	Mozambique	56.0	54.8	43	26	37.9
171	Burundi	50.5	50.8	22	45	58.4
172	Mali	35.3	73.6	35	43	72.8
173	Burkina Faso	43.4	75.2	58	34	61.2
174	Niger	38.7	83.5	41	40	61.4
175	Sierra Leone	57.5	—	43	27	57.0

Source: Charts adapted from Human Development Report, United Nations Development Programme, 2003 from http://hdr.undp.org/reports/global/2003/.

To illustrate this discrepancy, the United Nations Development Program monitors human development worldwide, publishing the *Human Development Report.* The report compares countries based on adult illiteracy, access to a viable water source, children underweight for their age, and the percentage of the population living on less than $1 per day. Table 2-2 compares countries in the low-human-development category on those dimensions.

Rostow model of economic development: A model of economic development in which each stage of development is a function of productivity, economic exchange, technological improvements, and income.

Traditional society: Economic development stage in which the economy is dominated by agriculture, minimal productivity, and low growth in per capita output.

2-4b Economic Development: The Rostow Modernization Model

Economic development can be explained in terms of productivity, economic exchange, technological improvements, and income. Economic growth requires advancing from one stage to another. According to the **Rostow model of economic development,** [13] the modernization stages are

- Traditional society
- Transitional society
- Take-off
- The drive to maturity
- High mass consumption

Traditional Society Countries in the **traditional society** stage are characterized by an economic structure that is dominated by agriculture. Minimal productivity occurs, and only a few exchange transactions take place. Economic change and technological improvements are not sufficient to sustain any growth in per capita output, which is low.

Transitional Society (Pre-Conditions for Take-Off) The **transitional society** stage is characterized by increased productivity in agriculture, and modern manufacturing begins to emerge. In manufacturing, low productivity remains the norm.

Transitional society: Economic development stage in which there is increased productivity in agriculture; manufacturing begins to emerge.

Take-Off During **take-off,** growth becomes the norm and improvements in production lead to the emergence of leading sectors. Income rises across the board, and a new class of entrepreneurs emerges.

Take-off: Economic development stage in which growth becomes the norm, income rises, and leading sectors emerge.

The Drive to Maturity In the **drive to maturity** stage, modern technology is fully adopted in all economic activity, and new leading sectors emerge. The economy demonstrates the technological and entrepreneurial skill to produce anything it chooses to. The economy looks beyond the country's border for development.

Drive to maturity: Stage of economic development in which modern technology is applied in all areas of the economy.

High Mass Consumption In the age of **high mass consumption,** leading sectors shift toward durable goods (Figure 2-13 presents an advertisement for Aeneas Williams Dealerships, aimed at a high mass consumption society). A surge occurs in per capita income and there is increased allocation to social welfare programs. The masses can afford goods beyond food, clothing, and shelter.

In the United States and most other industrialized, developed countries, the focus of the economy is shifting toward services, which currently account for most of the output. All companies, however small, are impacted by changes in the international economic environment, by the availability of raw materials in developing countries, by disruptions in important labor markets, and by the stability of international and local financial institutions. The local bakery and the mom-and-pop hardware store are affected, among others, by national and international economic cycles, by prices of raw materials from developing countries, by the local labor market, and by consumer income. Large multinational companies are also affected by developments in the economy, in the international

High mass consumption: Stage of economic development in which leading sectors shift toward durable goods and an increased allocation to social welfare programs.

Figure 2-13
In a high mass consumption society, the masses can afford vehicles like the ones shown in this advertisement for Aeneas Williams Dealerships.
Source: Courtesy of The Marketing Exchange.

Marketing Illustration 2-2

Haggling Uptown in a Slow Economy

With the economy gone sour and customers holding on to their wallets, retailers report that customers are bargaining more, even at sleek stores in Manhattan's SoHo, in Miami's design district, and in West Hollywood designer showrooms; at chain electronic retailers; and in upscale department stores where haggling is not a practice managers like to talk about. How much can you shave off the price of an item? Here are some examples:

Roseanne Hirsch shopped at the upscale Manhattan department store Bloomingdale's for furniture for her new Park Avenue apartment. She found two ultrasuede Louis XIV couches originally priced at $5,600, marked down to $3,360, and bought them for $1,785 a piece, saving $1,575 for each. She suggests that consumers should ask how much more the retailer can take off the price—that the price is still too high.

P. J. Casey, owner of the C.I.T.E. SoHo store in Manhattan, specializing in mid-century modern furniture, sold an $18,000 desk-and-credenza set for $9,000 when a customer offered her $9,000 cash for it. According to her, the store was unable to sell one single piece of furniture without coming down on price since the September 11 terrorist attacks.

Guido Maus, owner of Lili Marleen, a TriBeCa antiques shop, charged a couple $12,000 for a table with a $17,000 price tag—a gesture he made to them even before they asked for a discount.

Deanna Jackman, a Saks Fifth Avenue customer in Beverly Hills, California, had a salesman put a pair of Chanel evening shoes off the shelf for a month, until the price came down from $775 to $400.

From the consumer's perspective, it never hurts to ask. Retailers are fervently promoting their merchandise and discounting prices and often providing their offering free to the right person. Celebrities commonly trade their marquee appeal for free or discounted favors, or the celebrity may simply ignore the invoice. Diamond sellers, jewelers, florists, chefs, and caterers angled to get a piece of Donald Trump's wedding to supermodel Melania Knauss, many offering their goods free. Graff, a diamond dealer, offered a 15-carat engagement ring for half the price. Jean-Georges Vongerichten, whose four-star restaurant is a tenant in a Trump property, was selected as chef for the wedding and provided filet mignon with green peppercorn sauce and steamed shrimp for the calorie-conscious among the 500 guests—all free. This is not a small gesture: A typical prix fixe dinner at Jean-Georges is about $87 without wine.

Sources: Alex Williams and Eric Dash, "At Celebrity Nuptials to Die for, Vendors Give Themselves Away," *The New York Times* (January 13, 2005): A1; Terry Pristin and Marianne Rohrlich, "Latest Word in Luxury Is Haggling," *New York Times* (October 16, 2002): A2.

labor markets, and in consumer spending in the different markets where they operate. The next section addresses the impact of the economy on consumer income and spending.

2-4c The Economy and the Consumer

The economy affects consumer income and spending patterns. In periods of economic growth, consumers give in to their materialistic drive, purchasing products they may or may not need. During the 1980s, in the era of the Yuppie, companies were competing for the disposable income of the upward-mobile, upper middle class. This was the time of the Rolex watch, Armani suit, and Gucci loafers; it was also the time when stores such as the Sharper Image and other trendy shops sold designer garbage bags, birthday-control pills, nose-shaped tissue dispensers, and other useless products at high prices.

In a slow economy, when companies reduce their workers' hours and the nation's payrolls shrink by thousands of jobs monthly, consumers tend to be more cautious with their expenditures. They "deliberate over a purchase for weeks and then decide against it."[14] Retailers, who are already offering blanket sales all year long for their products, need to cut prices even further, as customers do not respond to their promotions unless they perceive that they are truly getting a great deal. As Marketing Illustration 2-2 illustrates, even upscale stores encourage shoppers to bargain shop in a slow economy.

The distribution of income across social class categories has important implications for marketing decisions. Upper class consumers are less likely to be affected by economic cycles; their purchase patterns remain constant as they continue to purchase products and services such as high-fashion clothing, gourmet food, cleaning services for their McMansions (see Marketing Illustration 2-1), exotic vacations, and country-club memberships.

TABLE 2-3 Average Annual Expenditures of Consumers: A Comparison for Different Household Income Levels

Expenditures	Household Income: $5,000–$9,999	Household Income: $20,000–$29,999	Household Income: $50,000–$69,999	Household Income: Over $70,000
Food	$3,485	$4,349	$6,548	$8,874
Housing	$6,775	$9,595	$15,276	$23,695
Personal Care	$300	$432	$655	$915

Source: From *Consumer Expenditure Survey, 2002,* U.S. Department of Labor, Bureau of Labor Statistics (February 2004): Report 974.

Figure 2-14
Protecting natural resources is an important societal concern.

Middle-class consumers are more vulnerable during economic downturns and could experience job loss or the threat of job loss; consequently, they are more likely to reduce consumption, limiting purchases to necessities. The lower class consumers are most likely to be affected by economic slowdown because part-time jobs and/or jobs requiring a lower skill level are likely to be cut.

Table 2-3 illustrates annual expenditures of consumers for different household income levels. Housing is by far the greatest expense for all income levels; across the board, expenses for necessities such as food and personal care products and services decrease as a proportion of income as household income increases, allowing households with higher income to spend more on entertainment, education, and vacations, and to save for the future.

2-4d The Economy and Natural Resources

As mentioned earlier in Section 2-4, the economic environment encompasses all the factors in the environment that affect the use of resources. Although many resources are renewable or recyclable (timber, for example), important natural resources, such as minerals, natural gas, and petroleum, are finite (protecting natural resources, such as the Smokey Mountains [see Figure 2-14], is an important priority). Increased control over these limited resources by national governments has led to higher prices for oil and the need to evaluate alternative energy sources and technologies.

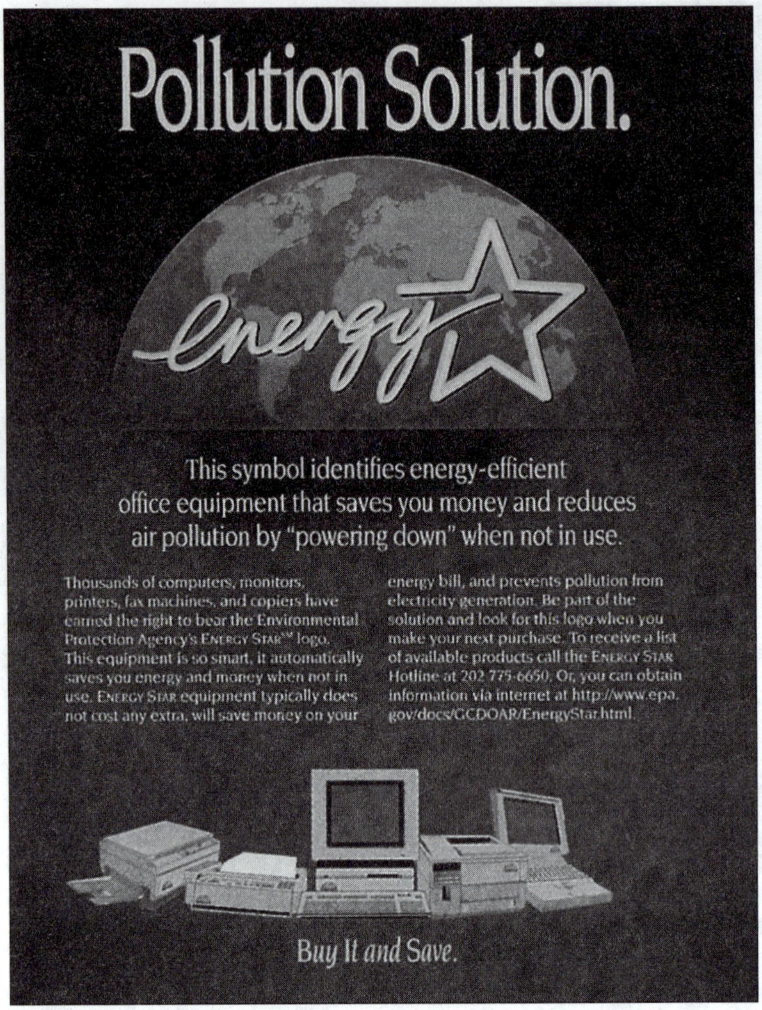

Figure 2-15
This advertisement highlights how purchasing energy-efficient office equipment not only saves money but also reduces air pollution.

Source: Courtesy of U.S. Environmental Protection Agency.

Other aspects of the natural environment have important repercussions on the economy and on the overall quality of life of consumers. Pollution in the form of greenhouse gases has led to global warming, dying coral reefs, and an overall change in the ecological equilibrium of oceans; chemical spills and nuclear waste are compromising our water supply; and landfills are overflowing with packaging material, much of which is not biodegradable (see Figure 2-15, which highlights the importance of purchasing energy-efficient office equipment). Some of these environmental concerns are directly attributable to marketing efforts to create products that are convenient or attractive for consumers, such as excessive packaging that helps products stand out on supermarket shelves, the use of nonbiodegradable Styrofoam in packaging to protect products or for cups used to hold hot beverages, and convenient, disposable diapers, among others. Marketing is also attempting to demarket (slow down or reduce) the use of environmentally harmful products. For example, fast-food companies have decided to limit the use of Styrofoam cups and containers, replacing them with paper bags and cardboard. Many products are now offered in environmentally friendly, recyclable packaging; in fact, many companies provide incentives for consumers who recycle their packages.

Topography, hydrology, climate, population, and environmental quality determine the status of a particular country as a viable trade partner. Topography is important because it determines access to the market and affects distribution decisions. For example, Holland has a flat terrain, allowing for efficient transportation. On the other hand, a mountainous terrain restricts access to markets. The Andes, for example, allow local consumers only minimal access, which can be accomplished only at great company expense. Hydrology

Figure 2-16
Man-made canals in the Netherlands allow for quick and inexpensive access to markets.

determines access to local markets as well. Ocean access allows for the affordable shipping of goods to the local target market. Rivers and lakes offer access as well as potential for the development of agriculture and manufacturing. Hydroelectric power is essential for local development. In general, economic development is related to hydrology. In the Netherlands, the topography was altered to increase access by creating an effective network of man-made canals that cross the country in every direction allowing for easy access to markets (see Figure 2-16). Climate is also an essential determinant of economic development. Arid lands, such as the desert lands of the Sahara and the Southwestern United States, are inhabitable only at a very high cost. Excessive rain and hurricane activity often lead to flooding and the destruction of the local infrastructure.

One relevant aspect of the natural environment is the scarcity of natural resources, and especially raw materials, in light of today's high population growth. High population growth in spite of limited natural resources has led to famine and precipitated conflict in Ethiopia, Somalia, Rwanda, and Burundi in Sub-Saharan Africa. In these markets, the overall infrastructure is insufficient and cannot meet the basic needs of the population. The concentration of population in large cities of millions of inhabitants, such as Mumbai (Bombay), Mexico City, and Cairo, has taxed the infrastructure and impeded the optimal functioning of business. Most importantly, today, the world's population exceeds 6 billion and is growing rapidly, especially in developing countries. Table 2-4 illustrates the high annual population growth in low- and middle-income countries, compared to that of high-income countries. The population growth rate is highest for the developing countries of South Asia and Sub-Saharan Africa.

2-5 The Technological Environment

Technology is the primary driver of change in the environment. Our lives are changing dramatically and at a faster pace due to technological change. Just in the past decade, the pharmaceutical industry has created numerous miracle drugs: For example, Celebrex has greatly improved the quality of life of people with arthritis in spite of its greatly debated health side effects, and Viagra has revolutionized the sex life of older men. Magnetic Resonance Imaging (MRI), laser, and endoscopic instruments have revolutionized diagnostics and treatment in medicine (see Figure 2-17). The Internet has become an important venue for communication with a company's target market, as well as an effective retailing venue. The computer has changed our daily lives, from the manner in which we communicate in

TABLE 2-4 Population Growth Trends

	Population	Annual Growth	Population Age Composition		
	(2002)	(2002–2015)	(0–14)	(15–64)	(65+)
Low-middle income countries	**5,232.4**	**1.2**	**31.2**	**63.1**	**5.7**
East Asia & Pacific	1,838.3	1.4	26.3	67.2	6.5
Europe/Central Asia	472.9	0.5	20.9	67.9	11.2
Latin America /Caribbean	524.9	1.3	30.9	63.6	5.5
Middle East/ North Africa	305.8	2.6	35.3	60.7	4.0
South Asia	1,401.5	12.0	34.2	61.2	4.6
Sub-Saharan Africa	688.9	12.7	43.8	53.3	3.0
High-income countries	**966.2**	**0.7**	**18.3**	**67.3**	**14.4**

Source: World Development Indicators, *World Development Report 2004,* World Bank Group, http://econ.worldbank.org/wdr/wdr2004.

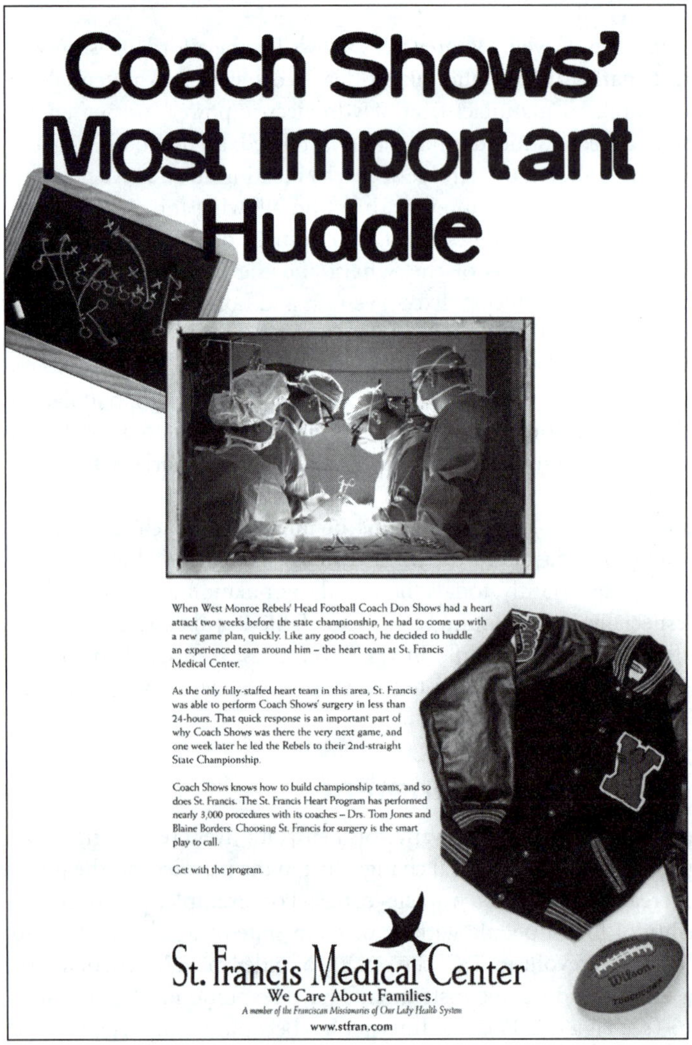

Figure 2-17
Advances in pharmaceutical knowledge and medical procedures are critical to saving lives.

Source: Courtesy of Newcomer, Morris and Young.

	Year			
Company	2000	2001	2002	2003
Ford Motor Company	$6.80	$7.27	$7.63	$7.50
General Motors Corp.	$6.60	$6.06	$5.55	$5.70
Pfizer	$4.44	$4.40	$4.70	$7.13
IBM	$4.35	$4.55	$4.71	$5.07
Microsoft	$4.06	$4.66	$5.26	$4.67
Intel	$4.00	$4.58	$5.16	$4.36

TABLE 2-5

Corporate Expenditures in Research and Development, 2000–2003
(in billions of dollars)

Sources: David Rotman, Jessica Gorman, Patric Hadenius, and Peter Fairley, "Special Report: R&D 2004," *Technology Review,* vol. 107, no. 10 (December 2004): 60–65; Tim Studt and Jules J. Duga, "Smaller Increase Forecast for U.S. Research Spending," *Research & Development,* vol. 44, no. 1 (January 2002): F3–F8.

our work and home environment, to the manner in which we distribute documents, obtain approvals, and share the latest photographs of our loved ones. Hand-held computers are allowing us to handle such communication without having to physically access our desktops. And cellular phones allow us to communicate from anywhere on the planet.

Technological change is taking place rapidly in all domains of human endeavor. Companies are under pressure to come up with new and better products, with new technologies, to gain advantage over competitors, or simply to keep up. Table 2-5 illustrates the amount spent by corporations in research and development. The continued growth of research and development spending is largely attributed to industry's realization that structural and operational changes are not the only road to profitability. Continued investment in research and especially in development is required for long-term survival.[15]

Research and development spending is also funded by the federal government and by universities and nonprofit research centers. Excellent business conditions in the 1990s, a strong economy, and enhanced tax revenues fueled a federal budget surplus, thus potentially easing some past pressures on government support of research and development. Furthermore, the budget surpluses eased the cost of money and effectively reduced the costs of investing in research and development.[16]

The United States spends more on research and development than any other country in the world. In the year 2002, federal spending on research and development was estimated to be $75.5 billion, industry spending about $195 billion, and universities' and research centers' support was estimated at $15.4 billion, for a total of $285.9 billion.[17] More recently, however, a troubling trend emerged: Corporate research and development spending is on the decline. This trend cuts across industries. For example, the top spender, Ford Motor Company, cut its budget by $200 million, while Siemens cut its spending by $900 million in 2003, with subsequent cuts in 2004. Worldwide, information technology hardware accounts for the highest level of the research and development expenditures, followed by the automotive sector and the pharmaceutical industry, as illustrated in Figure 2-18.

It is essential for the marketing department to work closely with research and development to ensure that the firm as a whole pursues a market orientation (see Chapter 1, "Scope and Concepts of Marketing"). The marketing department should ensure that the new products and services and all innovations are directed at effectively meeting the needs of consumers, and that research and development maintains a constant market focus.

2-6 The Political Environment

Business must constantly scrutinize the political environment, which includes federal and local government policies as well as labor and political action groups that could have an impact on their operations. Multinational corporations have an even greater burden. They

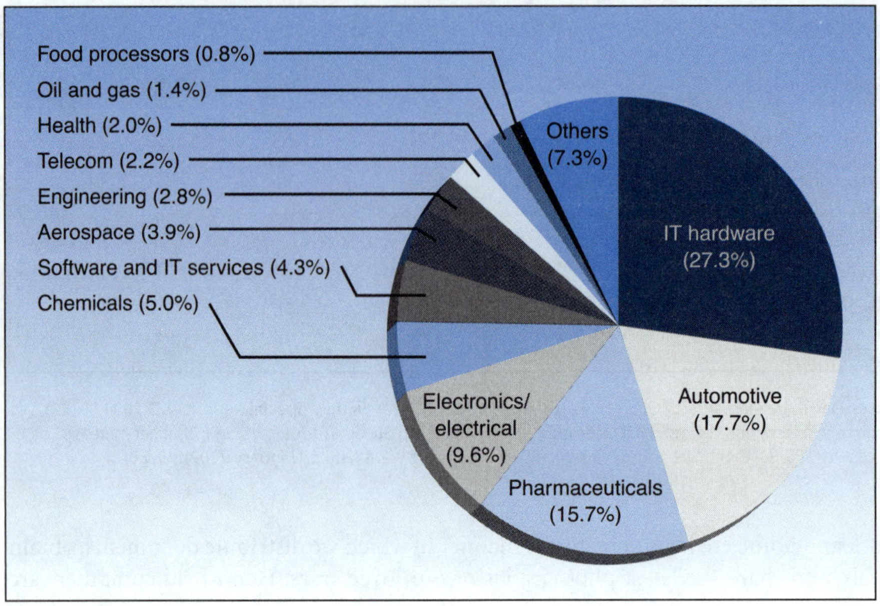

Figure 2-18
Research and Development Expenditures by Industry

Sources: David Rotman, Jessica Gorman, Patric Hadenius, and Peter Fairley, "Special Report: R&D 2004," *Technology Review,* vol. 107, no. 10 (December 2004): 60–65; Tim Studt and Jules J. Duga, "Smaller Increase Forecast for U.S. Research Spending," *Research & Development,* vol. 44, no. 1 (January 2002): F3–F8.

must evaluate political developments in the host country of operations, as well as in the home country where the parent company is headquartered. The next section addresses the different types of political risks that currently confront businesses.

2-6a Risks Related to Economic Performance

A poor economic performance and forecast are likely to lead to greater levels of risk for companies. Of particular concern are high inflationary rates and high unemployment rates, both of which could lead to higher taxes, regulatory restrictions, an increasingly active labor movement, and even political instability.

During downturns in the economy, federal, state, and local governments often resort to increasing taxes to provide a source of valuable revenue. The government may also reduce expenditures that facilitate industry performance; for example, the government may spend less on improving the transportation infrastructure, it might reduce expenditures for the military, or it may limit lucrative industry contracts on government-subsidized economic development projects.

2-6b Risks Related to Government Economic Policy

Government elections, especially elections in which a change in the governing party occurs, usually signal a change in policies in general. The new policies may increase or decrease tax burdens, or tighten or loosen industry regulations. For example, when the November 2002 elections took place, the Republican victory across the board set the stage for a pro-business agenda. Corporations quickly brought their wish lists to the new administration; among the topics considered after the elections were[18]:

- New tax cuts
- New laws governing terrorism insurance and a government-backed insurance program
- Resolution of asbestos-related lawsuits
- New limits on medical malpractice lawsuits and punitive damages
- Opening the Arctic National Wildlife Refuge in Alaska to drilling
- Repealing a Depression-era regulation law limiting the consolidation of the electricity industry

- Overhauling the bankruptcy code to make it difficult for borrowers to avoid paying credit card bills
- Overhauling Social Security

2-6c Risks Related to Labor and Action Groups

From labor unions to political action groups, many political forces, in addition to the government, can greatly impact a company's operations. In many countries, labor unions are very powerful and can readily influence national policies. In the United States, labor unions have lost some ground in recent years due to a history of abuses and due to a strong economy that ensured solid bonuses for workers. Unions in the United States are organized under the umbrella of the American Federation of Labor—Congress of Industrial Organizations (AFL-CIO), which represents more than 13 million workers.

Action groups can also affect company operations. For example, Exxon recently was the victim of a "Boycott Esso" (Exxon's name outside the United States) campaign aimed at United States' environmental policies. Groups such as the Public Citizen, associated with Ralph Nader, and other consumer groups are constantly monitoring companies to identify issues that may be of interest to consumers and those taking a stand.

Companies have some control over the actions of labor and action groups. Although they cannot control market demand and derived demand for labor, companies can provide severance packages that are fair, as well as invest in the services of job placement businesses in an effort to seek placement for the employees who have been terminated. In addition, to avoid negative public sentiment, companies should be politically neutral and keep some distance from politics. Being too closely associated with an administration or political party could result in a negative attitude toward the company and its products.

2-6d Risks Related to Terrorism

Terrorist attacks against business interests culminated in the United States with the September 11, 2001 attack on the World Trade Center in New York City. In recent years, terrorist attacks have been steadily increasing in frequency. Organizations or businesses with a United States connection alone were hit 206 times in 2000, up from 169 in 1999. Internationally, private-sector facilities were attacked 384 times, up from 276 in 1999, while only 17 government facilities and 13 military facilities were similarly hit around the globe. Terrorism was most lethal in Asia in the year 2000, with 281 of the 405 international victims perishing there. Africa had the second highest total, with 73 dead.[19]

The events of September 2001 have exponentially altered the trend of those statistics. In a choreographed operation, terrorists hijacked four planes that took off within minutes of each other and crashed into each of the World Trade Center's twin towers, as well as the Pentagon. Experts evaluated these attacks as the culmination of a 20-year trend toward assaults aimed to kill many people in technically complex operations. A blow to the financial nerve center of capitalism, the September 11 events disrupted financial operations worldwide, displaced hundreds of businesses in the area and beyond, and, for the first time ever, stopped all travel in U.S. airspace. An "attack on the world's . . . superpower, undertaken as a consequence of specific American alliances and actions,"[20] represents a form of corporate terrorism with the greatest of scopes.

Companies have some control, however, in reducing their likelihood of becoming victims of terrorism by training employees in terrorism avoidance, such as briefing personnel on what to expect when in high-risk areas. Companies can also purchase insurance against terrorist acts from private insurance companies. For example, Cigna International's International Specialty Products & Services offers insurance products that cover kidnapping, detention (kidnapping without asking for ransom), hijacking, evacuation, business interruption and extra expenses, product recall expenses, and expenses arising from child abduction (such as hiring private investigators or posting rewards for information).[21] The

TABLE 2-6

Country Risk Scores

Country	Ranking	Risk Score (Max.= 100)	Political Risk (Max.=25)	Economic Performance (Max.=25)
Luxembourg	1	99.78	24.81	25.00
Norway	2	99.70	24.88	24.85
Switzerland	3	97.69	25.00	22.72
United States	4	97.39	24.48	23.01
Denmark	5	95.97	24.15	21.85
Sweden	6	95.32	24.57	20.78
United Kingdom	7	94.48	24.64	19.87
Czech Republic	39	69.78	19.36	10.50
Saudi Arabia	44	66.59	15.40	10.00
China	50	62.77	16.83	12.12
Iran	79	45.65	11.34	6.96
Vietnam	73	46.63	10.93	7.55
Cuba	181	16.00	3.06	10.11
Iraq	183	7.13	1.02	5.28
North Korea	184	6.55	0.00	5.38
Afghanistan	185	6.39	1.32	0.00

Source: "Country Risk—Results & Methodology," *Euromoney* (March 2004): 1.

private and public sectors have learned to deal more effectively with terrorism. The terrorist bombing of the London underground in July 2005 only affected traffic for one day due to efficient efforts to restore operations.

A company has several resources at its disposal to evaluate country risk. The Department of State, the Department of Commerce, and other governmental and nongovernmental agencies provide data on country political risk that are current and continually updated to reflect new developments in each country around the world (see an example of country risk evaluation in Table 2-6).

Summary

1. *Provide an overview of the marketing microenvironment and all of its components.* A major function of marketing is to develop a company's customer base. Potential customers must be identified, targeted with appropriate marketing strategies, and persuaded to purchase a company's goods or services. While this task may appear to be rather simple, it becomes daunting when the company's microenvironment is considered. Strengths and weaknesses in internal company dynamics, current and potential customers, and suppliers and competing firms can influence how successfully the marketing function is performed. It is the responsibility of the marketing department to manage these various components of the microenvironment, addressing their weaknesses and focusing on their strengths in a manner that is congruent with the company's marketing and organizational goals.

2. *Provide an overview of the socio-demographic and cultural environment components of the macroenvironment and related trends.* The socio-demographic and cultural environment comprises elements such as demographics (statistics that describe the population, such as gender, age, ethnicity, income, education) subcultures and cultural values, and all other elements in the environment related to consumers' backgrounds, values, attitudes, interests, and behaviors. Socio-demographic trends that will impact marketing in the future include a slower population growth rate, an aging population, and a more diverse population. Because individuals are waiting longer to get married and are having smaller families than in the past, the U.S. population is not expected to grow as fast during the twenty-first century as it did during the twentieth century. While the growth is slower, the average age of the American population will increase. This is primarily due to advances in medical knowledge. In addition, the diversity of the U.S. population will increase due primarily to higher birth rates among minorities than among the Caucasian population. Continuing immigration is also a factor in this increase in diversity.

3. *Address the economic and natural environment components of the macroenvironment and the topic of economic development.* The economic environment encompasses all the factors in the environment that affect the use of resources, including the limited natural resources, the production of goods and services, and the allocation of goods and services to individual and organizational consumers. Marketing is an important driver of the economy; in turn, the economy has a profound impact on marketing decisions and on consumers, determining consumer income and spending, borrowing decisions, and savings—which, in turn, affect the economy. There is a large degree of interdependence between the economies of the world, regardless of whether they are those of developing countries, countries with emerging markets, or developed countries. Economic development is a function of productivity, economic exchange, technological improvements, and income, and, according to the Rostow modernization model, societies must go through different phases to achieve a developed state. These phases are traditional society, transitional society, take-off, drive to maturity, and high mass consumption.

4. *Examine changes in the technological environment component of the macroenvironment.* Technology is the primary driver of change in the environment. Companies are under constant pressure to develop new and better products, with new technologies, to gain advantage over competitors, or simply to keep up. The continued growth of research and development spending is largely attributed to industry's realization that structural and operational changes are not the only road to profitability. The United States spends more on research and development than any other country in the world. In the year 2002, federal spending was estimated to be $75.5 billion, industry spending about $195 billion, and university and research center support was estimated at $15.4 billion, for a total of $285.9 billion spent on research and development.

5. *Address the political environment component of the macroenvironment and discuss indicators of political risk and company approaches to political risk management.* Businesses must constantly scrutinize the political environment, which includes federal and local government policies and labor and political action groups that could have an impact on their operations. Companies can experience political risks attributed to economic performance, to government economic policy, to labor and action groups, and to corporate terrorism.

Key Terms

big emerging markets (BEMs) (p. 41)
countries with emerging markets (p. 41)
cultural values (p. 39)
culture (p. 38)
demographics (p. 34)
developed countries (p. 40)
developing countries (p. 41)
distributors (p. 31)
drive to maturity (p. 43)
elements of culture (p. 39)
emerging markets (p. 40)
empty nesters (p. 38)
Generation X (p. 36)
Generation Y (p. 35)
high mass consumption (p. 43)
macroenvironment (p. 28)
McMansions (p. 36)
microenvironment (p. 28)
norms (p. 39)
older boomers (p. 36)
Rostow model of economic development (p. 42)
seniors (p. 38)
socio-demographic and cultural environment (p. 34)
take-off (p. 43)
traditional society (p. 42)
transitional society (p. 43)
younger boomers (p. 36)

Discussion Questions

1. Comment on the following statement: "Strengths and weaknesses in internal company dynamics, current and potential customers, and suppliers and competing firms can influence how successfully the marketing function is performed." How do suppliers impact the company's ability to optimally address consumers' needs?
2. Compare Generation X-ers with young boomers. Can marketers target them similarly? Explain.
3. For each of the following products, discuss how a company would market to each of the age groups and ethnic groups mentioned Section 2-3a, "The Socio-Demographic and Cultural Environment":
   a. Lawn service
   b. Hiking boots
   c. Mexican restaurant
   d. Condoms
   e. Ski resort in Colorado
   f. Mayoral political candidate
4. Economic interdependence exists today between countries of different levels of development. Assume that China and India experience a downturn in their economies. How could companies in the United States be affected by changes in the economies of these countries?
5. What are the factors driving up the costs of technology? Why is there a need for constant emphasis on research and development and technological change?
6. Describe indicators of political risk. Examine current events and identify some of the political risks that companies could encounter.
7. How can companies reduce political risk?

Review Questions

True or False

1. The political and legal environment is NOT a component of the macroenvironment.
2. To evaluate competitive forces, it is important to take into consideration several layers of competition.
3. Marketing managers do NOT typically consider the limited company's resources.
4. Generation Y is a segment of consumers who spend heavily on clothing, automobiles, college education, and rental apartments.
5. Cultural norms are defined as beliefs about a specific mode of conduct or desirable end-state that guide the selection or evaluation of behavior.
6. Since the United States became such a powerful leader in information technology, the fluctuations in the economy in the rest of the world barely affect its domestic market.
7. Countries in Central and Eastern Europe are considered as emerging markets, which both grow rapidly and have great potential.
8. Middle-class consumers are the least likely to be affected by downturns in the economy.
9. Private industry is accountable for all the research and development spending in the United States.
10. Companies have no control over the activities of labor and political action groups.

Multiple Choice

11. Which of the following categories relate to the microenvironment?
    a. strengths and weaknesses of the company
    b. consumers and suppliers
    c. middlemen, facilitators of marketing functions, and competitors
    d. all of the above
12. The elements of socio-demographic and cultural environment are
    a. federal and local government.
    b. expenditures for different household items.
    c. labor and action groups.
    d. none of the above
13. Which of the following consumer segments are more likely to have large proportions of disposable income and would tend to purchase luxurious items?
    a. empty nesters
    b. older boomers
    c. seniors
    d. none of the above
14. The characteristics of the high mass consumption modernization stage are
    a. leading sectors shifting toward durable goods.
    b. surge in per capita income.
    c. increased allocation to social welfare programs.
    d. all of the above

15. What stage of economic development in the Rostow model is characterized by the adoption of modern technology in all economic activity?
- **a.** the transitional stage
- **b.** the traditional stage
- **c.** the take-off stage
- **d.** the drive-to-maturity stage

16. Protecting natural resources is an important societal concern. The most appropriate action is
- **a.** demarketing the use of environmentally harmful products.
- **b.** outsourcing the production of harmful products to other countries.
- **c.** providing more power to environmental protection agencies.
- **d.** none of the above

17. Most research and development spending takes place in the
- **a.** pharmaceutical industry.
- **b.** information technology hardware.
- **c.** chemical industry.
- **d.** automotive sector.

18. Which of the following is NOT a political risk that currently controls businesses?
- **a.** risk related to labor and political action groups
- **b.** risk related to competitive action
- **c.** risk related to terrorism
- **d.** risk related to government policies

19. During a period of poor economic performance, the government might reduce the expenditures that facilitate industry performance. What strategies are appropriate at this time?
- **a.** reducing the expenditures on the transportation infrastructure
- **b.** reducing the expenditures for the military
- **c.** limiting contracts on government-subsidized development projects
- **d.** all of the above

20. How could companies reduce the risk and/or costs of terrorism?
- **a.** by training their employees in terrorism avoidance
- **b.** by purchasing additional insurance against terrorism
- **c.** by considering the cultural, ethical, religious, and political issues of globalization
- **d.** all of the above

Notes

1. Chana R. Schoenberger, "A Valley Girl Grows Up," *Forbes*, vol. 170, no. 9 (October 28, 2002): 114.
2. Susan Greco, "How to Benchmark Sales-and-Marketing Budgets," *Inc.*, vol. 21, no. 2 (February 1999): 1c.
3. See Dana-Nicoleta Lascu, Lalita A. Manrai, Ajay K. Manrai, and Ryszard Kleczek, "Interfunctional Dynamics and Firm Performance," working paper; and Ajay K. Kohli and Bernard J. Jaworski, "Market Orientation: The Construct, Research Propositions, and Managerial Implications," *Journal of Marketing*, 54 (April 1990), 1–18.
4. "Tale of Three Trends," *Monthly Labor Review*, vol. 125, no. 4 (April 1, 2002): 64.
5. "The Gen Y Budget," *American Demographics*, vol. 24, no. 7 (July/August 2002): S4.
6. "The Gen X Budget," *American Demographics*, vol. 24, no. 7 (July/August 2002): S5.
7. "The Younger Boomer Budget," *American Demographics*, vol. 24, no. 7 (July/August 2002): S6.
8. "The Older Boomer Budget," *American Demographics*, vol. 24, no. 7 (July/August 2002): S7.
9. "The Empty Nester Budget," *American Demographics*, vol. 24, no. 7 (July/August 2002): S8.
10. "The Senior Budget," *American Demographics*, vol. 24, no. 7 (July/August 2002): S10.
11. See Milton J. Rokeach, *The Nature of Human Values* (New York: The Free Press, 1973); and Jan-Benedict E. M. Steenkamp, Frenkel ter Hofstede, and Michel Wedel, "A Cross-Cultural Investigation into the Individual and National Cultural Antecedents of Consumer Innovativeness," *Journal of Consumer Research*, vol. 63 (April 1999): 55–69.
12. Michael J. Mandel, "In a One-World Economy, a Slump Sinks All Boats," *Business Week*, Industrial Technology Edition, no. 3738 (June 25, 2001): 38–39.
13. See Walt W. Rostow, *The Stages of Economic Growth: A Non-Communist Manifesto* (London and New York: Cambridge University Press, 1960); ———, "The Concept of a National Market and Its Economic Growth Implications," in *Marketing and Economic Development*, ed. P. D. Bennett (Chicago: American Marketing Association, 1965): 11–20; and ———, *The Stages of Economic Growth*, Second Edition (London: Cambridge University Press, 1971).
14. Terry Pristin and Marianne Rohrlich, "Latest Word in Luxury Is Haggling," *New York Times* (October 16, 2002): A2.
15. Tim Studt and Jules J. Duga, "Smaller Increase Forecast for U.S. Research Spending," *Research & Development*, vol. 44, no. 1 (January 2002): F3–F8.
16. Ibid.
17. Ibid.
18. Mary Williams Walsh, "Corporations Revise Wish Lists," *New York Times* (November 7, 2002): C1, C5.
19. Michael Gips, "Businesses Bearing Brunt of Terrorism," *Security Management*, vol. 45, no. 8 (August 2001): 18.
20. Ibid.
21. "Counter-Terrorism Driver Training May Thwart Executive Kidnapping," *Best's Review*, vol. 98, no. 2 (June 1997): 95.

Case 2-1: The House-Proud Consumers

- One in ten homeowners spends more than $5,000 a year on remodeling.
- More than 26 million homeowners reported undertaking a home-improvement project in 2003, spending $176 billion, or 2 percent of the nation's economy.
- More than 75 percent of homeowners report a home improvement within two years of having a child.

Home renovation has become a national pastime. Whether hiring contractors or as do-it-yourself mavericks, consumers are transforming their living quarters at a breakneck pace and with committed passion. Quality-of-life improvements are very high on people's lists since September 11, 2001. Before September 11, if consumers had an extra $15,000 to spend, they were likely to spend it on two weeks in Europe. Today they are putting in a media room or a steam shower. They have come to realize that $15,000 could buy major home improvements that they could have for years, not just weeks.

Young couples prepare rooms for their first child and then build an addition to accommodate family life with two children. Later, bright playrooms become teenagers' hangouts. Empty nesters reinvent the home as an expression of their tastes, comfort, and status, and then sell it to buyers who tear it apart to renovate to their own tastes. These individuals could move to a house in the Sunbelt that better fits their needs, but they might still have to renovate for a perfect fit—and spend $10,000 on a move and 6 percent in brokerage fees.

But renovation makes perfect sense. House prices have risen faster than the dollar-per-square-foot cost of renovating, which suggests that investing in your home is wise. The cost of buying a new home has escalated an average of 3.7 percent a year since 1994 (and double or triple that number in the country's hottest markets), while the cost of remodeling has gone up just 2.8 percent annually. Moreover, properties that are not properly maintained deteriorate. Kitchens and baths should be redone every 15 to 20 years to preserve the value of the house investment. Houses built in the 1960s had 1 1/2 baths, a small kitchen, and no family room, while today's new homes have three baths, great rooms, and master bedrooms you can land a plane in. The price of not keeping your home up-to-date is that it may eventually sell for significantly less than others of the same size, or it may linger on the market for months.

The house-proud constitute a very attractive target market for home-improvement stores, magazines, television programs, and contractors. These consumers rummage through expensive, glossy magazines for renovation and decoration inspiration—Kitchen and Bath, House and Garden, Southern Living, Coastal Living, and This Old House, spending hundreds of dollars on do-it-yourself books and videos, and call on friends and colleagues for contractor referrals. They tour appliance and furniture design showrooms, and rummage through tiles in tile specialty shops. In the evening, they are glued to Home and Garden Television (HGTV) programs such as This Old House, Weekend Warriors, Curb Appeal, and Before and After.

These glossy magazines, books, and programs present a cornucopia of styles and choices—fanciful, practical, cutting-edge, and neotraditional; Italian, British, Danish; stainless and distressed—and direct consumers to retailers where good taste in the form of mass-produced distinction and democratized connoisseurship is finally available to all, regardless of income and social class. Like the food revolution, the home design revolution is built on the paradox that what is special should be available for everyone's enjoyment and that good taste can at last shed its residue of invidious social differences.

Questions

1. Which demographic segments described in the text represent the best market for renovation businesses?
2. What types of industries and businesses can take advantage of this trend for renovation? How should each industry or business market itself to this group?
3. What is the economic motivation behind renovation? How does consumer income influence this decision? How does the economic cycle influence it?
4. What type of influences has the technological environment had on home renovation over the past 20 years? What technological advances might impact this market in the future?

Sources: A. O. Scott, "Interior Life," *The New York Times Magazine* (December 1, 2002): 19–20; Jean Sherman Chatzky and Lysa Price, "Home Remedies," *Money,* vol. 31, no. 5, (May 2002): 108–120; Sheila Muto, "Home & Family: Repairs and Improvements Totaled $233 Billion in 2003," *The Wall Street Journal* (January 13, 2005): D5.

Case 2-2 Munich Re: Changing the Industry after the September 11 Terrorist Attacks

Background

On September 11, 2001, apocalyptic images from the World Trade Center and the Pentagon inundated broadcast and print media around the world. The events of September 11 marked the beginning of new levels of vulnerability for businesses, for national and local governments, for the airlines, and for individuals. The insurance and reinsurance industries experienced the largest aggregate losses ever as a result of the attacks. Half a world away, in Munich, Germany, the world's largest reinsurance company, Munich Re (in German, Münchener Rück), suffered a loss of $1.84 billion as a result of the terrorist attacks on U.S. soil.[1] In an effort to adapt to the new, post-September 11 business environment and its challenges, the insurance and reinsurance firms were forced to change their entire marketing mix. One company that is undergoing a complete overhaul of its marketing strategy is Munich Re.

The Reinsurance Industry

Insurance firms rely on reinsurance firms to minimize losses, allowing for costs attributed to insurance losses to be distributed among multiple companies; the reinsurance industry makes it possible for insurance companies to take risks that they would not otherwise,[2] creating new opportunities for increased revenue and market share. The amount of risk assumed by reinsurers varies with the market. When the market is optimistic, reinsurers are more likely to assume greater risks; more capital is available, so the companies are capable of underwriting additional risk.[3] In 2001, the faltering state of markets worldwide depleted the reinsurance companies' capital; reinsurance companies were further confronted by the implications of the September 11, 2001, terrorist attacks. As a result, the reinsurance industry is exploring the different ways in which it can alter the mix of products offered to insurance firms all over the world and pricing strategies to most effectively operate in the present volatile environment.

Munich Re

Munich Re was founded in 1880 by Carl Thieme, who, with a vision far ahead of his time, created the reinsurance business. He convinced investors of the insurance companies' need for reinsurance as a means for redistributing risk (and loss) among insurance firms, thus allowing them to take advantage of opportunities that otherwise they could not afford to consider.[4] Munich Re is headquartered in downtown Munich, Germany, where it covers a couple of square blocks with impressive older and contemporary architecture. In front of its newest building, the tall figure of the Walking Man, by American artist Jonathan Borofsky, appears to leave the complex in a hurry (see Figure 2-19).

Inside the Munich Re complex, a Japanese garden offers an environment of meditation. Underground, all the buildings are connected with active corridors where color and light set a theatric stage; here, a second "downtown"—the downtown of Munich Re employees—exists in parallel to the bustling street, Leopoldstrasse. The environment projects a strong spirit of innovation, the very theme of Munich Re's corporate culture.[5] In addition to its quest for product innovation, Munich Re was the first German company to introduce English working hours in the nineteenth century, requiring shorter days from its employees and granting them greater leisure time; the company is also among a few in Germany that provide benefits such as access to a holiday home in the Alps and an onsite daycare—the Munich Re Giants Childcare Center.[6]

The Munich Re Product

With a dependable brand, international presence, diversified product offering, and 42 offices around the world, Munich Re has attracted customers and investors alike, and today it remains the largest reinsurance company in the world. The company offers several different types of insurance services, such as Alternative Risk-Financing and Risk-Transfer Solutions (ART), Agricultural Insurance, Managed Care Services, and Life Insurance. ART, including Finite Risk Reinsurance and Integrated Risk Management, supplements conventional reinsurance as a means of maximizing risk retention and discovering additional financial resources. This is an area that Munich Re has pioneered and that is especially in great demand today, after the September 11 events. Finite Risk Reinsurance allows the company to undertake more risk by using innovative financing techniques, rather than simply by transferring risk from the insured to the insurer.

Integrated Risk Management merges insurance risks with the risks involved in financial markets—for example, in currency fluctuation and in fluctuating interest rates. The objective of Integrated Risk Management is to achieve both the reinsurer's goals of the lowest possible risk and the client's goals of highest possible security and support.

Munich Re provides a number of other insurance services, covering all aspects of the economy. For example, Agricultural Insurance is a service that Munich Re has developed to protect commercial farmers in times of catastrophe and natural disaster. Its Managed Care Services, part of the Munich Re Health Division, are involved in evaluating each potential medical procedure that it insures to determine if, in fact, the procedure is essential. Finally, the company's Life Insurance services give the company access to final consumers—a different market than its traditional business-to-business market segments (its organizational consumers).

The September 11 Terrorist Attacks

Munich Re, much like other reinsurance companies, has had numerous challenges, many dealing with medical advances and genetics decoding, and others with natural disasters. More recently, Munich Re had to absorb the costs involved in the recall of Lipobay, a cholesterol-reducing drug that was linked to death among users; a large typhoon in Taiwan; and a chemical plant explosion in France.[7] Yet these losses were dwarfed by the September 11, 2001 terrorist attacks, when terrorists crashed passenger airplanes into the World Trade Center in New York, demolishing the twin towers and severely damaging the Pentagon in Washington, D.C. Total estimates for damages were between $10 and $12 billion; in addition to

Figure 2-19
The Munich Re Headquarters in Munich, Germany.

property costs and life insurance coverage, the insurance industry had to bear the costs for clean-up, replacement of items lost, and an array of other losses.[8] Original estimates were low, but by mid-September the major players of the reinsurance industry alone were expecting claims to total more than $3 billion for the disaster.[9] Munich Re's claims totaled $1.84 billion.[10]

Before September 11, 2001 terrorist attacks of this magnitude were inconceivable and were not considered in the calculations of premiums and the like. According to P. J. Crowley of the Insurance Institute of America, "There has never been a premium dollar collected to cover terrorism."[11] Reinsurance firms had to reconsider their stance on what coverage they would offer in the event of future terrorist attacks. For now, many insurance and reinsurance companies have included clauses in their policies that exclude the coverage of losses from any type of terrorism. Munich Re "was hit by the claims from September 11th more than other members of the reinsurance industry and thus it will have to make careful decisions concerning what to do about providing protection against terrorist claims."[12]

Today, Munich Re and most other insurers require exclusions in property insurance, for example; also joint ventures between state compensation and private insurance are becoming common.

Reinsurance companies consider four primary criteria of general risk insurability:

- Assessibility; most of the reinsurance companies have been lax in the past about ensuring that insurance companies have a clear (transparent) assessment of potential risk
- Randomness
- Mutuality
- Economic feasibility

After evaluating these risks, only a handful of companies have opted to provide terrorism risk coverage; however, if national governments agree to subsidize the industry, it is likely that more will join. These companies are:

- General Cologne Reinsurance (General Re); the company owns General Reinsurance Corporation, the market leader in the United States. General Re alone lost $1.7 billion from the September 11 attacks, but, for now, it continues to cover terrorist actions (although this might change in the future).

- Swiss Re, a challenger to Munich Re as the number-one reinsurance firm worldwide, also experienced substantial losses.
- Copenhagen Re, once a large and active player in the reinsurance business and a major competitor of Munich Re, ceased underwriting for two years as a consequence of the attacks and, as a result, has lost consumer confidence.

Changing the Marketing Mix at Munich Re

Compared to competition, Munich Re has handled the aftermath of September 11 well. After the attacks, insurance and reinsurance companies were reevaluated by Standard & Poor's to assess the appropriateness of rating that had been determined before September 11. The rating company agreed that their ratings of AAA/Stable were still appropriate for Munich Re, based on the company's performance by the end of 2001.[13]

In the wake of claims payout from the terrorist attacks, Munich Re found itself with less competition in the reinsurance industry as a number of smaller reinsurers had losses attributed to the September 11 attacks that caused them to leave the industry altogether.[14]

Subsequently, Munich Re experienced substantial losses: 557 million euros in 2002. Economic losses from natural catastrophes rose sharply due to heat waves, forest fires, severe floods in Asia and Europe, as well as tornadoes in the Midwestern United States.[15] Its ratings dropped from AA, further to A-plus.[16]

After deciding to underwrite more profitable businesses, however, Munich Re was able to rebound with a profit of 534 million euros ($646.4 million) in 2003.[17] This profit was gained in spite of severe natural hazard events, with the number of fatalities well above the average: More than 50,000 people were killed in natural catastrophes, such as more than 400 tornadoes in the Midwestern United States, California wildfires, hurricane Isabel, and snow and ice storms. In Europe, the company lost more than $13 billion due to the heat waves.[18] Ratings also dropped for most reinsurance companies because insurance companies today insist on having trigger clauses, which allow them to withdraw their business, demanding that a portion of the premiums be returned, or requiring the reinsurer to post collateral to help cover claims that the insurance companies may later present for payment.[19] As of 2005, Munich Re's rating is A+/Stable and the company is working on improving its Standard & Poor's rating from A+ to AA.[20]

Before September 11, 2001, no reinsurance company had ever considered terrorist actions of such magnitude when calculating Probable Maximum Loss (PML) for the properties insured. Insurance companies had to cover losses of more than 1,200 corporations housed in the World Trade Center complex, damage to the operating areas, loss of experienced employees, and destruction of business data and business income. More than 50 buildings were affected in addition to the World Trade Center, and 150,000 people were out of work permanently or temporarily.[21] These extreme circumstances led the reinsurance companies to change their marketing mix—especially the reinsurance product and its price.

According to Nicholas Roenneberg, senior executive manager, corporate underwriting/global clients division at Munich Re, if such a catastrophe had to happen, it did so at an opportune time for the company—when the company was renewing its policies for the year 2002 (most policies start at the beginning of the calendar year). At that point, the company placed all policy negotiations on hold so that it could reconfigure its marketing mix.

For the short term, Munich Re determined that terrorism was no longer insurable given the high risks, especially in high property concentrations. In these environments, it is impossible to estimate the frequency of such attacks and their total impact, thus presenting a situation in which an important criterion of general risk insurability—accessibility—cannot be met. In the long term, however, there may be some custom options for insurance for properties evaluated at more than 50 million euros (more than $50 million) on a case-by-case basis. Ultimately, all types of insurance options may be subject to negotiation. No terrorism exclusion, however, is imposed on life and personal accident insurance.

After the events of September 11, companies doing business with Munich Re were required to document all risks—many companies had not diligently met this requirement in the past. Transparency has become a most important criterion of insurability for Munich Re clients.

In terms of price, the company raised rates for aviation insurance by 80 percent; coincidentally, and to the advantage of Munich Re, aviation renewals were due on October 1, 2001, just after the September terrorist attacks. For property insurance, rates have gone up by 20 to 40 percent across the board.

With regard to promotion, the company has not changed its strategy substantially. It offers no advertising and no sponsorship. One of its main venues for communicating beyond its customer base is its website, which is comprehensive and well updated. Just after the September 11 attacks, the company undertook a tremendous public relations effort to inform shareholders about the impact of the attacks on the company's bottom line. The company increased the frequency of communication, particularly with large institutional investors; a preferred venue for such communication was telephone conferencing.

According to Christian Lahnstein, a specialist in genetic engineering law and liability law with Munich Re, there is an interest in the industry to learn from the experience of the September 11, 2001 events about the intervention of government in bailing out industries affected by disaster and about issues related to the equity of distribution of funds from the government and charitable sources. These findings may have an impact on the marketing mix of the company in the future.

Questions

1. Before analyzing the Munich Re case, address the political risk signals that brought about the September 11, 2001 terrorist actions. How can companies reduce their likelihood of becoming victims of terrorism?
2. As you conduct your case analysis, address the strategic changes to each element of the marketing mix at Munich Re as a result of the September 11 terrorist attacks.

Source: This case was developed by Jodie Applegate, Kristin DeYonker, Andrea Fuller, Dana Lascu, Brian Stroop, and Elise Woodling.

Notes for Case 2-2

1. "Re Costs $1.1B Loss," CNN.com Europe, http://europe.cnn.com/ (November 29, 2001): 1 (web); February 21, 2002.
2. "What Exactly Does a Reinsurer Do?" *Jobs and Career,* Munich Re, www.munichre.com/index.html (February 25, 2002): 1 (web).
3. "Finance and Economics: Premium Rates; Reinsurance," *The Economist* (February 9, 2002): 79.
4. "Profit Through Pioneering Spirit," *History,* Munich Re, www.munichre.com/index.html (February 24, 2002): 1 (web).
5. "Corporate Responsibility," *120 Years of Innovation,* Munich Re, www.munichre.com/index.html (February 24, 2002): 1 (web).
6. Ibid.
7. "Reinsurer Munich Re Posts US $1.06B Loss, Keeps Damage Estimates from Attacks," *Canoe Money,* www.canoe.ca/MoneyEarnings/nov29_munichre-ap.html (November 29, 2001): 1–2 (web); February 21, 2002.
8. September 2001, *Munchener Ruckversicherungs-Gesellschaft* (2001): 9.
9. "Reinsurers Double Terrorist Claims," *CNN Money,* http://money.cnn.com/2001/09/20/europe/insurance/index.htm (September 20, 2001): 1 (web); February 21, 2002.
10. "Munich Re Posts $1.1B Loss," http://europe.cnn.com/.
11. Dan Ackman, "Insurers Make a Claim on Taxpayers," Forbes.com, www.forbes.com/ (October 22, 2001): 1 (web); February 21, 2002.
12. Deborah Orr, "Risk Buster," Forbes.com, www.forbes.com/ (January 21, 2002): 1–2 (web); February 21, 2002.
13. "After the Terrorist Attacks: US Rating Agencies Affirm Their Top Rating for Munich Re," *Munich American News,* www.marclife.com/news01/mr100501.htm (October 5, 2001): 1 (web); February 21, 2002.
14. "Reinsurer Munich Re Posts US $1.06B Loss, Keeps Damage Estimate from Attacks," 2 (website: www.munichre.com).
15. Meg Green, "Extreme Weather Patterns Pose Greater Insurance Risk," *Best's Review,* vol. 104, no. 11 (March 2004): 69.
16. Ulrike Dauer, "Munich Re Reports Net Profits as Write-Downs, Claims Decline," *The Wall Street Journal* (May 27, 2004): A6.
17. Green, "Extreme Weather Patterns Pose Greater Insurance Risk."
18. "Munich Re: Reinsurer May Trim Holdings; Will Tie Dividends to Profits," *The Wall Street Journal,* (April 16, 2004): A7.
19. Stephen Searby and Wolfgang Rief, "Munich Re Group's 2004 Results in Line with Expectations; Ratings Unaffected," Standard & Poor (www2.standardandpoors.com, March 2005).
20. "11th September 2001: The Attack on the World Trade Center in New York from an Insurance Point of View," 2 (website: www.munichre.com).
21. Ibid.

Part 2

Marketing Foundation

Marketing Ethics, Regulations, and Social Responsibility

3

CHAPTER OBJECTIVES

1. Identify the ethical issues faced by marketers and discuss the pros and cons of each issue.
2. Discuss the legislation and regulatory agencies that impact marketing.
3. Describe the role of the Federal Trade Commission as it relates to marketing and discuss how it investigates complaints.
4. Discuss the role of the Better Business Bureau in regulating marketing activities.
5. Discuss the social responsibility of business firms and provide examples showing how a firm can demonstrate its social responsibility.

CHAPTER OUTLINE

Teenagers, a huge market for goods and services, spend more than $175 billion a year. This translates to $71.00 a week for males and $61.50 a week for females. However, it is not just their spending power that makes them attractive to marketers; it is the idea of developing brand loyalty. A study by Harris Interactive found that girls develop a brand preference for fragrances as well as cars, trucks, and vans when they are 12. When they are 13, they begin establishing brand preferences for designer apparel, portable electronics, and prestigious beauty products. Approximately two-thirds of the teens will continue buying their favorite brands, and 80 percent will try new products made by their favorite brands. In addition, teens tell others about their favorite brands, an average of 7.3 people compared to an average of 5.3 for adults.

If teens can be tied to a particular brand at a young age, then it is conceivable that they will be loyal to the brand for the rest of their lives. However, marketing to teens can be tricky. Teens are adventurous, easily excited, and eager to try new products, but their tastes can change overnight. They may want your brand today but your competitors' brands tomorrow.

According to Jarrod Moses, CEO and President of Alliance (a subsidiary of Grey Worldwide), "Teens are the most active target in the world. If you think you'll reach them by just throwing an ad on the WB, you'll be wrong. You can't look at TV as a primary vehicle. You have to build a lifestyle campaign. The traditional ways of advertising and marketing [do] not exist anymore."

According to Born to be Wired, a study by Yahoo! with Carat Interactive, among teenagers 13 to 18, 82 percent have computers, 62 percent have videogame consoles, 49 percent have cell phones, 32 percent have SMS, and 13 percent have PDAs. Reaching these teens requires using more nontraditional methodologies and less television. For example, Coke developed a Cokemusic.com campaign in which teens looked under bottle caps of specially marked bottles for a secret code. The code was then keyed into a website for points (called Decibels) and later redeemed for prizes. To reach teens with the information about the latest movies, New Line Cinema ran 15- and 30-second streaming video ads on AOL's Instant Messenger. Other companies have turned to in-game advertising on videogames.

While reaching teens is difficult, understanding teens may be even a greater challenge. In the Harris Interactive study, teens described themselves as independent, savvy, mature, sophisticated, influential, and brand-conscious. They have grown up with advertising and know good advertising from bad. They cannot be tricked into buying something just because it is supposed to be cool. According to Harris Interactive,

86 percent said they do not buy something simply because it is considered hot.

83 percent stated they do not buy brands just because they are popular.

75 percent noted they buy brands that reflect their style.

67 percent reported they buy brands that express their personality.

Advertising to teens requires nontraditional approaches and ads that are often cutting-edge. Not all critics approve of these methods of targeting teens. While not children, teenagers are not yet adults. Questions arise as to which goods and services are safe to promote to teens and which are not. In terms of advertising, debate centers on what is appropriate for teens and what is not? Certainly, advertising soft drinks would be appropriate, but questions were raised when 7-Eleven did it with an ad where a slurpee was used to freeze a teen's tongue in preparation for piercing it. Questions were raised when K-Mart advertised Joe Boxer underwear to teens. Was it appropriate to use teens in commercials for the underwear, and did such ads promote sexual activity?

Because of concerns of this type, the Canadian Marketing Association recently developed a code of ethics concerning marketing to teenagers. In part, it reads: "Marketers shall not portray sexual behavior appropriate to adults using teenagers or juvenile models or actors in marketing communications directed to teenagers. Marketers shall not suggest that a teen not consult, inform or obtain consent from a parent or guardian for a purchase." The code of ethics goes on to discuss privacy issues and what information can be obtained from young teens, ages 13–15, without their parents' permission, what information can be gathered only with parents' permission, and most importantly, how this information can be used.

Most of you were recently teenagers. What impact did marketing have on your behavior and your purchases? This chapter presents some of the ethical issues about marketing and resulting regulations.[1]

3-1 Chapter Overview

A primary goal of marketing is to develop a customer base that will desire and purchase a firm's products. In this process, marketing material is developed that will persuade consumers and other businesses about the firm's products. Ethical issues will arise about the material that is developed, as well as about how the marketing material is transmitted and even to whom it is transmitted, as was just discussed in the chapter-opening vignette. Section 3-2 discusses these ethical issues, presenting both criticism of and a defense for marketing to familiarize students with both sides of the issues.

Because companies and organizations do act in unprofessional and even illegal ways, a number of laws have been passed to protect consumers and businesses. Section 3-3 addresses the legal environment of business, described in Chapter 2, "The Environment of Marketing in the Twenty-First Century," as a component of the macroenvironment of the company. It is important to present the legal issues involved in marketing alongside ethics-related concerns and company self-regulation attempts. The section highlights the primary legislation that impacts marketing and the agencies that are responsible for regulating marketing activities. Of special importance to marketing is the Federal Trade Commission. This section closes with a discussion of industry regulatory agencies available through the Better Business Bureau.

Section 3-4 presents the positive side of the ethical issue—social responsibility. Firms are expected to act in a socially responsible manner. Two ways in which they can do this are cause-related marketing and green marketing. Both are discussed.

3-2 Ethical Issues in Marketing

Ethics: Philosophical principles that serve as operational guidelines for both individuals and organizations concerning what is right and wrong.

Morals: Personal beliefs or standards used to guide an individual's actions.

In understanding ethical issues in marketing, it is important to differentiate between ethics and morals. **Ethics** are philosophical principles that serve as operational guidelines for both individuals and organizations concerning what is right and wrong. **Morals** are personal beliefs or standards used to guide an individual's actions. Morals direct people as they make decisions about everything from personal conduct, to sexual behavior, to work activities, to family life, and interaction with other individuals. A person's feelings about companies can be based on his or her moral feelings. For example, numerous citizens believe the United States should not conduct business with countries that have a history of human rights violations or exploit child labor. Some will even boycott brands that operate in these countries.

Ethics help us as individuals and organizations to establish boundaries regarding acceptable and unacceptable conduct. Many leaders in organizations assert that they wish to be ethical in their decisions. Yet, recent events with companies such as Enron and WorldCom have spurred the need for a higher level of ethical behavior within corporations. The public is now demanding that companies, their leaders, and their employees act in an ethical manner. How are your ethics? Before proceeding any further with this chapter, take "The Top 10 Test" on marketing ethics found in Table 3-1.

Over the years, marketing has come under attack for questionable activities. Some of the major criticisms of marketing are listed in Table 3-2. It is important to examine these criticisms in an introductory course in marketing. While unfair and unethical behavior has occurred and will undoubtedly occur in the future, it is important to examine both sides of the issue and see how marketing can benefit society as a whole. If conducted in an ethical manner, marketing is not only a powerful force in the success of organizations, but it can also provide the opportunity for consumers to become more enlightened purchasers of goods and services.

3-2a Marketing Causes People to Buy More Than They Can Afford

Marketing critics have voiced the concern that marketing persuades individuals to purchase goods and services that they do not need and cannot afford. While it is true that millions of marketing dollars are spent to influence purchase decisions and sometimes people buy more than they should, the easy acquisition of credit and the overuse of credit cards makes it possible to overbuy.

The average number of credit cards per household is now 14.27, with an average balance of $7,034. Each year, more than 5 billion credit card offers are mailed to consumers.[2] But should all of the blame lie with credit companies? No, not anymore than it should be blamed on marketing. Overspending appears to be an epidemic, cultural change in our society caused by people seeking immediate gratification. Few are willing to save and make a purchase only when they have the cash. This tendency to live beyond one's means, however, has been exacerbated by the relatively easy escape offered by until-recently lenient U.S. bankruptcy laws (see Figure 3-1 on page 67). Based on recent legislation, consumers who have assets are forced to pay back some of their debts; however, the legislation requires credit card companies to rein in their reckless lending.[3]

3-2b Marketing Overemphasizes Materialism

Closely tied to the notion that people buy goods and services they cannot afford is the criticism that marketing has created a materialistic society. The debates center on one issue: Has the marketing of goods and services created an attitude of materialism, or has marketing merely responded to the materialistic desires of society?

Underlying this argument is the assumption that materialism is wrong. In response, those who defend this aspect of free enterprise suggest that materialism, like many other things, is bad only if carried to an extreme. In comparing developing countries with the United States and other developed countries with high-consumption cultures, it is easy to show how materialism has created a positive impact on society and the standard of living people enjoy.

3-2c Marketing Increases the Prices of Goods and Services

Does marketing increase the prices of goods and services? Yes, it does. There is no doubt prices would be lower if marketing were eliminated. But before we just cut marketing out, we must consider the following four factors: First, marketing creates intangible benefits for a product. Second, marketing provides information that allows consumers to become better informed. Third, a company can reduce its marketing efforts only if all the competitors within the industry do the same. Fourth, marketing is a significant contributor to the nation's GDP.

TABLE 3-1

The Top 10 Test of Right or Wrong

INTERACTIVE TABLE

Answer right or wrong to each of the following ethical situations. Be honest. Don't give the answer you think is right, but what you would do in that situation. No one will know your score.

1. *Share the Glory*—You're writing the monthly status report to the Board detailing the performance of your division. The talk in the corridor is about the incredible success resulting from an innovative strategic suggestion championed by a competitor in your division. Trouble is, you really dislike the guy. It's a personal thing. You deliberately fail to acknowledge his contribution and take all the glory yourself. Right or wrong?
2. *The Silent Kickback*—You're a consultant. A client, who trusts you implicitly, asks you to recommend a third-party vendor for a planned capital purchase. You provide a vendor recommendation but fail to mention that the vendor is going to commission you on the lead ... the classic 10-percent-off-the-top routine. Incidentally, the vendor in question does good work and there's no fiddling with the pricing structure because of your referral fee. You choose not to say anything to your client about the arrangement. Right or wrong?
3. *He's Not in Right Now*—You don't use voice mail. Your assistant, who screens your calls, informs you that Mr. Unhappy, who has been trying to track you down for the past week, is on the line. You have time to take the call. Courtesy alone dictates that you take it, but you choose to blow it off with any one of the common excuses (i.e., he's in a meeting, he's on the phone talking to London). Right or wrong?
4. *Promises Not Kept*—You run a research firm and recently sold a proposed industry study to a group of clients based on the guarantee that you'll be conducting interviews with 100 industry influentials. Because of timing and logistical difficulties, you complete only 75 of the interviews. However, you're still going to lose a ton of money on the deal. You priced the study too low to begin with, and it ended up absorbing more time than you had projected. Your clients, those who bought the study, have already prepaid and like the results even though you fell short of the guaranteed interview count. You choose to remain silent and not proportionally rebate your clients for the shortfall. Right or wrong?
5. *The Refund Not Refunded*—You're flying to meet a client in another city. At the last minute, you decide to extend the trip to visit a second client while you're on the road. The deal is that your clients always rebate you in full for travel expenses. You bill both clients for the full return airfare from your city to theirs, in spite of the fact that you were able to secure a multi-city, discounted fare and in the process made money on the deal. Right or wrong?
6. *The Money-Back Guarantee*—Your sales literature very clearly states that a dissatisfied customer is entitled to a full refund or credit irrespective of the reason or the cause. You do a job for a client but, because of contributory negligence on both sides, as well as a lack of clear definition and cause of the problem, your client chooses to pay you and let the matter drop. You believe that you went above and beyond the call of duty in addressing the client's needs. But you still don't offer a refund. Right or wrong?

Source: From "How Is Your Marketing Conscience?" by Alf Nucifora from *Fort Worth Press,* October 20, 2000. Reproduced with permission of the author. Alf Nucifora is a nationally syndicated marketing columnist and consultant. He can be contacted by phone at 404-816-6999 (Atlanta) or by email at alf@nucifora.com. His website is www.nucifora.com.

TABLE 3-2

Ethical Issues in Marketing

- Marketing causes people to buy more than they can afford.
- Marketing overemphasizes materialism.
- Marketing increases the prices of goods and services.
- Marketing capitalizes on human weaknesses.
- Marketing shapes inappropriate cultural values.
- Marketing uses deceptive and misleading techniques.
- Marketing violates consumer rights to privacy.

7. *The Plane Crash*—You're the marketing director of a major airline. One of your planes crashes because of airline negligence. You know that you have to expose the airline's insurance representatives to the next-of-kin as soon as possible in order to negotiate quick settlements. The longer the delay, the greater the risk that a class-action-suit attorney will get to them first and force protracted litigation, which, in turn, will result in higher settlement costs. It doesn't feel right to force a confrontation with the next-of-kin at their moment of greatest vulnerability, but you do it anyway. Right or wrong?
8. *The Name Dropper*—You and I meet for the first time. During the meeting, you ask me to provide names of friends and associates, people who might be prospects for your product or service. You subsequently write them a letter, and in the opening paragraph, you mention that the referral came from me. The problem is, you did it without my permission. When I gave you the names, I neglected (and you deliberately failed) to mention the issue. Right or wrong?
9. *The Fake Request for Approval (RFP)*—You're the head of a young, aggressive advertising agency, and you'd love to know how your competitors package and present themselves. Therefore, you fake an RFP for an imaginary account that's up for review, send it out, and specify that responses be mailed to a blind postal address. Your competition wastes precious time responding to a fictitious RFP, and you gain valuable insights into your competitors' psychology and marketing technique. Right or wrong?
10. *Fresh from the Faucet*—You're in the bottled water business. Unlike your competitors' products, your water doesn't come from a natural source. No gurgling springs for you. You take good old-fashioned town water, distill it, treat it, and package it with a fake, natural-sounding name, together with label artwork resplendent with waterfalls and bubbling brooks: A classic case of the reality not matching the perception. But it's great marketing. Right or wrong?

Results

- If you answered "right" to 0–1 of the situations: Congratulations! You make good ethical decisions.
- If you answered "right" to 2–3 of the situations: Congratulations! You tend to make good ethical decisions, but at times you are not sure what is the correct course of action.
- If you answered "right" to 4–10 of the situations: Ethics is an important issue that you will want to study further. It is important not only to recognize ethical situations, but also to make good ethical decisions.

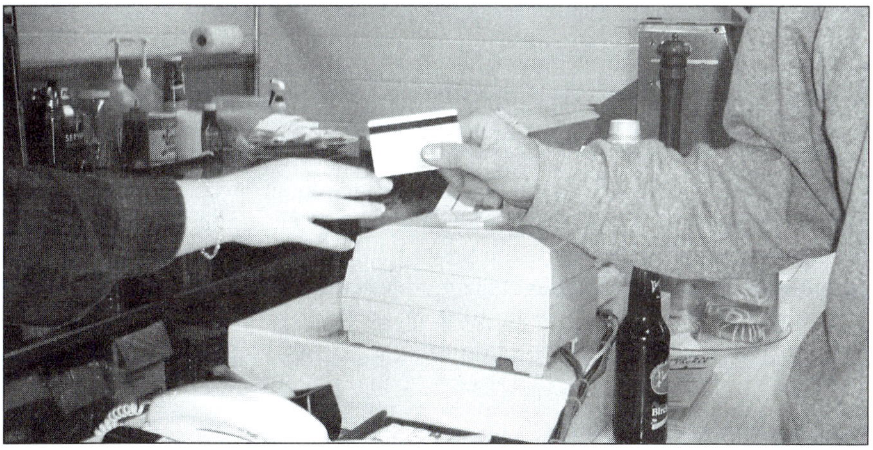

Figure 3-1
Overspending using credit cards is a national and international epidemic.

Figure 3-2
Advertising is an important component in building a strong brand for products like GMC trucks.
Source: Courtesy of The Marketing Exchange.

Marketing can be used to create intangible benefits for goods and services. Consider the case of Nike shoes, GMC trucks (see Figure 3-2), Levi jeans, McDonald's restaurants, Tide detergent, American Express credit cards, and Southwest Airlines. Each of these brands conveys a meaning beyond the product category. Nike, Jaguar, and Levi can command higher prices because of the brand name, which is the result of their marketing effort. McDonald's and Southwest Airlines enjoy a large market share in their respective industries because they have been able to position themselves in a highly competitive market as the low-cost provider. Tide and American Express are highly recognizable names because of intensive advertising. Consumers purchase these brands and many others because of intangible benefits such as the trust and quality that stands behind the name. Consumers know that every time they purchase Tide, it will perform.

Through marketing, consumers have the opportunity to become better informed. Marketing can provide consumers with knowledge about specific brands as well as product categories. Until Rogaine advertisements appeared, consumers had no idea that there were products that could be used to prevent hair loss. Until Rogaine targeted some of its ads to females, consumers thought the product was only for men. Other forms of marketing communications such as point-of-purchase displays, product labels, and salespeople can provide valuable information to consumers to assist them in making wiser decisions.

Figure 3-3
Advertising provides important information to consumers, such as this ad for Family Care, informing consumers about its after-hours clinic.

Source: Courtesy of Newcomer, Morris and Young.

For example, the advertisement for Family Care in Figure 3-3 provides information about its after-hours clinic for individuals who may be sick on the weekends or in the evenings.

Firms within highly competitive industries such as soft drinks, automobiles, and athletic shoes would like to reduce the size of their marketing budget. But if competitors do not reduce their marketing budget, it will be difficult for a firm to remain competitive with the firms in the industry. Table 3-3 provides a list of the top six brands in the car and light truck industry by market share. Notice that the top six automobile brands are in the top 12 brands in total U.S. expenditures in advertising. Subaru, shown in the advertisement in Figure 3-4, ranks 88th in spending at $126.6 million, far behind the top six brands. See Table 3-4 on page 71 for a list of the top 25 megabrands and how much each spends on advertising alone. It is interesting to note that in the top 12 brands in terms of advertising spending, seven are automobile brands, three are telecommunications companies, one is a restaurant, and one is a department store.

Within the vehicles category, if Ford chose to reduce its advertising expenditure, it is highly likely it would lose market share unless Chevrolet, Toyota, Dodge, Honda, and Nissan also reduced their advertising spending. If all of these brands did agree to reduce their advertising expenditures, then it is likely they would face collusion charges for restraint of free trade. We do not want competitors making agreements among themselves that will in any way hinder the free market system.

Advertising in the United States alone totaled $231.3 billion, which is about 2.4 percent of the United States GDP. This does not include dollars spent on promotions, personal selling, and other forms of marketing communications. Traditionally, advertising accounts for about 25 percent of all marketing dollars. This means that the total marketing-related expenditures are around $912 billion, or 9.5 percent of the GDP. Eliminating marketing would create a tremendous loss of jobs and create a serious blow to the nation's GDP.

TABLE 3-3
Comparison of Market Share to Advertising Expenditures for Car and Light Truck Brands

Brand	Market Share for Top Car and Light Truck Brands		U.S. Advertising Expenditures by Brand	
	Percent	Rank	Total (millions)	Rank
Ford	19.2%	1	$655.9	4
Chevrolet	15.6%	2	$780.4	3
Toyota	8.8%	3	$568.3	7
Dodge	7.3%	4	$499.2	9
Honda	6.0%	5	$452.5	11
Nissan	3.7%	6	$428.1	12

Source: Adage.com (www.adage.com, November 2, 2002).

Figure 3-4
In terms of megabrands, Subaru ranks 88th in total ad spending at $126.6 million.

Source: Reprinted with the permission of Subaru of America, Inc.

3-2d Marketing Capitalizes on Human Weaknesses

A sensitive ethical issue in marketing is the promotion of goods or services of a highly personal nature or during times of human vulnerability. For example, after the terrorist attacks of September 11, 2001, it was felt that some companies utilized patriotic themes to promote sales rather than to display genuine concern for the situation and victims of the attacks. Funeral homes and other similar services have been accused of taking advantage of grieving loved ones to encourage purchases beyond an individual's means.

In terms of personal services, marketers have been criticized for promoting the idea that happiness depends on physical attractiveness.[4] Appearance is a critical issue, especially to females. To create an advertisement that feeds on insecurities about looks is considered by some to be unfair. To illustrate, consider the various ads for weight loss programs. Most display both "before" and "after" pictures, with the person, usually a female, looking forlorn in the "before" photo while the "after" shot depicts a much happier person.

In addition to weight loss programs, companies also offer consumers who are unhappy with their appearance services such as abdominoplasty (tummy tuck), electrolysis (hair removal), breast enhancements, and liposuction. All of these services are based on dissatisfaction with one's physical appearance. Critics say these efforts create unrealistic goals regarding personal appearance, and cause people to examine self-worth in an unfair, shallow, and sexist manner.

Recently, men have been attracted by this desire to enhance their physical appearance as well as their desire to improve their sexual performance. Hair coloring products, hair transplants, face-lifts, penile enlargement programs, and Viagra advertisements all feed on a person's insecurities. The issue here is similar to the first one that was raised about materialism: Is marketing driving human behavior or just responding to human desires (i.e., is

TABLE 3-4

Top 25 Megabrands and Advertising Expenditures

Rank	Megabrand	Industry	Advertising Expenditure (millions)
1–5	AT&T	Telecommunications	$996.6
	Verizon	Telecommunications	$824.4
	Chevrolet	Vehicles	$780.4
	Ford	Vehicles	$655.9
	McDonald's	Restaurants	$635.1
6–10	Sprint	Telecommunications	$620.4
	Toyota	Vehicles	$568.3
	Sears	Department stores	$511.5
	Dodge	Vehicles	$499.2
	Chrysler	Vehicles	$474.2
11–15	Honda	Vehicles	$452.5
	Nissan	Vehicles	$428.1
	Cingular	Telecommunications	$411.4
	Macy's	Department stores	$381.0
	Volkswagen	Vehicles	$365.9
16–20	Home Depot	Specialty stores	$347.3
	K-Mart	Discount stores	$338.1
	Wal-Mart	Discount stores	$329.4
	Target	Discount stores	$313.4
	JCPenney	Department stores	$308.4
21–25	IBM	Computers and software	$305.5
	Microsoft	Software	$302.0
	Burger King	Restaurants	$298.3
	Best Buy	Electronic stores	$266.0
	Visa	Credit cards	$251.9

Source: Adage.com (www.adage.com, November 2, 2002).

marketing responding to society's preoccupation with personal appearance, or is marketing taking advantage of a person's insecurities)?

3-2e Marketing Shapes Inappropriate Cultural Values

In terms of marketing's influence on cultural values, several issues are at stake. For example, marketing has been attacked for promoting products that are not good for public consumption. Alcohol and tobacco especially are believed to have a negative impact on people, and on society as a whole. This has led some activists to object to the advertising of these products. The first issue here is one of free speech and free enterprise. As long as the firms are not violating the law (e.g., selling to minors), then why shouldn't companies have the same right to market their products as any other organization?

The second issue is more philosophical. Does the promotion of such products shape cultural values, and if so, then is it ethical to encourage individuals to consume a product (e.g., tobacco) that is known to be harmful to their health and results in millions of dollars of health-care costs? If marketing, and especially advertising, indeed shapes cultural values, then it would appear that marketing should be regulated and controlled. The difficulty lies in the decision about who should determine what is appropriate and what is not appropriate. If, however, marketing just reflects the morals and values of our cultural environment, then regulating marketing would not be helpful in shaping cultural values.

To understand this dilemma better, consider the marketing of personal products such as condoms, feminine hygiene items, male sex enhancement drugs, bras, and underwear. In the 1960s, none of these products were advertised on television. Now all are advertised. Is this change a reflection of changing social and cultural values, or has the promotion of these types of products molded social and cultural values to a point where this is now acceptable?

Many citizens believe that advertisements are becoming more offensive. Sex and nudity are the most troubling and controversial issues. For example, Calvin Klein has been highly criticized for the level of nudity and sexual suggestiveness in its advertisements. Calvin Klein has a history of pushing sex and nudity to the limit. More recently, it has been cited for the manner in which children are used in its promotions. The objections began when 15-year-old Brooke Shields was featured in a Calvin Klein ad proclaiming "Nothing comes between me and my Calvins." People not only objected to Calvin Klein using a 15-year-old, but also objected to the sexual innuendos of a 15-year-old not wearing underwear. Viewers protested even stronger about a series of Calvin Klein television ads featuring underage girls being asked about their bodies. At the same time, a series of magazine ads featured partially clothed young models posing in sexy and suggestive ways to expose their underwear. Many magazine editors refused to run the print advertisements, and some television stations objected to the television commercials. Because of the complaints, the FBI investigated Calvin Klein to see if the magazine models were indeed 18-years-old.

Later, in an attempt to sell children's underwear, Calvin Klein decided to prepare a large billboard in Times Square to accompany a series of magazine advertisements. The billboard promoting its line of children's underwear was to show two 6-year-old boys arm wrestling and two girls about the same age jumping on a sofa. All were to be clad only in their underwear. Based on public opinion and strong objections from conservative groups, psychologists, and even the mayor of New York that such advertisements bordered on child pornography, Calvin Klein canceled the proposed billboards.[5]

Calvin Klein is not the only company using sex to sell its products. It is used overtly or subtly in many ads because it helps sell products. But in discussing the use of sex in marketing material, it must be kept in mind that what is offensive to one individual or group may not be to another (see Figure 3-5). In a nation that proclaims freedom of speech and expression, this is a very controversial issue. Company leaders must decide if they are going to use marketing material that contains sexuality or nudity. If so, then they must examine how their customers will view the ads. Ultimately, it is the customers who decide if the advertisements are acceptable and, as long as using sexuality in ads increases sales, companies will continue to use it.

An especially controversial area of marketing is that of advertising to children. Advertisers spend more than $12 billion a year on marketing products to children ages 4–12. More than $2 billion is spent on print advertising, $2.5 billion each for TV and radio advertising, and the remaining $5 billion is used for public relations and marketing of events attended by children. To snag these children, advertising agencies and marketing managers are hiring child psychologists. They want to know what kids think and how best to reach them.

Why are children such an attractive market? Sheer numbers, for one thing. There are 18.9 million kids under the age of 5, another 19.5 million between the ages of 5 and 9, and another 20.1 million between the ages of 10 and 14. More importantly, the income of the 36 million kids between the ages of 4 and 12 is $31.7 billion. That is an average of $16.31 per child per week (see Figure 3-6). With only 8 percent of this money being saved, there is a lot to spend. In addition, these children influence another $565 billion of their parents'

Figure 3-5
Sexuality is a primary theme in many Guess brand advertisements.

Source: Courtesy of Guess and Creative Director Paul Marciano.

Figure 3-6
Children demand the promoted Teletubby and Barney products, and parents give in and purchase them.

money on products such as video games, stereo systems, vacation destinations, computer equipment, yard furniture, and cars.[6]

Are children a fair target for marketers? Children have not reached maturity and do not have the reasoning power of adults. It is difficult for children to distinguish between fact and fiction. They are easily influenced and misled. They develop strong feelings toward products at a very early age and, by the early teenage years, insist upon designer clothes and brand-name products. While some would like to ban all advertising to children, others would like no restrictions at all, claiming First Amendment rights. Somewhere between these two extremes is the right answer.

3-2f Marketing Uses Deceptive and Misleading Techniques

For many consumers, the statement that "salespeople cannot be trusted" applies to more than just car salespeople. From the business-to-business perspective, many buyers feel that every salesperson will say and promise anything to make a sale. Often the relationship becomes almost adversarial, pitting buyers against sellers. While it is true that some salespeople do use deceptive and misleading statements to sell, most do not. It is not in their best interests to do so. Salespeople rely on word-of-mouth communications from current customers to attract new business as well as repeat business. Dishonesty will be punished by consumers who will make purchases elsewhere, tell others to avoid the business, and file complaints with agencies such as the Better Business Bureau. The long-term benefits of being honest far outweigh the short-term benefits of high-pressure and deceptive sales tactics.

For the business-to-business sector, more serious ethical issues include gifts and bribery. To influence sales, purchasing agents and other decision makers within a company are often the recipients of gifts, meals, entertainment, and even free trips. From a personal ethics standpoint, many concerned leaders wonder if personal gifts should be accepted if they are designed to influence a business decision.

Closely tied with the issue of receiving gifts is one that is even more complex and difficult. In many countries, bribery is an accepted practice. To obtain government permits and business contracts, it is a common practice to offer bribes. Without them, permits and business contracts are not granted or are very difficult to obtain. In Germany and France, the government actually permits companies to write off bribes as tax deductions. Dealing with these ethical issues is a major concern for business-to-business operations and businesses operating in the international environment.[7]

Bait and switch: A marketing tactic in which a retailer promotes a special deal on a particular product and then, when consumers arrive at the store, the retailer attempts to switch them to a higher-priced item.

In the retail area, a marketing tactic occasionally used is bait and switch. When using **bait and switch,** retailers promote a special deal on a particular product and then, when the consumer arrives at the store, they attempt to switch the consumer to a higher-priced item. Often, advertised specials are stripped-down versions of a product or the low end of a product line. Once the consumers are in the store, salespeople will attempt to switch them to a better, pricey model. This tactic becomes illegal under two conditions. The first is when the retailer does not stock enough of the sale item, with the intention of not having it in stock when the consumer arrives. The second is when the salespeople use undue pressure to influence the customer to switch. As you can see, the second would be hardest to prove.

Deceptive or misleading advertising is even more difficult to judge. When does an advertisement become misleading or deceptive? For example, a Botox ad promised that use of the product would reduce all wrinkles, while the FDA had approved the product for use only between a person's eyebrows. Further, the ad did not tell viewers that the result is temporary and that, for lasting results, injections of Botox have to be taken every three to four months.[8] Certainly, regulator authorities have concluded that this particular ad is deceptive and misleading. Section 3-3 includes a more detailed explanation of the standards used in determining if an advertisement is deceptive or misleading.

Another concern is ads that are legally not deceptive or misleading, but clearly are biased. For example, consider the numerous ads for cologne and perfume. Many promote the idea that you will become instantly appealing to members of the opposite sex and that your dream mate will suddenly discover you. Most people would consider these events unlikely to occur, but the message is still there. Use the cologne or perfume and you will become more sexually attractive. How far can an advertiser go with themes like this before it becomes misleading? As you can see, that question is difficult to answer, as everybody will have a different opinion about where that point is.

3-2g Marketing Violates Consumer Rights to Privacy

The more marketers understand about you as a consumer, the more efficient they can become in developing marketing material that will influence your purchase behavior. Although age, gender, income, and education are important pieces of information, if marketers can learn about your hobbies, interests, attitudes, and opinions, then it will be easier to design a message that will attract your attention. If marketers know where you shop and what you purchase, then the picture of you becomes even clearer. To learn all of these things about you, the marketer must gather information. That is where the right to privacy issue comes into play. Consumers want to protect their personal information, but marketers need it to promote their goods and services.

Where do marketers typically obtain information? Information comes from many different sources. For example, magazines sell their subscription lists. A firm that sells camping supplies would like to purchase subscription lists from magazines about camping so it can send direct-mail pieces and catalogs to people that like camping. By targeting people who like camping, costs can be reduced and the material will be received by people who are more likely to buy. Other sources of information include warranties that are filled out when purchasing a new product, surveys sent by magazines or other companies, credit card companies, banks, and schools.

The information-gathering source that has raised the most controversy lately is the Internet. Through "cookies," information can be gathered from your computer about what sites you have visited, how long you were at each site, and any other activity you conducted while on the Internet. This information becomes extremely valuable to marketers in understanding your habits, interests, and purchases. Tied in with demographic data, this information is a goldmine for marketers.

In discussing this controversy, it must be kept in mind that marketers are interested in groups of people who fit a certain pattern, not individuals. It is not cost effective to market to every person with a different marketing message; however, it is cost effective to market to a group of consumers who have the same interests, habits, and purchase behavior. For example, the goal of the company that sells camping supplies is to obtain a database of people who would be inclined to purchase camping supplies. From this information, the company can better understand this group's thinking, interests, and attitudes, which can be used in preparing marketing communications material. Although it is important to protect the privacy of consumers, it is also important for consumers to understand how marketers are using the information. For an interesting view of a new radio chip technology that could enhance marketing communications but that could also raise concerns about consumer privacy, see Marketing Illustration 3-1.

3-2h Marketing's Role in Society

While the criticisms of marketing have an element of truth, it is necessary to realize that marketing is an important ingredient of society and does perform a valuable role. Although marketing's primary function is to promote the purchase and consumption of goods and services, consumers have the opportunity to gather information that will allow them to make better decisions.

It is also important to remember that some marketing tactics may be legal, but are still perceived by a large segment of society to be unethical or in bad taste. When one is making marketing decisions, it is important to keep in mind that individuals, groups, states,

Marketing Illustration 3-1

Radio Chip Technology

It was only a pair of tennis shoes, but they were embedded with an RFID, which stands for radio frequency identification. When Andrea returned to the store six months later, she was greeted by a different salesperson, who asked her how she liked her shoes. How did the sales clerk know they were purchased here? Why was she treated better than the other customers? How did they know she had bought two other pairs for her children? How did this store know so much about her? While this scenario is fictitious, it illustrates the concerns consumers have about the most recent technology that has the ability to invade their privacy. The RFID chip is the size of a pencil tip and can be placed on any product. Radio signals can be sent to a special receiver that can track the product's movement.

Radio frequency chips are now being produced that can be individualized with electronic product codes that will allow for individual tracking of each chip. Procter & Gamble, Wal-Mart, and Unilever use the chips to track shipments of merchandise. By the end of 2005, Wal-Mart's top 100 vendors must use RFID chips on all shipments. Through this technology, Wal-Mart anticipates a boost in sales of 1 percent. Maybe that doesn't sound like much, but for Wal-Mart that translates to an extra $2.5 billion.

The excitement, however, to manufacturers is the potential use in and on packages of products. Putting the chips in packages would make it possible for retailers, or manufacturers, to develop in-store promotions and ads aimed at individual consumers based on their previous purchases or items currently in their shopping cart. Coupons for competing products or offers for complementary products could be offered. When it comes time to check out, instead of using the current optical product code scanners, the radio frequency chips could be used, which would result in almost instantaneous checkout.

For homes, the chips could be programmed to develop an electronic shopping list as soon as a product is used. It could be used to produce coupons and other promotions from competing brands. The potential is there for it to program ovens, microwaves, and other kitchen appliances with complete cooking instructions.

Right now, the cost of these chips makes their widespread use prohibitive. Current costs are $1 a chip; however, within three years, the cost is expected to drop to 5 cents. The cost of the ID chip readers is also expected to fall from the current $1,000 to less than $100. It is this drop in costs that has some consumer groups concerned about privacy and the way businesses will use the technology. The potential is there to track your every purchase, regardless of where it is purchased.

Sources: Simon Cooper, "Who's SPYING on You?" *Popular Mechanic,* vol. 182 (January 2005): 56; Daniel B. Wood, "Radio ID Tags Proliferate, Stirring Privacy Debates," *Christian Science Monitor,* vol. 97 (December 15, 2004): 14–16; Jack Neff, "A Chip over Your Shoulder?" *Advertising Age,* vol. 73 (April 22, 2002): 4–5.

nations, and societies differ in their beliefs about what constitutes both ethical and unethical behavior, and about what should be considered legal or illegal (see Figure 3-7). To help guide marketers in making ethical decisions, the American Marketing Association (AMA) adopted the code of ethics in Table 3-5 (see page 78 and 79).

3-2i Individual Roles in Marketing Ethics

When thinking about individuals and ethical decisions that each person faces, one should consider the two extremes. At one extreme are marketing decisions that are viewed as unethical only by a few individuals because they do not have a serious impact on other people, firms, or society. At the other extreme are marketing decisions that are viewed as unethical by most people and do have a potentially lasting and serious impact on individuals, firms, or society.

Figure 3-8 provides a useful framework for examining how someone in marketing would make a decision that can carry some ethical ramifications. For purposes of illustration, suppose you are the marketing director of a video game company that wants to market a new video game to male teenagers, ages 13–18. While the game has some violence, the sexy attire of the female characters disturbs you. When you are preparing the marketing material for the game, your dilemma is how sexy to make the ads. More importantly, is using sex appeal even appropriate for this age group?

As illustrated in Figure 3-8, your decision is influenced by your personal background and experiences. If you grew up in a liberal environment where sexuality was discussed,

Figure 3-7
Beliefs about ethical and unethical behavior and what is considered legal and illegal vary from country to country and across cultures within a country.

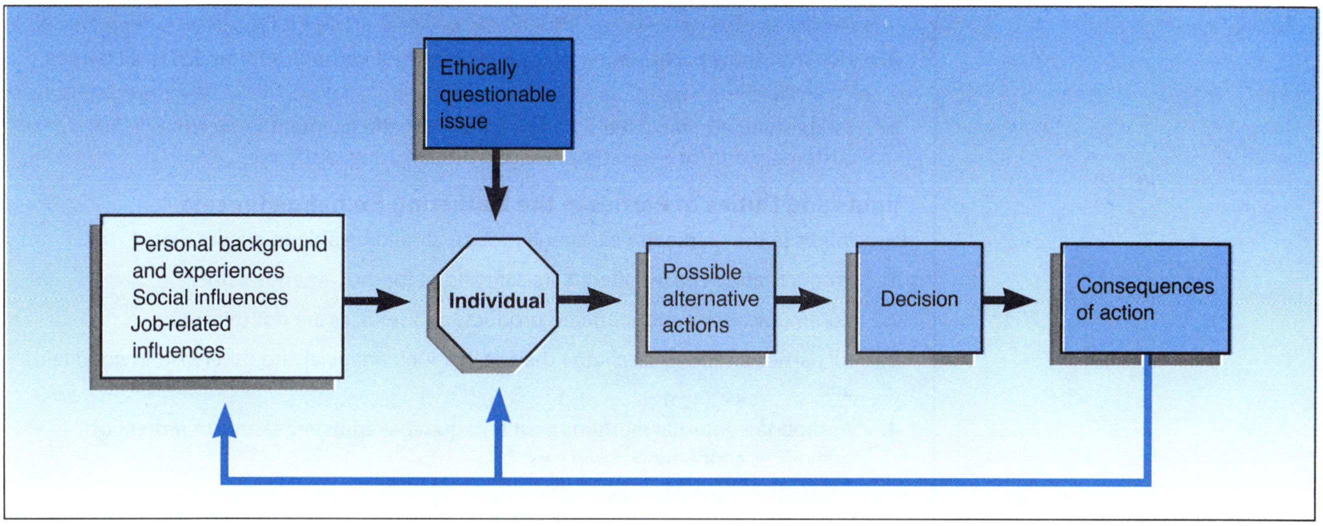

Figure 3-8
A Framework for Ethical/Unethical Decision Making

INTERACTIVE FIGURE

you may not see an ethical dilemma at all. But if you grew up in a religious or conservative environment where sexuality was a taboo subject, you may feel sexuality is not an appropriate marketing appeal for young teenagers. If you are the parent of a teenage boy or a teenage girl, your feelings may be different than if you are 25 and have no children.

While society and its views will have an influence on your decision, a more relevant influence will be the forces within your company. For example, if you were just appointed the marketing director and your career will be influenced by the sales of this video game, your decision may be different than if you've been with the company for 20 years and have proven your ability to make good decisions. A major difficulty for employees in these situations is the attitude and beliefs of the company. For example, if the CEO of this video game company feels it is not ethically wrong to use sex appeal, then you will have less latitude to make a decision.

In most ethical decisions, there are consequences to the decision. In this situation, your decision will impact the success of this video game. While there is no guarantee that using sex appeal will increase sales, you suspect that teenage boys ages 13 to 18 would be more inclined to pay attention to such an advertisement. However, if you take a stand and say no,

TABLE 3-5

The American Marketing Association's Code of Ethics

Members of the American Marketing Association (AMA) are committed to ethical professional conduct. They have joined together in subscribing to this Code of Ethics embracing the following topics:

Responsibilities of the Marketer

Marketers must accept responsibility for the consequences of their activities and make every effort to ensure that their decisions, recommendations, and actions function to identify, serve, and satisfy all relevant publics: customers, organizations, and society.

Marketers' professional conduct must be guided by:

1. The basic rule of professional ethics: not knowingly to do harm;
2. The adherence to all applicable laws and regulations;
3. The accurate representation of their education, training, and experience; and
4. The active support, practice, and promotion of this Code of Ethics.

Honesty and Fairness

Marketers shall uphold and advance the integrity, honor, and dignity of the marketing profession by:

1. Being honest in serving customers, clients, employees, suppliers, distributors, and the public;
2. Not knowingly participating in conflict of interest without prior notice to all parties involved; and
3. Establishing equitable fee schedules, including the payment or receipt of usual, customary, and/or legal compensation or marketing exchanges.

Rights and Duties of Parties in the Marketing Exchange Process

Participants in the marketing exchange process should be able to expect that:

1. Products and services offered are safe and fit for their intended uses;
2. Communications about offered products and services are not deceptive;
3. All parties intend to discharge their obligations, financial and otherwise, in good faith; and
4. Appropriate internal methods exist for equitable adjustment and/or redress of grievances concerning purchases.

It is understood that the above would include, but is not limited to, the following responsibilities of the marketer:

In the area of product development and management,

- Disclosure of all substantial risks associated with product or service usage;
- Identification of any product component substitution that might materially change the product or impact on the buyer's purchase decision;
- Identification of extra-cost added features.

Source: Reprinted by permission of American Marketing Association.

will those in the company, especially your boss, respect your decision, or will you soon be looking for another job? Your decision and the consequences that occur as a result will then become part of your personal experience that will be used in future decisions.

3-3 Marketing Regulations

Because of the ethical issues discussed in Section 3-2, the federal and state governments of the United States have passed a number of laws to protect consumers from unethical corporate practices. These laws pertain to price fixing, free enterprise, food quality, fair inter-

In the area of promotions,

- Avoidance of false and misleading advertising;
- Rejection of high-pressure manipulation;
- Avoidance of sales promotions that use deception or manipulation.

In the area of distribution,

- Not manipulating the availability of a product for purpose of exploitation;
- Not using coercion in the marketing channel;
- Not exerting undue influence over the reseller's choice to handle the product.

In the area of pricing,

- Not engaging in price fixing;
- Not practicing predatory pricing;
- Disclosing the full price associated with any purchase.

In the area of marketing research,

- Prohibiting selling or fund raising under the guise of conducting research;
- Maintaining research integrity by avoiding misrepresentation and omission of pertinent research data;
- Treating outside clients and suppliers fairly.

Organizational Relationships

Marketers should be aware of how their behavior may influence or impact the behavior of others in organizational relationships. They should not demand, encourage, or apply coercion to obtain unethical behavior in their relationships with others, such as employees, suppliers, or customers:

1. Apply confidentiality and anonymity in professional relationships with regard to privileged information;
2. Meet their obligations and responsibilities in contracts and mutual agreements in a timely manner;
3. Avoid taking the work of others, in whole or in part, and represent this work as their own or directly benefit from it without compensation or consent of the originator or owner;
4. Avoid manipulation to take advantage of situations to maximize personal welfare in a way that unfairly deprives or damages the organization of others.

Any AMA members found to be in violation of any provision of this Code of Ethics may have his or her Association membership suspended or revoked.

est rates, product safety, protection of children, deceptive advertising, and a variety of other issues. Table 3-6 lists the major federal legislation, along with a description of each.

Two overriding principles are behind the legislation mentioned in Table 3-6. First is the objective of ensuring free trade and open competition among firms. Second is the need to protect consumers from unscrupulous actions of business firms. As businesses grew in size during the 1800s, the federal government realized that, if left unchecked, these businesses would create monopolies and eventually dominate the marketplace. With no competitors, the large businesses could dictate prices, distribution, and access to goods and services. Consumers would be forced to pay the price charged or do without, especially if no substitutes existed.

TABLE 3-6

Major Federal Legislation Impacting Marketing Activities

Legislation	Description
1890—Sherman Antitrust Act	Prohibits trusts, monopolies, and activities designed to restrict free trade.
1906—Federal Food and Drug Act	Created the Food and Drug Administration and prohibits the manufacture and sale of falsely labeled foods and drugs.
1914—Clayton Act	Prohibits price discrimination to different buyers, tying contracts that require buyers of one product to also purchase another item, and combining two or more competing firms by pooling ownership or stock.
1914—Federal Trade Commission Act	Created the Federal Trade Commission to address antitrust matters and investigate unfair methods of competition.
1936—Robinson-Patman Act	Prohibits charging different prices to different buyers of the same merchandise and requires sellers that offer a service to one buyer to make the same service available to all buyers.
1938—Wheeler-Lea Amendment	Expanded the power of the FTC to investigate and prohibit practices that could injure the public, as well as false and misleading advertising.
1946—Lanham Act	Established protection of trademarks.
1966—Fair Packaging and Labeling Act	Requires that manufacturers provide a label containing contents, who made the product, and how much of each item it contains.
1972—Consumer Product Safety Act	Established the Consumer Product Safety Commission, which sets safety standards for products and ensures that manufacturers follow safety standard regulations.
1976—Hart-Scott-Rodino Act	Requires corporations wanting to merge to notify and seek approval of the government before any action is taken.
1990—Children's Television Act	Limits the number and times advertisements can be aired during children's programs.

To prevent monopolies and trusts that could restrict trade, the Sherman Antitrust Act was passed in 1890. This was followed in 1914 by the passage of the Clayton Act and in 1936 by the Robinson-Patman Act. These last two acts were designed to prevent price discrimination by sellers. When businesses could no longer form monopolies or large trusts, they controlled buyers by using "tying contracts" and price discrimination. Charging small businesses more for the same merchandise and forcing them to buy an entire line of merchandise allowed the manufacturers to choose who would be allowed to purchase from them. The Clayton Act and Robinson-Patman Act prevented this type of behavior.

To protect consumers from unethical, deceptive, and misleading marketing tactics, the Federal Food and Drug Act, the Federal Trade Commission Act, the Wheeler-Lea Amendment, the Fair Packaging and Labeling Act, the Consumer Product Safety Act, and the Children's Television Act were passed. While the focus of each piece of legislation was slightly different, the overarching principle of each was to ensure that consumers were treated fairly and protected from deceptive marketing practices.

TABLE 3-7

Primary Federal Agencies Involved in Regulating Marketing Activities

Agency	Responsibility
Food and Drug Administration (FDA)	Regulates and oversees the manufacturing, distribution, and labeling of food and drugs.
Federal Communications Commission (FCC)	Regulates the television, radio, and telephone industries.
U.S. Postal Service (USPS)	Responsible for mail delivery and investigating mail fraud schemes and any other illegal marketing activities using the mail system.
Bureau of Alcohol, Tobacco, and Firearms (BATF)	Oversees the manufacture, sale, and distribution of tobacco and alcohol.
Federal Trade Commission (FTC)	Primary agency responsible for ensuring free trade among businesses and investigating false, deceptive, or misleading claims in advertising and other types of marketing communications.
Consumer Product Safety Commission (CPSC)	Sets safety standards for products used by consumers in or around their home.

Passing laws to prevent monopolies and to protect consumers did not ensure that businesses would comply. Using federal authorities, state authorities, and the court system became too burdensome. Therefore, a number of federal agencies were created to ensure that laws were upheld. Table 3-7 lists the primary agencies along with a description of each agency's responsibilities. These various agencies were given the authority to set standards, investigate cases of wrongdoing, and punish those who did not comply. While all are important, we will discuss only the FDA and the FTC because they are the most relevant to marketing.

3-3a The Food and Drug Administration

The Food and Drug Administration (FDA) has the responsibility of overseeing the sale of all food and drug products. Before a drug can be used by physicians or sold to the public, the FDA must approve it. Strict tests and guidelines are used to ensure that there are no detrimental side effects. Occasionally, the FDA will allow doctors to use a drug under test conditions to measure its impact and side effects before it is released for public use.

For food products, the FDA is responsible for ensuring that food is safely processed and packaged. Because labels were often misleading, the Fair Packaging and Labeling Act was passed in 1966 (see Figure 3-9). This law requires that all food products have a label stating every ingredient in an order that corresponds to its relative content.

Phrases such as "contains 220 calories per serving" have to be explained in terms of what constitutes a serving size. Often, the typical serving size that an individual eats is not the same as that designated by a manufacturer. For example, a low-fat granola cereal that states it has 220 calories and three grams of fat per serving size is required to state on the label that a serving size is only two-thirds of a cup, not the two or three cups a typical person may eat at a meal.[9]

For those who like smoothies, see Table 3-8 for content information about the various brands and types. You may be surprised at the differences in calories, fat, sugar, and protein content.

Figure 3-9
To protect consumers from misleading labels, the Fair Packaging and Labeling Act, passed in 1966, sets standards for what should be on a label.

TABLE 3-8 Calories, Fat, Sugar, and Protein Content of Smoothies

Brand	Name	Serving (ounces)	Calories	Fat (grams)	Sugar (grams)	Protein (grams)
Dunkin Donuts	Orange-Mango	16	65	0	27	0
	Kahlua Coolatas	16	400	19	42	1
Saratoga	Smoothies Berry	16	120	0	25	1
	Fruit for Thought	16	130	0	30	1
Snapple Whipper	Snapple Wild	10	150	0	37	0
Baskin & Robbins	Nonfat Cappuccino	16	210	0	43	6
	Mocha Cappuccino Blast	16	290	12	40	6
Starbuck's	Wild Berry Tazzi	16	250	1	50	2
	Coffee Frappuccino	16	250	3	NA	4
Smoothie King	Youth Fountain	20	267	1	NA	3
	Raspberry Sunrise Fruit	20	335	1	NA	3
	Peanut Power	20	502	21	NA	3
7-Eleven	Fruit Cooler Strawberry	12	270	1	41	1
	Fruit Cooler Orange	12	280	1	48	1
Friendly's	Raspberry Sorbet	16	300	0	69	1
Ben & Jerry's	Cappachillo Cooler	22	320	0	68	20
	Real Fruit	22	380	0	57	0
	Doonesberry	22	630	40	60	18

Source: Andrea Platzman, "Smoothies: The Best of Drinks, the Worst of Drinks," *Environmental Nutrition,* vol. 22 (August 1999): 5.
Note: NA = not applicable.

3-3b The Federal Trade Commission

The agency with the most impact on marketing is the Federal Trade Commission (FTC). In addition to ensuring free trade among businesses, the FTC is responsible for investigating claims of false, deceptive, or misleading marketing communications. Deceptive or misleading marketing communications can stem from any type of marketing source, such as advertising, billboards, direct mail, corporate literature, oral and written communications by salespeople, or corporate Internet materials. The Wheeler-Lea Amendment, passed in 1938, gave the FTC authority to investigate claims of false advertising and prohibit any marketing practice that might injure the public or in any way be deceptive.

A firm can violate this law even when the company did not expressly intend to deceive or mislead consumers. According to the FTC, an advertisement or marketing communication is deemed to be deceptive or misleading when:

1. A substantial number of people, or the "typical person," is left with a false impression or misrepresentation that relates to the product; or
2. The misrepresentation induces people, or the "typical person," to make a purchase.

A violation is deemed to have occurred if one or both conditions are met. Businesses as well as individuals can sue under the guidelines of the FTC.[10]

When investigating complaints, the FTC does not consider subjective or puffery claims to be a violation. **Puffery** exists when a firm makes an exaggerated claim about its goods or services, without making an overt attempt to deceive or mislead. Terms normally associated with puffery include words such as "best," "greatest," and "finest." For example, in the advertisement in Figure 3-10, the headline reads "The Best Seat in the House." The FTC sees this as puffery and would take no action. When Ol'Man states that its deer tree stand is the "most comfortable," the "easiest to use," and the "highest quality," these are all statements of puffery. However, when Ol'Man states it is the "safety leader," then it becomes deceptive and misleading if indeed the Ol'Man tree stand is not the safety leader. It must be able to back up this type of statement. Obviously, there is quite a bit of gray area when a claim about a false or misleading statement is made.

Puffery: When a firm makes an exaggerated claim about its goods or services, without making an overt attempt to deceive or mislead.

The FTC can receive a complaint from any of the following sources:

- Consumers
- Businesses
- Congress
- The media
- The FTC itself

Each entity can raise concerns about what appears to be an unfair or deceptive practice by a particular business, group of businesses, or even an industry. In the beginning, FTC investigations are often confidential, but they do not have to be. This protects both the FTC and the company being investigated if no violation has occurred. However, if the FTC believes a law has been violated, the first step in resolving the issue will be to issue a *consent order.* If the company agrees to the consent order, it agrees to stop the disputed practice but does not admit any guilt. Most investigations of the FTC end with a signed consent order.

An example of this process involved two companies that collected extensive information from high school students that was to be shared with colleges, universities, and other education-related services. These companies—the National Research Center for College and University Admissions (NRCCUA) and American Student List (ASL)—distributed questionnaires in high schools, collecting from students information such as their name, address, gender, GPA, academic and occupational interests, athletic interests, extracurricular interests, ethnicity, and religious background. Both firms claimed that this data collection request was funded by colleges and universities and that the data would be shared with educational institutions. The FTC found both claims to be false. Although the data were shared with educational institutions, they were also sold to commercial firms for marketing purposes. In

Figure 3-10
This advertisement by Ol'Man uses puffery in the statements "The Best Seat in the House," "Most Comfortable," "Easiest to Use," and "Highest Quality."

Source: Courtesy of Newcomer, Morris and Young.

addition, commercial entities provided financial support to both companies. Because neither of these facts was shared with the high school students or the schools, the FTC found the marketing approach to be misleading and deceptive.

Both companies signed a consent order agreeing that information collected in the past would not be sold to any commercial firm. They also agreed to properly disclose in future data collection efforts that the companies were also supported by commercial entities and that the data could be sold to commercial firms for marketing purposes. By signing the consent agreement, both firms agreed to stop the potentially "deceptive and misleading practices," while not admitting they were guilty of breaking any FTC regulations.[11]

If a consent agreement cannot be reached, the FTC may issue what is called an *administrative complaint.* A formal proceeding similar to a court trial is held before an administrative law judge. Both sides submit evidence and testimony to support their case. At the end of the administrative hearing, the judge makes a ruling. If the judge feels a violation of the law has occurred, a *cease-and-desist order* is prepared. This order requires the company to immediately stop the disputed practice and refrain from any similar practices in the future. If the company is not satisfied with the decision of the administrative law judge, it can appeal the case to the full FTC commission.

The full commission holds a similar type of hearing, where evidence and testimony can be presented. The full commission can issue a cease-and-desist order if it believes the company is guilty or dismiss the case if it feels the administrative judge and earlier rulings were incorrect. Companies not satisfied with the ruling of the full FTC commission can

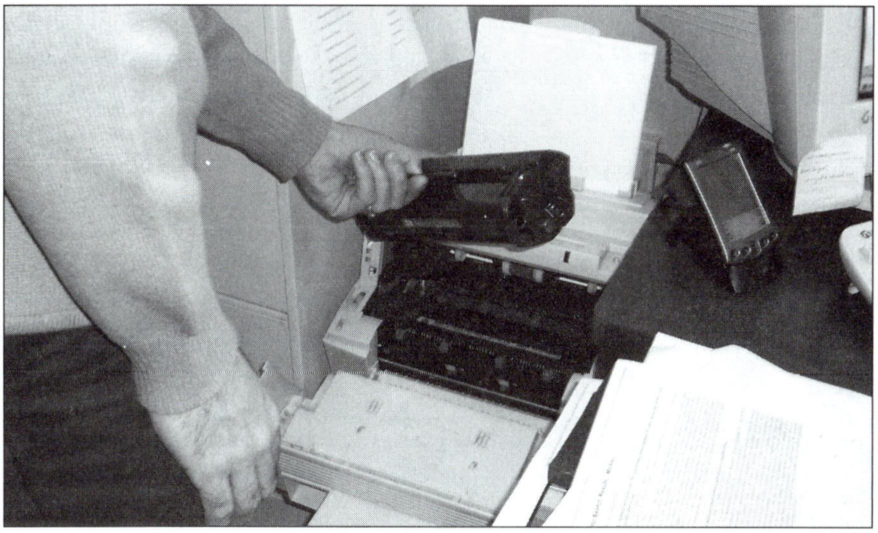

Figure 3-11
The FTC ordered E-Babylon, Inc. to pay a $40,000 civil penalty as part of its consent agreement for misleading and deceptive marketing practices for its inkjet cartridges.

appeal the case to the U.S. Court of Appeals and even up to the U.S. Supreme Court. The danger in appealing to the Court of Appeals is that the Court has the power to provide consumer redress (i.e., the power to levy civil penalties).

A complaint does not have to go to the Court of Appeals, however, for civil penalties to be assessed. The FTC has the power to do so also. For example, E-Babylon, Inc. agreed to pay a $40,000 civil penalty as part of its consent agreement. The FTC accused E-Babylon, Inc. of misrepresenting its products as being new, brand-name inkjet cartridges, when in fact they were either remanufactured or generic cartridges (see Figure 3-11). In addition, E-Babylon, Inc. advertised that any dissatisfied customer could receive a "no questions asked" refund, but in reality, customers had an extremely difficult time in obtaining refunds. Further, E-Babylon, Inc. did not comply with the FTC's Mail Order Rule because it did not advise customers who purchased its products that they had the right to cancel their orders and receive a refund if E-Babylon, Inc. could not ship the merchandise on time. Lastly, E-Babylon, Inc. was ordered to pay redress to all consumers who were entitled to refunds either under the FTC's Mail Order Rule or E-Babylon, Inc.'s money-back guarantee. Rather than risk a greater penalty by appealing to the court system, firms like E-Babylon, Inc. will usually agree to consent orders.[12]

In more severe instances of deceptive or misleading advertising, the FTC can order a firm to prepare corrective advertising. These situations are rare and occur only when the FTC feels that discontinuing a false advertisement will not be a sufficient remedy. In ordering corrective advertising, the FTC concludes that consumers believed the false or misleading information, and the goal of having the company issuing corrective ads is to bring consumers back to a neutral state that existed prior to the misleading ads.

Corrective advertising orders are rare but were utilized by the FTC following a judgment against Volvo Cars of North America. The company had created an advertisement showing a row of cars being destroyed by a monster truck as it ran over them. Only the Volvo was not smashed. Upon investigation, the FTC discovered that the Volvo automobile had been altered with steel bars to prevent it from being crushed. The FTC concluded that the ad would cause consumers to believe that Volvo was a safer automobile than it actually was. Consequently, the FTC not only ordered Volvo to discontinue the ad, but also to run a new advertisement explaining how the car had been altered in the previous commercial.[13] The FTC seldom orders corrective ads because in most cases, it is extremely difficult to eliminate the impact of a misleading ad and take consumers back to a neutral point.

The FTC rules cover every aspect of marketing communications. Regardless of the type of communication, unfair or deceptive marketing communications are prohibited. Marketers must be able to substantiate claims through competent and reliable evidence (see Figure 3-12). If endorsers are used, their statements must be truthful and represent

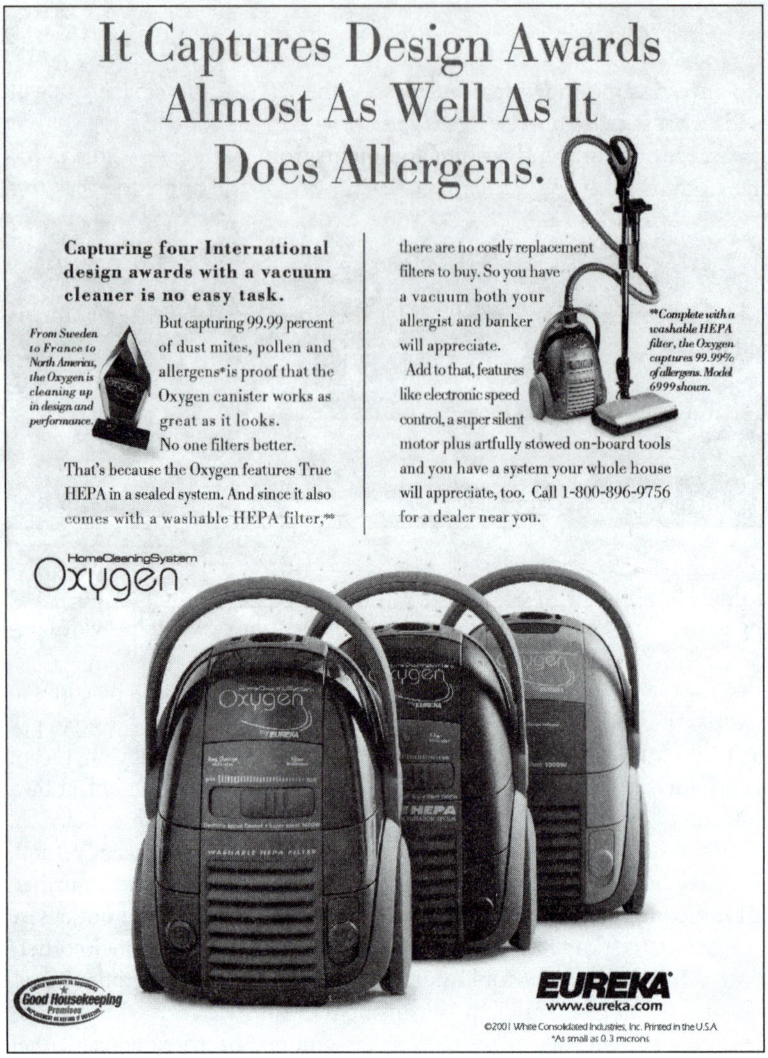

Figure 3-12
Eureka's claims that it has won awards for design are substantiated in this advertisement.
Source: Courtesy of Eureka.

their experiences or opinions. If expert endorsements are used, their statements must be based on legitimate tests performed by experts in the field. All claims must reflect the typical experience that a customer would expect to encounter from the use of the product or service, unless the advertisement clearly and prominently states otherwise.[14]

One of the keys to FTC evaluations of advertisements and marketing communications is the idea of *substantiation*. Firms must be able to substantiate (e.g., prove or "back up") any claims made. Failure to do so can result in some form of FTC action. For example, a consent order was issued to Dr. Robert M. Currier for his testimony for SNORenz, a product that was promoted to help people reduce snoring and reduce symptoms of sleep apnea, a potentially life-threatening breathing disorder. The FTC alleged that Dr. Currier made numerous false and unsubstantiated claims that he had conducted a study that proved SNORenz was an effective treatment for snoring. The FTC found no substantiation that SNORenz would reduce snoring and also found that SNORenz was not intended to treat sleep apnea. An interesting aspect of this case is that Dr. Currier is a surgical doctor of osteopathic medicine with a specialty in eye disorders; he has not had any specialized training in disorders of the throat. So in addition to not being able to support the claims he made for SNORenz, Dr. Currier was not even an expert in the area he claimed in the advertisement.[15]

If a firm makes a claim about its product, it must be able to substantiate that claim. If a firm says, "Brand X reduces the symptoms of the common cold," it must be able to prove that Brand X does indeed reduce the symptoms of the common cold. In this case, an independent study would be the best substantiation. If the company performs the study itself, it must be very careful to follow good scientific procedures. The FTC examines company-sponsored research more closely than research by an independent firm.

In addition to investigating individual businesses, the FTC can also investigate an industry and provide what is called a *trade regulation ruling*. Normally, the FTC will hold a public hearing and accept both oral and written arguments from companies in the industry concerned. The Commission will then make a ruling that would apply to every firm within an industry. As with other rulings by the FTC, decisions can be challenged in the U.S. Court of Appeals.

In 1984 and 1994, an FTC investigation into the pricing practices of the funeral home industry resulted in a trade regulation ruling. Under this trade regulation ruling, funeral homes are required to provide an itemized list of charges. They must provide the price along with a detailed description of the product or service. As part of the itemization, the ruling required all funeral homes to disclose to their customers the following four statements:

1. Consumers have the right to select only the goods and services they desire.
2. Embalming is not always required by law.
3. Individuals desiring cremation of a loved one can use alternative containers for the remains other than those furnished by the funeral home.
4. The only fee that a consumer is required to pay is the nondeclinable basic service fee.[16]

The purpose of a trade regulation ruling is to prevent collusion or conspiracy among firms in an industry and to ensure that consumers have freedom in making decisions. While funeral homes in this case did not overtly collude, their practices restricted consumer choice, and their unwillingness to offer options and an itemized list of expenses was deemed to be unfair and misleading to consumers. See Marketing Illustration 3-2 for the FTC's efforts to decrease spam emails.

Marketing Illustration 3-2

The FTC and Spamming

The FTC has been in the forefront in the battle of spam emails that plague everybody's email inboxes, but very little progress has been made. Although a law meant to curb spamming went into effect on January 1, 2004, consumers and businesses have seen little impact. One reason for this lack of progress is the law itself. The new law, called the CAN-SPAM Act of 2003, does not make spamming illegal. Instead, it regulates how bulk emails are to be sent out and what must go on the subject line. Further, it requires companies to offer recipients an "opt out" option on every email.

While the law has teeth—violators can be assessed penalties of $11,000 per violation—massive problems exist in the investigation stage. First, there is the problem of identifying and locating the spammer. Second, if the spammer can be located, it is difficult to gather sufficient evidence to prove the person was responsible for sending the email. In many cases, spammers use false email addresses or may even hijack the email accounts of a business. Third, the reward offered to people for turning spammers into the FTC is not sufficient in comparison to the risks and consequences. In many cases, the spammer is a friend, business associate, or relative.

Congress as well as consumers have urged the FTC to create a do-not-spam list similar to the do-not-call list for telephones. The FTC is resisting this move because it would be too difficult to enforce. The FTC receives more than 300,000 pieces of spam per day! Investigating each one would take tremendous manpower. Afraid that a do-not-spam list would not greatly diminish spamming, the FTC is looking at other approaches.

The first approach is to reward whistleblowers with rewards of up to $300,000. However, no budget has been allocated for this, at least at this point in time. The second approach is to punish spammers when they are caught. This has been and will continue to be very difficult. The third approach is to encourage entrepreneurial businesses to build filters and other types of programs that will prevent spammers from getting through. Thus, the FTC currently is relying more on businesses to fight the spamming epidemic than on regulations and enforcement by the FTC.

Sources: "FTC: 'Can Spam" Law Only a Mild Deterrent," Fox News (http://www.foxnews.com/story/0,2933,110910,00.htm, February 10, 2004); "FTC Fights Spam with Carrot and Stick," *Asisonline.org* (December 2004): 30; "FTC Wants the Public to Help Slam Spam, Response (November 2004): 6.

3-3c Industry Regulations

Because of the volume of complaints, the federal regulatory agencies would have a difficult time investigating them all if it were not for the industry regulatory system. While the various industry regulatory agencies have no legal power, they can reduce the load on the FTC and the legal system. Many allegations or complaints about unfair and deceptive marketing practices are handled and settled within the advertising and business industry. Although various industry agencies exist for monitoring marketing activities, the three most common are (1) the Better Business Bureau, (2) the National Advertising Division, and (3) the National Advertising Review Board.

The Better Business Bureau (BBB) is a venue available to both consumers and businesses. Unethical business practices or unfair treatment can lead to the filing of complaints against a business with the BBB. The BBB will compile a summary of charges leveled against individual firms. While the charges are not investigated, they are kept on record for potential customers who want to learn about a particular business. When asked by an individual or business, the BBB will provide a carefully worded report that will raise cautionary flags about a firm that has received a great number of complaints, as well as state the general nature of the complaints.

When complaints about advertising are received, the BBB refers them to the National Advertising Division (NAD) of the BBB. The NAD will collect information and evaluate data concerning the complaint to determine whether the complaint is legitimate. In most cases, the NAD is looking for evidence of substantiation. If the firm's advertising claim is substantiated, then the complaint is dismissed. If it is not, the NAD will negotiate with the business to modify or discontinue the advertisement. Recently, Southern LINC filed a complaint with the NAD that an advertisement by Nextel was false and misleading. Nextel had advertised "only Nextel Direct Connect, the digital two-way feature, offers instant contact with the push of a button." Nextel argued that the claim was rate-plan related and exclusive to Nextel. However, because Southern LINC offered the same digital two-way feature, NAD ruled that Nextel's advertisements were false and misleading and could not appear in future advertising. Based on the NAD decision, Nextel discontinued the exclusive claim.[17]

When a complaint is not resolved by the NAD or the advertiser appeals the decision, it goes to the National Advertising Review Board (NARB). The NARB is composed of advertising professionals and prominent civic representatives. If the NARB rules that the firm's advertisements are not substantiated, it then issues an order for the firm to discontinue the advertisements. This would be very similar to the consent order by the FTC, but is issued by this private advertising board. If the firm being accused refuses to accept the NARB ruling, then the matter is turned over to the FTC or an appropriate federal regulatory agency.

The NARB has been involved in numerous business versus business disputes. Recently, Meril Limited, the manufacturer of Heartguard and Frontline, filed a complaint against Pfizer and its new product called "Revolution." Pfizer claimed Revolution could protect dogs and cats from fleas, ticks, and other external parasites as well as heartworm and gastrointestinal parasites. Meril Limited has made the same claim, but only if the consumer uses both Heartguard and Frontline. Meril's case against Pfizer was based on Pfizer's claim that Revolution was not a pesticide. Legally, according to EPA law, Revolution was not classified as a pesticide. However, Meril presented survey research to the NARB that the phrase "not a pesticide" suggested to consumers that the product was safe when, in reality, Pfizer could not support the implication that pesticides were safe for animal consumption. While the NARB agreed that the Revolution product by Pfizer was not technically a pesticide, it determined that the phrase "not a pesticide" was misleading to consumers since in consumers' minds a "pesticide is an agent used to kill pests." Because Revolution is a product designed to kill pests, consumers would therefore be led to believe that the product is a safe pesticide. This interpretation was based on the FTC idea of what a "typical person" would be led to believe, not on what is technically or, in this case, legally correct. The typical person would not be privy to such a specialized meaning of the word "pesticide."[18]

Seldom does the NARB refer a case to the Federal Trade Commission. In fact, it has done so only four times in the past 25 years. The last was a case dealing with Winn-Dixie, which made direct price comparisons with competitors in its advertisements. The NARB found that Winn-Dixie was using prices that were sometimes 90 days old. The NARB ruled that any price comparisons made in an advertisement by Winn-Dixie must use prices that are no more than seven days old. The decision to forward the case to the FTC was made when Winn-Dixie refused to modify its ads and accept the NARB ruling.[19]

3-4 Social Responsibility

Consumers today expect companies to act responsibly and to be good citizens. In a 2002 survey, 83 percent of Americans indicated that it is important for corporations to support the needs of society.[20] This can be done by producing environmentally safe products, by controlling for emissions and wastes that contaminate the environment, or by becoming involved in meeting the social needs of society. In the past, most corporations fulfilled the requirement of meeting the needs of society through philanthropy. Then, in 1984, American Express promised to donate one cent for the Statue of Liberty restoration project for every cardholder transaction. In three months, $1.7 million was donated. Transactions rose by 28 percent, and new card applications rose by 17 percent.[21] It was a whopping success for the Statue of Liberty restoration effort as well as for American Express. It was also the beginning of a movement from philanthropy to cause-related marketing (see Figure 3-13).

Figure 3-13
This advertisement by Plum Creek shows its commitment to social responsibility. Although Plum Creek provides timber for the lumber industry, it is committed to preserving hunting, fishing, and outdoor recreation habitats.

Source: Sample print advertisement courtesy of The Miles Agency and Alliance One Advertising, Inc.

3-4a Cause-Related Marketing

Cause-related marketing: A long-term partnership between a nonprofit organization and a corporation that is integrated into the corporation's marketing plan.

Writing a check to a local charity or even a national charity is not cause-related marketing, but rather philanthropy. **Cause-related marketing** is a long-term partnership between a nonprofit organization and a corporation and is integrated into the corporation's marketing plan. Both parties must benefit from the relationship for it to be an effective cause-related marketing effort (see Figure 3-14).

The Cone/Roper Corporate Citizenship Survey found, shortly after the events of September 11, 2001, that 81 percent of Americans would switch brands to help support a cause if price and quality were equal, and 92 percent indicated they felt more positive about a corporation that supported a cause. This was up from 81 percent in March of 2001.[22]

To be successful with a cause-related program, the firm must demonstrate a genuine support for a cause. If it does not, and if customers suspect a firm is using the nonprofit cause to benefit itself, it will backfire. To ensure that a cause-related program will work, a firm first must align itself with a cause that fits its mission and its products. Avon's support for breast cancer research is a logical fit. Likewise, Wal-Mart's commitment to children with disabilities fits with its image of diversity and caring for the local community.

How companies promote the cause is extremely important. If they spend $3 million to advertise their $100,000 donation, as Philip Morris did after the September 11 terrorist attacks, consumers will see it as exploitation. If they mention it in their advertising, on point-of-purchase displays, and in their facility but do not make it a big deal, consumers will accept it. Consumers are looking for a genuine relationship between the nonprofit organization and the company, not a gimmick by the corporation to boost its sales. One method of demonstrating this genuineness is getting employees involved. If employees do not support and believe in the cause, the public will be suspicious of the motives. Employees of corporations with legitimate cause-related programs are 38 percent more likely to say they are proud of their employer than employees who work for a corporation that is not involved with a cause.[23] For a study on cause-related marketing in New Zealand, see Marketing Illustration 3-3.

3-4b Green Marketing

Green marketing: The development and promotion of products that are environmentally safe.

Cause-related marketing is one way a company can demonstrate its social responsibility; green marketing is another. **Green marketing** is the development and promotion of products that are environmentally safe. Although almost all Americans support the concept of green marketing, few really support it with purchases. For example, more than 11,000 different products have the U.S. Environmental Protection Agency's ENERGY STAR label for energy efficiency. More than 40 percent of consumers recognize the label, but only a small percentage demand the label when making a purchase. Despite advances in technology, a study by Roper found that 42 percent of consumers interviewed still believe that "environmentally safe products don't work as well" as regular products (see Figure 3-15).

Figure 3-14
A partnership between a local supermarket, a health-care provider, and a health-care insurance company offers children free shots.

Source: Courtesy of Ukrop's Super Markets, Inc.

Give Your Child a Free Shot at Good Health

School is just around the corner, so give your child a shot at good health by taking advantage of FREE SHOTS FOR TOTS. Ukrop's has partnered with Bon Secours Richmond Health System, Cigna HealthCare of Virginia, and WTVR Channel 6 to provide free, standard school mandated shots, pneumonia and chicken pox vaccine for babies, pre-schoolers and kindergartners. In addition, Hepatitis B will be available for anyone 19 years of age or younger. All families are welcome to participate. Please bring your child's complete shot records. Back by popular demand, Bon Secours will provide up to 35 school entry physicals for any child who is uninsured!

Check out the Ukrop's locations and dates listed below:

Friday, August 1st	Ashland	3pm-7pm
Saturday, August 2nd	Colonial Heights	8am-12pm
Friday, August 8th	Laburnum	3pm-7pm
Saturday, August 9th	Chippenham Crossing	8am-12pm

For more information, call (804) 378-7009 or any of the pharmacy locations listed above.

Marketing Illustration 3-3

It Pays to Be Nice: A Report from New Zealand

A survey by Stillwater/ACNielsen in New Zealand supports the benefits of cause-related marketing. Most surveys examine purchase intentions; this survey also examined actual purchase behavior. While 74 percent of the respondents said they would change brands if a similar brand supported a worthy cause, 41.7 percent actually did purchase a good or service because of cause-related marketing. Another 84 percent agreed that cause-related marketing did change their perception of a brand. Other findings of interest in the New Zealand study include:

- Females are more likely to support a cause than males.
- Causes that benefit children, health, education, or animals received the highest scores.
- Animal-related causes are higher for the younger age groups.
- Child-related causes are the highest for the 45- to 54-year-old age group.
- Companies that sponsored local causes received higher scores than those that supported national or international causes.
- Respondents were skeptical of businesses that used the name of the charity but gave only a minimal contribution.

Source: Jill Ford and Helen Flanner, "It Pays to Be Nice," *NZ Marketing Magazine,* vol. 21 (May 2002): 21.

Figure 3-15
The U.S. Environmental Protection Agency encourages businesses and institutions to use products that are efficient and protect the environment.

Source: Courtesy of U.S. Environmental Protection Agency.

Global warming has received considerable press lately. Fifty-eight percent of Americans agree that there has been a global warming, and 50 percent believe it is serious. Yet, consumers are reluctant to turn off lights and drive more fuel-efficient cars. Furthermore, fewer than 1 percent would even consider a hybrid gas-electric car such as the Toyota Prius.[24]

The key to successful green marketing is the same as developing a strong brand name for any product. First, the product must be of high quality. While marketing may be able to entice some people to purchase, a poorly built product will eventually lose. Consumers will not continue to purchase poorly built products to support the environment. While in the past green marketing products such as laundry detergents were inferior, such is not the case anymore.

Second, the cost of producing green products must be reduced. This has been a challenge because of the lack of acceptance by the public. Companies are reluctant to invest huge dollars in research on green products that may not do well in the marketplace. This will change, however, if companies continue to have success with green products. Phillips Lighting recently introduced the "Marathon" fluorescent light bulb that has a longer life and lower operating costs. It has done very well in the marketplace.

The last key to successfully marketing green products is to make these green products attractive to the public. If products like Pepsi and Coke can be made "sexy" through shrewd marketing and advertising techniques, so can products that are environmentally friendly. Companies that recognize this opportunity and jump on it now will build an advantage for the future when the world's petroleum supply and other natural resources do become a factor. At the rate of current consumption, the cost of producing environmentally friendly products such as synthetic carpet will someday be cheaper than carpet made with petroleum chemicals.

Summary

1. *Identify the ethical issues faced by marketers and discuss the pros and cons of each issue.* A number of ethical issues have been raised concerning marketing. First, marketing causes people to buy more than they can afford. While some would feel this overspending is the result of marketing, others would claim marketing is just responding to what consumers want. Second, marketing overemphasizes materialism. Again, while some would argue that marketing creates materialism, others would say marketing is merely responding to materialistic desires. Third, marketing increases the prices of goods and services. While this is true, marketing also provides information so consumers can make intelligent consumption decisions. Fourth is the criticism that marketing capitalizes on human weaknesses. Marketers would argue that they are just responding to personal needs. Fifth, critics would suggest that marketing shapes and encourages inappropriate cultural values. Marketers would contend that marketing responds to current cultural values and would not be effective in promoting desires that do not conform to cultural values. Sixth, marketing uses deceptive and misleading advertising. While some marketers do use deceptive and misleading advertising, agencies such as the FTC have been created to protect consumers. Lastly, critics contend that marketing violates consumers' right to privacy. While marketers do gather personal information, it is used to better market to people's needs.

2. *Discuss the legislation and regulatory agencies that impact marketing.* A number of laws have been passed to protect consumers and to ensure free trade among businesses. Antitrust legislation includes the Sherman Antitrust Act, Clayton Act, Robinson-Patman Act, and the Hart-Scott-Rodino Act. Legislation to protect consumers includes the Federal Food and Drug Act, the Federal Trade Commission Act, the Wheeler-Lea Amendment, the Fair Packaging and Labeling Act, the Consumer Product Safety Act, and the Children's Television Act. These laws were passed to prevent misleading and deceptive marketing practices and ensure honest labeling of foods, drugs, and safe products for consumer use.

From these acts, a number of agencies were established, including the Food and Drug Administration; the Federal Communications Commission; the U.S. Postal Service; the Bureau of Alcohol, Tobacco, and Firearms; the Federal Trade Commission; and the Consumer Product Safety Commission. Each of these agencies is responsible for regulating business and investigating activities of wrongdoing.

3. *Describe the role of the Federal Trade Commission as it relates to marketing and discuss how it investigates complaints.* The role of the FTC is to investigate activities that restrict free trade and claims of misleading or deceptive marketing communications. Complaints can be filed by consumers, businesses, Congress, the media, or the FTC itself. An advertisement or marketing communication is said to be deceptive or misleading if the typical person is misled. Any claims made by a company must be substantiated in some way. If the FTC finds that a violation has occurred, it can issue a consent order or a cease-and-desist order. It can also levy civil penalties. Appeals from the FTC go to a federal court of appeals.

4. *Discuss the role of the Better Business Bureau in regulating marketing activities.* The BBB is a private organization that encourages good business practices but also keeps a record of complaints registered against businesses in its area. Complaints about advertising are referred to the BBB's National Advertising Division (NAD) or the

National Advertising Review Board (NARB). Complaints not settled by the NAD are referred to the NARB. Both operate similar to the FTC, but without obligatory power. However, in most cases decisions by the NAD or NARB are followed.

5. *Discuss the social responsibility of business firms and provide examples of how a firm can demonstrate its social responsibility.* Businesses are expected to behave in a socially responsible manner and be supportive of societal needs. This social responsibility can be met through cause-related marketing programs or green marketing programs.

Key Terms

bait and switch (p. 74)
cause-related marketing (p. 90)
ethics (p. 64)
green marketing (p. 90)
morals (p. 64)
puffery (p. 83)

Discussion Questions

1. Marketing to teenagers has raised a number of ethical issues, as was discussed in the chapter-opening vignette. Do some research on the Internet or with an electronic database to find articles that discuss the ethical issues in marketing to teenagers.
2. Pick one of the ethical issues presented in Section 3-2. Talk to 10 people you know of various ages, genders, and ethnic backgrounds. Summarize how each felt about the issue you picked.
3. Pick one of the ethical issues presented in Section 3-2. Discuss how you feel about the issue. Find articles that either support or refute your view on the Internet or from an electronic database.
4. Read Marketing Illustration 3-1 about radio chip technology. What are the benefits of using RFID? What are the dangers? Do some additional research and discuss what you learned.
5. Pick one of the pieces of legislation listed in Section 3-3. Research its background and the impact it has on business.
6. Access the website of the Federal Trade Commission at www.ftc.gov. Review the press releases and past decisions. Find one that interests you to discuss.
7. If you came across an advertisement that you thought was misleading and wanted to report it, would you report it to the FTC or the NAD? Why?
8. Read Marketing Illustration 3-2 about the FTC and spamming? What is your view of spamming? What approach do you think the FTC should take? Would you be willing to turn in a friend, relative, or business associate who was violating the law? How much of a reward would it take?
9. What is your opinion of cause-related marketing? What causes do you support? Do you modify your purchase decisions based on causes a company supports?
10. What is your attitude toward green marketing? Name the last product you purchased because of green marketing. How much impact does green marketing have on your purchase behavior?

Review Questions

True or False

1. Ethics help individuals and organizations to establish boundaries regarding acceptable and unacceptable conduct.
2. Morals are personal beliefs or standards used to guide an individual's actions.
3. Marketing has been criticized for creating a materialistic society.
4. Bait and switch tactics used by retailers provide more product options to the consumer.
5. Personal information gathered through the Internet should allow marketers to advertise specific products of interest to each individual.
6. To determine whether a company used deceptive or misleading advertising, the Federal Trade Commission will examine the company's intentions to design a deceptive and misleading ad.
7. The FTC does not have the power to levy civil penalties; only the U.S. Court of Appeals has this power.
8. Decisions by the National Advertising Division or National Advertising Review Board cannot be appealed to the FTC or to the Federal Court system.
9. Historically, green marketing has not been successful because green products were considered to be of inferior quality.
10. Cause-related marketing is a strategy used to promote a product line by advertising donations made to nonprofit organizations.

Multiple Choice

11. Easy consumer credit is partially to blame for which of the following criticisms of marketing?
    a. Marketing causes people to buy more than they can afford.
    b. Marketing increases the prices of goods and services.
    c. Marketing capitalizes on human weaknesses.
    d. Marketing violates consumers' rights to privacy.
12. Which of the following is an example of the criticism that marketing shapes inappropriate cultural values?
    a. an advertisement for weight-loss programs
    b. an advertisement offering a complete computer system for only $299
    c. an advertisement for Rogaine, a hair-growth product
    d. an advertisement for birth control pills
13. Which of the following statements defines the marketing role in society?
    a. Marketing uses unethical methods to lure customers.
    b. Marketing reduces tension between competing companies.
    c. Marketing has a limited commercial role.
    d. Marketing allows consumers to make better decisions.

14. The agency responsible for regulating the radio industry is the
a. Food and Drug Administration.
b. Federal Communications Commission.
c. Federal Trade Commission.
d. Consumer Product Safety Commission.

15. The legislation that prohibits false and misleading advertising is the
a. Fair Packaging and Labeling Act.
b. Lanham Act.
c. Wheeler-Lea Amendment.
d. Robinson-Patman Act.

16. The legislation that prohibits price discrimination to different buyers is the
a. Sherman-Antitrust Act.
b. Clayton Act.
c. Fair Packaging and Labeling Act.
d. Lanham Act.

17. When making a claim about a product, the FTC will look for
a. puffery statements.
b. substantiation of the claim.
c. a testimony of an expert witness.
d. overly complex claims.

18. Decisions by the National Advertising Division or National Advertising Review Board are
a. not binding, but most companies abide by decisions of the NAD and NARB.
b. binding only if ruled by the NARB.
c. as binding as rulings of the FTC.
d. none of the above

19. Advertisers engage in puffery
a. when the ad contains an obscene message.
b. when the ad makes reference to a competitor's product.
c. when the ad includes such words as "greatest," "finest," and "best."
d. when the ad is obviously designed to mislead.

20. If the FTC believes that a company used unfair or deceptive practices, the first step in resolving the problem will be to issue a(n)
a. consent order.
b. administrative complaint.
c. cease and desist order.
d. judgment for approval by the Federal Court.

Notes

1. Jim McElgunn, "Those Tricky Teens," *Marketing Magazine*, vol. 107 (September 2, 2002): 18; Theresa Howard, "Kmart Aims for Teens Appeal with Joe Boxer Line, Edgy Ads," *USA Today*, (July 31, 2002): Money, 03b; Theresa Howard, "7-Eleven's Yucky Yuks Target Teens," *USA Today* (August 26, 2002): Money, 07b; Valarie Seckler, "Teens as Brand Ambassadors," *WWD: Women's Wear Daily*, vol. 188, no. 107 (November 18, 2004): 12; Kenneth Hein, "The Age of Reason," *Brandweek*, vol. 44, no. 39 (October 27, 2003): 24.
2. Paul J. Lim, "Credit Squeeze," *U.S. News & World Report*, vol. 132 (June 17, 2002): 38–39.
3. Michael Schroeder, "Tough on Debtors, Bankruptcy Bill Advances to Bush," *The Wall Street Journal* (April 15, 2005): A2.
4. D. Kirk Davidson, "Marketing This 'Hope' Sells Our Profession Short," *Marketing News*, vol. 32 (July 20, 1998): 6.
5. Andy Newman, "Calvin Klein Cancels Ad with Children Amid Criticism," *New York Times*, (February 18, 1999): 9; Suzanne Fields, "Calvin Klein Ads Again Use Kids and Sex to Sell," *Philadelphia Business Journal*, vol. 18 (March 5, 1999): 47; Kirk Davidson, "Calvin Klein Ads: Bad Ethics, Bad Business," *Marketing News*, vol. 29 (November 6, 1995): 1–12.
6. Faye Rice, "Superstars of Spending," *Advertising Age*, vol. 72 (February 12, 2001): 9c.
7. Brian Marchant, "Bribery and Corruption in the Business World," *Credit Control*, vol. 18, no. 7 (1997): 27–31.
8. Lisa Stein, "Furrowed Brows," *U.S. News & World Report*, vol. 133 (September 23, 2002): 18.
9. "Portion Sizes Growing Out of Control," *USA Today Magazine*, vol. 128 (April 2000): 10–11.
10. James A. Calderwood, "False and Deceptive Advertising," *Ceramic Industry*, vol. 148 (August 1998): 26.
11. Federal Trade Commission Press Release, "High School Student Survey Companies Settle FTC Charges," Federal Trade Commission Website (www.ftc.gov/opa/2002/10/student1r.htm, November 6, 2002).
12. Federal Trade Commission Press Release, "On-Line Sellers of Inkjet Cartridge Refills Agree to Pay $40,000 Civil Penalty to Settle with the FTC," Federal Trade Commission Website (www.ftc.gov/ opa/ 2002/ebabylon.htm, November 6, 2002).
13. R. Serafin and G. Levin, "Ad Industry Suffers Crushing Blow," *Advertising Age*, vol. 61 (November 12, 1990): 1, 3.
14. Jack Redmond, "Marketers Must Be Familiar with FTC Guidelines," *Inside Tucson Business*, vol. 5 (March 18, 1996): 18–19.
15. Federal Trade Commission Press Release, "Eye Doctor That Purportedly Conducted Tests to Support the Efficacy of a Product to Treat Snoring Settles FTC Charges," Federal Trade Commission Website (www.ftc.gov/opa/2002/11/currier.htm, November 6, 2002).
16. "FTC Reviews Funeral Rules," Federal Trade Commission (www.ftc.gov/opa/1999/9904/fun-rule.rev.htm, November 7, 2002).
17. Sue Marek, "BBB Unit Rules on IDEN Ads," *Wireless Week*, vol. 8 (September 16, 2002): 36.
18. Mark LaRochelle, "False Pesticide Claim," *Consumers' Research Magazine*, vol. 83 (December 2000): 31.
19. "NARB Sends Winn-Dixie Complaint to FTC," *Advertising Age*, vol. 67 (December 23, 1996): 2.
20. Kevin T. Higgins, "Marketing with a Conscience," *Marketing Management*, vol. 11 (July/August 2002): 12–16.
21. Beth Armknecht Miller, "Social Initiatives Can Boost Loyalty," *Marketing News*, vol. 36 (October 14, 2002): 14–15.
22. Ibid.
23. Higgins, "Marketing with a Conscience."
24. Jacquelyn A. Ottman, "Green Marketing," *In Business*, vol. 24 (July/August 2002): 30–31.

Case 3-1 The New Video Game

Normally, the initial marketing meeting for a new video game was not a big deal. However, this one was different, for a number of reasons. Sales had been flat; combined with increased costs, profits had been down for the past two quarters. With the Christmas season approaching, Brad knew this was an opportune time to push a new product. Sales could be generated quicker than at any other time of the year. The last two new video games had fallen under projected sales. Fingers were pointed at the marketing department, especially at Brad since he was the marketing manager, a position he had held for the past three years. But the CEO stood up for Brad, suggesting that maybe R&D had not done their homework in creating games that would appeal to the company's young male market.

Feeling some heat to produce a winner, Brad slid into his seat beside Amy, the new public relations director. She had made a huge impression on the management team in the four months she had been there. She was attractive, witty, and, with a double degree in marketing and public relations from the University of Georgia, well qualified for the position she held. She had already earned the respect of the CEO and other top management personnel with the way she handled a recent negative press situation.

Across the table were the Vice President of R&D, Stewart Hanks, and two of the "techies" from the video game division. At the head of the table was Alex Olfermayer, the CEO. He had been with the company for 23 years and had served as CEO for the past seven. During his tenure, the company had grown from $3 million in annual sales to more than $9 million.

Brad turned his attention to Mr. Hanks, who explained the newest video game. It was based on the game player rooting out terrorists from around the world before they destroyed major American targets like the Pentagon and the White House. The terrorists were not easily identifiable and, if innocent people were killed, then the probability of the terrorists hitting American targets increased. Time and skill would be needed to beat the terrorists before the ultimate disaster hit, the assassination of the president.

Just listening to the description of the new game got Brad excited. As the video game team went through a simulated version of some of the graphics, Brad looked over at the CEO. He could see that he was also impressed. Brad had a gut feeling this was going to be a big winner.

When the presentation was over, the CEO expressed his enthusiasm for the game. Brad joined in the discussion, telling the group this would be an easy marketing sell. Turning to Amy, he asked her opinion.

With a solemn look on her face, she replied, "Our competitor is already developing a similar game, but they are at least a month ahead of us."

"When is their game coming out? They've beat us with the last three games, they're not beating us this time!" Mr. Olfermayer snapped.

"I don't know," Amy replied.

"Can you find out?"

"How do you know they are producing a similar game?" Brad asked before Amy could reply to the CEO's question.

"I know somebody who works over there."

"You need to get us the scoop on what is going on over there and when they plan to introduce their version. We have to make sure our game is better," the CEO replied.

"He's not going to tell me confidential information like that. He just happened to let it slip about this new game. It was just by accident I found out."

Looking at Amy, the CEO narrowed his eyes. "You find out about this game so we can beat them. We are not losing on another game." Turning to Brad, he continued as he stood up to leave the room. "You understand what I am saying, don't you?"

"Yes, sir."

Feeling the tension in the room, the R&D staff quickly slipped out behind the CEO. For a few minutes, neither Amy nor Brad spoke.

Turning to Amy, Brad asked, "Can you get the information?"

"It will cost $10,000."

"That's blackmail."

"How bad do you want it?" Amy replied coolly.

"Not bad enough to pay someone $10,000. It would be my head if an auditor ever found something like that, and I'm not going to Mr. Olfermayer with that type of request."

Standing up, Amy looked down at Brad, a sly grin on her face. "If $10,000 is too risky for you, then I'd settle for the associate marketing director's position."

"I already have someone in that position."

"So, what does that matter?" Amy replied as she walked out of the room.

Never in his 12 years of working in a marketing department, in three different companies, had Brad experienced anything like this. Looking out the window, he noticed his wife and two kids coming toward the building. He had almost forgotten this was his youngest child's birthday. He couldn't afford to lose his job, at least not right now.

Questions

1. What options does Brad have for dealing with this situation? What are the ethical implications for each option?
2. If you were in Brad's spot, what would you do? Would your actions be different if quitting was not an option right now because of family concerns and financial obligations?
3. What is your evaluation of Amy and her approach to Brad's dilemma?
4. Although Amy does not report to you, should you have a talk with her boss about her? Should you talk with the CEO about Amy? What are the consequences of each action?
5. If Brad would make the decision to either give Amy the $10,000 or fire his current associate and give her the position, what would be the consequences of the decision?
6. Discuss the ethical implications of the newly proposed game.

Case 3-2 The Ottawa Renegades

In 1996, the Ottawa Rough Riders CFL franchise folded. For 98 years, the city of Ottawa had hosted the Rough Riders. When it folded, fans were embittered and stuck with useless season tickets. Then in 2001, Brad Watters suggested bringing football back to Ottawa. He had successfully brought lacrosse to Toronto, silencing skeptics who said Canadians would never attend a lacrosse game. Nonetheless, he made the team and the sport highly popular in Toronto. He offered something different: a brutal game, cheap tickets, and loud music. Yet, winning back jilted fans from the defunct Rough Riders would require a unique balance of novelty and nostalgia.

"The biggest challenge," said Watters, "was convincing the public we were not a fly-by-night organization." The fans had been burned already when Chicago millionaire Horn Chen had purchased the Rough Riders. Without setting foot in Ottawa, he purchased the team, later tried to sell the team, and then, when no buyers came forward, he just dismantled it.

When Watters announced he was bringing a CFL team back to Ottawa, fans demanded it be named the Rough Riders. However, the previous owner, Horn Chen, demanded $250,000 for the use of the name. "We could still buy it back," said Watters, "but we really wanted to separate ourselves from the [previous] organization." Instead of negotiating with Chen for use of the name, Watters decided to conduct a radio poll. Five names were put up for vote: Renegades, RiverMen, Raftsmen, Beavers, and Bureau-Cats. Renegades won by a landslide. While die-hard Rough Riders were unhappy with the vote and felt it was rigged, the voting brought a high level of attention to the new team.

Using his experience with the Toronto Rock lacrosse team, Watters pumped nearly $2 million into stadium renovations. A new video board was installed, luxury suites were renovated, the press box was remodeled, and the Beaver Lodge was constructed. The Beaver Lodge was an open-air bar located in the end zone. For $49 a ticket, a fan could buy a seat in the lodge and be served food by a waitress wearing a Renegades helmet. If the fan was real lucky, he or she might pick off a stray football thrown or kicked beyond the end zone of the field. With a capacity of 450 fans, the lodge was sold out for every home game. It was a way to bring the bar/nightclub experience into the stadium and lure young people from the Elgin Street bars into the game. According to Watters, "the older people seem to still accept the CFL. But we want to get the 21 to 35 demographic coming out and having a good time. That's who the lodge is targeted at."

To ensure that the stadium was filled, One on One Communication of Toronto designed a clever advertising campaign using humor. The first advertisements showed the front of a lawn cut to look like a football field with a bride and groom being doused in Gatorade. In addition to television ads, full-color ads were placed in the *Ottawa Citizen* and *Ottawa Sun*. Similar ads were placed on 200 city buses. The impact of this initial advertising blitz was the purchase of more than 13,000 season tickets.

With a new team, a new owner, a remodeled stadium, and an aggressive marketing campaign, it was time to put the finishing touches on this new CFL team. It was time to develop a cause-related marketing program that would speak strongly to the Ottawa community that this team was part of the community and here to stay. It needed to be a program that the fans would support and would fit with the image of the Ottawa Renegades football team. Especially important was reaching the younger fans, the 21- to 35-year-old group. To be successful, management also knew that employees would have to believe in the cause.

Questions

1. Using the Internet, locate four possible cause-related marketing programs that would fit well with the Ottawa Renegades and their target market.
2. Evaluate each of the cause-related programs you chose in the previous question. What are the advantages and disadvantages of the program?
3. Which cause-related program would you recommend? Justify your selection.

Sources: Nate Hendley, "Ottawa Renegades Ready to Romp," Marketing Magazine, vol. 107 (July 8, 2002): 4; Judy Trinh, "Touchdown!" Profit, vol. 21 (October 2002): 64–65; David Chilton, "Vanishing Teams," Marketing Magazine, vol. 107 (January 13, 2002): 26–27.

Consumer Behavior

4

CHAPTER OBJECTIVES

1. Identify the elements of a consumer behavior model.
2. Describe the different social influences that have an impact on consumer behavior.
3. Describe the different psychological influences that have an impact on consumer behavior.
4. Address the five stages of the consumer decision-making process.
5. Describe variations in consumer decision making based on whether consumers engage in extensive, limited, or routine problem solving.

CHAPTER OUTLINE

Cheri has style. Far removed from her deceased parents' midwestern farm home and an artist by training, she started exhibiting her contemporary artwork in galleries throughout the Southeast a year ago and has acquired quite a following. She can never produce enough pieces to keep up with demand.

Her artistic talent is also reflected throughout her home and in her impressive wardrobe. She recently built a 3,000-square-foot home on a lake with part of her substantial inheritance. The house is located 60 miles from her studio downtown in a medium-sized Southeastern city. She designed the home of her dreams with a competent local architect. On the mantle in her living room, one of her lively paintings dominates and dictates the colors of the room. Cheri had the living room rug designed to be identical to the painting and paid $6,500 for a local interior design outfit to create it. She bought an antique grandfather clock for $10,200 and placed it in the center of the living room. The adjoining kitchen combines expensive stainless steel appliances with granite countertops and IKEA cabinets. The dining room is IKEA cheap chic, defined by functionality and simplicity. Her bedrooms are primarily furnished with IKEA furniture and inherited antiques.

Cheri's most valued possession in her home, next to her artist's home mini-studio with its state-of-the-art instruments and tools, is her wardrobe. Her designer clothes are dominated by black and gray Donna Karans and Armanis bought from a local boutique, Bridgetts, for about $1,000 per suit. Her casual clothes come primarily from local discounters, T. J. Maxx and Marshalls, and from Wal-Mart. She also purchases many of her everyday clothes from the local Junior League thrift shop, sometimes for as little as $2 per item.

Food shopping is not much of a challenge for Cheri; the only supermarket that is close to her home is Food Lion, a lower-priced supermarket. She purchases virtually all her food at this store in one Sunday-afternoon trip when she loads the trunk of her VW Passatt station wagon with groceries. She uses newspaper coupons on almost every item she purchases. Whenever she can, she purchases the Food Lion store brand, rather than the national brand, for additional savings.

4-1 Chapter Overview

Product evaluations and purchase decisions dominate our lives as consumers. We define who we are through consumption. Cheri's decisions to live in a 3,000-square-foot home and to wear designer clothes, as well as her decision to cut coupons and purchase store brands, are all part of a broader plan that requires daily planning and decision making. The plan involves projecting an image to the outside world, to others who see her on the street, and to her friends who visit her at home. It also involves cutting costs in areas that are not readily visible to others. This chapter will suggest that, like Cheri, consumers cannot be placed neatly into the categories that the chapter introduces. Individual motivations, interests, attitudes, and upbringing create complex individuals who may not be easily categorized (see Figure 4-1). The chapter introduces a basic model of consumer behavior in Section 4-2, noting the personal and social (interpersonal) influences on behavior. Section 4-3 addresses social influences such as cultures and subcultures, social class, individual roles and status, family and households, and reference groups in developing attitudes, interests, opinions, and behavior. Section 4-4 addresses psychological influences, such as motivation, perception, learning, beliefs and attitudes, personality, and lifestyle. The five stages of the consumer decision-making process—problem recognition, information search, alternative evaluation, purchase, and post-purchase behavior—are described in Section 4-5. Finally, Section 4-6 offers insights into variations in decision processes attributed to the extent of problem solving involved in the purchase and the level of consumer involvement.

Figure 4-1
Consumers are complex individuals who are influenced by many factors, such as culture, social class, families, and reference groups.

4-2 A Consumer Behavior Model

Marketing managers extensively scrutinize consumer behavior. From national department stores to local convenience stores, from large consumer-goods manufacturers to small service providers, businesses strive to acquire timely information about their target consumers. Learning why consumers behave in a particular manner and how their behavior changes over time is essential to the company's bottom line. First, social influences, such as culture and subculture, social class, individual roles and status, family makeup, and reference groups are instrumental in shaping individual attitudes, interests, opinions, and behavior. In the chapter-opening vignette, Cheri is apparently a single woman living alone and working on her career as an artist. It can be assumed that she is upper middle class, with upper-class tastes, but a middle-class budget. While she can afford a large home, unique furnishings, and a haute-couture wardrobe, she buys other products at discount stores or thrift stores.

Psychological influences also affect consumer behavior. Individual motivation, perception, learning, personality, and lifestyles, as well as beliefs and attitudes, are likely to influence how consumers behave. Cheri, in our example, has grown up in a materialistic culture and probably has well-to-do friends. She buys products that her friends or those that she aspires to have as friends approve of and pays for them using a large amount of her discretionary income. She lives the lifestyle she aspires to, while cutting costs by purchasing less visible products from cheaper sources.

Marketers need to understand what motivates consumers like Cheri in their purchase behavior. What motivates them to purchase certain brands and shop at certain stores? What messages do consumers want to convey about themselves through the products they purchase? Figure 4-2 illustrates the different influences exerted on consumer behavior.

4-3 Social Influences on Consumer Behavior

The social influences examined in this chapter are culture, social class, role and status, families and household, and reference groups. Culture is recognized as having an important influence on consumption and consumer behavior in general. Cultural influences are

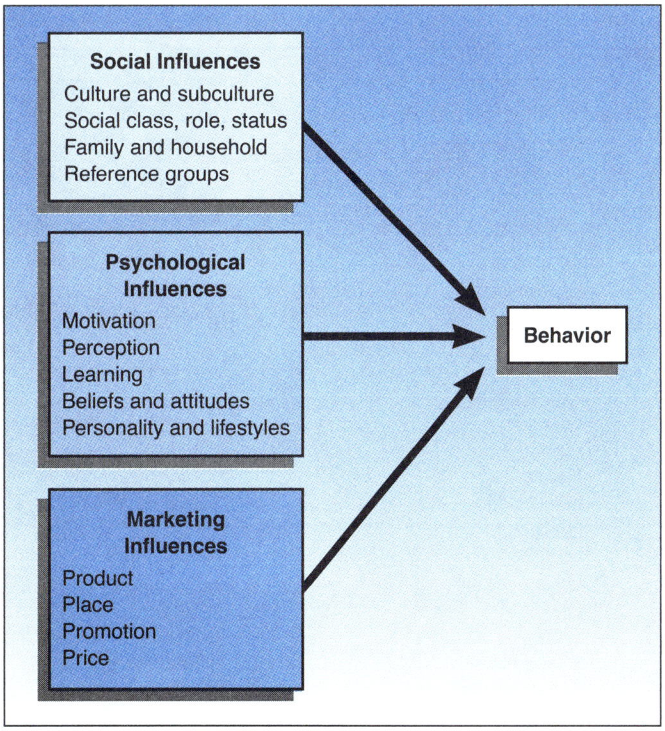

Figure 4-2
Model of Consumer Behavior

Source: Adapted from George Fisk, "Reflection and Retrospection: Searching for visions in Marketing," *Journal of Marketing,* 1999, Vol. 63 (1), pp. 115–121; William O. Bearden, R. E. Netemeyer, and Jesse E. Teal, "Measurement of Consumer Susceptibility to Interpersonal Influence", *Journal of Consumer Research,* 1989, Vol. 15, pp. 473–81; Dana N. Lascu, William O. Bearden and Randall L. Rose, "Norm Extremity and Interpersonal Influences on Consumer Conformity", *Journal of Business Research,* 1995, Vol. 32, pp. 201–12; J. Paul Peter and James H. Donnelly, Jr., *Marketing Management: Knowledge and Skills,* 7th Edition, (Boston, MA: McGraw-Hill Irwin).

Culture: A continuously evolving totality of learned and shared meanings, rituals, norms, and traditions among the members of an organization or society.

Values: Important elements of culture defined as enduring beliefs about a specific mode of conduct or desirable end-state.

Terminal values: Values related to goals.

Instrumental values: Values related to processes whereby one can attain certain goals.

Acculturation: The process of learning a new culture.

Assimilation: Adapting to and fully integrating into the new culture.

expressed in the consumption of goods and services, in homes, offices, stores, and marketplace sites, with differences noted across various subcultures.[1] Similarly, social class, role, and status influence the types of goods and services consumers purchase. Friends and family are also likely to affect individuals' consumption, the brands that they purchase, the frequency of purchase, the prices they are willing to pay, the stores where they purchase their goods, and the service establishments they select, as well as the media that they are exposed to.

4-3a Cultural Influences on Consumer Behavior

Culture—a society's personality—is defined as a continuously changing totality of learned and shared meanings, rituals, norms, and traditions among the members of an organization or society. **Values** are important elements of culture; they are defined as enduring beliefs about a specific mode of conduct or desirable end-state that guides the selection or evaluation of behavior, and are ordered by importance in relation to one another to form a system of value priorities.[2] Values guide individuals' actions, attitudes, and judgments, which are derived from and continuously modified through personal, social, and cultural learning, ultimately affecting their product preferences and their perception of products. Cultures are set apart by their *value systems*—the relative importance or ranking of values. Western cultures (North American and Western European) place more stress on success, achievement, and competitiveness, whereas Eastern cultures are more likely to be concerned with social welfare. Examples of universally held values are provided in Figure 4-3 and are attributed to Rokeach.[3] According to this classification, values can be related to goals (**terminal values**) or to the processes whereby one can attain those goals (**instrumental values**).

Values are learned from those with whom individuals are in contact: family, friends, teachers, clergy, politicians, and the media. The United States is a melting pot of different cultures that have blended together to create the American culture with its own values and beliefs. Learning a new culture, which most immigrants must do when they come to the United States, is known as acculturation. **Acculturation** encompasses interaction with the American culture and adaptation to the culture, and it includes the **assimilation** of a new culture, maintenance of the new culture, and resistance to both the new and old cultures. Acculturation does not necessarily mean abandoning all home country traditions; that is,

Figure 4-3
Instrumental and Terminal Values

Source: Adapted from Milton J. Rokeach, *The Nature of Human Values* (New York: The Free Press, 1973).

INTERACTIVE FIGURE

Instrumental Values (the means by which terminal values are achieved) →	Terminal Values (goals reached by means of instrumental values)
Ambitious	A comfortable life
Broadminded	An exciting life
Capable	A sense of accomplishment
Cheerful	A world at peace
Clean	A world of beauty
Courageous	Equality
Forgiving	Family security
Helpful	Freedom
Imaginative	Inner harmony
Independent	Mature love
Intellectual	National security
Logical	Pleasure
Loving	Salvation
Obedient	Self-respect
Polite	Social recognition
Responsible	True friendship
Self-controlled	Wisdom

it does not mean complete assimilation of the new culture. For example, recent Asian-Indian immigrants to the United States are less likely to be assimilated in this culture because they maintain their original religious practices, language, food consumption, housing, and friendship patterns, as well as contact with India.[4] Although Indian Americans are not easily assimilated, they are, nevertheless, acculturated in the U.S. culture.

Consumer acculturation refers to contact with a new culture and the resulting change for consumers in terms of their approach to consumption in the new environment.[5] Asian-Indian consumers, for example, consume fast food, shop at supermarkets, root for their favorite baseball team, and, overall, successfully integrate in the U.S. culture, without necessarily being assimilated.

Subcultures **Subcultures** are components of the broad culture. They are groups of individuals with shared value systems based on ethnicity or common background. Subcultures could be based on regional differences: Southern consumers have different lifestyles than Midwest consumers. Case 4-1 at the end of this chapter examines an Eastern Shore subculture and its impact on consumer behavior.

Subcultures: Groups of individuals with shared value systems based on ethnicity or common background.

Subcultures are often based on ethnicity or nationality: Italian Americans maintain many of their home-country traditions and strong ties to the old country. Or subcultures can be based on religion—an important element of culture. Among the important ethnic and national subcultures in the United States are African Americans, Hispanics, and Asian Americans.

The African-American subculture makes up 12.7 percent of the total U.S. population. African Americans are younger than the rest of the U.S. population, with a large percentage living in cities. They spend proportionately more than the dominant culture on products such as clothing, personal care, and furnishings, but less on medical care, food, education, and leisure activities. They are also more brand loyal and less likely to be innovators and try out new products during the introduction stage of the product lifecycle.

The Hispanic subculture makes up 13 percent of the U.S. population and is the largest and fastest growing subculture in the United States. More than half of Hispanics are of Mexican origin, with the rest coming from Central and South America and Puerto Rico. While Hispanics do not constitute a homogeneous group, they do share a number of traits: the Catholic religion, the Spanish language, traditional and conservative values, and male dominance. Hispanics are brand conscious and brand loyal, and they adopt primarily well-established brands.

The Asian-American subculture, which is 4 percent of the U.S. population, is the most heterogeneous subculture, consisting of ethnic and national groups with different languages and traditions—Chinese, Asian Indian and Pakistani, Filipino, Japanese, and Korean are examples. They are more affluent than the dominant culture and most other ethnic and national groups. They value education and quality brands and tend to be brand loyal (see Figure 4-4).

Religious subcultures are important for marketers because **religion** defines a society's relationship to the supernatural and, as a result, determines dominant values and attitudes. Religious beliefs are important determinants of consumer behavior since they influence purchase motivation, consumption preferences, purchase patterns, personal customs, and business practices. Attitudes toward authority, family, and peers, as well as attitudes toward material possessions, cultural values, and norms, among others, can all be traced to religion.

Religion: A way of defining a society's relationship to the supernatural and, as a result, determining dominant values and attitudes.

Religion is linked to cultural behaviors of the different subcultures that have an impact on marketing. For example, the Protestant religion stresses hard work and frugality and is linked to the development of capitalism and economic emancipation. Such attitudes may have created the opportunity for do-it-yourself stores and discounters. In other examples, Judaism, with its disdain for ignorance and sloth, stresses education. Jewish consumers in the United States are an important target market for educational and professional development. Islam dictates social etiquette between the genders and discourages the consumption of pork products and alcohol. The Hindu religion encourages a family orientation and

Figure 4-4
This advertisement, featuring Chinese actress Zhang Ziyi, is directed at the Asian-American subculture.

Source: Courtesy of Bozell Worldwide, Inc. as agent for the National Fluid Milk Processor Promotion Board.

discourages the consumption of animal products—beef, in particular. Firms targeting these consumers need to be aware of the religious constraints of Muslims and Hindus and offer goods and services that address their special needs. For example, fast-food restaurants find that they can better serve their Asian-Indian consumers by offering ample choices of vegetarian food. Vegetarian options may also serve Jewish consumers since they do not compromise consumer kosher requirements. Keeping kosher requires, among others, the separation of milk products and meat products and of the implements used to serve or process them; vegetarian products are pareve—neutral, with regard to kosher requirements.

There are, of course, other subcultures that represent important market segments: the different age groups previously described in Chapter 2, "The Environment of Marketing in the Twenty-First Century"—Generation X, Generation Y, young boomers, and older boomers—represent different subcultures. Similarly, gay and lesbian consumers represent an important subculture, and an important and influential market. Marketing Illustration 4-1 describes the gay and lesbian subculture.

Social class: Relatively permanent divisions within society that exist in a status hierarchy, with the members of each division sharing similar values, attitudes, interests, and opinions.

4-3b Social Class, Role, and Status Influences on Consumer Behavior

The position of individuals in society can be defined in terms of social class. **Social class** is defined as relatively permanent divisions within society that exist in a status hierarchy, with the members of each division sharing similar values, attitudes, interests, and opinions.

Marketing Illustration 4-1

Gay and Lesbian Consumers

Marketers in the 1960s were described as myopic for not being aware of the importance of the mature market—the segment of older consumers with the largest disposable income. In the new millennium, a large percentage of marketers remain myopic to another substantial and well-off market: the gay and lesbian consumer market. With a buying power close to $450 billion and a median household income of $65,000 (compared to $40,800 for all U.S. households) and with 9 out of 10 being registered voters, the majority of whom vote in presidential elections, this market is substantial and active. In terms of other demographics, more than half are in committed partnerships (58 percent of lesbians and 43 percent of gay men), and almost 13 percent report having children in the home, which is noteworthy, since only 29.6 percent of U.S. households include children under age 18.

Only 6 to 7 percent of people in the United States self-identify as gay and lesbian; yet, marketing to the gay and lesbian market will effectively reach many more consumers, including those who are not out, or those who are gay-friendly. As gay and lesbian relationships are increasingly accepted as a norm, and quickly becoming part of the mainstream media, Fortune 500 companies appear to be slowly following suit.

Among the companies that regularly advertise to gay and lesbian consumers and sponsor exhibits at gay and lesbian expos are American Airlines, America Online, Merrill Lynch, Chase Manhattan, British Airways and Virgin Atlantic, Levi Strauss, American Express, IBM, Saab, and Anheuser-Busch. Those companies that actively target gay and lesbian consumers have been able to reap substantial rewards: Gay and lesbian consumers have a fierce loyalty to a brand they identify as supportive.

Researchers have uncovered a number of behavioral traits of the gay and lesbian subculture of importance to marketers:

- A large percentage of lesbian consumers dine out, attend musical and theatrical performances, visit nightclubs and museums, and join health clubs.
- Lesbian consumers are avid mail-order buyers—95 percent of the female readers of *OUT* magazine have ordered products via mail and phone.
- Gay consumers spend significantly more on travel, and they strongly prefer warm-weather destinations.
- Gay consumers are likely to embrace new technology early in the product lifecycle.

With regard to financial services, while the general market is most interested in retirement savings and financing children's education, gay and lesbian consumers focus on establishing and managing joint ownership of assets.

Gay and lesbian consumers find the privacy and anonymity of the web appealing: The web is an ideal venue for marketing to gay and lesbian consumers.

Sources: C. J. Prince, "Rolling Out the Red Carpet for Gay Consumers," *Advocate*, vol. 26, no. 4 (February 19, 2002), www.advocate.com; "A Snapshot of Gay and Lesbian Lives," *Advocate*, vol. 16, no. 1 (November 6, 2001), www.advocate.com; Howard Buford, "Understanding Gay Consumers," *Gay & Lesbian Review*, vol. 7, no. 2 (Spring 2000): 26; "Mainstream Marketers Are Now Courting Lesbians as Consumers," *About Women & Marketing*, vol. 9, no. 9 (September 1996) (Newsletter).

Social class is evaluated as a combination of occupation, education, income, wealth, and personal values, which have a direct impact on consumption. Children are initially socialized in their parents' social class, engaging in activities characteristic of that class. Marketing Illustration 4-2 offers a description of the social classes in America. Cindy Crawford grew up in the cornfields of Illinois with ambitions of becoming an engineer. Today, she is a supermodel living a celebrity life as a jetsetter. Nevertheless, she has not lost all traces of her background and social class, and to her, it is an advantage to be seen as the girl next door that others can relate to.

How do different social classes consume differently? The PBS Social Class in America site has a Chintz or Shag game, which offers illustrations of consumption by social class. The old money class, according to the site, prefers threadbare rugs, antiques and duck decoys as displays, original paintings by recognized artists, a television set not in the living room, and an elk hound for a pet. Wall-to-wall shag carpeting, bowling trophies, beer posters, a corduroy recliner, a 27-inch color TV in an armoire, a gun rack, and a pit bull qualify one for the trailer park. (See Figure 4-5 on page 105 for an illustration of furnishings of the lower upper class.)

In addition to differences in good and service preferences and consumption, each social class has other distinctive traits. For example, the upper classes have a broader social circle beyond their immediate community and family, whereas lower classes are more restricted to their home environment and to family life. Upper classes also participate more

Marketing Illustration 4-2

Social Classes in America

Upper Upper Class (Old Money)
The upper upper social class is composed of the wealthiest 1 percent of the U.S. population. Most people in this class inherited their money and spend it without display. They are educated in private preparatory schools and the best colleges in the United States. They are socially concerned and self-actualized, freely deviating from class norms. They own expensive homes with original antique furniture and artwork by internationally recognized artists. They engage in inconspicuous consumption, dressing down and paying others to purchase goods for them.

Lower Upper Class (New Money)
The lower upper social class is composed of the next wealthiest Americans, comprising 2 percent of the U.S. population. Members of this class have college degrees, although not necessarily from the best colleges. They earned their new money, primarily through businesses, and like to show that they have it by spending on luxury items. They frequently buy new products and technologies before the rest of Americans and, thus, are classified as innovators. They value business, politics, and social concerns. They engage in conspicuous consumption and constitute prime markets for exclusive gated communities, luxury automobiles, and designer clothes.

Upper Middle Class (Professional)
The upper middle social class comprises 12 percent of the U.S. population. Members of this social class earn their money through successful careers founded on professional and graduate degrees. They live graciously, entertaining friends, but are careful to buy quality products. They value family and home and invest in children's education.

Lower Middle Class (White Collar)
The lower middle social class comprises 30 percent of the U.S. population. Members of this class earn their money through skilled and creative jobs founded on technical training, and sometimes, a college diploma. They could be construction contractors, salespeople, and clerical workers. They compose the price-sensitive market, value homes and neighborhoods, and adhere to norms and standards. People in the lower middle class work hard, attend church, obey laws, and value home and family. Therefore, they can be most effectively reached with conservative messages. And because they have many obligations but a limited income to meet those obligations, they read self-improvement and how-to information.

Upper Lower Class (Blue Collar)
The upper lower social class comprises 35 percent of the U.S. population. They work at manual jobs that can be acquired with moderate skills and education—they are skilled and semi-skilled manual workers. They live routine lives, have limited social interaction, and spend impulsively on national brands. People in the upper lower class engage in unchanging activities, live in dull surroundings, and rely on relatives for socialization and support.

Lower Lower Class (Unskilled or Unemployed)
The lower lower social class comprises 20 percent of the U.S. population. They make their money through unskilled work, or through underground jobs and illegal activities. Alternatively, they are unemployed and on welfare. They have minimal skills and education, buy impulsively and on credit, get their kicks wherever they can, and reject middle-class morality. They often live in substandard housing, and their homes have used, substandard furniture.

Sources: Linda P. Morton, "Segmenting Publics by Social Classes," *Public Relations Quarterly*, vol. 44, no. 2 (Summer 1999): 45–46; Richard P. Coleman, "The Continuing Significance of Social Class to Marketing," *Journal of Consumer Research*, vol. 10, no. 3 (December 1983): 265–280; Eugene Sivadas, "A Preliminary Examination of the Continuing Significance of Social Class to Marketing: A Geodemographic Replication," *Journal of Consumer Marketing*, vol. 14, no. 6 (1977): 463–479.

in activities outside the home, such as theater performances, than lower classes, which engage in physical activities for recreation.

Roles: The activities people are expected to perform according to individuals around them.

Individuals' positions within a group can also be defined in terms of role and status. **Roles** are based on the activities people are expected to perform according to the individuals around them. In traditional families, women are expected to stay at home and take care of the daily functioning of the household. Women are traditionally assigned to the role of mother and maid. In a more modern rendition of this traditional role, women play the role of soccer moms, carpool drivers, and PTA (Parents Teachers Association) activists.

In many developing countries, this traditional role is in fact law. In the most traditional Islamic countries, such as Saudi Arabia, women are not allowed to drive and not permitted to be in public if unaccompanied by a male relative. In these countries, women's business activities are channeled toward interaction in a women-only environment. Personal services can be performed only by individuals of the same gender. For example, women can bank only at women's banks, can have their hair done only by other women, and so on. In less-traditional Islamic countries, such as Pakistan, women share responsibility with men in business. It is noteworthy, however, that women play a more limited role politically, where only a few hold notable positions, and when they do, it is often by virtue of their father's position.

Figure 4-5
Lower upper class furnishings might include gilded Louis XVI antiques.

In today's modern society, women focus on careers, assuming the roles of professionals and managers, and leaving traditional chores to individuals who are considered competent to handle them: maids, daycares, and personal shopping services. Gender roles are not as clearly defined, especially for the upper middle class. Children and the household become the responsibility of both parents who take turns in fulfilling the roles that traditionally have been assigned to women. Today's modern society also accepts that the world is not populated only by heterosexual married households. Single parents and gay parent families raise children, adopting the roles that best meet the needs of the children and the family as a whole.

Status is defined as the esteem that society bestows upon a particular role. The role of soccer mom is, unfortunately, lower than the role of district manager; a woman playing both roles will probably not stress the role of soccer mom in her professional circles for fear of lessening her status of district manager. Status defines what products we consume and how we behave. Related to one's background is one's concern with status, or status concern—maintaining it or acquiring it—and with material possessions, or materialism. Individuals' concern with status is related to the values placed on symbols of status and on the attainment of high status. Often, the products consumed convey messages about the consumer in the same way that language does.[6] Driving a Mercedes or a Porsche advertises that one is a successful professional. The Mercedes station wagon is a typical family automobile for this upper middle class professional, as illustrated in Figure 4-6.

Status: The esteem which society bestows upon a particular role.

Status—like social class, to which it is related—is easier to transcend in industrially developed countries than in developing countries. In the United States, the Protestant ethic of hard work has led to centuries of individual prosperity and, at the individual level, status advancement. In the United States, it is not perceived as shameful for prominent politicians and business people to refer back to their humble beginnings.

More recently, however, status and social class have become more dynastic than dynamic. The past two decades have seen a substantial increase in inequality in America, with real incomes of households in the lowest fifth (the bottom 20 percent) growing by 6.4 percent, and the income of the top 1 percent growing 184 percent. And the rise in inequality did not come with a commensurate rise in mobility; in fact, social sclerosis is evident for the middle and lower income population. Clear evidence in this regard is provided in the political arena. In a country where every child aspires to be a president, it appears that the political elite have become a self-perpetuating elite, with prominent

Figure 4-6
The Palo Alto Taxi—the Mercedes Benz station wagon with children's car seats—is an important accoutrement of the upper middle class.

politicians in their recent family pedigree coming from the blue-blooded world of private schools and ultra-select Ivy League societies. And, surprisingly, nobody complains that dynastic ties are proliferating, social circles are interlocking, and mechanisms of social exclusion of the vast majority are strengthening.[7]

4-3c Family and Household Influences on Consumer Behavior

The family exerts probably the most influence on consumers. Consumers continue to purchase the brands they grew up with. Somebody growing up with Ford automobiles will probably continue to purchase them as an adult. If mother always bought a Butterball turkey for Thanksgiving dinner, her adult daughter will probably continue the Butterball tradition for her family. And should marketers attempt to change these traditions, they are most likely going to encounter substantial resistance.

Marketers are also interested in how decisions are made in the family. Traditionally, food shopping has been the domain of women, while automobiles have been the domain of men. Those roles are greatly changing today, with men often taking charge of household purchases in households with dual-career couples. For decades, models of family decision making equated family decisions with husband-wife decisions, and excluded or ignored the role of children. More recently, however, the influence of children has received ample attention from marketers, especially when the decision centered on less-expensive products and those products designed for the child's personal use.[8] Yet, children's documented buying power and influence on family purchase decisions extend beyond these products. Children are important influencers when it comes to decisions regarding family vacations, the family automobiles, and the new television set. Children even determine the brands of products used in daily consumption, such as food and grooming products. In a family household, there may be other decision makers, in addition to the family itself. The residential cleaning service may determine the brands of cleaning products and furniture polish. The family pet may have a preference of one brand of food over another.

Finally, in nonfamily households, roommates bring with them the consumption traditions of their own families and backgrounds. These household members exert an important influence on the types of products and services consumed by an individual.

4-3d Reference Groups

Reference groups are defined as groups that serve as a point of reference for individuals in the process of shaping their attitude and behavior. **Associative reference groups** are groups that individuals belong to. As a member of a group, an individual will adopt the group's behaviors, engage in similar activities, and purchase similar brand names as referent others in the group. For example, members of a sorority are likely to dress similarly, with a preference for the same brand names and retailers. **Dissociative groups** are groups that individuals want to dissociate from through their behavior. For example, lesbians are rarely dressed in pretty, frilly dresses, and they reject the make-up and accessories that are characteristic of heterosexual women. They tend to dissociate from the more traditional, submissive females through their style, which is simple, assertive, and natural. **Aspirational groups** are groups that individuals aspire to join in the future—by virtue of education, employment, and training, for instance. Aspirational groups are very important determinants of consumer behavior. Business students aspiring to work on Wall Street will acquire products that fit with their new profile—leather briefcase, designer suit, executive pen set, and other products associated with their coveted professional position.

For Cheri in the chapter-opening vignette, Donna Karan and Armani outfits, expensive antiques, and the house on the lake reflect her desire to be accepted by refined locals of taste and means in the town where she recently moved. In cases in which her products are visible and conspicuous, as in the case of clothing or the home itself, Cheri readily spends large amounts of money to signal her preferences to her aspirational group. She

Reference groups: Groups that serve as a point of reference for individuals in the process of shaping their attitude and behavior.

Associative reference groups: Groups that individuals belong to.

Dissociative groups: Groups that individuals want to dissociate from through their behavior.

Aspirational groups: Groups that individuals aspire to join in the future—by virtue of education, employment, and training, for example.

purchases products that are privately consumed, such as food, at a discount from off-price retailers. In her public consumption, Cheri distances herself from her associative group, her family on the farm in the Midwest.

4-4 Psychological Influences on Consumer Behavior

Consumer behavior is likely to be influenced by the following psychological factors: motivation, perception, learning, beliefs, attitudes, personality, and lifestyles. The field of psychology has extensively examined these dimensions and their influence on individual behavior.

4-4a Motivation

Consumers are motivated by needs and wants. Needs were defined in Chapter 1, "Scope and Concepts of Marketing," as basic human requirements. People are motivated to seek products and services that satisfy their needs, and marketers attempt to address consumer needs with the different goods and services they offer. A need becomes a want when it is directed to a particular product—wants are shaped by one's culture. We may have a physiological need, such as something to drink, that can become a want—a desire for a particular brand: Coke. When a need is not satisfied, it becomes a **drive** (or **motive**), which is defined as a stimulus that encourages consumers to engage in an action to reduce the need. Figure 4-7 illustrates motivation as a process that moves consumers from a latent need (hunger) to the behavior that satisfies that need (going to a restaurant).

Drive (or **motive**): A stimulus that encourages consumers to engage in an action to reduce the need.

Consumers first experience a latent need, such as the need for food. The unsatisfied need becomes a drive or motivation to reduce hunger. The need then translates into a want: a sandwich wrap. The consumer then has a specific goal—searching in his or her memory for various wrap sources—and decides to go to Wawa, a popular gas station convenience store. The behavior that reduces hunger involves eating the Wawa wrap.

One popular theory of motivation, Maslow's theory of needs, explains individuals' motivation to engage in particular behaviors as a function of needs arranged in a hierarchy from the most urgent to the least urgent. Consumers need to satisfy their most urgent needs, such as food and drink, before they can satisfy higher-level needs. As soon as they satisfy their lower needs, their higher needs become more pressing.

The Maslow hierarchy of needs is illustrated in Figure 4-8. The most basic needs are physiological: the need for food, water, and sleep. At the next level are safety needs, such as the need for shelter and protection from danger or harm. Love, social, or belonging needs are at the following level—the need to be accepted by one's group, family, and friends. Once in a group, individuals crave self-esteem—status and appreciation, respect from others. Finally, individuals need self-actualization, the need to accomplish and realize their own

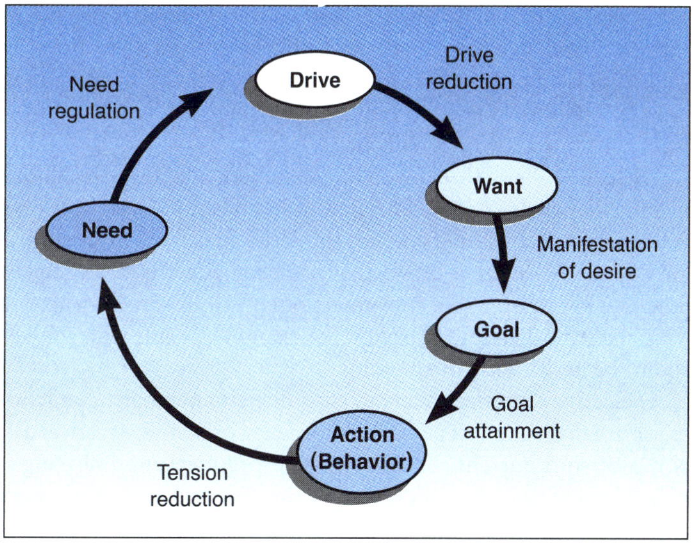

Figure 4-7
Motivation as a Process
Motivation moves consumers from latent need through stages of increasing specificity to the behavior that satisfies the need.

INTERACTIVE FIGURE

Figure 4-8
Maslow's Hierarchy of Needs

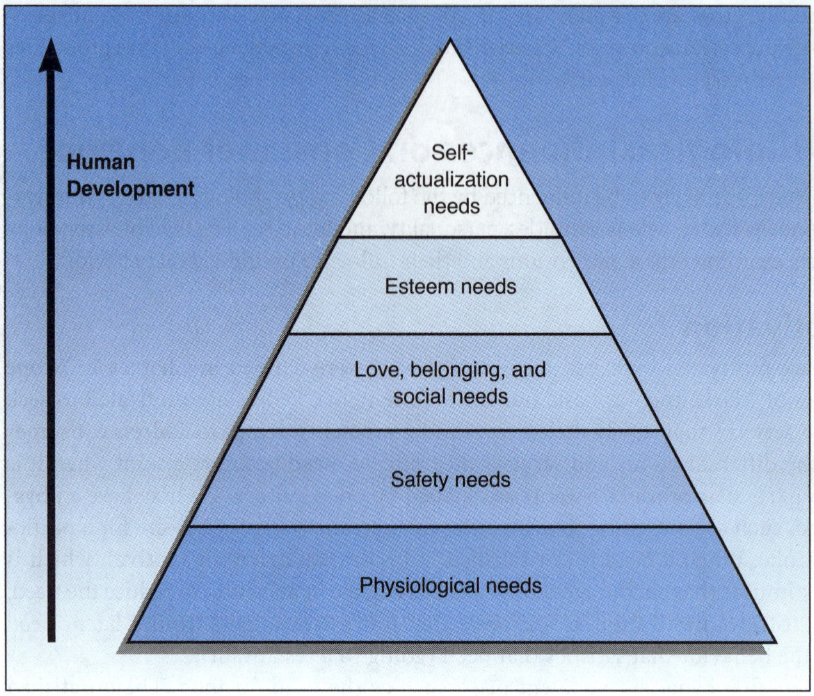

potential. Products can satisfy a number of needs at the same time. Cheri in our example has a strong social need: She needs to belong to an aspirational group defined as locals of taste and means. In order to satisfy this need, she purchases visibly consumed products, such as expensive antiques and top designer brands that are popular with this aspirational group.

Consumers can satisfy thirst needs with a can of Pepsi or iced tea, they can satisfy hunger needs with a steak or a Snickers bar, and they can satisfy safety needs with the right brand of tires. The Goodyear tires in Figure 4-9 clearly address consumers' need for safety, offering "freedom from worry."

Perception: The manner in which people collect, organize, and interpret information from the world around them to create a meaningful image of reality.

4-4b Perception

Perception is defined as the manner in which we collect, organize, and interpret information from the world around us to create a meaningful image of reality. Individuals form different images of the same stimulus because of differences in the perceptual processes. One such difference is attributed to **selective exposure**—the stimuli that consumers choose to pay attention to. Individuals are exposed to numerous advertisements every day: They see television and newspaper ads and billboards, and they listen to advertising on radio. Clearly, most consumers could not possibly retain all the information from these different sources. Advertisers need to create advertising that stands out from the multitude of messages consumers see on a daily basis.

Selective exposure: The stimuli that consumers choose to pay attention to.

Selective distortion: Consumers adapting information to fit their own existing knowledge.

Selective distortion involves consumers adapting the information to fit their own existing knowledge or beliefs. A new brand of soup advertising on television would need to make sure that consumers do not think the ad is for a competitor's offering—for example, for Campbell's Soup, a brand that has been advertised on television for decades. After a purchase has been made, consumers often will distort information to make it conform to their current beliefs and behavior. For example, people who smoke tend to distort messages about the health risks of smoking.

Selective retention: Remembering only information about a good or service that supports personal knowledge or beliefs.

Selective retention refers to consumers remembering only information about a good or service that supports personal knowledge or beliefs. An advertisement that does not support a person's current concepts is easily forgotten. A purchasing agent listening to a salesperson may remember only the portions of the conversation that reinforce his or her

Figure 4-9
This advertisement for Aquatred 3 assures consumers that these tires perform well, even in wet weather.
Source: Courtesy of Goodyear Tire & Rubber Co.

Learning: Change in individual thought processes or behavior attributed to experience.

Cues: Stimuli in the environment, such as products or advertisements, that create individual responses.

Stimuli: Cues in the environment, such as products and advertisements, that create individual responses.

Response: An attempt to satisfy an individual drive.

Reinforcement: Learning achieved by strengthening the relationship between the cue and the response.

current beliefs about the vendor. To overcome selective retention, marketers must provide information that makes their good or service stand out from that of competitors, and to get beyond selective retention usually involves repeating the message over and over until the target audience makes the new information part of its current knowledge and belief structure.

4-4c Learning

Learning is defined as a change in individual thought processes or behavior attributed to experience. It involves **cues** or **stimuli** in the environment, such as products and advertisements, which create an individual response. **Response** is defined as an attempt to satisfy an individual drive. Cheri in our example has a drive to satisfy a social need—the need to be accepted locally by upscale consumers. Her response to this drive is conditioned by cues in the environment that confirm or reject her choices. Cheri may find it rewarding to see celebrities wearing outfits by her preferred designers, to note that these designers are available only in the most exclusive local shop, and especially, that her aspirational group approves of these designers. The outcome of these desirable cues is a reduction in the drive, known as **reinforcement**—referring to the reinforcement of the learning process, achieved by strengthening the relationship between the cue and the response. Repeated reinforcement creates a habit. Marketers are keen on making their brands habitual purchases.

4-4d Attitudes and Beliefs

Attitudes: Relatively enduring and consistent feelings (affective responses) about a good or service.

Attitudes are defined as relatively enduring and consistent feelings (affective responses) about a product or service. A consumer may like Starbucks, Bose speakers, and Intel processors, and dislike fast food, loud music in restaurants, and intrusive salespeople. Cheri in the chapter-opening vignette has a positive attitude toward brands such as Donna Karan and Armani—she likes their neutral colors and conservative yet sleek designs. She also likes Donna Karan, the designer herself, because Karan is a tough New Yorker-type with whom she can identify. Finally, she likes it that Donna Karan associates with celebrities like Barbra Streisand, who epitomize high style and New York chic.

Attitudes are difficult to change; therefore, changing attitudes about brands can be quite challenging, depending on how strong the attitudes are. The more firmly held the attitude, the more difficult it is to change. The advertisement in Figure 4-10 attempts to change consumers' attitudes about ready-made soups, suggesting that they can be both delicious and nutritious.

Beliefs: Associations between a good or service and attributes of that good or service.

Beliefs are associations between a product and attributes of that product. Examples of such beliefs are the following: "Starbucks sells strong coffee," "Bose speakers are a product of advanced German technology," "Intel processors only exist in quality computers," or "Fast food and smoking cause heart attacks." Marketers attempt to create positive attitudes toward their goods and services and to create beliefs that link their brands to desirable

Figure 4-10
This advertisement attempts to change consumers' attitudes about ready-made soups, suggesting that they reduce the risk of cancer.
Source: Courtesy of Campbell Soup Co.

attributes. For example, many consumers believe that Volvo and Mercedes automobiles are among the safest and most durable automobiles on the road (see Figure 4-11).

Consumers also believe that sports utility vehicles (SUVs) are very safe; this is true simply by virtue of their size and elevation of the cabin. Hummers are especially popular in this category and, given a choice, consumers would probably feel safest in this tank.

Cheri believes that Food Lion provides basic food of reliable quality. She believes that the Food Lion brand is just as good as any other national brand and that it provides a better value for one's money than competing national brands.

Personality: An individual's unique psychological characteristics leading to specific response tendencies over time.

4-4e Personality and Lifestyles

Personality is defined as an individual's unique psychological characteristics leading to specific response tendencies over time. Brands are often positioned to appeal to consumers with a particular personality. For example, high-performance automobiles, such as Porsche and Maseratti, and Rossignol skis attempt to appeal to high-sensation seekers looking for adventure and fun. Variety seekers are a good market to target when introducing a new brand and/or a new product. Retailers target impulsive consumers, placing impulse items close to the register. Consumers who are more impulsive will buy those products rather than rigidly sticking to the products on the shopping list.

Lifestyles: Individuals' style of living as expressed through activities, interests, and opinions.

Cheri in our example appears to have high self-esteem. She feels positively about herself and creates the atmosphere in her home that provides her with comfort and projects the image she desires. She is constantly monitoring herself, ensuring that she projects the right image to others by purchasing the right visible brands. As an individual who engages in extensive self-monitoring, Cheri is probably more influenced by image advertising than informational advertising and responds positively to appeals that emphasize style.

Psychographics: Categorization of consumers according to lifestyles and personality.

Lifestyles refer to individuals' style of living as expressed through activities, interests, and opinions. Marketers have made numerous attempts to categorize consumers according to lifestyles—this categorization and measurement is known as psychographics. **Psychographics** incorporate lifestyle and personality dimensions, as the following example illustrates.

Innovators: Psychographic group of individuals who are successful, sophisticated, and receptive to new technologies.

SRI Consulting Business Intelligence provides a popular classification of lifestyles: The VALS 2 typology categorizes respondents based on resources and on the extent to which they are action oriented. VALS 2 categorizes consumers as:

Thinkers: Psychographic group of individuals who are educated, conservative, and practical consumers who value knowledge and responsibility. They look for durability, functionality, and value.

- **Innovators**—They are successful, sophisticated, and receptive to new technologies. Their purchases reflect cultivated tastes for upscale products.
- **Thinkers**—They are educated, conservative, practical consumers who value knowledge and responsibility. They look for durability, functionality, and value.

Figure 4-11
Volvo has consistently advertised itself as a *safe* and *durable* automobile. The one in the photograph has more than 150,000 miles and is used daily.

Achievers: Psychographic group of individuals who are goal-oriented, conservative, committed to career and family, and favor established, prestige products that demonstrate success to peers.

Experiencers: Psychographic group of individuals who are young, enthusiastic, and impulsive. They seek variety and excitement, and spend substantially on fashion, entertainment, and socializing.

- **Achievers**—They are goal-oriented, conservative consumers committed to career and family. They favor established prestige products that demonstrate success to peers.
- **Experiencers**—They are young, enthusiastic, and impulsive consumers who seek variety and excitement, and spend substantially on fashion, entertainment, and socializing.
- **Believers**—They are conservative, conventional consumers who focus on tradition, family, religion, and community. They prefer established brands, favoring American products.
- **Strivers**—They are trendy, fun-loving consumers who are concerned about others' opinions and approval. They demonstrate to peers their ability to buy.
- **Makers**—They are self-sufficient consumers who have the skill and energy to carry out projects, respect authority, and are unimpressed by material possessions.
- **Survivors**—They are concerned with safety and security, focus on meeting needs rather than fulfilling desires, are brand loyal, and purchase discounted products.

Knowledge about consumers' lifestyles is important. Marketers who learn about and adapt to changing consumer attitudes, interests, and opinions will have an advantage in the marketplace. Cheri is a successful artist with means, refined tastes, and social ambition; within the VALS 2 categorization, she could be categorized as an innovator. She is also a practical consumer who does not pay premium prices for food items, favoring store brands rather than established national brands.

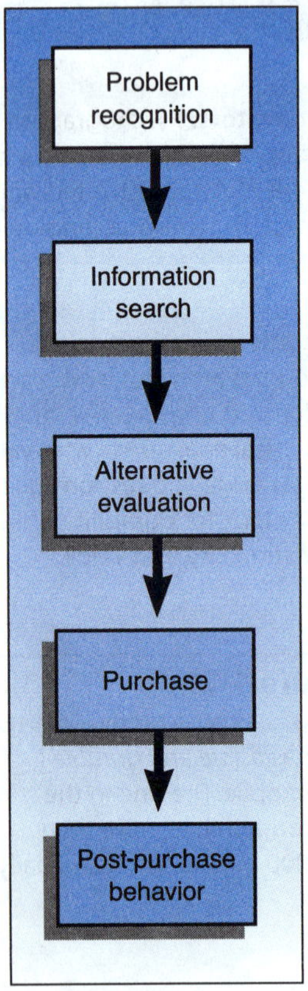

Figure 4-12
The Consumer Decision-Making Process

INTERACTIVE FIGURE

4-5 The Consumer Decision-Making Process

We have addressed the different influences on consumer behavior—social influences and psychological influences. We are now going to examine the consumer decision-making process, addressing each of the five stages: problem recognition, information search, alternative evaluation, purchase, and post-purchase behavior, as illustrated in Figure 4-12. It should, however, be mentioned that not all consumers go through each stage every time they make a purchase and that certain stages may take more time and effort than others, depending on the type of purchase decision involved—as will be seen later in this section.

Let us, once again, use Cheri from the chapter-opening vignette to illustrate different examples of consumer decision making. Cheri is planning to entertain at Thanksgiving and has to engage in a number of purchases. On her most urgent shopping list, she has a new faucet for her guest bathroom, replacing the original faucet, which is a bit too basic for a transitional style bathroom. She also needs to purchase a turkey and the appropriate trimmings. These purchase decisions will be used to illustrate her decision-making processes, from problem recognition, to purchase, to post-purchase experiences.

4-5a Problem Recognition

The consumer decision process starts when the consumer realizes that he or she has a particular need triggered by the difference between the *actual state* and a *desired state.* In the case of the guest bathroom faucet, Cheri has realized that her current faucet is too plain and that it does not convey her sense of style, which is reflected throughout the downstairs entertainment area. Her need for a new faucet is triggered *externally:* She has seen faucets with Victorian and contemporary designs at the homes of many of her friends, in stores, and in restaurant bathrooms. (The advertisement in Figure 4-13 may, for example, suggest to her that she really needs to have a faucet that makes a statement in this room as well). She does not exactly know what she wants, but she knows that she wants something other than what she currently has in her guest bathroom.

Her need to have a Thanksgiving dinner party is triggered *internally:* She has the need to socialize with new acquaintances from her new environment. She has a social need to belong to this group of individuals.

Figure 4-13
Seeing an advertisement for sinks, such as this one by Delta, could trigger a need for Cheri to purchase a new bathroom faucet for her guest bathroom.

Source: Courtesy of Delta Faucets.

4-5b Information Search

Consumers may search for extensive information about the product, comparing the features and prices of competing brands while searching for different sources from which to purchase the product. They could engage in an *internal information search,* thinking back to the different places where they have seen the product displayed or experiences that they themselves had with the good or service. If consumers have previously bought a product (or a particular brand), these consumers could simply engage in a repeat, habitual purchase, buying the same brand at the same store.

As previously mentioned, Cheri is a regular customer at Food Lion. Based on her experience, she knows that the store will carry some brand—any brand—of fresh turkey, canned cranberries, stuffing, and walnuts for the stuffing. She also has seen pumpkin pie sold at the store. Cheri's mother always used to shop at the last minute for products for the Thanksgiving dinner and she always delivered a great meal; her mother was never keen on brand names—any brand of turkey was acceptable, as long as it was fresh. When the time comes, Cheri will spend about half an hour at Food Lion buying all the products she needs for the dinner.

Consumers could also engage in an *external information search,* taking time to read published information about the product, going through manufacturer or retailer brochures, or searching the Internet. In her search for a new faucet, Cheri would most likely

Believers (pg. 112): Psychographic group of individuals who are conservative, conventional, and focus on tradition, family, religion, and community. They prefer established brands, favoring American products.

Strivers (pg. 112): Psychographic group of individuals who are trendy and fun loving. They are concerned about others' opinions and approval, and demonstrate to peers their ability to buy.

Makers (pg. 112): Psychographic group of individuals who are self-sufficient. They have the skill and energy to carry out projects, respect authority, and are unimpressed by material possessions.

Survivors (pg. 112): Psychographic group of individuals who are concerned with safety and security. They focus on meeting needs rather than fulfilling desires, are brand loyal, and purchase discounted products.

go to specialty stores that specialize in bathroom and kitchen fixtures and appliances and to large home improvement stores to see what brands are available. She would also read magazines such as *Kitchen and Bath,* looking for specifics about faucets. She is planning to spend quite some time to make sure that she gets the right product at the right price.

It is important for marketers to be aware of the information sources that their target consumers use. For bathroom sinks, for example, the most useful sources are those controlled by the manufacturer and its channel of distribution: Consumers rely on salespeople and manufacturer brochures for information. For turkey purchases, consumers are more likely to rely on retail advertising and on word-of-mouth communication for information. Marketers do not control the latter. Advertisements strategically placed in magazines where consumers would search for information can trigger a need to purchase, for example, additional insurance during pregnancy (see Figure 4-14).

4-5c Alternative Evaluation

In evaluating product alternatives, consumers compare the different brands and retailers in order to make sure that the good or service they purchase best meets their needs. Often, this step occurs simultaneously with information search. For new product purchases, the alternative evaluation step is very important. Consumers typically use about five evaluation criteria in deciding on the brand that they are going to purchase. Among these criteria are those that a product must meet. For example, the faucet that Cheri is going to purchase

Figure 4-14
Advertisements by Cigna strategically placed in magazines where consumers would search for information can trigger a need to purchase additional insurance during pregnancy.
Source: Courtesy of Graciela Iturbide.

must be stylish and unlike most of the other faucets on the market. There are no trade-offs for style and uniqueness. Other important criteria are performance and ease of use. In other respects, Cheri is flexible: Prices for faucets range between $20 and $130, but she is willing to go much higher. She is also flexible with regard to the location of the retailer and is willing to order the product so that it would be conveniently delivered home.

In her search, Cheri finds brands such as Moen, FHP, Delta, Grohe, and Hansgrohe. The Moen and FHP brands appear to be rather simple, similar to the faucets that one can find in any public toilet. Grohe, a German manufacturer, seems to have more interesting designs in general, but its sink faucets are unremarkable. Cheri is particularly interested in the Philippe Stark models sold by Hansgrohe, another German manufacturer, under the brand name Axor and the Our Victorian brand sold by Delta.

Cheri finds out that the Axor faucet costs about $670 at the different specialty stores. She tries to find the brand at a lower price on the Internet, without success. All the sites direct buyers to retailers and none offer discounts. One such distributor is Duravit (www.duravit.com), in Germany, which sells the complete Stark line, including toilets, sinks, and accessories. Lowe's, a home-improvement store, does not carry the Stark collection. Home Depot, another large home-improvement store, can obtain it at a lower price—$458. Cheri finds out that, if she orders the product at Home Depot, the store can put in a rush order so that the faucet can be installed before the Thanksgiving party.

It is possible, however, that the alternative evaluation step may not be part of the decision-making process. For habitual purchases, consumers rely on their memory of a previous purchase and product experience and quickly decide which brand to purchase. Cheri has organized many Thanksgiving dinners, even when she used to live in a small city apartment while attending the Institute of Fine Arts in New York. While not a habitual purchase, a turkey is a turkey . . . with some caveats. First, her convection oven would choke on anything larger than 20 pounds. Second, she would not consider buying a frozen turkey—her mother fervently believed that they could pose a health danger because they tend not to defrost evenly. And trimmings are trimmings—the store brand is just as good as any other competing national brand. Cheri thought that she could stop at the natural food store to purchase a farm-raised turkey on the way home from her studio in the city, but quickly dismissed the idea. It involved complex logistics; moreover, she believed that the turkey would probably not be as plump and juicy if it is not fed the right hormones.

It is important for marketers to understand the consumer evaluation process and focus on the more important attributes. For products where brand names are established, it makes sense to advertise the brand and to focus on its differentiating features in the message. The Tree Top apple juice advertisement in Figure 4-15 emphasizes the Tree Top brand name, while also stressing that the product is 100 percent pure and made from Washington State apples.

4-5d Purchase

There are two important aspects to the purchase process: the *purchase intention* and the *actual purchase.* A number of consumer behavior models address the purchase intention and the purchase as two separate steps. Consumers may decide on a particular brand, as well as on the outlet where the product will be purchased. These decisions reflect their purchase intentions. However, between the point where the purchase intention was formed and the actual purchase, there can be many intervening factors that could impede the purchase. The individual may have second thoughts about the brand or the importance of the purchase altogether. In our example, Cheri may decide that it is too expensive to purchase a new faucet and that she would be better off saving the money to purchase a new outfit. Or she may decide to buy the turkey from the natural food store, rather than from Food Lion, to make sure that she will serve the highest quality product—she can also share the information with her guests. If she were to purchase the turkey from Food Lion, then she would be reluctant to share information about the product's source with her guests.

Figure 4-15
This advertisement focuses on the recognizable Tree Top brand name, as well as on the characteristics—100 percent pure and Washington State apples.

Source: © Tree Top, Inc., 2002, Yakima, WA. Created by Cole & Weber / Red Cell, Seattle, WA.

Alternatively, she may go to Home Depot with her best friend to make the faucet purchase. Upon a closer examination, however, her friend may notice that the Axor faucet does not spray water evenly; Cheri then could decide to purchase the Victorian style Delta faucet, which costs only $179. The job of marketers is to make sure that purchase intentions are translated into purchase behavior. Having a competent salesperson that will handle the order quickly, an appealing store environment with pleasant lighting, and beautiful shiny fixtures could help the consumer to advance from intention to purchase.

4-5e Post-Purchase Processes

The marketing task is not complete at the point where the client purchases the product. As mentioned in Chapter 1, "Scope and Concepts of Marketing," satisfaction and dissatisfaction are important determinants of whether consumers will purchase the brand again. Marketing managers need to persuade consumers that they purchased a quality, reliable product that addresses the needs consumers identified in the problem recognition stage as well as, or better than, the competition. Marketers must also address consumers' feelings of anxiety related to losing the freedom to purchase other products—products that may or may not compete with those of the manufacturer.

Expectations and Satisfaction As previously explained, consumers anticipate product performance based on their experiences, as well as information received from the media and from other consumers. They have **expectations** that influence the evaluation of good or service quality and predict how the product will perform on the market. Cheri expects that the Delta faucet she ultimately purchased will be of very high quality—**quality** refers to overall product quality, reliability, and the extent to which it meets consumers' needs. She expects that the faucet will perform well, and, more importantly, it will look lovely in her guest bathroom.

Expectations: Anticipated product performance based on consumers' experiences, on information received from the media, and from other consumers.

Quality: Overall good or service quality, reliability, and the extent to which it meets consumers' needs, has the greatest impact on satisfaction.

If a good or service performs better than expected, then consumers are likely to be satisfied. If satisfied, consumers are likely to purchase the good or service in the future. If performance matches expectations, consumers are somewhat satisfied (psychologists refer to this as "satisficing"—meaning that the consumer is satisfied, but would switch to another good or service without much persuasion). If expectations are greater than performance, then there is a gap between expectation and performance: Consumers are likely to be dissatisfied with the product and may never purchase it again. These consumers are expected to engage in negative word-of-mouth communications about the product and the firm and switch to a competitor in the future.

If Cheri is satisfied with the Delta brand faucet, she may, in the future, spend thousands of dollars to purchase an entire Victorian style bathroom suite, from the formidable, wall-anchored toilet, to the geometric bathtub marvel, to the modest yet unique shower. If she is dissatisfied, she may return the product to the retailer for a full refund or just badmouth the brand to her friends if she does not want to go through the return process.

Cognitive Dissonance and Buyer's Regret **Cognitive dissonance** is an anxiety feeling of uncertainty about whether or not the consumer made the right purchase decision. This feeling is especially strong if the purchase is important and expensive, and if the consumer does not have the option of returning the product if he or she is not satisfied with it. **Buyer's regret** is related to cognitive dissonance, in that it is also a feeling of anxiety; the anxiety is related to the consumer's loss of freedom to spend money on other products. Spending $458 on a faucet will limit the amount that Cheri can spend when her favorite retailer, Bridgetts, has its end-of-year sale.

Cognitive dissonance: An anxiety feeling of uncertainty about whether or not the consumer made the right purchase decision.

Buyer's regret: A feeling of anxiety related to the consumer's loss of freedom to spend money on other products.

An important task of marketers is to reduce cognitive dissonance and buyer's regret by reassuring consumers that they made the right purchase. Post-purchase installation, service, and warranties, as well as advertisements and direct-mail communications, all serve to reduce consumers' cognitive dissonance and dispel any concerns the consumers may have about the purchase. Such communications may compare the brand favorably with competing brands and stress attributes that are important to the consumer. For example, Cheri would be delighted to receive a note from Delta congratulating her on her purchase or a telephone call from Home Depot reassuring her that it stands behind the Delta brand. Table 4-1 summarizes the consumer decision-making process for Cheri in the purchase of the faucet and the Thanksgiving turkey.

4-6 Variations in Decision Making

In the process of making purchase decisions, consumers can engage in extensive problem solving, going carefully through each of the steps of the consumer decision-making process. In this case, consumers will spend substantial amounts of time searching for information about the different brands and outlets where the product may be purchased. **Extensive problem solving** is typical for **high-involvement purchases** (products that have a high personal relevance). For example, most consumers purchasing furniture and décor products will engage in extensive problem solving because, for most, it will be a high-involvement purchase decision, as Figure 4-16 on page 119 illustrates.

Extensive problem solving: Consumer decision making that involves going carefully through each of the steps of the consumer decision-making process.

High-involvement purchases: Purchases that have a high personal relevance.

TABLE 4-1 Cheri's Decision-Making Process for a Faucet and a Turkey

Stage	Faucet	Turkey
Problem recognition	The need for a new faucet was triggered externally because of faucets Cheri had seen with Victorian and contemporary designs at the homes of many of her friends, in stores, and in restaurant bathrooms.	Cheri's need to have a Thanksgiving dinner party was triggered internally because she had the need to socialize with new acquaintances from her new environment.
Information search	In her quest for a new faucet, Cheri searched externally for information at specialty stores and large home improvement stores to see what brands were available. She also read magazines such as Kitchen and Bath, looking for specifics about faucets.	Cheri conducted an internal search based on her memory of her mother shopping at Food Lion at the last minute for products for the Thanksgiving dinner. Her mother was never keen on brand names—any brand of turkey was acceptable, as long as it was fresh.
Alternative evaluation	Cheri located several brands of faucets and spent considerable time evaluating each brand. Price, quality, and appearance were the major criteria she used.	Cheri spent very little time evaluating the various brands of turkey. In fact, she never paid any attention to the brand name. She based her evaluation on the size and the appearance of the turkey.
Purchase	After careful consideration, Cheri purchased the Victorian style faucet made by Delta and sold at Home Depot.	Cheri purchased the turkey from Food Lion, since that was the retailer she used for groceries and where she was purchasing her other food items.
Post-purchase evaluation	Cheri experienced both cognitive dissonance and buyer's regret. She worried her friends would not like the style she picked out and, if they didn't, she didn't have the money to buy another new set.	Cheri spent very little time evaluating the turkey purchase because it tasted good and her company enjoyed it.

Cheri, in our example, considers a faucet a high-involvement purchase since the faucet selected is important in projecting her sense of style to her aspirational group. She wanted the faucet to be unique, unlike all the other products on retailers' shelves and in her acquaintances' bathrooms. Cheri went through extensive problem solving when purchasing the Delta faucet, spending large amounts of time and energy to learn about the different faucet brands available on the market.

Limited problem solving: Consumer decision making that involves less problem solving. This type of decision making is used for products that are not especially visible, nor too expensive.

Consumers can engage in **limited problem solving** for products that are not especially visible or too expensive. In deciding to purchase the turkey at Food Lion, Cheri wanted to minimize the amount of time and effort dedicated to the purchase. While buying a turkey was not quite a routine purchase, her once-a-year experience provided enough information to her that she did not need to ask around where she would find a reasonable product. She may have looked at the weekly advertisements from other supermarkets to note whether they offered a greater discount, and she may have examined different brands of fresh turkey at Food Lion. Beyond that, her decision process was relatively simple: She selected the turkey brand, found the right size turkey, and purchased it.

Routine problem solving: Consumer decision making whereby consumers engage in habitual purchase decisions involving products that they purchase frequently.

Consumers can also engage in **routine problem solving**. Consumers engage in routine problem solving for habitual purchase decisions involving products that they purchase frequently. Consumers routinely purchase Tropicana juice, Yoplait yogurt, Granola cereal, Eggo waffles, Colgate toothpaste, and other similar brands. Consumers do not need to compare these brands with alternative product offerings if these brands have provided a

Figure 4-16
Inside Indigo recognizes that most consumers purchasing furniture and décor products engage in extensive problem solving because it will be a high-involvement purchase decision.

Source: Sample print advertisement courtesy of The Miles Agency and Alliance One Advertising, Inc.

satisfactory consumption experience for many years. Routine problem solving is typical for **low-involvement products** (products with limited personal relevance, such as eggs, cheese, and other convenience goods).

Low-involvement products: Products with limited personal relevance.

Finally, consumers are greatly affected by **situational influences.** When purchasing products for personal private consumption, consumers are more likely to purchase discounted products or to buy store brands. When purchasing products with friends, consumers tend to engage in more limited problem solving in making their purchase decision. And, when purchasing a product for gift giving, consumers are likely to engage in extensive problem solving, both with regard to the brand and the retailer, ensuring that the product is impeccably packaged and presented. Marketers need to take note of consumers' situational influences and to steer their decision accordingly. Salespeople in boutiques and department stores often take special care to ensure that products targeted for gift giving are attractively wrapped and presented. For a review of the variations in decision making, see Table 4-2.

Situational influences: Influences that are attributed to the purchase situation.

TABLE 4-2

Variations in Decision Making

Picture	Purchase Situation	Decision-Making Method
Faucet	Cheri spent several days and a lot of time choosing just the right bathroom faucet.	Extensive problem solving
Turkey	Cheri examined the various turkeys at Food Lion and, after several minutes, picked the one that she thought would be the best.	Limited problem solving
Candy bar	As Cheri was checking out, she noticed the rack of candy bars and picked out her favorite.	Routine problem solving
Stereo	Wanting to get the right stereo, Cheri spent several weeks looking in stores and catalogs and on the Internet before she made a purchase.	Extensive problem solving
Soft drink	Thirsty, Cheri went to the soda machine and bought Diet Coke, the same brand she almost always purchases.	Routine problem solving
McDonald's arches	Cheri was hungry but did not have much time. She thought about which fast-food restaurants were on her way to work, and since McDonald's was on the right side of the street and there did not appear to be a long line of cars at the drive-up window, she chose it.	Limited problem solving

Summary

1. *Identify the elements of a consumer behavior model.* The consumer behavior model addresses the influence of social and psychological factors that impact consumer behavior. Social influences, such as culture, subcultures, social class, roles, status, families, households, and reference groups, are instrumental in shaping individual attitudes, interests, opinions, and behavior. Psychological influences, such as motivation, perception, learning, personality, and lifestyles, as well as beliefs and attitudes, are likely to influence how consumers behave.

2. *Describe the different social influences that have an impact on consumer behavior.* Among the social influences that affect consumer behavior are culture, social class, role and status influences, family and household influences, and reference group influences. Culture includes the totality of learned and shared meanings, rituals, norms, and traditions among the members of an organization or society. Values are particularly important in that they guide individuals' actions, attitudes, and judgments and thus affect behavior. Values are learned from those with whom individuals are in contact: family, friends, teachers, clergy, politicians, and the media. Learning a new culture is known as acculturation. Subcultures are components of the broad culture; they are groups of individuals with shared value systems based on ethnicity or common background. Among the important ethnic and national subcultures in the United States are the African-American subculture, the Hispanic subculture, and the Asian-American subculture. Social class, role, and status influences also have an important impact on consumer behavior. In the United States, the social classes are the upper class, consisting of upper uppers (old money) and lower uppers (new money); the middle class, consisting of upper middle class (professionals) and lower middle class (white collar); and the lower class, consisting of upper lower class (blue collar) and lower lower class (unskilled and unemployed). Additional social influences are exerted by one's family and household, as well as by reference groups, especially by aspirational reference groups that one would like to belong to.

3. *Describe the different psychological influences that have an impact on consumer behavior.* Consumer behavior is influenced by motivation, perception, learning, attitudes, beliefs, personality, and lifestyles. Consumers are motivated by needs and wants, which create a drive to engage in behavior. In the hierarchy of needs, physiological needs, such as food and water, are the most basic. They are followed by safety needs and social needs—for love and belonging. At the higher levels are the need for self-esteem and status in society, and at the highest level, the need for self-actualization—the need to accomplish and realize one's full potential. Perception is the manner in which we perceive the world around us, the manner in which we notice advertisements and products in a store. Learning, which involves changes in individual thought processes or behavior attributed to experience, influences consumer behavior. Attitudes and beliefs involve developing feelings about products and associations between a good or service and attributes of that good or service. Finally, individuals' enduring traits and responses to stimuli around them (personality) and individuals' style of living as expressed through activities, interests, and opinions (lifestyles) also influence consumer behavior. Marketers have devised modalities to cluster individuals based on personality and lifestyle through psychographic measurement.

4. *Address the five stages of the consumer decision-making process.* The stages of the consumer decision-making process are problem recognition, information search, alternative evaluation, purchase, and post-purchase behavior. Problem recognition develops when there is a difference between the actual state and a desired state. It can be triggered externally, by advertising, store displays, or by observing others consuming a product; or internally, through an individual need. Consumers could search for information internally, by searching their own memory about a product experience, or externally, by consulting magazines or salespeople. After evaluating the different brand and retail outlet alternatives, consumers typically develop the intention to purchase a product; barring any intervening events or concerns, the consumer engages in the purchase. After purchase, marketers need to ensure that consumers will be satisfied with their purchase by offering guarantees and prompt post-purchase service and by ensuring that the product functions optimally. They also have to reduce consumers' cognitive dissonance (the anxiety that consumers associate with the concern that they may not have bought the best product) and buyer's regret (the regret for the loss of freedom to purchase other products with the money).

5. *Describe variations in consumer decision making based on whether consumers engage in extensive, limited, or routine problem solving.* Depending on the product purchased, consumers could engage in extensive problem solving, where they will go through each stage of the decision-making process. This is typical for products of high personal relevance—high-involvement products—that may have been expensive and/or may be closely tied to the consumer's self-image. Limited problem solving takes place in the case of products that are not especially expensive or important (low-involvement products), and only minimal problem solving takes place for routine purchase decisions, many of which are habitual.

Key Terms

acculturation (p. 100)
achievers (p. 112)
aspirational groups (p. 106)
assimilation (p. 100)
associative reference groups (p. 106)
attitudes (p. 110)
beliefs (p. 110)
believers (p. 113)
buyer's regret (p. 117)
cognitive dissonance (p. 117)
cues (p. 109)
culture (p. 100)
dissociative groups (p. 106)
drive (or motive) (p. 107)
expectations (p. 117)
experiencers (p. 112)
extensive problem solving (p. 117)
high-involvement purchases (p. 117)
innovators (p. 111)
instrumental values (p. 100)
learning (p. 109)
lifestyles (p. 111)
limited problem solving (p. 118)
low-involvement products (p. 119)
makers (p. 113)
perception (p. 108)
personality (p. 111)
psychographics (p. 111)
quality (p. 117)
reference groups (p. 106)
reinforcement (p. 109)
religion (p. 101)
response (p. 109)
roles (p. 104)
routine problem solving (p. 118)
selective distortion (p. 108)
selective exposure (p. 108)
selective retention (p. 108)
situational influences (p. 119)
social class (p. 102)
status (p. 105)
stimuli (p. 109)
strivers (p. 113)
subcultures (p. 101)
survivors (p. 113)
terminal values (p. 100)
thinkers (p. 111)
values (p. 100)

Discussion Questions

1. What are the primary subcultures in the United States based on nationality and ethnicity? Can you identify other subcultures, based on age and geographic location?
2. How can these additional subcultures you have identified be targeted most efficiently by marketing managers?
3. What social class does each of the following individuals belong to?
   - A successful carpenter who makes $85,000 annually and lives in an upper middle class neighborhood. Explain.
   - A medical resident who makes $38,000 annually and lives in student apartments. Explain.
4. Identify your reference groups. What groups do you belong to (associative groups)? What types of products do you consume based on these affiliations? What groups do you aspire to belong to? What products do you consume or purchase by virtue of this projected affiliation?
5. Take the VALS 2 typology (www.sric-bi.com/VALS/) test. What psychographic category do you belong to? Are your friends in the same category? How do you explain the differences?
6. Identify a low-involvement product and a high-involvement product that you have recently purchased. Attempt to reconstruct the consumer decision-making process involved for each product.

Review Questions

True or False

1. The consumer behavior model is based on social influences, such as culture, subculture, social class, individual roles and status, and family.
2. Values are defined as a continuously changing totality of learned and shared meanings, rituals, norms, and traditions among the members of society.

3. The lower upper class accounts for 2 percent of the U.S. population; the class earned new money through business ventures and are most likely to show off their possessions.
4. Consumers are motivated by needs and wants.
5. Selective retention involves consumers adapting the information to fit their own existing knowledge or beliefs.
6. A consumer's personality is expressed through activities, interests, opinions, and lifestyle.
7. The customer decision-making process consists of five stages: defining the desired social status, seeking information, searching for the best discounts, making the purchase, and post-purchase behavior.
8. The consumer decision process starts with the consumer realizing that a particular need is triggered by the difference between the actual state and the desired state.
9. Alternative evaluation is a necessary step in the decision-making process for all purchases.
10. When purchasing low-price products for personal private consumption, consumers tend to follow the extensive problem-solving pattern.

Multiple Choice

11. Which of the following categories relate to the psychological influences of consumer behavior?
    a. family and households
    b. personality and lifestyles
    c. individual roles and status
    d. culture and subculture
12. Which of the following categories relates to subculture?
    a. ethnicity and nationality
    b. age groups
    c. religion
    d. all of the above
13. Which of the following statements defines status?
    a. the products people consume and individuals' behavior
    b. activities people are expected to perform
    c. emphasis on the individual materialistic perception of success
    d. a and b
14. Which of the following are reference groups?
    a. aspirational groups
    b. family and household groups
    c. dissociative groups
    d. all of the above
15. Reinforcement in the context of the learning process refers to
    a. strengthening the relationship between the cue and the response.
    b. change in the contents in an advertisement.
    c. applying more aggressive direct sales techniques.
    d. all of the above
16. Which of the following characteristics describes the psychographic profile of the VALS group called "Survivor"?
    a. focused on meeting needs rather than fulfilling desires
    b. sophisticated
    c. goal oriented
    d. b and c
17. When making a purchase, what information source do consumers typically use?
    a. internal and/or external information sources
    b. internal information sources
    c. external information sources
    d. none of the above
18. Different factors could interfere and prevent the purchase in the __________ phase of the purchase process.
    a. purchase intention
    b. actual purchase
    c. post-purchase
    d. a and b
19. Which of the following statements describes cognitive dissonance?
    a. dissatisfaction with product performance
    b. consumers trying out a different brand each time when making a purchase
    c. anxiety feelings of uncertainty about the right purchase decision
    d. none of the above
20. The purchase of a new suit or dress will normally require
    a. extensive problem solving.
    b. situational problem solving.
    c. limited problem solving.
    d. routine problem solving.

Notes

1. Lisa Penaloza and Mary C. Gilly, "Marketer Acculturation: The Changer and theChanged," *Journal of Marketing,* vol. 63, no. 3 (July 1999): 84–104.
2. See Milton J. Rokeach, *The Nature of Human Values* (New York: The Free Press, 1973); and Jan-Benedict E. M. Steenkamp, Frenkel ter Hofstede, and Michel Wedel, "A Cross-Cultural Investigation into the Individual and National Cultural Antecedents of Consumer Innovativeness," *Journal of Consumer Research,* vol. 63 (April 1999): 55–69.
3. Rokeach, *The Nature of Human Values* (1973).
4. Raj Mehta and Russell W. Belk, "Artifacts, Identity and Transition," *Journal of Consumer Research,* vol. 17 (March 1991): 398–411.
5. Penaloza and Gilly, "Marketer Acculturation," 84–104.
6. David K. Tse, Russell W. Belk, and Nan Zhou, "Becoming a Consumer Society: A Longitudinal and Cross-Cultural Content Analysis of Print Ads from Hong Kong, the People's Republic of China, and Taiwan," *Journal of Consumer Research,* vol. 15 (March 1999): 457–472.
7. "Special Report: Ever Higher Society, Ever Harder to Ascend—Meritocracy in America," *The Economist,* vol. 374, no. 8407 (January 1, 2005): 35.
8. Ellen Foxman, P. Tanshuaj, and K. Ekstrom, "Family Members' Perception of Adolescents' Influence on Family Decision Making," *Journal of Consumer Research,* vol. 15 (March 1989): 482–491.

Case 4-1 The Eastern Shore Lifestyle

Far from the rustle and bustle of vibrant East Coast cities, the Eastern Shore is the tranquil southern area of the Delmarva Peninsula, separated by the 24-mile-long Chesapeake Bay Bridge-Tunnel from mainland Virginia. With its small marinas owned by local historic towns, boat ramps, and stretches of farmland, the Eastern Shore is a destination for bird watchers, bicycle enthusiasts, and fishermen (see Figure 4-17). At the southern tip of the peninsula lies the town of Cape Charles, founded in 1884 as a planned community by railroad and ferry interests. The town thrived for more than half a century because anyone who traveled up and down the Eastern Shore had to pass through it—up to two million people arrived annually by train or car to catch the steamer or ferry to or from Norfolk. After World War II, however, the ferry terminal relocated south of town and the trains stopped carrying passengers. The Chesapeake Bay Bridge-Tunnel, which opened in 1964, provided access to the mainland, and a new highway bypassed the town. Since 1953, when the last ferry left, time has virtually stopped in the area.

Dwellers of the Eastern Shore are passionate about their heritage, or about their newly adopted home, respectively. They drive automobiles with Virginia lighthouse license plates and have the ubiquitous ES as part of the license plate number. Boats abound in the driveways, garages, and marinas, and every day that the bay waters are reasonably calm, fishing takes priority over all other activities.

Life on the Eastern Shore is decidedly casual for locals and visitors alike. In the spring, summer, and fall, the small communities experience a substantial influx of tourists, and the Chesapeake Bay Bridge-Tunnel makes millions of dollars by charging a toll of $12 in each direction to offer access to the Eastern Shore. Friendly neighbors greet each other and visitors from other states on the street and on the boardwalks, and chat about the weather and the tide schedules. Dress is informal—with the exception of Sunday mornings—even for bankers.

Recently, the entire Eastern Shore has been experiencing a renaissance. Cape Charles, for instance, changed from a down-on-its-luck outpost in the Mid-Atlantic into one of the Mid-Atlantic's hottest second-home real estate markets in just a few years. The main force behind the town's new economic revival is a developer named Richard S. Foster, who developed Bay Creek, a massive gated community and resort destination that surrounds and overshadows the existing town, which is a grid of American Foursquare and Sears homes. The old town itself has only about 650 houses, a number that until recently had not changed for 60 years. In the near future, however, Bay Creek plans to have 2,500 homes, retail shops and restaurants, a 100-room hotel and spa, a beach club on the Chesapeake, tennis courts, a pool, a community center, two 18-hole golf courses (an Arnold Palmer and a Jack Nicklaus course), a replica of a historic lighthouse, and 113 acres of artificial lakes.

In other changes, the national wildlife refuge has a state-of-the-art visitor center that the ranger on duty believes to be the most advanced in the country. A longtime merchant has furnished a turn-of-the-century general store as a museum. A Library of Congress staffer has created a gift shop that would be at home in Georgetown or Manhattan. A food retailer, Stingray's, has turned a truck stop into something of a gourmet restaurant, serving soda fountain food, as well as fresh crab-stuffed flounder and Chateauneuf du Pape French wine. A Washington, D.C., chef has opened a true gourmet restaurant in a Victorian mansion, and a coffee shop developed by a resettled Californian offers French pastries that taste almost like French pastries should.

Figure 4-17
Tranquil town on the Eastern Shore.

These changes have resulted in substantial socio-demographic transformations in the region. Many long-established locals are selling their homes, either to take advantage of the increasing real estate prices, or because they can no longer afford the high taxes and the prices charged by increasingly expensive repairpersons. Others who can afford to do so remain in their ancestral homes, enjoying the relaxed lifestyles. Often, the ones who do leave the region are African Americans, in the lower socio-economic strata of society.

By contrast, the newcomers tend to be upper middle class consumers with a weekend home and retirees. They purchase the older homes and renovate them to twenty-first-century standards. As a result, houses and commercial buildings that were falling apart five years ago now sell for $400,000 or more. New homes with a British West Indies architecture cost about $1 million, while Bay Creek neighborhoods in Cape Charles cost from $350,000 to more than $2 million for a condominium.

These transformations of the Eastern Shore have important implications for social and psychographic changes in the region. They also create opportunities for entrepreneurs interested in serving this region.

Questions

1. Describe the social factors that might influence the different consumers on the Eastern Shore.
2. Assume that you are opening a grocery store in the area. How do you plan to meet the needs of the different consumer lifestyles on the Eastern Shore?
3. Discuss the various psychological influences that are creating conflicts between the old-time residents and the new residents of the Eastern Shore. Can these two groups enjoy life together, or will the old-time residents have to depart to resume their current lifestyle?
4. What other types of businesses would do well on the Eastern Shore?

Sources: Tim Neville, "Waking Up Cape Charles," *The New York Times* (September 3, 2004): C1; Nancy and Richard Woodworth, *Inn Spots & Special Places/Mid-Atlantic* (West Hartford, CT: Wood Pond Press, 2000); www.baycreek.com.

Case 4-2 The New Immigrants

Cities on the East and West Coast and in the southern United States boast large numbers of immigrants who have come to this country in search of the American dream. Motivation for immigration includes survival, economic improvement, and the pursuit of religious and political ideology.

Immigration from developing countries often brings honor to immigrants' extended families left behind in the home country. Often immigrants accumulate money in the United States and remit large proportions to those left behind, ensuring their relative economic prosperity. In addition to the substantial remittance to the home country, many immigrants attempt to save money at the same time, in order to be able to afford a quality education for their children. These circumstances are likely to create a rejection of American materialist values at first; successful immigrants, however, covet the American dream of a large home and expensive car as their economic situation improves.

Immigrants attempt to fit in their new environment, quickly learning the language and the local traditions. They participate in the social life of their newly adopted country, watching television programs, reading popular books, and shopping in the impressive malls and supermarkets that are omnipresent on the American landscape. Their children integrate quickly, often preferring American pastimes and food to those of their parents' homeland.

The new immigrants also maintain many of the traditions and related objects from their home country. For example, Indian immigrants build household shrines, and decorate their homes with Indian artifacts and replicas of Indian landmarks. Latin American and Jewish immigrants often bring with them the objects of their prayer room from their home country. Often, the immigrants use videos to teach children about traditions. For special occasions, immigrants wear traditional clothing from their home country: Indian women wear saris, Sub-Saharan African women wear booboos, North African women may wear a gallabeya (a long dress with traditional embroidery), and German men may wear lederhosen.

New immigrants have strong preferences for food from the home country—hence, the numerous prosperous ethnic supermarkets cropping up in ethnic neighborhoods. When celebrating traditions of their newly adopted country, they often add a component of home-country celebrations. For example, Indians celebrating Thanksgiving may also serve masala dosa as an appetizer and sambar on the side. French immigrants may serve the traditional turkey cut in pieces and prepared as part of a cassoulet, with beans and sausages. Italian immigrants may also have vegetarian pasta as a side dish. Romanian immigrants may serve stuffed cabbage as a first course, before the turkey. Jewish immigrants may start the Thanksgiving dinner with a first course of matzo ball soup. Moroccan immigrants may serve couscous with raisins as a side dish. And Dutch immigrants may serve erwte soup—a winter vegetable soup—as a first course.

Questions

1. How do immigrants from developing countries affect the role and status of family left behind in the home country?
2. Describe how American and home-country cultures influence new immigrant behavior.
3. How can marketers best meet the needs and address the drives of these consumers?
4. Discuss the various psychological factors that would influence an immigrant's purchase of an automobile.
5. Pick one immigrant group discussed in this case and search for additional information about the group's characteristics. How can this additional information help marketers be more effective in reaching them?

Source: Raj Mehta and Russell W. Belk, "Artifacts, Identity, and Transition: Favorite Possessions of Indian Immigrants to the United States," *Journal of Consumer Research*, vol. 17 (1991): 398–411.

Business-to-Business Behavior

5

Chapter Objectives

1. Identify the types of goods and services that businesses purchase.
2. Identify the types of business customers.
3. Explain the concepts of derived and joint demand and why they are important for the business-to-business market.
4. Identify the types of buying situations and when each is used.
5. Describe the concept of the buying center and the different roles employees can play.
6. Discuss the factors that influence business-to-business buyer behavior.
7. List the seven steps in the business-to-business buying process and explain what occurs in each step.

Chapter Outline

Techies refer to it as 802.11; others know it as Wi-Fi. For those who do not recognize either, Wi-Fi stands for wireless fidelity and is a wireless means of Internet access. A Wi-Fi base station is connected to a high-speed Internet connection such as DSL, cable modem, or T1 line. Then, using radio waves, Internet signals are sent from the base station to wireless computers.

Worldwide use of Wi-Fi networks is expected to grow from 42 million users in 2003 to 600 million by 2007. Approximately 47 percent of Wi-Fi users are in the United States, 35 percent in Western Europe, and 17 percent in Asia-Pacific. This market is growing so rapidly that suppliers are scrambling to meet the demand.

Microsoft, Intel, and T-Mobile were the early pioneers for this technology. In the beginning, all three companies faced an important marketing decision. They could market the product to consumers who could use it around the house with the base station plugged into the home's DSL or modem. However, users could not stray too far from the house or the signal would be lost. While the consumer market was seen as important, all three companies saw another market opportunity, perhaps a larger market: businesses.

With an eye on the consumer market, salespeople from T-Mobile approached Schlotzsky's Deli with the idea of installing this new technology in its restaurants. Using Austin, Texas, as a test market, Wi-Fi was installed in several Schlotzsky's locations. The plan was to keep the service quiet until all of the kinks were worked out, then expand nationwide. But Wi-Fi users detected Schlotzsky's signal and, according to Schlotzsky's CEO John Wooley, "people started showing up with their laptops."

Almost simultaneously, T-Mobile approached Starbucks with the same idea. Seeing the opportunity for patrons to use their laptops while they drank a cup of coffee, Starbucks immediately signed up for the new technology (see Figure 5-1).

Realizing the potential, T-Mobile approached other businesses. The concept was sold to Borders bookstores and was installed in 400 stores. United, American, and Delta were convinced this was a good thing to purchase for their frequent-flier clubs, so the wireless system was installed in more than 100 airports. A smaller, rival company, Surf and Sip, has sold the wireless technology in smaller markets to coffee shops, hotels, and stores. Bongo Wireless, another wireless network provider, has more than 700 locations. Love's Travel Stops & Country Stores has installed Wi-Fi at more than 100 of its truck stops because more truckers are carrying Wi-Fi devices to be able to communicate with their families as

Figure 5-1
Coffeehouses have become popular for consumers who like to bring their laptops and work in a relaxed atmosphere.

well as the corporate office. Truckstop.net has installed an additional 500 HotStops throughout the United States. The number of hotspots at commercial establishments is expected to grow from 71,000 in 2003 to more than 477,000 in 2007.

While the consumer market was noteworthy, the business market offered a better opportunity for this new technology. However, reaching these businesses required different marketing methods, and convincing businesses they should purchase this new technology required a different marketing approach. The effort has paid off with sales over $1.7 billion.[1]

5-1 Chapter Overview

While the marketing of goods and services to businesses has some similarities to the marketing of goods and services to individual consumers, there are also some significant differences. This chapter addresses those differences. Section 5-2 begins with a discussion of the various types of goods and services purchased by businesses. They range from multimillion-dollar projects such as new buildings to low-cost items such as paper clips and copy paper.

Section 5-3 presents the different types of business customers and the way businesses determine demand for their products. In the consumer market, if a firm wishes to stimulate demand, it can offer a price discount, coupons, or some other promotion to encourage consumers to make a purchase. A supplier of raw materials, such as lumber to a furniture factory, cannot stimulate demand just by offering some type of special deal because the amount of lumber a furniture factory will buy depends on how much furniture it sells to retail stores, who in turn sell the furniture to consumers.

Section 5-4 examines the business-to-business purchase process itself. In many situations, more than one person is involved in the purchase decision, with each performing a different role. Some will be instrumental in making the decision, whereas others provide information or work out the details of the purchase. The section concludes with a discussion of the various factors that influence how individuals act within the business-to-business purchasing process and what affects the purchase decision that is made.

The last section of the chapter, Section 5-5, identifies the seven steps of the business purchase process. The buying process begins with the identification of a need, goes through identifying potential vendors, and ends with the selection of a vendor who can meet the company's need.

5-2 Types of Business Goods and Services

In understanding business buyer behavior, it is helpful to identify the types of goods and services that businesses purchase. They include major equipment, buildings and land, accessory equipment, fabricated and component parts, process materials, maintenance and repair parts, operating supplies, raw materials, goods for resale, and business services. Each of these requires a slightly different marketing approach and is purchased by a different kind of customer.

5-2a Major Equipment, Buildings, and Land

The purchase of buildings, land, and major equipment such as factory machines, mainframe computers, and robotic equipment requires considerable time and thought. Top management is almost always included in the decision and often in the selection process because the cost of these items is normally quite high. These types of purchases are often the result of strategic decisions made by top management, and financing is almost always a consideration, since few companies would have the cash to pay for them. In the case of major equipment, leases are often examined as an option since that may be more cost effective than a purchase. From a seller's standpoint, these types of purchases require a long period of time, often several months, as well as the involvement of the top management of the selling company.

5-2b Accessory Equipment

Accessory equipment consists of items used by a business but usually not directly involved in the production or sale of the firm's products. For example, accessory equipment would include furniture, office equipment such as personal computers, copy machines, forklifts, and vehicles such as a company truck. The sensor equipment sold by Sensormatic to prevent shoplifting (see Figure 5-2) would be accessory equipment for a retail store. These items are not purchased on a regular basis and therefore require some extra effort when the purchase is made. Because most are not high-ticket items, top management is not normally involved in the selection but may be involved in the final approval. This would likely depend on the ticket price. For a fax machine, top management probably would not be involved, but for a company truck that may cost $30,000, it may be. At a minimum, a vice president will probably be involved in the truck purchase. As with major equipment, leases are sometimes considered rather than a purchase. For example, rather than purchase copy machines or a fleet of cars, these items may be leased.

5-2c Fabricated and Component Parts

Fabricated and component parts are identifiable products that are incorporated into another product. For example, in automobiles, component parts include the spark plugs, the battery, the radio, and the tires. These parts are not made by the automobile manufacturer

Figure 5-2
This advertisement by Sensormatic promotes its anti-shoplifting equipment to retail stores. For a retail store, this would be an example of accessory equipment needed to operate its facility.

Source: Reprinted by permission of Sensormatic.

but are purchased from outside vendors and installed on the vehicle. Fabricated parts are a type of component part; however, the difference is that the fabricated parts are not as easily identifiable. For instance, most computer manufacturers use fabricated parts in building their computers. The processor, the CD-ROM drive, and the speakers used in your computer were all purchased from various vendors. Your computer manufacturer just assembled them into a computer for you. Unless you are a computer wizard, the only fabricated part you can probably identify is the Intel Pentium processor. The sink shown in Figure 5-3 is a component part used in the construction of kitchens by building contractors.

Because fabricated and component parts become a part of a finished product, quality and dependability become important issues. If the motherboard on your computer or the radio in your automobile is of inferior quality, then it will reflect on the product being purchased. If you purchased a Mercedes, your expectations of radio quality would likely be different than if you purchased a Yugo. Therefore, Mercedes is likely to purchase a higher quality radio or stereo system. The key is to match the quality of the component part to the quality of the finished product.

The second important factor is dependability. If the stereo installed in your Mercedes is not dependable, then Mercedes will spend time and money replacing it. Ford found itself in a costly situation with Firestone tires that were installed on new Ford vehicles. The recall of all of the vehicles to replace the Firestone tires not only cost Ford a lot of money, but it also damaged Ford's reputation, even though Ford did not manufacture the tires. The Firestone

Figure 5-3
FHP is promoting its line of sinks for building contractors to use in the construction of homes and business facilities.

Source: Sample print advertisement courtesy of The Miles Agency and Alliance One Advertising, Inc.

Figure 5-4
Cement is a process material used in the construction of buildings and other products.

situation was also a major factor in the ouster of Ford's CEO at the time, Jacques Nasser. Consumers blamed Ford for purchasing defective tires for its new vehicles, and Nasser was blamed for the way he handled the situation.[2]

5-2d Process Materials

Process materials are used in the manufacture of other products but lose their identity. Process materials include items such as cement, aluminum, steel, plastic, and wire (see Figure 5-4). Because process materials are used in the building of other products, specifications are an important issue. The metal and plastic used in building a clothes dryer must meet certain grade, quality, and durability specifications. The grade of electrical wire required varies depending on whether it is used for the switch on the dryer's console or the cord that is plugged into the home's 220-volt electrical outlet.

As with fabricated and component parts, quality and cost are important issues. Because process materials lose their identity, any defects will be directly attributed to the manufacturer. But it is also the case that, since they lose their identity, they achieve a commodity status with buyers. The electrical wires used in the GE clothes dryer can be purchased from a number of firms that manufacture electrical wiring. The quality is often the same, so factors such as price, deals, and dependable delivery become more important in the purchase decision. GE would be inclined to go with the lowest cost as long as the firm can provide quality and dependable delivery of the wire. However, if another company offers GE a special deal on wire, GE may be willing to switch vendors. All of this is said with the understanding that dependable delivery is crucial. If the wire is not delivered to the GE factory in a timely manner, it could cause a shutdown of the assembly line and cost GE money. Therefore, buyers often build in penalties or fines if a supplier's failure to deliver their materials causes a shutdown of an assembly process.

5-2e Maintenance and Repair Parts

Items such as oil, grease, filters, gears, switches, and motors are maintenance and repair parts. These items are needed to keep a machine running or to repair a machine when it is broken. Maintenance items are normally kept in stock and are replenished on a regular basis. As with process materials, maintenance items are often commodity products with no or little brand-name recognition. Because the brand of grease used on a machine is usually not a factor in the purchase decision, price becomes an important determinant.

Repair parts are not usually kept in stock unless they are items that break down often or may be extremely critical to an operation. For example, a mill that uses a large number of electrical motors will usually keep motor parts on hand so that a motor can be repaired quickly. It may even keep spare motors that can be switched out while the broken one is being repaired.

For accessory equipment that a firm purchases, instead of the buyer taking care of the repairs and keeping repair parts on hand, it may opt for a maintenance contract. Copiers are an excellent example. With the purchase of a Minolta copier, a business may also purchase a three-year maintenance agreement whereby Minolta agrees to maintain the copier and repair anything that is broken. These maintenance contracts are especially important for technical equipment requiring a specialized knowledge to repair.

5-2f Operating Supplies

Operating supplies tend to be low-cost items a company needs for day-to-day operations. Light bulbs, paper, pencils, paper clips, and cleaning chemicals would be examples. These types of products are purchased on a regular basis by the purchasing department's staff or secretarial staff. Price and convenience are usually the most important criteria in purchasing. Little effort or time is devoted to purchasing operating supplies.

5-2g Raw Materials

Raw materials are supplied by the agriculture, fishing, mining, and timber industries. Raw materials must go through some type of manufacturing process before they can be used in building a product. Timber must be cut into some type of board or chips at a sawmill before it can be used. Minerals must be mined and impurities taken out before the minerals can be used. Corn, wheat, and other agricultural products must be cleaned and processed before they can be used as ingredients in other products.

Raw materials are purchased in bulk based on some type of grading process. The price a farmer will be paid for wheat is determined by the grade and quality of the wheat. When it is sold, it loses its identity, as it is often mixed with grain from other sources. The mill that grinds the wheat into flour has no idea what farmer's wheat is used but does know the grade and type of wheat. Because the wheat has no brand identity, brokers, agents, and distributors are often used (see Figure 5-5). General Mills does not want to deal with every farmer to purchase wheat for its needs. Therefore, it will deal with a broker or distributor who has purchased wheat from a number of sources and pooled it together.

For a company like General Mills, the two most important factors in purchasing an ingredient like wheat are the price and a dependable supply. Because wheat is graded by quality, General Mills will tend to go with the supplier who offers the best price with an acceptable level of quality and delivery.

Because of the commodity nature of raw material, the Internet has gained in popularity as a mode of purchasing. In Asia, a website by the name of asiafurniturehub.com has been set up for furniture manufacturers. Companies wanting to either buy or sell raw

Figure 5-5
Wheat is a raw material that food manufacturers purchase through brokers and distributors.

materials to build furniture can use the site. Buyers can use the exchange at no charge, but sellers must pay a one-time fee of $10,000.[3]

5-2h Goods for Resale

Wholesalers and distributors: Middlemen that purchase goods from a manufacturer for resale to other members of the channel.

As you will learn in future chapters, wholesalers, distributors, and retailers purchase many goods for the purpose of resale. **Wholesalers and distributors** are middlemen who purchase goods from a manufacturer for resale to other members of the channel. In most cases, wholesalers and distributors sell to retail outlets. But in recent years, retailers have started buying directly from the manufacturer to reduce costs.

Manufacturers who are producing goods for end-user consumption must understand the consumer market. For example, to be successful, Reebok must understand what consumers want in shoes, even though it does not sell directly to consumers but through retail shoe stores. In addition, Reebok must understand that shoe retailers are not particularly concerned about selling a specific brand, but in selling shoes. If Reebok's advertising can increase the sales for a retail store, then the store will display and push Reebok products. However, if consumers walking in are demanding Skechers, then shoe stores will feature Skechers. Reebok may have to offer shoe stores larger discounts or other incentives to encourage them to give a higher priority to Reebok shoes. You can quickly see that if Reebok does this, then other shoe manufacturers may have to counter with their own set of incentives and deals.

The same philosophy applies to wholesalers or distributors. Because their goal is to earn a profit, they will push the brand that benefits them the most. Suppose an office supply distributor carries multiple brands of staplers. Unless there is demand for a specific brand by the retail stores, the distributor will push the brand that generates the highest profits and sales for them. As a result, pricing and trade deals become significant components of the selling process of goods for resale.

5-2i Business Services

Business services consist of professional services and operating services. Professional services would include legal counsel, medical services, CPAs, auditing services, and consulting services. Operating services would include the telephone service, Internet provider, insurance carrier, lawn care service, janitorial service, and shipping services. Professional services tend to be hired for a particular situation or on retainer when they are needed. Operating services tend to be hired on contract to supply the service on a continual basis for a fixed period of time. For many companies, these types of services are let out for bid on a routine basis, often once a year (see Figure 5-6).

In recent years, there has been a trend to outsource some of a company's operation to outside vendors. For example, large companies that have a cafeteria will often contract with an outside vendor such as Marriott to operate the food service for them. Other companies have outsourced human resource functions, IT functions, and payroll. By so doing, they feel they will obtain better service at a lower cost than if they did it themselves.

Marketing of a service to another business is a greater challenge than marketing a good because the business cannot see the service prior to making the purchase. Personal relationships and trust become more important. If the members of an office complex decide that they want to hire a service to take care of their lawns, they must make a decision on proposals submitted and the work they believe the service will provide. Because of this risk of not knowing how well a service will perform, most companies do not switch service providers unless they are unhappy with their current provider. Seldom will coming in with a lower price be enough unless the price is substantially lower than the company's current vendor. Even then, the company may have doubts whether the new service provider can provide the same service level at such a reduced price. Read Marketing Illustration 5-1 to see how airlines are targeting business travelers.

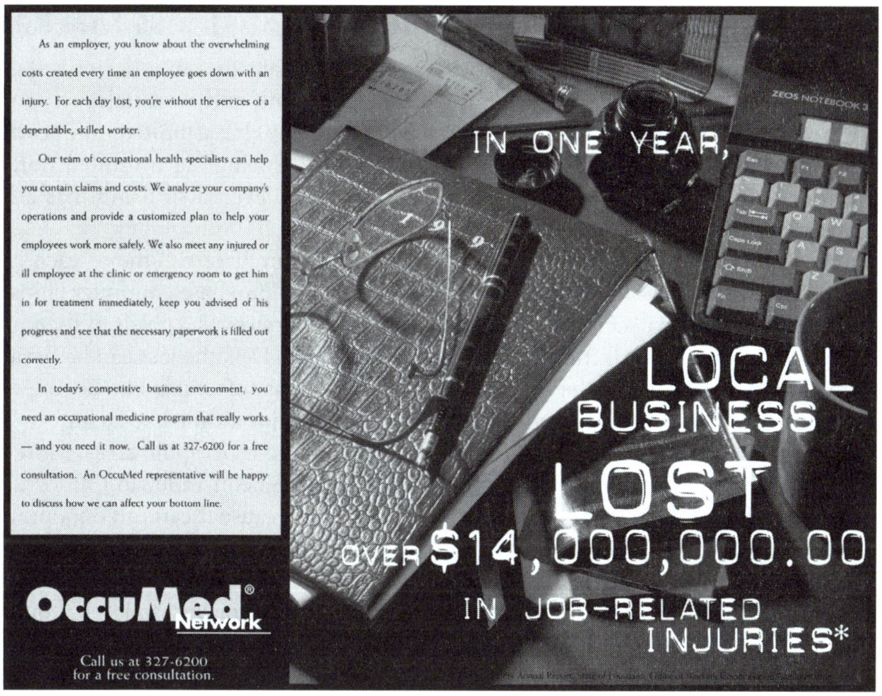

Figure 5-6
This advertisement by OccuMed promotes its occupational medicine program and is directed at businesses.

Source: Courtesy of Newcomer, Morris and Young.

Marketing Illustration 5-1

Selling Airline Travel to Business Travelers

Traditionally, business travelers flew almost exclusively with the major carriers, while low-cost airlines fought over the leisure traveler. Led by the discount king airline, Southwest Airlines, that situation is quickly changing. Twenty-three percent of all business travelers now use one of the discount carriers, with another 19 percent anticipating an increase in their usage of discount airlines.

To reach the business traveler, Southwest Airlines launched a $38.5 million ad campaign aimed at business travelers. Titled "MacGregor," these ads depicted a group of businesspeople gathering for a conference call, only to reach MacGregor's voice mail. The punch line is that MacGregor is ready to enter the conference room in person. The tagline reads, "Business travel is back." Another series of ads pointed out that Southwest capped its business walk-on fares, which was the minimum fare for many of the other airlines. In addition, Southwest created SWABiz, which is a business booking system that allows users to track ticket purchases, traveler whereabouts, and average one-way fares.

Not wanting to lose its business passengers to the low-cost carriers, American Airlines launched an advertising campaign that showed eight American planes flying between New York and Los Angeles with the tagline "Schmooze in NY, pitch in LA, scout in NY, cast in LA." The ad points out that American has more daily flights between New York and Los Angeles than any other airline. The goal of the campaign was to highlight the convenience of American, which is important to business travelers. The ad also points out the benefit of first class and business class seats. In addition, American, Delta, and the other airlines slashed the prices of their business fares. While not as low as Southwest's fares, the newer fares are much more attractive to cash-strapped corporations.

Understanding the business traveler is not easy, and airlines have struggled to find the best marketing approach. A recent survey of business travelers indicated they are not swayed by prices only. They want an airline with the best schedule and fewest stops. They want assigned seats. They want frequent flyer programs that give them upgrades and overseas tickets. They want automatic booking. But they do not want to pay exorbitant prices for these amenities.

The battle between the discount airlines and the major carriers for business travelers is sure to intensify in the future, especially with the major carriers slashing business travel prices. Will the lost revenue due to cheaper fares generate enough additional passengers to cover the cost? Only time will tell.

Sources: Michael Arndt, "The Big Airlines' Loyal Fans," *Business Week* (October 25, 2004): 112–113; Jennifer Michels, "What Road Warriors Want," *Travel Agent,* vol. 318 (October 4, 2004): 30–31; Sean Callahan, "Airlines Feel Turbulence in Biz Travel," *B to B,* vol. 87 (September 9, 2002): 1, 28.

5-3 Characteristics of Business-to-Business Markets

Business-to-business markets differ from consumer markets in a number of ways. Fewer buyers, larger purchase volume, geographic concentrations, and a formal buying process are the major differences. A manufacturer of computer chips has a limited number of computer manufacturers who will buy its computer chips. Boeing has a limited number of businesses that will purchase its commercial jumbo jets. Even a steel mill has a limited number of buyers of its products.

Because there are a limited number of buyers, the purchase volume of each is much higher. Dell, IBM, and other computer manufacturers will purchase computer chips by the thousands and will expect volume discounts and other services as a result of the purchase. If a computer chip manufacturer loses a large account like Dell, the loss can be devastating to the business. Because of the high cost of airplanes, a manufacturer like Boeing will not even start production until it receives an order from a major airline like Delta.

It is very common for businesses to cluster in specific geographic areas. Most people know that the computer industry is concentrated in the Silicon Valley in California. That makes it easier for a company selling component parts because it can call on a number of companies within the valley. It is not unusual for these suppliers to build offices and factories around their market. This has occurred around Wal-Mart's office in Bentonville, Arkansas. Because of the size of Wal-Mart and the size of the orders it places, a number of companies such as Procter & Gamble have built offices nearby to service the Wal-Mart account. A similar scenario has occurred with Del Monte and its supplier of corrugated boxes used to ship Del Monte's food items. The supplier of Del Monte boxes has built a facility close to each Del Monte factory.[4]

5-3a Types of Customers

In developing an understanding of business buyer behavior, it is helpful to examine the different types of customers available to a business. They include manufacturers, wholesalers, retailers, government agencies, and nonprofit organizations. These customers are highlighted in Figure 5-7.

Not all of the customer types are viable customers for the different types of goods and services discussed in Section 5-2. Table 5-1 provides a summary of each customer type and the types of goods and services each would likely purchase.

Manufacturers are involved in producing goods for resale. They take raw materials, process materials, and component parts and combine them into a new good to be sold to consumers or other businesses. A manufacturer of jeans will need sewing machines, cutting machines, and other types of equipment in order to make the jeans. It will also need cloth, buttons, zippers, thread, and other material to make the jeans. To supply these

Figure 5-7
Organizational and Business Customers

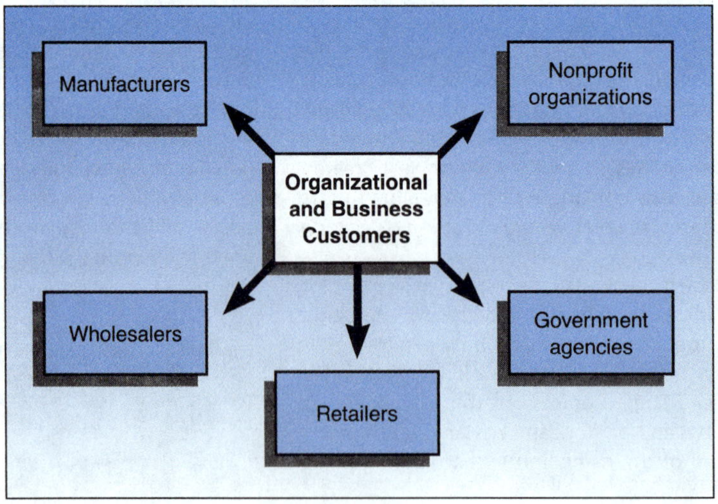

TABLE 5-1 Types of Customers and Types of Goods and Services They Are Likely to Purchase

Types of Goods or Services	Manufacturers	Wholesalers	Retailers	Government	Nonprofit Organizations
Major equipment	X	X	X	X	X
Accessory equipment	X	X	X	X	X
Fabricated and component parts	X				
Process material	X				X
Maintenance and repair parts	X	X	X	X	X
Operating supplies	X	X	X	X	X
Raw materials	X				X
Goods for resale		X	X		
Business services	X	X	X	X	X

important ingredients, the manufacturer must choose reliable suppliers, and suppliers would like to gain exclusive contracts with the manufacturer to increase the size of the order. This arrangement is desirable for the manufacturer as well because it can obtain quantity discounts. However, there is a risk. Suppose the supplier of zippers cannot meet the demand. In that case, the production of jeans stops, or the manufacturer has to quickly contact another supplier. For this reason, some manufacturers prefer dealing with more than one vendor, dividing the orders among them. They lose, however, the quantity discounts and may not receive the same level of service they would if they dealt with only one supplier.

Wholesalers purchase goods from a manufacturer and resell them to retailers or other distributors. Therefore, they do not purchase component parts, process materials, or raw materials. Because they serve as an intermediary between the producer and retailer, they will need some type of warehouse facility and offices. Forklifts and automated picking machines are primary needs. As retailers have grown larger, the need for wholesalers has diminished. However, in some industries, they still provide a valuable function of gathering goods from a number of suppliers and then making them available to retail outlets. For example, dealing with a few wholesalers who specialize in hardware supplies is more efficient for a retail store than having to deal with 200 or 300 different manufacturers. This is especially true for small retail chains or individual retail outlets. Only large retail operations like Home Depot, Lowe's, or True Value would have sufficient staff and purchase volume to make it feasible to deal with each manufacturer individually.

Because of the rise of large retail chains, many manufacturers are selling their goods directly to the retailer. Doing so reduces the costs of the goods because there are no middlemen who must earn a profit. It also is faster because the goods do not have to be shipped to a wholesaler, sorted, and then regrouped to be sent to a retailer. The reduced costs can be passed on to consumers by offering the merchandise at a lower price, or the retailer and manufacturer can use the reduced costs to increase profit margins. The disadvantage of this direct channel, however, is that, in most cases, the retailer will have considerably more manufacturers to deal with than if it used wholesalers.

Federal, state, and local governments represent huge opportunities for businesses. They purchase major equipment, land, and buildings. They purchase accessory equipment, maintenance supplies, repair parts, operating supplies, and business services. The major difference with government entities is the bidding process that must be used. Almost all governments have regulations that dictate how the bids have to be submitted, as well as the

Marketing Illustration 5-2

Effective Marketing to Institutions

When you think of business markets, often you may forget institutions. But think about the school you are attending. Think of all the goods and services it purchases: desks, computers, chairs, paint, lawn mowers, tractors, trucks, and even buildings. A similar situation exists at hospitals, nursing homes, daycare centers, police stations, libraries, government offices, and museums.

Suppose a furniture cataloger wants to market its products to these institutions. For a college, it can put a photo of college students on the front of the catalog. The same catalog can be used for high schools, but with high school students on the front. For a daycare center, the front can have a photo of children. For a library, it can show individuals within a library setting. The same catalog—but each with a unique front cover—can be used for all of the markets.

In selecting viable customers, a business has to be aware of uniqueness within each industry. For example, churches may have only two or three paid staff members but have many volunteers and a $200,000 budget. Schools receive their budgets based on the fiscal year, and so the best time to market them is beginning in July, not in February, when most of the money has already been spent. For doctors and teachers, the Internet is probably not the best marketing tool. Doctors are not on the computer much during office hours, and teachers are not usually receptive to email marketing material.

MCH, a list compiler, has 1.5 million institutions listed in its database and 5 to 6 million names. There are more than 7,000 hospitals with up to 65 names at each hospital, each with some type of buying responsibility. MCH believes that institutions are an ideal market for the catalog approach. Because of the funding situation in institutions, having a catalog on each person's desk ensures that, when money becomes available, those companies that have a catalog at the institution will have a chance to be a viable source.

Source: Alice O. Suman, "Institutions Are Businesses, Too," *Target Marketing,* vol. 25 (October 2002): 125.

manner in which the vendor is selected. For businesses willing to devote the time to submit bids, government contracts can be very lucrative.

Nonprofit organizations are similar to governments in the process they use to make purchases. Hospitals and schools are the two largest nonprofit institutions. In many locations, these two nonprofit organizations are the largest employers in the area. All need equipment, supplies, and services. See Marketing Illustration 5-2 for a review of effective institutional marketing.

5-3b Understanding Business-to-Business Demand

Derived demand: Demand for a good or service that is generated from the demand for consumer goods and services.

Demand for business goods and services is not as easy to determine as for consumer goods and services because of a concept called derived demand. **Derived demand** is the demand for a good or service that is generated from the demand for consumer goods and services. To illustrate, let's think about the demand for major appliances such as refrigerators, stoves, washers, and dryers. The number of appliances that a retail store like Sears will order depends on the demand it sees in the consumer market. If it is planning a big holiday promotion and the economy is doing well, it may see an increase in demand and will therefore place a larger order with the various appliance manufacturers, such as General Electric, Whirlpool, Maytag, and its own in-store brand, Kenmore.

The manufacturer's orders for metal, plastic, switches, motors, wires, and other parts used in the manufacturing of appliances depend on how many orders it receives from retailers such as Sears, Target, Wal-Mart, and other retailers that sell appliances. In turn, the suppliers of motors, electrical switches, metal, and plastic will order raw materials and processing materials based on the number of orders they receive from the appliance manufacturers. Thus, a company that makes plastic that is used in the manufacturing of major appliances depends on the demand that is derived all the way down from the consumer. The concept of derived demand is illustrated in Figure 5-8.

Because of derived demand in the business-to-business sector, it is much more difficult to predict demand and to control production the further distant a business is from the

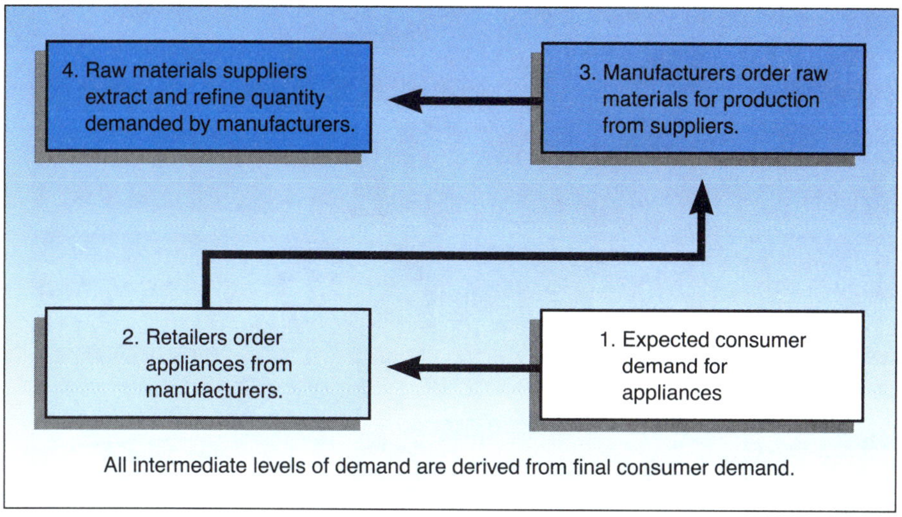

Figure 5-8
Derived Demand for Major Appliances

end user. The company that mines iron ore that is used for metal cannot stimulate demand by running an advertisement for metal. Consumers are not going to buy raw metal. The only way the demand can be stimulated is for other companies that utilize metal in their products to run ads, offer rebates, and create other special promotions for consumers.

Because of the concept of derived demand, businesses face a much more volatile sales situation than consumer markets. Fluctuations and swings in demand are common and can be extreme. This fluctuation and wide swing in sales are due to a concept called the **acceleration principle,** which states that an increase or decrease in consumer demand for a product can create a drastic change in derived business demand. For example, a small increase of 10 to 15 percent in the demand for major appliances can cause as much as a 200 percent increase in the demand for major equipment to boost production of the appliances. Unfortunately, the reverse is also true. A 10 to 15 percent decline in orders for appliances can cause a complete collapse in the demand for the machines and equipment used in the manufacturing of appliances.[5]

Acceleration principle: An increase or decrease in consumer demand for a product that can create a drastic change in derived business demand.

Another concept that is important in the business-to-business sector is joint demand. **Joint demand** means that the demand for one product is affected by the level of demand of another product. For example, the demand for operating system software is directly related to the demand for computers. If sales of computers decline, the demand for operating system software will also decline. While operating systems are sold independent of new computers, the vast majority of the operating systems are sold to computer manufacturers for installation on new computers. There is little a manufacturer of operating systems software can do to stimulate demand independent of computer demand.

Joint demand: Demand for one product that is affected by the level of demand for another product.

5-4 Business-to-Business Purchasing

In most cases, making purchases for a business is more complex than making personal purchase decisions. However, just like personal purchase decisions, not all business decisions are the same. Deciding on where to locate a plant or whether to build a $13 million building is certainly different than deciding where to purchase copier paper or ink pens. Purchase decisions vary because of the dollar value involved, the people involved in the decision process, and the amount of time spent making a decision. As would be expected, the decision on a $13 million building would involve more people and take more time than the decision about where to purchase copier paper.

5-4a Types of Buying Situations

While business purchases tend to be more formal than consumer purchases, they do vary in terms of the number of people involved, the amount of time spent on making the decision,

Figure 5-9
Because shelving at a retail store is not purchased on a regular basis, it is normally a modified rebuy purchase situation.

Source: Courtesy of Ukrop's Super Markets, Inc.

and the individuals who make the final decision. Business buying situations fall into one of three categories: new buy, modified rebuy, and straight rebuy.[6]

New buy situation: Purchases made by a business for the first time or purchases for which no one in the organization has had previous experience.

In a **new buy situation,** a business makes purchases for the first time. Land, buildings, and major equipment normally fit into this category. They are high-dollar purchases and will involve top management. It is not unusual for a new buy to take several months or even years. These complex decisions impact the strategic direction of the business and often require substantial research before a decision can be made.

Modified rebuy situation: Occasional purchases or purchases for which the members of the buying center have limited experience.

In a **modified rebuy situation,** a business makes occasional purchases. Modified rebuys occur in three different situations. The first is a situation in which the person making the purchase has limited buying experience with the good or service. It may be a vehicle or a forklift that is purchased every three to five years or shelving for a retail store. Because of the limited experience, time will need to be taken to develop specifications and to examine the possibilities. The process is not as complex, however, as the new buy primarily because it involves lower dollar purchases with less impact on the strategic direction of the company (see Figure 5-9).

A second situation that involves modified rebuys is dissatisfaction with the current vendor. It can be the supplier of aluminum to a factory that manufactures aluminum cans, or it can be the janitorial service for a large office building. The current vendor may not be reliable with delivery, the quality of work may not be up to the firm's specification, or the current vendor may have increased prices. Regardless of the reason for the dissatisfaction, the business decides to solicit bids from other vendors. In many cases, these new bids are compared to the current vendor's contract. Depending on the reason for seeking new bids, the current vendor may or may not be allowed to submit a new bid.

The third situation that causes modified rebuys is the end of a contractual relationship or an offer from a new firm that is substantially better than that of the current vendor. The firm is not dissatisfied with the current vendor but at the expiration of the contract may seek new bids. Government and nonprofit institutions are often required by regulation or bylaws to seek new bids at the end of each contractual period. The current vendor is allowed to rebid and often has the best chance of obtaining the contract unless the agency is required to go with the lowest bidder. This is often true for government entities.

Occasionally, a potential supplier will make an offer that is substantially lower than that of the current vendor. When this situation occurs, the firm may decide to open the contract for bid, allowing the current vendor as well as others to bid. Alternatively, the firm may go to the current vendor and see whether it can reduce its prices to meet the new offer that the firm has received. Or the firm may simply switch without giving the current vendor an opportunity to renegotiate. In all three cases, the firm making the purchase will have to study the specifications and spend some time making a decision. While not as involved as the new buy situations, these modified rebuys do require some effort and time in making the best decision.

The last purchase situation is the straight rebuy. In the **straight rebuy situation,** a business routinely purchases from a vendor without modifying specifications or without renegotiating new terms. Purchasing office supplies for a large office building is likely to fall into this category. Supplies are purchased from a chosen vendor on a regular basis through a phone call, email, fax, or personal sales call. For a selling firm, this is the best situation. The buyer does not consider other firms and, as long as the buyer is pleased with the service, purchases continue on a routine basis.

Straight rebuy situation: Routine purchases from a vendor without modifying specifications or without renegotiating new terms.

When one examines the types of goods and services firms buy in relation to the buying situation, typical patterns do emerge. For major equipment, buildings, and land, it is virtually always a new buy situation. These high expenditure, new situations will involve the CEO and other top management personnel. Accessory equipment will vary between the new buy situation and modified rebuys. The type will depend on the price of the accessory equipment and the experience the firm has with it. For some firms, purchasing a new company truck may be a rare occasion and therefore will involve the top management, whereas for other firms, it is a modified rebuy situation that involves only the purchasing department. Major factors in this decision are experience and cost relative to the size of a firm. For a small firm, the truck may be a major purchase and therefore a new buy situation. For a large firm that already owns 50 trucks, purchasing a new truck is not a major purchase, but neither is it a routine purchase that is made on a regular basis.

Fabricated and component parts, process materials, maintenance and repair parts, operating supplies, raw materials, and goods for resale all tend to be straight rebuy situations after a vendor is chosen. Companies develop relationships with a certain vendor or vendors, and they tend to remain in the relationship(s). It is difficult for a new vendor to receive an order, or to even be considered, unless the company becomes unhappy with its current supplier.

Business services vary widely across the three types of buying situations. For a consulting service that is rarely used, it would probably be a new buy situation. For legal services that are used on occasions when legal situations arise, it may be a modified rebuy situation. For telephone, Internet, and janitorial services, it is likely a straight rebuy situation. Keep in mind, however, that the cost of the service relative to the size of the company, the frequency of purchase, and the experience with the service being purchased determine what type of buying situation it is. For example, a factory with its own janitorial staff would be facing a new buy situation when deciding to use an outside vendor for the first time. But it would be a modified rebuy situation when contacting an outside vendor to come in once a year to clean the carpets, tile floors, and do other special tasks.

5-4b The Buying Center

Business-to-business buying decisions often involve more than one individual. The group of individuals who are involved in the purchase process is called the **buying center.** This can be as few as one individual in a family-owned business or as many as 20 or more in a large corporation. The size and roles of the various members of the buying center are determined by factors such as the dollar value of the purchase relative to the size of the company, the impact the purchase has on company operations, and the type of purchase situation. But within the buying group, regardless of size, there are five distinct roles. One individual can play multiple roles, or there can be a number of individuals within each role. The roles can also change over time and from one purchase situation to another. The roles in the buying center are gatekeeper, user, purchaser, decider, and influencer.[7]

Buying center: Group of individuals who are involved in the purchase process.

Gatekeeper: Individual who is responsible for the flow of information to the members of the buying center.

The **gatekeeper** is responsible for the flow of information to the members of the buying center. This can be a secretary who screens phone calls and salespeople wanting to see the purchasing agent or other members of the buying center. It can be a member of the purchasing department who is responsible for gathering and filtering information. It could even be the purchasing agent. Not only does the gatekeeper screen access to the members of the buying center, but he or she may also be the one asked to gather information for the group. By having control over information, the gatekeeper will have a large impact on the decision that is made.

User: An individual member of the buying center who actually uses the product or is responsible for the product being used.

An important member of the buying center is the user. The **user** is the individual who actually uses the product or is responsible for the product being used. On a factory floor, it could be the shop supervisor, the line supervisor, or in some cases, even one of the machine operators. The user's task is to provide information about the current product being used as well as the current vendor. For a factory that uses plastic in building its product, the user will know if the grade of plastic currently being used is causing problems on the assembly line. If so, this information can be relayed to other members of the group. If several vendors are being considered, the user will have some insight on the different grades, types, and durability of the plastics being considered from the vendors.

Influencer: A member of the buying center who influences the decision but may not necessarily use the product.

The **influencer** is someone who can influence the decision but may not necessarily use the product. It could be an engineer who knows the specifications that are required of specific process materials or fabricated parts. Through testing and information supplied by various vendors, the engineer could provide information as to which vendor is offering the best quality or the best materials. But the role of influencer can also be played by others in the company. It may be a vice president, someone from the accounting or business department, or a representative from the marketing area. Influencers are individuals who have some stake in the vendor selection and strive to influence the purchase decision.

Decider: The member of the buying center who makes the final decision.

The person who makes the final decision is the **decider.** This could be the president of the company, a vice president, the controller, the purchasing agent, the secretary, or even the janitor. The decider is the individual or individuals who make the decision on which vendor and which products to purchase. This may be a routine process that requires little or no input from others in the buying center if it is a straight rebuy situation. However, in a new buy situation, it may involve input from a large number of people and the actual decision is made by a group of individuals rather than just a single person.

Purchaser: The member of the buying center who makes the actual purchase.

The **purchaser** is the one who makes the actual purchase. In a large company, this usually is someone in the purchasing department. In a smaller company, it may be a secretary, the owner, the manager, or one of the other employees. Even for a large purchase, the president may make the decision, but it will likely be someone else who actually makes the purchase and works out the details of the purchase arrangement. In straight rebuy situations, the purchasing process may be automatic and just require a phone call or email message (see Figure 5-10).

Figure 5-10
The Buying Center

INTERACTIVE FIGURE

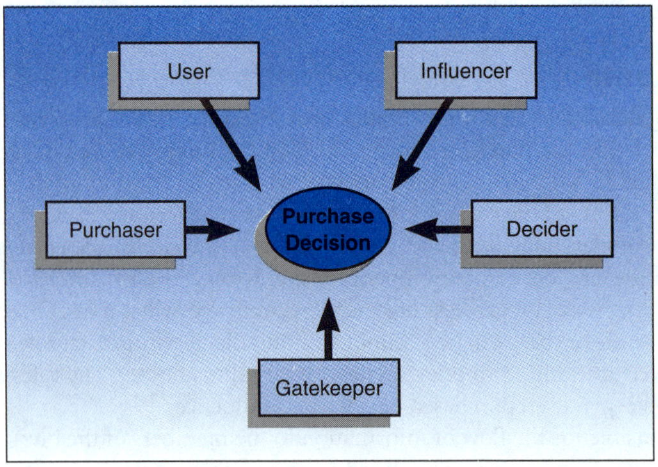

Figure 5-11
Purchasing a component part such as hydraulic pumps for the manufacturing of John Deere tractors would be a modified rebuy situation involving several members of the buying center.

To understand how the buying center operates, suppose John Deere wants to purchase a hydraulic pump for a particular line of its tractors. Let's assume that John Deere is dissatisfied with the current supplier, which makes this a modified rebuy situation (see Figure 5-11). Let us also assume that John Deere put the item out for bids and has received offers from nine different companies. The purchasing agent for John Deere may ask an associate to screen the bid proposals to make sure each is legitimate. In the screening process, the associate purchasing agent is to make sure that the bidder has the capability of supplying 1,750 pumps a month, is financially solvent, and has experience selling hydraulic pumps to large manufacturers like John Deere. In this capacity, the associate purchasing agent is serving as a gatekeeper because he or she will control the information that is forwarded.

Let's assume that three companies are screened out, leaving six. The bid information is then sent to John Deere's engineering department. The members of the engineering department look through the specification information and suggest that two firms be eliminated because they are not sure that the durability and quality of the firms' hydraulic pumps will meet John Deere's standards. While the decision to leave them in the pool or not is the purchasing agent's, the engineering department is serving the role of influencer by suggesting that two companies be dropped.

After accepting the information of the engineering department, the purchasing agent reduces the list to four viable vendors. Each is contacted, asked to make an oral presentation to John Deere, and asked to provide three hydraulic pumps for testing by John Deere's engineering lab. At the presentation are two engineers, the plant foreman, the vice president of operations, and the associate purchasing agent. Two weeks after the presentation by the vendors, the buying center meets to make a decision. The engineers report the findings of their laboratory tests. At this point, the engineers will probably try to influence the decision on which brand should be used. The other individuals in the group may agree and a joint decision is made to accept the brand chosen by the engineers. But it is highly likely that someone in the group will make a different choice and urge the group to purchase a different brand. At this point, the group can discuss each vendor and come up with a consensus, or someone in the group may take the role of the decider and make the final decision. The decider could be the plant foreman or the vice president of finance. It could even be the purchasing agent or one of the engineers, but this situation is not as likely. After the decision is made, the purchasing agent will be designated the purchaser and charged with the responsibility of working out the details of the contract.

5-4c Influences on the Purchase Process

The behaviors of each member of the buying center are influenced by a variety of organizational, individual, social, and temporary factors.[8] These factors influence the expectations of each member, the level of involvement in the purchase process, the role each person performs in the process, the person's level of participation in the decision, and the way the individual handles conflicting opinions (see Figure 5-12).

Because members of the buying center work within an organizational structure, a number of organizational factors impact purchase decisions and the roles an individual performs within the buying center. Especially important are the organization's goals and objectives. Decisions must be made within the framework of these goals and objectives. For example, Wal-Mart's goal of being the low-cost leader means that cost will be a major factor in purchase decisions. For Federal Express, a major goal is fast delivery of packages. Therefore, decisions are made relative to how they may impact the speed of delivery. While a purchase decision may be more cost effective, if it slows down the sorting process and packages do not reach customers in time, customer service may decline, causing a loss of business.

A company's organizational structure has an impact on the various buying center roles. In an organization with a centralized structure, decisions are made by a few individuals with others providing input or information. In a decentralized organization, decision making is moved down the organization, allowing more individuals to make decisions and be involved in decisions. Thus, in a decentralized organization, buying centers will tend to be larger, with buying center members participating more actively.

For many purchase situations, companies have a large number of options. Manufacturers who need to purchase nuts and bolts have hundreds of possible vendors, more than they have time to examine. To be able to eliminate possible vendors and narrow the list to a few that can be examined closely, most employees adopt some type of heuristic. **Heuristics** are decision rules adopted by individuals to make the decision process more efficient. For example, an individual within a buying center of a small manufacturer may decide that all large vendors should be eliminated. This decision could be based on his or her belief that a large vendor would not devote sufficient resources to a small account to provide good service and that, in an emergency, the vendor would neglect the small manufacturer to take care of larger clients.

Heuristics: Decision rules that individuals adopt to make a decision process more efficient.

Because of the large amount of information available from each vendor as well as independent information that is available, buying center members often adopt a heuristic called

Figure 5-12
Influences on the Business-to-Business Purchasing Process

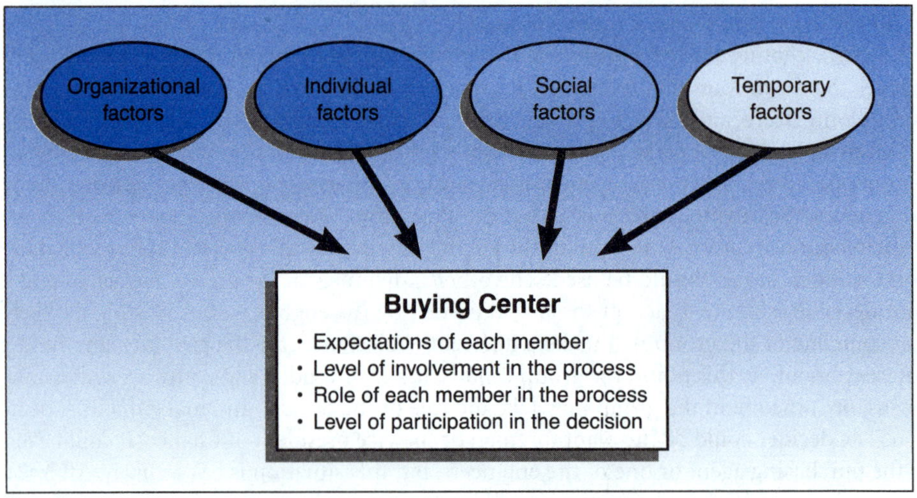

satisficing. **Satisficing** is the process of making a decision that is satisfactory, but not necessarily optimal. Often a buying center will make a decision when its members locate a vendor or arrive at a purchase decision that is satisfactory and meets the goals of the organization. It may or may not be the optimal solution. Individuals may feel making the optimal decision would require too much time or require additional resources and that the extra investment is not worth the possible payoff. Often, there is not time to solicit all the information needed before a decision must be made.[9]

Satisficing: Process of making a decision that is satisfactory, but not necessarily optimal.

Finances and budget constraints constitute organizational factors that impact the purchase decision. If engineers are involved in the buying center, it is not unusual for conflict to arise concerning which component parts or processes should be used. Engineers will push for the part or process that enhances the finished product, whereas the accountants will push for the lowest cost part or process that will get the job done. Again, the idea of satisficing will surface. If the $15 component part will suffice, then, from an accounting perspective, using it is wiser than using the $19 component part. The engineers will argue, however, that the $19 part will produce a superior product and fewer defects. However, if the $19 part will increase the cost of the product above the competition, the firm may have no choice but to use the $15 part. Financial constraints may restrict the company from using the better part.

While a number of individual factors influence each member of the buying center, the primary individual factors include personality traits, level of power, stakeholder interest, and personal objectives.[10] Each factor influences how an individual acts within the buying center and how he or she reacts to other members of the buying center.

An individual's personality traits are an important factor in determining how a person behaves and interacts with others. For example, a person who tends to be an extrovert will spend more time interacting with other members of the buying center than someone who is an introvert. However, an introvert is more likely to listen to a salesperson and gather more information than an extrovert. Another personality trait that is important is that of decisiveness. Some individuals are comfortable making decisions and recommendations, whereas others tend to be less decisive: They will wait and follow the recommendations of someone else. Decisiveness is closely tied with a person's level of risk taking and confidence. A person who is willing to take risks will be more likely to switch to a new vendor than someone who is risk averse. Individuals who have a high level of self-confidence will be more likely to share their opinion and persuade other members of the group that they are right, whereas a person who has a low level of self-confidence will tend to follow the recommendation of others. Table 5-2 summarizes these personality traits and ways they can impact the various members of the buying center.

In addition to personality traits, a person's level of power within an organization has an influence on how he or she behaves within a buying center. The higher-ranking a person is in an organization, the more legitimate power he or she will have in each of the buying center roles (see Figure 5-13 on page 145). Others within the group will have a tendency to follow his or her suggestions, ideas, and decisions. This power tends to be formal and is based on the person's position in the firm. For instance, a vice president's comments are more likely to be accepted by the buying group than the comments of a shop foreman or a supervisor. This formal power, however, can be an impediment to an open discussion about a vendor, even if the person with the formal power strives for it.

All organizations include individuals with informal power. These people have earned the respect of coworkers because of their expertise or ability to make good decisions. Such an individual might be the shop foreman or someone who does not have the formal power, but is highly respected by the other members of the buying center. Recommendations and comments made by this type of person will carry considerably more weight than others within the group.

TABLE 5-2 Personality Traits and Buying Center Functions

Personality Trait	Gatekeeper	User	Influencer	Decider	Purchaser
Degree of extroversion	A gatekeeper who is an extrovert is more likely to pass information on to other members of the buying center than an introvert.	A user who is an introvert will not be as likely to speak up about a purchase situation as would an extrovert.	An extrovert has more influence on a buying center than an introvert.	A decider who is an extrovert is willing to state his or her decision and is usually not as willing to listen to other viewpoints.	An extrovert purchaser is well liked by vendors and is likely to be very good at negotiations, but may not be as careful about details.
Degree of decisiveness	A gatekeeper with a high degree of decisiveness is inclined to make decisions about what information should be passed on to members of the buying center and what should be discarded.	A user who is decisive strives to have more influence on the purchase decision because he or she is using the product and will be more inclined to take a definite stand on specific brands or vendors.	Once an influencer has made a decision about the right product or vendor, someone who is high in decisiveness will make a forceful argument to the other members of the buying center, especially the decider.	A decider who is decisive is not as open to other views and is not as likely to be swayed by the opinion of the users or influencers in the buying center.	The purchaser who is high in decisiveness tends to dictate purchasing terms to vendors and is not as likely to compromise and work out details.
Level of risk taking	A gatekeeper who is risk averse tends to screen out all brands and vendors he or she perceives to be risky.	A risk-averse user will tend to stay with current vendors or brands and is reluctant to switch. Only strong evidence or a poorly performing vendor leads to switching vendors.	A risk-averse influencer tends to stay with the current vendor or brand and to persuade other group members to stay with known brands and vendors with a good record.	A decider who is risk averse is harder to persuade than someone who is willing to take risks.	A purchasing agent who is risk averse will stay with the current methods of purchasing and current terms.
Level of confidence	A gatekeeper with a high level of self-confidence will feel more comfortable in screening out information and vendors that he or she feels are not acceptable.	A user with a high level of self-confidence is more likely to argue for his or her view and insist that the buying center let the user make the decision.	An influencer with a high level of self-confidence strives to convince other members of the buying center that he or she is right.	A decider with a high level of self-confidence can be persuaded if given strong evidence but is less likely to change his or her mind once the decision is made.	A purchaser who has a high level of self-confidence takes the lead in the purchase negotiations.

Figure 5-13
Kevin Hade, Vice President of Sales and Marketing at Ukrop's Super Markets, Inc., has broad power in the chain's buying center.

Source: Courtesy of Ukrop's Super Markets, Inc.

Stakeholder interests and personal objectives are critical factors in how a person functions within the buying center.[11] A person who has a high level of stakeholder interest will be more inclined to be involved and more forceful in influencing the decision. To illustrate, suppose a major portion of a branch manager's evaluation is how well he or she reduces expenses. The more emphasis that is placed on reducing costs by management, the more active the branch manager will be in selecting the low-cost option. If this is coupled with personal objectives, such as his or her desire to become a vice president, then the incentive to be actively involved is even greater.

While we would like to believe that business purchase decisions are made on a rational basis and in terms of what is best for the firm, that is not always the case. Personal objectives such as seeking promotions, building a good reputation with the boss, or making a rival look bad will influence how a person acts within the buying center. Gifts or bribes offered by a salesperson can influence a purchase decision, especially in other countries where this practice is more common. See Marketing Illustration 5-3 for more details about how bribes are used in some European countries.

Employees tend to act in ways that will enhance their personal career and personal objectives. These actions may not always be visible to other members of the group but are closely connected with the concept of stakeholder interests. The more that individuals have at stake in a purchase decision, the higher will be their involvement and the more forceful they will be in the decision-making process. Even individuals who tend to be introverts will exert a stronger voice in deliberations and decisions if they have a high stake in the outcome of the decision and their job performance will be impacted by the purchase decision.

Closely tied with personal characteristics are social factors. Because individuals work within a social environment, social acceptance, norms, and rules of behavior will be factors in how members of the buying center interact with each other. Each person will have his or her own ideas of what is socially acceptable behavior and what is not. Each person will have his or her own ideas about how others ought to act and the roles they should perform within the group. Each business or organization tends to adopt over time a set of social norms. These **norms** are rules of behavior regarding the proper way to behave within the workplace. For example, most companies believe employees should treat others with respect and allow each person to express his or her views. With this open environment, better purchase decisions can be made. Although an open environment is ideal, social norms have developed in some companies that do not allow for open communication. Instead, it

Norms: Rules that dictate what is right or wrong, acceptable or unacceptable.

Marketing Illustration 5-3

Is Giving Gifts or Money to the Decider Okay?

As a salesperson operating in a transition economy, one of your primary tasks is to identify all the individuals in the buying group and those outside the buying group who might influence purchase decisions, such as brothers, cousins, and friends of the decision makers, and to offer the appropriate bribes to the right individuals. This is common procedure in many developing countries: The World Bank surveyed 3,600 companies in 69 countries and found that 40 percent of the firms paid bribes. This figure in industrial countries was 15 percent, and in the former Soviet Union, it increased to 60 percent.

The European Bank for Reconstruction and Development (EBRD), which encourages investments in the former Eastern bloc, has called Eastern Europe's pervasive bribe seeking a deterrent to foreign investment. To illustrate, a recent government crackdown in Romania resulted in investigations of nearly 1,100 teachers and doctors for taking bribes in return for issuing fake exam results and distributing medicine. During this crackdown, 4 government ministers, 4 state secretaries, 7 judges and prosecutors, 23 court bailiffs, 10 mayors, 3 generals, and 167 police officers came under investigation for corruption. Analysts suggest that corruption in many market economies is due to a legally and morally ambiguous environment, where individuals are likely to resort to devices, such as bribery and outright theft.

How do U.S. firms compete abroad when they must abide by the U.S. Foreign Corrupt Practices Act (FCPA)? The act makes it illegal for companies and their representatives to bribe government officials and other politicians or candidates to political office. The act also prohibits payment to third parties when the company has good reason to assume that part of that payment is being used for bribery purposes. U.S. multinational companies take such laws very seriously—some even address their commitment to reject bribery and other corruption in their mission statement (Caterpillar does so, for example)—even though forbidding these practices places U.S. firms at a disadvantage. In a number of high-profile cases, investigators found that illegal payments were made by U.S. firms operating in Canada, Colombia, Cook Islands, the Dominican Republic, Egypt, Germany, Iraq, Israel, Jamaica, Mexico, Niger, Nigeria, Trinidad, and Tobago. These payments ranged from $22,000 to $9.9 million and represented percentages of up to 20 percent of the business obtained. Seventeen companies have been charged under the FCPA, with fines ranging from $10,000 to $21.8 million.

Salespeople from the United States operating in a bribery-prone environment are becoming increasingly creative, often hiring firms whose task is to handle "relationships" with the buying group—while the salespeople maintain their head high and their spotless image. Is this ethical?

Sources: Jamal Al-Khatib, Christopher J. Robertson, and Dana-Nicoleta Lascu, *Journal of Business Ethics,* vol. 54 no. 1 (September 2004): 81–95; Dan Bilefsky, "To Join the EU, Romania Faces Many Hurdles; Graft and Rights Issues Make Outcome Uncertain; Warnings Rattle Optimists," *The Wall Street Journal* (September 20, 2004): A19; Jack G. Kaikati, George M. Sullivan, John M. Virgo, T. R. Carr, and Katherine S. Virgo, "The Price of International Business Morality: Twenty Years under the Foreign Corrupt Practices Act," *Journal of Business Ethics,* vol. 26, no. 3 (August 2000): 213–222.

may be expected that individuals with formal power will not be questioned and that others are expected to demonstrate their loyalty by showing support for these individuals. Social norms are created in companies by management over a period of time. Employees learn what is acceptable and what is not acceptable. These norms impact the buying center because they influence how individuals interact with each other.[12]

The last factor influencing purchase behavior is temporary situations. Because we live and work in a dynamic world, situations faced by businesses change daily. These changes impact purchase decisions. The terrorist attacks of September 11, 2001, changed a number of business decisions. A large number of companies grounded their salespeople and purchased video conferencing equipment to transact business. Email and telephones were used more frequently to contact clients and negotiate contracts. Shipments were delayed, rerouted, and modified to ensure employee safety. Other temporary factors such as declining sales, budget cuts, change in personnel, labor strikes, special interest groups, and vendor delivery problems can all impact purchase decisions. These temporary situations often force a buying center to make an alternate decision or one that is suboptimal.

To understand this organizational purchase decision process, examine Figure 5-14. During the first step, purchasing agents, engineers, users, and other members of the buying center bring their expectations to the process. These expectations are based on their

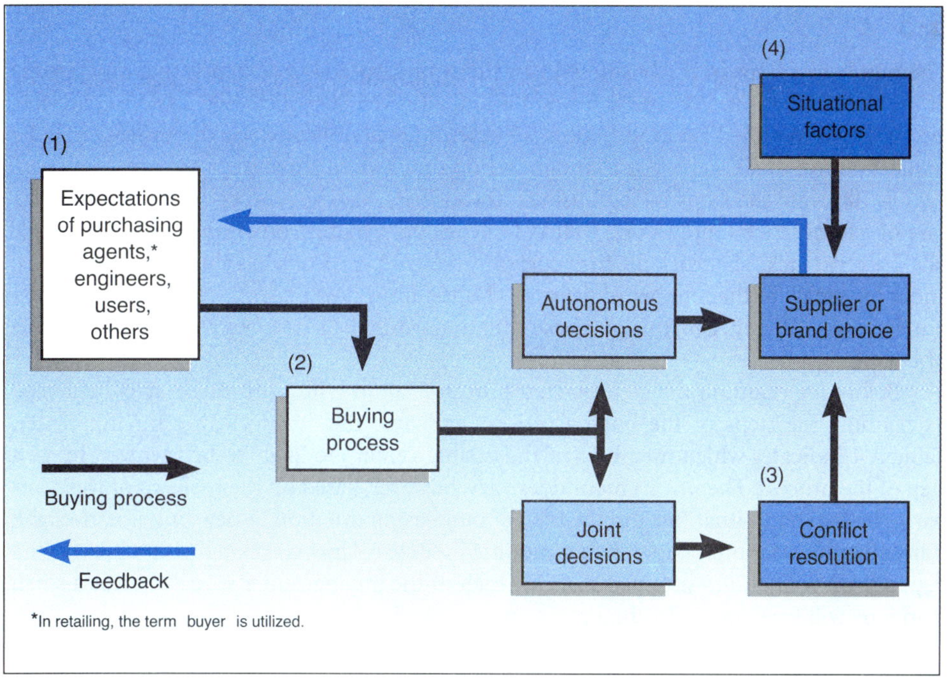

Figure 5-14
The Business-to-Business Purchase Decision Process

Source: Adapted from Jagish N. Sheth, "A Model of Industrial Buyer Behavior," *Journal of Marketing,* Vol. 37 (October 1973), p. 51. Reprinted by permission of American Marketing Association.

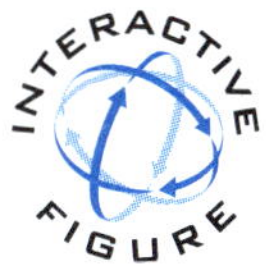

past experiences with the various vendors and their knowledge of the purchase decision that is to be made. Their expectations are also based on the individuals who will be involved in the purchase decision and their past behaviors.

In the second step, the responsibility for the decision is determined. Some decisions are autonomous, meaning that one person will make the decision, whereas others will involve multiple people and will be joint decisions. Factors determining who will be involved in the decision include, for example, the type of purchase decision, buying center makeup, social norms, relative cost of the purchase, and past experiences. Straight rebuy situations will tend to be autonomous, whereas new buys will tend to be joint decisions. Modified rebuys may go either way. If company executives or high-ranking personnel are in the buying center, joint decisions are less likely. Social norms that have been established and past experiences are usually followed unless they did not work in the past or someone specifically states "we are using a different method for making this decision." Lastly, as would be expected, the higher the cost, the more likely it will be a joint decision.

In the third step, conflict resolution will be required if members of the buying center have different opinions about the decision. Social norms and past experiences will determine the conflict resolution method that will be utilized. It can vary from an open debate about the various vendors to someone taking charge and telling others what the decision will be. During the fourth step, situational factors will be considered. These temporary factors will often force the group to make an alternate choice.

After the decision is made, members of the buying center will use the results to develop their expectations of future purchase decisions. If a member of the group was not allowed to express his or her opinion or was put down by others when he or she tried to speak, it is likely he or she will be less involved in the next decision. If a member of the group took an autocratic approach when it was supposed to be a joint decision, it is likely that fewer people will participate in the next decision, and the decision process may become autonomous. Over time, these experiences often become the social norms for the company, at least in terms of how the buying center operates.

5-5 The Business-to-Business Buying Process

The number of steps in the business-to-business process will vary, depending on the type of purchase situation. For a new buy situation, all seven steps listed in Table 5-3 are followed. For a modified rebuy situation, all seven may be followed, or the process may be reduced to five or six steps. For a straight rebuy, only two or three steps are involved.

To illustrate the steps in the business-to-business buying process, let us consider the case of a local office supply store, Dalton Office Supply, that is contemplating the purchase of a delivery truck. The truck the firm currently has is 12 years old, has almost 200,000 miles, and is too small for the number of deliveries Dalton must now make every day. Since the last purchase was 12 years ago, this purchase situation would be a new buy for the current staff of Dalton.

Before we examine the step-by-step process Dalton will go through, it is beneficial to examine the steps of the buying process and how they relate to the buying center. Table 5-4 indicates which members of the buying center are likely to be involved in each step of the process. The involvement does vary, however, based on the makeup of the company, the purchase situation, and the type of purchasing situation. A new buy situation will normally involve more people than a modified rebuy. A large company with a purchasing department will tend to use specialists for each of the buying center roles, whereas a small company will have one individual performing several roles.

For our Dalton Office Supply illustration, the user would be the truck driver. Because this is a local, two-store operation, the influencers are the two managers of the office supply stores. The decider will be the owner of Dalton, and the buyer is the assistant manager

TABLE 5-3

Buying Situation and Steps in the Buying Process

Step in Business-to-Business Buying Process	New Buy	Modified Rebuy	Straight Rebuy
1. Identification of needs	X	X	X
2. Establishment of specifications	X	?	?
3. Identification of feasible solutions	X	?	
4. Identification of feasible vendors	X	X	
5. Evaluation of vendors	X	X	
6. Selection of vendor(s)	X	X	
7. Negotiation of purchase terms	X	X	X

TABLE 5-4

Participation of Buying Center Members in the Buying Process

Step in Business-to-Business Buying Process	Gatekeeper	User	Influencer	Decider	Buyer
1. Identification of needs		X			
2. Establishment of specifications		X	X	X	X
3. Identification of feasible solutions	X	X	X	?	X
4. Identification of feasible vendors	X	X	X	?	X
5. Evaluation of vendors		X	X	?	X
6. Selection of vendor(s)		X	X	X	X
7. Negotiation of purchase terms					X

Figure 5-15
The purchase of a delivery truck is an important decision for a small business owner.

of the large store because he serves as the purchasing agent for both operations. The gatekeeper, in this illustration, is the assistant manager of the large store. In this purchase situation, he will serve both as the buyer and the gatekeeper (see Figure 5-15).

5-5a Identification of Needs

The first step in the business-to-business buying process is the identification of a need. Although advertising and marketing can create desires and needs for consumers, this phenomenon is not as likely to occur in the business environment. In most cases, needs are the direct result of a firm's operation. A bakery needs flour, sugar, and other ingredients to bake its products, and when these ingredients run low, it is time to purchase more. Manufacturers must keep an eye on all of the components and materials used in the production process to make sure they have a sufficient quantity on hand to keep production going. In these types of situations, the purchase process is normally just a straight rebuy. The supplier is notified, and products are shipped to the manufacturer. This is an ideal situation for the supplier because no other vendors or options are even considered. With this type of purchase situation, the company will skip to the last step and negotiate terms of the purchase.

Modified rebuy needs arise from dissatisfaction with the current vendor, a sales pitch by a potential vendor, or the need to purchase a product that is not purchased too frequently. The identification of a need with a new buy situation is the result of a strategic decision or the need to purchase a product that is seldom purchased.

5-5b Establishment of Specifications

The second step in the purchase process is the development of specifications. In straight rebuy situations, the specifications remain the same or are only slightly modified. In situations in which the specifications need a greater level of modifications, a firm will usually enter into the modified rebuy situation, which involves examining other alternatives and vendors.

To ensure that vendor bids can be compared, it is important to establish specifications. When each firm bids on the same set of specifications, a firm is able to compare bids and make a better decision. Sometimes firms are not sure what the specifications should be. This is especially true for new buy situations. For instance, a firm desiring to upgrade its computer system will often seek the help of vendors to establish the specifications. This makes the bidding process more difficult if the same specifications are not sent to every firm submitting a bid.

In setting the bid specifications, it is also beneficial to outline the decision criteria in advance. This will help ensure that the decision process is not biased toward a particular vendor. If buying center members set the criteria in advance, it is easier to compare vendor bids and choose the one that best meets the needs of the firm. If decision criteria are not set out in advance, one or two members of the buying center may choose a particular vendor and then try to persuade the group on selection criteria that will favor the vendor they prefer.

Almost all merchandise arrives in retail stores in some type of corrugated boxes. When selecting boxes, price, quality, and performance are common selection criteria. Most manufacturers, such as Hershey Foods and Coca-Cola, have added the specification that the box must be able to run through high-speed equipment without breaking down. Coca-Cola also wants a strategic relationship with the box supplier. For Del Monte Foods, the essential specification is the top-to-bottom compression strength. Because canned food is placed in boxes and then stacked on pallets for shipment, they must be able to withstand boxes and pallets stacked on top of each other.[13]

In choosing a truck, Dalton developed two sets of specifications. The first are the specifications for the truck; the second are the purchase criteria. In terms of minimum specifications, the truck must be one ton with a box bed, power lift, and a diesel engine. The criteria that would be used for selecting the truck are listed in Table 5-5. Notice that, in addition to the required specifications, Dalton has listed a number of specifications it will use to evaluate each vehicle. Dalton has also identified three additional criteria that will be used in the process. The first is the level of business the truck dealer does with Dalton. This is a common practice in business and is known as **reciprocity,** which means that a business will purchase from businesses that in turn patronize them. While it will not be the only criteria Dalton uses, it will favor a truck dealer that purchases office supplies from Dalton. Also used in the decision will be any personal experience the members of the buying center have had with the dealers. When this list is completed, the Dalton group is ready to move to the next step—identification of feasible solutions.

Reciprocity: Practice of one business making a purchase from another business that, in turn, patronizes the first business.

5-5c Identification of Feasible Solutions

At the third step in the process, a business needs to examine various ways of handling the need. The three most common are to purchase the product from an external business, produce the product itself, or lease it. Companies examining their shipping needs have the options of purchasing their own trucks, hiring an independent firm to ship the merchandise for them, or using a commercial service such as UPS.

Some decisions are more difficult. For example, Avon has several pieces of equipment used in the production of lipstick that are quite old and labor intensive. For $200,000 to $300,000, Avon can automate the machine and virtually eliminate the human operators. Avon must compare the labor savings of a new machine to the cost of the machine and the level of production that will result. For a high-production item, the labor savings will likely exceed the cost of the new machine. However, for a low-production item, Avon may be better off keeping the old machine, repairing it, and paying out more in labor.

TABLE 5-5

Dalton Truck Specifications

Required Truck Specifications	One-ton box truck
	Power lift
	Diesel engine
Truck Specifications to Be Evaluated	Fuel mileage
	Consumer report for quality
	Cost of repairs
	Warranty
	Price
Other Purchase Criteria	Level of business with Dalton
	Brand name (preference for American brand)
	Previous personal experience with dealership

Another option, especially for equipment, land, and buildings, is leasing. This is something Dalton Office Supply could consider. Instead of purchasing a new truck, Dalton could lease a vehicle. The advantages would include always having a newer model that can be used. Because maintenance is the responsibility of the dealer, the company can expense the cost of the lease out each month. Of course, the disadvantages include not owning the truck. In addition, if the mileage exceeds the lease limits, there is normally a penalty. Dalton must carefully calculate the total cost of owning the vehicle over the life of the truck versus the cost of leasing.

5-5d Identification of Feasible Vendors

If the decision to use an external source is made, then someone must contact possible vendors and ask them to submit bids. This is one of the tasks of the gatekeeper and, in the process of identifying possible vendors, he or she controls the information flow. If the gatekeeper does not like a particular vendor, that vendor may never be notified. However, some possible vendors may be left out by accident. Just the process of selecting and notifying possible vendors may cause some to be eliminated. For example, if the phone book is used, any vendor that did not have a Yellow Page ad may be eliminated. An out-of-town firm that may have the capability would not be included. If an industry directory is used, it may not be complete or may have wrong information.

After possible vendors have been located, then someone must screen the list for firms that are not feasible. In this process, firms that may not be able to meet production schedules or that are too small may be eliminated. For example, if the process is the construction of a \$20 million facility, small contractors with only a few employees do not have the capability of handling such a large job. Del Monte requires that all the vendors who supply corrugated boxes be located close to the Del Monte facilities because of the high cost of shipping box material a long distance.[14]

For Dalton, initial screening at this stage is to eliminate any trucks that do not have a diesel engine because that was set as a basic requirement. Suppose that, in gathering information about the various dealers, the assistant manager finds two dealers who have trucks that meet the specifications but not the criteria of being current customers of Dalton. One has never been a customer; the other used to be a customer but gradually reduced purchases to less than \$25 a month. Should these two possible vendors be eliminated? Suppose the dealer that has never been a customer has the lowest priced truck. Since the assistant manager has been charged with the responsibility of gathering a list of possible trucks, he would have to make a decision. He can leave these two dealers on the list, he can eliminate them, or he can ask someone else in the buying center for advice. It is unlikely that he would call a meeting of the entire buying center. Instead, if he wants advice on what he should do, he will go to one of the influencers or the decider. In this case, that would be one or both of the store managers or the owner of Dalton. The person or persons he would approach would depend a great deal on the organizational structure and the social norms for Dalton. If it is a company that encourages open communication and the owner is available, he may go straight to the owner and ask whether the dealers should be left on the list because the owner will ultimately make the decision. However, if the company social norms dictate a strong chain of command, then he will go to his boss, the store manager, for counsel.

With more business-to-business purchases occurring over the Internet, screening online vendors is a challenge. Buyers are concerned that they won't get the quality of products they order delivered at the right time. Sellers are concerned that they won't be paid. While some companies just do not do any business-to-business transactions over the Internet, most are looking for ways to screen businesses. For its vehicle leasing and logistics services, Ryder Systems, Inc. uses Instant Decision software developed by eCredit.com, Inc. to check the credit of businesses that initiate an online purchase from Ryder. The software uses company history as well as public information about the business to develop a credit rating. The price that Ryder will quote for its services is then based on the credit rating the software assigns. While not perfect, the software does allow Ryder to screen high-risk customers and charge them more if they want to lease a vehicle or use the logistics services.[15]

5-5e Evaluation of Vendors

Evaluation of vendors normally occurs at three levels. The first level is an initial evaluation screening of candidates. This evaluation screening is different from the screening in the previous step. Vendors who make this list are qualified and meet the minimum specifications. Screening at this level entails evaluating how well a vendor meets the specifications and purchase criteria identified in step two. One or two individuals within the buying center may perform this initial evaluation screening, or the whole group may be involved. The person or persons responsible will largely depend on how many vendors are on the initial list, the type of buying situation, and the relative cost of the purchase. If there are a large number of vendors, normally one or two individuals will be asked to pare down the list. If it is a new buy situation, more individuals will be involved in the initial screening process than if it is a modified rebuy situation. The same is true for the relative cost of the purchase. The greater the cost, the more people are likely to be involved. The purpose of this initial evaluation screening is to reduce the list of feasible vendors down to a smaller manageable list.

Suppose, in our Dalton example, that the assistant manager has a list of nine dealers and 12 possible trucks in the two towns where the company has offices. It is possible that everyone involved in the decision will want to be involved in this initial evaluation screening. However, it is more likely that the assistant manager and another person or two will be asked to narrow the list. The user—in this case, the firm's truck driver—may be asked to work with the assistant manager, or it may be one of the store managers, or both. It is unlikely that Dalton's owner will be involved with this initial screening.

The second level of evaluation is a vendor analysis. This is a formal evaluation of each vendor. Table 5-6 provides a vendor analysis for a supplier of denim cloth to a manufacturer of jeans. Each denim supplier will be evaluated on each of the seven criteria. This process will allow the jeans manufacturer to narrow down the list of feasible vendors to two or three.

For new buy situations, such as the case of Dalton Office Supply, all of the members of the buying center are usually involved. Involving everyone is especially important in new buy situations because no one has experience with the product being purchased, or the individuals involved have limited experience. Although members of the buying center at Dalton have all purchased vehicles for their private use, only one of the store managers has experience with purchasing a company truck. Using the truck specifications and purchase criteria listed in Table 5-5, the list of dealers will be further narrowed to only two or three dealers.

For modified rebuy situations, the number of members of the buying center who are involved in this vendor analysis will vary. If the situation involves a high-cost item or some-

TABLE 5-6

A Vendor Analysis for Denim Suppliers for a Jeans Manufacturer

	Excellent	Superior	Acceptable	Inferior
1. Speed of delivery	____	____	____	____
2. Handling of emergency and rush orders	____	____	____	____
3. Quality of denim material	____	____	____	____
4. Availability of different colors/styles	____	____	____	____
5. Handling of defective denim	____	____	____	____
6. Percent of denim that is defective	____	____	____	____
7. Purchase terms	____	____	____	____

thing that is purchased on an irregular basis or just occasionally, everyone may be involved. However, if the modified rebuy is due to dissatisfaction with the current vendor, the vendor analysis may be left to a couple of people. After the list is narrowed to two or three, then the rest of the buying center members may be involved. This would especially be true for the decider. He or she may not want to be involved until the list is pared down.

The last level of the evaluation process is the vendor audit or presentation. At this level, members of the buying center either visit the prospective vendor's site or have the prospective vendor make a presentation to the buying center. Typical questions asked during a vendor audit include:

- What are the vendor's production capabilities?
- What quality control mechanisms and processes does the vendor have in place? How closely does the vendor follow the processes?
- What is the defective material rate, and how does the vendor handle defective merchandise?
- What type of equipment is used, how old is the equipment, and how dependable is the equipment?
- What telecommunication and electronic data interchange (EDI) capabilities does the vendor have?
- Can the vendor handle order fluctuations?
- What is the financial stability of the company?
- How many customers does the firm have, and how many are competitors?
- What type of relationship does the vendor have with its suppliers? Will there be an interruption in supplies to the vendor that would impact the vendor's ability to fill orders?
- How stable is the vendor's labor pool? Will a strike or other labor problems cause an interruption in the ability to fill orders?

The primary purpose of the vendor audit is to ensure that the vendor has the capability of meeting the supply demands of the purchaser. If the vendor is supplying denim for a manufacturer of blue jeans, the manufacturer must be sure that the supply of denim will be met, that the quality meets its specifications, and that special orders can be filled quickly. Because the production of the blue jeans cannot occur without the denim material, supply capability is crucial (see Figure 5-16).

To ensure a regular supply of raw materials, as well as fabricated and component parts, a large number of buyers are using EDI technology with their vendors. **Electronic data interchange (EDI)** means that data from the manufacturer's production facility are sent directly to suppliers through computers. This allows the suppliers to see how much material is being used, which material is being used, and what level of inventory is left. By receiving data from the actual production process, the vendor knows what type, color, and style of material it needs to produce and when it needs to be sent to the manufacturer.

Electronic data interchange (EDI): A trust relationship that includes the sharing of data between the buying and selling firm.

This same technology is used at the retail level to ensure that store shelves remain stocked with the correct merchandise. These data can be extremely valuable to manufacturers not only in what needs to be produced and when it needs to be shipped, but in what is selling well and what is not. By monitoring actual sales of merchandise, the manufacturer knows which styles and colors are in high demand. This allows the firm to modify its production schedule to produce more of the items that are selling well and fewer of the items that are not selling. See Marketing Illustration 5-4 to review Wal-Mart's web EDI operation.

Instead of visiting the vendor's place of business, the vendor may make a presentation to the members of the buying center at their place of business. This is often the case with services, such as an advertising agency, a public relations firm, or a lawn service. For modified rebuy situations, this procedure is likely to be used. The same vendor questions will likely be asked, but the setting is different.

Figure 5-16
Jeans manufacturers depend on a regular supply of denim.

Dalton can handle the evaluation of vendors in a couple of different ways. When the list is narrowed down, a handful of members of the buying center may go to the dealers and test drive the trucks. When the list has been further narrowed down to two or three trucks, the owner and the rest of the members of the buying center may go to the dealers and examine the trucks, or perhaps just the owner will go with one other person. Instead, the owner may request that the dealers bring the trucks to the office supply store so everyone has a chance to look at them.

5-5f Selection of Vendor(s)

Before a final selection is made, the business must decide whether it will go with one vendor or more. For Dalton, because only one truck will be purchased, only one vendor will

Marketing Illustration 5-4

Wal-Mart's Web EDI

Wal-Mart built its retail empire largely upon its EDI technology and was the first retailer to utilize EDI to reduce costs and to manage inventory and logistics more effectively. Now, EDI is the lifeblood of most retail business operations as purchase orders and other key information are shared with each retailer's supply base. Traditionally, EDI transactions have all been handled on private lines called value-added networks (VANs).

Now, Wal-Mart is once again pushing the technology, this time to web EDI. With web EDI, all transactions are handled over the Internet instead of on the traditional VANs. Wal-Mart has now mandated that all of its 14,000 suppliers use web EDI for the $217 billion worth of transactions that are conducted each year. While suppliers can choose to hook up with Wal-Mart by any approach and with any vendor, Wal-Mart has chosen iSoft to handle its end of the web EDI. For vendors who need help, iSoft is willing to help suppliers move to an Internet-based EDI. The agreement iSoft has with Wal-Mart is that it will help any supplier link for just a $300 annual support fee.

For suppliers, a tough choice lies ahead: Either switch to web EDI or lose the Wal-Mart account. For some suppliers, the cost of acquiring and supporting the web EDI may not be worthwhile. For others, to survive, they will have no choice. For most suppliers, switching will not be a cost savings. For Wal-Mart, it will be a huge savings. It will mean dealing with over 14,000 suppliers using a common Internet-based EDI technology instead of maintaining a long bank of VANs, faxes, and telephones. The cost of installing and bringing online the web EDI system was recovered within just a few months.

Sources: Anthony Adshead, "Web EDI Forces Suppliers to Change Tactics," *Computer Weekly* (July 1, 2003): 8; Richard Karpinski, "Wal-Mart Pushes Web EDI," *B to B*, vol. 87 (October 14, 2002): 15.

be selected. But for a supplier of raw materials or component parts, the decision is more complicated. The advantage of choosing one vendor is lower prices through quantity discounts, but the disadvantage is that a greater risk occurs if, for some reason, the one supplier cannot fill all of the orders or is late with the shipment. If the business has an EDI relationship with its vendors, then having more than one supplier creates a higher risk in terms of data exchange. Sharing production schedules and sales data with suppliers assumes a high level of trust between the parties concerned. If more than one vendor is involved with a particular product, maintaining a high level of trust becomes much more difficult. Each vendor is vying for a larger share of the business and can easily see from data it receives how much of the business it has and how much is being given to the competition. For this reason, if more than one vendor is used, EDI relationships are either not established or are established with only the primary vendor. The business may use another vendor for a small amount of the raw material or component parts just to ensure a safe backup to the primary vendor.

In the past, the U.S. military used a large number of vendors to supply its maintenance, repair, and operations materials. To reduce operating and inventory-carrying costs and create better efficiencies in ordering, the Defense Logistics Agency (DLA) decided to go with just one bidder. After evaluating six bids, the five-year, $59 million-per-year contract was awarded to SupplyCore, Inc. of Rockford, Illinois. A year later, SupplyCore, Inc. won a five-year, $35 million-per-year bid to supply materials to all of the U.S. military bases in Japan. Shipments, which took 9 to 12 months in the past, arrive within 50 days, now at a savings to the DLA of $590,000 a year.[16]

5-5g Negotiation of Purchase Terms

In most purchase situations, the last step, negotiation, is merely a formality because most of the purchase terms have already been worked out during the evaluation and selection process. But for those terms that have not been agreed upon, it will be the responsibility of the buyer to negotiate. Payment method, due date, size of order, delivery schedule, and method for handling defective merchandise are a few of the terms that will be agreed upon at this stage. After a contract or agreement has been reached, the unsuccessful bidders are informed that the bidding process has been concluded and that a vendor has been chosen.

While the buying process is over at this point for members of the buying center, evaluation of the purchase process occurs. It may be a formal evaluation, or it may be informal. Users will evaluate the decision based on the criteria used in the selection process. If the new vendor meets everyone's expectations, then for products used on a regular basis the company will move to a straight rebuy situation with the vendor. For both the buyer and seller, this relationship is the most desirable and, as long as it remains satisfactory for both parties, it will continue.

For products that are in the modified rebuy situation, the results of the purchase will be remembered by those involved, and the next time the product has to be purchased, the chosen vendor will have a greater chance of being selected. If Dalton purchases a Ford truck and is pleased with the truck's performance, then Dalton will be more likely to purchase a Ford truck the next time. Even in a modified rebuy situation, this will save members of the buying center a considerable amount of time.

For new buy situations, the results of the current purchase are of little value. If it is another 12 years before Dalton purchases another truck, it is likely that the company will spend the same amount of time during the purchase process. Most of the members of the buying center will be new, and the makes, models, and vehicle dealers will have all changed. It is very likely that the dealer the truck was purchased from will have a new owner, so there is no longer any guarantee of the same level of satisfaction. If the dealership is still owned by the same individual, personnel at the dealership have probably changed. That is why, for new buy situations, firms go through all seven steps, and decisions can take anywhere from a few weeks to a few years.

Summary

1. *Identify the types of goods and services that businesses purchase.* Businesses can purchase major equipment, buildings and land, accessory equipment, fabricated and component parts, process materials, maintenance and repair parts, operating supplies, raw materials, goods for resale, and business services.

2. *Identify the types of business customers.* The types of business customers include manufacturers, wholesalers and distributors, retailers, governments, and nonprofit organizations.

3. *Explain the concepts of derived and joint demand and why they are important for the business-to-business market.* The demand for many business-to-business products is dependent, or derived, on the demand for consumer products. The demand for parts that are used in the manufacturing of a washing machine is derived from the consumer demand for washing machines. With joint demand, the demand for a product is dependent on the supply of other products used in the manufacturing of a product. For example, the demand for electrical switches for washing machines will be affected by the supply of the other parts used in the construction of the washing machines. For business-to-business markets, joint and derived demand determine the demand for a product. Often, there is little a business-to-business firm can do to modify demand for its products.

4. *Identify the types of buying situations and when each is used.* Types of buying situations include new buy, modified rebuy, and straight rebuy. Organizations purchasing a product for the first time or products with which no one has any relevant experience are involved in a new buy situation. In a modified rebuy situation, a product is purchased infrequently and the organization has little experience with the product, or the organization is dissatisfied with its current vendor or receives an attractive offer from another firm it wants to consider. Modified rebuys can also occur at the end of a contract period. Straight rebuy situations occur when orders are placed with the current vendor without considering any other vendors.

5. *Describe the concept of the buying center and the different roles employees can play.* Many buying decisions within a business are joint decisions and involve more than one person. Members of the buying center can play the roles of gatekeeper, user, influencer, decider, and purchaser. The gatekeeper is responsible for filtering information to the other members of the buying center. The user is the individual who actually uses the product or oversees its use. Influencers are individuals who have a significant influence on the decision but do not actually make the decision. The decider is the individual who makes the final decision. The purchaser is the one who negotiates the terms of the contract and actually makes the purchase.

6. *Discuss the factors that influence business-to-business buyer behavior.* The behaviors of each member of the buying center are influenced by a variety of organizational, individual, social, and temporary factors. These factors influence the expectations of each member, the level of involvement in the purchase process, the role each person performs in the process, the person's level of participation in the decision, and the way the individual handles conflicting opinions. The organizational factors include the corporate goals and objectives, the firm's organizational structure, and the finances and budget of the firm. Individual factors that influence each member of the buying center are personality traits, level of power, stakeholder interest, and personal objectives. Each factor influences how an individual acts within the buying center and how he or she reacts to other members of the buying center.

Closely tied with personal characteristics are social factors. Because individuals work within a social environment, social acceptance, norms, and rules of behavior will be factors in how members of the buying center interact with each other. Temporary factors, such as declining sales, budget cuts, changes in personnel, labor strikes, special interest groups, and vendor delivery problems, can all impact purchase decisions. These temporary situations often force a buying center to make an alternate decision or one that is suboptimal.

7. *List the seven steps in the business-to-business buying process and explain what occurs in each step.* The first step in the business-to-business buying process is identification of needs. They can be routine needs, such as those that are part of a manufacturing process, or rare needs, such as a new building. Once the need has been recognized, the next step is the establishment of objectives. For rebuy situations, this is routine and is the same that has been ordered in the past. For modified and new buy situations, time will need to be taken to determine both the product and purchase specifications. During the third step, feasible solutions are evaluated. They often include leasing and outsourcing or using an alternate material. After the decision is made to purchase the product, potential vendors are contacted. Once the list of possible vendors is narrowed down to a smaller, manageable list, evaluation of each vendor occurs. A vendor analysis and vendor audit are often a part of this evaluation. Based on the results of the evaluation, a vendor is selected. The last step is the negotiation of terms with the vendor.

Key Terms

acceleration principle (p. 137)
buying center (p. 139)
decider (p. 140)
derived demand (p. 136)
electronic data interchange (EDI) (p. 153)
gatekeeper (p. 139)
heuristics (p. 142)
influencer (p. 140)
joint demand (p. 137)
modified rebuy situation (p. 138)
new buy situation (p. 138)
norms (p. 145)
purchaser (p. 140)
reciprocity (p. 150)
satisficing (p. 143)
straight rebuy situation (p. 139)
user (p. 140)
wholesalers and distributors (p. 132)

Discussion Questions

1. Read the opening vignette about Wi-Fi. In terms of commercial locations, where are the hotspots for Wi-Fi in your area? How do each of the locations benefit from offering Wi-Fi to customers or patrons? What are the drawbacks?
2. From the list of goods and services purchased by a business, identify at least one example from each category for each of the following types of businesses:
   a. Bakery
   b. Manufacturer of electric leaf blowers
   c. Pizza restaurant
   d. Tree removal service
   e. Wholesale distributor of hardware supplies
3. Read Marketing Illustration 5-1 about selling airline travel to business travelers? Using a database search engine, investigate the current status of business travelers in relation to discount airlines and major carriers. If you know of a businessperson who does considerable traveling, discuss with him or her the issues involved in business travel and how he or she makes a decision about which airline to use.
4. Discuss how the concepts of derived demand and joint demand would be relevant to each of the following suppliers:
   a. Supplier of sand to a concrete mixing company
   b. Lumberyard that supplies lumber and other building materials for home construction companies
   c. Supplier of wire that is used in building electrical motors
   d. Food processing factory that makes tomato paste that is sold to other businesses making various types of foods
   e. Company that mines iron ore
5. For each of the following situations, discuss what type of buying situation it is and identify who might serve in each of the buying center roles:
   a. Construction of a new 10,000-square-foot addition to a current 40,000-square-foot factory
   b. Purchase of a new photographic developing machine for a commercial photographic developing service
   c. Purchase of furniture for a new office complex that has just been built
   d. Because of dissatisfaction with the last vendor, the selection of a new company to supply the flour used in baking pizza crusts for the retail food market
   e. The ordering of an extra 5,000 electrical switches used in the manufacturing of electrical space heaters that are sold to retail stores
6. Do some research on the impact of the terrorist attacks of September 11, 2001, on business-to-business markets. What types of business-to-business markets were adversely affected? What business-to-business markets benefited from the terrorist attacks in terms of increased sales?
7. Read Marketing Illustration 5-3 about selling in international markets and the use of gifts and bribes. How do you stand on this issue? Is it ethical for salespeople working in another country where gifts and bribes are used to utilize the same methods? What may happen if they don't follow the local customs? What may happen if they do, in terms of U.S. laws?
8. Do some research on web EDI. Who else uses it—in addition to Wal-Mart? What are the advantages and disadvantages of web EDI?
9. How important is the Internet in identifying possible vendors? Are companies located through the Internet viable vendors? How can a business determine whether a business is legitimate?
10. Assume you have been given the responsibility of searching the Internet for viable companies for each of the following purchase situations. Use the Business-to-Business section under Business and Economy at Yahoo. Locate five feasible companies and discuss why each is a viable company.
    a. Fresh fish for a retail grocery store
    b. Circuit boards for a computer manufacturer
    c. Electric motors to be used in electrical leaf blowers
    d. Translation services for a company wanting to do business in Argentina
    e. Shipping company to transport grain to South America

Review Questions

True or False

1. Top managers normally participate in the purchase of major equipment, buildings, and land.
2. To reduce the cost of a finished product, a manufacturer may use fabricated and component parts of inferior quality.
3. The most efficient channel of selling goods to consumers consists of a manufacturer, a wholesaler, and a retailer.
4. Derived demand is the demand generated from the demand for consumer goods or services.
5. It is not unusual for a new buy to take several months or even several years.
6. Purchasing office supplies for a large corporation is classified as a straight rebuy.
7. In the business-to-business purchasing process, the gatekeeper is responsible for screening the decisions made by the buying center.
8. The user is the individual who actually uses the product or is responsible for the product being used.
9. If a group of engineers provides test data or information on quality and reliability, they can decide which vendor to choose.
10. EDI technology allows data from the manufacturer's production facility to be sent directly to suppliers and vendors.

Multiple Choice

11. Retailers, wholesalers, and distributors purchase goods for the purpose of resale. Which of the following statements is correct?
- **a.** Retailers are not concerned with selling a particular brand.
- **b.** Wholesalers and distributors will push the brand that benefits them the most.
- **c.** a and b
- **d.** none of the above

12. The fluctuations and wide swing in sales can be explained by the acceleration principle. The principle addresses which of the following?
- **a.** A small increase in the demand for a good can cause a huge increase in demand for production equipment.
- **b.** A 10 to 15 percent decline in orders can cause a complete collapse in the demand for the raw materials used in making a product.
- **c.** a and b
- **d.** none of the above

13. Business-to-business markets differ from customer markets in all of the following aspects EXCEPT
- **a.** fewer buyers.
- **b.** large purchase volume.
- **c.** geographic concentration.
- **d.** informal buying process.

14. The number of batteries supplied to a Ford plant directly relates to the number of other engine components supplied to assemble a particular model. This is an example of
- **a.** derived demand.
- **b.** joint demand.
- **c.** straight rebuy.
- **d.** direct demand.

15. A modified rebuy occurs in which of the following situations?
- **a.** limited buying experience with the product
- **b.** dissatisfaction with the current vendor
- **c.** switch to a new vendor by the end of the contractual relationship
- **d.** all of the above

16. Heuristics are decision rules adopted by the members of a buying center to
- **a.** make the decision process more efficient.
- **b.** select vendors based on location.
- **c.** avoid errors in vendors' evaluation.
- **d.** none of the above.

17. Satisficing is a heuristic decision rule that
- **a.** requires consideration of all known information in the final decision.
- **b.** satisfies the expectations and strategies of the top managers.
- **c.** is satisfactory but not necessarily optimal.
- **d.** satisfies the requirements for easy manufacturing.

Notes

1. Michelle Kessler, "Growing Wi-Fi Services Cast Wide Net," *USA Today* (November 14, 2002): Money, 03b; Ephraim Schwartz, "Coffee Black, No Wi-Fi," *InfoWorld*, vol. 24 (November 4, 2002): 24; Reed E. Hundt, Newman Stagg, and John E. Richards, "Wi Fi Goes to Washington," *McKinsey Quarterly*, vol. 4 (2002): 150–153; Kate Maddox, "Report Predicts Surge in WiFi Use," *B to B*, vol. 88 (December 8, 2003): 4; Kathryn Ward, "Double-Duty WiFi," *Convenience Store News*, vol. 40 (November 22, 2004): 82 82.
2. David Kiley, "While CEOs Take Beating, Ford's Scores with Spots," *USA Today* (July 29, 2002): Money, 04b.
3. "Asian B2B Internet Platform Up and Running," *Furniture Today*, vol. 25 (April 9, 2001): 38.
4. Will Mies, "Buyers Say Corrugated Suppliers Bring Value, But Business Reinvestment Warrants Concern," *Pulp & Paper*, vol. 76 (July 2002): 38–42.
5. Eugene F. Brigham and James L. Pappas, *Managerial Economics*, 2nd ed. (Hinsdale, IL: Dryden Press, 1976).
6. Patrick J. Robinson, Charles W. Faris, and Yoram Wind, "Industrial Buying and Creative Marketing," *Marketing Science Institute Series* (Boston: Allyn & Bacon, 1967).
7. Patricia M. Doney and Gary W. Armstrong, "Effects of Accountability on Symbolic Information Search and Information Analysis by Organizational Buyers," *Journal of the Academy of Marketing Sciences*, vol. 24 (Winter 1996): 57–66; Kenneth E. Clow and Donald Baack, *Integrated Advertising, Promotion, & Marketing Communications* (Upper Saddle River, NJ: Prentice-Hall, 2002): 196–199.
8. Frederick E. Webster, Jr., and Yoram Wind, "A General Model for Understanding Organizational Buyer Behavior," *Marketing Management*, vol. 4 (Winter/Spring 1996): 52–57; Clow and Baack, *Integrated Advertising, Promotion, & Marketing Communications*, 196–199.
9. Herbert Simon, *The New Science of Management Decisions* (Upper Saddle River, NJ: Prentice-Hall, 1977).
10. Webster and Wind, "A General Model for Understanding Organizational Buyer Behavior," 52–57; Doney and Armstrong, "Effects of Accountability on Symbolic Information Search and Information Analysis by Organizational Buyers," 57–66.
11. Phillip L. Dawes and Don Y. Lee, "Information Control and Influence in Emergent Buying Centers," *Journal of Marketing*, vol. 62 (July 1998): 55–69.
12. Marvin E. Shaw and Phillip R. Costanzo, *Theories of Social Psychology*, 2nd ed. (New York: McGraw-Hill, 1982).
13. Mies, "Buyers Say Corrugated Suppliers Bring Value, But Business Reinvestment Warrants Concern," 38–42.
14. Ibid.
15. Bob Violino, "Building B2B Trust," *Computerworld*, vol. 36 (June 17, 2002): 32–33.
16. Peter Provenzano, "Military Orders Sole Supplier," *Government Procurement*, vol. 10 (August 2002): 24–25.

Case 5-1 Briggs & Stratton

Briggs & Stratton is the world's number one maker of air-cooled gasoline engines used in lawn mowers, garden tillers, and other lawn equipment. Sales of these small gasoline engines account for about 86 percent of the total sales for Briggs & Stratton, which was $1.95 billion last year.

Briggs & Stratton manufactures all of its 3- to 25-horsepower small engines in the United States. Factories are located in Alabama, Georgia, Kentucky, Missouri, and Wisconsin. It also has joint ventures with companies in China, India, and Japan. The headquarters for Briggs & Stratton is located in Wauwatosa, Wisconsin.

A major component part of the gasoline engine is the spark plug. With the contract up for its current supplier, the Briggs & Stratton purchasing department in Wauwatosa, Wisconsin, decided to put the contract up for bid. At the current production level, Briggs & Stratton purchased about 2 million spark plugs a year. Because of the size of the contract, Senior Vice President Paul Neylon and Vice President and General Manager of the Small Engine Division, Joe Wright, were asked to participate in the initial discussion.

The first decision that had to be made was who would be included in the vendor decision. At the first meeting, the group agreed that both Neylon and Wright should be involved in the decision. Neylon suggested, given the size of the contract, that Senior Vice President and CFO James Brenn should also be involved in the purchase decision—at least at the stage of selecting the vendor. While the foreign joint ventures in China, India, or Japan would not be directly affected by the decision, Neylon suggested that the Vice President of International Operations, Michael Scheon, and the Vice President of European Operations should also be involved. His rationale for inclusion was that any changes in major suppliers in the United States would have ripple effects in the international operations and the same vendor chosen for the United States would be in the bidding for the international production facilities. Wright disagreed, saying that the Far-East facilities are different because of the joint ventures and that the factories there tend to utilize local vendors, not American firms.

V. P. Wright felt strongly that the buying center group should also include the plant managers at each of the five manufacturing facilities, an engineer from each facility, and the Vice President of Distribution, Sales, and Service, Curtis Larson. He wanted to know firsthand from each facility if there were any problems with the current vendor and what factors were important in the selection of a vendor. He also felt Larson was important because he could relay information about service problems with the engines and about whether the spark plug was a contributor to any service recalls or warranty repairs.

Leaving the final decision of who should be included in the buying center group to Joe Wright, attention was turned to the possible vendors. Wright suggested they consider Autolite, Robert Borsch Corporation, ACDelco, NGK, Champion, Spitfire, and Kingsborne. Each of these brands had a good reputation, was dependable, and was large enough to handle the Briggs & Stratton account.

"We will need to develop the vendor analysis criteria as well as a vendor audit list for the site visit," suggested Neylon. "But the most critical decision is: Do we go with just one vendor, or do we use two or three? With five plants, we could potentially use up to five vendors. By allowing each plant the freedom to use a different vendor, we don't have such a high risk if there are problems with one vendor in meeting our production schedule. We could easily contact one of the others to fill in any slack."

Wright countered that he felt that strategy was not cost effective. First, he didn't like the idea of each manufacturing facility choosing the brand of spark plugs. Second, he felt that by consolidating to one vendor, the company could negotiate a better price. Ordering 2 million from a single vendor would certainly be cheaper than breaking down the order to 400,000 from several vendors. Third, given the EDI relationship the company has with its current vendor, Wright did not want to share production data with four or five different vendors.

Although Neylon understood, he felt strongly that it was too risky to go with just one vendor. "At least use another vendor at one of the plants to ensure a backup vendor," he suggested.

Wright could see this was going to be a very difficult decision and would take a long time to accomplish. It was also a very critical decision that had significant ramifications for the entire company. He first would have to decide on how many people he wanted in the buying group and who they would be. He then would have to decide on the vendor analysis criteria and the vendor audit checklist. Lastly, he would have to decide about how many vendors to use.

Questions

1. Who should be in the buying center for this decision? Discuss which roles you think each person should play.
2. Develop a list of criteria you think should be included in the vendor analysis.
3. Develop the vendor audit checklist that should be used when the buying center visits the facilities of the spark plug manufacturer.
4. Should Briggs & Stratton use only one vendor or more than one? Justify your recommendation. What are the advantages and disadvantages to your decision?

Source: Fictitious case based on *Hoover's Company Profiles* of Briggs & Stratton Corporation, January 7, 2005.

Case 5-2 Baldor Electric

Baldor Electric is a manufacturer of industrial electric motors, controls, and drives that power products ranging from industrial pumps to giant rock tumblers. Baldor produces both AC and DC motors as small as 1/50 horsepower and as large as 1,500 horsepower. Baldor sells its products primarily to OEMs (original equipment manufacturers) in the agricultural, food processing, heating, air conditioning, and semiconductor industries and to independent distributors for resale as replacement parts.

Baldor has 22 factories in Germany, the United Kingdom, and the United States. Products are sold in more than 60 countries through Baldor affiliates in Australia, Europe, Latin America, and the Pacific Rim region. Sales during 2003 were $561.4 million, down from a high of $621.1 during 2001.

Baldor's primary manufacturing facility is in Fort Smith, Arkansas. This state-of-the-art facility has won several awards for innovative design and automation. The new automated manufacturing system for Baldor's electric motors has shortened lead times for new products and has given the company greater flexibility in product design. The new winding system virtually automates the whole process of winding coils, welding, insulating stator laminations, testing, and inserting the coil winding into the motor housing. The new automated line has shortened the time it takes to build a stator from 3 hours to 25 minutes.

In 1983, Baldor developed a series of energy-efficient electric motors called the "Super-E" series, but customers were not willing to pay the 20 percent premium price for the new motors. However, with energy costs on the rise and businesses facing a tough economy, Baldor has decided to launch a nationwide campaign to demonstrate the lifetime savings of the Series-E motors over the conventional motors. According to John McFarland, Baldor President and CEO, "A 30-hp motor can consume over $22,000 in electricity if operated continuously for a year. Installing a Super-E premium efficient motor can reduce the electricity cost by nearly $1,200 per year. That's close to the purchase price of a new Super-E motor."

To help customers understand the benefit of the Super-E motor, Baldor has produced a business card CD that will calculate the costs for various sizes of electric motors. In operating an electrical motor, approximately 97 percent of the lifetime costs are for electricity, while only 3 percent are for the actual motor, installation, and repair. The premium costs of buying a Series-E motor that can cut electrical costs about 9 percent per year can be erased in 12 to 18 months.

"One of our biggest challenges," according to McFarland, "is to grab the attention of the person at our customer plants who has to pay the electric bill."

To do this, Baldor Electric hired NKH&W, an advertising firm in Kansas City, to develop an advertising campaign. Using the tagline "Baldor, the answer for an energy-driven economy," NKH&W developed an ad campaign aimed at financial decision makers at the industrial companies that use electric motors. The campaign used print ads, point-of-purchase displays, product brochures, CD promotions, and a direct-mail piece. The print ad ran in industrial magazines such as *Purchasing, Consulting and Specifying Engineering, Design News,* and *Industrial Distribution.* The only piece left out of NKH&W's advertising plan was a direct email component. Company officials strongly believed that an email campaign directed at chief financial officers who paid the firm's electric bill would be successful. NKH&W, however, did not have that expertise. Its research did produce five possible vendors: Quris, Inc., iPost, Zynergy, Blue Ink Solutions, and Aviatech. The websites of each firm were given to the Vice President of Marketing at Baldor, Randall P. Breaux. Choosing the right one would be tough because Breaux did not know a lot about email marketing approaches.

Questions

1. How should Mr. Breaux evaluate the websites of each of the email marketing firms?
2. What criteria should be used? Develop a vendor analysis checklist.
3. Examine each of the following websites. Evaluate each, using the vendor analysis checklist you developed in Question 1.
   a. Quris, Inc (www.quris.com)
   b. iPost (www.ipost.com)
   c. Zynergy (www.zynergy.com)
   d. Aviatech (www.aviatech.com)
4. Which agency do you think is the best for Baldor? Justify your answer.

Sources: Baldor Electric Company, *Hoover's Company Profiles* (January 7, 2005); "New Campaigns," *B to B*, vol. 86 (June 25, 2001): 10; Larry Maloney, "Baldor's Energy Crusade," *Design News*, vol. 56 (September 3, 2001): 43; Miles Budimir, "Automation Comes to Winding Lines," *Machine Design*, vol. 74 (September 5, 2002): 88.

Marketing Segmentation

6

CHAPTER **OBJECTIVES**

1. Identify the rationale for adopting a target marketing strategy.
2. Identify the bases for consumer segmentation and offer company application examples.
3. Identify the requirements necessary for effective market segmentation.
4. Describe the three targeting strategies that companies use.
5. Describe the six positioning strategies that companies can use to position their brands in the minds of target consumers.

CHAPTER **OUTLINE**

The image of Internet users has changed substantially over time. Originally, they constituted a homogeneous segment of geeky white guys (GWGs) who enjoyed hacking, technophiles who had enough money to acquire clunky desktops and snail-paced 14.4 modems. "They were overwhelmingly male, overwhelmingly young, and overwhelmingly college educated," says Humphrey Taylor, chairman of the Harris Poll, which has been tracking the Internet audience ever since 1995.

Since then, the web community has exploded. Attracted by the increasingly affordable technology, the online population looks more and more like the country as a whole. For example, the number of women online has surpassed that of men. From wealthy suburbanites to retirees in rural areas, to people with a lower income, modest education, and blue-collar jobs—everybody in the United States surfs the web.

A new phenomenon is developing—a behavioral divide between web veterans and web newcomers. Old-timers (upscale veteran web surfers) have bookmarked a handful of favorite sites, and their web sessions are more efficient. Consequently, they spend much less time online. Time-pressed, sophisticated urban couples and elite suburban families tend to view the web as a transactional arena where they can gather information or buy big-ticket items. They patronize news, travel, and financial sites; for them, the Internet is just another information tool or purchase venue. Consumers at the lower end of the socioeconomic ladder are more likely to regard the Internet as a kind of home digi-plex: an entertainment center for fun and games, where they can surf a variety of entertainment and sweepstakes sites.

Another development is a growing gender gap on the Internet: While both men and women engage in banking, instant messaging, and in downloading music, they differ in other respects. Men are more likely to go online to buy stocks, get news, compare products, buy products, bid at auctions, and visit government websites; whereas women are more likely to send email, play games, score coupons, and get information on health, jobs, and religion. This gender gap forms early in the teenage years.[1]

6-1 Chapter Overview

With the exception of very narrow markets, one single company, however large its resources and capacity, cannot possibly serve all customers. Consumers are too numerous, and their needs and wants are too diverse. At one point in its early years, the Internet served primarily one type of consumer: male, highly educated technophiles. Advertising and selling on the Internet to this consumer were relatively easy—he was easy to target with high-tech products and banking and investment services. Today's Internet surfers are diverse: women, men, and children, white and blue collar, and of different ethnicities.

The chapter-opening vignette suggests that there may be different consumer segments that businesses can approach through the Internet and that they have to do so using different strategies. Among these segments are old timers (upscale veteran web surfers who perceive the web as a transactional arena where they can gather information, buy big-ticket items, or use it for all banking needs) and newcomers to the web (lower-class consumers who regard the Internet as an entertainment center for fun and games). Another way to slice the Internet pie is by gender: men who go online to buy stocks, get news, compare products, buy products, bid at auctions, and visit government websites, and women who send email, play games, score coupons, and get information on health, jobs, and religion.

Just like the Internet, the entire marketplace is diverse: Consumers have unique needs and different attitudes, interests, and opinions. Given this diversity, it is important for companies to focus on those segments that they can serve most effectively and to design goods and services with these segments in mind—that is, to engage in **target marketing.**

> **Target marketing:** The process of focusing on those segments that the company can serve most effectively and designing products, services, and marketing programs with these segments in mind.

Companies use target marketing to:

1. Identify segments of consumers who are similar with regard to key traits and who would respond well to a product and related marketing mix (market segmentation)

2. Select the segments that the company can serve most efficiently and develop products tailored to each (market targeting)
3. Offer the products to the market, communicating through the marketing mix the products' traits and benefits that differentiate the products in the consumer's mind (market positioning)

Market segmentation, targeting, and positioning constitute the focus of this chapter. Section 6-2 focuses on market segmentation, identifying the requirements for successful segmentation and the bases for segmentation. Section 6-3 addresses the three strategies used in targeting: differentiated, concentrated, and undifferentiated. Finally, Section 6-4 addresses the different approaches to positioning brands in relation to other competing products, based on product traits and benefits that are relevant to the consumer.

6-2 Market Segmentation

The marketplace consists of consumers with unique needs and preferences. Firms find that it is difficult to satisfy all consumers; consequently, they simplify their marketing task by appealing to those consumers whose needs are most effectively met by their own offering. Market **segmentation** involves identifying consumers who are similar with regard to key traits, such as product-related needs and wants, and who would respond well to a similar marketing mix.

Segmentation: The process of identifying consumers and/or markets that are similar with regard to key traits, such as product-related needs and wants, and that would respond well to a product and related marketing mix.

It is important to realize that not all market segments are financially feasible to explore because they are either too small or their characteristics are not that different from the population as a whole or other market segments. As will be illustrated in Chapter 7, "Marketing Research," most companies conduct some type of segmentation study to identify profiles of different types of consumers that the company could target. Marketing managers are especially interested in identifying those segments composed of consumers who are heavy product users. For example, KitchenAid-sponsored research suggested that the company should focus on "the culinary-involved" consumers, a segment of heavy users of kitchen appliances. The company successfully targeted these consumers, and its sales experienced a double-digit increase.[2] For other product examples, income may be the primary basis for segmentation. Luxury brands are targeted at high-income consumers. Yet, other products are targeted at the mass market—the manufacturer mass-produces the product, promotes it, and distributes it widely to the mass market. But even these products need to be appropriately targeted, as Figure 6-1 illustrates. The following section addresses the different bases for identifying market segments that share similar needs and wants.

6-2a Levels of Segmentation

As mentioned in the preceding paragraphs, the marketplace consists of consumers with unique needs and preferences. Individual buyers have unique product needs, and a company that has all the resources available at its discretion—including time—can potentially target each prospective buyer individually. However, for most firms, that is a difficult and costly proposition. It is virtually impossible to satisfy every consumer, and thus companies will simplify their marketing task by appealing to those consumers whose needs are most effectively met by their own offering. Some firms may not even segment the market at all, marketing to the masses. Figure 6-2 identifies the three levels of segmentation: mass marketing, segment marketing, and micromarketing.

Mass marketing is the shotgun approach to segmentation. It involves identifying the product-related preferences of most consumers in order to then target the product broadly to all consumers with the maximum likelihood of success. Mass marketing allows firms to subsequently target these consumers while incurring minimal costs; the outcome of this strategy is ultimately low prices for the consumer or high profit margins for the seller. Mass marketing by itself is a rather difficult proposition in industrialized markets, where consumers are highly differentiated in their preferences. In the aggregate, there is a move from

Mass marketing: The process of identifying the product-related preferences of most consumers in order to then target the product broadly to all consumers with the maximum likelihood of success.

Figure 6-1
Even for commodity-type products like milk, it is important to understand the market segments that need to be reached with advertising and what type of message will appeal to each market segment.

Source: Courtesy of Bozell Worldwide, Inc. as agent for the National Fluid Milk Processor Promotion Board.

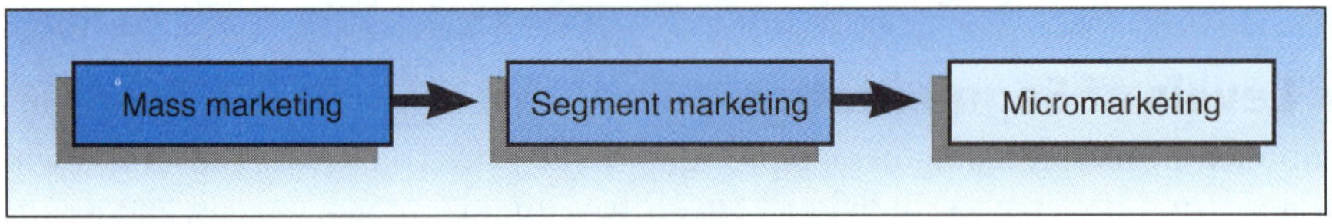

Figure 6-2
Levels of Segmentation

INTERACTIVE FIGURE

Segment marketing: A process that involves identifying consumers who are similar with regard to key traits, such as product-related needs and wants, and who would respond well to a similar marketing mix.

Micromarketing: A process that involves a microanalysis of the customer and customer-specific marketing.

mass marketing to micromarketing. But, for individual firms, a mix of strategies is necessary: for example, Procter & Gamble uses more precise segmentation approaches that coexist with mass marketing. In developing countries, however, mass marketing plays a key role—a central role in some areas.[3]

Segment marketing involves identifying consumers who are similar with regard to key traits, such as product-related needs and wants, and who would respond well to a similar marketing mix. For example, BMW offers the Mini to young consumers who have just finished college, the 300 series to young professionals, and the 500 and 700 series to mid-level professionals and families. Section 6-2 in this chapter focuses primarily on segment marketing.

Micromarketing involves a microanalysis of the customer, and it involves customer-specific marketing. Micromarketers need more information about prospective customers than mass marketers; therefore, they utilize databases to create and update customer information in a searchable form.[4] In its most extreme form, micromarketing involves market-

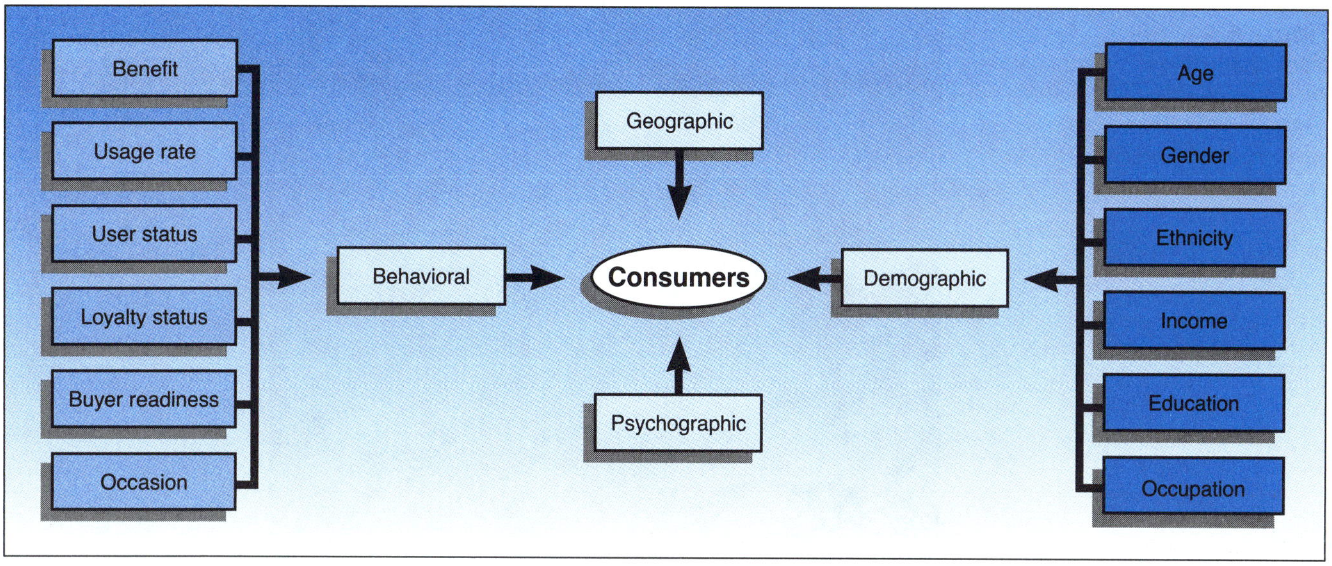

Figure 6-3
Bases for Segmentation

ing to the individual, in effect, customizing the marketing mix to the needs of that individual. As such, micromarketing is more a targeting strategy than a segmentation strategy, unless it is a question of identifying the individuals who make it profitable for the firm to tailor its offerings.

6-2b Bases for Segmentation

The purpose of segmentation is to identify clusters of consumers that respond in a similar fashion to a company's marketing strategies. Identifying individual market segments will enable the company to produce products that meet the precise needs of target consumers with a marketing mix that is appropriately tailored for those segments. The company typically conducts extensive marketing research to identify such segments.

In the process of analyzing consumer demand and identifying clusters of consumers that respond similarly to marketing strategies, firms must identify those bases for segmentation that are most relevant for their goods or services. Figure 6-3 identifies the bases for segmentation that companies could use in the process of analyzing their markets.

Demographic Segmentation Demographics are statistics that describe the population, such as age, gender, race, ethnicity, income, education, occupation, social class, lifecycle stage, and household size. There are many differences among consumers with regard to demographic variables. The following examples demonstrate how these differences have important implications for marketing.

Two major **demographic segmentation** variables are age and lifecycle stage. As individuals age and enter different lifecycle stages, their product preferences also change.

Demographic segmentation: The process of identifying market segments based on age, gender, race, income, education, occupation, social class, lifecycle stage, and household size.

In Chapter 2, "The Environment of Marketing in the Twenty-First Century," an age categorization of socio-demographic groups examined Generations X and Y, baby boomers, empty nesters, and seniors. Each of these categories has been identified as a viable target segment for certain products. For example, Generation Y consumers tend to spend more on entertainment and television sets, while baby boomers and Generation X consumers' spending has a family focus. The needs and preferences of each segment vary substantially. Generation Y consumers, for instance, have grown up in a media-saturated, brand-conscious world. The intense marketing efforts aimed at Generation Y have taught them to assume the worst about companies trying to coax them into buying something. Consequently, advertisements meant to look youthful and fun may come off as merely opportunistic, as PepsiCo's "Generation Next" campaign was viewed. This group of consumers responds better to humor, irony, and the "unvarnished" truth, as Sprite has done

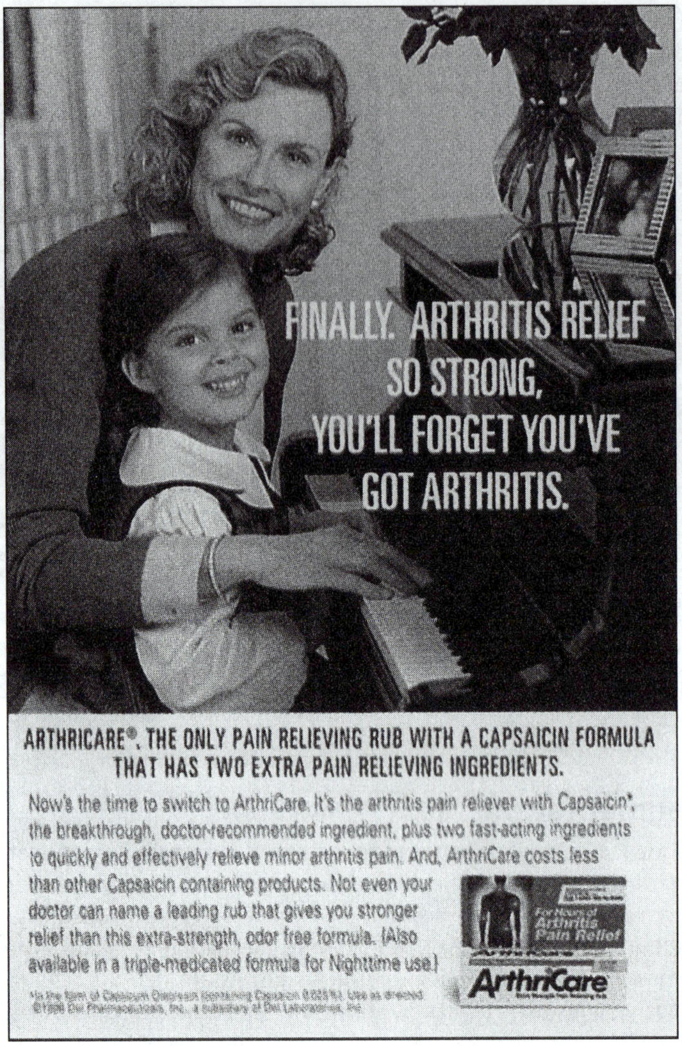

Figure 6-4
Many products, such as ArthriCare, are marketed based on a person's age or lifecycle stage.
Source: Reprinted by permission of Del Labs.

with advertisements that parody celebrity endorsers and carry the tagline, "Image is nothing. Thirst is everything. Obey your thirst."[5] These consumers tend to be more blasé and less susceptible to influence.

Baby boomers, who are in a different lifecycle stage, have different interests and concerns. As baby boomers enter the 55- to 74-year-old age category, it is expected that there will be a surge in the number of affluent households, with incomes over $100,000. These consumers have already demonstrated a penchant for trying to delay the aging process. As they move into their 60s, they will almost certainly avail themselves of such cosmetic procedures as Botox shots to erase wrinkles, skin treatments at health spas, and highly personalized health-care services (to illustrate, see Figure 6-4—ArthriCare is targeted to this segment). Even periodic house calls by a doctor to check on health status may not be a stretch for this market.[6]

Products such as clothing, cosmetics, and hair products are among the obvious products that are tailored based on a person's gender. Companies may elect to target either men or women with their products. Yet, often success in one category may compel the company to target the other gender. For example, clothing brands such as Liz Claiborne and DKNY, which have traditionally targeted women, find their men's lines to be increasingly successful. Alternatively, clothing brands such as Armani, which have traditionally targeted men, are quickly becoming established in women's fashions.

Even Nike, a company that has traditionally targeted hardcore sports guys, is now attempting to actively court women. Nike has recently plunged into the yoga market with everything from shoes to balance boards. The company's still-unfolding women's initiative is considered to be its most important strategic undertaking of the new millennium: Every new resource allocation at Nike now is considered with at least one eye toward the female consumer. Although women's products have been generating less than 20 percent of Nike's overall sales, the company's goal is to double that number in the next few years. Nike is planning to target women very differently than it targets men. The company is in the process of opening new retail stores, called Nike-Goddess, where the company can display its array of products in a carefully designed, exclusive environment.[7]

Targeting men and women with different products and marketing strategies makes good business sense. Women are receptive to different messages than men and have different interests than men. One illustration of these differences is in Internet usage (see Table 6-1). Notice that each gender is subdivided into five different market segments. When various market segments are identified, descriptive names are often given to each group. For instance, the male Internet segment that has a high level of computer usage and likes to use the Internet to research investments and locate software is called "Bits and Bytes." This segment has a special interest in computers, and most of their hobbies are computer related, so calling this market segment "Bits and Bytes" makes sense. However, the female group that uses the Internet for chats and a personal web page is called "Social Sally." Their lives revolve around making friends, and the Internet is a means of socializing. Understanding the broad differences between men and women and the differences between the behavioral segments within each gender category helps marketers target these segments more efficiently. The marketing message designed for the "Bits and Bytes" male segment will look different than the marketing message designed for the "Social Sally" segment.

As seen in Chapter 4, "Consumer Behavior," subcultures constitute important markets of consumers with shared value systems that are based on ethnicity and/or common backgrounds. Marketing managers increasingly focus on individual ethnicities, directing their marketing efforts to meet their specific needs. For example, J. P. Morgan Chase focuses its marketing efforts on multicultural market segments. Its corporate branding campaign targets Hispanics in New York and Texas with Spanish-language TV, radio, and print advertising, and is actively targeting Asian consumers. Met Life estimates that ethnic consumers account for about 30 percent of the company's retail business, including insurance and retirement products, and focuses its marketing efforts on these segments. MasterCard International launched a television campaign on Spanish-language networks, which adapted its "Priceless" general-market effort with new Spanish-language commercials. And

TABLE 6-1

Male and Female Segments on the Internet

Male Segments	Usage Situations	Favorite Materials
Bits and Bytes	Computers and hobbies	Investments, discovery, software
Practical Pete	Personal productivity	Investments, company listings
Viking Garner	Competing and winning	Games, chat, software
Sensitive Sam	Help family and friends	Investments, government information
World Citizen	Connecting with world	Discovery, software, investments
Female Segments	**Usage Situations**	**Favorite Materials**
Social Sally	Making friends	Chat and personal web page
New Age Crusader	Fight for causes	Books and government information
Cautious Mom	Nurture children	Cooking and medical facts
Playful Pretender	Role-play	Chat and games
Master Producer	Job productivity	White pages, government information

Source: Scott M. Smith and David B. Whitlark, "Men and Women Online: What Makes Them Click?" *Marketing Research,* vol. 13, no. 2 (Summer 2001): 20–25.

Marketing Illustration 6-1

The High-Income Consumer

In the past, it was easier to identify who was wealthy and who was not. Being invited to the right parties meant that one's fortune qualified for the wealthy status. Today, wealth is not displayed as readily and is not as readily identifiable. Consider Jeffrey Cohen: He commutes by train daily to his job at Information Builders Inc., a family-owned computer software company employing 900 people in New York City. He drives a modest car, lives in a good though hardly fashionable neighborhood, hates the opera, and loves professional wrestling; in other words, his life does not resemble Robin Leach's *Lifestyles of the Rich and Famous*. Today's high-income consumer segment consists of a dynamic range of individuals with very different preferences and spending habits. Many of them are conservative spenders who have accumulated wealth through saving.

An important trait of affluent consumers is that they are difficult to reach because of their ability to build screens to block out unwanted information; companies have difficulty reaching these very busy people. Partnerships with swank sporting events, exclusive private parties, and luxurious sweepstakes constitute one effective approach to reach them. Examples are sponsorships of the ATP tennis tournament, the Mercedes Golf Championship in Hawaii, and the CARTFEDEX Series motor sports races. Altruism also motivates affluent consumers. Prior to the annual Mercedes-Benz golf championship in Hawaii, national dealers invited Mercedes owners and prospective buyers to participate in national and local tournaments. The entry fee for the tournaments was donated to the March of Dimes.

Most affluent consumers expect value and unique features for the money they spend. Silversea Cruise Line attracts seasoned travelers with its unique global itineraries and all-inclusive price structure. Members of the Silversea's Venetian Society are also offered special complimentary land excursions designed to reflect the culture of the countries they are visiting. Past events have included a Turkish wedding, Greek street fairs, and wine tasting in a French chateau.

Affluent consumers expect special rewards in return for their patronage. Merrill Lynch's Cash Management Account (CMA) Visa Signature Reward program targets its best customers while also encouraging loyalty. This program gives one point for every dollar spent on the CMA debit card. More popular awards are golf sessions with professional golfer Tom Layman, custom cruise packages, race car driving lessons with Richard Petty, and tours of the Galapagos Islands, as well as custom suits and ties.

How should firms most effectively market to these consumers? A study recently attempted to discern spending patterns of the elite affluent, defined as those with a net worth of more than $10 million, compared to the merely rich. The study suggests that reaching these markets through direct marketing is not effective because fewer than one in four open their own mail. Instead, the elite affluent are most effectively reached through publications such as *Elite Traveler*, which reaches them on private jets and yachts and in professional sports locker rooms.

Sources: Sandra O'Loughlin, "Clearly, These Are Consumers Worth Banking On," *Brandweek*, vol. 45, no. 6 (February 9, 2004): 1; Jeanie Casison, "Wealthy and Wise," *Incentive*, vol. 173, no. 1 (January 1999): 78–81.

Washington Mutual, which already advertises in Spanish and Chinese, plans to create new campaigns in Vietnamese and French.[8]

Product price is often a determinant of whether the company will target higher- or lower-income consumer segments. In general, luxury designers target their products at high-income consumers. Bvlgari, Fendi, Hermès, Prada, and Escada brands retail for prices prohibitive for middle- and lower-income consumers. The converse is not necessarily true: Lower-priced products do not necessarily appeal only to lower-income consumers. Wal-Mart consumers come from all economic strata of society, all with the same goal: to get value at everyday-low prices. Marketing Illustration 6-1 offers a glimpse at the main characteristics of high-income consumers: desire for uniqueness and diversity.

Psychographic segmentation: The use of values, attitudes, interests, and other cultural variables to segment consumers.

Psychographic Segmentation Demographics are closely linked to **psychographic segmentation,** which includes lifestyles, values, attitudes, interests, and opinions. It is difficult to describe psychographics without demographics. Cultural variables such as religion, norms, and even language influence consumer product preferences as well.

One vehicle for segmenting consumers psychographically that was addressed in detail in Chapter 4, "Consumer Behavior," is the VALS typology provided by SRI Consulting Business Intelligence. The VALS typology (www.sric-bi.com/VALS/) categorizes respondents based on resources and on the extent to which they are action oriented. The VALS psychographic categories and their descriptors are listed in Table 6-2.

TABLE 6-2
VALS Psychographic Categories

VALS Category	Characteristics
Innovators	Successful, sophisticated, and receptive to new technologies, their purchases reflect cultivated tastes for upscale products.
Thinkers	Educated, conservative, and practical consumers, they value knowledge and responsibility and look for durability, functionality, and value.
Achievers	Goal-oriented, conservative, and committed to career and family, they favor established, prestige products that demonstrate success to peers.
Experiencers	Young, enthusiastic, and impulsive, they seek variety and excitement, and spend substantially on fashion, entertainment, and socializing.
Believers	Conservative, conventional, and focusing on tradition, family, religion, and community, they prefer established brands, favoring American products.
Strivers	Trendy and fun loving, they are concerned about others' opinions and approval.
Makers	Self-sufficient, they have the skill and energy to carry out projects, respect authority, and are unimpressed by material possessions.
Survivors	Concerned with safety and security, they focus on meeting needs rather than fulfilling desires, are brand loyal, and purchase discounted products.

Marketing managers must understand the psychographic and demographic makeup of their **target market** in order to effectively address its needs. Ukrop's Super Markets in Virginia use a different appeal to consumers in the various neighborhoods where they have stores. Their merchandise mix varies in order to best address the needs of each neighborhood. For example, in their upscale neighborhoods, they carry exclusive French cheeses, such as Chaumes, Morbier, and Roquefort. In their more bohemian neighborhoods, they carry a wider selection of natural foods. And in their ethnic neighborhoods, they attempt to carry products that appeal to the respective consumers. Figure 6-5 illustrates the store's kosher refrigerated selection.

Target market: Consumers and/or markets that are similar in aspects relevant to the company.

Figure 6-5
The refrigerated section at Ukrop's offers kosher products to a large Jewish community living in the neighborhood.

Source: Courtesy of Ukrop's Super Markets, Inc.

Figure 6-6
Francis Tetard, a high-sensation seeker, in his airplane, Bébé Jodel.

Another example of a psychodemographic segment is the high-sensation seeker. High-sensation seekers thrive on high stimulation and hedonic consumption. Their behavior translates into a windfall for manufacturers of high-risk products and entertainment—and even for the armies of psychologists, psychiatrists, and geneticists who specialize in sensation seekers. Medical research has found that the traditional attribution of high-sensation seeking to high testosterone levels is, in fact, a myth and that people hooked on thrills have a low cortisol level, which is remedied promptly by high excitement. Marvin Zuckerman, a professor of clinical psychology who has studied high-sensation seekers for four decades and developed well-known psychometric measures for sensation seeking, has identified certain common characteristics of the sensation-seeking market. High-sensation seekers drive fast, are drawn to excitement and to exciting people, and, "in every aspect of their lives, they are looking for the latest thing."[9]

Francis Tetard, a professional living in the Montpellier region in Southern France, epitomizes the high-sensation seeker. He has traversed continents in search of excitement, flying into blazing volcanoes and speeding through banana plantations in Central Africa. He spends his free time as staff of the local Aero Club, flying gliders, planes, and helicopters. His current personal excitement arsenal includes a helicopter, a glider, and his almost-family-member historic airplane, Bébé Jodel (see Figure 6-6). When Francis is not airborne, surveying the sea, canyons, mountains, beaches, and lakes in the region, his secondary passion is tinkering with the respective high-sensation facilitators.

Yet another psychodemographic market segment that is a political force, but also an important and loyal market segment, is the New Right, a core constituent of the political right. See Marketing Illustration 6-2 for a review of the New Right market segment.

Behavioral Segmentation Behavioral segmentation is used to identify clusters of consumers who seek the same product benefits or who use or consume the product in a similar fashion. Behavioral variables include benefits sought, user rate, usage status, loyalty status, buyer-readiness stage, and occasion.

Benefit segmentation: The process of identifying market segments based on important differences between the benefits sought by the target market from purchasing a particular product.

Benefit segmentation is defined as the process of identifying market segments based on important differences between the benefits sought by the target market from purchasing a particular product. Marketers who understand the motivation behind consumer purchases will be able to send the appropriate message to the relevant market segments. In the previous example in Table 6-1, classifying men and women using the Internet, the benefit sought by each segment is different. "Bits and Bytes" men use the Internet to find out more

Marketing Illustration 6-2

The New Right: An Important Market Segment

The New Right is a core constituent of the political right. It differentiates itself from traditional conservatism by being far more militant, concerned with social conservatism—with family and morality issues—and is more religious. The New Right emerged as a result of concerns with national security, of anxieties related to economic well-being and morality. The humiliation America has experienced at the hands of less technologically advanced militants who decimated military barracks in Saudi Arabia and collapsed the World Trade Center were perceived by the New Right as directly linked to the decaying moral fabric of the United States. The Clinton years were perceived by the New Right as the apogee of moral decay. The New Right is anti-elite, anti-intellectual, and against big government; it is socially nostalgic, and it believes in material blessings for those who love the Lord and live right.

The New Right is an important market segment that cannot be ignored. It is a substantial economic power that believes in accumulating wealth and displaying material possessions. According to Jerry Falwell, "Ownership of property is biblical. Competition in business is biblical. Ambitious and successful business management is clearly outlined as a part of God's plan for His people."

One very original business that was created with this market in mind was Heritage Village, USA, in South Carolina. The symbolism of the name suggested religion, patriotism, and a sacred, simple community. The village combined religion with consumption: Its mall lured consumers to shop in an ethereal environment of floating clouds. Related sites appealing to this market segment are those that celebrate the history of the Civil War or American history in general. Colonial Williamsburg is a popular reminder of the simple life on the new continent.

Efforts to target the New Right have met with an enthusiastic response. In addition to responding positively to religious and history-related appeals, the New Right consumers have responded well to businesses that do not allow the sale of alcohol and those that are closed on Sunday, allowing their employees a day of rest.

Source: Thomas C. O'Guinn and Russell W. Belk, "Heaven on Earth: Consumption at Heritage Village, USA," Journal of Consumer Research, vol. 16, no. 2 (September 1989): 227–239.

about the latest computer models and software, to keep up with their hobbies, and to manage their investments. The "Viking Garner" segment seeks opportunities to chat with others and to play games. "Social Sally" women seek similar benefits: making friends and chatting, as well as sharing their news with friends and relatives through their web page. "New Age Crusaders" use the Internet to fight for their causes and to find related books and government information.

Usage rate segmentation is defined as the process of segmenting markets based on the extent to which consumers are nonusers, occasional users, medium users, or heavy users of a product. Segments of consumers identified as heavy users of a product category would constitute prime target markets for new brands in the category. For example, Taco Bell introduced the Grilled Stuft Burrito backed by an advertising campaign with the tag line "Ooh, fajitas," and Border Bowls, with beans and salad topped with meat and cheese, to its heavy users—consumers between the ages of 18 and 34, who wanted "the beef to be beefier, the beans to be chunkier, the restaurants to be cleaner, and the service to be faster," according to company research.[10]

Usage rate segmentation: The process of segmenting markets based on the extent to which consumers are nonusers, occasional users, medium users, or heavy users of a product.

User status segmentation is defined as the process of determining consumer status—as users of competitors' products, ex-users, potential users, first-time users, or regular users. While the ideal consumer may be considered to be the regular user, companies should not limit their marketing efforts to just reinforcing the user behavior of this market. While it is true that introducing a product for the first time to a market of nonusers will create enormous and costly challenges for the company, in that it has to educate consumers about the product and convince them to buy, it is also true that such markets may present great potential. In the previous example, Taco Bell decided to promote the Border Bowl to markets other than its traditional 18- to 34-year-olds; in the process, it managed to attract a nontraditional customer: the 50-year-old male. Overall, the company was able to achieve 9 to 10 percent same-store gains.[11]

User status segmentation: The process of determining consumer status—as users of competitors' products, ex-users, potential users, first-time users, or regular users.

Loyalty segmentation is defined as the process of segmenting the market based on the degree of brand preference, commitment, retention, allegiance, and the extent to which

Loyalty segmentation: The process of segmenting the market based on the degree of consumer loyalty to the brand.

consumers engage in repeat purchases.[12] Very loyal consumers are very valuable to companies; these are the consumers that the company does not need to persuade to buy its products. Marketing managers strive to create consumer loyalty by offering consistently high-quality goods and services. Marketers also tie the consumer to the brand by offering loyalty programs that direct individual consumer's consumption to the company. For example, airlines and hotel chains ensure consumer loyalty by offering rewards tied to the extensive use of that airline or hotel chain. And supermarkets offer various promotions only to consumers who use their loyalty cards frequently.

Buyer-readiness stage segmentation: The process of segmenting the market based on individuals' stage of readiness to buy a product.

Buyer-readiness stage segmentation is defined as the process of segmenting the market based on individuals' stage of readiness to buy a product. For LASIK (laser-assisted) surgery aimed at correcting hyperopia, myopia, and astigmatism, the market can be segmented into consumers who are not aware of the service, consumers who are aware of it and may need it in the future, consumers who are aware of it but will never need it, consumers who are interested to find out more about LASIK surgery, consumers who would like to have the surgery but cannot afford it, and consumers who intend to have the surgery, among others. A company such as Virginia Eye Institute, a heavy promoter of this type of surgery, will need to create different promotion campaigns for each viable segment. Examples of such campaigns are awareness campaigns for those who do not know about this type of surgery or about the fact that Virginia Eye Institute offers this surgery, informational campaigns for consumers who might want additional information, and persuasive campaigns for those who are still debating about whether they should have this type of surgery.

Occasion segmentation: The process of segmenting based on the time or the occasion when the product should be purchased or consumed.

Occasion segmentation is defined as segmentation based on the time or the occasion when the product should be purchased or consumed. For example, champagne is normally consumed to celebrate a special occasion, on New Year's Eve, or at Sunday brunch. Cosmetics companies increase their advertising, promoting extensively before Mother's Day. Different types of candy are promoted for special occasions. For Halloween, candy is sold in large packages that include small portions. And for Valentine's Day, candy is presented in red, heart-shaped packages (see Figure 6-7). Table 6-3 summarizes the various behavioral segmentation strategies.

Geographic segmentation: Market segmentation based on geographic location, such as country or region.

Geographic Segmentation

Geographic segmentation is defined as segmentation based on geographic location, such as region, state, or city. Small companies typically limit their marketing to segments within the proximity of the firm. Large companies may elect

Figure 6-7

Valentine's Day display at the local supermarket.

Source: Courtesy of Ukrop's Super Markets, Inc.

TABLE 6-3

Behavioral Segmentation Strategies

Behavioral Segmentation	Definition	Typical Categories
Benefit segmentation	Market segments based on important differences between the benefits the target market seeks from purchasing a particular product	Varies
Usage rate segmentation	Market segments based on the extent, or quantity, to which consumers use a product	Nonusers Occasional users Medium users Heavy users
User status segmentation	Market segments based on the current usage of a product	User of competing brands Ex-user Potential user First-time user Regular user
Loyalty status segmentation	Market segment based on the degree of brand preference, commitment, retention, and allegiance to a brand	No loyalty Low loyalty Medium loyalty High loyalty
Buyer-readiness stage segmentation	Market segments based on individuals' stage of readiness to buy a product	Consumers who are not aware Consumers who are aware of it but will never need it Consumers who are aware of it and may need it in the future Consumers who are interested and want to learn more Consumers who are ready to purchase
Occasion segmentation	Market segments based on the time or the occasion when a product should be purchased or consumed	Varies

to target various regional segments differently, based on regional preferences. For example, Coke and Pepsi taste differently in different parts of the United States and in the world—sweeter in the South of the United States, and with a stronger lemon flavor in Europe.

Often, firms are organized geographically, with different divisions specializing in particular markets. In other examples, Stihl, a manufacturer of chainsaws, sells its products primarily to individual consumers in the southeastern United States and to professional loggers in the northwestern United States. The planners of the Louisiana Folklife Festival would use geographic segmentation to target ads to people in Louisiana and surrounding states close to Monroe (see Figure 6-8).

Multiattribute segmentation: The process of segmenting the market by using multiple segmentation variables.

Multiattribute Segmentation

Multiattribute segmentation is defined as a process that uses multiple bases for segmenting consumers. For instance, companies rarely use only demographic variables in their segmentation approaches. Typically, they also add psychographic and behavioral variables to the demographic information to determine the

Figure 6-8
In promoting the Louisiana Folklife Festival, a geographic segmentation strategy was used, placing the ads in media outlets in the geographic area surrounding Monroe, Louisiana.

Source: Sample print advertisement courtesy of The Miles Agency and Alliance One Advertising, Inc.

best approach to reach their target market. For example, Reynolds aluminum foil is targeted to women ages 24 and above—women who cook, or at least store food, that is.

Many management-consulting firms have come up with systems for segmenting consumers using multiple bases for segmentation: demographics, psychographics, and behavior. Two very popular classification systems based on ZIP code are PRIZM (offered by the firm Claritas) and ACORN (offered by ESRI Business Information Solutions). PRIZM was the first lifestyle segmentation system and is still widely used. Based on the principle of "birds of a feather flock together" (i.e., that people of similar demographic and lifestyle characteristics tend to live near each other), PRIZM assigns every neighborhood in the United States to one of 62 clusters. Each cluster describes the predominant demographics and lifestyles of the people living in that neighborhood. Among the classifications used by PRIZM are rural, small town, second cities, suburbs, urban, and upper market, middle market, and lower market in terms of social rank—based on income, household wealth, education, occupation, and home value.

ACORN is based on the same principle. According to the ACORN classification, one of the authors of this text lives in an area referred to as Twentysomethings, described as "still unsettled, this market is just completing college or starting their first, postgraduate job. Most are single, mobile, city dwellers, who are young, active, and urban. Education is the key to this small market's success. Rent is generally below average. This is the second-ranked market for fast food, and they are also dieters. They read books, but the media of choice is television."[13] Most of the author's colleagues in the business school live in areas classified as Upper Income Empty Nesters and Prosperous Baby Boomers. To find out how your ZIP code is classified, refer to ESRI's website (www.esribis.com).

6-2c Segmenting Business Markets

Business markets can be segmented based on similar variables as used with the consumer market: geographic location, behavioral dimensions such as benefits sought, user status and usage rate, buyer-readiness stage, degree of loyalty, and other adapted dimensions. For example, instead of demographics, segmentation can take place based on firm size and industry sector.

A recent study identified four behavioral segments of business markets:[14]

- The **relationship-seeking segment** consists of relatively sophisticated service-users who believe that the user-provider relationship is very important. This segment has a "realistic" level of expectations for the service requirements and does not expect to pay a low price—these consumers understand the trade-off between service levels and price.
- The **price-sensitive segment** is looking for low prices but also has low service requirements; it wants the work done at the lowest possible cost.
- The **high-expectation service segment** is the most demanding and needs extensive customer focus, placing considerable demands on service providers while demanding low prices.
- The **customer-focus needs segment** is prepared to pay for higher-than-average service that is tailored to meet users' needs.

Relationship-seeking segment: Business segment that consists of relatively sophisticated service users who believe that the user-provider relationship is very important. They have a "realistic" level of expectations for the service requirements and do not expect to pay a low price.

Price-sensitive segment: Business segment that looks for low prices but that also has low service requirements; these users want the work done at the lowest possible cost.

High-expectation service segment: Business segment that is the most demanding and needs extensive customer focus, placing considerable demands on service providers while demanding low prices.

Customer-focus needs segment: Business segment that is prepared to pay for higher-than-average service that is tailored to meet the users' needs.

6-2d Requirements for Successful Segmentation

Identifying the bases that the company will use for segmentation is important. Equally important is ensuring that the segments are large enough to warrant investment, that they are relatively stable over time, and that they are going to respond to the company's marketing efforts. In order for segmentation to be effective, marketing managers need to assess the measurability, substantiality, stability over time, accessibility, and actionability of the market segments.

Measurability is defined as the degree to which individual market segments are easy to identify and measure, or the ability to estimate the size of market segments. In highly industrialized countries, such as the United States, it is relatively easy to measure or estimate market segments. Government and marketing data are readily available to help companies in the process of making decisions: Census data are reasonably accurate, television viewing data can be relatively easily collected with the cooperation of cable companies, and shopping behavior can readily be evaluated by linking UPC data to loyalty cards' use.

Measurability: The ability to estimate the size of a market segment.

Yet, even in our data-rich environment, marketers will find that important segments may not be fully measurable. For example, a company advertising to Hispanic consumers can only partially estimate its reach in markets where there is a large seasonal and unregistered migrant population. Companies targeting their products to gay and lesbian consumers find that only about 6 percent of the population self-identifies as gay and lesbian. Limiting targeting strategies to the self-identified segment ignores the large closeted gay and lesbian segment.

Substantiality is defined as the degree to which a segment is large enough and profitable enough to warrant investment. After measuring the size of a market segment, the company needs to determine whether the segment is large enough to earn a decent return on its investment. For example, it would not make sense for a retailer to position itself as specializing in selling clove cigarettes because the market for clove cigarettes is very limited, even in large cities.

Substantiality: The extent to which the market is large enough to warrant investment.

Figure 6-9
Leopard skins that were once prominently displayed now are placed on a child's bed, out of visitors' view.

Stability: The extent to which preferences are stable, rather than changing, in a market segment.

Accessibility: The ability to communicate with and reach the target market.

Actionability: The extent to which the target market segment is responsive to the marketing strategies used.

Differential response: The extent to which market segments respond differently to marketing strategies.

Stability is defined as the degree to which segment consumer preferences are stable over time. This is an important consideration in an environment where products are in different lifecycle stages and where preferences are continuously changing. For decades until the late 1980s, dealers of artifacts and antiques prominently displayed elephant tusks and rare leopard skins in Fifth Avenue and 57th Street store windows in Manhattan. Chinatown retailers experienced brisk sales of ornately carved elephant tusks. However, a change in public opinion took place after the U.S. government and various international organizations revealed the cruelty of these trades and stressed the distinct possibility that these animals may become extinct. The movie and book *Gorillas in the Mist*, also popular in the 1980s, further convinced consumers that the trade in rare animals is cruel. The trade in objects made from rare animals fell out of favor with the consuming public, and this once-substantial market segment quickly diminished (see Figure 6-9).

It is important to note that segments do change with time, especially early in the product lifecycle or when new technologies appear. As discussed in the chapter-opening vignette, the traditional segments of Internet users changed substantially after the technology became more affordable and computers were bought by the mass market.

Accessibility is defined as the ability to communicate with and reach the target market. Some markets cannot be accessed with marketing communications. A large proportion of children cannot easily be reached through marketing communication. Many children spend their weekdays in daycares that have a policy not to expose children to television programming. At home, their parents may decide not to allow them to watch television programs and show them, instead, educational videos. In their everyday lives, these children may never be exposed to children's advertising.

Working mothers are also difficult to target: Most have little time to watch television and read women's magazines. They spend their free time catching up on home chores and tending to their spouse and/or children, rather than in front of the television set or leafing through nonessential magazines. Marketers often can reach them only relatively late during the consumer decision-making process, when they are already at the store and they may have already made their purchase decision.

Actionability is defined as the extent to which marketers are capable of designing effective programs that can effectively serve the market segment. An important question that marketing managers must ask is whether they can effectively serve the market segment. Do they have the product that the market needs? Are they pricing it based on the needs of the market? Can they deliver on time? A small manufacturer of low-priced cigarettes in Virginia found it very difficult to compete effectively with Philip Morris and other established lower-priced brands such as Bailey's cigarettes. Cigarette retailers asked for high slotting fees to place the product on their limited cigarette shelf space or simply refused to carry the brand. Instead, the company found that its strategy was actionable in Russia, where the appeal of "Made in Virginia, U.S.A." worked very well with target consumers, and retailers were eager to have yet another cheap brand that would appeal to Russian consumers.

Differential response is defined as the extent to which market segments are easy to distinguish from each other and respond differently to company marketing strategies. If consumers are similar and/or have identical preferences—and this is hardly ever the case—there is no need for target marketing. Even the market for olive oil is carefully segmented based on consumer preferences with regard to country of origin, whether the oil is extra virgin or mild, and the oil's flavor and use (see Figure 6-10).

6-3 Target Marketing Decisions

Companies that have ample resources can, and often do, address the needs of all segments of consumers. Procter & Gamble and Kraft attempt to target all consumers with the products they sell, filling the supermarket and discount store shelf space with what seemingly are competing brands and saturating the media with their communication, meeting all related needs of target consumers at a nice profit. Other companies with sufficient

Figure 6-10
Olive oil market segments have distinct preferences: virgin, extra virgin, Italian, and Greek.

Source: Courtesy of Ukrop's Super Markets, Inc.

resources choose to focus on one well-established brand, improving it continuously, offering alternatives under the same umbrella brand name. Boeing uses such a strategy and, to date, it has only one true direct competitor—Airbus Industries. Not all companies have the resources of the companies mentioned here. Frequently, small and medium-size businesses are quite successful by best addressing the needs of one segment, or a niche. One common trait of all these companies is that they research very closely their consumers, and target and position their products accordingly.

Companies can use three main strategies to target their markets: differentiated, concentrated, and undifferentiated.

6-3a Differentiated Marketing Strategy

Differentiated marketing: A targeting strategy identifying market segments with different preferences for a particular product category and targeting each segment with different brands and different marketing strategies.

Companies that use a **differentiated marketing** strategy identify, or even create, market segments that want different benefits from a product and target them with different brands, using different marketing strategies. Some companies have the necessary resources to offer at least one product to every conceivable market segment. Procter & Gamble, for example, offers a variety of laundry detergents to consumers all over the world: Bold, Cheer, Dreft, Era, Febreze Clean Wash, Gain, Ivory Snow, and Tide. To European consumers, the company offers Ace, Alfa, Ariel, Bold 2 in 1, Bonux Biomat, Dash, Daz, Dreft, Fairy, Moher, Tide, Tix, and Vizir.[15] Each of these laundry detergents appeals to a different market: consumers who want a detergent that has an excellent cleaning ability, consumers who need whitening, consumers who need fabric softening agents in the washing process, consumers who need a product for sensitive fabrics or for babies' sensitive skin, and consumers who may be allergic, to name a few.

Such strategies, whereby companies offer brands for every market segment, require significant resources on the part of the company. It is much more costly to develop a marketing strategy for each market segment than to address a single segment, or to offer only one brand targeted at all consumers.

6-3b Concentrated Marketing Strategy

Concentrated marketing: The process of selecting only one market segment and targeting it with one single brand.

Not all companies can afford to offer something for everyone. Not all companies desire to meet the needs of all consumers in the marketplace. In fact, many companies select only one market segment and target it with one single brand, using a **concentrated marketing** strategy. Mont Blanc, a company manufacturing pens and fountain pens, offers a relatively

Figure 6-11
Tree Top uses a concentrated marketing strategy with this advertisement directed to mothers of infants.

Source: © Tree Top, Inc., 2002, Yakima, WA. Created by Cole & Weber / Red Cell, Seattle, WA.

limited product selection that it markets using the same theme—"the art of writing"—to all consumers worldwide. The product is targeted at the professional class. Tree Top also uses a concentrated marketing strategy, focusing primarily on mothers of infants (see Figure 6-11).

Companies that cannot afford to compete in a mature market with an oligopoly may choose to pursue a small segment—a niche. This option may be the only one available for the company's limited resources. Retailers often use a niche strategy. For example, the Body Shop caters to consumers who are environmentally concerned and who want to purchase natural products that have not been tested on animals. Marketing Illustration 6-3 offers insights into niche markets for hair-care products.

Undifferentiated marketing: A targeting strategy aiming the product at the market using a single strategy, regardless of the number of segments.

6-3c Undifferentiated Marketing Strategy

An **undifferentiated marketing** strategy is one in which the product is aimed at the entire market using a single marketing strategy. The company using this strategy chooses to ignore differences between consumers and offers the entire market one single brand. Many bulk products are aimed at all consumers, regardless of demographics, psychographics, and

Marketing Illustration 6-3

Niche Hair-Care Markets

Many hair-care companies are adding premium-priced niche products to their traditional product lines in order to increase their profit margins. New startup beauty product companies have followed suit. Brocato Blonde, from the startup company Beautopia, is targeted specifically to blondes. This product adds volume and shine to naturally blonde hair that is often fine, fragile, and limp. Hair that is blonde by chemical processing requires moisturizing. The five products in the Brocato Blonde line address all of these needs. Consumers have responded with phenomenal orders, pushing sales into the millions of dollars.

Marketing to children is another niche area that marketers in the hair-care sector hope will grow to a full-fledged market segment. Some estimates already place the children's personal care market at more than $213 billion, which includes both professional and final consumer sales. According to a Salomon Brothers report, this niche market will continue to grow at an annual rate of 8 percent yearly and has a promising future. Because the average 10-year-old receives nearly $15 of allowance and chore money every week, it is expected that, annually, kids age 4 to 12 will spend more than $35 billion a year buying products that satisfy their needs and desires. It should be noted that these are children of the baby boomers, also known as echo boomers. An important trait of the members of this market segment is their desire to look their best; it is thus expected that a large portion of their spending will go for fashion and grooming.

Professional hair-care lines for children are already experiencing some demand. Among the brands targeted at this niche market are Sea Critters, which sets itself apart with its see-through plastic tubes featuring a toy inside, and Jungle Care. Industry insiders tout Jungle Care as the market leader. Beginning with a basic line of four products, and 10 more currently in the process of rolling out, the Jungle Care product line has carved a solid niche for itself. According to Alice Cherry, director of consumer marketing at Jungle Care, the company has been able to establish itself quickly because of its company philosophy. Jungle Care does not simply manufacture adult shampoo and say that it is made for kids. The company feels that there should be products made for children's specific needs, which are different from adult requirements. Its philosophy also centers on children as the salon customers of the future, and they are treated as such. The result is that children respond.

Source: Barbara Jewett, "State of the Professional Haircare Market," *Global Cosmetic Industry,* vol. 164, no. 6 (June 1999): 50–56.

behavioral differences. For branded products, this is difficult to achieve: Even salt brands offer low sodium and kosher versions.

Using an undifferentiated strategy offers the company economies of scale in manufacturing and promotion and the ability to cut costs. Although this strategy may appear as the most obviously efficient, marketers are aware that segment needs may be better served by tailoring the offering to the market. In that sense, manufacturers of branded products will benefit from using a differentiated strategy, if they can afford it; if not, they can offer a concentrated strategy, meeting the needs of a target segment more efficiently than they would those of the entire market.

6-4 Positioning the Brand

Positioning entails placing the brand in the consumer's mind in relation to other competing products, based on product traits and benefits that are relevant to the consumer. Such a process involves identifying competitors, determining how the competitors are perceived and evaluated by target consumers, determining the competitors' positions in the consumers' mind, analyzing the customers, selecting the position, and monitoring it.[16]

There are six approaches to the positioning strategy: attribute/benefit positioning, price/quality positioning, use or applications positioning, product user positioning, product class positioning, and competitor positioning.[17]

6-4a Attribute/Benefit Positioning

Procter & Gamble focuses on product attributes and benefits to position many of its products within a single product category. An **attribute/benefit positioning** strategy

Attribute/benefit positioning: Positioning that communicates product attributes and benefits, differentiating each brand from the other company brands and from those of competitors.

uses product or service attributes and benefits to position it in the consumers' mind relative to competitors' products and services. The following are examples of product positioning by P&G:[18]

- Bold is positioned as a powder laundry detergent with fabric softening and pill/fuzz removal.
- Cheer, in powder or liquid, with or without bleach, is positioned as protecting against fading, color transfer, and fabric wear.
- Dreft is positioned as a detergent that removes tough baby stains and protects garment colors.
- Gain, as a liquid and powder detergent, is positioned as having exceptional cleaning and whitening abilities.
- P&G's premium product, Tide, in powder or liquid, with or without bleach, is positioned as a laundry detergent with exceptional cleaning, whitening, and stain removal abilities.

Such precise positioning, which is reflected in the company's communication with its respective segments, clearly differentiates each brand from the other company brands and from those of competitors such as Unilever and Colgate-Palmolive.

6-4b Price/Quality Positioning

Price/quality positioning: A strategy whereby products and services are positioned as offering the best value for the money.

The **price/quality positioning** strategy positions goods and services in terms of price and quality. Manufacturers such as Toyota, Daewoo, and Philips, as well as retailers such as Wal-Mart and Sears, emphasize the value aspect of their offerings. Alternatively, goods and services can be positioned at the other end of the price/quality continuum, as the best product that money can buy. In addition to stressing high price and high quality, such positioning also entails an exclusive distribution or access, an expert sales force and service, and advertising in publications aimed at an upscale market. Mercedes-Benz claims that, in a perfect world, everyone would drive a Mercedes. Kempinski Hotels and Resorts, an upscale German chain, "reflects the finest traditions of European hospitality, luxurious accommodation, superb cuisine and unrivalled facilities—complemented by impeccable service."[19]

6-4c Use or Applications Positioning

Use or applications positioning: The process of marketing a very precise product application that differentiates it in consumers' minds from other products that have a more general use.

How a product is used or the various applications of a product are often used to position products in the **use or applications positioning** strategy. Procter & Gamble's Era is positioned as a high-technology detergent that pre-treats and washes fabrics to suspend dirt. This very precise application differentiates it in consumers' minds from other laundry detergents that have a more general use.

Sometimes, the uses or applications differ from one market to another: A bicycle manufacturer would most likely position its offerings in Asia and Europe as efficient transportation machines, whereas, in the United States, it would position them as high-performance recreation instruments.

6-4d Product User Positioning

Product user positioning: A positioning strategy that focuses on the product user, rather than on the product.

The **product user positioning** strategy focuses on the product user, rather than on the product. The marketing mix for the Hummer is targeted at the individual who wants to go places where trucks and cars do not have access. All product descriptions and advertising emphasize this aspect. The Hummer itself has the aspect of a tank that is about to climb impossible terrain. GE Monogram appliances are aimed at those who have a Hatteras yacht, Barcelona chairs, and Noguchi tables. Phoenix Wealth Management is positioned to appeal to the woman who gives her broker investment ideas, who is taking her company public, or who earns more than her CEO husband. The Skeeter boat in Figure 6-12 is positioned as the best boat for bass fishermen.

Figure 6-12
Skeeter Performance Fishing Boats uses a product user positioning strategy with this advertisement directed to bass fishermen.

Source: Courtesy of Newcomer, Morris and Young.

6-4e Product Class Positioning

Pizza Hut has used the approach that it is the best dine-in pizza establishment. It wants to be in the dine-in pizza product class, not the delivery business. Products using a **product class positioning** strategy differentiate themselves as leaders in a product category, as they define it. Milk, for most people, is considered a breakfast drink. For others, milk is consumed with cookies, by children, after school. To increase sales, the milk industry wants to reposition its product to be consumed at any time of the day, for any reason. Thus, it does not want consumers to put milk in the breakfast drink category; the milk industry wants milk to be a beverage (see Figure 6-13). The danger, of course, of such a strategy is that now milk must compete with soft drinks, coffee, tea, and other drinks, instead of breakfast drinks like orange juice.

Product class positioning: A strategy used to differentiate a company as a leader in a product category, as defined by the respective companies.

6-4f Competitor Positioning

When a firm compares its brand with those of competitors, it uses a **competitor positioning** strategy. Some comparisons are direct. Others are subtle. When Airbus asks readers of *The Financial Times* if they would be more comfortable with two or four engines when they are up in the air, it makes an implicit reference to Boeing, which has only two engines.

Competitor positioning: The process of comparing the firm's brand, directly or indirectly, with those of competitors.

All positioning, ultimately, is relative to competition, only not always explicitly so. Even symbols hint at competition: Merrill Lynch is bullish on the market (it is portrayed

Figure 6-13
To boost sales, the milk industry would like consumers to consider milk a beverage that can be consumed anytime, rather than just at breakfast.

Source: Courtesy of Bozell Worldwide, Inc. as agent for the National Fluid Milk Processor Promotion Board.

by the bull); all other competitors are probably wimps. The *New York Times*' positioning as "all the news that's fit to print" ultimately states that, if it is not published there, it is not newsworthy. (This, of course, may be problematic because the paper is sold in many markets where the New York Metro section has minimal relevance to readers.) The advertisement in Figure 6-14 uses a competitor positioning strategy. In the advertisement, Welch's compares its white grape juice to apple juice, stating that white grape juice is easier for infants to digest.

6-4g Positioning Maps

Positioning is all about perception—it is in the consumer's mind and is the consumer's perception of a brand relative to the competition. Brands can be mapped on a positioning map based on their attributes, allowing them to be compared relative to other brands with which they are competing. A company should ask the following questions, according to Trout and Ries:[20]

1. What place does a product occupy in most consumers' minds?
2. What place does the company want to occupy?
3. What competitors does the company have to defeat to occupy the position it desires?

Figure 6-14
Welch's is using a competitor positioning strategy in this advertisement by comparing its white grape juice to apple juice.

Source: Courtesy of Welch Foods, Concord, MA.

4. Does the company have the resources to attain this position?
5. Can the company persist until it gets there?
6. Are the company's tactics supporting its positioning objectives?

Let us assume two attributes, price and strength of automobiles, where strength is defined as a tank-like quality which offers the consumers the comfort (justified or not) that they will survive any collision. We are using only two attributes because they are easier to map than multiple attributes. However, marketers use three-dimensional maps routinely to position their brands. The two attributes, price and strength, will be mapped on the x and y axes, respectively, as shown in Figure 6-15.

We have four quadrants. The Hummer has the highest price and strength as perceived by consumers. The Volvo also occupies a position, albeit a less-prominent one, in the high-price/high-strength quadrant. This position was achieved with extensive advertising over decades of Volvo attempting to convince buyers of the strength of its automobile. Jeep lies in the lower-price/high-strength quadrant. It is sturdy but more affordable than the Hummer or the Volvo. The BMW M-Class is a very expensive and tiny automobile, which, with its soft-top, can be easily flattened by a collision with just about any sports utility vehicle. It occupies the low-strength/high-price quadrant. The Dodge Neon is cheap but also not very sturdy, compared with a Hummer, for example; therefore, it occupies the low-price/low-strength quadrant.

Figure 6-15
Positioning Grid

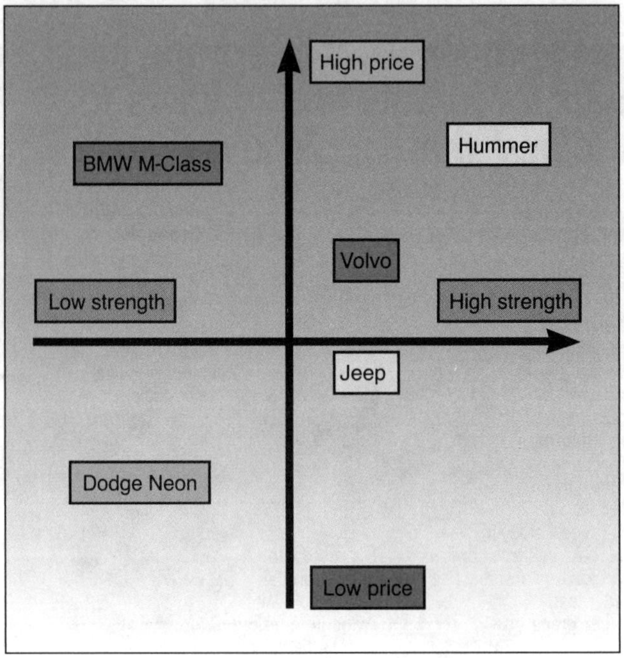

An automobile manufacturer can use this map in many ways: to determine its position on this positioning map or on another map with different attributes. It can also use the map to determine where, in the consumers' minds, it should position its new models. By mapping all competing brands on the price-strength dimensions, the company can identify gaps that are not addressed by competitors and offer a new model that fits in the respective position. Alternatively, if the company determines that the automobile is in an undesirable quadrant, from the consumers' point of view, it can advertise itself as occupying a different position—as long as that position is plausible. For example, the Dodge Neon probably wants to maintain its position as low-price; however, assuming that buyers want a higher-strength position, it can communicate (advertise) its performance in collisions, assuming that the respective record supports a higher-strength position.

Summary

1. *Identify the rationale for adopting a target marketing strategy.* Target marketing is used to identify segments of consumers who are similar with regard to key traits, who would respond to a particular marketing mix (i.e., to segment the market); to select the segments that the company can serve most efficiently and develop products tailored to each (i.e., to target the market); and to offer the products to the market, communicating through the marketing mix (i.e., positioning) the product traits and benefits that differentiate the product in consumers' minds.

2. *Identify the bases for consumer segmentation and offer company application examples.* Consumers are segmented based on the following variables: demographics, which are statistics that describe the population, such as age, gender, ethnicity, education, income, and occupation; psychographics, which refer to values, attitudes, interests, and other cultural variables used to segment consumers; geographical location; and behavior. Behavior segmentation is composed of using variables such as usage rate and user status, loyalty status, and the benefits sought from purchasing the product or service. Business segments are based on some of the same criteria, with some adaptation. For example, demographic variables for businesses may consist of company size and industry sector. In addition, other behavioral variables could be used in the case of businesses. Examples are relationship-seeking segments, which consist of relatively sophisticated service users who believe that the user-provider relationship is very important but have realistic expectations for the service requirements and do not expect to pay a low price; price-sensitive segments, which consist of businesses that are looking for low prices but also have low service requirements; high-expectation service segments, which are the most demanding, need extensive customer focus, and place considerable demands on service providers while demanding low prices; and customer-focus needs segments, which are prepared to pay for higher-than-average service that is tailored to meet these users' needs.

3. *Identify the requirements necessary for effective market segmentation.* For segmentation to be effective, segments must be easy to measure, stable over time, accessible via marketing communication and distribution, actionable through marketing strategies, and able to respond differentially from other segments to a company's marketing strategy.

4. *Describe the three targeting strategies that companies use.* These strategies are differentiated marketing, whereby companies address the needs of different segments by offering them different brands and using different marketing mix strategies; concentrated marketing, whereby companies address a single consumer segment that is large and stable enough to warrant the investment; and undifferentiated marketing, whereby a company can reap the benefits of standardization by using the same strategy to market to all consumers.

5. *Describe the six positioning strategies that companies can use to position their brands in the minds of target consumers.* Companies can position products by focusing on product attributes or benefits; by positioning the brand as a high-price/high-quality product or as the best value for the money; by positioning the brand based on use or applications; by positioning the brand based on traits of product users; or by positioning it as the best product in its class.

Key Terms

accessibility (p. 176)
actionability (p. 176)
attribute/benefit positioning (p. 179)
benefit segmentation (p. 170)
buyer-readiness stage segmentation (p. 172)
competitor positioning (p. 181)
concentrated marketing (p. 177)
customer-focus needs segment (p. 175)
demographic segmentation (p. 165)
differential response (p. 176)
differentiated marketing (p. 177)
geographic segmentation (p. 172)
high-expectation service segment (p. 175)
loyalty segmentation (p. 171)
mass marketing (p. 163)
measurability (p. 175)
micromarketing (p. 164)
multiattribute segmentation (p. 173)
occasion segmentation (p. 172)
price/quality positioning (p. 180)
price-sensitive segment (p. 175)
product class positioning (p. 181)
product user positioning (p. 180)
psychographic segmentation (p. 168)
relationship-seeking segment (p. 175)
segmentation (p. 163)
segment marketing (p. 164)
stability (p. 176)
substantiality (p. 175)
target market (p. 169)
target marketing (p. 162)
undifferentiated marketing (p. 178)
usage rate segmentation (p. 171)
use or applications positioning (p. 180)
user status segmentation (p. 171)

Discussion Questions

1. Demographics and psychographics are often used in the process of conducting multiattribute segmentation. You have been hired by a new gardening magazine to identify the different market segments that the magazine could target. Conduct your segmentation analysis.
2. Describe the different bases for behavioral segmentation. What are some of the relevant behavioral market segments that the prospective gardening magazine could target?
3. Marketing managers use a number of criteria to ensure effective segmentation. Assume that you are working for a manufacturer of children's hair-care products. What are the criteria that you would use for effective segmentation?
4. Describe the principal targeting strategies. Go to the Procter & Gamble home page (www.pg.com). What targeting strategy does the company use? Explain.
5. Go to ESRI's web page (www.esribis.com) and enter the following ZIP codes: 23220, 90210, 10022, and 23229. What makes of automobiles would sell well in these target markets? Explain. What other product categories should be targeted to these markets?
6. What are the six positioning strategies? What strategies does Mercedes USA use for its U.S. market? Does Mercedes use different strategies for its international markets? (Go to the other English-language Mercedes sites to answer this question.)
7. For each of the positioning strategies discussed in Section 6-4, identify a brand that uses the respective strategy. Explain your choice.

Review Questions

True or False

1. Market segmentation is defined as identifying the segments of consumers who are similar with regard to key characteristics and who would respond well to a product and related marketing mix.
2. The purpose of segmentation is to identify all consumers' needs and develop a specific marketing strategy for each segment.
3. User status segmentation is defined as the process of segmenting the markets based on the extent to which consumers are nonusers, occasional users, medium users, or heavy users of a product.
4. Multivariable segmentation is based on benefits sought and usage status.
5. Measurability for successful segmentation is defined as the degree to which an individual market segment is easy to

identify and measure, or the ability to evaluate the market segment's size.

6. Stability, as a basis for successful segmentation, is defined as the degree to which the segments are large enough to warrant the investment.

7. Companies that use a differentiated strategy identify or even create market segments that want different benefits from a product and target them with different brands.

8. A company that pursues a small market segment—a niche—is engaging in differentiation.

9. A company that offers a brand that is positioned as an advanced-formula detergent that can suspend dirt engages in product user positioning.

Multiple Choice

10. Which of the following categories relate to selecting segments that the company can serve most efficiently and developing a product mix tailored to each segment?
    - **a.** market segmentation
    - **b.** market targeting
    - **c.** market positioning
    - **d.** all of the above

11. Demographic segmentation includes which of the following categories?
    - **a.** motivation
    - **b.** user status
    - **c.** income
    - **d.** none of the above

12. Companies that attempt to provide skin-treatment products for baby boomers are engaged in which of the following types of segmentation strategies?
    - **a.** behavior segmentation
    - **b.** multiattribute segmentation
    - **c.** segmenting business markets
    - **d.** demographic segmentation

13. Two popular classification systems based on ZIP codes are PRIZM and ACORN. They aid in _____ segmentation.
    - **a.** behavior
    - **b.** geographic
    - **c.** multivariable
    - **d.** occasion

14. In segmenting business markets, the relationship-seeking segments are characterized as
    - **a.** seeking low prices and accepting low service levels.
    - **b.** understanding the trade-off between service levels and price.
    - **c.** demanding low prices but extensive customer service.
    - **d.** accepting higher prices to address their own specific needs.

15. Which strategy would offer the best value for the money spent on goods and services?
    - **a.** price/quality positioning
    - **b.** use or application positioning
    - **c.** product user positioning
    - **d.** competitor positioning

Notes

1. Michael J. Weiss, "Online America," *American Demographics*, vol. 23, no. 3 (March 2001): 53–60.
2. Alison Stein Wellner, "Culinary Feat," *American Demographics*, vol. 23, no. 3 (March 2001): S16.
3. Jack Neff, "P&G Chief: We Need A New Model—Now," *Advertising Age*, vol. 75, no. 46 (November 15, 2004): 1–2.
4. Michael R. Pearce, "Succeeding with Micromarketing," *Ivey Business Quarterly*, vol. 62, no. 1 (1997): 69–72.
5. Joyce M. Wolburg and James Pokrywczynski, "A Psychographic Analysis of Generation Y College Students," *Journal of Advertising Research*, vol. 41, no. 5 (September/October 2001): 33–52.
6. Peter Francese, "Older and Wealthier," *American Demographics*, vol. 24, no. 10 (November 2002): 40–41.
7. Dale Buss, "Nike's Feminine Side," *Potentials*, vol. 35, no. 10 (October 2002): 16–20.
8. Mercedes M. Cardona, "Segment Marketing Grows as Tool for Financial Services Leaders," *Advertising Age*, vol. 71, no. 48 (November 20, 2000): S1, S11.
9. Sharon Begley, "Researchers Delve into the Darker Side of Scary-Ride Junkies," *The Wall Street Journal* (May 31, 2002): B1.
10. Bob Sperber, "Taco Bell Builds Beyond Border Bowls," *Brandweek*, vol. 43, no. 40 (November 4, 2002): 6.
11. Ibid.
12. Rebekah Bennett and Sharyn Rundle-Thiele, "A Comparison of Attitudinal Loyalty Measurement Approaches," *Journal of Brand Management*, vol. 9, no. 3 (January 2002): 193–209.
13. See www.infods.com/freedata/.
14. Bill Merrilees, Rohan Bentley, and Ross Cameron, "Business Service Market Segmentation," *Journal of Business and Industrial Marketing*, vol. 14, no. 2 (1999): 151–164.
15. See www.pg.com.
16. Adapted from David A. Aaker and Gary J. Shansby, "Positioning Your Product," *Business Horizons*, vol. 25, no. 3 (May/June 1982): 56–62.
17. Ibid.
18. See www.pg.com.
19. See www.kempinski.com.
20. Jack Trout and Al Ries, *Positioning: The Battle for Your Mind* (New York: McGraw-Hill, 2000).

Case 6-1 The World—Vegas Style

Before 1990, the word "elegance" was never used in the same sentence as Las Vegas. The dominant traits of an earlier Las Vegas were excess and tackiness, not elegance. Vegas was about ogling long-legged cocktail waitresses in Daisy-Duke tights, eating thick steaks, drinking scotch, and wearing fashions such as furs on the mistress and jackass slacks on the Dunes golf course.

In an attempt to outgrow its tacky past and create fantasy excursions to faraway places, Las Vegas has created an opulent international oasis in the desert. Evocative of Italy, the $1.8 billion, 3,000-room Bellagio Hotel opened in October 1999; followed by the $950 million, 3,700-room Mandalay Bay, recreating the South Seas; the Venetian, with 6,000 rooms at a cost of $1.3 billion; the $760 million, 2,900-room Paris–Las Vegas; and a 2,600-room Arabian-themed Aladdin. It is projected that the city will add 10,600 additional hotel rooms by 2007.

Las Vegas visitors today can choose between a gondola ride through an indoor canal ($12), a trip to the top of the Eiffel Tower ($8), or an expensive dinner at the Wolfgang Puck eateries, which make Vegas one of the best restaurant cities in the United States. Inspired by the Bellagio Hotel's shows *O* (Cirque du Soleil) and *Mystére*, the new Paris hotel has put on its own French musical, *Notre Dame de Paris*.

A unique city in the middle of the desert, Las Vegas draws numerous visitors attracted to gambling opportunities, conferences, entertainment, and the Strip's new hotels (see Figure 6-16 for the magical Las Vegas skyline). Las Vegas does not share its visitors with any other attraction: They are captivated and captured by gambling, attending shows, and shopping within the environment. It is a marketer's dream that resort mogul Steve Wynn would like to capture yet again, through Le Reve (in French, "the dream")—a $2.4 billion, 2,700-room preeminent luxury hotel and destination resort. An additional 1,500-suite tower expansion will open in 2007, and a 142-acre hotel, casino, and residential resort complex will begin construction in 2008.

Le Reve will be the most expensive resort ever built in Las Vegas, topping the $1.8 billion Bellagio. Built on the site of the old Desert Inn at the north end of the Strip, Le Reve will be comparable in size to Bellagio, featuring 2,700 rooms, an 111,000-square-foot casino with 2,000 slot machines and 136 table games, an 18-hole golf course, a water-based entertainment complex, a Ferrari and Maserati dealership, and an art gallery featuring works from Wynn's collection. Wynn has already built key hotels in Vegas—most recently, the Bellagio, which houses his impressive art collection.

Who is the target market for these grandiose plans? Most likely, the yuppies who are expected to take their morning stroll in Bellagio's botanical garden, splendid with blooms. These are the consumers who marvel at original paintings in the hotel's art museum, who dine in French restaurants, and who buy gowns they will wear proudly to a black-tie fund-raiser in Middle America.

Figure 6-16
Las Vegas skyline at night.

Questions

1. Describe the different visitor market segments that Las Vegas appeals to. Use demographic, psychographic, behavioral, and geographic bases for segmentation in creating your descriptions.
2. What are the target markets of the new international hotels in Las Vegas? Go to the Bellagio Hotel and Casino site, www.bellagio.com, to find out more information about the hotel's target market.
3. What types of targeting strategies are these international hotels using?
4. What is the positioning strategy that the new hotel, Le Reve, will be using to attract its visitors?

Sources: Tony Illia, "Vegas Readies Itself for Yet Another Boom," *ENR*, vol. 253, no. 21 (November 29, 2004): 17; Richard Corliss, "Spotlight on . . . Las Vegas," *Time*, vol. 155, no. 7 (February 21, 2000): 132; Andrew Baby, "Just a Dream?" *Barron's*, vol. 82, no. 41 (October 14, 2002): 29; www.1st100.com.

Case 6-2 Bubba's Organic Borscht

Karl Marx, a former advertising executive with a major East Coast ad firm, is interested in opening an ethnic café in his parents' hometown, Phoenix, Arizona. He is thinking of calling it Bubba's Organic Borscht, stressing the organic nature and the origins of the food he would serve—southern and Jewish (as in grits and gefilte fish).

One of the more important considerations for Karl is locating close to his parents' home in Phoenix, in an area known as Moon Valley, close to Scottsdale, a luxury destination for tourists and retirees. He found an ideal location for his café in a shopping center located on the corner of 7th Street and Thunderbird Avenue. The shopping center is dominated by a gourmet shop, AJ's Fine Foods (www.ajsfinefoods.com). It also has a small bank office, a Mail Boxes, Etc. office, and not much else that Karl noted. The shopping center is diagonally across the Pointe Tapatillo, a famous Hilton resort property that draws clients from all over the United States. Although it may appear unlikely that resort clients would descend the hill and cross a busy street to come to the restaurant, the idea is not far-fetched: Getting around anywhere in the resort demands some effort going uphill or downhill. And hotel residents may want to get away from the typical hotel fare, opting for ethnic variety.

Bubba's Organic Borscht would be open for lunch and dinner, and it would have on its menu many items from the southeastern United States region. Grits would be a staple for lunch, biscuits would be served with every meal, and the smell of baked apple pie and pecan pie would always permeate the café. The café would have two kitchens, one for dairy and one for meat, in keeping with kosher requirements—while the café would not position itself as a kosher café to the Moon Valley market (its primary target market), Karl intended to promote it as such to the greater Phoenix Jewish community (its secondary target market). In keeping with the kosher requirements, the café would not carry some of the traditional southern foods, such as bacon and ham, which are considered treif (biblically prohibited food).

It was important for Karl to understand more about Moon Valley residents. It was his impression that the neighborhood looked very much like East Coast suburbia, but with a requisite swimming pool in the back yard. Karl had free access to ACORN and ESRI Business Information Solutions (www.esribis.com), which helped him obtain more data on the neighborhood where he planned to open his café. By entering the ZIP code of Moon Valley, 85022, he found out that this area is populated by enterprising young singles, described as follows: "These ambitious people with a head start and the promise of success are especially active, dine out frequently, and spend money on furniture, small appliances, and apparel. Over half are under the age of 35. With high labor force participation rates, they tend to rent videos and use personal computers at work and at home. Media preferences include *Entertainment Weekly* and the *Wall Street Journal*."

He also obtained some information on the market demographics at the ACORN website, listed in Table 6-4, and now he is ready to plan his targeting and positioning strategies.

Questions

1. Describe the different market segments that Bubba's Organic Borscht appeals to, using demographic, psychographic, behavioral, and geographic bases for market segmentation.
2. Given the existing market segments that might respond well to Karl's new café, what is the targeting strategy that Karl should use?
3. Assume that the café's neighbor, AJ's Fine Foods, also serves its ready-made gourmet food on a rather small patio. How should Bubba's Organic Borscht position itself from this nearby competitor?

Source: www.esribis.com.

TABLE 6-4 Moon Valley (ZIP 85022) Demographics

	ZIP 85022	National		ZIP 85022	National
General Statistics			***Population by Gender***		
Total population	46,912	295,628,353	Male	49.0%	49.1%
Number of households	21,198	111,572,974	Female	51.0%	50.9%
Population by Race			***Income Figures***		
White	86.2%	73.6%	Median household income	$53,235	$48,124
Black	2.2%	12.5%	Household income under $50K	46.8%	51.1%
Asian Pacific Islander	3.1%	4.2%	Household income $50K–$100K	30.7%	31.0%
Other	8.5%	8.7%	Household income over $100K	22.5%	17.4%
Housing Figures					
Average home value	$178,339	$206,430			

Marketing Research

7

CHAPTER
OBJECTIVES

1. Define marketing research, provide a description of its scope, and offer examples of each type of research conducted in marketing.
2. Describe the steps involved in the marketing research process.
3. Introduce the concept of decision support systems for marketing and describe the sales forecasting process.

CHAPTER
OUTLINE

In a bear market and stagnant economy, luxury products typically do not sell well among middle and upper middle class consumers. There is one exception: the Hummer. General Motors can barely keep up with demand. Its supply is only six days ahead of demand in a market where 10 times that amount is ideal. Even more impressive, the product is selling without any incentives—no piling of rebates and no free financing for this make. What lends so much appeal to this great heavy monster (it weighs three tons, one ton more than the Ford Explorer) and gas guzzler? The Hummer attracts attention. Robert Fishelson feels like a movie star in his Hummer. He has young teenybopper girls yell out of their windows at him. He has owned 15 Corvettes in the past and never got so much attention. Bill Kramer owned an Escalade, a Mercedes, and a Jaguar, but his Hummer H2 draws more looks and questions than any other vehicle he has ever owned.

The Hummer offers protection. Consumers who buy this make often echo the opinion "I can protect my family: If someone bumps into me, they're dead."

In addition, the Hummer helps break stereotypes and tradition. Female buyers with kids in the car feel that "no one is going to look at me as a soccer mom." Men feel like they are putting on a Superman outfit.

The Hummer helps people show strength. After the September 11, 2001 attacks, people feel that they are at war and need to be protected.[1]

7-1 Chapter Overview

Why is the Hummer such a successful product? What are the consumer motivations behind the Hummer vogue? What is General Motors doing to create such strong demand for its gas-guzzling tank? Not much; the product is selling itself without any of the typical incentives that automobile retailers are accustomed to offering and that consumers have come to expect. The reality is that the Hummer appears to be the right product offered at the right time, when consumers feel vulnerable and have a strong safety need. And it doesn't hurt that the car also addresses their self-esteem needs.

The marketing of successful products like the Hummer requires a thorough understanding of the product's target market. Numerous marketing plans fail due to an incomplete understanding of the market. Critical to this understanding is marketing research.

This chapter defines marketing research in Section 7-2 and examines its broad scope within marketing across all components of the marketing mix (product, place, price, and promotion) in Section 7-3. Section 7-4 addresses the marketing research process and the different steps involved in defining the research problem, developing a research plan, collecting information, conducting primary research, and interpreting the results. Section 7-5 addresses the decision support systems used in marketing and how they can help marketers forecast sales.

7-2 Defining Marketing Research

Marketers need to constantly monitor the different forces affecting their operations and the products they sell. Marketing information, which should constitute a basis for all executive action, must be taken into consideration to improve the chances of success in a complex marketing environment. An important caveat is that such information needs to be carefully evaluated and viewed in light of the purpose for which it was collected. Complex environmental factors complicate the task of marketing researchers, who should have not only an expertise in the most advanced techniques of scientific inquiry, but also a profound understanding of the markets under investigation.

Was the success of the Hummer in the chapter-opening vignette a surprise to the company? Probably not. General Motors most likely engaged in extensive marketing research that found that a staple of recent wars would appeal to consumers—thereby addressing different consumer needs such as protection, self-esteem, and self-actualization.

Figure 7-1
Market research helps Lincoln-Mercury market its vehicles by understanding who purchases the vehicles and why each is purchased.

Source: Courtesy of The Marketing Exchange.

Not all products perform as predicted in the marketplace. Mazda engaged in extensive marketing research in order to come up with a product that would appeal to young consumers just out of college—the Mazda Miata. The company found out very quickly that its primary market was not the intended younger consumer, but rather, middle-aged men. Companies such as Ford Motor Company perform extensive research to find out exactly who purchases their various brands of automobiles and why (see Figure 7-1).

Research does not provide all the answers, but it does provide solid information that marketing managers can use to make intelligent decisions. **Marketing research** involves the systematic design, collection, recording, analysis, interpretation, and reporting of information pertinent to a particular marketing decision facing a company.

Marketing research: The systematic design, collection, recording, analysis, interpretation, and reporting of information pertinent to a particular marketing decision facing a company.

7-3 The Scope of Marketing Research

Marketing research addresses both broad and specific issues that are relevant to the company and its operations. It ranges from monitoring developments in the marketing environment—or general **marketing intelligence**—to anticipating a product's performance in the marketplace, to evaluating consumers' specific brand-related or advertisement-related attitudes. Figure 7-2 highlights the scope of marketing research and the components of marketing research that will be examined in this section.[2]

Marketing intelligence: Results obtained from monitoring developments in the firm's environment.

Figure 7-2
The Scope of Marketing Research

INTERACTIVE FIGURE

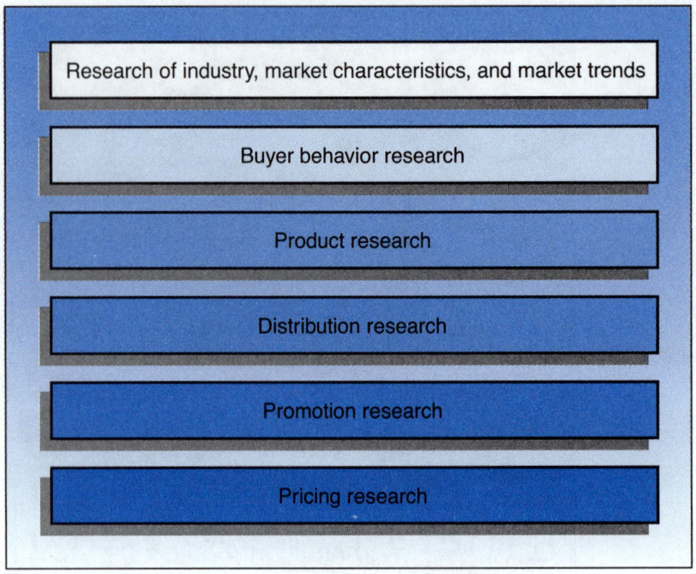

7-3a Research of Industry, Market Characteristics, and Market Trends

Studies of industry trends, market characteristics, and market trends are conducted regularly by marketing research suppliers, such as ACNielsen, and shared with subscribers. In a recent study, for example, ACNielsen found that consumers are too tired to clean and prepare dinner. ACNielsen examined data regarding convenience-oriented product categories and found that, indeed, semiprepared food and products that offer cleaning convenience are among the top industry sellers.[3]

Why would such data and information be valuable? First, understanding industry and market characteristics and trends will tell a firm what products should be produced and how those products should be marketed. For instance, ACNielsen's research indicated that firms producing cleaning products should produce products that offer consumers cleaning convenience. The research also indicated that firms should use convenience-oriented advertisements to promote the products. A company like Pillsbury can focus advertisements on how easy it is to make its brand of muffins.

7-3b Buyer Behavior Research

Buyer behavior research: Research examining consumer brand preferences, brand attitudes, and brand-related behavior.

Buyer behavior research examines consumer brand preferences and brand attitudes. To offer an example, DuPont performed research with more than 85,000 respondents to identify consumer perceptions of its DuPont Lycra brand. The company found that 64 percent of the consumers interviewed perceived clothing made with DuPont Lycra to be of better quality, 45 percent indicated that they wanted stretch-type clothing in their wardrobe, and a total of 30 percent actually asked for Lycra apparel.[4] By classifying each respondent based on his or her demographic background, DuPont was also able to see what types of consumers were the most likely to purchase Lycra. As a result of this buyer behavior research, DuPont launched an advertising campaign to promote Lycra apparel to men and women ages 21–49 with a household income of more than $35,000, and to teenage girls between the ages of 12 and 17.[5]

Brand awareness research: Research investigating how consumers' knowledge and recognition of a brand name affects their purchasing behavior.

In another example, a Nielsen study found that higher-income households are more likely to purchase at warehouse clubs—they make 37 percent of their purchases there—while lower-income households are more likely to shop at dollar stores. Interestingly, there is an even household income distribution for Wal-Mart (see Table 7-1).

In developing strong brands, brand-name recognition and awareness are important. A component of buyer behavior research, called **brand awareness research,** investigates how

TABLE 7-1

Household Purchases at Warehouse Clubs, Dollar Stores, and Wal-Mart

	Distribution of Dollar Sales		
Household Income	Warehouse Club	Dollar Store	Wal-Mart
$70,000+	37%	9%	18%
$50,000–69,999	22%	13%	18%
$40,000–49,999	13%	11%	14%
$30,000–39,999	11%	15%	17%
$20,000–29,999	10%	22%	20%
<$20,000	7%	29%	16%

Source: ACNielsen, "Leveraging Consumer Insights to Drive Retail Sales: Who Shops Where?" *Facts, Figures and the Future* (www.factsfiguresfuture.com, November 8, 2004).

consumers' knowledge and recognition of a brand name affects their purchasing behavior. Such studies are often conducted by companies to assess the position of their brands in the marketplace relative to the competition. For example, the International Research Institute on Social Change launched a study of luxury goods in the United States. A total of 3,000 respondents were interviewed in person at home and were asked about their familiarity, at least by name, with a set of 34 luxury brands. They were asked the following question: "Here is a list of luxury brands. Please indicate which ones you know at least by name." The researchers found that, in the United States, global brands of crystal and fine china such as Daum, Christofle, and Bvlgari were relatively unknown. Consequently, consumers were less likely to indicate an intention to purchase these brands.[6] Because of this low brand awareness, Daum, Christofle, and Bvlgari realized that if they were going to be successful in the United States, they would first have to launch an advertising campaign to build brand awareness. Only then would consumers consider purchasing the brands.

Consumer segmentation studies: Research conducted to identify market segment profiles.

Other useful studies that belong to this category are **consumer segmentation studies,** which are conducted to identify profiles of different consumers that the company could target. Marketing researchers often attempt to identify those segments composed of consumers who are heavy product users. To illustrate, KitchenAid commissioned a battery of ethnographic studies, which found that consumers weren't interested in the appliance for the appliance's sake. They were interested in what the appliance could do for them and how it could help them prepare delicious food and be able to entertain friends and family. To confirm and quantify these results, KitchenAid commissioned a segmentation study that found that the company should focus on "the culinary-involved," a segment of consumers who were heavy users of kitchen appliances, and who believed in using the best products for their homes. These "wannabe chefs" are passionate about cooking, and most importantly to KitchenAid, the segment cuts across all demographic groups. It isn't confined to upper income households. As a result of the consumer segmentation study, KitchenAid's advertising agency created an advertising campaign featuring a picture of lemon soufflé pancakes drizzled in lemon sauce and topped with raspberries. Beneath the picture were images of the large and small appliances that helped to prepare the dish. Six months after the campaign was launched, sales for both the KitchenAid countertop and major appliances were showing double-digit growth.[7] The segmentation study provided the right information about who purchased KitchenAid products and what type of advertising approach would appeal to them.

Faced with stagnating sales, the milk industry conducted research to see how much milk girls drank and how much they should drink. Using this information, the Bozell Agency developed the advertisement in Figure 7-3. Because of Britney Spears's popularity with young girls, she was used in the advertisement to get their attention and to encourage them to drink milk so their bodies would have the correct amount of calcium.

Figure 7-3
Buyer behavior research determined that 9 out of 10 girls do not get enough calcium and that they should drink four glasses of milk per day. As a result of this research, Bozell Agency designed this ad with Britney Spears to encourage girls to drink more milk.

Source: Courtesy Bozell Worldwide, Inc. as agent for the National Fluid Milk Processor Promotion Board.

7-3c Product Research

Most product research is directed to new product development. A brief overview will be given in this section, but a more thorough discussion is found in Chapter 8, "Product Strategies." Typical product research includes:

- Concept development
- Competitive product studies
- Brand-name generation
- Product packaging design
- Product testing
- Test marketing

Concept development research: Concept tests that evaluate the product/service offering and the related marketing mix in light of the different target markets.

Concept development research studies evaluate the viability of a new product and the composition of the other marketing mix elements in light of the product's intended target market. Activities research includes investigating the feasibility of a new product idea through generating a concept statement, determining technical feasibility for the concept, testing the concept with customers, and defining the product and target market. In the U.S. consumer packaged-goods industry, it is estimated that a company spends at least $20 million to introduce a new product and that about 80 percent of the products fail.[8] With such

Figure 7-4
When American Cyanamid created a new herbicide-tolerant crop production system, the company used brand-name studies to narrow the 600 possible names down to the one that was chosen—Clearfield.

a high cost to develop new products and such a high failure rate, it is essential that companies test the product concept before they ever start investing money into actual product development.

Brand-name generation involves the development and testing of brand names and logos. These studies are used not only by companies manufacturing consumer goods, where their importance is obvious, but also by industrial marketing companies and agricultural goods companies. For example, when American Cyanamid Company created a new herbicide-tolerant crop production system, it used a research firm that started out with 600 possible names and then narrowed the list to 30, which were then tested for linguistic appropriateness. After the company decided on the Clearfield brand, it tested the brand for six different crops (see Figure 7-4). Testing showed the Clearfield name and logo to be meaningful, credible, appropriate, memorable, and likable.[9]

The annals of marketing are replete with examples illustrating the importance of testing a global brand name in all the countries where the product is to be sold. Rolls-Royce planned on marketing its Silver Mist model in German-speaking countries, only to find out before the launch that "mist" means "dung" in German.[10] Sunbeam Corporation, however, entered the German market without testing the name of its product, Mist-Stick, before introduction.[11] As you would expect, the product did not do well.

Product testing estimates product performance and preference in a given market, while **competitive product studies** are helpful in determining the overall product strategy for the product, the price that the market will bear for the respective product category, and the promotion that is appropriate in light of the competition. **Product packaging design** studies help firms determine consumers' reactions to various package designs, the extent to which the package adequately communicates information to the consumer, and the distribution implications of packaging decisions.

After a product has been developed, many companies will use test markets to fine-tune the marketing approach that will be used and to make modifications in the product itself. **Test marketing** involves testing new product performance in a limited area of a target market to estimate product performance in the overall market. In the late 1990s, Procter & Gamble test-marketed Swiffer, a new disposable mop. Based on sales in the test markets, P&G decided to launch the Swiffer mop in all of the company's major markets.[12]

More recently, after conducting additional product research using focus groups, P&G introduced the Swiffer Sweep+Vac, a small, battery-operated vacuum cleaner with a Swiffer mop attached. P&G found that people would go on their hands and knees to wipe up

Brand-name generation: The testing of brand names and logos.

Product testing: Studies that estimate product preference and performance in a given market.

Competitive product studies: Studies that help in determining the overall product strategy for the product, the price that the market will bear for the respective product category, and the promotion that is appropriate in light of the competition.

Product packaging design: Studies that evaluate consumers' reaction to a package, the extent to which the package adequately communicates information to the consumer, and the distribution implications of the package.

Test marketing: Evaluating product performance in select markets that are representative of the target market before launching the product.

the pile of dirt that was left behind after mopping with a dry Swiffer cloth. But the new product was then quickly recalled because it presented a potential fire hazard.[13] Perhaps the company focused too much on what consumers wanted, rather than on product performance.

7-3d Distribution Research

Channel performance and coverage studies: Studies investigating whether existing channels are appropriate for the marketing task at hand.

Examples of distribution research are **channel performance and coverage studies,** which investigate whether existing channels are appropriate for the marketing task at hand. Channel performance and coverage studies are usually the first steps that the company undertakes in the process of channel design. The analysis involves identifying the threats, opportunities, strengths, and weaknesses that will influence channel performance and viability. Research should evaluate competitors' share of existing channels, the relative profitability of each channel, the coverage of the market served, and the cost of each channel function. Research should also evaluate likely changes in buying patterns, potential competitive entrants, long-run cost pressures, and new technologies such as the Internet or multimedia retail kiosks. Research should assess what customers are seeking from the various channels by asking the following questions:

- What service attributes do the target customers value?
- How can we use the differences in preferences to segment customers with similar needs?
- How well do the available channels meet the needs of each market segment?[14]

Plant/warehouse location study: A study that evaluates the appropriateness of plant or warehouse location to ensure that it is in accordance with the needs of the company.

To evaluate the appropriateness of plant or warehouse locations to the needs of a company, a **plant/warehouse location study** can be used. Such research evaluates variables such as the cost of transportation, real estate, and labor costs, as well as the availability of power sources and tax rates. Also important in the analysis is the proximity to the customer. Although it may seem like a minor detail, plants and warehouses located in the wrong places can add considerable costs to the price of a product and create a situation in which a company cannot compete effectively. A major reason Wal-Mart has been so successful is its understanding of distribution costs and the need to minimize the costs through optimal locations of its distribution systems.

7-3e Promotion Research

Promotion research evaluates, among other factors, the extent to which the company effectively communicates with the market, the extent to which certain promotional strategies are appropriate for a particular market, and the extent to which the media used are appropriate for the intended message. In this section, a brief overview of the primary evaluation methodologies will be presented, with more detailed coverage following in Chapter 13, "Integrated Marketing Communications."

Studies of premiums, coupons, and deals: Studies that determine the appropriateness and effectiveness of premiums, coupons, and deals for a given target market.

Studies of premiums, coupons, and deals determine the appropriateness and effectiveness of these types of promotions for a given target market. For example, Promotions Decisions Inc., a Cincinnati-based research firm, uses the Coupon Prophet Model to compare coupon redeemers and nonredeemers using detailed consumer information gained from frequent shopper data. The company then analyzes prior purchase behavior to identify those segments that responded well to couponing strategies.[15]

Advertising effectiveness research: Studies conducted to examine the effectiveness and appropriateness of advertisements aimed at individual markets.

Advertising effectiveness research is frequently conducted to examine the effectiveness and appropriateness of advertisements aimed at individual markets. Advertising effectiveness can be evaluated by measuring viewers' recall of an advertisement, their attitude toward the ad, and the extent to which the ad persuaded the consumer to purchase the sponsor's product. Marketing Illustration 7-1 addresses a situation in which advertising has been highly effective in creating demand for a drug by the patients, not the doctors.

Marketing Illustration 7-1

Overly Effective Advertising

Women walk into clinics asking for Prempro, a hormone-replacement drug, not because they might have hot flashes or because they may be interested in preventing bone loss, but because they want to look like Patti LaBelle and Lauren Hutton. They used to ask for Vioxx because they wanted to skate lithely around a rink, like Dorothy Hamill. Increasingly, drugs are perceived much like discretionary products that consumers can use or throw away on a whim.

It is estimated that 8.5 million Americans request and obtain specific prescriptions after seeing or hearing ads for particular drugs. And pharmaceutical companies eagerly advertise—to the tune of $2.7 billion annually—their products, prodding patients to "ask your doctor about..." the company's new and superior brand.

Pharmaceutical companies have already figured out how to push drugs with doctors, offering talks and sumptuous dinners to them, and taking them to exotic lands to describe the advantages of their drugs over those of their competitors. In their new, well-researched advertising campaigns, they are creating demand with patients, asking patients to request a particular drug from their doctor. The doctor can, of course, refuse to prescribe the coveted brand—but at the risk of losing the patient.

Source: Erin N. Marcus, "When TV Commercials Play the Doctor," *New York Times* (January 3, 2003): A19.

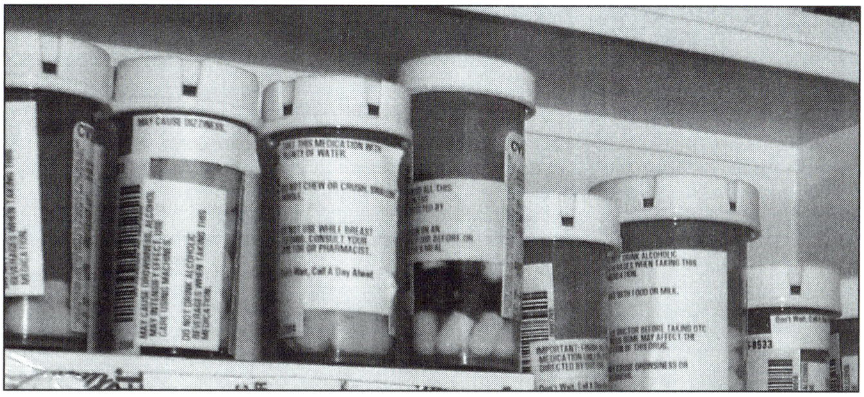

Figure 7-5
Prescription drugs are often readily prescribed.

(Figure 7-5 exemplifies the outcome of consumer demand: The owner of these drugs, a middle-aged woman who closely follows advertising, asked her doctors, after an accident, for every imaginable pain pill in common advertisements—and had most of them prescribed.)

Media research is an important component of promotional research. Identifying the media that best fits with the company's target market and the company's advertising needs ensures that advertising dollars are well spent. It is critical that the product's target market match the viewing audience of the media being used.

Media research: Studies that evaluate media availability and the appropriateness of the medium for a company's message.

Nielsen Media Research is an important research provider in this category. It uses the National People Meter service to provide audience estimates for all national program sources, including broadcast networks, cable networks, Spanish-language networks, and national syndicators. It also provides local Nielsen ratings for television stations, regional cable networks, and Spanish-language stations in each of the 210 television markets it serves. An example of media research on African-American television audiences is presented in Marketing Illustration 7-2.

Sales force compensation, quota, and territory studies: Different studies pertaining to personal selling activities; they are crucial in helping to determine the appropriate sales and incentive strategies for certain markets.

Other promotion-related research studies may address personal selling activities. Examples of such studies are **sales force compensation, quota, and territory studies,** which are crucial in helping to determine the appropriate sales and incentive strategies for

Marketing Illustration 7-2

African-American Television Audiences

Nielsen Media Research identifies African Americans as the largest minority segment of the U.S. television household population—12 percent of the 102 million households. African Americans generally watch more television than any other segment of the population; for prime-time viewing—8–11 P.M., Monday–Saturday, and 7–11 P.M. on Sunday—African-American homes watch more television than all other U.S. homes, across all age groups (see Figure 1).

Figure 1
Prime Time Television Watching Behavior (8–11 P.M. Monday–Saturday; 7–11 P.M. Sunday)

Source: National People Meter Sample, September 22, 2003, through May 30, 2004

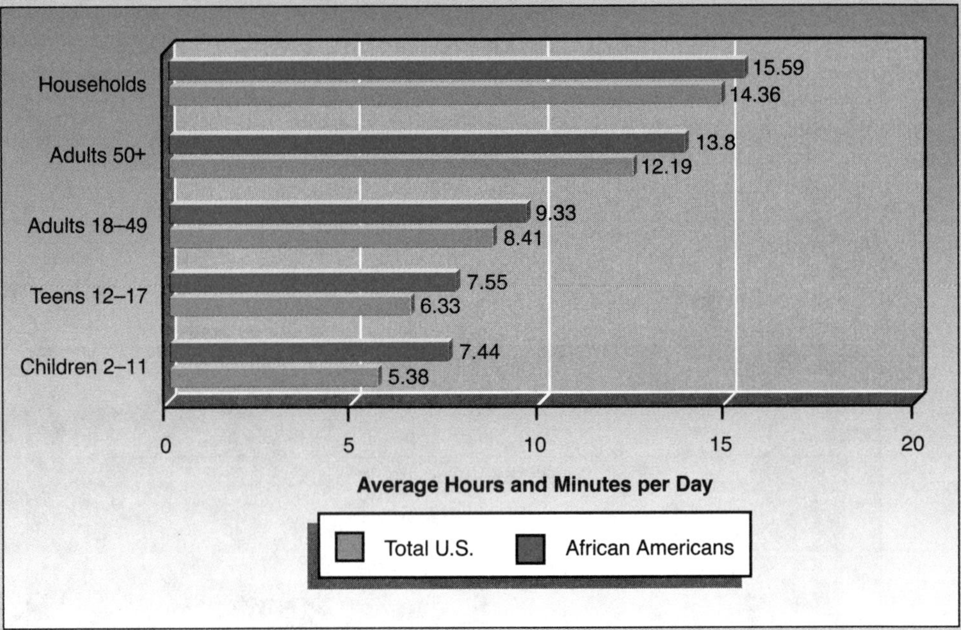

Market potential studies: Studies conducted to evaluate the potential of a particular market.

Sales potential studies: Studies forecasting optimal sales performance.

Sales forecasts: Projected sales for a particular territory.

Cost analyses: Methods used for projecting the cost of research.

Profit analyses: Studies that estimate product profit in specific markets.

Price elasticity studies: Studies examining the extent to which a particular market is price sensitive.

Competitive pricing analyses: Pricing studies that determine the price the market will bear for the respective product category based on a survey of competitors' prices.

certain markets. Sales force studies will also determine the performance of salespeople by territories, which will guide sales managers in placing salespeople in territories and redeploying salespeople to territories that may have greater potential.

7-3f Pricing Research

There are numerous examples of pricing research. Pricing is a key determinant in research studies attempting to project demand, such as **market potential studies, sales potential studies,** and **sales forecasts.** Pricing research is also an important determinant in **cost analyses, profit analyses, price elasticity studies,** and **competitive pricing analyses.**

Today, product quality is important, but the dealmaker is often the price tag. A decade ago, consumers were attracted by store atmosphere, the assortment of brand names, and customer service. To buy a brand name, one had to shop in a department store, and that alone carried cachet—to be a discount shopper meant being lumped with the proletariat. Today, research reveals that the once-mysterious ways of merchandising have been reduced to a single element: price. According to Marshal Cohen, co-president of NPD Fashionworld, a company tracking retail sales, you could be at a dinner party on Fifth Avenue and millionaires will be talking about what deals they were able to get at Wal-Mart.[16] Much of the recent pricing research confirms that shoppers' economic status does not determine where they shop; they just don't want to pay a lot for that muffler, or sweater, or digital camera.[17] Pricing research can help companies find the optimal price that will help meet the company's pricing objectives—even when it comes to canned fruits and vegetables (see Figure 7-6).

Table 1 shows the highest-rated prime-time television programs in African-American television households for the 2003–2004 television season, excluding specials. In addition, TNT, Lifetime, and Nick at Night are also very popular with African Americans, primarily because they are late-night TV watchers, and at that time, there is more to watch on cable.

TABLE 1

Highest-Rated Prime-Time Television Programs in African-American Television Households, 2003–2004

Rank	Program	Network	Household Rating %
1	American Idol—Wednesday	FOX	19.9
2	American Idol—Tuesday	FOX	18.9
3	Girlfriends	UPN	17.5
4	Eve	UPN	17.1
5	Half And Half	UPN	16.8
6	America's Next Top Model 2	UPN	15.9
7	My Wife and Kids	ABC	14.9
8	The Parkers,	UPN	14.7
9	All of Us	UPN	14.6
10	NFL Monday Night Football	ABC	14.1

Sources: american/programsAA.html, January 2005; Gerry Khermouch, "Hard to Hold: Hispanic & African American," *Brandweek,* vol. 30, no. 19 (May 10, 1999): s28–s32.

Understanding pricing is essential for marketers. Consumers' need for a deal and price competition must be aligned with businesses' need to make a profit and with all of their other marketing mix strategies.

Figure 7-7 reviews examples of the various types of research discussed in this section. It also highlights the operational and managerial uses of the research, as well as the strategic use of the information.

Figure 7-6
Pricing research helps determine the optimal price that will meet the company's pricing objective—even for products such as canned fruits and vegetables.

Source: Courtesy of Ukrop's Super Markets, Inc.

7-4 The Marketing Research Process

The marketing research process follows the steps outlined in Figure 7-8 on page 201. The first step in the process is to define the issue or problem faced. The second step is to examine secondary data for relevant information. If the problem cannot be solved with secondary data, then a primary research study needs to be conducted. This is the third step. The fourth step involves analyzing the data, making recommendations, and implementing the findings of the research.

Marketing research may be done with in-house staff or through a marketing research firm. Using an in-house staff reduces the cost of the research, and staff members normally have a better understanding of the problem being researched and how it needs to be done. However, they are likely to lack the marketing research expertise that an outside vendor would have. It is because of this expertise that most companies look to outside vendors, especially for major research projects.

Marketing Research	Operational Uses	Managerial Uses	Strategic Uses
Industry and market research	Evaluate industry and market trends.	Modify product attributes and promotion to meet changes in the industry and market.	Ensure that the company is producing the product desired by consumers.
Buyer behavior research	Understand why, how, and when consumers purchase the product.	Modify the promotional approach to ensure that the message matches the needs and interest of the target market.	Ensure that the product is being promoted to the correct target market in the correct manner.
Product research	Review current product features.	Assess new product features.	Use computerized design to devise new products.
Distribution research	Monitor supply-demand imbalances.	Manage supply-demand imbalances.	Strengthen distribution channels.
Promotion research	Evaluate effectiveness of promotions such as advertising, sales promotions, and trade promotions.	Adjust promotional methods and media outlets to ensure that the target market is being reached.	Ensure that the product is being correctly promoted.
Pricing research	Measure consistency and accuracy.	Adjust prices to reflect elasticity.	Ensure long-run competitiveness.

Figure 7-7
Summary of Marketing Research

Exploratory research: Research conducted early in the research process that helps further define a problem or identify additional problems that need to be investigated.

Research approach: The method used to collect data.

Descriptive research: All research methods observing or describing phenomena.

7-4a Problem Definition

The first step in the marketing research process requires that marketing managers and marketing researchers define the research problem and jointly agree on the research objectives. It is possible that the marketing manager does not have a clear idea of the research problem that needs to be investigated. For example, the marketing manager may be aware that the Hummer in the chapter-opening vignette is selling well, but may be concerned about how consumers will react in the future to the automobile's high gas consumption when there are many Hummers on the road. Or the marketing manager may express concerns about public attitudes toward General Motors if accident reports in the future suggest that Hummers demolish most automobiles in a collision, causing fatalities. To help in defining a marketing problem, researchers often conduct **exploratory research,** which is research conducted early in the research process to assist researchers in defining a problem or identifying additional problems that need to be investigated.

In understanding the issue to be examined, researchers will also discuss the **research approach** that will provide the best answer. Marketers have two approaches that can be used: descriptive research and causal (experimental) research. **Descriptive research** involves

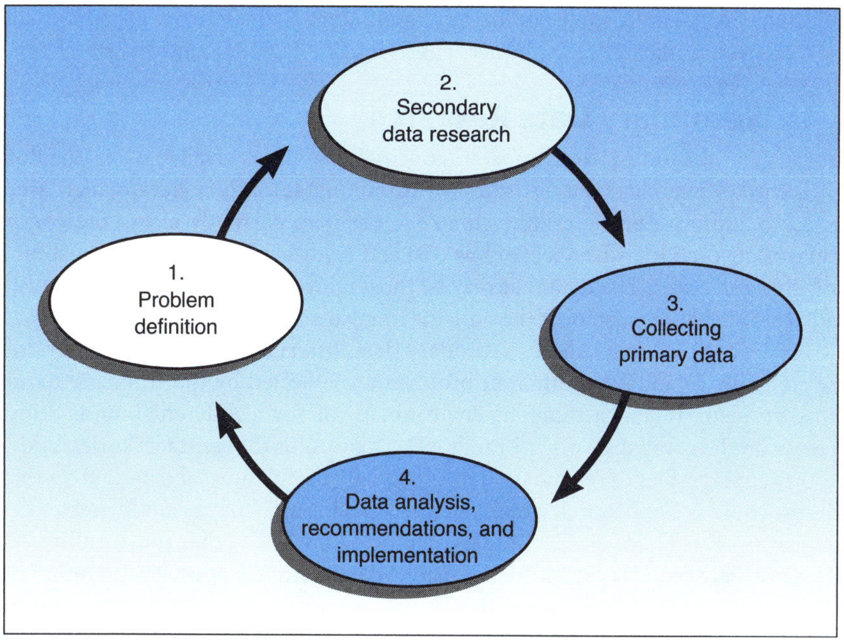

Figure 7-8
The Marketing Research Process

observing and/or describing a phenomenon. For example, descriptive research could involve collecting information about consumer attitudes toward the Hummer. Such research could describe demographically Hummer owners, or describe their lifestyles, or it could compare Hummer-owner attitudes to those of consumers who do not own a Hummer. The chapter-opening vignette is an example of descriptive research that the *New York Times* conducted about the Hummer. The research found that owners perceive the Hummer as a product that attracts attention, that offers protection, that helps women break soccer-mom stereotypes, and that helps owners show strength. **Causal (experimental) research,** however, examines cause-and-effect relationships. For example, a causal research study could test whether increases in the price of gas would lead to decreases in sales for the Hummer.

Causal (experimental) research: Research that examines cause-and-effect relationships.

It should be noted that this first step is extremely important. Paying to do high-quality research on the wrong problem can be an expensive mistake. Managers must note that there is a fine line between identifying problems too broadly—"How do consumers feel about the Hummer?"—and too narrowly—"Will enough consumers buy the Hummer if gasoline prices increase by 25 cents per gallon? One dollar per gallon?" At ten miles per gallon, the Hummer H2 can be expensive to operate even for those who can afford to pay $50,000 for this automobile.

It is safe to assume that GM has already evaluated this causal relationship: Its Hummer H3, launched in 2005, is almost 17 inches shorter than the H2, and gets 20 miles per gallon, double the amount of the Hummer H2.[18]

Let us assume that marketing managers at General Motors would like to explore consumer attitudes about the Hummer.The Hummer was touted as a vehicle that can go places where trucks and cars aren't supposed to.[19] This positioning primarily appeals to rugged individuals in search of adventure. Let us assume that GM is contemplating creating an awareness campaign about the Hummer that stresses its safety features instead. Would a focus on safety have a broader appeal? Would GM be able to sell more vehicles if the Hummer is positioned as a safe automobile? Let us also assume that GM hired KD Research to conduct marketing research on the Hummer. Suppose together, GM and KD Research come up with the following research question: "Will a safety positioning increase consumer demand for the Hummer?" The question itself suggests a cause-and-effect relationship (i.e., safety positioning results in an increase in consumer demand). The objective of the research, then, is to conduct *causal research* to determine whether there is such a relationship. If it does not increase the costs too much, nor interfere with the primary research objective, GM would also like to identify respondent characteristics of individuals who are most likely to purchase the Hummer. This is a secondary, *descriptive research* objective.

7-4b Secondary Data Research

Secondary data: Data collected to address a problem other than the problem at hand.

Internal secondary data: Data previously collected by a company to address a problem not related to the current research question.

External secondary data: Data collected for purposes other than the problem at hand.

Researchers first must determine if any information is available on the topic being researched. Researchers should start by examining **secondary data,** which are data collected to address a problem other than the problem currently facing the company. Secondary data offer the advantage of low cost and ready availability; data collection also takes less time and effort. The data that may be most relevant to the researcher's study, however, will most likely not exist, or if they do, they may be dated or unreliable.

There are two categories of secondary data. **Internal secondary data** are collected by the company to address a different problem, or collected by the company to address the same problem, but in a different environment or for a different brand. Prior research reports on the company's other brands, sales figures for different territories, and inventory reports are examples of secondary data. Especially useful internal data sources that General Motors could use to research whether a safety positioning may result in greater demand for the Hummer would be similar studies conducted on GM's other sports utility vehicles.

External secondary data are defined as data collected by an entity not affiliated with the company. Table 7-2 lists a number of reliable sources for data that companies may use in the early stages of their research. Local libraries, for example, have readily available general interest and business publications. Most university libraries that have a business school are likely to carry the trade publications and marketing journals listed. Many of the government sources listed in Table 7-2 are readily available online. The marketing organizations listed can also provide access to relevant data at a reasonable fee.

For its research on the effectiveness of consumer safety appeals, GM may consult a number of marketing articles published in the *Journal of Consumer Research* over the years. The *Journal of Marketing and Public Policy* may also be a reasonable source for articles that address consumer attitudes toward wasteful consumption—relevant to the marketing of the Hummer, considering that it is a gas guzzler. Other sources for information would be *American Demographics,* which may have articles addressing consumer lifestyle trends, and the government source, *Monthly Retail Sales & Inventories,* which may reveal sales trends for sports utility vehicles.

Valuable secondary data can be provided by marketing research firms, such as ACNielsen, which offer extensive information to subscribers on different markets, products, and topics. (Table 7-3 on page 204) lists the top 10 U.S. research firms in terms of sales revenue.) For example, a marketing research firm could tell GM the market share for every brand of SUV and how the Hummer compares to each brand. The research firm would probably have studies on why consumers choose SUVs and how they go about making their purchase decision.

An examination of ACNielsen will provide an excellent example of the many marketing research services available to a company. These services are listed in Table 7-4 on page 204. One service, Consumer*Facts, could be useful to GM in an assessment of the demographic profile of its target market. Consumer*Facts offers information on household purchase behavior and demographic profiles on an all-outlet basis. The service provides category and brand details for more than 1,000 product categories (dollar sales, dollar share, number of buying households, percent household penetration, buying rate, and purchase frequency). The most valuable information to GM might be the insights that the research company can provide into consumer demographic trends.[20]

Quality secondary data will help companies further refine problems and objectives, and, if necessary, even redefine them. But even the highest quality secondary data alone usually do not provide an answer to a specific research problem. Effectively addressing a research problem requires the collection of primary data. For the Hummer, secondary data can help General Motors identify consumer trends and trends in the automotive industry, but they would not help the company answer the question "Will a safety positioning

TABLE 7-2

External Secondary Data Sources

General Interest and Business Publications

American Demographics
Business Horizons
Business Week
Forbes
Fortune
Harvard Business Review
Newsweek
Time
U.S. News & World Report

Trade Publications

Advertising Age
Adweek
Brand Marketing
Brandweek
Catalog Age
Chain Store Age
Discount Store News
Marketing
Marketing Management
Marketing News
Marketing Research
Mediaweek
Sales & Marketing Management
Stores
Target Marketing

Academic Marketing Journals

Journal of Advertising
Journal of Business Research
Journal of Consumer Research
Journal of Consumer Marketing
Journal of Consumer Psychology
Journal of Macromarketing
Journal of Marketing
Journal of Marketing and Public Policy
Journal of Marketing Research
Journal of Retailing
Journal of Services Marketing
Marketing Science
Psychology & Marketing

Marketing Organizations

Academy of Business
Academy of Marketing Science
Advertising Research Foundation
American Academy of Advertising
American Marketing Association
American Psychological Association
Association for Consumer Research
Center for Service Marketing
Chartered Institute of Marketing
Direct Marketing Association
Institute for the Study of Business Markets
Interactive Marketing Institute
Marketing Research Association
Marketing Science Institute
Medical Marketing Association
Sales & Marketing Executives Association
Society for Marketing Advances

Government Sources

Advance Monthly Sales for Retail and Food Services
Annual Retail Trade Survey
Annual Survey of Manufacturers
Census of Wholesale Trade
Current Industrial Reports
Monthly Retail Sales & Inventories
STAT-USA/Internet
Statistical Abstract of the United States
U.S. Census Bureau

TABLE 7-3

Top 10 Marketing Research Firms Operating in the U.S.

Marketing Research	Country	Web Address
1. VNU Inc.	U.S.A./Netherlands	vnu.com
2. IMS Health Inc.	U.S.A.	imshealth.com
3. Information Resources	U.S.A.	infores.com
4. Westat, Inc.	U.S.A.	westat.com
5. TNS U.S.A.	U.K.	tns-global.com
5. TNS London	U.K.	tns-i.com
5. TNS NFO	U.S.A.	nfow.com
6. The Kantar Group	U.S.A.	kantargroup.com
7. Arbitron Inc.	U.S.A.	arbitron.com
8. NOP World US	U.S.A.	nopworld.com
9. Ipsos	U.S.A.	ipsos-na.com
10. Synovate	U.S.A.	synovate.com

Source: "Top 50 U.S. Research Firms," *Marketing News*, vol. 38, no. 11, (June 15, 2004): Supplement, H4–H44.

TABLE 7-4

ACNielsen Syndicated Services[21]

ACNielsen AdEx International	Chain-Level Trading Areas
Account Shopper Profiler	Store-Level Trading Areas
Intended User Survey	Consumer Marketplace Report
Cross Outlet Facts	A.C. Nielsen Convenience Track
Fresh Foods Consumer Panel	A.C. Nielsen Homescan
Fresh Foods Syndicated Reports	Homescan Basket*Facts
Consumer*Facts	Homescan New Product*Facts
Channel Facts	Market*Track International Panorama
Panel*Views	Retail Account Reports
Promotion Planner	SCANTRACK Services
Strategic Planner	SCANTRACK Ethnic Services
Super SCANTRACK	A.C. Nielsen SCANTRACK In Store Conditions Service
SPINS Natural Track	SCANTRACK Key Account Causal
Syndicated Trade Marketing Services	

Primary data: Data collected for the purpose of addressing the problem at hand.

Data collection instruments: The instruments used to collect data, such as a questionnaire, a paper-and-pencil measure, or an electronic measurement device.

Contact methods: Methods used for approaching study respondents.

Reliability: The extent to which data are likely to be free from random error and yield consistent results.

Validity: The extent to which data collected are free from bias.

strategy increase consumer demand for the Hummer?" The company must collect primary data to address its research problem. The process of collecting primary data is examined in the next section.

7-4c Collecting Primary Data

Most marketing research projects involve the collection of **primary data,** which is information collected for a specific purpose: to address the problem at hand. Collecting primary data requires substantial expertise in both instrument design and administration and, as a consequence, it is expensive and time consuming. Collecting quality primary data requires a concerted effort on the part of marketing managers and researchers to identify the appropriate research approaches, **data collection instruments,** sampling plans, and **contact methods** that are capable of providing primary data of high **reliability** and **validity** that best address the research problem and research objectives.

The Research Methodology When collecting primary data, researchers can use two different methods: qualitative research or quantitative research. **Qualitative research** typically involves a small number of respondents answering open-ended questions. Results are usually subjective because the researcher must interpret what respondents are saying. Alternatively, qualitative research could also involve observation that is not systematically structured, but open to a subjective analysis. **Quantitative research**, however, is a more structured approach involving responses that can be summarized or analyzed with numbers. Descriptive and causal research approaches discussed in Section 7-4a would utilize a quantitative research methodology, while exploratory research would typically use the qualitative methodology. It is interesting to note that, in certain countries, such as France and Italy, there is a preference for qualitative data as a complement to quantitative data, whereas in others, such as Germany, the United States, and Scandinavian countries, quantitative data are deemed as most valuable.

Qualitative research: Research that involves a small number of respondents answering open-ended questions.

Quantitative research: A structured type of research that involves either descriptive research approaches, such as survey research, or causal research approaches, such as experiments in which responses can be summarized or analyzed with numbers.

Qualitative research has been particularly useful either as a first step in studying marketing phenomena—when conducting exploratory research—or as one of the methods of exploring the problem at hand using multiple methods. Among the more popular qualitative research approaches are focus group interviews, depth interviews, and observation.

Focus group interviews typically involve from 6 to 12 participants recruited to meet some previously decided characteristics—for instance, ethnic background, certain age groups, social class, and use of certain products—and a moderator who guides the discussion based on a certain discussion agenda. Frequently, representatives of the sponsor observe the group's deliberations through a one-way mirror or on closed-circuit television. A video camera or tape recorder may also be used to record the group's deliberations on a certain topic of interest to the sponsor. The participants are typically given a small financial reward for participating in the study, or products such as free product samples, food, and so on.

Focus group interviews: A qualitative research approach investigating a research question, using a moderator to guide discussion within a group of subjects recruited to meet certain characteristics.

Researchers for General Motors could use focus groups to address GM's research question. They could identify a group of eight individuals in a broadly defined target market—consumers who can afford to purchase the Hummer at a minimum price of $50,000 (for a Hummer H2). A moderator will start by probing for consumer attitudes about SUVs, as well as about consumer perceptions of the Hummer and its safety. Then, their conversation would be guided by the moderator to address the likelihood that they would purchase this make if they knew that the Hummer is one of the safest passenger vehicles on the road.

Another approach that is helpful for collecting qualitative data is the depth interview. **Depth interviews** are one-on-one attempts to discover consumer motivations, feelings, and attitudes toward an issue of concern to the sponsor, using a very loose and unstructured question guide. They are typically used if the issue under study is a complex behavioral or decision-making consideration or an emotionally laden issue. Professional interviewers are typically well trained in keeping the respondent focused on the problem addressed and in handling complex interviewing situations. In addition to guiding respondents to address the problem investigated, interviewers can demonstrate the product and its features, and further probe into issues that are relevant to the research.

Depth interviews: A qualitative research method involving extensive interviews aimed at discovering consumer motivations, feelings, and attitudes toward an issue of concern to the sponsor, using unstructured interrogation.

Depth interviews can take place in person—these are referred to as personal interviews. There are cheaper alternatives to personal interviews: For instance, Computer Assisted Telephone Interviewing (CATI) is a telephone data collection method whereby the interviewer sits in front of a computer terminal, reads the questions on the screen, and promptly enters the answers.

Using interviewers to conduct research is very expensive and more time consuming than other research methods; however, the data they collect are normally more robust because interviewers can further address issues that come up during the interview. Consequently, the method offers insights that quantitative research approaches cannot provide.

Observational research (or **observation**) is a particularly useful research approach for gathering qualitative data. It is defined as a research approach in which subjects are observed interacting with a product and reacting to other components of the marketing mix and the environment. Numerous approaches are used in observational research. One

Observational research (or **observation**)**:** A research approach whereby subjects are observed interacting with a product and reacting to other components of the marketing mix and the environment.

Naturalistic inquiry: An observational research approach that requires the use of natural rather than contrived settings because behaviors take substantial meaning from their context.

Ethnography: The study of cultures.

method, known as **naturalistic inquiry,** is an observational research approach that requires the use of natural rather than contrived settings because behaviors take substantial meaning from their context.[22] The researcher is directly involved in the data collection, as a participant in the group whose verbal and nonverbal behaviors are observed. The analysis performed by the researcher is inductive, rather than deductive; that is, unlike in conventional research methods, the researcher does not rely on previous theory in the process of developing hypotheses, but rather, develops theories from the data. **Ethnography**—the study of cultures—is largely based on naturalistic inquiry. Both academic researchers and practitioners have used this approach to better understand consumers and consumer motivations. This technique is frequently used by researchers who attempt to increase the validity of their studies by acquiring an intimate knowledge of a culture's daily life through personal observation.[23] An example of qualitative observational research would involve a researcher joining a club of Hummer enthusiasts and noting their comments and reactions to changes in the Hummer product line.

Quantitative research methods are structured research approaches involving either descriptive research, such as observation, survey research, and content analysis, or causal research approaches, such as experiments. Observation, previously noted as a type of qualitative research, can also be quantitative when the subjects are *systematically* observed interacting with a product and reacting to other components of the marketing mix and the environment. An example of a quantitative observational method is the study of garbage (garbology). Garbology studies could examine if consumers' reported diet matches the packages identified in their garbage bins.

Physiological instruments can also be used as an observation method to measure a respondent's involuntary responses to stimuli. An instrument called a pupillometric meter can be used to measure eye movements as well as dilation of a person's pupil. Another instrument, the psychogalvanometer, attached to a respondent's fingers can measure an individual's perspiration level. These instruments are often used in advertising research to measure the physiological reaction to particular ads. Some researchers believe these instruments are more accurate than verbal or written responses where a respondent may give researchers the socially acceptable answer. For instance, in measuring the impact of nudity in an ad, respondents may indicate on a paper-and-pencil test that they don't even notice nudity in an ad anymore, while a physiological test may indicate otherwise. Physiological instruments are good for evaluating an individual's level of arousal to ads and other marketing material. They are also good for packaging research—not only to measure physiological reaction but to track eye movement across the package. Such research helps marketers identify whether people are paying attention to the ad and if they are focusing on the brand name and logo.

Content analysis: Method that assesses the content of advertisements in a medium with verbal and/or visual content.

Content analysis is a quantitative methodology that entails counting the number of times preselected words, themes, symbols, or pictures appear in a given medium such as a print advertisement or any medium with verbal and/or visual content. One area where content analysis is used extensively is advertising research, in an attempt to discover emerging themes and patterns. General Motors could conduct a content analysis study to identify the advertising themes and approaches used by competitors to advertise sports utility vehicles. Marketing Illustration 7-3 offers an example of a questionnaire that may be used in such a study (more information about questionnaire design will be provided later in this section). Survey respondents would be asked to complete the questionnaire as they examine SUV advertisements. The data would then be entered for all the SUV ads, and means would be calculated to determine to what extent SUV ads have the traits outlined in the questionnaire presented.

Survey research: Descriptive research that involves the administration of personal, telephone, or mail questionnaires.

Survey research, another example of widely used descriptive research, typically involves the administration of *structured* questionnaires in a personal interview, by telephone, or by mail. The use of the questionnaires assumes that respondents are both capable and willing to respond to the questions. The cheapest survey method is mail questionnaires; however, this method has a very high nonresponse rate. Many mail surveys are discarded, even if they come from establishments that consumers patronize. The most

Marketing Illustration 7-3

Content Analysis Study

Please look at each ad and indicate to what extent you believe the ad appears to have the following characteristics by circling the corresponding number, as follows:

1 = if the ad DOES NOT AT ALL HAVE the respective characteristic
2 = if the ad DOES NOT HAVE the respective characteristic
3 = if you are NOT SURE if the ad has the respective characteristic
4 = if the ad HAS the respective characteristic
5 = if the ad DEFINITELY HAS the respective characteristic

The ad appears to be:

• Interesting	5	4	3	2	1
• Funny	5	4	3	2	1
• Seductive	5	4	3	2	1
• Joyful	5	4	3	2	1
• Scary	5	4	3	2	1
• Colorful	5	4	3	2	1
• Dull	5	4	3	2	1
• Spartan	5	4	3	2	1
• Stressing practicality	5	4	3	2	1
• Stressing safety	5	4	3	2	1
• Stressing excitement	5	4	3	2	1
• Stressing adventure	5	4	3	2	1

Now, please fill in the following information:
The ad features ___ people.
The age of the driver is ___ years.
The ad is for a _______________(list make of vehicle).

expensive survey method is the personal interview—a method that provides very valuable data. Such an interview would be highly structured, compared to the depth interview discussed in the qualitative research approach section. However, even a structured personal interview allows the interviewer to probe into issues that the respondent may raise or to answer questions, thus providing valuable additional information to the researcher. Cheaper alternatives to the personal interview are Computer Assisted Telephone Interviewing (CATI), whereby a telephone interviewer in front of a computer terminal reads the questions on the screen and promptly enters the answers. Telephone interviews can also be automated, prompting the respondent to enter the appropriate response by pushing a number on the telephone keypad.

Causal (experimental) research looks at cause-and-effect relationships, eliminating or controlling for other extraneous factors that may be responsible for the results, and eliminating competing explanations for the observed findings. It requires the use of matched groups of subjects who are subjected to different treatments, to ascertain whether the observed response differences are statistically significant.

An example of an experiment that General Motors researchers could conduct to test whether a safety positioning strategy would increase consumer demand for the Hummer may involve a study of prospective buyers in two cities: Seattle and Miami. Let us assume that prospective buyers subscribe to *Architectural Digest,* a magazine targeted at consumers of luxury goods. GM will advertise the Hummer in *Architectural Digest* using different ads. The ads aimed at prospective buyers in Seattle would emphasize safety, while the ads aimed at prospective buyers in Miami would emphasize adventure. Subsequent to the advertising campaign, General Motors could compare the two cities with regard to dealer inquiries about the Hummer. In comparing the results between responses in the two cities, the researchers would need to determine whether other extraneous factors may contribute to the research results. Could consumers in Seattle be more adventurous and more interested in higher-risk sports, thus accounting for a lower response to the safety campaign? Could readers of *Architectural Digest* be more conservative and not very interested in adventure? Could readers in Miami be significantly older than those in Seattle and not too interested in adventure? By asking questions relating to these concerns in the questionnaire, researchers will be able to rule out these extraneous factors if no significant differences are found. If so, then any differences in the dealer inquiries following the ads would be due to the advertisements. Although difficult to do, causal research provides marketers with reliable data. Figure 7-9 summarizes the various research methods that can be used in collecting primary data.

Open-ended questions: Questions with free-format responses that the respondent can address as he or she sees appropriate.

Semantic differential scale: Scale that is anchored by words with opposite meanings.

Likert scale: A scale that is anchored by "strongly disagree" and "strongly agree" statements.

Data Collection Instruments Although electronic measurement devices are used to collect data, most data are collected using some type of questionnaire with either paper-and-pencil forms or a computer. In developing a questionnaire, researchers must come up with an appropriate format that will accurately collect the data. The questionnaire could use **open-ended questions,** which allow respondents to use their own words in responding to the questions. Alternatively or in addition, the questionnaire could use *forced-choice questions,* which include the possible responses of which respondents must select one. Examples of the latter are the **semantic differential scale,** a scale anchored by words with opposite meanings (good . . . bad, important . . . not important); and the **Likert scale,** anchored by "strongly disagree" and "strongly agree" statements. Clear instructions, preferably with examples, would help respondents in filling out the questionnaire appropriately.

Figure 7-9
Primary Data Research Methods

INTERACTIVE FIGURE

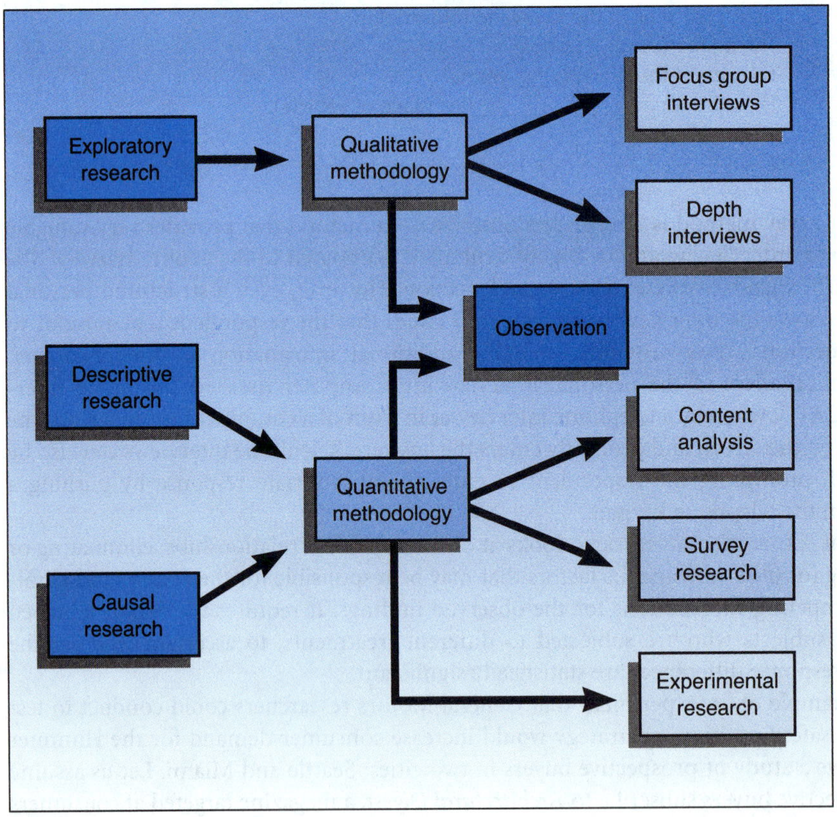

Marketing Illustration 7-4

Sample Consumer Research Questionnaire

Please indicate the extent to which you agree or disagree with the statements below by circling 5 if you strongly agree, 4 if you agree, 3 if you neither agree nor disagree, 2 if you disagree, and 1 if you strongly disagree with the statement. Please answer *every* question; the questionnaire cannot be used unless you do so.

1.	I seek adventure and fun in most of my spare time.	5	4	3	2	1
2.	My life is rather dull.	5	4	3	2	1
3.	I rarely have time for fun; I work during most of my spare time.	5	4	3	2	1
4.	In purchasing a car, my primary concern is access to inaccessible places.	5	4	3	2	1
5.	In purchasing a car, my primary concern is adventure.	5	4	3	2	1
6.	In purchasing a car, my primary concern is status.	5	4	3	2	1
7.	In purchasing a car, my primary concern is safety.	5	4	3	2	1
8.	I like to drive fast; I would love to drive a race car.	5	4	3	2	1
9.	The Hummer is one of the safest vehicles on the road.	5	4	3	2	1
10.	The Hummer is an automobile designed for rough roads.	5	4	3	2	1
11.	The Hummer offers excitement to drivers.	5	4	3	2	1
12.	The Hummer attracts attention on the road.	5	4	3	2	1
13.	The Hummer demands respect on the road.	5	4	3	2	1
14.	The next automobile I will purchase will be a Hummer.	5	4	3	2	1

The Likert scale is used in Marketing Illustration 7-4. Note the detailed explanation of the numbers to be circled.

The questionnaire in Marketing Illustration 7-4 could be used by General Motors to identify what type of consumer is likely to buy a Hummer. The questionnaire could also help the company determine how the target market, as well as other consumers, perceive the Hummer. Is it the explorer, the high-sensation seeker, who is more likely to state that the next automobile he or she will buy will be a Hummer, or is it the person who is concerned about safety?

A semantic differential questionnaire is illustrated in Figure 7-10. Notice that in this case, the respondent is asked to evaluate a particular color console television brand along 12 criteria. The respondent is also asked to evaluate the leading competitor and the ideal rating for a color console television. Charting all three measures on one graph allows researchers to determine how well their brand compares to the leading competitor and the ideal brand.

Sampling Plan The sampling plan calls for the marketing manager and researcher to jointly decide on the **sample** selected for the study—a segment of the population selected for the study and considered to be representative of the total population of interest. The population of interest, in the case of General Motors' Hummer, is its target market: consumers with higher household income, who can afford to purchase a vehicle whose base price is around $50,000.

Sample: A segment of the population selected for the study and considered to be representative of the total population of interest.

The chapter-opening vignette identified this target population to consist of individuals keen on owning a vehicle that stands out, one that provides status to its driver. Prospective Hummer drivers are individuals who pursue distinctive products, who have a strong need for self-esteem and being noticed—indeed, appreciated—for their choices. A sample selected from a population of individuals with a household income of $125,000 and who want distinctive products is appropriate for a study involving the Hummer. Alternatively,

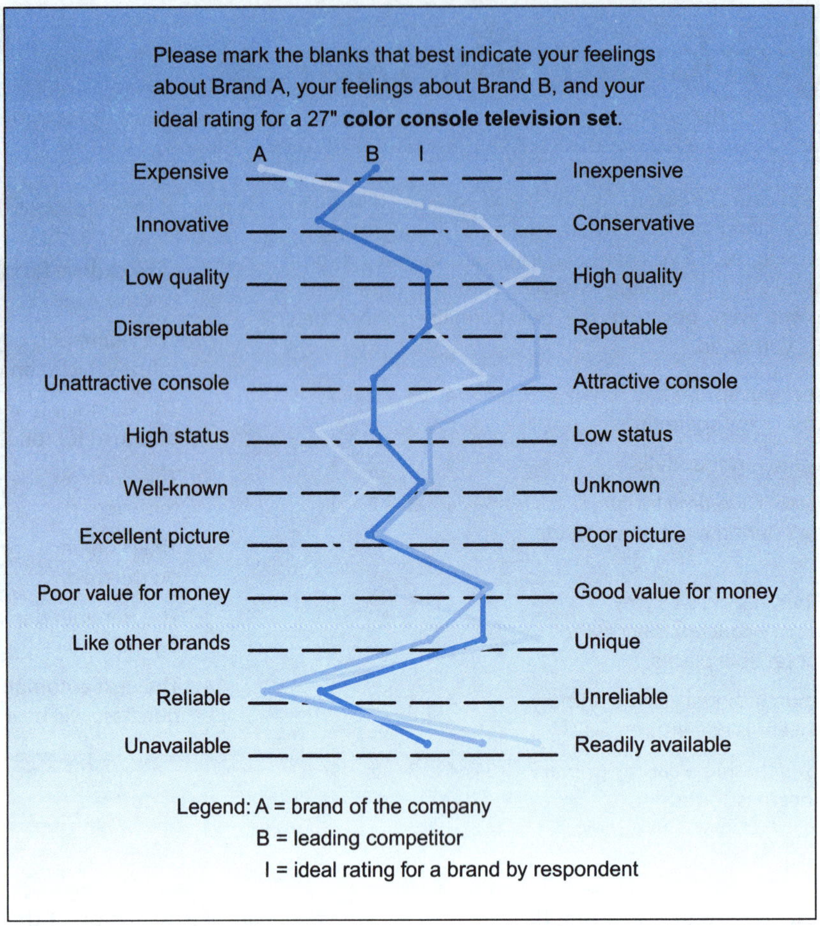

Figure 7-10
A Semantic Differential for a Color Television

the study population could consist of Hummer dealers, who understand the attitudes, interests, and opinions of the target population. A sample of dealers, then, could be interviewed.

Among sampling decisions are the selection of the **sampling unit**—determining who will be included in the survey. Should the researcher interview anybody in the household, including children? Should the researcher interview only the driver? Should the sample include people from all over the United States or just certain regions? Should the sample include individuals from other countries? Or should Hummer dealers be included in the sample? If so, should all dealers be surveyed, or should a sample of dealers be selected? If so, how will they be selected?

Researchers must also decide on the **sample size**—determining how many individuals will be surveyed. Ideally, a larger sample should be chosen to ensure that accurate results are obtained. The **sampling procedure**—determining how the sampling units will be selected—is also important. The most representative sample of a particular population is a **random probability sample,** in which each individual selected for the study has a known and equal chance of being selected. A less representative but easier method of selecting a sample would be to use a **convenience sample,** which is composed of individuals who are easy for the researcher to contact. For the Hummer, that might be individuals who own an SUV, regardless of brand. It might be individuals who have a GM credit card. For both sampling units, it would be relatively easy to obtain names, addresses, and telephone numbers. Another sampling method that does not pose much effort for the researcher is a **judgment sample,** which is a sample of individuals thought to be representative of the population. An example of a judgment sample could be owners or managers at each of the Hummer dealerships. In a consumer research project on fashion, it might be all of the designers who participate in a particular fashion show.

- **Sampling unit:** The individuals or groups included in the study.
- **Sample size:** The number of study participants.
- **Sampling procedure:** The procedure used in the selection of sampling units.
- **Random probability sample:** A sample in which each individual selected for the study has a known and equal chance of being included in the study.
- **Convenience sample:** Sample composed of individuals who are easy to contact for the researcher.
- **Judgment sample:** A sample of individuals thought to be representative of the population.

The most critical criterion in selecting a sampling technique is how well the sample represents the population. While the ideal is to use a random probability sample, it is not always practical. It would be extremely difficult and costly for KD Research to randomly select individuals in the United States, especially if they want only the opinions of individuals with incomes above $125,000. As long as the sample selected represents the population being studied, a convenience or judgment sample is adequate.

The last decision researchers must make, in terms of sampling, is the **sampling frame**—the list from which sampling units are selected. Examples of sampling frames are mailing lists or telephone books. For a list of the dwellers in a subdivision where the prices of homes start at $500,000, researchers may contact a neighborhood organization, or they may check property records of the respective city or county. For KD Research, they could use the list of GM credit card holders or buy a mailing list of individuals who own SUVs or who have incomes above $125,000. Once the sampling frame is chosen, then researchers normally develop some type of random selection method within the sampling frame. For instance, suppose KD Research has 450,000 names in the sampling frame. If researchers want to survey 2,000 individuals, they may select every 225th name to contact. Figure 7-11 reviews the sampling decisions that must be made.

Sampling frame: The list from which sampling units are selected.

Collecting Data Data can be collected using the various contact methods, such as mail, email, Internet, telephone, and personal interview. Table 7-5 addresses the advantages and disadvantages of each type of contact method. For decades, the traditional forms of data collection have been mail, telephone, and personal interviews. New methods attributed to the technological revolution—methods that became especially popular starting with the 1990s—are email and Internet contact methods.

The best method for a research study is a function of researcher needs, the size of the sample desired for the study, the amount of data needed, and other considerations. For a very large sample, using a mail and email questionnaire is appropriate. If a large amount of data needs to be collected, then a mail questionnaire would be the best contact method. Alternatively, if researchers want to further probe into a particular response, personal interviews offer more flexibility. A higher response rate is obtained with a personal or a telephone interview than with other methods.

In the case of the General Motors' study of prospective Hummer buyers, the research company, KD Research, needs to decide on the research approach that will be used; this decision, in part, will determine the appropriate contact method. For example, if the company decides to use the sample consumer research questionnaire in Marketing Illustration 7-4, then a mail, email, or Internet survey would be appropriate. The company could also conduct personal interviews with prospective Hummer buyers, or a focus group interview, as described in Section 7-4c.

After the instrument is designed and the sample is selected, the researcher or research team is ready to collect the primary data. This expensive undertaking can be eventful. The data collectors need to be briefed appropriately. Researchers must decide how **nonresponse**—defined as the inability or refusal by a respondent to participate in the study—should be handled. In some instances, it makes sense to go back and identify the traits of the respondents who refused to participate in order to compare them with those of respondents who participated to be sure the sample who responded is the same as those who did not respond. For mail surveys, the nonresponse rate can be very high, as much as 90 percent or even more. So for valid research, it is essential that individuals who participated in a study represent the population being studied and are not different from individuals who did not participate.

Nonresponse: The inability or refusal by a respondent to participate in a study.

7-4d Data Analysis, Recommendations, and Implementation

Data collected should be coded, entered into the analysis program, and analyzed. Researchers will tabulate the results and put them in a form that is meaningful and that will answer the problems introduced in the beginning of the research process. To understand these last three steps in the research process, study Figure 7-11.

Figure 7-11
The Sampling Plan

INTERACTIVE FIGURE

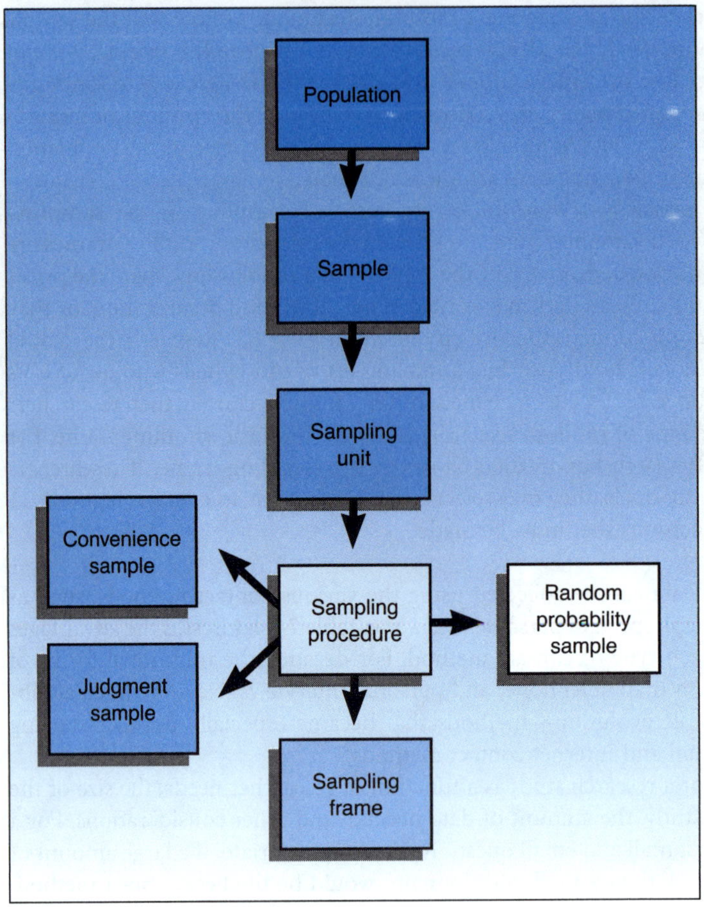

TABLE 7-5

Advantages and Disadvantages of Different Contact Methods

Method	Advantages	Disadvantages
Mail	Inexpensive No interviewer effects Large amounts of data Reasonable sample control	Slow Low response rates Lack of flexibility
Email	Inexpensive No interviewer effects Reasonable amount of data Fast Reasonable sample control	Low response rates Lack of flexibility
Internet	Inexpensive No interviewer effects Reasonable amount of data Fast	Low response rates Not much flexibility Poor sample control
Telephone	Reasonable cost Few interviewer effects Reasonably fast Reasonable response rates Reasonable sample control	Lower amounts of data Higher cost than mail, email, and Internet
Personal and focus group interviews	High flexibility High response rate Large amounts of data Reasonably fast High sample control	Expensive Large interviewer effects

Notice in the first step of the analysis that 500 questionnaires were collected and that each questionnaire was numbered from A001 to A500. Each response was then coded and tabulated. The results of the tabulations appear on the right upper portion in Figure 7-12. Notice that, out of the 500 respondents, 300 drink coffee, and 270 drink coffee in the morning.

The lower portion of Figure 7-12 presents some of the analysis of the data. For instance, because 500 respondents took the survey and 300 said they drink coffee, we can say that 60 percent of the respondents drink coffee. Notice that 142 said they drink coffee two or more times per day. Because we know that 300 drink coffee, we can say that 47 percent of coffee drinkers consume coffee two or more times per day (142 divided by 300). Likewise, we can say that 90 percent of the coffee drinkers consume coffee in the morning. (Supermarkets offer an extensive array of coffee choices to meet consumers' coffee drinking needs—see Figure 7-13.)

Based on this research and the analysis, a possible recommendation could be that the coffee industry and individual firms need to increase the advertising geared toward non-coffee drinkers because 40 percent of the sample does not drink coffee. For those who drink coffee, advertising could focus on drinking coffee in the afternoon, the period with the lowest consumption.

1. Do you drink coffee?	Yes	01	300
	No	02	200
2. In general, how frequently do you drink coffee? (Check only one answer.)	Two or more times per day	03	142
	Once per day	04	84
	Several times per week	05	42
	Once or twice per week	06	20
	One to three times per month	07	12
	Never	08	200
3. During what time of day do you drink coffee? (Check all answers that apply.)	Morning	09	270
	Lunchtime	10	165
	Afternoon	11	100
	Dinnertime	12	150
	Evening	13	205
	None	14	200

Coding: Questionnaires numbered A001 to A500. Each response is labeled 01 to 14 (e.g., Morning is 09, Evening is 13.) Question 3 is a multiple-response question.

Tabulation: Total responses are shown above right.

Analysis: Sixty percent drink coffee. About 28 percent drink coffee two or more times daily (representing 47 percent of all coffee drinkers); almost 25 percent of coffee drinkers (74 people) consume coffee less than once per day. Ninety percent of coffee drinkers consume coffee in the morning; only one-third consume it in the afternoon.

Recommendations: The coffee industry and individual firms need to increase the advertising geared toward noncoffee drinkers, as well as infrequent coffee drinkers. Emphasis should also be placed on lifting coffee consumption during afternoon hours.

Implementation: New, more aggressive advertising campaigns will be developed, and the annual media budgets devoted to increasing overall coffee consumption will be expanded. One theme will stress coffee s value as an afternoon pick-me-upper.

Figure 7-12
Data Analysis, Recommendations, and Implementation of Findings for a Study on Coffee

INTERACTIVE FIGURE

Figure 7-13
Research can help supermarkets determine the appropriate coffee flavors for their coffee drinking shoppers.

Source: Courtesy of Ukrop's Super Markets, Inc.

Implementation of the findings might include a more aggressive advertising campaign that is aimed at noncoffee drinkers. This would require an increase in the media budget and could also require an additional study to see what media outlets would be the best for reaching noncoffee drinkers. For the current coffee drinkers, to stimulate additional consumption, the theme that coffee is "an afternoon pick-me-upper" could be used.

7-5 Marketing Decision Support Systems

Marketing decision support systems (MDSS): A coordinated collection of data, systems, tools, and techniques, complemented by supporting software and hardware designed for the gathering and interpretation of business and environmental data.

Marketing decision support systems are defined as a coordinated collection of data, systems, tools, and techniques, complemented by supporting software and hardware designed for the gathering and interpretation of business and environmental data.

Ideally, a marketing decision support system should be:

- *Computerized*—Having a computerized support system is now possible even for small and medium-sized businesses due to the increase in the capability of personal computers to perform more and more complex tasks.
- *Interactive*—Managers can use online instructions to generate on-the-spot reports, without assistance from a programmer, who will be involved only in system updating and training.
- *Flexible*—Managers can access and integrate data from a variety of sources and manipulate the data in a variety of ways (producing averages and totals, sorting the data, etc.).
- *Discovery-oriented*—Such systems should produce diagnostics that reveal trends and identify problems.

A number of areas lend themselves well to marketing decision support systems (MDSS). A common use is that of sales forecasting. The more complex the techniques used in forecasting sales, the more their efficiency can be improved in an MDSS environment. Nevertheless, input obtained from using the simpler methods (sales force composite estimates, jury of executive opinion, and the Delphi method) can be used to cross-validate the estimates given by the more sophisticated forecasting techniques (time series and econometric models).

Sales force composite estimates: Research studies in which sales forecasts are based on the personal observations and forecasts of the local sales force.

Forecasts from **sales force composite estimates** are based on the personal observations and "hunches" of the sales force. Salespeople are in close contact with the consumer and,

Figure 7-14

Researchers use store scanners to assess market share, as well as to track current sales of products.

Source: Courtesy of Ukrop's Super Markets, Inc.

therefore, are in the best position to find out about consumer desires and overall changing market trends. Forecasts from the **jury of expert opinion** are based on the opinions of different experts about future demand. The experts' opinions are then combined, and an aggregate demand estimation is offered. Another method, the **Delphi method,** entails asking a number of experts to estimate market performance, aggregate the results, and share this information with these experts. This process is repeated several times, until a consensus is reached.

Jury of expert opinion: An approach to sales forecasting based on the opinions of different experts.

Delphi method: A method of forecasting sales that involves asking a number of experts to estimate market performance, aggregating the results, and then sharing this information with the said experts; the process is repeated several times, until a consensus is reached.

Among the more sophisticated forecasting techniques are time series methods, which use data of past performance to predict future market demand. Typically, these methods give more weight to more recent developments. They assume that the future will be similar to the past. Econometric methods, however, take into account different deterministic factors that affect market demand—factors that may or may not depend on past performance trends. **Time series and econometric methods** are dependent on the availability of historical data. For markets where historical data are unavailable, such as developing countries, it is appropriate to estimate demand *by analogy*, noting responses of markets with similar relevant characteristics, markets with similar levels of economic development, markets with similar cultural characteristics, and so on.

Time series and econometric methods: Methods that use the data of past performance to predict future market demand.

The **analogy method** is an estimation method that relies on developments and findings in markets that are relatively similar. For example, to estimate the anticipated adoption rate of cellular phones in Latvia, it may be appropriate to identify the proportion of new adopters in a more advanced country in the Baltics—Estonia, which is more developed—where cellular phone service is widely available, but which shares a similar history and similar geopolitics with Latvia. This is an example of *country performance analogy.* However, to estimate the adoption rate of Internet service in Sri Lanka, it may be appropriate to evaluate the adoption rate of computers in Sri Lanka. This is an example of *product performance analogy.*

Analogy method: A method for estimation that relies on developments and findings in similar markets or where the product is in the same lifecycle stage.

Important forecasting methods for retailers and other channel members involve **point-of-sale (POS)-based projections,** which are performed with the help of store scanners, such as those used by Ukrop's Super Markets in Figure 7-14. Research suppliers increasingly use store scanners to assess market share and other relevant market dimensions. Weekly or biweekly store audits reveal the movement of goods within the store and from warehouses.

Point-of-sale (POS)-based projections: Market projections based on the use of store scanners in weekly and biweekly store audits.

Summary

1. *Define marketing research, provide a description of its scope, and offer examples of each type of research conducted in marketing.* The chapter offers examples of each type of research conducted in marketing. Marketing research involves gathering information for marketing decisions. It is wide in scope, covering industry research, market traits and trends, buyer behavior, and the marketing mix. Examples of product research are product testing, product package studies, and competitive product analysis. Distribution research covers areas such as channel performance and coverage and plant/warehouse location studies. Promotion research has a wide scope, with studies of premiums, coupons, and deals; advertising effectiveness; media research; and sales force analyses. Pricing research involves studies projecting demand, as well as market potential studies, sales potential studies, cost analyses, and profit analyses, among others.

2. *Describe the steps involved in the marketing research process.* The first step of the research process involves defining the research problem and setting the research objectives; this is usually done in conjunction with the research team and the marketing managers initiating the research. The development of the research plan involves deciding on the information sources—primary and secondary—and determining the appropriate research approach. The research approach may involve collecting qualitative data, using focus groups or observation methods, or collecting quantitative data, using descriptive (surveys, content analyses) or causal research methods (experimental research). They, in turn, determine the contact methods: mail, email, Internet, telephone, and personal interviews. The sampling plan must be determined: selecting the sampling procedure, sample size, frame, and unit. Finally, the researcher must collect, analyze, and interpret the information.

3. *Introduce the concept of decision support systems for marketing and describe the sales forecasting process.* Decision support systems represent a coordinated approach to collecting and interpreting business and environmental data. Methods used in sales forecasting are sales force composite estimates, which are based on the personal observations or hunches of the sales force; jury of expert opinion, which involves the aggregate opinions of different experts about future demand; the Delphi method, which entails asking a number of experts to estimate market performance, aggregate the results, share the information with the experts, and repeat the process several times until a consensus is reached; time series and econometric models, which use data of past performance to predict future market demand; the analogy method, which is an estimation method that relies on developments and findings in markets that are relatively similar; and point-of-sale-based projections, which perform sales forecasts with the help of store scanners.

Key Terms

advertising effectiveness research (p. 196)
analogy method (p. 215)
brand awareness research (p. 192)
brand-name generation (p. 195)
buyer behavior research (p. 192)
causal (experimental) research (p. 201)
channel performance and coverage studies (p. 196)
competitive pricing analyses (p. 198)
competitive product studies (p. 195)
concept development research (p. 194)
consumer segmentation studies (p. 193)
contact methods (p. 204)
content analysis (p. 206)
convenience sample (p. 210)
cost analyses (p. 198)
data collection instruments (p. 204)
Delphi method (p. 215)
depth interviews (p. 205)
descriptive research (p. 200)
ethnography (p. 206)
exploratory research (p. 200)
external secondary data (p. 202)
focus group interviews (p. 205)
internal secondary data (p. 202)
judgment sample (p. 210)
jury of expert opinion (p. 215)
Likert scale (p. 208)
market potential studies (p. 198)
marketing decision support systems (p. 214)
marketing intelligence (p. 191)
marketing research (p. 191)
media research (p. 197)
naturalistic inquiry (p. 206)
nonresponse (p. 211)
observational research (or observation) (p. 205)
open-ended questions (p. 208)
plant/warehouse location study (p. 196)
point-of-sale (POS)-based projections (p. 215)
price elasticity studies (p. 198)
primary data (p. 204)
product packaging design (p. 195)
product testing (p. 195)
profit analyses (p. 198)
qualitative research (p. 205)
quantitative research (p. 205)
random probability sample (p. 210)
reliability (p. 204)
research approach (p. 200)
sales force compensation, quota, and territory studies (p. 197)
sales force composite estimates (p. 214)
sales forecasts (p. 198)
sales potential studies (p. 198)
sample (p. 209)
sample size (p. 210)
sampling frame (p. 211)
sampling procedure (p. 210)
sampling unit (p. 210)
secondary data (p. 202)
semantic differential scale (p. 208)
studies of premiums, coupons, and deals (p. 196)
survey research (p. 206)
test marketing (p. 195)
time series and econometric methods (p. 215)
validity (p. 204)

Discussion Questions

1. Using the example of the Hummer, describe the types of promotion-related research that could be conducted that would help the company more effectively promote its brand.
2. You have been hired by Procter & Gamble to conduct a study that investigates whether consumers are likely to purchase a new product: Dero Lux. P&G envisages the product as a quality detergent to be used only on the highest quality fabrics—silk, wool, and fine cotton blends. Take this study through all the steps of the research process and elaborate in detail on the investigation.
3. What is the difference between qualitative and quantitative research approaches? Give examples of each.
4. Design a content-analysis questionnaire that evaluates the portrayal of women in advertising.
5. Going back to the Dero Lux example in Question 2, explore different methods for forecasting sales for the new brand.

Review Questions

True or False

1. Channel performance and coverage studies are examples of distribution research.
2. Focus group interviews typically involve randomly selected groups of people who share their opinion about a product in front of TV cameras.
3. Observation is a type of research approach in which subjects are observed interacting with a product and reacting to other components of the marketing mix and the environment.
4. Exploratory research is conducted early in the research process; it is the research that helps to further define a problem or identify additional problems that should be investigated.
5. Observational analysis is a quantitative method that counts the number of times preselected words, themes, symbols, or pictures appear in a given media with verbal or visual content.
6. The questionnaires that use open-ended questions are based on semantic differential scales or Likert scales.
7. Marketing researchers should eliminate nonresponse cases—defined as the inability or refusal of respondent to participate in a study—because they do not provide conclusive information.

Multiple Choice

8. Marketing research addresses which of the following issues?
   a. monitoring developments in the market environment
   b. anticipating product's performance in the marketplace
   c. evaluating customer-specific brand-related or advertisement-related attitudes
   d. all of the above
9. _______ research examines consumer brand preferences, brand attitudes, and brand-related behavior.
   a. Buyer behavior
   b. Purchase-related
   c. Brand loyalty
   d. Brand management
10. Advertising effectiveness research measures which of the following?
   a. viewers' recall of an advertisement
   b. viewers' attitude toward the ad
   c. the extent to which the ad persuaded the consumer to purchase the product
   d. all of the above
11. Which of the following categories relate to pricing research?
   a. cost analysis and profit analysis
   b. price elasticity studies
   c. competitive price analysis
   d. all of the above
12. Naturalistic inquiry is a method used in observational research in which information is gathered using
   a. one-on-one interviews with loose and unstructured questions.
   b. natural rather than contrived settings.
   c. an analysis of verbal and nonverbal behavior.
   d. b and c
13. Which of the following types of research looks at cause-and-effect relationships and eliminates other extraneous factors that may be responsible for the results?
   a. observation
   b. content analysis
   c. descriptive research
   d. experimental research
14. Which of the following categories is used to determine who should be included in the marketing survey?
   a. sampling unit
   b. sampling procedure
   c. sampling size
   d. sampling frame
15. Which of the following methods asks a number of experts to estimate the market performance and then aggregates the results and shares this information with the same experts, repeating the procedure until a consensus is reached?
   a. jury of executive opinion
   b. analogy method
   c. Delphi method
   d. time series model

Notes

1. Danny Hakim, "Detroit's Hottest Seller Is Its Biggest Gas Guzzler," *New York Times* (November 2, 2002): B1, B3.
2. This section is organized based on a framework provided in a table in Thomas C. Kinnear and Ann R. Root, eds., *1988 Survey of Marketing Research: Organization, Functions, Budgeting, and Compensation* (Chicago: American Marketing Association, 1989): 43.
3. See www.acnielsen.com.
4. Kim Thuy Balin, "DuPont Lycra Goes Global," *Sporting Goods Business,* vol. 32, no. 5 (March 28, 1999): 16.
5. Ibid.
6. Bernard Dubois and Claire Paternault, "Observations—Understanding the World of Luxury Brands: The 'Dream' Formula," *Journal of Advertising Research,* vol. 35, no. 4 (July/August 1995): 69–74.
7. Alison Stein Wellner, "Culinary Feat," *American Demographics,* vol. 23, no. 3 (March 2001): S16.
8. "Special Report: New Products," *Ad Age International* (April 13, 1998): 17–20.
9. Erika Rasmusson, "Growing a Global Brand," *Sales and Marketing Management,* vol. 151, no. 8 (August 1999): 17.
10. Charlotte Clarke, "Language Classes," *Marketing Week,* vol. 20, no. 17 (July 24, 1997): 35–39.
11. David Ricks, *Big Business Blunders* (Homewood, IL: Dow Jones Irwin, 1983).
12. James I. Steinberg and Alan L. Klein, "Global Branding: Look Before You Leap," *Brandweek,* vol. 39, no. 43 (November 16, 1998): 30–32.
13. Deborah Ball, Sarah Ellison, and Janet Adamy, "Just What You Need!: It Takes a Lot of Marketing to Convince Consumers What They're Lacking," *Wall Street Journal* (October 28, 2004): B1; "Procter & Gamble Co.: Vacuum Cleaner Is Recalled for Posing Possible Fire Hazard," *Wall Street Journal* (November 29, 2004): 1.
14. Erin Anderson, George Day, and V. Kasturi Rangan, "Strategic Channel Design," *Sloan Management Review,* vol. 38, no. 4 (Summer 1997): 59–69.
15. See www.promotiondecisions.com.
16. Constance L. Hays, "One-Word Shoppers' Lexicon: Price," *New York Times* (December 26, 2002): C1, C3.
17. Ibid.
18. Karen Lundegaard, "Macho Lite: Latest Crop of SUVs to Hit the Streets; Toyota Introduces Vehicle to Battle Smaller Hummer, Emphasizing Gas Mileage," *The Wall Street Journal* (February 10, 2005): D1.
19. See www.HUMMER.com.
20. See www.acnielsen.com.
21. Ibid.
22. See Yvonna S. Lincoln and Egon G. Guba, *Naturalistic Inquiry* (Beverly Hills: Sage Publications, 1985); Laura A. Hudson and Julie L. Ozanne, "Alternative Ways of Seeking Knowledge in Consumer Research," *Journal of Consumer Research* (March 14, 1988): 508–521.
23. Jerome Kirk and Marc L. Miller, *Reliability and Validity in Qualitative Research* (Beverly Hills: Sage Publications, 1986).

Case 7-1 The Complex World of Trademarks

A new party supply retailer in southern Maryland, close to Washington, D.C., registered its name as Paper-Max. The store sells party supply paper products of all colors and textures to consumers living in the bedroom communities of Washington, D.C. Soon after opening, a friend of the owner, Don Levy, came into the store and recommended that the store change its name and logo to look less like the name and logo of Office-Max—an office supply superstore. Don said that he had heard that Office-Max had sued CARMAX for having a similar name, and that Bailey's Irish Cream (a liquor manufacturer) sued the maker of Bailey's cigarettes, a small manufacturer of cheap cigarettes in Virginia, for using the Bailey's name for a product in a similar product category—a vice product.

The store manager, Marc Johnson, thought long and hard about this new problem that he had not foreseen when he decided to name his new store. CARMAX is a retailer of used cars; if Office-Max sued the car retailer, then the likelihood that it would sue Paper-Max would be even higher because Paper-Max is in the paper product business. Marc decided to bring in a local marketing research firm, KD Research, to find out whether trademark litigation was something he should worry about.

KD Researchers told Marc that it is already not wise that he used the letter "X" in the store name. It is well known that "X" names, with their emphasis on tech-sounding prefixes and suffixes, are potentially subject to trademark infringement claims, especially because there are many known brand and store names with these prefixes and suffixes. KD Research proposed to conduct a research study to find out whether there was any likelihood that consumers might confuse Paper-Max with Office-Max. Such a research study would have to meet very strict standards. The minimum standards for surveys in litigation are found in the *Manual for Complex Litigations,* published by the Federal Judicial Center. They include these criteria:

- The population was properly chosen and defined.
- The sample represented that population.
- The data were accurately reported.
- The data were analyzed against statistical principles.
- The questions asked were clear and not misleading.
- Proper interviewing procedures were followed.
- The process ensured objectivity; for example, the interviewers were not aware of the purpose of the survey.

These standards call for careful analysis. Among the important decisions are determining which company's customers and prospects should be surveyed. Typically, it is the older company's customers who are thought to be most likely to be confused by the new company's use of the similar name. Such surveys are problematic if the population is too broadly or narrowly defined. In *Schwinn Bicycle Co. v. Ross Bicycles Inc.,* a case involving exercise bicycles, the court disregarded a survey of fitness professionals; they were not considered representative of the general consuming public.

Marketing researchers who prepare surveys for litigation have to develop thick skins, as the opposing side always finds ways to attack their work. Typically, the opposing side will take one or both of two positions: They will hire their own expert to critique the survey or retain an expert to conduct a counter survey. When a survey is attacked, the opposition's expert will usually point out its "fatal flaws." In briefs opposing the survey, attorneys have called the researcher on the other side "intellectually dishonest." So when an attorney hires a researcher, he or she probably will call for a "bulletproof survey," which may or may not be possible, unless unlimited funds are available.

Marc thought long and hard about this dilemma. He could not really afford a lawsuit. He thought it might help him to conduct such a study to share with managers of any long-established stores with a "Max" suffix to convince them that there was no likelihood that their clients would believe that his store, Paper-Max, was affiliated with their stores. But he could not afford the steep fee of $14,000 that KD Research would charge to conduct such a survey.

Questions

1. How is it possible that Paper-Max could be confused with Office-Max? Can you think of other retailers whose names end in "Max"?
2. List the names of other brands of products or retailers that are somewhat similar.
3. Design a research study that will investigate the likelihood of consumer confusion between Paper-Max and Office-Max. Who is your population? Who will be included in your sample, and how will you select the sample? What type of research will you conduct? The case mentions that surveys are typically used to assess the likelihood of confusion. Design a survey that would address your research question.

Source: Gabriel Gelb, "Litigation Surveys Have Special Rules," *Marketing News,* vol. 35, no. 20 (September 24, 2001): 26.

Case 7-2 Starting a Modeling Agency

Karen Johnson is contemplating starting a modeling agency in Flagstaff, Arizona. She has previously worked for two top New York modeling agencies and believes that she has sufficient experience, both as a model and as a modeling agency employee, to create a successful agency of her own. Because Flagstaff is somewhat off the beaten path of these agencies, her scouting capabilities in this remote location and her connections in the fashion world may prove to be valuable for her new enterprise.

Although Karen has a feel for what fashion magazines and the fashion industry want in a model, she would like to create a better match between her models and the industry by creating for her models portfolios of photographs that present the prevailing "look"—what is considered to be the in-look. To better define the in-look, she has hired KD Research to perform a content analysis on the most recent advertisements that appeared in last month's issues of *Vogue*, *Elle*, and *Cosmo*.

KD Research recruited judges to fill out the questionnaire in Table 7-6. Each ad in the three magazines was evaluated separately by three judges.

The researchers then attempted to identify the characteristics that were the most prevalent in the ads. They calculated the averages for all the advertisements; Table 7-7 shows the results.

The leading traits of the women portrayed in the current ads were soft, poised, confident, youthful, calm, warm, cool, elegant, daydreaming, good girl, seductive, pensive, and proud.

Questions

1. Advise Karen on the prevailing "look" that she should create for her models.
2. Evaluate the research process that KD Research used.
3. In determining what individuals Karen should target for her modeling agency, she again wants to hire KD Research. Outline a research approach for KD Research. Be sure to include all of the components discussed in Section 7-4c, especially the sampling plan.

TABLE 7-6 KD Research Questionnaire

Please look at each ad and indicate to what extent you believe that THE WOMAN IN THE AD appears to have the following characteristics by circling the corresponding number, as follows:

1 = if the ad/woman DOES NOT AT ALL HAVE the respective characteristic
2 = if the ad/woman DOES NOT QUITE APPEAR TO HAVE the respective characteristic
3 = if the ad/woman APPEARS TO HAVE the respective characteristic
4 = if the ad/woman HAS the respective characteristic
5 = if the ad/woman DEFINITELY HAS the respective characteristic.

The woman in the ad appears to be					
Soft	5	4	3	2	1
Cool	5	4	3	2	1
Seductive	5	4	3	2	1
Scornful	5	4	3	2	1
Kitten-like	5	4	3	2	1
Optimistic	5	4	3	2	1
Maternal	5	4	3	2	1
Loving	5	4	3	2	1
Practical	5	4	3	2	1
Proud	5	4	3	2	1
Comical	5	4	3	2	1
Calm	5	4	3	2	1
Superior	5	4	3	2	1
Elegant	5	4	3	2	1

(a total of 30 adjectives)

The woman in the ad appears to be					
Caucasian	5	4	3	2	1
African American	5	4	3	2	1
Hispanic	5	4	3	2	1
Asian	5	4	3	2	1
The woman is looking at					
People	5	4	3	2	1
An object	5	4	3	2	1
Nothing	5	4	3	2	1
The reader	5	4	3	2	1

*The woman's age is approximately*____ ***years.***

TABLE 7-7

Prevalent Characteristic Averages

Emotion/Expression	Mean	Standard Deviation
Soft	3.264	1.035
Poised	3.256	1.004
Confident	3.058	1.072
Youthful	3.019	1.124
Calm	3.001	.898
Warm	2.977	1.042
Cool	2.975	1.037
Elegant	2.968	.93
Daydreaming	2.947	1.099
Good girl	2.946	1.016
Seductive	2.901	.959
Pensive	2.857	1.013
Proud	2.854	.947
Sexy	2.826	.988
Sophisticated	2.821	.961
Sexual	2.791	.976
Loving	2.786	.976
Self-loving	2.781	.921
Snobbish	2.756	1.115
Natural	2.743	.983
Smiling	2.731	1.135
Humble	2.686	1.031
Happy	2.679	1.007
Sassy	2.678	.958
Mannequin	2.672	.991
Demure	2.670	1.064
Anxious	2.641	.954
Tease	2.623	.937
Stiff	2.603	.977
Superior	2.529	.874
Socialite	2.521	.982
Coy	2.496	.884
Reluctant	2.456	.951
Emotionless	2.438	1.175
Nostalgic	2.432	.837
Caucasian	3.704	1.373
Hispanic	1.745	1.096
African American	1.314	.818
Asian	1.290	.67
Nothing	2.706	1.679
Reader	2.495	1.813
People	1.867	1.279
Object	1.832	1.153

Part 3

Marketing Mix Strategies

Product Strategies

8

CHAPTER OBJECTIVES

1. Define and classify products into relevant categories.
2. Address issues related to branding, such as the brand name, mark, logo, and character; brand sponsor; and brand strategy decisions.
3. Address product packaging and labeling issues.
4. Analyze the different dimensions of the product mix.
5. Describe the new product development process and the different degrees of product newness.
6. Examine the new product diffusion process and the different categories of product adopters.
7. Address the different stages of the product lifecycle.
8. Examine the challenges involved in managing the product portfolio.

CHAPTER OUTLINE

Mick Jagger, Keith Richards, Charlie Watts, Ron Wood, and Brian Jones belong to a brand that is as much in demand today as it was 40 years ago: the Rolling Stones. The veteran rock band has managed to fill and rock the house at New York's Madison Square Garden, the Los Angeles Forum, and Toronto's Air Canada Centre, surviving more than four decades in a fickle, trend-driven, cutthroat, turbulent, insanely competitive music industry. Today, the Rolling Stones, "the greatest rock 'n' roll band in the whole world ever," according to former President Bill Clinton and millions of others, are the most successful rock band in history, having generated more than $1.5 billion in revenues—and that is only since 1989.

The Stones are, in fact, a brand, and their brand management skills are the reason for their remarkable success. From the beginning, the Rolling Stones positioned themselves clearly. They were not the Beatles, nor the Beach Boys—they were different: a little rougher, more in your face. Their formula was simple, consisting of Keith Richards's guitar riffs and Mick Jagger's affected, tough vocals. And it paid for them to be a differentiated brand that stayed true to their original formula: They were able to maintain their loyal followers and gain new, younger, ones. For older followers, the 60-something Stones continue to perform with the energy and attitude of 18-year-olds and, in so doing, turn back the older crowd's personal clock. The younger followers pursue an attitude (the Stones' brand character) that talks adeptly to timelessness and timeliness.

The skilled brand manager, lead singer Mick Jagger, understood the importance of the band's (brand's) consistency in their core product—their music—and beyond, in their concerts, merchandising, and advertising. Everything carries their instantly recognizable tongue/lips logo, reasserting the brand's stance and impertinence. Mick Jagger is actively involved in every aspect of their tours and related merchandising, insisting on ultimate approval on everything right down to the T-shirt design and the signage outside the concert stadium.

The Stones also seek business partnerships that are harmonious with their own, both in stature and shared relevance with their target audience—among their partners are Sheryl Crow, Anheuser-Busch, Microsoft, Sprint, and E*Trade.[1]

8-1 Chapter Overview

The Rolling Stones have survived for more than four decades in an environment that creates challenges for most of those involved in the music industry—an industry described in the chapter-opening vignette as fickle, trend-driven, cutthroat, turbulent, and insanely competitive. The Stones' survival is attributed to a clear differentiation of their brand from that of the competitors, and consistency—staying true to their winning core product formula—over time. Most other similar music brands have not encountered the same resonant appeal over time. Twisted Sister, Front 242, Cyndi Lauper, and Sisters of Mercy have held a fraction of the music audience's attention for a fraction of the Stones' time. Like most products, they have advanced through the product lifecycle rapidly, from introduction to decline in a couple of years. This chapter will address product-related issues—from new product development decisions, to challenges presented by new product launch decisions, to issues involving managing the product mix and the product portfolio in line with the company strategy and the demands of different consumers.

Section 8-2 provides a product definition and addresses the different product dimensions and classifications. Section 8-3 addresses product decisions regarding branding, logos, trademark protection, and brand strategy. Section 8-4 addresses the packaging and labeling decisions of the firm, and Section 8-5 examines product mix management decisions and issues related to product length, width, and depth. Section 8-6 addresses the new product development process and new product-related decisions. Section 8-7 addresses product diffusion and the different types of adopters, and Section 8-8 addresses the product lifecycle stages—introduction, growth, maturity, and decline. Section 8-9 addresses issues related to the management of the product portfolio.

8-2 Product Definition and Classification

A Rolling Stones performance, merchandise sold at the concert, hair highlights at the Frederic Fekkai hair salon, a burger at Burger King, and landscaping by the local landscaping service are all examples of products. A **product** is defined as any offering that can satisfy consumer needs and wants. As mentioned in Chapter 1, "Scope and Concepts of Marketing," products include goods, which refers to tangible products, and services, which refers to intangible activities or benefits that individuals acquire, but that do not result in ownership, and ideas and experiences that consumers perceive as valuable because they fulfill their needs and wants.

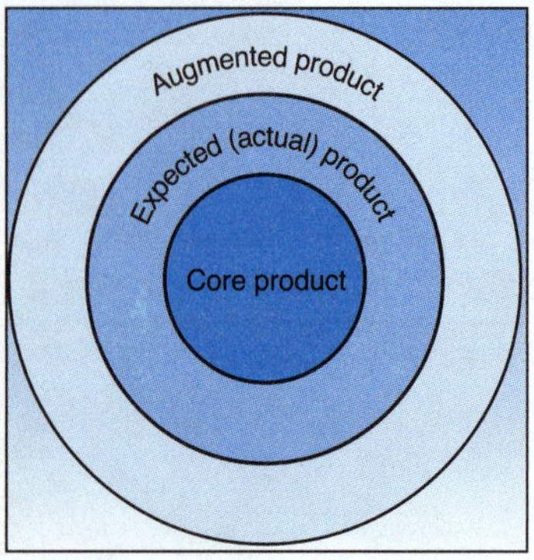

Figure 8-1
The Core, Expected, and Augmented Product

- **Product:** Any offering that can satisfy consumer needs and wants.
- **Core product:** The fundamental benefit, or problem solution, that consumers seek.
- **Expected** (or **actual**) **product:** The basic physical product, including styling, features, brand name, and packaging, that delivers the benefits that consumers seek.
- **Augmented product:** A product enhanced by the addition of extra or unsolicited services or benefits, such as a warranty, repair services, maintenance, and other services that enhance product use, in order to prompt a purchase.

8-2a Core, Expected, and Augmented Products

Products can be conceptualized at three levels, as illustrated in Figure 8-1.[2] The **core product** is the fundamental benefit, or problem solution, that consumers seek. An individual who purchases aspirin is actually buying relief from headaches. Another individual buying an automobile is purchasing transportation. Another individual purchasing a massage is buying relief from muscle ache. Relief and transportation are the fundamental benefits that the respective consumers are seeking.

The **expected** (or **actual**) **product** is the basic physical product, including styling, features, brand name, and packaging, which delivers those benefits. An individual purchasing a massage at her health club also expects to have a gentle masseuse with magic fingers, calming music, clean sheets, and clean covers. The consumer purchasing the automobile expects it to have comfortable seats, a reasonable radio with a CD player, power steering, and, in North America, air conditioning and automatic transmission.

The **augmented product** is a product enhanced by the addition of extra or unsolicited services or benefits to the consumer in order to prompt purchase—such as warranty, repair services, maintenance, and other services that enhance the product's use (see Figure 8-2). Most of the competition today takes place in the augmented product arena. A children's dentist provides a Mermaid toothbrush and fun-colored gel, sends a birthday card with a smiling cartoon character, and has toys ready for the tots in the waiting room. Some automobile dealers offer breakfast and a free carwash every Saturday. When all competitors offer extra or unsolicited services or benefits, that augmented product becomes the expected product. Turn-down hotel service, where the bed is arranged for sleeping and a chocolate mint is placed on the pillow, becomes the expected product. Liquid washing detergents are expected to have a measuring cap indicating amounts required for different size loads.

Figure 8-2
In this advertisement by Community Trust Bank, augmented services such as no monthly service fee, no per check charges, no charge for first order of checks, and plus overdraft advantage are being promoted to differentiate the bank from its competitors.

Source: Sample print advertisement courtesy of The Miles Agency and Alliance One Advertising, Inc.

8-2b Product Durability

Durable goods are defined as tangible products that have a prolonged use. Automobiles, appliances, and furniture are examples of durable goods that last over many years of use. Most definitions suggest that durable goods are goods that have a life of more than two years. **Nondurable goods** are defined as tangible products that are consumed relatively quickly and purchased on a regular basis that last less than two years. Examples of non-durables are food, clothing and shoes, gasoline, and heating oil, among others. Services are defined as intangible activities or benefits that individuals acquire, but that do not result in ownership. Examples of services are medical care and legal, accounting, and marketing services. Services are further examined in Chapter 9, "Services Marketing."

8-2c Product Classification

Marketing managers have classified consumer products into four basic categories,[3] based on the level of risk attributed to the purchase and the amount of effort involved in purchasing the product.

Convenience goods are relatively inexpensive and frequently purchased products. Relative to the other three categories, convenience goods are considered to have the lowest level of perceived risk and purchase effort. Examples of convenience goods are bread, milk, beer, and snacks. Among examples of convenience goods are **impulse goods,** which are goods bought without any earlier planning, such as candy, gum, and magazines. Retailers place these goods conveniently within reach of the checkout aisle. However, for those consumers who cannot resist candy, supermarkets are now offering candy-free checkout aisles (see Figure 8-3). Other examples of convenience goods are **staples,** which are products that are bought routinely, such as milk, cheese, bread, and soap; and **emergency goods,** which are purchased to address urgent needs, such as candles, lanterns, and bottled water when a hurricane is announced, and salt and snow shovels when snow is in the forecast.

Preference goods are defined as convenience goods that become differentiated through branding and achieve some degree of brand loyalty. Preference goods are higher risk and higher in terms of purchase effort compared with convenience services. To indicate that a preference exists, the term "favorite" can be attached to the product category. For example, if one's favorite cola is Pepsi, one will most likely shop only in larger stores that are more likely to sell the brand than in smaller stores that could have an exclusive arrangement with Coke.

Shopping goods are defined as goods that consumers perceive as higher risk goods, which they are willing to spend a greater amount of purchase effort in searching for and evaluating. Among examples of shopping goods are home appliances, clothing, and furniture. Shopping goods can be classified further based on their degree of homogeneity.

Durable goods: Tangible products that have a prolonged use.

Nondurable goods: Tangible products that are consumed relatively quickly and purchased on a regular basis; they last less than two years.

Convenience goods: Relatively inexpensive and frequently purchased products.

Impulse goods: Goods bought without any earlier planning, such as candy, gum, and magazines.

Staples: Goods that are bought routinely, such as milk, cheese, bread, and soap.

Emergency goods: Goods purchased to address urgent needs.

Preference goods: Convenience goods that become differentiated through branding and achieve some degree of brand loyalty.

Shopping goods: Goods that consumers perceive as higher risk but for which they are willing to spend a greater amount of purchase effort to find and evaluate.

Figure 8-3
Ukrop's Super Markets offer a candy-free checkout experience.

Source: Courtesy of Ukrop's Super Markets, Inc.

Figure 8-4
Rissy Lyn frames are one-of-a-kind, handmade creations—specialty goods sold at Henri Bendel, New York City, and other specialty boutiques nationwide. For additional information on Rissy Lyn and her creations, visit her website (www.rissylyn.com).

Source: Courtesy of Rissy Lyn, "dream, wish, inspire, and create!"

Homogeneous shopping goods: Goods that vary little in terms of physical characteristics or functions.

Heterogeneous shopping goods: Goods that vary significantly in terms of functions, physical characteristics, and quality, and that require a physical evaluation by the buyer.

Specialty goods: Goods that reach the ultimate in differentiation and brand loyalty in that only the chosen brand is acceptable to the consumer.

Brand: A name, design, symbol, or a combination thereof that identifies the product and/or the seller and that is used to differentiate the product from competitors' offerings.

Brand equity (or **brand franchise**)**:** Brands with high consumer awareness and loyalty.

Homogeneous shopping goods are goods that vary little in terms of physical characteristics or functions; consequently, the buyer does not necessarily need to evaluate the item physically. **Heterogeneous shopping goods** are products that vary significantly in terms of functions, physical characteristics, and quality, and require a physical evaluation by the buyer.

Specialty goods are goods that reach the ultimate in differentiation and brand loyalty, where only the chosen brand is acceptable to the consumer. These goods are conceptualized as high risk and are distinguished from shopping goods primarily in terms of higher purchasing effort. Consumers are willing to wait, search high and low, and not settle for anything less. Examples of specialty goods are gourmet foods, such as aged Gouda cheese and Mousse Royale paté; designer clothes, such as Dana Buchman knits and Hugo Boss suits; and other goods, such as Dunhill cigarettes and Rissy Lyn frames (available from Henri Bendel in New York—see Figure 8-4). The following is a summary of the classification categories of products:

1. Convenience goods are relatively inexpensive and frequently purchased products (examples: bread, milk, beer, and snacks).
   - Impulse goods are goods bought without any earlier planning (examples: candy, gum, and magazines).
   - Staples are products that are bought routinely (examples: milk, cheese, bread, and soap).
   - Emergency goods are purchased to address urgent needs (examples: medicine, bandages, candles, lanterns, and bottled water when a hurricane is announced).
2. Preference goods are goods that become differentiated through branding and achieve some degree of brand loyalty (examples: Coke, Pepsi, Nike shoes, and Levi jeans.)
3. Shopping goods are goods that consumers perceive as higher risk goods, which they are willing to spend a greater amount of purchase effort in searching for and evaluating (examples: home appliances, clothing, and furniture).
4. Specialty goods are goods that reach the ultimate in differentiation and brand loyalty, where only the chosen brand is acceptable to the consumer (examples: BMW car, Rolex watch).

8-3 Branding

One of the most important roles played by marketing involves branding the product. Branding adds value to products, as it makes products appear more distinctive and valuable.

A **brand** is defined as a name, design, symbol, or a combination thereof that identifies the product and/or the seller, and is used to differentiate the product from competitors' offerings. A brand also serves as a guarantee to consumers that the product will be identical each time consumers purchase it, with the same features, design, and performance.

All products benefit from branding—from turkeys (Butterball) to eggs (Eggland's Best), to oranges (Jaffa and Sunkist), to couscous (Near East), to beer (Michelob and Corona), and to cereal (Total and Cheerios). Brands that have high consumer awareness and loyalty are said to have high **brand equity** (or **brand franchise**). Brand equity (or franchise) is defined as a set of brand assets and liabilities linked to a brand and its name and symbol, adding or subtracting from the value provided by a product or service to a firm and/or to that firm's customers. Brand loyalty is an essential asset of brand equity. The epitome of brand equity is the Harley-Davidson aficionado who wears the Harley symbol as a tattoo.[4] Brand equity entails a strong brand identity and it allows firms to charge premium pricing for the product.

Marketers have attempted to evaluate brand equity and establish the actual value of the brand. A widely accepted brand value ranking is compiled by Interbrand with the help of data from Citibank and currently is considered the most valuable indicator of the financial health of the global elite. The ranking is determined by a collation of brand strength (based on factors such as leadership and market stability), financial and analyst reports, revenue, and profit figures.[5]

Table 8-1 ranks the top 20 brands in terms of brand equity worldwide. Coke, for example, has lost substantial brand value: It appears to be vulnerable because it has a single product offering, and the brand reached its peak in Europe and Latin America.[6] In particular, it has not recovered from recent employee lawsuits over diversity issues, fizzling bottler relations, plunging demand for syrup that forced a production stoppage, and a disastrous product recall in Belgium.[7]

The important branding decisions involve deciding on the brand name, mark, logo, and character; the brand sponsor; and the brand strategy. These elements help to create the **brand image,** defined as the consumer perception of the particular brand. Consumers associate certain brand characteristics with a particular brand—marketers, through advertising, can help in forming that brand image through appropriate positioning strategies.

Brand image: The consumer perception of the particular brand.

Brand name decisions include the selection and protection of the brand name. Brand sponsor decisions involve determining if the brand should be sold as a manufacturer brand, also known as a national brand; a dealer brand, also known as a private label brand; or a generic brand. The brand can be licensed or co-branded. Brand strategy decisions center on creating brand extensions or line extensions, or using or creating family brands, new brands, or multibrands.

TABLE 8-1

The Leading Brands of the World

Brand	Brand Value, 2004 (billions of dollars)	Brand Value, 1999 (billions of dollars)
1. Coca-Cola	$67.29	$83.84
2. Microsoft-Windows	$61.37	$56.65
3. IBM	$53.79	$43.78
4. General Electric	$44.11	$33.50
5. Intel	$33.50	$30.02
6. Disney	$27.11	$32.28
7. McDonald's	$25.00	$26.23
8. Nokia	$24.4	$20.69
9. Toyota	$22.67	$12.31
10. Marlboro	$22.13	$21.05
11. Mercedes-Benz	$21.33	$17.78
12. Hewlett-Packard	$20.97	$17.13
13. Citibank	$19.97	NA
14. American Express	$17.68	$12.55
15. Gillette	$16.72	$15.89
16. Cisco Systems	$15.95	NA
17. BMW	$15.89	NA
18. Honda	$14.87	$11.10
19. Ford	$14.47	$33.20
20. Sony	$12.76	$14.23

Sources: Jane Bainbridge, "Global Forces," *Marketing* (July 20, 2000): 24–25; "The Global Brand Scoreboard: The 100 Top Brands," *Business Week* (August 2, 2004): 68–71.
Note: NA = Not applicable

8-3a Brand Identity

Selecting the instruments that identify the brand—that is, the brand name, the brand mark, the brand logo, and the brand character—constitutes very important decisions. A **brand name** is defined as the part of a brand that can be spoken; it may include words, letters, or numbers. Toyota, McDonald's, Coach, and Delta Airlines are all examples of brand names. Successful brand names have the following characteristics:

Brand name: The part of a brand that can be spoken; it may include words, letters, or numbers.

- They are easy to pronounce, memorable, and distinctive. Celebrex, Taco Bell, and Gateway are memorable names that are easy to pronounce. A distinctive fun name with a memorable alliteration is Jolly Green Giant.
- They suggest product traits and/or benefits—for example, Hefty bags suggest product strength (see Figure 8-5). Kentucky Fried Chicken relates the type of product sold and the style in which it is cooked (i.e., in a southern fashion). Among brand names that are indicative of product traits and benefits are Skin-so-Soft, Pampers and Huggies, Lean Cuisine and Healthy Choice, Taster's Choice, Sinutab, and Head & Shoulders.
- They should also be easy to translate into other languages. A number of international market research firms help companies test their names in international markets. In international marketing, the wrong brand name can make or break a product—as will be seen in Chapter 17, "International Marketing."

Brand mark: The part of a brand that can be seen but not spoken.

In addition to the brand name, there are other means for product identification. For example, a **brand mark** is part of the brand that can be seen but not spoken. For McDon-

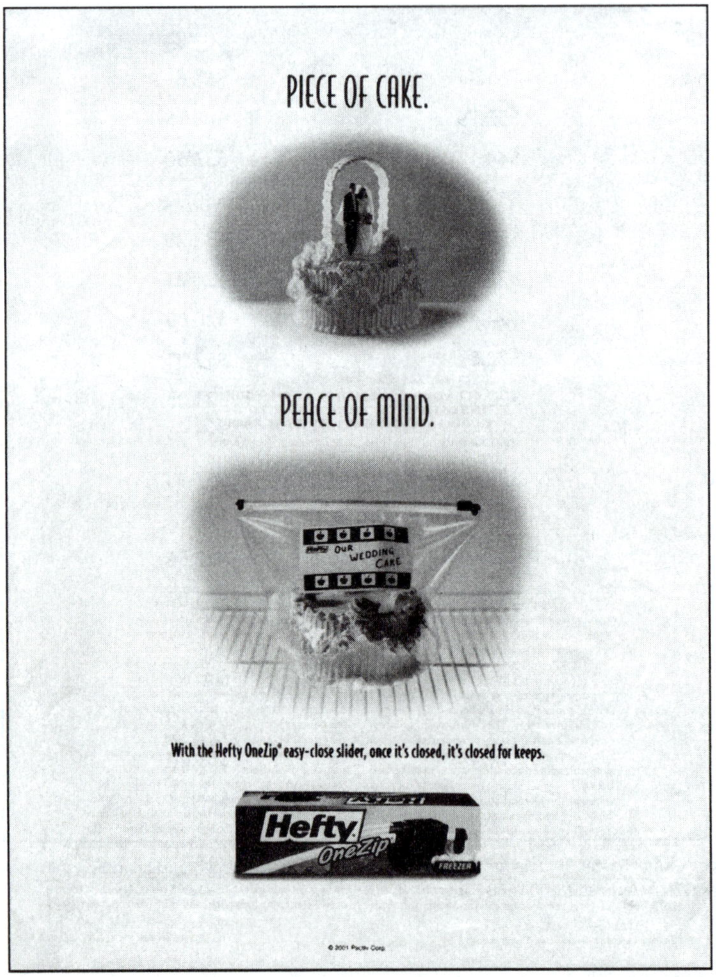

Figure 8-5
By using the brand name of "Hefty," the product attribute of strength is suggested, as this ad portrays.
Source: Reprinted with kind permission from Pactiv Corporation.

ald's, the brand mark is the golden arches. A **brand logo** is a distinctive mark, sign, symbol, or graphic version of a company's name used to identify and promote its product. The Gateway logo is the cube with black and white patches. The Pepsi logo is the half-white, half-blue circle with a white curved dividing line. The Rolling Stones' logo is the well-known red lips and tongue. A **brand character** (or **trade character**) is a character that personifies the brand, such as Tony the Tiger for Kellogg's Frosted Flakes and Ronald McDonald for McDonald's. These elements together help to build the brand's identity and are valuable and well-protected trademarks. The Rolling Stones' brand character is depicted by its logo in motion; at their recent concerts, they had an ethereal female creature riding on the tongue; arguments can be made for using both the mouth and tongue or simply one or the other in playing the role of brand character. A **trademark** consists of words, symbols, marks, devices, and signs that are used in trade to indicate the source of the goods and to distinguish them from the goods of others. A trademark is legally registered with the United States Patent and Trademark Office for use by a single company. A **servicemark** is the same as a trademark, but it identifies and distinguishes the source of a service, rather than a good. The terms *trademark* and *mark* are used to refer to both trademarks and servicemarks. Rights for a federally registered trademark can last indefinitely, as long as the owner continues to use it and continues to apply for renewal. A **patent** is the grant of a property right to the inventor. New patents are valid for 20 years from the date on which the patent was filed, and, under special circumstances, they can be extended beyond the 20 years. Patents and trademarks are issued by the United States Patent and Trademark Office, and they are effective only in the United States and its territories and possessions. It is the responsibility of the firm to protect its trademarks and patents.[8] Internationally, firms must apply with the national governments for protection.

The next section addresses some of the challenges firms encounter when protecting their valuable brands and related trademarks and patents.

Brand logo: A distinctive mark, sign, symbol, or graphic version of a company's name that is used to identify and promote the company's product.

Brand character (or **trade character**)**:** A character that personifies the brand.

Trademark: Words, symbols, marks, and signs that are legally registered for a single company's use.

Servicemark: Words, symbols, marks, and signs that are legally registered for a single company's use that identify and distinguish the source of a service.

Patent: The grant of a property right to the inventor.

8-3b Protecting the Brand

Brand names are valuable assets to a company, as established in Section 8-3, which addressed brand equity. Companies pay millions to protect their brand names from dilution by registering them anywhere they are present and defending them in court. Companies are proactive, rather than reactive, primarily because counterfeit merchandise harms the brand's reputation and its value, as well as company profits.

In many parts of the world, brands are readily counterfeited. To illustrate, Yiwu, a city five hours from Shanghai, China, is one of the largest wholesale centers of China, where 200,000 distributors purchase up to 2,000 tons of goods daily. It also is China's counterfeit capital, where counterfeit products bearing established brand names—such as Procter & Gamble's Safeguard soap and Rejoice shampoo, Gillette razor blades, and other brands belonging to companies such as Philip Morris, Anheuser-Busch, Prada, Robert Bosch, Kimberly-Clark, and Nike—are sold at a fraction of their genuine counterparts' cost.[9] Counterfeiters in China range from manufacturers of shampoo and soap in back rooms to large state-owned enterprises and/or joint-venture partners making their profits selling knockoffs of soft drinks and beer, to factories producing car batteries, motorcycles, and even mobile CD factories with optical disc machines. These products are distributed all over the world, including the United States.[10]

Examples of counterfeiting are design counterfeiting and brand-name counterfeiting. Design counterfeiting includes copying designs or scents; this practice is quite common and risk free. Many companies replicate the polo-style shirt with a design that approximates the polo rider. The design of women's Peugeot watches is close to that of the Rolex Oyster Perpetual. Unknown perfume manufacturers suggest that their brand is similar in scent to a particular brand of perfume, which they name in their product packaging and advertising. At the next level is brand-name counterfeiting. Purses with names such as Prada, Fendi, and Louis Vuitton are sold practically on the steps of the actual retailer on Fifth Avenue in New York City, as are fake Rolex watches. Counterfeit products even make it to flea markets all over the United States. Companies work diligently to develop a strong brand identity, so they do not want to see counterfeiters use their brand name.

Several factors contribute to the counterfeiters' success. First, consumers are very willing to purchase counterfeit goods. Studies have shown, for example, that a large proportion of consumers are likely to select a counterfeit apparel item over a genuine good when there is a price advantage, primarily because function risks are low for apparel, whereas prestige gains are high.[11] In this sense, products that are visible and/or consumed publicly are more likely to be in demand than products that are less visible and/or consumed publicly. Second, the spread of advanced production technology (affordable, quality, color-copying machines), as well as production lines supplied by pirates, makes it possible for counterfeiters to make perfect replicas of the original products. Frequently, neither the manufacturer nor the consumers can tell fakes from the real product.[12] Third, supply chains are not adequately controlled. Traders use Internet chat rooms and unauthorized dealership networks to sell the products and mix counterfeit products with legitimate products sold on the secondary gray market.[13] Finally, governments in many developing countries are reluctant to crack down on counterfeiters, especially when state-owned enterprises are involved in the operations. In the case of China, for instance, local governments hesitate to crack down on product pirates because they create thousands of jobs and keep the local economy going.[14]

Companies have used a number of strategies to combat counterfeiting. Lobbying the U.S. government, as well as the governments allowing counterfeiting, is a first step. Alternatively, companies could engage in a concerted action to combat counterfeiting by changing a product's appearance to differentiate authentic products from fakes. Budweiser embedded special images in its beer bottles that appear only when the product is chilled, rendering them difficult to copy. Microsoft included holograms on its software boxes and inside user manuals, but pirates quickly learned the trick.[15] But the most successful attacks have been launched with the cooperation of governments of developing countries. In China, for example, a raid was launched by seven battery makers, including Gillette, Energizer, and Panasonic, with the help of 200 government agents, on 21 factories in a southwestern city. As a result of the raid, a total of 150 pieces of manufacturing equipment and 3 million counterfeit batteries were confiscated.[16]

8-3c Brand Sponsor Decisions

Brand sponsor decisions involve determining if the brand should be sold as a manufacturer brand, also known as a national brand; a dealer brand, also known as a private label brand; a retailer brand; wholesaler brand; distributor brand; or as a generic brand. Brand sponsor decisions also involve determining if the brand can be licensed or co-branded.

Manufacturers' brands (or national brands): Brands owned by a manufacturer.

Private label brands: Reseller (wholesaler or retailer) brands.

Branding today is more complex than ever. In the past, **manufacturers' brands** (or **national brands**), defined as brands owned by a manufacturer, dominated retail shelves. Today, **private label brands,** defined as reseller (wholesaler or retailer) brands, abound on the retail shelves. Alongside the national megabrands, such as Procter & Gamble and Rubbermaid, there is now an increasingly large mix of store brands. According to the Private Label Manufacturers Association, store brands currently account for one out of five items sold at supermarkets, drug chains, and mass merchandisers in the United States, accounting for $48.8 billion in sales in 2001.[17]

Private label brands are much more profitable for retailers, compared to manufacturers' brands. Of these, the most profitable for retailers are, of course, store brands. For consumers, private label brands represent a guarantee of quality at a lower price; consequently, they increase store loyalty and patronage. Among successful private label brands are K-Mart's Jaclyn Smith, Martha Stewart, and Kathy Ireland, which appeal to working- and middle-class mothers; Target's Honors brand; Kohl's Sonoma brand; Nordstrom's Classiques; and Macy's Cellar brand. In recent years, groceries and canned goods represented the product category where consumers were most willing to try store brands, according to Table 8-2, which ranks the product categories of products that consumers are most willing to buy under private label.

TABLE 8-2

Percentage of Consumers Willing to Buy Private Labels

Product Category	2001	2002	2004
Groceries and canned goods	66%	71%	72%
Greeting cards	71%	69%	67%
Snacks	NA	67%	69%
Domestics	76%	66%	66%
Health and beauty aids	49%	59%	54%
Men's apparel	62%	58%	56%
Beverages	46%	57%	56%
Women's apparel	53%	56%	54%
Intimate apparel	59%	55%	58%
Children's apparel	59%	54%	57%
Candy	NA	53%	46%
Toys	59%	50%	54%
Film	55%	52%	59%
Cosmetics	45%	42%	43%
Consumer electronics	49%	40%	42%
Camera	35%	39%	41%
Computer/ Entertainment software	43%	33%	38%

Sources: Mike Duff, "Top Brands 2002: Private Label—Drop-Off Begs Question, How Much Is Too Much?" *DSN Retailing Today*, vol. 41, no. 20 (October 28, 2002): 37, 43; Mike Duff, "Private Label Hits Its Stride," *DSN Retailing Today* vol. 43, no. 20 (October 25, 2004): 35–38.
Note: NA = not applicable.

Battle of the brands: The conflict between manufacturers and resellers to promote their own brands.

Generics: Products that emphasize the product, rather than the brand of the manufacturer or reseller.

In terms of in-store marketing strategy, retailers are aggressively promoting their own brands, placing them typically side-by-side with the national brands, offering consumers the choice of the purchase of the retailer's brand at a lower price. Often, even the packaging is quite similar to that of the manufacturers' brands. This is an example of the **battle of the brands,** defined as a conflict between manufacturers and resellers to promote their own brands. In this battle, manufacturers' advantage lies in the consumers' preference for the manufacturer's brand. But to build this preference requires extensive expenditures on advertising. For example, in Central Virginia, the Ukrop's Super Market brand is seen at the same level as, if not better than, national brands (see Figure 8-6).

Retailers, however, have substantial bargaining power in this battle. They control the shelf space and manage it much like real estate, promoting their own brands by placing them, as mentioned, side-by-side with competing national brands to stress the price difference and offer consumers the option to purchase the product at a lower price. They have central displays with their own brands, creating convenience for consumers looking for that particular product category (see Figure 8-7, illustrating a prominent Ukrop's brand display).

Generics, products that emphasize the product, rather than the brand of the manufacturer or reseller, represent the third brand category. They are rarely, if at all, advertised; there is minimal expense associated with their manufacturing, packaging, and distribution; and their shelf location is confined to the bottom shelves in low-traffic areas. This strategy allows them to be significantly cheaper than branded product alternatives. Generics are popular in the drug industry, where the cost of certain brand-name products is often prohibitive for individuals living on low fixed incomes. Marketing Illustration 8-1 addresses recent developments in generic drugs.

Figure 8-6
Ukrop's private label orange juice competes well on both price and taste with national brands.

Source: Courtesy of Ukrop's Super Markets, Inc.

Figure 8-7
Ukrop's private label rolls have their own prominent display in the supermarket.

Source: Courtesy of Ukrop's Super Markets, Inc.

Marketing Illustration 8-1

The Drug Industry Dilemma

Generics constitute a serious challenge to brand-name drugs. Generic drugs are very popular with consumers and in great demand at pharmacies. Whenever prescriptions permit substitutes, most informed consumers demand generics. Generic drugs are chemical replicas of brand-name medicines, and they usually cost much less than the patented drugs they copy—at least they used to cost much less, until recently.

Currently, the prices of generic drugs are increasing twice as rapidly as those of brand-name drugs and are quickly catching up with them. There are a number of reasons accounting for their rapid increase in price. Many patents for brand-name drugs have recently expired, and generic drug manufacturers tend to charge more when the generic versions first enter the market. The generic drug industry is consolidating, leaving fewer companies to compete for this lucrative market. In addition, wholesalers and retailers (pharmacies) found that they can simply charge more for generics and that the generics still cost less than the brand-name medicine.

Generic drug manufacturers have additional advantages: The government is actively attempting to help generic drugs reach the market faster by limiting the brand-name drug maker to one automatic patent extension on any drug as it disputes its patent rights.

Brand-name drug manufacturers encounter yet another challenge: cross-border shopping. Many consumers take shopping trips to Canada and Mexico, where they can buy cheaper drugs because the respective governments place caps on drug prices and because the American dollar has more buying power in Canada and Mexico. While drug manufacturers and pharmacies are unhappy about this phenomenon, regulators do not seem ready to crack down on buyers, who tend to be older and on limited incomes. Furthermore, UnitedHealth Group, a large health insurer, recently promised the American Association of Retired Persons (AARP) that it would reimburse members for prescriptions filled overseas.

Sources: Milt Freudenheim, "As Patents on Popular Drugs End, Costs for Generics Show a Surge," *New York Times* (December 27, 2002): A1, C2; "A New Source for Discount Prescriptions," *New York Times* (December 26, 2002): A29.

Licensing: A process that involves a licensor, who shares the brand name, technology, and know-how with a licensee in return for royalties.

Licensing involves the owner of the brand name allowing a manufacturer or a reseller to sell the product under the owner's brand name in return for a licensing fee. Bayerische Motoren Werke AG (BMW) created quite a buzz when it bought the Rolls-Royce name, without the product, for $60 million. BMW then agreed to license the rights to Volkswagen. This followed Volkswagen's agreement to purchase Rolls-Royce and Bentley cars for more than $700 million from Vickers PLC, a deal in which VW outbid BMW. The licensing agreement enabled Volkswagen to manufacture and distribute Rolls-Royce automobiles only until 2002, when BMW took control of Rolls-Royce production.[18] The first Rolls-Royce was built in 1904[19] and it took the company many years to develop this reputable brand that stands for excellence in the automotive industry. Licensing the Rolls-Royce name offered the licensee an instant brand name of the highest resonance.

Numerous brands are licensed in the clothing industry. Oleg Cassini, Pierre Cardin, and Bill Blass have almost lost their cachet as high-quality exclusive brands due to extensive licensing. Barney, Teletubbies, Bob the Builder, and other popular children's programs have successfully licensed their popular brand names to create equally popular toys. Keds, a shoe manufacturer, has acquired the licenses for Tommy Hilfiger and Levi's shoes. Joseph Aboud, a high-couture clothing brand, was licensed to mid-price bed linen products. Eskimo Pie ice cream has become a successful international brand through licensing.

It should be mentioned that it is not only manufacturers' brands that are licensed. Private label brands are also sold under license. For example, K-Mart's Martha Stewart line was licensed to Sears in Canada.[20]

Co-branding: Using the brands of two different companies on one single product.

A fourth brand strategy is **co-branding,** which involves using the brands of two different companies on one single product. For example, American Express co-brands with Delta Airlines to offer the Delta Skymiles Credit Card; Kellogg is currently co-branding with Disney in the United Kingdom, using Mickey Mouse and Winnie the Pooh on its products. Breyer's Ice Cream Parlor brands are co-brand offerings, with Almond Joy, Klondike, Reese's, Oreo, and Hershey's. And Esso (Exxon) co-brands with Disney in Europe (see Figure 8-8)

Figure 8-8
What do the Lion King and the tiger in your tank have in common? Apparently quite a bit—you need the tiger to take you to the lion … or something to that effect. In Europe, Esso (Exxon) co-brands with Disney.

Co-branding can be a profitable strategy for firms. In one example, Jack Daniel's co-branded a line of grilling sauces with H. J. Heinz. Because Jack Daniel's stands for Southern heritage, original high-quality craftsmanship, and flavor, and because grilling and barbecue also have longstanding roots in the South, it was believed that this relationship would create the synergy needed for success: The Jack Daniel's grilling sauce line has captured 12 percent of the premium barbecue sauce segment since the product's introduction.[21]

8-3d Brand Strategy

In deciding on brand strategy, a company has a number of options. **Line extension** involves extending the existing brand name by introducing new product offerings in an existing product category. Examples of line extensions are new flavors. For instance, Celestial Seasonings introduced a raspberry-flavored Green Tea, in addition to its already existing Green Tea. Pepsi introduced lime flavors for Diet Pepsi and regular Pepsi. St. Francis Hospital created a new Kids Surgery Suite designed "especially for kids" (see Figure 8-9). New product forms are also popular line extensions. Most detergents introduced liquid versions that they sell in addition to the traditional powder versions. Added ingredients, such as Palmolive dish detergent with antibacterial soap, or removed ingredients, such as low-fat versions of products, are also examples of line extensions. Size can also be varied: Dove ice cream now offers bite-size versions of its very popular ice cream.

Line extension: The process of extending the existing brand name by introducing new product offerings in an existing product category.

Companies must be careful when attempting line extensions: In the process, they could sabotage their core brand. Any extension called ultra, plus, or extra may be problematic. The introduction of Alka-Seltzer Plus, for example, was very successful—at the expense of the Alka-Seltzer brand.[22]

Another strategy involves introducing **brand extensions**—that is, using an existing brand name to introduce products in a new product category. The assumption, for brand extensions, is that the brand is quite successful and enjoys substantial consumer franchise.

Brand extensions: The use of an existing brand name to introduce products in a new product category.

Figure 8-9
This advertisement for the St. Francis Kids Surgery Suite promotes a line extension service designed especially for children.
Source: Courtesy of Newcomer, Morris and Young.

In fact, if a brand is well known and enjoys substantial consumer franchise, it is only natural for firms to attempt to leverage that into new products. Many strong brands, such as Disney and Taco Bell, have transformed themselves into megabrands through brand extensions.[23] Kodak disposable cameras, Crest toothbrushes, and Porsche apparel and sunglasses are all examples of brand extensions.

It is important to note that the wrong extension could create damaging associations that may be expensive to change. Moreover, the decision usually involves an important strategic growth thrust, thus causing the company to lose substantial time and resources and to miss important opportunities.[24]

Family branding (or **blanket branding**): Branding strategy whereby one brand name is used for more than one product.

A third strategy is **family branding** (or **blanket branding**), whereby one brand name is used for more than one product. Kodak uses its name for all the products it sells, whether film, cameras, or other related products. Stihl sells chainsaws for individual use and industrial use under the same brand name. Volvo sells automobiles and trucks under the Volvo umbrella name. And the Rolling Stones sell tickets, T-shirts, and other paraphernalia under their well-known brand name.

Multibranding: Using different brand names for products that the firm sells in the same product category.

The reverse of this strategy is **multibranding,** which involves using different brand names for products that the firm sells in the same product category. For example, Procter & Gamble sells an array of products in the laundry detergent category, positioned to address every imaginable laundry need: Tide, Bold, Cheer, Dreft, and Era, among many others.

New brands: New brands in new product categories for the firm.

Yet another strategy involves creating **new brands** in new product categories for the firm. This strategy is often pursued through acquisitions. For example, when Kraft bought Jacobs Suchard, it expanded into the chocolate product category—a category consistent with its cookies and crackers. In the process, it acquired the Toblerone brand, as well as other famous European chocolate brands—Milka and Suchard—that are certain to make their way to store shelves in the United States one day. Thus, through the purchase, Kraft went into a new product category, acquiring new brands.

8-4 Packaging and Labeling

An important feature of the product is the package. **Packaging** is defined as all the activities involved in designing the product container. Packaging is a very important product feature whose cost ranges from less than 10 percent for a simple plastic wrap to more than 50 percent for a fancy golden mirror that is part of a purse-size compact powder or an elaborate lipstick package. The package contains and protects the product during shipping, handling, and storage.

Packaging: All the activities involved in designing the product container.

The primary package may be a single container or wrapper—this is the immediate package. Bread, for example, is wrapped in one single plastic container. Almond Joy and Snickers bars are wrapped in a single wrapper. The primary package may also be enclosed in a secondary package. For example, Toblerone bars are wrapped in an aluminum wrapper and then in the distinctive triangle-shaped yellow box. Chewing gum is wrapped in a primary package for individual pieces of gum and a secondary package that holds five or ten pieces of gum. An important consideration in designing the package is its storage. For example, products in round packages cannot be efficiently stored on the store shelves and result in substantial wasted space for the retailer, which manufacturers must take into consideration when designing the package. Ocean Spray recently heavily promoted its new square package that now fits in home refrigerator doors, saving valuable space.

The shipping package is usually a larger corrugated box that contains a number of products and protects them during shipping and storage. For Almond Joy, a shipping package contains 40 Almond Joy bars.

The package contains the product label, which performs the following functions:

- Identifies the product or brand—it carries the brand name, logo, and brand mark.
- Describes the product in terms of ingredients and/or components, weight, or volume. For food products, the label contains nutritional facts, such as calories, fat, cholesterol, sodium, carbohydrates, sugars, and protein based on serving size, and number of servings per package.
- Informs consumers when the product expires and classifies the product based on quality and/or size.
- Identifies the manufacturer and/or the distributor and has the Universal Product Code for easy inventory processing and scanning.
- Promotes the product. The label advertises the product to the consumer every time the consumer handles it. It is the last brand communication that reminds the consumer to purchase the product when it runs out.
- Directs the consumer on product use, offering recipes for food products, or instructions on assembly and safety.

The information that cannot be communicated in the label due to space restrictions can be included in an insert within the package. Inserts include information on assembly and safety in different languages, or they could include, for drugs, for example, information on ingredients and side effects.

Packaging is a very important marketing function that must be appropriately coordinated with the company's marketing mix. Consumers expect that, if they pay $200 for a one-ounce bottle of perfume, the package will be unique and plush, not just functional. And they react positively to innovative packaging ideas: The Hershey's kiss is one unique package that consumers are fond of.

Consumers also expect a package to resist reasonable stress in handling, while maintaining an attractive appearance. However, they also expect that packaging should not be excessive. In response to this expectation, more and more consumer product manufacturers are attempting to cut down on waste and pollution by offering a product in a single primary package, rather than multiple packages. For example, Uncle Ben's rice is no longer packaged separately, in a secondary package, next to the seasoning package. It is placed directly in the box. Similarly, the Manischewitz matzo meal, used as bread and seasoning for frying or for making matzo balls, is now simply offered in a cardboard container, rather than in one-use size secondary packages.

8-5 The Product Mix

Product mix: The complete assortment of the products that a company offers to its target consumers.

Product line: The related brands the company offers in the same product category.

Product length: The total number of brands in the product mix—all the brands the company sells.

Product width: The total number of product lines the company offers.

Product depth: The number of different offerings for a product category.

Product consistency: The extent to which the different product lines are related, use the same distribution channels, and have the same final consumers.

The product offering of a firm is usually diversified into various products to ensure a more stable income over time. The **product mix** is defined as the complete assortment of the products that a company offers to its target consumers and has a number of important dimensions. One important dimension of the product mix is the **product line,** which consists of the related brands in the same product category. Companies use different line strategies to achieve market share and profitability goals. For example, companies engage in line extensions to target consumers who otherwise cannot afford a particular product. In the fashion realm, for example, numerous top-line designers attempt to increase their profits by targeting the masses with bridge offerings (secondary, more affordable lines): Escada with Laurel, Ann Klein with Ann Klein II, Donna Karan with DKNY, Armani with Emporio Armani, and so on.

Other important product dimensions are the **product length,** which is the total number of brands in the product mix or all of the brands sold by the company; the **product width,** which is the total number of product lines the company offers; and the **product depth,** which is the number of different offerings for a product category. To illustrate these product dimensions, we will use the example of Unilever (www.unilever.com), one of the largest consumer product companies in the world. Although Unilever is organized primarily into two divisions—the foods division and the personal care division—the company has a number of product lines that are addressed as separate strategic business units. Let us assume that Table 8-3 comprises all the Unilever brands. The total product length, then, is 22. Counting the different product lines (culinary products, frozen foods, ice cream, margarine, tea, detergents, deodorants, shampoos, personal care, oral care, and fragrances), the total product width is 11. To explain product depth, Lipton tea comes in at least three variants: Lipton Yellow Label, Lipton Ice Tea, and Lipton Brisk. The depth of the tea category (the Lipton brand), therefore, is 3. Product depth for the tea line is thus calculated by adding all the variants under the Lipton brand.

Another important dimension of the product mix is **product consistency,** the extent to which the different product lines are related and use the same distribution channels and have the same final consumers. The Unilever brands are consistent within each of the company divisions: the foods division and the personal care division.

8-6 New Product Development

To maintain their competitive advantage and to ensure survival and growth, companies must develop and introduce new goods and services that meet the needs of their markets. New product development is a costly and risky process that involves the firm at all levels. The following are examples of risks and difficulties companies face when developing new products:

- Competitors could appropriate the good/service idea and deliver the final good or service to the market more swiftly, economically, and with stronger company backing (brand reputation, financial support) than the initial good/service developer.
- Target consumers might not respond as anticipated to the offering because it does not meet their needs, because they cannot afford it, and/or because they prefer to

TABLE 8-3

Unilever Products Aimed at the U.S. Market

Product Area	Brand Names
Culinary products	Ragu Spaghetti Sauces
	Hellmann's Mayonnaise
	Knorr Soups
Frozen foods	Gordon's Tenders
Ice cream	Breyers
	Ben & Jerry's
Margarine	I Can't Believe It's Not Butter
Tea	Lipton
Detergents	Snuggle
Deodorants	Sure
	Dove
Shampoos	SunSilk
	ThermaSilk
	Organics
Personal care	Dove
	Vaseline Intensive Care
	Pond's
Oral care	Mentadent
	Close-Up
Fragrances	Valentino
	Cerruti
	Calvin Klein

adopt a product later in the product lifecycle stage, when the product is proven and more affordable.

- The government might impose restrictions on product-testing procedures.

Figure 8-10 illustrates the product development process. At each step, the process can be either terminated or restarted for each individual product idea. Consequently, a product will go through each stage, or at least through some of the stages, in order to reach the product launching stage. Throughout the product development process, maintaining a strong market orientation is important: A thorough understanding of consumers' needs and wants and of the competitive situation and the nature of the market is critical to product success.[25]

8-6a Generating New Product Ideas

The first step in the new product development process is generating new product ideas—that is, systematically searching for ideas for new products. Depending on the products provided and/or company philosophies, ideas will be sought using different strategies. Most firms are driven by the marketing concept, and their product development decisions are based on identifying the needs, wants, and desires of consumers. For technology-driven firms, the focus is more likely to be on the product itself, and thus the research and development division may be responsible for developing product ideas. Even in this second instance, however, products are developed with the needs of the consumer in mind.

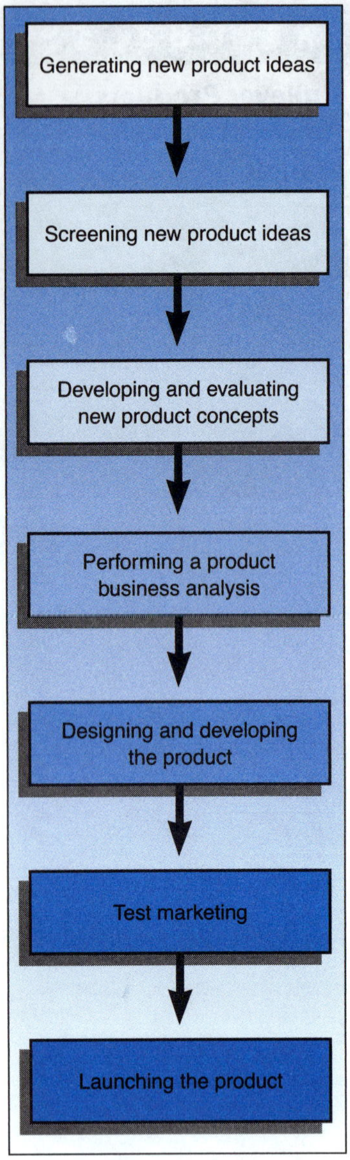

Figure 8-10
Steps in the New Product Development Process

INTERACTIVE FIGURE

Companies use multiple sources for ideas. The most obvious sources for ideas are consumers. As salespeople interact with consumers, the company's customer service employees can be queried about customers' reactions to products and about product preferences and needs. Marketing research firms can collect data on consumer preferences as well. They can conduct qualitative research with consumers to explore and identify their needs, gripes, complaints, and hassles.[26]

Internal idea sources—within the company—are also useful. Company idea schemes, even though they tend to focus on cost reduction through process streamlining, waste reduction, and productivity improvement, can also be a good source for ideas. Internal brainstorms can generate innovative ideas. Brainstorming sessions represent a venue for conducting internal qualitative research and may also be used in the process of generating product ideas.[27]

Suppliers and channel members could provide important input. For example, in the cosmetics and toiletries industry, many innovations are driven by raw materials, the properties they bestow on formulations, and the beneficial claims that are associated with their inclusion in formulations.[28] Competition represents an obvious source for ideas. Products that are in the test market phase or that are just being launched are always vulnerable to having their ideas copied. Other sources of ideas are consultants, nonprofit research laboratories, universities, and research firms.

8-6b Screening New Product Ideas

In the process of screening new product ideas, the goal is to ensure that the product fits well with the target consumers' needs, as well as with the overall mission of the organization.[29] At this stage, a checklist is usually developed to screen out product ideas that do not meet these criteria.

In the screening process, the following should be taken into consideration:[30]

- The product to be developed should be superior, delivering unique benefits to users, rather than a "me-too" undifferentiated product. Such superiority is derived from design, features, attributes, specifications, and product positioning.
- The target market should be a large, attractive, growth market, where the product is perceived as important, where demand for it has been stable over time, and where customers are profitable and price-insensitive.
- There should be a fit between the new product requirements and the resources, skills, and experiences of the firm with regard to management capabilities, technical support, research and development, manufacturing skills, sales and distribution skills, and the firm's channel of distribution.

8-6c Developing and Evaluating New Product Concepts

The next stage, developing and evaluating concepts, entails developing product concepts and determining how consumers will view and use the product. This information can be determined by having the target consumers test the idea to gauge its usefulness.[31] Typically, the process involves developing a detailed description of the product and asking prospective consumers to evaluate it and to indicate their willingness to purchase the hypothetical product. Most often, this is done using a focus group of representative target consumers.

One method that is frequently used at this stage is conjoint analysis. In this method, respondents receive descriptions of different hypothetical products with varying levels of the same attributes, which they are then asked to rank. Analysts can determine the ideal combination of attributes, ascertain the importance of each attribute, and, assuming the data were collected from a sufficiently large sample of the target population, estimate market share.

The creation of new products may range from the substitution of a cheaper material in an existing product to a better way of marketing, distributing, or supporting a product

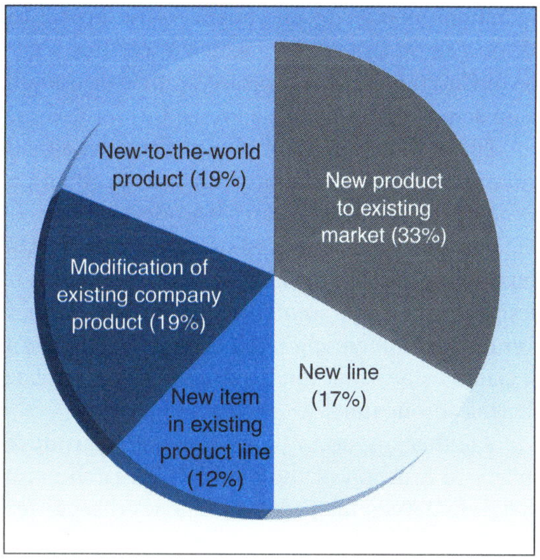

Figure 8-11
Types of New Products

INTERACTIVE FIGURE

or service.[32] **Degree of product newness** refers to the extent to which a good or service is new to the market. The creation of new products can be accomplished using different strategies. The marketing literature uses various classifications for different categories of innovation. At a basic level, new goods and services can be classified in one of the five categories highlighted in Figure 8-11.[33]

Degree of product newness: The extent to which a product or service is new to the market.

Another popular classification organizes innovation into the *radical, dynamically continuous,* and *continuous categories.* **Radical innovations** (or **discontinuous innovations**) create new industries or new standards of management, manufacturing, and servicing, and they represent fundamental changes for consumers, entailing departures from established consumption.[34] Examples of relatively recent radical innovations are the Internet and endoscopy. **Dynamically continuous innovations** do not significantly alter consumer behavior, but they represent a change in the consumption pattern. Cellular telephones are an example of such an innovation. **Continuous innovations** have no disruption on consumption patterns and involve only product alterations, such as new flavors, or a new product that is an improvement over the old offering. They usually are congruous, in the sense that they can be used alongside the existing systems. For example, a new Microsoft Windows version will work with computers that are only a few years old or older computers with enhanced capacity. Most of the innovations taking place today are continuous.

Radical innovations (or **discontinuous innovations):** Innovations that create new industries or new standards of management, manufacturing, and servicing, and that represent fundamental changes for consumers, entailing departures from established consumption.

Dynamically continuous innovations: Innovations that do not significantly alter consumer behavior but represent a change in the consumption pattern.

Continuous innovations: Innovations that have no disruption on consumption patterns and involve only product alterations, such as new flavors or a new product that is an improvement over the old offering.

8-6d Performing a Product Business Analysis

Performing a product business analysis should include calculating projected project costs, return on investment, and cash flow and determining the fixed and variable costs for the long term.[35] However enthusiastic the target consumers' response, if these figures do not fit the company budget, the project will be high risk. For many product categories, product price is a critical characteristic. At this stage, it is important to identify the price level at which revenue or profit best fit the manufacturer's goals.[36]

8-6e Designing and Developing the Product

At the next stage, designing and developing the product, product prototypes are developed. It is important that product prototypes precisely match the concept description developed in the concept development and evaluation stage. If the company strays from the initial description, it is crucial that the revised product description be tested first.[37] The product now acquires a name, a brand identity, and the marketing mix is developed. The cross-functional team developing the product—research and development, engineering, operations, marketing, and finance—must come together for this process.[38] This team must be focused on the project in such a way that a large percentage of team members' time is devoted to this particular project, rather than to other projects. It also is important that the team acts as a unit, focusing on the project itself, rather than on departmental interests.[39]

For multinational companies, it is advisable that coordination takes place across subsidiaries, or in conjunction with international partners. Companies such as Boeing and Motorola coordinate research and development activities globally by establishing worldwide information systems to coordinate product and design development. For example, in developing the Boeing 777, the company used real-time computer-aided technology to design components jointly with Japanese partners.[40] Companies also tend to encourage communication among research and development facilities in different countries. Procter & Gamble and Unilever, for example, require extensive communication and information sharing among units.[41]

Product design: The aesthetic traits, style, and function of the product.

Another important consideration is **product design**, defined as the aesthetic traits, style, and function of the product. Research points to the importance of design and aesthetics in developing products. The IPod is particularly popular and has substantial brand franchise, especially because of its sleek, minimalist design. Currently, the firm is focusing its efforts into transforming the IPod into a veritable fashion statement, offering IPod tattoos, so one can change the look of the MP3 as often as one changes clothes.[42]

8-6f Test Marketing

Test marketing a product can provide a good indication of how the product will be received when it is in the marketplace, but this stage can also be expensive, time consuming, and open to competitive sabotage.[43] The following are test-marketing options firms can use to evaluate the reaction of the market to their product. Because 8 out of 10 products fail, **simulated test marketing** is often used to reduce the risks a company would incur in terms of marketing, sales, and capital expenses, in terms of cannibalization of the original brand through line extension, and in terms of competitive reaction to the new product.[44] Among the simulated test-marketing research systems used today are LITMUS, which is used especially for new packaged goods, consumer durables, and services; ASSESSOR, which is used for packaged goods; BASES, which is used primarily for food and health and beauty products; and ESP, which is used primarily for packaged goods.[45]

Simulated test marketing: Test marketing that simulates purchase environments in that target consumers are observed in the product-related decision-making process.

To illustrate, the LITMUS simulated test-marketing study[46] recruits about 600 representative consumers who participate in a research study in a central facility in a number of markets. After responding to questions about their product-related attitudes and purchase behavior, the consumers in the sample view advertising of the new brand and of competitive brands that are embedded in a television program. The respondents then comment on the television program and the advertising and then proceed to a simulated store stocking test brands and competitive brands where they can buy the products at a substantial discount. The proportion of individuals purchasing the test brand is then used to estimate product trialability.

Usually conducted by a research firm in industrialized countries, controlled test marketing involves offering a new product to a group of stores and evaluating the market reaction to it (consumer reaction as well as competitive reaction). In the process, different aspects of the marketing mix are varied—price, in-store promotion, placement in the store, and so on. A more informal **controlled test marketing** involves simply asking a number of stores to carry the product for a fee; depending on the outcome, the manufacturing firm may decide to produce the product on a larger scale, or not.

Controlled test marketing: Offering a new product to a group of stores and evaluating the market reaction to it.

Commercialization (pg. 243): Stage in the new product development process when the product is introduced to the market.

A number of important decisions are involved in the full-blown actual test marketing, in which the product and related marketing mix are tested in a large test-market area. Companies at this stage must decide on the cities that are most appropriate for testing the product, based on the availability of retailers and other necessary distribution and logistics service providers, and on the availability of the infrastructure needed to conduct the test market, such as the necessary media, research firms, direct-mail providers, and so on. For companies selling financial products and for companies that cannot afford large-scale testing in the marketplace, test marketing may be limited to direct mail. For example, MasterCard continuously tests new products by using direct mail. This strategy also appeals to service providers from developing countries.

Although test marketing can provide valuable information for the manufacturer, anticipating product performance in the short run, its usefulness is often questioned given the high expense it necessitates. In a rapidly changing competitive environment, being first in the market constitutes an important competitive advantage addressed earlier—the first-mover advantage. As such, the company is the first to attract consumers and to commit channel members for its new product. A company is also vulnerable to competitive reaction during the test-marketing stage. On one hand, competition could appropriate the product idea and be the first to offer the product to the market. On the other, competition could sabotage the new brand, cutting prices for all competitive offerings.

Test marketing, nevertheless, can be a reliable predictor of market share, costs, and profitability and a tool to assess and compare between alternative product strategies; yet, surprisingly, this tool is frequently overlooked in marketing.[47] Among errors to avoid in test marketing are incorrect forecasts, unrealistic market conditions, and choice of the wrong test market.[48]

8-6g Launching the Product

Launching the product, also known as **commercialization,** involves introducing the new product to the market. Strategies for launching the product have an impact on later product performance. Products launched using a successful strategy have a higher rate of success and score high ratings on profitability, technical success, and positive impact on the company.[49] Quality of launch is characterized by the following, in order of impact: high service quality, on-time shipment and adequate product availability, quality sales force and enough sales effort and support, quality of promotion, and sufficient promotional effort.[50]

An important decision is the timing of the new product launch. Companies often attempt to gain the first-mover advantage by being the first to launch the new product. Alternatively, they could engage in later entry. The advantage of later entry is that a firm's competitors would have to incur the costs of informing the market about the new product and its features. Also, the company could market the product as a "me-too" product, reducing advertising costs significantly.

Figure 8-12 illustrates the new product development process used by Coors Brewing Company. The company stresses the role of research and development, as well as the involvement of the other functional areas of the company, in most steps of the process. As the figure indicates, part of the process involves evaluating the overall product portfolio balance.

As many companies have found out over time, planning and timing are crucial elements of new product development. Poor planning and timing can lead to product failure. In an effort to portray beer as a pure drink, Philip Morris decided to offer clear beer. Consumers, however, did not buy into this concept, as they did not buy into the concept of a clear cola.

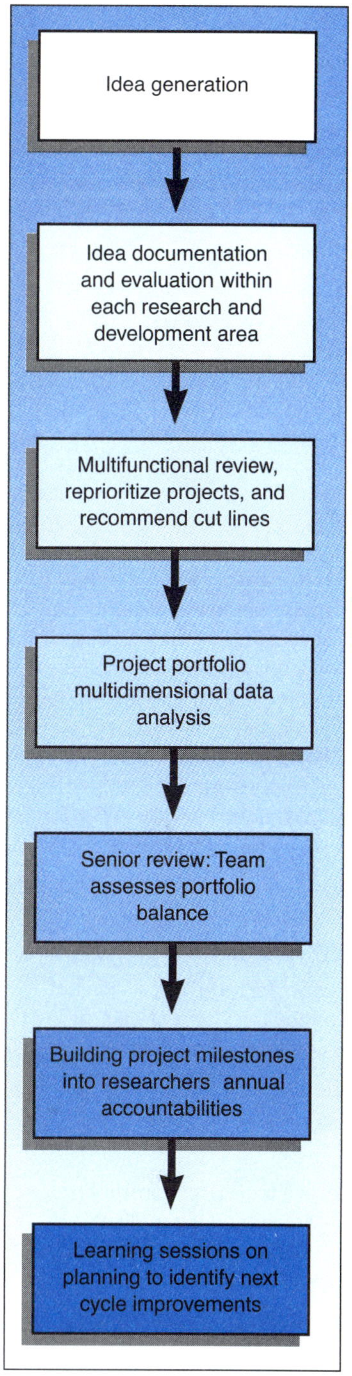

Figure 8-12
The New Product Development Process

Source: "Applying Total Quality to R&D at Coors Brewing Company," by Hugo Patino from *Research Technology Management,* vol. 40, no. 5 (September/October 1997): 32–36. Reprinted by permission of Industrial Research Institute.

INTERACTIVE FIGURE

8-7 New Product Diffusion

Product diffusion refers to the manner in which consumers accept new products and the speed of new product adoption by various consumer groups. A number of factors influence the speed of product adoption.[51] First, the new product must offer a *relative advantage* compared to the other offerings available on the market and must be *compatible with the needs of consumers.* In addition, the good/service use must be observable (or communicable to others) and have a high *trialability* (for example, consumers can try the product on a limited basis, by renting it, for instance).

Figure 8-13
New Product Adoption

INTERACTIVE FIGURE

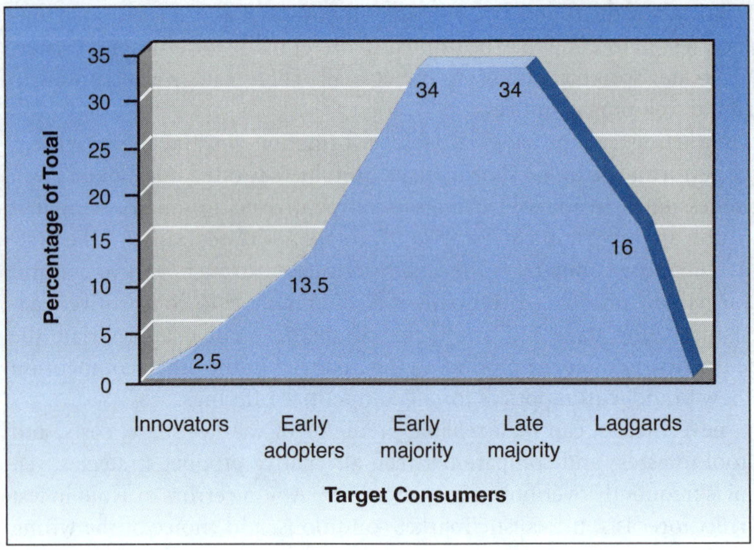

Innovators: Psychographic group of individuals who are successful, sophisticated, and receptive to new technologies.

Early adopters: Consumers who purchase the product early in the lifecycle and are opinion leaders in their communities.

Early majority: Consumers who are more risk averse but enjoy the status of being among the first in their peer group to buy what will be a popular product.

Late majority: Consumers with limited means likely to adopt products only if the products are widely popular and the risk associated with buying them is minimal.

Laggards: Consumers who are the last to adopt new products and who do so only in late maturity.

Product lifecycle (PLC): The performance of the product in terms of sales and profit over time.

Target consumers can be segmented based on the manner in which they adopt new products throughout the respective products' lifecycle. The segments and their characteristics, also shown in Figure 8-13, are as follows:

Innovators—These few risk takers (2.5 percent of the total market) can afford to pay the higher purchase price charged by companies during the introduction stage of a new product. They are willing to accept risk, and they like to be known as the first to try out product concepts among their peers.

Early adopters—The next consumers to purchase the product tend to be opinion leaders in their communities who take risks, but with greater discernment than innovators. They constitute about 13.5 percent of the total population.

Early majority—These consumers, who account for 34 percent of the total market, are more risk averse than individuals in the first categories but enjoy the status of being among the first in their peer group to buy what will be a popular product.

Late majority—These consumers, who account for 34 percent of the total market, are individuals of limited means who are likely to adopt products only if the products are widely popular and the risk associated with buying them is minimal. The products themselves are much more affordable at this stage.

Laggards—These consumers, who account for 16 percent of the total market, are the last to adopt new products and often do so reluctantly. In general, laggards are risk averse and very conservative in their spending.

8-8 The Product Lifecycle (PLC)

After new products are launched, marketing managers need to ensure that their products perform well on the market for a very long time—long enough to generate sufficient profits that can be used to finance other items in the product portfolio. Products pass through distinct stages in their evolution, during which sales and profits rise and fall. In this evolutionary process, products require different marketing strategies at each stage. The **product lifecycle** (PLC) is defined as the performance of the product in terms of sales and profit over time. The product lifecycle can apply to a product category or to a particular brand. The traditional product lifecycle is illustrated in Figure 8-14. The characteristics of each stage are further explained in Table 8-4, in terms of industry sales, profits, price, promotion, competition, and target market.

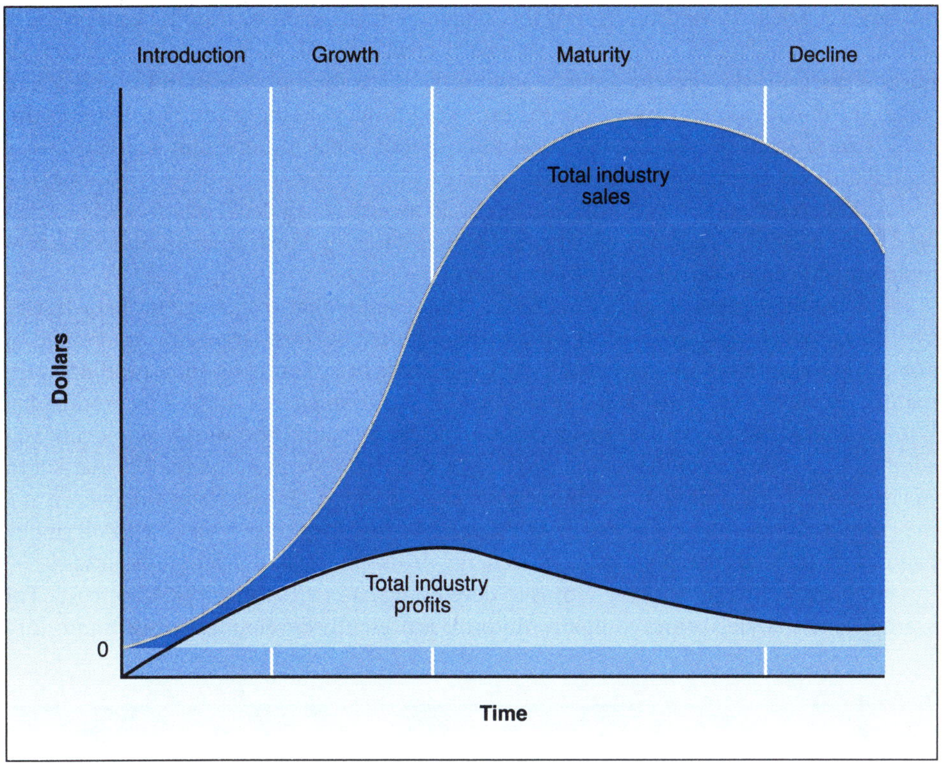

Figure 8-14
The Traditional Product Lifecycle

The **product introduction stage** is the product lifecycle stage when the product is available for purchase for the first time. During this stage, products are developed in industrialized countries and supported by a firm's substantial research and development budgets and by highly skilled product research teams. To quickly recover the high costs of product development and launching, a firm markets products in industrialized countries to consumers who can afford the high prices that need to be charged. The firm at this stage still has control of the market: It is the only manufacturer or one of the few manufacturers of the product.

Product introduction stage: Stage in the product lifecycle when the product is available for purchase for the first time.

In the introduction stage, firms—or the one firm first introducing the product—have negative or very low profits. They are attempting to recover the high product-development costs. Sales are low, but increasing. And the company (companies) spends heavily on promotion in order to encourage product innovators to adopt the product and on developing a viable distribution channel for the product, if such a channel is not yet established. Smart phones are currently in this stage.

The **growth stage** is the product lifecycle stage characterized by increasing competition, with new product variants offered to the market, as well as rapid product adoption by

Growth stage: Stage in the product lifecycle characterized by increasing competition, with new product variants offered to the market, as well as rapid product adoption by the target market.

TABLE 8-4 Product Lifecycle (PLC) Strategies

PLC Stage	Industry Sales	Industry Profit	Product Price	Promotion	Target Competition	Market
Introduction	Low	Low	High	High	Low	Innovators
Growth	Increasing	Increasing	Decreasing	High	Increasing	Early adopters and early majority
Maturity	High and stable	Decreasing	Lower	Decreasing	High	Early and late majority
Decline	Decreasing	Decreasing	Low	Low	Decreasing	Late majority and laggards

the target market. Toward the end of this stage, the focus is on developing economies of scale in the manufacturing process. A standard is reached and, subsequently, price competition is intense. Sales increase rapidly, and profits reach their peak toward the end of this stage. The in-car video is currently in the early growth stage, as more and more parents discover that it creates a magical back-seat atmosphere, replacing constant toddler drama. Digital cameras are in the late growth stage.

Although the goal of every company is rapid growth, the growth rate should be managed appropriately, based on company resources. Marketing Illustration 8-2 describes how rapid growth can be detrimental to companies.

Maturity stage: Stage in the product lifecycle characterized by a slowdown in sales growth as the product is adopted by most target consumers and by a leveling or decline in profits primarily due to intense price competition.

Usually the longest stage in the product lifecycle, the **maturity stage** is characterized by a slowdown in sales growth as the product is adopted by most target consumers, and by a leveling or decline in profits primarily due to intense price competition. A product in the maturity stage in the United States is Red Bull, an Austrian energy drink. The product has systematically taken over the energy drink marketing around the world. The drink was adopted by consumers in the rest of Europe in the early 1990s and took the U.S. market by storm in 1997. Today, it is in nearly every retail shop in the United States (Tennessee and the Dakotas are among the few states without it). In less than three years, Red Bull single-handedly created and then propelled the energy drink category to $75 million in sales.[52]

At maturity, manufacturing moves to developing countries to save on labor costs. For example, the U.S. electronics company Motorola is presently developing software and chips

Marketing Illustration 8-2

Rapid Growth Does Not Always Equal Success

Americans' use of cell phones has increased at such rapid rates that wireless networks are becoming overloaded. Consumers increasingly complain about calls that are inaudible or cut off. Often, consumers have difficulty making contact and need several attempts in order to hear the telephone ring at the other end. This situation is likely to become even more problematic in the future, as features such as digital photography and Internet games become more popular.

In the past 10 years, there has been an impressive growth in cell phones and related wireless services. While the U.S. market is far behind that of many other countries in Europe in terms of cellular phone adoption, it is remarkable that 56 percent of all U.S. households have wireless telephone subscriptions. Typical in the late growth stage, the prices of cell phones and wireless services have plunged, making cellular service attractive to increasingly larger numbers of consumers. Today, using the cellular phone costs an average of 11 cents per minute, compared to 56 cents in 1995. For companies, this means a decline in average revenue per customer from $74 a month in 1995 to $61 per month currently. It may be argued that more profits can be made given the volume, but because cellular phones need more and more cash input to create wireless networks that can handle the call volume, cellular companies have yet to invest the amount needed for efficient operations.

As a consequence, a total of 61 percent of wireless subscribers have called customer service centers at least once a year to complain about their cellular phone—a level higher than for any other product. It is unlikely that, in the near future, cell phone companies will have fewer complaints. Some deficiency can be attributed to the product itself: A cell phone is much like a glorified radio, subject to interference from building walls, sunspots, or the weather, and there will always be a trade-off between mobility and call quality. Furthermore, unlike conventional telephone systems, in which customers are hard-wired to the network, wireless systems rely on a mesh of thousands of antennae and cellular relay stations that can easily be flooded with an increase in calling volume. After the September 11, 2001 terrorist attacks, the sheer number of calls shut down local wireless networks.

It is hoped that recently introduced cellular phone capabilities, such as text messaging and the transmission of digital photos, will ultimately generate the revenue needed to give wireless companies the financial support for upgrading the systems. But systems, as well as individuals, need to adapt to the technology. As of 2005, the nation's wireless operators have set standards that enabled multimedia services interoperability across carriers' networks. Text messaging took off after operators agreed to text messaging interoperability. It is likely that multimedia messaging will also take off because subscribers can exchange photos and media content without regard to network boundaries. Essential, however, is the rapid consumer adoption of the technology. Consumers with picture phones are not quite sure to whom they can send a picture message because they don't know what type of handset lies at the other end.

Sources: Simon Romero, "Cell Phone Service Hurt by Success," *New York Times* (November 18, 2002): A1, A17; Jason Ankeny, "The Apps on Tap for 2005," *Wireless Review*, vol. 21, no. 12 (December 2004): 14–17.

in Poland,[53] while Siemens and Intel Corp. manufacture their semiconductors in Thailand.[54] Products at maturity do not need as much promotional support; the cash they generate is used to promote products in the introduction and growth stages, as Section 8-9 will illustrate. Examples of products in this category are television sets, hi-fi equipment, and video cameras, among others.

Products in the **decline stage** are rapidly losing ground to new technologies or product alternatives. Sales and profits are rapidly declining at this stage, and the firm is likely to cut back on production, distribution, and promotional support. Alternatively, management may decide that it is not worthwhile to maintain the product on the market because the costs of even minimal product maintenance are high. Firms still have to pay the costs of manufacturing and distributing the product; among these costs are those of maintaining the sales staff, of managing the distribution channel, of maintaining shelf space (slotting fees and other expenses), and so on. Dropping the product has many costs associated with it, in addition to the overall losses that it incurs in the divestiture of equipment and physical manufacturing facilities: The company may have dissatisfied employees and formerly loyal consumers.

Decline stage: Stage in the product lifecycle where products are rapidly losing ground to new technologies or product alternatives, and, consequently, sales and profits are rapidly declining.

Products vary in the length of time needed for them to go through the lifecycle. Although most products go through the traditional lifecycle, fashion, fads, and styles, for instance, have a much shorter cycle (see Figure 8-15). For example, a **style** is defined as a general form of popular expression that could last for a longer period of time—even decades—or that could be cyclical in nature. The transitional home is an example of a style. It has traditional elements, such as molding and traditional mantle pieces, as well as modern bathrooms and kitchens. Louis XV is a furniture style characterized by slightly curved legs for chairs and tables. Current Louis XV designs are rendered in dark wood; the original style was popular gilded, white, or a combination thereof. The black-tie dress style for men has been a constant for more than a century, with small variations.

Style: A general form of popular expression that could last for a longer period of time and/or that could be cyclical in nature.

A **fashion** is defined as a current style. In the 1960s, polyester leisure suits and Nehru jackets became popular, followed by bell-bottom pants. In the 1980s, the more dressy yuppie look became popular. In Germany, hip-hop fashion is taking the country by storm. A **fad** is a fashion that quickly becomes very popular and just as quickly disappears. An example of a fad is tooth jewelry. Another example is Tickle Me Elmo, which had a very short duration—just one pre-Christmas sales season. Marketing Illustration 8-3 demonstrates how toy makers are attempting to revive popular toys.

Fashion: A current style.

Fad: A fashion that quickly becomes very popular and just as quickly disappears.

8-9 Managing the Product Portfolio

The **product portfolio** is defined as the totality of products managed by the company as separate businesses. Product portfolio decisions are an important aspect of strategic

Product portfolio: The totality of products the company manages as separate businesses.

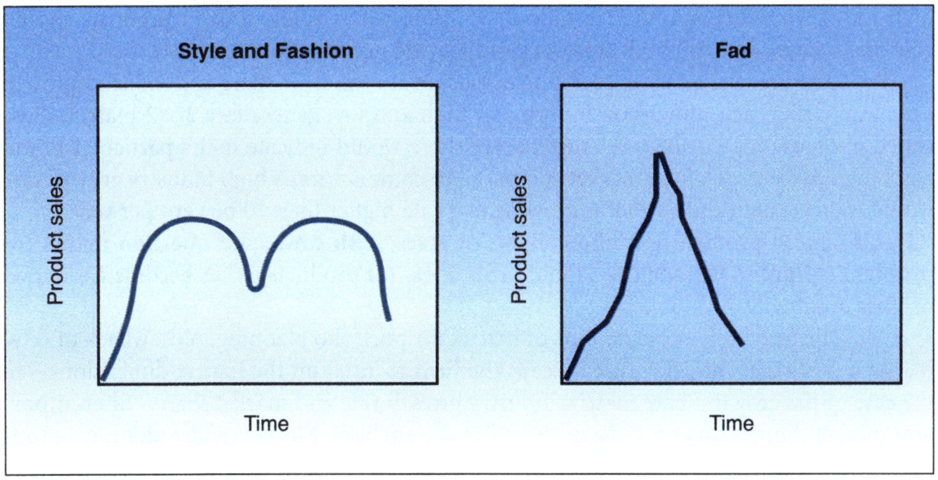

Figure 8-15
Style, Fashion, and Fad—Product Sales over Time

INTERACTIVE FIGURE

Marketing Illustration 8-3

Oldies as Goodies

Toy manufacturers have a certain degree of influence in reviving popular toys. While leading toy manufacturers, such as Mattel, typically bring about 400 new toys to market every year, they often capitalize on oldies to create excitement for a popular toy-selling season—Christmas. During the recent recession, Batman, Barbie, G.I. Joe, Monopoly, and Play-Doh were prime sellers. According to a spokesman for a leading toy manufacturer, toy mega-hits are unpredictable. In an uncertain economy, extending the brand provides a safety net. Moreover, the cost of developing, manufacturing, and advertising a new toy is very high. Developing a new Barbie, for example, costs about $1 million, including the packaging, the hair, the clothes, and the advertising. For a totally new doll, the cost could be as much as $10 million. The cost of making a new radio-controlled toy that retails for more than $60 is about 30 times the cost of recycling an older version.

The market for toys tends to be unpredictable because children are notoriously fickle consumers. One of the few promising toys of a recent holiday season was Chicken Dance Elmo—when you touched his toe, he sang "C'mon, everybody, let's do the Chicken Dance." Interestingly enough, the toy was also popular with teenagers and buyers in their twenties. It was a fad.

Among other industry characteristics, toys based on movies start out red hot and subsequently fizzle out. Spider-man toys initially did well following the movie's release, but not for long, suggesting that this was a fad. Toys based on television shows last the longest because preschoolers like to watch these shows over and over again. Barney, Teletubbies, Bob the Builder, and Thomas the Tank Engine have been doing very well for years.

Source: Tracie Rozhon, "Toy Makers Hope Children Will See Oldies as Goodies," *New York Times* (November 16, 2002): B1–B2.

Growth-share matrix: Portfolio matrix developed by the Boston Consulting Group and one of the most popular bases for evaluating company product portfolios; it assumes that, to be successful, a company should have a portfolio of products with different growth rates and different market shares.

Stars: High-share, high-growth products that create profits but require additional investment.

Cash cows: Products with high market share and slow growth that generate large amounts of cash, in excess of the reinvestment required to maintain market share.

Question marks (or problem children): Low market share and high-growth products that require more cash investment than they generate.

Dogs: Products with low market share and slow growth.

Product-market matrix (p. 249): A matrix used to identify future products and opportunities for companies.

planning, as will be seen in Appendix A, "The Marketing Plan: A Strategic Marketing Perspective." Companies periodically review their different businesses and make decisions on whether to acquire new ones or divest those that might be unprofitable or that do not represent a good fit with the company. For example, Pepsi Co. decided to focus more on the Pepsi and Frito Lay brands and divest the restaurant business by spinning off its fast-food restaurants, Taco Bell, Kentucky Fried Chicken, and Pizza Hut. As we have seen in earlier examples, Kraft bought Jacobs Suchard and thus acquired the popular chocolate brands Toblerone, Suchard, and Milka, and the very popular European coffee brand Jacobs. Unilever decided to enter the gourmet ice cream business by acquiring Ben & Jerry's. These are all portfolio decisions that involve substantial resource allocations. Companies must constantly re-evaluate their portfolios to make sure that they are appropriately allocating their resources to ensure firm success. Two models exist to evaluate portfolios: the growth-share matrix and the product-market matrix.

The **growth-share matrix** was developed by the Boston Consulting Group in the 1970s and remains one of the most popular bases for evaluating company product portfolios. The assumption of the matrix is that a company should have a portfolio of products with different growth rates and different market shares in order to be successful—high-growth products require cash inputs to grow, whereas low-growth products should generate excess cash, and both types of products are needed simultaneously.[55]

Products are evaluated on two dimensions: relative market share and industry growth rate. Evaluating each dimension in terms of high and low generates a 2 x 2 matrix, illustrated in Figure 8-16. A high relative market share would indicate that a particular brand has a high percentage of the market compared to competitors. A high industry growth rate would indicate an industry that is growing at a rate higher than 10 percent per year.

A balanced product portfolio consists of **stars, cash cows,** and **question marks** (or **problem children**). Companies should drop **dogs.** All products either become cash cows or dogs eventually.

Most firms do rely on some type of matrix for portfolio planning. A drawback of relying on a particular model is that it keeps the firm focused on the matrix dimensions—in the case of the growth-share matrix, industry growth rate and market share. Other important market dimensions could be neglected in the analyses. Moreover, abandoning a prod-

Relative Market Share

Industry Growth Rate	High	Low
High	**SBU Designation:** Star **Marketing Strategy:** **Stars** are high-share, high-growth products. A star creates profits, but it may require additional investment. If it maintains a high share, it will become a cash cow when growth stops. An example of a star is the Kodak EasyShare digital camera. Digital cameras are still in the growth stage, and Kodak EasyShare is among the brands that hold a substantial market share—it is a star.	**SBU Designation:** Question mark **Marketing Strategy:** **Question marks** or **problem children** are low market share and high-growth products that require more cash investment than they generate. If the cash is not supplied, they are likely to become dogs; even when the cash is supplied, if they simply hold their share, they become dogs when the growth stops. This product is a liability unless it gains substantial market share through aggressive investment. An example of a question mark is the introduction of Kraft's Milka in the United States. Milka is a cash cow in most of Europe; in the United States, the company is introducing it at select stores—Target and small gourmet shops are the only stores that carry it, in this author's experience. In the growing gourmet chocolate market, where brands such as Godiva and Ghirardelli appear to hold the lead, Milka may be a solid contender, if Kraft invests enough cash in the brand.
Low	**SBU Designation:** Cash cow **Marketing Strategy:** **Cash cows** are products with high market share and slow growth. They generate large amounts of cash, in excess of the reinvestment required to maintain market share. This excess should be invested in other products in the portfolio. Many of Procter & Gamble's products are cash cows: Tide, Bold, Cheer, for example.	**SBU Designation:** Dog **Marketing Strategy:** **Dogs** are products with low market share and slow growth; they may show an accounting profit, but the profit must be reinvested to maintain share, leaving no excess cash. The product is essentially worthless. Total decided to produce cereals to compete with the Quaker Oatmeal brands. While the product gained some loyalty among consumers, Quaker was the favored national brand, and store brands remained the preferred cheaper alternative for consumers. The company decided to pull the brand off the shelves, selling it for less than half price.

Relative market share is an SBU's market share in comparison to the leading competitors in the industry. Industry growth rate is the annual growth of all similar businesses in the market (such as sugarless gum).

Figure 8-16
The Boston Consulting Group Matrix

INTERACTIVE FIGURE

uct because it has become a dog may be premature: The dog could quickly become a star if the target market is actually becoming a niche market.

Another approach to evaluating products is the **product-market matrix,**[56] which helps companies identify future products that should be considered for its portfolio. Figure 8-17 identifies four strategies depending on market saturation and contingent on the firm's ability and desire to introduce new products.

The following is a brief summary of each strategy with corresponding examples:

- **Market penetration** is defined as selling more products to present customers without changing the product. Approaches include increasing the usage rate of current customers and attracting competitors' customers. Improving product visibility through promotion and through securing better shelf space are two strategies that could be used to this end. Kodak is attempting to penetrate the market further by creating bundles of films, selling a combination of 36-exposure and

Market penetration: The process of increasing the usage rate of current customers and attracting competitors' customers to sell more products to present customers without changing the product.

Figure 8-17
The Product-Market Opportunity Matrix

Source: Adapted from H. Igo Ansoff, "Strategies for Diversification," *Harvard Business Review,* vol. 35 (September–October 1957): 113–124.

INTERACTIVE FIGURE

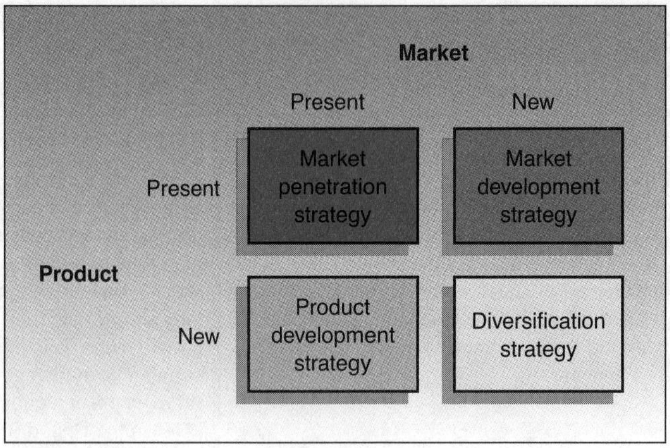

24-exposure films in one package. Research has demonstrated that consumers who buy products in larger packages are likely to consume more; this strategy, thus, might increase consumption.

Market development: The process of developing new markets for the company's existing product or creating new product uses.

- **Market development** is defined as increasing product sales by developing new markets for the company's existing product or by creating new product uses. Kodak going international is an example of such a strategy. For example, if the U.S. government allows access to the Cuban market for U.S. firms, Kodak will enter this market, engaging in market development.

Product development: The process of developing new products to appeal to the company's existing market.

- **Product development** is defined as developing new products to appeal to the company's existing market. Developing Kodak brand cameras is an example of such a strategy. Kodak attempts to sell a new product, the Kodak camera, to its original film market.

Diversification: Opportunity for expansion involving developing or acquiring new products for new markets.

- **Diversification** is defined as developing or acquiring new products for new markets. Kodak may also rely on its good name to sell Kodak cameras to Fuji film consumers. In this situation, it is engaging in diversification by new product development. In an earlier example, Kraft decided to diversify into popular European chocolate brands by acquiring Jacobs Suchard. It should be noted that Kraft diversified in a related industry: Kraft sells primarily food products, and cookies constitute a large proportion of its total product mix. Cookies and chocolate are related, as snacks. Thus, this is an example of diversification by acquisition.

Summary

1. *Define and classify products into relevant categories.* A product, an offering developed to satisfy consumer needs, can be conceptualized at three levels. The core product is the fundamental benefit, or problem solution, sought by consumers. The expected or actual product is the basic physical product, including styling, features, brand name, and packaging, which delivers those benefits. The augmented product is a product enhanced by the addition of extra or unsolicited services or benefits to the consumer in order to prompt purchase, such as warranty, repair services, maintenance, and other services that enhance product use. In terms of durability, products are classified as durables (tangible products that have a prolonged use, such as automobiles and appliances), nondurables (tangible products that are consumed relatively quickly and purchased on a regular basis), and services (intangible benefits or activities that individuals acquire but that do not result in ownership). Consumer products are classified into convenience goods, preference goods, shopping goods, and specialty goods. Convenience goods are inexpensive and purchased frequently, and include impulse goods that are bought without earlier planning; staples, which are bought routinely; and emergency goods, which are bought to address urgent needs. Preference goods are convenience goods that become differentiated through branding and achieve some degree of brand loyalty. Shopping goods are perceived as higher risk goods that consumers are willing to spend a greater amount of purchase effort in searching for and evaluating. Specialty goods are highly differentiated and enjoy high brand loyalty, such that they are the only brand acceptable to the consumer.

2. *Address issues related to branding, such as the brand name, mark, logo, and character; brand sponsor; and brand strategy decisions.* A brand is a name, design, symbol, or a combination thereof that identifies the product and/or the seller, and is used to differentiate the product from competitors' offerings. Brand marks are part of the brand that can be seen but not spoken, and a brand logo is a distinctive mark, sign, symbol, or graphic version of a company's name, used to identify and promote its product. A brand character or trade character is a character that personifies the brand, such as Tony the Tiger for Kellogg's Frosted Flakes and Ronald McDonald for McDonald's. These together help to build the brand's identity and are valuable and well-protected trademarks. A trademark consists of words, symbols, marks, and signs that are legally registered for use by a single company. Counterfeiting, ranging from direct copying to design counterfeiting, is flourishing due to improved technology, inadequate channel control, lax enforcement locally and worldwide, and consumer demand. Brand sponsor decisions involve determining if the brand should be sold as a manufacturer brand (a national brand), a dealer brand (a private label brand, a retailer brand, a wholesaler brand, or a distributor brand, depending on whether it is a retailer or wholesaler selling the product under its own name), or a generic brand. Brand sponsor decisions also involve determining if the brand can be licensed or co-branded. Brand strategies involve extending the existing brand name by introducing new product offerings in an existing product category, such as new flavors, colors, or sizes (known as line extensions); brand extensions, using an existing brand name to introduce products in a new product category; family (blanket) branding, whereby one brand name is used for more than one product; multibranding, which is using different brand names for different products that the company sells in the same product category; and creating new brands in new product categories for the firm.

3. *Address product packaging and labeling issues.* Packaging addresses all the activities involved in designing the product container. The primary package may be a single container or wrapper; this is the immediate package. The secondary package may enclose the primary package. The shipping package contains a number of products and typically consists of a corrugated box used for shipping. The package contains the product label, which identifies the product or brand. It carries the brand name, logo, and brand mark; describes the product in terms of ingredients and/or components, weight, or volume; informs consumers when the product expires; classifies the product based on quality and/or size; identifies the manufacturer and/or the distributor; and has the Universal Product Code for easy inventory processing and scanning. The package also promotes the product because the label advertises the product to the consumer every time the consumer handles it.

4. *Analyze the different dimensions of the product mix.* The product mix is the complete assortment of products that a company offers to its target consumers. The product line consists of the related brands in the same product category. Other important product dimensions are the product length (the total number of brands in the product mix), the product width (the total number of product lines the company offers), and the product depth (the number of different offerings for a product category).

5. *Describe the new product development process and the different degrees of product newness.* The new product development process starts with idea generation, inside and outside the company. The next step involves idea screening using predetermined criteria, followed by concept development and evaluation. Product business analysis determines the extent to which the product is likely to be viable. In the next stage—product design and development—product prototypes are developed and evaluated by target consumers. Test marketing involves great expense on the part of the company; it also leaves the company vulnerable to competitive idea theft. The final stage—launching—requires significant commitment to the product and to the target market. There are different types of new products: products that are new to an existing market or new to an existing company; new lines (i.e., new products or product lines to a company, but for a company already operating in that market); new items in an existing product line for the company; modifications to an existing company product; and innovations.

6. *Examine the new product diffusion process and the different categories of product adopters.* The new product diffusion process involves the following stages: innovators, early adopters, early majority, late majority, and laggards. Product diffusion begins when innovators try the product during the introduction stage of the product lifecycle. If the product is successful, then early adopters will start using it. These are opinion leaders who others will follow. The early majority is ready to try the new product after it is established and prices have come down. The late majority purchases the product only during the mature stage of the PLC when competition is high, prices are lower, and product differentiation has occurred. The laggards resist the new product and buy only when older alternatives are not available.

7. *Address the different stages of the product lifecycle.* The first stage of the product lifecycle is the introduction stage, when the product is first introduced to the market. The product most likely has no or only minimal competition, and it is targeted to innovators who are willing to try new products and spend substantial amounts for the product. The firm has negative profits in the sense that it is attempting to recover product development costs. In the growth stage, sales and profits are increasing rapidly, and more and more competitors are offering the product. In the maturity stage, there is a slowdown in sales growth as the product is adopted by most target consumers and as profits level off or decline primarily due to intense price competition. Products are rapidly losing ground to new technologies or product alternatives in the decline stage. Sales and profits are rapidly declining, and the firm is likely to cut back on production, distribution, and promotional support.

8. *Examine the challenges involved in managing the product portfolio.* The product portfolio consists of the totality of products managed by the company as separate businesses. A popular matrix used for portfolio assessment is the Boston Consulting Group growth-share matrix. Its assumption is that a company should have a portfolio of products with different growth rates and different market shares in order to be successful. The matrix consists of cash cows, which are products with a high market share and slow growth that generate large amounts of cash, in excess of the reinvestment required to maintain market share; dogs, which have a low market share and slow growth; question marks or problem children, which are low market share and high-growth products that require more cash investment than they generate; and stars, which are high-share, high-growth products that create profits but may require additional investment. A product-market opportunity matrix is used to identify future products that companies should consider for their portfolio. Companies have the option to pursue one of four strategies: market penetration, which involves selling more products to present customers without changing the product by increasing usage rate of current customers and attracting competitors' customers; market development, which involves developing new markets for the company's existing product or by creating new product uses; product development, which involves developing new products to appeal to the company's existing market; and diversification, which involves developing or acquiring new products for new markets.

Key Terms

augmented product (p. 226)
battle of the brands (p. 233)
brand (p. 228)
brand character (or trade character) (p. 231)
brand equity (or brand franchise) (p. 228)
brand extensions (p. 235)
brand image (p. 229)
brand logo (p. 231)
brand mark (p. 230)
brand name (p. 230)
cash cows (p. 248)
co-branding (p. 234)
commercialization (p. 243)
continuous innovations (p. 241)
controlled test marketing (p. 242)
convenience goods (p. 227)
core product (p. 226)
decline stage (p. 247)
degree of product newness (p. 241)
diversification (p. 250)
dogs (p. 248)
durable goods (p. 227)
dynamically continuous innovations (p. 241)
early adopters (p. 244)
early majority (p. 244)
emergency goods (p. 227)
expected (or actual) product (p. 226)
fad (p. 247)
family branding (or blanket branding) (p. 236)
fashion (p. 247)
generics (p. 233)
growth-share matrix (p. 248)
growth stage (p. 245)
heterogeneous shopping goods (p. 228)
homogeneous shopping goods (p. 228)
impulse goods (p. 227)
innovators (p. 244)
laggards (p. 244)
late majority (p. 244)
licensing (p. 234)
line extension (p. 235)
manufacturers' brands (or national brands) (p. 232)
market development (p. 250)
market penetration (p. 249)
maturity stage (p. 246)
multibranding (p. 236)
new brands (p. 236)
nondurable goods (p. 227)
packaging (p. 237)
patent (p. 231)
preference goods (p. 227)
private label brands (p. 232)
product (p. 226)
product consistency (p. 238)
product depth (p. 238)
product design (p. 242)
product development (p. 250)
product introduction stage (p. 245)
product length (p. 238)
product lifecycle (PLC) (p. 244)
product line (p. 238)
product-market matrix (p. 249)
product mix (p. 238)
product portfolio (p. 247)
product width (p. 238)
question marks (or problem children) (p. 248)
radical innovations (or discontinuous innovations) (p. 241)
servicemark (p. 231)
shopping goods (p. 227)
simulated test marketing (p. 242)
specialty goods (p. 228)
staples (p. 227)
stars (p. 248)
style (p. 247)
trademark (p. 231)

Discussion Questions

1. Identify 10 brand characters and 10 brand logos. What makes these characters and logos memorable?
2. Try to think of brand names for medicine that you do not normally take. What traits of these brand names made them memorable?
3. Go to Unilever's home page (www.unilever.com) and access the brands sold to consumers in the United States. Comment on the product depth, width, and length, as well as on product consistency.
4. How could Unilever take advantage of opportunities in each of the four quadrants of the product market matrix? Give examples in each category.
5. What are the activities involved at each stage of the new product development process? Where are most new products developed?
6. Many products are advertised in the United States as "new and improved." What does this description mean in terms of new product classifications?
7. Recall the last time you remember a product launch that was accompanied by aggressive advertising. What brand was advertised? What traits of the introductory communication campaign do you recall?
8. Describe the product lifecycle and the activities involved at each stage. Offer examples of products at each of the four stages.
9. Differentiate between a fad and a fashion. Can a fashion be really a fad? When can marketing managers find out whether this is the case? Can marketing managers influence fashion and fads? Explain.

Review Questions

True or False

1. The expected, actual product is enhanced by the addition of extra and unsolicited services or benefits to the consumer, which help promote the purchase.
2. As a subgroup of convenience goods, impulse goods are those products bought routinely, such as groceries.
3. Manufacturing brands are also sold as private labels.
4. Licensing involves the owner of the brand name allowing a manufacturer or reseller to sell the product under the owner's brand name in return for a licensing fee.
5. Packaging has a minimal influence on the product's purchase price.
6. Companies' success depends on internal research and brainstorming sessions to generate new product ideas.
7. Products launched with a well-determined strategy have a higher rate of success and score high in profitability, technical success, and positive effect on the company's performance.
8. Innovators and early adopters constitute the majority of consumers throughout the lifecycle of a product.
9. The maturity stage of the product lifecycle is characterized by increasing competition, with new product variations offered to the market, and rapid market adoption.

Multiple Choice

10. Which of the following categories is indicative of high consumer awareness and loyalty?
    a. brand equity
    b. brand franchise
    c. brand identity
    d. a and b
11. Which of the following categories characterize brand names? Brand names
    a. are easy to pronounce and memorize.
    b. suggest product benefits.
    c. are easy to translate into other languages.
    d. all of the above.
12. The battle of the brands is defined as
    a. a conflict between manufacturers and retailers to promote their own brands.
    b. a similarity in packaging of manufacturers' and retailers' brand products.
    c. the selling of the retailer brand at a lower price than the national brand.
    d. all of the above.
13. Which of the following categories is related to the product mix?
    a. product length
    b. product width
    c. product depth
    d. all of the above
14. The product introduction stage is characterized by
    a. negative or low profits.
    b. low but increasing sales.
    c. promotions to encourage product innovators.
    d. all of the above.
15. Which of the following groups in the growth-share matrix is characterized by low market share and high-growth products that require more cash investment than they generate?
    a. cash cows
    b. dogs
    c. question marks (or problem children)
    d. stars

Notes

1. Ian Mirlin, "The World's Greatest Rock 'n' Roll Brand," *Marketing Magazine*, vol. 107, no. 43 (October 18, 2002): 16.
2. Theodore Levitt, "Marketing Success through Differentiation—Of Anything," *Harvard Business Review* (January–February, 1980): 83–91.
3. Casey Donoho, "Classifying Services from a Consumer Perspective," *The Journal of Services Marketing*, vol. 10, no. 6 (1996): 33–44.
4. Robert W. Pimentel and Kristy E. Reynolds, "A Model for Consumer Devotion: Affective Commitment with Proactive Sustaining Behaviors," *Academy of Marketing Science Review*, vol. 1 (2004): 1; David A. Aaker, *Managing Brand Equity* (New York: Maxwell Macmillan International, 1991).
5. Jane Bainbridge, "Global Forces," *Marketing* (July 20, 2000): 24–25.
6. Ibid.
7. Kate MacArthur, "Coke Crisis: Equity Erodes as Brand Troubles Mount," *Advertising Age*, vol. 71, no. 18 (April 24, 2000): 3, 98.
8. See www.upsto.gov.
9. Dexter Roberts, Frederik Balfour, Paul Magnuson, Pete Engardio, and Jennifer Lee, "China's Pirates: It's Not Just Little Guys—State-Owned Factories Add to the Plague of Fakes," *Business Week*, Issue 3684 (June 5, 2000): 26, 44.
10. Ibid.
11. Peter H. Bloch, Ronald F. Bush, and Leland Campbell, "Consumer 'Accomplices' in Product Counterfeiting," *Journal of Consumer Marketing*, vol. 10, no. 4 (1993): 27–36.
12. Ibid.
13. Ibid.
14. Ibid.
15. Roberts, Balfour, Magnuson, Engardio, and Lee, "China's Pirates: It's Not Just Little Guys—State-Owned Factories Add to the Plague of Fakes," 26, 44.
16. Ibid.
17. Mike Duff, "Top Brands 2002: Private Label—Drop-Off Begs Question, How Much Is Too Much?" *DSN Retailing Today*, vol. 41, no. 20 (October 28, 2002): 37, 43.
18. Michelle Wirth Fellman, "Just the Name, Thanks: Why Beemer Bought Rolls," *Marketing News*, Vol. 32, no. 19 (September 14, 1998): 6.
19. See www.rolls-royce.com.
20. Duff, "Top Brands 2002: Private Label—Drop-Off Begs Question, How Much Is Too Much?" 37, 43.

21. Lisa Marchese, "Brand Schizophrenia: Today's Epidemic," *Brandweek*, vol. 43, no. 38 (October 21, 2002): 28.
22. Jon Berry, "Brand Equity: How Much Is Your Brand Worth?" *Brandweek*, vol. 34, no. 26 (June 28, 1993): 21–24.
23. Ibid.
24. David Aaker and Kevin Lane Keller, "Consumer Evaluations of Brand Extensions," *Journal of Marketing*, vol. 54, no. 1 (1990): 27–41.
25. Robert G. Cooper, "New Products: What Distinguishes the Winners?" *Research Technology Management*, vol. 33 (November/December 1990): 27–31.
26. Scott M. Davis, "Bringing Innovation to Life," *Journal of Consumer Marketing*, vol. 14, no. 5 (1997): 338–361.
27. Gordon A. Wyner, "Product Testing: Benefits and Risks," *Marketing Research*, vol. 9, no. 1 (Spring 1997): 46–48.
28. Patrick Love, "Driving Productivity in Product Innovation," *Management Services*, vol. 45, no. 1 (January 2001): 8–13.
29. Lisa Susanne Willsey, "Taking These 7 Steps Will Help You Launch a New Product," *Marketing News*, vol. 33, no. 7 (March 29, 1999): 17.
30. See Cooper, "New Products," 27–31.
31. Willsey, "Taking These 7 Steps," 17.
32. Nicholas Valery, "Survey: Innovation in Industry: Industry Gets Religion," *The Economist*, vol. 350, no. 8107 (February 20, 1999): S5–S6.
33. Robert G. Cooper, "Debunking the Myths of New Product Development," *Research Technology Management*, vol. 37, no. 4 (July/August 1994): 40–50.
34. See Michael-Jorg Oesterle, "Time-Span Until Internationalization: Foreign Market Entry as a Built-in-Mechanism of Innovations," *Management Review*, vol. 37, no. 2 (1997): 125–149.
35. Willsey, "Taking These 7 Steps," 17.
36. Wyner, "Product Testing," 46–48.
37. Robert S. Doscher, "How to Create New Products," *Target Marketing*, vol. 17, no. 1 (1994): 40–41.
38. Willsey, "Taking These 7 Steps," 17.
39. Robert G. Cooper, "How to Launch a New Product Successfully," *CMA*, vol. 69, no. 8 (1995): 20–23.
40. Shaoming Zou and Aysegul Ozsomer, "Global Product R&D and the Firm's Strategic Position," *Journal of Marketing*, vol. 7, no. 1 (1999): 57–76.
41. Ibid.
42. Lianne George, "Style—An iPod Interface-Lift," *Macleans*, vol. 117, no. 47 (November 22, 2004): 56.
43. Willsey, "Taking These 7 Steps," 17.
44. Kevin J. Clancy and Robert S. Shulman, "It's Better to Fly a New Product Simulator than Crash the Real Thing," *Planning Review*, vol. 20, no. 4 (July/August 1992): 8–16.
45. Ibid.
46. The LITMUS test is the creation of Kevin J. Clancy, who describes the procedure used in Clancy and Shulman, "It's Better to Fly a New Product Simulator," 10–16.
47. Tamer S. Cavusgil and Ugur Yavas, "Test Marketing: An Exposition," *Marketing Intelligence and Planning*, vol. 5, no. 3 (1987): 16–20.
48. Ibid.
49. See Cooper, "Debunking the Myths," 40–50.
50. Ibid.
51. See Everett M. Rogers, *Diffusion of Innovations*, 3rd edition (New York: Free Press, 1983).
52. Kenneth Hein, "Bull's Market," *Brandweek*, vol. 42, no. 22 (May 28, 2001): 21, 23.
53. Milton Keynes, "Motorola Chooses Poland for New Site," *Corporate Location*, European Edition (May/June 1998): 7.
54. Faith Hung, "Consortium Looks to Build Thailand Fab—Siemens, Intel and Macronix Want to Jumpstart Country's Semi Industry," *Electronic Buyers' News*, Issue 1214 (June 5, 2000): 4.
55. See www.bcg.com.
56. H. Igor Ansoff, "Strategies for Diversification," *Harvard Business Review*, vol. 35 (September–October 1957): 113–124.

Case 8-1 The SUV Challenge

Jonathan Smith, working for BRAM Research, a medium-sized consulting firm specializing in new product development, has just heard from one of the leading sports utility vehicle (SUV) manufacturers. The company needs him to come up with a concept of an SUV that would be attractive to consumers concerned with the negative opinion generated by this product category. Jonathan was not up-to-date on product-related opinions. He knew that environmentalists were unhappy about the SUV fuel consumption rates, but that was about all. He turned to his research team and to the current press: Both had ample amounts of information to share.

First, he found that SUVs made winter drivers overconfident. Towing companies reported seeing a lot of them rolled over. Police departments believe that accidents are caused by the overconfidence of these drivers. Sports utility vehicles require even more careful driving on slippery roads than regular cars do because they have a propensity to roll over when a driver swerves and because they also require long distances to stop. Antilock systems of SUVs have longer stopping distances than cars so that they lessen the possibility of rollovers. Also, SUVs are more likely to inflict greater damage on other automobiles because they are heavier and their bumpers, engines, frame rails, and hoods are higher. When a light truck hits a car, the occupant of the car is 29 times more likely to die than the person in the truck; these statistics are potentially even higher for an SUV.

Excessive consumer overconfidence is amply reinforced by advertising. The Chevy Blazer is promoted as prepared for the worst of Mother Nature in Colorado snowstorms and in midwestern downpours. Similarly, the Land Rover Discovery is promoted as an automobile that makes the whole idea of canceling school because of the weather seem unnecessary.

SUVs have also been recently linked to terrorism by encouraging U.S. dependence on foreign oil. And the Evangelical Environmental Network stirred a national debate with the provocative question in a *Christianity Today* advertisement that showed an image of Jesus in prayer juxtaposed with a photo of a crowded highway. The ad called upon Christians to drive fuel-efficient automobiles because the decision is ultimately about values. The ad asked "What would Jesus drive?"

However, the greatest threat to SUVs—the factor that propelled Smith's client to seek his help—is that regulators have taken aim at SUVs because SUVs were found to pose a danger to other passenger cars. Some automakers have already taken steps to make SUVs safer for other drivers and for their own occupants, and for good reasons: SUVs are the cash cow of an otherwise marginally profitable industry.

Jonathan Smith gathered his team in the conference room and started an initial brainstorm session with a broad objective: to come up with a new, safer SUV, or to improve existing SUVs.

Questions

1. Is the SUV a fad, fashion, or style? Explain.
2. Assume that you are on Jonathan's team. Go through the following steps: Generate product ideas, screen the new product ideas, and develop and evaluate new product concepts. Comment on the degree of product newness for your selected new product concepts.

Sources: Danny Hakim, "A Regulator Takes Aim at SUVs," *New York Times* (December 22, 2002): BU1, BU10; Jim Motavalli, "An SUV and Ice: A Recipe for a Rollover," *New York Times* (February 14, 2003): D8.

Case 8-2 The Campina Product Mix

Campina is one of the leading dairy companies in the world and one of the few that produces only dairy products. A European company that remains close to its Dutch roots, Campina's image evokes picturesque Dutch cow pastures and healthy lifestyles. The company's history can be traced to Southern Holland, in the Eindhoven area; a dairy cooperative with the name "De Kempen" was created in 1947 and used the brand name "Campina." In 1964 the cooperative merged with another cooperative in the Weert region in Holland and formed Campina (named after a regional moor—its meaning is "from the land"). After several consecutive mergers—more recently, with Melkunie Holland—Campina Melkunie (or Campina, as it is informally known) became the largest dairy cooperative in the Netherlands.

In the Netherlands alone, Campina boasts 7,500 member dairy farmers. The farmers own the cooperative: Campina must buy all the milk the farmers produce, while the farmers must finance the cooperative and, in return, they obtain a yield of the products sold. Campina itself is a nonprofit organization. Member farmers receive all the company profits. They have voting rights in the company that are proportional to the amount of milk they deliver, and they are represented by the Members' Council, the highest managerial body of the cooperative.

The separation between Campina, the operating company, and its cooperatives is evident: Campina is headquartered in Zaltbommel, in an industrial park in southern Holland, and the dairies are located close to the consumers they serve, in different areas of the country.

Industry Trends

Among the main trends in the international dairy industry are the following:

Consolidation is a dominant trend of the dairy industry. The number of dairy companies is falling, and the production capacity of those that remain is increasing and becoming more efficient.[1] Yet, there are still companies that exist successfully in the $100 million to $200 million range of sales, surviving through a mix of ingenuity and innovation.[2]

The European Union (EU) remains the world's top dairy producer, manufacturer, and trader of dairy products; because the EU is a mature dairy market, the emphasis is on value growth and processing milk into products with high added value.[3] As such, Campina's strategy and general mission, "adding value to milk," fits well with this trend (see Figure 8-18). Of the world's top 25 dairy organizations, 14 have their headquarters in Europe.[4]

The degree of concentration varies significantly, however, from region to region. In Scandinavia and the Netherlands, a handful of major cooperatives dominate. In Greece, there are more than 1,000 dairy businesses, of which more than 700 make cheese. In Germany, the industry has changed from numerous small, localized firms to most milk processors either collapsing or merging. In France, the top five control 55 percent of milk production. And in Scandinavia, the major players wield even more control: In Denmark, MD Foods and Klover Maelk control 95 percent of milk production, and in Sweden, Arla handles 80 percent.[5]

Another important trend is the focus on convenience (a packaging issue) and on value-added nutrition for functional foods (a product ingredient issue). Changes include creating new packaging and unique containers for innovative products. For example, German-based Schwalbchen Molkerei has debuted Go! Banana, the first milk-energy drink made from fresh milk and real, pureed bananas, packaged in 330 ml Tetra Prisma cartons with fluted sides. Spain's Pascual Dairy offers the milk-based energy drink Bio Frutas in two flavors: Tropical and Mediterranean. German milk processor Immergut has introduced Drinkfit Choco Plus, a vitamin-fortified, chocolate-flavored milk in the same carton. The United Kingdom company Miller offers dual-compartment, side-by-side containers of refrigerated yogurt, while a new drinkable fruit yogurt from Nestle SA debuted in the United Kingdom under the name Squizzos, sporting Disney characters in a triangular-shaped package that is easy to tear, squeeze, and drink.[6]

Cheese is also presented in innovative packaging. Baars, a subsidiary of the BolsWessanen Group, a United Kingdom Dutch company, launched a smooth, flavorful medium/mature cheddar cheese, named Maidwell, that does not crumble; it is sold in an attractive, innovative, clear-plastic, resealable pack. Rumblers, a convenient all-in-one breakfast product manufactured by Ennis Foods Ltd., United Kingdom, is also available in an innovative package that holds cereal and fresh, semi-skimmed milk separately, all in one pack.[7]

Figure 8-18
Campina truck in Eindhoven.

Functional ingredients (health foods or ingredients that enhance the nutritional value of products) represent yet another important trend in the dairy industry: Dairy products represent the most important sector, accounting for 65 percent of sales in a sector that is very buoyant given the consumer interest in health and diet.[8] The leading companies in Europe in this domain are Campina Melkunie (the Netherlands), Nestle (Switzerland), and Danone (France).[9] Worldwide, Japan leads in the functional foods trend and is the only country with a regulatory policy on such foods: FOSHU (Foods for Specified Health Use).[10] There is a tradition of lactic acid bacteria culture drinks and yogurts in Japan, and many of these fermented drinks and yogurts contain other functional ingredients, such as oligofructose, calcium, and DHA, which is a polyunsaturated fatty acid derived from fish oil that is said to improve learning, lower blood pressure, help prevent cancer, and lower serum cholesterol.[11] And from Dairy Gold, Australia, comes Vaalia Passionfruit Smoothie, a low-fat milk-based drink containing 25 percent fruit juice, acidophilus and bifidus cultures, and insulin.[12]

Meeting Competitive Challenges at Campina: Adopting a Market Orientation

Historically, milk production has been supply driven, and excess milk was used to produce cheese and powder milk; this strategy led to excess cheese/commodities on the market and the need for subsidies. Campina initiated a change in this practice. In the past 15 years, the company has been demand driven: Farmers are assigned production quotas that they are not allowed to exceed.

In other attempts to adopt a market orientation, Campina decided to eliminate all milk powder production because milk powder is a low-margin commodity. Instead, the company is focusing on building the brand to ensure recognition by consumers as a value offering and as a quality brand name.

According to R. J. Steetskamp, Director of Strategic Business Development at Campina, the company examines consumer behavior to determine where to fit Campina products in consumers' lives. As such, Campina offers four categories of products:

1. *Indulgence products*—This category constitutes an important growth area for the company. Campina produces numerous milk-based desserts, with the exception of ice cream—primarily due to the product's seasonality and the logistics strategies involved in the transportation and storage of ice cream, which differ from those for the rest of the company's offerings (see Figure 8-19).
2. *Daily essentials*—This category includes Campina products that shoppers purchase routinely, such as milk, buttermilk, yogurt, coffee cream, butter, cheese, and others. Campina, using a strategy employed by all its competitors, also sells daily essentials under dealer (store) brands, rather than under its own brand name. For example, in Holland, it sells milk, plain yogurt, butter, Gouda cheese, and vla (chocolate or vanilla custard) under the Albert Heijn brand name. Albert Heijn is a dominant, quality supermarket chain in Holland that is owned by Royal Ahold—a large conglomerate that also owns supermarket chains in the United States (BI-LO, Giant,

Figure 8-19
Indulgence products.

Figure 8-20
Campina Daily Essentials
In the Netherlands, a vla dessert (a custard drink) is a daily essential.

and Stop & Shop). The company also sells daily essentials under dealer brands in Germany (see Figure 8-20).

3. *Functional products*—According to Mr. Steetskamp, this product category needs to be further explored and defined by the company. In this category are health foods and other milk-based nutritional supplements sold to consumers. DMV International is a Campina division that is present all over the world; it produces pharmaceutical products, food ingredients, and ingredients used to enhance the nutrition of consumers and their pets, such as proteins and powders with different functions. All of these products are milk-based, and many of them are well known. For example, Lactoval is a popular calcium supplement.
4. *Ingredients (food and pharmaceutical ingredients)*—This product category is targeted at other food product manufacturers, rather than at the individual consumers. The primary purpose of the food and pharmaceutical ingredients is to enhance the quality, taste, texture, and/or nutritive content of the products manufactured by Campina's clients. The company's Creamy Creation unit specializes in blending dairy and alcohol to make various cream liqueurs, leading to both healthy and indulgent drinks. In this category fall meal-replacement drinks and high protein drinks as well. With this category, Campina becomes a supplier to other manufacturers, rather than a product manufacturer distributing to supermarkets.

International Expansion at Campina

One of the most important undertakings at Campina in the last decade was to expand beyond the Netherlands. In its first expansion effort, the company bought Belgium's Comelco, another dairy cooperative. In Belgium, the company boasts the Joyvalle dairy products and milk brand and the Passendale, Père Joseph, and Wynendale cheese brands, all marketed under the Campina umbrella brand.

Campina expanded into Germany, purchasing a number of cooperatives: Sudmilch (Southern Germany), Tuffi (Western Germany), and Emzett (Berlin). In Germany, its primary brand is Landliebe; here, the company sells Landliebe milk, cream, and yogurts (seasonal, fruit, plain, and in different types of containers); different types of puddings including rice pudding, ice cream, cheese, and qwark (a traditional creamy cheese) plain or with fruit; yogurt

Figure 8-21
Offerings under the Mona umbrella brand.

drinks (with fruit flavors such as banana, cherry, lemon, peach, and orange); and different milk drinks with flavors such as vanilla and chocolate. The company also offers products such as coffee machines, cups, spoons, and others for purchase online at its site (www.landliebe-online.de). According to R. J. Steetskamp, the Campina name will be used as the umbrella brand for all the company products; the name comes from the Latin "from the land," and it is easily pronounced in all the different languages in Europe, the brand's target market. The only brands that will not be brought under the Campina umbrella brands, according to Mr. Steetskamp, are the Mona brand in the Netherlands (see Figure 8-21) and the Landliebe brand in Germany because both have high brand franchise with consumers in their respective countries. Interestingly, the Landliebe brand name is close in meaning to Campina, with both making reference to the land.

As a result of these acquisitions and mergers, according to Mr. Steetskamp, Campina is the market leader in Holland, Germany, and Belgium—as the company website states, "Campina is a household name in the Netherlands, Belgium and Germany."[13]

Campina has further expanded, with its own subsidiaries in the United Kingdom, Spain, Poland, and Russia, where it ultimately plans to use the Campina brand name (the Campina Fruttis brand is one of the most popular fruit yogurt brands in Russia).

Questions

1. Perform a product mix analysis for Campina. Calculate product length, width, and line depth and evaluate product consistency across the different lines. Refer to www.campina-melkunie.nl for additional brand information.
2. Attempt a comparison with U.S. dairy strategies: Go to your local grocery store chain and note the different brands of milk. Are indulgence products offered by the same company? (Most likely they are not.) Can you find one dairy cooperative that offers milk, butter, cream cheese, and sour cream? Explain the differences between Campina strategies and U.S. dairy cooperatives' strategies.

Notes

1. Sarah McRitchie, "Europe Shrinks to Expand," *Dairy Foods*, vol. 100, no. 1 (January 1999): 75–79.
2. Gerry Clark and Dave Fusaro, "Survival of the Smallest," *Dairy Foods*, vol. 100, no. 8 (August 1999): 48–55.
3. Ibid.
4. Ibid.
5. McRitchie, "Europe Shrinks to Expand," 75–79.
6. Ibid.
7. Ibid.
8. Ibid.
9. Ibid.
10. Donna Gorski Berry, "Global Dairy Food Trends," *Dairy Foods*, vol. 99, no. 10 (October 1998): 32–37.
11. Ibid.
12. Ibid.
13. See www.campina-melkunie.nl.

9

Services Marketing

CHAPTER OBJECTIVES

1. Discuss the impact of the services sector on the gross domestic product and what has led to the growth of the service sector.
2. Identify the four unique characteristics of services and how each impacts the marketing of services.
3. Explain the components of the purchasing process for services.
4. Identify the factors that impact the purchase decision during the pre-purchase phase of the purchase process.
5. Discuss the relevant elements of the service encounter and why they are important.
6. Describe the post-purchase evaluation of services and its impact on future purchase behavior.
7. Discuss how service quality is measured.
8. Describe an effective service recovery process.
9. Explain the importance of the customer value package and list the steps required to develop a customer value package.

CHAPTER OUTLINE

Digital camera sales have now surpassed traditional cameras, with 53 million digital cameras sold in 2004. Prices have fallen and automatic picture-taking technology has improved, allowing more families to purchase a digital camera. It makes for easy picture taking and sharing of pictures through email (see Figure 9-1).

But how does this technology impact photo-processing services that rely on people taking pictures and dropping off their film at the local drug store to be processed? Although many people purchase film at mass merchandisers like Wal-Mart, the highest percentage still take their film to a local drug store for photo processing. In fact, drug stores process 27 percent more rolls of film than they sell.

To remain competitive, drug stores have been forced to change the services they offer. Many now offer digital technologies that allow people to bring in rolls of film and receive not only prints, but also photos placed on a CD-ROM in digital format. Old family pictures can be converted to digital images. Walgreens and CVS Pharmacies now have one-hour digital imaging services.

But will the 28 percent of the households that have digital cameras destroy the photo-processing business? They will, unless photo-processing centers change the types of services they offer. Of those who use digital cameras, only 11.8 percent have prints made from the images, while 63 percent save, store, and keep their images in digital format and 16 percent email them to family and friends.

It is the 63 percent who save, store, and keep their images in digital format that has led to a whole new service industry: online photography. Sites like Snapfish, AOL You've Got Pictures, Shutterfly, and Ofoto offer people online photo services such as storage, sorting, editing, and printing of photos. These sites provide software that allows people to edit and touch up their images, or the service will do it for them. For individuals who want a print of a great snapshot, most online services will make a print and mail it to them. For those who like to share images, digital photos can be stored in a safe location for private viewing through a personalized website address, or they can be posted for public viewing that anyone can access. For individuals who like to take pictures with their cell phones, a new company called DotPhoto Inc. allows users to take photos with their camera-phone, email them directly to the service, and receive back 3″× 4″ prints for only 11 cents each.

With new technology inventions like digital cameras and camera-phones often come changes in services supporting that technology. Making prints from film is certainly entering the decline stage of the product lifecycle, but this decline has spurred a whole new industry, now in its growth stage: digital online photography services.[1]

Figure 9-1
Digital cameras make sharing pictures with family and friends easier and have also created a new online photography service industry.

9-1 Chapter Overview

Services are an integral part of the U.S. economy. They furnish the majority of jobs and contribute the major portion of the nation's gross national product (GNP). Some marketers would consider that marketing of goods and services are the same, whereas others will contend that it takes a different marketing approach. While it is true that the principles are the same, the unique characteristics of services discussed in Section 9-3 do make it apparent that the application of those principles may vary. Services face some unique challenges that often require a different approach.

Because of these differences between goods and services, the purchase process for services is described in Section 9-4. Understanding how services are purchased, consumed, and evaluated is critical to understanding how services are marketed. Section 9-5 presents the concept of service quality, how it is measured, and what happens when a service failure occurs. The last section, Section 9-6, discusses the services customer value package. Understanding service quality and the customer value package will make it easier for a service business to attract customers and to retain them.

9-2 The Service Sector

When you think of services, it is helpful to think of a continuum with pure services at one extreme and pure goods at the other extreme. A pure service does not have any type of good attached to it. Examples would include personal fitness training, legal services, medical services, and driver education instruction. A pure good is something that is sold without any type of service component attached, such as a computer CD, exercise equipment, socks, or gasoline at a self-serve convenience store. Most products fall somewhere between a pure service and a pure good. For example, a restaurant is a service because you are paying it to prepare the food (a good) for you. Computers are a good, but if you have difficulty with your computer, you can either call a toll-free number for assistance, contact the company using email, or call a local computer repair company. Figure 9-2 illustrates this goods and services continuum.

Figure 9-2
The Goods and Services Continuum

INTERACTIVE FIGURE

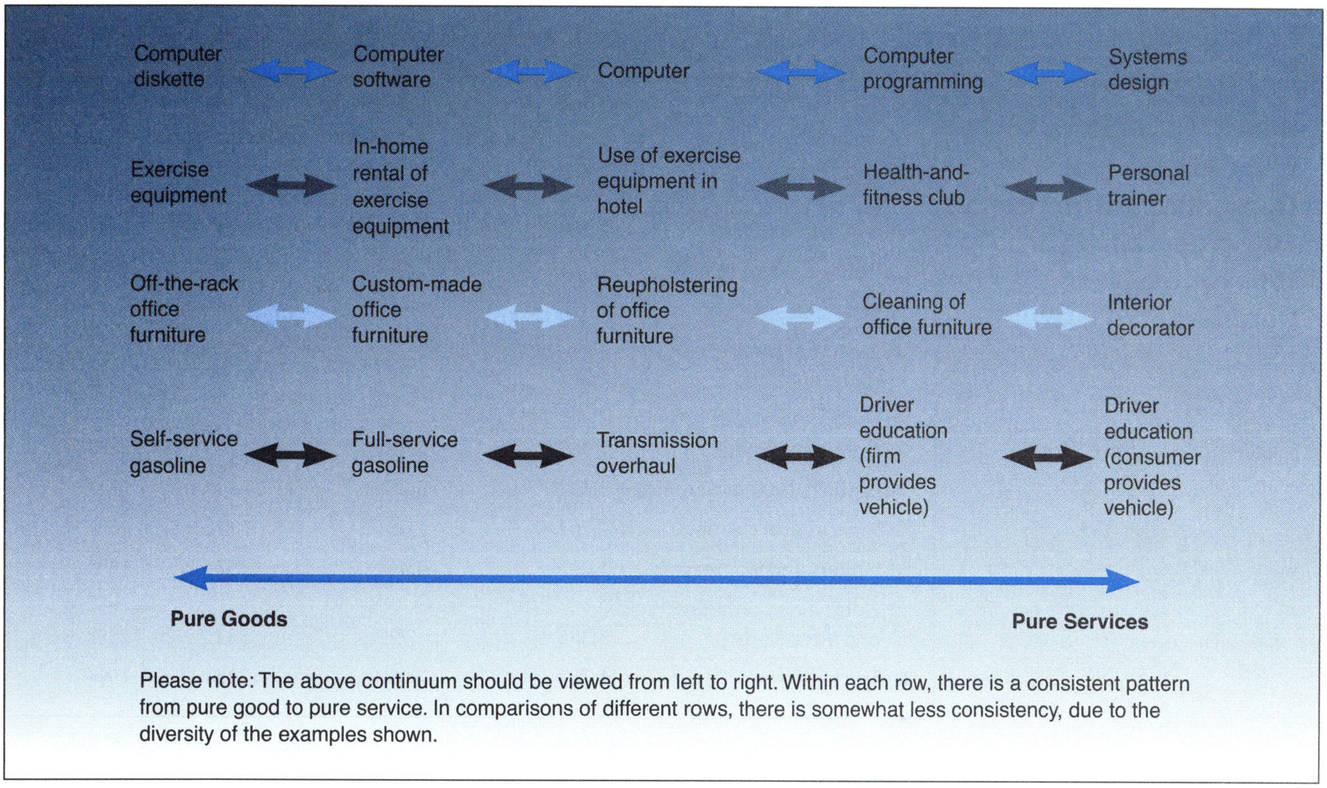

Services are a vital component of the United States economy, as well as that of most industrialized nations. The service sector in the United States accounts for 79 percent ($6.95 trillion) of the country's GDP and 77 percent of the total U.S. employment.[2] The preponderance of services in a nation's economy is typical of most developed countries in Western Europe and is growing in Asia. The service sector in China grew by 380 percent from 1978 to 2002, rising from 21.4 percent of the nation's GDP to 33.7 percent. Employment of Chinese in the service sector during the same time period grew from 48.90 million to 210.9 million.[3] The **gross domestic product (GDP)** is the sum of all goods and services produced within the boundaries of a country. For example, in the United States the GDP would include the production by American-owned firms as well as by foreign-owned firms. Goods and services produced by American-owned firms outside the country are not calculated in the United States' GDP.

Gross domestic product (GDP): The sum of all goods and services produced within the boundaries of a country.

Employment in the United States is expected to increase by 21.3 million jobs between 2002 and 2012.[4] The service sector is expected to furnish 58 percent of this growth, or a total of 12.9 million new jobs, with retail services accounting for an additional 3.1 million jobs. Approximately 62 percent of this growth in the service sector will be with service businesses that cater to other businesses, as well as to consumers. The fastest growth will be in the Internet, cable, and telecommunications industry; computer software industry; professional and business services; medical services; and employment services.[5] In order to learn more about the top 10 job growth occupations, see Table 9-1.

The service sector's rapid growth is primarily the result of nations shifting from a manufacturing-based economy to a service-oriented economy. A major stimulus in this shift is the movement to an information society spurred by the computer and advancements in telecommunications. Additional factors contributing to the growth of the service sector are an aging population, longer life expectancies, increased leisure time, higher per capita income, increased time pressure, more women in the workforce, sedentary lifestyles, changing social and cultural values, and advances in technology.[6] All of these factors have spurred the growth of various service industries.

The aging population and increase in life expectancy have spurred the need for medical services, nursing homes, and limited-care facilities. More females in the workforce has resulted in families with higher incomes, which translates into a larger discretionary

TABLE 9-1

What Are the Hot Occupations? The Top 10 Largest Growth Jobs for the Next Decade

Occupation	2002 Employment (000s)	2012 Employment (000s)	Change (000s)	Change Percent
1. Registered nurses	2,284	2,908	623	27%
2. Postsecondary teachers	1,581	2,184	603	38%
3. Retail salespersons	4,076	4,672	596	15%
4. Customer service representatives	1,894	2,354	460	24%
5. Food service and restaurant workers	1,980	2,444	454	23%
6. Cashiers (except gaming)	3,432	3,886	454	13%
7. Janitors and cleaners	2,267	2,681	414	18%
8. Waiters and waitresses	2,097	2,464	367	18%
9. Nurse aides, orderlies, and attendants	1,375	1,718	337	25%
10. Truck drivers	1,767	2,104	337	19%

Source: Daniel E. Hecker, "Occupational Employment Projections to 2012," *Monthly Labor Review*, vol. 127 (February 2004): 87–89.

Marketing Illustration 9-1

Eating Out: No Longer a Luxury

For many Americans, dining out or ordering take-out food is no longer a luxury. For many Americans, especially Generation Y, eating out has become an entitlement. According to Michael Allenson, principal at Technomic, a Chicago-based research firm that focuses on the food industry, for Generation Y "food is at the top of the scale in terms of what they're entitled to. It's a way of rewarding themselves. They may cut back in other areas, but not in food. They're less willing to compromise on 'that' than previous generations."

The good news for the restaurant industry is that the younger consumers are eating out and ordering take-out food at a much higher rate than older Americans (see Table 1). Generation Y, Americans ages 16 to 27, eat out on the average of 24 times a month, and 51 percent have ordered take-out within the past week. That number is in vast contrast to the swing generation, individuals 59 to 71, who eat out 16 times a month, with only 7 percent ordering take-out within the past week.

According to the Technomic study, the average ticket charge per meal for Generation Y individuals is $6 per person, which translates into $1,152 a year being spent on eating out. Clearly, Generation Y individuals eat many of their meals at fast-food outlets, whereas older Americans prefer to eat at higher-priced dine-in restaurants. Overall, Americans spend $884 per person per year eating out, which totals to $2,211 per household.

The same trend is occurring with minorities. African-American households increased their spending on eating out by 43.6 percent over the past five years and now average $1,517 a year, per household. During the same time period, Hispanic households increased their spending by 34.3 percent to $2,023 per household.

These trends are good news for the restaurant industry. If minorities continue to increase their spending and if the younger generations continue at their current pace, the restaurant industry should be a growth service for many years to come.

Source: Andrea Coombes, "Taking a (small) Bite Out of Savings," *CBS MarketWatch.com* (http://netscape5.marketwatch.com/news/story.asp, January 1, 2005); "Minorities Spending More Money on Eating Out, Entertainment, Research Shows," *Black Issues in Higher Education,* vol. 21 (September 9, 2004): 13.

TABLE 1

Eating Out Habits of Americans

Generation	Age	Number of Times Per Month Eat Out	Ordered Take-Out During Past Week
Generation Y	16–27	24	51%
Generation X	28–39	21	42%
Baby boomers	40–58	19	12%
Swing generation	59–71	16	7%

income to spend on luxury-type goods and services such as entertainment, dining out, vacations, and recreation. With both work and family responsibilities, individuals are stressed for time; consequently, goods and services that save time, such as housecleaning and lawn care, are in higher demand. This need to save time has also fueled growth in the restaurant industry, as discussed in Marketing Illustration 9-1.

Advances in technology have led to a rise in the demand for maintenance and computer-related services. Even automobiles have become more computerized, requiring skilled mechanics. The so-called "shade tree mechanic" who repairs his own car has become virtually obsolete. Because of cultural and social changes, society no longer places a stigma on individuals who hire someone else to take care of personal chores. Mothers are no longer seen as shirking their duty if they do not stay home with their children, cook the meals, and clean the house. Society no longer feels a man is neglecting his responsibilities when he hires someone to repair his car, mow his lawn, or repair his home.

The service sector is a critical component of our economy, and the successful marketing of services requires an understanding of how services are different from goods. Although the principles of marketing are the same, the application of those principles will be different for a service operation.

Figure 9-3
Characteristics of Services

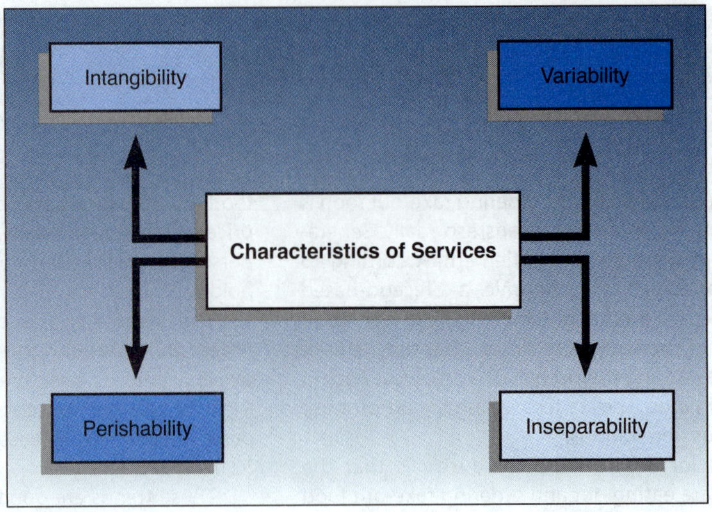

9-3 Characteristics of Services

Intangibility: The lack of tangible assets of a service that can be seen, touched, smelled, heard, or tasted prior to a purchase.

Perishability: The inability of a service to be inventoried or stored.

Inseparability: The simultaneous production and consumption of a service.

Variability: The unwanted or random levels of service quality customers receive when they patronize a service.

Services possess four inherent characteristics not found in goods: intangibility, perishability, inseparability, and variability (see Figure 9-3).[7] **Intangibility** refers to the lack of tangible assets that can be seen, touched, smelled, heard, or tasted prior to a purchase, and **perishability** refers to the inability of a service to be inventoried or stored. **Inseparability** refers to the simultaneous production and consumption of a service, and **variability** refers to the unwanted or random levels of service quality customers receive when they patronize a service. These characteristics create unique marketing challenges for services not only in terms of attracting new customers but also in retaining current customers.

9-3a Intangibility

Services vary in the degree to which they are intangible. Services such as a music concert, legal counsel, medical treatments, and a college education are highly intangible. The service cannot be seen, touched, smelled, heard, or tasted prior to the purchase. However, for each of these services, tangible items are used to perform the service. For example, for a musical concert, there are chairs, a stage, musical instruments, and loudspeakers. For legal services, clients see an office, desks, and law books. For a medical treatment, there are medical instruments and equipment. For a college education, there are the physical structures such as buildings and classrooms. But for all of these services, the actual outcome of the service cannot be seen until the service is performed or the event has taken place (see Figure 9-4).

Some services offer a tangible good with their service, but the service itself is still intangible because consumers are purchasing the service, not the good. For instance, restaurants offer food and a dentist uses crowns and other materials to perform his or her work. In the case of the restaurant, consumers are paying the restaurant to prepare the food for them. An evaluation of the service is based on how well the restaurant prepares the food. In the second case, patients are paying the dentist to repair a tooth, not just to supply the tooth crown and other materials. The quality of both services will be based on how well the service is performed.

Because of intangibility, consumers have greater difficulty in judging the quality of a service prior to a purchase. A good can be examined in advance, offering consumers some idea of what they are purchasing. Services are much more difficult to examine in advance. The haircut you receive at a beauty salon cannot be known until the beautician performs the work. This intangibility makes the purchase of a service a higher risk.

To reduce the risk consumers face, service firms strive to reduce the level of intangibility through the following strategies:

- Stress tangible cues.
- Use personal sources of information.
- Stimulate word-of-mouth communication.
- Create a strong corporate image.
- Encourage employees to communicate with customers.

To reduce intangibility, attorneys can feature tangible assets such as their building, their office, or other personnel in an advertisement. A college can feature its facilities, students, athletes, and professors. Using testimonials of students for a college and clients for an attorney can reduce the level of risk and intangibility. Personal sources of information and word-of-mouth communications are excellent ways of making a service appear more tangible. Employees should talk about the service. A beautician, through communicating with the customer, can reduce the intangibility of getting a haircut. An attorney, during an initial visit, can discuss the process he or she will use in handling the case. Because a service is intangible, communication becomes an important element in marketing the service. Although word-of-mouth communication from one customer to another is the best, anything a service can do to communicate with consumers about the service will help reduce the level of intangibility (see Figure 9-5).

Figure 9-4
Health care has a high degree of intangibility, so it is important to stress tangible assets and quality of care in advertisements.

Source: Courtesy of Newcomer, Morris and Young.

9-3b Perishability

The second characteristic of services is perishability. If a sweater does not sell today, a retailer can keep it and sell it at a later time; if the sale occurs much later, the retailer will sell it at a discount but, most likely, will still make a profit on it. This feature allows firms to mass-produce goods and store them in warehouses until consumers are ready to make a purchase. For services, this is not possible. A Delta Airlines flight that sells only 70 of the 160 seats will lose the revenue of the 90 empty seats. This revenue is lost forever. It cannot be sold at a later time.

Concerts and sporting events are live events. Fans have no choice as to when or where they can watch the events unless there are multiple performances. If they want to see a particular band, they must go where the performance is being held at the time it is occurring. Again, empty seats are lost revenue because they cannot be inventoried and sold later. To maximize revenue, sports teams, concerts, and airlines want to fill every seat.

Perishability can also cause the reverse situation. Demand can be greater than supply. In this situation, Delta Airlines does not have enough seats for everyone. Passengers are unhappy because they cannot book a particular flight. A Dallas Cowboys' game is sold out, and fans are unhappy because they cannot see a particular game. A Christina Aguilera con-

Figure 9-5
Office of an Art Text Translator
Translators in this specialized area do not promote their work: references from German publishers and the translator's name appearing in avant-garde publications represent the equivalent of a strong corporate image.

cert is sold out; fans wanting to see her performance either have to go to another location, hoping they will get a ticket, or forgo the opportunity of seeing her perform live. In every case, potential revenue is lost because of the fixed-seating capacities of each venue.

To reduce the negative impact of perishability, services can develop strategies to deal with fluctuating demand through simultaneously making adjustments in demand, supply, and capacity. The goal is to achieve parity among the three. At the optimum, demand will equal supply, which in turn will equal capacity.

Perishability for Christina Aguilera concerts can be managed in a number of ways. First, demand can be reduced through increasing ticket prices. As prices are increased, the number of people willing to pay the higher prices declines. Second, demand at various locations can be managed through a website that indicates sold-out concerts and locations where tickets are still available. This will shift demand to locations where empty seats are still available. Aguilera can manage the supply side of perishability by increasing the number of live concerts, thus allowing more people the opportunity to see her perform. The capacity component can be managed by finding larger facilities. Using all three components simultaneously, Christina Aguilera can maximize her revenue from the live concerts while providing fans the opportunity to see her perform. Her goal would be to fill every location to capacity with no empty seats and no fans turned away because the concert was sold out.

For a restaurant, the same principles apply. Demand can be managed through advertising, special promotions, and pricing. Having a higher dinner price will reduce demand during the evening dinner hours, while having a lower lunch price will stimulate demand at lunchtime. Advertising specials for breakfast meals will encourage people to eat breakfast at the restaurant. Supply can be managed by hiring part-time employees during meal times. Unlike the Christina Aguilera concerts, a restaurant does not have the ability to expand its capacity. The number of customers it can have at any one time is controlled by the seating capacity of the facility (see Figure 9-6).

Managing perishability is critical to the success of a service. When demand is less than supply, revenue is lost and the firm has excess capacity. A facility or equipment that is not used to capacity increases the total average unit costs to operate. For example, a movie theater that has a capacity of 175 will have a higher total average cost per customer to operate when the theater averages only 90 people per night, compared to 160 per night. Fixed costs remain the same, but the theater has fewer customers to spread the costs over.

When demand exceeds capacity, potential revenue is lost. Because the facility is filled or equipment is being used to its full capacity, businesses often do not worry about the customers that are turned away. But if customers cannot get tickets to a basketball game or an appointment with an attorney, they will seek other alternatives. The basketball fan may switch to another sport and never come back to watching basketball games, and the person seeking legal counsel may choose another attorney. In the long run, these lost customers

Figure 9-6
This restaurant's empty tables represent lost revenue for the owners. The loss is even greater if the wait staff is sitting idle.

can be detrimental to a firm that may need them during a later time, when demand is less than supply.

9-3c Inseparability

Goods can be produced in one location, warehoused in another, and then sold at a later time in a retail store; services cannot. For example, getting a cavity filled in a tooth involves a patient going to a dentist and being present while the service is being performed. Because the service must be performed and consumed at the same time, the quality of the service is highly dependent on the ability of the service provider and the quality of interaction between the service provider and the customer.

To reduce the importance of the customer-employee interaction, service firms look for methods of automating their service through the use of machines, computers, or other technology. The more that a service can be automated, the less it will be reliant on human performance, and the greater will be its availability to consumers. For example, banks now use ATMs to conduct business with customers. ATMs provide efficiency for the bank and convenience for the customer. To further reduce the interaction with bank personnel, most banks now offer online banking services (see Figure 9-7). With both the ATM and online banking, employees are not needed to perform the transaction at the time it is desired by customers. This not only increases the availability of banking services to customers to 24 hours a day, 7 days a week, but reduces the level of human interaction between bank personnel and customers. It also reduces the cost involved for a bank to handle transactions. Banks have estimated the average cost per transaction using a human teller to be \$2.50. The cost of a check transaction is \$0.68, a telephone transaction is \$0.35, an ATM transaction is \$0.27, and an online transaction is \$0.14.[8]

Realizing the benefit of online services, Citibank was the first financial institution to offer consumers consolidated personal account service—known as My Citi. Customers can log onto one account and conduct all of their banking transactions, pay credit card bills or obtain loans, obtain insurance and investment information, and use an online payment service. Through Travelers Insurance, online quotes and information on life, auto, and homeowners insurance can be gathered. Through Citigroup's subsidiary, customers can obtain free wireless access and portfolio tracking services, and through C2it, a Citibank system, customers can send payments to anyone via the Internet.[9] By offering all of these services on one consolidated online account, Citibank has effectively reduced the inseparability nature of its services.

Services such as hair salons have a more difficult situation because they have a high degree of inseparability. Customers are involved in the production of the service, other customers are usually present, and centralized mass production of the service is not possible. Because of the importance of the customer/service provider interaction, it is essential for services like hair salons to reduce any negative consequences that might be due to the inseparability. These negative consequences can be reduced by emphasizing the selection and training of employees. Training should include how to perform the service, as well as how to interact with customers. This training will increase the probability of a positive interaction between the customer and the beautician.

Hair salons also should have a process for managing customers because more than one customer usually will be in the facility at any one time. This process may include a receptionist greeting customers as they enter and notifying the particular beautician that the customer has arrived. The process may include providing a comfortable waiting area with appropriate reading material. While some customers are having their hair cut, others may be getting a shampoo or having their hair styled. To ensure that each customer is satisfied with the service, the hair salon must manage every step in the customer service process.

Because of inseparability, the number of customers that a hair salon can serve is limited to the time required for each haircut and the size of the facility. If a hair salon has six beauticians and six chairs, then only six customers can be served at one time unless other customers are under the hair dryer or waiting for a perm to set. A hair salon can reduce the

Figure 9-7
This advertisement by Ouachita Independent Bank features some of the bank's automated services, such as online banking, ATM cards, and debit cards with overdraft protection.

Source: Courtesy of Newcomer, Morris and Young.

negative impact of this inseparability and serve more customers by opening multiple sites. Because customers have to be present for the service, this strategy offers customers multiple sites to receive the service. The multiple-site strategy will also reduce the number of customers present at any one time in a facility. This should allow employees more time with each customer, increasing the quality of service and interaction with the customer.

9-3d Variability

The last unique characteristic of services is variability. Variability is primarily caused by the human element, although machines may malfunction, thus causing a variation in the service. Each employee will perform a service in a slightly different way with various levels of quality, and even the same employee will provide different levels of service from one time to another. For example, in getting a haircut, the outcome will differ if you use a different beautician each time you go to a salon. The outcome also will vary from one time to another even if the same person is cutting your hair. Although machines are much more reliable, differences in service can occur. If the computerized testing equipment at an auto repair facility does not operate properly, it may not detect a problem with an engine or it may misdiagnose the problem. However, when these problems do occur, the problems often are not with the computerized equipment but with the person operating the equipment.

While most variability is caused by the service provider, it also can be caused by a variance in the inputs. Computer consultants staffing hotlines face the challenge of dealing with the various levels of knowledge and expertise customers bring to the service process. The same would be true for a consulting service handling situations for various clients.

Because of this variability characteristic of services, standardization and quality control are the primary methods used to ensure a consistent level of quality across different service providers and across different service experiences with the same provider. A restaurant such as McDonald's will industrialize operations. In this context, **industrialization** refers to the use of machines and standardized operating procedures to increase the productivity and efficiency of a business. Hamburgers, French fries, and other foods are prepared in advance and put in warming bins. By mass-producing these items in advance, more customers can be served during peak demand times. Employees are also trained to follow a specific procedure in preparing each food item. Through standardization and industrialization, customers can expect the same quality of food and service at all of the McDonald's locations.

Industrialization: The use of machines and standardized operating procedures to increase the productivity and efficiency of a business.

Keep in mind that variability refers to unwanted or random variations in service quality. Thus, a restaurant like Outback Steakhouse will use industrialization and standardization procedures to improve productivity, but customers do not all want their food exactly the same. The cooking of steaks must be customized to meet the customer's desire, or a dish that has shrimp on it may be cooked without the shrimp upon a customer's request. Thus, customers at Outback want variability. They want food prepared differently. What they do not want is unwanted or random variability. Therefore, to reduce this unwanted or random variability, it is the responsibility of the wait staff to ask how food items are to be prepared. This will ensure that the particular requests of each customer are met and the unwanted variability in the service does not occur (see Figure 9-8).

Enterprise Rent-A-Car grew from $200 million to about $2 billion in revenue over the past decade to become the largest rental car company in the United States. But during that growth period, the quality of service slipped. Letters and phone calls from customers indicated that their expectations were not being met. The Enterprise Service Quality index, which had been developed to measure service quality at each of the branches, indicated that only about 65 percent of its customers were "completely satisfied." But more alarming was the wide range of scores: Over 28 points separated the branches with the highest service quality score from the branches with the lowest. This wide degree of variability troubled Enterprise management as much as did the average score of 65 percent. To ensure that cus-

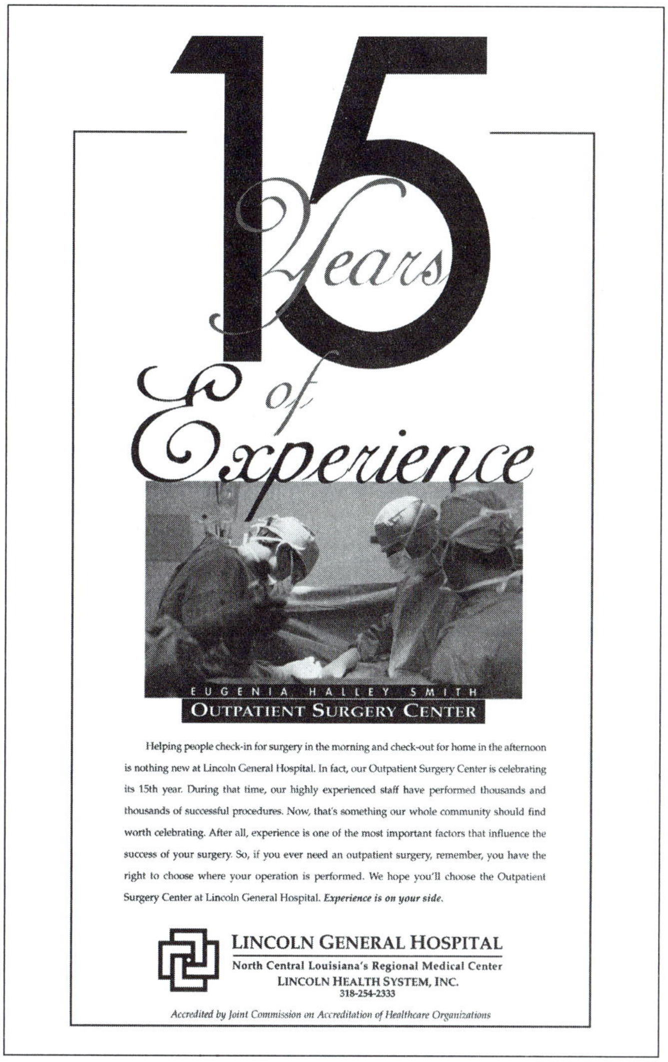

Figure 9-8
This advertisement by Lincoln General Hospital stresses the 15 years of experience of the hospital's outpatient surgery center. This experience will reduce the level of service variability.

Source: Courtesy of Newcomer, Morris and Young.

tomers received the same level of service at all of its locations, Enterprise took several steps. First, service quality was emphasized at training sessions, in the firm's correspondence with managers, and in its reports. Second, the score for each branch location was published monthly so everyone in the organization would know how they scored and how their score compared with other branches. Third, the Enterprise Service Quality index became a prominent factor in promotions. Branch managers whose facilities had seen rapid growth but had low service-quality scores were passed over for promotion in favor of managers who had received high service-quality scores. With management emphasis and support on improving quality and reducing variability, the average index moved to the high 70 percent range, with a range of only 11 percent between the highest and lowest.[10]

To be successful, service businesses must understand the characteristics of intangibility, perishability, inseparability, and variability. For examples of all four unique characteristics of services, see Table 9-2.

9-4 The Purchase Process for Services

Because of the unique characteristics of services, it is beneficial to examine the services purchase process. When you understand the process consumers use in choosing and evaluating a service, developing an effective marketing approach will be easier. The purchase process for services can be divided into three phases: the pre-purchase phase, the service

TABLE 9-2

Understanding the Unique Characteristics of Services

Intangibility

Definition: Lack of tangible assets that can be seen, touched, or smelled prior to the purchase

Business-to-business example: A professional janitorial service cannot be seen, touched, or smelled prior to the service. A firm hiring a professional janitorial service will have to rely on what the janitorial service tells it about the services to be performed.

Consumer example: The food at a restaurant cannot be seen, touched, or smelled prior to the service. The waiter or waitress can describe the food, and the restaurant may have a picture of the food on the menu or a written description of the particular dish, but consumers cannot actually see what will be served to them.

Strategies to reduce negative impact: Intangibility can be reduced by stressing tangible cues when marketing the service, using personal sources of information, stimulating word-of-mouth communications, creating a strong corporate and brand image, and encouraging employees to communicate with the customers during the service.

Perishability

Definition: Inability of a service to be inventoried or stored

Business-to-business example: The janitorial service cannot be inventoried or stored. Every day or week, depending on the contract, the service will have to be performed again. The same set of specifications will be performed each time the building is serviced.

Consumer example: The food is prepared when the customer places the order. Some food may be cooked in advance, but the actual order is prepared only after it is ordered. It cannot be inventoried or stored for a later time.

Strategies to reduce negative impact: The service firm has to develop strategies to deal with demand, supply, and capacity. The goal is for demand and supply to match, which should be close to the capacity of the firm. For example, when demand is high, the restaurant will need to expand supply by hiring additional wait staff and cooks.

encounter, and the post-purchase phase. During the pre-purchase phase, consumers evaluate alternatives, make a purchase decision, and finalize a brand choice. At some point after the decision is made, the consumer will move into the second stage, the service encounter, which is the actual interaction point between the customer and the service provider. Sometimes, the service encounter immediately follows the decision, while at other times, it may occur later. For example, when you are on vacation, deciding to patronize a particular restaurant and stopping to eat at the restaurant are virtually simultaneous. At other times, the decision to patronize a particular restaurant may be made hours or even days in advance. During the service encounter, the service is performed or provided to the customer. Because of the inseparability of services, what transpires at the time of consumption has a significant impact on the way customers evaluate the quality of the service and their future purchase decisions. The last phase of the services purchase process is the post-purchase evaluation, which begins upon completion of the service. During this phase, consumers make evaluations concerning the quality of service, their level of satisfaction or dissatisfaction, and future purchase intentions.

9-4a Pre-Purchase Phase

During the pre-purchase phase, consumers evaluate alternatives and make purchase decisions. A number of factors impact the evaluation and decision. These factors can be grouped into internal factors, external factors, firm-produced factors, and perceived risk. Table 9-3 lists each of these factors.

Inseparability

Definition: Simultaneous production and consumption of a service

Business-to-business example: The janitorial service cannot be separated from the individuals doing the service, and it must be performed at the customer's place of business.

Consumer example: The restaurant prepares the food for a customer when it is ordered. The customer consumes the food at the restaurant, and the customer's perception of quality will be partly due to the customer's interaction with the restaurant employees.

Strategies to reduce negative impact: It is important for the service firm to hire competent employees and then train them to perform the service. The service firm needs a process for managing customers so customers will have positive feelings about the interaction between employees and themselves. Inseparability can also be managed by having additional restaurant locations and by offering carryout and home delivery services.

Variability

Definition: Unwanted or random levels of service quality that customers receive when they patronize a firm

Business-to-business example: The quality of the service will depend on who does the work and how well they are trained.

Consumer example: The quality of service will depend on how well the cook prepares the food. Even the same cook may not prepare the food exactly the same way each time.

Strategies to reduce negative impact: Standardization and quality-control measures can reduce the variability of services. Standardization means that customers will tend to receive the same quality of service, regardless of who performs the service and when. In addition, if machines can be incorporated into the service, machines tend to be more consistent, in terms of quality production, than humans.

TABLE 9-3

Factors Impacting the Pre-Purchase Phase

INTERACTIVE TABLE

Internal Factors	1. Individual needs and wants
	2. Past experience
	3. Expectations of service alternatives
	4. Level of purchase involvement
External Factors	1. Competitive options available
	2. The social context of the purchase
	3. Word-of-mouth communications
Firm-Produced Factors	1. Promotions
	2. Price
	3. Distribution
Perceived Risk	1. Performance risk
	2. Financial risk
	3. Time-loss risk
	4. Opportunity risk
	5. Psychological risk
	6. Social risk
	7. Physical risk

Figure 9-9
When you choose a spring break location, the most important internal element in the decision will be what you want to do during the week: swim, ski, or hang out with friends.

Internal Factors For most purchase situations, internal factors are the most critical. Internal factors consist of individual needs and wants of the consumer, past experience, expectations of the service alternatives, and level of purchase involvement. To understand these elements, assume that you are looking for a vacation spot for spring break. The most important internal element in the decision will be your particular needs and wants. What do you want to do during spring break? What types of activities do you want to participate in? If you want to go swimming, then you will likely choose the beach or a lake. If you want to go scuba diving, you may choose a resort that teaches scuba diving or has excellent scuba facilities. If you are interested in nightclubs, you will choose a larger town, but if you want peace and quiet, you will choose an isolated, out-of-the way location. If you want to snow ski, you will look for a place in the mountains. If you want to explore another country, then you may choose Europe or someplace in South America (see Figure 9-9).

Your past experience will factor into this decision. If your past experience with a particular location was positive, then you will be more inclined to go back to the same place. If your past experience was negative, then it is highly probable that you will choose a different place for your spring break.

Your expectations of the various spring break locations will factor into your evaluation and decision. These expectations are based on, for example, past experience, word-of-mouth communications from others, and promotional materials produced by the various resorts and spring break locations. The higher the expectations you develop for a specific location, the greater the likelihood you will choose that location.[11] Of course, the reverse would also be true: The lower the expectations you have for a location, the less likely it will be chosen.

Involvement: The level of mental and physical effort a consumer exerts in selecting a good or service.

The last internal factor impacting your purchase decision in the pre-purchase phase is the level of your involvement. **Involvement** refers to the level of mental and physical effort exerted by a consumer in selecting a good or service.[12] In high-involvement purchase decisions, consumers spend considerable time searching for information, both internally and externally (see Figure 9-10). They are also inclined to spend more time in deliberating and weighing the various alternatives. In contrast, in low-involvement purchase decisions, consumers spend minimal time searching for information and in deliberation. In many cases, it becomes a habitual purchase that is performed with little thought. For example, selecting a video rental store would be considered a low-level-involvement situation and would involve very little thought or deliberation. In most cases, consumers patronize the video

Figure 9-10
Selecting an adult health-care facility for aging parents is a high-involvement decision that requires considerable time and effort in making the right choice.

Source: Courtesy of Newcomer, Morris and Young.

rental store closest to them or one they have patronized in the past. Unless you are going back to the same location for spring break, it is likely that selecting a spring break location will be a high-involvement decision that will require searching for information and then carefully evaluating the alternatives.

External Factors The external factors that influence the purchase decision during the pre-purchase phase are the competitive options available, the social context of the purchase, and word-of-mouth communications. Going back to our example of a place for spring break, your decision will be influenced by the competitive options available to you. Some options will come from your own memory, others from individuals around you, and others through your external search for information on the Internet or other sources such as an advertisement. If scuba diving is on your agenda for things to do, your options will be more limited because not all resorts and spring break locations are ideal for scuba diving.

For spring break, the social context of the purchase is usually very important. In fact, it may have a greater influence than even your own personal desires. If you want to spend spring break with college friends, a significant other, or family members, where you go will depend on where they want to go. Your choice will be more of a group decision than your individual decision unless you can convince everyone within your group to choose the location you desire.

Word-of-mouth communications are likely to have a significant impact on the purchase decision.[13] In the process of selecting a service, it is not unusual for consumers to ask other people for their recommendations or evaluations of specific vendors. Consumers feel that word-of-mouth communications from other people are more reliable than any company-sponsored communication, such as an advertisement. In choosing a spring break location, you will undoubtedly seek information from individuals who went on spring break last year. You will want to find out where they went, what they did, and how they liked it. You will especially want this information for locations that you are considering. While internal information may help you narrow the list of possible locations down to a smaller subset, external information can help you develop more concrete views of each location and influence your actual choice.

Firm-Produced Factors The firm-produced factors impacting the purchase decision include promotions, pricing, and distribution. From a consumer's viewpoint, firm-produced factors are the least reliable because consumers realize that the goal of the firm is to encourage and persuade consumers to purchase from it. From the service firm's perspective, firm-produced factors are its primary method of reaching consumers with information and persuading them to purchase its service.

Firms have several forms of promotion that can be used, such as advertising, sales promotions, and personal selling. Testimonials are especially useful for services (see Figure 9-11).

Service organizations can provide consumers with information that can be used as they make decisions about what service to purchase and which vendor to patronize. For spring

Figure 9-11
Judi Tal, a performer known for her exquisite interpretation of Israeli and Yiddish songs, uses client testimonials to communicate with her target market.

Source: Courtesy of Judith Tal de Boer.

break locations, advertising on college campuses and in newspapers in the area is an effective way to communicate with the target market. Television, magazine, and radio ads can be used during the winter months to encourage students to start thinking about spring break and to book their location early. Often, special deals encourage college students to act early.

Pricing is an important element of the pre-purchase evaluation process. Consumers often compare the prices charged by competing firms. For services, more so than for goods, prices are seen as an indicator of quality. An attorney who charges $100 per hour is normally perceived as more competent than an attorney who charges $75 an hour. A carpet-cleaning service that charges $29.99 per room will be seen as superior to one that charges only $19.99 per room. This does not, however, mean that consumers will choose the higher-priced firm. They may choose the lower price for one of several reasons. They may not have the money to pay a higher price. They may feel the higher-priced service is overpriced. They may rationalize that, although the service quality will not be as good, it is still a good value for the price being charged.

For services, **service distribution** is defined as the availability and accessibility of a service to consumers. It would include the firm's physical location, its hours of operation, and access availability. For example, a bank may operate several branches and place ATMs at various locations. Although actual bank hours are limited, customers have 24-hour-a-day access to their accounts through ATMs and online banking.

Service distribution: The availability and accessibility of a service to consumers.

Uncertainty: The probability that a particular outcome or consequence will occur.

Consequence: The degree of importance or danger of the outcome itself.

Perceived Risk The last factor in the pre-purchase phase is perceived purchase risk. Because of the unique characteristics of services, the purchase decision for services is perceived to be a higher risk than for goods.[14] Prior to a purchase, consumers will seek a means to reduce the risk involved in the decision, primarily through obtaining additional information. Consumers use the internal factors, external factors, and firm-produced factors just discussed to reduce this purchase risk.

Risk has two components: uncertainty and consequences.[15] **Uncertainty** is the probability that a particular outcome or consequence will occur. **Consequence** is the degree of importance or danger of the outcome itself. For example, there is risk in open-heart surgery. The uncertainty is the unknown probability of the surgery not being successful, and the consequence, if the surgery does not go well, is death or serious side effects. Although the seriousness of the consequences is high, because the procedure is now well developed and the probability of something going wrong during the surgery is low, most patients no longer view open-heart surgery as a high-risk medical procedure.

In the purchasing of services, there are seven types of risk. They are performance risk, financial risk, time-loss risk, opportunity risk, psychological risk, social risk, and physical risk (see Table 9-4). **Performance risk** is the chance that the service will not perform or provide the benefit for which it was purchased. For example, in the selection of a spring break location, there is the risk that the services the resort promises to provide are not available or are performed poorly. For an automobile repair service, performance risk would be the garage not fixing the problem properly.

Financial risk is the amount of monetary loss incurred by the consumer if the service fails. Money invested in personal tutoring that does not help a student is money poorly spent, or money lost. Money spent on a haircut that is not satisfactory is lost. In addition to the financial loss, there is the possibility of time loss. **Time-loss risk** refers to the amount of time lost by the consumer due to the failure of the service. If a consumer has to return to a garage to have his or her car repaired again because the problem was not taken care of the first time, then the consumer has lost the time required to drop off the vehicle and pick it up. In addition, the consumer could not use the vehicle during the time it is in the shop the second time it is being repaired.

Opportunity risk refers to the risk involved when consumers must choose one service over another. After a spring break selection is made, the opportunity to go to other locations is lost. You will never know if the other locations would have been better or worse. **Psychological risk** is the chance that the purchase of the service will not fit the individual's self-concept, and **social risk** is the probability that a service will not meet with approval

Performance risk: The chance that the service will not perform or provide the benefit for which it was purchased.

Financial risk: The amount of monetary loss the consumer incurs if the service fails.

Time-loss risk: The amount of time the consumer lost due to the failure of the service.

Opportunity risk: The risk involved when consumers must choose one service over another.

Psychological risk: The chance that the purchase of the service will not fit the individual's self-concept.

Social risk: The probability that a service will not meet with approval from others who are significant to the consumer making the purchase.

TABLE 9-4

Perceived Purchase Risk

Risk	Definition
Performance	The chance that the service will not perform or provide the benefit expected
Financial	The amount of monetary loss incurred if the service fails
Time-loss	The amount of time lost due to a service failure
Opportunity	The risk of losing other choices when one choice is selected
Psychological	The chance that the service will not fit the individual's self-concept
Social	The chance that the service will not meet the approval of others
Physical	The chance that the service will actually cause physical harm

from others who are significant to the consumer making the purchase. Choosing a resort that friends do not like is a high risk for the person who values friendships. Choosing a resort that does not meet with your self-concept is equally risky. The last type of risk that consumers of services face is physical risk. **Physical risk** is the probability that a service will actually cause physical harm to the customer. Medical procedures, such as plastic surgery, have physical risk.

Physical risk: The probability that a service will actually cause physical harm to the customer.

During the pre-purchase phase, consumers evaluate the type and extent of risk involved in the purchase decision. They will often compare service firms to see how much risk would be involved with each option. It is normally the uncertainty component being examined because the consequence component is usually the same. The first step most consumers take in reducing pre-purchase risk is to examine their own personal experiences. The tendency is to patronize service firms they have used in the past, since they know what type of service will be received. People tend to use the same hair stylist or barber because they know what to expect. Only if they are unhappy with the last haircut will they be inclined to switch.

To further reduce risk, consumers will often seek the opinion of others such as friends, relatives, business associates, or experts in the field. When looking for a dentist, consumers usually ask other people for recommendations. When looking for spring break locations, the opinions of others will be valuable. The higher the perceived risk, the more likely that the opinion of someone else will be sought. Consumers will sometimes seek service-produced sources of information during the deliberation stage or data collecting stage. Before deciding on a spring break location, you may collect information on several resorts. Common sources of information include advertising, promotions, and the Internet.

Service firms must be aware of the risk consumers perceive during the pre-purchase phase and take appropriate steps to reduce it. It is important to understand the difference between the uncertainty component and the consequence component. To reduce the uncertainty component, services must reduce the perceived probability of a service failure. It is important to recognize that the "perceived" risk may not be the same as the "actual" risk. Although the actual risk of a parachute not opening for a skydiver is extremely low, most consumers perceive the risk to be relatively high. Airlines face a similar problem in that it is statistically safer to fly than it is to drive one's own automobile, yet most people perceive flying to be riskier. In both cases, the perception is greater than reality, but consumer decisions are based on the perception, not reality. Therefore, firms must deal with reducing the "perceived" risk consumers have, regardless of what the actual risk may be (see Figure 9-12).

Communication is a key in reducing the uncertainty component of risk. Through advertising, brochures, and certification, the perceived probability that something will go wrong can be reduced. Having a strong brand name is extremely beneficial. Most travelers feel more comfortable eating at a brand-name restaurant such as Applebee's than at a restaurant with an unfamiliar name. The brand-name restaurant is perceived to be more

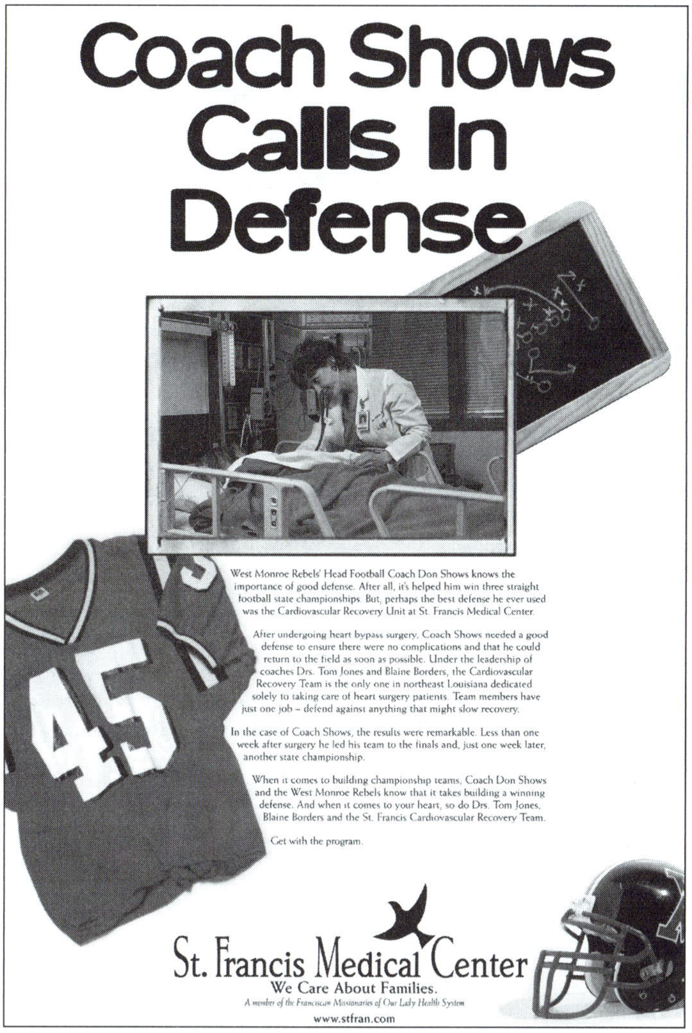

Figure 9-12
St. Francis Medical Center uses this advertisement about a local football coach's experience to reduce the perceived risk of heart bypass surgery.

Source: Courtesy of Newcomer, Morris and Young.

likely to have consistent quality at all of its restaurants. The traveler has no idea what to expect at an unknown restaurant.

Reducing the consequence component of risk is achieved by having quality control standards and procedures. Applebee's can reduce the consequence of food poisoning, or just a meal that tastes bad, by ensuring that all of its cooks and employees follow established quality control standards and specific operating procedures.

9-4b Service Encounter

Service encounter: The actual interaction point between the customer and the service provider.

The second stage of the service purchase process is the **service encounter,** which is the actual interaction point between the customer and the service provider.[16] In most cases, the service provider is a person, but it can also be a machine, as in the case of a bank's ATM. In most cases, the customer and service provider interaction are in person—as would be the case with a dental procedure; but it can occur over the telephone—as would be the case with a call center employee helping a customer with a computer problem. In all of these cases, the quality of the service encounter depends on the service environment and the service personnel or the service machine providing the service.

The service environment consists of the tangible elements of the facility, the facility's atmosphere, and other customers who are present at the time of the service. Tangible elements include, for example, the furniture, signs, brochures, and the equipment and tools being used to perform the service. Marketing Illustration 9-2 describes how important the table setting is for a restaurant.

Marketing Illustration 9-2

The Tabletop Sets the Environment

The next time you go to a restaurant, examine the tabletop. According to Joseph Durocher, the "elements of the tabletop should work together as an ensemble, improving the presentation of the food as well as enhancing the overall dining experience." The tabletop should be considered as a whole, not as individual pieces put on a table. To achieve this goal, Durocher offers restaurants several suggestions.

Setting the stage of this ensemble is the table covering. The selection must match the style of service being offered and the ambiance the restaurant wants to create. For example, in seafood and lobster restaurants, a plastic tablecloth that can be rolled up and tossed away makes sense. However, for a fine dining experience, a cloth table covering that can be removed after each guest would be more appropriate (see Figure 1). In terms of napkins, the high end includes cotton napkins that are soft to touch, readily absorb spills, and can be starched to create fancy shapes. At the other extreme are paper napkins. It is important that the napkin match the table covering in terms of visual and imagery appeal.

For most restaurants, except for the most deluxe establishments, flatware will be either stainless steel or plastic. When considering stainless steel, restaurant managers may decide that silver or gold-plated flatware will differentiate the restaurant from a competitor but it may not be a wise investment. For instance, if the restaurant is in a college town where students rip off tableware every fall for their dorm rooms and apartments, then plastic or a cheaper stainless steel flatware is best.

The dinnerware is one of the most important elements of the tabletop. According to Durocher, the dinnerware should be "the canvas upon which the chef paints the presentation" of food. For formal restaurants, white or embossed dinnerware is ideal, but for less formal establishments, colored or design dinnerware will fit nicely. In terms of size, it is important that the plate match the portions. A large plate at an establishment where small portions are served makes the restaurant look like it is skimpy, whereas smaller plates full of food give the impression of abundance.

Figure 1
This very clean tabletop in an informal café area of a supermarket has fresh flowers and all the necessary condiments.

Source: Courtesy of Ukrop's Super Markets, Inc.

The last selection of the tabletop is the glassware. Specialty glasses can dress up the tabletop and create the image or theme desired. Many restaurants have custom-designed glassware that customers can purchase and take home. If wine is served, then the glassware needs to match the selection of wine that is sold.

When choosing each element of the tabletop, managers need to try it personally. They may find that the spoon does not work well for the soup or that the fork slides down into the plate. The glassware may not feel comfortable to hold or may not match the table covering or the dinnerware. Because of the impact of the tabletop on a customer's overall experience with a restaurant, managers must be sure it all works together as an ensemble.

Source: Gail Bellamy, "Tips for Tabletops," *Restaurant Hospitality*, vol. 88 (July 2004): 84; "Eight Ways to Shine with Cloth Napkins," *Restaurant Business*, vol. 103 (December 15, 2004): 62; Joseph Durocher, "Set the Stage," *Restaurant Business*, vol. 100 (July 15, 2001): 97–98.

The atmospheric elements include such things as the office decor, the cleanliness of the facility, and intangible elements like noise, sound, and odors; atmospherics are further addressed in the discussion of the retail environment in Chapter 11, "Retailing Strategies." All of these elements impact how customers react to service situations. If a restaurant is cold, consumers are likely to have a lower evaluation of the service. If a dental office is dirty, it will affect patients' evaluation of the dental care they are to receive. If a bakery has the smell of freshly baked cookies, it will positively influence the consumer's evaluation of the pastry just purchased. In all of these cases, the evaluation of the service is impacted by intangible elements that are not part of the service itself. The actual service may be performed well, but customers can go away unhappy because of an intangible element.

If other customers are present during the service encounter, they can impact the quality of the environment. This is especially true for entertainment services such as sports, theme parks, movie theaters, and concerts. A rowdy or drunken fan can destroy the fun of

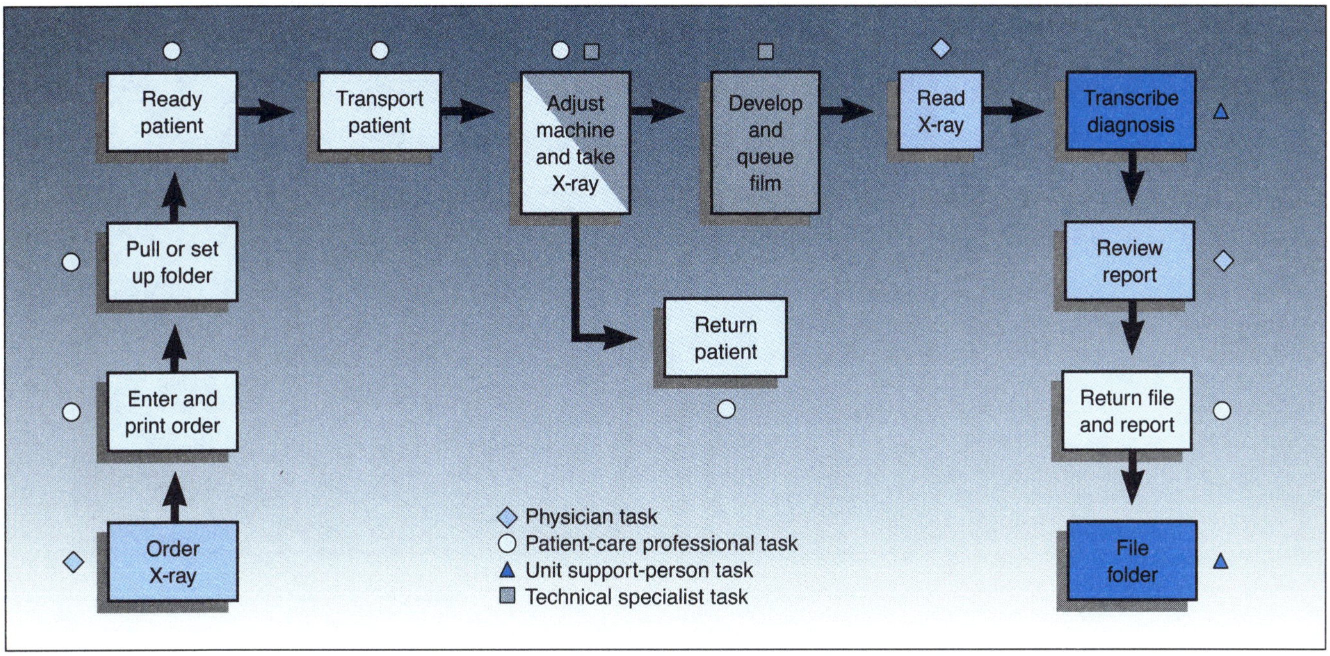

Figure 9-13
A Service Blueprint for an X-Ray
This service blueprint depicts the 13 steps involved in a typical hospital's X-ray process. The steps can be completed in less than one hour, and they require multiple employees. Without such a blueprint, the X-ray process would probably be less systematic, more time consuming, and less efficient.

Source: "Making Your Service Blueprint Pay Off!" by Stephen H. Baum from *Journal of Services Marketing*, (1990, vol. 4, p. 49). Copyright Emerald Group Publishing Limited. Reprinted by permission.

INTERACTIVE FIGURE

others watching a game. A customer talking at a movie theater can aggravate other viewers to the point they may not even stay for the whole movie.

In service encounters in which service personnel and customers have direct interaction, the conduct of the service personnel becomes a critical factor. If service personnel are polite and show genuine interest in the customer, their behavior will increase the level of customer satisfaction. If service personnel are indifferent or rude, their behavior can create customer dissatisfaction. The food at a restaurant can be excellent, but if the service is poor, it will reflect negatively on the entire experience. For many services, the conduct of the service personnel is as important or more important than the service itself.

To ensure a positive service environment, many firms use a concept called **blueprinting,** which is the process of diagramming a service operation.[17] Through blueprinting, every step in the purchase process, from the first contact the customer has with a firm to the completion of the service, is diagrammed. Through this blueprinting process, the firm can see how customers and the firm interact. They can see which steps are not being performed efficiently and where improvements need to be made. The blueprint shows at what times during the service the service environment, other customers, and service personnel are involved. By carefully blueprinting every step in the purchase process, a firm can manage the entire experience to increase the probability the customer has a positive experience. Figure 9-13 illustrates a blueprint for an X-ray process.

Blueprinting: The process of diagramming a service operation.

Each block in the blueprinting diagram is a "moment of truth" when the customer or patient interacts with the service. The total experience is the sum of each of the contact experiences or "moments of truth." If one link in the experience is bad, it will result in the negative evaluation of the whole experience. Customers will not remember the 10 steps that went right—only the one step where it went wrong. Del Powell, Southeast regional director for St. Paul Companies, summed the importance of the service encounter very succinctly when he stated, "People will forget what you say, they'll forget your slogans, they'll forget your advertising, and they'll forget your promises. But what they'll always remember is what it feels like to do business with you."[18]

9-4c Post-Purchase Phase

The third stage of the purchase process is the post-purchase phase. During this stage, customers will evaluate the quality of service and their level of satisfaction or dissatisfaction. For satisfied customers, future actions include repeat purchases, customer loyalty, and

Figure 9-14
The owner of Rayfield's Pharmacy, Mr. Rayfield, always chats with customers, making them welcome at his drug store, which is also a popular diner.

positive word-of-mouth communications. For dissatisfied customers, future actions include switching vendors and negative word-of-mouth communications.[19]

Technical service quality: The outcome of the service.

Functional service quality: The process whereby the service was performed.

Attribution theory: The process of deciding the cause of a service failure or poor service.

In evaluating service quality, consumers evaluate two components: the technical quality and the functional quality.[20] **Technical service quality** is the outcome of the service, and **functional service quality** is the process whereby the service was performed. For a restaurant, the technical service quality is the food and drinks that are served, while the functional service quality is the interaction with the people providing the service (see Figure 9-14). For both components, a consumer will compare the perceived level of service quality that was received to what was expected. If expectations are met or exceeded, then consumers are satisfied; if expectations are not met, then consumers are dissatisfied.

In cases in which expectations are not met, the level of customer dissatisfaction will be determined by how and where customers attribute the cause of the service failure or poor service. The process of deciding the cause of the poor service is called **attribution theory.**[21] Customers look at two factors in determining attribution: first, was the cause of the service controllable, and second, whether the firm could have prevented the service problem. If either factor is confirmed, then the customer will attribute the service problem to the firm and blame it for what occurred.

To illustrate, suppose you order some clothes over the Internet, and the package arrives two days late. If the delay is caused by bad weather, you are less likely to be dissatisfied because the Internet company does not have any control over weather conditions. However, if the package is delayed because the company failed to send it out in a timely manner, then it is likely that you will be dissatisfied because the company is at fault and the delay could have been prevented.

Customers who are dissatisfied with a service are likely to choose another firm the next time they purchase that particular service. Few customers actually voice a complaint to the manager or service personnel. The customer may be unhappy with the haircut or the food that was served at a restaurant but will usually not say anything to anyone at the service. In fact, research has shown that only 1 out of every 25 dissatisfied customers will voice some type of complaint.[22] The remaining 24 say nothing but demonstrate their dissatisfaction by either switching to a different firm, or by telling others about the poor quality service, or by doing both. The negative word-of-mouth can be devastating to a business because, on the average, an unhappy customer will tell between 10 and 11 other people about the bad experience.[23]

For customers who are satisfied, typical future behaviors include repeat purchases, firm loyalty, and positive word-of-mouth communications. Satisfied customers tend to patronize the same firm and, over time, become loyal to that firm. If a person likes the way a service mows the lawn or cleans the house, that person will continue to use the service. He or she may even engage in positive word-of-mouth communications, although usually it does not involve as many people as negative word-of-mouth communications. On average, a satisfied customer will tell only 3 others of his or her experience, instead of the 10 to 11 for customers who are dissatisfied.[24]

9-5 Service Quality

A critical component of future purchase behavior is the evaluation of the service a consumer receives. If customers are satisfied with the quality of service, they likely will patronize the firm again. If they are not satisfied, they likely will not patronize the firm in the future. Because future purchase behavior is largely determined by this service experience, it is beneficial to examine how a service business can measure service quality.

9-5a Measuring Service Quality

In making an evaluation of service quality, customers will compare the service they received to what they expected. This method of measuring service quality is called the **gap theory** because you are measuring the gap between expectations and customer evaluations of the service. Past research has indicated that consumers make this evaluation along the five dimensions of tangibles, reliability, responsiveness, empathy, and assurance.[25]

Tangibles refer to the service provider's physical facilities, equipment, and the appearance of employees. **Reliability** is the ability of the service firm to perform the service promised dependably and accurately. **Responsiveness** is the willingness of the firm's staff to help customers and to provide them with prompt service. **Empathy** refers to the caring, individualized attention the service firm provides each customer. **Assurance** refers to the knowledge and courtesy of the employees and their ability to inspire customers to trust and have confidence in the service provider. Marketing Illustration 9-3 discusses how to build trust in e-commerce interactions.

To illustrate these dimensions, suppose you have contacted a company to clean the carpets in your home. The tangibles are the appearance of the equipment being used and the personnel doing the work. If the equipment is old and worn, you may be inclined to believe that the quality of service the company provides is not as good as it would be for a company that has new, clean equipment. If the service is scheduled for 2:00 P.M. and the company shows up an hour late, the response will negatively impact your evaluation of the service quality. If, however, you called a company because of a water pipe break and service technicians are able to get out to your house in the afternoon or the first thing the next day, this quick response would have a positive impact on your evaluation. Employees who are knowledgeable and courteous will enhance your evaluation of the firm's service, whereas employees who do not know how to get particular stains out of your carpet or are rude will have a negative impact. In fact, a rude service technician can create a negative evaluation of the service even though the actual outcome of the service may be satisfactory. Empathy would be the caring, individualized attention the service provides. It may be moving some furniture for you at no additional cost, or it may be spending extra time on a particular spot in your carpet. How you evaluate the quality of service of the carpet-cleaning firm will be a summation of all five dimensions. The firm may do well on four of the five, but doing poorly on one dimension can create a negative overall evaluation of the service (see Figure 9-15).

In measuring service quality using the gap theory, a service firm has two options. First, it can ask consumers about their expectations prior to the service and then ask the same series of questions after the service. Subtracting the two scores will give a gap score for each dimension, as well as for the overall service. An alternative method of using the gap theory methodology is to ask customers to evaluate the service along the five dimensions as it relates to what they expected. For example, a question about empathy would read, "The service technician demonstrated he cared about me as a customer." This latter method requires surveying customers only once and will yield very similar results.

Gap theory: Method of measuring service quality that involves measuring the gap between expectations and customer evaluations of a service.

Tangibles: The service provider's physical facilities, equipment, and appearance of its employees.

Reliability: The ability of the service firm to perform the service provided in a dependable and accurate manner [service].

Responsiveness: The willingness of the firm's staff to help customers and to provide prompt service.

Empathy: The caring, individualized attention the service firm provides to each customer.

Assurance: The knowledge and courtesy of the employees and their ability to inspire customers to trust and have confidence in the service provider.

Marketing Illustration 9-3

Building Trust in E-Commerce Interactions

With a brick-and-mortar service operation, customers can see the facility, and they can see the employees. Developing a trusting relationship becomes much easier in this type of environment. It becomes more difficult if the service interaction is handled over the telephone or the Internet. Typical questions a potential customer would have of an e-commerce website include:

1. Will the business perform as stated?
2. Is the financial transaction secure?
3. Does the company use a cookie to gather information about me and my computer?
4. Is information about my transaction or even my computer being sold?
5. If I am dissatisfied, does the company have a warranty, and will it honor the warranty?
6. Will the merchandise be shipped on time, as ordered, and for the price quoted?

If an e-commerce site is to be successful, it must develop positive answers to these questions. To do so requires gaining the consumer's trust along two domains: web design and trust-building behavior.

The website design has an impact on a consumer's perception of the site's trustworthiness. Consumers look for any type of official seal of approval, a recognizable brand name, ease of navigation, and method of communication such as virtual communities, toll-free numbers, email or web-push technologies, and synchronous message boards where questions can be posted online to sales reps. Official seals of approval and known brand names add credibility to the site. An Enterprise Rent-A-Car website will gain immediate trust over a website of an unknown rental car company. Consumers expect some level of technology and ease of navigation as a sign of commitment by the firm to customer service. They want to see various methods of communication whereby they can contact the company for any reason. This helps ensure there is a solid, legitimate company behind the website and it is not a fly-by-night operation that will be gone tomorrow when the ordered merchandise does not arrive or malfunctions.

In terms of trust-building behaviors, the three major issues are privacy, risk security, and reliability. If cookies are used or information is sold, consumer trust will quickly diminish. If credit cards are used for purchases, consumers must feel the transaction will be handled securely. They also must feel that the firm is reliable and will deliver as promised.

Developing customer trust is more difficult for e-commerce companies, but without it, they will not succeed. If they use well-designed websites and engage in trust-building behavior, they can gain trust.

Sources: David Gefen and Detmar Straub, "Managing User Trust in B2C e-Services," *e-Service Journal*, vol. 2 (Winter 2003): 7–24; Scott A. Chadwick, "Communicating Trust in E-Commerce Interactions," *Management Communication Quarterly*, vol. 14 (May 2001): 653–658.

Figure 9-15
Performing well on all five dimensions of service quality is critical for a service such as Haik Humble Eye Center.

Source: Sartor Associates, Inc. for Haik Humble Eye Center.

Instead of using a gap analysis to measure service quality, a company can use internal measures. For airlines, internal measures are such items as the percentage of on-time flights, number of baggage claims, and number of customer complaints. This information has to be filed with the Department of Transportation on a monthly basis, so it is readily available. By tracking these measures over time, an airline can see whether its level of service is increasing or decreasing. It can also compare its data to that of other airlines to see how it stands. These comparative data are especially helpful because they will indicate areas for improvement. If an airline ranks first in the number of baggage claims per 1,000 passengers, then it needs to look at ways of improving its baggage-handling process. If it doesn't address the problem, passengers are likely to start flying on other airlines.

The advantage of using internal measures of service quality is that weaknesses as well as strengths can be identified. Weaknesses need to be improved to remain competitive, and strengths can be marketed as a reason to patronize the firm. The airline that ranks first in percentage of on-time flights can advertise this as proof of its dependable and reliable service.

9-5b Service Failure and Recovery

Service failures are defined as instances in which a service is either not performed at all or is poorly performed. Customers are not only dissatisfied, but they may be extremely angry. When service problems occur, customers are less likely to purchase from the firm again in the future and in many cases will tell others about the bad experience. For both reasons, services must develop methods for dealing with service failures.

Service failures: Instances in which a service is either not performed at all or is poorly performed.

Service firms must realize that a service failure does not automatically result in firm-switching behavior and negative word-of-mouth communications. Customers can be recovered. The manner in which service failures are handled will have a greater impact on future purchase behavior than the original bad experience. Firms often have a second chance to make things right. However, if a firm fails the second time around, the backlash is even stronger because the firm, in essence, has failed twice. This process of attempting to regain a customer's confidence after a service failure is called **service recovery.**

Service recovery: The process of attempting to regain a customer's confidence after a service failure.

A successful service recovery program can overcome most service failures and diminish the negative impact of the original poor or failed service.[26] The more quickly a service problem is handled, the more likely the customer can be recovered and will purchase from the firm again. If the service problem can be corrected at the time of the service encounter, the negative impact of the experience is almost always diminished. The longer it takes to correct the problem, the less likely it can be resolved satisfactorily and the less likely the customer will be to purchase again. Realizing this, Northwest Airlines now uses kiosks throughout the airport to notify passengers of cancelled flights with a selection of alternative flights they can take. The kiosk can also issue a "service recovery coupon," which is given to a Northwest agent for a pack that contains a meal voucher, a phone card, and a discount on future travel.[27] This system not only provides a quick response to the service problem but also provides passengers with the opportunity to select alternative solutions. See Marketing Illustration 9-4 for an example of BellSouth's service recovery program.

Employees should be trained to defuse the customer's anger as quickly and tactfully as possible. Normally, all this requires is attentive listening, admitting the firm made a mistake, and acknowledging the customer has a right to feel annoyed. Listening will allow customers to vent their anger and explain why they are unhappy. Admitting the firm made a mistake will offset any attribution directed to the firm. It is harder to be mad at someone who admits he or she made a mistake. By agreeing that the customer had a right to be upset and dissatisfied, employees demonstrate empathy and understanding. With this groundwork, the recovery process is ready to move into the resolution stage.

Many companies begin the resolution stage by asking the customer what the firm can do to correct the problem. Firms that have used this strategy are astounded at the reasonableness of customers and the solutions recommended. Customers seldom recommend drastic solutions. Often, they may suggest a partial refund or a coupon for a discount on

Marketing Illustration 9-4

BellSouth's Service Recovery Program

As a major supplier of cellular service, BellSouth has more than one million subscribers. While BellSouth is gaining 2,500 customers per day, it is also losing 500 customers a day. It costs approximately $350 to add a new customer, who then generates around $60 a month in revenue. The first step in regaining the 500 customers a day that leave was to find out why customers left. Research indicated the following reasons:

- No longer needed service—12 percent
- Company no longer pays the bill—18 percent
- Moved out of BellSouth's coverage area—24 percent
- Switched to the competition—34 percent
- Other reasons—12 percent

Realizing that the only viable market for its service recovery program was the 34 percent who switched to a competitor, BellSouth asked this group the key reasons why they left. The top three reasons were:

- BellSouth did something that upset me.
- BellSouth wouldn't issue a credit (50 cents) for a dropped call.
- BellSouth gave free phones to new subscribers, but not to me.

In this second survey, many of the former customers said they were willing to switch back to BellSouth but were under a contract with a competitor. They also indicated they wanted a free phone or free time as an incentive.

The third step in the service recovery plan was to mail each lost customer an offer to come back. BellSouth offered to give a 50-cent credit for dropped calls and either a free phone or free time. The direct-mail approach produced an 8 percent response rate and a 3 percent reactivation rate. If the direct-mail offer was followed by a phone call, the reactivation rate rose to 10 percent. This met BellSouth's goal when it started its service recovery program.

Source: Jill Griffin and Michael W. Lowenstein, "Winning Back a Lost Customer," *Direct Marketing*, vol. 64 (July 2001): 49–66.

another purchase. They may just want the service firm to correct the problem. Few customers will suggest solutions that are unreasonable.

After the customer has made a suggestion, the service employee is then ready to negotiate a viable solution to the problem. The goal of the resolution is twofold. First, the firm wants to eradicate the negative experience and change the dissatisfaction into some type of satisfaction. Second, the firm wants that customer to return and purchase again. With these goals in mind, the employee should negotiate a solution that satisfies the customer and is feasible for the firm.

If the problem cannot be corrected at the time it is discovered, then customers need to be informed. The customer needs to be kept up-to-date on the progress that is made. If the same employee can deal with the customer through the whole service recovery process, it will increase the chances of a positive outcome. In the business-to-business area, keeping customers informed through one contact person is very important. Too often, either the problem is passed around or it is assumed that the customer knows what is happening.

9-6 Customer Value Package

Dissatisfaction and poor service quality are not the only reasons customers switch firms. Customers can be satisfied with a service firm but switch because a competitor offers a better deal or is more convenient. Research has estimated that 65 to 85 percent of customers who switch firms were not dissatisfied with their last vendor.[28] See Figure 9-16 for a breakdown from one study on why customers leave. Because future purchase behavior is determined by more than customer satisfaction, service firms must look at ways to develop stronger relationships with their customers. The key to stronger relationships is in the concept of the customer value package, which is the perceived combination of factors that in the consumer's mind creates a superior value for him or her. The components of the **customer value package** are price, technical service quality, functional service quality, and company image.[29]

Customer value package: The best combination of price, technical service quality, functional service quality, and company image that provides value to the customer.

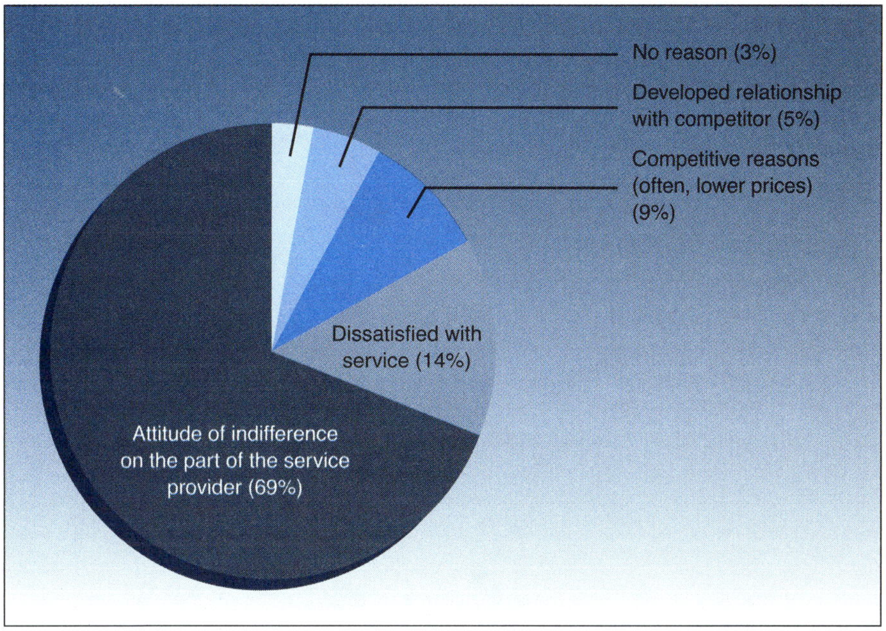

Figure 9-16
Why Customers Switch Firms

Source: Marc R. Okrant, "How to Convert '(3)'s and '(4)'s into '(5)'s," *Marketing News*, vol. 36 (October 14, 2002): 14–15.

Customers will patronize the firm that offers the best value. That value may be a lower price, superior technical quality, superior functional quality, or perceived company image. Customers weigh all four components of the value package and choose the service with the best combination. One consumer may choose a company that has adequate technical and service quality but a lower price, whereas other consumers may choose a different company they perceive to offer high service quality, although the cost is higher.

To develop and manage a customer value package, services will need to:[30]

1. Determine the relative weights customers place on each element of the value package
2. Determine the value package that will be offered
3. Develop business objectives and a mission statement that will incorporate the value package
4. Communicate the values to all company personnel
5. Develop plans to implement the value package
6. Monitor the environment for changes in customer value weights

To develop a customer value package, a service must first determine the relative weights customers place on each component. For many years, airlines believed that leisure travelers valued a high level of functional service quality. Although functional quality was important, price was more important. Based on this belief, Southwest Airlines launched a minimum service, low-priced airline. While other airlines have struggled, Southwest continues to thrive because it understands what value package most leisure travelers desire.

After a service has determined the relative weights customers place on each element of the service value package, the service must decide what value package they will offer. In addition to meeting the value package desired by customers, firms must examine their own resources and the competitive advantage they can develop. If a service has developed a high level of technical service quality, they will want to look for ways this advantage can be leveraged to produce value for the customer. Hilton, Four Seasons, and other high-end hotels are successful because they provide a customer value package that customers want. Although price is still a component of the value package, it is not as prominent as technical and functional service quality. Firms must carefully look at their target market and develop a value package that meets what their potential customers want (see Figure 9-17).

After the value package is developed, the service needs to incorporate the values into the company's business objectives and mission statement. If the company adopts a functional

Figure 9-17
Community Trust Bank's value package is based on its Freeplus Checking with overdraft advantage.

Source: Sample print advertisement courtesy of The Miles Agency and Alliance One Advertising, Inc.

service quality value, the mission statement should address the importance of customer-employee interaction. If the value package stresses price, the mission statement should promote the company's desire to be the low-priced leader. Putting the customer value package in the mission statement and business objectives conveys the message to both employees and customers that providing value to the customer is the driving force behind the company.

The fourth step is to communicate the value package to all employees in the company. They must know it, believe it, and follow it. If customer interaction is the key value being touted, every employee needs to be trained and rewarded for optimizing points of contact with customers. If technical service quality is the key value, then employees will want to emphasize outcome quality to ensure the highest possible level of service. Federal Express has clearly communicated to its employees, as well as to its customers, its guaranteed delivery time or there is no charge for the service.

The fifth step is to develop plans for how the customer value package will be implemented. In addition to communication with employees, external communication with current and future customers is important. If the service uses a distribution system, then the customer value package needs to be communicated to each member of the channel. The final step in the development of a customer value package is to monitor the marketplace for changes. Consumers may shift the weights placed on each component of the value package over time. Any change in the relative importance of the components may require the firm to shift its customer value package position.

Summary

1. *Discuss the impact of the services sector on the gross domestic product and what has led to the growth of the service sector.* The service sector in the United States accounts for 79 percent ($6.95 trillion) of the country's GDP and 77 percent of the total U.S. employment. Employment in the United States is expected to increase by 21.3 million jobs between 2002 and 2012, with the service sector furnishing 58 percent of this growth. The service sector's rapid growth is primarily the result of nations shifting from a manufacturing-based economy to a service economy. A major stimulus in this shift is the movement to an information society spurred by the computer and advancements in telecommunications. Additional factors contributing to the growth of the service sector are an aging population, longer life expectancies, increased leisure time, higher per capita income, increased time pressure, more female workforce participation, sedentary lifestyles, changing social and cultural values, and advances in technology.

2. *Identify the four unique characteristics of services and how each impacts the marketing of services.* Services possess four inherent characteristics not found in goods: intangibility, perishability, inseparability, and variability. Intangibility refers to the lack of tangible assets that can be seen, touched, smelled, heard, or tasted prior to a purchase, which renders a service relatively difficult for a consumer to evaluate prior to a purchase. Perishability refers to the inability of a service to be inventoried or stored. This means that one of the goals of marketing is to manage demand so it equals supply and capacity. Inseparability refers to the simultaneous production and consumption of a service, which requires marketing the service at the time and location of the service provider. Variability refers to the unwanted or random levels of service quality that customers receive when they patronize a service. Because of this variability, promises made in advertising and other marketing materials are not always kept; this reflects negatively on the service operation.

3. *Explain the components of the purchasing process for services.* The purchase process consists of three phases: the pre-purchase phase, the service encounter, and the post-purchase phase. During the pre-purchase phase, consumers evaluate alternatives, make a purchase decision, and choose a particular brand. At some point after the decision is made, the consumer will move into the second stage, the service encounter, which is the actual interaction point between the customer and the service provider. The last phase of the services purchase process is the post-purchase evaluation, which begins upon completion of the service. During this phase, consumers make evaluations concerning the quality of service, their level of satisfaction or dissatisfaction, and future purchase intentions.

4. *Identify the factors that impact the purchase decision during the pre-purchase phase of the purchase process.* During the pre-purchase phase, the factors that impact the purchase decision are internal factors, external factors, firm-produced factors, and perceived risk. Internal factors consist of individual needs and wants of the consumer, past experience, expectations of the service alternatives, and the overall level of purchase involvement. The external factors that influence the purchase decision during the pre-purchase phase are the competitive options available to consumers, the social context of the purchase, and word-of-mouth communications. The firm-produced factors impacting the purchase decision include promotions, pricing, and distribution. The types of perceived risk that can impact the purchase decision are performance risk, financial risk, time-loss risk, opportunity risk, psychological risk, social risk, and physical risk.

5. *Discuss the relevant elements of the service encounter and why they are important.* The service encounter is the actual interaction point between the customer and the service provider. The quality of the service encounter depends on the service environment and the service personnel or service machine providing the service. The service environment consists of the tangible elements of the facility, the facility's atmosphere, and other customers who are present at the time of the service. All of these components of the service encounter impact a customer's evaluation of the service being delivered, as well as the interaction between the customer and service personnel.

6. *Describe the post-purchase evaluation of services and its impact on future purchase behavior.* During the post-purchase phase, customers evaluate the quality of service and their level of satisfaction or dissatisfaction. For satisfied customers, future actions include repeat purchases, customer loyalty, and positive word-of-mouth communications. For dissatisfied customers, future actions include switching vendors and negative word-of-mouth communications.

7. *Discuss how service quality is measured.* In the process of evaluating service quality, customers will compare the service they received to what they expected along the five dimensions of tangibles, reliability, responsiveness, assurance, and empathy. Using this method of measuring service quality, companies can ask consumers about their expectations prior to the service and, subsequently, ask the same series of questions after the service. Subtracting the two scores will give them a gap score for each dimension, as well as for the overall service. An alternative method is to ask customers to evaluate the service along the five dimensions as it relates to what they expected. Instead of using a gap analysis to measure service quality, a company can use internal measures such as the number of lost baggage claims or percentage of on-time deliveries.

8. *Describe an effective service recovery process.* A successful service recovery program is designed to overcome service failures and diminish the negative impact of the original poor or failed service. The more quickly a service problem is handled, the more likely the customer can be recovered and will purchase from the firm again. Employees should be trained to defuse the customer's anger as quickly and tactfully as possible. Normally, all this requires is attentive listening, admitting that the firm made a mistake, and acknowledging that the customer has a right to feel annoyed. Once this is accomplished, it is time for the resolution stage. Many companies begin the resolution stage by asking the customer what the firm can do to correct the problem. Once the customer has made a suggestion, the service employee is then ready to negotiate a viable solution to the problem.

9. *Explain the importance of the customer value package and list the steps required to develop a customer value package.* Customers will patronize the service that offers the best value package of price, technical service quality, functional service quality, and firm image. To develop and manage a customer value package, services will need to (1) determine the relative weights customers place on each element of the value package, (2) determine the value package that will be offered, (3) develop business objectives and a mission statement that will incorporate the value package, (4) communicate the values to all company personnel, (5) develop plans to implement the value package, and (6) monitor the environment for changes in customer value weights.

Key Terms

assurance (p. 281)
attribution theory (p. 280)
blueprinting (p. 279)
consequence (p. 275)
customer value package (p. 284)
empathy (p. 281)
financial risk (p. 275)
functional service quality (p. 280)
gap theory (p. 281)
gross domestic product (GDP) (p. 262)
industrialization (p. 268)
inseparability (p. 264)
intangibility (p. 264)
involvement (p. 272)
opportunity risk (p. 275)
performance risk (p. 275)
perishability (p. 264)
physical risk (p. 276)
psychological risk (p. 275)
reliability (p. 281)
responsiveness (p. 281)
service distribution (p. 275)
service encounter (p. 277)
service failures (p. 283)
service recovery (p. 283)
social risk (p. 275)
tangibles (p. 281)
technical service quality (p. 280)
time-loss risk (p. 275)
uncertainty (p. 275)
variability (p. 264)

Discussion Questions

1. Do you own a digital camera? What percentage of your friends own a digital camera? Survey at least five individuals who have digital cameras. What do they do with the digital photos they take? Now that you've read the chapter-opening vignette, what types of service businesses do you foresee developing as a result of digital cameras?

2. The majority of new jobs in the future will be in the service sector. Using the Internet and an electronic database, locate articles that discuss future employment and the service sector. Will the service jobs in the future be primarily minimum-wage jobs at service businesses like restaurants, or will they be high-dollar jobs that require a college degree?

3. Select one item from the list of factors contributing to the growth of the service sector discussed in Section 9-2. Using the Internet and an electronic database, locate articles that discuss the factor selected. What types of service industries have benefited in the past, and what types of service industries will benefit in the future? What do you see in the future for the contributory factor you chose in terms of its impact on the service sector?

4. Read Marketing Illustration 9-1 about the current trends in dining out. Compare your eating-out habits with those of your parents and grandparents. What changes do you see among the three generations in terms of dining out, purchasing take-out, and eating at home? How has food that is purchased for home consumption changed?

5. For each of the following services, discuss the degree of intangibility, perishability, inseparability, and variability inherent in each service. Pick one service and discuss strategies for reducing the negative impact of each unique service characteristic.
   a. automobile repair service
   b. dentist
   c. photographer studio
   d. Chinese restaurant
   e. lawn service

6. Pick one of the following services. Discuss each factor of the pre-purchase phase and how it would impact your purchase decision.
   a. automobile repair service
   b. dentist
   c. photographer's studio
   d. Chinese restaurant
   e. lawn service

7. On your next dining-out experience, describe your service encounter experience. Discuss each element of the service encounter phase presented in Section 9-4b in terms of your experience. How did each element affect your evaluation of the service? In addition, read Marketing Illustration 9-2. Describe the tabletop environment at the restaurant you patronized. How did it impact your image of the restaurant and your evaluation of the service?

8. Identify a recent personal service failure situation in which the service was poor or not performed at all. Did you complain to anyone at the service? Why or why not? Have you told any of your friends, relatives, or others about the experience? How many have you told? Did the service make any attempt to make things right with you (i.e., use a service recovery process)? If so, describe the outcome. If not, what could the service have done to correct the situation?

9. Read Marketing Illustration 9-3. Pick two e-commerce sites that you have used in the past. Access each site and jot down what you like about the site in terms of building trust. Now access two new e-commerce sites you have never used before and evaluate each site in terms of building trust. What differences do you see? What website features do you connect with building trust?

10. Suppose you decide to purchase a year's membership at a fitness gym. What type of value package would you want? Describe how important each element of the customer value package would be to you. Locate three fitness centers or gyms in your area and evaluate them using your customer value package. Which facility would you choose? Why?

Review Questions

True or False

1. Since medical treatment of elderly patients requires special equipment and facilities, such a treatment cannot be characterized as a service.
2. Perishability is directly related to the demand for a particular service. Demand can be managed through advertising, special promotions, and pricing.
3. Variability is a unique characteristic naturally imbedded in most services.
4. Involvement refers to the level of mental and physical effort exerted by a consumer in selecting a good or service.
5. The service encounter is the actual interaction point between the customer and the service provider and consists only of tangible elements.
6. Gap theory measures the gap between customer expectations and customer evaluation of the service.
7. Alternatives to the gap analysis as a measure of service quality are internal measures performed by the company.
8. After service failure takes place, dissatisfied customers will be very reluctant to make another purchase from the same company.

Multiple Choice

9. What is the most critical group of factors that affect the pre-purchase phase?
   a. internal factors
   b. external factors
   c. firm-produced factors
   d. risk
10. The probability that a particular outcome will occur refers to which component of risk?
    a. uncertainty
    b. consequences
    c. opportunity
    d. performance
11. To ensure a positive service environment, many companies use the concept of blueprinting, which reveals
    a. every step in the purchase process.
    b. steps where the service is not performed in an efficient manner.
    c. how customers and service personnel interact in the environment.
    d. all of the above
12. In the post-purchase phase the customer evaluates the following components.
    a. technical service quality
    b. functional service quality
    c. financial benefits
    d. a and b
13. Negative word-of-mouth can be problematic: An unhappy customer is likely to share information regarding his or her bad experience with _____ people.
    a. 1–2
    b. 3–9
    c. 10–11
    d. 20 or more
14. The service staff's willingness to help customers and to provide prompt service is an example of
    a. validity.
    b. reliability.
    c. responsiveness.
    d. responsibility.
15. A customer value package is composed of
    a. price.
    b. company image.
    c. technical service quality and functional service quality.
    d. all of the above

Notes

1. Liz Parks, "Chains Draw Digital Customer, Grow Photo Share," *Drug Store News*, vol. 23, no. 18 (December 17, 2001): 77–78; Cliff Edwards, "No End in Sight to the Honeymoon with Digital," *Business Week* (January 10, 2005): 108; Joseph Tamowski, "Digital Photo Imaging: New Challenges, New Opportunities," *Progressive Grocer*, vol. 82 (August 1, 2003): 93–95.
2. *Department of Commerce, Bureau of Economic Analysis, BEA News Release* (February 28, 2002): 1–14; "Liberalizing Trade in Services," *CATO Journal*, vol. 19 (Winter 2000): 397–403.
3. "Service Industry to Grow in Share of China Economy," *Xinhua (China)* (January 8, 2004).
4. Daniel E. Hecker, "Occupational Employment Projections to 2012," *Monthly Labor Review*, vol. 127 (February 2004): 82.
5. Gene Koertz, "America's Jobs Are Changing," *Business Week* (January 24, 2000): 32; Jay M. Berman, "Industry Output and Employment Projections to 2012," *Monthly Labor Review*, vol. 127 (February 2004): 63.
6. David L. Kurtz and Kenneth E. Clow, *Services Marketing* (New York: John Wiley & Sons, 1998): 6.
7. Valarie A. Zeithaml, A. Parasuraman, and Leonard L. Berry, "Problems and Strategies in Services Marketing," *Journal of Marketing*, vol. 49 (1985): 33–46.
8. Joanna Stavins, "ATM Fees: Does Bank Size Matter?" *New England Economic Review* (January/February 2000): 13–25; Lisa Hochgraf, "Delivery Dance," *Credit Union Management*, vol. 22 (December 1999): 10–13; Sarah Rose, "The Best of the Web-Only Banks," *Money*, vol. 28 (July 1999): 125–127.
9. Eileen Colkin, "Citibank," *Information Week*, Issue 852 (August 27, 2001): 30–31.
10. Andy Taylor, "Driving Customer Satisfaction," *Harvard Business Review*, vol. 80 (July 2002): 24–25.
11. David L. Kurtz and Kenneth E. Clow, "Managing Consumer Expectations of Services," *Journal of Marketing Management*, Vol. 2 (Fall/Winter 1992–1993): 19–25.

12. Judith Lynne Zaichkowsky, "Measuring the Involvement Construct," *Journal of Consumer Research,* vol. 12 (December 1985): 341–352.
13. Keith B. Murray, "A Test of Services Marketing Theory: Consumer Information Acquisition Activities," *Journal of Marketing,* vol. 55 (January 1991): 10–25.
14. Ibid.
15. R. A. Bauer, "Consumer Behavior as Risk Taking," in *Dynamic Marketing for a Changing World,* ed. R. Hancock. (Chicago: American Marketing Association, 1960): 389–398.
16. Mary Jo Bitner, "Evaluating Service Encounters: The Effects of Physical Surroundings and Employee Responses," *Journal of Marketing,* vol. 54 (1990): 69–82.
17. G. Lynn Shostack, "Understanding Services through Blueprinting," in *Services Marketing and Management,* eds. T. Schwartz, D. Bowen, and S. Brown (Greenwich, CT: JAI Press, 1992): 75–90.
18. Caroline McDonald, "The Moments of Truth," *National Underwriter / Property & Casualty Risk & Benefits,* vol. 105 (July 9, 2001): 25.
19. Diane Halstead, Cornelia Droge, and M. Bixby Cooper, "Product Warranties and Postpurchase Service," *Journal of Services Marketing,* vol. 7, no. 1 (1993): 33–40; Mary Jo Bitner, "Evaluating Service Encounters: The Effects of Physical Surroundings and Employee Responses," *Journal of Marketing,* vol. 54 (1990): 69–82; William O. Bearden and Jesse E. Teel, "Selected Determinants of Consumer Satisfaction and Complaint Reports," *Journal of Marketing Research,* vol. 20 (February 1983): 21–28.
20. Christian Gronroos, *Service Management and Marketing* (Lexington, MA: Lexington Books, 1990): 37–39.
21. Valerie S. Folkes, Susan Koletsky, and John Graham, "A Field Study of Causal Inferences and Consumer Reaction: The View from the Airport," *Journal of Consumer Research,* vol. 13 (March 1985): 534–539.
22. David Lipton, "Now Hear This … Customer Complaints Are Not Bad if Viewed as Business-Building Occasions," *Nation's Restaurant News,* vol. 34 (August 29, 2000): 30–31.
23. John Disney, "Customer Satisfaction and Loyalty: The Critical Elements of Service Quality," *Total Quality Management,* vol. 10 (July 1999): S491–S497.
24. Barry Farber and Joyce Wycoff, "Customer Service: Evolution and Revolution," *Sales & Marketing Management* (May 1991): 44–48; 50–51.
25. A. Parasuraman, Valarie A. Zeithaml, and Leonard L. Berry, "SERVQUAL: A Multiple-Item Scale for Measuring Consumer Perceptions of Service Quality," *Journal of Retailing,* vol. 64 (Spring 1988): 12–40.
26. David L. Kurtz and Kenneth E. Clow, *Services Marketing* (New York: John Wiley & Sons, 1998): 400; Tor Wallin Andreassen, "From Disgust to Delight: Do Customers Hold a Grudge?" *Journal of Service Research,* vol. 4 (August 2001): 39–50.
27. Christ Woodyard, "Airlines Load Up on Self-Service Functions," *USA Today* (October 8, 2002): Money, 6b.
28. Joan O. Fredericks and James M. Salter, "Beyond Customer Satisfaction," *Management Review* (May 1995): 29–32.
29. Mokhtar Abdullah, Aamjad D. AlNasser, and Nooreha Husain, "Evaluating Functional Relationship Between Image, Customer Satisfaction and Customer Loyalty Using General Maximum Entropy," *Total Quality Management,* vol. 11 (July 2000): S826–S830.
30. Fredericks and Salter, "Beyond Customer Satisfaction," 29–32.

Case 9-1 First American Bank

Looking down his attendance list, Thomas Lauden, the Vice President of Marketing for First American Bank, checked off the names. Present were branch managers Brenda Neely and Charles Jones, Vice President of Retail Operations Kristen Hammersmith, Vice President of Consumer Loans Mingshing Liu, and marketing staff members Theresa Hanks and Ollie Jenkins. Lauden called this meeting to discuss the bank's marketing program. Because of declining profits and the emergence of two new banks in First American Bank's area, First American Bank's number of customers had actually declined for the first time in 30 years. Lauden began the meeting by presenting the financial statement for the past year for the 12 facilities in the First American Bank system. All but two had profits decline, and all but four had fewer customers.

Lauden continued by presenting data from the American Bankers Association, showing what customers value in a bank. Trust was at the top of the list, with 83 percent of the respondents indicating it was very important. Reasonable fees were second, competitive interest rates were third, convenience was fourth, financial strength fifth, and reputation sixth, followed by personal attention, up-to-date technology, investment expertise, and a wide range of products and services (see Figure 9-18).

Charles Jones was the first to speak. "We have no control over interest rates or fees really. Our fees are similar to those of other banks. So we can toss those out."

"I don't think we should toss them out if they are important," countered Theresa Hanks. "If they are important to customers, then we should discuss our fees in the marketing material."

"But what value is it if our fees are the same as those of every other bank? There is no value in promoting something that does not provide a competitive advantage for us or at least makes us stand out from the competition," Jones argued.

"I'm not so sure about that. Maybe our fees are the same and maybe our interest rates are the same, but how do people know that if we don't promote it?" Kristen Hammersmith interjected.

"So from this list, it would appear to me we ought to promote the idea of trust, that we have reasonable fees, competitive interest rates, convenience, and financial strength," Brenda Neely spoke up.

"But how do you promote trust? What can you say in an advertisement that conveys that message?" Jones asked.

Smiling, Lauden looked at Theresa Hanks and Ollie Jenkins as he replied, "That's what I pay my staff to figure out." Putting another slide on the overhead (see Figure 9-19), Lauden continued. "I think this slide is even more startling. When people were asked if their bank was committed to meeting their financial needs, look at the results. The younger the respondent, the less likely they were to agree. That means it's the younger generation that does not believe we are committed to meeting their financial needs."

"And they are our future customers," mused Kristen.

"The percentage of 24- to 35-year-olds is half of the percentage of retired people," Ollie pointed out. "In fact, the real problem appears to be the 24- to 45-year-old age group."

"Before we go any further," Lauden suggested, "let me show you the remaining two slides, which look at the overall percentages over time, since 1994 (see Figure 9-20). First is the statement that 'banks are committed to meeting your financial needs.' Notice that 31 percent strongly agreed in 1994, which dropped to a low of 17 percent in 1999, and is now up to 28 percent. For the statement that 'banks generally are objective about granting loans,' the percentage for strongly agree was 27 percent in 1994, which dropped to 19 percent in 1999, and is now at 21 percent."

"I thought we were doing a better job of granting loans to all of the different demographic groups," Mingshing Liu spoke. "But this information indicates that is not the perception."

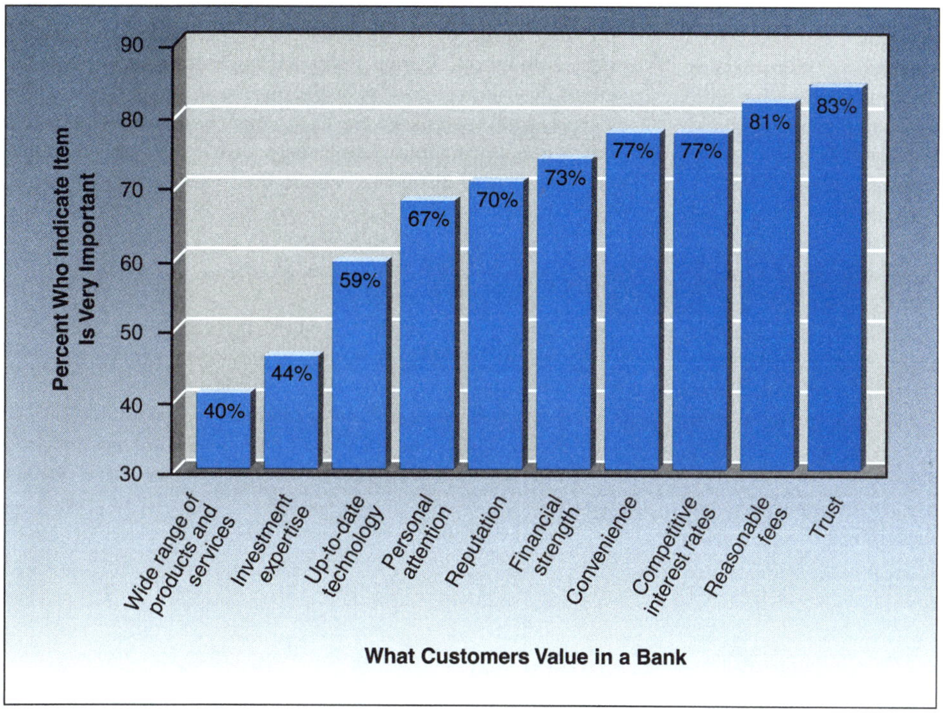

Figure 9-18
What Customers Value in a Bank

Source: "What Customers Value Most," *ABA Banking Journal*, vol. 93 (September 2001): 17.

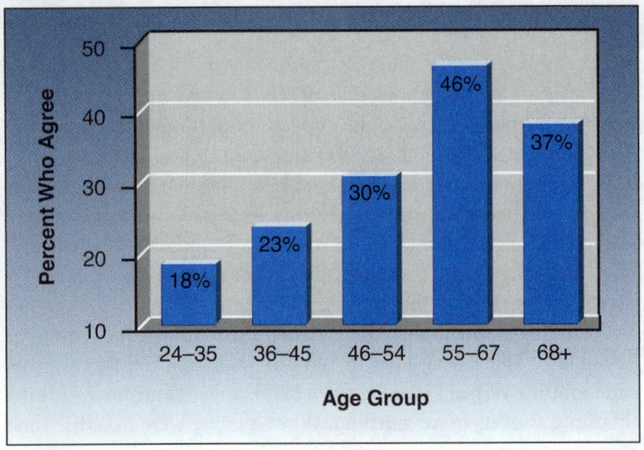

Figure 9-19
Banks' Commitment to Meeting Customers' Financial Needs by Age Category

Source: "Customer Views about Banks," ABA Banking Journal, vol. 93 (September 2001): 6–7.

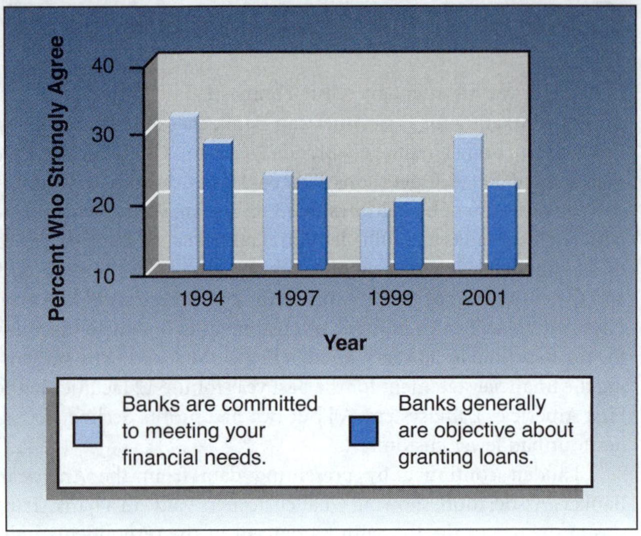

Figure 9-20
Perceptions about Banks

"Do you think we need to include more minorities in our marketing material?"

"That may be a good idea. Have we examined all of our marketing material to see how minorities, women, retirees, and even college students are represented?" Mingshing asked.

"We have, but not formally," Ollie replied.

"I don't think that is a real issue with us. What I do sense is that we are not attracting the under-30 individual, especially males. We seem to do better with females in that age category," Kristen pointed out.

"Do you think it's because they have higher expectations or maybe they are just harder to please? What do you think is the issue?" Liu asked.

Lauden responded, "I think they have options, especially Internet options that the older consumer does not have. I also believe they are not as interested in developing a personal relationship with their bank as are older consumers. Look who's in the lobby. Almost everyone out there is over 50. Look who's at the ATM, the drive-up window, and banking with us online. It's almost the opposite."

"I think Tom has a valid point," Charles spoke up. "If our goal is to reach the younger consumer, then we must promote the technology, the online access, the ATMs. That's what they want to see."

"And my experience from the loan area," Mingshing shared, "is that they are concerned about interest rates and reasonable fees. But before we go further on this, let me give you some information I found in my research. We are talking about gaining new customers, but shouldn't we be just as concerned about retaining our current customers? I read that it costs about six or seven times more money to get a new customer than to retain a current customer. I also read that the longer a customer stays with a company, the more profitable they become. They buy more and require less of our time. Here, let me show you some more interesting facts."

Moving to the overhead, Liu put up a slide with the following information:

- There is little correlation between satisfaction and retention.
- Sixty-five to 85 percent of defectors were satisfied with their previous service.
- For those dissatisfied, the primary reasons for leaving were failure to deliver a service as promised and being treated in an unprofessional manner.
- For those satisfied, the primary reasons for leaving were because of perceived better prices or a better value package from a competitor.

Liu continued, "As we develop our marketing plan, we need to think about our current customers and encourage them to stay with us. It makes no sense to spend our marketing budget trying to gain new customers if we are losing them as fast as we gain new ones. If the information I read is correct, we have to gain at least six new customers to just break even on the cost of losing one current customer."

"In the study you read, what was the key to retaining customers?"

"Contact with the bank."

"But how do you do that if 70 percent of our business is transacted at the ATM, drive-up, online, or by phone?" objected Hammersmith.

"That's the challenge," Liu countered.

"So, do we develop a marketing plan to seek new customers, or do we put our money into keeping our current customers?" Jenkins asked.

"Can we do both? Why does it have to be either or?" asked Neely.

Questions

1. How do the service characteristics of intangibility, perishability, inseparability, and variability fit into this discussion of marketing a bank?
2. Using all of the information presented in this case, what theme would you suggest for marketing of the First American Bank to the under-30 consumer? Why?
3. Can you target new customers and use the same set of ads to encourage current customers to stay with the bank? Why or why not?
4. What should the bank do about the customers they are losing?
5. If trust is an important value to bank customers, how can that message be conveyed to customers who bank primarily using the ATM, drive-up, or online facilities?

Sources: Thomas J. Healy, "Why You Should Retain Your Customers," *America's Community Banker,* vol. 8 (September 1999): 22–25; "What Customers Value Most," *ABA Banking Journal,* vol. 93 (September 2001): 17; "Customer Views about Banks," *ABA Banking Journal,* vol. 93 (September 2001): 6–7.

Case 9-2 Pasta House Company

When it comes to pasta, diners typically think of Olive Garden and Macaroni Grill, the two largest franchise operations in the Italian dine-in market segment. Other significant chain operations include Carrabba's Italian Grill, which is operated by Outback Steakhouse, and the Spaghetti Warehouse. Add to this mixture a host of local Italian restaurants in every neighborhood, and the result is a market segment that is becoming heavily saturated. This head-to-head competition will force some of the weaker operations into bankruptcy. Those that remain must find some way of remaining competitive.

For the national chains, Kathleen Pyle of Spaghetti Warehouse has made the observation that "people who frequent any kind of casual-dining chain are looking for consistency, value on the plate, and an acceptable flavor profile. They're looking for the reputation and reliability that a chain can deliver. Independents have a greater range in terms of pricing, and they can specialize for the market they are in."

While Spaghetti Warehouse has adopted a standardized approach offering the same menu and décor in all of its restaurants, the Olive Garden and Macaroni Grill have taken the opposite approach. Because of the large number of independents operating in each area, the Olive Garden and Macaroni Grill have chosen a strategy of tailoring their dishes to local tastes. They believe this will help them compete in each market more effectively.

In this mix of national chains and independents is a small chain of 28 restaurants called the Pasta House Co. Almost all of the restaurants are in or around St. Louis, Missouri. In fact, in one area of St. Louis, there are three restaurants within 10 minutes of each other. The goal of the Pasta House Co. is to saturate a market and become a part of the community through a program that J. Kim Tucci, President and founder of the Pasta House Co., calls "neighborhood marketing."

Neighborhood marketing includes a "Reading, Writing and Ravioli" program in the elementary schools. Co-sponsored with Coca-Cola, every child who reads a book and writes a report on it gets a free dish of spaghetti or ravioli with a salad and a Coca-Cola. Thus far, more than 400 schools and 4,000 teachers have participated with more than 6 million book reports submitted. To encourage teachers to participate, each participating teacher receives a 50 percent discount once a month on a meal at the restaurant.

For high school students, the Pasta House Co. sponsors art contests in which the student must use spaghetti in the art. Winners are selected from each high school, and prizes range from \$100 to \$1,000. For adults, the Pasta House Co. has a frequent-diner program, which now has more than 120,000 members. Members receive free spaghetti and a dessert on their birthday and for \$19.99 a special candlelit dinner for two on their anniversary. For every \$250 spent with the Pasta House Co., members receive a \$25 certificate that must be used at the location where they are members. This is to encourage local patronage and prevent competition among the various locations.

The stiff industry competition has made it difficult for the Pasta House Co. to expand beyond St. Louis. Two franchises located in Sacramento were forced to close because they were not profitable. An agreement with Tony Roma's in Mexico to open a Pasta House Co. facility expired because of financial instability in the country.

The Pasta House Co. built its success on offering great Italian food using a "neighborhood marketing" program. As it expands beyond St. Louis, it will encounter the same challenge faced by the Olive Garden, Macaroni Grill, and the Spaghetti Warehouse. While the Olive Garden and Macaroni Grill have modified each restaurant to fit the local community tastes, the Spaghetti Warehouse has not, believing that people want consistency and the same food prepared the same way in whatever Spaghetti Warehouse they patronize.

For the Pasta House, several tough decisions have to be made if it is going to be successful with its expansion program.

Questions

1. What has led to the success of the Pasta House Co.? What important facets of its program relate to the pre-purchase phase, the service encounter, and the post-purchase phase of the services purchase process presented in this chapter?
2. In terms of expanding beyond St. Louis, should the Pasta House Co. modify its approach for each community, or should it standardize its operation for all of its locations?
3. How important is the "neighborhood marketing" program to the success of Pasta House Co.? Should this program be replicated as part of the company's expansion plans? If so, how would it be done?
4. Because previous expansion attempts have failed, should the Pasta House Co. give up on expanding? Why or why not?
5. What customer value package do you believe the Pasta House Co. offers?

Sources: Bret Thorn, "Regional Powerhouse Chains: The Pasta House," *Nation's Restaurant News*, vol. 36 (January 28, 2002): 152–153; Jacqueline White Kochak, "Spaghetti Western," *Restaurant Business*, vol. 98 (April 15, 1999): 51–58.

10

Distribution Strategies

CHAPTER OBJECTIVES

1. Define distribution and identify the different channel functions and dimensions.
2. Identify issues related to channel management, such as channel organization, administration, and relationships.
3. Examine the different logistics functions.
4. Define wholesaling and identify the different functions of wholesaling.

CHAPTER OUTLINE

As a teenager, Kathleen King ended a fight with her father by telling him that, if she were living in the streets, she would survive. Her father challenged her to prove that she indeed could do so. Since then, Kathleen concentrated on developing Kathleen's Bake Shop, Inc., a successful bakery in fashionable Southampton, New York. Today, the bakery grosses just under $2 million from retailing cookies, pies, and other baked goods and wholesaling them to numerous New York area stores and beyond.

Kathleen grew up on a small farm just outside Southampton. As a young girl, she baked and sold cookies from the family's farm stand. After receiving a restaurant management degree, her parents asked her to move out of the house. She rented a bakery in downtown Southampton in 1979 for $350 a month and spent the winter perfecting her recipes and readying them for mass production. She then opened her doors when the summer crowd descended upon Southampton, and her all-natural (and high-cholesterol) cookies, pies, cakes, and other baked goods were an instant hit.

After a few years, Kathleen decided to follow her customers to Manhattan for the winter, where she eventually opened a bakery. However, her employees were twice held up at gunpoint, and once, thieves cut a hole in the store wall to enter. In 1989, she decided to focus her expansion efforts on wholesaling instead.

Today, around 75 percent of King's $1.5-million-a-year revenues come from wholesaling her goods to around 100 gourmet shops on Long Island, in New York City, and in other states. Gourmet shops are very popular, and most have an enticing bakery section (see Figure 10-1). She also closed a deal with a popular upscale grocery chain based in North Carolina—the Fresh Market. Among her numerous retail customers are the exclusive Balducci's and Canard & Co., and the very popular Amish Market in New York City, Sugar and Spice in Chappaqua, New York, and various gourmet shops and delis in New Jersey and Florida. Kathleen's Bake Shop is now named Tate's Bake Shop, in honor of her father. However, the products distributed still carry Kathleen's name. Her primary distributor is Bay View Distributing. And Kathleen has a popular cookbook on the market.[1]

10-1 Chapter Overview

In the chapter-opening vignette, Kathleen King attempted to open a bakery in Manhattan. The challenges she most likely encountered at the time were not limited to crime: Manhattan rents are exorbitant, and competition is fierce. Kathleen quickly realized that she

Figure 10-1
Gourmet shops often have attractive bakery displays, such as this one in Holland.

could have a presence in Manhattan and beyond, from Westchester to New Jersey, and all the way to North and South Carolina using a distribution channel. Kathleen's Bake Shop took on the role of manufacturer or producer. She sold her baked goods through a wholesaler, Bay View Distributing, to gourmet retailers in her target market. And she sold them directly to 17 Fresh Market gourmet grocery stores in North and South Carolina.

This chapter addresses issues related to distribution channels, physical distribution, and logistics, focusing on distributors and on the facilitators of the distribution process. Section 10-2 addresses the need for distribution channels and the different channel functions. Section 10-3 looks at the different channel dimensions, such as direct and indirect channels, channel length and width, and the intensity of distribution. Section 10-4 addresses channel management—in particular, channel organization and administration, management of conflict and power in the channel, and the modalities for establishing successful channel relationships. Section 10-5 addresses the different logistics functions, such as transportation, warehousing, inventory control, and order processing. Section 10-6 addresses the different categories of full-service and limited-service wholesalers and examines the different types of agents and brokers.

10-2 Distribution and the Channel Functions

Marketing managers understand that the planning of product distribution is among the most important tasks they need to undertake in order to ensure the market success of their products. **Distribution planning** is defined as the planning of the physical movement of products from the producer to individual or organizational consumers, and the transfer of ownership and risk. It involves transportation, warehousing, and all the exchanges taking place at each channel level. Distribution planning involves establishing the **channels of distribution,** defined as the totality of organizations and individuals involved in the distribution process who take title to or assist in the transferring of title in the distribution process from the producer to the individual or organizational consumer. The organizations or individuals involved in the distribution process are known as **intermediaries** (or **middlemen,** or **channel members**). The decision also involves identifying and managing other intermediaries involved in distribution (i.e., other entities that facilitate the distribution process, such as transportation firms, freight forwarders, and customs brokers for international distribution, for example).

The goal of intermediaries is to offer support for the activities involved in delivering products for the enhanced benefit of the customer. In that sense, intermediaries are active participants in the **value chain** (or **supply chain**), the chain of activities performed in the process of developing, producing, marketing, delivering, and servicing a product for the benefit of the customer. Intermediaries are components of the **value delivery chain,** which is composed of all the participants involved in the value chain. Today, many firms partner not just with the channel members or intermediaries, but also with their suppliers in order to provide optimal efficiencies that enhance profits, as well as customer benefits. Marketing Illustration 10-1 offers insights into successful supplier partnerships and addresses the drivers of an adaptive supply chain.

Using intermediaries entails relinquishing control over the marketing mix to a channel member. It also means paying for the channel member's services. Why do manufacturers use distributors to sell their products? Why do they not handle distribution themselves? The answer is that distributors cut down on the cost of distribution, while conveniently providing the desired assortment to consumers at a lower price. The following are the advantages of using intermediaries:

- *Intermediaries deliver convenience to consumers.* Intermediaries help distribute the product to a location that is convenient to the consumer.
- *Intermediaries carry and store the product.* Intermediaries distribute the product down the channel of distribution, and they store it in warehouses.

Distribution planning: The planning of the physical movement of products from the producer to individual or organizational consumers, and the transfer of ownership and risk; it involves transportation, warehousing, and all the exchanges taking place at each channel level.

Channels of distribution: The totality of organizations and individuals involved in the distribution process who take title to or assist in the transferring of title in the distribution process from the producer to the individual or organizational consumer.

Intermediaries (or **middlemen,** or **channel members):** The organizations or individuals involved in the distribution process.

Value chain (or supply chain): The chain of activities performed in the process of developing, producing, marketing, delivering, and servicing a product for the benefit of the customer.

Value delivery chain: The participants involved in the value chain.

Marketing Illustration 10-1

Adaptive Supply Chains

Close customer-supplier relationships trim costs and improve quality by disseminating quality-enhancing techniques across company boundaries and enlisting each supplier's technological expertise in design and manufacturing. Interdependency boosts speed, which is essential for increasingly faster product cycles. For example, in the automotive industry, building to order enables manufacturing to better respond to market conditions. The time lost between changes in customer preferences and in the firms' product mix disappears, and customer demand can be both anticipated and shaped by the sales system. Moreover, such a supply chain must be able to meet seasonal changes in consumer demand and the demand volatility for a particular product.

Value chain relationships are like a marriage. To illustrate, on a Saturday, Silicon Graphics executive Greg Podshadley called Rudy Gassner, a VP at AMP, an electrical and electronic connectors' manufacturer, at home to solicit his help. A connector made by an AMP competitor threatened product quality, shutting down the production line. Gassner sent his sales team to the distribution center. They found the connectors and even learned to use a complicated forklift to load the parts. Silicon Graphics soldered them onto circuit boards in California the next day. Gassner did this with zero paperwork, did not charge Silicon a premium for the service, and treated this as "an IOU to collect sometime."

Value chains are not just more cost efficient; they are also more adaptable. Just after September 11, 2001, the government contacted two global pharmaceutical companies about sending a large supply of antibiotics to New York. One company determined the feasibility of this request in 20 minutes and got the job. The other is currently attempting to overhaul its supply chain management process in order to ensure it does not miss out on such opportunities in the future.

What are the drivers of adaptive supply chains? (See Figure 1.)

Source: Ben Waller, "Market Responsive Manufacturing for the Automotive Supply Chain," *Journal of Manufacturing Technology Management*, vol. 15, no. 1 (2004): 10.

Figure 1
Drivers of Adaptive Supply Chains

Sources: Myron Magnet, "The New Golden Rule of Business," *Fortune*, vol. 129, no. 4 (February 21, 1994): 60–64; *2002 Report on Trends and Issues in Logistics and Transportation*, Cap Gemini Ernst & Young, Georgia Southern University.

INTERACTIVE FIGURE

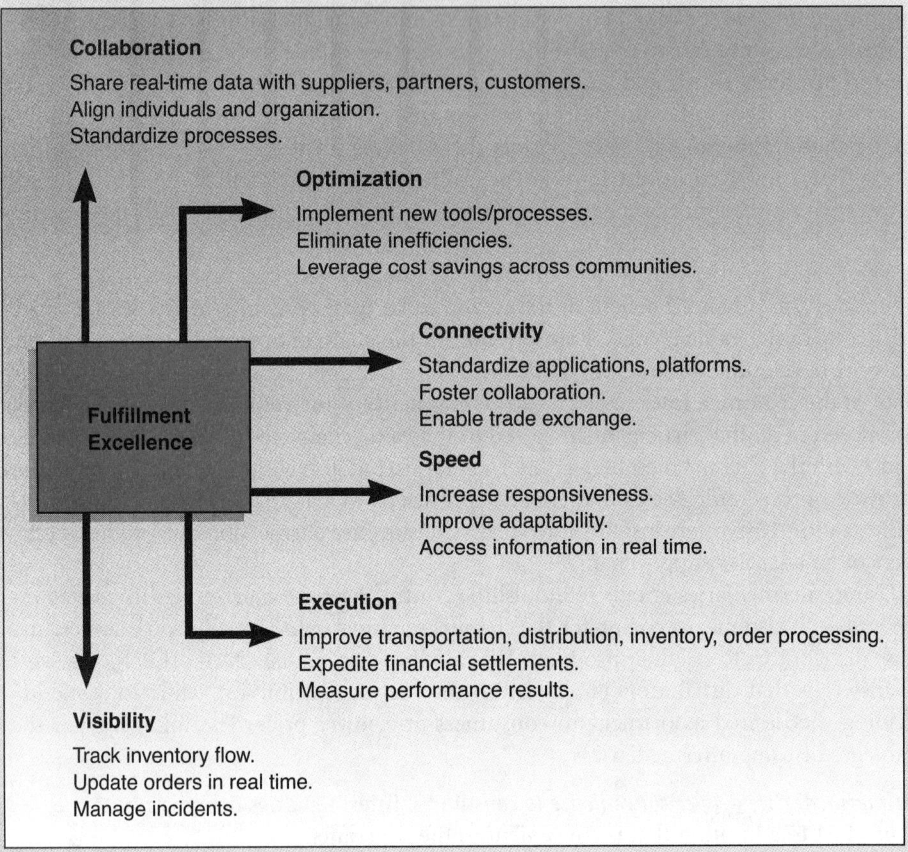

- *Intermediaries assume risk in the delivery process.* Intermediaries typically carry not just the title to the product, but also the risk for the product while it is in their possession, or even beyond.
- *Intermediaries reduce the cost of the product delivery process.* They reduce the number of transactions needed to deliver the product to the final consumer. Figure 10-2 illustrates how using a wholesaler can reduce the number of transactions, cutting down on the cost of transportation and handling. In the first scenario, there is no wholesaler; it would take 25 transactions to create an assortment of goods from each of the five manufacturers for each of the five retailers. Introducing a middleman in the second scenario reduces the number of transactions to 10. That, in fact, means fewer shipments are loaded, unloaded, and insured; fewer trucks are used in the transportation of the goods; and less paperwork is filled out by the firms.
- *Intermediaries provide an assortment for retailers and, ultimately, for consumers.* That is, the wholesaler takes the product from different manufacturers of narrow assortments and delivers it to retailers that can, as a result, provide a wider assortment to consumers.

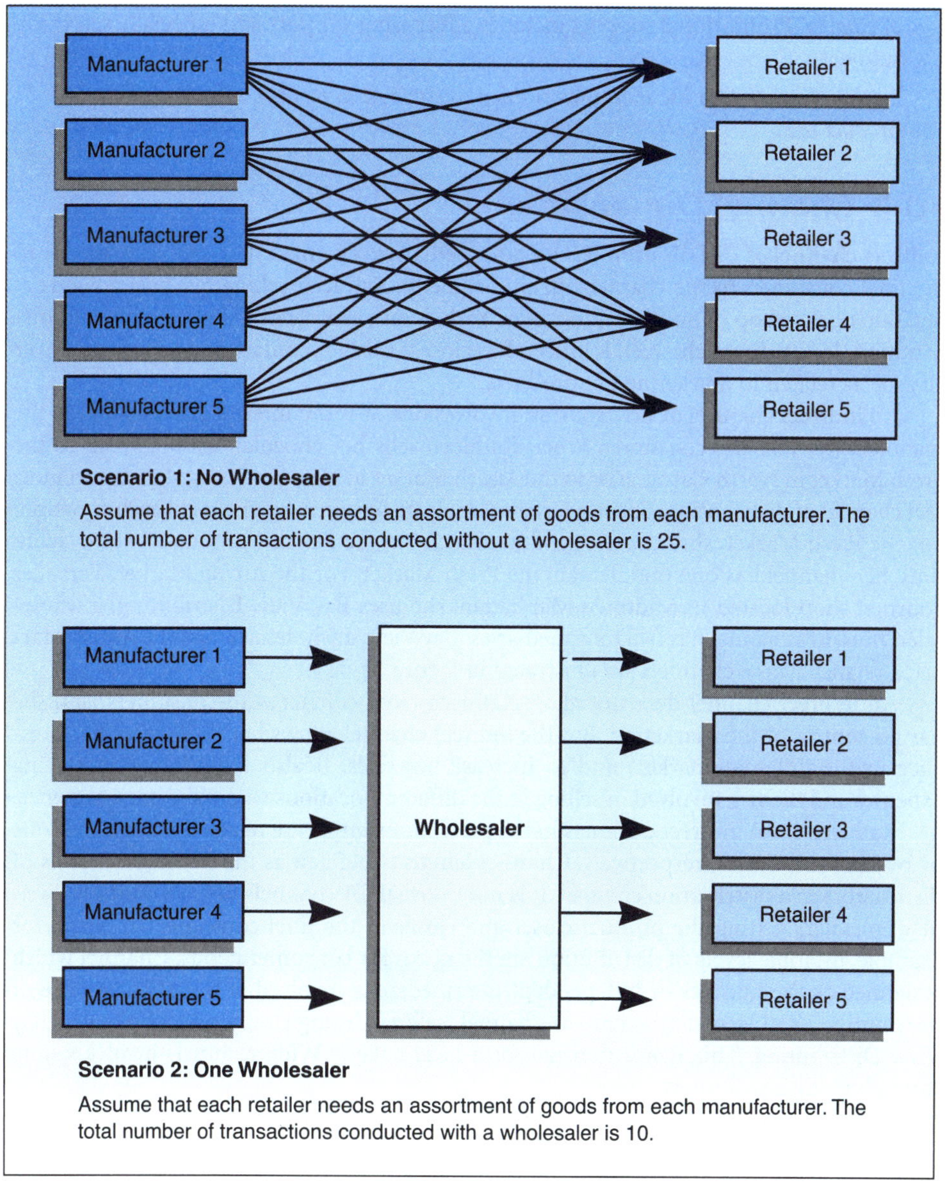

Figure 10-2
The Role of the Wholesaler in Reducing the Number of Transactions

INTERACTIVE FIGURE

- *Intermediaries buy products in bulk from manufacturers, at a discount.* By purchasing larger quantities on behalf of multiple retailers, the wholesaler can negotiate a discount for buying the product in bulk from each individual manufacturer. Then the middleman breaks bulk to sell smaller quantities to retailers.
- *Intermediaries conduct research for the manufacturer and the channel.* Intermediaries are close to retailers and have access to information about changing consumer needs and behavior. They offer important input into the product design, performance, pricing, and promotion. Intermediaries also identify prospective buyers.
- *Intermediaries provide credit to other channel members or to consumers.* This facilitates transactions. Often, retailers cannot pay wholesalers until the final sale is made; offering the option to pay for the product 30 days or longer after delivery increases the chances that the retailer will carry the product.
- *Intermediaries often provide service contracts.* Intermediaries handle many of the services consumers purchase along with the final product. In addition to service contracts, they also provide warranties for the products they carry if the manufacturer does not offer them.
- *Intermediaries often pay for part of the promotional expenditures of the manufacturer or retailer.* Promotional support includes advertising support and especially sales support.
- *Intermediaries often use their own trained salespeople to train retailers' sales staff on product use.*

10-3 Channel Dimensions

Direct channel of distribution: A channel that has no intermediaries; the manufacturer sells directly to the final consumer.

Indirect channel of distribution: A channel that involves one or more intermediaries between the manufacturer and the consumer.

Channel length: The number of levels of distributors in a distribution channel.

Channel width: The number of independent intermediaries involved at a particular stage of distribution.

Intensive distribution: A strategy that has as its purpose full market coverage, making the product available to all target consumers when and where consumers want them.

A **direct channel of distribution** has no intermediaries: The manufacturer sells directly to the final consumer. In the chapter-opening vignette, Kathleen selling her baked goods at her Tate's Bake Shop in Southampton, New York, is an example of a direct channel of distribution. In the direct channel, Kathleen has close customer contact and full control over all aspects related to marketing her products.

An **indirect channel of distribution** involves one or more intermediaries between the manufacturer and the consumer. When Kathleen sells her chocolate chip cookies to the Fresh Market in North Carolina or to the Amish Market in New York City, she uses an indirect channel of distribution. She has different intermediary arrangements in each situation. For the Fresh Market, she sells the product directly to the North Carolina 17-store chain; thus, her channel has one middleman, the Fresh Market. For the Amish Market, a smaller gourmet shop located in Midtown Manhattan, she uses Bay View Distributing, a wholesaler; thus, her channel has two intermediaries: Bay View, a wholesaler, and the Amish Market, a retailer. These channels are illustrated in Figure 10-3.

An indirect channel does not allow Kathleen close contact with consumers, and she has no control of the marketing. But the indirect channel allows her to increase her presence in the different markets and to increase her sales. It also reduces her marketing expenses and the risk involved in selling in the different locations where she has a presence.

Kathleen's two indirect channels in the previous example are relatively short, with one or two intermediaries, respectively. **Channel length** is defined as the number of levels of distributors in a distribution channel. It is not unusual for channels to have multiple levels of wholesalers getting the product closer and closer to the final consumer. In Japan, for example, multiple levels of distribution are the norm for consumer goods. **Channel width** is defined as the number of independent intermediaries involved at a particular stage of distribution. Kathleen uses a narrow channel, selling through only one wholesaler, Bay View Distributing. This is not unusual for a local bakery. Wide channels involve selling through many distributors.

In addition to channel length, companies need to decide on the number of intermediaries to use at each level of distribution. An **intensive distribution** strategy has as its pur-

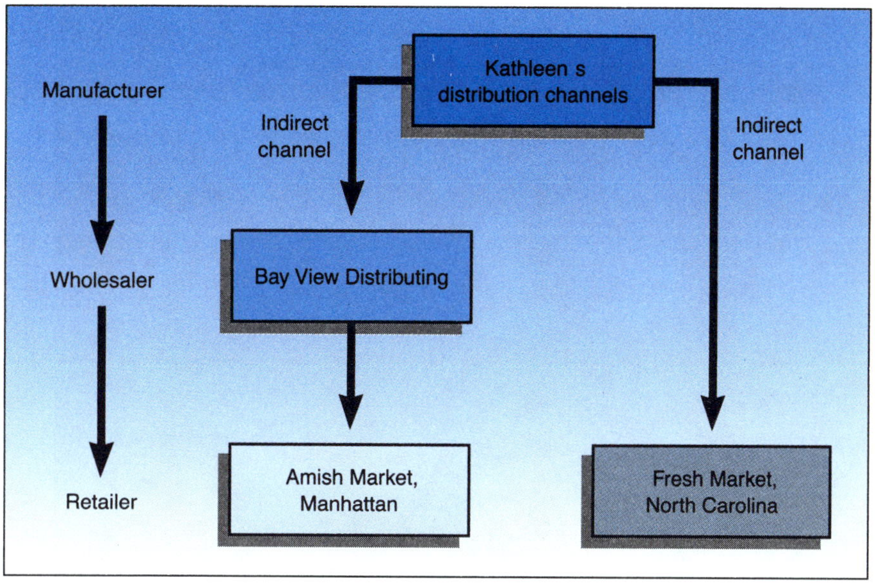

Figure 10-3
Two of Kathleen's Indirect Distribution Channels
Arrows indicate physical flow of goods and the flow of ownership.

INTERACTIVE FIGURE

pose full market coverage, making the product available to all target consumers when and where they want it. This type of distribution aims at achieving high total sales but is able to recover only low per-unit profits due to channel expenses. Staples, such as milk, colas, beer, toothpaste, and snacks, are distributed using an intensive distribution strategy (see Figure 10-4).

An **exclusive distribution** strategy has as a goal a high control of the intermediaries handling the product and thus of the marketing strategy by limiting their number to just one or two per geographic area. This type of distribution is intended to create prestige for the company's products and strong distributor support and service in return for high per-unit profit. Designer clothes, such as Prada, Escada, and Armani, and sleek electronics, such as Bang & Olufsen (www.bang-olufsen.com), are distributed to retailers using an exclusive distribution strategy.

Exclusive distribution: A strategy that has as a goal a high control of the intermediaries handling the product, and thus of the marketing strategy, by limiting them to just one or two per geographic area.

A **selective distribution** strategy lies in the middle between the two in terms of control, service, and profits. Firms using a selective distribution strategy have some control over the marketing strategy by limiting distribution to a select group of resellers in each area; at the same time, the company has a reasonable sales volume and profits (see Figure 10-5 on page 303). Kathleen uses a selective distribution strategy. Her goods are sold at a number of gourmet shops in Manhattan, but not at supermarkets such as D'Agostino's, nor even at Food Emporium, which is a bridge between a gourmet shop and a supermarket. However, her distribution is not restricted to Balducci's, a more exclusive gourmet shop where her goods are available.

Selective distribution: A strategy whereby firms have some control over the marketing strategy by limiting distribution to a select group of resellers in each area, while, at the same time, the company can achieve a reasonable sales volume and profits.

10-4 Channel Management

Numerous aspects of channel management need to be considered. First, the structure of the channel of distribution is important. Here, decisions must be made with regard to channel organization and administration, as well as channel strategies, such as vertical or horizontal integration. Second, channel relationships must be examined. The use of power in the channel and conflict management constitute important channel dynamics that can lead to the success or failure of the channel.

10-4a Channel Organization and Administration

A channel of distribution consists of one or more independent intermediaries, in which each is a separate entity whose goal, in a vacuum, would be resource or profit maximization. Taking the separate goals of each channel member into account, the outcome, within

Figure 10-4
The milk industry uses an intensive distribution strategy.

Source: Courtesy of Bozell Worldwide, Inc. as agent for the National Fluid Milk Processor Promotion Board.

Contractual channel arrangement: A contract between intermediaries that defines all the tasks that each channel member must perform with regard to production, delivery strategy and terms of sale, territorial rights, promotional support, the price policies of each intermediary, and contract length.

Administered channel arrangement: An arrangement between intermediaries such that a dominant member of the distribution channel in terms of size, expertise, or influence coordinates the tasks of each member in the channel.

Channel captain: The dominant member of a channel of distribution.

this narrow perspective, would be high margins at each level of distribution, minimal service, and, ultimately, prices that customers are unwilling to pay and service levels that customers are going to be dissatisfied with. The entire value chain needs to consider the different interests with a marketing perspective in mind: addressing the needs of the consumer. In this sense, a mechanism must exist that assigns marketing responsibilities and addresses channel-wide strategic objectives.

Channels of distribution adopting a **contractual channel arrangement** spell out in a contract all the tasks that must be performed by each channel member with regard to production, delivery strategy, terms of sale, territorial rights, promotional support, the price policies of each intermediary, and contract length.

Channels adopting an **administered channel arrangement** have a dominant member of the distribution channel in terms of size, expertise, or influence who coordinates the tasks of each channel member. The dominant member of the channel, known as the **channel captain,** can be at any level of the distribution channel. A manufacturer with a strong brand pull, such as Coca-Cola or Colgate-Palmolive, could be the channel administrator. Many powerful wholesalers, such as Supervalu, dealing with smaller manufacturers or retailers can act as channel captains. Influential retail chains, such as Wal-Mart and Home Depot, can take on the role of channel captain. Hybrid structures, such as Costco, a warehouse club that sells both to final consumers and resellers, also can administer the distribution channel.

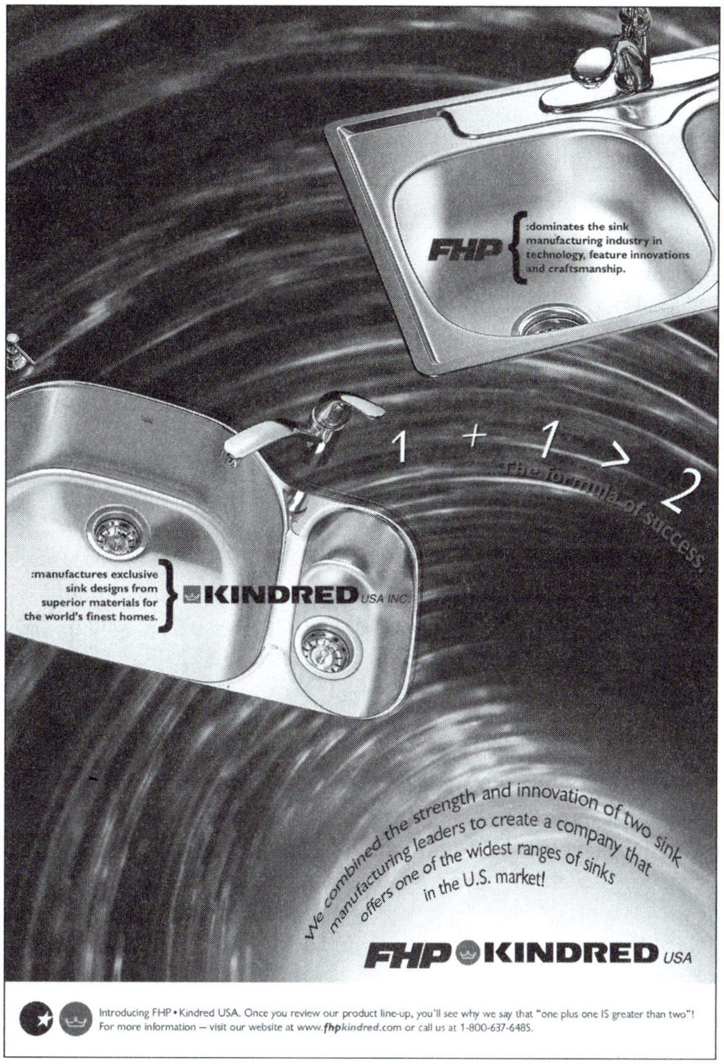

Figure 10-5
FHP Kindred uses a selective distribution strategy.

Source: Sample print advertisement courtesy of The Miles Agency and Alliance One Advertising, Inc.

A **dual channel of distribution** is employed by firms that use two different channels. For example, Kathleen uses a dual channel of distribution, selling (1) through a wholesaler to gourmet shops and (2) to the Fresh Market retail chain. In another example, the Donna Karan collection is distributed exclusively, whereas her bridge brand, DKNY, is distributed selectively. It is thus likely that two different channels are used to distribute the two brands: an exclusive distribution channel for the Donna Karan collection and a selective distribution channel for the DKNY brand.

A firm can also use a **multichannel distribution system**, also known as a **hybrid marketing channel.** Before the Internet, multichannel marketing was popular primarily in business-to-business environments. Today, the Internet has completely transformed direct marketing and companies' relationships with customers. By pairing email and the Internet with offline media, marketers can develop compelling campaigns that offer customers important advantages.[2] With multiple channels, customers have an expanding menu of purchase and communication options.

Channel members can strengthen their position in the channel through **vertical integration,** by acquiring or merging with an intermediary in the channel—a supplier or a buyer. Such integration offers the channel member more control in the channel. For example, Zara, a popular clothing retailer, makes more than half of its clothes in-house, rather than relying on a network of disparate and often slow-moving suppliers. Its competitor, H&M (Hennes & Mauritz), however, buys clothes from more than 900 firms.

Dual channel of distribution: The use of two or more channels of distribution to appeal to different markets.

Multichannel distribution system (or **hybrid marketing channel**)**:** The use of multiple (more than two) channels of distribution, thus offering customers multiple purchase and communication options.

Hybrid marketing channel (or **multichannel distribution system**)**:** The use of multiple (more than two) channels of distribution, thus offering customers multiple purchase and communication options.

Vertical integration: The acquisition or merger with an intermediary in the channel that is either a supplier or a buyer.

Starting with basic fabric dyeing, almost all of Zara's clothes take shape in a design-and-manufacturing center in Spain, with the sewing done by seamstresses from 400 local cooperatives. This setup allows designers to closely follow which items are in demand. They talk daily to store managers to discover which items are selling, and on the basis of this real-time data, they place their orders and ship the inventory directly to the stores twice a week. This procedure eliminates the need for warehouses and for keeping large inventories.[3]

Horizontal integration: An acquisition or merger with an intermediary at the same level in the distribution channel.

Vertical marketing systems (VMS): Intermediary marketing systems which consist of manufacturers, wholesalers, and retailers in the same channel who have partial VMS ownership acting as a unified whole.

Another strategy that increases intermediary strength in the market is **horizontal integration,** which would involve an acquisition or merger at the same level in the distribution channel. Examples of horizontal integration would be a manufacturer buying another manufacturer, a wholesaler acquiring another wholesaler at the same level in the distribution chain, or a retailer purchasing another retailer. This strategy, however, may trigger antitrust investigations and create long-term problems for the firms involved.

One of the most important developments in distribution for the past two decades has been the emergence of **vertical marketing systems (VMS),** which consist of manufacturers, wholesalers, and retailers in the same channel acting as a unified whole. Vertical marketing systems typically involve partial ownership. In an example, Ukrop's Super Markets, Inc. was a founding member of Richfood, a regional mid-Atlantic distributor; Supervalu bought Richfood in a successful horizontal integration bid, and Ukrop's owns a proportionately smaller stake in Supervalu. Vertical marketing systems benefit from greater coordination achieved through common ownership.

Horizontal marketing systems (HMS): Intermediaries at the same level of the distribution channel pooling resources and achieving partial ownership of the system, achieving economies of scale, and playing on their individual strengths.

Trading companies: Complex marketing systems that specialize in providing intermediary service and reducing risk through extensive information channels and financial assistance.

Keiretsus: Japanese families of firms with interlocking stakes in one another.

Pull strategy: A strategy whereby the manufacturer first focuses on consumer demand through extensive promotion, expecting that consumers will request the brand through the channel.

Push strategy: A strategy that focuses on intermediaries, providing the necessary incentives for them to cooperate in selling the product to the final consumer.

Horizontal marketing systems (HMS) consist of intermediaries at the same level of the distribution channel pooling resources and achieving economies of scale, thereby playing on their individual strengths. In a manufacturing example, Porsche is working with Harley-Davidson, the U.S. motorcycle icon, to help it develop low-noise, low-emissions motorcycles. Most recently, Porsche is helping Harley-Davidson develop its water-cooled Revolution engine.[4] At the wholesale level, Mitsui and Mitsubishi, large integrated trading companies, are using their bottling and distribution systems to bottle and distribute all Coca-Cola products in Japan. **Trading companies** are complex marketing systems specializing in providing intermediary services, risk reduction through extensive information channels, and financial assistance. Trading companies have been very successful in Japan and South Korea. Japanese trading companies have operations all around the world, ranging from finance to distribution, technology, mining, oil and gas exploration, and information. They act as intermediaries for half of Japan's exports and two-thirds of its imports. Currently, they are changing from pure traders to more financially sophisticated investment holding companies.[5] The biggest and the best of the traders are members of **keiretsus,** which are families of firms with interlocking stakes in one another. Here, the trading companies' role is to act as the eyes and ears of the whole group, spotting business trends, market gaps, and investment opportunities.[6] The top trading companies in Japan are Itochu Corp., Sumitomo, Marubeni, Mitsui, and Mitsubishi.[7]

10-4b Channel Relationships: Conflict and Power

Intermediaries sometimes disagree on channel goals, on their roles in the channel of distribution, and on the channel rewards. Channel members, for example, challenge each other directly through the strategies they use. Chapter 8, "Product Strategies," offered an illustration of one type of channel conflict: the battle of the brands, defined as a conflict between manufacturers and resellers to promote their own brands. Retailers, for example, are aggressively promoting their own brands, placing them side-by-side with manufacturers' brands, offering consumers the choice to purchase the retailer's brand at a considerably lower price.

Another area of conflict is the manufacturer's use of a **pull strategy,** whereby the manufacturer first focuses on consumer demand through extensive promotion, expecting that consumers will request the brand through the channel. The alternative, a **push strategy,** focuses on intermediaries, providing the necessary incentives for them to cooperate in marketing the product to the final consumer. Manufacturers typically use both strategies because using only a pull strategy would create conflict in the distribution channels.

Channel conflict can be reduced through the use of **relationship marketing,** the development of marketing strategies aimed at enhancing relationships in the channel. Businesses find that most of their sales are attributed to repeat business and that only one-fifth of their sales are new accounts. It is thus important to ensure that existing relationships are appropriately nurtured, ensuring customer retention.

Channel conflict can also be reduced through the appropriate use of power. **Reward power** refers to power over the channel members based on anticipation of special privileges, such as financial rewards for engaging in a particular desirable behavior. Reward power in the form of slotting fees offered by the manufacturer to the retailer will be exerted only as long as the slotting fees are paid. When the manufacturer ceases to pay slotting fees, the products will be removed from the retailer's shelf, unless other types of power exist concurrently. **Coercive power** refers to power over channel members based on the ability of one or more intermediaries to remove privileges for noncompliance. An example of coercive power involves the threat of elimination from the channel of distribution for noncompliance with a particular channel policy. Reward power and coercive power are less persuasive than the other forms of power because when the reward or coercion factors are removed, channel members' behavior reverts to one that is focused on individual goals.

Expert power refers to power over the other channel members based on experience and knowledge that a channel member possesses. For example, a wholesaler might have competent product maintenance staff capable of enhancing the reputation of the manufacturer's product and of enhancing satisfaction with the retailer due to their expert response. **Referent power** is among the most persuasive forms of power. It refers to power over the other channel members based on the close match in terms of values and objectives shared by members of the channel. Understanding that each channel member is acting in order to best serve final consumers at a fair profit can offer referent power to each member of the channel. **Legitimate power** refers to power over the other channel members by virtue of an intermediary's status or position in the channel. A channel captain has legitimate power over the other channel members by virtue of its position and role in the channel. Table 10-1 reviews the various forms of channel power.

Relationship marketing: The development of marketing strategies aimed at enhancing relationships in the channel.

Reward power: Power over the channel members based on an anticipation of special privileges, such as a financial reward for conducting a particular behavior.

Coercive power: Power over channel members based on the ability of one or more intermediaries to remove privileges for noncompliance.

Expert power: Power over the other channel members based on experience and knowledge that a channel member possesses.

Referent power: Power over the other channel members based on the close match in terms of values and objectives that members of the channel share.

Legitimate power: Power over the other channel members by virtue of an intermediary's status or position in the firm.

10-4c Establishing Successful Channel Relationships

In the process of setting up a firm's distribution activity in the target market, the firm will need to set up successful channel relationships. Particularly successful channel relationships are characterized by an atmosphere of openness between the customer and the

TABLE 10-1

Channel Power

Type of Power	Definition
Reward power	Power over the channel members based on the anticipation of special privileges
Coercive power	Power over channel members based on the ability of one or more intermediaries to remove privileges for noncompliance
Expert power	Power over the other channel members based on experience and knowledge that a channel member possesses
Referent power	Power over the other channel members based on the close match in terms of values and objectives that members of the channel share
Legitimate power	Power over the other channel members by virtue of an intermediary's status or position in the channel

Marketing Illustration 10-2

Unauthorized Marketing Channels

Assume that you can buy national brand-name cigarettes (Camel, Marlboro) in an outlet in Virginia for $17 a carton. Cigarette distributors in this state can sell the product at this low price because of the low, 2.5-cents-a-pack excise tax. In comparison, Washington State charges a $1.42-a-pack excise tax, amounting to $14.20 for a carton of cigarettes. If a retailer in Washington State were to charge $16 per carton, then it would be able to keep $2.80, which would not even cover the cost of the cigarettes. This discrepancy between a low-price market and high-price market—this time due to tax policy—creates opportunities for an unauthorized marketing channel. An enterprising individual could purchase cigarettes in Virginia for $17 and sell them in Washington State for $20 per carton, still well below cigarette prices in that market, and make a nice profit. This new, unauthorized retailer would hurt sales for the authorized channel.

A *gray market* refers to products purchased in a low-price market and diverted to other markets by means of a distribution system not authorized by the manufacturer. A low-price market is one where the products can be purchased for a lower price either because the company is in a competitive situation in which it must lower the price or because local taxes do not significantly increase the price of the products. Most often, however, gray market goods come from authorized dealers who get rid of excess inventory, selling the products to discounters.

In another example, the Netherlands is a low-price market for Similac, an infant formula manufactured by Abbott Laboratories. A 900-gram can of Similac sells for 5 euros, or about $7. A can of Similac weighing 850 grams (50 grams less than the can sold in the Netherlands) sells for about $22 in the United States. The reasons why Abbott Laboratories engages in the differential pricing of Similac may be numerous. First, it might be attempting to penetrate the market: Although the product is well known in the United States, it is not popular at all in Europe. Second, it is priced just less than the other local competing products. The company might be using a penetration-pricing strategy. Third, the Dutch government might have required the company to sell at a low price (unlikely, but possible). Consequently, the Netherlands constitutes a low-price market for Similac. If an entrepreneur decided to bring Similac from the Netherlands to sell it in the United States, he or she would be engaging in parallel imports and would have to sell the product on a gray market not authorized by the manufacturer.

provider, mutual trust, and a clear line of communication. The following steps are essential to successful channel relationships:[8]

1. Establish objectives and selection criteria. Because choosing a channel partner is a long-term decision, it is important to choose a partner that is likely to be a good match.
2. Identify qualified providers, with the help of consultants.
3. Express needs and wants. Here, issues such as integrating computer systems with that of the channel partner and other information-sharing needs should be expressed.
4. Evaluate bidders and select the partner, preferably after a site visit and interview.
5. Develop an integration plan. Because channel relationships involve many players, it is important to engage in system-wide integration.
6. Create a win-win relationship, based on continuous communication.
7. Measure and analyze performance.
8. Redefine the channel and individual goals and objectives.

Marketing managers must be aware of the fact that, even if the channel is a harmonious, conflict-free entity, challenges still threaten the stability of the channel. One such challenge is gray marketing, addressed in Marketing Illustration 10-2.

Logistics (or **physical distribution):** All the activities involved in the physical flow and storage of materials, semifinished goods, and finished goods to customers in a manner that is efficient and cost effective.

10-5 Logistics: Overview and Functions

Logistics (or **physical distribution**) is defined as all the activities involved in the physical flow and storage of materials, semifinished goods, and finished goods to customers in a manner that is efficient and cost effective. The logistics function can be handled by any

TABLE 10-2

Use of Logistics Information by Department

Task	Purchasing Department	Manufacturing Department	Marketing/Sales Department	Other Departments
Order status information	62.3%	14.8%	13.1%	9.8%
Tracking inbound shipments	61.9%	19.0%	6.3%	12.8%
Alerts on delayed shipments	58.2%	16.4%	15.6%	9.8%
Divergence of shipments	52.6%	21.5%	17.2%	8.7%
Tracking outbound shipments	17.6%	21.0%	42.9%	18.5%

Source: *2002 Report on Trends and Issues in Logistics and Transportation,* Cap Gemini Ernst & Young, Georgia Southern University.

entity in the distribution channel—the producer, intermediaries, or the customer. An important trait of distribution is that it should meet customers' needs in terms of convenient and timely access to the product at a fair cost. Different departments in the firm use logistics information. Table 10-2 examines the use of different types of logistics information by department.

Logistics costs account for as much as 10 to 35 percent of a company's gross revenues, and more than 10 percent of the GDP in the United States, making logistics the single highest operating cost.[9] When the U.S. Department of Commerce reported that 60 percent of all Fortune 500 companies' logistics costs are spent on transporting products, it became clear that money saved in this area is likely to lead to more affordable products for consumers.[10] These costs vary greatly by industry sector and by company size and location, as well as other factors. For example, retailers that need to offer wide assortments will spend more on logistics as transportation and storage costs increase. A critical decision in this regard is whether the manufacturer seeks to have an intensive, selective, or exclusive distribution. Logistics involve the following primary functions: transportation, warehousing, inventory control, and order processing, which will be addressed in the following sections.

10-5a Transportation

Transportation is an important factor that marketers must consider. The choice of transportation determines whether products arrive at their destination on time and in good condition. The cost of transportation is also an important consideration because transportation costs can increase the product price. Table 10-3 shows the breakdown of the primary modes of freight transportation: truck, railway, airways, waterways, and pipeline. Notice that, in terms of volume, the highest percentage of products is moved by rail (see Figure 10-6 for an illustration of volume distribution of the different transportation modes).

Trucks transport smaller shipments over shorter distances than the other freight carriers. Most local transportation is handled by truck, and thus trucks handle a substantial proportion (almost a third) of all traffic in the continental United States annually. Trucks offer high flexibility, taking products from the factory directly to the destination. Their rates are competitive with the other modes of intracontinental transportation in the United States, and they offer fast service on shorter routes compared to the other modes of transportation. Often, trucks are used in conjunction with other forms of transportation that

TABLE 10-3

Characteristics of Different Modes of Transportation

Mode	Flexibility (in terms of area coverage)	Cost	Speed	Product Examples	Volume of Domestic Traffic*
Truck	High	Higher	Higher	Perishables, clothing, cement, furniture, appliances, electronics, and automobiles	1,051
Rail	Higher	Medium	Lower	Coal, stone, cement, oil, grain, lumber, and automobiles	1,558
Air	Highest	High	High	Jewelry, perishables, electronics, semiconductors, wine, and spirits	15
Water	Low	High	Low	Coal, stone, cement, oil, grain, and automobiles	494
Pipeline	Low	Lower	Low	Oil and gas, chemicals, coal as a semi-liquid	616

Source: Statistical Abstract of the United States 2004–2005, U.S. Census Bureau.

*Volume of domestic yearly traffic within the continental United States; freight traffic in billion ton-miles, whereby a ton-mile is the movement of one ton (2,000 pounds) of freight for the distance of one mile.

Figure 10-6
Volume Distribution of Various Modes of Transportation

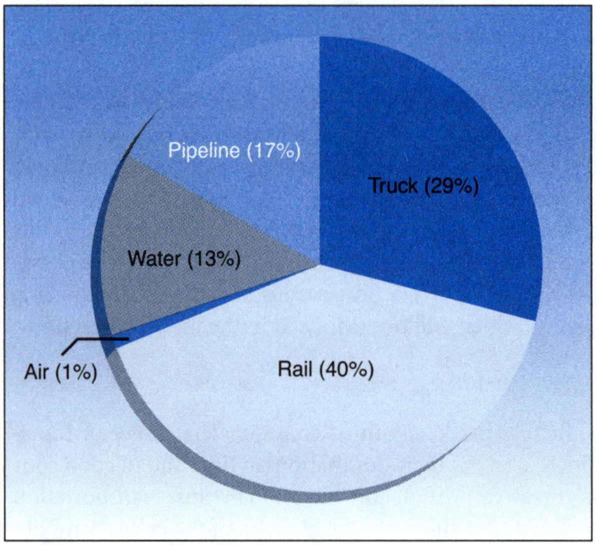

cannot take the product to the customer's doorstep, in what is referred to as inter-modal transportation, as will be seen in Section 10-5b. Trucks have capabilities, such as refrigeration and processing, which allow them to carry a wide array of products, from perishables to clothing, furniture, appliances, electronics, cement, and automobiles (see Figure 10-7).

Railways remain the primary mode for freight transportation in the United States intracontinentally, accounting for 40 percent of all domestic traffic. They transport over long distances high-weight, high-volume products that have a low per-pound value, such as coal, stone, cement, oil, grain, and lumber, but also more expensive products, such as large equipment and automobiles (Figure 10-8 illustrates a typical mode of transporting

Figure 10-7
Trucks are popular for making deliveries within the perimeter of a large metropolitan area.

Figure 10-8
Railways are a low-cost mode of transportation for shipping high-weight, high-volume products.

automobiles in Europe, where many road restrictions and high gasoline prices limit the use of the huge auto-transport trucks seen on U.S. highways). Railways are a low-cost mode of relatively low-speed freight transportation. They do not offer the flexibility that trucks do, however, because their mobility is restricted to areas designated for freight handling.

Air freight accounts for less than 1 percent of all intracontinental transportation in the United States. Air carriers offer high-speed, high-cost shipping that is ideal for perishable products, such as cut flowers; for low-volume, lower-weight, high-value products, such as jewelry and electronics; or for documents that necessitate prompt delivery. Companies such as Federal Express base their entire business on air transport, banking on their capability to take products to destinations overnight.

Tankers, barges, and other freighters in the inland and coastal waterways account for only 13 percent of the total domestic traffic volume. It should be mentioned, however, that water transportation is essential for international trade and accounts for a substantial proportion of international traffic. Waterways are used for transporting high-weight, high-volume products that have a low per-pound value, such as coal, stone, cement, oil, grain, lumber, and petrol, over long distances.

Pipelines are a low-cost mode of transporting liquid or semiliquid products from the source to the target market in a continuous manner, in which there are no interruptions (unless interruptions are voluntary), and intermediate storage is not necessary. Examples of pipelines are Basin, Bonito, and Capline for offshore and onshore crude oil; Harbor System and Wolverine Line for refined products; and the large, remote, and technically difficult pipeline, the Trans Alaska Pipeline,[11] a feat of engineering running from northern to southern Alaska across rough terrains and performing well in extreme weather conditions, transporting more than 1.4 million barrels of crude oil daily. Pipelines are typically owned by the producer, or by joint ventures, and they are expensive to maintain.[12]

Inter-modal transportation: Transportation using two or more different transportation modes—a combination of truck, rail, air, and waterways.

Firms often resort to **inter-modal transportation,** using two or more different transportation modes—a combination of truck, rail, air, and waterways. Inter-modal transportation has been greatly facilitated by containerization. For example, goods can be placed into containers at the factory, taken by truck to a train loading facility, transported to a port, and loaded aboard a ship; after crossing the ocean, the containers are loaded on a truck and transported to their final destination. All of these maneuvers can be accomplished using the initial containers, thus providing greater protection for the products, which do not have to be shifted individually from one vessel to another—and at lower cost because loading the individual products from/into vehicles is more expensive than using containers (see Figure 10-9).

10-5b Logistics Facilitators

Moving goods from the place of origin, normally a manufacturer, to the place of sale, normally the retailer, requires some type of facilitation. The two most common logistics facilitators are freight forwarders and the hub-and-spoke distribution center.

Freight forwarders: Specialized firms that collect shipments from different businesses, consolidate them for part of the distance, and deliver them to a destination, in what is typically a door-to-door service.

Freight forwarders are specialized firms that collect shipments from different businesses, consolidate them for part of the distance, and deliver them to a destination, in what is typically a door-to-door service. Many freight forwarders are adapting to fit the needs of their corporate consumers. Many pursue different value-added techniques, such as developing distinctive competencies in terms of geography, type of business, or specific commodities. For example, Kuehne & Nagel (www.kuehne-nagel.com) is well respected for its ability to expertly handle museum art and valuable exhibition material. The company has also developed expertise with respect to arranging trade fairs and art exhibits, as well as aid and relief for developing countries. Another freight forwarder, DHL (www.dhl.com), indicates particular expertise in several industry sectors, including health care, fashion, electronics, and live animals. Recently, DHL shipped 15 five-foot jellyfish to Australia.[13]

Hub-and-spoke distribution centers: Distribution centers designed to speed up warehousing and delivery, by channeling operations to one center (hub) that is particularly well equipped to handle the distribution of products to their destination.

Hub-and-spoke distribution centers are designed to speed up warehousing and delivery by channeling operations to one center (hub) that is particularly well equipped to handle the distribution of products to their destination. The idea of a hub location is to consolidate traffic from different origins and send it directly or via another hub to different destinations (nodes that are not destined as hubs are referred to as *spokes*), thus achieving economies of scale on hub-to-hub links. Such designs have been popular with airlines as well (Northwest, United, etc.), but a clear advantage of using them in the distribution network of a supply chain versus a direct airline flight from source to destination is that products, unlike passengers, are insensitive to how many hub stops they need to make. This makes it easier to achieve the goal of making the distribution channel more flexible and

Figure 10-9
Shipping containers significantly decrease the cost of transportation. The port of Rotterdam in the Netherlands, the largest port in the world, is a major container traffic hub. This container ship is embarking on a Transatlantic voyage.

responsive to customer needs.[14] Hub-and-spoke network designs have been used by Federal Express for a long time and are also used by UPS (www.ups.com), Norfolk Southern (www.nscorp.com), and Yellow Freight in some form or another.[15]

One company that takes advantage of this efficient hub-and-spoke distribution model is Carvel. Carvel is offering nationwide delivery for its ice cream cakes. It first promoted its overnight delivery in advertisements in the *New York Times* and the *Wall Street Journal*, listing an 800 number for FedEx delivery anywhere in the continental United States. In terms of logistics, the cakes are made at a Carvel store in Naples, Florida, packed in Styrofoam coolers with dry ice, and shipped within 48 hours via Federal Express. The cakes have a "no-melt" guarantee and stay intact in their packaging for about three days. The primary mail-order focus of this strategy is corporate gifts. In the recent past, a New York City promotion agency sent 100 cakes as holiday gifts to its clients, and customer reaction was very positive.[16]

10-5c Warehousing

Warehousing is defined as the marketing function whereby goods are stored, identified, and sorted in the process of transfer to an intermediary in the distribution channel or to the final consumer. **Inventory** is the amount of goods being stored. Warehousing is necessary when the speed of production does not match demand and/or consumption. For example, a wholesaler will get a break on price for bulk purchases, but may have to store products before there are enough retail orders or reorders. The concern, in this regard, is that the cost of storage is significantly lower than the price break the wholesaler received from purchasing the product in bulk, allowing for a profit. Or, the wholesaler may have to stock extra products to have them available for immediate delivery, in order to ensure customer satisfaction. If the product is not immediately delivered, the customer may order products from a different wholesaler in the future.

> **Warehousing:** The marketing function whereby goods are stored, identified, and sorted in the process of transfer to an intermediary in the distribution channel or to the final consumer.

> **Inventory:** The amount of goods being stored.

In other examples, many agricultural products, such as corn and wheat, are harvested at the end of the summer or in early fall. Making these products available at once will create excessive supply and depress prices. At the same time, customers are likely to demand these products throughout the year and, if the entire production is sold after harvest, these customers will seek the products from other suppliers. In yet other examples, products may be stored in anticipation of a price increase in order to obtain greater profits. For example, gas stations may store oil in anticipation of an oil shortage.

Companies can use different types of storage facilities. **Private warehouses** are owned or leased, and operated by firms storing their own products. They are used by intermediaries at all levels of distribution: manufacturers, wholesalers, and retailers. These intermediaries typically need to have storage on a regular basis. **Public warehouses** are independent facilities that provide storage rental and related services (see Figure 10-10). Public warehouses are used by firms that cannot afford to have their own facilities or that do not have a need for storage on a regular basis. International companies doing business in the United States periodically tend to use public warehouses rather than private warehouses. This is especially true in cases in which they have to store their products in customs-privileged facilities, such as foreign trade zones.

> **Private warehouses:** Warehouses that are owned or leased, and operated by firms storing their own products.

> **Public warehouses:** Independent facilities that provide storage rental and related services.

Distribution centers are computerized warehouses designed to move goods. They receive goods from different producers, take orders from buyers, and distribute them promptly. An example of one of the largest distribution centers for electronic components and computer equipment is the Phoenix, Arizona, based Avnet Inc. It has the capability of serving customers ranging from IBM to mom-and-pop shops in the embattled technology market, who demand to have zero-inventory. To keep a handle on inventory, to increase shipping capacity, and to reduce errors, the $2.14 billion company has rolled out Optum Inc.'s MOVE warehouse management system at its 400,000-square-foot Chandler, Arizona, logistics center. The software works in tandem with more than three miles of smart conveyance, 72 horizontal carousels, wireless data collection equipment, and bar code label printers. This distribution center handles distribution for more than 40,000 customers who do not want any inventory: They expect Avnet to control that.[17]

> **Distribution centers:** Computerized warehouses designed to move goods; they receive goods from different producers, take orders from buyers, and distribute them promptly.

Figure 10-10
Public warehouses facilitate storage for firms that cannot afford to own a private warehouse.

Foreign trade zone (FTZ): Tax-free area in the United States that is not considered part of the United States in terms of import regulations and restrictions. Also called a free trade zone.

In addition to the storage function, many warehouses engage in product assembly and packaging. This applies in particular to warehouses located in free trade zones. A **foreign trade zone (FTZ)** is a tax-free area in the United States that is not considered part of the United States in terms of import regulations and restrictions. Products can be shipped to an FTZ, stored and assembled there, and then be shipped to the United States or another country. Such products are not assessed duties and cannot be subjected to tariffs or quotas unless they enter the United States. An FTZ is considered to be an international area; merchandise in the FTZ, both foreign and domestic, is outside the jurisdiction of U.S. Customs.[18] FTZs are usually located in or near a port of entry and operated as a public utility by a public entity such as the Port of Portland, the Indianapolis Airport Authority, or the Crowfield Corporate Center in Charleston, South Carolina.[19] FTZs are used to show the product to customers, and pay duties only when the goods are sold;[20] to break bulk or store products and postpone the payment of duties until the product is shipped to the customer; and to assemble products (goods that are unassembled are cheaper to transport, and duties are assessed at lower rates for them than for assembled goods).

10-5d Inventory Control and Order Processing

Inventory control involves ensuring that there is a continuous flow of goods to customers that matches the quantity of goods with demand. Marketing managers need to understand how much inventory they need in order to address their customer needs within a reasonable amount of time and at low cost. In this sense, inventory control is especially problematic for seasonal production—for example, grain production linked to harvest—and for seasonal consumption, such as wool textiles in the winter.

Just-in-time (JIT) inventory system: Inventory system whereby a company reduces the amount of inventory by ordering products often and in lower quantities, thus creating flows, rather than stocks, of inventory.

Reducing inventory costs is essential. High inventories may result in products becoming stale. Alternatively, having a large stock of last year's models may hurt sales of new models, such as would happen with automobiles. In the case of overstock, products must often be liquidated at a low price and low profit; this may change customers' product price expectations in the future. One method for reducing inventory costs is by adopting a **just-in-time (JIT) inventory system,** whereby a company reduces the amount of inventory by ordering products often and in lower quantities—usually just enough for a few days of manufacturing—thus creating flows, rather than stocks, of inventory. This method allows for companies to substantially reduce their warehousing costs. It is essential that the company forecasts accurately its input needs; otherwise, if the supply is disrupted, the disruption could essentially cause the company to shut down operations.

Just-in-time logistics has been the purchasing managers' mantra for the past two decades and, indeed, was a profit center while commodity prices declined between the years 1985 and 2000. The assumptions of just-in-time management are based on a seamless transportation system and the ready availability of inputs from multiple sources. However, after the bursting of the tech bubble in the year 2000, none of these assumptions seem to apply. There is a shortage of commodities, such as steel, coal, and cement, and commodity prices are increasing. Capital investment has been inadequate over the past 10 years in the railroad, trucking, and shipping industries, resulting in transport bottlenecks and operations that simply demonstrate that transportation cannot keep up with the growth of international commerce.

For example, the Long Beach Port Director recently reported that 39 ships were waiting to be offloaded at Los Angeles and Long Beach, compared to a typical 2 to 4. All these developments may shake or even destroy the position of just-in-time logistics as a dominant management theory.[21]

The retail equivalent of JIT is the **quick response (QR) inventory system,** which creates a supply flow that more closely approximates consumer purchase patterns.

Important strides have been accomplished by linking suppliers' and customers' inventory systems. This was accomplished through electronic data interchange (EDI), an approach that allows different intermediaries to share standardized inventory information accomplished with the use of the Universal Product Code (see Figure 10-11) by all intermediaries, allowing firms to lower their inventory carrying costs and facilitating the flow of products. To illustrate, Wal-Mart is the only U.S. retailer selling the new Mary-Kate and Ashley One fragrance, by Coty. Coty uses a multichannel system that combines EDI to process orders electronically with Wal-Mart, exchanging messages with the retailer over the Internet, using EDI Internet transactions.[22]

Figure 10-11
Universal Product Codes facilitate inventory management.

Quick response (QR) inventory system: The retailing equivalent of the just-in-time inventory system that creates a supply flow that more closely approximates consumer purchase patterns.

A central aspect of inventory management is **stock turnover,** defined as the number of times per year that the inventory on hand is sold. The stock turnover annual rate is calculated as follows:

$$\frac{\text{Number of Units Sold per Year}}{\text{Average Inventory (units)}} \text{ or}$$

$$\frac{\text{Net Sales}}{\text{Average Inventory (\$ sales)}} \text{ or}$$

$$\frac{\text{Cost of Goods Sold}}{\text{Average Inventory (\$ cost)}}$$

Stock turnover: The number of times a year that the inventory on hand is sold.

A high stock turnover rate is a goal that allows companies to perform optimally in terms of inventory costs, but at the same time, companies do need to be careful that they do not run out of stock. Companies typically establish a **reorder point,** an inventory level at which new orders are placed.

Reorder point: An inventory level at which new orders are placed.

10-6 Wholesaling

Wholesaling encompasses all the activities involved in buying and handling the goods intended for sale to resellers or other organizational users. Wholesalers sell goods and services to manufacturers, to other wholesalers, to retailers, and to the government, or to nongovernmental organizations. As mentioned in Section 10-2, wholesalers provide the advantages of distributing the product down the channel of distribution to a location that is convenient to consumers, warehousing it in the distribution process. California Almonds, for example, are distributed all over the country by the wholesaler (see Figure 10-12). Wholesalers take risks for product obsolescence or theft, or even beyond. They reduce the number of transactions needed to deliver a wide product assortment to retailers and, ultimately, to consumers. They buy products in bulk from manufacturers at a discount and then break the bulk to distribute smaller quantities to retailers. Lastly, they conduct research for other channel members, provide service and credit to consumers and other channel members, and pay for promotional expenditures.

Wholesaling: All the activities involved in buying and handling the goods intended for sale to resellers or other organizational users.

10-6a Merchant Wholesalers

Merchant wholesalers are independent intermediaries who take title to and possession of products they distribute to resellers or organizational consumers. Merchant wholesalers constitute more than half of all wholesalers. There are two types of merchant wholesalers: full-service wholesalers and limited-service wholesalers.

Merchant wholesalers: Independent intermediaries who takes title to and possession of products distributed to resellers or organizational consumers.

Figure 10-12
Wholesalers provide important functions in the process of distributing products such as almonds from trees in California to grocery stores throughout the United States.

Source: Reprinted by permission of the Almond Board of California.

Full-service wholesalers: Independent intermediaries who provide a wide range of distribution tasks, such as product delivery, warehousing, sales force assistance, credit, research, planning, and installation and repair assistance, among others.

General merchandise wholesalers: Independent intermediaries who carry a broad product assortment, but low depth, in any one product line.

Specialty merchandise wholesalers: Independent wholesalers who carry a narrow product assortment but offer great depth in the product lines carried.

Rack jobbers: Wholesalers that manage the store shelves carrying their products.

Franchise wholesalers: Independent intermediaries affiliated with a manufacturer or wholesaler through a franchise contract.

Wholesale cooperatives: Voluntary chains of independent grocers pooling their resources and buying power and standardizing their marketing practices in a contractual agreement.

Limited-service wholesalers: Wholesalers who offer fewer services than full-service wholesalers, such as delivery and storage.

Full-service wholesalers provide a wide range of distribution tasks, such as product delivery, warehousing, sales force assistance, credit, research, planning, and installation and repair assistance, among others. Full-service wholesalers sell primarily to retailers, either to general merchandise retailers or to specialty stores. Examples of full-service wholesalers are general merchandise wholesalers, specialty merchandise wholesalers, rack jobbers, wholesale franchises, and wholesale cooperatives.

General merchandise wholesalers carry a broad product assortment, but low depth in any one product line. For example, a hardware wholesaler would carry most of the products sold in a general hardware store, such that the retailer would be able to obtain all the products it needs from this particular wholesaler. **Specialty merchandise wholesalers** carry a narrow product assortment but offer great depth in the product lines carried. For example, a seafood wholesaler on the Eastern Shore of Virginia would carry every type of seafood that fishing boats would bring in from the Chesapeake Bay and the coastal waters of the Atlantic Ocean.

Rack jobbers are wholesalers who manage the store shelves carrying their products, assemble the point-of-purchase displays, and determine product prices. They take title to the products they sell on consignment but are allowed to take unsold items back to the manufacturer or wholesaler selling the product. **Franchise wholesalers** are independent intermediaries affiliated with a manufacturer or wholesaler through a franchise contract. Examples include automobile retailers affiliated with the auto manufacturers carrying the brand (i.e., Mercedes contracts with dealers to carry its brand, offering the dealers exclusive distribution in their region of the country). In another example, Coca-Cola licenses bottlers worldwide to sell its product. **Wholesale cooperatives** consist of voluntary chains of independent retailers who pool their resources and buying power and standardize their marketing practices in a contractual agreement. An example of a wholesale cooperative is the Independent Grocers Alliance (IGA), which has a total of about 100 independent franchisees with worldwide retail sales of over $21 billion a year, and more than 4,400 supermarkets in 48 states in the United States and 43 countries.[23]

Limited-service wholesalers offer fewer services than full-service wholesalers. They may not provide distribution tasks such as sales force assistance, credit, research, planning, or installation and repair assistance, but they do normally provide delivery and storage. They sell perishables, such as seafood, construction materials, tobacco, dairy products, office supplies, and small business equipment.

Examples of limited-service wholesalers are **cash-and-carry wholesalers,** who carry a limited line of fast-moving goods. They travel to a wholesaler's location, pay cash for the merchandise, take physical possession of the product, and carry it directly to a retailer. They are paid on the spot—thus, they offer no credit or any other services. They are popular for perishable foods, for auto parts, for hardware, and for construction materials. **Truck wholesalers** (or truck jobbers, or truck and wagon wholesalers) take physical possession of the products and sell them from their truck or wagon on their regular sales route. They do provide merchandising and promotion support, but they do not offer credit, research, or other marketing services. Frito Lay and Mars sell chips and candy, respectively, using this type of wholesaler. **Drop shippers** (or **desk jobbers**) take title to, but not possession of, the product; they buy goods from suppliers and arrange to have them shipped directly to the reseller or organizational user. Drop shippers are popular for products that have high transportation costs, such as lumber and equipment, and where it makes sense to deliver the product directly to the consumer.

Mail-order wholesalers mail catalogs to businesses, take orders, and ship them to businesses. Business supplies, small office equipment, and specialty foods are sold using mail-order wholesalers. Table 10-4 summarizes the various types of wholesalers.

Cash-and-carry wholesalers: Wholesalers who carry a limited line of fast-moving goods; they travel to a wholesaler's location, pay cash for the merchandise, take physical possession of the product, and carry it directly to a retailer.

Truck wholesalers: Wholesalers who take physical possession of the products and sell them from their truck or wagon on their regular sales route.

Drop shippers (or **desk jobbers):** Wholesalers who take title to but not possession of the product; they buy goods from suppliers and arrange to have them shipped directly to the reseller or organizational user.

Mail-order wholesalers: Wholesalers who mail catalogs to businesses, take orders, and ship them to businesses.

TABLE 10-4

Merchant Wholesalers

Category	Type	Definition
Full-Service Wholesalers	General merchandise wholesalers	Carry a broad product assortment but low depth in any one product line
	Specialty wholesalers	Carry a narrow product assortment but offer great depth in the product lines carried
	Rack jobbers	Manage store shelves carrying their products, assemble the point-of-purchase displays, and determine product prices
	Franchise wholesalers	Independent intermediaries affiliated with a manufacturer or wholesaler through a franchise contract
	Wholesale cooperatives	Voluntary chains of independent retailers (such as grocers) who pool their resources and buying power and standardize their marketing practices in a contractual agreement
Limited-Service Wholesalers	Cash-and-carry wholesalers	Carry a limited line of fast-moving goods; travel to a wholesaler's location, pay cash for the merchandise, take physical possession of the product, and carry it directly to a retailer
	Truck wholesalers (truck jobbers)	Take physical possession of the products and sell them from their truck or wagon on their regular sales route; provide merchandising and promotion support, but do not offer credit, research, or other marketing services
	Drop shippers (desk jobbers)	Take title to, but not possession of, the product; buy goods from suppliers and arrange to have them shipped directly to the reseller or organizational user

Marketing Illustration 10-3

Why Does It Make Sense to Use Manufacturers' Agents Rather Than Your Own Sales Force?

Manufacturers' agents have many names, but the best way to define them is to think of them as outsourced providers of field sales services to multiple manufacturers of complementary products. When a company determines that an important element of its marketing plan is contacting its customers face-to-face on the customer's turf, it has three options:

1. Use nonsales company executives and managers who sell part-time.
2. Hire sales employees whose full-time job is to contact customers and service them.
3. Hire a manufacturers' agent.

Manufacturers' agents work on commission and pay their own expenses in return for a contractual agreement to be the exclusive "agent" of the manufacturers in a given territory, market, or for specific accounts. They offer the following advantages:

1. Predictable sales costs that go up and down with sales
2. Lower sales costs (the average industrial salesperson costs $150,000/year, which means that when producing $2,000,000 in new sales each year, the cost of sales would be 7.5 percent; a manufacturers' agent producing the same volume at a 5 percent commission costs $100,000)
3. Increased sales (the average industrial salesperson handles a territory for less than two years before he or she is promoted, transferred, or defects to a competitor; manufacturers' agents have a lifetime commitment to the territory)
4. Free consulting services because many agents have 15 to 20 years of corporate experience
5. No cost of training and turnover in sales personnel

Source: www.manaonline.org.

Agents: Intermediaries who represent buyers or sellers; they do not take possession of or title to the merchandise, and they work based on commission or fees.

Brokers: Intermediaries who bring buyers and sellers together; they do not take possession of or title to the merchandise, and they work based on commission or fees.

Manufacturers' agent (or manufacturers' rep.): Representative who works as the company's sales representative, representing noncompeting manufacturers in a particular market, and is paid on a commission basis.

Selling agent: Agent that holds an exclusive arrangement with the company, represents all its operations in a particular market, and acts as the sales and/or marketing department of the firm.

Purchasing agents: Agents with a long-term relationship with buyers who select, receive, and ship goods to buyers and are paid on a commission basis.

Commission merchant: Agent who takes possession of goods on consignment from the local markets and then sells them at a central market location.

10-6b Agents and Brokers

Agents represent buyers or sellers; they do not take possession of or title to the merchandise, and they work based on commission or fees. **Brokers** bring buyers and sellers together; they too do not take possession of or title to the merchandise, and they work based on commission or fees.

A **manufacturers' agent** (or **manufacturers' representative**) usually works as the company's sales representative, representing manufacturers in a particular market, and is paid on a commission basis. Manufacturers' agents can represent one or more noncompeting manufacturers. They are typically hired by small and medium-sized businesses that cannot afford their own field force, but then need the sales function covered. In that sense, they have a specified territory coverage and need to adhere to specific order-processing procedures. They are common for the clothing and furniture industries, as well as small electrics. Marketing Illustration 10-3 addresses the advantages of using manufacturers' agents.

A **selling agent** has an exclusive arrangement with the company, representing all of its operations in a particular market and acting as the sales and/or marketing department of the firm. Selling agents do not take title to the goods and are usually paid a percentage of sales. Given their broad responsibilities, their commission is higher than that of manufacturers' representatives. They are common for the clothing and furniture industries.

Purchasing agents have a long-term relationship with a buyer. They select, receive, and ship goods to buyers and are paid on a commission basis. Purchasing agents know their markets very well and are familiar with the needs of their customers. Examples of purchasing agents are smaller agents in Italy who purchase designer clothes that are not very popular in the United States but are regarded as solid in Europe. Purchasing agents scour the garment districts in Milan and Rome and bring the newest designs to U.S. buyers in the New York or West Coast garment districts or to another location in Europe.

A **commission merchant** takes possession of goods on consignment from the local markets and then sells them at a central market location. Commission merchants are prevalent for agricultural products, taking products from farmers and selling them to a central market, or for furniture, taking products from furniture manufacturing plants to a large central market that deals in furniture. Many such furniture markets are located in North Carolina.

Summary

1. *Define distribution and identify the different channel functions and dimensions.* Distribution planning is the planning of the physical movement of products from the producer to individual or organizational consumers, and the transfer of ownership and risk. It involves transportation, warehousing, and all the exchanges taking place at each channel level. It involves establishing the channels of distribution—the totality of organizations and individuals involved in the distribution process who take title or assist in the transferring of title in the distribution process from the producer to the individual or organizational consumer. It also involves identifying and managing other intermediaries involved in distribution (i.e., other entities that facilitate the distribution process, such as transportation firms, freight forwarders, and customs brokers for international distribution). The goal of intermediaries is to offer support for the activities involved in delivering products for the enhanced benefit of the customer. In that sense, intermediaries are active participants in the value chain (or supply chain), the chain of activities performed in the process of developing, producing, marketing, delivering, and servicing a product for the benefit of the customer. Channels of distribution perform the functions of distributing the product down the channel of distribution to a location that is convenient to consumers, warehousing it in the distribution process. They take risks for product obsolescence or theft, or even beyond. They reduce the number of transactions needed to deliver a wide product assortment to retailers, and, ultimately, to consumers. In addition, they buy products in bulk from manufacturers at a discount and then break the bulk to distribute smaller quantities to retailers. They also conduct research for other channel members, provide service and credit to consumers and other channel members, and pay for promotional expenditures.

Among channel dimensions are channel length (defined as the number of levels of distributors in a distribution channel) and channel width (the number of independent intermediaries involved at a particular stage of distribution). An intensive distribution strategy has as its purpose full market coverage, while exclusive distribution has as a goal a high control of the intermediaries handling the product, and thus the marketing strategy, by limiting their number to just one or two per geographic area. Selective distribution opts for some control over the marketing strategy by limiting distribution to a select group of resellers in each area; at the same time, the company has a reasonable sales volume and profits.

2. *Identify issues related to channel management, such as channel organization, administration, and relationships.* Intermediaries can opt for a contractual channel arrangement, which spells out in a contract all the tasks that must be performed by each channel member with regard to production, delivery strategy and terms of sale, territorial rights, promotional support, the price policies of each intermediary, and contract length. Intermediaries can also have an administered channel arrangement, which has a dominant member of the channel in terms of size, expertise, or influence that coordinates the tasks of each channel member—the channel captain. Firms can also use a dual channel of distribution, or multichannel distribution, appealing to different markets; this strategy is also known as multimarketing. Channel members can strengthen their position in the channel through vertical integration (by acquiring or merging with an intermediary in the channel—a supplier or a buyer). Alternatively, they can increase intermediary strength in the market through horizontal integration, which would involve an acquisition or merger at the same level in the distribution channel.

3. *Examine the different logistics functions.* Logistics involve the following primary functions: transportation, warehousing, inventory control, and order processing, as well as customer service, and plant, warehouse, and reseller location planning. In terms of transportation, firms must decide whether to ship products by truck, water, rail, air, or pipeline, or a combination of these methods—known as inter-modal transportation. These decisions depend on the type of product involved, on the urgency of delivery, and on how much the firm can afford to pay for the shipment. Companies must also decide on warehousing, which involves deciding where goods are stored, identified, and sorted in the process of transfer to an intermediary in the distribution channel or to the final consumer. There are different types of storage facilities that companies can use. Private warehouses are owned or leased, and operated by firms storing their own products. They are used by intermediaries at all levels of distribution: manufacturers, wholesalers, and retailers. These intermediaries typically need to have storage on a regular basis. Public warehouses are independent facilities that provide storage rental and related services. Public warehouses are used by firms that cannot afford to have their own facilities or that do not have a need for storage on a regular basis. Firms must also determine how to optimally manage their inventories. Inventory control involves ensuring that there is a continuous flow of goods to customers that matches the quantity of goods with demand. Reducing inventory costs is essential because high inventories may result in products becoming stale, or large stocks of last year's models may hurt sales of new models. One method for reducing inventory costs is by adopting a just-in-time (JIT) inventory system whereby a company reduces the amount of inventory by ordering products often and in lower quantities, thus creating flows, rather than stocks, of inventory. The retail equivalent of JIT is the quick response (QR) inventory system, which creates a supply flow that more closely approximates consumer purchase patterns. Important strides have been accomplished by linking suppliers' and customers' inventory systems. This was accomplished through electronic data interchange (EDI), an approach that allows different intermediaries to share standardized inventory information.

4. *Define wholesaling and identify the different functions of wholesaling.* Wholesaling encompasses all the activities involved in buying and handling the goods intended for sale to resellers or other organizational users. Merchant wholesalers are independent intermediaries who take title to and possession of products they distribute to resellers or organizational consumers. There are two types of merchant wholesalers: full-service wholesalers and limited-service wholesalers. Full-service wholesalers provide a wide range of distribution tasks, such as product delivery, warehousing, sales force assistance, credit, research, planning, and installation and repair assistance, among others. Examples of full-service wholesalers are general merchandise wholesalers, specialty merchandise wholesalers, rack jobbers, wholesale franchises, and wholesale cooperatives. Limited-service wholesalers offer fewer services than full-service wholesalers; they may not provide distribution tasks such as sales force assistance, credit, and research. Examples are cash-and-carry wholesalers, who carry a limited line of fast-moving goods, travel to a wholesaler's location, pay cash for the merchandise, take physical possession of the product, and carry it directly to a retailer; truck wholesalers (or truck jobbers, or truck and wagon wholesalers), who take physical possession of the products and sell them from their truck or wagon on their sales route; drop shippers (or desk jobbers), who take title to but not possession of the product; and mail-order wholesalers, who mail catalogs to businesses, take orders, and ship them to businesses. Agents represent buyers or sellers; they do not take possession of or title to the merchandise, and they work based on commission or fees. Brokers bring buyers and sellers together; they too do not take possession of or title to the merchandise, and they work based on commission or fees.

Key Terms

administered channel arrangement (p. 302)
agents (p. 316)
brokers (p. 316)
cash-and-carry wholesalers (p. 315)
channel captain (p. 302)
channel length (p. 300)
channel width (p. 300)
channels of distribution (p. 297)
coercive power (p. 305)
commission merchant (p. 316)
contractual channel arrangement (p. 302)
direct channel of distribution (p. 300)
distribution centers (p. 311)
distribution planning (p. 297)
drop shippers (or desk jobbers) (p. 315)
dual channel of distribution (p. 303)
exclusive distribution (p. 301)
expert power (p. 305)
foreign trade zone (FTZ) (p. 312)
franchise wholesalers (p. 314)
freight forwarders (p. 310)
full-service wholesalers (p. 314)
general merchandise wholesalers (p. 314)
horizontal integration (p. 304)
horizontal marketing systems (HMS) (p. 304)
hub-and-spoke distribution centers (p. 310)
hybrid marketing channel (p. 303)
indirect channel of distribution (p. 300)
intensive distribution (p. 300)
intermediaries (or middlemen, or channel members) (p. 297)
inter-modal transportation (p. 310)
inventory (p. 311)
just-in-time (JIT) inventory system (p. 312)
keiretsus (p. 304)
legitimate power (p.305)
limited-service wholesalers (p. 314)
logistics (or physical distribution) (p. 306)
mail-order wholesalers (p. 315)
manufacturers' agent (or manufacturers' representative) (p. 315)
merchant wholesalers (p. 313)
multichannel distribution system (p. 303)
private warehouses (p. 311)
public warehouses (p. 311)
pull strategy (p. 304)
purchasing agents (p. 316)
push strategy (p. 304)
quick response (QR) inventory system (p. 313)
rack jobbers (p. 314)
referent power (p. 305)
relationship marketing (p. 305)
reorder point (p. 313)
reward power (p. 305)
selective distribution (p. 301)
selling agent (p. 316)
specialty merchandise wholesalers (p. 314)
stock turnover (p. 313)
trading companies (p. 304)
truck wholesalers (p. 315)
value chain (or supply chain) (p. 297)
value delivery chain (p. 297)
vertical integration (p. 303)
vertical marketing systems (VMS) (p. 304)
warehousing (p. 311)
wholesale cooperatives (p. 314)
wholesaling (p. 313)

Discussion Questions

1. The chapter-opening vignette introduces Kathleen King as the owner of Kathleen's Bake Shop. Describe and categorize all the distribution activities she is involved in.
2. Assume that you are working for a large competitor of Kathleen's, one that would like to dominate this particular niche market—the gourmet bakery market. Devise a distribution plan for your company that would effectively compete with Kathleen in her target market.
3. The competing company you created in Question 2 needs to distribute its bakery goods all over the country. Assume that all the cookies are prepared at a large bakery on the outskirts of Greenwich, Connecticut. Your job is to determine the logistics involved in shipping the cookies to San Francisco, California; Oahu, Hawaii; and Boise, Idaho. What mode of transportation could you use for each destination? Which mode do you plan to use and why?

Review Questions

True or False

1. The goal of intermediaries is to offer support in delivering products by providing enhanced benefits to consumers.
2. A direct channel of distribution might have one or two intermediaries.
3. Channel length is defined as the number of independent intermediaries involved at a particular stage of distribution.
4. The channel captain is the dominant channel member in the administered channel arrangement.
5. Trading companies are complex marketing systems specializing in providing intermediary services, risk reduction, and financial assistance.
6. To eliminate conflicts in the distribution channels, manufacturers use both pull and push strategies to market products.
7. Because logistics can be handled by any entity in the distribution channel, operational expenses for logistics are rather low.

8. Inter-modal transportation is widely used in the era of modern logistics.

9. Due to the unpredictable demand for most goods, retailers cannot utilize just-in-time inventory systems.

Multiple Choice

10. Which of the following is a component of distribution planning?
- **a.** planning of the physical movement of products
- **b.** transfer of ownership and risk
- **c.** transportation, warehousing, and all exchanges at each channel level
- **d.** a, b, and c

11. Which of the following groups are drivers of an adaptive supply chain?
- **a.** collaboration and optimization
- **b.** connectivity and speed
- **c.** execution and visibility
- **d.** all of the above

12. Which distribution strategy aims at full market coverage, making products available to all consumers at the right place and the right time?
- **a.** intensive distribution
- **b.** exclusive distribution
- **c.** selective distribution
- **d.** contractual distribution

13. Multimarketing or selling through warehouse and retailer chains is an example of
- **a.** vertical integration.
- **b.** dual channel of distribution.
- **c.** horizontal integration.
- **d.** vertical marketing system.

14. Which type of power is based on a close match in terms of values and objectives shared by other channel members?
- **a.** coercive power
- **b.** expert power
- **c.** referent power
- **d.** legitimate power

15. Primary functions of logistics are
- **a.** transportation and warehousing.
- **b.** inventory control and order processing.
- **c.** customer service.
- **d.** a and b

Notes

1. Gail Buchalter, "Out of the Nest–Now," *Forbes*, vol. 149, no. 11 (May 25, 1992): 64; and www.tatesbakeshop.com.
2. Hallie Mummert, "Lessons in Multichannel Marketing," *Target Marketing*, vol. 27, no. 12 (December 2004): 39–41.
3. "Business: Floating on Air," *The Economist*, vol. 359, no. 8222 (May 19, 2001): 56–57.
4. Tim Burt, "Porsche Fires Revolution at Harley," *Financial Times* (July 14–15, 2001): 8.
5. "Japanese Trading Companies: The Giants That Refused to Die," *The Economist*, vol. 319, no. 7709 (1991): 72–73.
6. Ibid.
7. Ibid.
8. Adapted from Prabir K. Bagchi and Helge Virum, "Logistical Alliances: Trends and Prospects in Integrated Europe," *Journal of Business Logistics*, vol. 19, no. 1 (1998): 191–213.
9. Sue Abdinnour-Helm, "Network Design in Supply Chain Management," *International Journal of Agile Management Systems*, vol. 1, no. 2 (1999): 99–106.
10. Ibid.
11. Randy R. Irvin, "Pipeline Owners Must Reassess Utility of Undivided-Interest Ownership," *Oil & Gas Journal*, vol. 99, no. 30 (July 23, 2001): 60–65.
12. Ibid.
13. www.dhl.com.
14. Sue Abdinnour-Helm, "Network Design in Supply Chain Management," *International Journal of Agile Management Systems*, vol. 1, no. 2 (1999): 99–106.
15. Ibid.
16. Melissa Dowling, "Carvel Puts Its Ice Cream in the Mail," *Catalog Age*, vol. 10, no. 3 (March 1993): 12.
17. Brian Albright, "Better Distribution, Fewer Errors," *Frontline Solutions*, vol. 3, no. 13 (December 2002): 13–14.
18. George F. Hanks and Lucinda Van Alst, " Foreign Trade Zones," *Management Accounting*, vol. 80, no. 7 (January 1999): 20–23.
19. Ibid.
20. Ibid.
21. Steve Allen, "Inventory Crunch," *Barron's*, vol. 84, no. 52 (December 27, 2004): 35.
22. Ann Bednarz, "Internet EDI: Blending Old and New," *Network World*, vol. 21, no. 8 (February 23, 2004): 29–30.
23. See www.igainc.com.

Case 10-1 Shipping Doo Kingue

Doo Kingue, a baby mountain gorilla, is a member of one of the two most endangered ape families in the world. There are only approximately 655 mountain gorillas alive today, all living in the wild in the mountainous forests of northwest Rwanda, southwest Uganda, and the eastern Democratic Republic of Congo. Mountain gorillas in this region are constantly threatened by poaching, continuous encroachment on the national parks for agricultural use, extensive harvesting of wood for fuel, and a landmine landscape as a result of fighting between the different tribes in the region. Doo Kingue, whose tribe perished as a result of water contamination, was able to survive—barely—and is currently experiencing a difficult-to-treat pulmonary infection.

The Director of the Karisoke Research Center in Volcano National Park, founded by the late American anthropologist Dian Fossey in 1968, and run by the Dian Fossey Gorilla Funds, a United States nongovernmental organization, recently approached the National Zoo in Washington, D.C., and asked for help. The Center obtained permission from the regional government of Ruhengeri and the national government of Rwanda to send the gorilla to the National Zoo, provided the zoo took responsibility for shipping and hospitalization. John James, one of the directors of conservation and science at the zoo, is excited about having a mountain gorilla for its primate exhibit, and Doo Kingue seems like the ideal candidate.

John's plan is to work with one of the transportation companies doing business in Sub-Saharan Africa to bring Doo Kingue quickly and painlessly to Washington, D.C., and to start aggressive treatment on the pulmonary infection. Clearly, in this decision, time is of the essence. His staff is familiar with some of the companies that provide quick, reliable service for transporting animals. One of the companies he is considering is Animal Port Houston (www.pettransport.com), a company with expertise in the relocation of pets and animals, offering services that include housing, transporting, and preparing relevant health certificates and permits. Animal Port Houston is a member of the American Zoo Association (AZA), the International Animal Transportation Association (AATA), the International Pet and Animal Transport Association (IPATA), the American Association for Laboratory Animal Science (AALAS), the United States Animal Health Association (USAHA), and the U.S. Air Forwarders Association.

Another company that seems a viable candidate for the transportation job is Federal Express (www.fedex.com). FedEx has recently donated the use of its express transportation network to relocate six endangered polar bears from San Juan, Puerto Rico, to their permanent zoo homes. It flew the bears from San Juan to the FedEx Express Hub in Memphis onboard a DC-10 aircraft. Later in the day, the bears were transloaded to three other aircraft in Memphis to fly to their final destinations near Seattle, Washington; Detroit, Michigan; and Charlotte, North Carolina; respectively. FedEx Express used its customs clearance expertise to expedite the animals through U.S. Customs. John found out that FedEx Express has considerable experience in transporting animals, including elephants, rhinos, lions, and gorillas. The company even transported animals to the National Zoo. In December 2000, FedEx provided air transportation, ground support, and logistical expertise to deliver two giant pandas from Chengdu, China, to the National Zoo in Washington, D.C. In 2002, FedEx transported six rare white tigers from Memphis, Tennessee, to Bangkok, Thailand, to ensure that work could continue on an endangered species breeding program.

Questions

1. Weigh the advantages and disadvantages of using Animal Port Houston and FedEx Express to transport Doo Kingue to Washington, D.C.
2. Arrange for inter-modal transportation for Doo Kingue from Ruhengeri, Rwanda, to Kigali, the capital city of Rwanda, and to the United States. Note that none of these companies, nor any U.S. airlines, fly to Rwanda. Attempt a few routes by looking at airlines' websites, at the Animal Port Houston site, and the FedEx site to find out what markets they serve. Find out how animals can be transported from Dulles Airport to downtown Washington, D.C.

Sources: www.scienceinafrica.co.za; Paul R. Murphy and James M. Daley, "Profiling International Freight Forwarders: An Update," *International Journal of Physical Distribution Logistics Management,* vol. 31, no. 3 (2001): 152–168; www.fedex.com.

Case 10-2 The Complex World of Supervalu

Supervalu Inc. was selected as the 2003 Wholesaler of the Year by *PL Buyer* magazine, a leading industry publication covering the private label market. According to the magazine, Supervalu has demonstrated a top-down commitment to the creation of a truly superior, consumer-driven private label program. Supervalu is one of the largest companies in the United States grocery distribution channel. The company, which has 57,800 full- and part-time employees, is a Fortune 100 company—and growing—and is among Fortune's Most Admired Companies. With annual revenues in excess of $20 billion, Supervalu holds a leading market share position.

As of early 2003, Supervalu's retail store network, including licensed locations, totaled 1,391 stores in 40 states. Comprising the company's retail network were:

- 1,123 Save-A-Lot value stores—262 owned food stores, 778 licensed food stores, and 83 Deals—Nothing Over a Dollar general merchandise stores
- 208 price superstores, including Cub Foods, Shop 'n Save, Shoppers Food Warehouse, Metro, and Bigg's stores
- 60 traditional supermarkets, including Farm Fresh, Scott's Foods, and Hornbacher's stores

In addition to supplying its own retail store network, Supervalu also serves as primary supplier to approximately 2,490 retail grocery stores and 31 Cub Foods franchised locations, while serving as secondary supplier to an additional 1,400 stores.

Ukrop's Super Markets renewed a supply agreement with Supervalu in late 2002. The new five-year contract commits Supervalu to supplying products, including grocery, frozen, dairy, produce, meat, deli, bakery, general merchandise, and health and beauty care products, to the 27 Ukrop's Super Markets stores and one Joe's Market store—an upscale version of the Ukrop's Super Market.

Ukrop's has a close relationship with Supervalu. In addition to the supply agreement, Ukrop's also has a share in Supervalu. In 1999, Supervalu strengthened its Mid-Atlantic presence through its acquisition of Richfood Holdings. Ukrop's was one of the founding members of Richfood.

Questions

1. What type of wholesaler is Supervalu?
2. Describe vertical integration at Supervalu.
3. Describe horizontal integration at Supervalu.
4. What type of relationship do Ukrop's Super Markets have with Supervalu? Where is each company located in the channel of distribution?

Sources: www.prnewswire.com; www.supervalu.com.

11

Retailing Strategies

CHAPTER OBJECTIVES

1. Provide an overview and description of the general merchandise retailing category and offer examples and illustrations.
2. Provide an overview and description of the food retailing category and offer examples and illustrations.
3. Provide an overview and description of the nonstore retailing category and offer examples and illustrations.
4. Address issues related to retailer organization, retailing decisions in terms of merchandise and service mix, location, atmospherics, and future trends in retailing.

CHAPTER OUTLINE

"Showcased in magazines, attracting the attention of early product adopters, IKEA suited the benign technocracy and the ironic wink of the new economy. Where Pottery Barn and Restoration Hardware offer the comfort of a connection with the past, IKEA fabricates a connection with motion itself."[1] Through unique positioning, stressing functional design, and a merchandising strategy that revolutionized retailing in the United States since the 1970s, IKEA has penetrated urban homes and quickly become a dominant player in the furniture industry and beyond.

With its own brand assortment and significant product assortment beyond furniture, IKEA is becoming an important private-label player. In 2004, IKEA boasted $12,769.6 million in sales worldwide. In the United States, on a yearly basis, over 30 million consumers, referred to as "the many" or "the people with thin wallets," typically work their way through the labyrinth of IKEA stores in the United States and interact with the company's employees, called "coworkers." The company started with 5 stores in the United States in the 1990s, has 26 stores today, and is planning to add 40 more by 2013. Consumers in the United States are also effectively targeted with the IKEA catalog, which allows consumers to order by phone and mail. More recently, IKEA added the Internet as a retailing venue.

At first, IKEA offered basic products made out of solid pine with a Swedish look. Its merchandising strategy was unique, requiring the customer to assemble products, which lowered manufacturing costs. Products were sold in a flat package, which lowered transportation costs.

The company first targeted consumers who could not afford other furniture options, rather than the people who liked foreign travel and wine (i.e., the consumers who make up the early adopter segment and who shape American consumers' tastes). The Swedish company initially refused to adapt its beds and mattresses to fit American sheets, or its kitchen cabinets to fit American appliances. Even the glasses it sold were too small for American consumers' thirst. Consumers purchased vases to use as glasses. IKEA quickly found itself on the brink of abandoning operations in the United States.

However, with a renewed consumer focus, the company is today one of the most successful retailers in the United States. During the economic recession, its sales experienced a solid increase. How did IKEA manage a complete turnaround? With minimal change in the product line, the company shifted its profile from the bland functionality of prefab Utopia to trendsetting design (see Figure 11-1 for an illustration of IKEA design). In addition to its contemporary design, IKEA attempts to offer an attractive store environment, with bright, colorful displays alternating with romantic atmospherics. Strategically placed where parents might linger, little houses and playgrounds entertain very little people, while those between 37 and 48 inches can play in Smalland, a daycare that entertains children while parents fill out their order forms quietly. At lunch and dinner, consumers mob the store's cafeteria lines, sampling Swedish meatballs and salmon dishes, and sipping endlessly free refills of ligonberry juice. Merchandising strategies aimed at decreasing costs without sacrificing functionality or design, lively atmospherics, and a family focus have turned IKEA into a successful furniture store. Its designs are creatively combined in many contemporary homes. IKEA is considered a pioneer category specialist or category killer (i.e., a large retailer with a wide selection of merchandise in a single product category), the first in the furniture industry (see Figure 11-2 for a photo of a stylish IKEA armoire that fits the middle-class budget).[2]

Figure 11-1
The IKEA Akurum kitchen has a versatile and contemporary design.

11-1 Chapter Overview

The IKEA example in the chapter-opening vignette provides important insights into one of the oldest and most successful international specialty retailers. This chapter provides a definition of retailing in Section 11-2 and an overview and description of the different

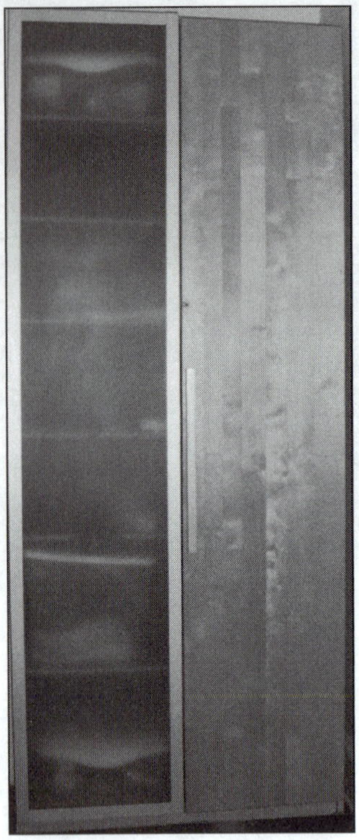

Figure 11-2
This IKEA armoire makes style affordable to the middle class.

retail formats—general merchandise retailing, food retailing, and nonstore retailing, with appropriate examples and illustrations—in Section 11-3. This section also offers a ranking of the top U.S. retailers and suggests that, although general merchandise and food retailers are predominant, these same retailers have a substantial nonstore retail presence. Section 11-4 addresses the organization of retailers into categories, with discussion of independent retailers, chain stores, franchises, and cooperatives, concluding that, although independent retailers outnumber all the other categories, chains account for about 60 percent of all sales. Section 11-5 addresses retailing decisions, such as merchandise mix, service mix, atmospherics, and location, and the last section, Section 11-6, addresses trends in retailing—namely, the shorter lifecycles, the ever-changing technology, the broadening competitive base, and retailers' international expansion.

11-2 Retailing Defined

Most consumers think of grocery stores and department stores as retailers because they are stores that sell products to consumers for final consumption. Yet, retailing has a much broader spectrum that includes vending machines, catalog stores, manufacturers' outlet shops, wholesale warehouses selling to consumers, your Amway salesperson, and Internet sites selling products. **Retailing** is defined as all the activities involved in the final stage of distribution—selling goods and services to final consumers for their consumption.

Retailing: All the activities involved in the final distribution—selling goods and services to the final consumers for their consumption.

Retailers perform the following distribution functions (also illustrated in Figure 11-3):

- *Creating convenience for consumers*—When retailers offer assortments of goods and services from different manufacturers, consumers do not have to go to each manufacturer's outlet or wholesaler distributing the manufacturer's product; instead, they shop at a conveniently located single retail outlet for the different products through transactions that the retailer facilitates.
- *Informing consumers*—Salespeople in the store, advertisements, and point-of-purchase displays all serve to inform consumers about the availability of products.
- *Serving the other channel members (manufacturers and wholesalers)*—Retailers place individual products, rather than bundles, on the shelves (i.e., they break bulk), mark product prices, store the products, and take ownership of the products, while assuming all related risks (theft, loss, etc.).

Figure 11-3
Key Retailing Functions

INTERACTIVE FIGURE

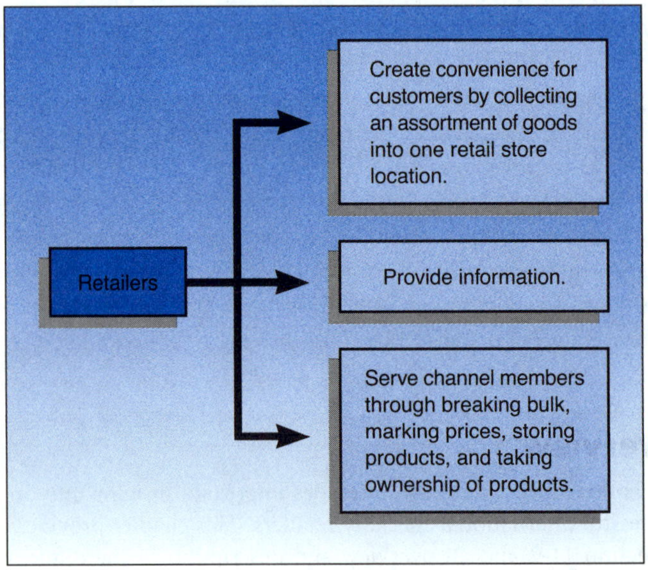

TABLE 11-1

Top 15 Global Retailers (ranked by sales)

Rank	Company	Sales (Million U.S.$)	Home-Country
1.	Wal-Mart Stores, Inc.	$250,681	U.S.A.
2.	Carrefour S.A.	79,653	France
3.	The Home Depot Inc.	64,816	U.S.A.
4.	Royal Ahold N.V.	63,360	Netherlands
5.	Metro A.G.	60,565	Germany
6.	Kroger Co.	53,791	U.S.A.
7.	Tesco PLC	50,343	U.K.
8.	Target Corp.	48,163	U.S.A.
9.	Rewe Group	44,275	Germany
10.	ITM Enterprises	43,394	France
11.	Costco Wholesale Corp.	42,546	U.S.A.
12.	Sears, Roebuck & Co.	41,124	U.S.A.
13.	Aldi Group	36,000	Germany
14.	Safeway, Inc.	35,552	U.S.A.
15.	Albertson's, Inc.	35,436	U.S.A.

Source: Jay McIntosh and Julie Kunkel, "Top 100 Global Retailers," *Chain Store Age*, vol. 80, no. 12 (December 2004): 73–78.

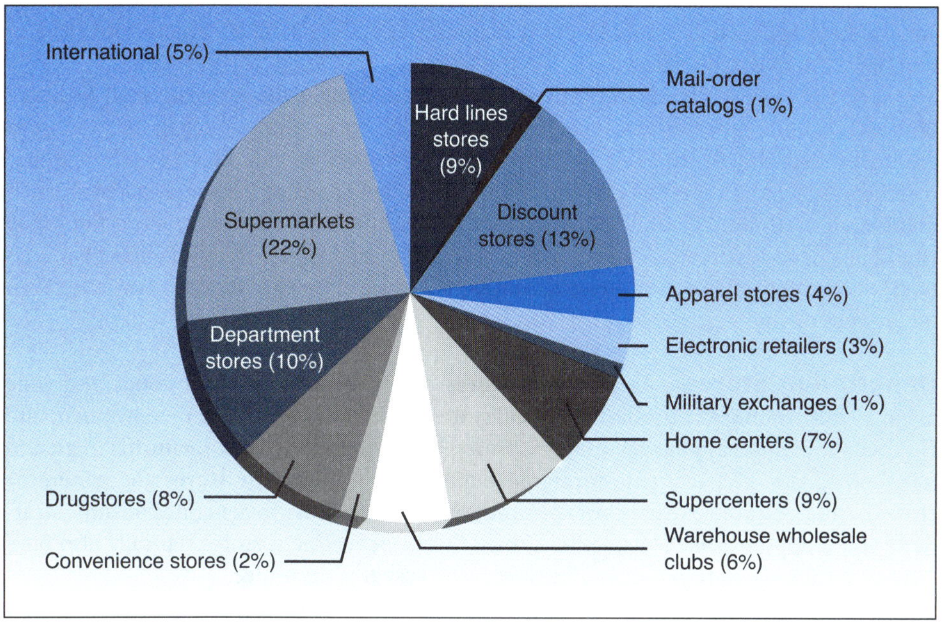

Figure 11-4
Top U.S. Retail Categories (based on sales)

Sources: Jay McIntosh and Julie Kunkel, "Top 100 Global Retailers," *Chain Store Age*, vol. 80, no. 12 (December 2004): 73–78; "State of the Industry: The Top 100 Retailers," *Chain Store Age* (August 2002): 3A–8A.

11-3 Retail Formats

The three main retail formats are general merchandise retailing, food retailing, and nonstore retailing. The top retailers in the world in terms of sales belong primarily to the first two categories—the top 15 retailers are listed in Table 11-1. However, many of the general merchandise retailers and food retailers also sell through their websites, placing them in the nonstore category as well.

Supermarkets constitute the largest category, accounting for 22 percent of total sales, followed by discounters, which account for 13 percent of sales, and by department stores, which account for 10 percent (see Figure 11-4).

The following subsections describe the retailers in each category (general merchandise retailing, food retailing, and nonstore retailing) and address the different variations for each retail format.

11-3a General Merchandise Retailing

General merchandise retailers are composed of specialty stores, department stores, general merchandise discount stores, off-price retailers, and catalog showrooms. Approximately 55 percent of all retail sales are made in this category.

Specialty stores: Retailers that offer a narrow product line and deep assortment.

Specialty Stores

Specialty stores offer a narrow product line and wide assortment. In this category are clothing stores, which are usually further specialized into women's, men's, or children's clothing stores, such as Gap, Victoria's Secret, and Acorn; bookstores, such as the local retailer of alternative books or the large Barnes & Noble's chain; toy stores, such as Toys "R" Us; office-supply stores, such as Office Max and Staples; home-improvement stores, such as Lowe's and Home Depot; and consumer electronics stores.

Category specialists (category killers): Large general-merchandise discount stores that carry a narrow variety of merchandise and a deep assortment.

The largest of these stores (i.e., Barnes & Noble, Toys "R" Us, Office Max, Staples, Lowe's, and Home Depot) offer a huge selection of products in the category in which they are specializing; these are known as **category specialists (category killers)** and carry a narrow variety of merchandise but offer a wide assortment. Traditionally located in suburbia, category specialists are now migrating to urban areas. In November 2004, a second Home Depot opened in mid-town Manhattan in New York City. Signs in the store offer delivery anywhere in the city for $21, and products are relatively down-sized to fit in tiny apartments and their tiny kitchens and bathrooms. A 110,000-square-foot Toys "R" Us store opened in Times Square and is one of the company's most successful retailtainment flagship stores. The bridge-and-tunnel people—those who commute to work in Manhattan—are also heavily courted: Home Depot is planning to open a 350,000-square-foot store in Red Bank, Brooklyn, in 2007.[3]

Specialty stores—chains in particular—are expanding at the expense of all forms of nonfood retailing. For example, specialty store chains are taking market share away from traditional department stores in the United States because they can offer a greater depth of merchandise within a product category. Shoppers looking for a new camera, stereo, kitchen utensils, or clothing will find more brands and selections in a specialty store than they would in a department store. Stores like the Indigo Company, featured in Figure 11-5, succeed because they offer a better selection of merchandise or hard-to-find unique items than other types of stores.

Department stores: General retailers that offer a broad variety of goods and deep assortments.

Anchor stores (generator stores): Stores situated at the end (anchor) positions in a mall to generate consumer traffic for the stores situated in between.

Department Stores

Department stores offer a broad variety of goods and wide assortments. Among the products they carry are the latest fashions for men, women, and children; household appliances and electronics; kitchenware; china; home furnishings; and toys and games. Department stores most often serve as **anchor stores** (or **generator stores**), situated at the end (anchor) positions in a mall in order to generate consumer traffic to the shopping mall. Outside the United States, department stores typically also have large supermarket sections, and some may even carry fresh produce.

It is typical for department stores to have numerous leased departments—sections that are centrally located in the store and that are leased to another retailer (see Figure 11-6). For example, cosmetics counters at most department stores are leased departments, where the cosmetics companies pay rent to be able to sell their products using their own sales staff. The Esteé Lauder counter at Nordstrom's department store is such an example: Its staff is hired, trained, and paid by Esteé Lauder. Leased departments create traffic for the department store, bringing in clients to purchase products that are complementary to the store's offerings. For example, 34 percent of all teenagers purchase their cosmetics at department stores, and because Esteé Lauder controls 42 percent of the cosmetics sold at department stores, having Esteé Lauder lease space makes good business sense.[4] Many customers who come to buy cosmetics will also purchase other products.

Figure 11-5
Specialty stores like the Indigo Company succeed because they offer consumers a greater depth of merchandise, as well as hard-to-find, unique items.

Source: Sample print advertisement courtesy of The Miles Agency and Alliance One Advertising, Inc.

Figure 11-6
This is a leased cosmetic department within a department store.

Department stores have suffered substantial losses in the past decade, mostly attributed to the rise in discount stores, off-price retailers, and category killers. The rental fee in malls tends to be higher than stand-alone facilities, and because of the large size of department stores, rent is a high-item expense for them. Discount stores, off-price retailers, and category killers can purchase large volumes of merchandise and sell it at a lower price than department stores, which puts a squeeze on the profit margins for department stores.

The Chapter 11 bankruptcy filing and eventual closing of the Ames Department Stores in the Northeast illustrate the saga many department stores have gone through.

Ames had been in business for 44 years and was positioned as a lower-priced department store, attempting to find a target market of working, blue-collar individuals. By positioning itself between the department stores of Sears and JC Penney and the discount stores like Wal-Mart, Ames believed it could thrive. After purchasing a couple of smaller department stores, it looked as though Ames could become a national chain. This did not happen, primarily because of Target and Wal-Mart. Both stores were larger and able to sell merchandise more efficiently. Consumers regarded Ames more as a discount store than a department store. With consumers fleeing department stores for cheaper-priced retailers, Ames was forced to file for Chapter 11 bankruptcy protection. Unable to obtain adequate financing for expansion, cash continued to dwindle until Ames made the decision in 2002 to close.[5] In good times, department stores do okay; in bad times, shoppers buy their merchandise at discount stores and category specialists. So, with each recession, more of the customer base of the department stores is eroded. The future of department stores is certainly a huge question mark.

General merchandise discount stores: Retailers that sell high volumes of merchandise, offer limited service, and charge lower prices.

All-purpose discount stores: General merchandise discount stores that offer a wide variety of merchandise and limited depth.

Off-price retailers: Retailers that sell brand-name and designer merchandise below regular retail.

General Merchandise Discount Stores

General merchandise discount stores sell high volumes of merchandise, offer limited service, and charge lower prices. Discount stores are divided into two categories: **all-purpose discount stores,** which offer a wide variety of merchandise and limited depth, and category specialists (category killers), which carry a narrow variety of merchandise and offer a wide assortment. The all-purpose category is dominated by stores such as Wal-Mart, K-Mart, and Target. Category specialists, also known as category killers or stores with category dominance, are large specialty stores that carry a narrow variety of merchandise and a wide assortment. Among examples of category specialists are office-supply stores, such as Staples, Office Max, and Office Depot (see Figure 11-7); home-improvement centers, such as Home Depot and Lowe's; bookstores, such as Borders; children's stores, such as Toys "R" Us; and furniture stores, such as IKEA, which dominate the modern, basic furniture market.

Off-Price Retailers

Off-price retailers sell brand-name and designer merchandise below regular retail prices. The products they sell may include overruns, irregular products, and products from previous seasons. Among examples of off-price retailers are the following:

- Factory outlet stores, for designers such as Ralph Lauren, Liz Claiborne, and Jones New York, and for porcelain manufacturers, such as Dansk and Royal Doulton

Figure 11-7
Office-supply category specialists have different sections created to look like a single store. The technology section is featured in this photo.

- Department store outlets, such as Off Fifth for Saks Fifth Avenue, Last Call for Neiman Marcus, or Nordstrom Rack for Nordstrom's. They carry products that did not sell at discounted prices in the respective department stores.
- Close-out retailers, with broad, inconsistent assortments, such as T.J. Maxx and Marshalls, or at the high end, Filene's Basement and Duffy's
- Single-price retailers, such as the Dollar Store

The largest off-price retailer is TJX Companies, with sales at $9.6 billion. TJX owns and operates T.J. Maxx, Marshalls, HomeGoods, A.J. Wright, Winners Apparel, and HomeSense in the United States and Canada, and T.K. Maxx in Europe.[6] Just as department stores are facing difficult times because of the large discount stores, so are off-price retailers. Many consumers find that prices are not that much cheaper and, with fewer stores, using the mass discounters is a lot more convenient. To counter this trend, Filene's Basement has launched a massive advertising campaign, instead of using word-of-mouth to build its business. With in-house resources, Filene's Basement created ads using animation and a jazzy jingle to lure consumers who want to buy designer clothes at good prices.[7]

Catalog Showrooms **Catalog showrooms** offer high-turnover, brand-name goods at discount prices. A typical format for a catalog showroom is one in which customers order from a catalog in the showroom where the product is displayed and then pick up the product at a designated location. The goods sold in this retail format are not always brand-name goods; they can be goods that have not sold through the company's catalog. Typically, customers receive a catalog, which is also available in the showroom; based on the offerings displayed in the catalog and in the showroom, they order the product they would like to purchase in the store and pick it up from a designated location, often in an unassembled state.

Catalog showrooms: Showrooms displaying the products of catalog retailers, offering high-turnover, brand-name goods at discount prices.

It should be mentioned that the catalog showroom in its pure form, where consumers shop from catalogs and where there is only one product sample on the shelves, has all but disappeared. An example of a failed catalog showroom that had survived for two decades is Service Merchandise. Such catalog showroom chains have not survived primarily because other discounters offered products at similar prices and without the inconvenience of a special order process. IKEA is an example of a catalog showroom that has changed with the times, offering easy access to products that can easily be carried by consumers, but maintaining the traditional order process for heavier or special-order products.

11-3b Food Retailers

Food retailers consist of conventional supermarkets, supercenters, warehouse clubs, and convenience stores. Stores in this category account for approximately 38 percent of all retail sales.

Food retailers: Retailers selling primarily food products.

Conventional Supermarkets **Conventional supermarkets** are self-service retailers with annual sales higher than $2 million and less than 20,000 square feet of store space. Conventional supermarkets, such as Kroger, Food Lion, Albertson, and Fry's, account for almost half of all supermarket sales and offer a one-stop grocery shopping opportunity to consumers. At the Ukrop's Super Market, consumers can purchase regular groceries, as well as fresh specialty products such as sushi and pannini sandwiches. Consumers who prefer to dine in can drop their children off for an hour at the on-site day care, which is available in a number of the stores, and go to the Ukrop's café for a relatively quiet hot lunch (see Figure 11-8). Subsequently, the entire family can shop for groceries and have the products carried to the family van by a courteous store employee.

Conventional supermarkets: Self-service food retailers with annual sales of more than $2 million and with an area of less than 20,000 square feet.

Superstores: Large retailers, such as combination stores or hypermarkets, that sell food, drugs, and other products.

Superstores **Superstores** are stores with more than 20,000 square feet of space and at least $17 million in sales. The superstore category includes **combination stores** (carrying food and drug products, as well as nonfood items that account for at least 25 percent of

Combination stores: Medium-sized retail stores that combine food and drug retailing.

Figure 11-8
The Ukrop's Super Market chain in Virginia is a successful and very busy supermarket that caters to a broad spectrum of consumers.

Source: Courtesy of Ukrop's Super Markets, Inc.

sales). A number of all-purpose general discount stores, such as Wal-Mart and K-Mart, have been transformed into superstores to facilitate one-stop shopping for consumers. In their new, enhanced formats, these stores are known as the Wal-Mart Superstore and Big K, respectively, and they carry an extensive food selection in addition to broad nonfood product lines. These stores are known as **supercenters** in the United States, or **hypermarkets** in Europe, and they combine supermarket, discount, and warehouse retailing principles.

> **Supercenters:** Stores that carry an extensive food selection and drug products, as well as nonfood items (which account for at least 25 percent of sales), combining supermarket, discount, and warehouse retailing principles.

> **Hypermarkets:** Very large retail stores in Europe that combine supermarket, discount, and warehouse retailing principles—similar to superstores in the United States.

Through its creative strategies, Wal-Mart has established itself as a market leader in the superstore category. One of its recent successes is the "smaller" neighborhood-focused offering. In order to address size restrictions in certain markets that do not allow combination stores larger than 100,000 feet, Wal-Mart developed what is known as an Urban 99 supercenter that is 99,000 square feet. In general, Wal-Mart has gone a long way as it has developed its food business, operating hypermarkets, supermarkets, and its familiar discount stores and supercenters. The company wants to establish itself as a best-in-class food merchandiser. Its stores do not have a large assortment of food for each category, but, in key food categories, the company has used its advances in distribution to make its supercenters price leaders on a market basket of food wherever the company competes.[8]

Warehouse Clubs or Wholesale Clubs

Warehouse clubs (or **wholesale clubs**) require members to pay an annual fee and operate in low-overhead, enormous warehouse-type facilities. They offer limited lines of brand-name and dealer-brand groceries, apparel, appliances, and other goods at a substantial discount (see Figure 11-9). They sell to final consumers who are affiliated with different institutions, as well as to businesses (when selling to businesses, they are wholesalers, rather than retailers). The top U.S. warehouse clubs are Sam's Club (part of Wal-Mart), Costco, and B.J.'s.

> **Warehouse clubs (or wholesale clubs):** Stores that require members to pay an annual fee and that operate in low-overhead, warehouse-type facilities, offering limited lines of brand-name and dealer-brand groceries, apparel, appliances, and other goods at a substantial discount.

Costco has planned an aggressive expansion for the next decade and will open up to 25 stores in the United States in the next five years. To date, there are 319 Costco stores in the United States, but the market probably can support double that amount. Costco is also experimenting with new store concepts.[9] For example, in 2004, the company opened its second home store, selling home furnishings. In addition, its online retailing arm, Costco.com, is doing very well, selling a broad product assortment, from appliances, books, DVDs, computers and peripherals, electronics and cameras, to caskets, furniture, pharmacy goods, office products, and many services (photo processing, travel, etc.), among others.

Convenience Stores

Convenience stores are small retailers located in residential areas convenient to consumers. They are open long hours (often 24/7); carry limited lines of high-turnover necessities, such as milk, coffee, soft drinks, beer, bread, medicine, and gasoline; and offer the possibility of a one-stop shopping experience. Formats of convenience stores vary from small, independent retailers to chains such as 7-Eleven (owned by the Japanese company Ito Yokado). A new convenience store chain that is particularly successful is Wawa, which sells gasoline at reduced prices and has healthy fast food, such as wraps and fresh sandwiches.

> **Convenience stores:** Small retailers that are located in residential areas, are open long hours, and carry limited lines of high-turnover necessities.

Figure 11-9
Wholesale clubs have an enormous amount of retail space and usually several aisles of refrigerated food items.

Figure 11-10
This convenience store in a fishing area sells, among other items, knives that fishermen can use.

In the United States alone, there are 124,500 convenience stores, generating annual revenues of $283 billion. Approximately 40 percent of their revenue comes from nonfuel items, such as in-store food, beverages, and merchandise. Among these nonfuel items, the number one category is cigarettes, accounting for 38.7 percent of the in-store sales. The number two category is nonalcoholic beverages, which generates 11.7 percent of sales. The major threats to convenience stores at this time are increased cigarette taxes and the rise of self-service gasoline stations at supercenters. Because cigarettes account for more than one-third of in-store sales, higher taxes mean lower sales. Since 59 percent of convenience store customers shop around for the lowest-priced gasoline, convenience stores have a difficult time competing with the large supercenters that want to sell gas. To compete, many convenience stores have added specialty services like a fast-food restaurant, a car wash, or a lube and oil service. Selling gas and a few emergency-type products is not enough to keep convenience stores profitable.[10] (See Figure 11-10.)

11-3c Nonstore Retailing

Nonstore retailing is extremely small compared to the other two categories but offers the potential of being the fastest growing. Internet retailing, or e-commerce, is the newest participant in this category and has the greatest potential for growth. Other components of nonstore retailing include vending machines, television home shopping, catalog retailers, and direct marketers.

Marketing Illustration 11-1

Online Shopping Deals: Great, But Retailers Are No Longer Giving Away the Store

In the recent past, retailers offered incredible deals to consumers for simply making a first purchase online. Drugstore.com offered a $50 gift and free shipping to consumers purchasing drugs through its site. Similar deep discounts and promotional gifts were the norm for the industry.

Today, however, offering such deals is no longer necessary. Over a recent Thanksgiving weekend, Internet sales (excluding airline tickets) amounted to $453.4 million, a 67 percent gain over the previous year. Internet sales are robust. Consumers are no longer just responding to discounts. They resort to the Internet as a convenient way to shop and compare prices.

Discounting still exists, however, with deep discounts for out-of-season products or odd sizes. Internet retailing serves as an effective inventory-clearing mechanism, especially for clothing. Among the websites that sell liquidated goods and excess inventory are Overstock.com and SmartBargains.com.

Most of the discounts, however, are smaller, in the form of coupons, rebates, and free shipping—similar to what brick-and-mortar stores are offering. Consumers can find deals by going through sites such as Amazing-Bargains.com, FatWallet.com, eDealFinder.com, and DealNews.com, which publish information about online discounts, coupons, and rebates.

To effectively compete with brick-and-mortar retailers, online retailers have reduced or waived shipping fees to keep customers from going offline. For example, Amazon.com reduced the minimum purchase for free shipping to $49 from $99, with a $25 minimum purchase for certain products; Buy.com offers free shipping with no minimum; and BarnesandNoble.com offers free shipping for two products going to the same address.

Online discounters often have great bargains for products only weeks after the same products are available in department stores. For instance, BlueFly.com, a discount site for luxury goods, offers Armani five-pocket jeans for $59.95, $60.00 below the manufacturer's suggested retail price; a Prada messenger bag for $299.00, compared to the manufacturer's suggested retail price of $550.00; and a Kenneth Cole Reaction quilted down jacket, for half its regular price—with shipping costs of only $5.95. Consumer-electronics retailers continue to aggressively discount notebook computers, portable DVD players, digital cameras, flat-screen televisions, and other popular electronics. And Etoys continues its discounting practice, especially at holiday time, when it lowers its price for more than 1,000 items, such as dolls, puzzles, action figures, selling many of them for a fourth of their regular prices.

Source: Amy Merrick, Kortney Stringer, and Ellen Byron, "Where the Deals Are This Weekend: Pre-Christmas Sales Emphasize Clothing, Electronics, and Toys; Using Free Gift Cards as a Lure," *Wall Street Journal* (December 16, 2004): D1; Barbara Whitaker, "Online Shopping Is Up, and Prices Can Still Be Down," *New York Times* (December 8, 2002): 10.

Internet retailing (or interactive home shopping or electronic retailing): Selling through the Internet using websites to increase market penetration and market diversification.

Internet Retailing **Internet retailing** (or **interactive home shopping** or **electronic retailing**) is quickly becoming an important retail format. The Internet retailing category includes both traditional retailers and the new dot-com companies (bricks and clicks, respectively). Traditional retailers are attempting additional market penetration through the Internet—making it convenient for loyal customers to purchase their products—as well as market diversification—expanding their market to consumers who otherwise would not normally shop in their particular retail establishment. Internet retailing provides opportunities for retail firms to define their market beyond their geographic target regions.

Internet consumers might encounter unethical Internet retailers. Whereas brick-and-mortar retailers can be sued in a local court of law for nonperformance, Internet retailers are sometimes elusive. The issue of the appropriate jurisdiction if problems arise further complicates the situation.

It should also be mentioned that most catalog retailers, such as IKEA, Eddie Bauer, Lands' End, and Spiegel, are now also selling through their own web pages. See Marketing Illustration 11-1 for more information on online shopping deals.

Vending machines: An interactive mode of retailing convenience goods.

Vending Machines With the advent of the Smart Card, **vending machines** have become more popular than ever (and, increasingly, more vending machines worldwide accept credit cards). Technology is now facilitating a more interactive consumer relationship, in which videos illustrate product use and provide more information. Vending machines are conveniently located close to consumers, allow for 24-hour access, and eliminate the need for salespeople. In the United States, they primarily sell beverages and food items. In Japan, they are very popular, and sell just about anything one can think of, including beer, sausage, rice, life insurance, eggs, cameras, pantyhose, and condoms. In Munich,

Germany, vending machines for fresh flowers are located in the center of town. In much of the rest of the world, with the exception of the United States and Canada, cigarettes are readily available in the streets at all times of the day. In most of Europe, condoms are sold in vending machines outside pharmacies.

Because of society's demand for convenience, the first Tiktok Easy Shop, a mini-mart–sized vending machine, was developed. Located in Washington, D.C., this first Tiktok Easy Shop was 200 square feet and offered over 200 items. With the use of a robotic arm, products can be fetched from one of 10 different shelves. The holding bin can hold up to 10 items before it is dispersed to the customer. In addition to candy, sandwiches, and beverages, the vending machine offers toothpaste, milk, aspirin, bread, diapers, razors, shampoo, motor oil, and a number of food items like bread, milk, and cereal. The giant vending machine is ideal for small spaces where a store cannot be built, such as busy pedestrian areas at railroad stations, office buildings, hospitals, and university dorms.[11]

Television Home Shopping The **television home shopping** category includes cable channels selling to consumers in their homes, infomercials, and direct response advertising shown on broadcast and cable television. The primary television shopping networks in the United States are the QVC and the Home Shopping Network. All sell products to consumers in a format that approximates that of a talk show with a primary focus on the product and on making the sale. Infomercials also have a talk-show format, often featuring celebrities or other appropriate spokespeople who, during half-hour-long television programs, attempt to sell a product. Television home shopping formats require consumers to contact the company through a telephone number flashing on the screen, or by sending a check to the company at an address listed on the screen.

Television home shopping: Retailing through cable channels selling to consumers in their homes, through infomercials, and by direct-response advertising shown on broadcast and cable television.

QVC, Inc. is the envy of many direct marketers and e-commerce retailers, with sales totaling $3.9 billion. Shipping charges are never disputed, repeat purchases account for a large portion of sales, and customers have a high level of trust in both the products being sold and the hosts presenting the merchandise. QVC watchers are extremely loyal, watching an average of 3.5 times a week. Repeat purchases from these individuals account for 44 percent of all QVC transactions. Between 180 and 200 items are shown each day, about nine per hour, with about 40 percent of the goods selling out when they are shown. The remaining 60 percent are moved to QVC's website.[12]

Interestingly enough, television home shopping ranks up there with the networks in terms of revenue. For example, QVC boasted the third largest revenue in 2004, just behind NBC and CBS, while HSN occupied the seventh place in the rankings (see Table 11-2).

TABLE 11-2

The Top 10 Networks: Ranking by 2004 Revenue
($million)

Rank	Network	2003	2004	Change
1	NBC	$4,461	**$5,062**	+13.5%
2	CBS	$4,050	**$4,449**	+9.9%
3	QVC	$3,845	**$4,150**	+7.9%
4	ABC	$3,190	**$3,325**	+4.2%
5	ESPN	$2,869	**$3,223**	+12.3%
6	Fox	$2,244	**$2,405**	+7.2%
7	HBO	$2,200	**$2,398**	+9.0%
8	HSN	$1,660	**$1,880**	+13.3%
9	TNT	$1,312	**$1,590**	+21.2%
10	Nick	$1,150	**$1,300**	+13.0%

Source: John M. Higgins, "Still Strutting After All These Years," *Broadcasting & Cable*, vol. 134, no. 50 (December 13, 2004): 20.

Direct-mail retailing: Retailing using catalogs and other direct mail, instead of brick-and-mortar stores.

Catalog retailers: Retailers selling products through mail catalogs.

Direct selling: Selling that involves a salesperson, typically an independent distributor, contacting a consumer at a convenient location (such as his or her home or workplace), demonstrating the product's use and benefits, taking orders, and delivering the merchandise.

Network marketing (or **multilevel marketing):** An alternative distribution structure, using acquaintance networks for the purpose of distribution.

Independent retailers: Retailers that operate only one outlet that is usually located conveniently close to the customer. The corner convenience mart, the ethnic grocer in suburbia, and the comic bookstore in a strip mall are all examples of independent retailers.

Retail chains: Two or more retail outlets that are commonly owned and that involve central purchasing and decision making.

Retail franchises: Franchises that result from a contract between franchisors (who could be manufacturers, wholesalers, or service providers) and a retail franchisee (an independent buyer or group of buyers), allowing the franchisee to own and operate one or more units of the franchise in return for franchise fees and royalties.

Retailer cooperatives: Associations of independent retailers who engage in centralized buying and promotion.

Catalog Retailing and Direct-Mail Retailing **Direct-mail retailing** refers to retailing using catalogs and other direct mail, instead of brick-and-mortar stores. Department stores and supermarkets often send direct mail to their valued customers to inform them about sales. Consumers can go to the store or order the advertised products by telephone or online.

Catalog retailers—retailers selling products through mail catalogs—are very popular in the United States. Numerous products are sold through catalogs. Gardeners ordering from one catalog retailer will find themselves on the list of many other catalog retailers—such as Heirloom Roses, Wayside Gardens, Edible Landscaping, and Mellinger's. Most gardening catalog retailers offer a colorful website as an alternative to the equally colorful catalog.

Catalogs and direct mail are especially popular with 30- to 39-year-olds because of the ease of shopping and the time crunch they face. More than half (52 percent) have purchased something from a catalog or direct mail in the past three months, 38 percent have purchased from a mail-order catalog, and 23 percent have purchased music or books through a mail-order club.[13] Even supermarkets send their loyal consumers direct mail.

Direct Selling In the **direct selling** retail format, a salesperson, typically an independent distributor, contacts a consumer at a convenient location (such as his or her home or workplace), demonstrates a product's use and benefits, takes orders, and delivers the merchandise. Retailers involved in direct selling are Avon Products, Nu Skin, and Mary Kay Cosmetics. Cutco knives, Electrolux vacuum cleaners, and encyclopedias are also sold through this venue. **Network marketing** (or **multilevel marketing**) is a variation on direct selling that involves signing up sales representatives to go into business for themselves with minimal start-up capital. Their task is to sell more "distributorships"—that is, to identify more sales representatives from their own personal network, to buy the product, and to persuade others to buy the product. Among the most successful network marketing firms are Amway, Herbalife International, and Equinox International.

11-4 The Organization of Retailing

Although more than two-thirds of the retail establishments in the United States are independently owned, retail chains and franchises are becoming more and more important. The primary ownership categories of retailers are:

- **Independent retailers,** which operate only one outlet that is usually located conveniently close to the customer. The corner convenience mart, the ethnic grocer in suburbia, the comic bookstore in a strip mall, the nice pastry shop with a faux-French name, and the large haute-couture shop on Main Street are all examples of independent retailers.
- **Retail chains** are composed of two or more outlets that are commonly owned and involve central purchasing and decision making. Retail chains account for more than half of all retail sales and are common in the case of department stores (Dillard's, Hecht's, Bloomingdale's, Macy's, and Nordstrom's, for example), category specialists (Lowe's, Home Depot, Toys "R" Us, IKEA), supermarkets (Kroger, Ukrop's, Albertson, Fry's, Food Lion), and specialty stores (Gap, Structure, The Limited, Williams and Sonoma), among others.
- **Retail franchises** result from a contract between franchisors (who could be manufacturers, wholesalers, or service providers) and a retail franchisee (an independent buyer or group of buyers), allowing the franchisee to own and operate one or more units of the franchise in return for franchise fees and royalties. Automobile dealerships and fast-food restaurants are examples of retail franchises.
- **Retailer cooperatives** are associations of independent retailers who engage in centralized buying and promotion; among examples are Ace Hardware Stores and various grocer cooperatives.

11-5 Retailing Decisions

Retailers need to make a number of important decisions in order to most effectively appeal to their target market. They need to determine the merchandise assortment, the types of services that need to be offered, the store characteristics likely to appeal to their target consumers, and the store location that is most appropriate for their customers.

11-5a The Merchandise Mix and the Service Mix

Retailers need to determine the optimal **merchandise mix**—that is, the product assortment and brands that will be carried by the store. Related to the merchandise mix is the **service mix**—the different types of services that will be offered to the retail customers. Decisions such as product assortment and service are important aspects of marketing that necessitate extensive evaluation on the part of retailers. To illustrate, Coplon's, a regional chain for upscale women's clothing with stores in select cities in the southeastern United States (Columbia, South Carolina; Richmond, Virginia; and Charlotte, North Carolina), boasts a large selection of designer fashions in each of the three cities. The store carries daywear, cocktail dresses, evening gowns, leisurewear, and accessories by designers such as Armani, Prada, Dolce & Gabbana, Escada, Laurel, Kate Spade, St. Johns, and other regional designers of distinction. An example of such a designer is Lana Marks, a Palm Beach company, which uses exotic skins for its handbags. They retail for about $4,000. Coplon's also offers exceptional service. Distinguished, middle-aged female sales clerks who are impeccably dressed approach customers as soon as they enter the store and help them in every decision aspect. The store hosts frequent trunk shows and puts together occasional in-store designer appearances.

Merchandise mix: The product assortment and brands that the store carries.

Service mix: The different types of services offered to retail customers.

In another example, Ukrop's Super Markets carries the typical supermarket fare that most of its competitors carry. In addition, it features gourmet products, such as specialty cheeses; dinner packages with complete entrée, dessert, and bread, waiting to be picked up and served on the dinner table; and hot gourmet food in its café. It has one section dedicated to natural foods and another to international foods, among others. In terms of customer service, Ukrop's staff actually takes customers to the location of the merchandise on the shelf and, if their groceries do not fit neatly in a small grocery bag, carries them to customers' automobiles.

Many retailers today attempt to increase their merchandise mix in order to become a one-stop shopping experience for consumers. In the process, they add products that are not related to the existing merchandise mix, which is known as **scrambled merchandising.** Scrambled merchandising expands a firm's competitors' base: A wine shop could add gourmet products and fresh bread from a local baker and produce from local farmers, thus competing with other gourmet stores, bakeries, and supermarkets. An antique dealer could carry designer pillows and sheets, thus competing with department stores. A home-improvement warehouse could carry furniture, thus competing with furniture stores. From the consumer's point of view, one-stop shopping is clearly an advantage. Inside Indigo, featured in Figure 11-11, carries small furniture items and home décor specialties, along with its clothing and jewelry lines.

Scrambled merchandising: Scrambled merchandising involves retailers adding complementary product categories not included in the existing merchandise mix and more services to create one-stop shopping convenience for target consumers.

Assuming that the retailer's traditional consumers do purchase the additional products added to the merchandise mix through scrambled merchandising, there is still the possibility that the same consumers may eventually become confused as to the precise business of the retailer. There is also the danger that the retailer will start into a never-ending spiral of retailing. To illustrate, suppose a supermarket adds a line of health and beauty aids to increase its profit margins. Drug stores, because they are losing customers now, will add a product to their merchandise line, such as greeting cards, stamps, magazines, and office supplies. Because of this, stationery stores are being threatened, so to remain competitive, they add gift items, toys, novelties, perfume, and inexpensive jewelry. Consumers no longer need to go to a stationery or gift store for gift specialties, so to maintain their customers, stationary and gift stores add candy, party supplies, a deli, and perhaps a small café. What do the supermarkets

Figure 11-11
Inside Indigo uses a scrambled merchandising strategy to boost its product line beyond apparel and apparel accessories.

Source: Sample print advertisement courtesy of The Miles Agency and Alliance One Advertising, Inc.

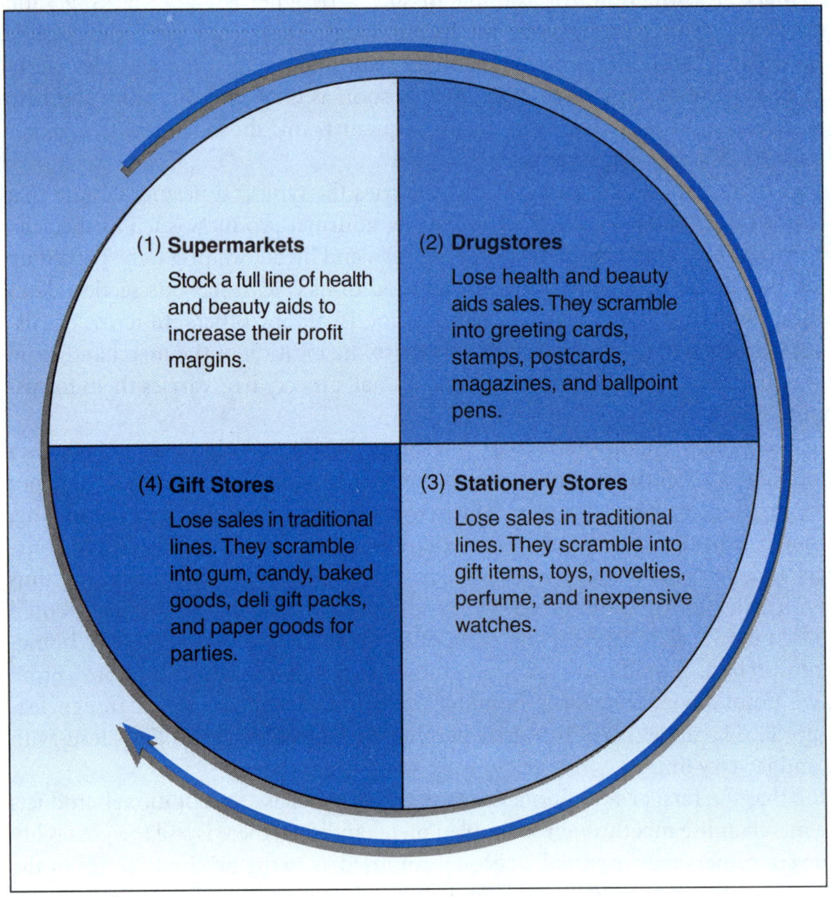

Figure 11-12
The Self-Perpetuating Nature of Scrambled Merchandising

Atmospherics: The general atmosphere of the store created by its physical attributes, including lighting and music tempo, the fixtures and other displays, colors, and store layout.

do now that some of their business is leaving? They need to add new scrambled merchandise. Figure 11-12 illustrates this self-perpetuating nature of scrambled merchandising.

11-5b Atmospherics

Atmospherics refer to the physical attributes of the store or nonstore retailer. For a brick-and-mortar store, atmospherics include lighting and music tempo, the fixtures

Marketing Illustration 11-2

Terminally Fabulous Websites

Websites have transformed the Internet into a Turkish bazaar, with noisy, cluttered pages of hyperventilated text shouting deals and casting a broad appeal that would maximize their revenue. But there are exceptions: user-friendly sites that open into an elegant and user-friendly atmosphere—with many belonging to hotels or hotel chains. Unlike Expedia, Travelocity, or Orbitz, these sites do not have to appeal to the masses; they take chances by focusing on design and daring visual effects accomplished with Flash technology that would waste valuable real estate on the other websites.

A leading pioneer of the terminally fabulous websites is Ian Schrager, the owner of a hotel chain for the sunglasses-after-dark set. IanSchragerhotels.com has a self-conscious, cool minimalist design. The site splash page is simple, with wide, gray borders and a miniature string of photographs with links to the different properties: Morgans, Royalton, Paramount, Hudson, Delano, Mondrian, Clift, St. Martins Lane, and Sanderson. It also has telegraphic links named "eat," "drink," "work," and "play" that direct readers to property descriptions and to sites that offer great shopping and dining tips. For example, it directs readers to the DailyCandy.com site, the advice bible for the urbane.

Before Ian Schrager's properties appeared online in the summer of 2002, the W hotels site, whotels.com, was by far the slickest. The W is part of the Starwood hotel brand, like the Sheraton and Westin. The site is aimed at a broader audience than the Schrager site, and it offers slide shows of the rooms, bars, and amenities.

Among other distinctive sites, Rosewood hotels has a quiet site, RosewoodHotels.com, with a Zen-type design and noise-free environment. Tablet Hotels, TabletHotels.com, is an Internet travel agency for hotels that meet rigorous specifications. The site has a tasteful design and captivating photography, and it categorizes hotels by name, destination, category, great deals, and "I Just Want to Get Away." Upon clicking on the link "I Just Want to Get Away," consumers are taken to a questionnaire where they can enter traits of the ideal getaway. If they check adjectives such as "pampering," "seduction," "adventure," and "unusual," the site suggests the Boulders in Arizona "for those with a burning desire to commune with the desert and spirits of the Native Americans, but who can't let go of their Gucci glasses or their stocked wine cellars."

Source: Bob Tedeschi, "Terminally Hip," *New York Times* (November 24, 2002): TR 8.

and other displays, colors, and store layout—in other words, all the store characteristics that create the overall mood and image for the store. For example, the Bloomingdale's department store is divided into what appears to be smaller boutiques. Individual designers or groups of designers have their own chambers, which are vividly lit. Perfumes are omnipresent, as are individuals ready to spray any of the passers-by with the newest olfactory attraction. Border's bookstore, a large category specialist specializing in book retailing, creates reading nooks with comfortable armchairs for quiet reading. The store also has a café where authors read passages from their newest books and where local bands play music.

For a web retailer, atmospherics consist of the home page and website characteristics such as overall design, product and department descriptions, and other features. Marketing Illustration 11-2 looks at some interesting websites that differentiate themselves through atmospherics.

11-5c Location

A critical decision for retailer success is location. It is important for a retailer to be located close to its customer base. Retail location determines in a large part the customer mix and the competition. In the past, most stores used to be located in **central business districts,** in the middle of busy downtowns, and often close to movie theaters and banks. In many urban areas, central business districts continue to thrive as the commercial and cultural heart of the city.

Secondary business districts are shopping areas that form at the intersection between two important streets, consisting primarily of convenience and specialty stores. **Neighborhood business districts** meet the needs of the neighborhood and tend to be located on a main street of a neighborhood; typically, they have a supermarket, a drug store, and several smaller retailers.

Central business districts: Business districts located in the commercial and cultural heart of the city, in the middle of busy downtowns, and close to movie theaters and banks.

Secondary business districts: Shopping areas, consisting primarily of convenience and specialty stores, that form at the intersection between two important streets.

Neighborhood business districts: Business districts that meet the needs of the neighborhood and that tend to be located on a main street of the neighborhood; typically, they have a supermarket, a drug store, and several smaller retailers.

Figure 11-13
Stores locate in shopping malls because of malls' appeal to shoppers. Correctly located, malls become a shopping mecca for consumers in an entire region.

Figure 11-14
Neighborhood shopping centers in Europe have a pedestrian zone; they are designed for a walking shopper, rather than for the driving public. Note the giant Pepsi point-of-purchase display outside one of the stores.

- **Shopping centers:** Groups of stores that are planned, developed, and managed as one entity.
- **Regional shopping centers:** Shopping centers that consist of at least 100 stores that sell shopping goods to a geographically dispersed market.
- **Community shopping centers:** Shopping centers with fewer than 40 retailers, containing a department store, a supermarket, and several smaller specialty retailers.
- **Neighborhood shopping centers:** Shopping centers that have between 5 and 15 retailers and that serve the neighborhood, providing convenience in the form of a supermarket, discount store, laundry service, and other smaller specialty stores.
- **Specialized markets:** Markets that contain specialty stores specializing in a particular product category.

Shopping centers consist of a group of stores that are planned, developed, and managed as one entity. **Regional shopping centers** consist of at least 100 stores that sell shopping goods to a geographically dispersed market; they tend to have three or four anchor stores or generator stores and several other retailers in between. Customers are drawn from the entire area to its stores (see Figure 11-13 for an illustration of a regional shopping center).

Community shopping centers have fewer than 40 retailers, with a department store, a supermarket, and several smaller specialty retailers. **Neighborhood shopping centers** have between 5 and 15 retailers and serve the neighborhood, providing convenience in the form of a supermarket, discount store, a laundry service, and other smaller specialty stores. In Europe, neighborhood shopping centers are likely to have a small pedestrian zone that cannot be accessed with automobiles; these neighborhoods are created for a walking, rather than a driving, shopper (see Figure 11-14). **Specialized markets** contain specialty stores specializing in a particular product category. An example is the diamond district in New York.

11-6 Trends in Retailing

Retailers operate in a rapidly changing environment. New retailers need to be innovative and proactive in order to survive; established retailers can easily fail if they do not keep up

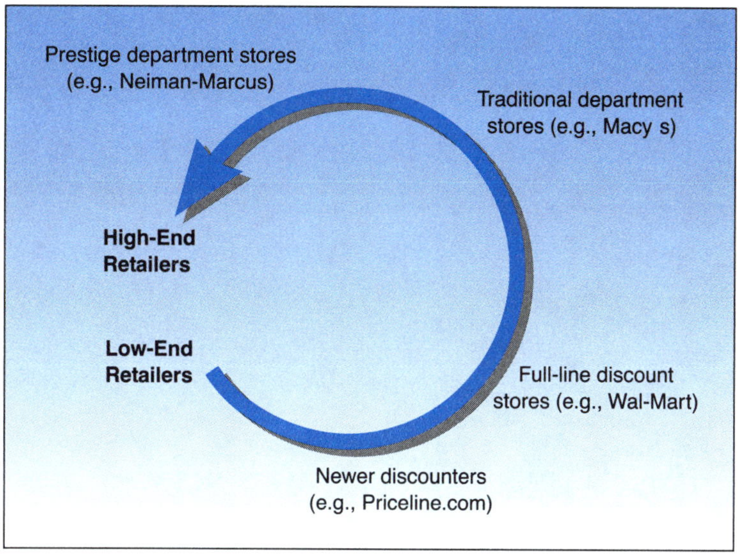

Figure 11-15
The Wheel of Retailing in Action

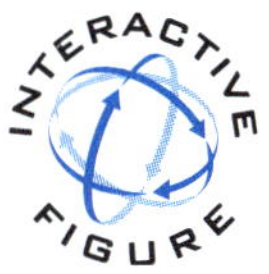

with retailing trends and practices. Moreover, the Internet has radically changed retailing practices. For existing retailers, it has created new possibilities for reaching old and new consumers, but it has also created new competition.

11-6a Shortening Retailer Lifecycles: The Wheel of Retailing

New forms of retailing are quickly emerging and rapidly reaching maturity. Whereas the department store took a century to reach maturity, new formats, such as warehouse clubs and Internet retailing, have reached or are quickly reaching maturity in less than a decade.

The **wheel of retailing** partially illustrates the evolution of retailing. It describes how stores that start out as innovative low-margin, low-cost, and low-price operations seek to broaden their customer base by adding services, upgrading facilities, and thus increasing costs and prices. In the process, they lose their initial customers, who move on to new low-priced retailers, and become conventional retailers. Ultimately, these conventional retailers fall off the wheel, as they are replaced with more innovative retailers climbing up on the wheel. The wheel of retailing is illustrated in Figure 11-15.

Wheel of retailing: Description of how stores add services and increase prices, thereby losing their initial customer base.

The wheel of retailing could explain the disappearance of many department stores, like Gimbels and Ames, that lost their middle-class customer base as they attempted to climb higher on the wheel. Another example is Bonwitt Teller, an upscale clothing specialty store that survived for decades until it decided to climb beyond the stratosphere of established high-end retailers, such as Bergdorf Goodman's and Henri Bendel; initially, all three were competing for the same consumers with robust bank accounts.

11-6b Technology-Based Developments

Technology is facilitating the retailing function, eliminating the need for salespeople, and increasing the accuracy of transactions. Pumping gas today is largely a self-service transaction, as is banking. Optical scanners have greatly facilitated the checkout process, ensuring accurate calculation, and facilitating inventory control. At many stores today, consumers can scan their own groceries and pay for them with credit cards, thus lowering the cost of human resources for the retailer.

The Internet, as mentioned earlier, enables traditional retailers to further penetrate their current market, offering convenience to loyal customers who purchase their products. It also allows them to diversify and expand their market to consumers who otherwise would not normally use the respective retail establishment, even to consumers in international markets interested in the retailer's offering.

Figure 11-16
This store offers an Asian olfactory and visual experience and, with the help of technology, auditory impressions that suggest that there is an elephant, rather than a tram, outside the door ready to take customers home after a day of shopping.

In other developments, retailers are attempting to use technology to create brand experiences. Shoppertainment is the logical blend of retailing and leisure that increases the guests' length of stay and, very importantly, the total spending on the retailer's premises. World retail brands and consumer product companies in the new millennium are aiming to create entertaining in-store environments that delight customers and increase the likelihood of repeat visits and spending. For retailers, experiential consumption is slowly becoming the norm worldwide (see Figure 11-16).

11-6c The Broadening Competitive Base

Retailers are facing increasing competition from competitors who are not in the same retail category. Part of this trend is attributed to scrambled merchandising, whereby retailers add unrelated goods in order to provide one-stop shopping convenience to consumers and increase their own profits. For example, in the past, gourmet coffee was available only at gourmet shops and coffee houses. Today, you can purchase gourmet coffee at gourmet shops, at gourmet coffee houses, at many supermarket chains, at wholesale clubs, at drug stores, and over the Internet. Consumers can purchase books at bookstores, at discounters such as KMart and Wal-Mart, at Internet sites such as Amazon.com, at supermarkets, and drug stores. Similarly, brand-name consumer electronics are no longer the realm of high-end specialty stores, as Marketing Illustration 11-3 explains.

11-6d International Expansion of Retailers

Retailers are rapidly expanding internationally to gain competitive advantage and to increase sales, profits, and overall firm performance. As they expand beyond their home-country borders, retailers also can take advantage of cost savings and learn from experiences in a way that could further enhance home-country operations. Tesco, the British retailer, for example, is using its stores in Central and Eastern Europe as a testing ground for ideas that are intended for application in the home market. The new Tesco Extra in Newcastle, U.K., is based on a Tesco hypermarket in Hungary.[14] Retailers from the United States are expanding in Latin America, Asia, and Europe. Wal-Mart, for example, has adopted an aggressive strategy for international penetration: Its purchase of the Asda Group (United Kingdom) has boosted its international sales to $25 billion, which is only a fraction of its total sales figure of $165 billion. Its ambition is for the international operations to account for a third of sales growth by 2004, which would mean $72 billion in revenue from international operations. Although some of this growth can be attributed to its Latin American operations, Wal-Mart's primary focus remains on Europe.[15]

Marketing Illustration 11-3

Discounters Expand Their Competitive Horizons with High-End Products

Shopping for consumer electronics at Wal-Mart or Kmart used to mean shopping for a no-name black box that had a plug attached to it and performed just fine. Consumers and manufacturers agreed that discounters were not respectable enough as outlets for their expensive and relatively upscale products.

However, today's Wal-Mart, Kmart, and Target are closing in on what used to be the realm of specialty retailers, stocking their shelves with the latest in consumer electronics, with brand names such as Panasonic and Sony. And these brands are flying off the shelves. Discounters are expanding their stock of electronic gadgets as well. Shopping for plasma TVs, MP3 players, and personal digital assistants no longer requires a trip to the mall, to Circuit City, or to Best Buy. Instead, consumers can add these brand-name products to the cart along with skim milk and canned veggies and check out with a successful one-stop shopping experience at their favorite discounter.

Specialty stores are taking these developments seriously. When the consumer electronics industry was growing, Wal-Mart and the other discounters did not hurt their business as much as they do now that the industry has reached maturity. Moreover, the wavering economy is holding spending in check, and consumers are flocking to discounters for bargains in all product categories. The result is that the difference between specialty stores and discounters is narrowing, and consumer electronics retailers accustomed to high profit margins on their electronic gadgets are likely to underperform. Indeed, Circuit City and Best Buy have experienced a substantial fall in sales compared to previous years.

The discounters' expansion into consumer electronics does not constitute the only attempt of the industry to expand its competitive horizons. As an example, discounters, as well as home-improvement stores, are expanding their garden section to compete with garden specialty shops, carrying high-end brands such as Jackson & Perkins for roses and what used to be special-order items, such as Brown Turkey figs, Nana pomegranates, and organic insecticides.

Source: Constance Hays, "Discounters Stalking High-End Territory," *New York Times* (December 14, 2002): B1, B14.

European retailers are expanding internationally as well. The top European grocery retailers are expected to command a 40 percent market share by 2005 in Europe; the five leading European retailers—Carrefour, Metro, Intermarché, Rewe, and Auchan—presently control a 25.4 percent share of the European grocery market.[16] In the process of internationalization, many retailers are subscribing to the current trend of consolidation in the food and general merchandise sectors. Examples of such consolidation are offered by Wal-Mart's acquisition of one of the largest United Kingdom grocery chains, the Asda Group; Royal Ahold's purchase of the Pathmark, Giant, and Stop & Shop chains in the United States; and the merger between two medium-sized French Wal-Mart lookalikes, Promodes and Carrefour, now present in all markets under the Carrefour name.[17]

Retailers expanding internationally must be aware of different regulations in the countries where they operate. Among some examples, regulations could restrict the expansion of superstores and hypermarkets (United Kingdom, France, and Belgium); limit the hours of operation to protect smaller stores (the Netherlands, Spain); require that stores locate in downtown areas (Germany); control disposal of packaging used for transportation (Germany); limit the use of promotional pricing (France, Germany);[18] and limit the period for sales to two weeks, twice a year (various countries in the European Union). French companies, for example, rarely offer an extra product free because the amount companies are allowed to give away is limited to 7 percent of the total value. In Germany, bundling offers, such as offering three products for the price of two, are illegal, and cash discounts to the consumer are limited to 3 percent.

Furthermore, retailers expanding internationally must be aware of different retail practices from one market to another. Consumers in the United States prefer to shop less frequently and purchase products in bulk, whereas consumers in Japan prefer to purchase products in smaller quantities, packaged individually. In Asia, store demonstrations are very popular, and in Japan and Korea, Saturday is a major shopping day, when shopping and attending the respective store demonstrations are a family affair. Consumers in Asia and the United Kingdom prefer products of the highest quality and are willing to pay the price. In Argentina and Saudi Arabia, consumers prefer to purchase food products at mom-and-pop stores, rather than at the supermarket, whereas in Mexico, consumers continue to go to farmers' markets for fresh produce. Even bugs on fruit are important to consumers in the Philippines; the bugs indicate that the fruit is ripe. Finally, in the United Kingdom, store name is a better indicator of quality for food products than brand name; hence, private labels are thriving for very popular stores.[19]

Summary

1. *Provide an overview and description of the general merchandise retailing category and offer examples and illustrations.* In the general merchandise retailing category are a number of retailers. Specialty stores, offering narrow assortments and deep product lines, are rapidly increasing their presence internationally. Department stores (general retailers that offer a broad variety of goods and deep assortments) are experiencing somewhat of a decline, whereas general merchandise discount stores are rapidly expanding, with great success. Wal-Mart, K-Mart, and Target, in particular, have made great strides in attracting consumers. Category specialists, specializing in one product category, are also very successful. Catalog showrooms, selling high-turnover, brand-name goods at discount prices, are going out of business, but of all catalog showrooms, the IKEA "model" has been the most enduring.

2. *Provide an overview and description of the food retailing category and offer examples and illustrations.* Food retailers include conventional supermarkets, which are dominated by national and regional chains. Superstores are large combination stores (food and drug); in the rest of the world, they are known as hypermarkets. Warehouse clubs are becoming very popular worldwide, and many U.S. retailers in this category are doing very well. Convenience stores abound, with many chains developing in conjunction with gas stations.

3. *Provide an overview and description of the nonstore retailing category and offer examples and illustrations.* Nonstore retailing is one of the areas with the highest growth and unlimited opportunities. Internet retailing has vastly expanded opportunities for small- and medium-sized retailers all over the world. Vending machines are increasing in sophistication and have different formats and capabilities in each market where they are available; the products they can carry also differ. Television home shopping is attracting more audiences, and today also offers opportunities to brick-and-mortar retailers to expand. Catalog retailers are still strong, expanding rapidly on the Internet. Direct selling and network marketing continue to gain ground, especially in developing countries.

4. *Address issues related to retailer organization, retailing decisions in terms of merchandise and service mix, location, atmospherics, and future trends in retailing.* In terms of organization, retailers can be independent, operating only one outlet that is usually located conveniently close to the customer; part of chains, which are composed of two or more outlets that are commonly owned; franchises, which result from a contract between franchisors and a retail franchisee; and cooperatives, which are associations of independent retailers who engage in centralized buying and promotion. Retailers need to make a number of important decisions in order to most effectively appeal to their target market. They need to determine the merchandise assortment that they should carry, the type of service that they should offer, the store characteristics likely to appeal to their target consumers, and the store location that is most appropriate for their customers. Among the trends in retailing are the shortening of the retailer lifecycle, with new forms of retailing quickly emerging and rapidly reaching maturity; technological changes that facilitate inventory control and the overall retail transaction, as well as access, facilitated by the Internet; broadening of the competitive spectrum, with many stores expanding beyond their traditional product mix; and rapid internationalization to take advantage of new opportunities and increase the retailers' bottom line.

Key Terms

all-purpose discount stores (p. 328)
anchor stores (or generator stores) (p. 326)
atmospherics (p. 336)
catalog retailers (p. 334)
catalog showrooms (p. 329)
category specialists (category killers) (p. 326)
central business districts (p. 337)
combination stores (p. 329)
community shopping centers (p. 338)
convenience stores (p. 330)
conventional supermarkets (p. 329)
department stores (p. 326)
direct-mail retailing (p. 334)
direct selling (p. 334)
food retailers (p. 329)
general merchandise discount stores (p. 328)
hypermarkets (p. 330)
independent retailers (p. 334)
Internet retailing (or interactive home shopping or electronic retailing) (p. 332)
merchandise mix (p. 335)
neighborhood business districts (p. 337)
neighborhood shopping centers (p. 338)
network marketing (or multilevel marketing) (p. 334)
off-price retailers (p. 328)
regional shopping centers (p. 338)
retail chains (p. 334)
retail franchises (p. 334)
retailer cooperatives (p. 334)
retailing (p. 324)
scrambled merchandising (p. 335)
secondary business districts (p. 337)
service mix (p. 335)
shopping centers (p. 338)
specialized markets (p. 338)
specialty stores (p. 326)
supercenters (p. 330)
superstores (p. 329)
television home shopping (p. 333)
vending machines (p. 332)
warehouse clubs (or wholesale clubs) (p. 330)
wheel of retailing (p. 339)

Discussion Questions

1. What are the primary functions of retailers involving consumers and channel members?
2. What is the difference between a specialty store and a category specialist? Can a specialty store also be a category specialist?
3. Hypermarkets are a dominant retailing format in Europe but not in the United States. What are hypermarkets? What type of U.S. retailer category do they most resemble?
4. Direct selling and network marketing are very popular today. What is the difference between the two categories of retailers, and how do they gain access to consumers?
5. Discuss the different types of retailer categories and offer examples of each.
6. Discuss the location decisions of retailers in your town. Identify the central business district. Is there more than one within a 40-mile radius? Where are the secondary business districts and the neighborhood business districts in your town? Where are the regional business districts?
7. What are some of the challenges that retailers face in international markets?

Review Questions

True or False

1. Category specialists offer great product depth and narrow product breadth.
2. Off-price retailers sell brand-name products and designer merchandise of lower quality than those available in department stores.
3. Convenience stores gain more and more profitability in the United States because they offer efficient shopping and, by shopping at convenience stores, consumers can avoid huge crowds at the malls.
4. In the Internet age, television home shopping does not have much popularity.
5. Independent retailers typically operate just one outlet that is located conveniently close to consumers.
6. Scrambled merchandising describes the mix of assortments and brands in one particular product category carried by the retailer.
7. Regional shopping centers consist of fewer than 40 retailers with a department store, a supermarket, and several smaller specialty stores.
8. The wheel of retailing illustrates how stores that start out as innovative low-margin, low-cost operations seek to broaden their customer base by adding services and increasing prices. In the process they lose their initial customer base and become conventional type retailers; soon they fall off the wheel as more innovative retailer chains replace them.
9. A reason for retailers to expand internationally is to increase sales and profits by taking advantage of new consumer markets.

Multiple Choice

10. Retailing involves which of the following activities?
    - a. creating convenience for consumers
    - b. informing consumers about retailer's prices
    - c. serving the other channel members by breaking bulk
    - d. all of the above
11. Which of the following retailer formats generates the highest revenue in the United States?
    - a. department stores
    - b. supermarkets
    - c. discount stores
    - d. warehouse wholesale clubs
12. Which stores most often serve as anchors in the mall, generating traffic for the stores situated in between?
    - a. all-purpose discount stores
    - b. category specialists
    - c. department stores
    - d. off-price stores
13. What type of retailer is a self-service retailer with annual sales higher than $2 million and less than 20,000 square feet of storage space?
    - a. supermarkets
    - b. superstore
    - c. combination stores
    - d. warehouse clubs
14. Which of the following retail formats serve the consumer at convenient locations, demonstrating the product's uses and benefits, taking orders, and delivering the merchandise?
    - a. direct mail retailing
    - b. scrambled merchandising
    - c. nonstore retailing
    - d. direct selling
15. Which of the following categories create atmospherics in a retail store?
    - a. lighting and music tempo
    - b. interior fixtures and displays
    - c. store layout and color selection
    - d. all of the above

Notes

1. John Leland, "How the Disposable Sofa Conquered America," *The New York Times Magazine* (December 1, 2002): 86–92, 96.
2. "IKEA Strategy Targets Big/Bigger/Best Stores," *DSN Retailing Today*, vol. 43, no. 21 (November 8, 2004): 28; Jay McIntosh and Julie Kunkel, "Top 100 Global Retailers," *Chain Store Age*, vol. 80, no. 12 (December 2004): 73–78; Mercedes M. Cardona, "IKEA, Circuit City Stores Go Bilingual," *Advertising Age*, vol. 76, no. 1 (January 3, 2005): 19.
3. Bernadette Casey, "Make Room for Big Box Outside Big Apple," *DSN Retailing Today*, vol. 44, no. 1 (January 10, 2005): 9.
4. Faye Brookman, "US Letter," *Soap, Perfumery & Cosmetics*, vol. 71, no. 1 (January 1998): 17; Howard Rudnitsky and Julie Androshick, "Leonard Lauder Goes Scalloping," *Forbes*, vol. 158, no. 14 (December 16, 1996): 96–100.
5. Mike Duff, "Discount Veteran Ames to Liquidate After 44 Years," *DSN Retailing Today*, vol. 41, no. 16 (August 26, 2002): 1, 27.
6. "The TJC Companies, Inc.—the Fabric of Diversity," *Black Collegian*, vol. 32, no. 2 (February 2002): 128.
7. Lisa Van der Pool, "Filene's Basement Breaks First Ads in Two Years," *Adweek New England Edition*, vol. 38, no. 15 (April 9, 2001): 3.
8. Mike Duff, "Building Up EDLP Food by Being 'Best in Class,'" *DSN Retailing Today*, vol. 43, no. 17 (September 6, 2004): 40.
9. Doug Desjardins, "Costco Still Bullish on Growth at Home and Abroad," *DSN Retailing Today*, vol. 43, no. 3 (February 9, 2004): 4–5.
10. Ken Clark, "Fighting for Foot Traffic," *Chain Store Age*, vol. 78, no. 10 (October 2002): 44–45; Margaret Sheridan, "Convenient Location," *Restaurants & Institutions*, vol. 112, no. 22 (October 1, 2002): 67–71.
11. Neal Learner, "Vending Machines That Match the Minimart," *Christian Science Monitor*, vol. 94, no. 239 (November 4, 2002): 16.
12. Matthew Haeberle, "Loyalty Reigns at QVC," *Chain Store Age*, vol. 78, no. 10 (October 2002): 72.
13. Barbara White-Sax, "Appealing to the Time-Crunched 30s," *Drug Store News*, vol. 21, no. 9 (June 7, 1999): 78–81.
14. Alexandra Jardine, "Retailers Go on International Shopping Trip," *Marketing* (January 20, 2000): 15.
15. Kerry Capell and Heidi Dawley, "Wal-Mart's Not-So-Secret British Weapon; It's Using Its Asda Unit for an All-Out Assault on Europe," *Business Week*, no. 3665; Industrial/Technology Edition (January 24, 2000): 132.
16. "European Consolidation," *Progressive Grocer*, vol. 79, no.1 (January 2000): 22.
17. For a discussion of these mergers, see Allyson L Stewart Allen, "Ensure Success by Studying Europe's Lessons," *Marketing News*, vol. 34, no. 4 (February 14, 2000): 11; "Global Retailing in the Connected Economy," *Chain Store Age*, New York, vol. 5, no. 12 (December 1999): 69–82.
18. See Brenda Sternquist, *International Retailing* (New York: Fairchild Publications, 1998); and David Reed, "Country Practice," *Marketing Week*, vol. 20, no. 4 (July 3, 1997): 45–49.
19. Terry Hennessy, "International Flavors," *Progressive Grocer*," vol. 78, no. 8 (August 1999): 67–73.

Case 11-1 Defining Competition at Ukrop's Super Markets

Ukrop's Super Markets, Inc., a family-owned supermarket chain in Virginia, has proven that it is, in fact, possible to compete with the national supermarket chains and the Wal-Marts of the world—a daunting task for regional, family-owned grocers. Ukrop's is proving that it can not only compete but also maintain a dominant presence in its chosen Virginia markets. Ukrop's employs more than 5,600 people, has 27 stores, three manufacturing facilities and a distribution center, and annual sales of $699 million. The retailer is the supermarket sales leader in Richmond, distancing itself from competitors with a third of the market share.

However, retailers are increasingly competing with other food retailers—not just supermarkets. Mass merchandisers, warehouse club stores, supercenters, convenience stores, and drug stores sell grocery items. When these stores are taken into consideration, Ukrop's Super Markets has 23.8 percent of the market share, according to Bobby Ukrop, the chain's CEO.

Ukrop's is continuously expanding in areas other than traditional supermarket fare. In 1976, Ukrop's purchased Richmond's premier pastry shop, and now Ukrop's offers bread, rolls, donuts, bagels, decorated cakes, pies, and pound cakes. In 1989, Ukrop's opened a new store concept that included a grill and cafe, chilled prepared foods, European pastries, a flower shop, and a pharmacy; it also began preparing "ready-made" dishes, today offering more than 400 varieties.

More recently, Ukrop's decided to enter into the banking business in a partnership with the National Commerce Bank of Memphis, Tennessee, creating First Market Bank. Ukrop's Super Markets owns 49 percent interest in First Market Bank, which today has 24 full-service offices (18 contained within the supermarkets and six traditional branch locations) with more than $700 million in assets. First Market Bank is now the largest local bank in Richmond; three of the previously existing banks were sold to financial institutions in Charlotte.

Ukrop's has also created the renowned Carryout Catering program, following an industry trend of substantial annual supermarket catering sales of $800 million nationwide.

"If you do the right things for the right reasons, good things will happen," asserts Jim Ukrop, the chain's chairman. "We've been lucky to be in the right place at the right time."

Questions

1. Is Ukrop's engaged in scrambled merchandising? Explain. Will this help Ukrop's compete more effectively, or will it create greater overhead and reduce profits?
2. How has Ukrop's broadened its competitive base? Who are its new competitors? How similar are the new competitors with the retailer's old competitors?
3. Advise Bobby Ukrop about new possible related areas where the company could expand in the future. How does it stay ahead of Wal-Mart and the other large chain stores?

Sources: Bob Ingram, "Catering, Supermarket Style," *Supermarket Business,* vol. 54, no. 8 (August 1999): 71–75; "Retail Entrepreneurs of the Year: Joseph Ukrop/Jacqueline Ukrop/James Ukrop/Robert S. Ukrop, *Chain Store Age,* vol. 77, no. 12 (December 2001): 42–43.

Case 11-2 The "Real" Bergdorf Customer—Core Consumer Versus Aspirational Consumer

Economic distress caused by a volatile stock market, job insecurity, terrorism, and the threat of war has affected all consumers, from the well-heeled luxury shopper to the rubber-soled bargain hunter at Wal-Mart. Yet, these two ends of the market are, in fact, the healthiest; it is the middle market that is suffering most. Sales of inexpensive items and luxury brands remain strong—a trend that economists have dubbed "the hourglass effect."

For high-end specialty market retailers, the outlook is promising: According to the U.S. Census Bureau, there are 15.1 million households with an annual income in excess of $100,000. One in 7 households today earns at least $100,000, versus 1 in 11 a decade ago. Of this segment, the sub-segment of luxury consumers, according to Michael Calman, Senior Vice President of Marketing for Bergdorf Goodman's, a luxury specialty store on Fifth Avenue in Manhattan, may not be shopping or socializing quite as often, but when they do, they are even more selective on their purchases, especially in apparel. The well-dressed woman who pays full price for Hermes and Yves St. Laurent bags and Manolo Blahnik shoes also frequents luxury purveyors like Piaget and Harry Winston, where $8,000–$120,000 watches are still selling very well.

The segment of luxury consumers who have been most hurt by the downturn in the economy are those who want to be part of the luxury world, for whom spending $1,000 on a handbag or $2,000 for a watch is a big purchase. These wealthy wannabes are having to make do with the luxury brands they find at discount warehouse clubs like Costco, where high-end watches and even Ralph Lauren apparel are common. This aspirational consumer prefers to purchase accessories, such as sweaters, ties, bags, and jackets, which together constitute the least expensive way to create an image and can be seen.

Luxury retailers are wooing the wealthy via in-store events and promotions, often with a charity tie-in, to make them feel special. Beauty parties and luncheons with fashion designers facilitate the shopping experience at Bergdorf Goodman's, where a relaxing atmosphere sets the tone. Offering special services, such as personal shoppers and in-store concierges, is considered more important than ever.

Luxury consumers are spending money on products with high endurance and timeless appeal: This consumer may wear Old Navy jeans with Gucci loafers, with a mindset that suggests "Just because I'm rich enough to afford it doesn't mean I'm stupid enough to spend it." And luxury consumers are eager to participate in loyalty programs where the rewards are interesting enough. Neiman Marcus offers a snakeskin-patterned Nokia phone cover, a trip to Los Angeles or a movie premiere with *Instyle*, a photo shoot with Annie Liebovitz, or one of six automobiles (among them, a Volkswagen Beetle and a BMW convertible). And Bergdorf Goodman's offers a first-class trip to Sweden's Ice Hotel or complimentary tickets to the Tony Awards.

Questions

1. A focus on a retailer's core consumer is important in the long term. How does this case demonstrate that?
2. Who are the competitors of high-end luxury specialty stores such as Bergdorf Goodman's and Neiman Marcus in difficult economic times?
3. What retailers would be in a position to market themselves to the aspirational consumers who want to display their luxury class but cannot afford it?
4. What is the best method of marketing to the aspirational consumer? What is important in terms of merchandise and service mix? What about the atmospherics? How important is the location of the store?

Sources: Sandra Dolbow, "Catering to the Well-Heeled," *Brandweek*, vol. 43, no. 39 (October 28, 2002): 26–29; Amanda Beeler, "Heady Rewards for Loyalty," *Advertising Age*, vol. 71, no. 34 (August 14, 2000): s8.

12

Pricing Strategies

CHAPTER OBJECTIVES

1. Define pricing and examine the external and internal influences on pricing decisions.
2. Examine the different price objectives: sales-based, profit-maximization, product-quality leadership, and status-quo.
3. Address the pricing strategies: cost-based, demand-based, competition-based, and combination pricing.
4. Address strategic marketing applications in relation to pricing, such as price variability, price psychology, price discounting, and pricing in relation to the marketing mix.
5. Address strategies that companies use to change prices.

CHAPTER OUTLINE

According to Marshal Cohen, Co-President of NPD Fashionworld, shoppers' economic status no longer determines where they shop. Price has become one of the most important considerations for consumers, who are now more educated than ever. Consumers were once attracted by the atmosphere, assortment, and customer service available at department stores. They also knew that department stores were the only places where they could purchase brand-name merchandise, and department stores alone carried a cachet. Today, the mysterious ways of merchandising have been reduced to one dimension: price. Consumers will not pay full retail price at department stores. In fact, consumers of all economic strata of society shop at discounters that stack the brand-name merchandise high and offer minimal service.

The exodus from department stores to bare-bones discounters has accelerated in the past five years. "Consumers are laser-beam–focused on finding the best value," says analyst Emme P. Kozloff of Sanford C. Bernstein & Co. "And the absolute best value is a (wholesale) club."

On a sultry June afternoon in Plano, Texas, the bargain hunters are out in force for the grand opening of a new Sam's Club, and shoppers are swirling around a 20-carat, $1.2 million diamond, snacking on fresh Alaska salmon, and scoping out good deals. With most retailers enduring the worst sales drought in a decade, the likes of Sam's, where consumers and businesses pay annual fees ranging from $30 to $100 to shop, are still packing them in. The clubs' formula of ultralow prices and deals on selected upscale merchandise is helping Sam's (part of Wal-Mart Stores), Costco Wholesale, and BJ's Wholesale Club steal business from just about every other retailing segment. And the addition of fresh food and gasoline is bringing customers in more often. Renovations and the addition of quality brand-name merchandise, such as Waterford crystal, Birkenstock sandals, Ralph Lauren sheets, and Grohe bathroom fixtures, aimed at higher-income customers continue to bring consumers to these clubs—and successfully so: ACNielsen found that higher-income households (those with incomes higher than $70,000) constitute 37 percent of all warehouse club shoppers.[1]

Price deals are drawing consumers in droves to McDonald's for its 99-cent Big 'n' Tasty burger, to discounters and other retailers slashing prices to keep up with them, and to automobile dealerships that advertise their markup as lower than competition. Price-cutting strategies (such as the clearance sale illustrated in Figure 12-1) have proven successful with today's deal-prone consumer.[2]

Figure 12-1
Today's deal-prone consumers are looking for storewide sales, clearance sales, price reductions, and any other type of pricing incentive that will result in a good bargain.

12-1 Chapter Overview

Consumers demand low prices. Manufacturers and all other intermediaries in the channel of distribution must focus on cutting costs and maintaining high quality to address consumers' needs. If they do not, consumers will defect to competitors. Department stores will be replaced with discounters, and one brand will be replaced with another that performs similarly and has a similar design.

Pricing is a central marketing strategy element due to its effect on product positioning, market segmentation, demand management, and market share dynamics.[3] Setting prices is a complex undertaking. Numerous internal and external variables, such as the nature of the product, the location of production plants, the type of distribution system used, and the economic climate, must be evaluated before determining the final price of products and services.[4]

This chapter addresses challenges that firms face internally when setting prices. It also addresses the impact of the competitive, political and legal, and economic and financial environment on firm pricing decisions. Section 12-2 offers a definition of pricing and addresses external and internal influences on pricing. Section 12-3 addresses the different price objectives: sales-based, profit-maximization, product-quality leadership, and status-quo objectives, as well as other objectives involving pricing. Section 12-4 examines the cost-based, demand-based, competition-based, and combination pricing strategies. Section 12-5 addresses strategic marketing applications in relation to pricing, such as price variability, pricing psychology, price discounting, and pricing in relation to the marketing mix, while Section 12-6 examines issues related to changing the price.

12-2 Influences on Pricing Decisions

Price is defined as the amount of money necessary to purchase a good or service. Everything and everyone has a price. A marketing manager's price is his or her salary, which accounts, in part, for the individual's ability, work experience, education, and training. CEOs of large multinationals have a much higher price than foremen in an industrial supply firm. A hamburger has a price, which captures various costs incurred in obtaining and processing the ingredients, in paying for distribution costs, for the franchise royalties, space rent, and advertising. Pets have a price, from a $100 spaying fee for an adorable half-breed street puppy from the local SPCA to $14,000 for a superb Hyacynth Macaw parrot.

Price: The amount of money necessary to purchase a good or service.

As the chapter-opening vignette suggests, in today's economy, price plays an essential part. Many products are standardized in the mature marketplace of the United States, and competition stands ready to chip away at company profits by offering the same product at a lower price. A business can use its pricing strategy wisely in order to reach its objectives and maximize its revenue. In fact, price is the only element of the company's marketing mix that produces revenue; product, place, and promotion, the other elements of the marketing mix, represent costs to the firm. This section addresses the different influences on price decisions: external influences and internal influences.

12-2a External Influences on Price

The primary external influences on price are consumers, economic influences, intermediaries' influences, competitive influences, and the government.

Law of demand: Economic law whereby consumers are believed to purchase more products at a lower price than at a higher price.

Consumer Influences on Price Consumers play an important role in determining the final price of products. According to the **law of demand,** consumers purchase more products at a lower price than at a higher price. For each price the company may charge, there will be a different level of demand. This relationship is illustrated in the **demand curve,** which portrays the number of units bought for a particular price in a given time period. Figure 12-2a shows the demand curve for most products: As price increases, the quantity demanded decreases. Marketing managers can influence the price-quantity

Demand curve: Curve that portrays the number of units bought for a particular price in a given time period.

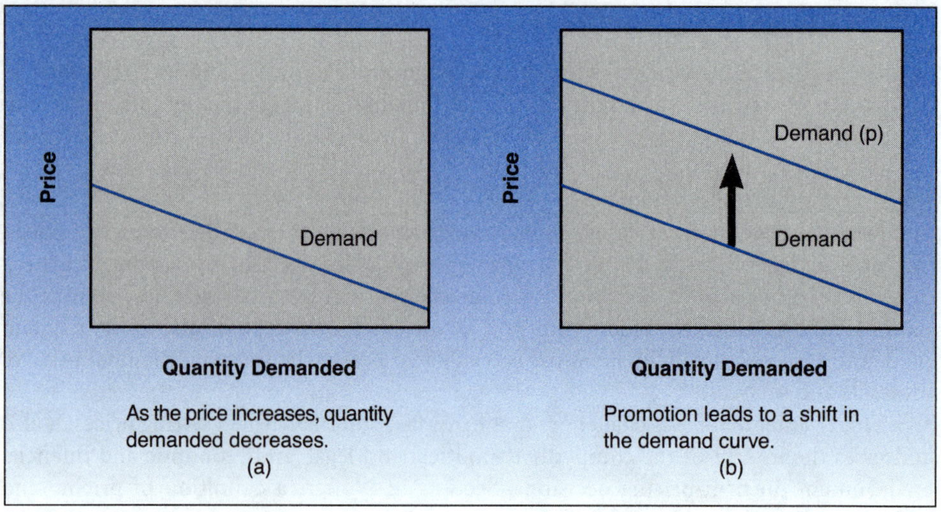

Figure 12-2
Demand Curves
(*a*) Demand curve for most products. (*b*) Demand curve shift as a result of promotion.

INTERACTIVE FIGURE

demanded relationship to a certain extent. For example, they could increase promotion for the product. This would lead to an increase in the quantity demanded, as illustrated in Figure 12-2b, causing a shift in the entire demand curve.

However, consumers may or may not be sensitive to price changes. For example, introducing a high excise tax on cigarettes has not led to a change in cigarette demand in any of the 50 states, regardless of the tax imposed.[5] Cigarette users view cigarettes as necessities and are thus not likely to give up smoking as a result of price increases. Demand for cigarettes is inelastic; it does not respond to price changes. **Price elasticity** is defined as buyer sensitivity to a change in price. The formula for calculating price elasticity is

Price elasticity: Buyer sensitivity to a change in price.

$$\text{Price Elasticity of Demand} = \frac{\text{Percent Change in Quantity Demanded}}{\text{Percent Change in Price}}$$

or

$$\text{Price Elasticity of Demand} = \frac{\dfrac{\text{Quantity 1} - \text{Quantity 2}}{\text{Quantity 1}}}{\dfrac{\text{Price 1} - \text{Price 2}}{\text{Price 1}}}$$

The formula calculates the percentage change in demand for each percentage change in price. Demand is elastic if a small change in price results in a large change in demand (see Figure 12-3a). For cigarettes, demand is inelastic; that is, for a small change in price, there is only minimal, if any, change in the quantity demanded (see Figure 12-3b).

If consumers believe that products are relatively similar and there are many product substitutes, they are less likely to purchase at high prices. Thus, for these consumers, demand is elastic. Marketers who understand elasticity price their products and run their promotions accordingly (see Figure 12-4). Delta Airlines, for example, offers deeply discounted fares for consumers to fly across country in October or February because the airline understands that, for these consumers, demand is elastic. They are more likely to travel if airfares are discounted. Business travelers, however, must travel on short notice and their travel cannot be postponed until prices are lower. For these consumers, who cannot purchase tickets far in advance, Delta Airlines maintains high prices during these months, in spite of the seasonal slowdown in the business.

In addition to economic considerations, other consumer behavior-based determinants explain price-related behavior. For example, deal-prone consumers are more likely to

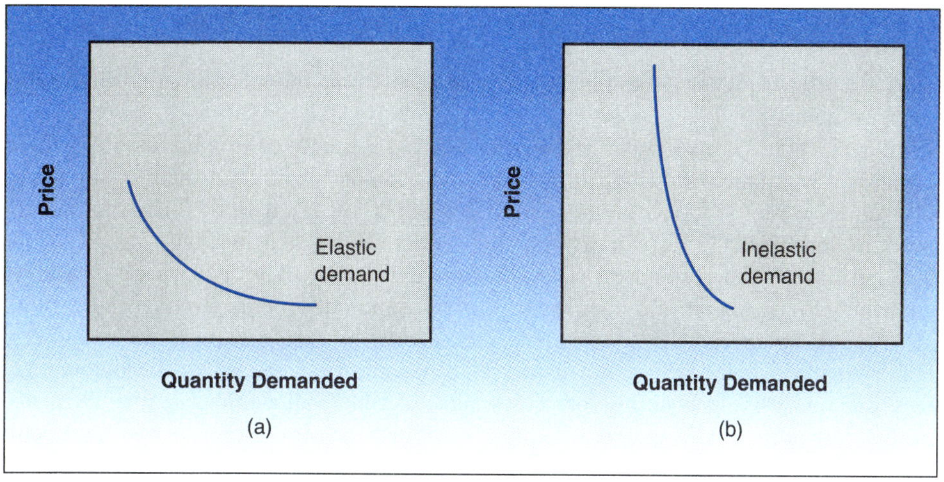

Figure 12-3
Demand Elasticity
(*a*) Elastic demand.
(*b*) Inelastic demand.

Figure 12-4
Products like the On Time wildlife feeders face an elastic demand curve.

Source: Courtesy of Newcomer, Morris and Young.

respond to deals than consumers who are not deal-prone. Similarly, consumers loyal to a brand will purchase that brand even if prices increase—up to a point. Consumers loyal to a retailer will pay higher prices for the privilege of shopping there because they prefer special treatment.

For example, Ukrop's Super Markets offer extra services to consumers shopping there: Employees carry the products to the shopper's automobile and load them in the trunk. Consumers who ask about the location of a product are taken to the aisle that has the product, and the employee will pick up the product off the shelf for them. In spite of the fact that Ukrop's charges higher prices, the stores are busy at all hours. Ukrop's consumers are willing to pay higher prices for the extra service and atmosphere (see Figure 12-5).

A company's pricing decisions are also influenced by customer profitability and customer retention. As addressed in Chapter 1, "Scope and Concepts of Marketing," companies are increasingly focusing on customers' lifetime value—that is, the estimated profitability of the customer over the course of his or her entire relationship with the company. Customer lifetime value in essence determines each customer's profit and loss (P&L).[6] Three primary success drivers for marketing programs are customer profitability, customer profit potential, and the likelihood of retention:[7]

Customer profit: Profit measure calculated as revenue minus costs for that particular customer.

Customer profit—Many companies are starting to calculate profit for each of their customers. Customer profit is calculated as revenue minus costs for that particular customer, and it is a measure of past performance. In general, it is believed that a profitable customer needs to be retained, and much of a firm's efforts are concentrated on customer retention, based on the assumption that acquiring new customers takes much more effort and cost than retaining old customers. Under this assumption, a particularly valuable customer is one who has had a profitable relationship with the company.

Customer profit potential: An estimate of the individual's contribution to a company's bottom line.

Customer profit potential—Customer profit potential is an estimate of the individual's contribution to a company's bottom line. This figure is obtained by comparing estimated potential using external data predictors such as demographics, psychographics, and summarized credit data by geographic location to actual profit. When estimating customer profit, the company should also find out who currently is not profitable but looks like they should be.

Retention: The ability of the firm to maintain a particular customer over time.

Retention—Customer retention adds value to the enterprise at practically exponential rates. A two-point improvement in retention, for instance, from 82 percent to 84 percent, adds 6 percent to current value.

Figure 12-5
Consumers are willing to pay higher prices at Ukrop's because of superior customer service, attractive atmosphere, and higher product quality.

Source: Courtesy of Ukrop's Super Markets, Inc.

Economic Influences on Costs and Price Economic factors, such as inflation, recession, and interest rates, affect pricing decisions because they affect the cost of producing a product. An inflationary environment places strong pressures on companies to lower prices; often, pricing competitively may mean that companies are not producing a profit. During inflationary periods, firms often find that they must decide between maintaining a competitive presence in a market and weathering the downside of the economic cycle or abandoning the market, which is a high-cost, high-risk proposition.

The cost of materials, supplies, and labor are among the many costs that are not within a firm's control. For example, several factors affect the cost of gasoline at any time. Price increases can be caused by rising crude oil costs (the raw material that accounts for 40 percent of the retail price for gas). Political turmoil in one or more oil-producing countries can be a factor behind the drop in supplies and rise in costs. The Iraq war led to unprecedented increases in the price of oil and a leap in the price of energy worldwide. The price can also be affected by the risk premium accompanying the political or economic uncertainty in the Middle East. Environmental regulations, such as the Tough Clean Air Act requirements for reformulated gasoline and the proliferation of distinct fuel blends, can create price increases. Similarly, summer is the time of both the highest motor fuel demand and of the imposition in metropolitan areas of costly environmental regulations designed to fight smog. In Europe, consumers are paying high prices for gasoline due to very high taxes and high oil prices (see Figure 12-6). On the other side, gas prices could be lowered by opening parts of Alaska's Arctic National Wildlife Refuge and other U.S. sites to oil exploration and drilling.[8]

Intermediaries' Influences on Price As seen in Chapter 10, "Distribution Strategies," intermediaries attempt to have some level of control over their own markups, while at the same time, taking into consideration the price that consumers are willing to pay. Intermediaries are becoming more and more efficient at inventory management, using just-in-time delivery methods, quick-response inventory systems, and electronic data interchange, which allow intermediaries to lower their inventory carrying costs and facilitate the flow of products. The use of computerized distribution centers and efficient intermodal transportation using containers also cut intermediary costs.

These developments in channel management and logistics have had a moderating influence on the price that consumers pay for products. Distribution prices have also been kept in check by the fact that consumers are now willing to do with less service in return for a lower product markup at the retail checkout aisle.

Figure 12-6
Gasoline prices in Europe are very high due to high taxes and oil prices; by comparison, gasoline prices in the U. S. are a bargin.

Competitive Influences on Price Competitive forces constitute important determinants of firm pricing strategies. Pricing strategies must take into consideration both the competitive environment and the firm's position relative to competition. Firms can control prices only if their product is in the early stages of the product lifecycle and they are one of the market leaders. During maturity, the competitive field is broad, characterized by products that are relatively similar, based on the prevalent standard. In this type of market, individual firms have little control over price. Therefore, the goal of firms at this stage is to keep product prices low, by, for example, moving production to a low-labor-cost country. In the maturity stage, companies can still maintain some control over price if their products are well differentiated and have a high degree of brand franchise. Finally, in certain markets, such as utilities, prices are regulated by the government to ensure access to the services for all consumers. Utilities can also be owned and operated by the government. In planned economies, such as those of China, North Korea, and Cuba, the government sets most prices.

Pure competition: Market that consists of many buyers and sellers, where no buyer or seller can control price or the market.

An economics perspective describes four different types of markets based on competition. **Pure competition** characterizes a market that consists of many buyers and sellers, where no buyer or seller can control price or the market. In this environment, marketing plays a minimal role. Because sellers can sell as much as they want and buyers can buy as much as they need, perfect market information is available to both buyers and sellers, and the product sells for about the same price in the marketplace. Although pure competition is difficult to accomplish in the marketplace, commodities are examples of products sold in the environment that come closest to pure competition.

Monopolistic competition: Market that consists of many buyers and sellers and products that vary greatly in the same product category.

Monopolistic competition characterizes a market that consists of many buyers and sellers and products that vary greatly in the same product category. Products are differentiated based on price, style, flavor, and other characteristics important for the final consumer. An example in this category is coffee, which sells under many brands, such as Maxwell House, Folgers, Eight O'Clock, Taster's Choice, Starbucks, store brands, regional distributor brands, and even ethnic brands, such as Vassilaros and Venizelos. These brands are clearly differentiated, and price changes for one brand may not lead to a change in pricing strategy for another. Figure 12-7 illustrates how Skechers uses price, style, and brand image to differentiate its brand.

Oligopolistic competition: Market that consists of few sellers who dominate the market.

Oligopolistic competition characterizes a market that consists of a few sellers who dominate the market. Change in the strategy of one seller is going to directly affect the other sellers in the marketplace. The automobile industry and the airline industry are characterized by oligopolistic competition. In terms of pricing, the airlines follow very similar pricing strategies. The airlines charge similar prices for the same type of consumer: leisure traveler, business traveler, or off-peak traveler. For example, if one airline lowers prices to attract travelers in the low season, then, typically, all the airlines follow suit.

Pure monopoly: Market that consists of only one seller.

Pure monopoly characterizes a market that consists of only one seller. This seller could be the government, for planned economies, or a government-owned utility company, in the case of market economies. An example of a government-owned monopoly in the United States is the U.S. Post Office. Other examples of monopolies are private regulated monopolies, such as local power companies, and unregulated monopolies, as in the case of pharmaceutical companies' drugs that are under patent protection. Regulated monopolies are often required to maintain lower prices to ensure access to the good or service to all consumers. Unregulated monopolies can charge any price the market will bear, but often they do not do so because the need brand-loyal consumers, or because of concern that the government may interfere.

The Government's Influence on Price The government plays an important role in pricing. The government has enacted legislation to protect competitors, channel members, and consumers from unfair pricing strategies. Among examples of areas where the government becomes involved in the pricing strategies of the firm are the following:

Price discrimination: The practice of charging different prices to different buyers of the same merchandise.

- **Price discrimination**—Legislation such as the Robinson-Patman Act prohibits charging different prices to different buyers of the same merchandise and requires

Figure 12-7
Because hiking boots compete in a monopolistic market, companies like Skechers can use price, style, and brand image to differentiate their product from competing brands.

Source: Courtesy of Skechers USA.

sellers that offer a service to one buyer to make the same service available to all buyers.

- **Resale price maintenance**—Manufacturers are prohibited from requiring retailers to charge a particular price for a product. They are allowed, nevertheless, to print a suggested retail price on the product package or attached label. Manufacturers can, however, use an exclusive distribution channel that allows them some level of control over the retailer marketing strategy, including pricing.
- **Price fixing**—Legislation such as the Federal Trade Commission Act and the Sherman Antitrust Act addresses all types of unfair competition, including price fixing—an agreement between channel members at the same level in the channel of distribution to charge the same price to all customers. Companies are frequently scrutinized for their price-fixing practices: Christie's and Sotheby's, the most prominent auctioneers of art and antiques, have recently paid large fines, and their reputations have suffered greatly after they were found to engage in price fixing.
- **Deceptive pricing**—There are many examples of pricing strategies that sellers use, such as stating prices or price savings, that may mislead consumers or that are not available to consumers. Firms are prohibited from engaging in deceptive pricing by the Sherman Act, the Clayton Act, the Wheeler-Lea Act, the Federal Trade

Resale price maintenance: Manufacturers requiring retailers to charge a particular price for a product.

Price fixing: Agreement among channel members at the same level in the channel of distribution to charge the same price to all customers.

Deceptive pricing: Strategy used by sellers who state prices or price savings that may mislead consumers or that are not available to consumers.

Marketing Illustration 12-1

Dumping as a Competitive Threat

Dumping—selling products below cost to get rid of excess inventory and/or to undermine competition—is an important factor affecting pricing decisions. A typical example of dumping involves a foreign company that enjoys high prices and high profits at home as a result of trade barriers against imports. The company uses those profits to sell at much lower prices in foreign markets to build market share and suppress the profitability of competitors with open home markets. Dumping can cause injury to an established industry in a particular market.

The United States Department of Commerce, the government branch responsible for determining whether products are dumped on the U.S. market, considers that dumping takes place if products are priced only minimally above cost, or at prices below those charged in the producing country. Dumping challenges and charges abound. China, Japan, and South Korea have often been challenged for dumping products in the United States and Europe. As established by the World Trade Organization, after determining that price discrimination did indeed occur and that a particular local industry was injured by the dumping activity, governments are entitled to impose antidumping duties on the merchandise. Similar to these are countervailing duties, which are imposed on subsidized products imported into the country. Such subsidizing could, for example, take the form of government aid in the processes of production and/or distribution.

Enforcement of antidumping regulation is particularly intense when the economy is not faring well and when price competition is high. In the recent past, the United States Department of Commerce and the International Trade Commission scrutinized numerous importers' pricing practices, using strict criteria to determine whether the importer had committed price discrimination and, if so, if it resulted in injury to a particular local industry. Electronics, textiles, and steel, among others, originating in countries from Japan to Russia to Mexico, have been at the center of antidumping action in the past few decades.

Source: Greg Mastel, "The U.S. Steel Industry and Antidumping Law," *Challenge*, vol. 42, no. 3 (May/June 1999): 84–94.

Predatory pricing: Pricing strategies used to eliminate small competitors and to deceive consumers.

Dumping: Selling products below cost to get rid of excess inventory and/or to undermine competition.

Price confusion: Strategies to confuse consumers so that they do not quite understand the price that they ultimately have to pay.

Unit pricing: Pricing that allows consumers to compare among prices for different brands and for different package sizes of the different brands.

Commission (FTC), and various state laws. Unfair pricing tactics include predatory pricing, bait-and-switch tactics, and price confusion strategies. **Predatory pricing** is charging prices below cost to eliminate small competitors. One way to do this is through **dumping,** which is selling products below cost to get rid of excess inventory and/or to undermine competition (Marketing Illustration 12-1 addresses the influence of dumping on product prices). Bait-and-switch strategies advertise items at a low price; however, when customers arrive, they are told that the store is out of stock, and the retailer attempts to sell them a higher-priced item. The last type of unfair pricing is **price confusion,** which firms use to confuse consumers, so that they would not quite understand the price that they ultimately have to pay. Examples of the latter abound: AT&T Wireless charges for calls that go unanswered for more than 30 seconds; New York theaters charge a "theater restoration fee" or a "facilities fee"; some hotels charge a "connectivity fee" for access to the phone and the Internet, and another fee for safes, whether or not the phone, the Internet, or the room safe are used.[9]

Many states also require retailers to engage in **unit pricing**—that is, pricing that allows consumers to compare between prices for different brands and for different package sizes of the different brands. Table 12-1 addresses different examples of federal government legislation that affects pricing.

The government may also affect pricing through protectionist strategies that protect national industries from international competitors. This, in turn, leads governments of those competitors to retaliate, with a negative effect on price for all. Government protectionism adds to the final price paid by consumers. For example, the costs of protectionism for the European consumer are as high as 7 percent of the gross domestic product of the European Union—some $600 billion.[10] To illustrate, the EU's banana-import restrictions cost European consumers up to $2 billion a year or about 55 cents per kilogram of bananas. Since the United States has retaliated with punitive tariffs on $191 million of European imports, the

TABLE 12-1

Major Legislation Impacting Pricing

Legislation	Description
1890—Sherman Antitrust Act	Prohibits trusts, monopolies, and activities designed to restrict free trade. Bans predatory pricing (i.e., charging prices below cost to eliminate small competitors).
1914—Clayton Act	Prohibits price discrimination to different buyers, tying contracts that require buyers of one product to also purchase another item, and combining two or more competing firms by pooling ownership or stock. Bans predatory pricing.
1914—Federal Trade Commission Act	Created the Federal Trade Commission (FTC) to address antitrust matters and investigate unfair methods of competition. Addresses price fixing and price advertising.
1936—Robinson-Patman Act	Prohibits charging different prices to different buyers of the same merchandise and requires sellers that offer a service to one buyer to make the same service available to all buyers.
1938—Wheeler-Lea Amendment	Expanded the power of the FTC to investigate and prohibit practices that could injure the public and false and misleading advertising. Addresses price advertising. Bans bait-and-switch advertising.
1966—Fair Packaging and Labeling Act	Requires that manufacturers provide a label containing the contents, what company made the product, and how much of each item it contains. Allows for fair price comparisons.

cost of the EU's banana regime is even higher.[11] In other examples, European beef farmers receive large subsidies, while tariffs of up to 125 percent are imposed on beef imports; in addition, the European Union has a ban on hormone-treated beef from the United States. The costs incurred by European beef consumers for subsidies, tariffs, and other restrictions amount to $14.6 billion a year in the form of higher prices and taxes, or around $1.60 per kilogram of beef.[12] In spite of the Uruguay round of trade liberalization and the strides made by the World Trade Organization, protectionist actions continue to increase the costs of goods, and hence the price for the final consumer. The cost of protectionism is high in the United States as well, especially in service industries such as shipping and banking.[13]

12-2b Internal Influences on Price

Internal factors, such as the firm size, the organizational structure, and the industry focus, determine who in the company makes pricing decisions. In smaller organizations, it is usually the owner or the top managers who decide on pricing. In larger organizations, pricing is decided by the brand manager or negotiated in a business-to-business setting. In a market-oriented company, pricing is determined based on information shared with the marketing department by the other functional areas, such as finance, engineering, research and development, or sales. In fact, these departments may be allowed to have direct input in pricing decisions.

Costs are also important determinants of price. In pricing their products, companies need to take into consideration all product costs, as well as to obtain a fair rate of return

Fixed costs: Costs that do not vary with the amount of output.

Variable costs: Costs, such as raw materials, packaging, and shipping costs, that vary with the amount of output.

on investment. A company has **fixed costs,** which are costs that do not vary with the amount of output, such as building rental, maintenance, and the costs of the permanent staff. It also has **variable costs,** which vary with the amount of output, such as raw materials, packaging, and shipping costs. Together, variable costs and fixed costs make up total costs at a particular level of production. Production costs typically fall as a function of experience: As companies acquire more experience, they realize economies of scale. This leads to lower prices and increased sales volume, ultimately leading to greater profits for the company.

12-3 Setting Pricing Objectives

Firms set their pricing objectives in line with the company goals. Thus, different firms in the same industry may have different pricing objectives predicated on firm size; in-house capabilities; and focus on profit, sales, or government action. Sales-based objectives focus on increasing sales volume, profit-based objectives focus on the total return on investment, and status-quo objectives focus on maintaining a good relationship with customers, channel members, and regulatory bodies. Companies may elect to have more than one goal.

Penetration pricing: Pricing strategy whereby firms initially price the product below the price of competitors to quickly penetrate the market at competitors' expense and acquire a large market share, and then gradually raise the price.

A firm that focuses on sales-based pricing objectives attempts to increase its sales volume and its market share relative to competitors. The premise of this strategy is that sales growth will lead to dominance in the marketplace achieved at low per-unit cost. Companies often introduce new products with sales-based objectives in mind. For example, in order to achieve high sales, a company may resort to **penetration pricing,** whereby firms price the product at first below the price of competitors to quickly penetrate the market at competitors' expense and acquire a large market share, and then gradually raise the price. Compaq was able to quickly capture the European market by using this strategy. In the Netherlands, for example, Compaq offered deals unmatched by any brand-name competitor and coupled this pricing strategy with excellent warranties and support. This strategy can be used when consumers are sensitive to price, as well as when the company has achieved economies of scale in manufacturing and distribution, and can afford to sell the product at lower prices. Those low prices must be low enough to keep out competition.

Skimming: Pricing strategy whereby the product is priced higher than that of competitors.

A firm that focuses on profit-maximization pricing objectives attempts to recover the costs of product development quickly, while simultaneously providing value to consumers. Companies estimate the demand and costs at different prices and will select the price that will produce the maximum profit, or return on investment. Companies often introduce new products with profit-maximization objectives in mind. For example, they may use a **skimming** strategy, whereby the product is priced above that of competitors. The focus of the company is on immediate profit, rather than on long-run performance. This strategy is most effectively used early in the product lifecycle when competition is minimal (once there is substantial competition, there is a high likelihood that competitors will undercut the price) or when there is a high degree of brand loyalty. In general, consumers responding to skimming strategies are more concerned with quality, uniqueness, and status, rather than price. In turn, the product's image and quality must warrant the product's high price.

Product-quality leadership objectives do not necessarily mean that the company is reaping the highest potential profits. In this case, the company is not estimating the demand and costs at different prices and selecting the price that yields the maximum profit, or return, on investment; rather, the company is charging a high price to cover the costs of producing a very high quality product and the costs of related research and development.

Firms may set status-quo–based objectives when they are facing too much competition, when they want to refrain from disrupting the channel with changes, or when they do not want to be scrutinized by the government. Such objectives are used to minimize the impact of competitors, government, or channel members and to avoid sales decline. This strategy does not mean that the firm does not change prices—it must match competitors' price reductions if it wants to keep its customers, for example. It should be noted that status-quo–based objectives could be adopted only in the short term, to weather a partic-

Marketing Illustration 12-2

Low-Cost Leadership Can Be Expensive

The Ford Focus is the eleventh best-selling automobile in the United States, a cornerstone of Ford's product line, and one of the 10 best cars in the U.S. auto industry, according to *Car and Driver* magazine. Pitched as a first purchase for young people, and endorsed by William Clay Ford, Jr., the company's chief executive and Ford family scion, as comparable with Ford's Model T, the Focus is today also vulnerable to the aggressive lemon laws of Arkansas, Kansas, and Ohio. The Ford Focus has had several safety recalls since its introduction in 1999 and is the subject of five defect investigations by federal regulators, making it the second most recalled automobile in the industry.

What are the implications to the Ford Motor Company, in addition to its battered reputation on the quality front? First, its dealers are not happy: Although they are pocketing the extra profits from repairs paid for by Ford, they are losing customers for their automobiles, and their job to persuade consumers to purchase Ford automobiles is increasingly more difficult. In order to reassure new customers, Ford is now offering 100,000-mile power-train warranties for new models. The standard bumper-to-bumper warranty is three years or 36,000 miles for most vehicles. This adds further to the Ford Focus costs and to Ford's troubles, from plummeting market share, to the ravaging effect of a price war, to lowered credit ratings. In the end, low-price leadership for Ford became a high-cost proposition.

Source: Danny Hakim, "A Low-Cost Model Is a Big Headache for Ford," *New York Times* (November 6, 2002): C1, C7.

ular condition or challenge. In the long term, companies must be proactive, rather than reactive, to be able to optimally meet the needs of their target consumers.

Companies may pursue other objectives with their pricing strategies. A nonprofit restored local theater and architectural gem may charge just enough to be able to maintain the building and the antique Wurlitzer organ that emerges from the platform on Saturday nights for performances with the help of restoration experts. Different establishments may choose not to charge senior citizens for services, or charge them a reduced rate, to ensure their participation in certain events. Other companies may decide that one particular brand they offer will be a low-cost leader. It should be noted, however, that low-cost leadership can be a problematic strategy if the product is not backed by adequate performance, as Marketing Illustration 12-2 demonstrates.

A firm must coordinate its pricing strategy with its product image positioning, with product design and performance characteristics, and with its promotion and distribution strategy in order to optimally address target market needs. For example, it needs to decide how the product price fits with prices for the entire product line and how the price compares with prices of the direct competition. Coordinating pricing strategies with the overall marketing strategy is complex. Price is a flexible element of the marketing mix that can be changed quickly to respond to new market developments, unlike the product, the distribution, and the promotional strategies, which cannot be changed as quickly. It is important to note that the pricing strategy also poses the most challenge to the firm. Even companies that de-emphasize price in their positioning, opting for a quality positioning, for example, need to be mindful of how they use price to communicate. A price that is not high enough may cause consumers to question the product quality. Pricing the product too high may cause consumers to switch to competitors. In fact, pricing even slightly higher than direct competitors—competitors who also use a quality-positioning strategy—can lead to a substantial loss in market share. And pricing any product too low, regardless of positioning, may cut severely into profits, cause consumers to question product quality, and bring about a dumping inquiry from the government.

12-4 Pricing Strategies

Pricing strategies can be cost-based, demand-based, competition-based, or, when these approaches are integrated, the strategy may involve combination pricing.

Cost-based pricing: Pricing strategy whereby the firm sets the price by calculating merchandise, service, and overhead costs and then adds an amount needed to cover the profit goal.

Price floor: The lowest price a company can charge to attain its profit goals.

12-4a Cost-Based Pricing

In **cost-based pricing,** the firm sets the price by calculating merchandise, service, and overhead costs and then adding an amount needed to cover the profit goal. Cost-based pricing is relatively easy to calculate because there is no need to take into consideration the estimated price elasticity of demand or the reaction of competitors to price changes. Moreover, costs are easier to estimate than demand elasticity, competitive reactions, and market conditions. The firm's goal is to obtain reasonable profits, using a specified **price floor,** that is, the lowest price a company can charge and attain its profit goals. The cost-based pricing techniques are cost-plus, markup, traditional break-even analysis, and target profit pricing.

Cost-Plus Pricing Cost-plus pricing is relatively simple: It involves adding a target profit to total costs. Let us assume that a "boutique" nursery selling unique plants tailored to business customers' needs in the Eastern United States incurs the following costs and has the following goals:

Variable Cost	$100 per plant
Fixed Costs	$30,000
Number of Plants Produced	4,000
Desired Profits	$20,000

$$\text{Price} = \frac{\text{Fixed Costs} + \text{Variable Costs} + \text{Profit}}{\text{Number of Units Produced}}$$

$$\text{Price} = \frac{30,000 + (4,000 * 100) + 20,000}{4,000} = \$112.50 \text{ per plant}$$

As in other cost methods, this method evaluates profits as a function of costs, and the price is not linked to demand. There is no accounting for excess capacity, and there is no attempt to lower costs because profits remain the same regardless of costs. This strategy is appropriate for custom-made products, such as furniture and other unique items, equipment, and other similar goods. Typically, the nursery gets orders for a number of plants from customers, calculates the price using the cost-plus method, and sends invoices to the businesses placing the order after calculating the total costs.

Markup Pricing Markup pricing is a variant of cost-plus pricing, with a markup used to cover selling costs and profits. Using the example of the nursery (see Figure 12-8), markup pricing uses the following formulas: First, the unit cost is calculated; next, the markup price is calculated, as in the following:

$$\text{Unit Cost} = \text{Variable Cost per Unit} + \frac{\text{Fixed Costs}}{\text{Units Produced}} = \$100 + \frac{\$30,000}{4,000} = \$107.50$$

Assuming that the nursery would like to have a 10 percent markup (.10), then the price would be calculated as follows:

$$\text{Markup Price} = \frac{\text{Unit Cost}}{1 - \text{Markup Percentage}} = \frac{\$107.50}{1 - .10} = \$119.44$$

This yields a profit of \$11.94 per plant (\$119.44 – 107.50).

This method has the shortcomings of other cost-based methods that calculate profits as a function of costs and where price is not linked to demand. If the company does not meet its sales target, then its unit costs will be much higher—this method assumes costs remain the same. The markup method makes sense only if the company meets its sales target. And yet, the method is widely used. Translators, accountants, contractors, and many other service providers use this strategy to determine price. It is a method commonly used for pricing at the different levels of the channel of distribution as well. It is a popular method for a number of reasons. First, costs are easier to calculate than demand. Second, this method is based on costs, which are more stable than demand. Third, expenses, trade discounts, and markdowns are expressed as a function of sales or unit prices—and so are markups. Fourth, competitive price data are readily available, while cost data are not—markup pricing thus facilitates comparison with competition. Lastly, when all competitors use this method, prices tend to be more similar. Thus, price competition is minimized.

Figure 12-8
Nurseries and flower shops are especially profitable in early spring when consumers are eager to get back to gardening.

Break-Even Analysis Break-even analysis identifies the number of units the company needs to sell, or the total number of dollars it needs to make on sales, in order to break even with regard to costs, given a particular price. If the sales exceed the break-even quantity, the company earns a profit; if sales come short, the company has a loss. The break-even point can be calculated in terms of the number of units sold or in terms of sales dollars. Let us assume that an art book publisher is planning on publishing a catalog for a new contemporary art exhibition that will travel to numerous museum venues (see Figure 12-9). The publisher incurs the following costs and has the following goals:

Variable Cost	\$15 per book
Fixed Costs	\$130,000
Price of Each Book	\$70
Desired Profits	\$40,000

$$\text{Break-Even Point (number of units)} = \frac{\text{Fixed Costs}}{\text{Unit Price} - \text{Variable Costs per Unit}}$$

$$\text{Break-Even Point (number of units)} = \frac{\$130{,}000}{\$70 - \$15} = 2{,}364 \text{ books (units)}$$

$$\text{Break-Even Point (sales dollars)} = \frac{\text{Fixed Costs}}{1 - \dfrac{\text{Variable Costs per Unit}}{\text{Price}}}$$

$$\text{Break-Even Point (sales dollars)} = \frac{\$130{,}000}{1 - \dfrac{\$15}{\$70}} = \$165{,}456$$

Figure 12-9
Art books, especially exhibition catalogs, are often produced in small numbers at a loss. The city or state where the sponsoring museum is located may cover these costs.

The break-even point can also be calculated by taking into account the amount of profit targeted by the firm:

$$\text{Break-Even Point (number of units)} = \frac{\text{Fixed Costs} + \text{Desired Profit}}{\text{Unit Price} - \text{Variable Costs per Unit}}$$

$$\text{Break-Even Point (number of units)} = \frac{\$130,000 + \$40,000}{\$70 - \$15} = 3,091 \text{ books (units)}$$

$$\text{Break-Even Point (sale dollars)} = \frac{\text{Fixed Costs} + \text{Desired Profit}}{1 - \dfrac{\text{Variable Costs per Unit}}{\text{Price}}}$$

$$\text{Break-Even Point (sale dollars)} = \frac{\$130,000 + \$40,000}{1 - \dfrac{\$15}{\$70}} = \$216,365$$

Break-even analysis is used by many types of businesses, including intermediaries at different levels of the channel of distribution. The company can create a break-even chart, which shows the total cost and total revenue expected at different sales volume levels.

Break-even analysis has many of the shortcomings of cost-based pricing: It does not take into consideration demand, and it assumes that customers will purchase at the given price, that no purchase discounts will need to be offered over time, and that costs can be fully assessed *a priori*.

Target Profit Pricing Target profit pricing is used by capital-intensive firms, such as automobile manufacturers and public utilities, which must make a reasonable return on investment that is typically approved by the different regulatory commissions. The formula used to calculate target profit pricing takes into consideration a standard volume of production that the firm is expected to achieve. For most firms, that target is more than 90 percent of plant capacity. Assume that a motorcycle company has invested $120,000,000 for a new manufacturing plant with a 30 percent target return on investment (ROI). In its first year, its production was 70,000 units. Its average total costs for each motorcycle are $8,500 per motorcycle at a production level of 70,000 units.

Investment Cost	$120,000,000
Target ROI	30 percent
Standard Volume (number of units per year)	70,000
Average Cost per Unit	$8,500

To calculate the selling price for the motorcycle, the firm uses the following formula:

$$\text{Price} = \frac{\text{Investment Cost} \times (\text{Target ROI Percentage} + 1)}{\text{Standard Volume (units per year)}} + \text{Average Costs per Unit (at standard volume)}$$

$$\text{Price} = \frac{\$120{,}000{,}000 \times 1.30}{70{,}000} + \$8{,}500 = \$10{,}728.57 \text{ (selling price)}$$

Target profit pricing is likely to understate the selling price for firms with low capital investments. It also assumes a standard volume that may not be achievable by the firm or, if achieved, does not account for the possibility that there may not be enough demand for the units.

12-4b Demand-Based Pricing

Demand-based pricing takes into consideration customers' perceptions of value, rather than the seller's cost, as the fundamental component of the pricing decision. As such, price is considered as part of the marketing mix before assessing the costs involved. While cost-based pricing is product driven, demand-based pricing is consumer driven. For demand-based pricing, firms identify a **price ceiling,** which is the maximum amount that consumers are willing to pay for a product. The ceiling is contingent on the elasticity of demand, which itself is contingent on the availability of product substitutes and urgency of need. Demand estimates are much less precise than cost estimates because they are based on research of consumers' willingness to pay for the product at different price levels and on consumers' perceptions of product value. In highly competitive situations, firms need to lower prices, which, in turn, requires companies to keep costs low. When there is minimal competition, firms can afford to increase prices and obtain high profits from sales.

One example of demand-based pricing is **modified break-even analysis,** which combines break-even analysis with an evaluation of demand at various price levels, assuming that, as the price increases, demand will decrease in an elastic demand environment, where there are many product substitutes and competition is intense. It should be noted, however, that demand estimates are not always going to be on the mark, so this approach, while taking into consideration likely demand, is not as precise as the cost-based, traditional break-even approach. Another approach is price discrimination, in which one higher-priced product is offered to inelastic segments, and lower prices are offered to elastic segments. Discrimination could be based on consumers' ability to pay, the product features, time or season, or place. These issues are further addressed in Section 12-5e on pricing segmentation.

Key to demand-based pricing is the fact that today's consumers demand value—high-quality products at a fair price. Most consumers demand deals; they are no longer

Demand-based pricing: Pricing strategy that takes into consideration customers' perceptions of value, rather than the seller's cost, as the fundamental component of the pricing decision.

Price ceiling: The maximum amount that consumers are willing to pay for a product.

Modified break-even analysis: Analysis that combines break-even analysis with an evaluation of demand at various price levels, assuming that, as the price increases, demand will decrease in an elastic demand environment, where many product substitutes are available and competition is intense.

willing to pay high department store prices, and they refuse to pay the retail price in general. Offering deals is expected. The McDonald's Big 'n' Tasty burger at 99 cents is a favorite of consumers, drawing great numbers to the franchise. In fact, most fast-food restaurants have a few popular items on the menu for 99 cents or one dollar.

The Wal-Mart every day low price (EDLP) strategy is a clear winner and is adopted by companies that understand that consumers do not want to wait for a sale—they want deals on everything they buy, all the time (see Figure 12-10). And consumers have made it clear that they are willing to forgo service if that means being able to purchase quality products at lower prices—hence, the popularity of warehouse clubs, as illustrated in the chapter-opening vignette.

12-4c Competition-Based Pricing

Many firms choose to use competitors' prices, instead of demand or product costs, in order to determine the prices of their products. This method is useful when firms compare themselves to relatively similar companies with similar products that have similar demand patterns and similar costs. Competition-based pricing may mean that the firm prices its products at the level of competition, above the prices of competition, or below the prices of competition. Pricing at the level of competition does not lead to competitive retaliation because it does not affect competitors. Pricing below competition, however, is likely to elicit some level of competitive response.

Figure 12-10
This advertisement for Zeagler Music promotes the idea that the company's cymbals are priced using every day low pricing.

Source: Sample print advertisement courtesy of The Miles Agency and Alliance One Advertising, Inc.

In an oligopoly, typically one firm, or a few firms, tend to be the first to announce price changes, and the rest of the firms follow. This is known as **price leadership.** These firms tend to be the market leaders with well-accepted leadership positions in the industry.

Price leadership: The tendency of one firm or a few firms to be the first to announce price changes, with the rest of the firms following.

Another form of competition-based pricing is **bid pricing,** which involves competitive bidding for a contract, whereby a firm will price based on how it believes competitors will price, rather than based on demand or costs. The firm that bids lowest typically wins the contract. Most project development for U.S. development bodies such as the U.S. Agency for International Development, and for international bodies, such as the World Bank and the United Nations Development Program, are contracted using competitive bidding. The federal, state, and local governments, as well as numerous other organizations, require competitive bidding, which gives each bidding company one single chance to make an offer.

Bid pricing: Pricing that involves competitive bidding for a contract, whereby a firm will price based on how it believes competitors will price, rather than based on demand or costs.

12-4d Combination Pricing

Combination pricing is often used in practice. Firms might use cost-based pricing in order to establish the lowest acceptable price—the price floor—and then use demand and competition-based approaches when pricing their products for intermediaries, or for the final consumer. For example, a manufacturing firm might determine the maximum price that consumers are willing to pay for its products—the price ceiling—and then work backward to the product cost in order to determine the target profit it should achieve, while still allowing for reasonable markup pricing for the different levels of channel intermediaries.

12-5 Strategic Marketing Applications

This section addresses price variability, pricing psychology, price discounting, and pricing in relation to the overall marketing strategy and the other elements of the marketing mix.

12-5a Price Variability and Marketing Strategy

Consumers prefer and expect prices to be relatively stable for the most part. **Customary pricing,** whereby a firm sets prices and attempts to maintain them over time, is a strategy used to address this expectation (see Figure 12-11). One of the primary reasons for increasing prices is inflation; in this case, manufacturers are forced to pass price increases on to the final consumer. Another reason is excessive demand; in this situation, increasing prices in order to lower demand may work against the firm at some point, when consumers move on to competitors who charge lower prices, or to more distant product substitutes. And, when the cost of ingredients increases, manufacturers prefer to alter product size, or the product ingredients, rather than alter the price. Candy in the checkout aisle has relatively constant prices over time. Likewise, milk prices have not increased in years.

Customary pricing: Pricing strategy whereby a firm sets prices and attempts to maintain them over time.

Certain products, however, are priced to change. Prices at gas stations change almost daily, in direct response to changes in crude oil costs, or to changes in driving behavior—in the summer, the cost of gas goes up. Gas stations practice **variable pricing,** changing their prices in response to changes in cost or demand.

Variable pricing: Strategy of changing prices in response to changes in cost or demand.

Flexible pricing is a strategy that allows a firm to set prices based on negotiation with the customer, or based on customer buying power. For example, this deal-prone author haggles for everything from the price of a cake in a pastry shop that is about to close at the end of the day, to the price of a designer bracelet that stayed too long in a clothing store window, to the price of antiques in an exposed store on the eve of a hurricane. When purchasing a large quantity of goods, or when purchasing expensive merchandise, the consumer is likely to yield substantial savings from negotiations.

Flexible pricing: Pricing strategy that allows a firm to set prices based on negotiation with the customer, or based on customer buying power.

No-haggle pricing is a strategy that is aimed at consumers who are averse to negotiation, but who want, nevertheless, to have some sort of low-price guarantee. In the automobile industry, where prices are traditionally set based on negotiations, Saturn was the first to advertise itself as haggle-free. In the automobile resale business, CARMAX pioneered the concept of haggle-free secondhand automobile retailing, with great success.

No-haggle pricing: Pricing strategy that is aimed at consumers who are averse to negotiation, but who want, nevertheless, to have some sort of low-price guarantee.

Figure 12-11
Companies like Delta Faucet use a customary pricing strategy.
Source: Courtesy of Delta Faucets.

12-5b Pricing Psychology and Marketing Strategy

Psychological pricing refers to setting prices in order to create a particular psychological effect. One of the dimensions involved in psychological pricing is the **reference price,** the price that consumers carry in their mind for a particular product or brand. Reference prices can be created and/or influenced by previous purchase experiences, by advertising, or by the manufacturer's suggested retail price or list prices, for example.

Price is often used as a signal for quality: Consumers tend to believe that higher prices are associated with better quality, especially in cases in which quality is difficult to evaluate—for unknown brand names, for example. **Prestige pricing** is a strategy based on the premise that consumers will feel that products below a particular price will have inferior quality and will not convey a desired status and image. To support prestige pricing, retailers tend to use a psychological tool known as **even pricing** (setting selling prices at even numbers) in order to contrast with **odd pricing,** which sets prices at below even dollar values to give the impression that the product is not expensive. Upscale retailers, such as Saks Fifth Avenue and Neiman Marcus, use even pricing for most of their products; they use odd pricing only for those products they place on sale. Odd pricing is used to give the impression that consumers are getting a great value: A dishwashing machine that costs $995 is expensive, but it will not be perceived as expensive as one that is $1,000. Odd pricing typically has decimal prices that end in .99, .97, or .95—as in $999.99, $19.97, or $27.95 (see

- **Psychological pricing:** Setting prices to create a particular psychological effect.
- **Reference price:** The price that consumers carry in their mind for a particular product or brand.
- **Prestige pricing:** Strategy based on the premise that consumers will feel that products below a particular price will have inferior quality and will not convey a desired status and image.
- **Even pricing:** Setting selling prices at even numbers.
- **Odd pricing:** Setting prices at below even dollar values.

Figure 12-12 (left)
Ukrop's is using odd pricing—59 cents for each item—in this advertisement for its frozen vegetables.

Source: Courtesy of Ukrop's Super Markets, Inc.

Figure 12-13 (above)
Even pricing is preferred in Europe.

Figure 12-12). The odd/even pricing strategies are not used in many markets. In Europe, even pricing is preferred because it facilitates calculations (see Figure 12-13).

12-5c Price Discounting and Marketing Strategy

Price discounting involves reducing the price for purchasing larger quantities, for responding to a promotion, for paying cash, or responding earlier than a particular set time. There are a number of examples of discounts. One example is the *quantity discount.* Consumers as well as intermediaries typically get a price break when they purchase larger quantities of a particular product. Purchasing a mega pack of Huggies diapers results in a per-unit price that is almost half of that paid for a small package. Purchasing a package of eight Bounty paper towel rolls is significantly cheaper than purchasing eight separate rolls of identical size. These are examples of **multiple-unit pricing,** whereby consumers get a discount to purchase a larger quantity with the purpose, ultimately, to increase sales volume. The goal of the firm is for consumers to respond to the price incentive by purchasing the product, and then to increase consumption—use more paper towels for more household chores or change the baby more often.

Middlemen can benefit from *trade discounts* for selling or storing the product, *seasonal discounts* for purchasing the product in the off-season, or *cash discounts,* such as a 5 percent reduction in price for paying within two weeks. Consumers can also benefit from seasonal discounts, such as by going to a resort in the off-season. Or they can qualify for a *trade-in allowance* for turning in their old product when they purchase a new one; for example, they could receive a trade-in allowance for trading in an old automobile.

Another form of price discounting is **promotional pricing,** which reduces prices temporarily to increase sales in the short run (see Figure 12-14). Special event sales, cash rebates, low or zero-interest financing, and free maintenance are all examples of promotional pricing strategies. One strategy that retailers use and that manufacturers find problematic if it involves their brand is **loss-leader pricing,** whereby the firm advertises a product at a price that is significantly less than its usual price in order to create traffic in the stores for consumers to purchase higher-margin products. Eggs for 50 cents before Easter and turkeys for 40 cents a pound before Thanksgiving are examples of loss leaders. The problem with loss-leader pricing and with promotional pricing in general is that it can hurt the brand in the long term: Consumers will expect to find the brand at the reduced price and will refuse to purchase it at its regular price. Also, if the product is available for a very low price, consumers may come to question its quality relative to the competitors' product.

Price discounting: Strategy that involves reducing the price for purchasing larger quantities, responding to a promotion, paying cash, or responding earlier than a particular set time.

Multiple-unit pricing: Pricing whereby consumers get a discount to purchase a larger quantity with the purpose, ultimately, to increase sales volume.

Promotional pricing: Strategy that reduces prices temporarily to increase sales in the short run.

Loss-leader pricing: Pricing whereby the firm advertises a product at a price that is significantly less than its usual price in order to create traffic in the stores for consumers to purchase higher-margin products.

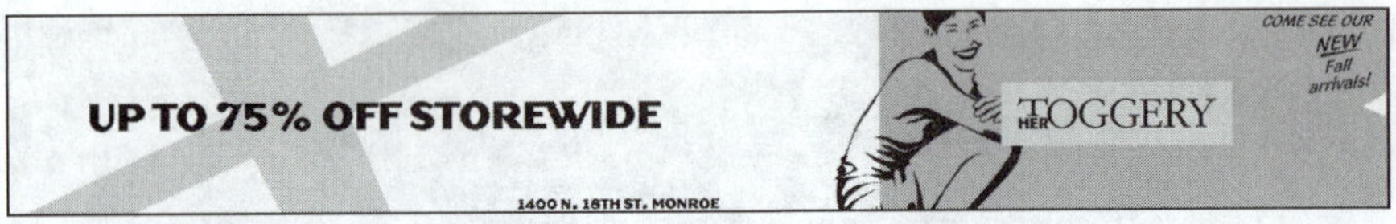

Figure 12-14
Both "Her Toggery" and "The Toggery," which is a men's store, use the promotional pricing strategy of an "Up to 75 percent off storewide" sale to attract customers.

Source: Sample print advertisement courtesy of The Miles Agency and Alliance One Advertising, Inc.

12-5d The Product and Pricing

With regard to the product component of the marketing mix, pricing can be used for numerous purposes. **Product line pricing** involves creating price differences between the different items in the product line, such that specific price points are used to differentiate between the items in the line. For example, instead of selling products for one price, using one version of a product, the firm may select to identify different market segments and price products differently for the respective segments. Segmented pricing, in this case, adjusts prices to allow for differences in the products. For example, designers offer collection lines (Ralph Lauren, Anne Klein) at higher prices and the bridge lines (Polo, Anne Klein II) at lower prices. The differences between the prices of the different lines are easily observable—thus, the price points are distinct: Ralph Lauren shirts retail for more than $55, whereas Polo shirts can be bought for less than $40. Anne Klein jackets cost at least $400, whereas Anne Klein II jackets retail for less than $400. As these examples illustrate, product line pricing is popular in the clothing industry, where designs are greatly differentiated (see Figure 12-15).

With multiple product lines, companies can appeal to different market segments, increasing their profit opportunities. Problematic with product line pricing is the likelihood that markdowns taken on the higher-price merchandise will blur the distinction between the two different lines.

Other product-related dimensions of pricing include **accessory pricing,** which addresses pricing of accessories and other optional products sold with the main product. Examples of accessories for a bed set are neck pillows, decorative pillows, valances, and other products that have the same design and that would look lovely when used with the main product. **Captive-product pricing** involves pricing of products that must be used with the main product. Examples of captive products that a company may sell are the camera docks that must be used with a digital camera in order to load the photographs on the computer, the software that must be installed in order to download the photographs, and the printer paper needed to print the photographs. **Byproduct pricing** involves pricing of

Product line pricing: Pricing that involves creating price differences between the different items in the product line, such that specific price points are used to differentiate among the items in the line.

Accessory pricing: Pricing of accessories and other optional products sold with the main product.

Captive-product pricing: Pricing of products that must be used with the main product.

Byproduct pricing: Pricing of byproducts that are of low value in order to get rid of them.

Figure 12-15
Product line pricing is common for clothing.

byproducts that are of low value in order to get rid of them. Examples of byproducts are the wood chips produced after shredding the wood of a felled tree; these chips can be treated with insecticide and used as mulch.

Bundling refers to the pricing of bundled products sold together. For example, a company can sell a product, warranty, delivery, and installation together in one bundle. Another example is the QE 2 transatlantic cruise, which includes return air, transportation to London from Southampton, and a week's stay in London, all for an amount that could be used to purchase a nice little car.

Bundling: Pricing of bundled products sold together.

12-5e The Place and Pricing

Distribution can increase product delivery costs and hence the cost of a product. **Geographic pricing** is defined as pricing that accounts for the geographic location of customers. Most IKEA merchandise is cheaper in Europe than in the United States; Levi's jeans are much more expensive in Europe than in the United States; Similac, the baby formula manufactured by Abbott Laboratories, sells in Holland for a fraction of its cost in the United States; cigarette prices in Washington state are much higher than in Virginia—all for different reasons. Geographic pricing takes into consideration the cost of distribution, as well as other factors, such as taxes, competitors who benefit from government subsidies, and consumer demand.

Geographic pricing: Pricing that accounts for the geographic location of customers.

In geographical pricing, companies must take into consideration the customers' ability to pay. Often customers do not have access to currency that is acceptable for payment; in these situations, companies have to resort to countertrade. Marketing Illustration 12-3 addresses the challenges presented by countertrade.

In addition to geographic pricing, place, time, and seasons can be used in pricing segmentation. For an example of place segmentation, seating behind home plate is more expensive than seating in the nosebleed section of the outfield in baseball stadiums. In other examples, daytime performances at the theater are cheaper than evening performances; summer rates tend to be higher than off-season winter rates for beach resorts.

12-6 Changing the Price

Companies often find that they have to make pricing changes in order to remain competitive. In inflationary times, they must pass along costs to consumers. When competition is intense and competitors are slashing prices, the company must go along with the price cuts in order to avoid losing customers. Cutting prices, however, is not always the solution: In addition to diminishing profit margins, such strategies might bring about price wars with competitors trying to hold on to their market share, crippling the entire industry.

Companies can use a number of methods to pass on increases in costs to the consumers. First, the company can communicate openly the reason for the price increase. Gas companies rely on the media to communicate this information. Because the media are perceived as more or less unbiased, this type of communication is very valuable. The gas companies themselves do not need to justify the price increase to the consumer. Retailers can also communicate price increases to consumers; in times of shortage due to drought or other natural phenomena, retailers will communicate the reason behind the high prices of produce. Another method for increasing prices is to do so without the consumer immediately noticing: by eliminating price promotions, by adding more expensive items to the product line and eliminating cheaper ones, and by changing ingredients and lowering the quantity, without altering the package.

One important concern of the firm is the reaction of competitors to product price changes. Usually, if more than one competitor follows suit in lowering the price, all the others will follow suit. If more than one competitor follows suit in raising the price, it is uncertain whether the others will do so, leaving the firm that initiated the price increase at a disadvantage, unless the firm repositions itself as a higher-quality prestige brand.

Marketing Illustration 12-3

International Pricing Challenges: Countertrade

Developing countries face a significant shortage of hard currency reserves. Hard currency is currency that is accepted for payment by any international seller; soft currency is currency that is kept at a high artificial exchange rate, overvalued, and controlled by the national government. Countertrade involves selling a product to a buyer and agreeing to accept, in return for payment, products from the buyer's firm or from the trade agency/institution of the buyer. Countertrade is on the increase worldwide. It is estimated that the percentage of the total world trade financed through countertrade transactions is just more than 20 percent. Many developing countries rely heavily on countertrade in their international trade activity; for example, as much as 70 percent of Russian industrial activity involves barter.

A typical countertrade exchange today would involve a seller from a developed, industrialized country and a buyer from a developing country where hard currency is scarce and tightly controlled by national institutions, such as the Central Bank and the Ministry of Foreign Trade. Usually, firms in the developing country are unable to secure bank loans that would finance imports of products deemed to be unessential, such as consumer products. In many developing countries (even in countries with greater access to hard currency—primarily due to the export of natural reserves, such as oil and diamonds), governments actually mandate countertrade as a form of payment for firms purchasing imported goods.

Often, countertrade is conducted with the help of countertrade brokers because it is rare that a perfect match can exist for product exchanges and because the exchanges themselves are complex. Exchanges could range from paying sausages to rock stars for their performances, to bringing French high fashion to Russian consumers by selling quality Russian crystal to Saudi merchants. In the second example, the barter of French high fashion for Russian crystal is mediated by Swedish parties, who pay cash to the French couturiers.

Numerous companies specialize in brokering barter deals. Located in many financial centers, such as London and New York, as well as in countries that have traditions of brokering barter agreements, such as Sweden, these brokers can put together intricate exchanges. Among the major U.S. corporate barter firms doing large-volume business are the New York firms of Atwood Richards, Inc., Active International, Global Marketing Resources, Media Resources International, and Tradewell, Inc. These barter agents or brokers, known in the trade as commercial trade exchanges, number approximately 400 in the United States and typically utilize extensive computerized databases to locate and match demand and supply.

The different types of countertrade usually involve monetary exchange to a certain degree. Barter can be traced as a form of exchange for centuries. It involves a simple, nonmonetized exchange of goods and/or services between two parties. Although no money is involved in the exchange, the parties calculate the value of the goods in a particular currency and attempt to achieve value parity for the exchanged goods. Another type of countertrade is performed through compensation, which involves payment in products and in cash, usually in a mutually agreed-upon convertible currency. The firm compensated using this system is at lesser risk—especially if the proportion of cash is high—than the firm that is entirely dependent on the sale of the products it receives from the trading partner. Yet another type is known as counterpurchase or parallel barter. It involves two exchanges that are paid for in cash. The seller agrees to purchase products that usually are unrelated to its business from the buyer and sell them on international markets. The purchase could be for the total sum of the products sold or for a fraction thereof. The exporter agrees to buy goods from a shopping list provided by the importer; the list typically consists of light manufactures and consumer goods. In one example, Volkswagen sold 10,000 cars to the former East Germany and agreed to purchase, over a period of two years, goods for the value of the automobiles, from a list of goods provided by the East German government. Another illustration of counterpurchase is the classic countertrade example whereby PepsiCo sold its syrup to Russia in the late 1960s; the export agreement stated that PepsiCo would subsequently import Stolichnaya vodka to be sold in the United States.

Source: Sam C. Okoroafo, "Determinants of LDC-Mandated Countertrade," *International Marketing Review*, vol. 5 (Winter 1988): 16–24; David Woodruff, *Money Unmade: Barter and the Fate of Russian Capitalism* (Ithaca, NY: Cornell University Press, 1999); Janet Aschkenasy, "Give and Take," *International Business*, vol. 9, no. 8 (September 1996): 10–12; Richard E. Plank, David A. Reid, and Frank Bates, "Barter: An Alternative to Traditional Methods of Purchasing," *International Journal of Purchasing and Materials Management*, vol. 30, no. 2 (Spring 1994): 52.

Summary

1. *Define pricing and examine the external and internal influences on pricing decisions.* Price is the amount of money necessary to purchase a good or service. Among external influences on price are consumers, who, according to the law of demand, purchase more products at a lower price than at a higher price. Economic factors, such as inflation, recession, and interest rates, also affect pricing decisions because they affect the cost of producing a product. An inflationary environment places strong pressures on companies to lower prices. Firms then find that they must decide between maintaining a competitive presence in a market and weathering the downside of the economic cycle or abandoning the market, which is a high-cost, high-risk proposition. The costs of materials, supplies, and labor are among the many costs that are not within a firm's control. Intermediaries also affect product prices, as does competition. In a competitive environment where there is pure competition, the effect is not as great as in an oligopolistic environment. Yet another external influence on the firm is exerted by the government, which takes action against unfair pricing practices, such as price discrimination, resale price maintenance, price fixing, and various deceptive pricing practices. Deceptive practices include predatory pricing, which involves charging prices below cost to eliminate small competitors (dumping to get rid of excess inventory is an example of predatory pricing); bait-and-switch tactics, which involve advertising items at a low price, telling customers they are out of stock, and then trying to sell them a higher-priced item; and price confusion, which is a strategy used to confuse consumers with regard to the actual price. Among internal factors influencing pricing are firm size and costs, such as fixed and variable costs, which are important determinants of price.

2. *Examine the different price objectives: sales-based, profit-maximization, product-quality leadership, and status-quo.* Sales-based pricing objectives focus on increasing the sales volume. One way a company can increase sales for its company is through penetration pricing, selling the product for a low price in order to gain market share. Profit-based objectives focus on the total return on investment. With this strategy, a company introducing a new product can use a skimming strategy, pricing the product high in order to recoup investments quickly in the early stages of the lifecycle. Product-quality leadership pricing objectives establish prices based on the performance and image of the product. Status-quo objectives focus on maintaining a good relationship with customers, channel members, and regulatory bodies. This strategy cannot be maintained for long, but it is useful, especially if the company is under scrutiny from the government or competition. Companies may elect to have more than one objective.

3. *Address the pricing strategies: cost-based, demand-based, competition-based, and combination pricing.* For cost-based pricing, a firm sets the price by calculating merchandise, service, and overhead costs and then adding an amount needed to cover the profit goal. Cost-based pricing is easy to calculate because it does not take into consideration the price elasticity of demand or the reaction of competitors to price changes. The cost-based pricing techniques are cost-plus, markup, target, price-floor, and traditional break-even analysis. Demand-based pricing takes consumers' perceptions into account, as well as their potential response to the product at different price levels. For demand-based pricing, firms identify a price ceiling, which is the maximum amount that consumers are willing to pay for a product; this amount is contingent on the elasticity of demand, which itself is contingent on the availability of product substitutes and urgency of need. Demand estimates are less precise than cost estimates because they are based on consumers' willingness to pay for the product at different prices and on consumers' perceptions of value. In competitive situations, firms need to lower prices and thus need to keep costs low. When there is minimal competition, firms can increase prices and obtain high profits. Many firms use competitors' prices, instead of demand or product costs, in order to determine the prices of their products. This approach is useful when firms compare themselves to similar companies with similar products that have similar demand patterns and similar costs. Pricing at the level of competition does not lead to competitive retaliation since it does not affect competitors. Pricing below competition, however, is likely to elicit some level of competitive response. Companies can also use combination pricing, or a combination of these strategies.

4. *Address strategic marketing applications in relation to pricing, such as price variability, price psychology, price discounting, and pricing in relation to the marketing mix.* With regard to price variability, companies can use customary pricing, keeping the same price over time. They can also use variable pricing, changing their prices in response to changes in cost or demand, and flexible pricing, which allows a firm to set prices based on negotiation with the customer, or based on customer buying power. Psychological pricing refers to setting prices in order to create a particular psychological effect. Price is often used as a signal for quality; as such, prestige pricing is a strategy based on the premise that consumers will feel that products below a particular price will have inferior quality and will not convey a desired status and image. To support prestige pricing, retailers use even pricing, setting selling prices at even numbers, in order to contrast with odd pricing, which sets prices at below even-dollar values to give the impression that the product is not expensive. Price discounting involves reducing the price for purchasing larger quantities, for responding to a promotion, for paying cash, or responding earlier than a particular set time. The goal in price discounting is for consumers to respond to the price incentive by purchasing the product, and then to increase consumption in the long term. Middlemen can benefit from trade discounts, seasonal discounts for purchasing the product in the off-season, or cash discounts for paying within a specified period. Consumers can also benefit from seasonal discounts, or they can qualify for a trade-in allowance for turning in their old product when they purchase a new one. Promotional pricing reduces prices temporarily to increase sales in the short run; loss-leader pricing, whereby the firm advertises a product at a price that is significantly less than its usual price in order to create traffic in the stores for consumers to purchase higher-margin products, may pose problems to the brand in the long term.

With regard to the marketing mix, product dimensions of pricing are accessory pricing, which addresses pricing of accessories and other optional products sold with the main product; captive-product pricing, which involves pricing of products that must be used with the main product; byproduct pricing, which involves pricing of byproducts that are of low value in order to get rid of them; and bundling, which refers to pricing of bundled products sold together. Place dimensions are geographic pricing, defined as pricing that accounts for the geographic location of customers, and place, time, and season pricing segmentation.

5. *Address strategies that companies use to change prices.* Companies often find that they have to make pricing changes in order to remain competitive. In inflationary times, they must pass along costs to consumers. When competition is intense and competitors are slashing prices, the company must go along with the price cuts in order to avoid losing customers. Companies can use a number of methods to pass increases in costs on to the consumers. First, the company can communicate openly the reason for the price increase. Retailers and manufacturers can also communicate price increases to consumers. In times of shortage due to drought or other natural phenomena, retailers will communicate the reason behind the high prices of produce. Another method for increasing prices is to do so without the consumer immediately noticing: by eliminating price promotions; by adding more expensive items to the product line and eliminating cheaper ones; and by changing ingredients and lowering the quantity, without altering the package.

Key Terms

accessory pricing (p. 368)
bid pricing (p. 365)
bundling (p. 369)
byproduct pricing (p. 368)
captive-product pricing (p. 368)
cost-based pricing (p. 360)
customary pricing (p. 365)
customer profit (p. 352)
customer profit potential (p. 352)
deceptive pricing (p. 355)
demand-based pricing (p. 363)
demand curve (p. 349)
dumping (p. 356)
even pricing (p. 366)
fixed costs (p. 358)
flexible pricing (p. 365)
geographic pricing (p. 369)
law of demand (p. 349)
loss-leader pricing (p. 367)
modified break-even analysis (p. 363)
monopolistic competition (p. 354)
multiple-unit pricing (p. 367)
no-haggle pricing (p. 365)
odd pricing (p. 366)
oligopolistic competition (p. 354)
penetration pricing (p. 358)
predatory pricing (p. 356)
prestige pricing (p. 366)
price (p. 349)
price ceiling (p. 363)
price confusion (p. 356)
price discounting (p. 367)
price discrimination (p. 354)
price elasticity (p. 350)
price fixing (p. 355)
price floor (p. 360)
price leadership (p. 365)
product line pricing (p. 368)
promotional pricing (p. 368)
psychological pricing (p. 366)
pure competition (p. 354)
pure monopoly (p. 354)
reference price (p. 366)
resale price maintenance (p. 355)
retention (p. 352)
skimming (p. 358)
unit pricing (p. 356)
variable costs (p. 358)
variable pricing (p. 365)

Discussion Questions

1. Demand for certain products is price inelastic. Think about some goods and services that you would purchase at practically any price. Would most consumers purchase those products, regardless of how much they cost?
2. Demand for most products is price elastic. Think about something that you would purchase in a greater quantity, or more frequently, if the price was lower. Would most consumers purchase more of those same products if their prices were significantly lower?
3. On a continuum where pure monopoly is at one end and pure competition is at the other, where would you place automobiles? Airlines? Telephone companies? Clothing manufacturers? Beer manufacturers? Explain.
4. When Wawa gas stations were first introduced to the market, they had the cheapest gasoline of all competitors. Wawa also had the highest quality sandwich wraps for sale, better than those of most restaurants, at about the same price. What pricing strategy did Wawa use to introduce its gasoline business? What strategy did it use to introduce its wraps?
5. Recall your recent shopping experiences. What product accessories have you bought? How were they priced relative to the main product? What captive products have you bought? Have you ever bought byproducts?
6. As you read in Chapter 8, "Product Strategies," Rissy Lyn frames are one-of-a-kind, handmade frames sold at Henri Bendel, New York City, and at other specialty boutiques nationwide. Visit the Rissy Lyn website at www.rissylyn.com for more information about Rissy Lyn products. What types of psychological pricing strategy would you advise the company to use for its products?
7. Assume that Rissy Lyn's company decided to sell its products through a distributor. What type of promotional pricing could Rissy Lyn offer to the distributor?

Review Questions

True or False

1. According to the law of supply and demand, consumers purchase fewer products at a lower price than at a higher price.
2. The demand curve portrays the number of units bought for a particular price in a given time period.
3. Monopolistic competition characterizes a market that consists of many buyers and sellers, where no buyer or seller can control price or the market.
4. Legislation such as the Robinson-Patman Act prohibits charging different prices to different buyers of the same merchandise and requires sellers that offer a service to one buyer to make the same service available to all buyers.
5. Predatory pricing and dumping are examples of price fixing.
6. In pricing their products, companies need to take into consideration all product costs, as well as to obtain a fair rate of return on investment.
7. Skimming involves firms initially pricing the product below the price of competitors to quickly penetrate the market at competitors' expense and acquire a large market share, and then gradually raise the price.
8. In cost-based pricing, the firm sets the price by calculating merchandise, service, and overhead costs and then adds an amount needed to cover the profit goal.
9. Cost-plus pricing is a variant of cost-based pricing, with a markup used to cover selling costs and profits.

Multiple Choice

10. A market that consists of few sellers who dominate the market is a(n)
    a. pure monopoly.
    b. example of monopolistic competition.
    c. oligopoly.
    d. monopoly.
11. A market that consists of many buyers and sellers and products that vary greatly in the same product category is a(n)
    a. pure monopoly.
    b. example of monopolistic competition.
    c. oligopoly.
    d. monopoly.
12. Manufacturers are prohibited from requiring retailers to charge a particular price for a product; they are thus prohibited from
    a. price discrimination.
    b. price fixing.
    c. resale price maintenance.
    d. engaging in odd pricing.
13. The price that consumers carry in their mind for a particular product or brand is known as
    a. referent pricing.
    b. reference pricing.
    c. referral pricing.
    d. none of the above
14. Which of the following is an example of prestige pricing?
    a. odd pricing
    b. even pricing
    c. cost-plus pricing
    d. all of the above are examples of prestige pricing
15. A strategy whereby the firm advertises a product at a price that is significantly less than its usual price in order to create traffic in the stores for consumers to purchase higher-margin products is known as
    a. loss-leader pricing.
    b. reference pricing.
    c. odd pricing.
    d. none of the above

Notes

1. A.C. Nielsen, "Leveraging Consumer Insights to Drive Retail Sales: Who Shops Where?" *Facts, Figures and the Future* (www.factsfiguresfuture.com, November 8, 2004)
2. Constance Hays, "One-Word Shopper's Lexicon: Price," *New York Times* (December 26, 2002): C1, C3; Wendy Zellner, "Warehouse Clubs: When the Going Gets Tough . . ." *Business Week*, Industrial/Technology Edition, No. 3741 (July 16, 2001): 60.
3. Terry Clark, Masaaki Kotabe, and Dan Rajaratnam, "Exchange Rate Pass-through and International Pricing Strategy: A Conceptual Framework and Research Propositions," *Journal of International Business Studies*, vol. 30, no. 2 (1999): 249–268.
4. Virginia Citrano, "The Right Price," *CFO*, vol. 8, no. 5 (May 1992): 71–72.
5. Macki Sissoko, "Cigarette Consumption in Different U.S. States, 1955–1998: An Empirical Analysis of the Potential Use of Excise Taxation to Reduce Smoking," *Journal of Consumer Policy*, vol. 25, no. 1 (March 2002): 89–107.
6. Ravi Dhar and Rashi Glazer, "Hedging Customers," *Harvard Business Review*, vol. 81, no. 5 (May 2003): 86–92.
7. Sam Koslowsky, "The Marketing Cube," *Journal of Financial Services Marketing*, vol. 6, no. 2 (December 1, 2001): 164–171.
8. Ben Lieberman, "Why Chicagoans Are Paying More for Gas at the Pump," *Chicago Sun-Times* (February 17, 2003): 53.
9. Jennifer Bayot, "Fees Hidden in Plain Sight, Companies Add to Bottom Line," *New York Times* (December 28, 2002): A1, B4.
10. "Finance and Economics: Europe's Burden," *The Economist*, vol. 351, no. 8120 (May 22, 1999): 84.
11. Ibid.
12. Ibid.
13. Ibid.

Case 12-1 Rethinking the Travel Agency

Jodie Malcom, the owner of a small travel agency in Norfolk, Virginia, is concerned that her target market, a niche consisting of church groups visiting European capitals, is slowly dwindling. Demand for next summer, typically the high season for her target market, is practically zero. Gone are the days of two-week-long cruises down the Danube, with a stop in each capital. There is no interest in the Mediterranean tours, nor in the Paris-London-Madrid luxury tours. One reason may be the economy. Another may be concerns over attitudes toward Americans in general.

Jodie's traditional market segment has learned from other tourists and from many local and national newspapers that Europeans are verbally attacking Americans on the street, opposing the U.S. military policies around the world and, especially, in Iraq. Newspapers advise: If you're heading overseas, be prepared to have discussions with people who think America is the devil. If the past 100 years were widely considered the American Century, this new century is rapidly shaping up as the Anti-American Century. From Spanish plazas, to Berlin taxicabs, American tourists are being quizzed, grilled, and even spat on by people who do not approve of American foreign policy.

In order to maintain a hold on her target market, Jodie has to devise new strategies. First, she has to rethink destinations; second, she must offer basement rates to her customers simply to get them to travel again. One possibility would be to organize tours in the Caribbean using cruise lines, which are offering great deals to draw passengers. Norwegian Cruise Line has cut the price of three-night cruises to $169, Carnival is selling seven-day trips for $299, and Holland America, a premium line that commands higher prices, has cut rates on week-long cruises to $399. As a travel agent, Jodie could book these same cruises for 20 percent less if she is able to organize groups of at least 20. She could then split the discount with the passengers and offer them a rate that is even more appealing than the rates they would obtain if they were to book the cruise directly.

In terms of destinations, Jodie is attempting, for now, to focus on the Caribbean. In due time, she may attempt a number of attractive Central American destinations, such as Costa Rica, and Equador. These areas are particularly friendly toward American tourists, and they are perceived as safe. Jodie can take advantage of her increasingly attractive relationship with American Airlines for all of these destinations. American Airlines is presently repositioning itself as the top provider of travel value that offers a great low fare. Like most airlines, American has seen revenue fall substantially, as consumers have a strong preference for low fares when they do travel. In 1998, 22.7 percent of all passengers were high-fare-paying business travelers who produced over 36 percent of the revenues. Today, business travelers represent only 13.4 percent of the market, generating only 20 percent of the industry revenue. With its new substantial cuts, American is attempting to increase its volume substantially, and if possible, make a profit while doing so.

With all the information and documentation in place, Jodie is ready to prepare package offers for church groups of 20 from the greater Norfolk area. From her understanding, the main concerns of her market are safety and price.

Questions

1. Jodie pays herself a salary of $55,000 and her assistant $34,000. Her additional fixed office expenses, which include rent, are $18,000 annually. Assuming that she will distribute the cruise groups equally over the different cruise lines, and assuming that she gets a 20 percent discount, which she splits with passengers, how many groups would she have to organize annually in order to break even?
2. How many groups would Jodie have to book if she wanted to earn $10,000 profit for the agency?
3. What psychological pricing tools do you advise Jodie to use? Specifically, what prices should she charge?
4. From Section 12-2, discuss the various influences that will impact Jodie's pricing decisions.

Sources: Marco R. Della Cava, "Ugly Sentiments Sting American Tourists as Europeans Cite Frustrations with U.S. Policy," *USA Today* (March 4, 2003): 1–2; Gene Sloan, "Cruise Lines Are Forced to Bail Again," *USA Today* (March 4, 2003): 10b; Dan Reed, "American Wants to Get the Low-Fare Word Out," *USA Today* (March 4, 2003,): 8A.

Case 12-2 The Business Side of Exhibition Catalogs

Karen Kaminer, a talented curator and art businesswoman with noteworthy art exhibitions on her resume, is in the process of planning a traveling exhibition of German expressionist painters throughout the United States. She has received commitments, pending adequate insurance, for a number of paintings.

To date, Karen has received financial support commitments from two nonprofit foundations—the Goethe Institute and the Institut fuer Auslandsbeziehungen—to underwrite the cost of transportation of the art pieces from different museums and private lenders to the museums where the art will be exhibited. She is still working with museums to ensure their commitment. She has been able to secure only a handful of venues for the exhibit: the Virginia Museum of Fine Art, in Richmond, Virginia (a smaller museum, with a reasonable contemporary art collection, but with only a handful of expressionist pieces), and a small museum in New York City specializing in German and Austrian art. She has also been able to persuade one other museum in the Midwest to host the exhibition.

Furthermore, Karen needs to cover two additional costs. One is the cost of the exhibition catalog, which she will author. She will have 4,000 copies printed and delivered at a cost of $30 each. Her total cost for the catalog will be $120,000.

Another is the cost of insurance. This latter cost is likely to present the most problems. According to Lisa Dennison, a deputy director of the Solomon R. Guggenheim Museum in New York and its chief curator, "the rising value of art, coupled with the escalating cost of insurance premiums are making these . . . shows prohibitive . . . . This, along with falling attendance, has been one of the most serious repercussions of September 11." The art lost in and around the World Trade Center, about $10 million worth of pieces by Calder, Miro, and Lichtenstein, may constitute just a fraction of what could be lost in another massive attack. Collectors also fear for their art, and some insist that museums obtain extra insurance before they agree to lend their art.

Karen's total insurance bill will be around $18,000 ($13,000 for the New York museum and $5,000 for the other two museums). Her personal additional expenses are $27,000. She has negotiated to receive $62,000 from the three museums, regardless of exhibit attendance. Now she must decide the price that she should charge the museums for the catalogs.

Questions

1. If Karen's fixed expenses are $120,000 for the catalog, $18,000 for insurance, and $27,000 for personal expenses, how much must she charge the museums for the catalog in order to break even?
2. If Karen wanted to make a total of $100,000—which includes the $62,000 that she was able to negotiate with the museum—how much would she have to charge the museum for the catalogs?
3. What are some of the shortcomings of the methods you used to calculate the prices of the catalogs in Question 1? And in Question 2?
4. From Section 12-4, discuss each of the major methods of pricing as it would relate to Karen's pricing of the catalog. Which method should she use? Why?

Source: Carol Vogel, "Fear of Terror a Complication for Art Exhibits," *New York Times* (February 25, 2003): A1, A20.

Part 4

Marketing Communications

Integrated Marketing Communications

13

CHAPTER OBJECTIVES

1. Discuss the concept of integrated marketing communications.
2. Identify the various marketing communication elements.
3. List the stages of integrated marketing communications.
4. Identify the elements of communication and the importance of AIDA.
5. Discuss the various factors that impact the relative mix of communication elements in an integrated marketing communications plan.
6. Explain various methods for measuring the effectiveness of marketing communication.

CHAPTER OUTLINE

"What did you say? Would you please repeat that?"

"Huh?" "What?"

These statements, followed by a blank stare, may indicate that your intended listener was not aware that you were speaking to him or her, and quite likely, the listener was not your grandmother. It may have been your father, mother, an aunt, an uncle, or a close friend. According to the Hearing Industries Association, 6 million Americans wear hearing aids, and an additional 6 million need them, but either won't get one or do not realize they need one. Among adults 18 and older with impaired hearing, only 22 percent wear a hearing aid, and for seniors 65 and older, only 39 percent are willing to wear a hearing aid.

Why is there such a strong resistance to hearing aids when we will readily purchase eyeglasses or contacts? The reason is the psychological, social, and age stigma connected with hearing aids. Research has indicated that people think of hearing loss in terms of aging, being feeble, and incompetence. They don't want to admit to themselves or to others that they are getting older or have a hearing problem.

This negative image associated with hearing aids presents a huge challenge to marketers because not only do individuals who need hearing aids deny they need them, but often they will develop a negative attitude to the product and will tune out or ignore any marketing communication. According to Kruskopf Olson of Kruskopf Olson Advertising, "Audiologists have a hard job because they're selling a product nobody wants to admit they need." How do you market a product under these circumstances? For years, Beltone used product-oriented advertisements to promote its hearing aids, telling consumers about the latest technologies. But telling consumers about the latest product innovations is of no value if they are unwilling to admit they even need a hearing aid.

Barbara VaSomeren, Director of Business Communication for Beltone, stated, "We need to destigmatize hearing devices. Hearing loss is totally natural, and taking care of it should be a lifestyle health issue." To get this idea across, Beltone developed a series of 15- and 30-second advertisements that focus on the sounds of life "that should not be missed," such as "children speaking or waterfalls flowing."

In-Tune Hearing Centers, which are located inside Pearle Vision Centers, adopted a humorous approach. In-Tune developed a print campaign with taglines such as, "After one visit, you'll be hearing voices," "We're turning the hearing aid industry on its ear," and "You can take all of this super high-tech computer stuff and stick it in your ear."

Marketing a product that consumers do not want to admit they need is a challenge that requires more than just running a few television or print ads. As you will see in this chapter, a successful marketing campaign involves integrating TV ads, print ads, and other types of marketing communication so consumers receive the same message from every source. When this was done for hearing aids, the most effective approach was the combination of telemarketing and direct mail. The worst was when only print or only television advertising was used.[1]

13-1 Chapter Overview

The fourth component of the four *P*s of marketing is promotion. **Promotion** refers to all forms of external communications directed toward consumers and businesses with an ultimate goal of developing customers. In recent years, marketers have been pushing to integrate all forms of promotion, or communication, to ensure that the company speaks with one voice. Section 13-2 presents the concept of integrated marketing communications (IMC), as well as the principal components of an IMC program. Marketing communications are based on an understanding of the communication process, which is discussed in Section 13-3.

Promotion: All forms of external communications directed toward consumers and businesses with an ultimate goal of developing customers.

For an effective IMC plan, a firm must decide which elements of communication it needs to use to communicate effectively with customers. The relative mix of promotional elements will vary depending on the objectives that the firm would like to achieve and the budget that has been allocated for marketing. Section 13-4 discusses the communication mix and the elements that influence how the marketing package is developed.

Evaluation is an important component of marketing communications. While it is difficult to measure the exact impact of marketing, it is important to determine how effective the communications are in order to ensure that marketing expenditures are not wasted. Section 13-5 presents a brief overview of various evaluation techniques that can be used. The chapter closes with Section 13-6, which addresses global marketing communications.

13-2 Integrated Marketing Communications

Integrated marketing communications (IMC): The coordination and integration of all marketing communication tools, avenues, and sources within a company into a seamless program designed to maximize the communication impact on consumers, businesses, and other constituencies of an organization.

While some marketing experts would argue that the integrated marketing communications (IMC) approach is a recent phenomenon, others would argue that it has been around for a long time. The latter view is supported by marketing articles, which for years have promoted the idea of coordinating all of the marketing functions and activities. While the concept may have been discussed in marketing articles, few companies practiced IMC until recently. Integrated marketing communications has now become the key term and key guiding principle in developing marketing communications. What is **integrated marketing communications (IMC)**? It is the coordination and integration of all marketing communication tools, avenues, and sources within a company into a seamless program designed to maximize the communication impact on consumers, businesses, and other constituencies of an organization.

Because of stagnant circulation, the *Stanford Advocate,* one of Connecticut's largest daily newspapers, decided to develop an integrated marketing communications campaign aimed at boosting its image and its circulation. Print advertisements were created by Re:think Group Brand Communications to run in the *Advocate* as well as other local publications. At the same time, outdoor billboards and transit posters appeared in the Stanford area. Television ads were run on the local Stanford Cable Channel, and 15-second radio spots were launched. From all of these venues, people in Stanford heard the message "Don't miss a day. Don't miss a thing."[2] By integrating all of these messages and using multiple mediums, the company ensured that practically everyone in the Stanford area was exposed to an advertisement. Integrating all of these forms of communication resulted in a greater impact than using a different message in each medium or broadcasting messages at different times. See Marketing Illustration 13-1 for more information about using multiple media for a marketing communications campaign.

Figure 13-1
Coyote Wild's message that it is the source for "fine home interior furnishings, accents, and gifts" must be communicated to employees and stakeholders as well as customers.

Source: Sample print advertisement courtesy of The Miles Agency and Alliance One Advertising, Inc.

Customers, both individuals and businesses, are better informed, more price conscious, and more demanding of quality, service, convenience, and speed than in the past. Reaching these potential customers requires a consistent marketing message at every customer contact point. IMC is a holistic approach that involves everyone in the company articulating the same message. For this integration to work, it must occur at three levels. First, there must be open communication vertically within the company, from the employees who interact with customers and perform the day-by-day work to the CEO. Second, there must be horizontal communication, across functional areas and departments. Third, there must be communication to customers and stakeholders who have an interest in the company (see Figure 13-1).[3]

IMC involves communicating to four primary groups: customers, channel members, employees, and stakeholders. Customers can be consumers, businesses, governments, institutions, and other entities that purchase a firm's products. Channel members include wholesalers, distributors, retailers, and any other middlemen involved between the producer and the customer. Employees include every individual who works in an organization, not just those in the marketing department. Stakeholders are individuals or groups with a stake in a company's welfare, such as shareholders, investment bankers and institutions, special interest groups, and government agencies.

Marketing Illustration 13-1

Multichannel Marketing

Multichannel marketing is the process of making goods and services available to customers in the distribution channel that are best for the customer and using the types of communication programs that are best for the customers. In terms of distribution, typical questions are:

- How much emphasis should be placed on each channel of distribution?
- How much emphasis should be placed at the retail level?
- How much reliance should there be on a traditional sales force?
- How much emphasis should be placed on e-commerce?

As companies ponder these questions, they must ask the questions in relation to where customers want to make the purchase. Because of information technology, customers are now in control of the marketplace. They have more sources of information and more places they can make purchases.

In terms of marketing communications, typical questions that should be asked are:

- How do customers want to receive product information?
- Where do customers look for product information?
- How much information do customers want?
- What type of information do customers want?

As companies ponder these questions, they must think about the many ways customers gather information from different sources and integrate it into a single picture in their minds. To make this process easier, companies need to offer information to customers in locations where they can easily access it and easily process it with other information that is obtained.

Multichannel marketing involves providing multiple channels for customers to purchase a product and multiple avenues of communication for customers to gather information. Integrating both the distribution and the communication will result in greater sales and lower costs as customers shift to lower-cost distribution channels and increase their purchases through having multiple-channel access.

Multichannel marketing: The marketing of a product through two or more channels.

Source: Don E. Schultz, "Multichannel: New Term, Old Challenges," *Marketing News*, vol. 36, no. 9 (April 29, 2002): 10; Joseph B. Myers, Andrew Pickersgill, and Evan S. Van Metre, "Steering Customers to the Right Channels," *McKinsey Quarterly*, vol. 4 (2004): 36–47.

13-2a Communication Venues

An organization has many potential venues of communication. Traditionally, the promotional mix included advertising, sales promotion, trade promotion, personal selling, and public relations. With an integrated approach, other components of communication have also become important, such as the Internet, databases, and direct marketing. Viable venues for communication are traditional mediums (radio, television, newspapers, and magazines), as well as the Internet, billboards, transit signs, store signage, and company stationery.

Practically every organization uses some type of advertising to promote its products. **Advertising** is any form of paid communication directed to an organization's customers and/or other stakeholders. Outlets for advertising include the traditional media, such as radio, television, magazines, newspapers, and billboards, as well as the Internet and nontraditional outlets, such as streamers pulled by airplanes and sponsorships of football bowl games and NASCAR events. Advertising has a major advantage: It is able to reach a large number of people with a single message. While cost may be high (as much as $2 million for a 30-second Super Bowl TV spot), the relative cost per person reached is very low. While a direct-mail piece to a consumer may cost as much as $2 per person, a TV advertisement that costs $250,000 but reaches 2.5 million people costs only 10 cents per person (see Figure 13-2). Advertising will be discussed in more detail in Chapter 14, "Advertising, Sponsorships, and Public Relations."

Advertising: Any form of paid communication directed to an organization's customers and/or other stakeholders.

Whereas advertising is aimed primarily at customers, public relations is aimed at the general public and stakeholders of an organization. **Public relations (PR)** addresses issues faced by an organization and represents the organization to the public, media, and various stakeholders. The public relations department normally handles any event that occurs that has a direct or indirect impact on the public or stakeholders. If an accident occurs at a factory, the public relations department will deal with the media and provide information to

Public relations (PR): A communication venue that addresses issues an organization faces and represents the organization to the public, media, and various stakeholders.

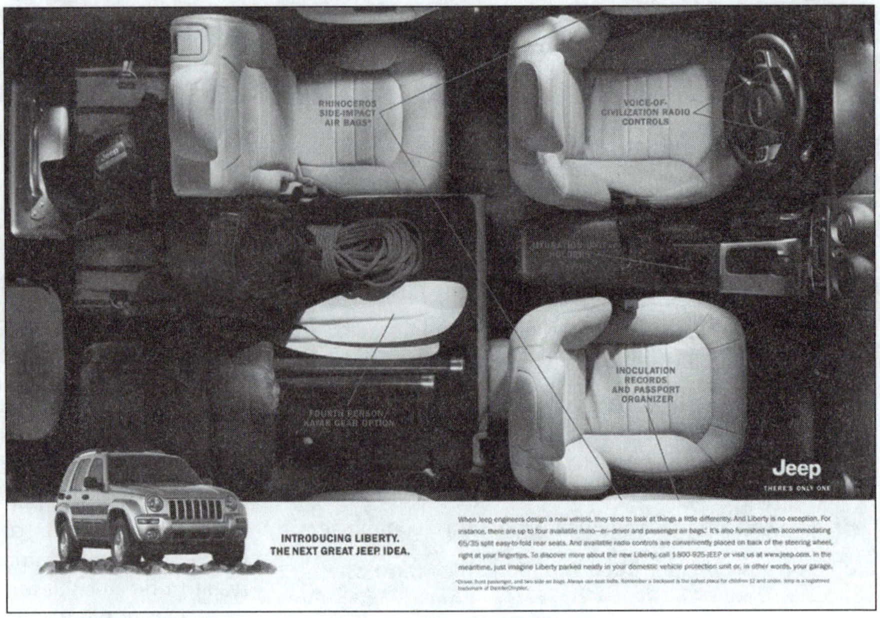

Figure 13-2
This advertisement introducing the Jeep Liberty is a cost-effective method of reaching millions of consumers.

Source: Courtesy of PentaMark Worldwide, a division of BBDO Worldwide Network on behalf of DaimlerChrysler.

the public. If a new product is introduced, it is the responsibility of the PR department to send out a news release. If the quarterly earnings are above or below the projection, it is the PR department that deals with Wall Street and other investors.

Publicity: A form of public relations produced by the news media but not paid for or sponsored by the business concern.

Publicity is usually an outcome of public relations that is produced by the news media and is not paid for or sponsored by the business involved. A newspaper article about Enron, Coca-Cola, Gap, or any other organization would be publicity. The company has no control over what is being said. It is the responsibility of the PR department to monitor the media, as well as the environment that surrounds a firm—especially the macroenvironment—for events that may have an impact on the organization. Businesses should monitor articles that are written about the firm. Rather than react to events, it is better if a business is prepared for them and can act proactively. If a strike in South America is going to interrupt the supply of coffee to Starbucks, the PR department can alert Starbuck's management so another source of coffee beans can be contacted or an alternate plan can be developed. If an article is going to appear in the *Wall Street Journal* about the labor practices of a company, then the firm can be better prepared to counter possible misconceptions. Public relations will be discussed further in Chapter 14.

Sales promotions: Incentives to encourage end users or consumers to purchase a product.

Trade promotions: Incentives directed toward channel members to encourage them to purchase, stock, or push a product through the channel.

To stimulate sales, companies will often use either sales promotions or trade promotions or both. **Sales promotions** are incentives used to encourage end users to purchase a product. **Trade promotions** are incentives directed toward channel members to encourage them to purchase, stock, or push a product through the channel. Both are short-term tactics used by firms to stimulate sales, demand, or inquiries. Sales promotions include offers such as coupons, premiums, sweepstakes, and contests. Most sales promotions offer some type of price incentive or additional gift or merchandise to encourage consumers to make a purchase. Coupons offering $1.00 off a bottle of shampoo or 50 cents off a box of cereal are found in almost every Sunday newspaper across America. According to Watts NCH Promotional Services, marketers distributed 314 billion coupons during a recent year. Consumers redeemed 3.6 billion of the coupons (1.15 percent) for a combined savings of $3 billion. The most popular coupons are for food products, accounting for 40 percent of all the coupons distributed and 55 percent of all the coupons redeemed (see Figure 13-3).[4]

Trade promotions involve channel members. Similar to consumer promotions, trade promotions are designed to encourage immediate activity. It may be a discount or price-off offer if a retailer will purchase a certain number of cases of cereal by the end of the month. It can be an offer for a free case of motor oil if the retailer will purchase 20 cases within the following 30 days. It may be a commitment to pay 75 percent of the cost of a retailer's

Figure 13-3
This coupon is a sales promotion, offering 55 cents off a Diet Pepsi or Caffeine-Free Diet Pepsi multipack or 2-liter bottle.

Source: Courtesy of Pepsi-Cola Company.

advertisement in a newspaper if the manufacturer's product is prominently featured. Because of intense competition among manufacturers for retail shelf space, trade promotions have become extremely important in the marketing of products. Manufacturers spend about 14 percent of their total sales on trade promotions. For food manufacturers, this percentage is higher (16 percent). The amount spent on trade promotions has increased dramatically from $8 billion in 1980 to more than $85 billion today.[5]

Personal selling is an important component of marketing, especially for companies that sell to other businesses, the government, or institutions. It is also important for consumer products, such as real estate, insurance, and high-ticket items like automobiles and furniture. **Personal selling** is a direct communication approach between the buyer and seller with the express purpose of selling a product. In most cases, personal selling takes place between two individuals, but it can also take place between teams of individuals. With large corporate purchases, it is not unusual for the selling organization to use a team approach in selling its products. Even with consumer sales, teams may be used, but it is usually with the buyer, in the form of a couple or family. Home and automobile purchases are normally joint decisions, and vacations may involve the entire family. The first part of Chapter 16, "Personal Selling, Databases, and Direct Marketing," discusses personal selling.

Personal selling: A direct communication approach between the buyer and seller with the express purpose of selling a product.

Table 13-1 contrasts advertising, the publicity component of public relations, personal selling, and sales promotion on factors such as audience, message, cost, sponsor, flexibility, control over the content and placement of the message, credibility, and major goal. An example is also given of each type of promotion as it would relate to a Sony CD player.

TABLE 13-1 Characteristics of Major Forms of Marketing Communication

Factor	Advertising	Publicity Form of Public Relations*	Personal Selling	Sales Promotion
Audience	Mass	Mass	Small (one-to-one)	Varies
Message	Uniform	Uniform	Specific	Varies
Cost	Low per viewer or reader	None for media space and time; can be some costs for media releases and publicity materials	High per customer	Moderate per customer
Sponsor	Company	No formal sponsor (media are not paid)	Company	Company
Flexibility	Low	Low	High	Moderate
Control over Content and Placement	High	None (controlled by media)	High	High
Credibility	Moderate	High	Moderate	Moderate
Major Goal	To appeal to a mass audience at a reasonable cost, and to create awareness and favorable attitudes	To reach a mass audience with an independently reported message	To deal with individual consumers, to resolve questions, to close sales	To stimulate short-run sales, to increase impulse purchases
Example	Television ad for a Sony CD player for use in cars	Magazine article describing the unique features of a Sony CD player for use in cars	Retail sales personnel explaining how a Sony CD player for cars works	A coupon for $15 off a Sony CD player

*When public relations embodies advertising (an image-related message), personal selling (a salesperson describing his or her firm's public service efforts to college students), and/or sales promotion (distributing special discount coupons to low-income consumers), it takes on the characteristics of those promotional types. However, the goal would be more image-related than sales-related.

Database marketing: The collection, analysis, and use of large volumes of customer data to develop marketing programs and customer profiles.

Direct marketing: The promotion of a product directly from the manufacturer or seller to the buyer without any middlemen involved in the transaction.

Internet marketing: The promotion and sale of products through the Internet.

Computer technology has facilitated the development of customer databases, which can be used for database marketing programs and direct marketing programs. **Database marketing** refers to the collection, analysis, and use of large volumes of customer data to develop marketing programs and customer profiles. **Direct marketing** is the promotion of a product directly from the manufacturer or producer to the buyer without any middlemen involved in the transaction. Because of the development of computerized customer databases, most direct marketing today utilizes the information stored in company or commercial databases. Both approaches have gained prominence with the increased use of computer technology. The last part of Chapter 16 will present more details about how database marketing is being used today.

The rise of computer technology has also given birth to **Internet marketing,** which is the promotion and sale of products through the Internet. According to PEW Research Center, 78 percent of Americans ages 18–39 have access to the Internet. The percentages decline for older Americans, from 71 percent for individuals 40–49 to 17 percent for seniors 69 and older. But to marketers, more importantly, 65 percent of Internet users have purchased something online.[6] These percentages are expected to rise in the future as people become more comfortable with the Internet and more comfortable with making Internet purchase transactions. Internet marketing is really in its infancy, and companies are still experimenting with the best approaches. As the Internet itself matures, the marketing techniques now being used will undoubtedly lose ground to new approaches, new techniques, and new methods of reaching consumers. Because of the impact the Internet currently has on mar-

Figure 13-4
This individual frequently purchases computer parts, airline tickets, and even Dutch food online.

Source: Courtesy of Hendrik Opstelten.

keting and the tremendous impact it could have in the future, all of Chapter 18, "Internet Marketing," is devoted to this topic (see Figure 13-4).

13-2b Stages of Integrated Marketing Communications

It is important to realize that IMC is more than a marketing plan or a marketing function. It should be an organization-wide process. According to a study by American Productivity & Quality Center (APQC) of Houston of the best-integrated marketing firms, it takes time to develop a true IMC culture. The APQC found that organizations go through four stages in developing an IMC system.[7] The first stage involves identifying, coordinating, and managing all forms of external communication. The goal is to bring all of the company's brands and divisions under central control. During this stage, the organization makes certain that all advertisements, public relations activities, promotional materials, personal selling approaches, flyers, and any other material directed to customers use the same logos, themes, and colors. It is important that every form of external communication has the same message and the same look.

In the second stage, the firm should extend the scope of communication to include everyone touched by the organization. External communications now should match all internal messages sent to employees. External communications made during public relations announcements or with outside advertising agencies should be consistent with what is being communicated internally. It is important to make sure channel members such as distributors, retailers, dealers, and product package designers are hearing and seeing the same message. By the end of this stage, every person who comes into contact with an organization should see one overall theme.

During stage three, information technology becomes prominent and is applied to IMC programs. Databases are developed to include every customer's activities, purchases, and interactions with the company. While a number of companies have made it through the first two stages, few have made it to stage three. It is during this stage that the customer information that has been gathered is used to make product and promotion decisions.

The last stage of IMC development occurs when the organization treats IMC as an investment and not as a departmental function. Companies that have reached this stage, such as Dow Chemical, Federal Express, and Hewlett-Packard, have taken the customer databases and used them to establish individual customer values. Customers are not equal: Some customers have the potential for making large purchases, whereas others do not.

Some customers are likely to become brand loyal, whereas others will not. Using the customer value concept, the organization can develop individualized marketing approaches that will maximize the return on effort. It makes good business sense to expend the most energy on customers who are likely to yield the highest sales potential.

13-3 The Communication Process

The key to successful marketing is communication. Someone must send a message, and someone must hear and understand the message. The challenge is developing a message that will get the attention of consumers or businesses and that will then move the recipient to respond in the desired manner. With all of us being bombarded by hundreds of marketing messages each day, getting noticed is difficult. Then, if a message is noticed, will the message be interpreted correctly, in the manner the advertiser or business intended? Examine the advertisement in Figure 13-5. What message do you think the advertiser wants to convey? Examine the advertisement in Figure 13-6. What message is it conveying? Have a fellow classmate, relative, or friend look at the two ads. What do they see? Did you have the same reaction? Ask a couple of other people to examine the ads. Was their reaction consistent with yours and those of your friends or relatives? If so, the advertisers created effective advertisements that convey a single message—if, in fact, that was the message the advertisers wanted you to receive. If each of you interpreted the ads differently, you now realize the challenge that advertisers and marketers face in creating effective communication.

Figure 13-5
What message does this Guess advertisement convey?

Source: Courtesy of Guess and Creative Director Paul Marciano.

Figure 13-6
What message does this advertisement for The Toggery convey?

Source: Sample print advertisement provided courtesy of The Miles Agency and Alliance One Advertising, Inc.

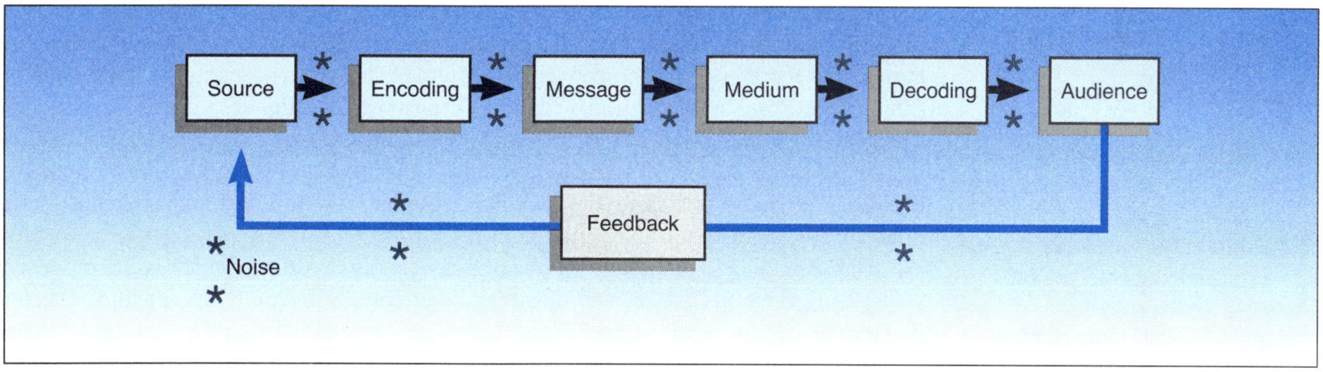

Figure 13-7
The Channel of Communication

INTERACTIVE FIGURE

13-3a Model of Communications

Marketing communications function similarly to other types of communication between two parties. Someone sends a message; someone else receives it. With marketing, however, the message does not always have to be sent through a person. It can be sent using television, radio, magazines, or billboards. The channel of communication contains a series of six sequential stages, as illustrated in Figure 13-7.

Figure 13-8
The Bozell Agency created this "Got Milk?" advertisement for the milk industry to encourage consumers to drink more milk.

Source: Courtesy of Bozell Worldwide, Inc. as agent for the National Fluid Milk Processor Promotion Board.

Source: The organization that originates a marketing communication message.

Encoding: The process of transposing the objective or goal of a marketing communication concept into an actual marketing communication piece, such as an advertisement, brochure, or sign.

Message: The completed marketing communication piece.

The message begins with a **source,** which is the organization that originates a marketing communication. The source can be the company itself, or it can be the advertising agency that represents the company. For the "Got Milk?" advertisement in Figure 13-8, the source is the Bozell Agency, hired by the milk industry to develop the advertising campaign. The goal of the campaign was to encourage consumers to drink more milk. With the rise in popularity of soft drinks and other types of drinks, the consumption of milk had declined. To reverse this trend, the milk industry hired the Bozell Agency to create a series of ads to stimulate interest in drinking more milk.

The second step in the communication process is **encoding,** which is the process of transposing the objective or goal of a marketing communication concept into an actual marketing communication piece such as an advertisement, brochure, or sign. With the "Got Milk?" campaign, the creative staff working on the milk industry account wanted to convey the message that drinking milk is fashionable and cool. Therefore, they chose a series of celebrities that are well liked by consumers and not only showed them with a glass of milk, but also with a white milk mustache. In addition, copy was added to explain the importance of drinking milk and the fact that milk is a good source of calcium for bones.

When the encoding process is complete, a message has been created. The **message** is the completed marketing communication piece. It may be a 30-second advertisement for television, a point-of-purchase display for a retail store, an interactive website, or a direct-mail offer. If the message is done well, it will embody the objectives and goals of the creatives who developed it. The advertisement in Figure 13-8 is one of a series of messages created for the milk industry by the Bozell Agency.

Once the message has been created, it must be sent to the consumer. The **medium** is the venue used by the source to send a marketing communication message to its intended audience. The medium may be television, radio, a magazine, the Internet, an envelope, or a sign on the side of a city bus. The choice of medium is very important because, if the intended audience does not receive or see the marketing message, they cannot react to it. For the Bozell Agency, magazines were chosen as the primary medium for its series of print "Got Milk?" advertisements.

Medium: The venue the source uses to send a marketing communication message to its intended audience.

As a consumer picks up a magazine and notices the milk advertisement, **decoding,** the process of interpreting the meaning conveyed in a marketing message, begins. One consumer may look at the advertisement, notice the attractive female, and think that milk will promote good looks. That is not the message that was intended. Another person may notice the advertisement and think that drinking milk is cool. If that was the message intended in the original encoding process, then effective communication has taken place. If the consumer thinks that not only is milk cool to drink, but that it is an excellent source of calcium, then the agency has effectively communicated the message that was intended.

Decoding: The process of interpreting the meaning conveyed in a marketing message.

The **audience** is defined as the individuals who observe a marketing communication and decode the message. It is the individuals who see the ads during a television show, or in a magazine, or on a billboard. It is the shopper who sees a point-of-purchase display in a grocery store. It is the person at home who receives a direct-mail piece offer. For effective communication to take place, the audience who receives the marketing communication needs to match the audience for which it was designed. If the "Got Milk?" ad shown in Figure 13-8 was intended for females, 15 to 30 years old, and 80 percent of those who saw the advertisement were males over age 50, the advertisement did not reach its intended target: The message the agency wanted to send to the 15- to 30-year-old female was never received.

Audience: The individuals who observe a marketing communication and decode the message.

The last step in effective communication is **feedback,** which is the response of the audience to the message. For the "Got Milk?" advertisement, the feedback may be the increased consumption of milk or a more positive attitude toward drinking milk. If the sale of milk increases after the launch of the milk ads, then the agency knows that the message was heard and that consumers responded positively. To see if the message was interpreted correctly, the agency will need to interview viewers of the ad to see what they thought about the ad and what message they thought the ad conveyed. For advertising and many types of marketing communications, feedback is informal and indirect, making it difficult for marketers to know how effective the communication was, or even if the intended audience received the message. For personal selling, however, the salesperson can watch the buyer and listen to his or her reaction. Feedback is immediate, allowing the salesperson to modify the message to ensure that the decoding is taking place as intended.

Feedback: The response of the audience to the message.

The last factor in the channel of communication is **noise,** which is anything that interferes with the audience receiving the message. It can occur anywhere along the channel of communication. It may be someone talking during the airing of a radio advertisement. It may be someone getting something to eat during a television commercial. It may be that the model in the "Got Milk?" ad distracts a viewer and he or she does not even notice the written message in the ad. It may be a shopper thinking about a work situation and not listening to what a salesperson is saying. Noise prevents the audience from seeing a marketing communication message or from correctly comprehending the intended message.

Noise: Anything that interferes with the audience receiving the message.

One form of noise that impacts the effectiveness of ads is advertising clutter. In many magazines, there are more pages devoted to advertisements than to the magazine's content. In television, more than 15 minutes of each hour is spent with advertisements or public service announcements. ABC had the highest proportion, with 15:16 minutes per hour, followed closely by NBC at 15:06 minutes. CBS and Fox were both under 15 minutes, but not by much, at 14:01 and 14:34, respectively. Even cable channels are becoming filled with ads, averaging more than 14 minutes per hour. ESPN had the least clutter of the cable channels at 11:13 minutes, while USA had the highest of the cable channels at 14:24. Not only are viewers concerned about so many commercials, but advertisers are as well. A study by the

Marketing Illustration 13-2

Advertising on the Plane: A Dream Captive Audience

Because of advertising overload all around us, advertisers are aggressively seeking permission to advertise on airlines, while passengers are in flight. So far, only two airlines have given way to this pressure, Virgin Atlantic and JetBlue. However, because of the slowdown in flying and financial difficulties, other airlines may soon follow.

What advertisers want is the opportunity to advertise on the in-flight shows and over the in-flight television. This captive audience is an advertiser's dream. The median annual income of airline travelers of major carriers is $93,822, with about 40 percent of the passengers being professionals, managers, executives, or other influential consumers. For some of the shuttle services, such as Delta's, the numbers are even better. More than 25 percent of these passengers earn more than $250,000 a year, with a median annual income of $181,498.

Delta does not sell in-flight advertising, but it does sell ad space on the plastic covers of magazines distributed on-board, the in-flight entertainment guides, snack bags, boarding passes, ticket jackets, and e-ticket confirmation itinerary inserts. American Airlines sells advertising on its headset packages and plans to allow advertisers to provide sample CDs and DVDs for premium-class passengers. Over $360 million was spent on these types of ad placements and promotions during 2001.

With such a dream audience available and a financially struggling airline industry, it won't be long until advertising on airlines while in-flight will be no different than the advertising you see around you every day.

Source: Felicia Williams, "Air Travel Now a Fully Developed Medium," *B&T Weekly*, vol. 54 (November 12, 2004): 14–15; Pamela Paul, "Advertisers Climb on Board," *American Demographics*, vol. 24, no. 9 (October 2002): 30–32.

Cabletelevision Advertising Bureau indicated that there is an enormous difference in the viewer's ability to recall ads between the first ad in a series and the fourth or fifth ad in the series.[8] To avoid this high level of ad clutter, advertisers are aggressively seeking the opportunity to advertise on airlines, while passengers are in flight. Read Marketing Illustration 13-2 for more information.

13-3b AIDA Concept

The ultimate goal of marketing communication is for the audience to respond in some manner. It may be to make a purchase, to enter a contest, to call a toll-free number, or to shop at a retail store. One method of reaching these goals is to design marketing communication using the AIDA concept.[9] **AIDA** is an acronym that stands for *attention, interest, desire,* and *action.*

AIDA: An acronym that stands for *attention, interest, desire,* and *action.*

Before consumers or a business can be influenced to make a purchase, the marketer must get their attention. If it's a salesperson making a sales call, then a smile, a handshake, and a friendly greeting can gain the buyers' attention. If it's a television commercial, the viewers' attention might be gained by having the volume louder; having a sexy, attractive person appear on the screen; playing a familiar tune; or using a tranquil scene. For a print ad, attention may be garnered through a unique, psychedelic array of colors; a large, bold headline; an eye-catching scene; or a well-known celebrity. To get viewers' attention, the advertisement in Figure 13-9 for Ouachita Independent Bank, designed by the Newcomer, Morris and Young agency, used a Dachshund in full color to contrast with the black and blue ink used in the rest of the ad.

Once the marketer has the person's attention, the next step is to develop interest. The attractive model, the Dachshund, or a familiar tune may catch your attention, but if you don't stop and read the advertisement, the message will not be received. Taglines and written or verbal copy must then express the concept or idea that the advertiser wishes to express, in order to develop your interest in the product. The advertisement for Ouachita Independent Bank used the headline "Here's the Long and Short of It" to tie in with the picture of the Dachshund and the content copy of the ad. The agency that designed the ad is hoping the headline, with the picture, will garner your attention long enough that you will be interested in reading the rest of the ad. A salesperson has an advantage over adver-

Figure 13-9
This advertisement for Ouachita Independent Bank captures viewers' attention by showing a Dachshund in full color, in contrast to the rest of the ad, which is in black and blue.

Source: Courtesy of Newcomer, Morris and Young.

tising because once the salesperson has your attention, he or she can adjust the sales presentation to build interest in the product and answer any questions you may have.

Once a person's interest has been gained, the third step is to build desire. A purchasing agent for a large company may have four or five vendors from whom he or she can purchase raw materials. The salesperson has to convince the purchasing agent why his or her company should be selected. In contrast, it is more difficult for an advertiser to present a message that will lead the viewer from just being interested in the product to wanting to purchase it. A representative at Ouachita Independent Bank talking about the benefits highlighted on the ad would have an easier time developing desire than if someone just read the advertisement itself.

The last step in this process is action. This is the actual decision to make the purchase. For the purchasing agent, it may be signing a contract with a supplier. For the person seeing the Ouachita Independent Bank ad, it may be going to the bank and securing a home equity loan.

The amount of time a person will spend in each step will vary widely. For high-involvement decisions such as purchasing furniture, clothes, or a vehicle, it may take a marketer a long time to develop desire. For candy bars, simply using a point-of-purchase display near the checkout stand may be enough to urge someone to make a purchase. The time from attention to action may be only a few seconds. If it takes longer, the person is likely to decide that the candy bar is too fattening and that he or she can get by without it.

Figure 13-10
Using the AIDA Concept to Sell an Exercise Bike

Attention → Interest → Desire → Action

AIDA Concept	Retail Sales Situation	Television Advertisement
Attention	A store sign offering $25 off catches your attention.	A well-built young man appears on the screen wearing only shorts.
Interest	A sign by the exercise bike highlights the low cost and features of the bike.	You have been wanting an exercise bike, and this is a model you have not seen before, so you want to see what it looks like and what features it has.
Desire	You sit on the bicycle, and it feels more comfortable than any others you have tried.	After seeing the TV ad, you check the Internet to see where the closest retail store is located and what the website says about the bike.
Action	When a salesperson tells you that the bike can be purchased now and, if for any reason, you don t like the bike, you can return it within 30 days for a full refund, you decide to purchase it.	Having thought about the exercise bike, you see another advertisement. You decide this is the right bike and make a decision to purchase it, using the toll-free number listed on the TV screen.

Figure 13-10 summarizes the use of AIDA for an exercise bicycle in a retail sales situation and with a television advertisement.

13-4 The Communication Mix

In developing an integrated marketing plan, the marketing manager must decide on the relative mix of communication tools. How much will be spent on advertising? How much will be spent on trade promotions and sales promotions? How much will be spent to support personal selling? Will sponsorships be used, or will the company use database marketing? How will the Internet be utilized? The answer to these questions depends on a number of factors that will be discussed in this section. But first, it is interesting to examine how current marketing budgets are used (see Figure 13-11). Because of the pervasive nature of advertising, students tend to believe that most of a company's marketing budget is spent on advertising. This is not true. In fact, only about 25 percent of all marketing dollars is spent on advertising. The remaining 75 percent is spent on trade promotions and sales promotions, with trade promotions using up 50 percent of the budget and sales promotions the other 25 percent.

13-4a Business Versus Consumer Marketing

The communication mix for business-to-business marketing tends to be different than for consumer marketing. Business-to-business marketing relies more on personal selling, trade promotions, and telephone marketing, whereas consumer marketing relies more on advertising and sales promotion. Because businesses are more concentrated and make larger volume purchases, using a salesperson makes sense. One salesperson may account for annual sales in the millions of dollars. Also, because of the high volume of a single purchase, it is important to use the best means of communication: personal selling. For consumers, however, it would not be financially feasible to use a salesperson, except for large ticket items. Advertising can reach more people with a message at a much lower cost per person.

Figure 13-12 provides a more detailed breakdown of some of the major forms of communication spending, excluding personal selling and promotions. Notice that 52.6 percent

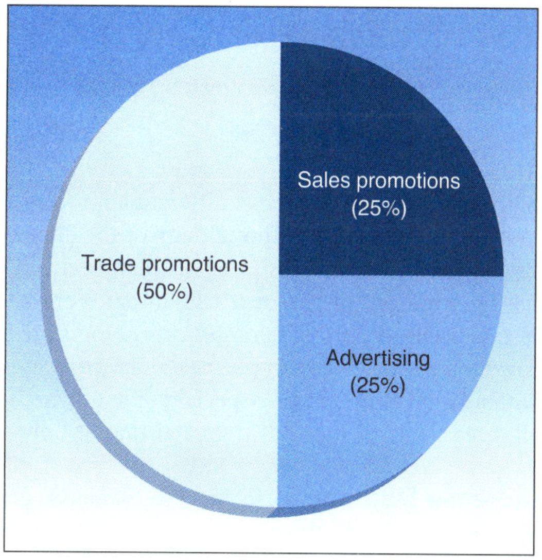

Figure 13-11
How Marketing Dollars Are Used

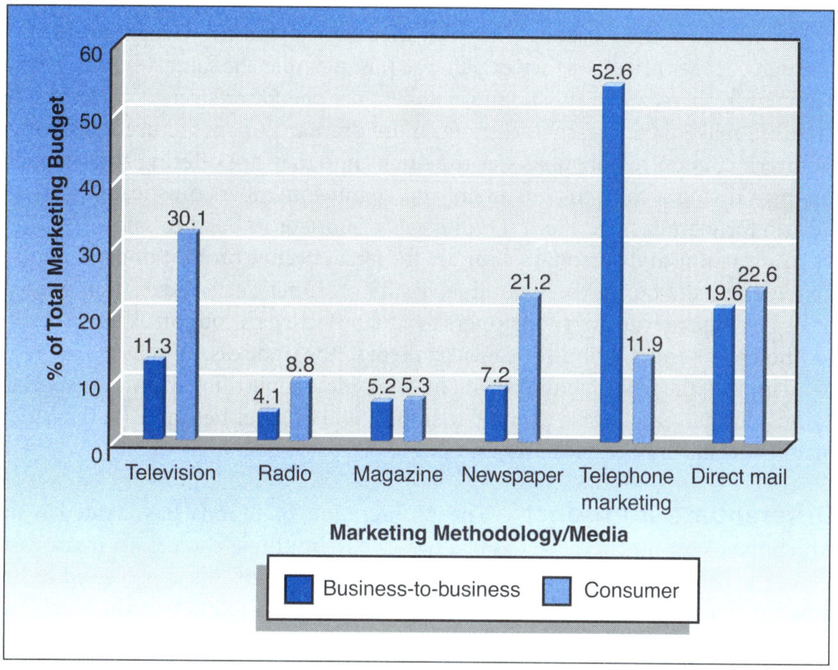

Figure 13-12
A Comparison of Business-to-Business and Consumer Marketing Expenditures

Source: "2004 Marketing Fact Book," *Marketing News*, vol. 38 (July 15, 2004): 10–15.

of all business-to-business expenditures is for telephone marketing, while 30.1 percent of all consumer expenditures is spent on television advertising.

13-4b Communication Objectives

A major factor in how marketing dollars are allocated and the mix of communication tools is what the firm wishes to accomplish. An IMC plan is often oriented toward a single objective. It is possible, however, for a program to accomplish more than one objective at a time, but this may be confusing to potential customers. Communication objectives can be classified into these six major categories:

- Increase demand
- Differentiate a product

- Provide information
- Build brand equity
- Reduce purchase risk
- Stimulate trial

Each objective requires a different approach, and each requires a different mix of communication elements. Although any of the communication elements, such as advertising, can be used to accomplish any of the objectives, other forms of communication such as sales promotions or personal selling may work better for a specific objective. The optimal results occur when the communication tools are used together, integrating them into one common theme. For example, to reduce purchase risk, a firm may use advertising coupled with a $2-off coupon and a special point-of-purchase display. The combined effect of using all three elements together is greater than if only one was used.

Figure 13-13
This advertisement by Haik Humble Laser Center strives to differentiate the center's brand name by stressing new laser vision correction technologies that are available to patients and by using an endorsement from pro-football quarterback Doug Pederson.

Source: Sartor Associates, Inc. for Haik Humble Eye Center.

Increase Demand To increase demand, firms usually turn to trade and sales promotions. Offering wholesalers and retailers trade promotions such as price discounts, quantity discounts, and bonus packs encourages them to purchase more of a product because they can increase their margins. For example, if a manufacturer of picture frames offers retail stores a 10 percent discount on purchases made by October 1, many of the stores will boost their orders. They can then either pass the savings on to the customer through cheaper prices, or they can charge the customer the same amount, increasing their profit by 10 percent. In most cases, retailers use the latter strategy. Retail prices stay the same. To make the increase in demand more dramatic, manufacturers may offer a manufacturer's coupon to consumers at the same time they are offering the channel discount. Giving a discount to both consumers and channel members drastically reduces the profit margin for manufacturers, but it will create a short-term burst in sales.

Advertising and personal selling are the least effective promotional elements to directly increase demand but can serve a valuable support function. An advertisement on television or in a newspaper can alert consumers to a manufacturer's coupon. A direct-mail piece sent to wholesalers and distributors can alert them to the trade discount being offered. For more of an impact, the manufacturer could have its salespeople offer customers special trade discounts. In these situations, channel members will often either increase the order they had planned or make a special purchase.

Differentiate a Product The proliferation of brands has created a situation in which most consumers as well as businesses have multiple choices. In many cases, there is very little actual difference between the various brands. If this is perceived to be so by the buyer, then price becomes the determining factor. To avoid situations in which buyers make purchase decisions entirely on price, companies strive to differentiate their product from the competitors'. Benefits and features not available from competitors are stressed. If there are few or no actual differences, companies will often strive to create a psychological difference. The best communication tool used to differentiate a product is personal selling. A salesperson has the opportunity to explain a product's features and benefits. The message can be tailored to each buyer, and questions can be answered. For business-to-business markets and high-end consumer products that use salespeople, this method is very effective once the salesperson has the ear of a prospective buyer. But in situations in which personal selling is not possible, a product can be differentiated effectively through advertising. Through an ad, a firm has the opportunity to highlight a product's features and benefits and to show how a particular brand differs from competing brands. The Haik Humble Laser Center advertisement in Figure 13-13 highlights a free seminar individuals can attend that will explain the new S3 VISX technology used in laser vision correction.

Trade promotions and sales promotions are not effective in differentiating a product, unless the differentiation is based on price. If a brand is positioned as the low-cost option, then using trade promotions and consumer promotions can be valuable. But if the differentiation is to be based on a benefit or feature, then using numerous trade and sales promotions can actually make it more difficult to differentiate a product. If Pringles chips are promoted as not being greasy, but the company uses coupons extensively, consumers are likely to see Pringles as a cheap brand of potato chips rather than a brand that has been differentiated in another way.

Provide Information Salespeople and advertising are most effective at providing potential customers with information. Salespeople are able to modify the information to meet the needs of individual customers. A retail salesperson can provide a shopper with information on washing machines and features of each brand. A field salesperson can inform clients about a special upcoming sale or a new product recently introduced. Advertising is also an excellent means of providing information. Retailers use advertising on a regular basis to inform customers of their location, their operating hours, and the brands they carry. Advertising can be used to promote special events like a Labor Day sale; the introduction of a new brand, such as Vanilla Coke; or the grand opening of a new business (see Figure 13-14). Trade and sales promotions are not good venues for providing information because each offers some type of incentive to encourage action on the part of the consumer or business.

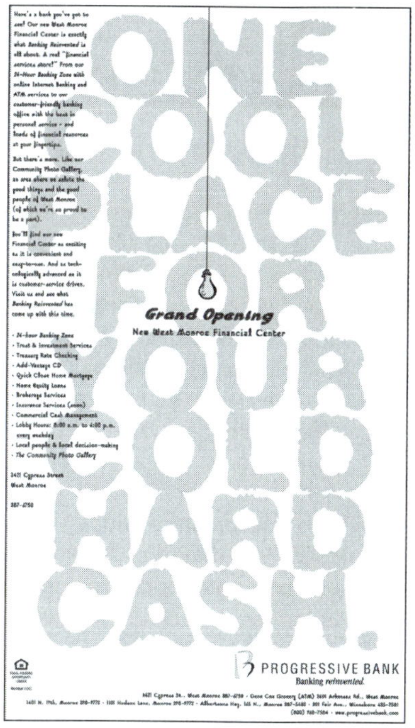

Figure 13-14
The objective of this advertisement is to provide information about the grand opening and services of the new West Monroe Financial Center.

Source: Courtesy of French Creative Group, Monroe, LA.

Build Brand Equity For long-term survival, brands must develop a certain level of brand equity that allows them to stand apart from competitors. As mentioned in Chapter 8, "Product Strategies," brand equity (or franchise) is defined as a set of brand assets and liabilities linked to a brand and its name and symbol, adding or subtracting from the value provided by a product or service to a firm and/or to that firm's customers.

Brand equity is built on two foundations: quality and awareness. The quality must match or exceed the relative price being charged. For example, the quality of food served at McDonald's does not match that of food served at Outback Steakhouse or Ruby Tuesday's, but it meets the standard relative to the price. If McDonald's did not produce quality fast-food items, it could not stay in business. Part of McDonald's brand equity, however, is not only its food, but also its service, convenience, and standardization.

The other factor in building brand equity is awareness. Although awareness does not equate to brand equity, you cannot have a high level of brand equity without awareness. McDonald's, Campbell's Soup, Wal-Mart, Nike, Toyota, and Kodak are all well known and have a high level of awareness. K-Mart, Enron, and WorldCom are also well known but, because of quality issues, they lack a high level of brand equity.

About the only way to develop a high level of brand awareness is through advertising. Television, radio, and print advertising are major avenues for making people aware of a particular brand. For many brand ads, little information is given. The focus is not on differentiating the product, but on building an awareness of the brand name and reminding consumers of the brand. The goal is to build a strong brand name. If awareness and a brand name are backed by quality products, then brand equity will develop. Brand equity is important from a company perspective because it equates to loyal customers. Marketing Illustration 13-3 discusses a unique form of brand equity—or the epitome of brand equity—cult brands.

Reduce Purchase Risk Reducing purchase risk is important for new products and for gaining new customers of current products. Personal selling is the best communication tool to accomplish this objective, offering the salesperson the opportunity to answer objections and explain features that will reduce the buyer's perceived risk. If safety is a factor, the salesperson can explain the safety features. If performance is a factor, the salesperson can explain the performance features and how the product will provide the benefits the customer wants.

Other communication tools that can reduce purchase risk are sales and trade promotions. Both are effective because they offer the buyer an incentive, normally a price reduction, to make the purchase. A 25-percent discount reduces purchase risk. With sampling,

Marketing Illustration 13-3

Cult Branding

What is cult branding? It is a brand that obtains a unique, almost cult-like following. Such brands have the uncanny ability to bind individuals to their cause, to their brand, with an exceptional loyalty not seen with any other type of brand. Apple, Harley Davidson, Linux, and eBay are brands that have reached this unique status with consumers.

The classic example of a cult brand is Harley Davidson. To celebrate Harley Davidson's 100th birthday, more than 250,000 Harley riders rode into Milwaukee, Wisconsin, the home of Harley Davidson. The Harley Owners Group has 886,000 members and organizes rides, training, courses, social events, and charity fund-raisers. Owning a Harley means belonging to a unique society of bikers. It is not the Hell's Angels of the past, but professionals, such as lawyers, doctors, and businesspeople.

In other examples of cult brands, more than 85,000 Apple Computer fans make a pilgrimage each year to the MacWorld Expo in San Francisco to see the latest Apple gadgets and to pay homage to Steve Jobs. Whether Jobs is there in person or is viewed on a giant screen, every word of his speech is cheered. After all, it was Steve Jobs who brought the computer to ordinary people and who developed an operating system that anyone could use.

How does a brand build a cult-like following? First, the brand is different from its rivals. It provides a unique identity for its members that makes them different from mainstream society. Often it is a brand that has faced a life-and-death situation but has been yanked from the grave. Such brands are underdogs, large enough to be worth fighting for, but small enough that if you don't join the cause, the big guys will stomp on them.

Source: Diane Brady, Robert D. Hof, Andy Reinhart, Ihlwan Moon, Stanley Holmes, and Kerry Capell, "Cult Brands," *Business Week* (August 2, 2004):. 64–67; Rob Schwartz, "Cult-tural Marketing," *Adweek*, vol. 45 (November 29, 2004): 13.

purchase risk can be reduced even further: If a potential customer can use a gym free for a week, then the risk of making a purchase is greatly reduced. The customer has a good idea of the benefits of membership and can more readily tell if it is a lifestyle fit.

While advertising can be used to reduce purchase risk, it is not too effective. Viewers know that the ad is going to promote a product and its features, so it will have little effect on their perceived risk of making a purchase. In rare cases, however, an advertisement may point out a feature or statistic that will be effective in reducing purchase risk. The airlines have tried to reduce the perceived risk of flying for passengers who are afraid by pointing out that it is statistically safer to fly than to drive. The advertisements have virtually no impact on perceived risk because of the consequence of an accident: People who fear flying may think that they would be one of those statistics.

Figure 13-15
Free samples create substantial traffic in retail stores.

Stimulate Trial To build new brands and to rejuvenate stagnant brands, companies will want to stimulate trial. Consumer promotions are the best means of accomplishing this objective. Coupons, sweepstakes, contests, and sampling are excellent methods of getting someone to try a product. Food manufacturers will often offer free samples of their food at grocery stores so people can try it (see Figure 13-15). If they like it, there are coupons readily available that allow the consumers to purchase the product at a reduced price.

Trade promotions are relatively ineffective in stimulating trial. Wholesalers and retailers are reluctant to try new products unless they know consumers will buy them. The trade incentive would have to be substantial, reducing the wholesaler's and retailer's risk before they would stock an item that no one may buy. For established brands like Procter & Gamble, General Foods, and Kellogg's, retailers are more likely to take the risk because they know that these companies thoroughly test a product in advance, and their history indicates that they have solid products. But even in these cases, the retailer will want the manufacturer to tie the trade promotion into some type of sales promotion or advertising.

Advertising and personal selling have moderate success in stimulating trial. Advertising could create interest in the product, but stimulating trial would be slow. If advertising is tied with sales promotions, then its effectiveness will increase dramatically. The same is true for personal selling. A salesperson has some impact on stimulating trial, but it really takes a trade or sales promotion offer for the buyer to go ahead and make a purchase. Philips Belgium found a unique method for stimulating trial of its new Philishave Cool Skin shaver, which proved to be very successful. Philips Belgium created traveling shaving stations complete with barber chair, sink, and Cool Skin hostesses. The portable shaving stations were set up in malls, movie theaters, department stores, and other high-traffic areas. People who bought the shaver onsite received a free shaving kit stocked with Nivea skin products, as well as a Philishave Cool Skin towel. The promotion generated 4,600 trials, with 25 percent of those who tried the shaver purchasing it.[10] Table 13-2 summarizes the relative strength of each communication element for each of the communication objectives.

INTERACTIVE TABLE

Communication Objectives and Communication Elements — TABLE 13-2

Communication Objective	Advertising	Trade Promotions	Sales Promotions	Personal Selling
Increase Demand	Slow, takes time	Excellent for encouraging distributors and retailers to purchase more; impact is immediate and short term	Excellent for encouraging end users to request the product; impact is immediate and short term	Good for items that are sold almost entirely by field salespeople, but poor for retail sales, since the salesperson is dependent on someone coming into the store
Differentiate a Product	Excellent	Poor, because differentiation is almost always based on price, not product features	Moderate for encouraging end users to request the brand, but may create price-related differentiation rather than differentiation based on product features	Excellent, since the salesperson has the ability for two-way communication and can often demonstrate how the product is different from that of a competitor
Provide Information	Excellent	Poor, since it depends on the type of trade promotion, and the trade offer normally overshadows the information	Poor, since it depends on the type of sales promotion, and the promotional offer normally overshadows the information	Excellent, since there is two-way communication and the buyer can ask questions
Build Brand Equity	Excellent	Poor, since most trade promotions focus on some type of price incentive	Poor, since most sales promotions focus on some type of price incentive	Moderate, since salespeople's primary goal is to sell a product, not to build its equity
Reduce Purchase Risk	Poor, since advertising can reduce risk only through talking about the features and benefits of the product	Good, since wholesalers and retailers can receive price incentives to make a purchase	Good, since sales promotions can reduce the financial risk; excellent if the firm can use sampling or trial purchase incentives	Excellent, since the salesperson has an opportunity to answer questions and demonstrate the product
Stimulate Trial	Moderate to good success if tied with a sales promotion	Poor, because of so many new products being introduced	Excellent, through offering consumers some type of incentive	Moderate success because of ability to answer questions and demonstrate the product

13-4c Push/Pull Marketing Strategies

Push/pull marketing strategies relate to how manufacturers market their products. With a push marketing strategy, the manufacturer attempts to push the product through the channels with the belief that if the product is available in retail outlets, consumers will purchase it. With a pull marketing strategy, the manufacturer builds product demand at the consumer level with the belief that consumers will go to retailers and demand that the product be stocked. Manufacturers seldom use either one or the other; instead, they use a combination. Thinking of push/pull marketing strategies along a continuum provides a better understanding of how they work together and what types of communication elements are best suited for each. Manufacturers who place the greatest emphasis on a push strategy will primarily use trade promotions and personal selling. Trade promotions provide incentives to channel members to stock an item and to push it through the channel. Personal sales calls on retailers and wholesalers will then enhance this process. For a pull strategy, the emphasis will be on advertising and sales promotions. Advertising builds awareness and brand identity, and sales promotions offer consumers incentives to try the product. Table 13-3 summarizes these relationships.

In the past, pharmaceutical companies relied exclusively on a push strategy. Samples of new drugs were given to physicians and advertisements were taken out in medical journals. The goal was to get physicians to prescribe the drug for their patients. Recently, however, drug companies have turned to a pull strategy. Viagra, produced by Pfizer, relied heavily on this strategy. Using television and print ads with Bob Dole and other celebrities, Pfizer encouraged patients to talk to their doctor about Viagra. After taking note of Viagra's success, Pharmacia sunk $130.4 million into promoting its arthritis drug, Celebrex. Drug companies are still providing samples to physicians but have moved a large amount of their marketing money into consumer advertising with the goal of building demand with patients, who will then request the drug from their physician.[11]

13-4d Product Lifecycle

The stage of the product lifecycle has a strong impact on marketing communications and the elements used. During the introductory stage, the goals of businesses introducing a new product are to promote industry demand and brand awareness, and to stimulate trial. Advertising works best for promoting industry demand and building awareness. For a business-to-business product, personal selling will also work well. Sales promotions are important to stimulate trial purchases. Normally, trade promotions will not work because channel members are uncertain about the projected consumer demand.

When the product moves to the growth stage, marketing dollars continue to be spent on advertising, but the objective is to develop brand preference and to differentiate the product from the competition, rather than build industry demand, unless the company has substantial market share. When Nintendo owned 80 percent of the video game market, expanding the industry demand was a logical objective since Nintendo would get 80 percent of the new business. Because of increasing demand, dollars are shifted from sales promotions to trade promotions. With growing consumer demand, companies will spend more on encouraging channel members to push their brand rather than the competition's. Since consumers want the product, there is little need for sales promotion offers.

TABLE 13-3

Communication Elements and Push/Pull Marketing Strategies

Push Strategy ←		→ Pull Strategy
Low ←	*Advertising*	→ High
High ←	*Trade Promotions*	→ Low
Low ←	*Sales Promotions*	→ High
High ←	*Personal Selling*	→ Low

Marketing Illustration 13-4

The Battle to Satisfy the Teen Thirst

While the baby boom generation feasted on cola drinks, today's teen population is turning to noncolas and new-age drinks. The battle to satisfy this portion of the population's thirst is intense, and it should be. With money to spend, this group spends most on apparel, consumer electronics, food away from home, and drinks. Because of taste desires of teens, new-age and noncola beverages doubled in sales in just two years, from $65 million to $130 million. The growth is the result of the characteristics of the new drinks that appeal to teens—new, edgy, and offering a legal buzz.

Mountain Dew and Sprite were the pioneers in teen-focus marketing. Manufacturers of SoBe joined the fight for market share. Using its website (www.sobebev.com) and "Team Lizard," the company launched a teen-based promotional contest offering prizes such as a Motorola pager, an MP3 player, and a dirt bike. In addition to advertising and the website, promotions included retail point-of-purchase displays. To keep pace, Pepsi first purchased SoBe, then launched its own noncola, lemon-lime drink called Sierra Mist. Dr. Pepper/7Up upped its noncola line for teens to include 7Up, Sunkist, Sun Drop, and Hawaiian Punch. Though not introducing a new product, Coca-Cola used NBA star Grant Hill to promote its Sprite brand in an effort to reach urban youth.

The teen market is attractive for two reasons. First, the growth in the soft drink industry is in the noncola category. Second, this group has not yet developed brand loyalty, and each company is hoping to get that loyalty—it hopes for a lifetime. With the high level of consumption of soft drinks, loyalty gained at age 15 turns into a lot of dollars.

Source: Libe Goad, "Non-Colas Quench Teen's Developing Thirsts," *Drug Store News*, vol. 23, no. 6 (April 23, 2001): 35.

When the product hits maturity, competition becomes intense. About the only way a company can increase market share is to take it away from the competition. In this environment, expenditures in all four areas are high. Advertising is needed to differentiate the product. Trade promotions are needed to encourage channel members to place a greater emphasis on a particular brand. Sales promotions are needed to encourage consumers to choose a particular brand over the competition. Personal selling is needed to highlight the advantages of one brand over another. Refer to Marketing Illustration 13-4 and Figure 13-16 for information about the battle to satisfy the thirst of today's teens.

The reverse situation occurs when the product moves into the decline stage. It does not make sense to advertise, use trade or sales promotions, or personal selling. Firms reduce their marketing expenditures with the idea of pulling out of the market and discontinuing the product. Table 13-4 summarizes the marketing communication elements as they relate to the product lifecycle.

Figure 13-16
Because of the spending power of teens, suppliers of soft drinks, energy drinks, and new-age drinks battle fiercely for the teen dollar and allegiance.

TABLE 13-4 Marketing Communications and Product Lifecycle

Marketing Communication Element	Stage of the Product Lifecycle			
	Introductory Stage	*Growth Stage*	*Maturity Stage*	*Decline Stage*
Advertising	Moderate, to develop awareness of a new product and build industry demand	High, to develop brand name and brand awareness	High, to differentiate the product from the competition	Low, because demand is declining and a new product or technology has taken its place
Trade Promotions	Low, because consumers are not familiar with the new product, and for retailers, it would be a high risk	Moderate, since consumers are demanding the product, and manufacturers do not need a high level of trade promotion to push their product	High, to encourage channel members to stock and push the firm's product	Low, because with declining demand, there is no need to encourage channel members to stock the product
Sales Promotions	High, to encourage trial usage of the product	Low, since consumers are demanding the product, and few sales incentives are needed for purchasing	High, to encourage consumers to choose a particular brand over the competition	Low, because sales promotion incentives will not encourage consumption
Personal Selling	High for business-to-business salespeople because they can explain the new product, but low for consumer products since the salesperson would have to wait for the customer to come to them	Moderate, since salespeople serve primarily as order takers with consumers and businesses demanding the product	High, to encourage customers to purchase a particular brand	Low, because few people or businesses want the product

13-4e Communication Budget

Developing a communication budget is difficult: It is challenging to identify the benefits and effectiveness of the various communication methods. While the previous discussion provides companies with an idea of the relative amounts to be spent on each type of marketing communication, it does not provide much help in terms of determining the overall budget. For this task, firms use a variety of methods, such as

- Objective and task
- Percent of sales
- Historical
- Comparative parity
- Executive judgment
- All you can afford

Companies using the **objective-and-task method** first identify communication goals such as target audience reach, awareness, comprehension, or even sales. Research is conducted to determine the cost of achieving the respective goals. Then the necessary sum is allocated based on the estimated cost to achieve each objective. This method is the most popular one used by multinational corporations in the process of deciding on their advertising budgets because it takes into consideration firms' strategies.[12] Most marketing experts also see it as the most sound method, since the budget is built on what it costs to achieve an objective.

Objective-an Method of de communicati first identifies the communication goals, such as target audience reach, awareness, comprehension, or even sales.

The **percent-of-sales method** determines the total budget allocated to communication based on past or projected sales. This method is difficult to adopt for firms entering new markets or introducing a new product because no past sales data are available. The problem with this method is that it causes advertising expenditures to decline as sales decline; at this point, the company should increase advertising spending, not reduce it. This method is appropriate for stable markets where sales do not fluctuate considerably or where sales are slowly increasing. For firms with a long presence in a particular international market, this method is used by almost half of the companies, with firms in Brazil and Hong Kong using it the most.[13]

Percent-of-sales method: Method of determining a communications budget based on past or projected sales.

Firms using the **historical method** base the communication budget on past expenditures, usually giving more weight to recent expenditures. The percent-of-sales method utilizes the historical method as a first step, if the percentage allocated to advertising is based on past, rather than on projected, sales. This method is not recommended for firms in an unstable economic, political, or competitive environment or where sales show wide fluctuation. It is based on the premise that past marketing expenditures have been sufficient to accomplish the firm's goals and that future expenditures should continue at the same level.

Historical method: Method of determining the communications budget based on past expenditures, usually giving more weight to more recent expenditures.

The **competitive-parity method** uses competitors' level of communication spending as benchmarks for a firm's own advertising expenditure. This approach is used in highly competitive markets to ensure that established firms maintain their market share. In the automobile industry, soft drink industry, and many other mature industries, firms spend about the same amount of money on marketing as their competitors. For firms entering a new market or a new industry, the method will indicate how much will have to be spent to be competitive. If a new soft drink company wants to compete on the same level as Coke and Pepsi, it will have to spend about the same amount, or more, to gain recognition. For brands that are not well established, this may be a dangerous strategy: The payoff to reach the breakeven point may take so long that a new brand can never be profitable. The more serious problem with this approach is that it suggests that a firm's goals and strategies are identical with those of competitors, which, most likely, is not the case. Table 13-5 provides comparisons of spending by major companies within the telecommunications, automobile, restaurant, department store, and discount store industries.

Competitive-parity method: Method of determining a communications budget that uses competitors' levels of communication spending as benchmarks for a firm's own advertising expenditure.

In the **executive-judgment method,** executive opinion is used in determining the communication budget. This is based on the philosophy that executives know the industry, know what is happening with the competition, and most importantly, know the future strategic direction of the firm. The danger is that, unless these executives have a marketing background, the budget may not be grounded on a solid marketing foundation.

Executive-judgment method: Method of determining the communications budget using executive opinion.

The last method is used by most small and medium-sized enterprises entering a new market without the large budgets of Fortune 500 corporations. The **all-you-can-afford method** best suits the financial limitations of these firms. Unfortunately, this approach completely ignores strategic issues and the competition. More seriously, when tough economic times hit, the marketing dollars are usually cut first. When this situation occurs, it creates a downward spiral that gains momentum over time. As communication budgets are cut, demand falls, causing another reduction in the communication budget, which, in turn, further reduces demand. In time, the company declares bankruptcy and wonders what happened to its customers.

All-you-can-afford method: Method of determining a communications budget that uses whatever funds are available after all other expenses are paid.

TABLE 13-5

Advertising Spending by Major Firms in Selected Industries

Industry	Firm	2003 Total U.S. Advertising (overall rank)
Telecommunications	AT&T	$479 million (68)
	Verizon	$1.67 billion (11)
	Sprint	$1.07 billion (30)
	MCI	$517 million (64)
Automobiles	Ford Motor Co.	$2.23 billion (6)
	General Motors	$3.43 billion (1)
	Toyota Motor Corp.	$1.68 billion (10)
	Honda Motor Corp.	$1.14 billion (26)
	Nissan Motor Co.	$1.30 billion (19)
	DaimlerChrysler	$2.31 billion (5)
Restaurants	McDonald's	$1.37 billion (16)
	Burger King	$525 million (62)
	Wendy's	$386 million (88)
Retail	Sears	$1.63 billion (12)
	JCPenney	$1.03 billion (33)
	Wal-Mart	$678 million (48)
	K-Mart	$413 million (81)
	Target	$1.08 billion (29)

Source: "U.S. Company Revenue Per 2003 Ad Dollar" (January 13, 2005); www.adage.com.

13-5 Measuring Communication Effectiveness

Measuring the effectiveness of marketing communications is a difficult task. While the ultimate goal of marketing communications is to increase sales or demand, it is not always easy to determine what contributed to sales growth or caused a sales decline. This is especially true if a firm uses an IMC approach. Is the sales growth or decline due to advertising, trade promotions, sales promotion, or personal selling, or is it attributable to other factors, such as price, quality, or service? Given the strong inter-functional relationship between marketing and production, finance, and other corporate areas, it is not easy to determine cause and effect. Nevertheless, companies demand greater accountability for their market expenditures. They want to know that the amounts spent on advertising, promotions, and personal selling benefit the company and contribute to the bottom line (i.e., the firm's profit).

While addressing different techniques for evaluating marketing communications, it is important to stress that the evaluation method should match the communication objective. For example, if the communication objective is to increase demand, then the evaluation must involve a method of measuring demand. If the communication objective is to build brand equity, it must measure brand equity. It is also important, if possible, to use more than one measuring technique. Just as using more than one marketing communication element enhances the overall impact, using more than one evaluation technique will yield a more accurate evaluation of the impact of marketing communications.

13-5a Evaluating Advertising

Advertising is difficult to evaluate for a number of reasons. First, the impact of advertising is often delayed. A consumer or a business may see an advertisement a number of times before acting. The AIDA concept discussed in Section 13-3b indicates that it takes time to move consumers from the attention stage to the action stage. It may be a matter of days, weeks, months, or years before the cycle is complete. Also, the more an individual observes an advertisement, the more likely the ad and the brand name will be stored in the person's memory. Second, advertising is often used to accomplish communication objectives that are not directly related to sales, such as building brand equity. Just as human relationships take time to develop, so does building brand equity. Third, because advertising is directed to mass audiences, it is difficult to determine who has seen the ad and who has not, and, for those who saw it, whether or not they comprehended it. Last, because advertising impacts the attitude and feelings of viewers, only subjective and indirect measures can be used to find out what consumers are thinking. The primary tests used to evaluate advertising are:

- Concept tests
- Copy tests
- Recall tests
- Recognition tests
- Attitude tests

Concept tests are used before an advertisement is developed or in the early stages of development. The purpose of concept tests is to find out whether the target market likes the concept of the ad or marketing approach. For example, if an agency wanted to develop a series of advertisements promoting electrical cars as environmentally friendly, it could use a concept test to see whether this approach is effective. The company might learn that the person who would consider purchasing an electric car is not concerned about pollution. With ad production costs now averaging $343,000 for a 30-second television commercial, it is better to find out if an idea works before an advertisement is produced rather than later.[14]

Copy tests are similar to concept tests but are conducted with either finished ads or ads in the last stages of production. The goal of copy tests is to obtain the reaction of the target market. If positive, then the ad is ready for final production and launching. If the reaction is negative, the ad can be pulled or modified. While production costs are lost at this stage, it is better to stop rather than spend $10 million on a campaign that is not effective.

Recall tests are used after an advertisement has been launched. The most common recall tests are **day-after recall (DAR)** tests. With the DAR method, individuals are called the day after a new advertisement appears and asked what ads they remember from the previous day. For unaided DAR tests, no hints are given. For aided DAR tests, the individuals may be asked whether they remember any ads for tennis shoes, thus prompting them as to the category. An alternative to recall tests is **recognition tests.** With this approach, consumers are shown a series of ads and asked whether they recognize any.

While recall tests and recognition tests will give an agency an idea of what percentage of an audience saw an advertisement, they do not tell the agency whether the audience liked the ad. To measure people's impression of an advertisement, **attitude tests** are conducted. Attitude tests vary widely, but all have the primary goal of measuring reaction to an advertisement. By knowing how viewers feel about an advertisement, an agency is in a position to improve the advertisement in order to obtain a more positive reaction. Gaining a high-recall score for an advertisement that consumers do not like will not benefit a client, so attitude tests are an important component of the evaluation.

Treetop can use several approaches to evaluate the advertisement in Figure 13-17. Since the ad is already developed, it is too late for concept testing. Because there are five ads in this series, copy testing is effective before the launch of the ad campaign. Copy tests would allow Treetop's advertising agency to evaluate the target market's reaction to this advertisement as well as the campaign concept. Since this ad is targeted to mothers of young children, especially babies, it is important to make sure that the participants selected

Concept tests: Evaluations of the content or concept of an advertisement and its potential impact on viewers; conducted in the very early stages of ad development or while the ad is in the concept stage.

Copy tests: Evaluations of a completed or nearly completed advertisement.

Recall tests: Evaluation procedures whereby participants are asked about their recall of specific advertisements.

Day-after recall (DAR): Advertising evaluation method of calling individuals the day after a new advertisement appears and asking them what ads they remember from the previous day.

Recognition tests: Evaluation procedures whereby participants are shown a series of advertisements and asked whether they have seen them before.

Attitude tests: Evaluation procedures of participants' attitudes toward a particular advertisement.

Figure 13-17
Treetop can use several methods of evaluating this advertisement, such as copy tests, recall tests, recognition tests, and attitude tests.

Source: © Tree Top, Inc., 2002, Yakima, WA. Created by Cole & Weber / Red Cell, Seattle, WA.

for the copy tests match the target audience of the advertisement. Although it is called a copy test, both the visual as well as the copy are evaluated.

After the Treetop advertising campaign is launched, recall tests can measure how many people recalled seeing the ad. Since it is a magazine advertisement, a recognition test could also be used. With the recognition tests, participants would be given copies of the magazines in which the Treetop ad appeared and asked whether they recognized the advertisement. Both the recall and recognition tests would give Treetop an idea about the impact of the ad. Based on the AIDA concept, the ad needs to garner attention. The creative staff working on the advertisement believed that the unusual visual of an apple swinging in a baby swing would catch the attention of someone looking at the magazine, especially young mothers. Recall and recognition tests can verify if this is the case.

To measure the audience's feelings toward the ad, an attitude test could be used. The attitude test measures how well new mothers liked the ad and whether it had a favorable impact on their attitude toward Treetop apple juice. Attitude tests are important because they allow a firm to obtain rough measures on the "interest" and "decision" component of AIDA. Even purchase behavior (action) could be measured by asking respondents if the ad

TABLE 13-6

Advertising Evaluation Techniques

Concept Tests	Evaluations of the content or concept of an advertisement and its potential impact on viewers; conducted in the very early stages of ad development or while the ad is in the concept stage
Copy Tests	Evaluations of a completed or nearly completed advertisement
Recall Tests	Evaluation procedures whereby participants are asked about their recall of specific advertisements
Recognition Tests	Evaluation procedures whereby participants are shown a series of advertisements and asked whether they have seen them before
Attitude Tests	Evaluation procedures of participants' attitudes toward a particular advertisement

influenced their purchases of apple juice. For a summary of advertising evaluation techniques, see Table 13-6.

While these tests tend to be subjective in terms of measuring the effectiveness of advertising, they do provide information as to the impact of an advertising campaign. Most agencies will take measurements over time to see if scores are increasing or decreasing. For example, recall tests may be conducted the first week of each quarter to measure over time what percentage of an audience recalls seeing the advertisement. If the recall percent increases over time, the agency is making progress. If not, then the agency needs to modify the advertisement or use alternate placement. The ad may be fine, but if it is on a television show that the target audience does not watch, it will not be effective.

13-5b Evaluating Trade and Sales Promotions

Evaluating trade and sales promotions is typically easier because of the nature of these types of promotion and the types of communication objectives they are designed to meet. While each type of trade or sales promotion may have a unique method for measuring its effectiveness, the major evaluation methods include:

- Changes in sales
- Inquiries
- Number of responses
- Redemption rate

Because of the short-term impact of promotions, changes in sales are usually immediate or occur over a short period of time. A trade offer made to wholesalers and retailers will normally result in increased orders within days of the offer. The same is true for coupons and other forms of sales promotions. When Pizza Hut sends out a coupon offer with the newspaper, sales will increase immediately, and within two to three weeks, the impact of the coupon is virtually gone.

Direct marketing techniques involve some type of call to action. Advertisements will sometimes encourage people to call a toll-free number or access a website. These inquiries can be counted and even categorized. If proper coding techniques are used, a company can know the source of every inquiry, if it was a television ad or a magazine ad. Inquiries are used more extensively in the business-to-business sector because a business may not have enough information to make a purchase and may seek additional details.

Redemption rates and the number of responses can be used to evaluate a promotional activity. Coupon redemption rates evaluate the success of a coupon promotion. The number of people who enter a contest will give an agency an idea of how successful the contest was. The same techniques can be used for trade promotions.

13-5c Evaluating Personal Selling

Personal selling is normally evaluated by sales because salespeople are hired to sell a product. But firms can use other measures. Sometimes, the number of new customers obtained is useful as a means of evaluation and important for firms that want their salespeople to be involved in gaining new customers. Part of a salesperson's job is to service current accounts. If salespeople are paid a commission on sales, they may be reluctant to devote much time to current accounts if they do not produce additional sales. For example, once a business purchases a copier, it is unlikely to purchase another one soon. The salesperson may not want to spend time on a business that has already purchased; he or she will move on to the next potential customer. To ensure that salespeople service accounts after a sale is made, firms can use customer retention and level of customer satisfaction as evaluation measures. The effectiveness of these two methods depends on the weight management places on them: If pay raises or bonuses are tied to customer retention and/or satisfaction, then salespeople will spend time servicing the account.

13-6 Global Communications

Standardization: The process of using the same product and marketing approach across countries.

Adaptation: The process of modifying the product and marketing approach for each country.

IMC is an international trend, commonly referred to as a GIMC or a globally integrated marketing communications program. Although the goal is still the same (to coordinate marketing efforts), the challenges are greater due to national and cultural differences. In the past, marketers had two different strategies for international companies: standardization and adaptation. **Standardization** is the process of using the same product and marketing approach across countries. **Adaptation** is the process of modifying the product and marketing approach for each country. With standardization, the goal is to generate economies of scale in production while creating a global product using the same promotional theme. The language would be different, but the marketing message would be the same. With adaptation, the goal is to modify the product and marketing message to better fit with each country's culture, with the idea of better meeting each target market's needs.

The GIMC approach is easier to apply when a company has relied on standardization. However, GIMC can and should be used with either standardization or adaptation.[15] To reduce marketing costs, careful coordination of marketing efforts should occur across countries. Even when a firm uses an adaptation strategy, subsidiaries can learn from each other—synergy can occur between countries. More importantly, learning can occur.

In terms of marketing, perhaps the best philosophy to follow is "think globally but act locally." To fully utilize the power of GIMC, marketing messages should be designed with a global theme in mind, so the same general message is heard worldwide. At the same time, when marketers design or encode messages for local markets, they should have the freedom to tailor or alter the message to the local culture and the target market. In other words, Pepsi may wish to portray a global image around a theme of "Generation Next," but how the final message is conveyed to each country may vary. Development of a GIMC is the final extension of an IMC plan. With its completion, companies are able to compete more effectively both at home and abroad.

Summary

1. *Discuss the concept of integrated marketing communications.* Integrated marketing communications is the coordination and integration of all marketing communication tools, avenues, and sources within a company into a seamless program designed to maximize the communication impact on consumers, businesses, and other constituencies of an organization. IMC is a holistic approach that involves everyone in the company articulating the same message. There must be open communication vertically within the company, horizontally across functional areas and departments, and outward to customers and stakeholders who have an interest in the company. IMC involves communicating to four primary groups: customers, channel members, employees, and stakeholders.

2. *Identify the various marketing communication elements.* The marketing communication elements include the traditional promotional mix of advertising, sales promotions, trade promotions, personal selling, and public relations. But with the integrated approach, other components of communication have also become important, such as Internet, database, and direct marketing. Possible communication outlets include traditional venues such as radio, television, newspapers, and magazines, but also the Internet, billboards, transit signs, store signage, and company stationery.

3. *List the stages of integrated marketing communications.* The four stages of developing an IMC culture within a company include (1) identifying, coordinating, and managing all forms of external communication; (2) including everyone touched by the organization into the communication, both internal communication as well as external communication; (3) using information technology prominently to develop databases of customer activities, purchases, and interactions with the company; and (4) treating IMC as an investment and not a departmental function.

4. *Identify the elements of communication and the importance of AIDA.* The six steps in communication are the source, encoding, message, medium, decoding, and audience. For communication to occur, the source, which for IMC is normally a business or an ad agency, encodes what it wants to communicate into a message, which is transmitted to an audience via some channel such as a television or POP (point-of-purchase) display. The audience, or potential customer, sees the message and decodes the message. If the decoded message matches the encoded message, accurate communication has occurred. Feedback from the audience back to the sender alerts the sender to the success of the message and what, if anything, needs to be modified for future messages. Noise is anything that interferes with the delivery of the message from the source to the audience. AIDA is an acronym for attention, interest, desire, and action. It is the process of developing customers, taking them through the stages of getting their attention, building interest in the product, building desire for the product over competitors, and encouraging them to act, ultimately, to purchase.

5. *Discuss the various factors that impact the relative mix of communication elements in an integrated marketing communications plan.* The factors that impact the relative mix of an IMC campaign include business versus consumer market, communication objective, push/pull strategy, product lifecycle, and communication budget. Business markets tend to rely more on personal selling, whereas consumer markets rely more on advertising. The communication objectives include increasing demand, differentiating a product, providing information, building brand equity, reducing purchase risk, and stimulating trial. The IMC mix will vary depending on which objective is primary. For push strategies, firms will rely more on trade promotions and personal selling, whereas for pull strategies, advertising and consumer promotions are used. The relative IMC mix will vary with each stage of the PLC, with the maturity stage requiring the highest level of all components of the IMC mix. The overall communication budget determines how much is available to divide among the various elements.

6. *Explain various methods for measuring the effectiveness of marketing communication.* The primary tests used to evaluate advertising are concept tests, copy tests, recall tests, recognition tests, and attitude tests. Concept tests are used before an ad is produced. Copy tests are used on completed or nearly completed ads. Recall and recognition tests are used to measure the awareness of an advertisement, and attitude tests are used to measure viewers' opinions of ads. Trade and sales promotions are evaluated through measuring changes in sales, number of inquiries, number of responses, and redemption rate. The primary method for evaluating salespeople is sales. However, new customers, customer retention rate, and customer satisfaction are also used.

Key Terms

adaptation (p. 406)
advertising (p. 381)
AIDA (p. 390)
all-you-can-afford method (p. 401)
attitude tests (p. 403)
audience (p. 389)
competitive-parity method (p. 401)
concept tests (p. 403)
copy tests (p. 403)
database marketing (p. 384)
day-after recall (DAR) (p. 403)
decoding (p. 389)
direct marketing (p. 384)
encoding (p. 388)
executive-judgment method (p. 401)
feedback (p. 389)
historical method (p. 401)
integrated marketing communications (IMC) (p. 380)
Internet marketing (p. 384)
medium (p. 389)
message (p. 388)
multichannel marketing (p. 381)
noise (p. 389)
objective-and-task method (p. 401)
percent-of-sales method (p. 401)
personal selling (p. 383)
promotion (p. 379)
public relations (PR) (p. 381)
publicity (p. 382)
recall tests (p. 403)
recognition tests (p. 403)
sales promotions (p. 382)
standardization (p. 406)
source (p. 388)
trade promotions (p. 382)

Discussion Questions

1. Read the opening vignette about hearing aids. Do you know of someone who should buy one, but doesn't. Why? What other products fit into the same category as hearing aids, in terms of consumers needing them but being reluctant to purchase them. What is the best approach to market these types of products?
2. Pick a well-known restaurant, such as Pizza Hut, McDonald's, Outback Steakhouse, or Olive Garden. Discuss how the restaurant integrates all of its marketing messages. What common theme is used? What types of IMC elements are used? Access the firm's website. Is the website consistent with the television, radio, and other media advertising?
3. Think about purchasing a new car. Identify all of the venues, such as television, radio, magazines, and so on, that you would use to gather information about the various models and list them. In a second list, include any sources of information an automobile dealer may use to communicate with you but that you would not pay any attention to. What are the most effective means of communicating with you? Where would the automobile dealer be wasting money?
4. Record an advertisement from TV. Show it to five people. Ask each one what message is being conveyed. Did the advertiser do a good job of communicating? Do you think the message was decoded accurately? Do you think the advertiser did a good job of encoding the message?
5. Pick a magazine ad that you like. Show it to five people. Ask each one what message is being conveyed. Did the advertiser do a good job of communicating? Do you think the message was decoded accurately? Do you think the advertiser did a good job of encoding the message?
6. Think about the last major purchase you made. Go through the AIDA concept in terms of what the brand did to get your attention, build interest, build desire, and promote action.
7. Read Marketing Illustration 13-2. How do you feel about advertising on airplanes? For the airlines, what are the pros and cons of selling advertising time and space on airplanes?
8. Leaf through your favorite magazine. From the list of possible communication objectives, find an example of an advertisement to illustrate each one. Which objectives tend to appear the most in your magazine? Why?
9. Read Marketing Illustration 13-3. Why are brands such as Apple and Harley Davidson able to attract such devoted customers? What other brands would you classify as cult brands? Why? Do cult brands just occur, or can a company create a cult brand? What can a company do to create a cult brand or at least move a brand in that direction?
10. Create three columns on a piece of paper with the headings (1) Recognize, (2) New, and (3) Not sure. As you watch each advertisement during a 30-minute television show, put a hash mark in the correct column based on whether it was an ad you recognize as having seen before, a new ad, or an ad you are not sure you have seen before. What was the total number of ads aired during the show? Write down the top five ads you recall seeing. What did you like or dislike about each? Do you remember where they were in the sequence of the ad block? Does it make a difference where they are located in the sequence? Why or why not?

Review Questions

True or False

1. Promotion refers to those forms of external communications that provide information about discounts or special offers and are aimed at increasing sales revenues.
2. In order to be efficient, the integrated marketing communications approach requires direct communications with the firm's primary competitors.
3. The process of encoding begins with the interpretation of the meaning conveyed in the marketing message.
4. The abundance of different communication channels and prolific advertising facilitate the communication process and allow customers to select the right message.
5. Marketing managers allocate at least 75 percent of the marketing budget for advertising since advertising has the most direct impact on sales.
6. Most business-to-business marketing expenditures are spent on direct mail and print advertising, whereas the greater part of consumers' marketing expenditures are for advertising on TV channels.
7. The best approach to differentiate the company's product involves creating a psychological difference through massive sales promotion with readily available coupons.
8. The broad implementation of information technology allows measuring the effectiveness of advertising with reasonable accuracy.

Multiple Choice

9. What is the best description of integrated marketing communications?
   a. seamless programs designed to maximize the communication effect
   b. coordination and integration of all marketing communications tools
   c. coordination and integration of all marketing resources
   d. all of the above
10. Which of the following descriptions refers to multichannel marketing?
   a. multiple channels for customers to purchase a product
   b. multiple avenues of communication to gather information
   c. integration of both distribution and communication channels
   d. none of the above

11. Which of the following descriptions relates to public relations?
- **a.** paid communications to the customers and other stakeholders
- **b.** events with direct or indirect effect on the public or stakeholders
- **c.** encourage end users to purchase the product
- **d.** all of the above

12. The promotion of a product directly from the manufacturer or producer to the buyer without any middleman involved in the transaction is known as
- **a.** personal selling.
- **b.** database marketing.
- **c.** direct marketing.
- **d.** Internet marketing.

13. The last step in the communication process, feedback, is the most efficient and informative element in which of the following?
- **a.** personal selling
- **b.** Internet selling
- **c.** direct selling
- **d.** none of the above

14. After seeing an advertisement on TV, a consumer checks the Internet to find the closest retail store or searches for more information on the web. According to the AIDA concept, these actions belong to which step?
- **a.** attention
- **b.** interest
- **c.** desire
- **d.** action

15. Which of the following categories are often used as objectives in the integrated marketing communications plan?
- **a.** increasing demand and product differentiation
- **b.** providing information and building brand equity
- **c.** reducing purchase risk and stimulating trials
- **d.** all of the above

Notes

1. Dawn Iacobucci, Bobby J. Calder, Edward Malthouse, and Adam Duhachek, "Did You Hear?" *Marketing Health Services,* vol. 22, no. 2 (Summer 2002): 16–20; Aaron Baar, "GN Resound Targets Boomers," *Adweek Midwest Edition,* vol. 42, no. 39 (September 24, 2001): 6; David Goetzl, "Beltone Sees Big Market in Graying Baby Boomers," *Advertising Age,* vol. 70, no. 15 (June 5, 1999): 3–4; Dawn Iacobucci, Bobby J. Calder, Edward Malthouse, and Adam Duhachek, "Psychological, Marketing, Physical, and Sociological Factors Affecting Attitudes and Behavioral Intentions for Customers Resisting the Purchase of an Embarrassing Product," *Advances in Consumer Research,* vol. 30, no. 1 (2003): 236–240.
2. Kristen Rountree, "Daily Promotes New Sections," *Adweek,* vol. 39, no. 37 (September 16, 2002): 5.
3. Lelia Zoby, "Modern Communication: Share Thy Craft!" *Communication World,* vol. 18, no. 1 (December 2000/January 2001): 28–30.
4. Natalie Schwartz, "Clipping Path," *Promo, SourceBook 2005,* vol. 17 (2005): 15; "Coupon Distribution and Redemption Up in 2001," *Marketing Magazine,* vol. 107, no. 19 (May 13, 2002): 19.
5. Al Urbanski, "Trade Promo Lowdown," *Progressive Grocer,* vol. 82 (March 1, 2003): 45–46; Walter Heller, "Promotion Pullback," *Progressive Grocer,* vol. 81, no. 4 (March 1, 2002): 19; Paul Crnkovich, "New Image Evolving for Trade Spending," *Brandweek,* vol. 41, no. 16 (April 17, 2000): 32.
6. Mark Dolliver, "People Keep Expanding Their Internet Activity," *Adweek,* vol. 45 (April 19, 2004): 35; Pat Friessen, "Three-Part Harmony," *Target Marketing,* vol. 24, no. 5 (May 2001): 71–74.
7. Don Schultz, "Invest in Integration," *Industry Week,* vol. 247, no. 10 (May 19, 1998): 20.
8. Chuck Ross, "NBC Blasts Beyond the 15-Minute Barrier," *Advertising Age,* vol. 71, no. 33 (August 7, 2000): 304.
9. E. K. Strong, Jr., "Theories of Selling," *Journal of Applied Psychology,* vol. 9 (1925): 75–86.
10. Stephanie Thompson, "Grab a Coffee and a Shave on the Go," *Brandweek,* vol. 40, no. 17 (April 26, 1999): 53.
11. Christine Bittar, "High Anxiety: Patents Expire, Success Wanes," *Brandweek,* vol. 43, no. 24 (June 17, 2002): S64.
12. Nicolaoes E. Synodinos, Charles F. Keown, and Lawrence W. Jacobs, "Transnational Advertising Practices: A Survey of Leading Brand Advertisers in Fifteen Countries," *Journal of Advertising Research,* vol. 29, no. 2 (April/May 1989): 43–50.
13. Ibid.
14. Robert Goldrich, "Perry Explains Overtime Anomaly," *Shoot,* vol. 41, no. 49 (December 8, 2000): 49–50.
15. Stephen J. Gould, Dawn B. Lerman, and Andreas F. Grein, "Agency Perceptions and Practices on Global IMC," *Journal of Advertising Research* (January/February 1999): 7–26.

Case 13-1 Swanson Imports

Swanson Imports is a retailer specializing in fine home furnishings, accents, and gifts, with merchandise from around the world. The store also offers interior home design and consultation with two interior designers on staff. The retail store is located in a southern midwestern town of 150,000. While sales have been adequate, the owner, Katie Swanson, would like to see the store grow. Over the past four years, sales growth has averaged just 2.4 percent annually, which has not kept up with the increased cost of goods sold and utilities.

Katie had been handling her own advertising, dealing directly with the local newspaper and running ads on a weekly basis. A television station had contacted her about advertising, but Katie felt its prices were too high. She had thought about radio but wasn't sure it would work for her store. Realizing she needed professional help if she were to boost sales to the level she wanted, Katie decided to hire the Marshall Advertising Agency.

After getting a brief history of the advertising Katie had used in the past, Brenda Marshall of the Marshall Agency asked Katie to describe her typical customer in terms of demographics. "It is a female, probably around 35 or so. We get men into our store, but only about 25 percent of our customers are men. I'd say about half of the females who shop here work. Most are involved in social clubs and are prominent in charities in the area. Family income probably averages around $75,000 a year. Many of our customers are either professionals or wives of professionals like lawyers, doctors, or dentists. Almost all own their own homes, with many of the homes in the $200,000 plus range."

With a good picture of the customer in mind, Brenda suggested that the first thing the agency needed to do was measure awareness of the store. This would involve calling 500 phone numbers in the area, randomly, to find out how many people knew about the store and what they knew about it. Once that information was gathered, they would be ready to develop an IMC campaign. While Katie agreed the information was important, she was disappointed because she was hoping they would get started with an ad campaign immediately. Instead, Katie was to return in 30 days, after the survey was complete.

When Katie returned to the agency, Brenda Marshall handed her the results of the telephone survey. Using information obtained from a local marketing research firm, the agency contacted 320 people who fit the target group Katie had described. Here are the results of the survey:

- 18 percent named the store, unaided, when asked about a location for purchasing home furnishings.
- 62 percent said they recognized the store's name when it was mentioned.
- 28 percent of the sample had been to the store.
- 13 percent of the sample had made a purchase at the store.

Katie stared in disbelief at the survey results. It was not what she expected.

After giving Katie time to digest the numbers, Brenda started: "We need to decide on the objective of the ad campaign, but first, let me explain what these numbers mean. The recognition test indicated that almost two-thirds of your target market recognized the name of your store, yet it was alarming that it was not on the top of their minds. Only 18 percent named your store in an unaided recall test. Three of your competitors had unaided recall scores of 65 percent, 48 percent, and 35 percent. While your sales have been adequate, you have a tremendous potential to grow. Since only 28 percent of the sample had ever been in your store, that means 72 percent of your target market does not know what you have to offer. If we could get half of that 72 percent into your store, your sales could double."

Katie's eyes lit up. She had no idea that such a small number of her potential target market had actually been in the store. Her enthusiasm grew as Brenda continued. "Your success rate is really good, if you can get them into your store. Of the 28 percent of the sample who had visited your store, 13 percent had made a purchase. That is almost 50 percent. So, you can see if we double the number of customers, your sales should also double."

"I am so glad I decided to hire a professional agency," Katie said excitedly. "Where do we go from here?"

Brenda replied, "First, we must decide on the communication objective. It will guide the rest of the IMC plan."

Questions

1. Looking at the communication objectives listed in Section 13-4b of this chapter, which communication objective would you identify for the initial integrated marketing communications campaign?
2. Based on the IMC objective you identified in Question 1, what IMC elements would you use? What would be the relative mix of advertising, sales promotions, and personal selling?
3. Brenda Marshall knows that doubling sales will take time and sequential IMC campaigns. Explain the AIDA concept in terms of the Swanson Imports store and the IMC campaign that the Marshall Agency would have to develop. Describe, for each step of the AIDA concept, what type of communications the Marshall Agency should design to ensure that the majority of the Swanson Imports' target market reaches that step. For example, for the *attention* component, what type of communications is needed to ensure that the majority of the target market is aware of Swanson Imports?

Case 13-2 International House of Pancakes (IHOP)

The International House of Pancakes, more widely known as IHOP, had earnings of $40.29 million on a total revenue of $1.35 billion. It owns or franchises a total of 1,164 restaurants. The restaurant, with headquarters in Glendale, California, is now headed by Julia A. Stewart, formerly of Applebee's. As part of her strategic development direction for the restaurant, Ms. Stewart is examining the creative side of the restaurant's advertising business.

In 1999, Kirshenbaum Bond & Partners West won the $20 million IHOP creative account. The creative account involved creating, designing, and developing the ads for IHOP's advertising campaigns. The purchasing of media time is handled by a media buying specialist, Horizon Media of Los Angeles, with help from regional shops around the country. The new ads developed by Kirshenbaum did not follow the traditional advertising mold of IHOP. Instead, they took viewers behind the scenes to IHOP's kitchens to show how food was made. New characters called "Old Fashioned Syrup," "Strawberry Syrup," and "Mr. Pancake" were introduced. The ads were a cross between *America's Funniest Home Videos* and *Hard Copy*. According to Nigel Carr, Kirshenbaum's managing partner, "IHOP has a very loyal customer base, but it has a base of people who have strong memories of the brand but haven't been there recently." Carr felt these former customers "just needed to be reminded" through advertising about what they had experienced at IHOP. "We all felt very strongly that IHOP is a magical, whimsical place that lives in people's minds, even if they hadn't been there recently."

While the approach was novel and different, sales results were not. IHOP was disappointed with the results at the end of the contract and sought a new creative ad agency. Heil-Brice Advertising of Glendale, California, was chosen and given $30 million to handle the account. Instead of the whimsical, behind-the-scenes approach of the former agency, Heil-Brice developed a series of ads featuring vignettes of everyday life using the tagline "any time's a good time for IHOP." One spot showed a young boy teaching his grandfather how to ride a scooter. The two end up at the local IHOP to eat and talk about their experience. In addition to the everyday-life vignettes, Heil-Brice developed brand-image spots to support the breakfast, lunch, and dinner meals that IHOP serves. According to Susan Hernandez, Vice President of Marketing for IHOP, the former ads focused on the food products produced by IHOP. What was needed, she felt, was brand promotion. "I think that the best restaurant advertising does, in fact, reinforce the brand as well as drive traffic into the restaurants. The whole idea is to focus on the strengths of the brand, that friendly, warm, nostalgic feeling, and make it relevant to the lives of consumers."

When Julia Stewart became CEO of IHOP, she wanted to renegotiate the creative contract with Heil-Brice Advertising. The ad agency was not interested in a new contract. After talks between the two parties failed to settle their differences, both decided it was best to sever their relationship. That meant IHOP would have to look for a new ad agency to handle the creative side of its advertising. After 150 ad agencies pitched their offers to IHOP, the choice was narrowed down to 21 contenders. After careful review, IHOP settled on three finalists: McCann-Erickson of Los Angeles; Young & Rubicam of Irving, California; and Venables, Bell, & Partners of San Francisco.

Websites

McCann-Erickson Worldwide Group: www.mccann.com
Young & Rubicam, Inc.: www.yandr.com
Venables, Bell, & Partners: www.venablesbell.com

Questions

1. Examine the websites of the three finalists for the creative work of each advertising agency. Based on your knowledge of IHOP, list the strengths and weaknesses of each agency to handle the advertising of creative business for IHOP. (Handling the creative work means the agency is responsible for creating the ads.)
2. It is important to use an agency that has some experience with restaurants but that does not represent a competitor. It would be a conflict of interest if the agency also represented one of IHOP's competitors. Which agency do you think has the best experience to work with IHOP? Why?
3. Which agency would you select for IHOP? Justify your answer.
4. What advertising team would you use to promote IHOP. Should IHOP focus on its breakfast specialty, or should it focus on offering a complete menu, not just breakfast? Justify your answer.

Source: Kenneth Hein, "IHOP Steaks a Claim for Menu Options," *Brandweek*, vol. 45 (April 26, 2004): 14; Al Stewart, "IHOP Narrows Creative Review to 3 Calif. Shops," *Adweek Western Edition*, vol. 52, no. 26 (June 24, 2002): 5; Gregg Cebrzynski, "New IHOP TV Spots Are Warm and Friendly, Not Sappy," *Nation's Restaurant News*, vol. 35, no. 4 (January 22, 2001): 16; Gregg Cebrzynski, "IHOP Corp. Breaks 'Pretty Different' Advertising Campaign," *Nation's Restaurant News*, vol. 33, no. 38 (September 20, 1999): 4.

Advertising, Sponsorships, and Public Relations

14

CHAPTER OBJECTIVES

1. **Identify the various types of advertising.**
2. **Discuss the selection process for choosing an advertising agency.**
3. **Describe the appeals that can be used in designing an advertisement.**
4. **Differentiate between the three types of message strategies.**
5. **Identify the various ad executions that are available.**
6. **Discuss the advantages and disadvantages of the primary media.**
7. **Describe the current use of sponsorships.**
8. **Identify the role of public relations in integrated marketing communications (IMC).**

CHAPTER OUTLINE

Imagine: All the cookies you can eat! This is heaven. Now all you need is some milk to wash them down. Great! A giant refrigerator, full of milk cartons. But wait, they're empty. Every carton is empty! This isn't heaven; it's the other place.

This scenario, the first in a series of 40 television advertisements for the "Got Milk?" campaign, was the brainwork of Goodby, Silverstein, & Partners of San Francisco. Because milk consumption had declined from 29 gallons per year per person to 23 gallons between 1980 and 1993, the California Milk Processor Board turned to advertising to boost consumption.

Jeff Manning and Jeff Goodby went to work. Since everybody knew that milk was good for them, advertising that fact was not going to boost sales. To determine how important milk was, they decided to go one week without milk. From that, the deprivation strategy was born. Without milk, there was no cereal, there was nothing to drink with cookies, and so forth.

An entire series of television ads was created using the deprivation theme, in which the main character found out too late there was no milk. The first ad, titled "heaven," was launched in 1993. Another ad shows a toddler in a highchair with her milk bottle and a cat drinking milk at his bowl. The out-of-milk father looks from the cat to the baby. Using the music from *The Good, the Bad, and the Ugly,* the baby, afraid her milk is about to go, says, "I don't think so, baldy."

In addition to the original set of TV commercials, the Bozell Agency created the celebrity "milk mustache" campaign in 1999. While the ad agency, Goodby, Silverstein, & Partners, based its ads on the deprivation theme, Bozell went with the health theme. National research had found that if a mother drinks milk, her children are twice as likely to drink milk. Further, it showed that the primary reason women ages 25 to 49 drink milk is for calcium, which they hope will prevent bone disease later in life. Based on this research, a series of milk mustache ads were produced by the Bozell Agency similar to the ad in Figure 14-1 featuring the Dixie Chicks.[1]

14-1 Chapter Overview

Advertising is an important component of integrated marketing communications (IMC). In this chapter, we examine the role of advertising, as well as the process of developing advertisements. Section 14-2 begins with a discussion of the impact of advertising from an advertiser's viewpoint. While we can see advertising all around us and know it is a pervasive element of our society, companies who purchase advertising want to know it works.

Section 14-3 presents the different types of advertising, which fall into two broad categories: product advertising and institutional advertising. Section 14-4 provides a brief overview of advertising agencies. The various types of agencies are presented as well as a description of how a company selects an advertising agency.

Section 14-5 provides a synopsis of the creative design process. The section discusses the types of appeals, message strategies, and executions available to creatives (the individuals who design ads). Section 14-6 discusses the media selection process and the advantages and disadvantages of the primary media, such as television, radio, newspapers, and magazines. It is important that ads appear when and where a firm's target market will see them. The chapter concludes with a discussion of sponsorship marketing in Section 14-7 and public relations in Section 14-8.

14-2 The Impact of Advertising

Advertising is all around us. We see it on television, hear it on the radio, and read it in newspapers and magazines. It is on billboards, the side of buses, and even in public bathrooms. No matter where we go, advertising is there. But the big question that must be asked is, does it work?

In 1969, Condon Bush used his mother's recipe to develop the first can of Bush's Best Baked Beans. Through hard work and perseverance, that first can of baked beans

Figure 14-1
The "milk mustache" theme produced by the Bozell Agency has effectively boosted milk consumption.

Source: Courtesy of Bozell Worldwide, Inc. as agent for the National Fluid Milk Processor Promotion Board.

Figure 14-2
Because of a savvy advertising program, Bush's beans are now the market leader in the baked beans category.

produced a small family business. Primarily using a push strategy, the Bush family was able to grow their business into the No. 3 spot in the baked beans category, behind ConAgra's Van Camp's and Campbell's baked beans. But the family finally made the decision in 1993 to use advertising to promote their product, with the objective of growing even more. Because they did not believe in advertising, convincing them to give advertising a try was a big challenge.

Jay Bush, grandson of the company's founder, was selected to be the company's spokesperson. The first ad featured Jay explaining to consumers that the baked beans tasted so good because they were prepared according to an old family recipe, a secret recipe known only to Duke, the family dog. The ad ends with Duke conveying the idea that, with him knowing the secret, the recipe may not be a secret much longer. The ad was so successful that in just one year, Bush's market share in the baked beans category nearly tripled. It now has a 50 percent share of the $470-million-a-year baked bean market, compared to only 24 percent for Van Camp's and 7.5 percent for Campbell's. A major reason for Bush's success is that it spends about $14 million a year on advertising, compared to less than $1 million for Van Camp's and Campbell's combined.[2] Now the Bush family is a strong believer in the benefits of advertising and even sponsored GSN's "Dog Days of Summer" which consisted of a half-day block of a double-dog-dare game show called Dog Eat Dog. It consisted of a fun-in-the-sun pool party/barbecue, dog antics, and sunbathers performing belly flops and cannonballs for 'bean-counter judges' (see Figure 14-2).[3]

TABLE 14-1

Revenue per Advertising Dollar of Expenditure

Category	U.S. Revenue per Ad Dollar	
Automotive	Ford Motor Co.	$46.30
	General Motors Corp.	$39.04
	Honda Motor Co.	$35.24
	DaimlerChrysler	$31.42
	Toyota Motor Corp.	$31.09
	Volkswagen	$27.46
	Nissan Motor Co.	$23.32
Computers and Software	Dell	$50.64
	IBM	$39.16
	Hewlett-Packard	$32.49
	Intel	$19.41
	Microsoft	$19.26
Food	Altria Group	$30.74
	ConAgra	$23.19
	Nestle	$18.45
	Sara Lee Corp.	$18.30
	Campbell Soup	$11.03
	Kellogg	$9.88
	General Mills	$9.57
Personal Care	Kimberly-Clark	$24.91
	Unilever	$8.37
	Colgate-Palmolive	$7.10
	Procter & Gamble	$6.58
	Gillette Co.	$5.64
	L'Oreal	$3.48
	Estee Lauder Cos.	$3.26
Retail	Wal-Mart	$307.96
	Kroger	$87.96
	Albertson's	$75.92
	Lowe's Cos.	$61.23
	Safeway	$59.09
	Home Depot	$56.37
	Kmart	$56.29
	Target	$44.46

Source: "U.S. Company Revenue Per 2003 Ad Dollar," *Adage* (www.adage.com, January 13, 2005).

One measure of advertising's impact is comparing revenue to ad expenditures. Table 14-1 shows the U.S. corporate revenue per dollar of advertising expenditures for a few select industries. Notice that, in the automotive category, Ford is the leader with $46.30 of revenue for every dollar of advertising that is spent. Close behind is General Motors at $39.04 and Honda at $35.24. In personal care products, Kimberly-Clark's revenue per ad dollar expenditure is considerably higher than its closest competitor, Unilever ($24.91 for Kimberly-Clark compared to $8.37 for Unilever). The company with the highest revenue per advertising dollar is Wal-Mart, at $307.96 of revenue for every dollar spent on advertising. Its closest competitor is Kroger, at $87.96.

Although examining the revenue generated per advertising dollar is one measure of the impact of advertising, it does not tell the whole story. Does it produce market share? Table 14-2 provides a list of the top cookie brands, their advertising expenditures, and their market share. Nabisco Oreos has 13.2 percent of the market and ranks first among cookies in ad expenditures at $32.8 million. In comparison, Nabisco Snackwells, which spends $700,000 in advertising and ranks eighth among the cookie brands in ad spending, has a market share of only 2.2 percent. The last column of the table shows the cost for each market share point. For each market share point, Nabisco Oreos spends $2,048,000. In comparison, Pepperidge Farm spends only $860,000 for each market share point for their distinctive brand. Of course, Pepperidge Farm has only 3.4 percent of the market compared to Nabisco Oreo's 13.2 percent. If Pepperidge Farms wants to increase its market share, the company may have to double or triple ad spending. Industry wide, the top brands will spend, on the average, $2 million for each market share point, whereas the bottom brands have to spend almost $3 million for each market share point. Clearly, the top cookie brands are obtaining greater impact for their advertising dollars than the other brands.

The amount of money spent on advertising varies widely among different types of industries. For example, amusement parks spend close to 10 percent of their income on advertising, whereas grocery stores spend only 1 percent of income on advertising. The category with the highest percentage is real estate agents, who spend 14 percent of their income on advertising. Table 14-3 provides information on other industries and the percentage of their income that goes to advertising.

If, after all of the hard data just presented, you still have any doubt about the impact of advertising, just look around at the clothes people are wearing. Look through a magazine such as *Glamour* or *GQ*. Look carefully at the apparel ads both in magazines and on television. Ask a parent of a junior high school girl what impact advertising has on her selection of clothing for school. Even preteens are brand conscious (see Figure 14-3).

TABLE 14-2

Top Eight U.S. Cookie Brands by Market Share and Advertising Expenditures

Brand	Market Share (percentage)	Advertising		
		Expenditures	*Rank*	*Cost per Market Share point*
Nabisco Oreos	13.2%	$32.8	1	$2,048,000
Nabisco Chips Ahoy	9.0%	$18.8	2	$2,100,000
Keebler Chips Deluxe	3.4%	$ 3.3	6	$ 970,000
Pepperidge Farm Distinctive	3.4%	$ 2.9	7	$ 860,000
Nabisco Newtons	3.3%	$11.4	3	$3,460,000
Keebler Fudge Shoppe	2.7%	$ 5.1	4	$1,800,000
Nabisco Teddy Grahams	2.4%	$ 4.4	5	$1,830,000
Nabisco Snackwells	2.2%	$ 0.7	8	$ 310,000
Top 8 Brands	*39%*	*$79.3*	—	*$2,033,000*
Remaining brands	*61%*	*$179.7*	—	*$2,946,000*
Total for industry	100%	$259	—	$2,590,000

Source: "Top 10 U.S. Cookies in 2003," *Adage* (www.adage.com, January 13, 2005).

TABLE 14-3

Advertising-to-Sales Ratios for Select Industries

Industry	Ad Dollars as a Percent of Sales
Amusement parks	9.6%
Beverages	9.0%
Dolls and stuffed toys	11.2%
Eating places	3.2%
Food products	11.1%
Grocery stores	1.0%
Men's clothing	3.3%
Motion pictures, videotapes	12.5%
Perfume and cosmetics	7.2%
Real estate agents	14.0%
Women's clothing	2.7%

Source: "2004 Advertising to Sales Ratios for 200 Largest Ad Spending Industries," *Adage* (www.adage.com, January 13, 2005).

Today's parents are fighting with preteen kids who want to wear slinky spaghetti-strap tops, low-slung jeans that reveal a bare midriff, and short skirts—fashions that many parents believe are not suitable for teens, let alone preteens.

Marketing Illustration 14-1 describes in more detail the belly button culture and advertising's role in it. But as some fashion experts point out, the same parents who are fighting the fashion trends of their children today were battling for the right to wear denim as children. According to Cylin Busby, senior editor at *Teen* magazine, "It comes up [with] every single generation—with miniskirts, with cutoff jeans. Each generation pushes the envelope."[4]

14-3 Types of Advertising

Advertising can be classified into two broad categories: product advertising and institutional advertising. Both categories can be used to accomplish the communication objectives discussed in Chapter 13 "Integrated Marketing Communications." It is important for marketers to remember that advertising is just one component of the communication mix, and it must fit into the overall IMC objectives and not drive the marketing campaign. Too many marketers fall into the trap of thinking that advertising can solve all of their problems and thus put it into a lead role. For some IMC campaigns, advertising should be in a lead role, but for others, it needs to provide a supporting role.

Product advertising: Advertising designed to promote a firm's brand.

Figure 14-3
Preteens are susceptible to advertising, demanding particular brands for their clothing and lunch bags.

14-3a Product Advertising

Most advertising falls into the product advertising category. **Product advertising** is any advertisement that is designed to promote a firm's brand. It can be targeted to end users or channel members. Product advertising can be further subdivided into the following categories:

- Brand
- Informative
- Persuasive
- Pioneer
- Comparative

Marketing Illustration 14-1

The Belly Button Fad

Some say it started with Shania Twain, others claim it was Britney Spears, yet others credit advertising. While arguments ensue about where it started, no one doubts the significance of the belly button fad. Eager to be noticed among myriads of advertisements, Levi-Strauss, mLife, and JCPenney jumped on the opportunity.

Advertising agency Ogilvy & Mather produced a television spot entitled "belly button" that showed people's stomachs, paying careful attention to their navels. The ad started with an older woman's belly and, with each succeeding scene, the person got younger, until the last scene showed a woman who had just given birth. As the doctor prepared to cut the umbilical cord, the voiceover explained that people were meant to live wireless lives and that AT&T with mLife could make that a reality.

Advertising agency TBWA\Chiat\Day developed a 30-second TV spot for Levi-Strauss that focused on young women dressed in Levi's Superlow jeans. The camera panned on their bare midriffs and singing belly buttons with vocals by Jamie-Lynn (Sigler) Discala, who plays Tony Soprano's daughter, Meadow, in the HBO series *The Sopranos*. According to Anna Brockway, Levi's Director of Marketing, "The belly button spot is a lighthearted ad that showcases Superlow jeans as a confident, sexy, fun way to make a statement."

Eager to boost "Back to School" sales in a sagging economy, an advertisement produced for JCPenney featured a curly-haired preteen admiring her outfit—low-rider jeans and a crop trop—in front of a mirror. Her mother came in and explained that the daughter could not go to school like that. Rushing over to her daughter, she yanked the girl's jeans down another inch or so. "There, that's better," she exclaimed. Because of a strong negative reaction by parents, JCPenney quickly pulled the ad, afraid it would damage "Back to School" sales, instead of boosting them.

In Louisiana, State Representative Danny Martiny introduced a bill to get rid of low-riding jeans and exposed underwear. While most laughed at the idea of a fashion police, parents, school districts, and conservatives continued their battle. But the bare midriff has become a common site at colleges, high schools, and even junior highs. Fueled by fashion, advertising, and celebrities, low-riding jeans, skimpy tops, and miniskirts have remained fashionable.

While advertising did not initiate the "belly button" fad, it certainly is taking advantage of the phenomena to attract attention to ads and to boost sales for their clients. However, as in the case of JCPenney, advertisers have to be careful not to push the fashion envelope too far, especially with teen and preteen targets.

Sources: Margarita Bauza, "Skimpy School Wear Frustrates Parents," *The Detroit News*, (http:www.detnews.com/2004/schools/0405/28-a01-164586.htm, May 26, 2004); Michelle Krupa, "Bill Would Ban Low-Riding Pants," *New Orleans Times-Picayune*, (April 22, 2004): F3; Justin M. Norton, "TBWA\C\D Debuts Singing Belly Buttons for Levi's," *Adweek Eastern Edition*, Vol. 42, No. 25 (June 18, 2001): 25–26; Christine Champagne, "Launching Mobility," *Shoot*, Vol. 43, No. 8 (February 22, 2002): 26–27.

In examining the different types of product advertising, you must keep in mind that a good advertisement may have components from more than one category. These categories exist only for the purpose of discussion and to assist you in understanding how advertisements are created.

Brand advertising: An advertisement designed to promote a particular brand with little or no information in the advertisement.

Brand advertising is designed to promote a particular brand and typically provides little or no information in the advertisement. Figure 14-4 is an advertisement for Aeneas Williams Dealerships. The ad does not provide any information about the product other than placing the various automobile brand names down the left side of the advertisement. The primary goals of brand advertising are to develop a strong brand name and to build brand awareness. Recall from Chapter 13 "Integrated Marketing Communications," that to develop brand equity, a firm must first build a high level of brand awareness. Brand advertising can accomplish this goal.

Informative advertising: An advertisement designed to provide the audience with some type of information.

Informative advertising is designed to provide the audience with some type of information. It may be a retail store informing the public of its address, phone number, or operating hours. Figure 14-5 for Zeagler Music is such an advertisement. It provides the phone numbers of the store and informs consumers that Zeagler Music has electric Fender guitars starting at $199. Product manufacturers will sometimes produce informative ads that tell consumers which retail stores carry their brands.

Persuasive advertising: An advertisement designed to persuade viewers' thinking in some way.

The most common form of product advertising is **persuasive advertising,** which is designed to persuade viewers' thinking in some way. The advertisement for Skeeter boats in Figure 14-6 on page 420 is designed to persuade fishermen that owning a Skeeter boat is one of life's breathtaking experiences. The ad creatives wanted to add validity to their state-

Figure 14-4
This advertisement by Aeneas Williams Dealerships is an example of brand advertising.

Source: Courtesy of The Marketing Exchange.

Figure 14-5
This advertisement for Zeagler Music is an example of informative advertising.

Source: Sample print advertisement courtesy of The Miles Agency and Alliance One Advertising, Inc.

Figure 14-6
This advertisement for Skeeter Performance Fishing Boats is an example of persuasive advertising.
Source: Courtesy of Newcomer, Morris and Young.

ment so they used the Bass Masters Classic Official Sponsor logo indicating that Skeeter is an official sponsor of the Bass Masters Classic. Additional detail is then provided in the ad copy to back up the tagline used in the advertisement.

Pioneer advertising: An advertisement designed to build primary demand for a product.

The least-used type of product advertising is pioneer. With **pioneer advertising,** the goal is to build primary demand for a product. It is normally used only in the introductory stage of the product lifecycle (PLC). Because the product is new, consumers have to be convinced to buy it. After the product moves into the growth stage of the PLC, advertisers have to switch to another type of advertising, unless they are the industry leader. Even in those cases, they have to be careful because pioneer advertising builds demand for the product category, which means the ad will also help the competition. Pfizer used pioneer advertising when it introduced Viagra. The first ads were designed to build demand for the product—the Viagra name was not even mentioned. Men with impotency problems were just encouraged to see their physician and told that there was a drug available that would help.

Comparative advertising: An advertisement that compares the featured brand with another brand, either named or implied.

The last type of product advertising is **comparative advertising,** which compares the featured brand with another brand, either named or implied. Advertisers have to be careful with comparative ads to ensure that they do not violate the Lanham Act. The ads must compare similar products, and any claims made in the advertisement must be substantiated. Because companies do not like to see their brand being ridiculed in an ad or shown to be inferior, most companies examine comparative ads very closely to ensure that they are not violating the law. Comparative ads can be successful, however, especially for new

Figure 14-7

This advertisement for Glenwood Regional Medical Center is an example of institutional advertising.

Source: Sample print advertisement courtesy of The Miles Agency and Alliance One Advertising, Inc.

brands. When a new brand is compared to a well-known brand, the new brand will gain recognition and brand equity. Seeing the two brands together in the same ad encourages consumers to see the two brands as equals.

14-3b Institutional Advertising

Institutional advertising is designed to build the corporate reputation or develop goodwill for the corporation. Seldom is a brand name mentioned in the advertisement and often the corporate name is a minor component of the ad. The advertisement in Figure 14-7 for Glenwood Regional Medical Center highlights the heart care that is available to patients in the communities surrounding Glenwood.

Institutional advertising: Advertising designed to build the corporate reputation or develop goodwill for the corporation.

Institutional ads can also be public service announcements and cause-related promotions. For example, the advertisement in Figure 14-8 is a public service ad by Glenwood Regional Medical Center providing information about what people can do to prevent encephalitis. Both public service ads and cause-related advertising enhance a brand's goodwill with the public, if the ads convey genuine concern. As was presented in Chapter 3 "Marketing Ethics, Regualtions, and Social Responsiblility," it is important for companies to demonstrate that they care about society and the environment. Consumers also believe that firms should be involved in supporting good causes. Thus, most companies will designate part of their advertising budget to institutional advertising.

Figure 14-8
This advertisement by Glenwood Regional Medical Center is an example of a public service ad.

Source: Sample print advertisement courtesy of The Miles Agency and Alliance One Advertising, Inc.

14-4 Advertising Agencies

Because of an advertising agency's expertise, most companies and even many nonprofit organizations will hire an external advertising agency. All types and sizes of advertising agencies exist. At one extreme is the highly specialized, boutique-type agency that offers only one specialized service, such as television ad production, or that serves only one type of client. For example, G & G Advertising of Albuquerque, New Mexico, specializes in advertising to Native Americans, a market that is estimated at 10 million people.[5] At the other extreme is the full-service agency that provides all of the advertising services as well as assistance in the other components of IMC, such as sales and trade promotions, public relations, sponsorships, direct marketing, database marketing, and so forth.

In addition to advertising agencies, other types of firms are closely related to, and work with or assist, advertising agencies. They include media service companies that negotiate and purchase media packages (called "media buys") for companies. Media production companies specialize in producing the actual advertisements. Most of these companies are in the area of broadcast production, such as television or radio. Many small advertising firms will use the services of a media production agency to produce the ad after it has been created. Direct marketing companies and database marketing companies handle every aspect of a direct or database marketing campaign or just handle designated components of it. Some companies handle only trade promotions, handle only sales promotions, or handle both. Within this category are highly specialized agencies that handle nothing but contests and sweepstakes or coupons. A number of public relations firms can handle all aspects of public relations or just components of public relations, such as an event-marketing program, a cause-related program, sponsorships, or crisis management. Many companies will use the services of a public relations firm when a crisis occurs or for specific events that the company does not have the public relations expertise to handle.

A recent trend in advertising introduced by the Young & Rubicam Advertising Agency is the "whole egg theory." This theory is based on advertising agencies moving from selling a client's products to helping the client achieve success in the marketplace. The key to this change is using an integrated marketing approach by offering a full spectrum of services to both business and consumer clients. Thus, as companies move toward an IMC approach, agencies such as Young & Rubicam are able to handle more of the IMC functions beyond advertising. Often, this is done through subsidiary boutique firms or on a subcontracting basis. For instance, Young & Rubicam may hire another firm to handle the sales promotion component of an IMC account it has or use one of its own subsidiary firms. It is important that advertising agencies be able to work with every aspect of a firm's integrated marketing campaign.[6]

The decision to hire an advertising agency is based on the belief that the agency can provide services and assistance beyond the firm's own capability. With most products in the maturity stage of the product lifecycle, advertising is key in the process of developing brand awareness, brand equity, and brand preference. Advertising agencies can provide a number of services, such as:

- Identification and development of a brand's target market(s)
- Business-to-business marketing expertise
- Brand and image development
- Planning, preparing, and production of advertisements
- Planning and purchasing of media time and space
- Integration of advertising with other components of the IMC
- Assistance in developing other components of the IMC

Choosing an advertising agency is a difficult task. Major criteria that should be used in the selection process include:

- Size of the agency
- Relevant experience of the agency
- Conflicts of interest
- Creative reputation and ability
- Ad production capability
- Media planning and purchasing capability
- Other IMC services available

The agency needs to match well with the firm in terms of size. A small agency would have difficulty handling the demands of a large client, and a large agency would have difficulty in meeting the needs of a small client. A good rule of thumb is that the account should be large enough that it is important to the advertising agency, but small enough that the loss of that account would not have a major detrimental impact on the agency.

It is important for the agency to have experience relevant to the client's needs, but not represent a competing firm—which would constitute a conflict of interest. For example, in the selection of the Miles Agency to handle the advertising for Inside Indigo, the agency had relevant experience with retail but did not represent a direct competitor (see Figure 14-9). The Miles Agency's other retail clients are clothing stores, The Toggery and Her Toggery. A

Figure 14-9
The Miles Agency, which handles the advertising for Inside Indigo, has relevant experience with retail but does not represent any retailers who directly compete with Inside Indigo.

Source: Sample print advertisement courtesy of The Miles Agency and Alliance One Advertising, Inc.

conflict of interest would occur if the Miles Agency represented a retail outlet that sold home furnishings, gifts, and accessories similar to what is sold at Inside Indigo.

Because of advertising clutter, clients want an agency that can design ads that will be noticed and accomplish the communication objective for which they were designed. An agency's creative reputation and ability provide one measure of how successful an agency is in creating successful ads. The type and number of awards will tell you what the advertising industry thinks of the agency's creative ability. Although awards do not always translate into effective advertisements, in most cases there is a strong relationship between winning awards and writing effective ads.

Ad production capability as well as media planning and purchasing capability should be evaluated. However, it must be kept in mind that many agencies will work with production firms and media buying firms in accomplishing these tasks. It is not essential that the ad agency itself have these capabilities. What is important is that the finished product is of acceptable quality and that media time and space are purchased efficiently.

The last criterion in the agency selection process is the availability of other IMC services. Just as with ad production and media buying, many agencies will work with boutique shops to produce trade promotions, sales promotions, public relations material, and other IMC material. The key is to work with an agency that understands the importance of integration and will be sure that the advertising produced is fully integrated with the other IMC materials that are produced, whether the agency or another firm does it.

Account executive: The key representative of the advertising agency to the client company.

Creatives: Individuals who actually design the advertisements.

The advertising **account executive** is the key representative for the advertising agency to the client company. This individual is actively involved in soliciting the account, finalizing details of the contract, and managing the advertising campaign. Many times, the account executive will help a client define its advertising message and integration with the firm's IMC campaign.

Creatives are the individuals who actually design the advertisements. These individuals usually work for the advertising agency but can also be freelancers. Many firms will use freelance creatives to assist with projects, to help during peak times, and to provide a new spark or idea to an advertising campaign. It is important for the creative and account executive to work together as a team. The account executive knows what the client wants to accomplish, and the creative has the task of creating an advertisement that will get attention, be comprehended, and most importantly, produce results. In Section 14-5, we will provide a brief overview of the creative process and how creatives work.

14-5 Creative Design

The creative design process begins with information obtained from the account executive about the objectives of the advertisement or the ad campaign, the target audience, and any message themes that should be included. The advertising objective would be related to the communications objectives discussed in Chapter 13, "Integrated Marketing Communications." For example, if the communication objective were to build brand equity, then the advertising objective would be to increase brand awareness by 25 percent over the four months of the advertising campaign. If the brand already has a high awareness, then the objective may be to increase brand preference for the product by 10 percent over the four months of the advertising campaign. Notice that with advertising objectives, the objective needs to be specific, measurable, and have a specific time frame.

In addition to the advertising objective, the creative needs to know who the target audience will be in terms of demographics and psychographics. Demographic information such as age, gender, ethnicity, income, education, and geographic region is essential. A brand awareness advertisement aimed at teenage females is going to be designed differently than one aimed at females over age 60. Psychographics will provide information about the target audience's attitudes, interests, and opinions. This information is as important as the demographics. If the creative knows the target audience likes outdoor activities such as hiking, boating, and fishing or that they believe in protecting the environment, this information will help in designing an effective ad. The more the creative knows about how the audience thinks

Marketing Illustration 14-2

Docker Sells Jeans to Generation X-ers

"I don't want high-waisted 'grandma' jeans. I want to be hip, and yet I don't want to look like Britney Spears." This statement was not made by a 12-year-old preteen, or a 17-year-old teen, or even a 23-year-old young female; it was made by 44-year-old Mary Young, a singer-bookkeeper from Florence, Alabama. Ms. Young's views are shared by many women age 30 and over. These females originally shied away from super-low jeans as the fads of pop stars and teen idols, but with the enduring popularity of lower waistlines, these older consumers have modified their position. They now want lower waistlines—just not the hip-slung look of a teenager.

The 45 million Generation X-ers were born between 1965 and 1978. This generation grew up in broken homes with stepfamilies and split custody. Television has always been a part of their lives, portraying a world of violence, unrest, and prosperity. While contraception led to a more liberal view of sex, about the time Generation X hit puberty AIDS and other sexually transmitted diseases warned them of great dangers.

Generation X-ers are media savvy and understand the power of media as well as its ability to distort reality. They treat the media with irony and irreverence. Marketers can use advertisers to reach them, but advertisments need to be more informative than persuasive. This generation especially likes websites that allow them to gather product information for themselves.

Armed with an understanding of what Generation X women wanted, Dockers for Women launched a "Three fits so we all fit in" campaign. Dockers for Women offers three waist options: the "classic" high waistline fit, the "favorite" slightly below the natural waist fit, and the "nouveau," an inch or so lower fit. To support this launch, Dockers for Women used television advertising supported by a print ad campaign. Dockers also developed an interactive website that explained each of the waist options. With the new Dockers for Women jeans line and creative advertising campaign, Generation X women could maintain their "hipness" and "youthful appeal."

Source: Georgia Lee, "The Great Waist Debate," *WWD: Women's Wear Daily*, vol. 188 (October 1, 2004):14; Linda P. Morton, "Targeting Generation X," *Public Relations Quarterly*, vol. 48 (Winter 2003), 43–45; Theresa Howard, "Ads Follow Gen Xers to Suburbs," *USA Today* (October 26, 2004): Money 07b.

and behaves, the easier it is for him or her to design an effective ad. See Marketing Illustration 14-2 to discover how understanding the audience has helped clothing manufacturers market to Generation X women.

In advertising campaigns, message themes are often carried over from one ad to another and even from one campaign to another. Allstate Insurance, in Figure 14-10, uses the message theme "You're in good hands" in every campaign and with almost every advertisement. UPS has the theme "Moving at the speed of business." Reebok had a series of advertisements that featured its DMX technology. The message theme is a method of ensuring that ads and campaigns are connected and that consumers hear a consistent message.

Once the creative has the background information from the account executive, he or she is ready to start working on the ad or the ad campaign. The next set of decisions involves the appeal, the message strategy, and the execution. While these decisions will be discussed independently, the creative normally makes the decision about each simultaneously, as they are interrelated.

14-5a Advertising Appeals

The **advertising appeal** is the design a creative will use to attract attention to and interest in an advertisement. The six primary types of appeal are:

Advertising appeal: The design a creative will use to attract attention to and interest in an advertisement.

- Emotional
- Fear
- Humor
- Sex
- Music
- Rational

The appeal chosen will depend on the objective of the ad, the message theme to be used, the target audience, and how the creative wants to convey the message to the intended

Figure 14-10
Allstate uses the message theme "You're in good hands" in all of its advertisements.

Source: Courtesy of Allstate Insurance Company.

audience. Almost every product can be advertised using any of the six appeals, and often an advertisement will use two or three appeals together.

For instance, in creating advertisements for the milk industry, Goodby, Silverstein, & Partners used a deprivation approach with a humor appeal. Bozell, however, used a variety of appeals in its print ads. Some ads used an attractive, sexy model, as in Figure 14-11. Others used a rational approach in talking about the importance of milk in providing calcium. Some used an emotional approach—see Figure 14-1, the "Got Milk?" ad with the Dixie Chicks.

Emotional appeals are an excellent method of building brand preference and brand loyalty. The goal is to build a bond between the brand and the consumer, just as you would between two people. Most of the Effie Award winners, which are presented by the New York chapter of the American Marketing Association, use some type of emotional appeal. The most common emotional appeals focus on the consumer's life and feelings.[7] Because of the capacity to use both sight and sound, television is the best medium for emotional appeals. Facial expressions, body language, and voice inflections can all be used to demonstrate feelings.

Fear appeals are used for many products such as insurance, fire alarms, deodorant, and mouthwash. With insurance, the fear focuses on what happens if an accident occurs and the person is not insured. With deodorant, the fear focuses on social rejection. Fear appeals work because they increase viewer's attention, interest, and persuasion. Many viewers will remember an ad with a fear appeal better than one with a rational, upbeat argument.[8] But advertisers have to be careful to use the right level of appeal. If the fear level is too low, viewers will not pay attention to the ad; on the other hand, if it is too high, then they will tune the ad out or switch channels. The most effective fear ads are somewhere in between.[9] See Figure 14-12 for an illustration of this concept.

Figure 14-11

The Bozell Agency used sex appeal in this advertisement for the milk industry.

Source: Courtesy of Bozell Worldwide, Inc. as agent for the National Fluid Milk Processor Promotion Board.

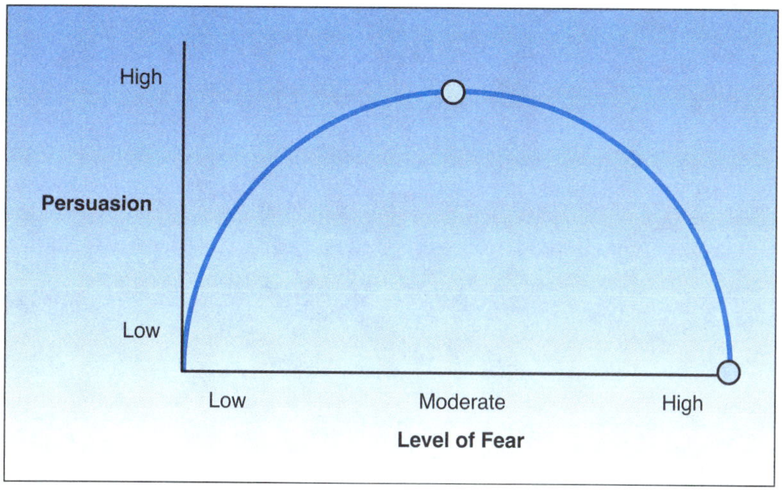

Figure 14-12

The Relationship between Fear Intensity and Persuasion

Persuasion through fear is most effective at moderate intensity. High levels of fear may cause consumers to block out the message.

Intrusion value: The ability to break through clutter and gain a person's attention.

Humor is used in about 30 percent of all advertisements because it has proven to be one of the best approaches to garnering viewers' attention and keeping their interest.[10] It has **intrusion value,** which means it has the ability to break through clutter and gain a person's attention. People like to laugh, and they enjoy watching ads that are humorous. Humor provides a way to escape from reality through a comedic view of life. The danger of using humor is that it can overpower the product and the intended message. To be effective, the humor has to grab the viewer's attention and hold it throughout the ad. But if the humor is too strong, then the viewer will remember the ad but have no idea of what brand is being advertised or of the message being conveyed. It is important to tie the humor to the brand and the message.

Many advertisers use sex appeals for a wide variety of products. Research has shown that sex and nudity in an advertisement increases viewer attention, regardless of the gender of the audience or the gender of the models in the ad. The danger, however, is that brand recall for ads with sex appeal is usually lower. Thus, while sex appeal gains attention, it appears that, if it is not done tactfully, the sex appeal may interfere with the person remembering the brand being advertised or the message being conveyed.[11] Sex appeals work best for products that are in some way related to sex. For instance, the advertisement by Guess in Figure 14-13 is an effective use of sex appeal because the clothes being advertised are designed to enhance a person's personal, sexual appearance. Using sex appeal to sell tools, office furniture, or life insurance will not be as effective, because these products do not have a natural relationship with sex.

Music is an important component of broadcast ads because it helps to gain people's attention and link them emotionally to the product being advertised. Music, like humor, has a strong intrusion value and can capture the attention of an individual who is not paying any attention to the TV or the radio. With a music appeal, the primary thrust of the ad is the song. The visuals and the copy support the song. With this type of appeal, advertisers like to use popular tunes that people have already developed an affinity for with the hope that the same feelings will be transferred to the product being advertised. The difficulty is the cost, which averages $250,000 per song. However, for an extremely popular song such as Jimi Hendrix's "Are You Experienced," the price tag can skyrocket to $7 million. Microsoft paid $12 million for the Rolling Stones' song "Start Me Up."[12]

Figure 14-13
Guess effectively uses sex appeal in many of its advertising campaigns.
Source: Courtesy of Guess and Creative Director Paul Marciano.

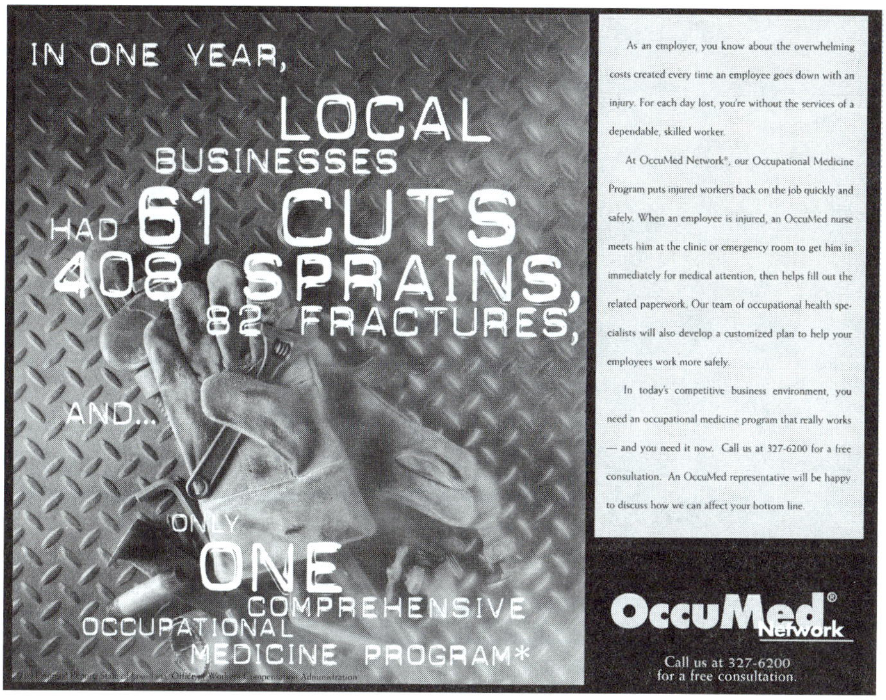

Figure 14-14
This business-to-business advertisement by OccuMed Network uses a rational appeal.

Source: Courtesy of Newcomer, Morris and Young.

Rational appeals are used in many advertisements, especially in print ads and for business-to-business ads. The premise of a rational appeal is that consumers will stop, look at the ad, and be interested in reading the copy or listening to what is being said. Unfortunately, with the large number of ads everyone is exposed to on a daily basis, it is much harder to get a person's attention using a rational appeal. However, if a person is interested in a product, then the rational appeal is the most effective means of conveying information and promoting the product's benefits. It is also an effective means of advertising high-involvement products about which consumers may want to obtain additional information. If a consumer will stop and pay attention to an ad using a rational appeal, the chances are very good that the information will be understood and become a part of the person's memory. Figure 14-14 illustrates a business-to-business advertisement using a rational appeal.

14-5b Message Strategies

The **message strategy** is the primary tactic an advertisement will use to deliver a message. The message strategy is *what* is being said, while the appeal is *how* it is being said. For example, a person may say "look at that" and by the inflection of the person's voice relay fear, shock, love, emotion, or just a matter-of-fact, rational statement with no emotion. Message strategies fall into three categories: cognitive, affective, and conative.

> **Message strategies:** The primary tactic an advertisement will use to deliver a message.

Cognitive message strategies are the presentation of rational arguments or pieces of information to consumers. The message focuses on key product attributes or important customer benefits. Shoes with DMX technology may be described as comfortable. A fishing boat may be featured as being designed for bass fishing with oversized storage, livewells for fish, built-in coolers, and ergonomically designed cockpits with backlit controls. With a cognitive message strategy, creatives assume the audience will read or listen to the ad, pay attention to the message, and cognitively process the information. The goal is to develop a positive attitude toward the brand by presenting a rational argument about the product's attributes or benefits.

> **Cognitive message strategies:** The presentation of rational arguments or pieces of information to consumers.

As would be expected, the cognitive message strategy works well with a rational appeal. However, often advertisers will use an emotional, fear, or sexual appeal to get the person's attention, and then use a cognitive message to explain the product's benefit. With this contrasting approach, the visual element and/or the headline is normally used to grab attention;

Figure 14-15
This advertisement by Purina Dog Chow uses a cognitive message strategy with a humor appeal.
Source: Reprinted by permission of Carl Furuta Studio, Inc., Los Angeles, California.

- **Affective message strategies:** Messages designed to invoke feelings and emotions within the audience.
- **Conative message strategies:** Messages designed to elicit some type of audience behavior, such as a purchase or inquiry.
- **Advertising execution (pg. 431):** The manner in which the advertisement will be presented.
- **Animation (pg. 431):** Advertising execution that involves the presentation of an advertisement using drawn or personified characters or computer-enhanced or modified imagery.
- **Rotoscoping (pg. 431):** The process of placing drawn characters digitally into live television footage.
- **Slice-of-life execution (pg. 431):** Advertising execution that involves presenting a problem and a solution within the framework of the advertisement.

then the body of the ad is used to explain the product. Purina Dog Chow used this strategy in Figure 14-15. The visual contains a humorous appeal, while a cognitive message strategy explains the benefit of Purina Dog Chow.

Affective message strategies are designed to invoke feelings and emotions within the audience. They are based on the belief that if consumers react emotionally to an advertisement, their response will affect their attitude toward the ad, which will then be projected toward the brand. An advertisement that elicits a feeling of warmth and love within the viewer will usually create a liking for the ad, which will enhance positive feelings toward the product. Affective emotions can work in the reverse as well. An advertisement that creates anger or disgust will create a negative feeling toward the ad and, in turn, a negative feeling toward the brand. Affective message strategies are used in conjunction with emotional, fear, humor, sex, and music appeals. Seldom will an affective message strategy be coupled with a rational appeal. Figure 14-16 illustrates how an affective message strategy builds a favorable attitude toward the brand.

Conative message strategies are designed to elicit some type of audience behavior, such as a purchase or inquiry. They are normally tied with a trade or sales promotion that is offering a coupon, a price-off, or some other special deal. An advertisement for Cheerios with a 50-cent coupon and an opportunity to enter a special sweepstakes would be a conative message strategy because the goal of the ad is to have consumers purchase a box of Cheerios and to enter the contest. The advertisement in Figure 14-17 by the Breast Center of Glenwood Regional Medical Center uses a conative message strategy. The ad encourages women to ask their doctor about a Mammotome or to call the Glenwood HealthSource for more information. An emotional and fear appeal is used to send the message by combining a photo of a young, attractive female with the fact that about 1 out of 8 women will be diagnosed with breast cancer.

14-5c Execution

The **advertising execution** is defined as the manner in which the advertisement will be presented. It is like the setting in a movie scene. What the actor says is the message strategy, and how he or she says it is the appeal. The types of ad execution include:

- Animation
- Slice-of-life
- Dramatization
- Lifestyle
- Testimonial
- Demonstration
- Fantasy
- Presentation

Animation is defined as the presentation of an advertisement using drawn or personified characters or computer-enhanced or modified imagery. Animation was originally used by advertisers with low budgets who could not afford actors or the budget required to produce a commercial. But today, it has become a highly popular method of creating an ad. A technique called rotoscoping makes animation more interesting to viewers. **Rotoscoping** is defined as the process of placing drawn characters, such as Bugs Bunny, digitally into live sequences with people, such as Michael Jordan. It allows personifications like the Pillsbury Doughboy to be placed in live television scenes.

A **Slice-of-life execution** involves presenting a problem and a solution within the framework of the advertisement. Most slice-of-life ads involve the four steps of (1) encounter, (2) problem, (3) interaction, and (4) solution. A typical slice-of-life commercial may show a little girl in a white dress playing while the wedding party is preparing (the encounter). The dress becomes stained with a drink or by her falling in a mud puddle (the problem). But have no fear—a special detergent comes to the rescue. A voiceover explains the power of this special detergent to get out even tough stains (the interaction). Finally, the dress comes out

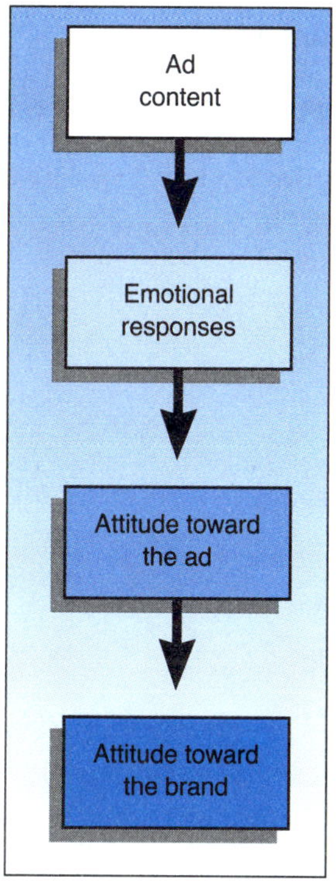

Figure 14-16
The Mediating Effect of Emotions on Communication Cues and Attitude toward the Brand
Emotional responses evoked by advertising may, in turn, affect consumers' attitudes toward the advertised brand.

INTERACTIVE FIGURE

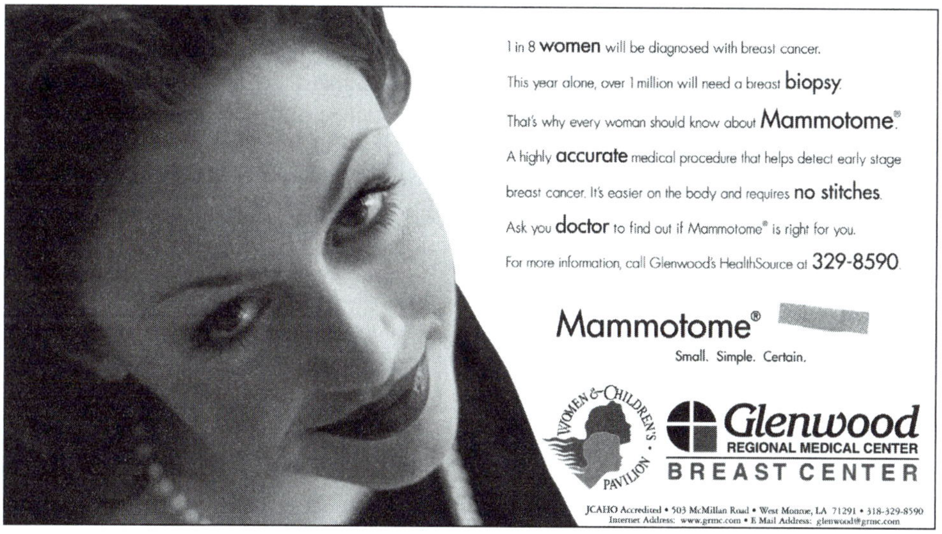

Figure 14-17
This advertisement by the Breast Center of Glenwood Regional Medical Center uses a conative message strategy.

Source: Sample print advertisement courtesy of The Miles Agency and Alliance One Advertising, Inc.

Figure 14-18
This Skechers advertisement uses a lifestyle execution to convey the message that young people who purchase Skechers footwear will fit in socially.
Source: Courtesy of Skechers USA.

Dramatization: An advertising execution that is a form of slice-of-life execution but uses a higher level of excitement, where the suspense builds to a crisis.

Lifestyle execution: An advertising execution that portrays the product fitting into a person's current or desired lifestyle.

Testimonial execution: An advertising execution that uses an individual, such as a celebrity, an ordinary person, or a customer, endorsing the product.

Demonstration execution: An advertising execution that shows how a product works.

sparkling white, and the little girl is able to march down the wedding aisle looking like a little princess (the solution).

Dramatization is a form of slice-of-life execution but uses a higher level of excitement, where the suspense builds to a crisis. Oglivy and Mather Ad Agency created an ad for Dunlap tires that used a dramatization execution. The commercial opened in the closing seconds of a boys' rugby match with the score at 23–22. The losing team is awarded a penalty kick right in front of the opponent's goal post with a chance to win the game. The kick is to be made by young Rupert Williams, but the challenge is that the field is extremely muddy. As the boy prepares for the kick, the sports commentator says, "He could slot this one with his eyes closed, but he's taking his time. He wants to be sure." As the boy approaches the ball, he loses his footing on the muddy field, and the ball just dribbles a few feet. A different voiceover then announces, "Because you never think about grip until you lose it. Think Dunlop tires."[13]

A **lifestyle execution** portrays the product fitting into a person's particular lifestyle. It can be that person's current lifestyle or a projected, desired lifestyle. An advertisement for a bicycle may show the rider in rugged, mountainous terrain, enjoying the beauty and peace of nature. The advertisement in Figure 14-18 uses a lifestyle execution, with Skechers being a part of these people's social group.

The **testimonial execution** uses an individual, such as a celebrity, an ordinary person, or a customer, to endorse the product. A **demonstration execution** shows how a product works. Both types of executions are used frequently in business-to-business and service ads. In business-to-business ads, a customer talking about the benefits of a good or service is an effective means of providing credibility and an endorsement for the brand. Because of the unique characteristics of services discussed in Chapter 9, "Services Marketing," testimonies are an excellent method of reducing a service's intangibility. Demonstration executions allow an advertiser to demonstrate the attributes of a product and how it can benefit the consumer or business. This technique provides an excellent execution for explaining complex products as well as demonstrating the benefits of a product. Cleaning chemicals often use a demonstration execution to show how well they work under difficult situations.

A **fantasy execution** is designed to lift the audience beyond the realm of reality. Love, sex, and romance are the most common fantasy themes. Perfume and cologne manufacturers often use a fantasy approach to illustrate the benefit of their brand. Services such as cruise lines and resorts will use a fantasy approach to entice the audience into thinking about how the service can provide a romantic interlude into their lives.

Fantasy execution: An advertising execution designed to lift the audience beyond the realm of reality.

The last execution, **presentation,** is the portrayal of a product in a straightforward, matter-of-fact way. It is a radio announcer talking about the attributes of a particular brand of ceiling fan and why someone should purchase that brand. Because radio lacks a visual element, the presentation format works well. It is not used as often with television because of competition with other ads that use livelier and more interesting approaches. Business-to-business ads often use this approach with print ads, frequently with no visual or with only a picture of the product. The major portion of the ad is a presentation about the product's attributes and benefits.

Presentation: An advertising execution that portrays a product in a straightforward, matter-of-fact way.

While any appeal or any message strategy can be used with any execution, some combinations work well together. For example, a fear appeal works well with an affective message strategy and a slice-of-life or dramatization execution. A humor appeal works nicely with an affective message strategy and either animation or slice-of-life execution. If a creative wanted to use a testimonial execution, it would work best coupled with a cognitive or conative message strategy and a rational appeal. However, an emotional or sexual appeal could also be used, depending on the product and the message that is to be conveyed. The goal of the creative is to use the best combination of appeal, message strategy, and execution that will convey the intended message in a way that gets the attention of audience members and persuades them to act.

14-6 Media Selection

Media selection is a critical component of advertising. If the correct medium is not selected, the target market will not hear the message. Understanding the target audience in terms of media behavior is important. Just as research is conducted to understand consumer behavior in terms of purchasing products, research must be conducted to understand media behavior. How much time is allocated to each medium, such as radio, television, newspapers, and so forth? More important, if the members of a particular target market watch TV, which shows do they tend to watch?

14-6a Media Choices

Figure 14-19 presents the breakdown by media of the $236.9 billion spent on advertising media buys for 2002. Notice that newspapers account for 18.6 percent of all advertising expenditures, and television accounts for 24.7 percent of all ad spending if the cable and broadcast television totals are combined. Broadcast TV consists of the major national networks like ABC, CBS, NBC, Fox, UPN, and WB. Cable TV consists of all of the other channels, such as ESPN, the Home Shopping Network, CNN, and the Travel Channel. Direct mail also accounts for 19.4 percent of ad spending, with a large portion of direct mail in the business-to-business advertising sector.

The use of the various media differs across countries. Table 14-4 shows a breakdown of advertising by media for North America, Europe, and Japan. Figure 14-20 on page 435

Figure 14-19
U.S. Ad Spending by Media, 2002

Source: "Coen's Spending Totals for 2002," *Adage.com* (www.adage.com, January 14, 2005).

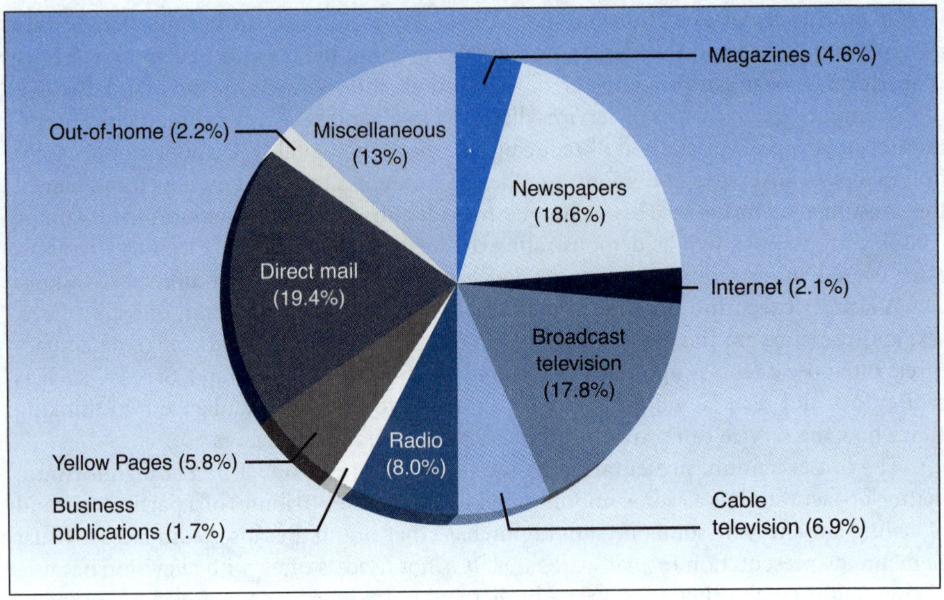

TABLE 14-4

Advertising Expenditures (in billons) by Medium for North America, Europe, and Japan

Media	North America	Europe	Japan
Newspapers	44.02	28.50	7.88
Magazines	14.33	13.54	2.97
Television	52.69	25.15	13.41
Radio	17.89	3.89	1.33
Outdoor	4.34	4.57	3.71
Internet	4.88	0.75	0.59
Directories	13.77	3.41	1.24
Direct mail	46.07	15.89	2.77

Sources: "Global Adspend Trends: Global TV Advertising," *International Journal of Advertising*, Vol. 22, No. 4 (2003), 567–568.

provides a breakdown of those expenditures as a percentage of the total ad expenditures for that particular area. Notice that almost 40 percent of advertising in Japan is via television, whereas it is about 26 percent of the advertising expenditures for North America and Europe. Other noticeable differences are for magazines, radio, outdoor, and direct mail. Magazines are used more extensively in Europe; radio and direct mail are used more in North America; and outdoor is used more in Japan.

14-6b Broadcast Media

Reach: The number of people, households, or businesses in a target audience exposed to a media message at least once during a given time period.

Broadcast media consist of television and radio. Television provides excellent opportunities for creating effective advertisements because both visual images and sounds can be incorporated simultaneously. Television also has the advantage of having high **reach**, defined as the number of people, households, or businesses in a target audience exposed to a media message at least once during a given time period. Just one television advertisement can reach millions of consumers. For example, an advertisement on *Crime Scene Investigators (CSI)* during a recent week reached 19,377,000 households, and an advertisement on *Desperate Housewives* reached 16,578,000 households. Each week, Yahoo! TV publishes the Nielsen ratings for the top 20 shows at http://tv.yahoo.com/nielsen/. For more information about Nielsen ratings, what they mean, and how they are used, see Marketing Illustration 14-3 on page 436.

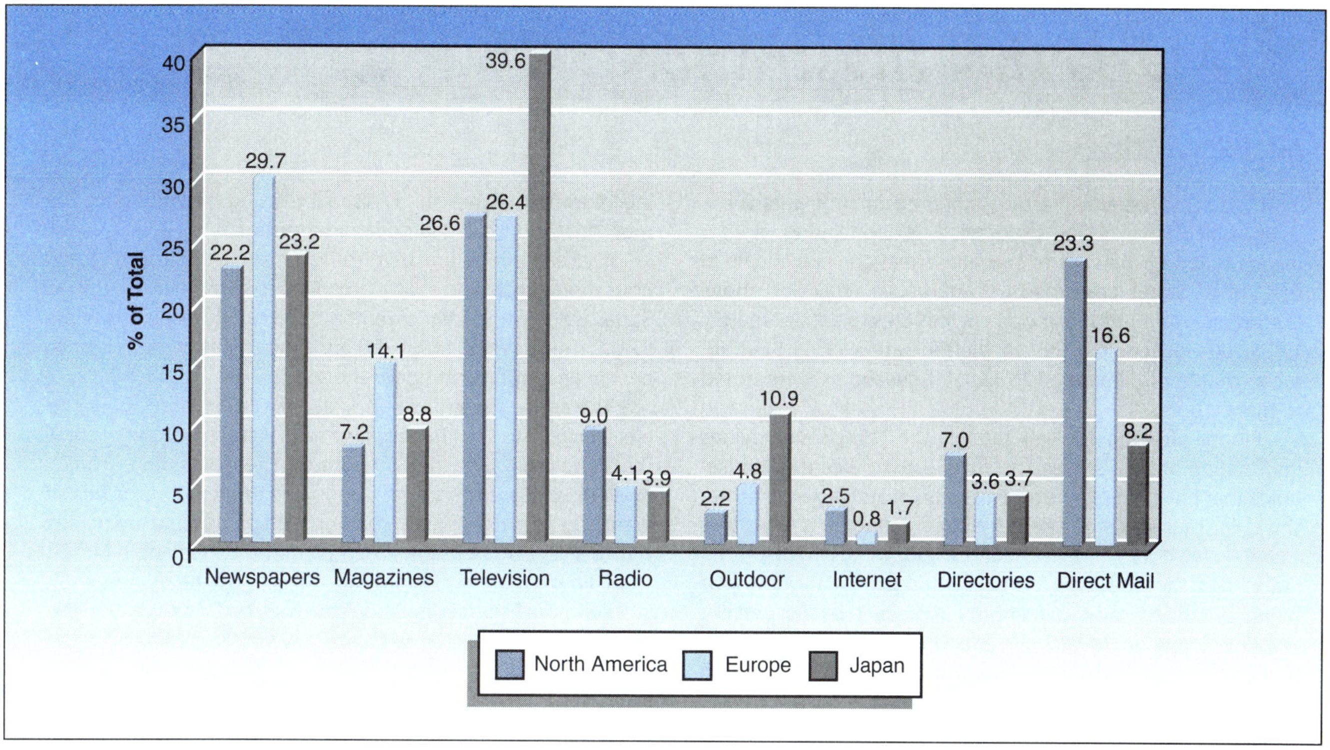

Figure 14-20
Advertising Expenditures as Percent of Total Ad Spending for North America, Europe, and Japan

Source: "Global Adspend Trends: Global TV Advertising," *International Journal of Advertising*, Vol. 22, No. 4 (2003): 567–568.

Because of television's high reach potential, the cost per contact is very low, despite the relatively high cost of one TV advertisement. For example, a 30-second ad on *CSI* costs $310,324. But if 19,377,000 people watch the show, then the cost per thousand is only $16.00. The **cost per thousand (CPM)** is the cost of reaching 1,000 members of a media vehicle's audience. Super Bowl ads cost a whopping $2.4 million, but based on the 48 million people who watch them, that is a CPM of only $50.00. Table 14-5 lists some of the major prime-time television shows and the cost for a 30-second ad, and Figure 14-21 on page 437 presents the cost of advertising during the Super Bowl from Super Bowl I in 1967 to 2005.

Cost per thousand (CPM): The cost of reaching one thousand members of a media vehicle's audience.

Clutter remains the primary problem with television advertising, especially on network programs. Most television networks now have 14 to 16 minutes of advertising per hour. Within each commercial break, between 8 and 15 commercials are packed together. Many viewers simply switch channels during long commercial breaks or use the time to get something to eat or go to the bathroom. Because of the large number of commercials per ad segment, messages at the beginning or near the end of the break have the best recall. Those in the middle often have virtually no impact.[14]

Television commercials have short life spans. Most ads last only 15 or 30 seconds, with an occasional 45- or 60-second ad. In addition to the high cost of media time, producing a television ad is expensive, averaging $245,000 for a 30-second spot. But it is not unusual for an agency to spend up to $1 million on producing an outstanding ad. Because of the high frequency of television advertisements, wear-out occurs fast (i.e., the ad quickly loses its ability to hold the viewers' interest). Consequently, agencies have to constantly produce new ads. Often, a series of advertisements will be produced so they can be rotated. Another tactic advertisers use is to create a 30- or 45-second spot and then make 15-second ads from the larger one. All of these tactics create variety and are designed to prevent wear-out from occurring so quickly.

While radio may not have the glamour appeal of television, it does offer the advantage of intimacy. Listeners can develop an affinity with the DJs and other radio personalities. This closeness grows over time, especially if the listener has a conversation with the DJ

Marketing Illustration 14-3

Nielsen Ratings

Nielsen ratings are an estimate of the audience watching a particular television program. A Nielsen rating of 11.5 means that 11.5 percent of the households or individuals in the United States are tuned to a particular television show. Currently, a rating of 1, or 1 percent, equates to approximately 1,055,000 households. Thus, a Nielsen rating of 11.5 would mean that approximately 12,132,000 households were tuned to that station.

Along with the Nielsen ratings, the company provides information on the "share." The share is the percent of households that have the television on and are watching a particular show. For example, suppose the Nielsen rating for a show was 11.5 percent. If only 60 percent of the households in the United States had the television on when this particular show was being broadcast, then dividing 11.5 percent by 60 percent would yield a share of 19.2 percent, which means that of those households that had the television on, 19.2 percent of them were tuned into this particular show.

Nielsen TV ratings and share are important in the advertising marketplace because they are used to determine advertising rates. The higher the Nielsen TV ratings a show gets, the more that show can charge for advertising.

Nielsen ratings are determined from a sample of 5,000 households that represent a broad cross-section of the United States. If you compare the demographics of the Nielsen sample to U.S. Census data, they are very similar. This is important to ensure an accurate rating for shows.

The actual rating is done with a "People Meter." This is an electronic box that sits on top of the TV. It records every show that is watched and when the TV is on. There are different lights to allow each person in the household to record his or her TV watching. The ratings are also done with diaries that are mailed out to select households. When compared, the People Meters yield almost identical ratings for shows as do the diaries.

For more information about the Nielsen TV ratings, you can go to Nielsen Media Research at www.nielsenmedia.com.

Source: "What TV Ratings Really Mean," and "Ratings 101," Nielsen Media Research, www.nielsenmedia.com, January 14, 2005.

TABLE 14-5

Prime-Time Advertising Cost per 30-Second Ad

Network	Show	Advertising Cost
NBC	*Friends*	$473,500
	Will & Grace	$414,500
	ER	$404,814
	Scrubs	$360,950
	Coupling	$316,400
	Good Morning Miami	$279,813
	Law & Order	$266,220
	Frasier	$252,067
CBS	*Survivor*	$390,367
	CSI	$310,324
	Everybody Loves Raymond	$301,640
Fox	*24*	$292,200
	The Simpsons	$249,067
ABC	*Monday Night Football*	$272,867
	The Bachelor	$253,940

Source: Richard Linnett "TV Show with the Highest-priced Ads: Friends," *Adage.com* (www.adage.com, September 15, 2003).

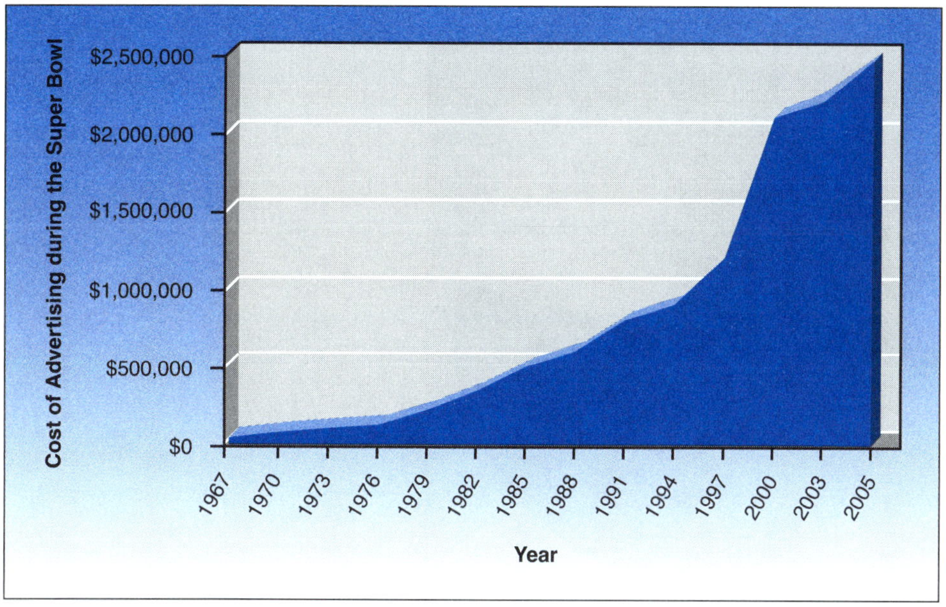

Figure 14-21
Cost of a 30-Second Advertisement during the Super Bowl

Source: Ronald Geskey, "Is Advertising in the Super Bowl A Good Media Buy or an Ego Trip?" Press Release of 2020: Marketing Communications LLC, January 14, 2005; Wayne Friedman, "Second DOWN," *Advertising Age*, Vol. 72, No. 36 (September 3, 2001): 3–4.

INTERACTIVE FIGURE

during a contest or when requesting a song. The bond that develops means the DJ will have a higher level of credibility, and goods or services that are endorsed by the DJ will be more readily accepted.

In addition to providing intimacy, radio is also mobile. People can take radios with them wherever they go. They can listen while at the beach, at home, at work, or on the road in between. No other medium has the power to stay with an audience quite like radio. For business-to-business advertisers, radio provides an opportunity to reach businesses during working hours when businesspeople are likely to be listening to the radio. Even more important is the transit time to and from work when a businessperson is more likely to pay attention to an ad, especially if he or she is stuck in traffic snarl.

Radio stations tend to have definable target markets based on their formats, such as talk radio, country music, rock, pop, oldies, and so forth. This means that a company that wants to advertise on country music stations can find stations all across the country. Recently, Campbell's Soup used radio to promote its Chunky Soup and its tie-in with the National Football League. It advertised on radio stations with primarily male audiences and strong sports programming, using professional football players praising Chunky Soup.[15]

Another major advantage of radio is the flexibility and the short lead time for producing commercials. An ad can be recorded and placed on the air within a few days and sometimes within hours. Ads can also be changed quickly. This is especially helpful in the retail sector, where a store may want to change the items featured as being on sale.

Radio has some disadvantages, in addition to the lack of a visual element. Like television, the short exposure time of most radio advertisements makes it difficult to comprehend what has been said. This is especially true for radio, because people are often involved in other activities, such as working on a computer or driving a vehicle. In many cases, the radio is simply background noise used to drown out other distractions.

For national advertisers, producing a national radio advertisement is challenging because there are few large radio conglomerates and national networks available. To place a national advertisement requires contacting a large number of stations and companies that may own a handful of radio stations. As a result, 78 percent of all radio advertising is for local businesses, with the remaining 22 percent being national ads (see Figure 14-22). Only .1 percent of ad revenue is from network radio shows. Radio ads cost only $5 to $200 per spot, with stations in large cities with large audiences charging higher rates.

For a summary of the advantages and disadvantages of television and radio advertising, see Table 14-6.

Figure 14-22
Breakdown of Radio Advertising Revenue

Source: "Coen's Spending Totals for 2002," *Adage.com* (www.adage.com, January 14, 2005).

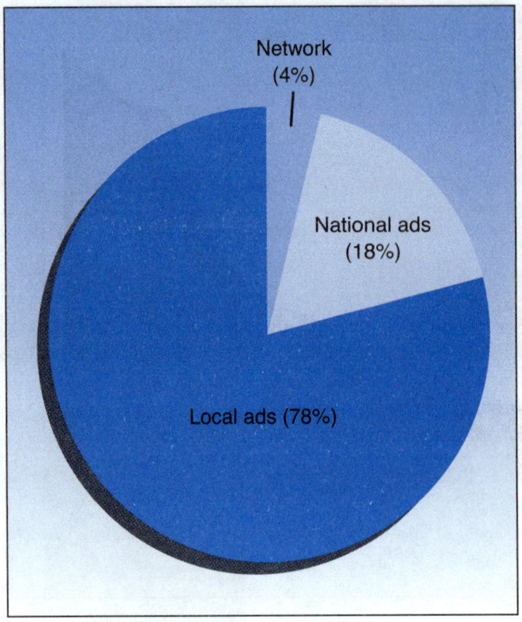

14-6c Print Media

The primary print media are newspapers, magazines, the Yellow Pages, business publications, and direct mail, which account for 50.1 percent of the total expenditures on advertising (see Figure 14-19).[16] The largest percentages go for direct mail and newspapers, 19.4 percent and 18.6 percent, respectively. Direct mail will be covered in Chapter 16 "Personal Selling, Databases, and Direct Marketing," while the other print media will be presented in this section.

Retailers rely heavily on newspapers because they offer geographic selectivity (i.e., access to the local target market area). Sales, retail hours, and store locations are easy to pro-

TABLE 14-6
Advantages and Disadvantages of Broadcast Advertising

Television	
Advantages	***Disadvantages***
1. High reach	1. High level of clutter
2. High frequency potential	2. Low recall
3. Low cost per contact	3. Short ad duration
4. High intrusion value	4. High cost per ad
5. Creative design opportunities	
6. Segmentation through cable channels	
Radio	
Advantages	***Disadvantages***
1. High recall potential	1. Short ad duration
2. Segmented target markets	2. Low attention
3. Flexibility and short lead time in ad production	3. No national audience
4. Intimacy with DJs	4. Difficulty in buying national time
5. Mobility of radios	5. Target duplication in large metropolitan areas
6. Excellent for local businesses	
7. Low cost per contact	

Figure 14-23
This newspaper advertisement for The Toggery and Her Toggery promotes an upcoming trunk show featuring clothing by Robert and Audrey Talbott.

Source: Sample print advertisement courtesy of The Miles Agency and Alliance One Advertising, Inc.

mote in a newspaper ad. Newspapers have relatively short lead times, which allow retailers the flexibility to change ads frequently and keep ads current. They can quickly modify an ad to reflect recent events or to combat a competitor's actions. The ad for The Toggery and Her Toggery in Figure 14-23 informs consumers about an upcoming trunk show.

Newspapers tend to have a high level of credibility because people rely on newspapers for factual information in stories. This carries over to a greater level of credibility for newspaper advertisements. Because readers take time to read a newspaper, they tend to pay as much attention to advertisements as to news stories. This increased audience interest allows advertisers to provide more copy detail in their ads.

Newspapers do have some limitations. Except for geographic selectivity, it is difficult to target an advertisement to a specific market segment. Newspapers have a short life span. Once read, most newspapers are discarded. If readers do not see an ad when they first read the paper, it probably will go unnoticed, since it is unlikely they will pick up the paper a second time. Compared to other print media, newspaper ads have poor production quality. There are few color ads, because they are expensive, and photos and copy tend to be more difficult to read. Creatives do not have as much freedom to create wild, lavish advertisements, since newspapers tend to be more conservative. Newspaper editors are very concerned about offending readers with risqué ads. Just as with radio, it is difficult to purchase national ad space, and because of their local nature, newspapers are a better medium for local businesses than national firms.

Magazines have become a preferred advertising medium for many products. Research by ACNielsen indicated that people who viewed magazine advertisements were more likely to purchase the product. Research by Millward Brown concerning the cost effectiveness of magazine advertising indicated that magazine advertising is three times more cost effective than television advertising.[17] Of course, television executives debate the validity of both studies. In any case, magazines do provide an excellent medium for advertising.

A major advantage of magazines is the ability to precisely target audience segments. Specialized magazines aimed at specific target markets are more common than general readership magazines. Advertising in these specialized magazines allows advertisers to reach a greater percentage of their audience. Individuals reading *Modern Bride* will pay more attention to ads about weddings than someone reading *People*, so advertising wedding products in *Modern Bride* is likely to be more effective.

Most magazines offer high-quality color reproduction capabilities that allow creatives more freedom in designing advertisements. Color, headlines, and unusual images can be used to attract attention. Magazines such as *Glamour, Elle,* and *Cosmopolitan* will use scratch and sniff ads to entice women to smell a particular brand of perfume or cologne.

Magazines have a long advertising life beyond the immediate issue. They are often read and re-read by subscribers, which means ads are often seen more than once. Magazine ads last beyond the current issue with people reading the magazine in a doctor's office or the waiting room of a Jiffy Lube. Weeks and even months later, individuals may see an advertisement. In the business-to-business sector, trade journals are often passed around to several individuals or members of the buying center and sometimes kept on file for later reference. As long as the magazine lasts, the advertisement is still there to be viewed. This opportunity for repeat viewings is attractive to advertisers.

Magazines are facing some tough times, however. Because of the Internet and television, magazines lost 61 million readers in the 18 to 49 age category in just one year—a decline of 5.9 percent. Of the 200 magazines examined, 56 gained readers and 144 lost readers.[18] As with other media, clutter is becoming a greater problem for magazines. For example, a recent 318-page issue of *Glamour* contained 195 pages of advertising and only 123 pages of content. It is easy for ads to be lost in those situations. See Table 14-7 for a list

TABLE 14-7 Top 15 Magazines Ranked by Total Net U.S. Revenue

Rank	Magazine	Total Net U.S. Revenue (millions)	Ad Revenue (millions)	Ad Revenue as Percent of Net U.S. Revenue	Parent Company
1	*People*	$4,514	$744	16.5%	Time Warner
2	*Parade*	$2,197	$613	27.9%	Advance Publications
3	*Good Housekeeping*	$1,900	$402	21.2%	Hearst Corp.
4	*Motor Trend*	$1,079	$133	12.3%	Primedia
5	*Reader's Digest*	$835	$242	28.9%	Reader's Digest Association
6	*Better Homes & Garden*	$808	$654	80.9%	Meredith Corp.
7	*Family Circle*	$788	$302	38.3%	Gruner & Jahr USA
8	*PC World*	$760	$96	12.6%	International Data Group
9	*BuinessWeek*	$668	$336	50.3%	McGraw-Hill Cos.
10	*EDN*	$601	$35	5.8%	Reed Elsevier
11	*Woman's Day*	$531	$319	60.1%	Hatchette Filipacchi Media US
12	*Shape*	$516	$110	21.3%	American Media
13	*TV Guide*	$365	$382	104.7%	Gemstar-TV Guide International
14	*Men's Health*	$355	$109	30.7%	Rodale Press
15	*Newsweek*	$354	$431	121.8%	The Washington Post Co.

Source: "Top 25 Magazine Companies," *Adage.com* (www.adage.com, January 15, 2005).

of the top 15 magazines, in terms of net revenue, advertising revenue, and ad revenue as a percentage of net revenue. As the table indicates, advertising revenue is a significant component of a magazine's total gross revenue.

Magazines require long lead times, often six months. That makes it difficult to modify ads and to keep ads current. Because of the long life of a magazine ad, people may still see it several months after it appears in the magazine. That means a creative has to think ahead 6 to 12 months when designing an ad to decide what type of appeal might work.

Most people use the Yellow Pages to locate a phone number or the address of a local business. But with the rise of the Internet, more people are using Yahoo! or other search engines to locate phone numbers and addresses. Yet, for local businesses, the Yellow Pages are essential, especially for service and specialty businesses. Someone looking for an air conditioning repair service, an automotive parts store, or a plumber is likely to look in the Yellow Pages. For these types of businesses, having a Yellow Page ad can be effective. The ad has a long life, with many phone books still being used even after a new one comes out. See Table 14-8 for tips on how to get the most from a Yellow Page ad.

The Yellow Pages do not permit advertisers much flexibility and allow very little creative design freedom. Most ads are standard and are often designed by the Yellow Pages' creative department, not an advertising agency. Ads are costly and often have limited exposure. Only individuals looking for a specific product category will ever see a Yellow Page ad. Yet, despite these major flaws, more money is spent on Yellow Page advertising than on magazine advertising. The primary reason is that almost every business will have a listing in the Yellow Pages, even if it's just a telephone number, and many will go ahead and put in some type of ad. While the cost per business is relatively low, the volume of businesses that place ads in the Yellow Pages is huge. More businesses place ads in the Yellow Pages than in any other media, broadcast or print.

TABLE 14-8

Getting the Most Out of a Yellow Page Ad

Facts (from Statistical Research, Inc.)	
1. 28.8 percent of people interviewed purchased goods/services from the Yellow Pages.	
2. 90 percent contacted one or more businesses advertised.	
3. 48 percent said the Yellow Page ad influenced their decision.	
4. 34 percent were first-time customers of the business.	
Rule 1: Remember what you're selling.	The goal of a Yellow Page ad is to get the person to make a phone call. Design the ad with that idea in mind.
Rule 2: Include a unique, powerful, benefit-based headline.	Almost 90 percent of Yellow Page ads do not have a headline. In the headline, put the benefit that customers want and what you do well.
Rule 3: Be persuasive quickly.	Readers do not spend time studying ads. Get your points down, shorten them, and drive them home quickly.
Rule 4: Understand what persuades readers and what doesn't.	Persuade customers to call by describing real benefits to them, then back your benefits with a guarantee or warranty. Think of it from the customer's perspective.
Rule 5: Size and looks do matter.	The larger ads do elicit more phone calls. A test of three different-size ads yielded 1,382 calls for the large, 443 for the medium, and 241 for the small. Going over three-fourths of a page, however, does not yield greater results.

Source: Adams Hudson, "How to Make Yellow Pages Ads Pull More Leads," *Air Conditioning Heating & Refrigeration News,* Vol. 210, No. 13 (July 24, 2000): 14–15.

Outdoor advertising primarily involves billboards, but also signs on cabs, buses, park benches, sports arenas, and blimps flying over a major sports stadium. Retailers are major users of outdoor advertising, especially billboards, because it is a convenient method for informing consumers about store locations and hours of operation. A major advantage of billboard advertising is its long life and low cost per impression. A billboard sign along a major highway can be seen by thousands of people every day. Every person who travels by a billboard has the potential of being exposed to the message. Many billboard companies now provide "rotation" packages in which an ad moves to different locations throughout a town during the course of the year, thereby increasing the reach of the ad.

A primary disadvantage of outdoor advertising is the short exposure time. Drivers must pay attention to the traffic as they speed by an outdoor ad, so they have only a couple of seconds to gather the message. As a result, billboards cannot contain much information, and what is on the billboard must be easy to read, easy to understand, and easy to remember.

For a summary of the advantages and disadvantages of print media, see Table 14-9.

TABLE 14-9

Advantages and Disadvantages of Print Advertising

Advantages	Disadvantages
Newspapers	
1. Excellent for local businesses	1. Poor buying procedures
2. High flexibility	2. Short life span
3. High credibility	3. Poor quality reproduction
4. Strong audience interest	4. Limited ad design creativity possible
Magazines	
1. High target audience segmentation	1. Declining readership
2. High reader interest	2. High level of clutter
3. High color quality	3. Long lead time to design ad
4. Long life	4. Little flexibility
5. Multiple frequency	5. High cost
Yellow Pages	
1. Excellent for local businesses	1. No creative design freedom
2. Long life	2. Limited exposure
3. Product segmentation	3. High cost
	4. No flexibility
Outdoor	
1. Geographic selectivity	1. Short exposure time
2. Excellent for local ads	2. Only brief messages can be used
3. Low cost per impression	3. Limited audience segmentation
4. High frequency	4. Clutter along roads

14-7 Sponsorships

Sponsorship marketing involves a company paying a fee to an event, person, or organization in exchange for a direct association with that event, person, or organization. North American companies spent $11.2 billion on sponsorships ranging from an event like a Little League baseball tournament or a local fall festival to the naming rights of a professional sports arena.[19] Figure 14-24 provides a breakdown of various types of sponsorships. Notice sports comprise 68.8 percent of all sponsorships, totaling $7.7 billion.

Sponsorship marketing: Marketing that involves a company paying a fee to an event, person, or organization in exchange for a direct association with that event, person, or organization.

In choosing a sponsorship, it is important to match the audience profile with the company's target market. A firm whose primary customers are females should examine opportunities to sponsor events that involve females, such as a female softball team, the WNBA, or a beauty pageant. It is also important to make sure the image of the event matches the image the company wants to project. A tuxedo or formal gown retailer sponsoring a dance or beauty pageant is a better fit than sponsoring a rodeo or wrestling tournament.

One of the most effective sports sponsorships has been NASCAR, which has grown from primarily beer, auto parts, and tobacco sponsors in the 1970s to include a wide range of consumer products, business-to-business products, and Internet brands today. According to Performance Research, 72 percent of NASCAR fans buy products that support the sport, and 40 percent of the fans will switch their brand loyalty to NASCAR-related brands. The sport has seen a 97 percent increase in attendance since 1990 to 6.5 million fans, with women now making up 38.5 percent of the fans. In addition, the sport generates strong Nielsen TV ratings. A recent Daytona 500 race scored a Nielsen rating of 10 with a 24 percent market share.

Such lucrative ratings and fans' support cost sponsors money. The annual rate to endorse a top-notch driver has risen from $6,000 in 1963 to $3 million in 1987 to $15 million today. The price tag of a primary sponsorship slot on a race car ranges from $8 million to $15 million. In one year, it is estimated that the racing teams and the racetracks combined produced $558 million in sponsorships.[20]

Recently, companies have been paying big money for naming rights to ballparks and stadiums. The average annual price is $1.28 million. More than 50 stadiums now carry the names of companies. Some of the stadiums, with the corresponding price tags, are:[21]

- America West Arena, Phoenix (NBA Suns, NHL Coyotes), $26 million for 30 years
- Coors Field, Denver (MLB Rockies), $15 million, indefinite
- Delta Center, Salt Lake City (NBA Jazz), $25 million for 20 years
- Fleetcenter, Boston (NBA Celtics, NHL Bruins), $30 million for 15 years
- Minute Maid Park, Houston (MLB Astros), $100 million for 30 years
- Staples Center, Los Angeles (NBA Clippers, Lakers, NHL Kings), $116 million for 20 years

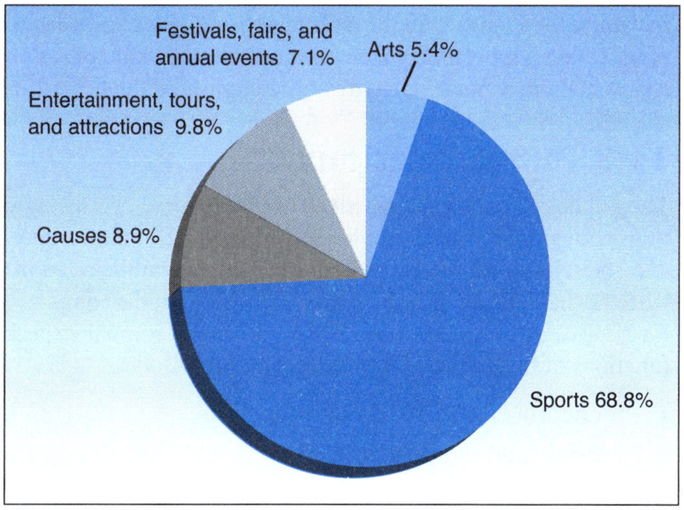

Figure 14-24
Breakdown of North American Sponsorships

Source: "Events & Sponsorships," *Marketing News*, vol. 38 (July 15, 2004): 18.

Marketing Illustration 14-4

Personal Sponsorships: The Newest Trend in Sponsorships

Grappling with ways to get the attention of consumers, a few companies are experimenting with personal sponsorships. The most notable examples of personal sponsorship are Chris Barrett and Luke McCabe of Haddenfield, New Jersey. In the spring of 2002, the pair approached First Bank USA and convinced the company to pay them $40,000 toward their first year in college in exchange for always wearing the bank's logo. When the two students walk around campus, the First Bank USA logo is on everything from their clothes to their backpacks and surfboards.

"It was a great opportunity for us," says Robert Filak, Vice President of Marketing at First Bank USA. "What better way than to have two cool students, normal guys, spread our message?" The result has been that First Bank USA is now a credit card brand that other students recognize and trust.

Meltem Tekeli operates Sponsor Direct Online, a marketplace for buying and selling personal sponsorships. According to Tekeli, "Where the marketing relationship used to be a one-way transaction—companies selling to consumers—now it has become more of a dialogue. People are over stimulated so companies need to take a different approach. They need to listen to consumers, and what consumers are saying to companies is this: If you want our business, you have to reach out and help." Personal sponsorships, according to Tekeli, demonstrate a company's willingness to help.

Barrett and McCabe are not the only ones who obtained a personal sponsorship. Erika Armour and Nate Hughes convinced 17 local companies to give them $15,000 for their wedding. In exchange, the companies were acknowledged in the invitations and programs, and information about each company was included in a packet given to each wedding guest.

Is personal sponsorship a new trend or is it a fad? Time will tell.

Source: "Companies Get Personal with Corporate Sponsorships," *Potentials*, Vol. 35, No. 10 (October 2002): 10.

Some organizations have moved away from sports sponsorships and toward more cultural events, such as classical music groups, jazz bands, visual art exhibits, dance troupes, and theater performances. Cultural sponsorships are a good match for products that are sold to an upscale audience. For example, Credit Suisse sponsors the U.S. Equestrian Team and the individual performers for the Lincoln Center Theater. The company uses these cultural activities to help them establish long-term relationships and build goodwill with key clients, who get good seats at horse shows and theatrical performances.[22]

A few companies have even gone beyond both sports and cultural events in looking for that unique sponsorship opportunity that will make them stand out from all of the other companies. These companies believe they have found the secret, in personal sponsorships. Marketing Illustration 14-4 has more information on this newest trend in sponsorships.

As with the other marketing tools, the sponsorships should be integrated with the firm's advertising and IMC plan. The public should easily recognize the link between the person, group, or organization being sponsored and the company involved. It is also important to maximize the sponsorship through advertising, trade and sales promotions, and public relations. Unless a sponsorship is surrounded by some kind of supporting marketing effort, the sponsorship may not be effective at accomplishing the firm's IMC objectives.

14-8 Public Relations

The public relations department is responsible for overseeing publicity and communications with groups such as employees, stockholders, public interest groups, the government, and society as a whole. It is important that the public relations department work closely with the marketing department and be involved in the company's IMC effort to ensure that every piece of communication produced by the company speaks with one voice. The key functions of the public relations department include:

- Monitoring internal and external publics
- Providing information to each public that reinforces the firm's IMC effort

- Promoting sponsorships, event marketing efforts, cause-related marketing efforts, and other image-building activities
- Reacting to any news or emergencies that may occur that have an impact on the firm and the IMC effort being conducted

Often, major public relations efforts of a firm are handled by an external public relations firm for the same reasons that a firm hires an external advertising agency. In some cases, the advertising agency handles the PR function, but usually a separate firm is hired. Because the work of the PR firm is different, it is important that the PR firm understand the IMC effort of the client and how it fits into the picture. Special events, activities, and news releases produced by the PR firm must strengthen the firm's IMC effort.

PR departments monitor various internal and external constituencies, or stakeholders. A **stakeholder** is a person or group that has a vested interest in an organization's well-being. It can include employees, unions, stockholders, channel members, customers, the media, the local community, the financial community, the various government agencies, and special interest groups. The PR department is responsible for issuing news releases and information that is pertinent to each group. When approached by each stakeholder group with questions or requests for information, the PR department is responsible for providing the correct information and ensuring that it is consistent with the firm's IMC effort.

Stakeholder: A person or group that has a vested interest in an organization's well-being.

The PR department is also responsible for monitoring the actions and opinions of each group. The PR department should address any changes in attitudes, views, or concerns that develop.

One of the most important, and most difficult, tasks is the handling of negative publicity. A positive image that has taken years to build can be destroyed overnight. It is the PR department's responsibility to ensure that this does not happen. Crisis management and other techniques are used to help a firm cope with any circumstances that threaten the firm's image, regardless of the cause.

Many times a crisis contains the potential to improve the firm's position and image, if handled properly. For example, PepsiCo encountered some negative publicity about hypodermic needles being found in its products. The management team was quick to respond with photographs and video that demonstrated how bottles and cans are turned upside down while empty before they are filled with any soft drink and how it would have been impossible to put a needle into a soft drink. Pepsi's quick and positive response eliminated negative publicity and at the same time demonstrated to consumers the safety of its products. Unfortunately, the reaction of Ford and Bridgestone to the faulty tires on the new Ford Explorers was not handled as well. Instead of immediately seeking to correct the problem, both denied a problem existed and tried to blame it on tires that were not inflated correctly by consumers. The public did not buy the excuse, and the outcry against both companies was so strong that it cost them sales, damaged their images, and cost the CEO of Ford his job.

Crisis management involves either accepting the blame for an event and offering an apology, or refuting those making the charges in a tactful manner. Both Pepsi and Ford used the latter strategy. The public accepted Pepsi's explanation because it was supported by hard evidence but rejected Ford's explanation because they did not believe the entire problem was underinflated tires.

Instead of blaming drivers for not making sure the tires were inflated properly, Ford would have been wiser to accept the blame and have taken immediate steps to correct the problem. When 200 people in Belgium and France came down with nausea and dizziness from drinking Coke, CEO M. Douglas Ivester flew to Brussels and published a personal apology in Belgium newspapers for the problem. Coke set up special consumer hotlines and offered to pay the medical bills for anyone who got sick. Coke's investigation into the incident identified the cause of the illness as poor quality carbon dioxide and a fungicide that was used to treat the wooden pallets. According to Ivester, when a crisis occurs, the strategy should be the following: (1) be visible, (2) be sympathetic, and (3) be responsive.[23]

Summary

1. *Identify the various types of advertising.* Advertising can be divided into two primary types: product and institutional. Product advertising is any advertisement designed to promote a firm's brand. It can be targeted to end users or channel members. Product advertising can be further subdivided into brand, informative, persuasive, pioneer, and comparative advertising. Institutional advertising is designed to build the corporate reputation or develop goodwill for the corporation; it involves cause-related marketing and public service announcements.

2. *Discuss the selection process for choosing an advertising agency.* Choosing an advertising agency is a difficult task. Major criteria that should be used in the selection process include the size of the agency compared to the size of the client, the relevant experience of the agency in the client's product category, any conflict of interest in representing a competitor, the creative reputation and ability of the agency, the ad production capability of the agency, the media planning and purchasing capability of the agency, and other IMC services the agency can provide.

3. *Describe the appeals that can be used in designing an advertisement.* The advertising appeal is the design a creative will use to attract attention to and interest in an advertisement. The six primary types of appeal are emotional, fear, humor, sex, music, and rational. The appeal chosen will depend on the objective of the ad, the message theme to be used, the target audience, and how the creative wants to convey the message to the intended audience. Almost every product can be advertised using any of the six appeals, and an advertisement will often use two or three appeals.

4. *Differentiate between the three types of message strategies.* The message strategy is the primary tactic an advertisement will use to deliver a message. The three types of message strategies are cognitive, affective, and conative. Cognitive message strategies are the presentation of rational arguments or pieces of information to consumers. The message focuses on key product attributes or important customer benefits. Affective message strategies are designed to invoke feelings and emotions within the audience. They are based on the belief that if consumers react emotionally to an advertisement, their response will affect their attitude toward the ad, which will then be projected toward the brand. Conative message strategies are designed to elicit some type of audience behavior, such as a purchase or inquiry.

5. *Identify the various ad executions that are available.* The advertising execution is the manner in which the advertisement will be presented. It is like the setting in a movie scene. What the actor says is the message strategy, and how he or she says it is the appeal. The types of ad execution include animation, slice-of-life, dramatization, lifestyle, testimonial, demonstration, fantasy, and presentation.

6. *Discuss the advantages and disadvantages of the primary media.* Television has the advantages of offering high reach, high frequency potential, low cost per contact, high intrusion value, creative design opportunities, and segmentation through cable channels. The disadvantages of television are a high level of clutter, low recall, short ad duration, and high cost per ad. For radio, the advantages are high recall potential, segmented target markets, flexibility and short lead time in ad production, intimacy with DJs, mobility of radios, and low cost per contact. The disadvantages are a short ad duration, low attention, no national audience, difficulty in buying national time, and target duplication in large metropolitan areas. In the print media, newspapers offer the advantages of high flexibility, high credibility, and strong audience interest. Disadvantages are poor buying procedures, a short life span, poor quality reproduction, and limited ad design creativity. For magazines, the major advantages include high target audience segmentation, high reader interest, high color quality, long life, and multiple frequency. Disadvantages are a declining readership, high level of clutter, long lead time, little flexibility, and high cost.

7. *Describe the current use of sponsorships.* Sponsorship marketing involves a company paying a fee to an event, person, or organization in exchange for a direct association with that event, person, or organization. North American companies spent $11.2 billion on sponsorships, ranging from an event like a Little League baseball tournament or a local fall festival to the naming rights to a professional sports arena. Most sponsorships are in the area of sports. Recently, companies have paid big money for naming rights to ballparks and stadiums. The average annual price is $1.28 million, with more than 50 stadiums now carrying the names of companies. Beyond sports, some organizations sponsor cultural events, such as classical music groups, jazz bands, visual art exhibits, dance troupes, and theater performances.

8. *Identify the role of public relations in integrated marketing communications (IMC).* The public relations department is responsible for overseeing publicity and communications with groups such as employees, stockholders, public interest groups, the government, and society as a whole. It is important that the public relations department work closely with the marketing department and be involved in the company's IMC effort to ensure that every piece of communication produced by the company speaks with one voice. The key functions of the public relations department include: (1) monitoring internal and external publics; (2) providing information to each public that reinforces the firm's IMC effort; (3) promoting sponsorships, event marketing efforts, cause-related marketing efforts, and other image-building activities; and (4) reacting to any news or emergencies that may occur that impact the firm and IMC effort being conducted.

Key Terms

account executive (p. 424)
advertising appeal (p. 425)
advertising execution (p. 431)
affective message strategies (p. 430)
animation (p. 431)
brand advertising (p. 418)
cognitive message strategies (p. 429)
comparative advertising (p. 420)
conative message strategies (p. 430)
cost per thousand (CPM) (p. 435)
creatives (p. 424)
demonstration execution (p. 432)
dramatization (p. 432)
fantasy execution (p. 433)
informative advertising (p. 418)
institutional advertising (p. 421)
intrusion value (p. 428)
lifestyle execution (p. 432)
message strategy (p. 429)
persuasive advertising (p. 418)
pioneer advertising (p. 420)
presentation (p. 433)
product advertising (p. 417)
reach (p. 434)
rotoscoping (p. 431)
slice-of-life execution (p. 431)
sponsorship marketing (p. 443)
stakeholder (p. 445)
testimonial execution (p. 432)

Discussion Questions

1. Read the chapter-opening vignette. What is your evaluation of the milk advertisements? What other series of ads stands out in your mind? What makes them stand out? Why do you remember them?
2. Pick a topic in advertising that interests you. Using the Internet and a search engine, locate three articles on the topic. Summarize the findings of those three articles.
3. This chapter discussed the influence of advertising on fashion in both Marketing Illustration 14-1 and Marketing Illustration 14-2. After reading these marketing illustrations, do you think advertising influences fashion? Why or why not? What other product category does advertising influence? Why do you think so?
4. Look through a magazine. Classify each ad as product or institutional. Further classify the product ads as brand, informative, persuasive, pioneer, and comparative. Which type appeared most frequently? Why?
5. Pick one of the appeals listed in Section 14-5a. Find three advertisements that use the appeal. What did you like or dislike about the ads? Discuss the use of the appeal by advertisers.
6. Pick two of the ad executions listed in Section 14-5c. Compare and contrast the two in terms of suitability for specific goods and services and specific target audiences. Where would each work the best? Where would each not be as effective?
7. Make a chart of the media listed in Section 14-6. For one week, keep a diary of how much time you spend with each medium. Compare your diary with that of other students. What medium is the best for a marketer to reach you? What is the worst?
8. Look through a magazine. Pick out the five ads you like the best. Describe why you like them.
9. Name five television ads that stand out in your mind. What makes them stand out? Which ones did you like, and which did you not like?
10. Discuss your view of sponsorships. What types of sponsorships do you support? Does a company's sponsorship affect your purchase behavior?

Review Questions

True or False

1. The companies with the highest revenue per advertising dollar are the American-owned automakers Ford and General Motors.
2. Informational advertising is the most common form of product advertising.
3. If pioneer advertising worked successfully at the product introduction stage of the PLC, the same ad will most likely be effective in the growth stage.
4. Institutional advertising is designed to build corporate reputation or develop goodwill for the corporation.
5. With most products in the maturity stage of the PLC, advertising agencies are instrumental in the process of developing brand awareness, brand equity, and brand preference.
6. The advertisement execution defines the manner in which the advertisement will be presented.
7. An advertisement execution that presents a problem and solution within the framework of the advertisement is called slice-of-life.
8. Dramatization is the most effective execution type for business-to-business or service ads.
9. Sponsorship marketing involves a company paying a fee to an event, person, or organization in exchange for a direct association with the event, person, or organization.

Multiple Choice

10. What percentage of sales do real estate agents typically spend on advertising?
    a. more than 60 percent
    b. about 14 percent
    c. less than 1 percent
    d. 24 percent

11. The primary goal of brand advertising is to
a. build brand awareness.
b. develop a brand name.
c. provide detailed information about product features.
d. a and b

12. Comparative advertising is most successful in
a. building primary demand for a product.
b. introducing new brands.
c. developing goodwill for the corporation.
d. providing more information.

13. What should be a key consideration in creating an advertisement that will get attention and produce results?
a. advertisement objectives
b. demographic information
c. psychographics information
d. all of the above

14. Which of the following categories are the primary types of advertising appeal?
a. emotional, fear, humor
b. sex, music, rational
c. greed, self-confidence, comfort
d. a and b

15. Which of the following is a part of message strategy?
a. cognitive message strategy
b. affective message strategy
c. conative message strategy
d. all of the above

16. Why have magazines become a preferred advertising medium for many consumer products?
a. ability to precisely target audience segments
b. high-quality color reproduction capability
c. long advertising life beyond the immediate issue
d. all of the above

Notes

1. Rebecca Flass, "California Processors Vote to Continue 'Got Milk?'" *Adweek Western Edition,* vol. 51, no. 13 (March 26, 2001): 5; Alice Z. Cuneo, "New 'Got Milk?' Tactic: Got Health?" *Advertising Age,* vol. 70, no. 17 (April 19, 1999): 32; Sonia Reyes, "In Bid to Keep 'Got Milk?' Campaign Fresh, Milk Board Recalls Vintage Ads," *Brandweek,* vol. 42, no. 10 (March 5, 2001): 8; David Lipin, "The Dark Side," *Adweek Eastern Edition,* vol. 41, no. 10 (March 6, 2000): 26.
2. Stephanie Thompson, "Ads Boost Bean Business," *Advertising Age,* vol. 72, no. 9 (February 26, 2001): 2.
3. Becky Ebenkamp and Todd Wasserman, "Kids WB's Great Adventure; TNT and Fox's Evil Alien Plot," *Brandweek,* vol. 45 (July 26, 2004): 8.
4. Christina McCarroll, "Parents Gird for Midriff Wars with Preteen Set," *Christian Science Monitor,* vol. 93, no. 183 (August 15, 2001): 1.
5. "Ad Firm's Focus: Native Americans," *Editor & Publisher,* vol. 132, no. 28 (July 10, 1999): 28.
6. Beth Snyder and Laurel Wentz, "Whole Egg Theory Finally Fits the Bill for Y&R Clients," *Advertising Age,* vol. 70, no. 4 (July 25, 1999): 12–13.
7. Scott Rockwood, "For Better Ad Success, Try Getting Emotional," *Marketing News,* vol. 30, no. 22 (October 21, 1996): 4.
8. Jerry Olson and Thomas J. Reynolds, "Understanding Consumers' Cognitive Structures: Implications for Advertising Strategy," in *Advertising Consumer Psychology,* eds. L. Percy and A. Woodside (Lexington, MA: Lexington Books, 1983): 77–90.
9. Michael S. Latour and Robin L. Snipes, "Don't Be Afraid to Use Fear Appeals: An Experimental Study," *Journal of Advertising,* vol. 36, no. 2 (March/April 1996): 59–68.
10. Harlan E. Spotts and Marc G. Weinberger, "Assessing the Use and Impact of Humor on Advertising Effectiveness," *Journal of Advertising,* vol. 26, no. 3 (Fall 1997): 17–32.
11. Jessica Severn and George E. Belch, "The Effects of Sexual and Non-Sexual Advertising Appeals and Information Level on Cognitive Processing and Communication Effectiveness," *Journal of Advertising,* vol. 19, no. 1 (1990): 14–22.
12. Michael Miller, "Even Out of Context, the Beat Goes On (and On)," *Pittsburgh Business Times,* vol. 18, no. 18 (November 27, 1998): 12.
13. Bob Garfield, "One Slip, and It's All Over for Almost Great Tire Ad," *Advertising Age International* (May 1997): 16.
14. Chuck Ross, "Now, Many Words from Our Sponsors," *Advertising Age,* vol. 70, no. 40 (September 27, 1999): 18.
15. Stephanie Thompson, "Food Marketers Stir Up the Media," *Advertising Age,* vol. 70, no. 42 (September 11, 1999): 18.
16. "Coen's Spending Totals for 2002," *Adage.com* (www.adage.com, January 14, 2005).
17. Rachel X. Weissman, "Just Paging Through," *American Demographics,* vol. 21, no. 4 (April 1999): 28–29; "The Scoop on Magazine Advertising," *Florist,* vol. 33, no. 5 (October 1999): 16.
18. Tony Case, "Reading the Numbers," *Brandweek,* vol. 40, no. 35 (September 20, 1999): 64.
19. Christopher Moler, "Wanted: Not-For-Profit to Take Money . . ." *Parks & Recreation,* vol. 35, no. 9 (September 2000): 164–172.
20. Laura Petrecca, Wayne Friedman, Laura Q. Hughes, Alice Cuneo, David Goetzi, and Hillary Chura, "Nascar Sponsors Still on Track," *Advertising Age,* vol. 72, no. 9 (February 26, 2001): 4–5.
21. "Naming Rights," *Adage Special Report Sports Marketing,* S-12, October 28, 2002, (www.adage.com, January 5, 2003).
22. "Cultural Sponsorship Can Help Reach the Affluent," *Bank Marketing,* vol. 26, no. 10 (October 1994): 7.
23. "Coke's Hard Lesson in Crisis Management," *Business Week,* Issue 3636 (July 5, 1999): 102.

Case 14-1 The Neonatal Intensive Care Unit

In the past, hospitals, doctors, and other medical professions did not advertise or market their services. That has changed with increased competition among medical providers and increased medical costs. Patients are also becoming more concerned about medical treatment and will spend time shopping around for the best medical care. Pressure from insurance companies and increasing deductibles before the insurance kicks in have made patients more cognizant of cost.

Highland Regional Medical Center, like many other hospitals, began advertising its services in 1989. Its marketing budget grew from $80,000 to the current $2.1 million, which is just about the average for a hospital its size. Recent data indicate that hospitals spend an average of 0.77 percent of their net revenue on marketing. Highland's percentage for last year was 0.82 percent.

For more than 12 years, Highland had the only neonatal intensive care unit (NICU) in the region. With the other major hospital, First South Medical Center, installing an NICU, Highland was facing a new situation. The number of patients in its NICU had slowly declined and was now at about 73 percent of the previous usage. Because of the high cost of maintaining the NICU, Highland Regional had to develop a marketing plan to regain neonatal patients. While part of the marketing would have to be targeted to physicians, Highland Regional also recognized that it needed to do some public advertising.

The neonatal intensive care unit provides intensive care for newborn infants. They may be premature babies or infants born with some type of medical problem. A high level of staffing and expensive medical equipment, are required to maintain the personal level of care needed for the infants. Administrators at Highland Regional Medical Center knew they could not continue to fund the NICU at the current level unless they could increase the patient load. To do this, they turned to the advertising agency of Nelson, Mickelson, and Yost. It had a strong reputation in the area and represented a medical hospital in an adjoining state. Highland Regional did not see any conflict of interests because the other hospital was more than 200 miles away and did not draw from Highland's patient region.

Nelson, Mickelson, and Yost's first task was to gather more information about the situation with Highland and the NICU. Staff at Highland were quick to point out that their NICU had the highest level of accreditation, while the competitor's NICU did not. Ed Nelson, however, countered that patients may not understand the difference between Highland's top accreditation and the level three accreditation of First South. In terms of patients, Highland's patient load in the NICU had dropped 27 percent over the past five years. But in examining the number of NICU patients at First South, the ad agency found that the total number of NICU patients in the region had grown by 38 percent. Not only was Highland Regional Medical Center losing patients to First South, some were going to another county for treatment.

In examining media purchases within the hospital industry, Nelson, Mickelson, and Yost found the following data:

- 43 percent of the hospital's marketing budget goes for advertising.
- 37 percent of the advertising budget is used for newspaper and magazine ads, and 16 percent is used for television.

Questions

1. In advertising Highland Regional Medical Center's NICU, what should be the theme? Should the focus be on the NICU's highest level of accreditation? Would patients understand the difference, since the differences are based on technical criteria only the medical personnel would understand?
2. What type of appeal, message strategy, and execution should be used?
3. Design a print ad for the NICU using your answers to Questions 1 and 2.
4. What media should be used? Why?
5. What about sponsorships and public relations? Can they be used in this IMC campaign? If so, how?

Sources: "Findings," *Hospitals & Health Networks*, Vol. 76, No. 11 (November 2002): 72–73; Interview with Graham Morris of Newcomer, Morris, and Young, January 17, 2003.

Case 14-2 Mudd Jeans

In a recent survey, high school and college students were asked to name the pair of jeans that they were most likely to purchase. Here are the results:

- Levi's—12 percent
- Gap—7 percent
- Tommy Hilfiger—6 percent
- LEI—3 percent
- Express—3 percent
- Calvin Klein—3 percent
- Jnco—2 percent
- Mudd—2 percent
- Abercrombie & Fitch—2 percent

For Levi-Strauss, the survey vividly demonstrates what it already knows: It is losing the teen market. Brands such as Tommy Hilfiger, Gap, Express, Calvin Klein, and Mudd are eating away at Levi's market share in the $10.6 billion teen jeans market. In 1990,

Levi Strauss held 31 percent of the total market for jeans. It is now only 16.9 percent. Levi-Strauss has been passed by the VF Corporation (makers of Lee and Wrangler brands) as the number one jean manufacturer. The VF brands have gone from 17.9 percent of the total jean market in 1990 to 25.3 percent today.

While Levi's and VF have made strong attempts to corner the teen market, neither has been tremendously successful. According to Arun Jain, University of Buffalo marketing professor, teenagers don't care about the quality and workmanship that Levi has been emphasizing in its advertising. For teenagers, "it's all about image and not the way the fabric is cut."

Although only a small manufacturer in terms of market share, Mudd believes strongly that it can capture a significant component of the teen jeans market. Company marketing managers believe they offer the styles, image, and fashions teenagers want. According to Dick Gilbert, CEO of Mudd USA, "We found out we were very strong with 12- to 14-year-olds and just OK with 15- to 20-year olds." The challenge lies in creating ads that appeal to teenagers in both age brackets.

American Demographics conducted a survey to determine the most important rules to follow in advertising jeans to the teenage market. The results are in Table 14-10.

Access the Mudd jeans website at www.muddjeans.com. After studying the website and reading this case, assume you have been selected as the advertising agency for Mudd jeans to reach the 12- to 20-year-old market.

Questions

1. What is your evaluation of Mudd's website?
2. Based on the information in this case and the information on the website, what type of advertising campaign would you recommend for Mudd?
3. Should you use different ad campaigns for the 12- to 14-year-old age bracket and the 15- to 20-year-old age bracket?
4. How would you interpret the information provided by *American Demographics* concerning rules jean advertisers should follow for teenagers?
5. Discuss the creative design that you think would appeal to the teen market.
6. Discuss the media strategy that you think would be appropriate for the teen market.
7. Would you use any sponsorship programs? Why or why not?
8. Design a print advertisement for Mudd.

Sources: Scott Malone, "Mudd Grows Up," *WWD: Women's Wear Daily,* vol. 188 (August 26, 2004): 10; Christ Cobb, "Levi-Strauss Officials Hope for a Blue Explosion: How Will Public Relations Play a Role?" *Public Relations Tactics,* Vol. 6, No. 7 (July 1999): 1–4; Sandra Dolbow, "Assessing Levi's Patch Job," *Brandweek,* Vol. 41, No. 43 (November 6, 2000): 34–41; Mudd Jeans website, www.muddjeans.com, January 15, 2005

TABLE 14-10

Rules of Advertising to Teenagers

Rule	Percent of Survey Respondents Who Said:
Be honest.	65 %
Use humor; make me laugh.	52
Be clear.	45
Show the product.	43
Tell me something important about the product.	37
Don't use sex to sell.	31
Show situations that are realistic.	25
Have a great slogan or jingle.	24
Don't talk down to me.	22
Don't try too hard to be cool.	21
Use great music.	21
Show people/scenes I can relate to.	20
Show people my age.	19
Don't tell me what to do.	19
Show me things I've never seen before.	14
Don't butcher a song I like.	14
Show celebrities who use the product.	8
Show cute animals or babies.	6
Be sarcastic.	5
Show situations that are fantasy.	4

Sales and Trade Promotions

15

CHAPTER OBJECTIVES

1. Discuss the reasons for a shift in marketing expenditures to promotions.
2. Identify the various forms of sales promotions.
3. Identify the various types of coupons as well as distribution methods.
4. Explain the importance of in-store promotions in purchasing behavior.
5. Discuss the goals of trade promotions.
6. Identify the various types of trade promotions.
7. Discuss the issue of slotting fees.

CHAPTER OUTLINE

In the past, all Procter & Gamble had to do to sell a product was advertise it on television during one of the daytime soap operas. In fact, the formula was so successful that P&G not only became the title sponsor of CBS's *Guiding Light* and *As the World Turns*, but it purchased both shows. However, that was in the 1950s and 1960s. It's a different story today. During the past 10 years, the soap operas have lost, collectively, more than 2 million viewers. From an average Nielsen rating of 5.3 in 1991, most soaps now have Nielsen ratings around 2.0 or lower. *General Hospital*'s Nielsen rating is down to 2.0, the *Bold and Beautiful* is 1.4, *As the World Turns* is 1.8, the *Young and the Restless* is 2.3, *Guiding Light* is 1.3, and *Days of Our Lives* is down to 2.2.

Getting people, primarily females, to watch soap operas has become increasingly challenging. Two decades ago, the women who watched soaps viewed an average of four a day; that number is down to two a day now. This decline is due to more women in the workforce, the capability of recording shows on a VCR and watching them later, increased competition with soap-like shows in the evenings, and the ability to keep up with the plot via the Internet.

To attract viewers, some soap operas turned to using promotions (see Figure 15-1). NBC promoted a contest with the grand prize being a $10,000 cruise. The reaction was disappointing. But when NBC offered lunch with Luis and Sheridan, two characters on daytime soaps, the reaction was different. The winner, Debbie Bean, a 42-year-old Yellow Cab administrator from Elizabeth, New Jersey, nearly had a heart attack when she found out she had won. "They're hot," she said.

To promote *As the World Turns*, three of the show's young, new stars took part in an 11-day bus tour to 10 universities. The "Catch Us if You Can Tour" offered auditions at each college campus with about 15 students from each campus chosen for on-air scenes. CBS is also using contests and a fan event at Universal Studios to promote *The Young and the Restless.*

Sponsors like Colgate are getting involved through "Super Soap" promotions, including fan events at theme parks that include signage and product sampling of Total toothpaste. The Home Shopping Network offered items for sale that were used on the set of various soap operas, such as an engagement ring from *General Hospital* and a crystal ball from *All My Children.*

While P&G, Pfizer, Johnson & Johnson, and Kimberly-Clark still make up 37 percent of the daytime soap opera ads, the amount of advertising dollars they are willing to spend

Figure 15-1
With a drop in daytime soap opera viewing, soap operas are turning to sales promotions to win back viewers.

on these TV shows will continue to decline as long as the Nielsen ratings are dropping. Sales promotions may be the best way to win back viewers. Time will tell.[1]

15-1 Chapter Overview

Sales and trade promotions are a critical component of the integrated marketing communications effort. Over the past few decades, more and more dollars have been shifted from advertising to promotions. The next section of this chapter, Section 15-2, examines why this shift in spending has occurred.

Promotions can be divided into two types: sales promotions and trade promotions. Section 15-3 examines the major forms of sales promotion with a focus on couponing—the most pervasive sales promotion used. Not only are sales promotions used to stimulate sales, they are also used to generate store traffic because the final decision to purchase a particular brand is made inside the retail store. Section 15-4 examines in-store promotions that companies use to gain attention and to persuade consumers to make a purchase. The last section, Section 15-5, deals with trade promotions. While these tend not to be seen by most people, they are critical for pushing products through the channel and ensuring that products are on retail shelves so consumers can purchase them.

15-2 Promotions

In recent years, firms have shifted more of their communications budgets from advertising to trade and sales promotions. Trade promotions refer to offers made to channel members, whereas sales promotions are offers given to end users or consumers. Approximately 82.5 percent of all consumer marketing dollars are now being spent on promotions, compared to 40 percent 15 years ago. Only 17.5 percent of consumer marketing expenditures are now being spent on advertising. See Figure 15-2 for a breakdown of current overall consumer marketing expenditures.[2] This shift toward greater use of promotions has occurred for several reasons.[3]

First, promotions normally have an immediate impact on sales, whereas advertising takes a longer period of time. The impact is not only immediate, but is often quite dramatic in terms of increased sales.

A second reason for the shift to more promotions is increased brand proliferation and brand parity. Consumers and businesses have more choices today than ever before in their selection of a good or service. Most buyers see very little difference among firms and among various brands. For example, in choosing a restaurant, consumers may have some preferences, but they will patronize almost any restaurant and will often switch just for variety. The same can be said for purchasing a new pair of jeans. Consumers may have a preference but often buy the brand that offers the best price, style, or fit. In most clothes closets, you will find several brands of jeans.

A third reason for the increase of promotions is greater consumer acceptance of promotions and, in some instances, consumers' demand for special deals. The airline industry still struggles financially as travelers have become accustomed to price wars and low fares. Many travelers postpone travel until prices are reduced. Most automobiles are purchased with some type of factory rebate. Pizza coupons arrive in the mail regularly, and it is not unusual for consumers to buy whichever brand has a coupon. Most grocery stores have a price offer on either Coke or Pepsi products, and many consumers purchase the brand that is on sale. Many clothes are purchased only when they are on sale. A view of any Wednesday or Sunday newspaper indicates how many promotions are being offered to consumers on a regular basis.

A fourth reason for the increase in promotions is the declining impact of advertising. With remote controls and VCRs, consumers are zapping out many commercials. Those they do watch, view, or hear are quickly forgotten due to the high number of commercials they are exposed to each day. Because it is easier to stimulate action with a promotion than with advertising, many companies are shifting dollars to promotions. There are, however,

Figure 15-2
Consumer Marketing Expenditures: Promotions Versus Advertising

Source: "Upward Bound," *Promo*, vol. 17 (April 2004): AR3–AR5.

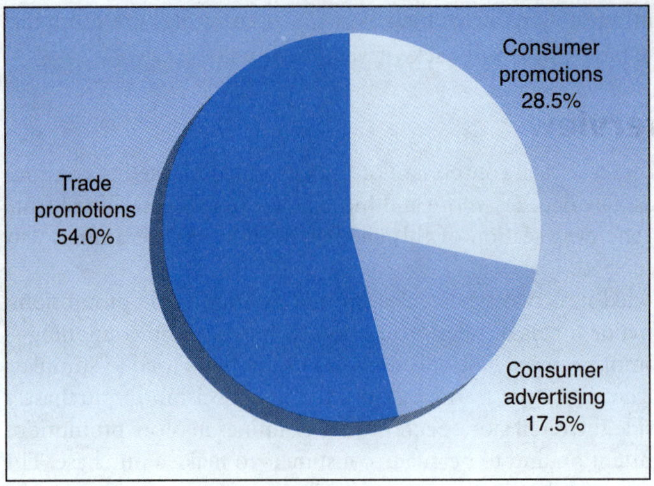

brand managers and marketing experts who believe such a shift may erode the brand equity that a firm has spent years in establishing. Recall from earlier chapters that brand equity is primarily built on advertising, and an over-reliance on promotions can erode brand image. Although advertising may not be as effective as in the past, it is still a critical component of the integrated marketing communications (IMC) package. Whatever promotions a company uses, they must be part of the company's IMC program and fit with the advertising that is being done.

15-3 Sales Promotions

Sales promotions are used to stimulate some type of activity on the part of a consumer or business. Most sales promotions are aimed at consumers, but sales promotions can also be targeted to businesses if the business is the final user of the product. For example, an office supply store may offer a business a special promotion to either make an immediate purchase or place a larger order. If the business purchases the office supplies for its own consumption, then the promotion is a sales promotion. If, however, it is reselling the office supplies, then it is a trade promotion.

Companies can use 10 primary types of sales promotions (see Figure 15-3). It is important that the sales promotions fit into the company's IMC effort and are part of the company's strategic thinking. If not, the message sent to consumers via a sales promotion may contradict the firm's IMC effort. For instance, if a firm wants to project an image of offering superior quality, using coupons on a regular basis conveys a different message to buyers. Mentally, one would say, "If this product is of such high quality, why do they always offer coupons?" Although coupons can be used, other sales promotion tools may do a better job of promoting the product while maintaining the higher image desired.

15-3a Coupons

Coupons: Sales promotion that offers customers some type of price reduction.

Coupons are an excellent strategy for stimulating sales, especially in the short run. The number of coupons has increased from 17 billion in 1970 to more than 336 billion today, which equates to more than 1,200 coupons for every person, including children.[4] Thus, a family of four would, on the average, receive close to 5,000 coupons each year either through the mail, on product packages, or in some form of print media such as newspapers. Approximately 85 percent of American consumers redeem coupons, although most are not avid coupon clippers.[5] Of 336 billion coupons distributed, only 2.7 billion, or 0.8 percent, were redeemed. This number is down from a 1.4 percent redemption rate in 2000.[6] Only 18.5 percent of consumers use coupons on a regular basis, and 23.3 percent rarely or never use coupons. Consumers who are concerned with saving money are the

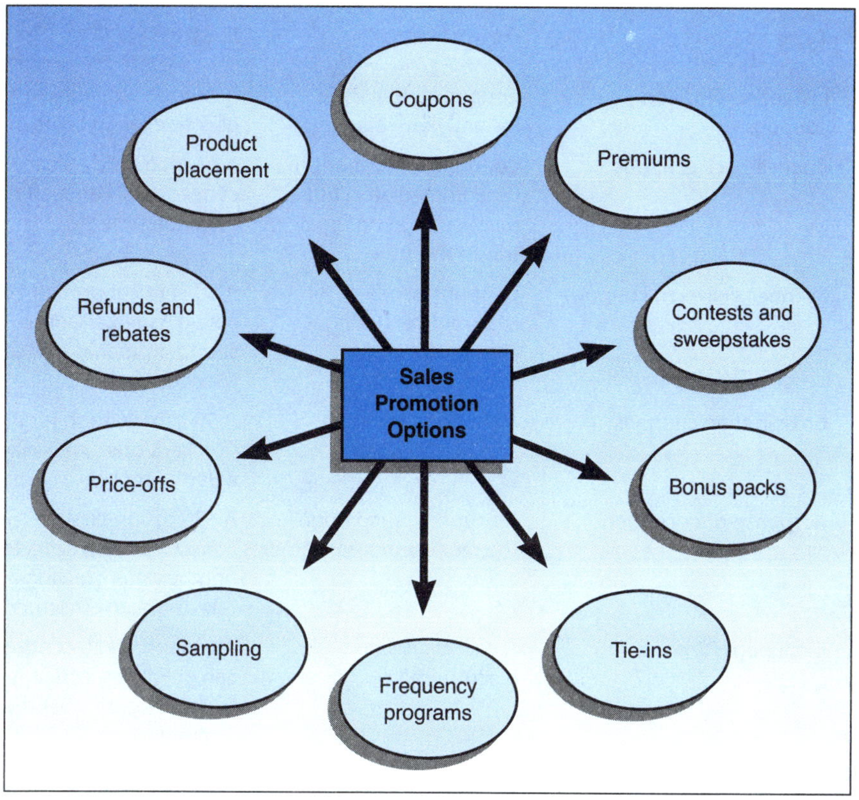

Figure 15-3
Sales Promotion Options

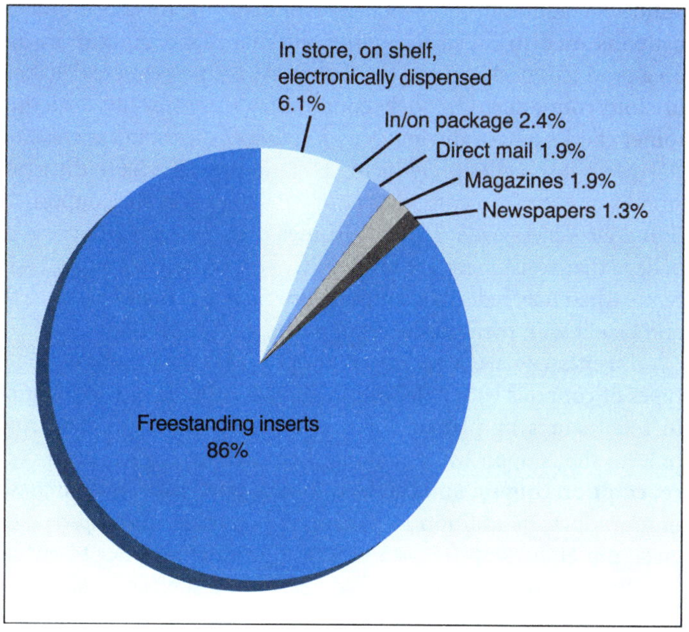

Figure 15-4
Coupon Distribution Methods

Source: Joseph Gatti, "Coupon Distribution Up, But Web Dispersal Still Scanty," *Direct Marketing* (October 1, 2003): 1–2.

most inclined to use coupons.[7] To encourage these individuals to use coupons, firms should use simple, straightforward messages that emphasize cost savings.[8]

Figure 15-4 identifies the various methods of distributing coupons and the percentage with which each is used. Manufacturers distribute approximately 80 percent of all coupons, and the primary method used is print media (89.2 percent). While magazines and newspapers themselves have coupons, 86 percent of all coupons are distributed via **freestanding inserts (FSI),** which are sheets of coupons distributed in newspapers, primarily on

Freestanding inserts (FSI): Sheets of coupons distributed in newspapers, primarily on Sunday.

TABLE 15-1 Types of Coupons

Type of Coupon	Definition	Example
Instant redemption coupons	Coupons that can be instantly redeemed	A coupon attached to a can of coffee for 50 cents off
Bounce-back coupons	Coupons that cannot be used immediately but must be used on the next trip to the store	A coupon inside a can of coffee for 50 cents off the next purchase
Scanner-delivered coupons	Coupons issued at the cash register during checkout	A 50-cent coupon for Folger's coffee issued after the shopper purchased a can of Maxwell House
Cross-ruffing coupons	A coupon placed on another product	A 50-cent coupon for Betty Crocker's cake icing placed on a Betty Crocker cake mix
Response-offer coupons	A coupon issued upon the request of a consumer	A $30 coupon issued to consumers who call a toll-free number after viewing a television advertisement
E-coupons (U-pons)	A coupon issued electronically	A coupon for 50 cents off a can of Folger's coffee issued to the consumer via the Internet

Sunday. In addition to the 89.2 percent distributed via print media, another 1.9 percent of coupons are distributed through direct mail, 2.4 percent more are distributed either in or on a product's package, and the remaining 6.1 percent are delivered in the retail store using in-store couponing, on-shelf couponing, electronically dispensed coupons when a customer checks out, or during free sampling of a product at the store.[9]

Most companies prefer using FSI and print media to distribute coupons because consumers must make a conscious effort to clip or save the coupon. Also, the coupon increases brand awareness even if the consumer does not actually use the coupon. Manufacturers believe that consumers are more likely to purchase a couponed brand and remember the name when they redeem a coupon, especially if it is an FSI, since they must clip the coupon and take it with them to the retail outlet.

Instant redemption coupon: A coupon that can be redeemed immediately while making a purchase.

Bounce-back coupons: Coupons that cannot be used until the next purchase.

Scanner-delivered coupons: Coupons issued at the cash register during checkout.

Cross-ruffing coupon: A coupon for one product placed on another product.

Businesses have a variety of coupons that can be used. Table 15-1 lists the different types of coupons with a definition and an example of each. Coupons are often distributed in retail stores by placing them on or near packages. The consumer can immediately redeem the coupon while making the purchase. This type of coupon is called an **instant redemption coupon** and can lead to trial purchases and purchases of additional packages of a product. In addition to placing the coupon on the package, coupons are sometimes given out along with free samples of a product in order to encourage consumers to try a new brand. Coupons may also be placed in dispensers near various products, which provide convenient access for customers. All of these methods are forms of instant redemption coupons because customers can use them immediately.

Bounce-back coupons are placed inside packages so that customers cannot redeem them at the time of the original purchase. This approach encourages repeat purchases because the coupon cannot be used until the next purchase. Another trend is to have coupons issued at the cash register during checkout. These are **scanner-delivered coupons** because they are triggered by an item being scanned, usually a competing brand. Scanner-delivered coupons are designed to encourage brand switching during the next shopping trip.

Another type of coupon is the **cross-ruffing coupon,** which is the placement of a coupon for one product on another product. For example, a coupon for a French onion dip

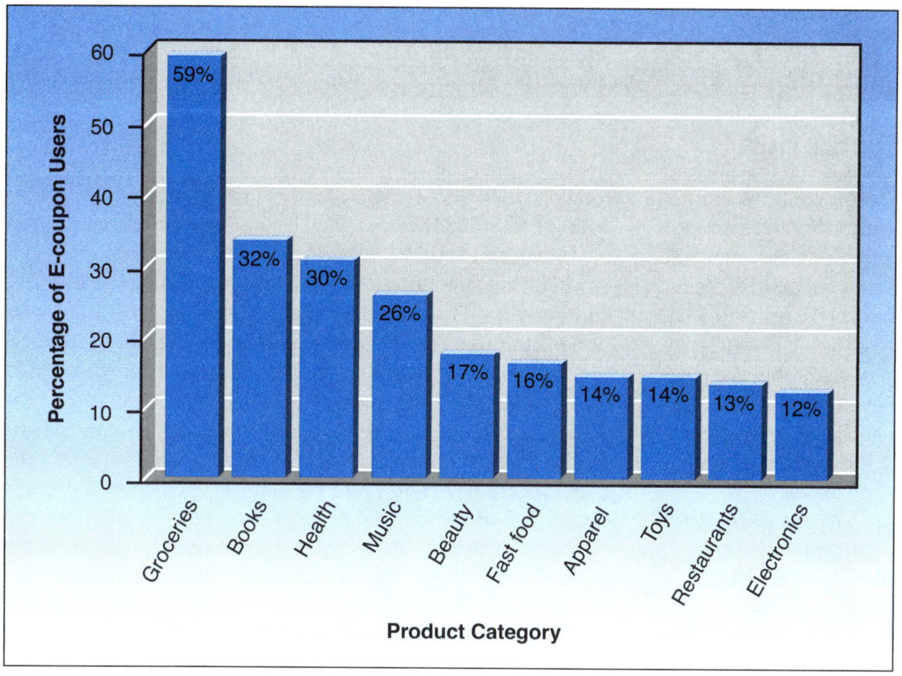

Figure 15-5
Percentage of E-Coupon Users by Product Category (Top 10 Categories)

Source: Alan J. Liddle, "Restaurants Tops in E-Coupon Redemption Derby," *Nation's Restaurant News*, vol. 34, no. 21 (May 22, 2000): 34.

might be placed on a package of potato chips. To be successful, cross-ruffing coupons must be used with products that fit together logically and that are normally purchased and consumed simultaneously. Occasionally, a manufacturer uses cross-ruffing to encourage consumers to purchase another one of its products or brands. For example, General Mills may place a coupon on a Honey Nut Cheerios box for another cereal, such as Golden Grahams or Wheaties. This type of couponing tactic encourages consumers to purchase within the same brand or family of products.

Response-offer coupons are issued following a request by a consumer. Requests may come through a 1-800 number, the Internet, or mail. Coupons are then mailed to the consumer or sent by Internet to be printed by the consumer. The coupon can also be faxed, which is a common method in the business-to-business sector. Office supply companies and other vendors use response offer coupons to invite business customers to make purchases or place orders. Firms also distribute coupons through their sales representatives, which allows for instant redemptions, since the salesperson also takes the order.

Response-offer coupons: Coupons issued following a request by a consumer.

E-coupons are any electronically delivered coupons. Most are delivered over the Internet and are printed by the consumer, but some, called U-pons, are delivered directly to the retail store's point-of-sales system. The first retailer to offer U-pons (paperless, Internet-delivered coupons) was Dick's Supermarkets. Coupons are sent to its 50,000 Savings Club members in Wisconsin and Illinois via the Internet. Consumers click on the coupons they want to use, and the amount of the coupon discount is then automatically deducted from the purchase price through the use of a frequent-shopper card that is presented at the store when they check out. The first year Dick's Supermarkets used U-pons, redemption rates for baby products averaged 36 percent; cheese and peanut butter, 30 percent; bread, 24 percent; prepared frozen foods, 22 percent; and cookies, 20 percent.[10] This is much higher than the standard 1 percent redemption rate from FSI.

E-coupons: Electronically delivered coupons.

E-coupon usage is still in its infancy, but preliminary data are encouraging for companies wanting to use the Internet to distribute coupons. A survey of Internet users found that e-coupons currently account for only 5 to 10 percent of all coupons redeemed, but 27 percent of all Internet users have used some type of e-coupon. The top e-coupon sites are Coolsavings.com and Mypoints.com. The top product categories are groceries (59 percent), books (32 percent), and health products (30 percent). Figure 15-5 identifies the top 10 categories for e-coupons.

Marketing Illustration 15-1

Coupon Fraud and Misredemption

More than 10 percent of all redeemed coupons are illegally reimbursed. The most common form of coupon fraud is mass cutting. This occurs when coupons are redeemed through a fraudulent retail outlet that does not exist, except at a mailbox set up by an illegal coupon ring. At 50 cents to $4.00 per coupon, mass cutting of coupons can be highly lucrative. Many times, these rings take advantage of charitable organizations and religious groups who think they are helping a worthy cause by sending in coupons to the mailbox to receive a percentage of the proceeds. Instead, they are actually aiding an illegal activity.

Counterfeiting occurs when coupons are copied by fraudulent retail establishments that usually exist only at post office boxes and then are sent to the manufacturer for reimbursement. The manufacturer is paying for coupons that were never used. Because many newspaper coupons are black and white, they are easy to counterfeit. Even color coupons are relatively easy to copy now using color copiers. They are not as lucrative, however, because of the cost of making a color copy.

The most recent form of coupon fraud involves downloading bogus coupons from the Internet. To most store clerks, these bogus coupons look legitimate. They tend to be for larger discounts and in some cases for free products. While some retailers will not accept any type of computer-generated coupon, most do. The challenge is for retailers and manufacturers to produce Internet coupons that cannot be altered.

Retailers are not normally involved in mass cutting or counterfeiting. They are, however, involved in the misredemption of coupons. For instance, a coupon for a can of soup states the size of can for which the discount applies. If the discount is used for another size, such as a 10-ounce can instead of the 20-ounce can, then misredemption has occurred. This may be due to an error on the part of the clerk who did not check the coupon carefully. It may also be that the clerk knew it was the wrong size of can but did not want to bother finding the correct size or risk making the customer mad by denying the coupon. Other times, clerks may honor coupons for merchandise that was not purchased when they take the coupon and subtract it from the customer's total without matching it to the actual product. Because the typical supermarket redeems more than 1,000 coupons per day, there is ample opportunity for errors, mistakes, and fraud.

Source: Jenny McTaggart, "Coupon Controversy," *Progressive Grocer*, vol. 82 (November 1, 2003): 26; Henry N. Nocella, "Clipping Coupon Fraud," *Security Management*, vol. 44, no. 12 (December 2000) 40–46.

More than 10 percent of all redeemed coupons are redeemed illegally or incorrectly. Marketing Illustration 15-1 discusses the issues of illegal coupon redemption, counterfeiting, and misredemption.

15-3b Premiums

Premiums: Sales promotion that offers customers free merchandise for making a purchase.

Premiums offer consumers some type of free merchandise for purchasing the product (see Figure 15-6). Cereal manufacturers have used prizes such as puzzles, games, and toys for years to entice consumers to purchase their brand of cereal. Banks have offered gifts such as personal organizers to small businesses that open an account with them. Premiums offer a major benefit not possible with coupons—customers pay full price for the product. If the premium is picked carefully, the premium can actually enhance a brand's equity.

Unfortunately, premiums tend to be used by regular customers, rather than new customers. Premiums are not as effective as coupons in encouraging trial purchases. If a firm wants to reward customers for their loyalty, offering premiums is one way of accomplishing this goal. Premiums can also be used to encourage customers to stock up, which would make promotional offers from competitors less attractive. For example, if Hollywood Tanning Salon offers consumers 2 free tans with the purchase of 10 tanning sessions, it accomplishes two major goals. First, it gets full price for the 10 sessions. Second, it encourages current customers to stay with the salon rather than switch to another firm offering a coupon.

To be effective, premiums must be attractive to the customer. If a free gift is being offered, the gift must be an item that is desirable and that reinforces the firm's IMC effort. For example, a firm that is marketing upscale products may want to offer a personalized gift such as an attaché case with the customer's name inscribed on it as the premium. Such a strategy would be appropriate for a private golf course soliciting new members.

Figure 15-6
This premium offered by Ukrop's Super Markets for a "2nd set free" from Richmond Camera is likely to increase customer demand for film development on Thursdays.

Source: Courtesy of Ukrop's Super Markets, Inc.

Figure 15-7
This advertisement by Oreck combines both a coupon and a premium in an overlay. Individuals who purchase the vacuum cleaner with the coupon also receive the iron as a premium.

Source: Reprinted by permission of Oreck.

Sometimes, premiums are used with another type of promotion, such as a coupon. This procedure of using two or more promotions in a single offer is called an **overlay**. The Oreck advertisement in Figure 15-7 illustrates the use of an overlay.

Overlay: The use of two or more promotions within the same promotional offer.

15-3c Contests and Sweepstakes

Contests and sweepstakes: Sales promotions that allow participants an opportunity to win free merchandise.

Both **contests and sweepstakes** allow participants an opportunity to win prizes. The difference between contests and sweepstakes is what a participant must do to win. In a contest, participants may be required to perform an activity or to make a purchase to be eligible to win. In a sweepstakes, participants do not need to make a purchase, and the winners are determined by a random drawing in which every entrant has an equal chance of being selected.

Whereas coupons appeal to price-conscious consumers, contests and sweepstakes appeal to individuals who enjoy higher levels of excitement and stimulation. Price-conscious consumers may not participate in contests and sweepstakes because they see the contests or sweepstakes as increasing the cost of the service.[11] To increase the effectiveness of a sweepstakes or contest, firms should emphasize the fun, fantasy, and stimulation aspect. Consumers enter contests and sweepstakes for the experience as well as the hope of winning. Contests should be structured to provide participants with a challenge as well as excitement.

AmeriSuites offered a sweepstakes in conjunction with its sponsorship of the Jaguar #12 car driven by Michael Lewis of the American Spirit Racing Trans-Am Series. The scratch-and-win cards offered more than 15,000 prizes to guests at AmeriSuites. The grand prize was a two-year lease on a new Jaguar X-type vehicle. Other major prizes included two three-night vacations for two at any AmeriSuite hotel, four sets of B. F. Goodrich tires, AmeriSuite certificates, Gatorz sunglasses, and Trans-Am series merchandise.[12] The advertisement in Figure 15-8 features a sweepstakes by Pepsi, featuring tie-ins with other companies such as Sony.

Figure 15-8
This advertisement by Pepsi promotes a sweepstake and features tie-ins with other companies.
Source: Courtesy of Pepsi-Cola Company.

Marketing Illustration 15-2

Kraft's Promotional Package

To maximize the effectiveness of promotion, Kraft has adopted a holistic approach across its various brands. According to Sarah Gleason, Vice President of Strategy and Marketing Services at Kraft, "Promotion is not just about planting seeds and waiting for them to sprout. [It is] not just about dropping a coupon. [It] requires internal sharing among leadership teams to cross-pollinate ideas: Public relations, advertising, and packaging must work in sync, guided by consumer insights and the core brand equity."

An excellent example of Kraft's holistic approach was the "Be a DiGiorno Delivery Guy" contest developed from the pizza's tagline "It's not delivery. It's DiGiorno." The contest was based on the idea that since DiGiorno was made fresh at home and not delivered, there was "nothing to do." Therefore, the instant-win sweepstakes offered $100,000 to do nothing; a Ford Mustang GT convertible, which winners did not have to drive; and a Hawaiian vacation, where the winner would do nothing. The sweepstakes was backed by a national TV/print advertising campaign, freestanding inserts on 10 million pizza boxes, and a telephone entry option. The integrated promotional campaign resulted in a 90 percent increase in sales for DiGiorno pizza and 18.1 percent of the frozen pizza market.

Another promotion that has been successful for Kraft is a tie-in with Nickelodeon, especially the "Slime Extravaganza" contest. Kids were invited to enter by mailing a postcard to Nickelodeon. The four winners received $1,000 and a chance for good-natured rebellion like dousing teachers and principals with green slime.

Source: Sonia Reyes, "Krafting the Total Promo Package," *Brandweek,* vol. 43, no. 27 (June 15, 2002): 24–28.

Both contests and sweepstakes are effective means for building customer traffic or generating interest in a firm's products. Retailers use them at a grand opening or at other special events to encourage consumers to visit the store. In an effort to stimulate inquiries about its new cars, Saab launched the "Ultimate Drive of a Lifetime" sweepstakes. Because more than 90 percent of the buyers of luxury cars research automobiles online, Saab required online registration to enter the sweepstakes. To promote the sweepstakes, ads were placed on auto, outdoors enthusiast, financial, news, and premium travel websites along with more general sites such as Forbes.com, Fortune.com, and concierge.com. Of the first 68,000 entries, 23,000 asked for more information on the new Saab vehicle.[13] For another example, see Marketing Illustration 15-2.

15-3d Bonus Packs

Bonus packs are additional merchandise offered at the same price or slightly higher price. For example, four bars of soap may be packaged together and sold for the price of three individual packages. Two containers of potato chips may be packaged together and sold for 50 percent more than the price of one container. The manufacturer's objective in developing a bonus pack is to entice consumers to switch to its brand from a competing brand or to entice current consumers to stock up so a competing brand's promotion is not attractive (see Figure 15-9).

Bonus packs: Sales promotion that offers customers some type of discount for purchasing multiple items.

If the bonus pack contained 25 percent or more additional product, research has indicated consumers were more likely to switch, especially if they believed the manufacturer was incurring the cost of the extra product. If the consumer believed the manufacturer increased the price to add the bonus product, then they were less likely to purchase the bonus pack. Almost 75 percent of all consumers believe that consumers will pay for the additional amount either directly or indirectly. Yet, 51 percent of consumers interviewed said they have purchased a bonus pack because they believed it was a good value, and 58 percent said they have tried a different brand to take advantage of a bonus pack promotion.[14]

Tie-ins: Sales promotion of two or more goods or services within the same promotional offer.

Intracompany tie-in: A sales promotion involving two or more distinct products within the same company.

15-3e Tie-ins

Promotional **tie-ins** include two or more goods or services within the same promotional offer. The tie-ins can be either intracompany or intercompany. An **intracompany tie-in**

Figure 15-9
Bonus pack advertisements in a grocery store weekly newspaper ad offer two 3-ounce packages of Esskay Chipped Beef for $3.00 and two 11-ounce packages of Esskay Creamed Chipped Beef for $5.00.

Source: Courtesy of Ukrop's Super Markets, Inc.

involves two or more distinct products within the same company. For example, Kraft, which has brands such as DiGiorno, Post, Oreos, and Life Savers, could place a 20 percent discount coupon for Oreos on its Post cereal boxes. An **intercompany tie-in** involves two different companies offering complementary products (see Figure 15-10). For example, the St. Louis Cardinals baseball team could provide a 50 percent off coupon to the nearby Gateway Arch with the purchase of an adult ticket to a Cardinals game.

Intercompany tie-in: A sales promotion involving two different companies offering complementary products.

Tie-ins can be an excellent means of stimulating demand for a particular product. They work best if consumers are offered some type of promotional incentive for a high-demand item if the low-demand item is purchased. Another approach is to offer a combination ticket in which the consumer gets two products for a reduced price. For example, tourists can save $10 with a combination ticket that allows them into both Busch Gardens and Adventure Island.

Intercompany tie-ins are more difficult to coordinate because two firms have to agree to the promotion. More lead time is needed because both companies will have to approve each detail of the joint promotion and each company must feel it is benefiting from the joint promotion. A unique tie-in promotion was developed between DaimlerChrysler Jeep and JCPenney for Penney's 100th anniversary. Old Toledo Brands developed a special Jeep line of apparel that included denim jeans, denim jackets, sports shirts, T-shirts, cargo pants, vests, outerwear, and hats. The Jeep apparel line was featured on JCPenney's website and in four JCPenney catalogs—workwear, outdoor apparel, big and tall, and Christmas. In addition to the special Jeep apparel, DaimlerChrysler developed a Jeep Jeans Wrangler vehicle with DuPont Teflon-coated seat covers, roll bars, and a JCPenney's 100th anniversary logo. Both the Jeep apparel line and the JCPenney anniversary Jeep vehicle were promoted in a joint sweepstakes with ads appearing in point-of-purchase displays in JCPenney stores, in the JCPenney Christmas catalog, and on AOL, Yahoo!, and MSN websites. The grand prize was the first Jeep Jeans Wrangler vehicle to roll off the assembly line. First prize was two all-expenses-paid trips to Camp Jeep. Second-place prizes were his and her Jeep mountain bikes. Third-place prizes were 50 water- and stain-resistant Jeep denim jackets.[15]

Tie-ins with movies have become more common. For instance, Revlon, Philips/Norelco, Ford, 7Up, and Omega watches had tie-ins with the latest James Bond movie. In addition, Revlon and Ford developed an intercompany tie-in, in which a Ford Thunderbird was featured in a Revlon television spot. The ad invited viewers to enter the Revlon contest in which they could win a Ford Thunderbird car.[16]

Figure 15-10
In this advertisement, Ukrop's is promoting an intercompany tie-in by offering a free 2-liter bottle of Coke with the purchase of any Ciabatta pizza.

Source: Courtesy of Ukrop's Super Markets, Inc.

15-3f Frequency Programs

Most sales promotion programs are of short duration and focus on boosting sales immediately, brand switching, or repeat purchase behavior. Few focus on developing brand loyalty and enhancing brand equity, which is the goal of frequency programs. **Frequency programs,** also called loyalty programs, are sales promotions aimed at current customers that are designed to build repeat purchase behavior and brand loyalty by rewarding customers for their patronage. Frequency programs have the following four characteristics:

Frequency programs: Sales promotions offered to current customers and designed to build repeat purchase behavior.

1. They require multiple purchases over a period of time.
2. There is a formal method for accumulating points or credits for purchases.
3. There is a standardized redemption process.
4. Rewards come in the form of additional goods, services, discounts, or cash when a certain number of points are accumulated.[17]

The first and perhaps the most popular frequency program is the frequent-flier program used by airlines. American Airlines launched the first such program in 1981. The other airlines quickly countered with their versions so as not to be at a competitive disadvantage. At first, the idea seemed great. Airlines gave away free seats. Minimal additional costs were accrued because the seats they gave away would have been empty anyway. The frequent-flier programs turned out to be more popular than expected. More than

22 million travelers have enrolled in some type of frequent-flier program. On the average, each traveler has joined 2.26 programs resulting in more than 50 million members. It is estimated that 70 percent of all business travelers are in one or more frequent-flier clubs.[18]

Figure 15-11
The Ukrop's Valued Customer card entitles buyers to weekly deals on the supermarket's products.

Source: Courtesy of Ukrop's Super Markets, Inc.

Successful frequency or loyalty programs require a strong brand name, which is built on brand equity and brand awareness. If customers join a frequency program because of the rewards being offered, the frequency program will fail. To succeed, customers' rationale for joining must be to receive a reward for their loyalty to a specific brand. A major problem with the airlines is that passengers are members of multiple frequent-flier programs and that the frequent miles given do not develop loyalty, but the frequent-flier miles are necessary to maintain patronage.

A successful frequency program ties customers to a firm because the firm provides quality products and rewards them for their loyalty. A recent survey by Frequency Marketing, Inc. of Milford, Ohio, found that 55 percent of Americans belong to at least one loyalty-type program. For households with incomes above $75,000, that participation jumps to 71 percent. From a business's perspective, the most interesting data are that 43 percent reported that membership in a frequency program led to more frequent purchases, and 16 percent reported that they purchased only one brand because of their membership. Once a customer joins a loyalty program, he or she tends to spend, on the average, 27 percent more with that company (see Figure 15-11).[19]

To obtain this type of success not only requires offering a quality product, but it also requires the right mix of rewards that match the firm's customer base. Probably the most successful frequency program is the American Express Membership Rewards program. Participants in this loyalty program spend four times more than a cardholder who is not enrolled. Original rewards included airline miles but now have expanded to more than 120 partners, such as hotels, merchandise, retailers, and movie tickets.[20]

15-3g Sampling

Sampling: Sales promotions that include the free delivery of an actual product or portion of a product.

Sampling is used primarily by food and beverage manufacturers, but can also be used by almost any type of good or service (see Figure 15-12). An attorney can use sampling by offering a free initial consultation. A fitness center can offer a trial membership for a week. A business-to-business firm could offer the use of a new machine for 30 days or samples of its products. The goal of sampling is to encourage consumers or businesses to try a new product. Often, coupons or other sales promotions are tied with sampling in an overlay to further increase the probability that a purchase is made.

Figure 15-12
Food stores often offer samples of food to consumers, increasing the traffic to the store and the probability that the consumer will purchase the product.

Source: Courtesy of Ukrop's Super Markets Inc.

Sampling was a major thrust of Coke's strategy during the introduction of Diet Vanilla Coke. Permission was obtained from 30 major retailers, such as Wal-Mart, Target, and CVS, to allow Coke samples to be distributed. In addition, ads appeared on television, radio, and billboards. The publicity effort included a concert by Cher and Cyndi Lauper in New York's Madison Square Garden. This united, integrated effort by Coke produced product sales of 1.7 million cases during the first four weeks, good for the No. 8 spot in soft drink sales at convenience stores and 2.7 percent of the overall market share for soft drinks.[21] The advertisement in Figure 15-13 is a form of sampling because NordicTrack's WalkFit is offered to consumers for a 30-day in-home trial.

Research by NFO WorldGroup found that 70 percent of the people who recalled receiving a free sample within the past year either "always" or "usually" looked at the product information that was included. Of those who recalled receiving a coupon with the sample, more than 50 percent said they redeemed the coupon. Although sampling is an expensive method of reaching consumers, if the sample also includes a coupon or some other type of promotional offer, it is an effective means of generating a trial purchase.[22]

15-3h Price-offs

Price-offs involve a reduction in the listed retail price of a product (see Figure 15-14). Price-offs are used to attract consumers, to reduce purchase risk, and to stimulate demand.

Price-offs: Sales promotion that offers a reduction of the retail price of a product.

Figure 15-13
This advertisement by NordicTrack offers consumers a 30-day home trial to sample the WalkFit.

Source: Reprinted by permission of ICON Health & Fitness, Inc.

Figure 15-14
Consumers follow closely the price-off deals at their favorite supermarkets.

Source: Courtesy of Ukrop's Super Markets, Inc.

Figure 15-15
This advertisement by Coyote Wild promotes its one-year anniversary sale of 15 percent off storewide and up to 75 percent off on selected items.

Source: Sample print advertisement courtesy of The Miles Agency and Alliance One Advertising, Inc.

Price-offs have the greatest impact on price-sensitive consumers and, unfortunately, also with current customers who would usually be willing to pay full price. From a firm's perspective, price-offs are an excellent tool for boosting sales because the impact is almost instantaneous. The disadvantage is that, if used too frequently, customers come to expect the reduced price and are not willing to pay full price for the product.

Retailers such as Coyote Wild (see Figure 15-15) use price reductions to attract shoppers into the store and to encourage them to make specific purchases. For example, during Thanksgiving the price of turkeys is reduced, often below cost, in the hope that the shopper will purchase other items. In some cases, the price reduction is used to remain competitive and to meet the prices of a competitor. It is also used to discourage customers from taking advantage of a promotion by a competitor. For example, if a particular brand of cookies launches a promotional campaign that includes a sweepstakes and coupons, a competitor may use a price-off strategy to discourage consumers from switching brands.

15-3i Refunds and Rebates

Rebates and refunds: Sales promotions that are a cash reimbursement to a customer for the purchase of a product.

Rather than use coupons to reduce the price of products, firms can use a rebate or refund. **Rebates and refunds** are cash reimbursements paid to consumers with some type of proof of purchase. Technically, a rebate refers to reimbursements for a durable good, whereas a refund refers to reimbursements for a soft good or service. However, the words are often used interchangeably today.

The primary objective of offering a refund or rebate is to reward individuals for the purchase of a product. Because the process involves mailing in proof-of-purchase documentation and waiting four to six weeks for the reimbursement, refunds and rebates are not as effective in stimulating a purchase. The exception, however, is in the automotive industry, where consumers expect to get a rebate. A recent study by J. D. Powers and Associates found that buyers expect to receive a discount of $3,000 or more on a new car. Among new car buyers, individuals who compared two or more models typically bought the less expensive model.[23] Because rebates have been overused in the industry, they are now expected by consumers and cannot be stopped unless all of the manufacturers are willing to discontinue the practice. Such a decision, however, would likely bring federal government action against the automobile industry for price fixing or price collusion.

The credit card industry has been very successful at using this type of sales promotion. The Discover card offers customers money back based on their usage of the card. General Motors has a similar plan for the credit card but instead of cash back, customers apply the rebate toward the purchase of a new GM car or truck. GM's program has been so successful that it signed up more than 5 million accounts in the first year.[24]

15-3j Product Placement

Product placement is a recent phenomenon that involves the placement of branded products in movies and television shows. Because of so much advertising clutter and the fact that many viewers tune out commercials, companies use product placement as a subtle way of advertising. The close-up of the product lasts only a few seconds, but is caught by most of the viewers. In the ESPN TV movie *The Junction Boys*, there were vintage scenes of Dr. Pepper soft drinks and General Motors automobiles. For Dr. Pepper, the movie had scenes of the soft drink as it appeared in the 1950s signage and billboards. General Motors used a vintage GM Suburban and Buick in the movie.[25]

Product placement: Sales promotion technique of placing branded goods or services in movies, on television shows, or in theatrical performances.

Another version of product placement is **branded media,** which is a movie or show that contains a brand name or logo with a storyline that intersects the brand's mission or current advertising campaign. An example is the movie *Castaway,* in which Tom Hanks plays a Federal Express executive trapped on a deserted island. The viewers receive the message about Federal Express but don't realize it. For FedEx, there is a strong, but subtle message that Fed Ex will get your package to its destination because in the film Tom Hanks keeps his sanity by knowing he will deliver the packages that have washed ashore.[26] In both branded media and product placement, the goal is to get the branded product before the audience in such a way that it is credible and does not appear to be a commercial.

Branded media: A movie or show that contains a brand name or logo with a storyline that intersects the brand's mission or current advertising campaign.

15-4 In-Store Promotions

Although shoppers may compile lists, written or mental, approximately 75 percent of all brand purchase decisions are made while in a retail store, and most shoppers walk out with twice the number of products they had planned on purchasing.[27] That means packaging, pricing, point-of-purchase displays (POP), and in-store promotions such as sampling and coupons are critically important in swaying consumers to purchase a particular brand. Advertising and sales promotions may get consumers to a retail store, but once in the store, shoppers add items to their shopping lists and switch brands because of a shelf display, a POP display, or product package.

Studies by the Point-of-Purchase Advertising Institute (POPAI) found that the cost of point-of-purchase displays per thousand impressions was about the same as for outdoor advertising, $6.50 per thousand. Compared to other media, POP displays are an excellent means of reaching consumers. As illustrated in Figure 15-16, the cost per 1,000 impressions for newspapers is $19.00; for television, $16.00; for magazines, $10.00; and for radio, $7.00. The difference was that POP displays generate anywhere from a 2 to 65 percent increase in sales, depending on the product category, the quality of the display, and the equity of the brand. The most effective POP displays are those that highlight a brand and a theme and

Figure 15-16
Cost Per 1,000 Impressions for Selected Media

Source: Michelle L. Kirsche, "POPAI Study Confirms Importance of POP Ads," *Drug Store News*, vol. 26 (October 11, 2004): 4–5.

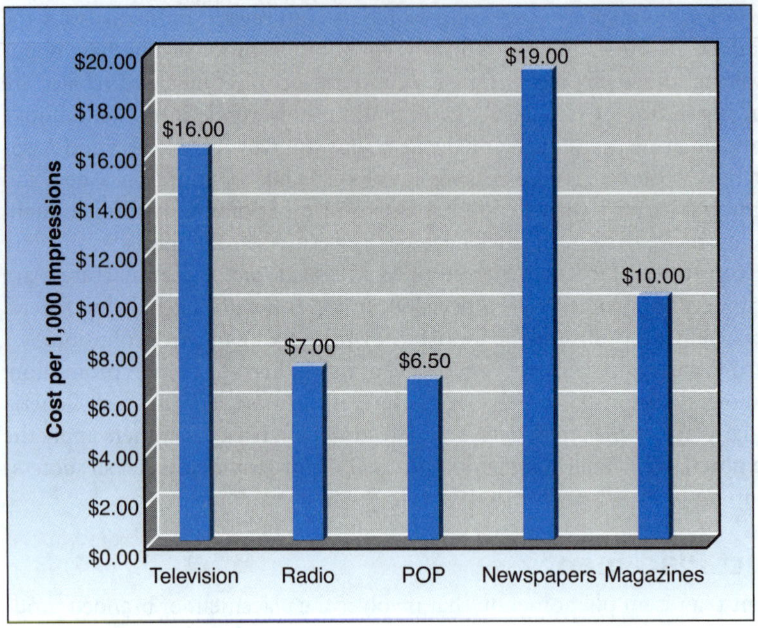

are consistent with the brand's IMC thrust (i.e., customers instantly recognize the POP display because they have seen advertising and other promotions with the same visuals, logo, graphics, or message).[28]

With so many purchase decisions made in the store, packaging becomes a critical piece of communication and is the last opportunity to convince a shopper to purchase a particular brand. The first task packaging has to accomplish is to attract the shopper's attention. That is not easy when a shopper strolling down an aisle scans more than 300-plus items per minute or one product per two-tenths of a second. The package must stand out and communicate the brand name and the most important assets quickly. Because consumers are walking down an aisle and scanning the shelves, brand equity and brand awareness become more important. Brands that consumers know are more likely to be seen and brands that are valued by customers have a better chance of being selected. Packaging can also be used to differentiate a product, as was the case with Heinz ketchup when the company introduced the EZ squirt containers.[29]

While packaging must attract attention, it must also protect the product and make it easy for retailers to stock. Odd-shaped packages may be attractive, but a hassle for retailers to place on shelves. It is also important to make sure the packaging stays fresh. Although it is important to maintain some consistency so shoppers can quickly recognize a brand, it is also important to change aspects of the package over time so that it will generate new interest. Just as ads can wear out over time, so can packaging design. See Marketing Illustration 15-3 for a discussion of packaging targeted to children and the four principles of successful package design.

15-5 Trade Promotions

Trade promotions are the expenditures or incentives used by manufacturers and other members of the marketing channel to help push their products through the channel. Trade promotions can be targeted toward retailers, distributors, wholesalers, brokers, or agents. The primary objective of trade promotions is to build relationships with other members of the marketing channel and to encourage them to sell the firm's products. When a retailer stocks a manufacturer's merchandise, consumers have the opportunity to buy the product. The same is true for distributors, wholesalers, brokers, or agents. It is a two-step process. The first step is convincing the channel member to stock the product; the second is to convince the channel member to push the product.

Marketing Illustration 15-3

Packaging for Kids

For children, packaging is an extremely important component of marketing. Studies have demonstrated that children can recognize brand logos before they can even read. Packaging professionals work diligently to find out what type of package attracts a child's attention and what type of package is needed to encourage repeat purchases. In this process, the package must also gain the trust of parents, especially the mother.

Researchers have discovered four important principles when it comes to packaging that resonates with children:

1. *Understand your market.* The package must be clear and targeted to the desired age group. For example, a package aimed at 3- to 10-year-old girls should use visuals and graphics that are warm and fuzzy, active and fun. However, for teenagers, the package needs to convey an image of cool, hip quality.
2. *Use their language.* Use and combine color, typography, symbols, shapes, and characters meaningful to the age and gender being targeted. For example, children respond to bold, bright, upbeat, friendly, warm, and fun hues such as red, blue, green, yellow, and orange.
3. *Capitalize on the power of the media.* If characters such as Bugs Bunny or Pokemon can be used, they provide an instant attraction. If not, using images, characters, and ideas from the media that kids see will help them identify with the package.
4. *Consider the package's nature.* For many products, the package is the product. For example, for cereals, children spend more time looking at the box than they do eating the cereal. A box that is fun and exciting makes the product inside fun and exciting.

Kraft Foods has embodied all of these principles with its Oscar Mayer Lunchables. The packages are brightly colored and attractive to kids. The clear plastic allows kids to see what is inside. The individual containers keep the different foods separate, yet allow the kids to assemble their own lunch. Lunch is fun, and packaging has increased that enjoyment!

Source: Allison Bardic, "Courting Kids," *The National Privisioner* (June 2003): 50–59; Paul R. Sensback, "Don't Kid Around with Kids' Packaging," *Marketing News*, vol. 34, no. 24 (November 20, 2000): 14.

Trade promotion expenditures have grown from $8 billion in 1980 to more than $546 billion today and account for 14 percent of sales. In 1990, trade promotions accounted for 35 percent of the marketing mix; today it accounts for 54 percent. While manufacturers and even retailers would like to see a reduction in trade promotion expenditures, it continues to grow as channel members continue to use trade promotions to push their products through to consumers.[30]

15-5a Goals of Trade Promotions

For manufacturers, the overarching goal of trade promotions is to increase sales of their brand. Retailers, however, seek to increase the market share of their stores and to boost sales of a product category. Retailers are less concerned with which brand sells the most as long as the product line sells. They will promote the brand that is demanded by their customers and which contributes the most to the retailers' gross profit. For example, it doesn't matter to the retailer which brand of athletic shoes sells as long as the retailer can sell the shoes to customers and they don't go to a competitor. To accomplish this, retailers will play one manufacturer against another to see which one will offer the best trade promotion and thus put them in a better situation to sell the merchandise to their customers.

From a manufacturer's perspective, trade promotion goals include:[31]

- Stimulating initial distribution
- Obtaining prime retail locations or shelf space
- Supporting established brands
- Countering competitive actions
- Increasing order size
- Building retail inventories

Figure 15-17
Manufacturers such as FHP rely on trade promotions to push their products through the distribution channel.

Source: Sample print advertisement courtesy of The Miles Agency and Alliance One Advertising, Inc.

- Reducing excess inventories of the manufacturer
- Enhancing channel relationships
- Enhancing the IMC program

Manufacturers such as FHP (see Figure 15-17) must use trade promotions to ensure that their products are in retail stores and are pushed through the distribution channel by the various channel members.

When a company introduces a new product, enters a new territory, or uses a new channel outlet, trade promotions are needed to push that product through the channel. Without any type of incentive, channel members are reluctant to add a new product. The same is true for obtaining prime locations and shelf space inside a retail store. A typical discount store, for instance, sells more than 40,000 products. Not all can have the best locations. In choosing how to display products and brands, retailers want to maximize their revenue and profits. For a manufacturer to obtain prime space or even more space than it already has requires some trade promotion incentives. This is even true for established brands. When a competitor offers a retail chain a trade incentive for extra shelf space, a manufacturer may have to match the competitor's offer just to maintain its current space. Keep in mind that the retailer's goals are sales and profits. If one manufacturer offers a discount on its brand and that brand sells as well as the competitor, then it makes sense for the retailer to offer more space to the discounted brand because the retailer will make more money.

Trade promotions are used to increase order sizes, to build retail inventories, and to reduce a manufacturer's excess inventory. By offering special trade deals, retailers or other channel members can be enticed to increase the size of their order. This serves two purposes. First, it encourages retailers to push the manufacturer's brand since they have a high inventory and, because of the trade incentive, they will probably earn more per item. Second, because of the higher retail inventory, it will reduce the amount of the product category retailers will order from the manufacturer's competitors.

Theoretically, trade promotions should enhance relationships with channel members and enhance the firm's IMC program. In reality, neither tends to happen. Retailers and other channel members tend to go with the vendor that offers the best trade promotions, and manufacturers and other channel members tend to use trade promotions to boost sales and prevent competitors from stealing market share, rather than use strategies related to a broader IMC effort. Much like sales promotions, trade promotions normally produce faster and more dramatic results. If sales are down, a trade promotion is often used to get back to the target level. If a competitor is encroaching on a firm's market share, trade promotion is used to counter the competitor's actions and to persuade channel members to stay loyal.

15-5b Types of Trade Promotions

Companies can use a variety of trade promotions, such as:[32]

- Trade allowances
- Trade contests
- Trade incentives
- Vendor support programs
- Trade shows

Choosing the correct trade promotion is an important decision. Each has its own set of advantages and disadvantages. The more a firm ties its trade promotion strategy to its IMC effort, the greater will be the impact of trade promotions, and in the long run, the less the firm will have to spend on trade promotions. Rather than use trade promotions as a reactive tool, if planned as part of the IMC, they can become a proactive method of pushing products through the channel.

Trade Allowances **Trade allowances** offer some type of financial incentive to channel members to motivate them to make a purchase. The most common trade allowances are off-invoice allowances, slotting fees, and exit fees. An **off-invoice allowance** is a financial discount or price-off on each case or item ordered. These types of trade allowances are common during holiday seasons and promotional seasons and are used to encourage retailers to purchase large quantities of various items. For example, a manufacturer may offer a 10 percent discount on fall apparel orders that are received by May 1st. In addition to a specified date, manufacturers may also place a minimum order size as a further condition. Off-invoice allowances are also used to encourage retailers to stock up on a particular brand and to meet a competitor's marketing actions. From the manufacturer's viewpoint, the problems with trade allowances are (1) channel members failing to pass along allowances to the consumers, (2) forward buying, and (3) diversions.

Trade allowan of financial inc channel meml them to make a purchase.

Off-invoice allowance: A financial discount or price-off on each case that a member of the distribution channel orders.

When manufacturers provide a trade allowance to a retailer, they would like to see that price reduction passed on to consumers so it will stimulate sales of their brand. More than 50 percent of the time, however, retailers do not pass the savings on to the consumer. Instead, they charge consumers the same price and pocket the allowance.[33] A tactic that retailers sometimes use to accomplish this is **forward buying,** which occurs when a retailer purchases excess inventory of a product while it is on-deal to be sold later when it is off-deal. During a "sale period," the savings will be passed on to the consumer, but when the sale is over, the retailer still has merchandise left that was purchased at a lower price, thus generating extra profits. The primary difficulty for the manufacturer is that new orders are then delayed because the retailer has excess inventory and does not need to buy for some time, creating an erratic production schedule for the manufacturer.

Forward buying: When a retailer purchases excess inventory of a product while it is on-deal to be sold later when it is off-deal.

When manufacturers offer deals that are not offered nationwide, retailers sometimes engage in a practice called diversion. **Diversion** occurs when a retailer purchases a product on-deal in one location and ships it to another location where it is off-deal. For example, a manufacturer may offer an off-invoice allowance of $5.00 per case for the product on the West Coast. A retailer like Wal-Mart or Target that normally purchases 50,000 cases a month may purchase an extra 50,000 or 100,000 cases on-deal and have them shipped to other parts of the country. This again allows the retailer to sell the merchandise at the regular retail price but earn higher margins because the merchandise was purchased at a lower price.

Diversion: A situation in which a retailer purchases a product on-deal in one location and ships it to another location, where it is off-deal.

Every year, thousands of new products are introduced, and retailers must make decisions about which items to stock and which not to stock (see Figure 15-18). The

Figure 15-18
To make room for new products, most retailers either have to reduce the shelf space allocated to current products or delete a current product from their inventory.

Source: Courtesy of Ukrop's Super Markets, Inc.

Slotting fees: Fees that retailers charge to stock manufacturers' brands.

typical supermarket, which carries 40,000 SKU (stock keeping units), must evaluate at least 10,000 new products per year. As a result, most retailers charge **slotting fees,** which are funds paid to retailers to stock new products. Retailers justify charging slotting fees because it costs them to add new products to their inventories and to stock the merchandise. If the product is not successful, the investment in initial inventory represents a loss, especially when the retailer has stocked a large number of stores. Also, adding a new product in the retail store means allocating shelf space to it. Since shelves are always filled with products, adding a new product means either getting rid of another brand or product or reducing the amount of shelf space allocated to other products. Regardless of which method is used, the retailer has both time and money invested when making the adjustment for the new product.

Slotting fees can cost a manufacturer as much as $25,000 per item per store, while some national chains charge slotting fees in the millions. Retailers believe that charging slotting fees reduces the number of new products being introduced, which in turn will reduce the number of new product failures. Although retailers are slow to admit it, another reason for supporting slotting fees is that this practice adds to their bottom line. Because most retailers have such low operating margins and markups, slotting fees provide additional funds to support retail operations. It has been estimated that 20 to 40 percent of the net profits earned by retailers come from slotting fees and other trade promotions.[34]

As would be expected, manufacturers oppose slotting fees and see them as a form of extortion. Because retailers control the channel and access to consumers, manufacturers have little choice but to pay the fees if they want their items on the store's shelves. Slotting fees virtually prohibit small manufacturers from getting their products on store shelves, since they cannot afford to pay millions of dollars to each large retail chain. Although some large retail operations have small vendor policies, getting merchandise on their shelves remains extremely challenging. If they are lucky enough to get shelf space, keeping it is another story. For example, one small manufacturer experienced a drop in sales from $500 per day to only $50 per day when its shelf space was reduced because a large, national manufacturer paid the store a large slotting fee to stock one of its new products.[35]

Exit fees: Monies paid to remove an item from a retailer's inventory.

Instead of slotting fees, some retailers charge **exit fees,** which are fees paid to remove an item from a retailer's inventory. This approach is often used when a manufacturer wants to introduce a new size of a product or a new version, such as a 3-liter bottle of Pepsi or the new Diet Vanilla Coke. Since Pepsi and Coke already have products on the retailer's shelves and have a strong brand name, adding a new version of their product is a much lower risk than adding an entirely new product. In these situations, retailers may ask for exit fees if the new version of the product fails or if one of the current versions must be removed from the inventory to make room for the new item.

Trade Contests In a trade contest, rewards are given to brokers, retail salespeople, retail stores, wholesalers, agents, or other channel members for achieving a specific goal. The goal can be achieving the highest sales within a specified time period, or it can be for all channel members to reach a minimum target level. For example, a hardware manufacturer can run a contest among its distributors and offer a grand prize to the distributor with the highest sales, with second- and third-place prizes for runners up. An alternative strategy is to offer prizes to all distributors who reach a certain level, perhaps 100,000 cases or $500,000 in sales. With this latter approach, the prize level is set at a point that only a small number of distributors can reach.

Spiff money: Monies or prizes awarded in trade contests.

Money or prizes awarded in trade contests are known as **spiff money.** The rewards can be cash or items such as luggage, a television, apparel, or a trip to an exotic place such as the Bahamas. Marketing Illustration 15-4 highlights trade contests sponsored by cruise lines. Contests can be held at any level of the distribution channel. Most contests are within an organization and not between rivals. The difficulty of contests at the retail level is that buyers in large organizations are often prohibited from participating in vendor contests because they create conflicts of interest and may unfairly influence the buyers' purchase

Marketing Illustration 15-4

Using Trade Contests to Stimulate Cruise Line Bookings

Demand for cruises has steadily increased for the past four years, creating intense competition among the various cruise lines. To attract guests, cruise lines have utilized a combination of advertising, consumer promotions, and trade promotions. For example, Carnival Cruise Lines launched a multimillion dollar advertising campaign titled "There Are a Million Ways to Have Fun." More than 6,500 television spots were purchased, supported by a strong print campaign. Royal Caribbean International developed an advertising campaign called "Get Out There" featuring people bundled up in heavy coats in cold climates, encouraging them to take a vacation to a warm climate.

In terms of consumer promotions, Silversea Cruise offered guests 50 percent off advanced bookings of their Mediterranean, northern Europe, and Far East cruises. Holland America offered guests free stateroom upgrades. Guests of the Norwegian Cruise Lines had opportunities to win numerous prizes. America West Steamboat offered free air fare between Seattle and Juneau for booking an Alaskan cruise.

Tied closely to the advertising campaigns and the consumer promotions were a number of trade promotions. Royal Caribbean International offered travel agents co-op versions of their TV and newspaper ads, as well as an email template. Norwegian Cruise Lines enrolled 5,500 agents into a "Sale of All Sails" promotion to win prizes based on their bookings. Each agent who booked with Holland America was enrolled in a trade contest with substantial prizes, including a free cruise with five veranda staterooms. Princess Cruise offered opportunities to win a West Coast cruise sail in a mini-suite. One such cruise would be given each day to an agent over a 90-day period.

Through the combination of advertising, consumer promotions, and trade promotions, advanced bookings of cruises for the summer of 2005 hit an all-time high! When travel agents had the opportunity to win prizes and cruises for themselves, their motivation to book cruises for specific airlines increased dramatically.

Source: "Cruise Selling Season Kicks Off with Agent Promotions and Optimism," *Travel Agent*, vol. 319 (January 3, 2005): 9.

decisions. Although the goal of the contest is to influence a buyer to make purchases, the buying organization does not want someone making purchases for 2,000 stores based on the buyer winning some sales contest.

Recently, the National Frozen & Refrigerated Foods Association ran an ice cream and frozen dessert display contest. The grand prize of $1,200 was awarded to Harris Teeter store No. 157 in Matthews, North Carolina, for a trio of extensive case-top displays running the length of the store aisle. Each display ran for two to three weeks and carried a different theme, such as a 1950s display with a carhop and Elvis. In addition to the grand prize, the association awarded 12 regional first- and second-place prizes worth $500 and $300, respectively, as well as 25 third-place prizes of $200. The ultimate goal of the contest was to boost sales of ice cream and frozen dessert items. During the 12 weeks of the contest, frozen dessert sales were up 7.2 percent, and ice cream sales were up 3.1 percent.[36]

Trade Incentives **Trade incentives** are similar to trade allowances; however, instead of price discounts, they involve the retailer performing some type of function in order to receive the allowance. The most common trade incentive is the CMA, or **cooperative merchandising agreement,** which is a formal agreement between the retailer and manufacturer to undertake a cooperative marketing effort. The agreement may involve advertisements produced by the retailer that features the manufacturer's brand. It may involve the retailer featuring the manufacturer's brand as a price leader in the store. It could involve the retailer emphasizing the manufacturer's brand in the display window, POP display, or special shelf display.

The advantage of the CMA agreement over trade allowances is that the retailer agrees to perform some function in exchange for the price discount. As would be expected, CMAs are popular with manufacturers because they are receiving some tangible benefit in exchange for the price discount. With a CMA, the manufacturer knows that either all of the

Trade incentives: Some type of financial incentive that involves the retailer performing some type of function in order to receive a trade allowance.

Cooperative merchandising agreement: A formal agreement between the retailer and manufacturer to undertake a cooperative marketing effort.

Figure 15-19
Because of CMAs, most grocery stores can keep at least one brand of soft drink on sale at all times.

Source: Courtesy of Ukrop's Super Markets, Inc.

price discount or a specified portion will be passed on to consumers. Perhaps the most important benefit, however, is that it allows the manufacturer to incorporate the CMA into the firm's IMC effort.

Calendar promotions: Promotional campaigns that retailers plan for their customers through manufacturer trade incentives.

A major benefit of a CMA for retailers is that it allows them to develop **calendar promotions,** which are promotional campaigns that retailers plan for their customers through manufacturer trade incentives. Through CMAs, retailers can schedule the time particular brands will be on sale. This allows them to alternate or rotate brands on sale such that, for their price-sensitive customers, at least one brand is always on sale (see Figure 15-19). While this may not be desirable from the manufacturer's viewpoint, it is for retailers. As stated earlier, retailers' interest is not in boosting the sales of a particular brand, but of the entire product category. By always having a brand on sale, retailers tend to sell more of that product category.

Instead of offering retailers price discounts, a manufacturer may offer a premium or bonus pack. For example, a manufacturer may offer a bonus pack of one case for each 20 that are purchased within the next 30 days. The bonus packs are free to the retailer and are awarded for either placing the order by a certain date, agreeing to a minimum-sized order, or both.

Often, manufacturers tie trade incentives to consumer sales promotions. For instance, Harley-Davidson motorcycles and Visa credit cards launched the Harley Dream Sweepstakes for consumers with a corresponding trade incentive program for retailers. At the consumer level, a new Big Twin motorcycle was awarded each week for 52 weeks. Holders of the Chrome Visa card received one entry into the sweepstakes for each dollar they spent but two entries per dollar for expenditures at participating Harley stores. To encourage Harley dealers to push the Chrome Visa credit card, Visa displays were placed on counters. For every customer who filled out the Chrome Visa card application and was approved by Visa, the dealers received a $20 credit toward Harley-Davidson merchandise for their store.[37]

Vendor Support Programs Manufacturers offer vendor support programs to support a retailer, wholesaler, or other channel member's programs. The most common vendor support program is the **cooperative advertising program,** in which the manufacturer agrees to reimburse retailers or other channel members for a portion of their advertising costs for featuring the manufacturer's brands in the ad. To receive the reimbursement, the retailer follows specific guidelines concerning the placement of the ad and its content. In almost all cases, no competing brands can appear in the ad, and in most cases, the manufacturer's brand must be prominently featured.

Cooperative advertising program: An arrangement whereby a manufacturer agrees to reimburse retailers or other channel members that feature the manufacturer's brands in the ad for a portion of their advertising costs.

One of the most well-known co-op advertising programs is by Intel Corporation. Almost everyone has seen the Intel symbol and logo in computer ads by various computer manufacturers. Intel spends about $750 million a year to promote the "Intel inside" theme. Intel offers a 6 percent co-op fund to all PC makers who place the Intel logo on their computers. Further, Intel allows a 4 percent fund accrual on the cost of print ads featuring the "Intel inside" logo and provides 2 percent for television and radio ads that include the Intel video or audio tag. This accrued co-op money can be used to pay up to 66 percent of the cost of a print advertisement and 50 percent of the cost of a broadcast ad. Intel cuts any payment in half for any advertisement that features a third-party logo of any type to ensure it is the only co-op brand featured in an ad. Approximately 1,400 PC makers worldwide, including the top 10 PC makers, take advantage of the Intel co-op advertising program.[38]

Co-op advertising programs benefit retailers because manufacturers pay a portion of the advertising costs. For most retailers, advertising national brands enhances the retailers' image and attracts customers to the stores. Manufacturers benefit because they gain additional advertising exposure at a reduced cost. More importantly, almost all co-op advertising programs are tied to sales, which means advertising costs are directly related to retail sales. Further, if retailers feature a particular manufacturer's brand in a store advertisement, they tend to encourage their in-store clerks and salespeople to push that particular brand. So the manufacturer not only benefits from the advertisement, but also from increased emphasis within the store.

Trade Shows In the business-to-business market, trade show expenditures are more than $12 billion a year, ranking third behind advertising and sales promotions. Manufacturers spend between $70,000 and $100,000 on airline tickets, hotels, entertainment costs, and booth fees to attend a major trade show. Retailers, however, pay only about $600 per person because their primary reason for attending is to see what products manufacturers are offering.[39]

Trade shows offer the opportunity for retailers and manufacturers to interact. Manufacturers are able to locate new potential customers as well as to develop stronger relationships with current customers. Occasionally, a deal may be consummated, but usually, it is a time for sharing information. Retailers have the opportunity to compare merchandise and develop contacts with multiple vendors within a very short time. Trade shows offer an excellent environment for buyers and sellers to meet.

While U.S. companies and attendees make few deals during trade shows, it is a different situation with international customers. First, international attendees tend to be senior executives with the power to make purchase decisions, not the salespeople and purchasing agents who normally attend from U.S. companies. Second, international attendees spend more time at each vendor's booth and gather more information. Third, many international attendees want to consummate deals or at least discuss purchase arrangements.[40]

Trade promotions are critical elements of marketing, especially within the distribution channel. Table 15-2 reviews all of the various forms of trade promotions.

TABLE 15-2

Forms of Trade Promotions

Trade Promotion Category	Type of Trade Promotion	Definition
Trade allowance (offer some type of financial incentive to channel members to motivate them to make a purchase)	Off-invoice allowance	A financial discount or price-off on each case ordered
	Slotting fees	Monies paid to retailers by manufacturers to stock new products in the retail store
	Exit fees	Monies paid to remove an item from a retailer's inventory
Trade contest		Rewards given to brokers, retail salespeople, retail stores, wholesalers, agents, or other channel members for achieving a specific goal
Trade incentives (involve the retailer performing some type of function in order to receive the allowance)	Cooperative merchandising agreement	A formal agreement between the retailer and manufacturer to undertake a cooperative marketing effort
Vendor support programs (offered by manufacturers to support a retailer, wholesaler, or other channel member's programs)	Cooperative advertising program	The manufacturer agrees to reimburse retailers or other channel members for a portion of their advertising costs for featuring the manufacturer's brands in the ad
	Trade shows	Shows where manufacturers can display products and meet buyers

Summary

1. *Discuss the reasons for a shift in marketing expenditures to promotions.* First, promotions normally have an immediate impact on sales, whereas advertising takes a longer period of time to produce an impact. Second, because of increased brand proliferation and brand parity, consumers and businesses have more choices today and see very little difference among firms and among various brands. Third, there is consumer acceptance of promotions, and in some instances, there is a demand for special deals before purchases will be made. Fourth, there is a decline in the impact of advertising. With remote controls and VCRs, consumers are zapping out many commercials, and those they do watch, view, or hear are quickly forgotten due to the high number of commercials they are exposed to each day.

2. *Identify the various forms of sales promotions.* Firms can use 10 different types of sales promotions. They include coupons, premiums, contests and sweepstakes, bonus packs, tie-ins, frequency programs, sampling, price-offs, refunds and rebates, and product placement.

3. *Identify the various types of coupons as well as distribution methods.* The types of coupons are instant redemption coupons, bounce-back coupons, scanner-delivered coupons, cross-ruffing coupons, response-offer coupons, and e-coupons. Distribution methods include print media; freestanding inserts (FSI); direct mail; on-, in-, or near-package; and other methods, such as in-store, fax, Internet, scanner-delivered, and sampling. The most common is FSI, which makes up 80 percent of all coupons.

4. *Explain the importance of in-store promotions in purchasing behavior.* Shoppers make approximately 75 percent of all brand purchase decisions while in a retail store, and most shoppers walk out with twice the number of products they had planned on purchasing. This means that packaging, pricing, point-of-purchase (POP) displays, and in-store promotions such as sampling and coupons are critically important in swaying consumers to purchase a particular brand.

5. *Discuss the goals of trade promotions.* For manufacturers, the overarching goal of trade promotions is to increase sales of their

brand. Retailers, however, seek to increase the market share of their stores and to boost sales of a product category. Retailers are less concerned with which brand sells the most as long as the product line sells. More specific goals of trade promotions include (1) stimulating initial distribution, (2) obtaining prime retail locations or shelf space, (3) supporting established brands, (4) countering competitive actions, (5) increasing order size, (6) building retail inventories, (7) reducing excess inventories of the manufacturer, (8) enhancing channel relationships, and (9) enhancing the IMC program.

6. *Identify the various types of trade promotions.* Companies have a variety of trade promotions that can be used, such as (1) trade allowances, (2) trade contests, (3) trade incentives, (4) vendor support programs, and (5) trade shows. Choosing the correct trade promotion is an important decision. The more a firm ties its trade promotion strategy to its IMC effort, the greater will be the impact of trade promotions, and in the long run, the less the firm will have to spend on trade promotions. Rather than use trade promotions as a reactive tool, if planned as part of the IMC, they can become a proactive method of pushing products through the channel.

7. *Discuss the issue of slotting fees.* Because retailers must make decisions about which items to stock and which not to stock, most retailers charge a slotting fee for new products. Slotting fees are funds paid to retailers to stock new products. Retailers justify charging slotting fees because it costs them to add new products to their inventories and to stock the merchandise. If the product is not successful, the investment in initial inventory represents a loss, especially when the retailer has stocked a large number of stores. Also, adding a new product in the retail store means allocating shelf space to it. Because shelves are always filled with products, adding a new product means either deleting another brand or product or reducing the amount of shelf space allocated to other products. Slotting fees can cost a manufacturer as much as $25,000 per item per store, with some national chains charging slotting fees in the millions. Retailers believe that, by charging slotting fees, they reduce the number of new products being introduced, which in turn reduces the number of new product failures. As would be expected, manufacturers oppose slotting fees and see them as a form of extortion. Since retailers control the channel and access to consumers, manufacturers have little choice but to pay the fees if they want their items on the store's shelves.

Key Terms

bonus packs (p. 461)
bounce-back coupons (p. 456)
branded media (p. 467)
calendar promotions (p. 474)
contests and sweepstakes (p. 460)
cooperative advertising program (p. 475)
cooperative merchandising agreement (p. 473)
coupons (p. 454)
cross-ruffing coupon (p. 456)
diversion (p. 471)
e-coupons (p. 457)
exit fees (p. 472)
forward buying (p. 471)
freestanding inserts (FSI) (p. 455)
frequency programs (p. 463)
instant redemption coupon (p. 456)
intercompany tie-in (p. 462)
intracompany tie-in (p. 461)
off-invoice allowance (p. 471)
overlay (p. 459)
premiums (p. 458)
price-offs (p. 465)
product placement (p. 467)
rebates and refunds (p. 466)
response-offer coupons (p. 457)
sampling (p. 464)
scanner-delivered coupons (p. 456)
slotting fees (p. 472)
spiff money (p. 472)
tie-ins (p. 461)
trade allowances (p. 471)
trade incentives (p. 473)

Discussion Questions

1. Read the chapter-opening vignette about soap operas and the use of promotions. Do you think this strategy will be successful? Why are the Nielsen ratings down for soaps? What can the producers do to boost ratings? What types of promotions should they use?
2. From the list of sales promotions provided in Section 15-3, discuss each sales promotion as it relates to your personal purchase behavior. Discuss things such as frequency of use, your attitude toward each, how these promotions impact your purchase behavior, and what types of design have an impact on you.
3. Pick one of the sales promotions identified in Section 15-3 that interests you. Use the Internet and an article database to locate more information about it. Write a summary of what you learn. How is it being used and what are the most successful strategies?
4. Pick one of the following types of products. Discuss how each of the sales promotions listed in Figure 15-3 could be used. Which ones would be most effective? Which ones would be least effective? Why?
   a. Pizza
   b. Hiking shoes
   c. Dental services
   d. Janitorial services for a business
   e. Video game
5. Keep a record of every sales promotion you receive in the mail, through email, see on the Internet or television, and hear on the radio. Put this data into a table for easy record keeping. Which promotions were the most prominent? Which were the least used? Discuss your impressions of the effectiveness of the promotions you were exposed to during the week.

6. The next time you are in a store, make a note of all of the promotions you see, especially point-of-purchase displays. Write a short report detailing the information. What promotions were the most effective? Why? Which promotions were not effective? Why?
7. In Section 15-4, it was stated that 75 percent of all product and brand purchases are not planned. What is your evaluation of this statistic? Talk to at least five other people about how closely they follow a shopping list and how many things they purchase that were not planned.
8. Read Marketing Illustration 15-4. Next time you go shopping, pay close attention to packaging. Did you see any packaging that stood out? Why did it stand out? Pick three items that you recently purchased. Discuss the packaging and what impact the package had on your purchase decision. What packages did you see that were clearly aimed for children?
9. Pick one of the trade promotions listed in Section 15-5b. Find additional articles and information about the trade promotion selected. Write a short report of your findings.
10. Read Marketing Illustration 15-4 about trade contests for travel agents who book cruises. Do you think this is a good approach? How would it impact an agent's behavior? Is it fair to consumers who are looking for a cruise? Would an agent push a particular cruise so he or she could enter a trade contest rather than find a cruise that is best for the consumer?

Review Questions

True or False

1. About 86 percent of all coupons are distributed via freestanding inserts (FSI).
2. Coupons placed inside packages so that customers cannot redeem them at the time of the original purchase are called cross-ruffing coupons.
3. Response-offer coupons are issued following a request by a consumer.
4. E-coupon usage is still in its infancy, but preliminary data are encouraging for companies wanting to use the Internet to distribute coupons.
5. The difference between contests and sweepstakes is that, in sweepstakes, participants may be required to perform an activity or to make a purchase to be eligible to win, whereas in a contest, participants do not need to make a purchase and the winners are determined by a random drawing in which every entrant has an equal chance of being selected.
6. Four bars of soap may be packaged together and sold for the price of three individual packages in a bonus pack.
7. The St. Louis Cardinals baseball team providing a 50 percent off coupon to the nearby Gateway Arch with the purchase of an adult ticket to a Cardinals game is known as an intracompany tie-in.
8. Frequency programs are sales promotions aimed at current customers that are designed to build repeat purchase behavior and brand loyalty by rewarding customers for their patronage.

Multiple Choice

9. A reduction in the listed retail price of a product used to attract consumers, to reduce purchase risk, and to stimulate demand is known as a
   a. rebate.
   b. price-off.
   c. promotional tie-in.
   d. none of the above
10. A movie or show that contains a brand name or logo with a storyline that intersects the brand's mission or current advertising campaign is known as
   a. trailer media.
   b. market media.
   c. cooperative media.
   d. branded media.
11. Expenditures or incentives used by manufacturers and other members of the marketing channel to help push their products through the channel are known as
   a. market promotions.
   b. rebate promotions.
   c. cooperative promotions.
   d. trade promotions.

Notes

1. David Finnigan, "Soap Sales Heat Up," *Brandweek*, vol. 43, no. 30 (August 19, 2002): 38–42; John Consoli, "What Women Don't Want? Soap Operas." *Adweek*, vol. 45 (November 1, 2004): 6.
2. "Upward Bound," *Promo*, vol. 17 (April 2004): AR3–AR5.
3. Jakki J. Mohr and George S. Low, "Escaping the Catch-22 of Trade Promotion Spending," *Marketing Management*, vol. 2 (1993): 30–39.
4. "Do Coupons Make Cents?" *Incentive*, vol. 177 (May 2003): 19.
5. Wayne Mouland, "Grocery Shoppers Still Keen on Coupons," *Marketing Magazine*, vol. 106 (June 4, 2001): 37.
6. "Do Coupons Make Cents?" *Incentive*, vol. 177 (May 2003): 19.
7. Kathleen M. Joyce, "Fast Clip," *www.PromoMagazine* (April 2003): 35, 43–44.
8. William C. LaFief and Brian T. Engelland, "The Effects of Optimal Stimulation Level of Value Consciousness on Consumer Use of Coupons and Contests," *Midwest Marketing Association 1995 Proceedings*, 83–87.
9. Joseph Gatti, "Coupon Distribution Up, But Web Dispersal Still Scanty," *Direct Marketing* (October 1, 2003): 1–2.
10. "Net Coupons Deliver High Redemption Rate," *Frozen Food Age*, vol. 47, issue 3 (October 1998): 63; "Replace Coupon Clipping with Clicking," *Chain Store Age*, vol. 74, issue 12 (December 1998): 226.
11. LaFief and Engelland, "The Effects of Optimal Stimulation Level of Value Consciousness on Consumer Use of Coupons and Contests," 83–87.
12. Libby Estell, "Summer Nights," *Incentive*, vol. 176, no. 8 (August 2002): 21.
13. Jean Halliday, "Saab Launches 9-3 Online Sweepstakes," *Automotive News*, vol. 77, no. 6009 (October 28, 2002): 22.

14. Larry J. Seibert, "What Consumers Think About Bonus Pack Sales Promotions," *Marketing News,* vol. 31, no. 4 (February 7, 1997): 9.
15. Sandra Dolbow, "Jeep Drives Penney's 100th," *Brandweek,* vol. 43, no. 23 (June 10, 2002): 12.
16. David Kaplan, "Revlon, 007 Hook Up," *Adweek Eastern Edition,* vol. 43, no. 41 (October 14, 2002): 4.
17. Patricia J. Daughtery, Richard J. Fox, and Frederick J. Stephenson, "Frequency Marketing Programs: A Clarification with Strategic Marketing Implications," *Journal of Promotional Management,* vol. 2, no. 1 (1993): 5–26.
18. Ibid.
19. Libby Estell, "Loyalty Lessons," *Incentive,* vol. 176, no. 11 (November 2002): 38–42.
20. Ibid.
21. Kenneth Hein, "Diet Vanilla Coke Debut Set to Pour, Backed by Radio, Outdoor, Sampling," *Brandweek,* vol. 43, no. 37 (October 14, 2002): 4.
22. "Read 'em and Reap," *Marketing News,* vol. 36, no. 18 (September 2, 2002): 3.
23. Joe Kohn, "Studies: Rebates Are Strong Poison," *Automotive News,* vol. 77, no. 6000 (September 2, 2002): 6.
24. David Sedgwick and Mary Connelly, "GM Sees Dollars in Its Mountain of Buyer Data," *Automotive News,* vol. 73 (May 17, 1999): 3–4.
25. Wayne Friedman, Hillary Chura, Jean Halliday, and David Goetzel, "ESPN, Dr. Pepper, GM in Timely Deal," *Advertising Age,* vol. 73, no. 43 (October 28, 2002): 43.
26. Maxine Retsky, "Story Lines Have to Follow Marketing's Laws," *Marketing News,* vol. 36, no. 21 (October 14, 2002): 12.
27. Julie-Anne O'Hagan, "Measurement: The Moment of Truth," *B&T Weekly,* vol. 54 (September 3, 2004): 23.
28. "POP Impact Quantified," *Frozen Food Age,* vol. 50, no. 2 (September 2001): 10; Michelle L. Kirsche, "POPAI Study Confirms Importance of POP Ads," *Drug Store News,* vol. 26 (October 11, 2004): 4–5.
29. Russ Napolitano, "Wrap Products Up in Creativity, Equity," *Marketing News,* vol. 36, no. 23 (November 11, 2002): 16.
30. "Upward Bound," *Promo,* vol. 17 (April 2004): AR3–AR5; Al Urbanski, "Trade Promo Lowdown," *Progressive Grocer,* vol. 82 (March 1, 2003): 45–46.
31. Kenneth E. Clow and Donald Baack, *Integrated Advertising, Promotion, & Marketing Communications* (Upper Saddle River, NJ: Prentice-Hall, 2002): 396–399.
32. Ibid., 378.
33. Philip Zerillo and Dawn Iacobucci, "Trade Promotions: A Call for a More Rational Approach," *Business Horizons,* vol. 38, no. 4 (July/August 1995): 69–76.
34. Jack J. Kasulis, "Managing Trade Promotions in the Context of Market Power," *Journal of the Academy of Marketing Science,* vol. 27, no. 3 (Summer 1999): 320–332.
35. Martin Hoover, "Supermarket 'Slotting' Leaves Small Firms Out," *Business Courier: Serving the Cincinnati-Northern Kentucky Region,* vol. 16, no. 25 (October 8, 1999): 3–4.
36. David Wellman, "Displays Power Adult Frozen Novelty Sales," *Frozen Food Age,* vol. 51, no. 4 (November 2002): 1–2.
37. Laurie Watanabe, "Duel at Dawn," *Dealer News,* vol. 33, no. 12 (November 1997): 59.
38. Bradley Johnson, "IBM Moves Back to Intel Co-op Deal," *Advertising Age,* vol. 68, no. 10 (March 10, 1997): 4.
39. Susan Greco, "Forgo the Trade Shows?" *Inc.,* vol. 23, no. 1 (January 2001): 104; Laurie Freeman, "B-to-B Marketing Communications Budgets Grow 14.5 Percent as Overall Spending Reaches $73 Billion," *Advertising Age's Business Marketing,* vol. 84, no. 5 (May 1999): S3–4.
40. Matthew Flamm, "Alien Influences," *Crain's New York Business,* vol. 15, no. 46 (November 15, 1999): 35–36.

Case 15-1 Trio City Plumbers, Inc.

In 1957, Ray and Ronald Newcombe founded Trio City Plumbers, Inc. Their primary focus was new construction until the 1970s, when they added the residential service operation. In 1982, they opened a retail store that sold plumbing parts and fixtures, primarily rare and hard-to-find plumbing repair parts that hardware stores and retailers like Home Depot and Lowe's did not carry. The store also carried the products used in the residential business. In 1986, Trio City Plumbers added the commercial service operation. Total revenue during this past year was $1.13 million. Figure 15-20 shows the percentage breakdown of Trio City's revenue.

Typical residential and commercial services provided by Trio City include:

- Repairs and remodeling of residential, commercial, and industrial plumbing
- Sewer and drain cleaning, repair, and replacement
- Pipeline locating and video inspection of interior pipes
- Water line replacement
- Floor furnace repair and replacement

At the retail level, Trio City sells drain products; toilet repair parts; bathtub faucets; faucet stems; kitchen faucets; lavatory faucets; and used, surplus, and overstocked plumbing fixtures. Trio City also purchases damaged merchandise, overstocks, and surplus plumbing parts and fixtures from local retailers to be resold.

In April, Trio City began a new pricing policy called "Flat Rate" pricing. In the past, service calls cost $49 per hour plus materials and labor. In most cases, customers had no idea how much the job would cost until it was finished and the plumber tallied the bill. With flat rate pricing, plumbers would diagnose the problem and quote a flat rate for the job inclusive of parts and labor. This policy is similar to what garages do when fixing someone's car when they provide a written estimate in advance of the work.

Trio City has used coupons in the past, published in the local newspaper, but that is the only sales promotion it has ever used. The coupon produced only a slight increase in sales, and the management at Trio City felt it was not worth the investment. They also know that whatever promotions are used need to fit well with all of the pieces of the business.

Questions

1. What type of sales promotion would you recommend for the residential service business? Why?
2. What type of sales promotion would you recommend for the commercial service business that would be compatible with the residential promotions? Why?
3. What type of sales promotion would you recommend for the retail store that would match with the commercial and residential service operation? Why?
4. How important are in-store promotions for the retail side of Trio City?
5. Develop a comprehensive promotion plan for Trio City that includes all elements of the business. How would you make sure it is integrated with the advertising program?

Figure 15-20
Breakdown of Trio City Plumbing, Inc.'s Revenue

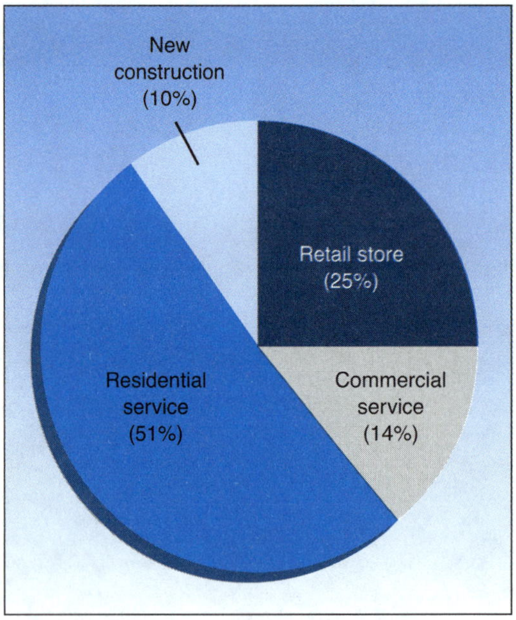

Case 15-2 Yonex

Yonex, originally Yoneyama Company, Ltd., was founded in Japan in 1946 by Minoru Yoneyama as a manufacturer of wooden floats for fishing nets. The business thrived until the introduction of plastic floats forced it out of business. At that time, Minoru Yoneyama vowed that his company would never again fail because it was left behind technologically.

Using his knowledge of wood crafting, the Yoneyama Company started building badminton racquets in 1957 under various brand names. In 1961, the first "Yoneyama" brand badminton racquet was produced, and two years later, Yoneyama Trading, Ltd. was established in Tokyo to distribute the Yoneyama racquets internationally.

The company's devotion to innovation attracted attention in 1969 when it introduced the first aluminum badminton racquet, the #700. Today, the Yonex badminton racquets are used by 80 percent of professional badminton players, and Yonex is the world's leading distributor of badminton racquets. Spurred by the success of its badminton racquets, Yoneyama entered the tennis racquet market in 1971. By 1973, the company's new logo "YY" and blue and green color combinations were common sights on both badminton courts as well as tennis courts. In 1978, Yoneyama introduced the first ultra-light badminton racquet. Then in 1980, it introduced the world's first "isometric" tennis racquet and the super-light R-7. Very quickly, Yoneyama became a powerful force in the tennis racquet market.

To more effectively expand internationally, Yonex Corporation established subsidiaries in the United States, the United Kingdom, Germany, Canada, Taiwan, and Hong Kong. Yonex continues to produce the most technologically advanced tennis and badminton racquets, which are used by both amateur and professional players. The company has also moved into producing technologically advanced golf clubs and equipment.

To push the sale of its tennis racquets, Yonex signed Anna Kournikova to a 10-year deal worth between $6 and $10 million. With her signing, Yonex is ready to expand its market share in the tennis racquet market. Its goal is to be the market leader. It recognizes that coupons are not an effective method to promote its tennis racquet because the message conveyed to consumers would conflict with its image as a technological leader. In addition to reaching adults, Yonex would like to focus on the youth market because, if it can win them over, it will have them for a lifetime. With recent ads by the tennis industry targeting young people appearing on the Cartoon Network, TBS, and TNT, Yonex believes that now is the time to develop a major offensive. With Kournikova signed and advertising in place, the only piece of the puzzle left is the sales and trade promotions that should be used.

Questions

1. Discuss each of the sales promotion options listed in Section 15-3 in terms of its effectiveness for Yonex tennis racquets, considering the company's position in the market and the current image that it wants to maintain.
2. What trade promotions should Yonex use to encourage sporting goods stores to stock its tennis racquets and to push them over other brands?
3. What sales promotional mix would you recommend for Yonex? Justify your position and discuss how you would use each sales promotional element you picked.

Sources: Mike Troy, "Tennis Industry Courts Kids to Push Entry-less Sales at Mass," *Discount Store News* vol. 36, no. 6 (March 17, 1997), 19; Terry Lefton, "Kournikova's Big Racket; Wizards Meet the MLB," *Brandweek,* vol. 41, no. 5 (January 31, 2000): 18; Yonex homepage (www.yonex.com, January 19, 2003).

Personal Selling, Databases, and Direct Marketing

16

CHAPTER
OBJECTIVES

1. Explain the different types of personal selling.
2. Discuss the various buyer-seller relationships.
3. Identify the steps in the selling process and briefly describe each step.
4. Explain the concepts of data warehousing and database management.
5. Identify the steps in developing a customer relationship management program.
6. Explain the concept of direct marketing and list the various methods of direct marketing.

CHAPTER
OUTLINE

Instead of using a real estate agent, Jay and Marcie decided to explore some new houses on their own. Using the Yellow Pages, real estate ads in the newspaper, and the Internet, they located three new construction communities that offered new homes for sale and encouraged new homebuyers to see what they had to offer.

Arriving at the first appointment, Jay and Marcie were shown a photo album of new homes that had just been built. Each was described in detail in terms of construction. The salesperson took great pride and stated several times that the company offered the best quality built homes in the area. Before taking them on a tour of three new homes in the gated community (see Figure 16-1) that were almost ready for the market, the salesperson pointed to plaques that hung on the wall, framing awards the company had recently won for innovative home design. As Jay and Marcie toured the three new homes on display, they were impressed. The homes were beautiful. The price was a little higher than they wanted to pay for a home, but as the salesperson pointed out the quality construction, he reassured them that the higher cost was a small price to pay for the quality that they would be receiving (see Figure 16-2). Thanking the salesperson for his time, Jay and Marcie drove to their next appointment.

Bringing the couple into her office, the next salesperson began asking Jay and Marcie questions about what they wanted in a house. As they talked, she took notes. Several times, she asked for clarification and for additional information. After 10 minutes of talking to them, she brought out a large book with photos of new homes that were being built or had been built. Turning the pages, she commented, "We have only two homes that I believe meet your requirements and fit the description of the type of house you are looking for. One is almost finished, the other is only about half done. Would you like to see them?" Excitedly, Jay and Marcie went with the agent to see the two homes. While probably not as nice as the homes they had toured earlier, both seemed to fit perfectly with what they wanted.

Since they had made a third appointment, Jay and Marcie felt obligated to keep the last one, although they doubted it could beat what they had just seen. Afraid they'd be late for the appointment, they skipped stopping for food, even though they were hungry. When they arrived, the office was locked, and the only people around were some construction workers working on one of the houses. The couple waited for almost 40 minutes before the

Figure 16-1
Gated communities are increasingly popular because they provide safety as well as a strong sense of community.

Figure 16-2
New homes are aggressively marketed for this and many other similar neighborhoods.

salesperson arrived. He never apologized for being late, other than making a comment that it had been a terrible day and that nothing seemed to be going right.

When asked about seeing new homes, the salesperson replied that the only ones available right now were about $50,000 above what the couple wanted to pay. He added, "The ones I told you about on the phone were sold a couple of months ago, but I figured you would like these better anyway. Let me show them to you." Without even asking for a response, he motioned for the couple to follow him for what they thought was a short distance. It turned out to be almost a two-block walk to the two new houses. Upon arriving, he discovered he had forgotten the keys. Shrugging his shoulders, he said, "I'll be right back. Just wait here!"

As he walked away, Jay looked over at Marcie, "I wonder how many homes he sells." Marcie shook her head as she replied, "What a contrast in salespeople!"

16-1 Chapter Overview

As the chapter-opening vignette relates, salespeople are essential in many transactions, especially for high-cost items like real estate. But they are also important when purchasing items at retail stores: They help customers locate merchandise, answer questions, and check out the products. Sales clerks at some retailers have to be hunted down, and they know very little about the merchandise being sold, while at other stores, the salespeople greet you as you walk in and are eager to assist you in finding just the right item.

Retail sales, however, are only part of the personal selling component of integrated marketing communications (IMC). Business-to-business sales make up a significant component of personal selling. While consumer and retail sales are discussed in this chapter, the primary focus of the personal selling component of the chapter is on business-to-business selling. Section 16-2 discusses personal selling in terms of the various types of personal selling, buyer-seller relationships, and the selling process. Section 16-3 examines the role of databases in the IMC and how they are used to support personal selling, customer service, and direct marketing. The concepts of data warehousing and data mining are presented, along with a recent database customer service program called customer relationship management. Because of advances in technology, databases have become a central component of business operations. The last section of the chapter, Section 16-4, discusses direct marketing. Firms have various methods of direct marketing that include mail, email, catalogs, the Internet, and the telephone.

Figure 16-3
An order taker in this retailing operation processes routine orders from customers.

16-2 Personal Selling

Personal selling is an important component of integrated marketing communications, especially for business-to-business transactions. Personal selling occurs in many situations ranging from the sales clerk at a local discount store helping a customer locate a particular item to the field salesperson for Boeing talking to airline companies, the Pentagon, or governments of other nations about purchasing airplanes. Personal selling offers one major advantage not found in the other forms of marketing: two-way communication. The seller is able to interact with the buyer to provide relevant information and to answer any questions or objections the buyer may raise.

Order takers: Salespeople who process routine orders from customers.

Order getters: Salespeople who actively generate potential leads and persuade customers to make a purchase.

Support personnel: Individuals who directly support or assist in the selling function in some manner, but do not process orders or directly solicit orders.

16-2a Types of Personal Selling

Personal selling staff can be classified into three broad categories: order takers, order getters, and support personnel. **Order takers** process routine orders from customers (see Figure 16-3), while **order getters** actively generate potential leads and persuade customers to make a purchase. **Support personnel** are individuals who directly support or assist in the selling function in some manner, but do not process orders or directly solicit orders.

Order takers can be seen in a variety of selling roles. In retailing, they operate the cash register, stock shelves, and answer basic questions from customers. Their role is to assist the customer and to be available when the customer is ready to make the purchase. In manufacturing, an order taker can be in the corporate office taking customer orders by telephone, fax, email, or the Internet. For a distributor, an order taker may go to retail stores and stock the shelves with the distributor's merchandise. In all of these cases, the order taker does not take an active role in seeking customers or persuading them to make a purchase. The merchandise is presold or selected by the customer. The order taker's task is to assist in completing the transaction.

Order getters, however, actively seek new customers and work to persuade customers to purchase more. In retail, a salesperson at a car dealer or a furniture store may be an order getter if part of his or her task is to convince customers to make a purchase. In retail situations in which salespeople are paid a commission, they are likely to be order getters because the more customers they can convince to make a purchase, the more the salespeople can earn. These salespeople are more likely to be involved in **cross-selling,** which involves the marketing of additional items with the purchase of a particular good or service. A salesperson at a clothing store may encourage a customer purchasing a new pair of pants to purchase a sweater to match it. A bank may encourage a customer opening a checking account to also open a safety deposit box or to apply for a home equity loan.

Cross-selling: The marketing of additional items with the purchase of a particular good or service.

Most order getters work in the business-to-business area as field salespeople. A **field salesperson** is involved in going to a potential customer's place of business to solicit business. Field salespeople can be used in the consumer market, but this is limited primarily to insurance, Amway, and Avon, all of which use a direct-marketing approach. Using salespeople in the business-to-business market is feasible because there are fewer buyers and each buyer tends to make a large volume purchase. Figure 16-4 highlights the primary differences between order takers and order getters.

Field salesperson: A salesperson who is involved in going to a potential customer's place of business to solicit accounts.

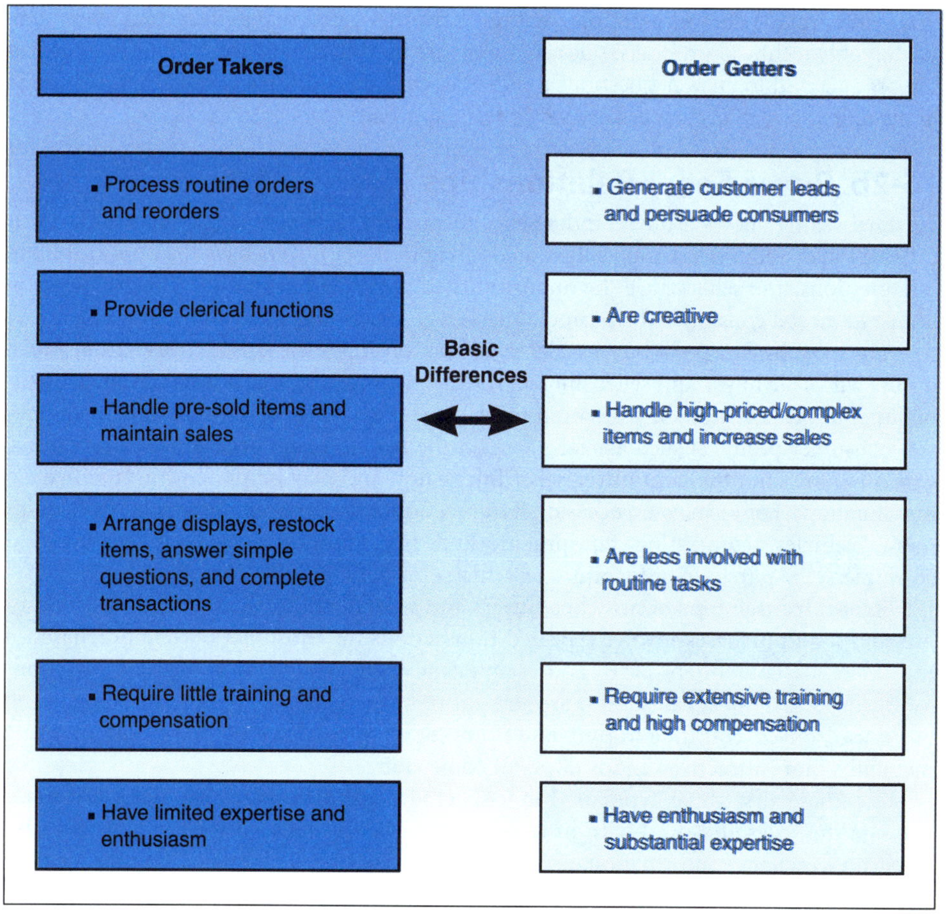

Figure 16-4
Contrasting Order Takers and Order Getters

Figure 16-5
FHP uses a variety of salespeople to push sinks through the channel. The company uses field salespeople to call on retail stores and both outbound and inbound telemarketers to solicit orders as well as to take orders.

Source: Sample print advertisement courtesy of The Miles Agency and Alliance One Advertising, Inc.

Outbound telemarketing: The process through which an order-getter salesperson calls prospects and attempts to persuade them to make a purchase.

Inbound telemarketing: The process through which an order-taker salesperson handles incoming calls from customers and prospects.

Missionary salesperson: A sales support person whose task is to provide information about a good or service.

Buyer-seller dyad: Two-way communication between a buyer and a seller.

Single transaction: Buyer and seller interacting for the purpose of a single transaction.

Occasional transactions: Transactions whereby buyer and seller interact infrequently in the process of making the transaction.

Repeat transactions: Buyer and seller interacting over multiple transactions.

Many companies are now using telemarketing to sell their products. If the company is calling customers and attempting to persuade them to purchase the product, this is called **outbound telemarketing** and is done by an order getter. If the company is manning telephones that customers call with orders, then it is **inbound telemarketing** and is handled by order takers. Both are used in the business-to-business market, as well as in the consumer market (see Figure 16-5).

The last category of salespeople is the support personnel. The most common support individual is the **missionary salesperson,** whose task is to provide information about a good or service. Pharmaceutical companies use missionary salespersons to distribute new drugs and provide doctors with information. The order getter makes the actual sales pitch. With highly technical products, sales engineers are used to discuss the technical aspects of the product and to answer questions a potential customer may have. Usually, this is done in conjunction with a salesperson using a team approach.

16-2b Buyer-Seller Relationships

Personal selling allows a buyer and a seller to interact. This two-way communication is called a **buyer-seller dyad** and is illustrated in Figure 16-6. Buyers have the opportunity to ask questions, and sellers have the opportunity to provide information. If the salesperson is able to meet a consumer (or business) need, a transaction is likely to occur.

The most basic type of buyer-seller dyad relationship is the **single transaction,** which occurs when the buyer and seller interact for the purpose of a single transaction. This situation may occur in new-buy situations in the business-to-business market and for expensive consumer products such as real estate. At the next level are **occasional transactions,** which require an infrequent buyer-seller interaction and may be present in modified re-buy situations. For businesses, occasional transactions may occur in the purchase of equipment, vehicles, computing equipment, and telecommunications equipment. For consumers, the purchase of furniture or vehicles may fall into this category.

Repeat transactions occur when buyers and sellers interact on a regular basis. Gasoline and food purchases involve repeated transactions for consumers, while purchases of raw materials, component parts, and maintenance supplies are often repeat transactions for businesses. In most cases, these are straight re-buy situations. For both consumers and businesses, buyers continue to purchase from the vendor as long as their needs are being met and a more attractive vendor does not come along.

For these first three types of buyer-seller dyad situations, transactions are made between the seller and dyad with little or no relationship between the two parties. They meet, they exchange information, and a transaction occurs. There is no commitment or loyalty from either side toward the other party. To ensure a greater commitment from buy-

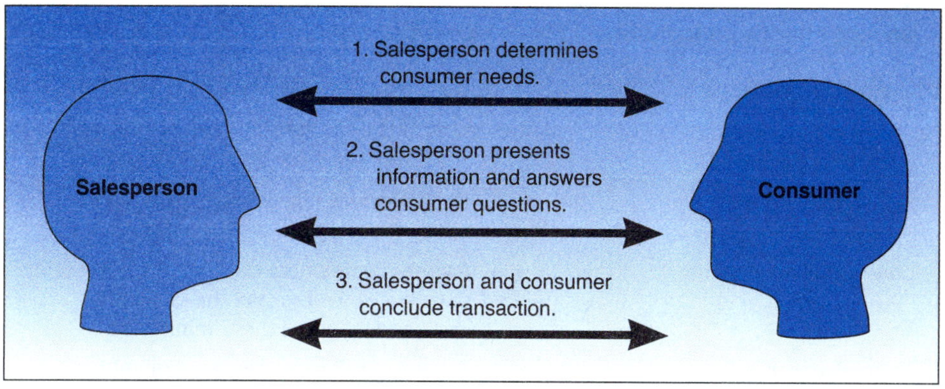

Figure 16-6
The Buyer-Seller Dyad

INTERACTIVE FIGURE

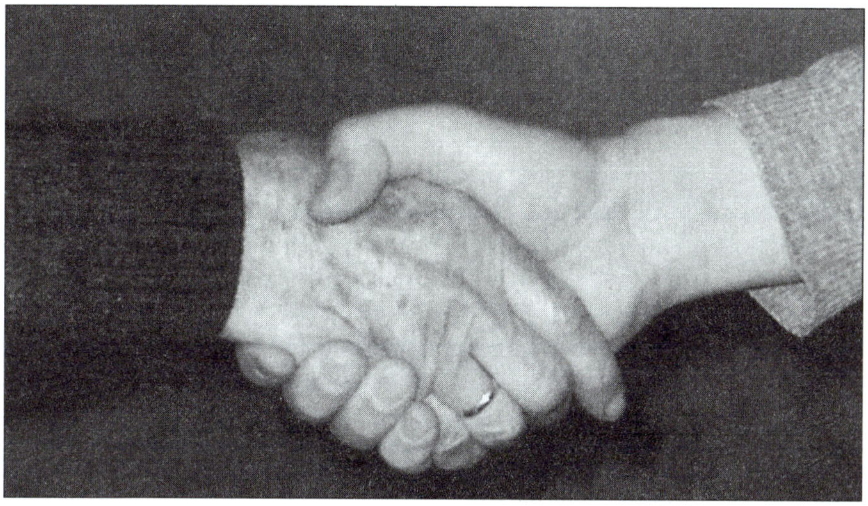

Figure 16-7
In many countries, a handshake is more valuable than a written contract.

ers, sellers will often attempt to move the dyad to a higher level, the contractual agreement. With a **contractual agreement,** a written agreement between the buyer and seller is established that states the terms of the interaction, costs, and length of the commitment. With a contractual agreement, both the buyer and seller benefit. Buyers are guaranteed a steady supply of a specific product at a predetermined price. Sellers benefit because the buying situation becomes a straight re-buy situation and does not require active selling. As long as they can meet the needs of the buyer, they are guaranteed a sale for the length of the contract and do not have to worry about a competitor taking their client away.

Contractual agreement: A written agreement between the buyer and seller that states the terms of the interaction, costs, and length of the commitment.

While contractual agreements represent a more involved form of dyad relationship, they may or may not involve trust. **Trust relationships** in a buyer-seller dyad are based on a mutual respect and understanding of both parties and a commitment to work together. In many countries outside the United States, trust relationships are expected, and company executives are insulted at the suggestion the agreement should be solidified through a written contract (see Figure 16-7).

Trust relationships: Buyer-seller dyads based on mutual respect and understanding of both parties and a commitment to work together.

At the next level is the **electronic data interchange (EDI)** relationship, which expands the trust relationship to include the sharing of data between the buying and selling firms. As illustrated in Chapter 10, "Distribution Strategies," EDI relationships are established between intermediaries. They take place when the buyer and seller electronically share information about production, inventory, shipping, and purchasing. Such relationships involve a high level of trust because the seller has access to all of the buying firm's production information, and the seller ships the materials automatically. Most EDI relationships are with single vendor sources, which sellers like because they know the customer is not making any purchases from a competitor, and as long as the customer is satisfied, they will keep the contract. Sellers also know that with EDI it is more difficult for the buyer to switch vendors because of the physical cost of hooking up with a new vendor.

Electronic data interchange (EDI): A trust relationship that includes the sharing of data between the buying and selling firm.

TABLE 16-1

Buyer-Seller Dyad Relationships

Buyer-Seller Dyad Relationship	Definition
Single transactions	The buyer and seller interact for the purpose of a single transaction.
Occasional transactions	The buyer and seller interact infrequently.
Repeat transactions	The buyer and seller interact on a regular basis.
Contractual agreement	A written agreement between the buyer and seller states the terms of the interaction, costs, and length of the commitment.
Trust relationship	The buyer-seller dyad is based on mutual respect and an understanding of both parties and a commitment to work together.
Electronic data interchange (EDI)	This trust relationship includes the sharing of data between the buying and selling firms.
Strategic partnership	The buyer and seller exchange information at the highest levels with the goal of collaboration.

Source: Kenneth E. Clow and Donald Baack, *Integrated Advertising, Promotion, & Marketing Communication* (Upper Saddle River, NJ: Prentice-Hall, 2002): 454.

Strategic partnership: Partnership in which the buyer and seller exchange information at the highest levels with the goal of collaboration.

At the highest level of the buyer-seller dyad interaction is the **strategic partnership.** With this approach, the buyer and seller share information at the highest levels. The goal of this relationship is to collaborate on plans to benefit both parties as well as the customers of the buying firm. In this type of relationship, the seller actively examines ways to modify its products to improve the position of the buying firm in the marketplace. Table 16-1 reviews these various levels of the buyer-seller dyad.

Personal selling, perhaps more than any of the other components of an IMC program, must be built on trust, honesty, and integrity. Regardless of the type of relationship between the buyer and seller, the buyer must have confidence that he or she is being given the correct and honest information. Yet, this is not always the case. Because of the lack of skill, pressure from sales managers, the desire to earn more money, and the need to meet a sales quota, salespeople may be tempted to use unethical techniques ranging from putting pressure on a buyer to make a purchase immediately to telling outright lies. While high-pressure techniques are not in the long-term best interest for a salesperson and the selling firm, lying and other forms of dishonesty are much worse.

It is important for salespeople to realize that receiving referrals, getting repeat business, and building a strong reputation are the keys to successful sales. Success is the result of salespeople being honest with buyers about their products, the products' attributes, and the benefits to the buyer. It is important for salespeople to believe in what they are selling. If they do not, it is impossible to present the product to potential buyers with passion and honesty.

Many salespeople are paid a commission on their sales to encourage them to concentrate on selling. Although a commission will certainly encourage a salesperson to push harder for sales, it can also be detrimental if unethical behaviors are used to obtain those sales. Marketing Illustration 16-1 discusses ethics and sales commissions for stockbrokers.

16-2c The Selling Process

The selling process consists of prospecting for leads, preparing a pre-sales approach, determining customer wants, giving a sales presentation, answering questions and objections, closing the sale, and following up. These steps are summarized in Figure 16-8. Order getters are involved in all seven steps, and order takers are involved in four or five of the steps.

Marketing Illustration 16-1

Ethics and Commission: Nancy Kurland's Story

Nancy Kurland was a single 26-year-old with a house payment to make. In just her first three months, sales as a stockbroker had not gone too well. Then her company gave her a new product to sell—a closed-end bond fund. She could earn 4 cents commission on each dollar sold. In addition, she could win a trip to Hawaii if her sales were high enough.

Nancy went to work calling clients and cold calling prospective ones. She told customers that the new closed-end bond fund was a conservative investment and that they did not have to pay any commission because it was a new issue. Although she did not sell enough to win a trip to Hawaii, she did sell a large number of the bonds, and clients were happy with the purchase—until three months later.

What Nancy had told her clients was true. They did not have to pay a commission on the purchase since it was a new issuance. What she had not told them was that the fund borrowed money to cover the expenses and that her company supported the stock in the open market. At the end of the three months, the stock dropped in value by 7 percent to pay a 3 percent underwriting fee and a 4 percent commission to Nancy.

As angry customers began to call, Nancy realized there was a big difference in being prudent and being honest. Although what she told clients was legally true, what she told them was not ethically right. She failed to disclose the 7 percent fee that would kick in after three months. Nancy realized that being honest with clients required providing them with all of the information, not just part of it. She also realized that gaining a commission at the expense of her clients was not an ethically wise decision.

Source: Nancy B. Kurland, "Ethics and Commission," *Business & Society Review*, vol. 104, no. 1 (Spring 1999): 29–34.

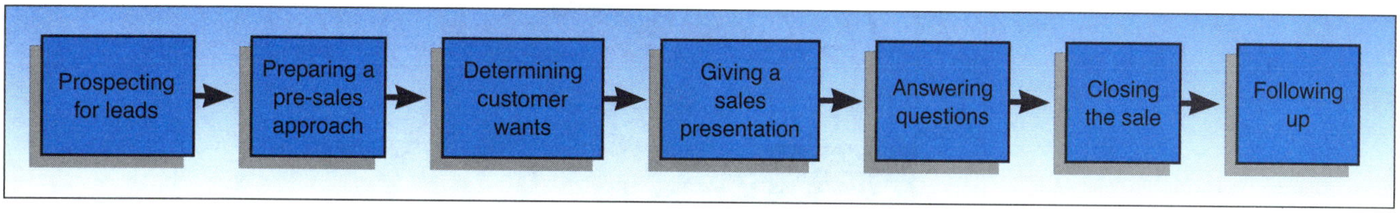

Figure 16-8
The Selling Process

Order takers do not prospect and often do not determine customer needs or follow up after the sale. Retail clerks may only answer questions and close the sale.

Prospecting for Leads The first step in the selling process is prospecting for leads. **Prospects** are potential customers who have a need for the product being sold and the ability to purchase the product.[1] For example, for a small electric motor manufacturer, prospects are all of the businesses that use small electric motors. They could be other manufacturers, they may be feed mills, they may be government organizations, or they could be distributors of electric supplies. While all of these firms could be potential customers, salespeople for the small electric motor manufacturer would have to find some way of locating the businesses that would offer the best opportunity for making a sale. The goal of prospecting is to develop a list of viable companies, or consumers, that would be the most likely to make a purchase.

Prospects: Potential customers of a firm.

Often, developing a list of potential customers can be the most difficult task in prospecting. Salespeople have several options, and the best method will depend on factors such as the type of product being sold, the expertise of the company, and the competition they face. One of the best sources for new customers is the firm's current customers. Often, they can provide the names of decision makers, influencers, and purchasing agents. Having a name and a referral often allows the salesperson to bypass the gatekeepers and talk directly with individuals who would be involved in the purchase decision (see Figure 16-9).

Commercial and government databases can provide potential customers. Commercial sources such as CompuServe, Discloser, Inc., and the Funk and Scott Index of Corporations and Industries can be used. Government sources include the Census of Business, the Census of Manufacturers, and the Standard Industrial Classification Code. Also, many marketing research firms sell information about companies that can be used. For example, one New

Figure 16-9
As this advertisement implies, successful sales begin by getting past gatekeepers, such as secretaries.

Source: Reprinted by permission of Barron's.

York–based research firm offers an online database of executives at 900,000 organizations in 172 countries. The company constantly updates the information and can provide information such as geographic location of the firm, names of company management personnel, job function, title, contact information, firm size and type, and organizational structure.[2]

A business can gather names and information from prospective buyers at trade shows. Most are excellent prospects because the primary reason they attend trade shows is to look at vendors and see what each vendor offers. Contacts can be obtained from advertising and Internet inquiries resulting from the business advertising its products and encouraging interested parties to make an inquiry. Names obtained through this method are almost always good prospects, since the potential customers are making the contact and want more information.

For small businesses and consumer services, networking can be used to become acquainted with potential customers. Professional, social, and business organizations are common places for networking. An insurance agent, for example, could develop valuable contacts through networking at the Chamber of Commerce, Kiwanis, Rotary, or other meetings of civic organizations. Business-to-business salespeople often join professional or trade associations in order to meet potential prospects.

The least-productive method of prospecting is cold canvassing, since the buyer knows little about the prospect and a lot of time is spent calling on prospects that have little or no interest. Because of the high cost of making a personal sales call, this method of prospecting is usually not cost effective. Instead of using a salesperson's time, some companies hire missionary salespeople to make cold calls; their task is not to make a sale but to leave information or a sample of the product. A salesperson would then call only on the ones the missionary salespeople identified as viable prospects.

The second part of prospecting is qualifying the leads. It is important to choose the prospects with the greatest potential or to rank them based on potential. Some questions that a small electric motor manufacturer may ask include:

1. What size of electric motors does the company use, and how many does it purchase each year?
2. Who is the company's current supplier?
3. How satisfied is the customer with its current supplier?
4. Does the company purchase from one vendor or multiple vendors?
5. Does the company fit with our current customer base, and do we understand the prospect's business so we can develop a relationship with the prospect?
6. How difficult will it be to get past the gatekeeper and talk with the engineers, users, and decision makers?
7. What criteria will the prospect likely use in making a decision?

Each potential customer can be classified into categories such as A, B, or C based on the responses to these questions. Although a salesperson may not have solid answers for each question, through research he or she can gather enough information to make an intelligent decision. For example, suppose a salesperson finds that a prospect purchases a large volume of electric motors in the size the manufacturer produces and that the prospect tends to use a single source vendor. Because of the high sales volume, this prospect is attractive, but key questions are who the current supplier is and how satisfied the prospect is with its current vendor. If the company is very satisfied, this prospect may be classified in the B or C category. However, if the company is not completely satisfied with its current vendor, then this prospect would immediately be placed in the A category and be among the first sales calls the salesperson will make. The better the job a salesperson does in qualifying prospects, the more effective he or she will be in generating sales because the salesperson will spend more time calling on prospects with the highest probability of making a purchase.

Preparing a Pre-Sales Approach In the pre-sales approach, the salesperson gathers information about the potential customer to determine the best sales approach. Useful information would include:

- Current vendor(s)
- Prospect's customers
- Customer needs
- Critical product attributes and benefits desired
- Relative mixture of price, service, and product attributes desired
- Trade promotions used in the past and planned in the future
- Expectations about use of sales promotions and advertising
- Risk factors in switching vendors

If the prospect's current vendor was not determined during the prospecting step, determining it during the second step is essential. Successful salespeople know their competitors, the approaches they are likely to use, and the reasons the customer chose the competitor. Armed with information about the competing firm the prospect is currently using, the salesperson is able to emphasize his or her company's strengths that are perceived as weaknesses for the current vendor. For instance, a salesperson may know that a current vendor has to ship products 1,500 miles by rail to reach the customer. With a facility only 200 miles from the customer, the salesperson is able to emphasize the importance of on-time delivery and how the closeness of the facility will ensure a steady supply without ever revealing that he or she knows the situation the current vendor faces.

Knowing who the prospect's customers are enhances the salesperson's ability to make an effective presentation. The salesperson would benefit from knowing which product attributes are most important to the prospect's customers and how the prospect will use the selling firm's products. For example, if you are selling dental supplies or equipment, it is important to understand the dentist's patient base. Does the dentist deal primarily with pediatrics or mature patients? How will your product or equipment benefit the patient? How will it improve the quality of dental care that the dentist will provide? Will the product make the dental practice more efficient or allow patients to be served faster. The more the salesperson understands about the dentist's practice and how the product will improve the dentist's practice, the more likely he or she will be to make a sale.[3]

In making a purchase decision, critical product attributes are evaluated from the perspective of the desired benefits. Knowing in advance what benefits are desired and what attributes the prospect will be examining allows the salesperson to have the correct information available. Closely tied with this knowledge is information about the relative mix of price, service, and product attributes. For some customers, price will be the critical purchase decision factor. For others, it will be a service component such as on-time delivery or the ability to handle large fluctuations in orders. Yet, for others, it may be some product attribute such as the stress strength of a cable or sheet of aluminum. By knowing the emphasis the prospect is likely to put on price, service, and product attributes, the salesperson is more likely to focus on the points of interest to the prospect and present the information in the correct manner.

Trade promotions are crucial elements of a complete IMC approach. With more than 50 percent of all marketing dollars spent on trade promotions, the salesperson needs to know what trade promotions the prospect expects and what the current vendor is providing. While all of the factors that have been discussed are important, it is not unusual for the final decision to be determined by the trade promotions being offered. Salespeople have to be careful here not to offer too much and make it difficult for their firm to earn a profit on the sale. However, if they don't offer enough, the prospect is not likely to consider the offer legitimate.

For buyers, switching vendors is a risk, depending on the level of relationship they have with the vendor. If it is only at the transaction level, then little risk is involved, and switching is done relatively easily. However, if it is a trust relationship, contractual agreement, or EDI relationship, then switching becomes more difficult and is normally done only if the firm is unhappy with the current vendor. To make a switch otherwise would require a demonstration of some benefit that is significantly superior to the current vendor. Price sometimes can make a difference. For example, if another vendor can offer a component part for 70 cents less and the prospect purchases 300,000 of these parts a year, that would be a savings of $210,000. But making the switch still involves a risk. If the new vendor does not supply the parts in a timely manner, the cost of downtime can quickly eat into the cost savings.

Determining Customer Wants If a salesperson has spent time and done a good job in the pre-sales approach, most of the information that is needed for the sales call has already been gathered. All that is needed during this step is confirmation of what the customer's needs are. The situation, however, is different for order takers. They do not make an initial contact with the customer and do not prospect or use a pre-sales approach. Their first knowledge and contact with the customer occur when the customer makes the contact. Before launching into a sales pitch, the salesperson should first determine the customer's needs.

When shopping for a boat, many buyers may not know what features they want or need. An in-house salesperson should begin by asking individuals questions about how they will use the boat. Will it be for fishing, leisure boating, or pulling skiers? How much boating will they do? Will it be for just the two of them, or will they be using it for entertaining others? If others, how many others? From these questions, the salesperson can

Figure 16-10
In selling a boat, the salesperson should first determine the customer's needs by asking the right questions.

Source: Courtesy of Newcomer, Morris and Young.

expand to presenting features such as engine size, engine type, and features of the models. By asking the right questions, the salesperson can determine the boat that will best meet the customer's needs and increase his or her chances of making a sale (see Figure 16-10).

In the chapter-opening vignette, the first salesperson skipped this stage and launched directly into the sales pitch without even determining what type of house Jay and Marcie wanted. Not only was time spent showing them houses that did not meet their need, but Jay and Marcie felt that the only thing the salesperson was interested in was making a sale. The second salesperson, however, took time to ask Jay and Marcie a number of questions. After she had gathered all of the information, she then offered to show them two houses that met their needs. You may recall the different marketing philosophies presented in Chapter 1, "Scope and Concepts of Marketing." The first salesperson in this chapter-opening vignette used the sales approach, whereas the second used the marketing approach. For most products, using a marketing approach is more effective than the sales approach.

Giving a Sales Presentation A salesperson can use four basic sales approaches:

- Stimulus-response
- Need-satisfaction
- Problem-solution
- Mission-sharing

Figure 16-11
In selling high-ticket items such as tractors, sales people need to use a higher-order sales such as need-satisfaction or problem-solution.
Source: Courtesy of Howard Berman.

Stimulus-response sales approach: Sometimes referred to as the canned sales approach, uses specific statements (stimuli) to solicit specific responses from customers.

Need-satisfaction sales approach: Sales approach aimed at discovering a customer's needs and then providing solutions that satisfy those needs.

Problem-solution sales approach: Sales approach that requires the salesperson to analyze the prospect's operation and offer a viable solution.

The **stimulus-response sales approach,** sometimes referred to as the canned sales approach, uses specific statements (stimuli) to solicit specific responses from customers. Often, the salespeople memorize the stimulus statements (the pitch), and offer memorized or scripted responses to specific questions they are asked. For instance, salespeople may ask prospects if they feel they are paying too much for their car insurance. Most prospects will answer yes (the stimuli), and the salespeople will then explain how they can save the prospects money on car insurance. If, by chance, prospects say no, the salespeople have another question already scripted that will lead into the sales pitch. This sales approach is common for telemarketers, retail sales clerks, and new field salespeople.

The **need-satisfaction sales approach** is aimed at discovering a customer's needs and then providing solutions that satisfy those needs (see Figure 16-11). This approach requires the salesperson to be skillful and to ask the right questions. The major difference with this approach is that the salesperson does not have a canned list of responses and questions that are designed to lead to the sales pitch. It is an excellent approach for in-house salespeople or order takers who are responding to a prospect's inquiry. Retail sales clerks of complex items like computers will often use this approach, as did the second salesperson in the chapter-opening vignette. Through asking the right questions, she was able to provide two homes that would meet Jay and Marcie's needs. Order getters also use this approach to amplify or clarify information they gathered in the pre-sales approach.

The **problem-solution sales approach** requires the salesperson to analyze the prospect's operation and offer a solution that is viable. With this approach, prospects often do not fully understand their needs. For example, they may know their computer system is inadequate for their e-commerce launch but not understand what is needed. The selling

TABLE 16-2

Selling Approaches

Type of Selling Approach	Definition	Example
Stimulus-response approach	Sometimes referred to as the canned sales approach, this approach uses specific statements (stimuli) to solicit specific responses from customers.	A telemarketer sells aluminum siding for a house, using a canned sales presentation.
Need-satisfaction approach	This approach is aimed at discovering a customer's needs and then providing solutions that satisfy those needs.	A salesperson at an electronics store questions a customer about how he or she will be using a camera before offering a particular brand of digital camera with the features that best meet the customer's needs.
Problem-solution approach	This approach requires a salesperson to analyze the prospect's operation and offer a viable solution.	With the help of computer specialists, a salesperson examines the computing needs of a new e-commerce business and then offers a computing network that will meet all of the customer's needs.
Mission-sharing approach	This approach involves two organizations developing a common mission and then sharing resources to accomplish that mission.	A supplier of fiberglass partners with a manufacturer of racing boats to produce a higher quality fiberglass that will withstand the high speeds of boat racing.

organization will often use a team approach in this case with engineers and computer experts assisting the salesperson in analyzing the problem and developing a feasible solution. This approach is common in new-buy situations and may be used with a modified rebuy situation.

The last approach, the **mission-sharing sales approach,** involves two organizations developing a common mission and then sharing resources to accomplish that mission. This requires the strategic partnership relationship that was discussed in Section 16-2b. In some ways, such a partnership resembles a "joint venture" project. With the increased pressure of global competition, firms have seen the need to cooperate on a higher level. Buyers and sellers that enter into a strategic partnership relationship can use this sales approach to ensure that both the buyer and seller are benefiting from the relationship. The goal is to work together for the benefit of both firms. Table 16-2 summarizes the four selling approaches.

Mission-sharing sales approach: Sales approach that involves two organizations developing a common mission and then sharing resources to accomplish that mission.

The primary factor in determining which approach is used is the form of a buyer-seller dyad. For transaction-type relationships, salespeople are likely to use the first two: stimulus-response and need-satisfaction. The reason the first salesperson in the chapter-opening vignette used the stimulus-response approach was that in almost every case he interacts with the customer for only one sale. He sees no need to develop a relationship or trust because it is highly unlikely the couple would ever buy a house from him again. The second salesperson chose the need-satisfaction approach because she felt she could increase her chances of making a sale by first understanding the couple's needs.

Additional factors that determine the selling approach are the dollar value of the sale and the role of personal selling in the IMC plan. If the dollar value of the sale is high, there is a tendency to shift to a higher-level sales approach. The same is true for IMC plans in which personal selling is prominent.

Answering Questions Few sales are closed immediately after the presentation. Prospects will have questions and doubts about making the purchase. Skillfully answering questions and addressing objections and doubts can make the difference between closing a sale and not closing a sale. The disadvantage of the stimulus-response sales approach is that if prospects raise questions not in the script, salespeople often are not prepared to provide an answer. In fact, most salespeople using this approach skip this step and move directly from the sales presentation to the closing. With the need-satisfaction approach, the salesperson will attempt to relate his or her responses to the needs that were identified earlier in the sales presentation. If this can be done successfully, a sale will often occur. With the problem-solution approach and the mission-sharing approach, few questions and objections are raised if the selling team has done a good job in understanding the problem and developing a joint mission.

A salesperson has six different methods he or she can use to overcome objections. They include:[4]

- Direct answer method
- Nondispute method
- Offset method
- Dispute method
- Comparative-item method
- Turn-around (boomerang) method

With the direct answer method, any objections or questions are met with direct responses. In the nondispute method, the salesperson avoids or delays any direct answers, or passively accepts the objection without providing an answer or disputing the prospect's claim. With the offset method, the salesperson accepts the objection but offsets it with information about the product's benefits or attributes. Often, the salesperson will use a demonstration, a comparison, or a testimonial to offset the objection.

With the dispute method, the salesperson confronts the objection directly, indirectly, or with a demonstration that shows that the objection is not true or is not founded on correct facts. With the comparative-item method, the prospect is shown two or more products, and when the prospect objects to one, the salesperson will immediately switch to another product to which the objection cannot apply. When using the turn-around, or boomerang, method, the salesperson converts the objection into a reason to make a purchase. For example, if the person says it's too expensive, the salesperson replies that the cost is the very reason it should be purchased.

Which method of handling questions and objections should be used depends on multiple factors, such as the buying situation, the personalities of both the buyer and seller, and the product being sold. Table 16-3 summarizes each of the methods of overcoming objections with an example of each.

Closing the Sale While closing the sale is the most important step, for many salespeople it is the most difficult step in the entire process, primarily because of the fear that the prospect will say no.

Closings can be classified into six different categories:[5]

- Straightforward close
- Presumptive close
- Arousal close
- Minor-decision close
- Single obstacle close
- Silent close

TABLE 16-3

Overcoming Objections

Method	Definition	Example
Direct answer	Objections or questions are met with direct responses.	"We produce all of the sizes you need, and we will make sure they meet your specifications."
Nondispute	Objections or questions are avoided, or the salesperson delays any direct answers, or passively accepts the objection without providing an answer or disputing the prospect's claim.	"I understand your concern, and it is legitimate." Without responding to the concern, the salesperson goes on, "Let me show you the different sizes we offer."
Offset	The objections or questions are offset with information about the product's benefits or attributes.	"I understand your concern, but let me show you all of the sizes we offer and how we go about ensuring that your specifications are met."
Dispute	Objections or questions are confronted directly, indirectly, or by demonstrating that the objection is not true or not founded on correct facts.	"Somebody gave you incorrect information. We can supply every size you use in your business, and we can meet those specifications. I am confident that our product is stronger than what you are currently using."
Comparative-item	The prospect is shown two or more products and, when the prospect objects to one, the salesperson immediately switches to another product to which the objection cannot apply.	"Since this particular brand does not have the size you need to fit with your product, let me show you this other brand. It comes in the size you need and will meet your specifications."
Turn-around (boomerang)	The salesperson converts the objection into a reason to make a purchase.	"I understand you can't afford it right now, but with what your competitors have just introduced, you cannot afford not to switch immediately. Any delay will cost you sales and future customers."

Source: Sean Dwyer, John Hill, and Warren Martin, "An Empirical Investigation of Critical Success Factors in the Personal Selling Process for Homogenous Goods," *Journal of Personal Selling & Sales Management,* vol. 20, no. 3 (Summer 2000): 152–161.

With the straightforward close, the salesperson asks for the order in a direct manner and, if necessary, summarizes the benefits for the prospect. With the presumptive close, the salesperson assumes the prospect is ready to buy and therefore asks a question in terms of how to write up the sale. A retail sales clerk may ask if the person would like to pay with cash, check, or money order. A field salesperson may ask how soon the customer wants the product shipped and in what quantity. With the arousal close, the salesperson appeals to the prospect's emotions or creates a sense of urgency. Insurance agents often appeal to taking care of loved ones before it is too late.

With the minor-decision close, the salesperson seeks approval of small-decision questions throughout the presentation. Then, when the purchase question is asked, the prospect has already responded yes to several smaller decision questions. If the prospect is almost ready to buy, but has just one objection, a salesperson can use the single obstacle close,

Marketing Illustration 16-2

Picking Up the Scent

While body language is not always reliable when it comes to selling, it can help. The important thing to remember, however, is not to become so wrapped up in watching body language that you miss the sale or fail to listen to what is being said. Body language can assist an astute salesperson in finding the answers to the following situations:

Who's Got the Power?

In business situations, the CEO or highest-ranking officer has the official power. But to determine who has the power to make decisions, study the other people in the room. The person with the most power is comfortable and relaxed with the CEO and usually sits across the table or room from the CEO, directly in the CEO's line of sight.

Who's Telling the Truth?

Buyers and sellers both know that the other party often embellishes the conversation, whether it is sales figures or attributes of a product. To see whether the person is telling the truth, watch the person's associates in the room. If they cringe, cough, or look uncomfortable, you know the speaker is embellishing what he or she is telling you.

Do They Like the Concept?

The way the person touches your product will tell you how much he or she likes it. A gentle, continual touch means the person likes it. Sitting the product down without further touching usually means he or she does not.

It's Time to Close the Deal?

While difficult to judge, arms folded across the chest means people are not convinced. Legs crossed at the ankles or hands folded together in the lap usually convey the same meaning. When the person changes positions, it usually means that the meeting is over or it's time to ask for the sale. Watch the eyes. If the person is looking directly at you, it's time to close. You've made a connection. If the person is looking away, it's time to close and try again later.

Source: Mark McCormack, "Picking Up the Scent," *New Zealand Management,* vol. 47, no. 4 (May 2000): 14–15.

which involves answering that one objection within the close. The last closing method is the silent close. With this close, the salesperson says nothing. The salesperson just waits and lets the prospect make the decision.

The best closing depends on a salesperson's personality and personal preference as well as the selling situation. Most salespeople tend to use a particular method more than the others, but may use all six. Most likely, however, they have two or three they tend to use most of the time. Marketing Illustration 16-2 discusses how body language can be a useful cue for a salesperson in knowing when to close as well as in gathering other important information.

Following Up Satisfied customers usually purchase again and in the business-to-business sector often develop a strong loyalty to a particular vendor. Unhappy customers, however, not only defect to a competitor but also spread negative word-of-mouth communications about the firm. Because it is much more cost effective to retain an old customer than to obtain new ones, follow-up is a critical component of the selling process. The difficulty is that, for many salespeople, it is the least-attractive component of the sale, especially if the salesperson is paid a commission. The salesperson does not want to spend time at activities that do not generate sales.

16-3 Databases

Databases have become an important component of IMC programs. They can be used for a variety of purposes, ranging from providing information to salespeople and other company personnel to direct marketing. Determining how the database will be used and who will be using it is crucial in the development process. The design of the database system, as well as the type of data that will be collected, are contingent on how the product is used and who will use it. Some typical applications for databases include:[6]

- Providing information about a firm's customers to internal personnel, such as the service call center, salespeople, and the marketing department
- Generating information about what customers purchase and why they make the purchase for the marketing department
- Providing purchase information and demographic information for direct-marketing programs
- Yielding information about the role of various members of the buying center for business-to-business transactions for field salespeople
- Tracking changes in purchasing behaviors and purchasing criteria used by customers for salespeople and the marketing department
- Storage of data about customers for a customer relationship management program

Service call centers need access to customer records when a customer calls. They need to be easily accessible and easy to understand. Customers expect a service call representative to know what they purchased and be able to answer questions about their account. Salespeople need the same information without waiting for a printout of a customer's purchase history or for an assistant in the firm to obtain the information. This is especially critical in preparing for a sales call and sometimes during a sales call. For a salesperson, direct access to customer information can make a difference.

Databases are important for marketing departments. Customer data help marketing personnel to understand what is being purchased and by whom. These data can be used to develop profiles of the firm's best customers and to determine the best target market for the various products sold by the firm. Databases are an important component of a direct-marketing campaign, which will be discussed in Section 16-4. They are also essential in tracking changes in purchase behavior, alerting marketing personnel to the need to either modify their product offering or alter their marketing communications material.

16-3a Data Warehousing

Data warehousing is the process of capturing and storing data within a single database that is accessible to internal personnel for a variety of purposes, such as marketing, sales, and customer service. Building a data warehouse involves understanding the various people and uses of the data. Too often, companies will develop a database only to find that they either have the wrong information, not enough information, or that the information cannot be accessed by the individuals who need it. Collecting the right information for a data warehouse is crucial.

Data warehousing: The process of capturing and storing data within a single database that is accessible to internal personnel for a variety of internal purposes, such as marketing, sales, and customer service.

Organizations have two sources of data: internal data and external data. Internal data come from customers, salespeople, service personnel, call center technicians, and others who have contact with customers. To make a database viable, every person who has contact with customers should be able to access information as well as add information. Most companies do not collect enough information about their customers, and company personnel are not trained to contribute information about customers that may be of value to someone else at a later time.

Names and addresses of customers are the most common form of internal data. Modern information technology techniques such as checkout scanners make it possible for nearly every business to track purchasing information and tie it in with names and addresses. Most retailers do not do this, and many business-to-business firms do not, but technology is available that allows for accurate tracking and recording of purchase data. Although the names, addresses, and phone numbers can be used for direct marketing, it is the purchase data that allow a marketing team to profile its customer base.

If scanner data for each customer are recorded, this history of what items the customer buys, which brands are purchased, how often purchases are made, and how much is purchased becomes valuable information. This information can be directly tied to a customer's name, address (especially ZIP code area), age, family size, and other bits of demographic information that can be obtained either from internal records or commercial sources such as surveys, credit reports, credit applications, and credit card companies.

In most cases, internal data are insufficient to develop an optimal data warehouse. Secondary data, such as psychographics, lifestyle, attitudes, interests, media habits, hobbies, and brand purchases, can be collected from external commercial database services. These data can be attached to purchase history to create a stronger profile of each customer.

For businesses that have primarily transactional relationships with their customers, as would be the case with most retailers, databases can still be useful in tracking purchase patterns. Using ZIP codes, commercial database services can provide retailers with information about customers in their area through a process known as neighborhood lifestyle clusters. These commercial services use information gathered from multiple services to generate information about purchase behaviors, media preferences, credit histories, attitudes, and interests of people who live within a neighborhood (see Figure 16-12).

Geocoding: The process of adding geographic codes to each customer record.

One method companies can use to enrich their internal data is called **geocoding,** which is the process of adding geographic codes to each customer record. Through geocoding, a business can add demographic information such as age, income, education, disposable income, net worth, number of children, race, employment, and whether the individual rents or owns a home. Lifestyle data, such as media habits, hobbies, interests, and opinions, can also be attached to the customer record. A number of firms can compile this type of information: All a firm has to do is supply the names and addresses of its customers. One

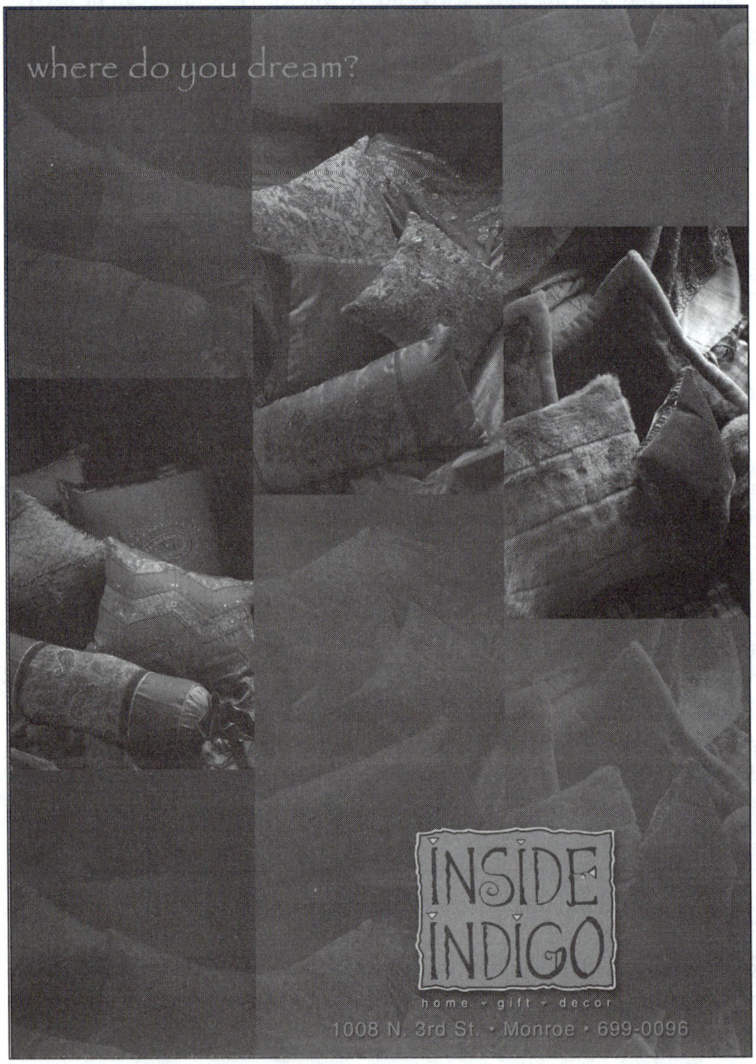

Figure 16-12
Retailers such as Inside Indigo can append data from commercial sources to their internal customer data to build a data warehouse for various marketing functions.

Source: Sample print advertisement courtesy of The Miles Agency and Alliance One Advertising, Inc.

such firm provides geocoding software, called CACI Coder/Plus, that allows a firm to append this information to its internal records, or it can have CACI perform this task.[7]

To illustrate the benefit of this information, suppose a business notices that its best customers are classified by CACI Coder/Plus as Enterprising Young Singles. This geodemographic group dines out frequently and spends money on small appliances, furniture, apparel, and video rentals. These customers are heavy users of personal computers, both at work and at home. They like to read *Entertainment Weekly* and *The Wall Street Journal*.[8]

To be effective, data warehousing has to be integrated with the other components of the IMC plan. One of the best examples of an integrated database system is the Education and Healthcare Division of Dell Computer Corporation. Dubbed the Integrated Generation Plan or the "Funnel Project," the integrated campaign features email, direct mail, events, and a monthly electronic newsletter designed to drive prospects to Dell's website. In addition, Dell collects the names of small-business owners, schools, and hospitals through trade shows, telemarketing, email, and direct mail. Using incentives, Dell is able to drive these contacts to the Dell website, where Dell collects more information about each person, such as job function and computing needs of the organization. With all of these data in one location, Dell is better able to reach these individuals. The best prospects are contacted by a salesperson from Dell, while other prospects are contacted through some type of direct-marketing campaign. Information gathered into Dell's database helps Dell to establish whether direct mail, direct email, or a telemarketer would constitute the optimal approach. Having names, job titles, and other pertinent information allows Dell to customize the message to best fit each person's needs. With the database information, Dell's response rate in its direct-marketing campaign is 3.4 percent for direct mail and 12 percent for targeted email, much higher than the industry average for direct-marketing campaigns.[9]

16-3b Data Mining

A major benefit of developing a data warehouse is the ability to perform data mining on the data. **Data mining** involves computer analysis of customer data to determine patterns, profiles, or relationships for the purpose of customer profiling or predicting purchase behavior. Data mining is similar to miners in the last century panning for gold. Instead of using a pan and sifting through dirt, rocks, and minerals, computers sift through thousands and sometimes millions of records searching for patterns and relationships that might help marketers to better understand customer purchase behavior.

Data mining: The process of compiling personal, pertinent, actionable information about the purchasing habits of current and potential consumers.

The most common use of data mining involves profiling of the firm's customers. Through developing profiles of current customers, the marketing team has a better idea of who is purchasing from the company and what they purchase. This information can be used to develop marketing programs aimed at prospects that meet the profile of the firm's best customers. It can also identify customers who may be in that second tier that the company should concentrate on because they match the profile of the firm's best customers, but not the purchase history. Because the customers are already purchasing from the firm, it is easier to encourage them to increase their purchases than it is to seek entirely new customers. Even hospitals are using this technology as competition for patients increases. By augmenting internal patient data with information from consulting firms like Solucient and CPM Consulting Group, hospitals can create profiles of individuals who are likely to need health care or will be selecting a health-care provider.[10] Marketing to this group is more cost effective than marketing to the entire general population.

Data mining will also suggest cross-selling opportunities that may exist with current customers. For example, Amazon.com collects data on every person who logs on to its site and makes a purchase. By mining purchase history and the material viewed, Amazon.com is able to determine a customer's preferences and, each time the person logs on, suggest new books or products that match the customer's interests (see Figure 16-13).[11]

Another use of data mining is to develop models that predict future purchase behavior based on past purchase activities. Rodale Press used this type of modeling to develop an understanding of Staples, Inc.'s best catalog customers. Through data mining, Staples, Inc.

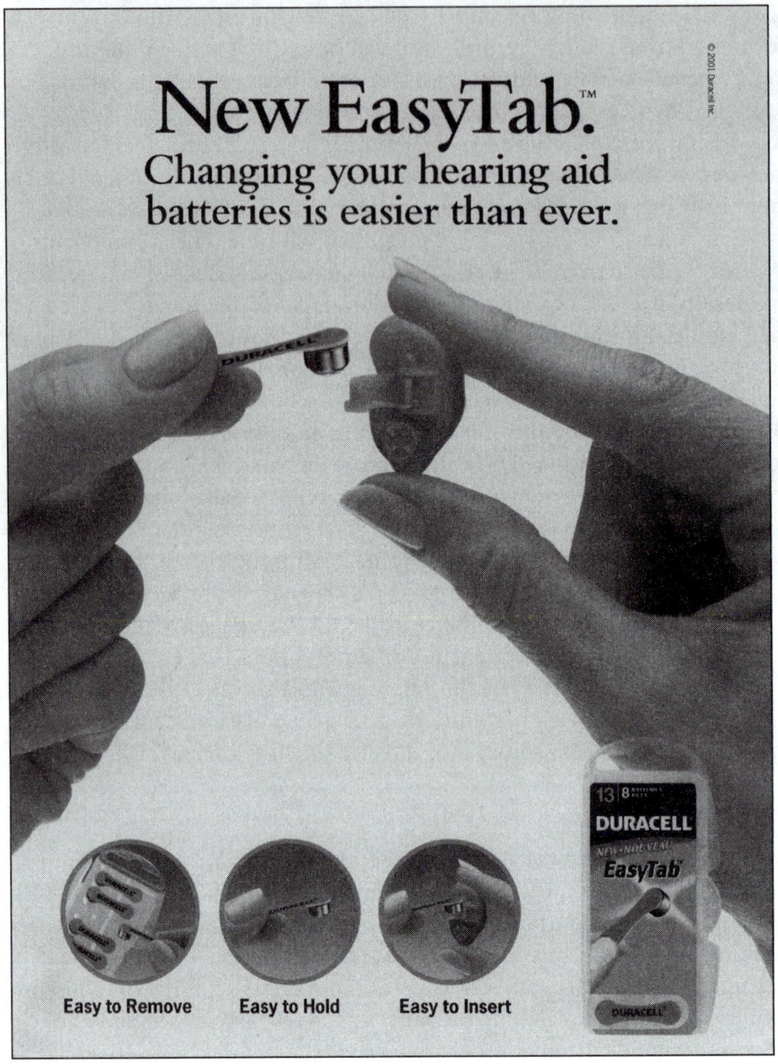

Figure 16-13
Data mining allows a company such as Duracell to profile the most likely customers for the new EasyTab product.
Source: Courtesy of Duracell.

was able to identify current customers who fit the profile of its best catalog customers and would be inclined to purchase from a catalog. By mailing catalogs to only this portion of the list, Staples reduced mailing costs and increased response rates. According to Tom Rocco, Vice President of Rodale Press publishing company, "Response modeling is an important part of the mailing program for many of the companies that rent our lists. They can tighten their mail programs to target the most likely respondents."[12]

Developing relationships with customers is an important ingredient in building brand loyalty as well as encouraging repeat purchase behavior. Through tying marketing efforts to information gained through data mining, companies can maximize their database marketing effort. **Database marketing** refers to marketing programs developed through information gathered from databases and targeted to specific customer segments. The example about Rodale Press and Staples, Inc. is an illustration of a database-marketing program. Figure 16-14 reviews the relationship between data warehousing, data mining, and database marketing.

Database marketing: The collection, analysis, and use of large volumes of customer data to develop marketing programs and customer profiles.

Customer relationship management (CRM): A database application program designed to build long-term loyalty with customers through the use of a personal touch.

16-3c Customer Relationship Management

A new trend in database application is a program called **customer relationship management (CRM),** introduced in Chapter 1, section 1-5e. The program is designed to build long-term loyalty with customers through the use of a personal touch. CRM programs go beyond the development of a database for traditional direct-marketing or personal selling

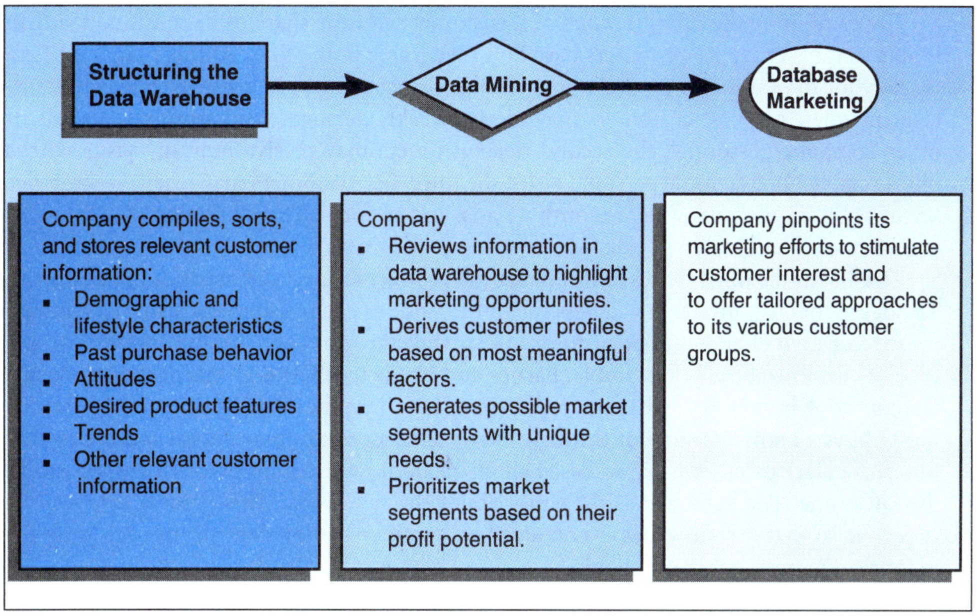

Figure 16-14
Applying Database Marketing

techniques. They also encompass product modifications to meet the needs of each individual customer.

Developing a CRM program requires four steps:[13]

1. Identify the organization's customers.
2. Differentiate customers in terms of their needs and value to the organization.
3. Interact with customers in a cost-effective and efficient manner.
4. Customize the product offering to meet individual customer needs.

Customer relationship management is based on the two tenets of (1) lifetime value of a customer and (2) share of the customer. The *lifetime value* of a customer is a measure of the value of a customer over the typical life span of a firm's customers. The first step in calculating the lifetime value of a customer is to multiply the average amount of money a customer spends with each purchase or visit, the number of purchases per year, and the average life span of a customer. The second step involves subtracting the costs of acquiring and servicing the customer from the number calculated in the first step and adding the value of any new customers that were received through referrals. Lifetime value calculations are based on the idea that customers are not of equal value to a company, even customers who spend the same amount of money. Because of acquisition costs, servicing costs, or customer referrals, customers can either gain or lose value.

In examining the lifetime value of its customers, a local janitorial service noticed that the cost of servicing a particular retail account was greater than what the janitorial service was earning from the account. Total direct and indirect costs were about $400 a month more than the income. But, as the janitorial service began to count the number of referrals that were obtained because of television ads that featured the retail account, it realized that it had picked up 17 new accounts in just 6 months. The total net earnings of those 17 accounts were more than $6,000 per month. Thus, in terms of lifetime value to the firm, this retail account was earning more than $600 a month ([6000/6] – 400).

The second tenet of CRM is that customers have different future potential value, based on the share of the customer. **Share of the customer** is the percentage (or share) of a customer's business that a particular firm has. For example, suppose a customer spends $3,000 per month with a particular supplier. If that $3,000 per month is only 17 percent of the total expenditures by the customer for that particular product, that customer has a high future potential value. If the supplier were the sole provider, that would equate to $18,000 a month in orders.

Share of the customer: The percentage (or share) of a customer's business that a particular firm has.

By combining the lifetime value of a customer with the share of the customer, a firm is able to rank-order its customers based on their value to the firm. At this point, the firm is ready for the third step in CRM: interacting with customers in a cost-effective and efficient manner. The best customers may receive weekly personal visits from salespeople or other company personnel, the second-tier customers may receive monthly visits with a phone contact between the personal visits, the third-tier customers may receive visits twice a year with phone contact on a monthly basis, and so forth. The marketing program that is designed should match the customers' value to the firm.

Tied with the third step is customizing the product to meet the needs of the customer. The degree of customization will depend on the value of each customer. Customers of high value receive a higher degree of customization, while those of low value may not receive any type of customization. For example, Barnes and Noble uses CRM to maximize its revenue from its book buyers. A database records buyers' long-term purchasing behavior. If the customer buys a book in a store or through the website, a prompt may appear indicating that this particular customer has purchased all of the books written by a certain author except the latest one. The customer is then told about the new book. This process can even be proactive so that the customer is contacted by email or some other means each time the author comes out with a new book.

Mitchell's of Westport is a high-end clothing store that has created an effective CRM program. The company has customer data available to the sales staff on each customer's preferences, sizes, and previous purchases. High-ticket purchases are followed up with thank-you notes; customers are notified of sales and given invitations to special events when specific products are available. This personalization has resulted in a high level of loyalty to the store. Even customers who have moved to new cities return to the store to buy clothing.[14]

16-4 Direct Marketing

Direct marketing: The promotion of a product directly from the manufacturer or seller to the buyer without any middlemen involved in the transaction.

Direct marketing is the promotion of a product from the producer directly to the consumer or business user without the use of any type of channel members. More than $200 billion a year is spent on some type of direct marketing.[15] Direct-marketing programs allow a producer or manufacturer of a product to develop direct links with potential customers as well as current customers. According to research conducted by Direct Marketing, 62 percent of direct marketing budgets are focused on prospecting for new customers, new contacts, or new business, whereas 38 percent is directed toward customer retention (see Figure 16-15).[16] Because channel members are bypassed, direct marketing normally allows a producer to earn greater profits. More importantly, it can help in developing a stronger brand loyalty with customers.

Figure 16-15
Focus of Direct Marketing Budget

Source: Richard H. Levey, "Prospects Look Good," *Direct*, vol. 16 (December 1, 2004): 1–5.

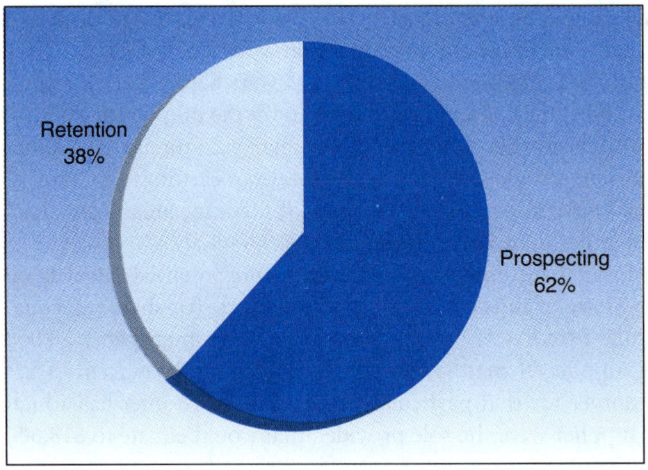

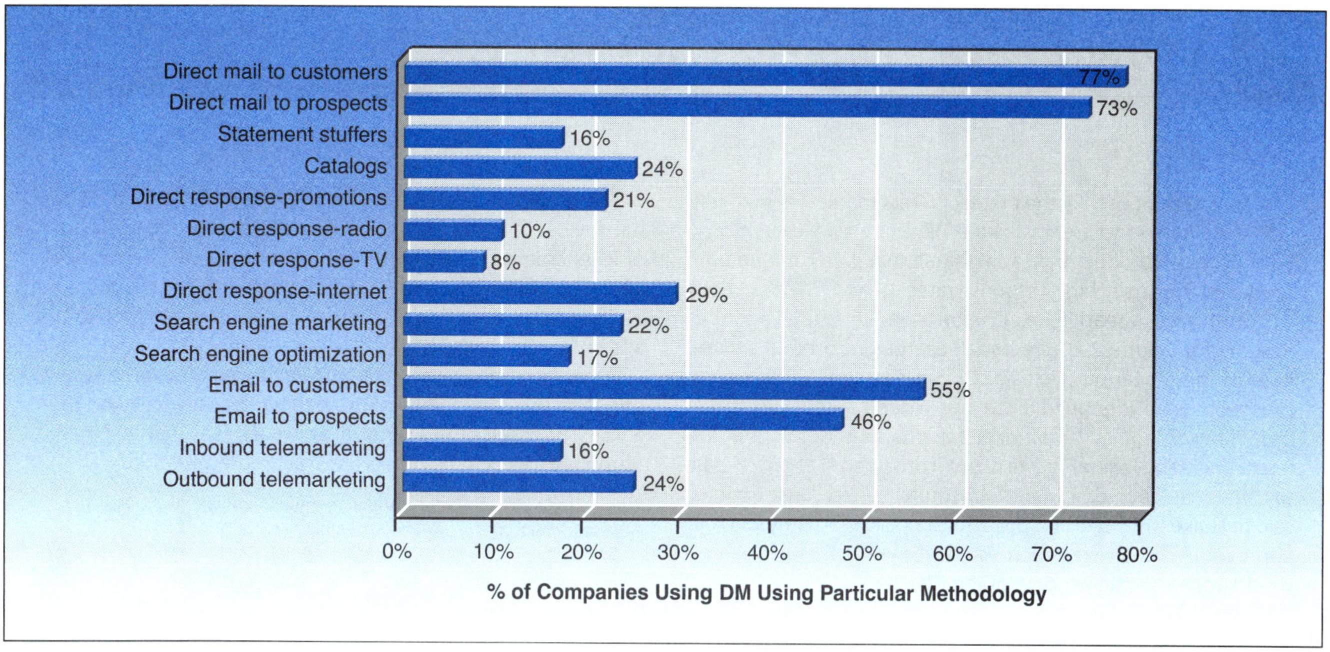

Figure 16-16
Direct Marketing Methods Used by Companies That Engage in Direct Marketing

Source: Richard H. Levey, "Prospects Look Good," *Direct*, vol. 16 (December 1, 2004): 1–5.

A key to a good direct-marketing program is the quality of information contained within the firm's database. Not only should it have the basic demographic information, but psychographic and purchase behavior information should also be available. Using this information, a direct-marketing program should begin by dividing each contact into one of three categories: buyers, inquirers, or prospects. Buyers are individuals who have purchased in the past, inquirers are individuals who have requested information, and prospects are individuals who fit the target profile but have not had any previous contact with the firm. The direct-marketing message that is designed will vary, depending on which group is being targeted.[17] Figure 16-16 provides information on the usage rate of the various methods of direct marketing by firms that use direct marketing.

Direct mail is the most common form of direct marketing. Of the companies that engaged in direct marketing, 77 percent mailed offers to customers and 73 percent mailed offers to prospects (see Figure 16-16). Direct mail can be used to generate leads, build interest, produce inquiries, and stimulate sales. A recent survey by *American Demographics* indicated that 77 percent of adults regularly read their direct mail and that 59 percent have read their direct mail during the past week. However, when it comes to reading every piece of direct mail, the percentages are much lower (9 percent). The most loyal group tends to be female (59 percent) and with household incomes of less than $30,000 (46 percent). Approximately 16 percent of the population will read direct-mail pieces related to products they would like to purchase or have considered purchasing. Again, this group tends to be female (61 percent), and almost one-third (28 percent) live in the Midwest.[18]

Direct mail offers marketers a major advantage: Its effects are measurable. The number of leads and orders can be easily tracked to direct-mail pieces, so a company can readily see how effective its direct-mail program is. Because of the relative ease of measuring results, direct mailing lends itself well to experimenting with different formats, colors, and designs to find the optimal mix. Marketing Illustration 16-3 highlights an unusual, but highly successful, direct-marketing program by a bank.

Two recent trends have enhanced the effectiveness of direct-mail programs. The first is database technology, especially data mining, which has made direct mail more effective. Database information can be used to narrow the list of prospects to those who are most likely to respond. Even commercial sources of data have more information within their database that allows for more precise targeting of the mail pieces.

Marketing Illustration 16-3

Three Boxes

Banks are not usually the greatest direct marketers, but First Trust Bank and Geneva State Bank are two exceptions. Both developed direct-mail campaigns that were unique and produced unusually high response rates.

Corporate Creative, a Charlotte advertising agency, designed a unique 3-D direct-mail campaign to build awareness of the 4-year-old First Trust Bank. The top 100 business prospects were identified. Each was mailed a series of three brown boxes labeled "traditional bank tool kit" but with a different message inside. The first box contained a child's 8-ball toy that was named "a magic substitute banker." Instructions said to shake the 8-ball and pose questions like "Will my loan be approved?" The answer, such as "Maybe" or "Ask again later," would appear in the window of the 8-ball.

The second box had a mirror with the label "large bank signal device." The instructions said it could be used to signal loan officers at large banks by reflecting sunlight off the windows of the traditional banker's tall buildings. The third box had a 12-inch crowbar, noting that it was the appropriate tool "to pry a loan from the large banks."

The prospects received a box each week for three weeks, and then the bank followed up with a telephone call and then a visit. The result of this unusual approach was that 30 percent of the prospects met with a First Trust representative.

Source: Bonnie McGeer, "Getting Attention—and Deposits—Via 3-D Mail," *American Banker,* vol. 167, no. 210 (November 1, 2002): 6A.

Digital direct-to-press: Printing technology that allows for the customization of each marketing piece.

The second trend is enhanced printing and digital technology that allows businesses to design one-on-one communication. Instead of running mass mailings that are impersonal, it is now possible to prepare mailers that are personalized. This technology is called **digital direct-to-press.** It is especially attractive in the business-to-business market because computers can be programmed to send a specific message to a printer. This gives the marketing team a high-quality one-of-a-kind piece to send to each potential customer, and each one can be adapted to the specific company being targeted. In the business-to-business sector, information about the firm's customers and the locations of its customers' offices can be included in the mailing.[19] The digital direct-to-press can also be sent to homes but is usually not cost effective. Personalizing each direct-mail piece is much more expensive than running mass offers with only a personalized cover letter. It takes a great deal of expertise to design a computer program that produces personalized messages.

Although the Internet has become very popular with consumers, catalogs are still an effective means of direct marketing, being used by 24 percent of the companies that engage in direct marketing (see Figure 16-16). Consumers can view catalogs at their leisure, and because most catalogs are kept for a period of time, they have a long shelf life. Days and even weeks after receiving a catalog, a consumer or business may refer to it for a purchase. One of the attractive features of catalogs is the soft sales approach.

Because of the high cost of printing and mailing catalogs, most catalog retailers have gone to more selective distribution lists. Database information about customers and potential customers is used to develop a mailing list of individuals who are the most likely to purchase merchandise through the catalog. Rather than one large catalog, many companies offer small, specialty catalogs that focus on a particular line of products like outdoor clothing, children's clothing, or kitchen merchandise.

Over the past few years, there has been a strong move to wed catalogs with a firm's Internet website. Often, consumers and businesses will examine a catalog but make the purchase either on the Internet or by telephone. According to Harvey Kanter, Vice President at cataloger Eddie Bauer, "There is no question that there is a crossover between the two channels. It's the richest customer to have. The catalog is not only a significant vehicle to drive its own business, but also for the customers to look and shop online. It's used as a tool in that regard. The Internet continues to grow as a percent of our direct business. We'll have over 50 percent penetration this year."[20] Many marketing experts believe that in the future, catalogs will take on a greater and greater role as a tool to drive customers to web-

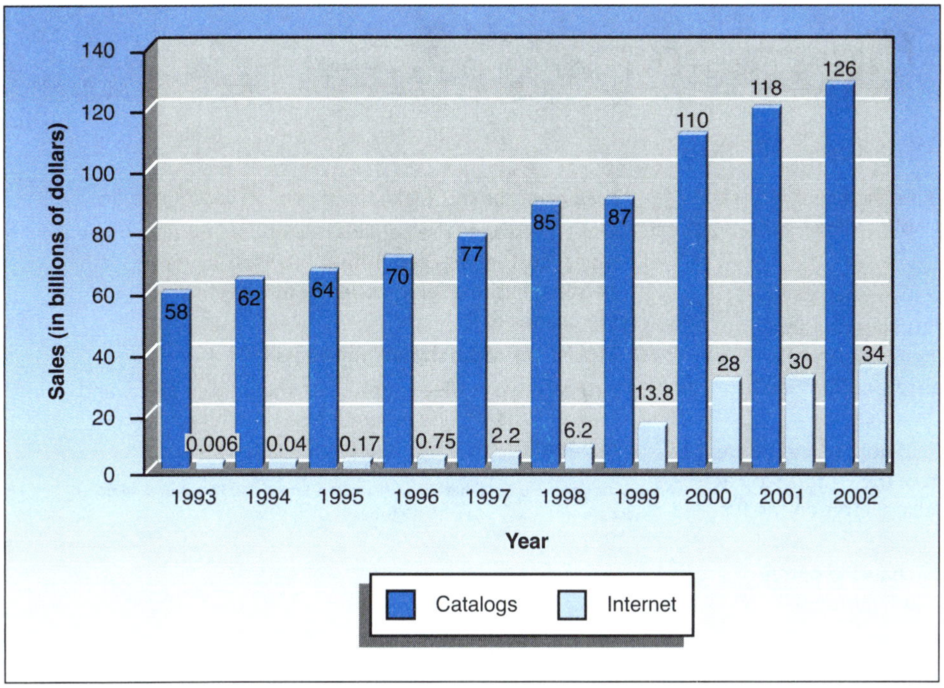

Figure 16-17
Catalog and Internet Sales

Source: Andrea Lillo, "Catalogs Feed Off Internet Growth" *Home Textiles Today*, vol. 21, no. 15 (December 16, 2002): 1, 6.

sites, where orders will be placed. Figure 16-17 compares catalog and Internet sales from 1993 through 2002.

Because individuals receive so many catalogs at home, companies are beginning to send catalogs to a person's workplace. Wolferman's English Muffins sent 200,000 catalogs to people at their offices, in addition to the 6 million that were sent to home addresses. This strategy makes sense based on surveys that indicate 75 percent of the goods sold on the web are ordered from a person's workplace. By sending catalogs to an individual's work, the company makes it very convenient for a customer to place an order using the catalog's website. Of the 90 billion pieces of direct mail sent to consumers, more than 500 million were sent to where they work.[21]

The Internet is a relatively new channel for direct marketing, which is still in the process of being developed. For most companies, the Internet is a place for consumers and businesses to get more information. While ordering capability may be in place, it is not the central thrust of the website. However, that is now changing with software such as Connectify Direct, NCR's Relationship Optimizer, and Prime Response Prime@Vantage, which allows a firm to create an interactive website. The software analyzes online purchases, clickstreams, and other interactions to develop personalized messages. In addition, the online behavior of a customer can be combined with demographic and psychographic data from either an internal database or an external database firm. Using all of this information, the software can suggest specific products the consumer is most likely to purchase. All of this analysis can occur while the person is still online. For example, a person who is looking at computer games and has purchased a certain type of game in the past may receive an offer for a new game that has just been introduced.

Using this type of technology, marketers can directly market to consumers and businesses on specific websites, which is being done by 29 percent of the companies engaged in direct marketing (see Figure 16-16). Marketers can also use the same technology with search engines. Direct-marketing ads can be placed on a search engine, or through the optimization software just discussed, the ad can be the result of a specific search and click-throughs. Marketing Illustration 16-4 offers tips on building a successful Internet direct-marketing program, regardless of which approach is being used.

Marketing Illustration 16-4

Internet Direct Marketing

Tim Choate, Chairman and CEO of FreeShop.com, offers the following tips on developing an online direct-marketing program:

1. *Acquire wisely.* Focus on the acquisition strategies that will result in the highest percentage of conversions and retentions. Typical acquisition strategies may include advertising on other websites, email responses, search engine listings, and media-directed venues.
2. *Keep it simple.* The first page must load quickly and be easy to navigate. If more than 25 percent of the visitors stop at the first page, then put your best-selling items on the first page.
3. *Try sampling.* Free or discounted merchandise or free shipping is an excellent method for luring browsers to the site.
4. *Keep them coming.* Make the shopping basket easy to use.
5. *Make it personal.* Use cookies to identify first-time users and repeat customers. Greet return browsers by name. Gather personal information by offering free or reduced merchandise.
6. *Make it fun.* Make the site fun to visit.
7. *Respect privacy.* Clearly articulate the privacy policy and make sure it is followed. Do not sell or share personal information without the approval of the customer.

Source: Kellee Harris, "What Direct Marketers Know That You Don't," *Sporting Goods Business*, vol. 33, no. 15 (October 11, 2000): 12.

In addition to website Internet programs, many companies are developing email direct-marketing campaigns. Notice from the survey conducted by Direct Marketing that email direct-marketing campaigns are second only to direct mail. Direct-marketing emails to customers are used by 55 percent of the firms, while 46 percent send email direct offers to prospects (see Figure 16-16). Email makes it possible for the company to deliver customized messages or promotions to customers similar to those sent in the mail. Recently, Williams-Sonoma Inc., a retailer of cookware and household goods, developed an email campaign with the objective of attracting customers into its retail store and to promote the Williams-Sonoma's online bridal registry. Approximately 5 percent of the customers contacted by email visited a local Williams-Sonoma store. This total was considerably higher than any direct-mail method the retailer had used before (see Figure 16-18).[22]

Automakers spend almost $300 million a year on direct marketing, with an increasingly higher proportion being spent on email campaigns. Nissan's Infiniti kicked off an advertising campaign to launch its new I35 sedan with an email blitz that involved sending one million emails to current owners and prospects, encouraging them to test drive the new sedan. A similar approach was used to promote the Mazda Tribute. Tied with a direct-mail campaign, the direct-marketing approach generated 25,000 Tribute vehicle sales as well as another 10,000 in other Mazda vehicles.[23]

Telemarketing has been an important medium for direct marketing, although legislation has altered its viability. Both consumers and businesses have grown impatient with telemarketers calling them at inopportune times and selling merchandise that is of no interest. Both the Federal Trade Commission and the Federal Communications Commission worked together to establish a federal do-not-call list that blocks telemarketing calls.

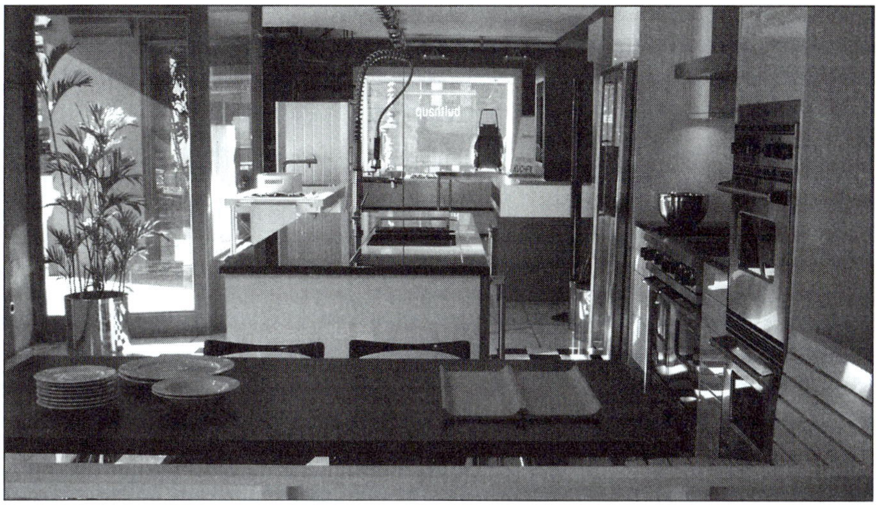

Figure 16-18
Retailers of cookware and household goods can benefit from email campaigns.

While the law stops some telemarketers, it exempts charities, political candidates, and businesses that already have a relationship with a customer. For example, if you have a credit card with Texaco, then Texaco can call you about other products, even if you are on the no-call list. Although the law has reduced the number of telemarketing calls, this approach remains a viable method of direct marketing.

In the business-to-business sector, telemarketing is a viable tool for reaching prospects. Field salespeople can spend $1,000 to $2,000 a week just in traveling costs to see only 10 prospects. Bonuses and commissions can cost a company from 5 to 7 percent of the orders taken. Telemarketers, however, cost only $35,000 a year and can make 250 calls a week, with no additional traveling expenses or hefty commissions.[24]

While the future of outbound telemarketing is uncertain, inbound telemarketing can be an important component of a direct-marketing campaign. Inbound telemarketers are used to support direct-marketing programs in other media, such as mail, email, catalogs, or television. It is important for companies to post toll-free numbers prominently and frequently in all direct-marketing and promotional materials in order to make sure consumers know where to go to gather additional information and place orders.

The mass media may be a part of a direct-marketing campaign. Compared to the other forms of direct marketing, mass media direct response offers tend to be used less, primarily because of a lower response rate. When used, the most common forms of mass media direct response marketing are television, radio, magazines, and newspapers. Television offers the advantage of access to a mass audience and is an excellent choice for products with a general appeal to the masses. Radio does not have the reach of television but still can be used to convey direct-marketing messages. However, unless toll-free numbers and web addresses are easy to remember and repeated frequently, consumers will have difficulty retaining the information, since in many cases, they are not in a situation in which they can write down the information. The print media, such as newspapers and magazines, are better for direct-marketing programs. Viewers can study ads and write down information.

Summary

1. *Explain the different types of personal selling.* Personal selling can be classified into three broad categories: order takers, order getters, and support personnel. Order takers process routine orders from customers, while order getters actively generate potential leads and persuade customers to make a purchase. Support personnel are individuals who directly support or assist in the selling function in some manner, but do not process orders or directly solicit orders. A field salesperson is an order getter who is involved in going to a potential customer's place of business to solicit business. If the company is calling customers and attempting to persuade them to purchase the product, this is called outbound telemarketing and is done by an order getter. If the company is manning telephones that customers call with orders, then it is inbound telemarketing, handled by order takers. A missionary salesperson, belonging to the last category of salespeople, provides information about a good or service.

2. *Discuss the various buyer-seller relationships.* The most basic type of buyer-seller dyad relationship is the single transaction, which occurs when the buyer and seller interact for the purpose of a single transaction. At the next level are occasional transactions that require an infrequent buyer-seller interaction and may be present in modified re-buy situations. Repeat transactions are at the third level; in repeat transactions, buyers and sellers interact on a regular basis. To ensure a greater commitment from buyers, sellers will often attempt to move the dyad to a higher level—the contractual agreement—which is a written agreement between the buyer and seller. While contractual agreements are a stronger form of dyad relationship, they may or may not involve trust. Trust relationships are based on mutual respect and understanding of both parties and a commitment to work together. At the next level is the electronic data interchange (EDI) relationship, which expands the trust relationship to include the sharing of data between the buying and selling firms. At the highest level of the buyer-seller dyad interaction is the strategic partnership. With this approach, the buyer and seller share information at the highest levels. The goal of this relationship is to collaborate on plans to benefit both parties as well as the customers of the buying firm.

3. *Identify the steps in the selling process and briefly describe each step.* The first step in the selling process is prospecting for leads. In this step, viable customers are identified and qualified. Step two is the pre-sales approach, in which the buyer gathers as much information as possible about the potential customer. In step three, the buyer determines the customer's needs in order to prepare the best selling approach and the strategy involved in presenting the product in its best light. Step four involves giving the sales presentation. Various methods can be used, depending on the ability and style of salespeople as well as the selling situation. Step five is answering any objections or questions the customer may raise. Step six is closing the sale. Various types of closings can be used, depending on the situation. The last step is the follow-up to ensure that the customer is satisfied with the sale.

4. *Explain the concepts of data warehousing and database management.* Data warehousing is the process of collecting, sorting, and retrieving relevant information about a firm's customers and potential customers. Through a process known as data mining, a company can gather useful information about its customers that can be used for profiling its best customers, developing marketing programs, and predicting future purchase behavior.

5. *Identify the steps in developing a customer relationship management program.* Customer relationship management (CRM) is a database application program designed to build long-term loyalty with customers through the use of a personal touch. The steps required to build a CRM program include (1) identifying the organization's customers, (2) differentiating customers in terms of their needs and value to the organization, (3) interacting with customers in a cost-effective and efficient manner, and (4) customizing the product offering to meet individual customer needs. Customer relationship management is based on the two tenets of (1) lifetime value of a customer and (2) share of the customer.

6. *Explain the concept of direct marketing and list the various methods of direct marketing.* Direct marketing is the promotion of a product from the producer directly to the consumer or business user without the use of any type of channel members. The typical direct-marketing venues include mail, catalogs, mass media, the Internet, email, and telemarketing.

Key Terms

buyer-seller dyad (p. 486)
contractual agreement (p. 487)
cross-selling (p. 485)
customer relationship management (CRM) (p. 502)
data mining (p. 501)
data warehousing (p. 499)
database marketing (p. 502)
digital direct-to-press (p. 506)
direct marketing (p. 504)
electronic data interchange (EDI) (p. 487)
field salesperson (p. 485)
geocoding (p. 500)
inbound telemarketing (p. 486)
mission-sharing sales approach (p. 495)
missionary salesperson (p. 486)
need-satisfaction sales approach (p. 494)
occasional transactions (p. 486)
order getters (p. 484)
order takers (p. 484)
outbound telemarketing (p. 486)
problem-solution sales approach (p. 494)
prospects (p. 489)
repeat transactions (p. 486)
share of the customer (p. 503)
single transaction (p. 486)
stimulus-response sales approach (p. 494)
strategic partnership (p. 488)
support personnel (p. 484)
trust relationships (p. 487)

Discussion Questions

1. Discuss a recent experience you had with a salesperson at a retail store. Was it a positive or negative experience? Which type of buyer-seller dyad was it?
2. Compare and contrast the various levels of buyer-seller relationships discussed in Section 16-2b in terms of your personal experience. Identify companies or salespeople you have interacted with for each type of relationship.
3. Pick a business that sells to another business, government, or institution. Discuss various ways a salesperson could prospect for new leads. What types of questions would be asked to qualify each lead?
4. For each of the following products and situations, which type of sales approach should be used?
   a. Selling kitchen appliances to a consumer in a retail store
   b. Selling car insurance to a consumer who stops at the office
   c. Selling liability insurance to a business on a cold call
   d. Selling accounting services to a large corporation
   e. Selling a new car to a consumer
   f. Selling a fleet of cars to a business for use by corporate personnel
5. Using a database or the Internet, do some research on answering objections in the selling process. Write a short paper on what you find.
6. Using a database or the Internet, do some research on closing a sale in the selling process. Write a short paper on what you find.
7. Using a database or the Internet, do some research on data mining. What did you learn?
8. Direct marketing is an effective means of reaching consumers. For the next week, keep a log of all of the direct-marketing pieces you receive through the mail, on the Internet, by email, in a magazine, or on television. Which direct-marketing pieces got your attention? Which were not effective?

Review Questions

True or False

1. Electronic data interchange (EDI) provides speed and accuracy in the sell-buy transactions; therefore, it is advisable that this system should be used with all potential buyers.
2. Occasionally, under the pressure of sales managers and the need to meet the sales quotas or desire to make more money, salespeople might use unethical techniques and persuade the customer in aggressive ways to make an immediate purchase.
3. The least-productive method of prospecting is cold canvassing because the buyer knows little about the prospect and a lot of time is spent on calling prospects with no interest.
4. With the presumptive close, the salesperson asks for an order in a direct manner and, if necessary, summarizes the benefits for the prospect.
5. Because it is more cost effective to retain current customers than to attract new ones, the follow-up is a critical component of the sales process.
6. Databases are important components of an IMC program and direct marketing campaign.
7. Data mining involves computer analysis of customer data to determine patterns, profiles, and relationships for the purpose of predicting purchase behavior.
8. Database marketing is a modern marketing program developed through information gathering from multisource databases and targeted to very broad customer segments.

Multiple Choice

9. Which category actively generates leads and solicits orders from prospects or customers?
   a. order takers
   b. order getters
   c. support personnel
   d. field salesperson
10. In which kind of buyer-seller relationship are the terms of interaction, cost, and length of commitment established in a written agreement?
    a. occasional transaction
    b. repeated transaction
    c. contractual agreement
    d. trust relationship
11. What information will be relevant to determine the best sales approach?
    a. current vendors
    b. critical product attributes
    c. expectations about sales promotion and advertising
    d. all of the above
12. Which sales approach, sometimes referred to as the canned sales approach, applies specific statements to solicit responses from customers?
    a. stimulus-response sales approach
    b. need-satisfaction sales approach
    c. problem-solution sales approach
    d. mission-sharing sales approach

13. Which method is applied when the salesperson confronts the customer objection directly, indirectly, or by a demonstration that the objection is not true or not founded on correct facts?
a. direct answer method
b. offset method
c. dispute methods
d. turn-around method

14. In the context of closing the sale, which category refers to the salesperson's appeals to the customer's emotions or attempts at creating a sense of urgency?
a. presumptive close
b. arousal close
c. minor-decision close
d. single obstacle close

15. Neighborhood lifestyle clusters based on ZIP codes are used by retailers to collect customer information about
a. purchase behavior and attitudes.
b. media preferences.
c. interest of people who lived in the neighborhood.
d. all of the above

16. Direct marketing is focused on which customer category?
a. buyers
b. inquirers
c. prospects
d. all of the above

Notes

1. Anthony J. Ubraniak, "Prospecting Systems That Work," *American Salesman*, vol. 48 (November 2003): 25–28.
2. Victoria Ocken, "Marking the Most of Online Databases," *Marketing News*, vol. 36, no. 20 (September 30, 2002): 17.
3. Roger P. Lewis, "Strategic Selling," *Proofs*, vol. 87 (November 2004): 54.
4. Sean Dwyer, John Hill, and Warren Martin, "An Empirical Investigation of Critical Success Factors in the Personal Selling Process for Homogenous Goods," *Journal of Personal Selling & Sales Management*, vol. 20, no. 3 (Summer 2000): 152–161.
5. Ibid.
6. Kenneth E. Clow and Donald Baack, *Integrated Advertising, Promotion & Marketing Communications* (Upper Saddle River, NJ: Prentice-Hall, 2002): 517.
7. Eric Cohen, "Database Marketing," *Target Marketing*, vol. 22, no. 4 (April 1999): 50.
8. Ibid.
9. Carol Krol, "Schools and Hospitals in Path of Dell's Funnel," *B to B*, vol. 87, no. 6 (June 10, 2002): 25.
10. Russell C. Coile, Jr., "Competing in a Consumer Choice Market," *Journal of Healthcare Management*, vol. 46, no. 5 (September/October 2001): 297–300.
11. Ibid.
12. Eric Cohen, "Database Marketing," *Target Marketing*, vol. 22, no. 4 (April 1999): 50.
13. "A Crash Course in Customer Relationship Management," *Harvard Management Update*, vol. 5, no. 3 (March 2000): 3–4.
14. Mary McCaig, "A Small Retailer Uses CRM to Make a Big Splash," *Apparel Industry*, vol. 1, no. 10 (October 2000): 30–34.
15. Alice Z. Cuneo, "Direct Spending for '02 Falls Short of Expectations," *Advertising Age*, vol. 73, no. 42 (October 21, 2002): 3.
16. Richard H. Levey, "Prospects Look Good," *Direct*, vol. 16 (December 1, 2004): 1–5.
17. Kellee Harris, "What Direct Marketers Know That You Don't," *Sporting Goods Business*, vol. 33, no. 15 (October 11, 2000): 12.
18. Sandra Yin, "Mail Openers," *American Demographics*, vol. 23, no. 10 (October 2001): 20–21.
19. Patrick Totty, "Direct Mail Gets a New Lease on Life," *Credit Union Magazine*, vol. 66, no. 4 (April 2000): 36–37.
20. Andrea Lillo, "Catalogs Feed Off Internet Growth" *Home Textiles Today*, vol. 21, no. 15 (December 16, 2002): 1,6.
21. Matthew Swibel, "Productivity Weakness Explained," *Forbes*, vol. 168, no. 16 (December 24, 2001): 38.
22. Jeff Sweat and Rick Whiting, "Instant Marketing," *Information Week*, vol. 746 (August 2, 1999): 34–37.
23. Jean Halliday, "Drives Sales Directly," *Advertising Age*, vol. 72, no. 43 (October 22, 2001): 22.
24. Nicole Ridgway, "Dialing for Dollars," *Forbes*, vol. 170, no. 11 (November 25, 2002): 226–227.

Case 16-1 National South Bank

National South Bank had been in business for more than 10 years and had expanded to a total of 11 facilities in three different towns. It was a locally owned and managed facility that had built a solid reputation for service, especially with the business community. The retail side of the business, which was directed to consumers, had done well, especially with the baby boomer generation.

National South was one of three locally owned banks, with total assets and facilities approximately equal to the other two locally owned banks combined. The difficulty National South faced was the large regional and national banks in the town. There were 18 of them, for a city with a population of 95,000 and a county population of slightly less than 160,000. Competition for customers was intense. But National South uncovered one area of town, on the north side, where the market seemed to be underserved. The area had grown rapidly during the previous five years, and a bank merger had reduced the number of facilities serving the north side. Eager to establish a presence in this area, National South built a large branch facility. It was now time to develop a marketing program for the branch's grand opening.

The first step National South took was to seek information from Claritas about the geodemographic makeup of the area. Using PRIZM, Claritas located the top market segments in the area that made up 90 percent of the population. These geodemographic groups are described in Table 16-4.

The second step for National South Bank was to hire a direct-marketing firm to handle the opening of the branch facility. National South recognized that it was in a delicate situation because it already had three other facilities in the town. Although it wanted new customers for the branch, it wanted to attract customers from competing banks, not have its current customers transfer their accounts to the new branch. While National South Bank was aware that some customers were likely to switch because the new location was more convenient for them, its objective was to ensure that the vast majority of customers were new. To attract these customers, the bank would have to offer some incentives. Some that were suggested included

- Free checking for six months
- Free safety deposit box for one year
- Free Internet banking for six months
- A free gift such as a kitchen appliance, briefcase, or makeup kit
- Reduced interest rate on a home equity loan

National South Bank recognized that it could not advertise these incentives on television or in the newspaper without upsetting its current customers, and it could not afford to offer these incentives to all of its current customers. By using a direct-marketing approach, National South felt that it could promote the new facility without very many of its current customers knowing what incentives were being offered.

The direct-marketing firm that was retained suggested that National South attempt a direct-mail campaign in the area surrounding the new facility, which could be followed up with a door hanger placed at each resident's home. Another suggestion was engaging in some tie-in partnerships with a few of the businesses in the area where they could place free direct-marketing pieces in the business and in the shoppers' bags as they checked out.

Questions

1. Which of the market segments would you suggest that National South Bank attract?
2. What incentives would you offer to each market segment selected in Question 1?
3. Design a direct-mail piece for National South Bank directed to one of the market segments.
4. Develop a direct-marketing program for National South Bank that would include the market segments you indicated in Question 1.
5. Do you think that National South Bank made the right decision in not offering free incentives in television and newspaper ads? Justify your answer.
6. How would you advertise this new branch facility without offending current customers at the other three facilities?

Source: Interview with Graham Morris of Newcomer, Morris, and Young (January 9, 2003); Claritas, Inc., http://cluster2.claritas.com, February 18, 2003.

TABLE 16-4

Geodemographic Groups

Source: *http://cluster2.claritas.com*

INTERACTIVE TABLE

Name	Size	Description	This PRIZM Cluster Is Most Likely to
Second city elite	30%	Upscale executive families Age group: 45+ Professional Household income: $67,800	Add a bathroom Own a laptop computer Own an Acura Read *Bon Appetit*
Upward bound	24%	Young, upscale, white-collar families Age group: Under 18, 35–54 Professional Household income: $62,100	Be very brand loyal Buy a new station wagon Have 401(K) plan Watch *The Tonight Show* Read *Vogue*
Middleburg managers	16%	Mid-level, white-collar couples Age group: 35–44, 65+ Professional/white collar Household income: $42,000	Own a laptop computer Have a home equity loan Watch the QVC channel Read *PC Magazine* Jog or run
Small-town downtown	12%	Older renters and young families Age group: 18–44 White collar/blue collar Household income: $22,800	Shop at Target Buy a VCR Have a school loan Watch MTV Read *Muscle and Fitness*
Southside city	8%	African-American service workers Age group: 18–34 Blue collar/service Household income: $17,000	Be pro-wrestling fans Buy gospel music Own a Mazda Watch BET Read *GQ*

Case 16-2 Selling Form/Label Combos

Most companies use separate forms to record orders, print packing labels, and print invoices. Not only is this process more time consuming, but it increases the chances of mistakes. Recent technology has allowed printing companies to develop a form/label combo, in which the purchasing form and label are all within one document. Manufacturers, distributors, mail-order companies, medical offices, and insurance companies like the new form/label combos. The primary advantages are convenience and reduction of shipping errors.

Although companies like the product, cost is a major stumbling block to adoption. Traditional purchase or invoice forms may cost a firm $600 and pressure-sensitive labels another $1,200. The affixed form/combo can cost up to $2,500 and if it is an integrated product that must be developed specifically for the firm, costs can go up to $6,000. So a firm is looking at $2,500 to $6,000, compared to $1,800 for its current method.

In a meeting of key salespeople, Digital Supply Forms, Inc. (DSF) sales manager Greg Fox asked for input on what could be done to boost sales of the form/label combo.

Mandall, a senior salesperson, began the dialogue. "You can't just walk in and talk about how this product is more convenient and will prevent errors. That won't work. You have to invest time and energy in learning the potential client's business operation. You have to walk through their business, or plant, or whatever it is, and see what they are currently doing. Once you see the problems they face, from their viewpoint, you can then start talking about how this combo will save them labor and costs in the long run, not the short run. If they are using different forms for picking products off of shelves, and packing them into their shipping containers, and then the actual packing label, they will immediately see the potential for error. You can also find out by that point how many shipments have problems and how much it costs them in direct costs to correct these problems. At this point, you have their interest, and you can start explaining to them how our product can meet their needs and save them money."

Warnez, another salesperson, added, "But the savings are only possible in the long run. They need to see that the initial cost may be more, especially if our computer people have to go in and develop the form that will work for them. But if they will make that investment, it will pay off. Another factor that you can throw in at this point is the goodwill gained with customers by not making errors."

Turning to Mandall and Warnez, Greg Fox asked, "What is the biggest objection companies have to this product?"

Both replied, almost simultaneously, "Cost." Mandall then continued, "If you can meet that objection, you've got a sale. But you better be prepared to show them, in black and white, with numbers why this form/label combo in the long run will save them money. The idea of reducing shipping errors is easy to get across. Every buyer I've talked to readily agrees with that."

Questions

1. What level of buyer-seller relationships discussed in Section 16-2b should DSF encourage with its salespeople?
2. Discuss the pros and cons of each of the sales presentation approaches. Which approach would you recommend?
3. What method of prospecting should DSF salespeople use to generate new leads? What questions should they ask to qualify their list of prospects?
4. How would you handle objections concerning the cost of the form/label combos?

Part

5

Marketing Expansion

International Marketing

17

CHAPTER OBJECTIVES

1. Address primary drivers of internationalization in the macroenvironment and the microenvironment.
2. Discuss the primary internationalization challenges and obstacles attributed to the cultural environment, to governments, to competition, and to the self-reference criterion.
3. Analyze the different levels of international involvement.
4. Address entry mode selection from a control and risk perspective.
5. Discuss the challenges presented by the international marketing mix to the international corporation.

CHAPTER OUTLINE

International marketing managers operating in unfamiliar environments need to have a thorough understanding of their target market if their marketing efforts are to be successful. Numerous marketing plans fail due to an incomplete understanding of the market. Companies selling consumer products are especially prone to experiencing difficulties in foreign markets. Many such examples exist. An American manufacturer of cornflakes tried to introduce its product in Japan but failed; the Japanese were simply not interested in the concept of breakfast cereals at the time. Also in Japan, Procter & Gamble (P&G) did not take into consideration women's needs for a thinner diaper due to the high frequency of changes and limited storage space, and a local competitor that provided thinner diapers in line with market demands quickly eroded P&G's market share. More recently, a Nike television ad depicted basketball star LeBron James in a videogame setting defeating a kung fu master and a pair of dragons, an important symbol of traditional Chinese culture. China banned the ad, considering it offensive.[1]

One way to ensure that such blunders are averted is to engage in a thorough market investigation. Marketers need to be aware of local rituals and traditions specific to the local culture in order to operate effectively in a particular country (see Figure 17-1 for an example).

Figure 17-1
In Rwanda, using both hands in a handshake conveys affection and respect.

17-1 Chapter Overview

This chapter introduces the challenges and opportunities facing firms engaging in international marketing. Section 17-2 explains why firms decide to go international, focusing on the macroenvironment drivers, such as economics, politics, and technology, as well as microenvironment drivers, such as consumer needs, competition, product lifecycle, standardization, economies of scale, and labor. Section 17-3 addresses the primary internationalization challenges and obstacles attributed to the cultural environment, to governments, to competition, and to the self-reference criterion. Section 17-4 addresses the different levels of international involvement—domestic marketing, export marketing, international marketing, and global marketing. Section 17-5 discusses the different international entry mode possibilities for the international firm from the least risk/least control option of indirect export, to the highest risk/control option of wholly owned subsidiaries. Finally, Section 17-6 addresses the challenges involved in deciding on the optimal marketing mix, given local market needs and company resources.

17-2 Why Firms Go International: Internalization Drivers

With a large, wealthy market available in the United States, why should firms go international? The United States constitutes one of the most important world markets, providing and consuming a high percentage of worldwide goods and services. Yet, for companies to achieve their full potential and prosper in the long run, it is crucial that they expand into international markets to take advantage of global market opportunities, to keep pace with competition, and to maximize the potential of their product mix. Global companies from small and large countries alike have achieved worldwide dominance. Companies from the Netherlands, a small country in Western Europe, have become giants of industry worldwide; among them are Philips (electronics) and Royal Ahold (retail). Companies from Japan, such as Mitsui and Mitsubishi (electronics, banking, and import-export, among others), Dentsu (advertising), Sony (see Figure 17-2), Panasonic (electronics), and Ito Yokado (retail), dominate their respective industries.

International companies such as General Motors, Mitsubishi, Microsoft, and Exxon earn profits greater than the gross domestic product of many developing countries, and their total market value is several times the size of their profits. Even successful small businesses can attribute their survival and/or success to international markets. Companies, in order to achieve their potential, must constantly monitor the international environment

Figure 17-2
Many Japanese companies, such as Sony, have developed worldwide dominance, especially in electronics and automobiles.

Source: © 2001 Sony Electronics, Inc. All rights reserved. Reproduction in whole or in part without written permission is prohibited. Sony, Dream On, and Mavica are trademarks of Sony.

for opportunities. Recently, privatization in countries where government monopolies have dominated for decades has made it possible for multinationals to compete for local airline, railway, and telecommunications industries. In the future, postal services might constitute the new competitive territory of international companies.

Few companies operate in an isolated, country-specific environment, and even fewer can effectively avoid international involvement. Local firms manufacturing for local consumers are dependent on equipment, parts, and/or raw materials originating abroad. They sell to clients and final consumers who have had exposure to international trade practices and to international products. A complete isolation from international influence is possible only for a closed environment, in countries such as North Korea, where consumers are shielded from international influence. Companies cannot avoid involvement in international marketing. Avoiding international expansion could mean losing market share to competitors and missing numerous opportunities created by changes in the international environment.

17-2a Drivers in the Macroenvironment

The macroenvironment provides several driving forces behind the international expansion effort. They include economic, political, and technology forces. Organizations that facilitate international trade and the development of transportation and telecommunication infrastructures are especially important. The following sections examine the drivers in the macroenvironment and the organizations that promote and facilitate international trade.

Economic Growth and Transition to a Market Economy Economic growth constitutes a very important driver of internationalization. Economic development in general and increased buying power—attributed to the emergence of a strong middle class in large markets, such as those of Brazil and India, for example—have created markets of potential for international brands. Economic growth has also opened markets that have been previously closed or that have limited international competition: A case in point is China, where consumers are no longer restricted with regard to their consumption and physical movement.

The transition of the former Eastern Bloc countries and other countries such as Vietnam and China to a market economy has also led to rapid economic development and has created important new markets for international brands. The deregulation and privatization of former government monopolies have also afforded important opportunities to international firms.

Regional Economic and Political Integration In addition to cultural similarities—language and religion, for example—economic and political integration play an important part in facilitating international trade. Regional agreements such as the North American Free Trade Agreement (NAFTA—a trade agreement between Canada, the United States, and Mexico), the Southern Cone Common Market (MERCOSUR—an agreement between Argentina, Brazil, Paraguay, Uruguay, Bolivia, and Chile), and the politically and economically integrated European Union are examples of successful attempts at lowering or eliminating barriers between member countries and promoting trade within the perimeter of each common market. The benefits of integration are bestowed on companies from nonmember states as well. Integration permits subsidiaries incorporated in the respective markets to benefit from free trade within the region and allows firms outside the integrated regions to conduct business within the common market without the impediments typically posed by crossing national borders—customs paperwork, separate tariffs for each country, and so on.

A company from the United States exporting products to multiple countries in the European Union, for example, will do the customs paperwork and pay the required customs duties only once, instead of applying for an import license and paying customs duties in every country where it exports products. A subsidiary of a company from the United States incorporated in any country of the European Union is a corporate citizen of the European Union. Consequently, the subsidiary does not have to pay duties when it crosses borders of European Union member states, nor foreign exchange costs, because all transactions are conducted in Euros.

Technology and the Transportation and Telecommunications Infrastructure Technology has created opportunities for firms involved in international business. In terms of media development, consumers worldwide are exposed to programming originating in other countries. Programming from the United States in particular dominates the international airways: *Baywatch* was followed by audiences worldwide, CNN is popular with businesspeople around the world, and NBC is eagerly exporting its mix of late-night comedy and news magazines to the rest of the world. Advertising also crosses borders, exposing consumers to brands from other countries. The web and the Internet have revolutionized the way many companies conduct business, offering, for example, small businesses instant and unlimited international exposure—something that bricks-and-mortar stores and traditional manufacturers have taken years to achieve.

Communication is reliable and instant. Telecommunication advances allow for teleconferencing with stakeholders across continents and efficient decision making.

The introduction of containers for international inter-modal (ship, truck, train) shipping greatly facilitates the transportation of physical goods. For passenger transport, efficient and rapid air travel has become more affordable, allowing for frequent interaction between expatriate or local employees and employees from the company headquarters.

Organizations Facilitating International Trade Several important international and local institutions promote international trade and offer important opportunities for international marketing operations, facilitating trade directly or promoting economic development. A brief overview of the primary trade organizations that facilitate international trade and development follow.

The World Trade Organization (WTO) Preceded by the General Agreement on Tariffs and Trade (GATT) and signed by 123 nations agreeing to promote trade and eliminate trade barriers, the World Trade Organization (WTO; www.wto.org) currently has 147 member countries from a world total of 192. The WTO is changing the way countries regulate international business in their territory and beyond. Its most important trait is that membership is predicated on full implementation and adherence to all agreements. Countries often must radically change their trade practices and, implicitly, their internal economic structures in order to gain membership. The WTO's main functions are providing assistance to developing and transitional economies, offering specialized help for export promotion through the International Trade Center, promoting regional trade agreements, promoting cooperation in global economic policymaking, reviewing members' trade policies, and engaging in routine notification when members introduce new trade measures or alter old ones.[2]

The Group of Eight (G8) Members of the Group of Eight (G8), the most industrialized countries, are Canada, France, Germany, Italy, Japan, Russia, the United Kingdom, and the United States. The group (which originally was known as the G7—excluding Russia) was organized during the 1970s' economic crisis as a forum for addressing economic and financial issues. The organization's yearly meetings involve heads of state, government ministers, and directors of central banks. The G8 currently addresses issues such as biotechnology and food safety, economic development, disarmament, arms control and nonproliferation, organized crime, drug trafficking, terrorism, environmental issues, digital opportunities issues, microeconomic issues, and trade.

The International Monetary Fund (IMF) and the World Bank The International Monetary Fund (IMF) (www.imf.org) and the World Bank (www.worldbank.org) were created in 1944 to address the need of global economic development, stability, and rebuilding after the Second World War and the 1930s' Great Depression. Both the International Monetary Fund and the World Bank are specialized agencies of the United Nations. Membership in the World Bank requires membership in the IMF. The goal of the IMF was to establish an innovative monetary system and an institution charged with monitoring it. The IMF is based on a system that encourages the unrestricted conversion of one currency to another by establishing a clear and unequivocal value for each currency.[3] The IMF comprises more than 180 member countries that are obligated to adhere to its charter of rights and obligations—or to leave the organization (as Cuba, Indonesia, and Poland have done in the past).[4] Traditionally, the IMF has played the role of lender of last resort; more recently, however, it has also assumed the position of mediator between debtors and creditors.

The World Bank is the largest international bank that sponsors economic development projects. The World Bank, headquartered in Washington, D.C. (see Figure 17-3) , employs international specialists in economics, finance, and industrial development. In addition, it has field offices in developing countries, overseeing projects in the areas of industry, health, and poultry and dairy production, among others. While, in the past, the World Bank's focus was industrial and infrastructure development, its current priorities lie primarily in the areas of health (it provided a $500 million umbrella loan for programs to combat

Figure17-3
The World Bank, headquartered in Washington, D.C., sponsors economic development projects worldwide.

HIV/AIDS in Sub-Saharan Africa) and information technology (in 2000, the World Bank awarded $1.5 billion in contracts to information-technology companies).[5]

Other Development Organizations A number of development banks with a regional focus also are instrumental in advancing economic development and in providing support for business and trade. Among the development banks are:[6] the African Development Bank (www.afdb.org); the Asian Development Bank (www.adb.org); the European Bank for Reconstruction and Development (www.ebrd.com), whose main goals are reforming and strengthening markets in the transition economies of Central and Eastern Europe; and the Inter-American Development Bank (www.iadb.org). All these banks attempt to improve the infrastructure in their target regions and to provide impetus for economic development. The United Nations (www.un.org) bodies, headquartered in Switzerland and the United States, promote the economic and financial welfare of developing countries, developing their industrial, communication, and transportation infrastructures.

Government Organizations Promoting international trade constitutes one of the more important tasks of the national and local governments of most countries. Many U.S. federal, state, and local government agencies promote the interests of U.S. businesses abroad, encouraging their international involvement in the form of export promotion or by providing foreign direct investment support. They also actively pursue foreign direct investment in the United States. Among the U.S. agencies supporting activities of international business are the U.S. Agency for International Development and the U.S. Department of Commerce, at the federal government level, as well as state and city economic development offices.

17-2b Drivers in the Microenvironment

A firm's microenvironment is a driving force behind international expansion. Converging consumer needs across nations, competition, product lifecycle, product development costs, economies of scale, standardization, and labor costs are the primary drivers in the microenvironment. The following sections discuss these drivers in more detail.

Converging Consumer Needs Consumers worldwide are loyal to international brands, such as Reebok sneakers, Levi's jeans, Coca-Cola, Heineken beer, and Ralph Lauren shirts (see Figure 17-4). Uniform consumer segments are emerging worldwide: the

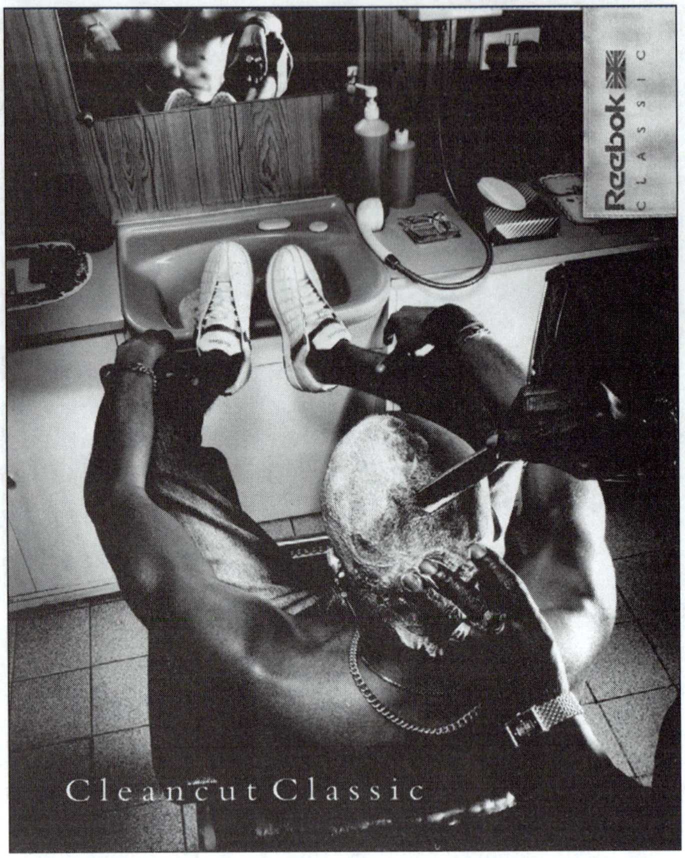

Figure 17-4
Consumers around the world are familiar with brands such as Reebok.
Source: Courtesy of Reebok.

younger generations in the United States and in Southeast Asia are loyal to the same soft drink brands, wear the same brands of clothing, listen to the same music, have the same idols, see the same television shows, and watch MTV for entertainment. During their international travels, consumers often purchase brands and services available in their own home country, which they are familiar with. These offerings tend to be successful international products. Alternatively, consumers who have traveled abroad bring with them product experiences and demand brands that may not be available in the home-country market. This generates pull demand, whereby consumers request the product from the retailers, who subsequently convey the request up the distribution chain to wholesalers, who would then order the product.

Firms facing similar consumers simultaneously demanding the same products can address the needs of these consumers, using a similar marketing strategy throughout the region. Entry in such uniform markets is facilitated by selling the same product regardless of market and by the use of the same advertising campaign, such as addressing Generation X in the United States, France, Malaysia, and El Salvador. Marketing Illustration 17-1 shows how worldwide music trends can produce uniform consumer segments.

Competition Competitive pressure is frequently a driver of internationalization. McCann Erickson, a leading advertising agency, follows one of its longtime clients, Coca-Cola, in every country where the company is present around the globe. McCann Erickson has been handling the Coca-Cola account in 89 countries since 1942.[7] That could mean that McCann Erickson may lose money in countries where it has only the Coke account. If McCann Erickson chose not to serve its client in a market, Coca-Cola might resort to the services of a competitor, and it might replace McCann Erickson with the competing advertising firm. McCann Erickson is like many firms: To remain competitive, it must expand internationally (see Figure 17-5).

Marketing Illustration 17-1

The World Is Dancing to World Beat

World Beat, a popular genre of music, is a mix of techno and Latin beats, hip-hop, and African or Arab beats, with a synthesized ethnic melodic touch. This music is marketed effectively to the World Beat consumer segment worldwide. Jessica, a 24-year-old Swede of African ancestry and a World Beat star in her home country, first launched her CD internationally in the Asia-Pacific region before introducing it elsewhere—with rapid success: Her album went gold instantly in South Korea and then began winning other markets around the world.

World Beat ranges from more traditional Europop groups such as Enigma with its haunting, sinful, seductive French whispers and interjections of Greek Orthodox church choir, to Alabina, a group whose Arabic-Latin music is heard even in U.S. supermarkets; Disidenten, a German group playing Arabic songs; and Gypsy Kings, a French group playing French music with a Latin beat. The late Israeli singer Ofra Haza attempted to bridge Israeli and Arab culture with her album *Shaday;* her song "Im Nin Alu," based on a seventeenth-century poem by Rabbi Shalom Shabazi, propelled her to international superstar status.

The market for World Beat is the world music consumer. This genre of music appeals across cultures and across age groups. In Europe and Africa, listeners range from teenagers to forty-somethings. In the United States, however, few mainstream songs are ever heard in a foreign language, with the exception of a few here in there that have a refrain in Spanish. Two record labels, Putumayo and World Music Network, have spent the past 10 years introducing U.S. listeners to world music. A promising album is *World 2004*, by a BBC disk jockey, which features performers from Venezuela, Israel, Cuba, Mali, and even the United States.

Sources: Author's interest; Ed Ward, "They Introduce America to World Music," *Wall Street Journal* (December 30, 2004): D8; "Jessica: Europop with Substance," http://iafrica.com (September 5, 2001).

Figure 17-5
To remain competitive, firms like Coca-Cola and Guess have to expand their market to other countries.

Product Drivers An important driver of international expansion is a firm's attempt to prolong the product lifecycle. Products that are in late maturity, or even in the decline stage, can change their position on the global product lifecycle by going into markets where the product is in high demand and in the growth stage. To illustrate this point, the cigarette industry is in either the late maturity stage or in the decline stage in many industrialized countries. By entering emerging markets where cigarettes are in the growth stage and consumers have increasing purchase power, such as China, India, and Eastern Europe, the cigarette industry is in fact prolonging its product lifecycle.

In addition, the costs of new product development are too high for firms to focus only on their home country. Nike, on the average, spends close to a year to develop, test, and manufacture new product designs that then last on the shelves in the United States for only six months. Despite the size and the purchase power of the U.S. market, it is unlikely that Nike would fully recover its product development costs and make a profit as well if it limited its sales to this country. This is especially true for companies at the forefront of technology (manufacturers of high-tech equipment and electronics, pharmaceutical firms, and others), which need to tap large markets for long periods to recoup costs and to make a profit; hence, for these companies, going international is not a choice—it is a precondition for survival.

PLC Maturity Stage During the maturity stage of the product lifecycle, the core product is likely to achieve a standard in a particular industry. Competitors—typically an oligopoly—respond to consumer needs by offering products whose components are interchangeable and which converge toward the brand experiencing the greatest consumer franchise (demand). During the maturity stage, firms also increasingly compete on price. Typically, they attempt to lower the product manufacturing costs by achieving economies of scale in production. Firms at maturity also move manufacturing operations and facilities abroad, to developing countries, in an attempt to take advantage of significantly lower labor costs.

Furthermore, international firms benefit from lessons they learn in the different parts of the world. Colgate-Palmolive, for example, developed its successful Axion paste for washing dishes for its Latin American market after noting that women washed dishes by hand, dunking their hands in a small tub with a few slivers of soap. The same product was then offered to consumers in Central and Eastern Europe after noting that they washed dishes using a similar method—and the product was a hit. Service providers such as Pizza Hut found that they were more successful with consumers in general, but especially with younger generations of consumers in Central and Eastern Europe, if they played pop music, on the rather loud side. As a result, they started entering new markets by partnering with radio stations and discos.

17-3 Internationalization Challenges and Obstacles

Companies attempting to establish and maintain an international presence are likely to encounter challenges and obstacles both from within the company and from outside. Aside from financial obstacles, which could prevent expansion locally, not just internationally, are challenges presented by a company's limited knowledge of a particular cultural environment and of local business practices.

17-3a The Challenging Cultural Environment

As discussed in Chapter 4, "Consumer Behavior," culture influences consumption. Culture is expressed in the consumption of numerous products in homes, offices, stores, and marketplace sites, with differences noted across various nations. Yet, the elements of culture—language and religion, among others—vary greatly from country to country.

Language Language poses a number of concerns to marketers. First, in terms of translation, the diversity of languages creates numerous difficulties for marketers operating internationally. Translation is expensive, especially in markets where multiple languages are spoken. For example, in India, there are more than 300 minor languages and 3,000 dialects. Only 15 distinct languages are widely spoken, however; Hindi, the official language, is spoken by 30 percent of the population, and English is widely used in administrative, commercial, and political life. To effectively communicate with this very promising multicultural market of approximately one billion, a firm's decisions on which language to use are crucial.

Problems could arise in the process of translation: Firms have placed the viability of their brands in jeopardy by relying on primary translations and not ensuring that either the product name is appropriate in a given culture or that the communication actually conveys the intended message. Many companies have made translation blunders, and the marketing literature is replete with examples, from the chocolate and fruit product sold under the

Marketing Illustration 17-2

International Body Language

In order to be effective, marketing managers must be aware of the following nonverbal modes of communication:

- *Proxemics* refers to the relationship between physical space and communication. A peculiar trait of American culture that surprises foreigners is the space around individuals (the "bubble"), which, if one violates, one must apologize. In Eastern Europe and Latin America, the bubble is unheard of. In these countries, even in polite society, it is not necessary to apologize for maneuvering too closely.
- *Postures, orientations*, and *oculesics* refer to one's positioning relative to others and the use/avoidance of eye contact during communication. In the United States, one should offer a firm and brief handshake while looking one's counterpart in the eye to portray a forthright attitude. This handshake is seen as aggressive in Asia, where a soft handshake, a humble posture, and avoidance of eye contact convey respect.
- *Chronemics* refers to the timing of verbal exchanges. Americans expect prompt responses. They are uncomfortable with a slow response and promptly fill in the silence. Other nationalities—the Japanese, for instance—prefer to use this "quiet time" as contemplation time, when they evaluate the message.
- *Kinesics* refers to the movement of the body in order to communicate. While communicating, Americans gesture little compared to other cultures, while the French and Italians use hand gestures frequently. Understanding the meanings of gestures is important to function efficiently. For example, the sign for "OK" used in the United States signifies zero in France, money in Japan, and is vulgar in parts of South America.
- *Paralinguistics* refers to emotional intonation, accents, and quality of voice. A louder, aggressive intonation denoting self-assurance in the United States is perceived as threatening or insulting by other cultures, where softness is equated with politeness. In West Africa, laughter indicates embarrassment, discomfort, or surprise.
- *Appearances* refers to physical attire and grooming. Cultures have their own expectations and norms regarding appropriate dress: Western business attire for men consists of a well-tailored dark suit, a conservative shirt and tie, and polished shoes. For women, it consists of a formal suit or a conservative dress and heels (Europeans allow for a more casual look and personal style than Americans). In the Middle East, depending on the country, men's business attire may consist of a *gallabeya* (a long, typically white garment) and a head cover, whereas women in business may have their hair covered, while wearing an equally long, conservative dress. In India, Pakistan, and Bangladesh, appropriate business attire for women may be the traditional *sari*, an exquisitely embroidered or designed material that is wrapped using a specific pattern. In Africa, women wear a gown with country-specific prints—a *bou-bou* (pronounced "boo-boo"), while men wear a short-sleeve shirt with a political party pin attached and a pair of slacks, with the exception of the most formal circumstances, when a coat and tie are worn.

Sources: Sami Abbasi and Kenneth W. Holman, "Business Success in the Middle East," *Management Decision*, vol. 31, no. 1 (1993): 55–59; David A. Ricks, *Blunders in International Business* (Cambridge, MA: Blackwell Publishers, 1993); Roger Colles, "Spain—A Hot Prospect," *Resident Abroad* (November 1993): 16–20.

name *Zit* in English-speaking countries, to the Fresca soda pop sold in Mexico (where, in slang, it means lesbian). Even if the same language is shared by different countries, marketers should be aware of differences in meaning: Procter & Gamble sells "nappies" in the United Kingdom, as opposed to "diapers"; the "boot" of the Ford automobile is actually its "trunk"; and housewives or househusbands who are "hoovering" in the United Kingdom may actually be "vacuuming" using an Electrolux vacuum cleaner.

It is important to communicate in the appropriate language with the target market in areas where multiple languages are used. Marketers selling their products in the United Arab Emirates will find that a significant proportion of consumers there do not speak the national language, Arabic. Guest workers in these countries are predominantly Indian, Pakistani, and Southeast Asian. In targeting these markets, firms would benefit from using English, which is widely understood and the main language used in business, rather than Arabic.

In international marketing, **nonverbal communication,** which includes body language, gestures, grimaces, eye contact, and even silence, is especially important. Silent communications, especially gestures, have different meanings across cultures, and marketing managers must be aware of them in order to avoid embarrassing or costly mistakes. Marketing Illustration 17-2 addresses nonverbal communication.

Nonverbal communication: All communication that is not written or spoken; includes body language, gestures, facial expressions, eye contact, and silence.

Religion Religion defines a society's relationship to the supernatural and, as a result, determines dominant values and attitudes. Religious beliefs are important determinants of consumer behavior. Purchase motivation; consumption preferences and patterns; customs and business practices; attitudes toward authority, family, peers, and foreigners; as well as attitudes toward material possessions, cultural values, and norms, among others, can all be traced to religion. Religion thus can be linked to cultural behaviors that have an impact on economic development and marketing. For example, the Protestant religion stresses hard work and frugality and is linked to the development of capitalism and economic emancipation. Judaism, with its disdain for ignorance and sloth, stresses education and has led to industrial development. Islam dictates social etiquette and consumption and bans the use of interest rates. It influences the relationship between men and women in society and in the workplace, discourages the consumption of pork products and alcohol, and requires procedures to reconcile Islamic banking laws with Western banking practices—by, for example, charging periodic fees, rather than interest. The Hindu religion encourages a family orientation and dictates a nine-tier class structure and strict dietary constraints, affecting the workplace hierarchy and discouraging the consumption of animal products—beef, in particular. Buddhism stresses sufferance and avoidance of worldly desires, thus, in principle, rejecting many aspects of marketing.

It is important to be aware of religious holidays, prayer requirements (Muslims are required to pray five times a day at specific times), and religion-mandated gender restrictions, such as the requirement that personal services should be performed only by individuals of the same gender. For example, women can bank only at women's banks in Muslim countries, can have their hair done only by other women, and so on. The genders typically do not interact in the very traditional Islamic countries except within the family.

Firms often must adapt their offering to the local culture to address consumers' religious concerns. Fast-food restaurants operating in Israel find that they can better serve their Jewish consumers by offering ample choices of vegetarian food, which does not compromise consumer kosher requirements. Keeping kosher requires, among others, the separation of milk products and meat products and implements used to serve or process them; vegetarian products are pareve (neutral, with regard to kosher requirements). In other examples the rituals of death, baptism, and marriage in the Eastern Orthodox religion are very involved and costly. For example, at an Eastern Orthodox funeral, tradition requires meals at the best restaurants the family can afford and offering quality brands of towels and other gifts to those involved in the funeral procession (see Figure 17-6).

Adapting Marketing Practices to Culture—Some Illustrations In general, many national and regional cultural differences require companies to adapt their marketing practices. With regard to advertising, substantial censoring occurs in many countries. In

Figure 17-6
The rituals at an Eastern Orthodox funeral can be involved and costly.

Saudi Arabia, women are not portrayed in advertisements. It is appropriate, however, to show the covered arms and wrists of a woman demonstrating product use. For magazines of Western provenance, censorship is enforced; for example, when such magazines are brought into the country by individuals, or when delivered by mail, any area of a woman's uncovered body and her face in photographs are blackened with a magic marker. In other Islamic countries, such as Malaysia, women should not be portrayed sleeveless, whereas in the streets of Turkey, one can actually see advertisements of women modeling bras.

In yet other examples, the United States has a driving culture. Students drive for six hours to be home for Thanksgiving, people easily drive 140 miles each way to their weekend houses, and a 45-minute daily automobile commute is not unusual. In the rest of the world, privately owned automobiles are used less—and mopeds and bicycles may replace them. For example, people use different means of transportation to purchase products and get about in their daily lives. In the United States, most marketing strategies address a driving public, the shopper who can park at a strip mall and load the contents of an extra-large shopping cart into the family van. In much of the rest of the world, things are quite different. For example, Western Europeans might take their bicycles (see Figure 17-7) to the supermarket and use automobiles only to drive to out-of-town destinations. In Central Asia and Sub-Saharan Africa, buses with crowded upper-level decks or trucks with protective bar grids are used for local and long-distance transportation. These consumers are likely to transport goods in crowded environments, where they must also keep their balance. A typical fast-food drive-through is not likely to be the most efficient means for serving these consumers. Marketing Illustration 17-3 notes the hazards of not understanding cultural differences.

17-3b Government Barriers

Local governments, especially governments in developing countries, keep tight control over international market entrants, permitting or denying access to international firms based on criteria that are deemed important for national industry and/or security considerations at a particular point in time. Among formal methods used by national governments to restrict or impede entrance of international firms in the local market are tariffs and barriers such as import quotas, or policies of restricting import license awards, foreign exchange restrictions, and local content requirements. However, member countries of the World Trade Organization, or members of regional economic integration agreements such as NAFTA and the European Union, find it very difficult to use tariffs as a means of restricting international

Figure 17-7
Cultural and behavioral differences exist throughout the world. In Bangladesh, buses with upper-level decks are a common means of transportation, whereas in Holland, bicycles are very common and, as in many countries in Europe, they have their own paths that parallel most roads.

Marketing Illustration 17-3

The Deal Gone Awry

Imagine you are in the middle of negotiations with a potential Turkish client in Istanbul, over lunch, at the Conrad Hilton Hotel. You go to the self-service buffet and pile some tasty pork chops on your plate from a plate clearly marked "pork." You ask the waiter to bring a bottle of wine and offer some to your potential Turkish client; he declines. Your products are known for their quality in Turkey and elsewhere in the world, and your client seems receptive to your price quote. After lunch, the potential client invites you to his home for coffee; you decline and state that you need to stay at the hotel to get some work done and bid him good-bye. You come back to the United States and find that you cannot reach your potential Turkish client. His secretary always claims he is not in, and he does not return your calls. What went wrong? You subsequently learn that, in Turkey, the dominant religion is Islam, and Islam bans the consumption of pork and alcohol. Could your lunch have turned off your client? Probably not too much, since he still seemed receptive to your offer as you were eating the "dirty animal" in front of him. Could he have been offended by your not going to his house for Turkish coffee? Even though you refused, you did not tell him that you really hate the stuff and that you were dreading spending even a few hours in 90-degree weather in a home that most likely was not air-conditioned. You were, after all, showing how dedicated you were to your job by staying home. Could the hotel staff have told him that you spent the evening next door, at another air-conditioned hotel, a former palace, having yet another bottle of wine?

Many companies find that their new foreign firm is about to collapse because they have failed to learn that country's customs, cultures, and laws. One study claims that two out of every three U.S. businessmen sent to Saudi Arabia are brought back home due to difficulties in adapting to the local culture, which obviously becomes very expensive for the companies involved. Using marketing strategies without understanding the local culture will quickly backfire. In the former Soviet Union, advertisements using the Marlboro Man did not produce much enthusiasm and did not initially enhance the adoption rate of the Marlboro brand. In spite of the popularity of movie and TV Westerns, a cowboy was perceived as the U.S. equivalent of a peasant—an uncultured, poor individual with a low status in society. In general, advertisements that promise prosperity, higher status, and overall advancement tend to be more successful in this market.

When marketers are armed with knowledge about the local culture, they are in a better position to communicate effectively with the target consumer.

Sources: Sami Abbasi and Kenneth W. Holman, "Business Success in the Middle East," *Management Decision*, vol. 31, no. 1 (1993): 55–59; Alan L. Gilman, "Stay Afloat in Foreign Expansions," *Chain Store Executive*, vol. 70, no. 5 (May 1994): 193.

expansion of companies in the countries' territories. Increasingly, they are using nontariff barriers, such as cumbersome procedures for import paperwork processing, delays in granting licenses, or preference given to local service providers and product manufacturing for all contracting work.

17-3c International Competition

Although competition can be a driver of internationalization, competitors can also erect barriers to new entrants in a market. They often do so by employing strategies such as blocking channels of distribution, binding retailers into exclusive agreements, slashing prices temporarily to prevent product adoption, or engaging in an advertising blitz that could hurt a company's initial sales in a market and cause it to retrench. With heavy competition from new and lesser brands in Asia, Central and Eastern Europe, North Africa, and the Middle East, Marlboro has created a strong defensive strategy for its cigarettes. It slashed prices by as much as a third and advertised heavily anywhere it was legal, especially on billboards in the center of different capital cities and towns in the provinces.

As an example, sales of Marlboro in southeastern Europe were hurt by various local competitors and, in particular, by a successful international brand, Assos, from Greece. Assos was rapidly gaining a leading position in a number of markets in the region when Marlboro went on the offensive, limiting Assos's market share to a point where the company was forced to abandon many of its markets. Marlboro effectively put in question the international expansion of many new European and Asian brands, as well as new brands from the United States (it decimated, for instance, sales of new brands of American cigarettes created specifically for the Russian market).

17-3d The Self-Reference Criterion

Of importance to international operations is the ability of the firm, and especially of its marketing program, to adapt to the local business environment in order to serve the needs of local consumers and to address the requirements of local government, industry, and channels of distribution. An impediment to adaptation is the **self-reference criterion,** defined as individuals' conscious and unconscious reference to their own national culture, to home-country norms and values, as well as to their knowledge and experience in the process of making decisions in the host country. Extensive self-reference can lead to a breakdown in communication between parties from different cultures. For example, consider an employee of a large multinational company from the United States conducting business in Japan; this employee has been trained by career counselors in the United States that looking one's counterpart in the eyes conveys directness and honesty is likely to be perceived as abrasive and challenging.

Self-reference criterion: Individuals' conscious and unconscious reference to their own national culture, to home-country norms and values, and to their knowledge and experience in the process of making decisions in the host country.

Domestic marketing: Marketing that is focused solely on domestic consumers and on the home-country environment.

17-4 Levels of International Marketing Involvement

All companies are affected by elements of the international marketing environment. In terms of international marketing involvement, however, companies have different degrees of commitment.

A company engaging in **domestic marketing** has the least commitment to international marketing. This company is focusing solely on domestic consumers and on the home-country environment. The home-country environment, however, is affected by developments in the international environment. Furthermore, the local company is directly affected by local competition, which could come from global companies. At the next level, **export marketing,** a firm could be involved in exporting indirectly, through orders from international clients, or directly, where the company actively seeks international clients. For both export marketers and domestic marketers, the international market constitutes an extension of the domestic market and is not given special consideration.

International marketing requires a focus on international consumers in a particular country or countries (when more countries are involved, it is referred to as **multinational marketing**). International marketing is the process of creation, production, distribution, promotion, and pricing of goods, services, ideas, and experiences for international markets. The international company is present in different countries with sales offices and subsidiaries, or is an active partner in strategic alliances with local companies; yet, its international activities are not coordinated across countries or across regions. **Global marketing** involves marketing across different countries without a national or regional focus. Global marketing is possible due to the emergence of global consumer segments and must be backed by efficient global allocation of company talent and resources.

Export marketing: Involvement in international marketing limited to the exporting function; although the firm actively seeks international clients, it considers the international market an extension of the domestic market and does not give it special consideration.

International marketing: The processes involved in the creation, production, distribution, promotion, and pricing of products, services, ideas, and experiences for international markets; these processes require a substantial focus on international consumers in a particular country or countries.

17-5 International Entry Mode Selection

The entry mode classifications offered in the following sections follow a general model of low to high control and risk, respectively—from indirect exporting to wholly owned subsidiary. That is, company control over operations and overall risk increase from the export entry mode to the wholly owned subsidiary entry mode. In general, companies tend to use the export mode in their first attempt to expand internationally and in environments that present substantial risk, and companies tend to approach markets that offer promise and lower risk by engaging in some form of foreign direct investment. There are, however, many exceptions: Companies that have been present for decades in attractive international markets, such as Airbus Industries and Caterpillar, continue to export to those markets rather than manufacture abroad. Similarly, many new small businesses find that they can manufacture products cheaply abroad and distribute them in those markets without making a penny in their home country; this is increasingly becoming a possibility for companies selling on the Internet.

Multinational marketing: Marketing in different countries without coordinating across operations.

Global marketing: International marketing activities that do not have a country or region focus and that are possible due to the emergence of global consumer segments and efficient global allocation of company talent and resources.

Indirect exporting: An export entry mode whereby a company sells its products in the company's home country to intermediaries, who, in turn, sell the product overseas.

Direct exporting: An export entry mode whereby a firm handles its own exports, usually with the help of an in-house exporting department.

Licensing: A process that involves a licensor, who shares the brand name, technology, and know-how with a licensee in return for royalties.

17-5a Exporting

Exporting can be either direct or indirect. **Indirect exporting** means that the company sells its products to intermediaries in the company's home country who, in turn, sell the product overseas. Using indirect exporting does not require market expertise or a long-term commitment to the international market. The company's risk is low; at most, it can lose a shipment. Among disadvantages are lack of control over the marketing of its products—which could ultimately lead to lost sales and a loss of goodwill that might affect the perception of the company and its brands in other markets where it has a greater commitment. Companies may use indirect exporting as a first step toward greater international involvement. It should be mentioned, however, that indirect exporting in the long term does not necessarily mean that the company is not committed to the market; it simply means either that the company does not have resources for greater involvement or that other markets need more resources. One of Europe's leading car makers, Germany's Volkswagen, operates through independent importers and distributors in Belgium, the Netherlands, Switzerland, and Austria, whereas in France, Germany, Italy, and Spain, which together account for 83 percent of European sales, it controls its wholesale operations directly.[8]

Companies engaging in **direct exporting** have their own in-house exporting expertise, usually in the form of an exporting department. Such companies have more control over the marketing mix in the target market. They can make sure that wholesalers and retailers observe the company's marketing policies by charging the suggested sale price, offering the appropriate promotions, and handling customer requests promptly and satisfactorily. More control, however, is expensive. The company carries the cost of the export department staff and the costs involved in selecting and monitoring middlemen involved in distribution—freight forwarders, shipping lines, insurers, merchant middlemen, and retailers—as well as other marketing service providers, such as consultants, marketing researchers, and advertising companies. One venue that opens new opportunities for direct exporting is the Internet. With a well-developed website, companies can now reach directly to customers overseas and process sales online. Catalog retailers and dot-com companies, such as Lands' End and Amazon.com, respectively, long ago made their first international incursions by exporting their products to consumers abroad and are rapidly expanding their international operations.

17-5b Licensing

Licensing, a popular international entry mode, presents more risks to the company but also offers it more control than exporting. Licensing involves a licensor and a licensee. The licensor offers know-how, shares technology, and often shares a brand name with the licensee. The licensee, in turn, pays royalties. The two approaches to licensing are licensing without the name and licensing with the name. A licensor licenses without the name when quality cannot be guaranteed or when the licensee does not allow the licensor sufficient control and scrutiny. For example, in the early 1970s, Italy's Fiat granted a license to Avto-VAZ, Russia's largest automobile manufacturer, to manufacture Lada, Russia's most popular automobile, and an important export to neighboring and other developing countries. Licensors can decide to adapt the names of their products when they have a greater confidence in the capability of the licensee's workforce. One example is Poland's Polski Fiat. Fiat was confident of the reliability of Polish manufacturing and did not require the use of a different name for the product. Today, Fiat no longer licenses the Fiat name to Polish manufacturers. It has set up a subsidiary with multiple operations, Fiat SpA, which manufactures many of the Fiats sold in Eastern Europe under the Fiat brand name (primarily lower-priced models, such as Fiat Punto and Seicento).

Licensing is a lower-risk entry mode that allows a company to manufacture a product all over the world for global distribution. Beverly Hills Polo Club, for example, conducts business in approximately 85 countries around the globe, producing apparel licensed under its own name and all licensed apparel for Harvard University, as well as Hype, Karl Kani, and

Blanc Bleu—a line that sells in upscale European retailers.[9] Licensing permits the company access to markets that may be closed or that may have high entry barriers. A downside of licensing is that it can produce a viable competitor in the licensee, who is well equipped to competently compete with the licensor. Simply training locals in company operations, particularly technology, can lead to the development of skills for future competitors.

17-5c Franchising

Franchising, a principal entry mode for the service industry, is the service industry's equivalent to licensing. The franchisor gives the franchisee the right to use its brand name and all related trademarks and its business know-how, such as secret recipes and customer interfacing techniques. The franchisor also may provide the franchisee with advertising and sales promotion support—all in return for royalties.

Franchising: The main international entry mode for the service industry, whereby the franchisor gives the franchisee the right to use its brand name and all related trademarks in return for royalties.

The popularity of U.S.-based franchises worldwide is undisputed. McDonald's Golden Arches decorate crowded Hong Kong streets, the picturesque Scottish countryside, elegant buildings in the downtown of centuries-old European cities (see Figure 17-8), and strip malls in Holland (where one franchise commissioned a giant Michael Jackson sculpture). Other fast-food franchises with an international presence include Pizza Hut, Kentucky Fried Chicken, and Burger King. Many of these franchises are adapted to the local market, serving spicy vegetarian dishes (and no beef) in India and Sri Lanka and beer and wine in Europe. Although some of the products might differ (as do the portions—gigantic in the United States, small in the rest of the world), the franchises look quite similar. They also offer the same courteous service, air conditioning, and toilets, and they run similar promotions.

Figure 17-8
This is an elegant McDonald's in elegant downtown Milan.

Surprisingly, some franchises are successful even if the premise of the service's primary offering (hamburgers) runs counter to the local culture (religious ban on eating beef). When a company sets up franchises, however, it is especially important to evaluate the market's acceptance of the offering. For example, Starbucks targeted Austria's coffee houses. Austria is a good market for coffee consumption, with an annual consumption of 56.8 gallons per person; there, it was believed that Starbucks would encounter many challenges, as it was unwilling to relax its global no-smoking policy, which is daring in a country with a high proportion of smokers. Also, the company's concept runs counter to an environment that perceives American coffee and the pace of life associated with American cafés as being different from the Austrian café business perfected over the course of 200 years[10]—the Kaffeehaus tradition. In spite of the negative predictions, Starbucks is doing very well in the market, opening a new franchise every month.

The advantages and disadvantages of a franchise system are similar to those of licensing. The franchisor experiences less risk and a higher level of control over operations and offerings to the target market. Franchising also is a method that allows for very rapid market penetration, which is especially important when new markets open their doors to foreign firms. On the downside, franchising can create future competitors who know the ins and outs of the franchise's operations. In fact, one hears many stories of former employees from fast-food restaurants who offer a precise replica of the original franchise, while charging lower prices. Ideas of franchises can also be copied. As soon as Esso (Exxon) stations in Europe started offering a Tiger Mart (convenience store affiliated with the Esso franchise), local competitors immediately set up their own versions that were even better adapted to local demands—selling, for example, potted flowers at discounted prices in affiliation with local growers.

17-5d Joint Ventures

Joint ventures often involve a foreign company joining with a local company, sharing capital, equity, and labor, among other items, to set up a new corporate entity. They could also be two foreign companies joining forces to create a third company in a country other than the home country of the two companies. Joint ventures are a preferred international entry mode for emerging markets. In developing countries, joint ventures are usually formed

Joint ventures: A corporate entity created with the participation of two companies that share equity, capital, and labor, among other things.

with the participation of an international firm and a state-owned enterprise. Developing countries welcome this type of investment as a way to encourage the development of local expertise, of the local market, and of the country's balance of trade—assuming the resultant production will be exported abroad.

The joint venture entry mode is not limited to developing countries. In Europe, joint ventures are popular but increasingly scrutinized. The European Commission of the European Union often investigates the impact of the joint venture on competition. One joint venture that the European Commission has recently examined involves the diamond giant De Beers Centenary AG (the world's largest diamond-mining company) and the French luxury goods company LVMH Moët Hennessy Louis Vuitton SA (which owns, among others, Christian Dior, Moët & Chandon, Louis Vuitton, and Donna Karan). The joint venture produces De Beers-branded jewelry and has opened a network of exclusive shops all over the world.[11]

Overall, 70 percent of all joint ventures break up within 3.5 years, and international joint ventures have an even slimmer chance for success.[12] Reasons for the failure of joint ventures are numerous. The failure of a partner can lead to the failure of the joint venture—as in the case of the joint venture between Bird Corp. of Dedham, Massachusetts, and conglomerate Sulzer Escher Wyss Inc., a subsidiary of Sulzer Brothers Ltd. of Switzerland. Although the joint venture performed well, Bird Corp. experienced serious problems with unsteady revenues and slim profits, leading to the failure of the joint venture.[13] Even a natural disaster or the weather could lead to failure. Zapata, a $93 million Houston, Texas, company involved in natural gas exploration, took a 49 percent share in a joint venture with Mexican investors with the goal of fishing on Mexico's Pacific coast for anchovies, processing them, and selling them as cattle and poultry feed. The weather system El Niño caused the anchovies to vanish, leading to the failure of the joint venture.[14]

A company can, to a certain extent, control its chances for success by carefully selecting the joint venture partner, realizing that a poor choice can be very costly to the company. Other factors that will increase the success of the international joint venture are the firm's previous experience with international investment and the proximity between the culture of the international firm and that of the host country. A greater distance erodes the applicability of the parent's competencies.[15]

Consortium: A company created with the participation of three or more companies; allowed in underserved markets or in domains where the government and/or the marketplace can control its monopolistic activity.

A special type of joint venture is a **consortium,** which involves three or more companies. An example of a successful consortium that involves some companies with a substantial percentage of government ownership is Airbus Industries. Airbus is an international consortium involving France (Aerospatiale with a 37.9 percent ownership), the United Kingdom (British Aerospace, with a 20 percent ownership), Germany (DaimlerChrysler DASA subsidiary, with a 37.9 percent ownership), and Spain (Construcciones Aeronauticas, with a 4.2 percent ownership). Most national governments and trade organizations are concerned with the monopoly effect that a consortium would create. In the case of Airbus, it was successfully argued that a single European country would not have the resources necessary to provide a challenge to Boeing, the U.S. manufacturer. In general, companies are allowed to set up consortia in the area of research and development, where they can share the cost of developing products that are at the forefront of technology.

17-5e Wholly Owned Subsidiaries

Wholly owned subsidiary: The entry mode that affords the highest level of control and presents the highest level of risk to a company; it involves establishing a new company that is a citizen of the country where the subsidiary is established.

Companies can avoid some of the disadvantages posed by partnering with other firms by setting up wholly owned subsidiaries in the target markets. The assumptions behind a **wholly owned subsidiary** are that the company can afford the costs involved in setting up a wholly owned subsidiary, that it is willing to commit to the market in the long term, and that the local government allows foreign companies to set up wholly owned subsidiaries on its territory. The company can develop its own subsidiary, which is costly, or it can purchase an existing company through acquisitions or mergers. The advantage of a wholly owned subsidiary is high control of all company operations in the target market—especially in handling revenue and profits.

Wholly owned subsidiaries also carry the greatest level of risk. A nationalization attempt on the part of the local government could leave the company with nothing—except a tax write-off. Problems could also arise when a company decides to acquire or merge with yet another unrelated company. In general, the company acquiring another or building its wholly owned subsidiary will not be able to share risks with a local partner, nor will it benefit from a partner's connections; it must build its own.

17-5f Branch Offices

The primary difference between subsidiaries and branch offices is that subsidiaries are separate entities, whereas **branch offices** are entities that are part of the international company. Companies that set up branch offices abroad often must engage in substantial investments. For example, Stihl, a German manufacturer of chainsaws, has a U.S. branch office in Virginia Beach that handles all company operations there. In addition to overseeing product sales, Stihl also ensures that servicing contracts are appropriately honored and that the representatives have adequate training. Branch offices of service providers typically engage in a full spectrum of activity in the domain of their specialization. The Chase branch offices in different European capitals handle the banking needs and credit to corporate and individual clients, in effect serving these markets the same way they serve the home markets. Branch offices, like subsidiaries, also offer companies a high level of control over operations and profits in international markets. In terms of risk, however, the company has invested much less in the market that can be lost in a government takeover attempt, compared to a subsidiary.

Branch offices: Offices that are part of the international company, rather than a new entity.

17-5g Strategic Alliances

Loosely stated, all joint ventures and licensing and franchising agreements are considered to be **strategic alliances** between companies attempting to reach joint corporate and market-related goals. This section addresses international corporate relationships that tend to be more short term in nature and that do not entail the same level of commitment as the previous categories. Such alliances crop up frequently and have various forms and degrees of "alliance." They vary from a contract manufacturing agreement that requires the contracting firm to provide raw material and training to the contracting factory in return for production that could last for two years, to an exchange of loyalty points (hotel, airline) between companies. The following are some examples of alliances:

Strategic alliances: Any type of relationship between one or more companies attempting to reach joint corporate and market-related goals; used to refer to most nonequity alliances.

- Manufacturing alliances cover many types of alliances, such as technological, engineering, and research and development alliances. A typical example of a manufacturing alliance is that between the U.S. company Motorola, Inc. and Singapore's Flextronics International, Ltd., whereby the Singapore-based electronics manufacturer would make billions of dollars' worth of Motorola products. At present, Flextronics has manufacturing contracts for infrastructure and cell phones, among others.[16] In another example, Porsche has engaged in different types of technical alliances with Harley-Davidson, the U.S. motorcycle icon, primarily helping it develop low-noise, low-emissions motorcycles.[17]
- Marketing alliances focus on all aspects of marketing. For example, Opel, the German subsidiary of U.S. auto manufacturer General Motors, signed a two-year contract to market its automobiles to 6.5 million America Online (AOL) subscribers in Germany by informing users about Opel and directing them to the Opel website.[18] The two companies created a marketing alliance involving mobile Internet. Opel equips its automobiles with mobile Internet connections, and AOL supplies content for the mobile service. Other marketing alliances focus on sales. For example, U.S.-based Northwest Airlines is in charge of all sales in the United States for the KLM Royal Dutch Airlines. Yet, other airline alliances focus on sales promotion. For example, Air France exchanges frequent-flyer mileage with Delta Airlines.

- Distribution alliances are common as well. Mitsui and Mitsubishi have set up distribution alliances with Coca-Cola in Japan for bottling and distributing all Coke products in this market.

17-6 The International Marketing Mix

While the marketing mix (i.e., the four *P*s) is the same in the international market, the application of each element may vary. Strategies that work in the domestic market will not always work in the international market.

17-6a Product

Product decisions in international markets involve two major issues: (1) standardizing the product offering across markets or adapting the offering to each market, and (2) developing a global brand or a local brand.

Global standardization: The standardization of products across markets and, ultimately, to the standardization of the marketing mix worldwide; more commonly called globalization.

Regional standardization: The use of a uniform marketing strategy within a particular region.

Global localization: The practice of global branding and localized marketing adaptation to differences in local culture, legislation, and even production capabilities.

Mandatory adaptation: The adaptation of products to local requirements so that the products can legally and physically function in the specific country environment.

Nonmandatory adaptation: The strategy of adapting a product to better meet the needs of the local market, without being required to do so.

Global standardization, the standardization of products across markets, has many arguments in its favor. From the global consumers' perspective, homogeneous interests are best addressed with one product strategy. From a firm's perspective, standardization allows the company to lower costs—passing the savings on to consumers. Ford attempted a global product approach to vehicle design and production, building "world cars."[19] Its first such experiment was the launch of the Ford Contour/Mercury Mystique in the United States and the Mondeo in Europe in 1993.[20] This attempt was followed by the marketing of the Ford Focus, which was successful on both sides of the Atlantic.

Regional standardization, a variation of global standardization, refers to the use of a uniform marketing strategy within a particular region—a strategy that is appealing to companies as regional market integration is gaining strength worldwide. For example, Pan-European brands are becoming common for U.S. multinationals, such as Procter & Gamble's Ariel detergent, its first Pan-European product (now present elsewhere).

In general, few goods and services can succeed through a purely global strategy; a degree of adaptation to local conditions is often imperative for company success. According to marketing experts, the idea of marketing a standardized product with a uniform marketing plan around the world remains purely theoretical. Although a product concept may be universal, it must still be adapted to differences in local culture, legislation, and even production capabilities.[21] **Global localization** involves global branding and localized marketing adaptation. For example, McDonald's hamburgers are adapted to the local culture. At its restaurants in New Delhi, where Indian consumers consider cows sacred and don't eat beef, McDonald's offers the Maharaja Mac (two all-mutton patties, special sauce, lettuce, cheese, pickles, onions on a sesame-seed bun).[22] Similarly, Volvo has a similar core product in every market; however, it offers air conditioning as a standard feature for the U.S. market.

To render products usable, manufacturers of appliances adapt their products to local requirements. One example of **mandatory adaptation** involves voltage—220 volts for Europe, whereas the U.S. standard is 110. Other such adaptations involve cycles (50 versus 60), electricity, telephone jacks, and television/VCR systems (NTSC in the United States, PAL, SECAM I, and SECAM II elsewhere in the world). Many global companies also adapt their offerings to better meet the needs of the local market, thus engaging in local, **nonmandatory adaptation.**

In terms of branding, a firm can use a private-label (retailer) brand. Private labels pose an increasing challenge to manufacturers' global or local brands. European food retailers, such as Sainsbury in the United Kingdom and Albert Heijn ("ah") in the Netherlands, as well as North American retailers, offer quality products with the "Sainsbury" and "ah" brands, respectively, packaged impeccably and positioned on the shelves side by side with popular multinational/national brands. A European case study[23] found that retailers compete primarily on price with their private-label brands, unless they are able to develop differentiated, high-quality store brands, thus creating consumer loyalty, which in turn translates to store loyalty.

For many products, country of origin is a critical purchase decision for consumers. **Country of origin** is defined as the country with which a particular good or service is associated. The country could be the **country of manufacture,** in the case of products, or the country where the company headquarters are located. The key to determining a product's perceived country of origin depends on which of the two (country of manufacture or home-country of the company) elicits the stronger association. For example, many of the appliances Philips sells are manufactured in Asia; however, the Philips headquarters are in the Netherlands. The country of origin for Philips appliances, then, is not the particular country in Asia where they are manufactured, but the Netherlands. A new, unknown brand, however, will be associated more strongly with the country of manufacture.

Country of origin: The country with which a particular product or service is associated.

Country of manufacture: The country in which a particular product is manufactured.

Advertisements often emphasize country-of-origin stereotypes. In the United States, Colombian coffee is touted as a certification of quality. Petrossian in New York stresses its reputation as the authentic retailer of Russian Beluga and Sevruga caviar. Toblerone chocolate stresses its European origins, but it is a Kraft (Jacobs Suchard) brand. Häagen-Dazs chocolate-dipped ice cream is really a product produced locally, in the United States; its name suggests an association with Europe, again affirming the quality association with European chocolate (see Figure 17-9).

Services also are stereotyped. Eastern European cosmeticians, for example, are very popular in the West (see Figure 17-10). Names such as Ilona of Hungary, Frederick Fekkai, and Erno Laszlo cosmetics are prominent on Madison and Fifth Avenues in New York. Tourists going to Eastern Europe often use the services of local beauticians or even go for extended stays to spas specializing in mud baths and life-renewal therapies.

Figure 17-9
The name Häagen-Dazs suggests that it is a European brand of ice cream; however, it is produced in the United States by a U.S. firm.

Source: Copyright © 2002 HDIP, Inc. Reprinted by permission of General Mills.

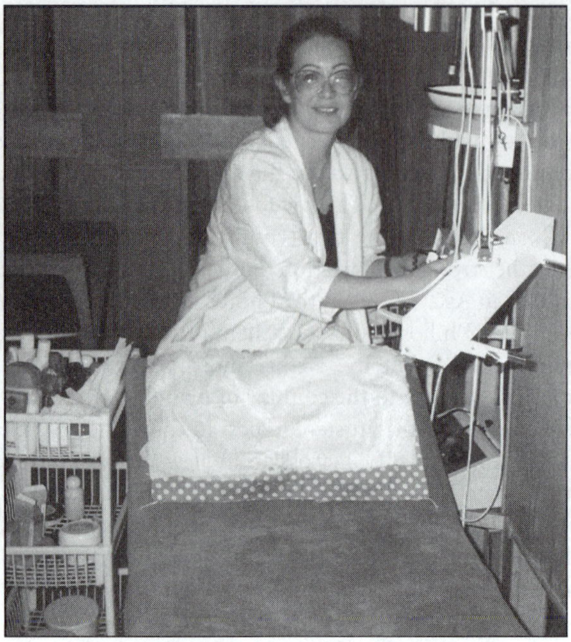

Figure 17-10
Polish beauticians are world famous. Using dated equipment and fresh natural products, and having impeccable dexterity, this beautician works wonders on tourists, as well as locals.

Figure 17-11
A waiter on the Champs Elysées graciously and competently serves beer on a busy July 14 (the French national holiday).

Unfortunate negative stereotypes also exist. French waiters have received unfair evaluations in the United States (see Figure 17-11).

17-6b Place (Distribution)

Entering a new market can be problematic for companies. In most cases, competitors already have a hold on existing channels and are thus likely to block them for new entrants. There are other obstacles to using established channels: For example, the amount charged by distributors could be so high that the company may be unwilling to use them. This was the case for Kraft in its attempt to enter the Hong Kong market. Distributors charged an exorbitant amount to distribute the brand. Kraft refused to pay the price but also faced barriers to entry on its own. A decade later, Kraft yielded, deciding to use the same overpriced distributors to sell its brand in Hong Kong and now China. The initial channel selection decision is very important. Once in a channel relationship, a company may be bound to that relationship and may not legally be allowed to change distributors.

Although building channels is very expensive, this strategy is necessary where no channels exist, or no channels conform to the needs of the company. When Coca-Cola decided to enter Eastern Europe, it found local state-enterprise channels that were selling Pepsi products operating with low efficiency, so it created its own channels that fit with the market structure, working with independent truck drivers.

In choosing a distribution channel, a firm can use home-country middlemen or foreign (host)-country middlemen. **Home-country middlemen** typically provide all marketing services for firms that do not wish to enter the foreign market and/or do not have the capability to do so. Companies relying on these middlemen relinquish control of the marketing mix to distributors in the foreign country. In international business, they would be **export merchants** who take title and possession to the exported goods.

Other examples of home-country middlemen are:

- **Export management companies,** which are highly specialized in certain industries, such as endoscopic instruments or networking products, and represent smaller companies in a region of the country. They also research markets, represent companies at trade shows, screen and select international distributors, and ship the company's product.
- **Trading companies,** common in Japan, have operations all around the world, ranging from finance to distribution, technology, mining, oil and gas exploration, and information. They act as intermediaries for half of Japan's exports and two-thirds of its imports.[24] The largest trading companies are Itochu Corp., Sumitomo, Marubeni, Mitsui, and Mitsubishi.[25] In the United States, export-trading companies are a consortia of smaller suppliers, service-oriented firms, multinational corporations, and quasi-public organizations or public entities.[26] In 1982, the U.S. Congress passed the Export Trading Company Act to encourage the formation of export trading companies to promote U.S. exports.
- Other home-country middlemen include home-country brokers and agents, who bring international buyers and sellers together in the company's home country and do not carry title to the product but are representatives of a manufacturer or buyers in the firm's home country.

Foreign-country middlemen can be placed in two broad categories: merchant middlemen, who are intermediaries that take title to and possession of the products they carry, and agents and brokers, who bring buyers and sellers together but do not carry title to and take possession of the products they deal with.

Retailing The text offers many examples that illustrate differences in international retailing practices worldwide. One of the main differences is that, in the United States, retailers address the needs of a public that is perpetually behind the wheel of an automobile. Internationally, that is quite different, as mentioned in Section 17-3a. Imagine daily mobility using slow public transportation, such as trams and busses, or a bicycle (see Figure 17-12). And imagine shopping in an environment where it very likely will rain most summers and sleet most winters: You are most likely not going to load up on groceries for the week in one shopping trip, nor will you buy a 10-gallon bottle of laundry detergent to carry through town. Marketers should consider mobility constraints when designing products for international markets.

17-6c Promotion

International companies must be prepared to face challenges to all of the elements of the promotional mix. While standardization is ideal, it is difficult to accomplish internationally.

In the case of advertising, the media infrastructure provides many challenges. A medium might not be considered appropriate for advertising. For example, newspapers might not constitute the appropriate medium for advertising a particular product in one country, or advertising on television may be prohibited altogether. The capability of the

Home-country middlemen: Middlemen in the home country who typically provide all marketing services for firms that do not wish to enter the foreign market and/or do not have the capability to do so.

Export merchants: Intermediaries who take title to and possession of the products they carry; they are responsible for shipping and marketing the products to the target market.

Export management companies: Companies specializing in the export function for companies in a particular industry.

Trading companies: Complex marketing systems that specialize in providing intermediary service and reducing risk through extensive information channels and financial assistance.

Foreign-country middlemen: Middlemen in the foreign country who are either merchant middlemen (intermediaries who take title to and possession of the products they carry) or agents and brokers (intermediaries who bring buyers and sellers together but do not carry title to and take possession of the products with which they deal).

Figure 17-12
The shopping public can be pedestrians, or they could be riding bicycles; retailers need to take into consideration the shopping needs of pedestrian or bicycling shoppers.

Figure 17-13
Outdoor umbrellas are practical and prominent modes of communication with consumers worldwide.

existing media to reliably reach the target consumer in the intended format and within the intended time frame is also important. Magazine or newspaper issues might not be printed on time, or publishers might accept more advertisements than they can print. The quality of the medium itself may be questionable. Local newspapers might not be of a high enough quality to print advertising for a global brand. Television stations might go off the air indefinitely at inopportune times, when a company's advertisement is scheduled to air. Advertising in a number of Islamic countries might not permit the portrayal of women, whereas in other countries (China, for instance) the media do not readily encourage the advertising of feminine hygiene products. Airtime might be limited; for example, the European Union allows only 12 minutes per hour for advertising on each television station.

Media formats may differ from one country to another. For example, using kiosks and fences for advertising posters is very common in many areas of the world. It is also common to advertise on the sides of private homes, on shopping bags, and on outdoor umbrellas (see Figure 17-13).

An interesting development is the extensive use of English in local advertising in order to stress a cosmopolitan attitude and to endow a good or service with status. Words such as "very quick" are used in advertising for a tire inflation service (*vulcanizacion*) in Ecuador and "super wonderful" to describe the travel bags sold by a company in Poland. This is also true for product brand names—for example, the Romanian-American University, American Gold for a brand of gold-plated jewelry—when the products or services really have nothing to do with the United States, Canada, or Mexico. Figure 17-14 shows an example of an advertisement, aimed at local consumers, using English in a non–English-speaking country.

Figure 17-14
This example illustrates the use of English in a German advertisement that wants to sell German consumers "Highspeed zu Lowcost" Internet service.

In another interesting twist, an advertiser might use English to show animosity toward a neighbor country in an environment where neither that country nor the advertiser use English to communicate. Figure 17-15 illustrates an advertisement for a Dutch brand of shoes that are guaranteed not to be German; the product is sold to Dutch consumers.

Advertisers encounter numerous restrictions in their efforts to deliver communication to consumers worldwide. Most regulations are imposed by national (host-country) governments. Alternatively, local firms have established traditions and self-imposed regulations that must be observed by newcomers to the local advertising scene. Advertising regulations may prohibit or limit comparative advertising, limit advertising to children (in France, the use of children as endorsers in advertising is limited, and the law prohibits the use of children's heroes as endorsers[27]), or could require advertisers (and all broadcasters) to keep the language pure—as, for example, in France.

Multinational corporations frequently experience negative publicity. In general, there is a negative perception of multinational firm dominance and globalization, as illustrated at the 1999 World Trade Organization meeting in Seattle, the G8 summits in Genoa, Italy, in 2001, and in Evian, France, in 2003. More recently, however, the theme changed to "food, not bombs" at the G8 meeting in Sea Island, Georgia, in 2004, and demonstrators decided to show anarchy in action by adopting nonviolent persuasion.[28]

McDonald's experienced a classic example of negative publicity in France. In response to Europe's decision to ban hormone-treated beef, the U.S. government imposed high import tariffs on French Roquefort cheese, Dijon mustard, and foie gras. The French retaliated by, among other means, vandalizing McDonald's restaurants. In their eyes, the company was a symbol of U.S. hegemony, globalization, multinationals, the power of the marketplace, and industrially produced food, at the expense of individuals' health and French peasants' livelihood.[29] In more recent examples, a McDonald's bus was torched in Hamburg, Germany, in protest against the United States.[30]

Figure 17-15
A Dutch brand guaranteed, in English, not to be German.

Positive publicity, although difficult to come by, is very valuable. Due to its independent nature, it is more credible than advertising. DaimlerChrysler received free positive publicity for its luxury Mercedes automobiles when a photograph of then U.S. Secretary of State, General Colin Powell, appeared at the wheel of a Mercedes on the front page of the *New York Times*, with the caption "Do you mind if I drive?" The paper published a follow-up story on Powell driving Jordan's King Abdulla's Mercedes.[31] Although the impact of such publicity is difficult to measure in terms of dollars and cents, marketing executives in Stuttgart, the home of Mercedes-Benz, can rest assured that their brand received significant exposure and a credible endorsement in the U.S. market.

International sales promotion activities must be adapted to local markets in order to comply with legal requirements. Even in economically and politically integrated markets, such as the European Union, sales-promotion–related legislation differs from one country to another. In Germany, for example, "buy one, get one free" offers are illegal. In France, premiums are restricted to 7 percent of the product's value, and in Belgium, retail sales can run for only a month, and prices cannot be cut below one-third their normal price.[32] Sweepstakes based on pure chance are deemed illegal in Holland,[33] Canada, Sweden, and Belgium,[34] whereas, elsewhere in the world, additional legal requirements for sales promotion strategies diverge. Puerto Rican law, for instance, requires rules for all promotions to be printed in both English and Spanish, and both versions must be printed in a general-circulation newspaper at least once a week for the duration of the campaign.

Figure 17-16
The theme of the World Fair in Hanover, Germany, was Humankind—Nature—Technology.

With regard to business-to-business promotion or international trade promotion, international trade shows are of particular prominence. Country and state governments are often involved in ensuring that national/local companies are represented at important fairs. In the United States, the Department of Commerce is actively involved in promoting U.S. companies abroad using trade shows as venues. Usually, the U.S. government shares the cost of the exhibits by sponsoring a national pavilion at the different fairs. The World Exposition (the World Fair) cuts across domains and is one of the most important venues for exhibiting new ideas, technology, and art in an environment where numerous countries are represented. The city of Hanover, Germany, hosted a recent World Fair—an exhibition of art, science, and culture (see Figure 17-16). The theme of the fair was "Humankind—Nature—Technology: A New World Arising," and its aim was to focus on creating guiding principles for living in the twenty-first century. Projects stemming from the Expo are taking place around the world, emphasizing the use of environmentally friendly technology. Expo 2005 is organized in Seto, Japan, in the Aichi Prefecture, and Expo 2010 will be organized in Shanghai, China.

In terms of personal selling, from a company perspective, hiring expatriates or locals is a function of the company's involvement in the market. The company's presence in the market—entry mode—and its commitment to the market are important considerations in determining (1) the size of the sales team and (2) the types of sales representatives the company employs. Companies primarily involved in exporting are likely to engage in only minimal international sales activity. An example of such an activity might be sending representatives to an international trade show to exhibit the firm's products.

Expatriates: Employees working in a foreign country.

Home-country national: An expatriate from the company's home country working in a foreign country.

Third-country national: An employee working in the country of assignment who is not a national of that country or of the country in which the corporate headquarters of the company for which he or she works is located.

Host-country national: A local employee who works in his or her home country for the international corporation.

The foreign sales force of the multinational corporation could include expatriates (home-country nationals and third-country nationals) and host-country nationals. **Expatriates** working in a particular foreign country belong to two categories: One category is the **home-country national,** who is successful as a sales representative in the home country but is assigned overseas. An example would be a Philip Morris U.S. employee engaging in sales in the company's Hong Kong operations. Representing the second category is the **third-country national,** a truly international salesperson who works in numerous countries. An example would be a Latin American salesperson who previously worked in sales in Italy and Spain calling on Colgate-Palmolive's trade accounts in Bulgaria. The local salesperson who works in his or her home country for an international corporation is a **host-country national.** An example would be the Hungarian brand manager, schooled in a U.S. university, working for Procter & Gamble (www.pg.com) in

Hungary. This individual understands the U.S. business environment, is well trained technically at an accredited U.S. institution, and is willing to return to his home country to work for a U.S. multinational firm.

Increasingly, international firms appear to prefer local employees to expatriates. Cost is only one consideration. Frequently, locals with similar levels of education and training are available for employment at a fraction of the cost of expatriates. Host-country nationals also speak the local language and often have a well-developed network within the local industry and government. And host governments restrict the number of foreign nationals working in the country; thus, host-country nationals also fit with the country's employment policies.

17-6d Price

Selling the product at the appropriate price for the market represents a challenge for many multinationals. The location of production facilities determines the extent to which companies can control costs and price their products competitively. Multinationals usually can afford to shift production to take advantage of lower costs and exchange rates, whereas small- to medium-size firms are often limited to exporting as the only venue for product distribution.[35] Companies can and often do price themselves out of the market in certain countries, especially if they do not shift production to a low-labor-cost, low-tax country. As an example, Marc Controls, in order to lower the price of its products, purchases raw materials in Korea, China, and India and ships them to the United States for manufacturing. Its products are competitively priced when sold on the German market, but they are considered overpriced in most of Asia.[36]

Among other factors, international and local competition often pose serious concerns to multinational firms. If competition can keep product prices low by manufacturing in a low-labor-cost country, firms must meet this challenge and maintain a low price, potentially at a loss. At a retail level, and especially in service environments, companies often are challenged by local competitors offering legal copycat products at a much lower price. For example, Pizza Hut is challenged in every market in Poland by a local pizza chain that offers almost identical products, such as Neapolitan pizza, at a fraction of Pizza Hut's offering. Another concern is posed by **parallel imports**—diverting products purchased in a low-price market to other markets by means of a distribution system not authorized by the manufacturer, otherwise known as a gray market.

Parallel imports: A distribution system not authorized by the manufacturer whereby the products purchased in a low-price market are diverted to other markets; also called gray market.

Firms also can face challenges from companies dumping products in their target market. Dumping is an important factor affecting pricing decisions. A typical example of dumping involves a foreign company that enjoys high prices and high profits at home as a result of trade barriers against imports. The company uses those profits to sell at much lower prices in foreign markets to build market share and suppress the profitability of competitors with open home markets.[37] According to the World Trade Organization, dumping should be condemned if it threatens to cause injury to an established industry in a particular market and/or if it delays the establishment of a viable domestic industry.[38]

Antidumping policies differ somewhat from country to country. China, according to its Antidumping and Anti-Subsidy Regulations set forth by the State Council, defines dumping as the subsidization of exports resulting in substantial injury, or the threat of substantial injury, to an established domestic industry, or substantially impeding the establishment of a comparable domestic industry.[39] According to the Chinese, dumping is involved if a product is sold at a price below its normal value, where normal value may be based on production costs plus reasonable expenses and profit, or on the comparable price in the exporting country for an identical or like product. If there is no comparable price for the product in the exporting country, reference is made to the price at which the exporter sells a similar product in a third country.[40]

Summary

1. *Address primary drivers of internationalization in the macroenvironment and the microenvironment.* Among the economic and political drivers of internationalization are organizations facilitating change, such as the World Trade Organization (WTO), whose primary mission is to facilitate trade, and the various development banks, such as the World Bank, the IMF, and the regional development banks. The primary mission of development banks is to promote economic development and prosperity, which, ultimately, will allow firms to become more involved in international trade. Other drivers of internationalization are regional political and economic integration, which facilitates the movement of goods within a broad, single, multinational market, and an improved telecommunications and transportation infrastructure. Drivers in the microenvironment are converging consumer needs, which allow firms to use a standardized—and thus cost-effective—marketing strategy. They also include competition, which requires that the market-share game be played internationally; the extension of the product lifecycle; long-term savings to offset high product development costs; standardization opportunities allowing for economies of scale; cheap labor abroad; and transfer opportunities.

2. *Discuss the primary internationalization challenges and obstacles attributed to the cultural environment, to governments, to competition, and to the self-reference criterion.* Companies operating internationally must deal with the complexities of language, adapting messages to different markets where there may be multiple languages and dialects. In many countries, nonverbal communication is important, and managers must be aware of the meanings of silence and postures. Religion also imposes restrictions on multinational firms in terms of holidays, behaviors, and religious practices. The government may erect other obstacles by limiting the repatriation of profits, requiring local participation in management, and limiting imports in order to support and promote local production. International competition will also erect barriers, especially if they were first present in the respective markets, blocking channels, and creating consumer loyalty. The self-reference criterion is also an obstacle in the sense that conscious and unconscious reference to one's own national culture, norms, and values may limit one's ability to function optimally in the new environment.

3. *Analyze the different levels of international involvement.* Domestic marketing, export marketing, international (multinational) marketing, and global marketing represent levels of increasing involvement in international marketing. Domestic marketing involves minimal international exposure, whereas global marketing involves a perspective that focuses on the world as the total market of the company such that marketing activities do not even have a country or regional focus.

4. *Address entry mode selection from a control and risk perspective.* The entry mode classifications offered in the chapter follow a general model of low to high control and risk, respectively—from indirect exporting (lowest risk, lowest control); to direct exporting, licensing, franchising, joint ventures, and consortia; to wholly owned subsidiaries (highest risk, highest control). The indirect export entry mode involves a company selling its products in the company's home country to intermediaries who, in turn, sell the product overseas. Direct exporting involves a firm handling its own exports, usually with the help of an in-house exporting department. Licensing involves a licensor, who shares the brand name, technology, and know-how with a licensee in return for royalties. Franchising is the main international entry mode for the service industry, whereby the franchisor gives the franchisee the right to use its brand name and all related trademarks in return for royalties. Joint ventures are corporate entities created with the participation of two companies that share equity, capital, and labor. Wholly owned subsidiaries involve establishing a new company that is a citizen of the country where the subsidiary is established. Finally, strategic alliances are relationships between one or more companies attempting to reach joint corporate and market-related goals.

5. *Discuss the challenges presented by the international marketing mix to the international corporation.* Among the decisions facing the company in its international operations are whether to standardize the product offering across each market (which is the most cost-effective approach) or whether to adapt it to each market. Companies must adapt to local markets in countries where local culture or legal requirements require adaptation. In other countries, companies often use a global localization strategy, where the brand name, logo, and other trademarked offerings remain the same, with partial adaptation of the offering to suit the local tastes. Internationally, companies face competition from private labels. Companies use different home-country and foreign-country middlemen to sell their products, depending on their international capabilities and desire for international involvement. If their involvement is low, then they use home-country middlemen, such as export merchants, trading companies, export management companies, or agents and brokers. If their involvement is higher, the companies are likely to use foreign-country middlemen, such as merchant middlemen, agents, and brokers. The company must also adapt its promotional and pricing strategies to local markets to ensure maximal performance. With regard to promotion, companies must understand the local media infrastructure and practices, and adapt accordingly. Companies also face challenges with regard to the management of the international sales force. They must recruit individuals who are best suited for international assignments. Finally, with regard to pricing strategy, companies face challenges from unauthorized distributors who engage in parallel imports, whereby the products purchased in low-price markets are diverted to other, higher price markets, and from competitors' dumping, which involves selling products below cost to get rid of excess inventory and/or to undermine the firm's operations.

Key Terms

branch offices (p. 535)
consortium (p. 534)
country of manufacture (p. 537)
country of origin (p. 537)
direct exporting (p. 532)
domestic marketing (p. 531)
expatriates (p. 542)
export management companies (p. 539)
export marketing (p. 531)
export merchants (p. 539)
foreign-country middlemen (p. 539)
franchising (p. 533)
global localization (p. 536)
global marketing (p. 531)
global standardization (p. 536)
home-country middlemen (p. 539)
home-country national (p. 542)
host-country national (p. 542)
indirect exporting (p. 532)
international marketing (p. 531)
joint ventures (p. 533)
licensing (p. 532)
mandatory adaptation (p. 536)
multinational marketing (p. 531)
nonmandatory adaptation (p. 536)
nonverbal communication (p. 527)
parallel imports (p. 543)
regional standardization (p. 536)
self-reference criterion (p. 531)
strategic alliances (p. 535)
third-country national (p. 542)
trading companies (p. 539)
wholly owned subsidiary (p. 534)

Discussion Questions

1. How does religion affect international marketing and international business operations in a target market?
2. Margaret Hogan is an international marketing manager planning to accept an assignment representing her company interests in Saudi Arabia, an Islamic country. What are some of the cultural elements that will have an impact on her performance? How can she best prepare for this assignment?
3. Discuss each type of entry mode, from exporting to wholly owned subsidiary, and address the risks and controls characterizing each entry mode.
4. What are some of the challenges involved in international advertising from the point of view of media availability and reliability?
5. Describe the different types of hires you could potentially make for your international operations. Who is your ideal international employee?
6. How does international trade promotion benefit international companies and target customers?
7. How could unauthorized distributors affect the price for the products you are intending for a particular high-price target market?

Review Questions

True or False

1. Converging consumer needs across countries represent a primary international driving force in the microenvironment.
2. When a particular product reaches maturity or decline, the product lifecycle cannot be prolonged by international expansion of the market.
3. Local governments in developing countries establish policies that foster and facilitate international trade and foreign direct investment.
4. Small companies can be more profitable by manufacturing and distributing the same products abroad without making a penny in their home countries.
5. Today licensing as an international entry strategy is a lower risk, lower control alternative.
6. Franchising allows rapid market penetration for services from foreign firms at low-risk levels.
7. Dumping is a pricing strategy whereby a company can sell the product below cost in foreign markets in order to stifle local competition.

Multiple Choice

8. Which international organization imposes significant changes on countries' internal economic structures as a requirement for membership?
   a. WTO
   b. IMF and World Bank
   c. The Group of Eight, G8
   d. United Nations
9. In nonverbal communication, chronemics refer to
   a. time differences between countries in the time zones.
   b. timing of verbal communications.
   c. perceptions of accuracy relevant to timing.
   d. (a) and (c).
10. Which action can be used to restrict international competition in the local market?
   a. blocking the channels of distribution
   b. biding retailers into exclusive agreements
   c. slashing prices temporarily to prevent product adoption
   d. all of the above
11. The self-reference criterion is defined as
   a. direct expression of feelings and emotions.
   b. confidence in quick decision making.
   c. individual conscious or unconscious reference to the native culture.
   d. self-awareness of strengths and weaknesses.

12. Which form of exporting of goods and services can be done with low risk and does not require market expertise or long-term commitment to the international market?
- **a.** indirect exporting
- **b.** direct exporting
- **c.** franchising
- **d.** direct mail

13. Which of the following decisions constitute key product decisions in international markets?
- **a.** standardizing the product offering across markets or adapting to each market
- **b.** developing a global brand or a local brand
- **c.** forming a strategic alliance or joint venture
- **d.** a and b

14. What restrictions may be encountered by advertisers when delivering communications to consumers worldwide?
- **a.** government regulations
- **b.** self-imposed traditions established by local firms
- **c.** limits to advertising imposed by local cultures
- **d.** all of the above

Notes

1. Brian Steiberg, "Advert Mailbox," *The Wall Street Journal* (December 15, 2004): 1.
2. See www.wto.org.
3. See www.imf.org.
4. Ibid.
5. Erin Butler, "New Directions for Investment in Developing Countries," *World Trade*, vol. 16, no. 6 (June 2001): 24–28.
6. Ibid.
7. Hillary Chura, "Coke Brands IPG as Global Ad Strategist," *Advertising Age*, vol. 71, no. 50 (December 4, 2000): 50.
8. Frank Bradley and Michael Gannon, "Does the Firm's Technology and Marketing Profile Affect Foreign Market Entry?" *Journal of International Marketing*, vol. 8, no. 4 (2000): 12–36.
9. Sherrie E. Zhan, "Choosing a Market Entry Strategy," *World Trade*, vol. 12, no. 5 (May 1999): 40–46.
10. "Starbucks Targeting Austria's Coffeehouses," *International Herald Tribune*, Frankfurt Edition (July 5, 2001): 12.
11. Brandon Mitchener and Deborah Ball, "EU Clears De Beers-LVMH Venture," *Wall Street Journal Europe* (July 6–7, 2001): 3.
12. Dave Savona, "When Companies Divorce," *International Business*, vol. 5, no. 11 (November 1992): 48–50.
13. Ibid.
14. Ibid.
15. Harry G. Barkema, Oded Shenkar, Freek Vermeulen, and John H. J. Bell, "Working Abroad, Working with Others: How Firms Learn to Operate International Joint Ventures," *Academy of Management Journal*, vol. 40, no. 2 (April 1997): 426–442.
16. "Motorola Scales Back Flextronics Outsourcing Deal," *International Herald Tribune*, Frankfurt Edition (July 4, 2001): 11.
17. Tim Burt, "Porsche Fires Revolution at Harley," *Financial Times* (July 14–15, 2001): 8.
18. Holger Schmidt, "Opel to Market Its Cars through AOL," *Frankfurter Allgemeine Zeitung*, no. 152/27 (July 4, 2001): 5.
19. Gary van Deursen, "The Globalization of Design," *Appliance Manufacturer*, vol. 43, no. 3 (March 1995): 10–11.
20. Ibid.
21. Cyndee Miller, "Chasing Global Dream," *Marketing News*, vol. 30, no. 25 (December 2, 1996): 102.
22. Ibid.
23. Ryan Mathews, "A European Case Study," *Progressive Grocer, Special Volume: Branding the Store* (November 1995): 8–9. The article discusses a study conducted by INSEAD on trends in the food industry in the U.K. and France.
24. "Japanese Trading Companies: The Giants That Refused to Die," *The Economist*, vol. 319, no. 7709 (1991): 72–73.
25. Ibid.
26. Lyn S. Amine, Tamer S. Cavusgil, and Robert I. Weinstein, "Japanese Sogo Shosha and the U.S. Export Trading Companies," *Journal of the Academy of Marketing Science*, vol. 14, no. 3 (Fall 1986): 21–32.
27. Ibid.
28. Anne Carrns and Nicole Harris, "Antiglobal Protesters Try New Tactics: Tea and Pudding; As Georgia Girds for the G-8, Groups Show Gentler Side; Anarchists Fixing Homes?" *The Wall Street Journal* (June 2, 2004): A1.
29. See Jon Henley, "Flip Flop," *The New Republic*, vol. 222, no. 1 (January 3, 2000): 24.
30. "La Vita Non Dolce," *The Wall Street Journal* (June 2, 2003): A16.
31. "How the General Put a Pedal to the Metal," *The New York Times* (February 26, 2001): A8.
32. Ken Gofton, "How Euro Rules Will Change SP," *Marketing* (October 5, 2000): 60–61.
33. Rob Furber, "Centre Shop," *Marketing Week*, vol. 22, no. 38 (October 1999): 51–54.
34. Warner Bernhard, "Crossing the Border," *Brandweek*, vol. 37, no. 48 (December 16, 1996): 37–38.
35. Virginia Citrano, "The Right Price," *CFO*, vol. 8, no. 5 (May 1992): 71–72.
36. Ibid.
37. Greg Mastel, "The U.S. Steel Industry and Antidumping Law," *Challenge*, vol. 42, no. 3 (May–June 1999): 84–94.
38. Ibid.
39. Lester Ross and Susan Ning, "Modern Protectionism: China's Own Antidumping Regulations," *The China Business Review*, vol. 27, no. 3 (May/June 2000): 30–33.
40. Ibid.

Case 17-1 The AvtoVAZ-GM Joint Venture

AvtoVAZ, or Automobile Factory of the Volga Region, also known as VAZ, was created in 1966 by the Soviet government. The government's goal was to create a venue for the mass production of affordable automobiles for Soviet consumers. The company was built by transplanting a defunct Fiat assembly plant from Italy to Togliatti, a small industrial town on the Volga River shores. AvtoVAZ's first car, the Zhiguli (better known in the West as Lada), was built based on Fiat 124, an automobile produced in Italy 20 years earlier. This first Lada was produced on April 19, 1970, and quickly became Russia's most popular passenger automobile. Its first model was VAZ 2101, which was endearingly called "kopeika" (the penny). It was considered to be of very high quality, and many of these models can still be seen on the road today. Over the years, the factory began to gain popularity as it strove to "supply Russian citizens with cars especially made for the tough Russian climate and harsh road conditions." During the Soviet era, AvtoVAZ quickly grew and expanded its production of the Lada. It later introduced Niva, a new model, in 1977 and Samara in the 1980s. These efforts allowed the company to move ahead of other competing Soviet automobile manufacturers AZLK, producer of Moskvich, a higher-end automobile, and AvtoGAZ, producer of the Volga, an automobile used primarily for government officials and functions.

After 1989, the end of Communism brought drastic changes to the political and economic environment. In addition to the breakup of the Soviet Union, the drive toward a new market economy placed substantial pressure on the old state-owned enterprises. AvtoVAZ needed to implement important changes in order to continue to compete in the new transition economy and to operate successfully in an unstable economic environment. The company privatized immediately after the fall of Communism—it was the first automobile company in Post-Soviet Russia to adapt to a market environment—and promptly lost its former government protection. It also became a target of corruption and mismanagement. At first, the Yeltsin government turned a blind eye to conflicts of interest and theft by corporate managers to win support for policies such as privatization. Today, Russia and AvtoVAZ are paying the price: Companies are held hostage by networks that rob the government of tax revenues, soak up cash needed for industrial modernization, and fuel organized crime.

In spite of the company's challenges, General Motors and the European Bank for Reconstruction and Development (EBRD), whose mission is to finance economic development projects in Eastern Europe, have created a new opportunity for AvtoVAZ: a $340 million joint venture to manufacture off-road vehicles in Togliatti. GM owns a 41.5 percent stake in the joint venture and invested $100 million; EBRD has a 17 percent stake and a $40 million investment, lending an additional $100 million; and AvtoVAZ contributed manufacturing facilities and intellectual property valued at $100 million, for a 41.5 percent stake. The new company produces the GM-branded Chevrolet Niva, aiming for a maximum yearly output of 75,000 vehicles, of which more than half are built for export. The new Niva is sold in Western Europe and to markets in Africa, Asia, Latin America, and the Middle East, where the old Niva was popular. In Germany, the Niva will be equipped with engines from Adam Opel.

The joint venture is attempting to maintain the price of the new cars below $10,000 (still beyond the reach of most Russian automobile buyers), but this requires dependence on domestic components. Lack of these components in sufficient volumes and at required quality levels has previously set back plans by Ford (U.S.) and Fiat (Italy) to produce for the Russian market. The Chevrolet Niva sports utility vehicle looks very attractive and has an impressive design. However, Russian consumers, in addition to balking at its price, still perceive it as being of lower quality: The automobile is assembled on the VAZ platform by VAZ workers. Also, the automobile body is produced at VAZ facilities—not at new GM facilities—so the Niva buyers do not expect the automobile finishing to be superior and last longer than that of the Niva ancestor, VAZ 21213. By 2005, the company had sold 53,053 Chevrolet Niva vehicles since the joint venture was established. In September 2004, the company started manufacturing an export version of the Niva, the Chevrolet Viva, which is essentially an Opel Astra with a cheaper engine.

Another product of the joint venture, the Opel Astra, designed for the tastes and pocketbooks of Western Europeans, began production at the Togliati plant in 2005. Prices for Astras start at $11,000. The company plans to produce at least 25,000 Astras a year in Russia; one hopes Russian incomes can keep pace.

Questions

1. Address the potential contribution of the GM–AvtoVAZ joint venture in creating competitive advantage for the AvtoVAZ.
2. What are some of the advantages and disadvantages of the GM-AvtoVAZ joint venture for GM?
3. Could GM have created a wholly owned subsidiary in Russia in order to gain greater control? What would have been its advantages and disadvantages?

Sources: Jason Bush and Ira Sager, "GM: On the Road to Russia," *Business Week* (January 19, 2004): 14; www.vaz.ru; *www.gm-avtovaz.com* (December 8, 2004); "GM-AvtoVAZ Starts Chevrolet Viva Car Assembly," *The Russia Journal* (www.russiajournal.com, August 9, 2004); Carol Matlack, "Anatomy of a Russian Wreck," *Business Week*, no. 3594 (September 7, 1998): 86b; "GM Seals AvtoVAZ Deal," *Country Monitor*, vol. 9, No. 27 (July 16, 2001): 8; "GM's Russian Partner," *Manufacturing Engineering*, vol. 126, no. 2 (February 2001): 20–22. This case was developed with the assistance of Maria Vornovitsky and Ramil Zeliatdinov.

Case 17-2 The Cultural Reinvention of Euro Disney

Euro Disney was launched in Europe in April 1992; since then, many name changes have been made with the purpose of distancing the company from bad publicity. After four different name revisions, the Disney Corporation settled on Disneyland Resort Paris. From the beginning, the Disney Corporation had the best of intentions for its European operation. After a successful opening of Disneyland Tokyo, the company was ready for its next international challenge. The company believed that locating the theme park in close proximity to Paris, France, would both ensure growth for Disney and offer an opportunity for it to incorporate different European cultures. In its first incarnation as Euro Disney, the company failed in many aspects of its marketing strategy. The French did not want the American dreamland to distract their children, economy, and country from their own successful entertainment and culture. In addition, Euro Disney failed to target the diverse tastes and preferences of a new continent of more than 300 million people. Addressing the needs for visitors from dissimilar countries, such as Norway, Denmark, and Germany on one hand, and Spain, Italy, and France on the other, was a challenge.

In addition, Disney's admission costs were 30 percent higher than a Disney World ticket in the United States, and the company refused to offer discounts for winter admissions. Furthermore, Euro Disney ignored travel lifestyles of Europeans, who are accustomed to taking a few long vacations, rather than short trips, which would fit with the Disney model. The company also neglected to consider national holidays and traditional breaks when Europeans were more likely to travel. Disney's failed marketing strategy for Euro Disney led to below-average attendance levels and product sales. The park was on the edge of bankruptcy in 1994, with a loss per year of more than a billion dollars. Changing strategies—as well as its name, to Disneyland Resort Paris—has led to increased revenues of more than 4 percent, with operating revenues increasing by $32 million to $789 million in 2004, and increased revenues of more than 5 percent in the first half of 2005.

With a full-scale change in the company's marketing direction, Disneyland Resort Paris has been successful in attracting visitors from many countries. Access was a priority for Disney. The company worked on access to the park via the fast train—the TGV; it also worked deals with the EuroStar and Le Shuttle train companies. In addition, Disney has worked deals with trains and airlines to reduce prices—a move that ultimately benefited all. The price for transportation to Disney has dropped by 22 percent since the park's opening. In 1992, the Walt Disney Company negotiated with Air France to make Air France the "official" Euro Disney carrier. For visitors from the United Kingdom, British Airways is the preferred carrier of Disneyland Resort Paris, and British Airways Holidays, its tour subsidiary, is the preferred travel partner.

Disney also adapted targeting strategies to individual markets to address the interests and values of different segments of European consumers. It placed representatives around the world with the task of researching specific groups of consumers and creating the best package deals for potential visitors. The new Disney offices were established in London, Frankfurt, Milan, Brussels, Amsterdam, and Madrid. Research results led to the tailoring of package deals that were in line with vacation lifestyles of the different European segments. In addition to the package deals, Disney offered discounts for the winter months and half-price discounts for individuals going to the park after 5:00 P.M.

To better accommodate its guests, Disneyland Resort Paris revised its stringent no-alcohol policy, allowing wine and beer to be served at its restaurants. The resort hotels also lowered their room rates and offered less expensive menu choices in their restaurants. The restaurants created more suitable food options, catering to different regional European tastes, but continued to offer large, American-size portions. Crepes and waffles are on the menu of almost every street stand in the park. Mickey Mouse and Donald Duck have French accents, and many rides were renamed to appeal to French visitors: in Adventureland, for example, Le Ventre de la Terre (Galleries under the tree), l'Ile au Tresor (Treasure Island), and La Cabane des Robinson (Robinsons' Cabin).

In an attempt to further target Europeans, Disney opened a Walt Disney Studios park where virtual tour guides are Jeremy Irons, Isabella Rossellini, and Nastassia Kinski speaking in their native tongues. The $533 million movie-themed park is a tribute to movie making—not just to Hollywood, even though it is modeled after an old Hollywood studio complex. Yet in France, montages show Disney characters speaking six different languages, and a stunt show designed by French stuntman Remy Julienne features cars and motorcycles that race through French resort town St. Tropez. Nevertheless, since its launch in 2002, the Studios park has underperformed, and visitors have complained that it does not have enough attractions.

Questions

1. How do the values and lifestyles of European consumers differ from those of consumers in the United States? Discuss the Disney failure to address European consumers' preferences.
2. A large proportion of the park's visitors come from Spain and Latin America. How can Disneyland Resort Paris appeal more effectively to this market? Design a new target marketing strategy aimed at the Spanish and Latin American market.

Sources: "REG-Euro Disney S.C.A. Interim Results," *Reuters*, (www.reuters.com, April 28, 2005); Christina Passariello, "Euro Disney Likely to Record Losses for the Next Few Years," *Wall Street Journal* (December 1, 2004): B3; Harriet Marsh, "Variations on a Theme Park," *Marketing* (London, May 2, 1996): 14; "Euro Disneyland SCA," International Directory of Company Histories, vol. 20 (1999): 209–212; "The Kingdom inside a Republic," *The Economist* (April 13, 1996): 66–67; Juliana Koranteng, "Euro Disney Revenues Rise," *Amusement Business* (August 6, 2001): 38; Barbara J. Mays, "French Park Still Negotiating for Airline Partnership," *Travel Weekly* (April 20, 1992); Barbara Rudolph, "Monsieur Mickey: Euro Disneyland Is on Schedule, but with a Distinct French Accent," *Time* (March 25, 1991): 48–49.

This case was originally developed with the assistance of Jessica DiTommaso.

Internet Marketing

18

CHAPTER OBJECTIVES

1. Identify the primary users of the Internet.
2. Discuss the benefits of Internet marketing.
3. Distinguish the Internet marketing functions.
4. Present the e-commerce components and incentives needed to encourage online purchasing.
5. Examine Internet branding and how it is accomplished.
6. Explain viral marketing.
7. List the steps in developing an Internet marketing strategy.

CHAPTER OUTLINE

Jill wants to purchase a new automobile, but she is leery of going to automobile dealers to gather information because of the high-pressure techniques some use. Like most Americans, Jill feels that the purchase of an automobile is a major decision that involves considerable time and effort to gather information and weigh all of the pros and cons of the various brands and models. Like a growing number of Americans, Jill decides to do her research on the Internet. She first goes to general sites that discuss and rank the various automobiles. She then focuses on specific brands, gathering information and examining photos of the exteriors as well as the interiors of various brands. By the time she shows up at the dealer showroom, Jill has already narrowed the list down to three models. Now it is time to test-drive each one.

Instead of going with the dealer's finance option, Jill will use the Internet to obtain the best financing terms. The same process will be used for insurance. Instead of just going down to the office of her current insurance vendor, Jill will look at policies and offers from various insurance companies and choose the one that best meets her needs.

Eric is the purchasing agent for a large Midwest business and has been assigned the task of locating a new piece of equipment for the plant and finding a better price for copper wire. Instead of calling a distributor, Eric gets on the Internet. After a few hours of searching business-to-business auction sites, he finds just the right piece of equipment the plant needs. Although the equipment is used, it can be purchased for only $68,000, versus $144,000 for new equipment.

For the copper wire, Eric locates three firms that he feels confident can meet the company's demand. Submitting the specifications that are needed by his company, he obtains three bids. Two out of the three are at a lower cost than his company is currently paying. Because of the critical nature of copper wire to the company's production process, Eric must be certain he is dealing with a legitimate firm that can meet the company's production schedule; a vendor audit is thus arranged with the top two candidates.

It is time for the Cox family to select a vacation spot. In the past, they would request literature from several vacation sites and stop by their local travel agent for information. Nowadays, they simply get on the Internet. Within hours, they have more information than they really need, and when the time comes to make reservations, they will use the Internet.

Andrew Cox is a vice president of a financial institution and travels about once a month to the corporate headquarters or to other corporate sites. He now makes airline reservations online the same way he makes hotel reservations and rental car reservations.

The Internet provides consumers with new ways of gathering information, making purchases, and communicating with each other. The Internet provides businesses with a new way of advertising their companies and their products and finding potential customers. Now even individuals living in small U.S. towns have access to the Internet and can book a train ride in Central Europe from their home computers (see Figure 18-1).

18-1 Chapter Overview

While marketing has been around for several decades, Internet marketing is a recent phenomenon. Because of increased usage of the Internet by both consumers and businesses, having a web presence has become important, and understanding how to maximize the marketing thrust of a website is even more important.

In Section 18-2, several types of Internet users are presented. Section 18-3 discusses the benefits of Internet marketing and functions that are possible with Internet marketing. Firms can do more than sell merchandise over the Internet. They can use it for a host of functions that can benefit consumers, other businesses, and even the firm's own employees. Section 18-4 is a presentation of e-commerce and includes a discussion of the components of an e-commerce website, incentives that are needed to encourage customers and businesses to make online purchases, and concerns that arise when operating in an inter-

Figure 18-1
You can book a bullet train ride in Europe from your laptop in Yuma, Arizona.

national environment. Section 18-5 discusses Internet branding from the perspective of new Internet firms and also for established, well-known brands. A unique form of Internet marketing, called viral marketing, is discussed in Section 18-6. The chapter concludes with a model for developing an Internet marketing strategy in Section 18-7.

18-2 Internet Users

Not since the invention of the automobile or computer has any single invention so radically transformed life and changed the way of doing business as has the development of the Internet. According to Nielsen/NetRatings, more than 452 million people around the globe are using the Internet, with 140 million of those in the United States. The average amount of time each person spends on the Internet is 25 hours a month, visiting an average of 59 different sites, going online an average of 30 times per month. Table 18-1 provides statistics on the 11 countries in terms of Internet penetration of the home market. People in Japan access the most unique domains each month, 76, while people in France spend the most time on the Internet, an average of 32 hours and 40 minutes per month. In terms of how long one page is viewed, Australians and the French spend the most time, an average of 55 seconds per page, while the Japanese spend the least, only 31 seconds per page.[1]

Not only has the Internet impacted personal lives, it has impacted how business is being conducted in the twenty-first century. To illustrate, you only need to examine the Internet sales of two companies: Dell Computers and Cisco Systems. Internet sales at Dell Computers average $18 million a day; for Cisco, Internet sales average $28 million per day. Other interesting facts about the Internet include the following:[2]

- There are more than 4 million websites, with 235,000 new ones being added each month.
- There are 200 million email boxes in the United States.
- People send more than 7 trillion emails each year in the United States.
- The average email user receives 31 emails per day.
- Business-to-business e-commerce in the United States totals $1.3 trillion per year.
- Businesses will place orders totaling $3 trillion per year worldwide via the Internet.
- Twenty-five percent of all business-to-business purchases are placed through some type of Internet connection.
- Internet retail sales account for almost 2.5 percent of all retail sales.

TABLE 18-1

Internet Penetration and Usage Statistics of the Home Market Per Month

Country	Average Unique Domains Visited per Person	Average Time per Person (hours and minutes)	Duration of Page Visit (seconds)	Active Digital Media Users (millions)
Australia	47	27:32	55	9.0
Brazil	43	25:27	55	10.9
France	73	32:40	41	15.5
Germany	69	28:49	39	29.5
Japan	76	14:57	31	36.6
The Netherlands	68	22:19	38	7.8
Spain	57	28:04	54	8.2
Sweden	38	21:41	41	4.6
Switzerland	72	28:19	40	3.3
United Kingdom	58	24:27	45	22.6
United States	54	30:20	53	139.5

Source: Compiled by the authors from Nielsen/NetRatings, www.nielsen-netratings.com, January 20, 2005.

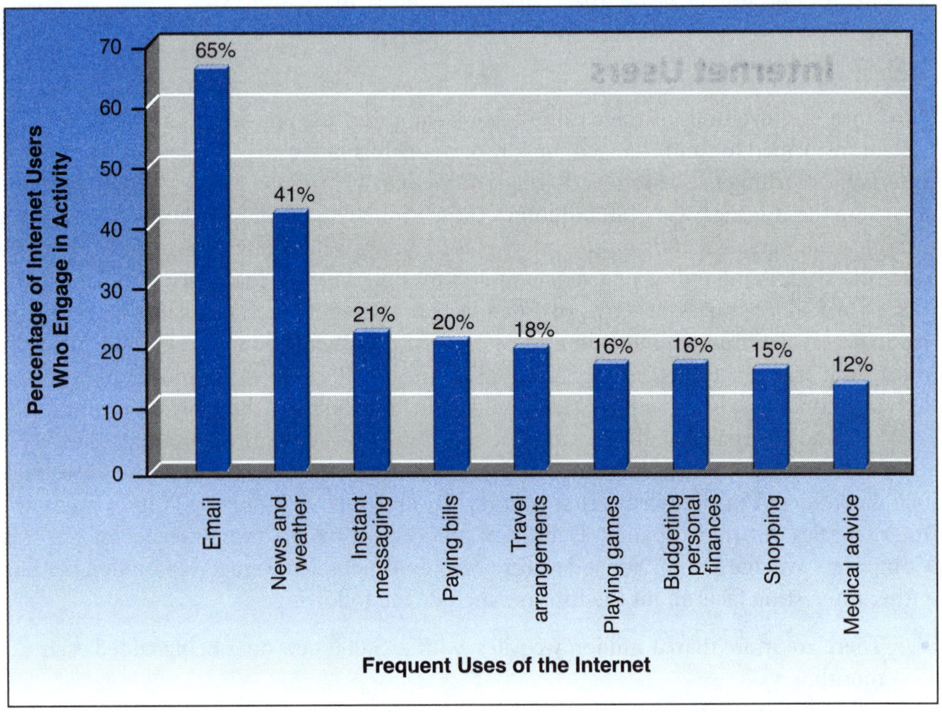

Figure 18-2
Internet Usage

Source: Linda Lyons, "Internet Use: What's Age Got to Do with It?" *The Gallup Poll Tuesday Briefing, The Gallup Organization*, (March 16, 2004).

A survey by the Gallup Organization provides some insight into how consumers are using the Internet.[3] As would be expected, the number one use is email. Sixty-five percent of Americans use the Internet frequently to send and receive email. Other frequent major uses of the Internet include obtaining news and the weather (41 percent), instant messaging (21 percent), paying bills online (20 percent), and making travel arrangements (18 percent). Figure 18-2 provides a breakdown of the top Internet activities.

How the Internet is used does vary by age. For instance, while 26 percent of individuals 30–49 said they use the Internet frequently to pay bills online, only 9 percent of U.S.

TABLE 18-2

Percentage of Respondents, By Age, Who Indicated They Frequently Use the Internet for the Stated Purpose

Internet Activity	18–29	30–49	50–64
Sending and receiving email	59%	69%	63%
Checking news and weather	40%	45%	33%
Using instant messaging	36%	18%	12%
Paying bills online	21%	26%	9%
Making travel arrangements	20%	18%	21%
Playing games	15%	18%	12%
Budgeting personal finances	17%	18%	12%
Shopping	10%	18%	11%
Finding medical advice	13%	11%	11%

Source: Linda Lyons, "Internet Use: What's Age Got to Do with It?" *The Gallup Poll Tuesday Briefing, The Gallup Organization* (March 16, 2004).

consumers 50–64 pay bills online. A similar pattern is seen for using instant messaging. Only 12 percent of U.S. consumers 50–64 use instant message frequently, while 36 percent of the individuals 18–29 use instant messaging on a frequent basis and 18 percent of individuals 30–49. Table 18-2 breaks down the Internet usage by age category.

A recent survey found that 22 percent of all Internet users are preteens and teens, with an additional 35 percent of the users being of college age. Generation X accounts for another 35 percent, and baby boomers or seniors account for only 8 percent.[4] In terms of income, 91 percent of individuals in the $75,000 to $99,999 income category use the Internet, compared to only 40 percent with incomes below $15,000. As would be expected, the higher the level of education a person has, the more likely that person is to use the Internet. Approximately 80 percent of the individuals with a college or post-graduate degree are Internet users, compared to 42 percent of individuals with a high school degree or less. In terms of ethnicity, the highest Internet usage is among Asian Americans (93 percent), and the lowest is among Hispanics (47 percent).[5] See Marketing Illustration 18-1 for information on Internet usage by Asian Americans.

Marketing Illustration 18-1

Asian Americans and Internet Usage

The heaviest ethnic users of the Internet are Asian Americans. In a typical day, 70 percent of the 5 million Asian Americans will get online. This is significantly higher than Caucasians at 58 percent, Hispanics at 48 percent, and African Americans at 39 percent.

As a group, Asian Americans have been online longer than any other ethnic group. Almost half of Asian Americans have been using the Internet for three or more years, and 80 percent have been online for two or more years. Asian Americans also stay online longer. Almost 40 percent of those who get online will spend two or more hours online, and about 15 percent will spend four or more hours online.

Asian Americans have enthusiastically embraced the Internet as a source of information both at work and at home. Compared to others, Asian Americans are more likely to use the Internet to gather information about financial matters, travel, and politics. They also use it more as a resource for school and work. In terms of gathering news online, 34 percent of Asian-American users get their daily news online, compared to 22 percent for whites, 20 percent for Hispanics, and 15 percent for African Americans.

For companies wanting to market to Asian Americans, the Internet offers a rich opportunity.

Source: Ronald Roach, "Survey: Asian Americans Are the Most Wired Ethnic Group," *Black Issues in Higher Education,* vol. 18, no. 24 (January 17, 2002): 44.

More and more U.S. workers are accessing the Internet from their workplace: 42 million workers or nearly 15 percent of all Americans get online. The average person logs on 43 times during a month, visits 35 sites, and spends an average of 22 hours and 38 minutes online. The places where workers surf include corporate information (49 percent), finance/insurance/investment (42 percent), travel (31 percent), telecom/Internet services (28 percent), and special occasions (27 percent). Nearly every website category has seen an increase in traffic; corporate information websites have grown the fastest, with a 49 percent increase in just one year.[6]

18-3 Internet Marketing

The Internet has transformed the way most businesses now operate. At the beginning, many businesses jumped onto the Internet and built websites because it was the thing to do. They were not sure how their site would be used or who would use their site. But as Internet usage has continued to increase dramatically, companies have come to realize that the Internet can provide substantial benefits to both customers as well as to the selling firm. Using this information, companies began developing the field of Internet marketing.

18-3a Benefits of Internet Marketing

The Internet provides numerous benefits for companies, which are highlighted in Figure 18-3. The most obvious use of the Internet is for sales. While online shopping accounts for only about 3 percent of retail sales, it is growing at a much faster pace than retail sales for bricks-and-mortar stores. In the United States, online sales are growing between 30 and 40 percent per year, compared to an average of 4 percent for offline retailers. Worldwide, the most concentrated online shopping is in the areas of computers, electronics, and travel, making up approximately 30 percent of total online retail sales.[7] As will be seen in Section 18-4, which discusses e-commerce, the Internet provides a new venue for shopping, which, if used appropriately, can mean a boost in sales for many companies.

The Internet allows for a dynamic, interactive communication environment. Advertising, sales promotions, trade promotions, and other integrated marketing communications (IMC) efforts are all static and directed toward consumers or other businesses. Only salespeople and the Internet have the capability of being interactive. By using attractive graph-

Figure 18-3
Company Benefits of Using the Internet in Marketing

INTERACTIVE FIGURE

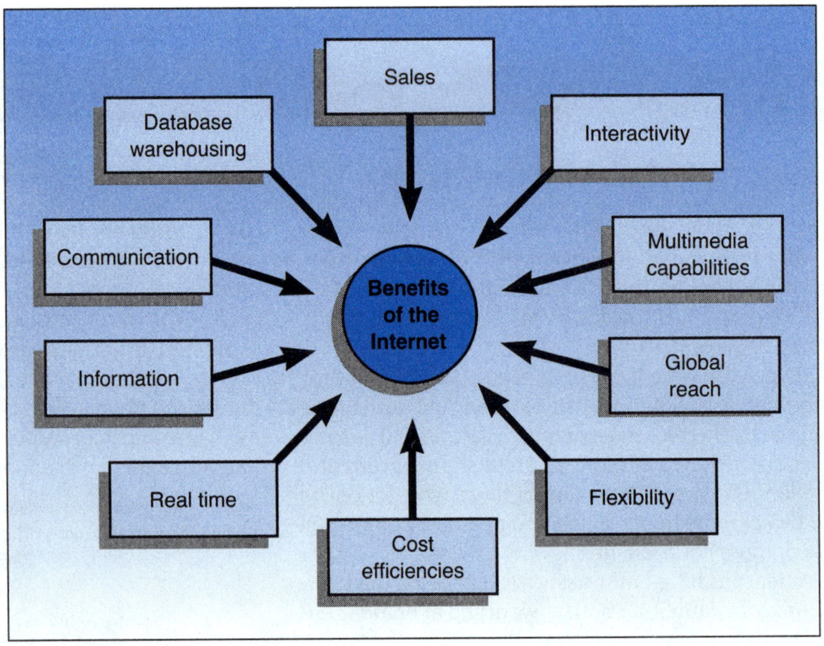

ics and menus, individuals can be guided throughout a website to the information they want. Yet, it can be done at the visitor's own pace. Visitors can skim some sections and read others. They can even bookmark the site or places in the site for future references. To encourage a visitor to explore deeper, interactive games and contests can be used.

The Internet provides a multimedia environment (see Figure 18-4). Sound, pictures, and even short videos can provide information or entertain. A live cam shot can be used for sites such as a college or resort to show a visitor what the actual campus or facility looks like. At a resort website, a multimedia presentation could show the different facets of the resort, such as the night club, the restaurants, the pool, the beach, and any other amenities that would be appealing. A big benefit of the Internet is that consumers (or businesses) can examine what they want to see, at the pace they want to see it, and as often as they want.

As the Internet continues to expand around the world, a company's website has an ever broader global reach. A company that used to sell its products within a 100-mile radius of its business can now sell its products anywhere in the world. Only imagination and logistics concerns separate a business serving the local community from one that sells to people in Spain, India, or Australia.

The Internet provides flexibility that is only available with salespeople. Content can be changed quickly, often within minutes or hours. New messages can be put up instantaneously. For instance, immediately after the terrorist attacks of September 11, 2001 many company websites had posted messages of sympathy. Many offered some type of assistance or help for the families of victims. The flexibility means that the Internet can virtually operate in real time. Ads can be placed on the Internet as soon as they are completed, not months later as would be the case with a magazine. A new product can be highlighted as soon as it becomes available and not have to wait until it passes through the channel and is stocked on store shelves.

The Internet provides an excellent medium to communicate with customers as well as prospects and to provide information to various constituencies. Customers can be provided passwords that will allow them to access website components that no one else can see. Pricing information and product production data, for instance, can be provided in such a manner. Information about a firm's products can be posted on the Internet, as well as shipping information and the location of retailers where the products can be purchased. Instead of a static, two-dimensional paper catalog, firms can develop an interactive Internet catalog that is more interesting to access and can provide more information.

A major advantage of the Internet that many companies have not fully realized yet deals with cost efficiencies. For example, most manufacturers spend approximately 20 to

Figure 18-4
The multimedia environment of the Internet provides an opportunity for individuals to view a site such as the residence of the Prince-Bishops of Wurzburg before they actually make their vacation plans.

30 percent of the final cost of their products on sales, marketing, and distribution. What makes the potential of the Internet so exciting is that these companies can establish a website and sell directly to customers, potentially reducing these costs to 10 to 20 percent. Even for bricks-and-mortar retailers, e-commerce provides an environment for gaining cost efficiencies. When products are shipped directly to customers instead of the retail store, the retailer can save the cost of packing, shipping, and transporting products to retail sites, where they have to be unpacked and stocked on shelves. Also, in most cases, handling and shipping costs can be charged to customers purchasing the product over the Internet.[8]

The last benefit of the Internet is also the most controversial. Because of Internet technology, information about individuals or businesses that visit the site can be gathered, with or without their knowledge. If used ethically, this information can help a firm do a better job of targeting its products to meet the needs of each person who accesses the website. This information can be added to the firm's database to build a more robust profile of its customers. For example, an individual who accesses the baseball equipment component of a sporting goods e-commerce site can be provided with a coupon or premium to encourage a purchase. If the individual accesses the same site on several occasions, the company can safely assume that the customer has a high level of interest in baseball.

18-3b Functions of Internet Marketing

Based on the benefits that a company is able to realize from the Internet, a firm can develop multiple functions. Although a number of functions can be accomplished, it is important for firms to realize that trying to do too many things with their websites can be a disaster for everyone. It is important to develop one or two primary functions that the firm can do and do well. Additional sites or links can be used for additional functions. Figure 18-5 highlights the various marketing functions available through the Internet.

The Internet provides an opportunity for business organizations to sell directly to consumers as well as to other businesses. (Marketing Illustration 18-2 highlights how companies can use the Internet to buy and sell industrial equipment to other businesses.) The

Figure 18-5
How the Internet May Be Utilized in Marketing

INTERACTIVE FIGURE

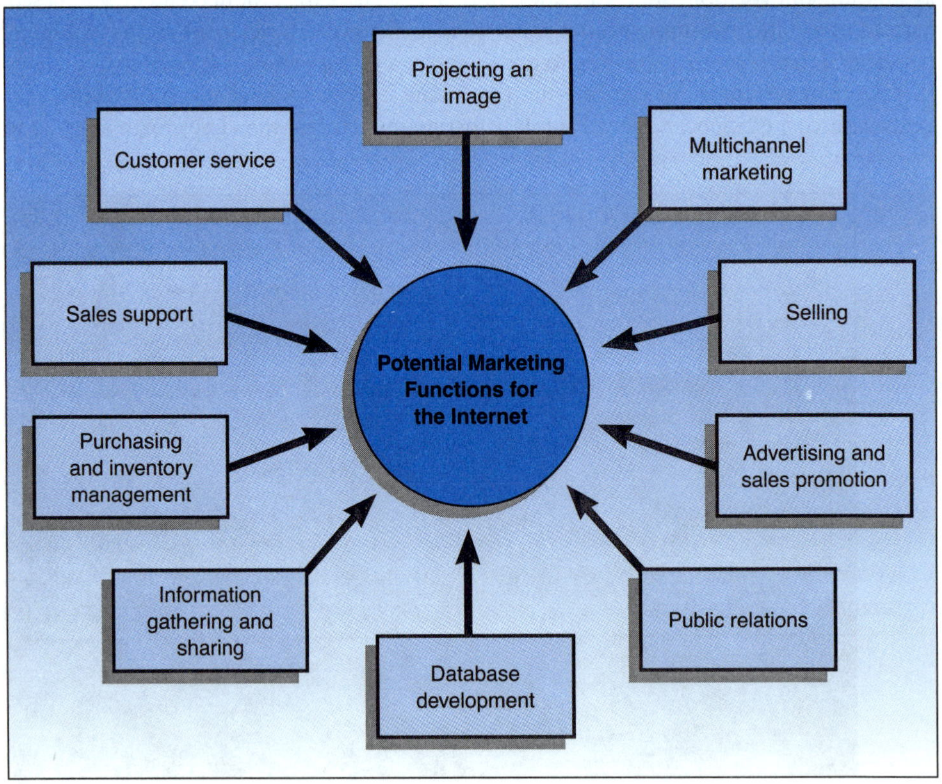

Marketing Illustration 18-2

Buying and Selling Industrial Equipment over the Internet

The auto industry is like many other manufacturers in that it requires a lot of heavy equipment to bend, machine, and join metals. To maintain efficiency, most manufacturers have a capital program to upgrade machinery on a regular basis. Used, outdated equipment would end up being scrapped or sold to a regional dealer or broker, who would try to sell it to another local manufacturer. This process usually meant that used equipment brought only a small fraction of its value. In addition, the whole process of upgrading equipment and disposing of old equipment was frustrating, time consuming, and inefficient.

Internet firms like Online Asset Exchange have drastically changed the way used industrial equipment is bought and sold. With the global reach of the Internet, buyers from any place in the world can be found. Surplus equipment that may not be state-of-the-art for one firm can be an upgrade for another firm.

Not only can the Internet bring buyers and sellers together, but it can also provide a multitude of functions needed to make the transaction happen. Appraisals, financing, shipping, escrow, and brokering can all take place over the Internet or with firms that can be quickly located on the Internet. Many sites, such as Online Asset Exchange, will provide these services or assist buyers and sellers in locating firms that will provide the services.

With the Internet, the surplus industrial equipment market is beginning to flourish. Used equipment being discarded in industrialized nations like the United States is also purchased by firms in developing countries such as Mexico, China, and countries in Africa.

Source: Lee A. Iacocca, "Buy and Sell Industrial Equipment over the Internet," *Motion Systems Distributor,* vol. 14, no. 4 (July/August 2000): 6.

Internet can be the only channel of sales, or it can provide a multichannel approach. A firm can still use wholesalers, distributors, and retailers. Many well-established retailers have found that the Internet provides an additional channel that consumers can use to make purchases. For manufacturers, it is more problematic, since they do not want to alienate their current channel members. This can occur if customers can buy directly from the manufacturer at a lower price. To prevent this potential conflict, manufacturers can either sell the products at the same price their channel member would or link consumers to a channel member's site when it comes to making a purchase. In this instance, the manufacturer uses its site to provide information.

The Internet is a logical place for advertising and sales promotions. The best location for sales promotion offers would be a firm's own website, but the best place for advertisements would be on other sites. Online advertising during this past year totaled $11.3 billion. By 2008, it is estimated that online advertising will reach $17.5 billion.[9] The primary benefit of online advertising is its effectiveness in developing a brand name, brand awareness, and brand equity. Whereas consumer products tend to advertise on websites related to the firm's products, business-to-business advertisers tend to spend online advertising dollars in more targeted formats, such as keyword search engines. Advertising through keyword searches has the ability to target an advertising message to users of the specific product being advertised and not just to the general business market.

Because of the wide use of banner ads, advertisers are becoming suspicious of their ability to reach consumers effectively. To ensure that Internet users notice ads, web designers are using fancier graphics, flashing images, and streaming videos. The first advance was to **interstitial ads**, which are Internet popup ads. Because the only way to get rid of an interstitial ad is to physically close it with the mouse or cursor, it has become quite controversial. Unfortunately, just as telemarketing yields results, the interstitial ad works significantly better than the traditional banner ad. This success has led advertisers to develop interstitials that work after a person leaves a website or even shuts off the computer. The ad will appear the next time the person logs onto the Internet.

Interstitial ads: Internet popup advertisements.

The newest types of ads are **rich media ads,** which are short video clips. Advertisers are currently spending about 8 percent of their online advertising dollars on rich media. Websites that are using the rich media ads claim they receive far less negative feedback about the rich media ads than they did about the popup ads.[10] Email advertisements are now

rich media ads: Media that uses audio and video formats, often using Macromedia Flash and Shockwave.

being created with full graphics and streaming videos that can be sent overnight to customers who were on a particular website. While the ethics of such advertising tactics are being debated, the fact is that they work.

In a worldwide Internet survey, individuals were asked to cite the most offensive form of advertising. Only 24 percent stated that Internet advertising was not intrusive or a turnoff; the remaining 76 percent did cite various types of Internet ads they thought were offensive. The biggest turnoffs were popup ads, named by 40 percent of the respondents. The next most disliked were email ads at 28 percent. Banner ads bothered only 8 percent of the sample.[11]

Cyberbait: A lure or attractive offer used to attract someone to an Internet site.

Attracting individuals or businesses to a website is often done through some type of lure or attractive offer, which is called **cyberbait.** Just as a worm or fishing lure is used to catch fish, cyberbait is some form of attraction that will draw people to a website. A common cyberbait used in the consumer market is sales promotions.

A popular cyberbait used to generate website traffic is some type of contest or sweepstakes. In using this approach, a firm must decide whether to have one major event or a number of smaller events. This situation can be compared to giving one person $100,000 or 500 people cash or merchandise worth $200. The large promotion attracts the type of person who enters a lottery or contest with the hope of winning the big prize. In contrast, smaller promotions often draw individuals who are more interested in the company's merchandise. For example, a sporting goods site could offer every person who buys something from its website a chance of winning $100,000, and the odds of winning may be 1 in 1,000,000. In contrast, the same company can offer free sporting goods, such as a fishing rod, baseball glove, or basketball, as prizes with the chances of winning being only 1 in 50. These two promotions would attract different types of potential customers.

Figure 18-6
Advances in technology and software development support interactive marketing on the Internet, which involves personalizing website content and products to the individual customer.

Source: Copyright © 2006 Atomic Dog Publishing and its licensors. All rights reserved.

To be effective in drawing attention to a website, promotions must be changed on a regular basis. For example, during one month, individuals who purchase merchandise may receive a free gift, such as a baseball with the purchase of any baseball equipment or a package of tennis balls with the purchase of any tennis equipment or clothing. The next month, they may have a 1 in 10 chance of winning a free gift that would be of greater value. In the third month, the promotion may change to receiving a third item free if the person buys two. Changing promotions encourages consumers to return to the site. Each promotion may also appeal to slightly different consumers. Thus, a coupon may appeal to one consumer, whereas a premium may be more appealing to another.

A major advantage of offering promotions is the opportunity for them to be used in database development. The Internet provides an ideal medium for gathering information about consumers or businesses that are visiting a site. While some information can be gathered without a person's consent, information that is more useful can be gathered through the individual voluntarily offering it. A short questionnaire can be attached to a sales promotion offer or consumers can be offered some free merchandise or an entry into a contest or sweepstake if they supply information about themselves. It is important to inform individuals providing this information as to how the data will be used. More and more consumers and businesses are becoming concerned about privacy issues and how companies are using information about them.

Interactive marketing: The process of individualizing and personalizing everything—from the website content to the products being promoted.

A recent trend that database development permits is **interactive marketing,** which is the process of individualizing and personalizing the website content, as well as the products being promoted (see Figure 18-6). NCR produces software called Relationship Optimizer and Prime Response that uses powerful data analysis techniques to personalize offers to customers. The NCR software analyzes customer interactions such as click-stream data traffic with any type of customer interaction with the firm, and combines it with demographic information from external or internal marketing databases. As the data are being processed, the software can launch complex interactive and personalized web and email campaigns.

Levi-Strauss uses software called Blue Martini E-Merchandising to customize its Levis.com and Dockers.com websites. The Home Shopping Network uses Edify's Smart Options software to track user preferences and suggest products based on the customer's past activities and current purchases. These technologies blur the line between selling and marketing because the messages and products a customer sees are based on past purchasing activities. These programs are designed to increase the odds that customers will see something they want, rather than being forced to wade through scores of products they have no interest in purchasing at a more standardized website.[12]

For business customers, the Internet provides an ideal method for purchasing and inventory management, sales support, and customer service. For many products, the ability to order directly over the Internet saves time for both the buyer and the seller. Through specialized software, computers can even take these orders without human intervention. For example, a sporting goods store may have its computer system set to order a new batch of footballs as soon as inventory reaches 50. Because the inventory is tied into the cash registers, no one needs to inform the manager that the supply is low and it is time to reorder. In addition, firms can check on the status of their order. They can find out when it will come off the assembly line, when it is loaded on a truck, and even where it is in shipment. Federal Express, UPS, and the U.S. Postal Service all have tracking software that allows someone to track a package and know exactly where it is.

The Internet can be used in various ways to support a company's sales efforts. The most common use of the Internet in the area of sales support is providing information about clients and products to the sales staff. The salesperson should be able to access all of the information the company has in its database about any given customer. In addition, data can be collected regarding the products that are being examined by individual customers who visit the company's website. This gives the salesperson insight regarding what products to pitch and how to make the sales approach. A well-designed database system that is integrated with the website can have all of this information added to the customer's profile.

The firm's website can be a valuable resource tool for salespeople who are making a sales call. While experienced salespeople may have complete knowledge of all of the products sold, new salespeople may not. The Internet can be used by the salesperson to provide the information a client is requesting. Often, this can be done in the client's office or within a short period of time. The Internet can also be used when a customer is ready to place an order. The order can be sent immediately, and the salesperson with access to the firm's database can inform the customer of the shipping date. If the item is out of stock, the salesperson is able to inform the customer that the item must be backordered.

The Internet is a very efficient and cost-effective way for companies to provide customer service. The key to effectively using the web to enhance customer service is found in the design of the website. The site must be easy for the consumer to use and provide some benefit over using the telephone. Speed is one primary benefit the Internet offers. Making it easier and faster to get the information encourages consumers to use a website. Providing additional information that is not normally provided over the telephone can be another advantage.

A major part of customer service is answering questions. Designed properly, a website can be a valuable resource for responding to common consumer inquiries. One method is to provide a series of responses to **FAQs,** or frequently asked questions people have about various items or services. These questions must be indexed or arranged by topics so customers can access answers quickly. Otherwise, consumers become frustrated and call a toll-free number instead. Another approach, still in its infancy, is computerized advisors created by companies like Kana Communications. Named Jill and Emily, this software uses focus groups, psychographics, demographics, and Bayesian mathematical models to create questions and answers with a human touch. See Marketing Illustration 18-3 for more information about Emily.

FAQs: Frequently asked questions people have about various items or services.

Many retailers now allow manufacturers to access their inventory through the Internet. Manufacturers are able to study which products are selling. They can also see which colors, sizes, and styles are the most popular. They can even find out which stores have the highest levels of sales. This information allows the manufacturer to modify or set production schedules in order to make sure retailers have a steady supply of just the right size, color, and so forth.

Marketing Illustration 18-3

Meet Emily

Instead of using the telephone to call and determine which flowers to purchase, consumers can get online and ask Emily. Using information gathered from focus groups, psychographics, demographics, and Bayesian mathematical models, Kana Communications created a software program that provides answers with a human touch.

To see how well Emily could pick flowers, Noshua Watson asked Emily what exotic, expensive bouquet should be purchased for a wife for her anniversary. After answering questions about who, what, why, and how much, Emily recommended red roses, a heart-shaped wreath with gardenias, and then more roses. Emily added that these choices "will definitely reveal the intensity of your feelings for your wife."

Noshua then told Emily that she hated roses and that roses would not be acceptable. Emily adjusted her choice. This time, Emily suggested white orchids, birds of paradise, and a bamboo plant.

Having received a satisfactory answer, Noshua then asked Emily what flowers she should send to her mom as an apology for not visiting her. Emily remembered that Noshua did not like roses and made her suggestion accordingly.

Source: Noshua Watson, "Hi, My Name's Jill. Can I Help You?" *Fortune,* vol. 142, no. 1 (June 26, 2000): 322.

While not a primary function of the Internet, public relations can be used successfully, especially on specific occasions. For example, after the terrorist attacks in the United States in September 2001, many firms posted messages of sympathy on their websites. Some offered special promotions or posted information about cause-related marketing efforts they were supporting on behalf of the victims. Even during normal times, most websites will have a link to a page about their cause-related marketing efforts. Note in the advertisement by Plum Creek Timber Company that the website is listed so that anyone interested in the environmental approach Plum Creek is using can gather additional information (see Figure 18-7).

18-4 E-Commerce

E-commerce: The selling of goods and services over the Internet.

A major use of the Internet is **e-commerce,** which is the selling of goods and services over the Internet. E-commerce and selling over the Internet can be performed in three ways, illustrated in Figure 18-8. The first method is made up of the bricks-and-mortar firms that do not have any presence on the Internet, in terms of e-commerce. These tend to be small firms with regional markets and products that do not lend themselves well to the Internet. In developed countries, bricks-and-mortar firms are a minority and are becoming an even smaller percentage of the total firms every year. However, in developing countries, this form of commerce is still the standard mode of operation.

Clicks-only firms: Organizations that sell only over the Internet.

In the 1990s, there was a huge burst of dot-com companies, or **clicks-only firms,** which are organizations that sell only over the Internet. While these firms may have an office somewhere, they do not have a bricks-and-mortar store that a customer can go to. Most shipments are made directly to the customer from the manufacturer or distributor. In many cases, these firms do not even own an inventory but drop ship directly from producer to the customer (see Figure 18-9 on page 562).

Bricks-and-clicks: Firms that operate both a bricks-and-mortar facility as well as an Internet e-commerce site.

Realizing the impact of the Internet and understanding that it is here to stay, bricks-and-mortar firms began adopting e-commerce websites. These firms, which operate both a bricks-and-mortar facility as well as an Internet e-commerce site, are known as **bricks-and-clicks.** These firms realize that e-commerce can provide customers with a different channel of making purchases and that it can be a valuable tool for providing information about the firms' products (see Figure 18-10 on page 562).

Brand-name retailers now realize that the Internet is not a threat to their retail operation, but rather, can be used to build brand loyalty and increase sales. JCPenney found that shoppers who purchased merchandise from all three channels (retail stores, catalog, and

Figure 18-7
In this public relations advertisement by Plum Creek Timber Company, Plum Creek emphasizes its concern for the environment. It also lists its website so that readers can gather additional information.

Source: Sample print advertisement courtesy of The Miles Agency and Alliance One Advertising, Inc.

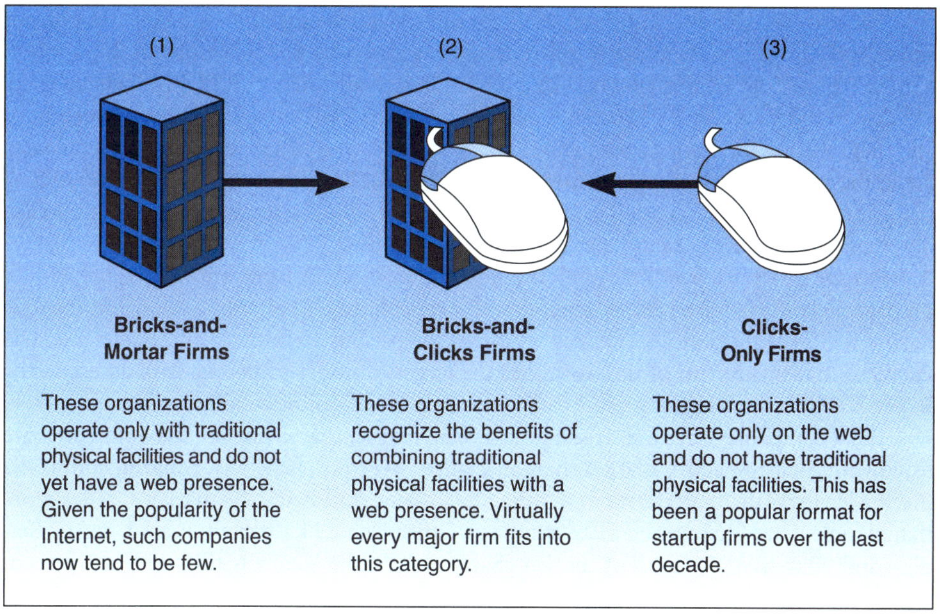

Figure 18-8
The Three Methods of Marketing and the Internet

INTERACTIVE FIGURE

Figure 18-9
Lands' End had already developed a strong brand name through its catalog business, so the company found it easy to make the transition to an Internet e-commerce company.

Source: © 2003 Lands' End, Inc. Used with permission.

Figure 18-10
Most banks have moved into e-commerce with their online banking services. Here, Ouachita Independent Bank notes that free Internet banking will be available soon.

Source: Courtesy of Newcomer, Morris and Young.

the Internet) spent more than $800 per year, on the average. Individuals who used only one channel spent an average of $200 per year.[13]

The growth of global Internet retail commerce has averaged an amazing 44 percent since 1999. In that year, global Internet retail revenue was $53.5 billion. In 2003 it was $232.5 billion (see Figure 18-11a). The two major retail categories of products sold are (1) tickets and travel and (2) computers, electronics, and software. Twenty-nine percent of all retail sales are for some type of travel arrangements, while 28.7 percent of all retail sales are in the areas of computers, electronics, and software. These two categories make up 57.7 percent of the total global retail online sales. See Figure 18-11b for a more in-depth breakdown of global Internet retail sales by product categories.

Europe generates over half of all online retail sales, at 52.1 percent (see Figure 18-11c on page 564). The United States generates 27.7 percent of global online sales, and the Asia Pacific region is third at 15.4 percent. What is surprising about the online sales for Asia Pacific is that this region of the world has the largest number of people with access to the Internet. These three regions generate 95.3 percent of all online retail sales.

What companies have the largest online retail market share? The top five companies are listed with their respective market share in Figure 18-11d on page 564. Amazon.com is the market leader with 2.3 percent of all online retail sales worldwide. Its market share is more than double that of the second place company, Office Depot (1.1 percent market share). Staples, and eBay have 0.9 percent market share, and Priceline.com is fifth with 0.5 percent market share.

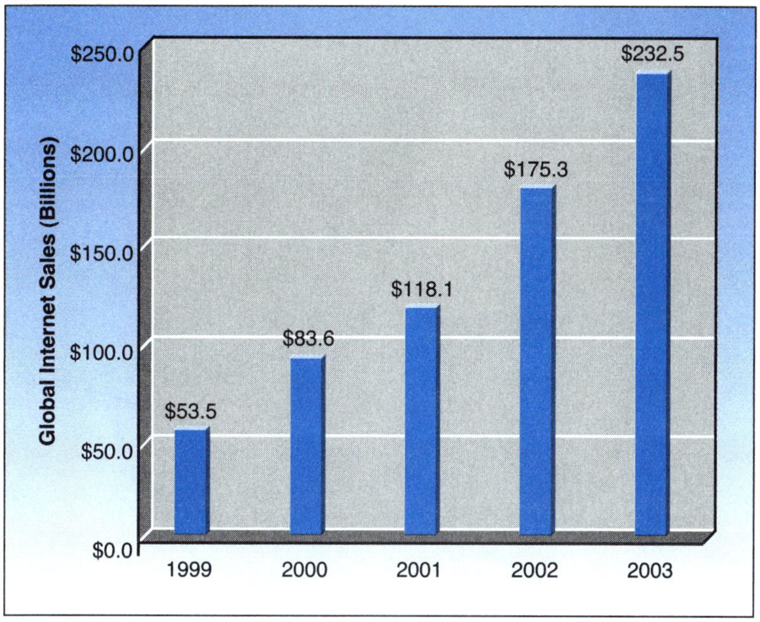

Figure 18-11a
Global Internet Retail Sales

Source: "Global Internet Retail," Internet Retail Industry Profile: Global (May 2004): 1–17.

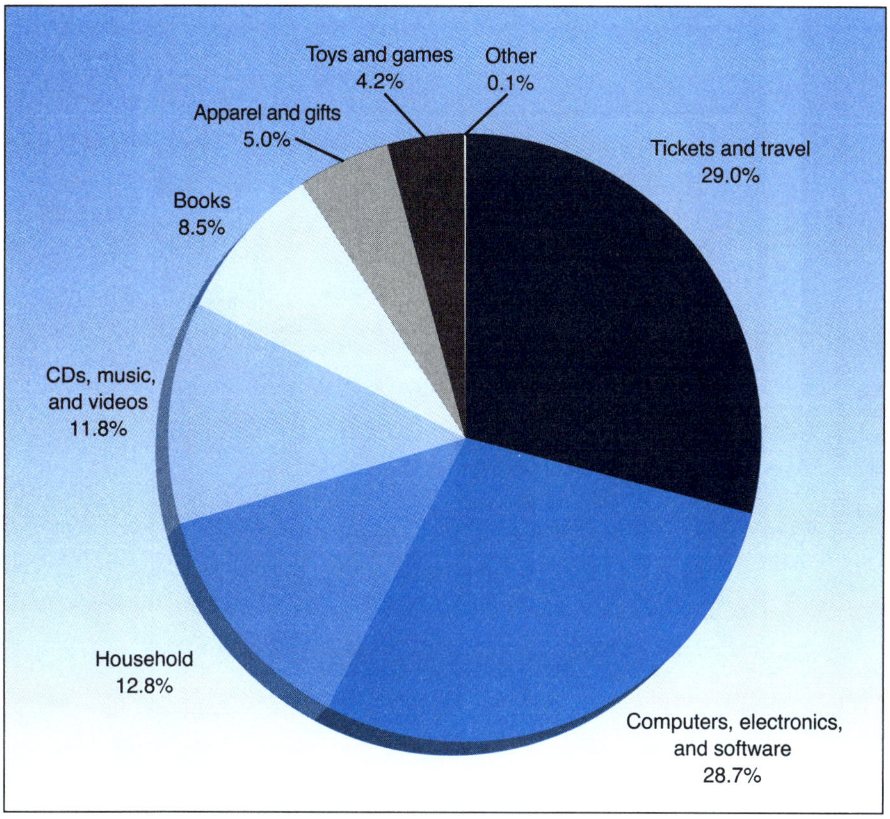

Figure 18-11b
Global Internet Retail Sales by Product Type

Source: "Global Internet Retail," Internet Retail Industry Profile: Global (May 2004): 1–17.

18-4a E-Commerce Components

An e-commerce site has three primary components: a catalog, a shopping cart, and a payment system. Bricks-and-clicks operations must have a fourth component: a location finder.

The catalog can be just a few items displayed on the main screen, or it can be a complex presentation of thousands of products embedded within multiple links and pages.

Figure 18-11c
Global Internet Retail Market Share by Region

Source: "Global Internet Retail," Internet Retail Industry Profile: Global (May 2004): 1–17.

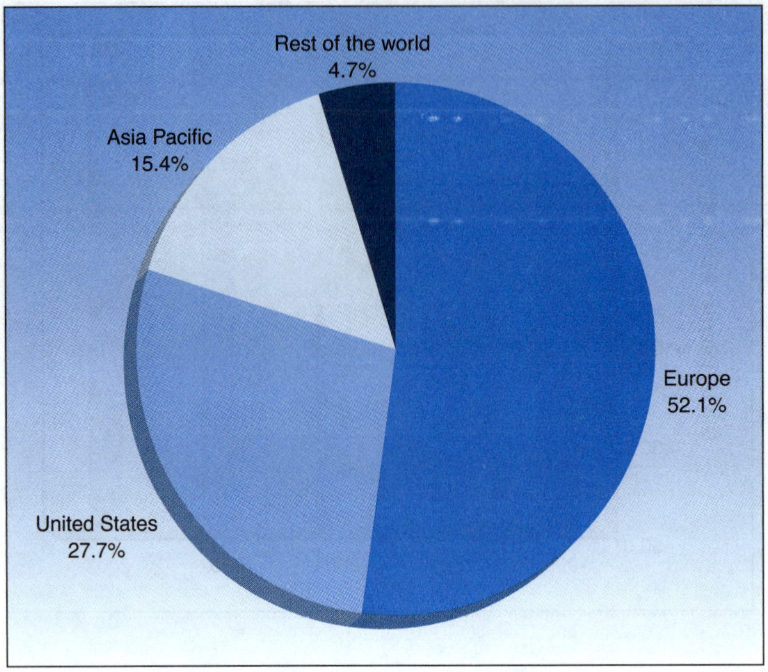

Figure 18-11d
Top Five Global Internet Retailers

Source: "Global Internet Retail," Internet Retail Industry Profile: Global (May 2004): 1–17.

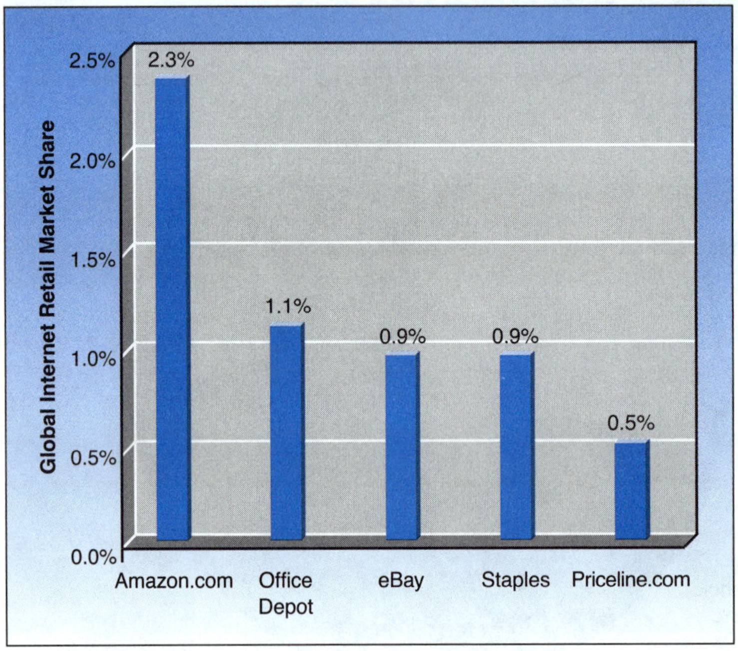

The type of catalog used is determined by how many products the firm sells and the objective of the website. For instance, if the website is to provide information, with most purchasing made in a bricks-and-mortar facility, then it will be designed differently from a website that is designed to entice web users to make an online purchase. In both cases, however, it is important for the site to be developed in such a way that consumers can easily find the products they want. Also, photos and detailed product information are important, and in some cases, short streaming videos can be used.

Each site must have some type of shopping cart to assist consumers as they select products. The shopping cart can range from just clicking a circle for an item when only a few products are offered to a more complicated shopping cart that keeps records of multiple purchases as well as previous purchases.

Each site must establish some way for customers to make payments for the items they purchase. For consumers, this is often a credit card system or one of the Internet services such as PayPal. For business-to-business operations, payments are normally made through a voucher system. In other situations, a bill is generated or a computerized billing system is used so that the invoice goes directly to the buyer. In more trusting relationships, the invoice is added to the customer's records without a physical bill ever being mailed.

For bricks-and-clicks operations, buyers need some way of finding the nearest location if the merchandise is not being shipped directly to them. For example, a consumer may examine clothes on the Internet but want to go to the retail outlet, where he or she can try on the clothes and then make the purchase. Vicinity Corporation produces software called SiteMaker and Business Finder that will display locations of the closest store, complete with a map and directions showing how to get there.[14]

For manufacturers such as Hewlett-Packard that do not sell directly to retailers but use other channel members, Vicinity SiteMaker will refer business customers to appropriate resellers. HP refers more than 100,000 customers each month to its closest reseller. This strategy has not only increased the loyalty of the reseller to HP but also has reduced the load on HP's call center. This results in major cost savings, since a human operator locating information and providing it to the customer is both slower and much more expensive. It is also more convenient for customers to use the SiteMaker locator software on HP's website. They can simply type in a ZIP code or address to gain access to location information. Further, a company can access the information at any time of the day, and no caller is forced to wait on hold for the next available HP company operator.[15]

18-4b E-Commerce Incentives

While online purchases are growing at a rapid rate, many consumers are still not sure about making online purchases for two reasons: security issues and purchase behavior habits. Many consumers are afraid to use credit cards because of the fear that their credit card number will be stolen. Others are concerned about fraud and dishonest e-commerce websites that will take their money and never ship the merchandise or ship poor-quality merchandise. In terms of purchasing habits, consumers feel more comfortable purchasing products from retail outlets because that is the way they have always shopped.

A brief view of history will provide an insight into these two concerns. When mail-order firms first encouraged ordering merchandise by telephone, consumers were fearful about giving out a credit card number to a stranger they couldn't see. Now, nearly everyone is willing to provide the information while placing orders on the phone. Also, not too long ago credit card holders expressed anxiety about various store employees stealing those numbers. Originally, customers were instructed to "take the carbon" from a credit card purchase to make sure it was torn into shreds in order to prevent an employee from using the credit card number later. The same pattern is likely to follow with Internet shopping. As consumers become accustomed to using the web, fears about giving out credit card information will be no greater than they are now for telephone orders or credit card store sales (see Figure 18-12).

Figure 18-12
In the past, consumers were fearful of providing credit card information over the telephone. Today, most people feel secure in doing it. Over time, the fear of providing credit card information over the Internet will also diminish.

The second issue is more difficult because it has strong ramifications regarding the future success of e-commerce. Consumers currently feel comfortable buying merchandise at retail stores and through catalogs. It will take time to change these habits, especially the preference for retail shopping. At the retail store, consumers can view and touch the merchandise. They can inspect it for defects and compare brands. Clothes can be tried on to make sure they fit. In addition, customers can see how clothing items look while being worn. As with any new technology, changing habits will require time and the right kinds of incentives, which are discussed in Section 18-5.

Figure 18-13
Why Consumers Purchase Online

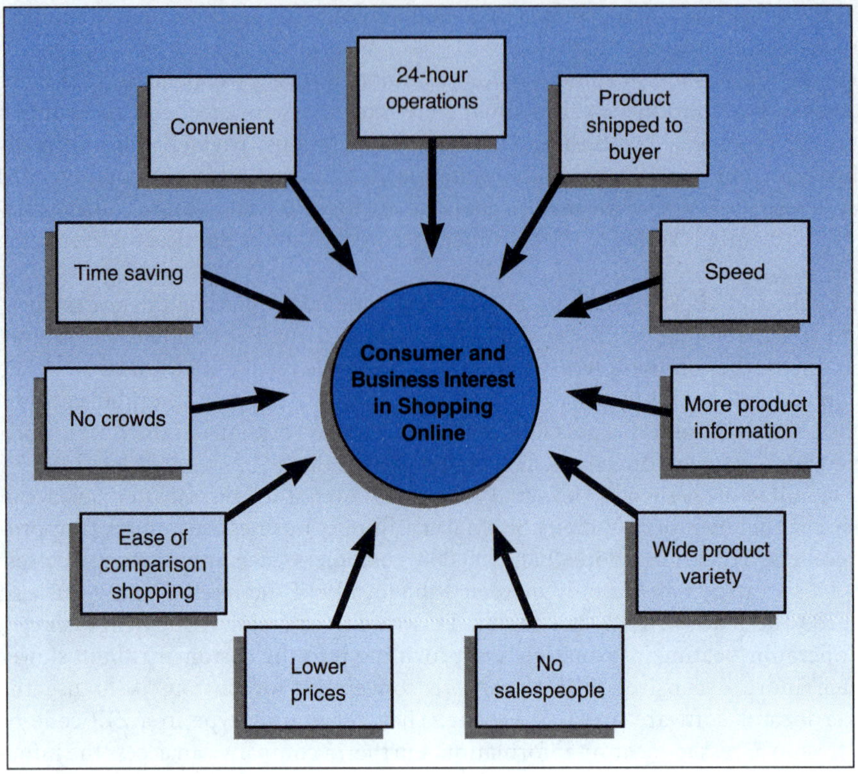

Before we examine ways to encourage consumers and businesses to shop online, it is helpful to review why anyone would shop online in the first place. Figure 18-13 provides a more complete list, but the most common reasons given are:

- 24-hour operations
- Convenience
- Time saving
- Lower prices
- No salespeople
- Speed

To encourage consumers and businesses to start making Internet purchases, a firm must provide some type of incentive. This is especially true for the long run. The incentives that can be used are financial incentives, convenience incentives, and value-added incentives.

To persuade an individual or business to change and make that first purchase online normally involves some type of financial incentive, which can be a reduced price, an introductory price, or some type of sales promotion, such as a coupon. Financial incentives are profitable for most firms because of the reduced costs of doing business online. Once the individual or company makes the switch, continuing the financial incentive may not be necessary because of the convenience or added-value features of e-commerce over traditional shopping methods.

Businesses are able to offer financial incentives because in most cases using the Internet to complete purchase transactions is cheaper than using traditional methods. E-commerce companies save money through lower telephone charges, since ordering is done over the Internet. Shipping costs are lower because, in most cases, buyers are charged a shipping and handling fee. Labor costs are saved from loading merchandise onto trucks, unloading them at a retail outlet, and then stocking the merchandise on store shelves. For business-to-business firms, additional savings occur if in the past a field salesperson was

Figure 18-14
A user-friendly and efficient website and a responsive customer service center streamline reservations at Las Vegas hotels.

used. The cost of the e-commerce transaction is considerably less than the $300 average cost per sales call for a salesperson.

Another major incentive that e-commerce can offer buyers is convenience. Instead of making a trip to a bricks-and-mortar location, a consumer or a business can place the order while remaining at home or at his or her place of business. More importantly, the order can be placed at any time, day or night. Seeking information about various products can be quicker and easier on the Internet than using *Consumer Reports,* talking to salespeople, or calling the manufacturer or a retailer. For businesses, ordering merchandise, supplies, and materials over the Internet can save purchasing agents considerable time. In addition to ordering, businesses can check on the status of their orders, shipment information, and even billing data. In most cases, doing so online is considerably quicker than making a telephone call. In this fast-paced world, convenience is a highly attractive incentive for many consumers and businesses (see Figure 18-14).

While financial incentives can encourage customers to switch to the Internet for their purchasing, it will take some type of value-added incentive (or convenience incentive) to make a more permanent change in purchasing habits. The added value may be personalization, where the firm becomes acquainted with the customer and his or her purchasing behaviors. Through specialized software, past purchase behavior can be tracked, allowing the Internet to automatically offer a customer special deals on merchandise he or she is most likely to purchase. For instance, a consumer going through the travel section of an online bookstore may see a popup banner advertising a special deal on a new travel book. In addition to instant banners, consumers and businesses may also receive emails offering new information and other special deals that are available. Again, these deals are based on past purchase behaviors contained within a database. These tools can make it much easier for e-commerce programs to create added values for customers.

Successful e-commerce begins with having the right website. It involves winning the trust of buyers, writing effective web content, protecting the firm from online fraud, and providing excellent post-sale customer service. See Marketing Illustration 18-4 for more details on how firms can build the right e-commerce website.

18-4c International Concerns

A major advantage of e-commerce over the bricks-and-mortar operation is the ability to reach customers everywhere in the world. Yet, 46 percent of the current companies with e-commerce capabilities turn away international orders, primarily because they do not have a way to ship the merchandise overseas or lack the necessary processes for international shipments. Therefore, while the Internet makes it possible for a company to sell items in an international marketplace, many companies are not prepared to go global. Specific obstacles to selling internationally include communication barriers, cultural differences, global

Marketing Illustration 18-4

Building the Right Website for E-Commerce Success

Building the right website is important. Here are a few suggestions on the major criteria:

How to Win Your Shoppers Trust

- Post your security statement.
- Post your privacy statement.
- Post third-party affiliations.
- Post testimonials.

How to Write Effective Web Content

- Put your best-selling products in a prominent place.
- Post the price, shipping/handling, and other fees clearly.
- Avoid colloquialisms. Write clearly so everyone can understand.
- Attract buyers by making the site easy to use.
- Set up a shopping cart system that is easy to use.

How to Protect Yourself from Fraud

- In your order form, always ask for the exact name and address of the person on the credit card.
- Ship the merchandise to the credit card address.
- Install transaction-tracking software to flag unusual orders.

How to Offer Post-Sale Customer Service

- Confirm the order as soon as you receive it.
- Follow up with a phone call or email when the item is shipped.
- Record all feedback, good and bad.

Source: Sue Salim, "E-Commerce Success Begins with the Right Web Site," *Selling* (October 2002): 6–7.

shipping problems due to a lack of sufficient infrastructure, and varying degrees of Internet capability in various countries.[16]

Before establishing an international presence, companies must examine how the merchandise will be shipped. For smaller products, air transport is normally affordable. DHL Worldwide Express, Federal Express, and UPS offer excellent shipping options to most countries throughout the world (see Figure 18-15). Larger products are normally shipped through some type of freight forwarder. Both express delivery and freight forwarding companies can provide valuable assistance in shipping to the various countries they serve. These companies offer specialized logistics software and also provide the proper documentation and forms to meet the regulations of each country. In addition, Internet companies must examine both export and import laws in the countries where they will be shipping merchandise to be sure they are meeting the legal requirements. The U.S. government as well as many shipping companies can provide information on export/import laws.

Payment mechanisms must be installed that allow for different payment methods. Each country is different not only in terms of the type of currency but in its methods of payment. For example, in Europe, debit cards are preferred to credit cards. Also, Europe has a high rate of credit card theft, which increases the risks associated with accepting them.

Another challenge in the international arena is developing websites that appeal to the audiences of each country. This entails adding information that would be needed by someone in another country, such as the country code for telephone numbers. It also requires removing or changing any colors, words, or images that might be offensive to a particular group of people in another country. Simply translating an English site into another language is not sufficient. The company must have someone who understands both the language and culture of the target area in order to ensure that no one is offended by a company's marketing efforts.

Probably the most difficult challenge companies currently face in the international market is the technical side of the e-commerce site. Software compatibility is a huge technical issue to be resolved. Countries vary in terms of how they handle e-commerce, and these various technologies must be merged into one system. Also, the bandwidth for handling Internet traffic varies considerably.

Figure 18-15
UPS is one of several shipping companies that can provide international shipments for firms wanting to sell merchandise globally.

Source: Copyright © 2005, United Parcel Service of America, Inc.

While it takes some effort, preparing a company for international commerce can be very worthwhile. Once equipped, small companies can effectively have the reach of any large international company. For example, Trebnick Systems is a printing business located near Dayton, Ohio. Trebnick employs 10 people, yet its website has attracted customers from Japan, Germany, Spain, and Ireland. Similarly, Greyden Press employs only 25 people but uses the Internet as a primary tool of operation. Customers can request quotes and submit jobs online. Most of the customers that Greyden serves are not located in Columbus, Ohio, where its facility is physically located. E-commerce allows small companies like these to expand their customer bases beyond their local regions.[17]

18-5 Internet Branding

Creating an effective online brand requires more than a website and e-commerce capability. It requires integrating online and offline branding tactics that reinforce each other. The most common method of building an online brand is through an offline technique called **brand spiraling,** which is the practice of using traditional and nontraditional media to promote and attract consumers to an online website. Advertisements on television, radio, newspapers, magazines, and nontraditional outlets such as shopping bags and specialty gifts given to customers should encourage people to visit the firm's website. The goals of these advertisements should be to generate traffic to the website and build brand awareness.

Brand spiraling: The practice of using traditional and nontraditional media to promote and attract consumers to an online website.

Adobe, a desktop publishing software company, uses billboards, the Internet, and print ads to drive traffic to its website. Print ads in magazines such as *Details, Spin, Wallpaper, Wired,* and *Adobe* target young 20- to 25-year-old professionals who do not have strong backgrounds in graphic arts but, for some reason, have jumped into desktop publishing. Once at the site, a person can test and try different versions of Adobe products.[18]

Companies with strong offline brands have an advantage and benefit from what is called a "halo effect." Consumers already have a positive feeling toward the brand, so developing a web presence is much easier. Selling over the Internet is easier because customers already trust the firm's bricks-and-mortar facility, and ordering merchandise over the Internet is viewed as an extension of the firm's retail operation. Customers are more likely to try new products that may be offered by the company on the Internet. These same customers are also more willing to provide information that can be used for greater personalization of messages. This halo effect results from the credibility of the firm's brand being transferred to an individual's evaluation of the website. Although Barnes & Noble and Toys "R" Us were late entrants into e-commerce, both companies have built successful Internet businesses because of the strength of their brand names.

A company such as Amazon.com, which was an Internet startup, had to use traditional advertising media to help develop its brand name. Branding cannot be created solely through advertising on the Internet. Amazon.com invested a half billion dollars in traditional media, in addition to its online advertising to become the global online retail market leader.[19]

However, companies have to be careful about spending too much on offline advertising. The former Pets.com company spent $14.7 million on television and mass-media advertising in just one quarter to acquire only 93,000 customers. That is a cost of $158.06 per customer. Because it sold heavily discounted pet food with low margins, the high cost of advertising and low return on customer acquisition ended up killing the company.[20]

An alternative approach was used by Graffiti, a young women's clothing store in East Northport, New York. Graffiti is one 2,100-square-foot store. Realizing the potential of e-commerce, Graffiti partnered with Barnes & Noble stores to distribute Graffiti value cards. The result was 130,000 new Internet customers in just one year. To keep the customers coming back to the site, Graffiti uses contests and special offers.[21]

18-6 Viral Marketing

Viral marketing: Preparing an advertisement that is tied to an email that one customer passes along to other potential buyers.

Internet technology has created a new form of marketing, called **viral marketing,** which is preparing an advertisement that is tied to an email. Viral marketing takes place as one customer passes along a message to other potential buyers. The name "viral" is derived from the image of a person being infected with the marketing message and then spreading it to friends like a virus. The major difference, however, is that the customer voluntarily sends the message to others. It is not done automatically.

Viral marketing messages can include actual advertisements for goods and services, hyperlinked promotions that take someone immediately to a website, online newsletters, or some type of sales promotion effort using a game or contest. Recent research indicates that 81 percent of recipients who receive a viral marketing message will pass it along to another person. Almost 50 percent pass it along to two or more people. The marketing message can be more deliberate, such as when an individual recommends something to a friend. It can also be transmitted passively, when the message is simply attached to an email. Because viral marketing works like a word-of-mouth endorsement, although through email, it tends to have greater credibility and allows for a rapid development of brand and product awareness at a low cost.[22]

Blue Marble, a company that offers viral marketing expertise, created a program for Scope mouthwash. Consumers could send a customized, animated email "kiss" to their friends. The attached marketing message reinforced the brand message that Scope brings people "kissably close." People who received the email kiss could forward the message to someone else. Blue Marble's tracking technology indicated that most people who received the message did forward the message to others.

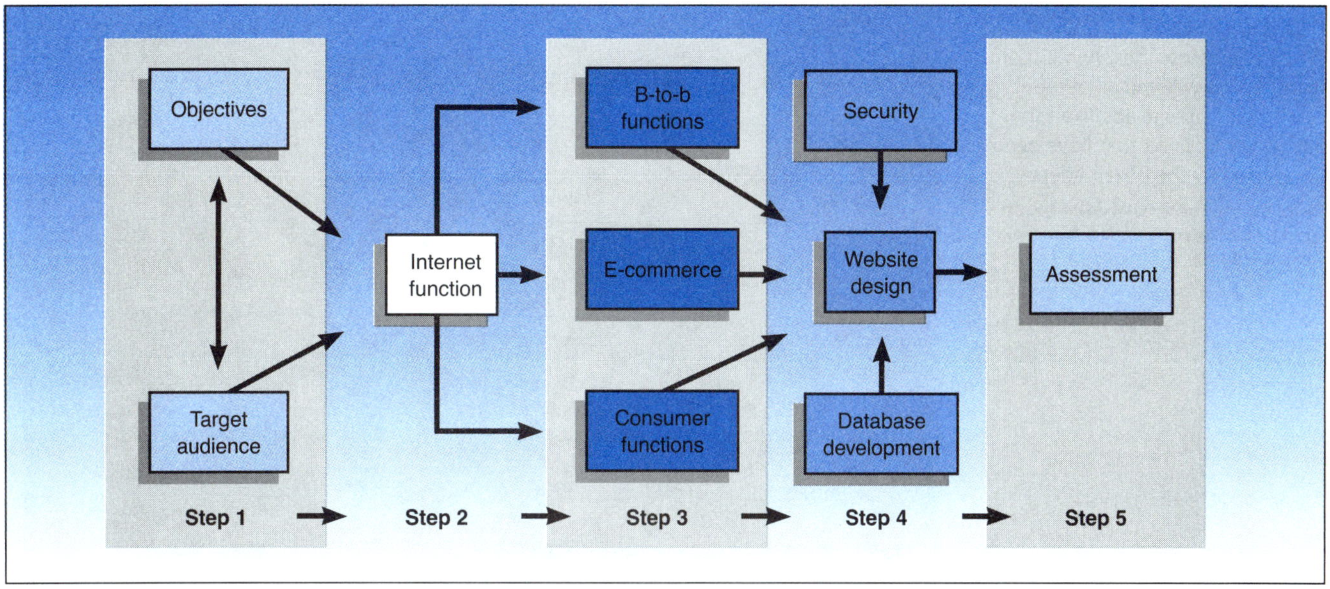

Figure 18-16
Developing an Internet Marketing Strategy
While the process for developing an Internet marketing strategy is shown sequentially, it must be an integrative process that involves personnel from all of the firm's departments.

To encourage consumers to pass a message along, many viral messages offer people some type of incentive. For instance, GreenTravel.com entered individuals who passed on its newsletter into a contest in which they could win an Osprey backpack.[23] For the viral message to be successful, individuals must have some type of incentive or reason for passing it to their friends or business associates. Because of the newness of this technology, it does not take much of an incentive for people to pass a message along, but as with other new forms of promotion, the more it is used, the more difficult it will become to attract attention and the more difficult it will become to solicit individuals who will pass messages along to others.

18-7 Internet Marketing Strategy

Internet marketing begins with a well-developed strategy. Figure 18-16 illustrates the five-step process. Although the process is illustrated as being sequential, it must be an integrative process that involves individuals from every department within a company—from the IT department to customer service.

The first step in the process is to make a decision on the audience that will be served and the objectives of the site. This decision lays the foundation for the development of the website and controls the functions of the website as well as the content. For example, access the following three milk websites to see how each one has a different objective and how each one is aimed at a different target audience:

- www.gotmilk.com
- www.whymilk.com
- www.got-milk.com

Notice that all of the celebrity mustache ads like the one in Figure 18-17 appear on the whymilk.com website.

The primary objective of companies developing websites is to better serve their customers, whether it is attracting new customers or servicing current customers. A survey by C&C Marketing Research found that, in terms of customers, the primary objective of an Internet marketing website was to attract new customers (67 percent). Other customer-related objectives cited were to build loyalty among existing customers (62 percent), improve customer service (58 percent), streamline business operations (48 percent), increase incremental sales of existing customers (47 percent), grow market share (47 percent), and enhance communication with customers (45 percent).[24]

Figure 18-17
When you access the whymilk.com website, you will find all of the celebrity mustache ads, like this Backstreet Boys ad, that have been developed by the Bozell Agency.

Source: Courtesy of Bozell Worldwide, Inc. as agent for the National Fluid Milk Processor Promotion Board.

Firms do have other reasons for Internet marketing beyond attracting and serving customers. Figure 18-18 provides a list of all of the other reasons given to C&C Marketing Research. But the top five reasons from this list are advertising (68 percent), lead generation (59 percent), brand building (51 percent), customer service (45 percent), and promotions (39 percent).[25]

The second and third steps in the process are to decide on the functions of the Internet website, which will be based on the objective or objectives that have been outlined. If the objective is to attract and service customers, then e-commerce will certainly be a primary function that will be used. If the firm has a business-to-business component, then typical functions to serve business customers may include purchasing and inventory management, sales support, and customer service. For the business-to-consumer component, typical functions may include selling, advertising and sales promotions, public relations, and information gathering and sharing.

The fourth step is the actual website design. Two components that are critical to the design, which are not really seen by customers, are the security and database development. Security is a critical issue web designers must consider. Customer information must be well guarded and protected. In addition, payment procedures must be encrypted to ensure that no one can see or steal the consumer or business's personal information. To maximize the impact of the website, it is essential that the site is tied into the database in such a way that

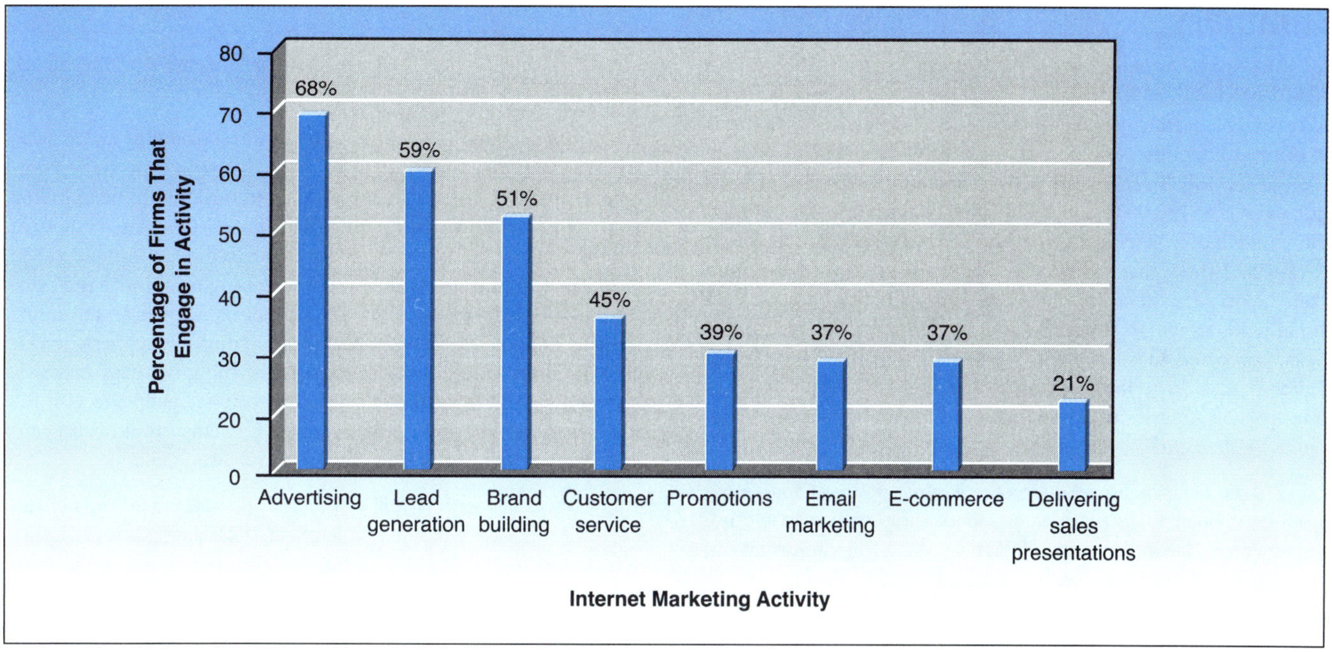

Figure 18-18
Reasons for Internet Marketing

Source: Ginger Conlon, "Ride the Wave," *Sales & Marketing Management*, vol. 152, no. 12 (December 2000): 67–73.

the information gathered can be added to the customer's profile. Software that has this capability can be purchased and can be used with both internal as well as external sources of additional data.

The last step in the process is assessment. As with any marketing venture, assessment is critical to success. Information about what is working and what is not working needs to be fed back to the organization so modifications can be made. This feedback can affect any step and any component in the process.

Internet marketing is here to stay, and successful firms must find ways to incorporate it into their strategic plans if they are to remain competitive. Most companies are able to generate additional revenue with their websites. Other benefits cited in the C&C Marketing Research study include increased productivity, reduced costs, and reduced cycle time for new product development. The Internet has resulted in more companies using multichannel approaches to the marketing of their products and a shifting of the percentages of their products sold in each channel.[26] Table 18-3 provides the complete results of this survey.

TABLE 18-3
How E-Business Has Impacted Companies

Category	Not at All	Somewhat	Significantly
Increased revenue	41%	47%	12%
Increased productivity	31%	45%	24%
Cut costs	41%	47%	12%
Reduced cycle time	44%	42%	14%
Changed percent of selling in each channel	47%	42%	11%
Altered selling and marketing of products	34%	51%	15%

Source: Ginger Conlon, "Ride the Wave," *Sales & Marketing Management*, vol. 152, no. 12 (December 2000): 67–73.

Summary

1. *Identify the primary users of the Internet.* A recent survey found that 22 percent of all Internet users were preteens and teens, with an additional 35 percent of the users being of college age. Generation X accounts for another 35 percent, and baby boomers or seniors account for only 8 percent. In terms of income, 91 percent of individuals in the $75,000 to $99,999 income category use the Internet, compared to only 40 percent with incomes below $15,000. As would be expected, the higher the level of education a person has, the more likely he or she is to use the Internet. Approximately 80 percent of the individuals with a college or post-graduate degree are Internet users, compared to 42 percent of individuals with a high school degree or less. In terms of ethnicity, the highest Internet usage is among Asian Americans (93 percent), and the lowest is among Hispanics (47 percent).

2. *Discuss the benefits of Internet marketing.* Internet marketing provides the benefits of sales, interactivity, multimedia capabilities, global reach, flexibility, cost efficiencies, real-time information, communication, and database warehousing.

3. *Distinguish the Internet marketing functions.* Based on the benefits a company can realize from the Internet, a firm can develop multiple functions. Although a number of functions can be accomplished, it is important for firms to realize that trying to do too many things with their websites can be a disaster for everyone. It is important to develop one or two primary functions that the firm can do and do well. Additional sites or links can be used for additional functions. Potential marketing functions include multichannel marketing, selling, advertising and sales promotion, public relations, database development, information gathering and sharing, purchasing and inventory management, sales support, and customer service.

4. *Present the e-commerce components and incentives needed to encourage online purchasing.* An e-commerce site has three primary components: a catalog, a shopping cart, and a payment system. Bricks-and-clicks operations must have a fourth component: a location finder. The catalog is a visual presentation of the merchandise to be sold. The shopping cart is some type of mechanism that allows a consumer to select merchandise and put it into a virtual shopping cart until he or she is finished making selections. For bricks-and-clicks operations, where individuals may want to locate or purchase from a bricks-and-mortar site, it is important to include a locator that will provide an address and a map to the facility.

While online purchases are growing at a rapid rate, many consumers are still not sure about making online purchases for two reasons: security issues and purchase behavior habits. Many consumers are afraid to use credit cards because of concerns that their credit card number will be stolen. Others are concerned about fraud and dishonest e-commerce websites that will take their money and never ship the merchandise or ship poor-quality merchandise. In terms of purchasing habits, consumers feel more comfortable purchasing products from retail outlets because that is the way they have always shopped. To encourage consumers and businesses to start making Internet purchases, a firm must provide some type of incentive. This is especially true for the long run. The incentives that can be used are financial incentives, convenience incentives, and value-added incentives.

5. *Examine Internet branding and how it is accomplished.* Creating an effective online brand requires more than a website and e-commerce capability. It requires integrating online and offline branding tactics that reinforce each other. The most common method of building an online brand is through an offline technique called brand spiraling, which is the practice of using traditional and nontraditional media to promote and attract consumers to an online website. Advertisements on television, radio, newspapers, magazines, and nontraditional outlets such as shopping bags and specialty gifts given to customers should encourage people to visit the firm's website. The goals of these advertisements should be to generate traffic to the website and build brand awareness.

Companies with strong offline brands have an advantage and benefit from what is called a "halo effect." Consumers already have a positive feeling toward the brand, so developing a web presence is much easier. Selling over the Internet is easier because customers already trust the firm's bricks-and-mortar facility, so ordering merchandise over the Internet is viewed as an extension of the firm's retail operation. Customers are more likely to try new products that may be offered by the company on the Internet. These same customers are also more willing to provide information that can be used for greater personalization of messages. This halo effect results from the credibility of the firm's brand being transferred to an individual's evaluation of the website.

6. *Explain viral marketing.* Internet technology has created a new form of marketing, called viral marketing, which is preparing an advertisement that is tied to an email. Viral marketing takes place as one customer passes along a message to other potential buyers. The name "viral" is derived from the image of a person being infected with the marketing message and then spreading it to friends like a virus. The major difference, however, is that the customer voluntarily sends the message to others. It is not done automatically.

7. *List the steps in developing an Internet marketing strategy.* A well-designed Internet marketing strategy begins with well-defined objectives that match the target audience of the website. The second step is to select the functions of the website, which are determined by the objectives and target audience. Possible functions include multichannel marketing, selling, advertising and sales promotions, public relations, database development, information gathering and sharing, purchasing and inventory management, sales support, and customer service. The third step is to divide the functions into business-to-business functions, e-commerce, and business-to-consumer functions. Step four is designing the website. As the site is being designed to meet the functions identified, it is vital that security be addressed to prevent hackers from entering a firm's computer system as well as protecting buyers' identities and personal information. Software needs to be purchased or developed to gather the desired database information. The last step is assessment, which should be a continuous process to examine how well the firm is meeting its objectives and stated functions.

Key Terms

brand spiraling (p. 569)
bricks-and-clicks (p. 560)
clicks-only firms (p. 560)
cyberbait (p. 558)
e-commerce (p. 560)
FAQs (p. 559)
interactive marketing (p. 558)
interstitial ads (p. 557)
rich media ads (p. 557)
viral marketing (p. 570)

Discussion Questions

1. Read the chapter-opening vignette. Have you used the Internet to research a product before making a purchase? If so, how much time did you spend conducting online research? How did the information influence your decision? Where did you make the final purchase?

2. Access Nielsen/NetRatings at www.nielsen-netratings.com. What information is available on the website? What websites are getting the most hits right now?

3. Pick 10 people of approximately the same age, gender, and ethnicity to interview about their Internet usage habits. Compare your findings to the information reported by Nielsen/NetRatings at www.nielsen-netratings.com.

4. Examine the benefits of the Internet listed in Section 18-3a. Discuss each one of them in terms of your use of the Internet.

5. Pick either the company you are presently working for or one that you have worked for in the past. Examine its website in terms of Internet marketing functions. Which functions is it fulfilling? How well is it performing those functions?

6. Pick one of the following product categories. Access five companies that operate in that particular industry. Compare and contrast each company in terms of the e-commerce components and incentives discussed in Sections 18-4a and 18-4b.
   a. Football equipment and fan memorabilia
   b. Cheerleading supplies and uniforms
   c. Dishes
   d. Jeans or another type of clothing

7. Pick one of the following product categories and access two companies that operate in that particular industry. Evaluate their websites based on the information provided in Marketing Illustration 18-4.
   a. Sports equipment and fan memorabilia
   b. Electronics such as radios, TVs, or stereos
   c. Household appliances such as electric mixers, toasters, or coffee makers
   d. Jeans or another type of clothing
   e. Shoes

8. Pick one of the following product categories. Access five companies that operate in that particular industry. Compare and contrast the Internet branding strategy being used and how well the Internet branding ties in with any offline advertising being done.
   a. Football equipment and fan memorabilia
   b. Cheerleading supplies and uniforms
   c. Dishes
   d. Jeans or another type of clothing
   e. Athletic shoes

9. Have you ever received a viral marketing message? If so, discuss your reaction to it. Whether you have received a viral marketing message or not, what are your feelings about it? What are the pros and cons of a company using viral marketing messages?

Review Questions

True or False

1. It is more likely that individuals with a college or a post-graduate degree are active Internet users than individuals with a high school degree or less education.

2. Most IMC involves one-way communications directed to consumers. Only salespeople and the Internet have the capability of being interactive.

3. The most effective way of advertising a company's brand name is the firm's own website.

4. The main business function of the Internet is to provide a cost-efficient customer service.

5. Due to the technological advantage of e-commerce, the most profitable retail channel is the Internet.

6. To encourage consumers and businesses to start making Internet purchases, a firm must provide some type of incentive.

7. Creating an effective online brand requires an attractive web page and efficient e-commerce capability.

8. Viral marketing takes place as one customer passes along a message to other potential buyers.

Multiple Choice

9. Which country boasts the highest average time per person spent on the Internet?
   a. the United States
   b. Switzerland
   c. France
   d. Spain

10. Which of the following categories provide the best potential for traditional retailers and producers?
   a. multimedia capabilities
   b. cost efficiencies
   c. real-time information
   d. database warehousing

11. Cyberbait is a lure or attractive offer that increases traffic on the website. Which of the following examples is cyberbait?
- **a.** free sporting goods such as a baseball glove with a purchase
- **b.** giving one special prize of $100,000 in cash
- **c.** a short questionnaire
- **d.** all of the above

12. A recent trend in database development is interactive marketing, defined as
- **a.** the exchange of instantaneous messages between seller and buyer.
- **b.** the broad global reach of the Internet.
- **c.** the process of individualizing and personalizing promoted products.
- **d.** all of the above

13. Although online purchases are growing at a rapid rate, many consumers are still not sure about making online purchases because of
- **a.** security issues and purchase behavior habits.
- **b.** competitive prices at the retail stores.
- **c.** enjoying shopping as a social event.
- **d.** (a), (b), and (c).

14. The objectives of an Internet marketing website involve
- **a.** attracting new customers.
- **b.** building loyalty among existing customers.
- **c.** improving customer service.
- **d.** all of the above.

15. Which website components not fully perceived by customers are critical to the design of a website?
- **a.** government regulations
- **b.** deciding on the functions of the Internet website
- **c.** the security and database development
- **d.** all of the above

Notes

1. Nielsen Netratings, www.nielsennetratings.com, January 20, 2005.
2. Al Nucifora, "Are You Preparing for the E-Business Revolution?" *Business First,* Louisville, vol. 16, no. 28 (February 11, 2000): 17; Don Jeffrey, "Survey Details Consumers Shopping Trends on the Internet," *Billboard,* vol. 111, no. 22 (May 29, 1999): 47–48; Al Nucifora, "There Are Lots of Good Reasons for All the Internet Hype," *Pittsburgh Business Times,* vol. 18, no. 42 (May 7, 1999): 20.
3. Linda Lyons, "Internet Use: What's Age Got to Do with It?" *The Gallup Poll Tuesday Briefing, The Gallup Organization* (March 16, 2004).
4. Don Jeffrey, "Survey Details Consumers Shopping Trends on the Internet," *Billboard,* vol. 111, no. 22 (May 29, 1999): 47–48.
5. Decision Analyst, Inc. (2001 data), www.nielsen-netratings.com, March 9, 2003.
6. Sara Cox Landolt and Lisa Hochgraf, "Surfing at Work Continues to Increase," *Credit Union Management,* vol. 24, no. 10 (October 2001): 47.
7. "Global Internet Retail," *Internet Retail Industry Profile: Global* (May 2004): 1–17; Fred Vogelstein, "E-Commerce," *Fortune,* vol. 146, no. 13 (December 30, 2002): 166.
8. Alan Mitchell, "Marketers Must Grasp the Net or Face Oblivion," *Marketing News,* vol. 22, no. 3 (February 18, 1999): 30–31.
9. Kate Maddox, "Online Advertising Will Grow in 2005," *B to B,* vol. 89 (December 13, 2004): 23.
10. Liane Cassavoy and Edward N. Alero, "Ads Get Flasher, More Personal," *PC World,* vol. 23 (February 2005): 22.
11. Don Jeffrey, "Survey Details Consumers Shopping Trends on the Internet," *Billboard,* vol. 111, no. 22 (May 29, 1999): 47–48.
12. Jeff Sweat and Rick Whiting, "Instant Marketing," *Information Week,* vol. 746 (August 2, 1999): 18–20.
13. Fred V. Vogelstein, "E-Commerce," *Fortune,* vol. 146, no. 13 (December 30, 2002): 166.
14. Karen E. Hussel, "New Service Helps Brand Clicks with Bricks," *Advertising Age's Business Marketing,* vol. 84, no. 11 (November 1999) 40–41.
15. Ibid.
16. Lynda Radosevich, "Going Global Overnight," *InfoWorld,* vol. 21, no. 16 (April 19, 1999): 1–3.
17. Todd McCollough, "Online Services Make Ordering, Billing, Printing a Snap," *Business First,* vol. 15, no. 24 (February 5, 1999): 19–20.
18. Beth Snyder, "Adobe Drive Aims to Build Image as a Web Company," *Advertising Age,* vol. 70, no. 41 (October 4, 1999): 28.
19. Robert Harvin, "In Internet Branding, the Offlines Have It," *Brandweek,* vol. 41, no. 4 (January 24, 2000): 30–31.
20. David Garfinkel and Kathleen Cholewka, "Making the Most of IT: How to Squeeze More Profits from the Web," *Sales & Marketing Management,* vol. 154, no. 3 (March 2002): 19–20.
21. Ibid.
22. Alf Nucifora, "Viral Marketing Spreads by Word of Net," *Business Journal,* Central New York, vol. 14, no. 18 (May 5, 2000): 25–26.
23. Ibid.
24. Ginger Conlon, "Ride the Wave," *Sales & Marketing Management,* vol. 152, no. 12 (December 2000): 67–73.
25. Ibid.
26. Ibid.

Case 18-1 Wood Creek Furniture

Wood Creek Furniture offers high-quality office furniture designed to effectively incorporate computers and accessory equipment into an executive or home office. The furniture is ergonomically designed for maximum comfort as well as usability. Several different pieces of furniture are offered, such as a computer desk, file cabinets, printer stands, bookcases, and the primary desk. The keyboard and monitor heights are adjustable on the computer desk to ensure maximum comfort. Computer cables are hidden from view, and shelving adds to the utility of the desk without sacrificing elegance.

The newest line of desks will accommodate a laptop computer with a docking station to connect to a network. The furniture has different configurations, which create easy access to the docking station. This allows for better use of space because it doesn't have to be dedicated to a CPU case. The furniture also can accommodate 17-, 19-, and 21-inch computer monitors if so desired. Wood Creek is one of the first manufacturers to provide custom furniture for wall-mounted flat screens, liquid crystal displays, and similar innovations.

In examining the marketing strategies for Wood Creek Furniture, the following facts are important:

- Few firms in this industry target home offices and small business owners.
- Personal selling is the primary marketing approach for competing firms, targeting corporate executives with high-end office furniture.
- Furniture dealers, such as Rocky Mountain Desk Corporation, are the major distribution outlets for high-end office manufacturers.
- Direct marketing is used by some office furniture manufacturers, but not extensively.
- The Internet is becoming a major source of information and purchasing for small business owners and home offices. Other high-end office manufacturers are not using the Internet, or if they are, they do so just to provide information and names for their sales staff to call on.

An analysis of the high-end computer office furniture market yields a unique opportunity for Wood Creek Furniture to access a new channel of direct distribution to small business owners and home offices through targeted catalog and Internet sales. The key to this opportunity is that no high-end computer office furniture manufacturer has aggressively pursued the small business owner and home office individual with a direct marketing approach. According to *Home Office Computing Magazine,* there are 36 million home offices in the United States, of which 26 percent have incomes higher than $100,000. There are approximately 15 million small businesses (businesses with fewer than 500 employees). Wood Creek feels that the top 10 percent of each of these markets are excellent targets for its products and that another 20 percent may have some interest in its products.

Wood Creek Furniture is now ready to develop a website and begin its Internet marketing business. The primary goal of the website is to reach the small business owner and the home office individuals. Wood Creek wants to pursue this direct channel while continuing to sell to furniture dealers. It is important that Wood Creek continues to serve these dealers and does not alienate them by selling directly to small businesses and home offices.

Questions

1. Using the steps outlined in Section 18-7 on developing an Internet marketing strategy, outline the objective(s) of the website and the target audience.
2. What Internet function(s) should the website fulfill (Step 2)?
3. Describe the e-commerce, business-to-business functions, and the consumer functions (Step 3).
4. Discuss the website design you think Wood Creek should use. How would you handle the security issue and database development (Step 4)?
5. How would you assess whether the website was effective (Step 5)?
6. Using either website development software, Word, or PowerPoint, design what you think the homepage of Wood Creek's website should look like.

Source: "Findings," Hospitals & Health Networks, vol. 76, no. 11 (November 2002): 72–73; Interview with Graham Morris of Newcomer, Morris, and Young, January 17, 2003.

Case 18-2 Selling Video Games

With two young children at home, Kyle and Aleecia Hendricks have seen firsthand the attraction of video games to kids. Not only their kids, but also almost every child they know plays video games and spends hours doing it. Wanting to start their own business, the Hendricks investigated the cost of opening a video game retail store. They soon found it was too expensive because of the capital needed for a building and the money needed for inventory. But in the process, Kyle did meet and have dinner with a representative of a video game distribution company. He suggested that the Hendricks should consider starting an online retail business (i.e., a clicks-only operation).

Before launching their online business, the Hendricks spent some time studying the habits of children. Although they had plenty of firsthand experience, they wanted to make sure that their experience (i.e., their children) was typical. Here are some of the facts that they learned about children, ages 5 to 18:

- Boys have an interest in sports, video games, music, cars, and girls.
- Mostly boys watch Japanese anime.
- Boys are crazy about superheroes, high-velocity fighting, and explosions.
- Boys need to be reached with a rich blend of print, broadcast, Internet, and event marketing.
- Boys are heavily involved in outdoor activities like skateboarding and indoor activities like playing video games and computer games and using the Internet.
- In terms of advertising, boys are picture-oriented, whereas girls tend to read the text.
- Girls (75 percent) say they love or like sports, compared to 85 percent for boys.
- Girls spend an average of 15 hours per week playing, watching, reading, talking, or thinking about sports, compared to 17 hours for boys.
- Girls play sports because they are interested in challenging themselves and being with friends, whereas boys play sports because they relish the competition.

Based on this preliminary information, the Hendricks decided to specialize in selling sports-related video games. Before launching their website, the Hendricks obtained two studies. One was a NeoPets Youth Study compiled by *Advertising Age*, and the other was a study by Taylor Research & Consulting Group. The results of these studies are shown in Table 18-4.

Questions

1. Using the steps outlined in Section 18-7 on developing an Internet marketing strategy, outline the objective(s) of the website and the target audience. Should the Hendricks market to both girls and boys or concentrate only on one gender?
2. What Internet function(s) should the website fulfill (Step 2)?
3. Describe the e-commerce and the consumer functions (Step 3).
4. Should the website be designed to reach parents, children, or both?
5. Discuss the website design you think the Hendricks should use. How would you handle the security issue and database development (Step 4)? How would you handle the ethical issue of marketing to kids?
6. How would you assess whether the website was effective (Step 5)?
7. To promote their website, the Hendricks know they need to have some offline advertising. Where would you suggest they advertise?
8. Using either website development software, Word, or PowerPoint, design what you think the homepage of the Hendricks' website should look like.

Sources: This case is based on Edmund O. Lawler, "Nonstop Action," *Advertising Age*, vol. 74, no. 7 (February 17, 2003): S-2; Rebecca Gardyn, "A League of Their Own," *American Demographics*, vol. 23, no. 3 (March 2001): 12–13.

TABLE 18-4

Youth Attitudes/Activities That Impact Video Game Sales

Attitude/Activity	Boys	Girls
"I like radio a lot."	21%	38%
"I like magazines a lot."	10%	18%
"I find TV quite educational."	21%	15%
"I find the Internet quite educational."	41%	35%
"Advertising on the Internet is very interesting."	44%	34%
"Professional athletes are quite convincing in ads."	22%	17%
Play sports/video games	85%	63%
Surf the Internet for sports-related stuff	49%	39%
Shop for sports, games, clothes, books, etc.	40%	38%
Watch sports on TV	92%	84%
Chat online or share messages with friends about sports	28%	25%
Play/practice for organized sports	68%	60%
Talk about or play sports for fun with friends	85%	75%

APPENDIX A

The Marketing Plan: A Strategic Marketing Perspective

Overview

The marketing plan is an essential element of the company strategic plan, an effort to maintain a fit between company objectives and capabilities and the continuously changing company environment. The approach to the marketing plan presented here addresses this important aspect of planning. You should first focus on corporate planning and, subsequently, on the marketing strategy.

A-1 Defining the Company's Mission Statement

Most organizations prominently articulate their mission statement. If your project involves creating a marketing plan for an existing business, check the company website to identify its mission statement. If you are creating your own new business, then articulate a mission statement that expresses the vision and principles of the company, a guide to what the company wants to accomplish in the marketplace. The mission should underscore the distinctive differentiating aspects of the business and the company's approach to its different stakeholders: consumers, employees, and society.

A-2 Identifying Company Goals and Objectives

A company's objectives stem from its mission statement. Objectives can be expressed in terms of profit, sales, market share, and return on investment, for example. Company objectives may be to enter new international markets or to increase market share in the national market. Alternatively, they may involve focusing on research and development in order to bring leading-edge technology to the marketplace. Objectives can also be expressed in terms of societal outcomes, such as increasing literacy or reducing world hunger, depending on the focus of the business.

As mentioned in Chapter 1, "Scope and Concepts of Marketing," the ultimate organizational goal is creating profit for the company and wealth for its shareholders. In that sense, increasing productivity and production volume, maximizing consumption, and as a result, increasing sales constitute primary objectives for the company, which can be accomplished with the appropriate marketing strategies. In the process of achieving organizational goals, companies offer quality and value to consumers and businesses, leading to a higher level of customer satisfaction. They compete to offer a wide variety of goods and services and a maximum number of choices for consumers. As they compete, they lower prices that consumers pay for their products in order to gain market share.

Based on your understanding of the company, what are the different goals and objectives it is pursuing? If working with a hypothetical company, you could think about the goals of competition in the process of identifying the goals and objectives of your company.

A-3 Managing the Business Portfolio

The third step in creating the marketing plan involves evaluating the different strategic business units of the company. At this stage, the company must identify the products that have great promise in the marketplace and need additional resources, the products that are performing well in a mature market, and those that are not, which must be divested. At this stage, establishing a strategic fit with the market is essential. The company may have the resources to support a particular strategic business unit, but if the unit does not fit with the company's long-term goals, or if selling the unit would generate resources that could be invested to further the company's goals, the company may consider selling this particular business. Companies periodically review their different businesses and make decisions on whether to acquire new ones or divest those that might be unprofitable or that do not represent a good fit.

In the analysis of the portfolio, you will benefit from using the growth-share matrix of the Boston Consulting Group and the product-market matrix introduced in Chapter 8, "Product Strategies" (especially Section 8-9, "Managing the Product Portfolio"). Place the different business units in the appropriate categories and comment on their position. Do they need additional resources? Are they performing optimally? Scrutinize them in terms of their market and financial performance and potential.

A-4 Strategic Business Unit (SBU) Planning

A-4a Developing the SBU Mission

Each business unit must develop its own mission statement, focusing on the strategic fit between strategic business unit (SBU) resources and the company goals with regard to its target markets. The SBU mission statement should be more specific than the corporate mission statement, focusing on the brand or product itself.

A-4b Conducting the SWOT Analysis

An important step in the analysis process involves identifying the company's strengths, weaknesses, opportunities, and threats (SWOT). First, examine the microenvironment of marketing, addressing its strengths and weaknesses; more specifically, examine strengths and weaknesses related to the company, consumers, suppliers, middlemen, other facilitators of marketing functions, and the competition (see Table A-1). Next, examine threats and opportunities in the socio-demographic and cultural environment, the economic and natural environments, the technological environment, and the political and legal environments (see Chapter 2, "The Environment of Marketing in the Twenty-First Century," and Chapter 3, "Marketing Ethics, Regulations, and Social Responsibility," and Table A-2).

A-5 The Marketing Plan

The marketing plan will focus on the strategic business unit you have selected: a good or service that you have proposed to analyze. It involves the following steps.

A-5a Identifying Marketing Objectives

Marketing objectives could be defined in terms of dollar sales or units sold, or in terms of market share. They can also be defined in terms of brand awareness or customer traffic, as would be the case for a retail operation.

A-5b Defining the Marketing Strategy

The marketing strategy involves identifying segments of consumers who are similar with regard to key traits and who would respond well to a product and related marketing mix (market segmentation); selecting the segments that the company can serve most efficiently and developing products tailored to each (market targeting); and offering the products to

TABLE A-1

Microenvironment SWOT Analysis

Microenvironment	List of Strengths	List of Weaknesses
Company		
Consumers		
Suppliers		
Middlemen		
Other facilitators		
Competition		

TABLE A-2

Macroenvironment SWOT Analysis

Macroenvironment	List of Threats	List of Opportunities
Socio-demographic and cultural environment		
Economic environment		
Natural environment		
Technological environment		
Political environment		
Legal environment		

the market, communicating through the marketing mix the product traits and benefits that differentiate the product in the consumer's mind (market positioning).

At this stage, you should clearly identify the different market segments, select the segments that represent the best fit with the company goals and objectives, and design the strategies aimed to serve these segments more effectively than competitors. Refer to Chapter 6, "Marketing Segmentation," in your analysis.

An important component of the marketing strategy is a competitive analysis. Identify and describe the products, markets, and strategies competitors are using and how your company or product is different. It is important to clearly identify the unique selling proposition or market that is being served.

A-5c Developing the Marketing Mix

After identifying the overall marketing strategy, you can proceed to develop the marketing mix—the four Ps of marketing (product, place, price, and promotion)—that the company can use to influence demand for its products:

- *Product*—Decide on design, features, brand name, packaging, and service components that will best meet the needs of the target market that has been identified. Refer to Chapter 8, "Product Strategies," and Chapter 9, "Services Marketing."
- *Place*—Decide on the types of channels used, market coverage, assortment, transportation and logistics, and inventory management that will be needed to move the product from production to the consumer or business customer. Refer to Chapter 10, "Distribution Strategies," and Chapter 11, "Retailing Strategies."
- *Price*—Decide on the price, discounts, and credit terms that will be used. Because of brand parity, pricing is an important decision variable in purchase decisions. Refer to Chapter 12, "Pricing Strategies."
- *Promotion*—Decide on advertising, personal selling, sales promotion, public relations, and publicity that the company should pursue. Although the nature of the product will have some impact on which method of promotion will be primary, it is also important to consider how competitors are promoting their product. Not only is it necessary to gain the attention of potential customers, it is also necessary to convince them concerning the superiority of the product being offered. Refer to Chapter 13, "Integrated Marketing Communications," Chapter 14, "Advertising, Sponsorships, and Public Relations," Chapter 15, "Sales and Trade Promotions," and Chapter 16, "Personal Selling, Databases, and Direct Marketing."

A-5d Marketing Implementation

Suggest how marketing plans can be turned into marketing action programs in order to accomplish the marketing objectives. For example, the marketing objective may be to increase awareness of a new product among the selected target market. Implementation may involve developing a series of television and magazine ads that promote this new product. Further, identify which television shows and which magazines would be the most effective in reaching the projected target market.

A-5e Marketing Control

Suggest the different procedures for evaluating the outcomes of the implemented marketing strategies and the corrective actions needed to ensure that the previously stated marketing objectives are met. For example, if the objective was to increase product awareness by 30 percent, the day-after recall (DAR) tests could be used to determine whether the objective has been reached. If not, the corrective action could be the purchase of additional television time or the development of a new advertising theme.

APPENDIX B

Careers in Marketing

Marketing is a popular major in most business schools and offers graduates a wide variety of career opportunities. The purpose of this appendix is to provide students with information about possible careers and marketing positions. Marketing positions can be organized into three categories: general marketing positions, positions in marketing communications, and sales positions.

B-1 General Marketing Positions

B-1a Marketing Management

Marketing managers are usually selected based on extensive work experience, especially in the case of larger firms. This advanced position requires major responsibility. However, with proper training in entry-level positions, graduates can quickly advance up the corporate ladder to the level of marketing manager.

B-1b Brand/Product Management

Brand/product managers are responsible for managing a brand or a particular product of a company throughout the brand/product lifecycle. Typically, these managers are responsible for segmenting the market and targeting and positioning the brands or products for which they are responsible. In effect, this manager is responsible for the brand or product as a strategic business unit and is in charge of overseeing the development, pricing, promotion, and distribution of the product. Most university graduates are expected to work in sales or other areas of the company, acquiring valuable experience before advancing to brand/product management. For more information about managing brands and products, refer to Chapter 8, "Product Strategies," and Chapter 9, "Services Marketing."

B-1c Marketing Research

Students interested in a marketing research career will benefit from extensive training in statistical methods and behavioral sciences. For analysts focusing on consumer goods firms, it is especially useful to have a background in psychology and psychometric measurement. Individuals working for a marketing research firm would have the title of marketing analyst or marketing researcher. Individuals could also specialize in developing and maintaining a database (i.e., they would be involved in database marketing). For more information about the tasks of marketing researchers, refer to Chapter 7, "Marketing Research."

B-2 Positions in Marketing Communications

B-2a Account Management

Account executives typically work for an advertising agency and are in charge of managing the advertising firm's relationship with existing and potential clients. They usually have at least three years' experience in lower-level advertising positions or in sales. Account executives are responsible for the day-to-day activities related to a particular account or set of accounts.

Account supervisors are in charge of managing the relationship of the advertising firm to the client; they typically have more work experience than account executives.

Management supervisors are responsible for coordinating the tasks of different account executives and account supervisors with the goals and objectives of top management. Management supervisors tend to be more seasoned managers.

Creative directors are in charge of the creative staff, coordinating the tasks of creative groups, broadcast production, and studio work. These individuals are typically not business majors; they tend to major in the liberal arts areas—often in art or graphic design.

Traffic managers are responsible for coordinating the work that has to be done for a client. They often will choose creatives and other agency personnel who will work on an account. Because they know the completion date, they will work with a schedule to ensure all of the work is finished on time.

It should be mentioned that graduates with a goal of working for an advertising agency are often recruited for positions involving managing traffic (the management of the ad production at different stages) or print production. The goal of most marketing majors going into advertising is to become account executives in three to five years after graduation. Often, they must accept lower-level jobs, such as account executive assistant, before they are placed in charge of an advertising account.

B-2b Media Management

Media planners are in charge of planning how often, where, and when advertisements will appear and in what media. These individuals tend to have a keen understanding of their client's business and are hired with some experience. Their goal is to match media with the ad's target market to ensure maximum effectiveness. Media buyers are in charge of actual space and time media purchases.

Media researchers are marketing researchers specializing in media. They research the effectiveness of particular media, trends in the media in general, and developments for individual media competitors.

B-2c Other Promotion-Related Positions

Numerous positions that do not center on advertising or media may appeal to marketing graduates. Direct marketing managers are in charge of a company's direct marketing efforts. For additional information on direct marketing, refer to Chapter 16, "Personal Selling, Databases, and Direct Marketing."

Event marketing managers are in charge of marketing particular events. In one example, sports marketing managers could focus on marketing a particular competition, such as the World Cup. Online marketing managers typically have an advertising focus, a sales focus addressing online retailing, or both.

B-3 Sales Positions

Most entry-level jobs for marketing degrees are in the area of sales. Many marketing graduates who decide to use sales as a stepping stone to other careers find that sales positions are particularly challenging and attractive and choose to remain in sales for the rest of their career. In many areas, salaries and commissions are particularly attractive, as is the freedom to be in charge of one's own territory. Order takers process routine orders from customers. Retail staff tend to operate as order getters, unless they are able to persuade the consumer to buy and close the sale. Order getters actively generate potential leads and persuade customers to make a purchase. In industrial sales, order getters tend to have a degree in engineering, as well as a Master of Business Administration. If they do not have a business degree, their companies are often likely to sponsor their best employee in the pursuit of this degree. Sales support personnel are individuals who directly support or assist in the selling function in some manner, but do not process orders or directly solicit orders. Examples of sales support staff are customer service representatives, who handle the service hotline of the company. For more information about the opportunities in sales, refer to Chapter 16, "Personal Selling, Databases, and Direct Marketing."

In addition to the marketing positions previously addressed, other types of positions fall in the realm of marketing. For example, graduates may elect to work for transportation and logistics companies or for a wholesaler. Chapter 10, "Distribution Strategies," contains additional information on the different types of opportunities. Graduates can also start out as assistants to buyers or purchasing agents, and then further advance to the position of buyer or purchasing agent for the company.

For information on careers in marketing, consult the following websites:

- American Marketing Association, *www.marketingpower.com*
- American Advertising Federation, www.aaf.org
- Marketing Jobs, www.marketingjobs.com
- Marketing and Sales Jobs, *www.nationjob.com/marketing*

Glossary

A

acceleration principle An increase or decrease in consumer demand for a product that can create a drastic change in derived business demand.

accessibility The ability to communicate with and reach the target market.

accessory pricing Pricing of accessories and other optional products sold with the main product.

account executive The key representative of the advertising agency to the client company.

acculturation The process of learning a new culture.

achievers Psychographic group of individuals who are goal-oriented, conservative, committed to career and family, and favor established, prestige products that demonstrate success to peers.

actionability The extent to which the target market segment is responsive to the marketing strategies used.

adaptation The process of modifying the product and marketing approach for each country.

administered channel arrangement An arrangement between intermediaries such that a dominant member of the distribution channel in terms of size, expertise, or influence coordinates the tasks of each member in the channel.

advertising Any form of paid communication directed to an organization's customers and/or other stakeholders.

advertising appeal The design a creative will use to attract attention to and interest in an advertisement.

advertising effectiveness research Studies conducted to examine the effectiveness and appropriateness of advertisements aimed at individual markets.

advertising execution The manner in which the advertisement will be presented.

affective message strategies Messages designed to invoke feelings and emotions within the audience.

agents Intermediaries who represent buyers or sellers; they do not take possession of or title to the merchandise, and they work based on commission or fees.

AIDA An acronym that stands for *attention, interest, desire,* and *action.*

all-purpose discount stores General merchandise discount stores that offer a wide variety of merchandise and limited depth.

all-you-can-afford method Method of determining a communications budget that uses whatever funds are available after all other expenses are paid.

analogy method A method for estimation that relies on developments and findings in similar markets or where the product is in the same lifecycle stage.

anchor stores (generator stores) Stores situated at the end (anchor) positions in a mall to generate consumer traffic for the stores situated in between.

animation Advertising execution that involves the presentation of an advertisement using drawn or personified characters or computer-enhanced or modified imagery.

aspirational groups Groups that individuals aspire to join in the future—by virtue of education, employment, and training, for example.

assimilation Adapting to and fully integrating into the new culture.

associative reference groups Groups that individuals belong to.

assurance The knowledge and courtesy of the employees and their ability to inspire customers to trust and have confidence in the service provider.

atmospherics The general atmosphere of the store created by its physical attributes, including lighting and music tempo, the fixtures and other displays, colors, and store layout.

attitude tests Evaluation procedures of participants' attitudes toward a particular advertisement.

attitudes Relatively enduring and consistent feelings (affective responses) about a good or service.

attribute/benefit positioning Positioning that communicates product attributes and benefits, differentiating each brand from the other company brands and from those of competitors.

attribution theory The process of deciding the cause of a service failure or poor service.

audience The individuals who observe a marketing communication and decode the message.

augmented product A product enhanced by the addition of extra or unsolicited services or benefits, such as a warranty, repair services, maintenance, and other services that enhance product use, in order to prompt a purchase.

B

bait and switch A marketing tactic in which a retailer promotes a special deal on a particular product and then, when consumers arrive at the store, the retailer attempts to switch them to a higher-priced item.

battle of the brands The conflict between manufacturers and resellers to promote their own brands.

beliefs Associations between a good or service and attributes of that good or service.

believers Psychographic group of individuals who are conservative, conventional, and focus on tradition, family, religion, and community. They prefer established brands, favoring American products.

benefit segmentation The process of identifying market segments based on important differences between the benefits sought by the target market from purchasing a particular product.

bid pricing Pricing that involves competitive bidding for a contract, whereby a firm will price based on how it believes competitors will price, rather than based on demand or costs.

big emerging markets (BEMs) Markets that present the greatest potential for international trade and expansion.

blueprinting The process of diagramming a service operation.

bonus packs Sales promotion that offers customers some type of discount for purchasing multiple items.

bounce-back coupons Coupons that cannot be used until the next purchase.

branch offices Offices that are part of the international company, rather than a new entity.

brand A name, design, symbol, or a combination thereof that identifies the product and/or the seller and that is used to differentiate the product from competitors' offerings.

brand advertising An advertisement designed to promote a particular brand with little or no information in the advertisement.

brand awareness research Research investigating how consumers' knowledge and recognition of a brand name affects their purchasing behavior.

brand character (or trade character) A character that personifies the brand.

brand equity (or brand franchise) Brands with high consumer awareness and loyalty.

brand extensions The use of an existing brand name to introduce products in a new product category.

brand image The consumer perception of the particular brand.

brand logo A distinctive mark, sign, symbol, or graphic version of a company's name that is used to identify and promote the company's product.

brand mark The part of a brand that can be seen but not spoken.

brand name The part of a brand that can be spoken; it may include words, letters, or numbers.

brand-name generation The testing of brand names and logos.

branded media A movie or show that contains a brand name or logo with a storyline that intersects the brand's mission or current advertising campaign.

brokers Intermediaries who bring buyers and sellers together; they do not take possession of or title to the merchandise, and they work based on commission or fees.

bundling Pricing of bundled products sold together.

buyer behavior research Research examining consumer brand preferences, brand attitudes, and brand-related behavior.

buyer's regret A feeling of anxiety related to the consumer's loss of freedom to spend money on other products.

buyer-readiness stage segmentation The process of segmenting the market based on individuals' stage of readiness to buy a product.

buyer-seller dyad Two-way communication between a buyer and a seller.

buying center Group of individuals who are involved in the purchase process.

byproduct pricing Pricing of byproducts that are of low value in order to get rid of them.

C

calendar promotions Promotional campaigns that retailers plan for their customers through manufacturer trade incentives.

captive-product pricing Pricing of products that must be used with the main product.

cash cows Products with high market share and slow growth that generate large amounts of cash, in excess of the reinvestment required to maintain market share.

cash-and-carry wholesalers Wholesalers who carry a limited line of fast-moving goods; they travel to a wholesaler's location, pay cash for the merchandise, take physical possession of the product, and carry it directly to a retailer.

catalog retailers Retailers selling products through mail catalogs.

catalog showrooms Showrooms displaying the products of catalog retailers, offering high-turnover, brand-name goods at discount prices.

category specialists (category killers) Large general-merchandise discount stores that carry a narrow variety of merchandise and a deep assortment.

causal (experimental) research Research that examines cause-and-effect relationships.

cause-related marketing A long-term partnership between a nonprofit organization and a corporation that is integrated into the corporation's marketing plan.

central business districts Business districts located in the commercial and cultural heart of the city, in the middle of busy downtowns, and close to movie theaters and banks.

channel captain The dominant member of a channel of distribution.

channel length The number of levels of distributors in a distribution channel.

channel performance and coverage studies Studies investigating whether existing channels are appropriate for the marketing task at hand.

channel width The number of independent intermediaries involved at a particular stage of distribution.

channels of distribution The totality of organizations and individuals involved in the distribution process who take title to or assist in the transferring of title in the distribution process from the producer to the individual or organizational consumer.

co-branding Using the brands of two different companies on one single product.

coercive power Power over channel members based on the ability of one or more intermediaries to remove privileges for noncompliance.

cognitive dissonance An anxiety feeling of uncertainty about whether or not the consumer made the right purchase decision.

cognitive message strategies The presentation of rational arguments or pieces of information to consumers.

combination stores Medium-sized retail stores that combine food and drug retailing.

commercialization Stage in the new product development process when the product is introduced to the market.

commission merchant Agent who takes possession of goods on consignment from the local markets and then sells them at a central market location.

community shopping centers Shopping centers with fewer than 40 retailers, containing a department store, a supermarket, and several smaller specialty retailers.

comparative advertising An advertisement that compares the featured brand with another brand, either named or implied.

competitive pricing analyses Pricing studies that determine the price the market will bear for the respective product category based on a survey of competitors' prices.

competitive product studies Studies that help in determining the overall product strategy for the product, the price that the market will bear for the respective product category, and the promotion that is appropriate in light of the competition.

competitive-parity method Method of determining a communications budget that uses competitors' levels of communication spending as benchmarks for a firm's own advertising expenditure.

competitor positioning The process of comparing the firm's brand, directly or indirectly, with those of competitors.

conative message strategies Messages designed to elicit some type of audience behavior, such as a purchase or inquiry.

concentrated marketing The process of selecting only one market segment and targeting it with one single brand.

concept development research Concept tests that evaluate the product/service offering and the related marketing mix in light of the different target markets.

concept tests Evaluations of the content or concept of an advertisement and its potential impact on viewers; conducted in the very early stages of ad development or while the ad is in the concept stage.

consequence The degree of importance or danger of the outcome itself.

consortium A company created with the participation of three or more companies; allowed in underserved markets or in domains where the government and/or the marketplace can control its monopolistic activity.

consumer complaints The registering of a problem with a good or service.

consumer retention The ability to retain consumers as customers in the future.

consumer segmentation studies Research conducted to identify market segment profiles.

contact methods Methods used for approaching study respondents.

content analysis Method that assesses the content of advertisements in a medium with verbal and/or visual content.

contests and sweepstakes Sales promotions that allow participants an opportunity to win free merchandise.

continuous innovations Innovations that have no disruption on consumption patterns and involve only product alterations, such as new flavors or a new product that is an improvement over the old offering.

contractual agreement A written agreement between the buyer and seller that states the terms of the interaction, costs, and length of the commitment.

contractual channel arrangement A contract between intermediaries that defines all the tasks that each channel member must perform with regard to production, delivery strategy and terms of sale, territorial rights, promotional support, the price policies of each intermediary, and contract length.

controlled test marketing Offering a new product to a group of stores and evaluating the market reaction to it.

convenience goods Relatively inexpensive and frequently purchased products.

convenience sample Sample composed of individuals who are easy to contact for the researcher.

convenience stores Small retailers that are located in residential areas, are open long hours, and carry limited lines of high-turnover necessities.

conventional supermarkets Self-service food retailers with annual sales of more than $2 million and with an area of less than 20,000 square feet.

cooperative advertising program An arrangement whereby a manufacturer agrees to reimburse retailers or other channel members that feature the manufacturer's brands in the ad for a portion of their advertising costs.

cooperative merchandising agreement A formal agreement between the retailer and manufacturer to undertake a cooperative marketing effort.

copy tests Evaluations of a completed or nearly completed advertisement.

core product The fundamental benefit, or problem solution, that consumers seek.

cost analyses Methods used for projecting the cost of research.

cost per thousand (CPM) The cost of reaching one thousand members of a media vehicle's audience.

cost-based pricing Pricing strategy whereby the firm sets the price by calculating merchandise, service, and overhead costs and then adds an amount needed to cover the profit goal.

countries with emerging markets Countries that are developing rapidly and have great potential.

country of manufacture The country in which a particular product is manufactured.

country of origin The country with which a particular product or service is associated.

coupons Sales promotion that offers customers some type of price reduction.

creatives Individuals who actually design the advertisements.

cross-ruffing coupon A coupon for one product placed on another product.

cross-selling The marketing of additional items with the purchase of a particular good or service.

cues Stimuli in the environment, such as products or advertisements, that create individual responses.

cultural values Beliefs about a specific mode of conduct or desirable end-state that guide the selection or evaluation of behavior.

culture A continuously evolving totality of learned and shared meanings, rituals, norms, and traditions among the members of an organization or society.

customary pricing Pricing strategy whereby a firm sets prices and attempts to maintain them over time.

customer expectations Anticipated good or service performance based on consumers' experiences, on information received from the media, and from other consumers.

customer lifetime value (LTV) The estimated profitability of the customer over the course of his or her entire relationship with a company.

customer profit Profit measure calculated as revenue minus costs for that particular customer.

customer profit potential An estimate of the individual's contribution to a company's bottom line.

customer relationship management (CRM) A database application program designed to build long-term loyalty with customers through the use of a personal touch.

customer relationship management (CRM) The holistic process of identifying, attracting, differentiating, and retaining customers.

customer value package The best combination of price, technical service quality, functional service quality, and company image that provides value to the customer.

customer-focus needs segment Business segment that is prepared to pay for higher-than-average service that is tailored to meet the users' needs.

D

data collection instruments The instruments used to collect data, such as a questionnaire, a paper-and-pencil measure, or an electronic measurement device.

data mining The process of compiling personal, pertinent, actionable information about the purchasing habits of current and potential consumers.

data warehousing The process of capturing and storing data within a single database that is accessible to internal personnel for a variety of internal purposes, such as marketing, sales, and customer service.

database marketing The collection, analysis, and use of large volumes of customer data to develop marketing programs and customer profiles.

day-after recall (DAR) Advertising evaluation method of calling individuals the day after a new advertisement appears and asking them what ads they remember from the previous day.

deceptive pricing Strategy used by sellers who state prices or price savings that may mislead consumers or that are not available to consumers.

decider The member of the buying center who makes the final decision.

decline stage Stage in the product lifecycle where products are rapidly losing ground to new technologies or product alternatives, and, consequently, sales and profits are rapidly declining.

decoding The process of interpreting the meaning conveyed in a marketing message.

degree of product newness The extent to which a product or service is new to the market.

Delphi method A method of forecasting sales that involves asking a number of experts to estimate market performance, aggregating the results, and then sharing this information with the said experts; the process is repeated several times, until a consensus is reached.

demand curve Curve that portrays the number of units bought for a particular price in a given time period.

demand-based pricing Pricing strategy that takes into consideration customers' perceptions of value, rather than the seller's cost, as the fundamental component of the pricing decision.

demands Wants backed by the ability to buy the good or service brand.

demarketing A company strategy aimed at reducing demand for its own products in order to benefit society.

demographic segmentation The process of identifying market segments based on age, gender, race, income, education, occupation, social class, lifecycle stage, and household size.

demographics Statistics that describe the population, such as age, gender, education, occupation, and income.

demonstration execution An advertising execution that shows how a product works.

department stores General retailers that offer a broad variety of goods and deep assortments.

depth interviews A qualitative research method involving extensive interviews aimed at discovering consumer motivations, feelings, and attitudes toward an issue of concern to the sponsor, using unstructured interrogation.

derived demand Demand for a good or service that is generated from the demand for consumer goods and services.

descriptive research All research methods observing or describing phenomena.

developed countries Highly industrialized countries that have well-developed industrial and service sectors.

developing countries Countries that are primarily agrarian and have low per capita income.

differential response The extent to which market segments respond differently to marketing strategies.

differentiated marketing A targeting strategy identifying market segments with different preferences for a particular product category and targeting each segment with different brands and different marketing strategies.

digital direct-to-press Printing technology that allows for the customization of each marketing piece.

direct channel of distribution A channel that has no intermediaries; the manufacturer sells directly to the final consumer.

direct exporting An export entry mode whereby a firm handles its own exports, usually with the help of an in-house exporting department.

direct marketing The promotion of a product directly from the manufacturer or seller to the buyer without any middlemen involved in the transaction.

direct selling Selling that involves a salesperson, typically an independent distributor, contacting a consumer at a convenient location (such as his or her home or workplace), demonstrating the product's use and benefits, taking orders, and delivering the merchandise.

direct-mail retailing Retailing using catalogs and other direct mail, instead of brick-and-mortar stores.

dissociative groups Groups that individuals want to dissociate from through their behavior.

distribution centers Computerized warehouses designed to move goods; they receive goods from different producers, take orders from buyers, and distribute them promptly.

distribution planning The planning of the physical movement of products from the producer to individual or organizational consumers, and the transfer of ownership and risk; it involves transportation, warehousing, and all the exchanges taking place at each channel level.

distributors Middlemen whose task is to ensure the convenient, timely, and safe distribution of the product to consumers.

diversification Opportunity for expansion involving developing or acquiring new products for new markets.

diversion A situation in which a retailer purchases a product on-deal in one location and ships it to another location, where it is off-deal.

dogs Products with low market share and slow growth.

domestic marketing Marketing that is focused solely on domestic consumers and on the home-country environment.

dramatization An advertising execution that is a form of slice-of-life execution but uses a higher level of excitement, where the suspense builds to a crisis.

drive (or motive) A stimulus that encourages consumers to engage in an action to reduce the need.

drive to maturity Stage of economic development in which modern technology is applied in all areas of the economy.

drop shippers (or **desk jobbers**) Wholesalers who take title to but not possession of the product; they buy goods from suppliers and arrange to have them shipped directly to the reseller or organizational user.

dual channel of distribution The use of two or more channels of distribution to appeal to different markets.

dumping Selling products below cost to get rid of excess inventory and/or to undermine competition.

durable goods Tangible products that have a prolonged use.

dynamically continuous innovations Innovations that do not significantly alter consumer behavior but represent a change in the consumption pattern.

E

early adopters Consumers who purchase the product early in the lifecycle and are opinion leaders in their communities.

early majority Consumers who are more risk averse but enjoy the status of being among the first in their peer group to buy what will be a popular product.

e-coupons Electronically delivered coupons.

electronic data interchange (EDI) A trust relationship that includes the sharing of data between the buying and selling firm.

elements of culture Elements such as language, religion, cultural values, and norms.

emergency goods Goods purchased to address urgent needs.

emerging markets Markets that are developing rapidly and have great potential.

empathy The caring, individualized attention the service firm provides to each customer.

empty nesters A segment of consumers between the ages of 55 and 64 with a large proportion of disposable income, who tend to purchase fancy automobiles, new furniture, and appliances.

encoding The process of transposing the objective or goal of a marketing communication concept into an actual marketing communication piece, such as an advertisement, brochure, or sign.

ethics Philosophical principles that serve as operational guidelines for both individuals and organizations concerning what is right and wrong.

ethnography The study of culture.

even pricing Setting selling prices at even numbers.

exchanges and transactions Obtaining a desired good or service in exchange for something else of value; involving at least two parties that mutually agree on the desirability of the traded items.

exclusive distribution A strategy that has as a goal a high control of the intermediaries handling the product, and thus of the marketing strategy, by limiting them to just one or two per geographic area.

executive-judgment method Method of determining the communications budget using executive opinion.

exit fees Monies paid to remove an item from a retailer's inventory.

expatriates Employees working in a foreign country.

expectations Anticipated product performance based on consumers' experiences, on information received from the media, and from other consumers.

expected (or actual) product The basic physical product, including styling, features, brand name, and packaging, that delivers the benefits that consumers seek.

experiencers Psychographic group of individuals who are young, enthusiastic, and impulsive. They seek variety and excitement, and spend substantially on fashion, entertainment, and socializing.

experiences Personal experiences that consumers perceive as valuable because they fulfill consumer needs and wants.

expert power Power over the other channel members based on experience and knowledge that a channel member possesses.

exploratory research Research conducted early in the research process that helps further define a problem or identify additional problems that need to be investigated.

export management companies Companies specializing in the export function for companies in a particular industry.

export marketing Involvement in international marketing limited to the exporting function; although the firm actively seeks international clients, it considers the international market an extension of the domestic market and does not give it special consideration.

export merchants Intermediaries who take title to and possession of the products they carry; they are responsible for shipping and marketing the products to the target market.

extensive problem solving Consumer decision making that involves going carefully through each of the steps of the consumer decision-making process.

external secondary data Data collected for purposes other than the problem at hand.

F

fad A fashion that quickly becomes very popular and just as quickly disappears.

family branding (or blanket branding) Branding strategy whereby one brand name is used for more than one product.

fantasy execution An advertising execution designed to lift the audience beyond the realm of reality.

FAQs Frequently asked questions people have about various items or services.

fashion A current style.

feedback The response of the audience to the message.

field salesperson A salesperson who is involved in going to a potential customer's place of business to solicit accounts.

financial risk The amount of monetary loss the consumer incurs if the service fails.

fixed costs Costs that do not vary with the amount of output.

flexible pricing Pricing strategy that allows a firm to set prices based on negotiation with the customer, or based on customer buying power.

focus group interviews A qualitative research approach investigating a research question, using a moderator to guide discussion within a group of subjects recruited to meet certain characteristics.

food retailers Retailers selling primarily food products.

foreign trade zone (FTZ) Tax-free area in the United States that is not considered part of the United States in terms of import regulations and restrictions. Also called a free trade zone.

foreign-country middlemen Middlemen in the foreign country who are either merchant middlemen (intermediaries who take title to and possession of the products they carry) or agents and brokers (intermediaries who bring buyers and sellers together but do not carry title to and take possession of the products with which they deal).

forward buying When a retailer purchases excess inventory of a product while it is on-deal to be sold later when it is off-deal.

franchise wholesalers Independent intermediaries affiliated with a manufacturer or wholesaler through a franchise contract.

franchising The main international entry mode for the service industry, whereby the franchisor gives the franchisee the right to use its brand name and all related trademarks in return for royalties.

freestanding inserts (FSI) Sheets of coupons distributed in newspapers, primarily on Sunday.

freight forwarders Specialized firms that collect shipments from different businesses, consolidate them for part of the distance, and deliver them to a destination, in what is typically a door-to-door service.

frequency programs Sales promotions offered to current customers and designed to build repeat purchase behavior.

full-service wholesalers Independent intermediaries who provide a wide range of distribution tasks, such as product delivery, warehousing, sales force assistance, credit, research, planning, and installation and repair assistance, among others.

functional service quality The process whereby the service was performed.

G

gap theory Method of measuring service quality that involves measuring the gap between expectations and customer evaluations of a service.

gatekeeper Individual who is responsible for the flow of information to the members of the buying center.

general merchandise discount stores Retailers that sell high volumes of merchandise, offer limited service, and charge lower prices.

general merchandise wholesalers Independent intermediaries who carry a broad product assortment, but low depth, in any one product line.

Generation X A segment of consumers between the ages of 25 and 34, whose focus is on family and children, striving to balance family with work, and outsourcing household chores and babysitting.

Generation Y A segment of consumers between the ages of 18 and 24 that spends substantial amounts on clothing, automobiles, and college education; they live in rental apartments or with parents.

generics Products that emphasize the product, rather than the brand of the manufacturer or reseller.

geocoding The process of adding geographic codes to each customer record.

geographic pricing Pricing that accounts for the geographic location of customers.

geographic segmentation Market segmentation based on geographic location, such as country or region.

global localization The practice of global branding and localized marketing adaptation to differences in local culture, legislation, and even production capabilities.

global marketing International marketing activities that do not have a country or region focus and that are possible due to the emergence of global consumer segments and efficient global allocation of company talent and resources.

global standardization The standardization of products across markets and, ultimately, to the standardization of the marketing mix worldwide; more commonly called globalization.

goods Tangible products, such as cereals, automobiles, and clothing.

green marketing The development and promotion of products that are environmentally safe.

gross domestic product (GDP) The sum of all goods and services produced within the boundaries of a country.

growth stage Stage in the product lifecycle characterized by increasing competition, with new product variants offered to the market, as well as rapid product adoption by the target market.

growth-share matrix Portfolio matrix developed by the Boston Consulting Group and one of the most popular bases for evaluating company product portfolios; it assumes that, to be successful, a company should have a portfolio of products with different growth rates and different market shares.

H

heterogeneous shopping goods Goods that vary significantly in terms of functions, physical characteristics, and quality, and that require a physical evaluation by the buyer.

heuristics Decision rules that individuals adopt to make a decision process more efficient.

high mass consumption Stage of economic development in which leading sectors shift toward durable goods and an increased allocation to social welfare programs.

high-expectation service segment Business segment that is the most demanding and needs extensive customer focus, placing considerable demands on service providers while demanding low prices.

high-involvement purchases Purchases that have a high personal relevance.

historical method Method of determining the communications budget based on past expenditures, usually giving more weight to more recent expenditures.

home-country middlemen Middlemen in the home country who typically provide all marketing services for firms that do not wish to enter the foreign market and/or do not have the capability to do so.

home-country national An expatriate from the company's home country working in a foreign country.

homogeneous shopping goods Goods that vary little in terms of physical characteristics or functions.

horizontal integration An acquisition or merger with an intermediary at the same level in the distribution channel.

horizontal marketing systems (HMS) Intermediaries at the same level of the distribution channel pooling resources and achieving partial ownership of the system, achieving economies of scale, and playing on their individual strengths.

host-country national A local employee who works in his or her home country for the international corporation.

hub-and-spoke distribution centers Distribution centers designed to speed up warehousing and delivery, by channeling operations to one center (hub) that is particularly well equipped to handle the distribution of products to their destination.

hybrid marketing channel (or **multichannel distribution system**) The use of multiple (more than two) channels of distribution, thus offering customers multiple purchase and communication options.

hypermarkets Very large retail stores in Europe that combine supermarket, discount, and warehouse retailing principles—similar to superstores in the United States.

I

ideas Concepts that can be used to fulfill consumer needs and wants.

impulse goods Goods bought without any earlier planning, such as candy, gum, and magazines.

inbound telemarketing The process through which an order-taker salesperson handles incoming calls from customers and prospects.

independent retailers Retailers that operate only one outlet that is usually located conveniently close to the customer. The corner convenience mart, the ethnic grocer in suburbia, and the comic bookstore in a strip mall are all examples of independent retailers.

indirect channel of distribution A channel that involves one or more intermediaries between the manufacturer and the consumer.

indirect exporting An export entry mode whereby a company sells its products in the company's home country to intermediaries, who, in turn, sell the product overseas.

industrialization The use of machines and standardized operating procedures to increase the productivity and efficiency of a business.

influencer A member of the buying center who influences the decision but may not necessarily use the product.

informative advertising An advertisement designed to provide the audience with some type of information.

innovators Psychographic group of individuals who are successful, sophisticated, and receptive to new technologies.

inseparability The simultaneous production and consumption of a service.

instant redemption coupon A coupon that can be redeemed immediately while making a purchase.

institutional advertising Advertising designed to build the corporate reputation or develop goodwill for the corporation.

instrumental values Values related to processes whereby one can attain certain goals.

intangibility The lack of tangible assets of a service that can be seen, touched, smelled, heard, or tasted prior to a purchase.

integrated marketing communications (IMC) The coordination and integration of all marketing communication tools, avenues, and sources within a company into a seamless program designed to maximize the communication impact on consumers, businesses, and other constituencies of an organization.

intensive distribution A strategy that has as its purpose full market coverage, making the product available to all target consumers when and where consumers want them.

intercompany tie-in A sales promotion involving two different companies offering complementary products.

intermediaries (or **middlemen,** or **channel members**) The organizations or individuals involved in the distribution process.

inter-modal transportation Transportation using two or more different transportation modes—a combination of truck, rail, air, and waterways.

internal secondary data Data previously collected by a company to address a problem not related to the current research question.

international marketing The processes involved in the creation, production, distribution, promotion, and pricing of products, services, ideas, and experiences for international markets; these processes require a substantial focus on international consumers in a particular country or countries.

Internet marketing The promotion and sale of products through the Internet.

Internet retailing (or interactive home shopping or electronic retailing) Selling through the Internet using websites to increase market penetration and market diversification.

intracompany tie-in A sales promotion involving two or more distinct products within the same company.

intrusion value The ability to break through clutter and gain a person's attention.

inventory The amount of goods being stored.

involvement The level of mental and physical effort a consumer exerts in selecting a good or service.

J

joint demand Demand for one product that is affected by the level of demand for another product.

joint ventures A corporate entity created with the participation of two companies that share equity, capital, and labor, among other things.

judgment sample A sample of individuals thought to be representative of the population.

jury of expert opinion An approach to sales forecasting based on the opinions of different experts.

just-in-time (JIT) inventory system Inventory system whereby a company reduces the amount of inventory by ordering products often and in lower quantities, thus creating flows, rather than stocks, of inventory.

K

keiretsus Japanese families of firms with interlocking stakes in one another.

L

laggards Consumers who are the last to adopt new products and who do so only in late maturity.

late majority Consumers with limited means likely to adopt products only if the products are widely popular and the risk associated with buying them is minimal.

law of demand Economic law whereby consumers are believed to purchase more products at a lower price than at a higher price.

learning Change in individual thought processes or behavior attributed to experience.

legitimate power Power over the other channel members by virtue of an intermediary's status or position in the firm.

licensing A process that involves a licensor, who shares the brand name, technology, and know-how with a licensee in return for royalties.

lifestyle execution An advertising execution that portrays the product fitting into a person's current or desired lifestyle.

lifestyles Individuals' style of living as expressed through activities, interests, and opinions.

Likert scale A scale that is anchored by "strongly disagree" and "strongly agree" statements.

limited problem solving Consumer decision making that involves less problem solving. This type of decision making is used for products that are not especially visible, nor too expensive.

limited-service wholesalers Wholesalers who offer fewer services than full-service wholesalers; they may not provide distribution tasks such as sales force assistance, credit, research, planning, or installation and repair assistance, but they do provide delivery and storage.

line extension The process of extending the existing brand name by introducing new product offerings in an existing product category.

logistics (or **physical distribution**) All the activities involved in the physical flow and storage of materials, semi-finished goods, and finished goods to customers in a manner that is efficient and cost effective.

loss-leader pricing Pricing whereby the firm advertises a product at a price that is significantly less than its usual price in order to create traffic in the stores for consumers to purchase higher-margin products.

low-involvement products Products with limited personal relevance.

loyalty segmentation The process of segmenting the market based on the degree of consumer loyalty to the brand.

M

macroenvironment Environment of the firm, which includes the sociodemographic and cultural environment, the economic and natural environment, the political environment, and the technological environment.

mail-order wholesalers Wholesalers who mail catalogs to businesses, take orders, and ship them to businesses.

makers Psychographic group of individuals who are self-sufficient. They have the skill and energy to carry out projects, respect authority, and are unimpressed by material possessions.

mandatory adaptation The adaptation of products to local requirements so that the products can legally and physically function in the specific country environment.

manufacturers' agent (or **manufacturers' representative**) Representative who works as the company's sales representative, representing noncompeting manufacturers in a particular market, and is paid on a commission basis.

manufacturers' brands (or national brands) Brands owned by a manufacturer.

market development The process of developing new markets for the company's existing product or creating new product uses.

market orientation A firm-wide focus on customer needs and on delivering high quality to consumers in the process of achieving company objectives.

market penetration The process of increasing the usage rate of current customers and attracting competitors' customers to sell more products to present customers without changing the product.

market potential studies Studies conducted to evaluate the potential of a particular market.

marketing The process of planning and executing the conception, pricing, promotion, and distribution of ideas, goods, and services to create exchanges that satisfy individual and organizational objectives.

marketing concept A marketing philosophy that assumes a company can compete more effectively if it first researches consumers' generic needs, wants, and preferences, as well as good- or service-related attitudes and interests, and then delivers the goods and services more efficiently and effectively than competitors.

marketing decision support systems (MDSS) A coordinated collection of data, systems, tools, and techniques, complemented by supporting software and hardware designed for the gathering and interpretation of business and environmental data.

marketing era Period from 1950 until the present, when the primary focus of marketing shifted to the needs of consumers and society.

marketing intelligence Results obtained from monitoring developments in the firm's environment.

marketing myopia The tendency of marketing efforts to focus on products/production or sales and ignore specific consumer needs or important markets.

marketing research The systematic design, collection, recording, analysis, interpretation, and reporting of information pertinent to a particular marketing decision facing a company.

markets All of the actual and potential consumers of a company's products.

mass marketing The process of identifying the product-related preferences of most consumers in order to then target the product broadly to all consumers with the maximum likelihood of success.

maturity stage Stage in the product lifecycle characterized by a slowdown in sales growth as the product is adopted by most target consumers and by a leveling or decline in profits primarily due to intense price competition.

McMansions Super-sized, expensive tract houses on relatively small lots in suburban neighborhoods.

measurability The ability to estimate the size of a market segment.

media research Studies that evaluate media availability and the appropriateness of the medium for a company's message.

medium The venue the source uses to send a marketing communication message to its intended audience.

merchandise mix The product assortment and brands that the store carries.

merchant wholesalers Independent intermediaries who takes title to and possession of products distributed to resellers or organizational consumers.

message The completed marketing communication piece.

message strategy The primary tactic an advertisement will use to deliver a message.

microenvironment Environment of the firm, which includes the company, its consumers, suppliers, distributors, and other facilitators of the marketing function and competition.

micromarketing A process that involves a microanalysis of the customer and customer-specific marketing.

missionary salesperson A sales support person whose task is to provide information about a good or service.

mission-sharing sales approach Sales approach that involves two organizations developing a common mission and then sharing resources to accomplish that mission.

modified break-even analysis Analysis that combines break-even analysis with an evaluation of demand at various price levels, assuming that, as the price increases, demand will decrease in an elastic demand environment, where many product substitutes are available and competition is intense.

modified rebuy situation Occasional purchases or purchases for which the members of the buying center have limited experience.

monopolistic competition Market that consists of many buyers and sellers and products that vary greatly in the same product category.

morals Personal beliefs or standards used to guide an individual's actions.

multiattribute segmentation The process of segmenting the market by using multiple segmentation variables.

multibranding Using different brand names for products that the firm sells in the same product category.

multichannel distribution system (or **hybrid marketing channel**) The use of multiple (more than two) channels of distribution, thus offering customers multiple purchase and communication options.

multichannel marketing The marketing of a product through two or more channels.

multinational marketing Marketing in different countries without coordinating across operations.

multiple-unit pricing Pricing whereby consumers get a discount to purchase a larger quantity with the purpose, ultimately, to increase sales volume.

N

naturalistic inquiry An observational research approach that requires the use of natural rather than contrived settings because behaviors take substantial meaning from their context.

need-satisfaction sales approach Sales approach aimed at discovering a customer's needs and then providing solutions that satisfy those needs.

needs Basic human requirements, such as food and water.

neighborhood business districts Business districts that meet the needs of the neighborhood and that tend to be located on a main street of the neighborhood; typically, they have a supermarket, a drug store, and several smaller retailers.

neighborhood shopping centers Shopping centers that have between 5 and 15 retailers and that serve the neighborhood, providing convenience in the form of a supermarket, discount store, laundry service, and other smaller specialty stores.

network marketing (or multilevel marketing) An alternative distribution structure, using acquaintance networks for the purpose of distribution.

new brands New brands in new product categories for the firm.

new buy situation Purchases made by a business for the first time or purchases for which no one in the organization has had previous experience.

no-haggle pricing Pricing strategy that is aimed at consumers who are averse to negotiation, but who want, nevertheless, to have some sort of low-price guarantee.

noise Anything that interferes with the audience receiving the message.

nondurable goods Tangible products that are consumed relatively quickly and purchased on a regular basis; they last less than two years.

nonmandatory adaptation The strategy of adapting a product to better meet the needs of the local market, without being required to do so.

nonresponse The inability or refusal by a respondent to participate in a study.

nonverbal communication All communication that is not written or spoken; includes body language, gestures, facial expressions, eye contact, and silence.

norms Rules that dictate what is right or wrong, acceptable or unacceptable.

O

objective-and-task method Method of determining a communications budget that first identifies the communication goals, such as target audience reach, awareness, comprehension, or even sales.

observational research (or observation) A research approach whereby subjects are observed interacting with a product and reacting to other components of the marketing mix and the environment.

occasion segmentation The process of segmenting based on the time or the occasion when the product should be purchased or consumed.

occasional transactions Transactions whereby buyer and seller interact infrequently in the process of making the transaction.

odd pricing Setting prices at below even dollar values.

off-invoice allowance A financial discount or price-off on each case that a member of the distribution channel orders.

off-price retailers Retailers that sell brand-name and designer merchandise below regular retail.

older boomers A segment of consumers between the ages of 45 and 54 that spends money on upgrading the family home, on taking vacations, and on ensuring children's education and independence.

oligopolistic competition Market that consists of few sellers who dominate the market.

open-ended questions Questions with free-format responses that the respondent can address as he or she sees appropriate.

opportunity risk The risk involved when consumers must choose one service over another.

order getters Salespeople who actively generate potential leads and persuade customers to make a purchase.

order takers Salespeople who process routine orders from customers.

outbound telemarketing The process through which an order-getter salesperson calls prospects and attempts to persuade them to make a purchase.

overlay The use of two or more promotions within the same promotional offer.

P

packaging All the activities involved in designing the product container.

parallel imports A distribution system not authorized by the manufacturer whereby the products purchased in a low-price market are diverted to other markets; also called gray market.

patent The grant of a property right to the inventor.

penetration pricing Pricing strategy whereby firms initially price the product below the price of competitors to quickly penetrate the market at competitors' expense and acquire a large market share, and then gradually raise the price.

percent-of-sales method Method of determining a communications budget based on past or projected sales.

perception The manner in which people collect, organize, and interpret information from the world around them to create a meaningful image of reality.

performance risk The chance that the service will not perform or provide the benefit for which it was purchased.

perishability The inability of a service to be inventoried or stored.

personal selling A direct communication approach between the buyer and seller with the express purpose of selling a product.

personality An individual's unique psychological characteristics leading to specific response tendencies over time.

persuasive advertising An advertisement designed to persuade viewers' thinking in some way.

physical risk The probability that a service will actually cause physical harm to the customer.

pioneer advertising An advertisement designed to build primary demand for a product.

plant/warehouse location study A study that evaluates the appropriateness of plant or warehouse location to ensure that it is in accordance with the needs of the company.

point-of-sale (POS)-based projections Market projections based on the use of store scanners in weekly and biweekly store audits.

predatory pricing Pricing strategies used to eliminate small competitors and to deceive consumers.

preference goods Convenience goods that become differentiated through branding and achieve some degree of brand loyalty.

premiums Sales promotion that offers customers free merchandise for making a purchase.

presentation An advertising execution that portrays a product in a straightforward, matter-of-fact way.

prestige pricing Strategy based on the premise that consumers will feel that products below a particular price will have inferior quality and will not convey a desired status and image.

price The amount of money necessary to purchase a good or service.

price ceiling The maximum amount that consumers are willing to pay for a product.

price confusion Strategies to confuse consumers so that they do not quite understand the price that they ultimately have to pay.

price discounting Strategy that involves reducing the price for purchasing larger quantities, responding to a promotion, paying cash, or responding earlier than a particular set time.

price discrimination The practice of charging different prices to different buyers of the same merchandise.

price elasticity Buyer sensitivity to a change in price.

price elasticity studies Studies examining the extent to which a particular market is price sensitive.

price fixing Agreement among channel members at the same level in the channel of distribution to charge the same price to all customers.

price floor The lowest price a company can charge to attain its profit goals.

price leadership The tendency of one firm or a few firms to be the first to announce price changes, with the rest of the firms following.

price/quality positioning A strategy whereby products and services are positioned as offering the best value for the money.

price-offs Sales promotion that offers a reduction of the retail price of a product.

price-sensitive segment Business segment that looks for low prices but that also has low service requirements; these users want the work done at the lowest possible cost.

primary data Data collected for the purpose of addressing the problem at hand.

private label brands Reseller (wholesaler or retailer) brands.

private warehouses Warehouses that are owned or leased, and operated by firms storing their own products.

problem-solution sales approach Sales approach that requires the salesperson to analyze the prospect's operation and offer a viable solution.

product Any offering that can satisfy consumer needs and wants.

product advertising Advertising designed to promote a firm's brand.

product class positioning A strategy used to differentiate a company as a leader in a product category, as defined by the respective companies.

product concept A marketing philosophy that assumes consumers prefer products that are of the highest quality and optimal performance.

product consistency The extent to which the different product lines are related, use the same distribution channels, and have the same final consumers.

product depth The number of different offerings for a product category.

product design The aesthetic traits, style, and function of the product.

product development The process of developing new products to appeal to the company's existing market.

product introduction stage Stage in the product lifecycle when the product is available for purchase for the first time.

product length The total number of brands in the product mix—all the brands the company sells.

product lifecycle (PLC) The performance of the product in terms of sales and profit over time.

product line pricing Pricing that involves creating price differences between the different items in the product line, such that specific price points are used to differentiate among the items in the line.

product line The related brands the company offers in the same product category.

product mix The complete assortment of the products that a company offers to its target consumers.

product packaging design Studies that evaluate consumers' reaction to a package, the extent to which the package adequately communicates information to the consumer, and the distribution implications of the package.

product placement Sales promotion technique of placing branded goods or services in movies, on television shows, or in theatrical performances.

product portfolio The totality of products the company manages as separate businesses.

product testing Studies that estimate product preference and performance in a given market.

product user positioning A positioning strategy that focuses on the product user, rather than on the product.

product width The total number of product lines the company offers.

product-market matrix A matrix used to identify future products and opportunities for companies.

production concept A marketing philosophy that assumes consumers prefer products that are easily accessible and inexpensive.

Production era Period between 1870 and 1930, when the primary focus of marketing was on producing the best products possible at the lowest price.

profit analyses Studies that estimate product profit in specific markets.

promotion All forms of external communications directed toward consumers and businesses with an ultimate goal of developing customers.

promotional pricing Strategy that reduces prices temporarily to increase sales in the short run.

prospects Potential customers of a firm.

psychographic segmentation The use of values, attitudes, interests, and other cultural variables to segment consumers.

psychographics Categorization of consumers according to lifestyles and personality.

psychological pricing Setting prices to create a particular psychological effect.

psychological risk The chance that the purchase of the service will not fit the individual's self-concept.

public relations (PR) A communication venue that addresses issues an organization faces and represents the organization to the public, media, and various stakeholders.

public warehouses Independent facilities that provide storage rental and related services.

publicity A form of public relations produced by the news media but not paid for or sponsored by the business concern.

puffery When a firm makes an exaggerated claim about its goods or services, without making an overt attempt to deceive or mislead.

pull strategy A strategy whereby the manufacturer first focuses on consumer demand through extensive promotion, expecting that consumers will request the brand through the channel.

purchaser The member of the buying center who makes the actual purchase.

purchasing agents Agents with a long-term relationship with buyers who select, receive, and ship goods to buyers and are paid on a commission basis.

pure competition Market that consists of many buyers and sellers, where no buyer or seller can control price or the market.

pure monopoly Market that consists of only one seller.

push strategy A strategy that focuses on intermediaries, providing the necessary incentives for them to cooperate in selling the product to the final consumer.

Q

qualitative research Research that involves a small number of respondents answering open-ended questions.

quality Overall good or service quality, reliability, and the extent to which a product meets consumers' needs; has the greatest impact on satisfaction.

quantitative research A structured type of research that involves either descriptive research approaches, such as survey research, or causal research approaches, such as experiments in which responses can be summarized or analyzed with numbers.

question marks (or problem children) Low market share and high-growth products that require more cash investment than they generate.

quick response (QR) inventory system The retailing equivalent of the just-in-time inventory system that creates a supply flow that more closely approximates consumer purchase patterns.

R

rack jobbers Wholesalers that manage the store shelves carrying their products, assemble the point-of-purchase displays, and determine product prices; they take title to the products they sell on consignment but are allowed to take unsold items back to the manufacturer or wholesaler selling the product.

radical innovations (or discontinuous innovations) Innovations that create new industries or new standards of management, manufacturing, and servicing, and that represent fundamental changes for consumers, entailing departures from established consumption.

random probability sample A sample in which each individual selected for the study has a known and equal chance of being included in the study.

reach The number of people, households, or businesses in a target audience exposed to a media message at least once during a given time period.

rebates and refunds Sales promotions that are a cash reimbursement to a customer for the purchase of a product.

recall tests Evaluation procedures whereby participants are asked about their recall of specific advertisements.

reciprocity Practice of one business making a purchase from another business that, in turn, patronizes the first business.

recognition tests Evaluation procedures whereby participants are shown a series of advertisements and asked whether they have seen them before.

reference groups Groups that serve as a point of reference for individuals in the process of shaping their attitude and behavior.

reference price The price that consumers carry in their mind for a particular product or brand.

referent power Power over the other channel members based on the close match in terms of values and objectives that members of the channel share.

regional shopping centers Shopping centers that consist of at least 100 stores that sell shopping goods to a geographically dispersed market.

regional standardization The use of a uniform marketing strategy within a particular region.

reinforcement Learning achieved by strengthening the relationship between the cue and the response.

relationship marketing The development of marketing strategies aimed at enhancing relationships in the channel.

relationship-seeking segment Business segment that consists of relatively sophisticated service users who believe that the user-provider relationship is very important. They have a "realistic" level of expectations for the service requirements and do not expect to pay a low price.

reliability [scale] The extent to which data are likely to be free from random error and yield consistent results.

reliability [service] The ability of the service firm to perform the service provided in a dependable and accurate manner.

religion A way of defining a society's relationship to the supernatural and, as a result, determining dominant values and attitudes.

reorder point An inventory level at which new orders are placed.

repeat transactions Buyer and seller interacting over multiple transactions.

resale price maintenance Manufacturers requiring retailers to charge a particular price for a product.

research approach The method used to collect data.

response An attempt to satisfy an individual drive.

response-offer coupons Coupons issued following a request by a consumer.

responsiveness The willingness of the firm's staff to help customers and to provide prompt service.

retail chains Two or more retail outlets that are commonly owned and that involve central purchasing and decision making.

retail franchises Franchises that result from a contract between franchisors (who could be manufacturers, wholesalers, or service providers) and a retail franchisee (an independent buyer or group of buyers), allowing the franchisee to own and operate one or more units of the franchise in return for franchise fees and royalties.

retailer cooperatives Associations of independent retailers who engage in centralized buying and promotion.

retailing All the activities involved in the final distribution—selling goods and services to the final consumers for their consumption.

retention The ability of the firm to maintain a particular customer over time.

reward power Power over the channel members based on an anticipation of special privileges, such as a financial reward for conducting a particular behavior.

roles The activities people are expected to perform according to individuals around them.

Rostow model of economic development A model of economic development in which each stage of development is a function of productivity, economic exchange, technological improvements, and income.

rotoscoping The process of placing drawn characters digitally into live television footage.

routine problem solving Consumer decision making whereby consumers engage in habitual purchase decisions involving products that they purchase frequently.

S

sales era Period between 1930 and 1950, when the primary focus of marketing was on selling.

sales force compensation, quota, and territory studies Different studies pertaining to personal selling activities; they are crucial in helping to determine the appropriate sales and incentive strategies for certain markets.

sales force composite estimates Research studies in which sales forecasts are based on the personal observations and forecasts of the local sales force.

sales forecasts Projected sales for a particular territory.

sales potential studies Studies forecasting optimal sales performance.

sales promotions Incentives to encourage end users or consumers to purchase a product.

sample size The number of study participants necessary to obtain a high reliability.

sample A segment of the population selected for the study and considered to be representative of the total population of interest.

sampling frame The list from which sampling units are selected.

sampling procedure The procedure used in the selection of sampling units.

sampling unit The individuals or groups included in the study.

sampling Sales promotions that include the free delivery of an actual product or portion of a product.

satisfaction A match between consumer expectations and good or service performance.

satisficing Process of making a decision that is satisfactory, but not necessarily optimal.

scanner-delivered coupons Coupons issued at the cash register during checkout.

scrambled merchandising Scrambled merchandising involves retailers adding complementary product categories not included in the existing merchandise mix and more services to create one-stop shopping convenience for target consumers.

secondary business districts Shopping areas, consisting primarily of convenience and specialty stores, that form at the intersection between two important streets.

secondary data Data collected to address a problem other than the problem at hand.

segment marketing A process that involves identifying consumers who are similar with regard to key traits, such as product-related needs and wants, and who would respond well to a similar marketing mix.

segmentation The process of identifying consumers and/or markets that are similar with regard to key traits, such as product-related needs and wants, and that would respond well to a product and related marketing mix.

selective distortion Consumers adapting information to fit their own existing knowledge.

selective distribution A strategy whereby firms have some control over the marketing strategy by limiting distribution to a select group of resellers in each area, while, at the same time, the company can achieve a reasonable sales volume and profits.

selective exposure The stimuli that consumers choose to pay attention to.

selective retention Remembering only information about a good or service that supports personal knowledge or beliefs.

self-reference criterion Individuals' conscious and unconscious reference to their own national culture, to home-country norms and values, and to their knowledge and experience in the process of making decisions in the host country.

selling agent Agent that holds an exclusive arrangement with the company, represents all its operations in a particular market, and acts as the sales and/or marketing department of the firm; selling agents do not take title to the goods and are usually paid as a percentage of sales.

selling concept A marketing philosophy that assumes consumers, if left alone, will normally not purchase the products the firm is selling, or not purchase enough products; as a result, consumers need to be aggressively targeted and approached with personal selling and advertising in order to purchase.

semantic differential scale Scale that is anchored by words with opposite meanings.

seniors A segment of consumers, age 65 and older, who live on fixed incomes and spend large amounts on home-related expenses and groceries.

service distribution The availability and accessibility of a service to consumers.

service encounter The actual interaction point between the customer and the service provider.

service failures Instances in which a service is either not performed at all or is poorly performed.

service mark Words, symbols, marks, and signs that are legally registered for a single company's use that identify and distinguish the source of a service.

service mix The different types of services offered to retail customers.

service recovery The process of attempting to regain a customer's confidence after a service failure.

services Intangible activities or benefits that individuals acquire, but that do not result in ownership, such as an airplane trip, a massage, or the preparation of a will.

share of the customer The percentage (or share) of a customer's business that a particular firm has.

shopping centers Groups of stores that are planned, developed, and managed as one entity.

shopping goods Goods that consumers perceive as higher risk but for which they are willing to spend a greater amount of purchase effort to find and evaluate.

simulated test marketing Test marketing that simulates purchase environments in that target consumers are observed in the product-related decision-making process.

single transaction Buyer and seller interacting for the purpose of a single transaction.

situational influences Influences that are attributed to the purchase situation.

skimming Pricing strategy whereby the product is priced higher than that of competitors.

slice-of-life execution Advertising execution that involves presenting a problem and a solution within the framework of the advertisement.

slotting fees Fees that retailers charge to stock manufacturers' brands.

social class Relatively permanent divisions within society that exist in a status hierarchy, with the members of each division sharing similar values, attitudes, interests, and opinions.

social risk The probability that a service will not meet with approval from others who are significant to the consumer making the purchase.

societal marketing concept A marketing philosophy that assumes the company will have an advantage over competitors if it applies the marketing concept in a manner that maximizes society's well-being.

socio-demographic and cultural environment A component of the macroenvironment that comprises elements such as demographics, subcultures, cultural values, and all other elements in the environment related to consumers' backgrounds, values, attitudes, interests, and behaviors.

source The organization that originates a marketing communication message.

specialized markets Markets that contain specialty stores specializing in a particular product category.

specialty goods Goods that reach the ultimate in differentiation and brand loyalty in that only the chosen brand is acceptable to the consumer.

specialty merchandise wholesalers Independent wholesalers who carry a narrow product assortment but offer great depth in the product lines carried.

specialty stores Retailers that offer a narrow product line and deep assortment.

spiff money Monies or prizes awarded in trade contests.

sponsorship marketing Marketing that involves a company paying a fee to an event, person, or organization in exchange for a direct association with that event, person, or organization.

stability The extent to which preferences are stable, rather than changing, in a market segment.

stakeholder A person or group that has a vested interest in an organization's well-being.

standardization The process of using the same product and marketing approach across countries.

staples Goods that are bought routinely, such as milk, cheese, bread, and soap.

stars High-share, high-growth products that create profits but require additional investment.

status The esteem which society bestows upon a particular role.

stimuli Cues in the environment, such as products and advertisements, that create individual responses.

stimulus-response sales approach Sometimes referred to as the canned sales approach, uses specific statements (stimuli) to solicit specific responses from customers.

stock turnover The number of times a year that the inventory on hand is sold.

straight rebuy situation Routine purchases from a vendor without modifying specifications or without renegotiating new terms.

strategic alliances Any type of relationship between one or more companies attempting to reach joint corporate and market-related goals; used to refer to most nonequity alliances.

strategic partnership Partnership in which the buyer and seller exchange information at the highest levels with the goal of collaboration.

strivers Psychographic group of individuals who are trendy and fun loving. They are concerned about others' opinions and approval, and demonstrate to peers their ability to buy.

studies of premiums, coupons, and deals Studies that determine the appropriateness and effectiveness of premiums, coupons, and deals for a given target market.

style A general form of popular expression that could last for a longer period of time and/or that could be cyclical in nature.

subcultures Groups of individuals with shared value systems based on ethnicity or common background.

substantiality The extent to which the market is large enough to warrant investment.

supercenters Stores that carry an extensive food selection and drug products, as well as nonfood items (which account for at least 25 percent of sales), combining supermarket, discount, and warehouse retailing principles.

superstores Large retailers, such as combination stores or hypermarkets, that sell food, drugs, and other products.

support personnel Individuals who directly support or assist in the selling function in some manner, but do not process orders or directly solicit orders.

survey research Descriptive research that involves the administration of personal, telephone, or mail questionnaires.

survivors Psychographic group of individuals who are concerned with safety and security. They focus on meeting needs rather than fulfilling desires, are brand loyal, and purchase discounted products.

T

take-off Economic development stage in which growth becomes the norm, income rises, and leading sectors emerge.

tangibles The service provider's physical facilities, equipment, and appearance of its employees.

target market Consumers and/or markets that are similar in aspects relevant to the company.

target marketing The process of focusing on those segments that the company can serve most effectively and designing products, services, and marketing programs with these segments in mind.

technical service quality The outcome of the service.

television home shopping Retailing through cable channels selling to consumers in their homes, through infomercials, and by direct-response advertising shown on broadcast and cable television.

terminal values Values related to goals.

test marketing Evaluating product performance in select markets that are representative of the target market before launching the product.

testimonial execution An advertising execution that uses an individual, such as a celebrity, an ordinary person, or a customer, endorsing the product.

thinkers Psychographic group of individuals who are educated, conservative, and practical consumers who value knowledge and responsibility. They look for durability, functionality, and value.

third-country national An employee working in the country of assignment who is not a national of that country or of the country in which the corporate headquarters of the company for which he or she works is located.

tie-ins Sales promotion of two or more goods or services within the same promotional offer.

time series and econometric methods Methods that use the data of past performance to predict future market demand.

time-loss risk The amount of time the consumer lost due to the failure of the service.

trade allowances Some type of financial incentive to channel members to motivate them to make a purchase.

trade incentives Some type of financial incentive that involves the retailer performing some type of function in order to receive a trade allowance.

trade promotions Incentives directed toward channel members to encourage them to purchase, stock, or push a product through the channel.

trademark Words, symbols, marks, and signs that are legally registered for a single company's use.

trading companies Complex marketing systems that specialize in providing intermediary service and reducing risk through extensive information channels and financial assistance.

traditional society Economic development stage in which the economy is dominated by agriculture, minimal productivity, and low growth in per capita output.

transitional society Economic development stage in which there is increased productivity in agriculture; manufacturing begins to emerge.

truck wholesalers Wholesalers who take physical possession of the products and sell them from their truck or wagon on their regular sales route.

trust relationships Buyer-seller dyads based on mutual respect and understanding of both parties and a commitment to work together.

U

uncertainty The probability that a particular outcome or consequence will occur.

undifferentiated marketing A targeting strategy aiming the product at the market using a single strategy, regardless of the number of segments.

unit pricing Pricing that allows consumers to compare among prices for different brands and for different package sizes of the different brands.

usage rate segmentation The process of segmenting markets based on the extent to which consumers are nonusers, occasional users, medium users, or heavy users of a product.

use or applications positioning The process of marketing a very precise product application that differentiates it in consumers' minds from other products that have a more general use.

user An individual member of the buying center who actually uses the product or is responsible for the product being used.

user status segmentation The process of determining consumer status—as users of competitors' products, ex-users, potential users, first-time users, or regular users.

V

validity The extent to which data collected are free from bias.

value The overall price given the quality of the product; perceived as important for the first purchase decision.

value chain (or **supply chain**) The chain of activities performed in the process of developing, producing, marketing, delivering, and servicing a product for the benefit of the customer.

value delivery chain The participants involved in the value chain.

value-based philosophy A philosophy that focuses on customers, ensuring that their needs are addressed in a manner that delivers a product of high quality and value, leading to consumer satisfaction.

values Important elements of culture defined as enduring beliefs about a specific mode of conduct or desirable end-state.

variability The unwanted or random levels of service quality customers receive when they patronize a service.

variable costs Costs, such as raw materials, packaging, and shipping costs, that vary with the amount of output.

variable pricing Strategy of changing prices in response to changes in cost or demand.

vending machines An interactive mode of retailing convenience goods.

vertical integration The acquisition or merger with an intermediary in the channel that is either a supplier or a buyer.

vertical marketing systems (VMS) Intermediary marketing systems which consist of manufacturers, wholesalers, and retailers in the same channel who have partial VMS ownership acting as a unified whole.

W

wants Needs that are directed at a particular product—for example, to meet the need for transportation, consumers may purchase an automobile or a bus ride.

warehouse clubs (or **wholesale clubs**) Stores that require members to pay an annual fee and that operate in low-overhead, warehouse-type facilities, offering limited lines of brand-name and dealer-brand groceries, apparel, appliances, and other goods at a substantial discount.

warehousing The marketing function whereby goods are stored, identified, and sorted in the process of transfer to an intermediary in the distribution channel or to the final consumer.

wheel of retailing Description of how stores add services and increase prices, thereby losing their initial customer base.

wholesale cooperatives Voluntary chains of independent grocers pooling their resources and buying power and standardizing their marketing practices in a contractual agreement.

wholesalers and distributors Middlemen that purchase goods from a manufacturer for resale to other members of the channel.

wholesaling All the activities involved in buying and handling the goods intended for sale to resellers or other organizational users.

wholly owned subsidiary The entry mode that affords the highest level of control and presents the highest level of risk to a company; it involves establishing a new company that is a citizen of the country where the subsidiary is established.

Y

younger boomers A segment of consumers between the ages of 35 and 44, whose focus is on family and home, who pay a large proportion of their income for mortgages, furnishings, pets, and children's toys.

Company/Product Index

Page numbers in italics identify illustrations. An italic *t* next to a page number (e.g., 204*t*) indicates information that appears in a table.

A

B

M

N

O

P

Z

Subject Index

Page numbers in italics identify illustrations. An italic *t* next to a page number (e.g., 169*t*) indicates information that appears in a table.

A

B

C

D

H

I

N

O

Q

R

S

T

U

V

W

X

Y

Z